THE

ABORIGINAL RACES

OF

NORTH AMERICA;

COMPRISING

BIOGRAPHICAL SKETCHES OF EMINENT INDIVIDUALS,

AND

AN HISTORICAL ACCOUNT OF THE DIFFERENT TRIBES.

FROM

THE FIRST DISCOVERY OF THE CONTINENT

TO

THE PRESENT PERIOD

WITH A DISSERTATION ON THEIR

Origin, Antiquities, Manners and Customs,

ILLUSTRATIVE NARRATIVES AND ANECDOTES,

AND A

COPIOUS ANALYTICAL INDEX

BY SAMUEL G. DRAKE.

FIFTEENTH EDITION,
REVISED, WITH VALUABLE ADDITIONS,

BY PROF. H. L. WILLIAMS.

They waste us; ay, like the April snow
In the warm noon we shrink away
And fast they follow as we go
Toward the setting day;
Till they shall fill the land, and we
Are driven into the western sea.—BRYANT.

NEW YORK.
HURST & COMPANY, PUBLISHERS.

PREFACE.

The history of the aboriginal races of the American Continent is an interesting study, not only to the people of this Union, but also to those of other lands, who regard them as the congeners of the nomadic hordes, which in times long past swarmed over the plains of now civilized Europe. In many respects there is a very close resemblance between the characters and final fate of all the primitive tribes and nations of the world — their mode of government, habits, customs, &c., being somewhat similar — and their recession before the onward march of civilization, as well as their final absorption or disappearance, following an inexorable natural law, which decrees the submission of the animal to intellectual development. From the study of past events alone can an opinion be formed of the causes which gave origin to them, and for this reason should every American citizen, who desires to understand the true history of his country, peruse with attention the records of the former owners of that soil, which ere long will no more give sustenance to any of their descendants.

No ordinary task is it for the faithful chronicler to trace the history of a people who have no written annals, and no written language; whose only records are of a pictographic character; and whose traditions are so vague and unconnected as to be very unreliable. Such are the difficulties he has to encounter anterior to the discovery of America by Columbus; and even subsequent to that period, owing to the unsettled condition of the country until within the last half century, years of research and comparison are rendered necessary in order to reconcile conflicting statements, and unravel the tangled web of confused narratives. Believing, however, that the end to be attained,—that of giving to the world a reliable history of the Indians of the North American

Continent — was one which justified the author in making any sacrifice of time and labor in its accomplishment, he, for many years, toiled unremittingly to accomplish this purpose; sparing neither trouble nor expense in the collection of facts and their sectional arrangement Whether he has succeeded in accordance with his hopes he does not pretend to say; leaving to the judgment of the intelligent reader the decision of the question, after a thorough and attentive perusal of the work.

The Indian has been traced through all his misfortunes, wanderings, and forced transmigrations, to his present home on the western shores of the Mississippi, where there is every prospect of his speedy absorption in the Anglo-Saxon current which is so steadily flowing toward the setting sun; and the last remnant of the race will soon in spirit, if not in words, echo the language of a poetic writer, who thus portrays the sole survivor as apostrophizing the Deity:

"Where is my home — my forest home? the proud land of my sires?
Where stands the wigwam of my pride? where gleam the council fires?
Where are my fathers' hallowed graves? my friends so light and free?
Gone, gone, — forever from my view! Great Spirit! can it be?"

CONTENTS.

BOOK IV.

Biography and History of the Southern Indians.

BOOK V.

BIOGRAPHY AND HISTORY OF THE IROQUOIS OR FIVE NATIONS, AND OTHER NEIGHBORING TRIBES OF THE WEST.

AN

ALPHABETICAL ENUMERATION

OF

THE INDIAN TRIBES AND NATIONS

AN attempt is made, in the following Table, to locate the various bands of Aborigines, ancient and modern, and to convey the best information respecting their numbers our multifarious sources will warrant. Modern writers have been, for several years, endeavoring to divide North America into certain districts, each of which should include all the Indians speaking the same, or dialects of the same, language; but whoever has paid any attention to the subject, must undoubtedly have been convinced that it can never be done with any degree of accuracy. This has been undertaken in reference to an approximation of the great question of the origin of this people, from a comparison of the various languages used among them. An unwritten language is easily varied, and there can be no barrier to innovation. A continual intermixing of tribes has gone on from the period of their origin to the present time, judging from what we have daily seen; and when any two tribes unite, speaking different languages, or dialects of the same, a new dialect is produced by such amalgamation. Hence the accumulation of vocabularies would be like the pursuit of an infinite series in mathematics; with this difference, however — in the one we recede from the object in pursuit, while in the other we approach it. But I would not be understood to speak disparagingly of this attempt at classification; for, if it be unimportant in the main design, it will be of considerable service to the student in Indian history on other accounts. Thus, the *Uchees* are said to speak a primitive language, and they were districted in a small territory south of the Cherokees; but, some 200 years ago, — if they then existed as a tribe, and their tradition be true, — they were bounded on the north by one of the great lakes. And they are said to be descended from the Shawanees by some of themselves. We know an important community of them is still in existence in Florida. Have they created a new language in the course of their wanderings? or have those from whom they separated done so? Such are the difficulties we meet with at every step of a classification. But a dissertation upon these matters cannot now be attempted.

In the following analysis, the names of the tribes have been generally given in the singular number, for the sake of brevity; and the word *Indians*, after such names, is omitted from the same cause. Few abbreviations have been used: — W. R., *west of the Rocky Mountains*; m., *miles*; r., *river*; l., *lake*; and perhaps a few others. In some instances, reference is made to the body of the work, where a more extended account of a tribe is to be found. Such references are to the Book and Page, the same as in the Index.

ABEKAS, probably Muskogees, under the French at Tombeckbee in 1750.
ABENAKIES, over Maine till 1754, then went to Canada; 200 in 1689; 150 in 1780.
ABSOROKA, (Minetare,) S. branch Yellowstone; lat. 46°, lon. 105°; 45,000 in 1834
ACCOKESAW, W. side Colorado, about 200 m. S. W. Nacogdoches, in 1805.
ACOMAK, one of the six tribes in Virginia when settled by the English in 1607.
ADAIZE, 4 m. from Nachitoches, on Lake Macdon; 40 men in 1805.
ADIRONDAKS, (Algonkin,) along the N. shore St. Lawrence; 100 in 1786.

AFFAGOULA, small clan in 1783, on Mississippi r., 8 m. above Point Coupé.
AGAWOM, (Wampanoags,) at Sandwich, Mass.; others at Ipswich, in 1620, &c.
AHWAHAWAY, (Minetare,) S. W. Missouri 1820, 3 m. above Mandans; 200 in 1805.
AJÓUES, S. of the Missouri, and N. of the Padoucas; 1,100 in 1760.
ALANSAR, (Fall,) head branches S. fork Saskashawan; 2,500 in 1804.
ALGONKIN, over Canada; from low down the St. Lawrence to Lake of the Woods.
ALIATAN, three tribes in 1805 among the Rocky Mountains, on heads Platte.
ALICHE, near Nacogdoches in 1805, then nearly extinct; spoke Caddo.
ALLAKAWEAH, (Paunch,) both sides Yellowstone, heads Big Horn r.; 2,300 in 1805.
ALLIBAMA, (Creeks,) formerly on that r., but removed to Red River in 1764.
AMALISTES, (Algonkins,) once on St. Lawrence; 500 in 1760.
ANASAGUNTAKOOK, (Abenaki,) on sources Androscoggin, in Maine, till 1750.
ANDASTES, once on S. shore Lake Erie, S. W. Senecas, who destroyed them in 1672.
APACHES, (Lapane,) between Rio del Norte and sources of Nuaces r.; 3,500 in 1817.
APALACHICOLA, once on that r. in W. Florida; removed to Red River in 1764.
APPALOUSA, aboriginal in the country of their name; but 40 men in 1805.
AQUANUSCHIONI, the name by which the Iroquois knew themselves.
ARAPAHAS, S. side main Canada River; 4,000 in 1836, on Kanzas River.
ARMOUCHIQUOIS, or MARACHITE, (Abenaki,) on River St. John, New Brunswick.
ARRENAMUSE, on St. Antonio River, near its mouth, in Texas; 120 in 1818.
ASSINNABOIN, (Sioux,) between Assinn. and Missouri r.; 1,000 on Ottawa r. in 1836
ATENAS, in a village with the Faculli in 1836, west of the Rocky Mountains.
ATHAPASCOW, about the shores of the great lake of their name.
ATNAS, (Ojibewas,) next S. of the Athapascow, about lat. 57° N., in 1790.
ATTACAPAS, in a district of their name in Louisiana; but 50 men in 1805.
ATTAPULGAS, (Seminoles,) on Little r., a branch of Oloklikana, 1820, and 220 souls.
ATTIKAMIGUES, in N. of Canada, destroyed by pestilence in 1670.
AUCOSISCO, (Abenaki,) between the Saco and Androscoggin River in 1630, &c.
AUGHQUAGA, on E. branch Susquehannah River; 150 in 1768; since extinct.
AYAUAIS, 40 leagues up the Des Moines, S. E. side; 800 in 1805.
AYUTANS, 8,000 in 1820, S. W. the Missouri, near the Rocky Mountains.

BAYAGOULA, W. bank Mississippi, opposite the Colipasa; important in 1699
BEDIES, on Trinity River, La., about 60 m. S. of Nacogdoches; 100 in 1805.
BIG-DEVILS, (Yonktons,) 2,500 in 1836; about the heads of Red River.
BILOXI, at Biloxi, Gulf Mex., 1699; a few on Red r., 1804, where they had removed.
BLACKFEET, sources Missouri; 30,000 in 1834; nearly destroyed by small-pox, 1838.
BLANCHE, (Bearded, or White,) upper S. branches of the Missouri in 1820.
BLUE-MUD, W., and in the vicinity of the Rocky Mountains in 1820.
BROTHERTON, near Oneida Lake; composed of various tribes; 350 in 1836.

CADDO, on Red River in 1717, powerful; on Sodo Bay in 1800; in 1804, 100 men.
CADODACHE, (Nacogdochet,) on Angelina r., 100 m. above the Nechez; 60 in 1820.
CAIWAS, or KAIWA, on main Canada River, and S. of it in 1830.
CALASTHOCLE, N. Columbia, on the Pacific, next N. the Chillates; 200 in 1820.
CALLIMIX, coast of the Pacific, 40 m. N. Columbia River; 1,200 in 1820.
CAMANCHES, (Shoshone,) warlike and numerous; in interior of Texas.
CANARSEE, on Long Island, N. Y., in 1610, from the W. end to Jamaica.
CANCES, (Kansas,) 1805, from Bay of St. Bernard, over Grand r., toward Vera Crux.
CANIBAS, (Abenaki,) numerous in 1607, and after; on both sides Kennebeck River.
CARANKOUA, on peninsula of Bay of St. Bernard, Louisiana; 1,500 in 1805.
CAREE, on the coast between the Nuaces and Rio del Norte; 2,600 in 1817.
CARRIERS, (Nateotetains,) a name given the natives of N. Caledonia by traders.
CASTAHANA, between sources Padouca fork and Yellowstone; 5,000 in 1805.
CATAKA, between N. and S. forks of Chien River; about 3,000 in 1804.
CATAWBA, till late, on their river in S. Carolina; 1,500 in 1743, and 450 in 1764.
CATHLACUMUPS, on main shore Columbia River, S. W. Wappatoo i.; 450 in 1820.
CATHLAKAHIKIT, at the rapids of the Columbia, 160 m. up; 900 in 1820.
CATHLAKAMAPS, 80 m. up Columbia River; about 700 in 1820.
CATHLAMAT, on the Pacific, 30 m. S. mouth of Columbia River; 600 in 1820.
CATHLANAMENAMEN, on an island in mouth of Wallaumut River; 400 in 1820.
CATHLANAQUIAH, (Wappatoo,) S. W. side Wappatoo Island; 400 in 1820.
CATHLAPOOTLE, on Columbia River, opposite the Cathlakamaps; 1,100 in 1820.
CATHLAPOOYA, 500 in 1820, on the Wallaumut River, 60 m. from its mouth.
CATHLASKO, 900 in 1820, on Columbia River, opposite the Chippanchikchiks.
CATHLATHLA, 900 in 1820, on Columbia River, opposite the Cathlakahikits.
CATHLATH, 500 in 1820, on the Wallaumut River, 60 m. from its mouth.
CATTANAHAW, between the Saskashawan and Missouri Rivers, in 1805.
CAUGHNEWAGA, places where Christians lived were so called.
CHACTOO, on Red River; in 1805, but 100; indigenous; always lived there.
CHAOUANONS, the French so called the Shawanese; (Chowans ?)
CHEEGEE, (Cherokees,) 50 to 80 m. S. of them; called also Mid. Settlement, 1780
CHEHAWS, small tribe on Flint River, destroyed by Georgia militia in 1817.
CHEPEYAN, claim from lat. 60° to 65°, lon. 100° to 110° W.; 7,500 in 1812.
CHEROKEE, in Georgia, S. Carolina, &c., till 1836; then forced beyond the Mississ.

CHESKITALOWA, (Seminoles,) 580 in 1820, W. side Chattahoochee.
CHIEN, (Dog,) near the sources Chien River; 300 in 1805; 200 in 1820.
CHIHEELEESH, 40 m. N. of Columbia River; 1,400 in 1820.
CHICKASAW, between heads of Mobile River in 1780; once 10,000; now in Arkansas.
CHIPPANCHIKCHIKS, 60 in 1820, N. side Columbia River, 220 m. from its mouth.
CHIKAHOMINI, on Matapony River, Va., in 1661; but 3 or 4 in 1790; now extinct.
CHIKAMAUGAS, on Tennessee River, 90 m. below the Cherokees, in 1790.
CHILLATES, 150 in 1820, on the Pacific, N. Columbia River, beyond the Quieetsos.
CHILLUKITTEQUAU, on the Columbia, next below the Narrows; 1,400 in 1820.
CHILTZ, N. of Columbia River, on the Pacific, next N. of the Killaxthocles.
CHIMNAHPUM, on Lewis River, N. W. side of the Columbia; 1,800 in 1820.
CHINNOOK, on N. side Columbia River; in 1820, about 400 in 28 lodges.
CHIPPEWAS, about Lake Superior, and other vast regions of the N., very numerous.
CHITIMICHA, on W. bank Miss. River in 1722; once powerful, then slaves.
CHOKTAW, S. of the Creeks; 15,000 in 1812; in 1848 in Arkansas.
CHOPUNNISH, on Kooskooskee River; 4,300 in 1806, in 73 lodges.
CHOWANOK, (Shawanese ?) in N. Carolina, on Bennet's Creek, in 1708; 3,000 in 1630.
CHOWANS, E. of the Tuscaroras in N. Carolina; 60 join the Tuscaroras in 1720.
CHRISTENAUX, only another spelling of KNISTENAUX, which see.
CLAHCLELLAH, 700 in 1820, on the Columbia River, below the rapids.
CLAKSTAR, W. R., on a river flowing into the Columbia at Wappatoo Island.
CLAMOCTOMICH, on the Pacific, next N. of the Chiltz; 260 in 1820.
CLANIMATAS, on the S. W. side of Wappatoo Island; 200 in 1820, W. R.
CLANNARMINIMUNS, S. W. side of Wappatoo Island; 280 in 1820, W. R.
CLATSOPS, about 2 m. N. of the mouth of Columbia River; 1,300 in 1820.
CLARKAMES, on a river of their name flowing into the Wallaumut; 1,800 in 1820.
CNEIS, on a river flowing into Sabine Lake, 1690; the COENIS of Hennepin, probably.
COHAKIES, nearly destroyed in Pontiak's time; in 1800, a few near Lake Winnebago.
COLAPISSAS, on E. bank Mississippi in 1720, opposite head of Lake Pontchartrain.
CONCHATTAS came to Appalousas in 1794, from E. the Mississ.; in 1801, on Sabine.
CONGAREES, a small tribe on Congaree River, S. Carolina, in 1701; long since gone.
CONOYS, perhaps Kanhawas, being once on that river; (Canais, and variations.)
COOKKOO-OOSE, 1,500 in 1806, coast of Pacific, S. of Columbia r., and S. of Killawats
COOPSPELLAR, on a river falling into the Columbia, N. of Clark's; 1,600 in 1806.
COOSADAS, (Creeks,) once resided near the River Tallapoosie.
COPPER, so called from their copper ornaments, on Coppermine River, in the north.
COREES, (Tuscaroras,) on Neus River, N. Carolina, in 1700, and subsequently.
CORONKAWA, on St. Jacintho River, between Trinity and Brazos; 350 in 1820.
COWLITSICK, on Columbia River, 62 m. from its mouth, in 3 villages; 2,400 in 1820.
CREEKS, (Muscogees,) Savannah r. to St. Augustine, thence to Flint r., 1730.
CREES, (Lynx, or Cat,) another name of the Knistenaux, or a part of them.
CROWS, (Absorokas,) S. branches of the Yellowstone River; 45,000 in 1834.
CUTSAHNIM, on both sides Columbia River, above the Sokulks; 1,200 in 1820.

DAHCOTA, or DOCOTA, the name by which the Sioux know themselves.
DELAWARE, (Lenna-lenape,) those once on Delaware River and Bay; 500 in 1750.
DINONDADIES, (Hurons,) same called by the French Tionontaties.
DOEGS, small tribe on the Maryland side Potomac River, in 1675.
DOGRIBS, (Blackfeet,) but speak a different language.
DOGS, the Chiens of the French. See CHIEN.
DOTAME, 120 in 1805; about the heads of Chien River, in the open country.

EAMUSES. See EMUSAS.
ECHEMINS, (Canoe-men,) on R. St. Johns; include Passamaquoddies and St. Johns.
EDISTOES, in S. Carolina in 1670; a place still bears their name there.
EMUSAS, (Seminoles,) W. side Chattahoochee, 2 m. above the Wekisas; 20 in 1820.
ENESHURES, at the great Narrows of the Columbia; 1,200 in 1820, in 41 lodges.
ERIES, along E. side of Lake Erie, destroyed by the Iroquois about 1654.
ESAWS, on River Pedee, S. Carolina, in 1701; then powerful; Catawbas, probably.
ESKELOOTS, about 1,000 in 1820, in 21 lodges, or clans, on the Columbia.
ESQUIMAUX, all along the northern coasts of the frozen ocean, N. of 60° N. lat.
ETOHUSSEWAKKES, (Semin.,) on Chattahoochee, 3 m. above Ft. Gaines; 100 in 1820.

FACULLIES, 100 in 1820; on Stuart Lake, W. Rocky Mount.; lat. 54°, lon. 125° W.
FALL, so called from their residence at the falls of the Kooskooskee. See ALANSARS.
FIVE NATIONS, Mohawks, Senecas, Cayugas, Onondagas, and Oneidas; which see.
FLAT-HEADS, (Tutseewas,) on a large river W. R.; on S. fork Columbia r.
FOLLES AVOINES, the French so called the Menominies.
FOND DU LAC, roam from Snake River to the Sandy Lakes.
FOWL-TOWNS, (Seminoles,) 12 m. E. Fort Scott; about 300 in 1820.
FOXES, (Ottagamies,) called Renards by the French; dispossessed by B. Hawk's war

GANAWESE, on the heads of Potomac River; same as Kanhaways, probably.
GAYHEAD, Martha's Vineyard; 200 in 1800; in 1820, 340.
GRAND RIVER, on Grand r., N. side L. Ontario; Mohawks, Senecas, and oth.; 2,000.

GROS VENTRES, W. Mississippi, on Maria River, in 1806; in 1834, 3,000.

HARE-FOOT, next S. of the Esquimaux, and in perpetual war with them.
HALLIBEES, a tribe of Creeks, destroyed in 1813.
HANNAKALLAL, 600 in 1820, on Pacific, S. Columbia, next beyond the Luckkarso
HASSANAMESITS, a tribe of Nipmuks, embraced Christianity in 1660.
HIHIGHENIMMO, 1,300 in 1820, from mouth of Lastaw River, up it to the forks.
HELLWITS, 100 m. along the Columbia, from the falls upward, on the N. side.
HERRING POND, a remnant of Wampanoags, in Sandwich, Mass.; about 40.
HIETANS, (Camanches,) erratic bands; from Trinity to Brazos, and Red River.
HINI, (Cadodache,) 200 in 1820, on Angelina r., between Red r. and Rio del Norte.
HITCHITTEES, once on Chattahoochee r.; 600 now in Arkansas; speak Muskogee.
HOHILPOS, (Tushepahas,) 300 in 1820, above great falls on Clark's River.
HUMAS, (Oumas,) "Red nation," in Ixsussees Parish, La., in 1805, below Manchak.
HURONS, (Wyandots, Quatoghies,) adjacent, and N. gt. lakes; subd. by Iroq., 1650.

ILLINOIS, "the lake of men," both sides Illinois r.; 12,000 in 1670; 60 towns in 170?
INIES, or TACHIES, [Texas ?] branch Sabine; 80 men in 1806; speak Caddo.
IOWAYS, on Ioway River before Black Hawk's war; 1,100 beyond the Mississippi.
IROQUOIS, 1606, on St. Lawrence, below Quebec; 1687, both sides Ohio, to Miss.
ISATIS, sometimes a name of the Sioux before 1755.
ITHKYEMAMITS, 600 in 1820, on N. side Columbia, near the Cathlaskos.

JELAN, one of the three tribes of Camanches, on sources Brazos, Del Norte, &c.

KADAPAUS, a tribe in N. Carolina in 1707.
KAHUNKLES, 400 in 1820, W. Rocky Mountains; abode unknown.
KALOOSAS, a tribe found early in Florida, long since extinct.
KANENAVISH, on the Padoucas' fork of the Platte; 400 in 1805.
KANHAWAS, Ganawese or Canhaways; on the River Kanhawa, formerly.
KANSAS, on the Arkansas River; about 1,000 in 1836; in 1820, 1,850.
KASKASKIAS, (Illin.) on a river of same name flowing into the Mississ.; 250 in 1797.
KASKAYAS, between sources of the Platte and Rocky Mountains; 3,000 in 1836.
KATTEKA, (Padoucas,) not located by travellers. See PADOUCAS.
KEEKATSA, (Crows,) both sides Yellowstone, above mouth Big Horn r.; 3,500 in 1805
KEYCHE, E. branch Trinity River in 1806; once on the Sabine; 260 in 1820.
KIAWAS, on Padouca River, beyond the Kites; 1,000 in 1806.
KIGENE, on the shore of Pacific Ocean in 1821, under the chief Skittegates.
KIKAPOO, formerly in Illinois; now about 300, chiefly beyond the Mississippi.
KILLAMUK, a branch of the Clatsops, on the coast of the Pacific Ocean; about 1,000
KILLAWAT, in a large town on the coast of the Pacific, E. of the Luktons.
KILLAXTHOCLES, 100 in 1820, at the mouth of Columbia River, on N. side.
KIMOENIMS, a band of the Chopunnish, on Lewis's River; 800 in 1820, in 33 clans.
KINAI, about Cook's Inlet, on the coast of the Pacific Ocean.
KITES, (Staetans,) between sources Platte and Rocky Mountains; about 500 in 182?.
KISKAKONS inhabited Michilimakinak in 1680; a Huron tribe.
KNISTENAUX, on Assinnaboin River; 5,000 in 1812; numerous; women comely.
KONAGENS, Esquimaux, inhabiting Kadjak Island, lat. 58°, lon. 152° W.
KOOK-KOO-OOSE, on the coast of the Pacific, S. of the Killawats; 1,500 in 1835.
KUSKARAWAOKS, one of six tribes on E. shore of Chesapeak in 1607; (Tuscaroras ?)

LAHANNA, 2,000 in 1820, both sides Columbia, above the mouth of Clark's River.
LAPANNE. See APACHES.
LARTIELO, 600 in 1820, at the falls of Lastaw River, below Wayton Lake.
LEAF, (Sioux,) 600 in 1820, on the Missouri, above Prairie du Chien.
LEECH RIVER, about 350 in 1820, near Sandy Lake, lat. 46° 9′ N.
LENNA LENAPE, once from Hudson to Delaware River; now scattered in the West.
LIPANIS, 800 in 1816, from Rio Grande to the interior of Texas; light hair.
LOUCHEUX, next N. of the Esquimaux, or S. of lat. 67° 15′ N.
LUKAWIS, 800 in 1820, W. of the Rocky Mountains; abode unknown.
LUKKARSO, 1,200 in 1820, coast of Pacific, S. of Columbia r., beyond the Shallalah.
LUKTONS, 20 in 1820, W. of the Rocky Mountains; abode unknown.

MACHAPUNGAS, in N. Carolina in 1700; practised circumcision.
MANDANS, 1,250 in 1805, 1200 m. fm. mouth of Misso.; 1838, reduced to 21 by sm. pox
MANGOAGS, or TUTELOES, (Iroquois,) Nottoway River, formerly; now extinct.
MANHATTANS, (Mohicans,) once on the island where New York city now stands.
MANNAHOAKS, once on the upper waters of the Rappahannock r.; extinct long ago
MARACHITES, (Abenakies,) on the St. John's; a remnant remains.
MARSAPEAGUES, once on Long Island, S. side of Oyster Bay; extinct.
MARSHPEES, (Wampanoags,) 315 in 1832; Barnstable Co., Mass.; mixed with blacks.
MASCOUTINS, or FIRE IND., betw. Mississ. and L. Michigan, 1665; (Sacs and Foxes ?)
MASSACHUSETTS, the state perpetuates their name.
MASSAWOMES, (Iroquois,) once spread over Kentucky.
MATHLANOBS, 500 in 1820, on an island in the mouth of Wallaumut River W. R.

Mayes, 600 in 1805, St. Gabriel Creek, mouth of Guadaloupe River, Louisiana.
Menominies, (Algonkins,) once on Illinois r.; now 300 W. Mississippi.
Messassagnes, 2,000 in 1764, N. of, and adjacent to, L. Huron and Superior.
Miamis, (Algonkins,) once on the r. of their name; now 1,500, beyond the Mississ.
Mikasaukies, (Seminoles,) about 1,000 in 1821; very warlike.
Mikmaks, (Algonkins,) 3,000 in 1760, in Nova Scotia; the Suriquois of the French.
Miksuksealton, (Tushepaha,) 300 in 1820, Clark's River, above great falls, W. R.
Minetares, 2,500 in 1805, 5 m. above the Mandans, on both sides Knife River.
Mindawarcarton, in 1805, on both sides Mississippi, from St. Peter's upward.
Mingoes, once such of the Iroquois were so called as resided upon the Scioto River
Minsi, Wolf tribe of the Lenna Lenape, once over New Jersey and part of Penn.
Missouries, once on that part of the River just below Grand r., in 1820.
Mitchigamies, one of the five tribes of the Illinois; location uncertain.
Mohawks, head of Five Nations; formerly on Mohawk r.; a few now in Canada.
Mohegans, or **Moheakunnuks**, in 1610, Hudson r. from Esopus to Albany.
Monacans, (Tuscaroras,) once near where Richmond, Virginia, now is.
Mongoulatches, on the W. side of the Mississippi. See **Bayagoulas**.
Montagnes, (Algonkins,) N. side St. Law., betw. Saguenay and Tadousac, in 1609.
Montauks, on E. end of Long Island, formerly; head of 13 tribes of that island.
Moratoks, 80 in 1607; 40 in 1669, in Lancaster and Richmond counties, Virginia.
Mosquitos, once a numerous race on the E. side of the Isthmus of Darien.
Multnomahs, (Wappatoo,) 800 in 1820, mouth of Multnomah River, W. R.
Munseys, (Delawares,) in 1780, N. branch Susquehannah r.; to the Wabash in 1808.
Muskogees, 17,000 in 1775, on Alabama and Apalachicola Rivers. See B. iv.

Nabedaches, (Caddo,) on branch Sabine, 15 m. above the Inies; 400 in 1805.
Nabijos, between N. Mexico and the Pacific; live in stone houses, and manufacture.
Nandakoes, 120 in 1805, on Sabine, 60 m. W. of the Yattassees; (Caddo.)
Nantikokes, 1711, on Nantikoke River; 1755, at Wyoming; same year went west.
Narcotah, the name by which the Sioux know themselves.
Narragansets, S. side of the bay which perpetuates their name; nearly extinct
Nashuays, (Nipmuks,) on that river from its mouth, in Massachusetts.
Natchez, at Natchez; discovered, 1701; chiefly destroyed by French, 1720.
Natchitoches, once at that place; 100 in 1804; now upon Red River.
Nateotetains, 200 in 1820, W. R., on a river of their name, W. of the Facullies.
Natiks, (Nipmuks,) in Massachusetts, in a town now called after them.
Nechacoke, (Wappatoo,) 100 in 1820, S. side Columbia, near Quicksand r., W. R.
Neekeetoo, 700 in 1820, on the Pacific, S. of the Columbia, beyond the Youicone.
Nemalquinner, (Wappatoo,) 200 in 1820, N. side Wallaumut River, 3 m. up.
Niantiks, a tribe of the Narragansets, and in alliance with them, p. 131.
Nicariagas, once about Michilimakinak; joined Iroquois in 1723, as seventh nation
Nipissins, (original Algonkins,) 400 in 1764, near the source of Ottoway River.
Nipmuks, eastern interior of Mass.; 1,500 in 1775; extinct. See p. 82, 104, 164, 275.
Norridgewoks, (Abenakies,) on Penobscot River. See Book iii. 303, 311.
Nottoways, on Nottoway River, in Virginia; but 2 of clear blood in 1817.
Nyacks, (Mohicans,) or **Manhattans**, once about the Narrows, in New York.

Oakmulges, (Muskogees,) to the E. of Flint River; about 200 in 1834.
Ocameches, in Virginia in 1607; had before been powerful; then reduced.
Ochees. See **Uchees**. — Perhaps Ochesos; 230 in Florida in 1826, at Ochee Bluff.
Oconas, (Creeks.) See Book iv. 369.
Ojibwas, (Chippeways,) 30,000 in 1836, about the great lakes, and N. of them.
Okatiokinans, (Seminoles,) 580 in 1820, near Fort Gaines, E. side Mississippi.
Omahas, 2,200 in 1820, on Elkhorn River, 80 m. from Council Bluffs.
Oneidas, one of the Five Nations; chief seat near Oneida Lake, New York.
Onondagas, one of the Five Nations; formerly in New York; 300 in 1840.
Ootlashoots, (Tushepahas,) 400 in 1820, on Clark's River, W. Rocky Mountains.
Osages, 4,000 in 1830, about Arkansas and Osage Rivers; many tribes.
Otagamies, (Winnebagoes,) 300 in 1780, betw. Lake of the Woods and the Mississ.
Otoes, 1,500 in 1820; in 1805, 500; 15 leagues up the River Platte, on S. side.
Ottawas, 1670, removed from L. Superior to Michilimakinak; 2,800 in 1820.
Ouiatanons, or **Waas**, (Kikapoos,) mouth of Eel r., Ind., 1791, in a village 3 m. long
Oumas, E. bank Mississippi in 1722, in 2 villages, quarter of a mile from the river.
Owassissas, (Seminoles,) 100 in 1820, on E. waters of St. Mark's River.
Ozas, 2,000 in 1750; on Ozaw River in 1780, which flows into the Mississippi.
Ozimies, one of the six tribes on E. shore of Maryland and Virginia in 1607.

Pacanas, on Quelquechose River, La.; 30 men in 1805; 40 m. S. W. Natchitoches
Padoucas, 2,000 warriors in 1724, on the Kansas; dispersed before 1805.
Padowagas, by some the Senecas were so called; uncertain.
Pailsh, 200 in 1820, on coast of the Pacific, N. Columbia r., beyond the Potoashs.
Palaches, a tribe found early in Florida, but long since extinct.
Pamlico, but 15 in 1708, about Pamlico Sound, in N. Carolina; extinct.
Pancas, once on Red River, of Winnipec l.; afterwards joined the Omahas.
Panis, (Tonicas,) 40 villages in 1750, S. br. Missouri; 70 villages on Red r., 1755.

PANNEH. See ALLAKAWEAH, 2,300 in 1805, on heads Big Horn River.
PASCATAWAYS, once a considerable tribe on the Maryland side Potomac River.
PASCAGOULAS, 25 men in 1805, on Red r., 60 m. below Natchitoches; from Florida.
PASSAMAQUODDIE, on Schoodak r., Me., in Perry Pleasant Point, a small number.
PAUNEE, 10,000 in 1820, on the Platte and Kansas; Republicans, Loupes, and Picts.
PAWISTUCIENEMUK, 500 in 1820; small, brave tribe, in the prairies of Missouri.
PAWTUCKETS, (Nipmuks,) on Merrimac River, where Chelmsford now is; extinct.
PEGANS, (Nipmuks,) 10 in 1793, in Dudley, Mass., on a reservation of 200 acres.
PELLOATPALLAH, (Chopunnish,) 1,600 in 1820, on Kooskooskee r., above forks, W. R
PENOBSCOTS, (Abenakies,) 330, on an island in Penobscot r., 12 m. above Bangor.
PENNAKOOKS, (Nipmuks,) along Merrimac r., where is now Concord, N. H., &c.
PEORIAS, 97 in 1820, on Current River; one of the five tribes of the Illinois.
PEQUAKETS, (Abenakies,) on sources Saco River; destroyed by English in 1725.
PEQUOTS, about the mouth of Connecticut River; subdued in 1637.
PHILLIMEES, (Seminoles,) on or near the Suane River, Florida, in 1817.
PIANKASHAWS, 3,000 once, on the Wabash; in 1780, but 950; since driven west.
PIANKATANK, a tribe in Virginia when first settled; unlocated.
PINESHOW, (Sioux,) 150 in 1820, on the St. Peter's, 15 m. from its mouth.
PISHQUITPAH, 2,600 in 1815, N. side Columbia River, at Muscleshell Rapids, W. R.
POTOASH, 200 in 1820, coast Pacific, N. mouth Columbia, beyond Clamoctomichs.
POTTOWATTOMIE, 1671, on Noquet i., L. Michigan; 1681, at Chicago.
POWHATANS, 32 tribes spread over Virginia when first discovered by the English.
PUANS, the Winnebagoes were so called by the French at one period.

QUABAOGS, (Nipmuks,) at a place of the same name, now Brookfield, Mass.
QUAPAW, 700 in 1820, on Arkansas r., opp. Little Rock; reduced by sm. pox in 1720.
QUATHLAHPOHTLES, on S. W. side Columbia, above mouth Tahwahnahiook River.
QUATOGHIE, (Wyandots,) once S. side L. Michigan; sold their lands to Eng. in 1707
QUESADAS. See COOSADAS.
QUIEETSOS, on the Pacific; 250 in 1820; N. Columbia r., next N. of the Quiniilts.
QUINIILTS, on coast of the Pacific, N. of Columbia r.; 250 in 1820; next the Pailshs.
QUINNECHART, coast Pacific, next N. Calasthocles, N. Columbia r.; 2,000 in 1820.
QUINNIPISSA are those called Bayagoulas by the Chevalier Tonti.
QUODDIES. See PASSAMAQUODDIE. — 3 Coll. Mass. Hist. Soc. iii. 181.

RAPIDS. See PAWISTUCIENEMUKS.
REDGROUND, (Seminoles,) 100 in 1820, on Chattahoochie r., 12 m. above Florida line.
REDKNIFE, so called from their copper knives; roam in the region of Slave Lake.
RED-STICK, (Seminoles,) the Baton Rouge of the French.
RED-WING, (Sioux,) on Lake Pepin, under a chief of their name; 100 in 1820.
RICAREE, (Paunees,) before 1805, 10 large vill. on Missouri r.; reduced by small pox.
RIVER, (Mohegans,) S. of the Iroquois, down the N. side of Hudson r.
ROUND-HEADS, (Hurons,) E. side Lake Superior; 2,500 in 1764.
RYAWAS, on the Padouca fork of the Missouri; 900 in 1820.

SACHDAGUGHS, (Powhatans,) perhaps the true name of the Powhatans.
SANKHIKANS, the Delawares knew the Mohawks by that name.
SANTEES, a small tribe in N. Carolina in 1701, on a river perpetuating their name.
SAPONIES, (Wanamies,) Sapona River, Carolina, in 1700; joined Tuscaroras, 1720
SATANAS, a name, it is said, given the Shawanees by the Iroquois.
SAUKE, or SAC, united with Fox before 1805; then on Mississ., above Illinois.
SAUTEURS, or FALL INDIANS of the French, about the falls of St. Mary.
SAVANNAHS, so called from the river, or the river from them; perhaps Yamasees
SCATTAKOOKS, upper part of Troy, N. Y.; went from New England about 1672.
SEMINOLES have been established in Florida a hundred years.
SENECAS, one of the Five Nations; "ranged many thousand miles" in 1700.
SEPONES, in Virginia in 1775, but a remnant. See SAPONIES.
SERRANNA, (Savannahs ?) in Georgia; nearly destroyed by the Westoes about 1670.
SEWEES, a small tribe in N. Carolina, mentioned by Lawson in 1710.
SHALLALAH, 1,200 in 1816, on the Pacific, S. Columbia r. next the Cookkoo-oosee.
SHALLATTOOS, on Columbia River, above the Skaddals; 100 in 1820.
SHANWAPPONE, 400 in 1820, on the heads of Cataract and Taptul Rivers.
SHAWANE, once over Ohio; 1672, subdued by Iroquois; 1,383 near St. Louis in 1820
SHEASTUKLE, 900 in 1820, on the Pacific, S. Columbia r., next beyond the Youitz.
SHINIKOOKS, a tribe of Long Island, about what is now South Hampton.
SHOSHONEE, 30,000 in 1820, on plains N. Missouri; at war with the Blackfeet.
SHOTO, (Wappatoo,) 460 in 1820, on Columbia River, opposite mouth of Wallaumut.
SICAUNIES, 1,000 in 1820, among the spurs of the Rocky Mountains, W. of the Rapids
SIOUX, discovered by French, 1660; 33,000 in 1820, St. Peter's, Mississ., and Misso. r
SISSATONES, upper portions of Red r., of L. Winnipec and St. Peter's, in 1820.
SITIMACHA. See CHITIMICHA.
SITKA, on King George III. Islands, on the coast of the Pacific, about lat. 57° N.
SIX NATIONS, (Iroquois,) Mohawk, Seneca, Onondaga, Oneida, Cayuga, Shawane.
SKADDALS, on Cataract River, 25 m. N. of the Big Narrows; 200 in 1820.
SKEETSOMISH, 2,000 in 1820, on a river of their name flowing into the Lastaw.

SKILLOOT, on Columbia River, from Sturgeon Island upward; 2,500 in 1820.
SKUNNEMOKE, or TUCKAPAS, on Vermilion River, La., 6 leagues W. of N. Iberia.
SMOKSHOP, on Columbia r., at the mouth of the Labiche; 800 in 1820, in 24 clans.
SNAKE. See ALIATANS, or SHOSHONEES.
SOKOKIE, on Saco River, Maine, until 1725, when they withdrew to Canada.
SOKULK, on the Columbia, above mouth of Lewis's River; 2,400 in 1820.
SOURIQUOIS, (Mikmaks,) once so called by the early French.
SOUTIES, (Ottowas,) a band probably mistaken for a tribe by the French.
SOYENNOM, (Chopunnish,) on N. side E. fork of Lewis's River; 400 in 1820; W. R.
SPOKAIN, on sources Lewis's River, over a large tract of country, W. Rocky Mts.
SQUANNAROO, on Cataract r., below the Skaddals; 120 in 1820; W. Rocky Mts.
STAETANS, on heads Chien r., with the Kanenavish; 400 in 1805; resemble Kiawas.
STOCKBRIDGE, NEW, (Mohegans and Iroquois,) collected in N. Y., 1786; 400 in 1820.
STOCKBRIDGE, Mass., (Mohegans,) settled there in 1734; went to Oneida in 1786.
ST. JOHN'S, (Abenakies,) about 300 still remain on that river.
SUSQUEHANNOK, on W. shore of Md. in 1607; that river perpetuates their name.
SUSSEES, near sources of a branch of the Saskashawan, W. Rocky Mountains.
SYMERONS, a numerous race, on the E. side of the Isthmus of Darien.

TACULLIES, "people who go upon water;" on head waters of Frazier's River, La.
TAHSAGROUDIE, about Detroit in 1723; probably Tsonothouans.
TAHUACANA, on River Brazos; 3 tribes; 180 m. up; 1,200 in 1820.
TALLAHASSE, (Seminoles,) 15 in 1820, between Oloklikana and Mikasaukie.
TALLEWHEANA, (Seminoles,) 210 in 1820, on E. side Flint River, near the Chehaws.
TAMARONAS, a tribe of the Illinois; perhaps Peorias afterwards.
TAMATLES, (Seminoles,) 7 m. above the Ocheeses, and numbered 220 in 1820.
TARRATINES, E. of Pascataqua River; the Nipmuks so called the Abenakies.
TATTOWHEHALLYS, (Seminoles,) 130 in 1820; since scattered among other towns.
TAUKAWAYS, on the sources of Trinity, Brazos, De Dios, and Colorado Rivers.
TAWAKENOE, "Three Canes," W. side Brazos r., 200 m. W. of Nacogdoches, 1804.
TAWAWS, (Hurons,) on the Mawme in 1780, 18 m. from Lake Erie.
TELMOCRESSE, (Seminoles,) W. side Chattahoochee, 15 m. above fork; 100 in 1820.
TENISAW, once on that river which flows into Mobile Bay; went to Red r. in 1765.
TETONS, (Sioux,) "vile miscreants," on Mississ., Misso., St. Peter's; "real pirates."
TIONONTATIES, or DINONDADIES, a tribe of Hurons, or their general name.
TOCKWOGHS, one of the six tribes on the Chesapeak in 1607.
TONICAS, 20 warriors in 1784, on Mississippi, opp. Point Coupé; once numerous.
TONKAHANS, a nation or tribe of Texans, said to be cannibals.
TONKAWA, 700 in 1820, erratic, about Bay St. Bernardo.
TOTEROS, on the mountains N. of the Sapones, in N. Carolina, in 1700.
TOTUSKEYS. See MORATOKS.
TOWACANNO, or TOWOASH, one of three tribes on the Brazos. See TAHUACANA.
TSONONTHOUANS, Hennepin so called the Senecas; by Cox, called Sonnontovans.
TUKABATCHE, on Tallapoosie River, 30 m. above Fort Alabama, in 1775.
TUNICA, (Mobilian,) on Red River, 90 m. above its mouth; but 30 in 1820.
TUNXIS, (Mohegans,) once in Farmington, Conn.; monument erected to them, 1840
TUSHEPAHAS, and OOTLASHOOTS, 5,600 in 1820, on Clark's and Missouri Rivers.
TUSCARORA, on Neus r., N. Carolina, till 1712; a few now in Lewiston, Niagara r.
TUTELOES. See MANGOAKS, or MANGOAGS.
TUTSEEWA, on a river W. Rocky Mts., supposed to be a branch of the Columbia.
TWIGHTWEES, (Miamies,) in 1780, on the Great Miami; so called by the Iroquois.

UCHEE, once on Chattauchee r., 4 towns; some went to Florida, some west.
UFALLAH, (Seminoles,) 670 in 1820, 12 m. above Fort Gaines, on Chattahoochee r.
UGALJACHMUTZI, a tribe about Prince William's Sound, N. W. coast.
ULSEAH, on coast of the Pacific, S. Columbia, beyond the Neekeetoos; 150 in 1820
UNALACHTGO, one of the three tribes once composing the Lenna Lenape.
UNAMIES, the head tribe of Lenna Lenape.
UNCHAGOGS, a tribe anciently on Long Island, New York.
UPSAROKA, (Minetare,) commonly called Crows.

WAAKICUM, 30 m. up Columbia River, opposite the Cathlamats; 400 in 1836
WABINGA, (Iroquois,) between W. branch of Delaware and Hudson r.
WACO, (Panis,) 800 in 1820, on Brazos River, 24 m. from its mouth.
WAHOWPUMS, on N. branch Columbia River, from Lapage r. upward; 700 in 1806.
WAHPATONE, (Sioux,) rove in the country on N. W. side St. Peter's River.
WAHPACOOTA, (Sioux ?) in the country S. W. St. Peter's in 1805; never stationary.
WAMESITS, (Nipmuks,) once on Merrimac River, where Lowell, Mass., now is.
WAMPANOAG, perhaps the 3d nation in importance in N. E. when settled by the Eng
WAPPINGS, at and about Esopus in 1758; also across the Hudson to the Minsi.
WARANANCONGUINS, supposed to be the same as the Wappings.
WASHAWS, on Barrataria Island in 1680, considerable; 1805, at Bay St. Fosh, 5 only.
WATANONS, or WEAS. See OUIATINONS.
WATEREES, once on the river of that name in S. Carolina, but long since extinct.
WATEPANETO, on the Padouca fork of the Platte, near Rocky Mts.; 900 in 1820.

WAWENOKS, (Abenakies,) once from Sagadahock to St. George River, in Maine.
WAXSAW, once in S. Carolina, 45 m. above Camden; name still continues.
WEAS, or WAAS, (Kikapoos.) See OUIATANONS.
WEKISA, (Semin.,) 250 in 1820, W. side Chattahoochee, 4 m. above the Cheskitaloas.
WELCH, said to be on a southern branch of the Missouri.
WESTOES, in 1670, on Ashley and Edisto Rivers, in S. Carolina.
WETEPAHATO, with the Kiawas, in 70 lodges in 1805, Padouca fork of Platte River.
WHEELPO, on Clark's River, from the mouth of the Lastaw; 2,500 in 1820; W. R.
WHIRLPOOLS, (Chikamaugas,) so called from the place of their residence.
WHITE, W. of Mississippi River; mentioned by many travellers.
WIGHCOMOCOS, one of the six tribes in Virginia in 1607, mentioned by Smith.
WILLEWAHS, (Chopunnish,) 500 in 1820, on Willewah r., which falls into Lewis's.
WINNEBAGO, on S. side Lake Michigan until 1832; Ottagamies, &c.
WOLF, Loups of the French; several nations had tribes so called.
WOKKON, 2 leagues from the Tuscaroras in 1701; long since extinct.
WOLLAWALLA, on Columbia r., from above Muscleshell Rapids, W. Rocky Mts.
WYANDOTS, (Hurons,) a great seat at Sandusky in 1780; warlike.
WYCOMES, on the Susquehannah in 1648, with some Oneidas, 250.
WYNIAWS, a small tribe in N. Carolina in 1701.

YAMACRAW, at the bluff of their name in 1732, near Savannah, about 140 men.
YAMASEE, S. border of S. Carolina; nearly destroyed in 1715 by English.
YAMPERACK, (Camanches,) 3 tribes about sources Brazos, del Norte, &c.; 1817, 30,000.
YANKTONS, in the plane country adjacent to E. side of the Rocky Mountains.
YATTASSEE, in Louisiana, 50 m. from Natchitoches, on a creek falling into Red r.
YAZOOS, formerly upon the river of their name; extinct in 1770.
YEAHTENTANEE, on banks St. Joseph's r., which flows into L. Michigan, in 1760.
YEHAH, above the rapids of the Columbia in 1820; 2,800, with some others.
YELETPOO, (Chopunnish,) 250 in 1820, on Weancum r., under S. W. Mountain.
YOUICOME, on the Pacific, next N. of the mouth of Columbia River; 700 in 1820.

BIOGRAPHY AND HISTORY

OF THE

INDIANS OF NORTH AMERICA.

BOOK I.

BOOK 1.

ORIGIN, ANTIQUITIES, MANNERS AND CUSTOMS, &c. OF THE AMERICAN INDIANS.

O could their ancient Incas rise again,
How would they take up Israel's taunting strain!
Art thou too fallen, Iberia? Do we see
The robber and the murderer weak as we?
Thou, that hast wasted earth, and dared despise
Alike the wrath and mercy of the skies,
Thy pomp is in the grave, thy glory laid
Low in the pits thine avarice has made.
We come with joy from our eternal rest,
To see the oppressor in his turn oppressed.
Art thou the God, the thunder of whose hand
Rolled over all our desolated land,
Shook principalities and kingdoms down,
And made the mountains tremble at his frown?
The sword shall light upon thy boasted powers,
And waste them as they wasted ours
'Tis thus Omnipotence his law fulfils,
And vengeance executes what justice wills.—COWPER

CHAPTER I.

Origin of the name Indian.—Why applied to the people found in America.—Ancient authors supposed to have referred to America in their writings—Theopompus Voyage of Hanno—Diodorus Siculus—Plato—Aristotle—Seneca.

THE name *Indian* was erroneously applied to the original man of America* by its first discoverers. The attempt to arrive at the East Indies by sailing west, caused the discovery of the islands and continent of America. When they were at first discovered, *Columbus*, and many after him, supposed they had arrived at the eastern shore of the continent of India, and hence the people they found there were called *Indians*. The error was not discovered until the name had so obtained, that it could not well be changed. It is true, that it matters but little to us by what name the indigenes of a country are known, and especially those of America, in as far as the name is seldom used among us but in application to the aboriginal Americans. But with the people of Europe it was not so unimportant. Situated between the two countries, India and America, the same name for the inhabitants of both must, at first, have produced considerable inconvenience, if not confusion; because, in speaking of an *Indian*, no one would know whether an American or a Zealander was meant, unless by the context of the discourse. Therefore, in a historical point of view, the error is, at least, as much to be deplored as that the name of the continent itself should have been derived from *Americus* instead of *Columbus.*

* So named from *Vesputius Americus*, a Florentine, who made a discovery of some part of the coast of South America in 1499, two years after *Cabot* had explored the coast of North America; but *Americus* had the fortune to confer his name upon both

It has been the practice of almost every writer, who has written about the primitive inhabitants of a country, to give some wild theories of others, concerning their origin, and to close the account with his own; which generally has been more visionary, if possible, than those of his predecessors. Long, laborious, and, we may add, useless disquisitions have been daily laid before the world, from the discovery of America by *Columbus* to the present time, to endeavor to explain by what means the inhabitants got from the old to the new world. To act, therefore, in unison with many of our predecessors, we will begin as far back as they have done, and so shall commence with *Theopompus* and others, from intimations in whose writings it is alleged the ancients had knowledge of America, and therefore peopled it.

Theopompus, a learned historian and orator, who flourished in the time of *Alexander* the Great, in a book entitled *Thaumasia*, gives a sort of dialogue between *Midas* the Phrygian and *Silenus*. The book itself is lost, but *Strabo* refers to it, and *Ælianus* has given us the substance of the dialogue which follows. After much conversation, *Silenus* said to *Midas*, that Europe, Asia and Africa were but islands surrounded on all sides by the sea; but that there was a continent situated beyond these, which was of immense dimensions, even without limits; and that it was so luxuriant, as to produce animals of prodigious magnitude, and men grew to double the height of themselves, and that they lived to a far greater age;* that they had many great cities; and their usages and laws were different from ours; that in one city there was more than a million of inhabitants; that gold and silver were there in vast quantities.† This is but an abstract from *Ælianus's* extract, but contains all of it that can be said to refer to a country west of Europe and Africa.‡ *Ælian* or *Ælianus* lived about A. D. 200.

Hanno flourished when the Carthaginians were in their greatest prosperity, but the exact time is unknown. Some place his times 40, and others 140, years before the founding of Rome, which would be about 800 years before our era.§ He was an officer of great enterprise, having sailed around and explored the coast of Africa, set out from the Pillars of Hercules, now called the Straits of Gibraltar, and sailed westward 30 days. Hence it is inferred by many, that he must have visited America, or some of its islands. He wrote a book, which he entitled *Periplus*, giving an account of his voyages, which was translated and published about 1533, in Greek.‖

Many, and not without tolerably good reasons, believe that an island or continent existed in the Atlantic Ocean about this period, but which disappeared afterwards.

---

* *Buffon* and *Raynal* either had not read this story, or they did not believe it to have been America; for they taught that all animals degenerated here. Many of the first adventurers to the coasts of unknown countries reported them inhabited by giants. *Swift* wrote *Gulliver's* Travels to bring such accounts into ridicule. How well he succeeded is evident from a comparison of books of voyages and travels before and after his time. *Dubartas* has this passage:—

"Our fearless sailors, in far voyages
(More led by gain's hope than their compasses),
On th' Indian shore have sometime noted some
Whose bodies covered two broad acres room;
And in the South Sea they have also seen
Some like high-topped and huge-armed treen;
And other some, whose monstrous backs did bear
Two mighty wheels, with whirling spokes, that were
Much like the winged and wide-spreading sails
Of any wind-mill turned with merry gales."
Divine Weeks, p. 117, ed. 4to, 1613.

† Ælian Variar. Historiar. lib. iii. chap. viii.

‡ Since the text was written, there has come into my hands a copy of a translation of Ælian's work, "in Englishe (as well according to the truth of the Greeke texte, as of the Latine), by *Abraham Fleming*." London, 1576, 4to. It differs not materially from the above, which is given from a French version of it.

§ Encyclopædia Perthensis.

‖ The best account of *Hanno* and his voyages, with which we are acquainted, is to be found in *Mariana's* Hist. of Spain, vol. i. 93, 109, 119, 122, 133, and 150, ed. Paris, 1725, 5 vols. 4to.

Diodorus Siculus says that some "Phœnicians were cast upon a most fertile island opposite to Africa." Of this, he says, they kept the most studied secrecy, which was doubtless occasioned by their jealousy of the advantage the discovery might be to the neighboring nations, and which they wished to secure wholly to themselves. *Diodorus Siculus* lived about 100 years before *Christ* Islands lying west of Europe and Africa are certainly mentioned by *Homer* and *Horace*. They were called *Atlantides*, and were supposed to be about 10,000 furlongs from Africa. Here existed the poets' fabled Elysian fields. But to be more particular with *Diodorus*, we will let him speak for himself "After having passed the islands which lie beyond the Herculean Strait, we will speak of those which lie much farther into the ocean. Towards Africa, and to the west of it, is an immense island in the broad sea, many days' sail from Lybia. Its soil is very fertile, and its surface variegated with mountains and valleys. Its coasts are indented with many navigable rivers, and its fields are well cultivated; delicious gardens, and various kinds of plants and trees." He finally sets it down as the finest country known, where the inhabitants have spacious dwellings, and every thing in the greatest plenty. To say the least of this account of *Diodorus*, it corresponds very well with that given of the Mexicans when first known to the Spaniards, but perhaps it will compare as well with the Canaries.

Plato's account has more weight, perhaps, than any of the ancients. He lived about 400 years before the Christian era. A part of his account is as follows:—"In those first times [time of its being first known], the Atlantic was a most broad island, and there were extant most powerful kings in it, who, with joint forces, appointed to occupy Asia and Europe: And so a most grievous war was carried on; in which the Athenians, with the common consent of the Greeks, opposed themselves, and they became the conquerors But that Atlantic island, by a flood and earthquake, was indeed suddenly destroyed, and so that warlike people were swallowed up." He adds, in another place, "An island in the mouth of the sea, in the passage to those straits, called the Pillars of *Hercules*, did exist; and that island was greater and larger than Lybia and Asia; from which there was an easy passage over to other islands, and from those islands to that continent, which is situated out of that region." * "*Neptune* settled in this island, from whose son, *Atlas*, its name was derived, and divided it among his ten sons. To the youngest fell the extremity of the island, called *Gadir*, which, in the language of the country, signifies *fertile* or *abounding in sheep*. The descendants of *Neptune* reigned here, from father to son, for a great number of generations in the order of primogeniture, during the space of 9000 years. They also possessed several other islands; and, passing into Europe and Africa, subdued all Lybia as far as Egypt, and all Europe to Asia Minor. At length the island sunk under water; and for a long time afterwards the sea thereabouts was full of rocks and shelves." † This account, although mixed with fable, cannot, we think, be entirely rejected; and that the ancients had knowledge of countries westward of Europe appears as plain and as well authenticated as any passage of history of that period.

Aristotle, or the author of a book which is generally attributed to him, ‡ speaks of an island beyond the Straits of Gibraltar; but the passage savors something of hearsay, and is as follows:—"Some say that, beyond the Pillars of *Hercules*, the Carthaginians have found a very fertile island, but without inhabitants, full of forests, navigable rivers, and fruit in abundance. It is several days' voyage from the main land. Some Carthaginians, charmed by the fertility of the country, thought to marry and settle there; but some say that the government of Carthage forbid the settlement upon pain of death, from the fear that it would increase in power so as to deprive the mother-country of her possessions there." If *Aristotle* had uttered this as a prediction,

* America known to the Ancients, 10, 8vo. Boston, 1773.

† Encyclopædia Perthensis, art. ATLANTIS.

‡ De mirabil. auscultat. Opera, vol. i. *Voltaire* says of this book, "On en fesait honneur aux Carthaginois, et on citait un livre d'Aristote qu'il n'a pas composé." *Essai sur les Mœurs et l'esprit des nations*, chap. cxlv. p. 703. vol. iv. of his works. Edit. Paris, 1817, in 8vo.

that such a thing would take place in regard to some future nation, no one, perhaps, would have called him a false prophet, for the American revolution would have been its fulfilment. This philosopher lived about 384 years before *Christ.*

Seneca lived about the commencement of the vulgar era. He wrote tragedies, and in one of them occurs this passage:—

> ————————" Venient annis
> Sæcula seris, quibus oceanus
> Vincula rerum laxet, et ingens
> Pateat tellus, Typhisque novos
> Detegat orbes; nec sit terris
> Ultima Thule."
>
> *Medea, Act* 3. v. 375.

This is nearer prophecy, and may be rendered in English thus:—" The time will come when the ocean will loosen the chains of nature, and we shall behold a vast country. A new Typhis shall discover new worlds: Thule shall no longer be considered the last country of the known world."

Not only these passages from the ancient authors have been cited and recited by moderns, but many more, though less to the point, to show that, in some way or other, America must have been peopled from some of the eastern continents. Almost every country has claimed the honor of having been its first discoverer, and hence the progenitor of the Indians. But since the recent discoveries in the north, writers upon the subject say but little about getting over inhabitants from Europe, Asia, or Africa, through the difficult way of the Atlantic seas and islands, as it is much easier to pass them over the narrow channels of the north in canoes, or upon the ice. *Grotius, C. Mather, Hubbard,* and after them *Robertson,* are glad to meet with so easy a method of solving a question which they consider as having puzzled their predecessors so much.

CHAPTER II.

Of modern theorists upon the peopling of America—St. Gregory—Herrera—T. Morton—Williamson—Wood—Josselyn—Thorowgood—Adair—R. Williams—C. Mather—Hubbard—Robertson—Smith—Voltaire—Mitchill—M'Culloch—Lord Kaim—Swinton—Cabrera.

St. Gregory, who flourished in the 7th century, in an epistle to St. *Clement,* said that beyond the ocean there was another world.*

Herrera argues, that the new world could not have been known to the ancients; and that what *Seneca* has said was not true. For that *God* had kept it hid from the old world, giving them no certain knowledge of it; and that, in the secrecy and incomprehensibility of his providence, he has been pleased to give it to the Castilian nation. That Seneca's prediction (if so it may be considered) was a false one, because he said that a new world would be discovered in the north, and that it was found in the west.† *Herrera* wrote about 1598,‡ before which time little knowledge was obtained of North America. This may account for his impeachment of *Seneca's* prophecy.

Thomas Morton, who came to New England in 1622, published in 1637 an account of its natural history, with much other curious matter. In speaking upon the peopling of America, he thinks it altogether out of the question to

* "S. Gregoire sur l'epistre de S. Clement, dit que passé l'ocean, il y a vn autre mond." (*Herrera,* I Decade, 2.) This is the whole passage.

† Ibid. 3.

‡ He died 27 March, 1625, at the age of about 66 years. His name was *Tordesillas Antonio de Herrera*—one of the best Spanish historians. His history of the voyages to, and settlement of America is very minute, and very valuable. The original in Spanish is very rare. *Acosta's* translation (into French) 3 v. 4to., 1660, is also scarce and valuable. It is this we cite.

suppose that it was peopled by the Tartars from the north, because "a people once settled, must be removed by compulsion, or else tempted thereunto in hopes of better fortunes, upon commendations of the place unto which they should be drawn to remove. And if it may be thought that these people came over the frozen sea, then would it be by compulsion. If so, then by whom, or when? Or what part of this main continent may be thought to border upon the country of the Tartars? It is yet unknown; and it is not like that a people well enough at ease, will, of their own accord, undertake to travel over a sea of ice, considering how many difficulties they shall encounter with. As, 1st, whether there be any land at the end of their unknown way, no land being in view; then want of food to sustain life in the mean time upon that sea of ice. Or how shall they do for fuel, to keep them at night from freezing to death? which will not be had in such a place. But it may perhaps be granted, that the natives of this country might originally come of the scattered Trojans; for after that *Brutus*, who was the fourth from *Eneas*, left Latium upon the conflict held with the Latins (where although he gave them a great overthrow, to the slaughter of their grand captain and many others of the heroes of Latium, yet he held it more safely to depart unto some other place and people, than, by staying, to run the hazard of an unquiet life or doubtful conquest; which, as history maketh mention, he performed.) This people was dispersed, there is no question, but the people that lived with him, by reason of their conversation with the Grecians and Latins, had a mixed language, that participated of both."* This is the main ground of *Morton*, but he says much more upon the subject; as that the similarity of the languages of the Indians to the Greek and Roman is very great. From the examples he gives, we presume he knew as little about the Indian languages as Dr. *Mather Adair*, and *Boudinot*, who thought them almost to coincide with the Hebrew. Though *Morton* thinks it very improbable that the Tartars came over by the north from Asia, because they could not see land beyond the ice, yet he finds no difficulty in getting them across the wide Atlantic, although he allows them no compass. That the Indians have a Latin origin he thinks evident, because he fancied he heard among their words *Pasco-pan*, and hence thinks, without doubt, their ancestors were acquainted with the god *Pan*.†

Dr. *Williamson*‡ says, "It can hardly be questioned that the Indians of South America are descended from a class of the Hindoos, in the southern parts of Asia." That they could not have come from the north, because the South American Indians are unlike those of the north. This seems to clash with the more rational views of Father *Venegas*.§ He writes as follows: "Of all the parts of America hitherto discovered, the Californians lie nearest to Asia. We are acquainted with the mode of writing in all the eastern nations. We can distinguish between the characters of the Japanese, the Chinese, the Chinese Tartars, the Mogul Tartars, and other nations extending as far as the Bay of Kamschathka; and learned dissertations on them, by Mr. *Boyer*, are to be found in the acts of the imperial academy of sciences at Petersburg. What discovery would it be to meet with any of these characters, or others like them, among the American Indians nearest to Asia! But as to the Californians, if ever they were possessed of any invention to perpetuate their memoirs, they have entirely lost it; and all that is now found among them, amounts to no more than some obscure oral traditions, probably more and more adulterated by a long succession of time. They have not so much as retained any knowledge of the particular country from which they emigrated." This is the account of one who lived many years among the Indians of California.

Mr. *William Wood*,‖ who left New England in 1633,¶ after a short stay, says, "Of their language, which is only peculiar to themselves, not inclining to any of the refined tongues: Some have thought they might be of the dispersed

* New Canaan, book i, pages 17 and 18. † Ibid. 18.

‡ In his Hist. N. Carolina, i. 216.

§ Hist. California, i. 60. His work was published at Madrid, in 1758.

‖ The author of a work entitled *New England's Prospect*, published in London, 1634, in 4to. It is a very rare, and, in some respects, a curious and valuable work.

¶ Prospect, 51.

Jews, because some of their words be near unto the Hebrew but by the sam rule, they may conclude them to be some of the gleanings of all nations, because they have words which sound after the Greek, Latin, French, and other tongues."*

Mr. *John Josselyn*, who resided some time in New England, from the year 1638, says, "The Mohawks are about 500: their speech a dialect of the Tartars (as also is the Turkish tongue)."† In another work,‡ he says, "N. England is by some affirmed to be an island, bounded on the north with the River of Canada (so called from Monsieur *Cane*), on the south with the River Monhegan or *Hudson's* River, so called because he was the first that discovered it. Some will have America to be an island, which out of question must needs be, if there be a north-east passage found out into the South Sea. It contains 1,152,400,000 acres. The discovery of the north-west passage (which lies within the River of Canada) was undertaken with the help of some Protestant Frenchmen, which left Canada, and retired to Boston about the year 1669. The north-east people of America, that is, N. England, &c., are judged to be Tartars, called Samoades, being alike in complexion, shape, habit and manners." We have given here a larger extract than the immediate subject required, because we would let the reader enjoy his curiosity, as well as we ours, in seeing how people understood things in that day. *Barlow*, looking but a small distance beyond those times, with great elegance says,—

> "In those blank periods, where no man can trace
> The gleams of thought that first illumed his race,
> His errors, twined with science, took their birth,
> And forged their fetters for this child of earth,
> And when, as oft, he dared expand his view,
> And work with nature on the line she drew,
> Some monster, gendered in his fears, unmanned
> His opening soul, and marred the works he planned.
> Fear, the first passion of his helpless state,
> Redoubles all the woes that round him wait,
> Blocks nature's path, and sends him wandering wide,
> Without a guardian, and without a guide."
>
> *Columbiad*, ix. 137, &c.

Reverend *Thomas Thorowgood* published a small quarto, in 1652,§ to prove that the Indians were the Jews, who had been "lost in the world for the space of near 2000 years." But whoever has read *Adair* or *Boudinot*, has, beside a good deal that is irrational, read all that in *Thorowgood* can be termed rational.

Reverend *Roger Williams* was, at one time, as appears from *Thorowgood's* work,‖ of the same opinion. Being written to for his opinion of the origin of the natives, "he kindly answers to those letters from Salem in N. Eng. 20th of the 10th month, more than 10 yeers since, *in hæc verba*." That they did not come into America from the north-east, as some had imagined, he thought evident for these reasons: 1. their ancestors affirm they came from the southwest, and return thence when they die: 2. because they "separate their women in a little wigwam by themselves in their feminine seasons:" and 3. "beside their god *Kuttand* to the S. West, they hold that *Nanawitnawit*¶ (*a god over head*) made the heavens and the earth; and some tast of affinity with the Hebrew I have found."

Doctor *Cotton Mather* is an author of such singular qualities, that we almost hesitate to name him, lest we be thought without seriousness in so weighty a matter. But we will assure the reader, that he is an author with whom we would in no wise part; and if sometimes we appear not serious in our introduction of him, what is of more importance, we believe *him* really to be so. And we are persuaded that we should not be pardoned did we not allow him to speak upon the matter before us.

---

* Ibid. 112. ed. 1764.
† His account of two voyages to New England, printed London, 1673, page 124.
‡ New England Rarities. 4, 5, printed London, 1672.
§ Its title commences, "*Digitus Dei: New Discoveries, with sure Arguments to prove*," &c.
‖ Pages 5 and 6.
¶ *Getannitowit* is god in Delaware.—*Heckewelder*

He says, "It should not pass without remark, that *three* most memorable things which have borne a very great aspect upon *human affairs*, did, near the same time, namely, at the conclusion of the *fifteenth*, and the beginning of the *sixteenth*, century, arise unto the world: the first was the *Resurrection of Literature;* the second was the opening of *America;* the third was the *Reformation of Religion*." Thus far we have an instructive view of the subject, calculated to lead to the conclusion that, in the dark ages, when literature was neglected and forgotten, discoveries might have been also, and hence the knowledge of America lost for a time. The reader must now summon his gravity. "But," this author continues, "as probably the *Devil*, seducing the first inhabitants of America into it, therein aimed at the having of them and their posterity out of the sound of the *silver trumpets* of the gospel, then to be heard through the Roman empire.* If the *Devil* had any expectation, that, by the peopling of America, he should utterly deprive any Europeans of the two benefits, *literature and religion*, which dawned upon the miserable world, (one just *before*, the other just *after*,) the first famed navigation hither, 'tis to be hoped he will be disappointed of that expectation."† The learned doctor, having forgotten what he had written in his first book, or wishing to inculcate his doctrine more firmly, nearly repeats a passage which he had at first given, in a distant part of his work; ‡ but, there being considerable addition, we recite it: "The natives of the country now possessed by the Newenglanders, had been forlorn and wretched *heathen* ever since their first herding here; and though we know not *when* or *how* these Indians first became inhabitants of this mighty continent, yet we may guess that probably the *Devil* decoyed those miserable salvages hither, in hopes that the gospel of the Lord Jesus Christ would never come here to destroy or disturb his absolute empire over them. But our Eliot was in such ill terms with the *Devil*, as to alarm him with sounding the *silver trumpets* of heaven in his territories, and make some noble and zealous attempts towards outing him of ancient possessions here. There were, I think, 20 several *nations* (if I may call them so) of Indians upon that spot of ground which fell under the influence of our *Three United Colonies;* and our *Eliot* was willing to rescue as many of them as he could from that old usurping *landlord* of America, who is, *by the wrath of God*, the prince of this world." In several places he is decided in the opinion that Indians are Scythians, and is confirmed in the opinion, on meeting with this passage of *Julius Cæsar:* "*Difficilius Invenire quam interficere*," which he thus renders, "It is harder to find them than to foil them." At least, this is a happy application of the passage. *Cæsar* was speaking of the Scythians, and our historian applies the passage in speaking of the sudden attacks of the Indians, and their agility in hiding themselves from pursuit.§ Doctor Mather wrote at the close of the seventeenth century, and his famous book, *Magnalia Christi Americana*, was published in 1702.

Adair, who resided 40 years (he says) among the southern Indians, previous to 1775, published a huge quarto upon their origin, history, &c. He tortures every custom and usage into a like one of the Jews, and almost every word in their language into a Hebrew one of the same meaning.

Doctor *Boudinot*, in his book called "The Star in the West," has followed up the theory of Adair, with such certainty, as he thinks, as that the "long lost ten tribes of Israel" are clearly identified in the American Indians. Such

---

* This, we apprehend, is not entirely original with our author, but borders upon plagiarism. *Ward*, the celebrated author of the "*Simple Cobler of Aggawam*," says of the Irish, "These Irish (anciently called *anthropophagi*, man-eaters) have a tradition among them, that when the Devil showed our Saviour all the kingdoms of the earth, and their glory, that he would not show him Ireland, but reserved it for himself. It is, probably, true; for he hath kept it ever since for his own peculiar: the *old fox* foresaw it would eclipse the glory of all the rest: he thought it wisdom to keep the land for a Boggards for his unclean spirits employed in this hemisphere, and the people to do his son and heir (the Pope) that service for which *Lewis* the XI kept his Barbor Oliver, which makes them so bloodthirsty."—*Simp. Cobler*, 86, 87. Why so much gall is poured out upon the poor Irish, we cannot satisfactorily account. The circumstance of his writing in the time of *Cromwell* will explain a part, if not the whole of the enigma. He was the first minister of Ipswich, Massachusetts, but was born and died in England.

† Magnalia Christ. Amer. b. i. ‡ Ibid. b. iii. § See Magnalia, b. vii.

theories have gained many supporters. It is of much higher antiquity than *Adair*, and was treated as such visionary speculations should be by authors as far back as the historian *Hubbard*, who wrote about 1680, and has this among other passages: "If any observation be made of their manners and dispositions, it's easier to say from what nations they did not, than from whom they did, derive their original. Doubtless their conjecture who fancy them to be descended from the ten tribes of the Israelites, carried captive by *Salamaneser* and *Esarhaddon*, hath the least show of reason of any other, there being no footsteps to be observed of their propinquity to them more than to any other of the tribes of the earth, either as to their language or manners."* This author was one of the best historians of his times; and, generally, he writes with as much discernment upon other matters as upon this.

That because the natives of one country and those of another, and each unknown to the other, have some customs and practices in common, it has been urged by some, and not a few, that they must have had a common origin; but this, in our apprehension, does not necessarily follow. Who will pretend that different people, when placed under similar circumstances, will not have similar wants, and hence similar actions? that like wants will not prompt like exertions? and like causes produce *not* like effects? This mode of reasoning we think sufficient to show, that, although the Indians may have some customs in common with the Scythians, the Tartars, Chinese, Hindoos, Welsh, and indeed every other nation, still, the former, for any reason we can see to the contrary, have as good right to claim to themselves priority of origin as either or all of the latter.

Doctor *Robertson* should have proved that people of color produce others of no color, and the contrary, before he said, "We know with infallible certainty, that all the human race spring from the same source,"† meaning *Adam*. He founds this broad assertion upon the false notion that, to admit any other would be an inroad upon the verity of the holy Scriptures. Now, in our view of the subject, we leave them equally inviolate in assuming a very different ground;‡ namely, that all habitable parts of the world may have been peopled at the same time, and by different races of men. That it *is* so peopled, we *know:* that it *was* so peopled as far back as we have any account, we see no reason to disbelieve. Hence, when it *was not* so is as futile to inquire, as it would be impossible to conceive of the annihilation of space. When a new country was discovered, much inquiry was made to ascertain from whence came the inhabitants found upon it—not even asking whence came the other animals. The answer to us is plain. Man, the other animals, trees and plants of every kind, were placed there by the supreme directing hand, which carries on every operation of nature by fixed and undeviating laws. This, it must be plain to every reader, is, at least, as reconcilable to the Bible history as the theory of *Robertson*, which is that of *Grotius*, and all those who have followed them.

When it has been given in, at least by all who have thought upon the subject, that climate does not change the complexion of the human race, to hold up the idea still that all must have sprung from the same source, (*Adam*,) only reminds us of our grandmothers, who to this day laugh at us when we tell them that the earth is a globe. Who, we ask, will argue that the negro changes his color by living among us, or by changing his latitude? Who have ever become negroes by living in their country, or among them? Has the Indian ever changed his complexion by living in London? Do those change which adopt our manners and customs, and are surrounded by us? Until these questions can be answered in the affirmative, we discard altogether that *unitarian* system of peopling the world. We would indeed prefer *Ovid's* method:—

> "Ponere duritiem cœpere, suumque rigorem
> Mollirique mora, mollitaque ducere formam
> Mox ubi creverunt, naturaque mitior illis
> Contigit," &c. &c.
>
> *Metamor.* lib 1. fab. xi.

* Hist. New England, 27. † Hist. America, book iv.

‡ Why talk of a theory's clashing with holy writ, and say nothing of the certainty of the sciences of geography, astronomy, geology, &c.?

That is, *Deucalion* and *Pyrrha* performed the office by travelling over the country and picking up stones, which, as they cast them over their heads, became young people as they struck the earth.

We mean not to be understood that the exterior of the skin of people is not changed by climate, for this is very evident; but that the children of persons would be any lighter or darker, whose residence is in a climate different from that in which they were born, is what we deny, as in the former case. As astonishing as it may appear to the succinct reasoner, it is no less true, that Dr. *Samuel Stanhope Smith* has put forth an octavo book of more than 400 pages to prove the *unity*, as he expresses it, 'of the human race,' that is, that all were originally descended from one man. His reasoning is of this tenor: "The American and European sailor reside equally at the pole, and under the equator." Then, in a triumphant air, he demands—"Why then should we, without necessity, assume the hypothesis that originally there existed different species of the human kind?"* What kind of argument is contained here we leave the reader to make out; and again, when he would prove that all the human family are of the same tribe, he says that negro slaves at the south, who live in white families, are gradually found to conform in features to the whites with whom they live!† Astonishing! and we wonder who, if any, knew this, beside the author. Again, and we have done with our extraordinary philosopher. He is positive that deformed or disfigured persons will, in process of time, produce offspring marked in the same way. That is, if a man practise flattening his nose, his offspring will have a flatter nose than he would have had, had his progenitor not flattened his; and so, if this offspring repeat the process, his offspring will have a less prominent nose; and so on, until the nose be driven entirely off the face! In this, certainly, our author has taken quite a roundabout way to vanquish or put to flight a nose. We wish he could tell us how many ages or generations it would take to make this formidable conquest. Now, for any reason we can see to the contrary, it would be a much less tedious business to cut off a member at once, and thus accomplish the object in a short period; for to wait several generations for a fashion seems absurd in the extreme. A man must be monstrously blind to his prejudices, to maintain a doctrine like this. As well might he argue that colts would be tailless because it has long been the practice to shorten the tails of horses, of both sexes; but we have never heard that colts' tails are in the least affected by this practice which has been performed on the horse so long.‡ Certainly, if ever, we should think it time to discover something of it! Nor have we ever heard that a female child has ever been born with its ears bored, although its ancestors have endured the painful operation for many generations—and here we shall close our examination of Mr. *Smith's* 400 pages.§

People delight in new theories, and often hazard a tolerable reputation for the sake of exhibiting their abilities upon a subject on which they have very vague, or no clear conceptions. Had Dr. *Smith* read the writings of Sir *Thomas Brown*, he could hardly have advanced such absurd opinions as we have before noticed; if, indeed, he were possessed of a sane mind. Dr. *Brown* was of the age previous to that in which *Buffon* lived. In speaking of complexion, he says, "If the fervor of the sun were the sole cause hereof, in Ethiopia, or any land of negroes, it were also reasonable that inhabitants of the same latitude, subjected unto the same vicinity of the sun, the same diurnal arch and direction of its rays, should also partake of the same hue and complexion, which, notwithstanding, they do not. For the inhabitants of the same latitude in Asia are of a different complexion, as are the inhabitants of Cambogia and Java; insomuch that some conceive the negro is properly a native of Africa; and that those places in Asia, inhabited now by

---

* Smith on Complexion, N. Brunswick, N. J. 1810, p. 11. † Ibid. 170, 171.

‡ The author pleads not guilty to the charge of plagiarism; for it was not until some months after the text was written, that he knew that even this idea had occurred to any one. He has since read an extract very similar, in Dr. Lawrence's valuable Lectures on Zoology, &c.

§ On reflection, we have thought our remarks rather pointed, as Mr. *Smith* is not a living author; but what called them forth must be their apology.

Moors, are but the intrusions of negroes, arriving first from Africa, as we generally conceive of Madagascar, and the adjoining islands, who retain the same complexion unto this day. But this defect [of latitude upon complexion] is more remarkable in America, which, although subjected unto both the tropics, yet are not the inhabitants black between, or near, or under either: neither to the southward in Brazil, Chili, or Peru; nor yet to the northward in Hispaniola, Castilia, del Oro, or Nicaragua. And although in many parts thereof, there be at present, swarms of negroes, serving under the Spaniard, yet were they all transported from Africa, since the discovery of Columbus, and are not indigenous, or proper natives of America." *

Hence it is evident, that 200 years before Dr. *Smith* wrote, the notion that situation of place affected materially the color of the human species, was very justly set down among the "vulgar and common errors" of the times.

Another theory, almost as wild, and quite as ridiculous, respecting the animals of America, as that advanced by Dr. *S. S. Smith*, seems here to present itself. We have reference to the well-known assertions of *Buffon* and *Raynal*, † two philosophers, who were an honor to the times of *Franklin*, which are, that man and other animals in America degenerate. ‡ This has been met in such a masterly manner by Mr. *Jefferson*, § that to repeat any thing here would be entirely out of place, since it has been so often copied into works on both sides of the Atlantic. It may even be found in some of the best English Encyclopædias. ‖

Smith ¶ does not deal fairly with a passage of *Voltaire*, relating to the peopling of America; as he takes only a part of a sentence to comment upon. Perhaps he thought it as much as he was capable of managing. ** The complete sentence to which we refer we translate as follows:—"There are found men and animals all over the habitable earth: who has put them upon it? We have already said, it is he who has made the grass grow in the fields; and we should be no more surprised to find in America men, than we should to find flies." †† We can discover no contradiction between this passage and another in a distant part of the same work; and which seems more like the passage Mr. *Smith* has cited:—"Some do not wish to believe that the caterpillars and the snails of one part of the world should be originally from an other part: wherefore be astonished, then, that there should be in America some kinds of animals, and some races of men like our own?" ‡‡

Voltaire has written upon the subject in a manner that will always be attracting, however much or little credence may be allowed to what he has written. We will, therefore, extract an entire article wherein he engages more professedly upon the question than in other parts of his works, in which he has rather incidentally spoken upon it. The chapter is as follows: §§—"Since many fail not to make systems upon the manner in which America has been peopled, it is left only for us to say, that he who created flies in those regions, created man there also. However pleasant it may be to dispute, it cannot be denied that the Supreme Being, who lives in all nature, ‖‖ has created about the 48° two-legged animals without feathers, the color of whose skin is a mixture of white and carnation, with long beards approaching to red; about the line, in Africa and its islands, negroes without beards; and

---

* "*Pseudodoxia Epidemica*: or Inquiries into very many Received Tenents, and commonly received Truths; together with the RELIGIO MEDICI. By *Thomas Brown*, Kt. M. D." Page 373, 6 edition, 4to London, 1672.

† After speaking of the effect of the climate of the old world in producing man and other animals in perfection, he adds, "Combien, au contraire, la nature paroît avoir négligé nouveau mond! Les hommes y sont moins forts, moins courageux; sans barbe et sans poil," &c.—*Histoire Philos. des deux Indes*, viii. 210. Ed. Geneva, 1781. 12 vols. 8vo.

‡ *Voltaire* does not say quite as much but says this:—"La nature enfin avait donné aux Americanes beaucoup moins d'industrie qu'aux hommes de l'ancien monde. Toutes ces causes ensemble ont pu nuire beaucoup à la population."—[*Œuvres*, iv. 19.] This is, however, only in reference to the Indians.

§ In his Notes on Virginia, Quer. vii.

‖ Perthensis, i. 637. (Art. AMER. § 33.)

¶ *Samuel Smith*, who published a history of New Jersey, in 1765, printed at Burlington.

** See Hist. N. J. 8.

†† Essai sur les Mœurs et l'Esprit des Nations. (Œuvres, iv. 18.)

‡‡ Ibid. 708.

§§ Œuvres, t. vii. 197, 198.

‖‖ Will the reader of this call *Voltaire* an atheist?

in the same latitude, other negroes with beards, some of them having wool and some hair on their heads; and among them other animals quite white, having neither hair nor wool, but a kind of white silk. It does not very clearly appear what should have prevented *God* from placing on another continent animals of the same species, of a copper color, in the same latitude in which, in Africa and Asia, they are found black; or even from making them without beards in the very same latitude in which others possess them. To what lengths are we carried by the rage for systems joined with the tyranny of prejudice! We see these animals; it is agreed that *God* has had the power to place them where they are; yet it is not agreed that he *has* so placed them. The same persons who readily admit that the *beavers* of Canada are of Canadian origin, assert that the men must have come there in boats, and that Mexico must have been peopled by some of the descendants of *Magog*. As well might it be said, that, if there be men in the moon, they must have been taken there by *Astolpho* on his hippogriff, when he went to fetch *Roland's* senses, which were corked up in a bottle. If America had been discovered in his time, and there had then been men in Europe *systematic* enough to have advanced, with the Jesuit *Lafitau*,* that the Caribbees descended from the inhabitants of Caria, and the Hurons from the Jews, he would have done well to have brought back the bottle containing the wits of these reasoners, which he would doubtless have found in the moon, along with those of *Angelica's* lover. The first thing done when an inhabited island is discovered in the Indian Ocean, or in the South Sea, is to inquire, Whence came these people? but as for the trees and the tortoises, *they* are, without any hesitation, pronounced to be indigenous; as if it were more difficult for nature to make men than to make tortoises. One thing, however, which seems to countenance this system, is, that there is scarcely an island in the eastern or western ocean, which does not contain jugglers, quacks, knaves, and fools. This, it is probable, gave rise to the opinion, that these animals are of the same race with ourselves."

Some account of what the Indians themselves have said upon the subject of their origin may be very naturally looked for in this place. Their notions in this respect can no more be relied upon than the fabled stories of the gods in ancient mythology. Indeed, their accounts of primitive inhabitants do not agree beyond their own neighborhood, and often disagree with themselves at different times. Some say their ancestors came from the north, others from the north-west, others from the east and others from the west; some from the regions of the air, and some fro under the earth. Hence to raise any theory upon any thing coming from them upon the subject, would show only that the theorist himself was as ignorant as his informants. We might as well ask the forest trees how they came planted upon the soil in which they grow. Not that the Indians are unintelligent in other affairs, any further than the necessary consequence growing out of their situation implies; nor are they less so than many who have written upon their history.

"In one grave maxim let us all agree—
Nature ne'er meant her secrets should be found,
And man's a riddle, which man can't expound!"
Paine's RULING PASSION.

The different notions of the Indians will be best gathered from their lives in their proper places in the following work.

Dr. *S. L. Mitchill*, of New York, a man who wrote learnedly, if not wisely, on almost every subject, has, in his opinion, like hundreds before him, set the great question, *How was America peopled?* at rest. He has no doubt but the Indians, in the first place, are of the same color originally as the north-eastern nations of Asia, and hence sprung from them. What time he settles them in the country he does not tell us, but gets them into Greenland about the year 8 or 900. Thinks he saw the Scandinavians as far as the shores of the St. Lawrence, but what time this was he does not say. He must of course make

* He wrote a history of the savages of America, and maintained that the Caribbee language was radically Hebrew.

these people the builders of the mounds scattered all over the western country. After all, we apprehend the doctor would have short time for his emigrants to do all that nature and art have done touching these matters. In the first place, it is evident that many ages passed away from the time these tumuli were begun until they were finished: 2d, a multitude of ages must have passed since the use for which they were reared has been known; for trees of the age of 200 years grow from the ruins of others which must have had as great age: and, 3d, no Indian nation or tribe has the least tradition concerning them.* This could not have happened had the ancestors of the present Indians been the erectors of them, in the nature of things.†

The observation of an author in Dr. *Rees's* Encyclopedia,‡ although saying no more than has been already said in our synopsis, is, nevertheless, so happy, that we should not feel clear to omit it:—"As to those who pretend that the human race has only of late found its way into America, by crossing the sea at Kamschatka, or the Straits of Tschutski, either upon the fields of ice or in canoes, they do not consider that this opinion, besides that it is extremely difficult of comprehension, has not the least tendency to diminish the prodigy; for it would be surprising indeed that one half of our planet should have remained without inhabitants during thousands of years, while the other half was peopled. What renders this opinion less probable is, that America is supposed in it to have had animals, since we cannot bring those species of animals from the old world which do not exist in it, as those of the tapir, the glama, and the tajactu. Neither can we admit of the recent organization of matter for the western hemisphere; because, independently of the accumulated difficulties in this hypothesis, and which can by no means be solved, we shall observe, that the fossil bones discovered in so many parts of America, and at such small depths, prove that certain species of animals, so far from having been recently organized, have been annihilated a long while ago."

Before we had known, that, if we were in error, it was in the company of philosophers, such as we have in this chapter introduced to our readers, we felt a hesitancy in avowing our opinions upon a matter of so great moment. But, after all, as it is only matter of honest opinion, no one should be intolerant, although he may be allowed to make himself and even his friends merry at our expense. When, in the days of *Chrysostom*, some ventured to assert their opinions of the rotundity of the earth, that learned father "did laugh at them." § And, when science shall have progressed sufficiently, (if it be possible,) to settle this question, there is a possibility that the *Chrysostoms* of these days will not have the same excuse for their infidelity. But as it is a day of prodigies, there is some danger of treating lightly even the most seemingly absurd conjectures. We therefore feel very safe, and more especially as it required considerable hardihood to laugh even at the theory of the late Mr. *Symmes*.

When we lately took up a book entitled "*Researches, Philosophical and Antiquarian, concerning the Aboriginal History of America*, by J. H. M'Culloh, Jr M. D." ‖ we did think, from the imposing appearance of it, that some new matters on the subject had been discovered; and more particularly when we read in the preface, that "his first object was to explain the origin of the men and animals of America, so far as that question is involved with the apparent physical impediments that have so long kept the subject in total obscurity." Now, with what success this has been done, to do the author justice, he shall speak for himself, and the reader then may judge for himself.

"Before we attempt to explain in what manner the men and animals of America reached this continent, it is necessary to ascertain, if possible, the circumstances of their original creation; for upon this essential particular depends the great interest of our present investigation. [We are not able to discover that he has said any thing further upon it.] It must be evident that we can arrive at no satisfactory conclusion, if it be doubtful whether the Creator of the universe made man and the animals but in one locality, from

* Or none but such as are at variance with all history and rationality.
† Archæologia Americana, i. 325, 326, 341, &c. ‡ Art. America
§ See Acosta's Hist. E. and W. Indies, p. 1. ed. London, 1604.
‖ Published at Baltimore, 1829, in 8vo.

whence they were dispersed over the earth; or whether he created them in each of those various situations where we now find them living. So far as this inquiry respects mankind, there can be no reasonable ground to doubt the one origin of the species. This fact may be proved both physically and morally. [If the reader can discover any thing that amounts to proof in what follows, he will have made a discovery that we could not.] That man, notwithstanding all the diversities of their appearance, are but of one species, is a truth now universally admitted by every physiological naturalist [That is, notwithstanding a negro be black, an Indian brown, a European white, still, they are all men. And then follows a quotation from Doctor *Lawrence** to corroborate the fact that men are all of one species.] It is true, this physiologist does not admit that the human species had their origin but from one pair; for he observes, the same species might have been created at the same time in very different parts of the earth. But when we have analyzed the moral history of mankind, to which Mr. *Lawrence* seems to have paid little attention, [and if our author has done it, we would thank him to show us where we can find it,] we find such strongly-marked analogies in abstract matters existing among nations the most widely separated from each other, that we cannot doubt there has been a time, when the whole human family have intimately participated in one common system of things, whether it be of truth or of error, of science or of prejudice. [This does not at all agree with what he says afterwards, 'We have been unable to discern any traces of Asiatic or of European civilization in America prior to the discovery of Columbus.' And again: 'In comparing the barbarian nations of America with those of the eastern continent, we perceive no points of resemblance between them, in their moral institutions or in their habits, that are not apparently founded in the necessities of human life.' If, then, there is no affinity, other than what would accidentally happen from similar circumstances, wherefore this prating about '*strongly-marked analogies*,' &c. just copied?] As respects the origin of animals, [we have given his best proofs of the origin of man and their transportation to America,] the subject is much more refractory. We find them living all over the surface of the earth, and suited by their physical conformity to a great variety of climates and peculiar localities. Every one will admit the impossibility of ascertaining the history of their original creation from the mere natural history of the animals themselves." Now, as "refractory" as this subject is, we did not expect to see it fathered off upon a miracle, because this was the easy and convenient manner in which the superstitious of every age accounted for every thing which they at once could not comprehend. And we do not expect, when it is gravely announced, that a discovery in any science is to be shown, that the undertaker is going to tell us it is accomplished by a miracle, and that, therefore, "he knows not why he should be called upon to answer objections," &c.

As it would be tedious to the reader, as well as incompatible with our plan, to quote larger from Mr. *M'Culloh's* book, we shall finish with him after a few remarks.

We do not object to the capacity of the ark for all animals, but we do object to its introduction in the question undertaken by Mr. *M'Culloh;* for every child knows that affair to have been miraculous; and if any part of the question depended upon the truth or falsity of a miracle, why plague the world with a book of some 500 pages, merely to promulgate such a belief, when a sentence would be all that is required? No one, that admits an overruling power, or the existence of God, will doubt of his ability to create a myriad of men, animals, and all matter, by a breath; or that an ark ten feet square could contain, comfortably, ten thousand men, as well as one of the dimensions given in Scripture to contain what that did. Therefore, if one in these days should make a book expressly to explain the cause of the different lengths of days, or the changes of the seasons, and find, after he had written a vast deal, that he could in no wise unravel the mystery, and, to close his account, declares it was all a miracle, such an author would be precisely in the predicament of Mr. *M'Culloh.*

* The celebrated author of Lectures on *Physiology, Zoology, and the Natural History of Man.*

We do not pretend that the subject can be pursued with the certainty of mathematical calculations; and so long as it is contended that the whole species of man spring from one pair, so long will the subject admit of controversy: therefore it makes but little or no difference whether the inhabitants are got into America by the north or the south, the east or the west, as it regards the main question. For it is very certain that, if there were but one pair originally, and these placed upon a certain spot, all other places where people are now found must have been settled by people from the primitive spot, who found their way thither, some how or other, and it is very unimportant how, as we have just observed.

Lord *Kaimes*, a writer of great good sense, has not omitted to say something upon this subject.* He very judiciously asks those who maintain that America was peopled from Kamskatka, whether the inhabitants of that region speak the same language with their American neighbors on the opposite shores. That they do not, he observes, is fully confirmed by recent accounts from thence; and "whence we may conclude, with great certainty, that the latter are not a colony of the former."† We have confirmation upon confirmation, that these nations speak languages entirely different; and for the satisfaction of the curious, we will give a short vocabulary of words in both, with the English against them.

English.	*Kamskadale.*	*Aléoutean.*‡
God	Nionstichtchitch	Aghogoch.
Father	Iskh	Athan.
Mother	Nas-kh.	Anaan.
Son	Pa-atch	L'laan.
Daughter	Souguing	Aschkinn.
Brother	Ktchidsch	Koyota.
Sister	Kos-Khou.	Angün.
Husband	Skoch	Ougünn.
Woman	Skoua-aou	Aï-yagar.
Girl	Kh-tchitchou	Ougeghilikinn.
Young boy	Pahatch	Auckthok.
Child	Pahatchitch	Ouskolik.
A man	Ouskaams	Toyoch.
The people	Kouaskou.	
Persons	Ouskaamsit.	
The head	T-Khousa	Kamgha.
The face	Koua-agh	Soghimaginn.
The nose	Kaankang	Aughosinn.
The nostrils	Kaanga	Gouakik.
The eye	Nanit	Thack.

After observing that "there are several cogent arguments to evince that the Americans are not descended from any people in the north of Asia, or in the north of Europe," Lord *Kaimes* continues,—"I venture still further; which is, to conjecture, that America has not been peopled from any part of the old world." But although this last conjecture is in unison with those of many others, yet his lordship is greatly out in some of the proofs which he adduces in its support. As we have no ground on which to controvert this opinion, we may be excused from examining its proofs; but this we will observe, that Lord *Kaimes* is in the same error about the beardlessness of the Americans as some other learned Europeans.

The learned Doctor *Swinton*,§ in a dissertation upon the peopling of Ameri-

* See his "*Sketches of the History of Man*," a work which he published in 1774, at Edinburgh, in 2 vols. 4to.

† Vol. ii. 71.

‡ The Aléouteans inhabit the chain of islands which stretch from the north-west point of America into the neighborhood of Kamskatka. It must be remembered that these names are in the French orthography, being taken from a French translation of *Billings's* voyage into those regions, from 1785 to 1794.

§ Doctor *John Swinton*, the eminent author of many parts of the *Ancient Universal History*. He died in 1777, aged 74.

ca,* after stating the different opinions of various authors who have advocated in favor of the "dispersed people," the Phœnicians, and other eastern nations, observes, "that, therefore, the Americans in general were descended from some people who inhabited a country not so far distant from them as Egypt and Phœnicia, our readers will, as we apprehend, readily admit. Now, no country can be pitched upon so proper and convenient for this purpose as the north-eastern part of Asia, particularly Great Tartary, Siberia, and more especially the peninsula of Kamtschatka. That probably was the tract through which many Tartarian colonies passed into America, and peopled the most considerable part of the new world."

This, it is not to be denied, is the most rational way of getting inhabitants into America, if it must be allowed that it was peopled from the "old world." But it is not quite so easy to account for the existence of equatorial animals in America, when all authors agree that they never could have passed that way, as they could not have survived the coldness of the climate, at any season of the year. Moreover, the vocabulary we have given, if it prove any thing, proves that either the inhabitants of North America did not come in from the north-west, or that, if they did, some unknown cause must have, for ages, suspended all communication between the emigrants and their ancestors upon the neighboring shores of Asia.

In 1822, there appeared in London a work which attracted some attention, as most works have upon similar subjects. It was entitled, "Description of the ruins of an ancient city, discovered near Palenque, in the kingdom of Guatemala, in Spanish America: translated from the original manuscript report of Capt. *Don Antonio Del Rio:* followed by a critical investigation and research into the *History of the Americans, by* Dr. *Paul Felix Cabrera,* of the city of New Guatemala."

Captain *Del Rio* was ordered by the Spanish king, in the year 1786, to make an examination of whatever ruins he might find, which he accordingly did. From the manuscript he left, which afterwards fell into the hands of Doctor *Cabrera,* his work was composed, and is that part of the work which concerns us in our view of systems or conjectures concerning the peopling of America. We shall be short with this author, as his system differs very little from some which we have already sketched. He is very confident that he has settled the question how South America received its inhabitants, namely, from the Phœnicians, who sailed across the Atlantic Ocean, and that the ruined city described by Captain *Del Rio* was built by the first adventurers.

Doctor *Cabrera* calls any system, which, in his view, does not harmonize with the Scriptures, an innovation upon the "holy Catholic religion;" and rather than resort to any such, he says, "It is better to believe his [God's] works miraculous, than endeavor to make an ostentatious display of our talents by the cunning invention of new systems, in attributing them to natural causes."† The same reasoning will apply in this case as in a former. If we are to attribute every thing to miracles, wherefore the necessity of investigation? These authors are fond of investigating matters in their way, but are displeased if others take the same liberty. And should we follow an author in his theories, who cuts the whole business short by declaring all to be a miracle, when he can no longer grope in the labyrinth of his own forming, our reader would be just in condemning such waste of time. When every thing which we cannot at first sight understand or comprehend must not be inquired into, from superstitious doubts, then and there will be fixed the bounds of all science; *but,* as Lord *Byron* said upon another occasion, *not till then.*

"If it be allowed (says Dr. LAWRENCE)‡ that all men are of the same species, it does not follow that they are all descended from the same family We have no data for determining this point: it could indeed only be settled by a knowledge of facts, which have long ago been involved in the impenetrable darkness of antiquity." That climate has nothing to do with the complexion, he offers the following in proof:—

* Universal History, xx. 162, 163.—See *Malone's* edition of *Boswell's Life Dr. Johnson* v. 271. ed. in 5 v. 12mo. London, 1821

† Page 30. ‡ Lectures on Zoology &c. 442. ed. 8vo. Salem, 1828.

"The establishments of the Europeans in Asia and America have now subsisted about three centuries. *Vasquez de Gama* landed at Calicut in 1498; and the Portuguese empire in India was founded in the beginning of the following century. Brazil was discovered and taken possession of by the same nation in the very first year of the 16th century. Towards the end of the 15th, and the beginning of the 16th century, *Columbus*, *Cortez*, and *Pizarro*, subjugated for the Spaniards the West Indian islands, with the empires of Mexico and Peru. Sir *Walter Ralegh* planted an English colony in Virginia in 1584; and the French settlement of Canada has rather a later date. The colonists have, in no instance, approached to the natives of these countries. and their descendants, where the blood has been kept pure, have, at this time, the same characters as native Europeans." *

The eminent antiquary *De Witt Clinton*† supposed that the ancient works found in this country were similar to those supposed to be Roman by *Pennant* in Wales. He adds, "The Danes, as well as the nations which erected our fortifications, were in all probability of Scythian origin. According to *Pliny*, the name of Scythian was common to all the nations living in the north of Asia and Europe." †

CHAPTER III.

Anecdotes, Narratives, &c. illustrative of the Manners and Customs, Antiquities and Traditions, of the Indians.

Wit.—An Ottaway chief, known to the French by the name of *Whitejohn*, was a great drunkard. Count *Frontenac* asked him what he thought brandy to be made of; he replied, that it must be made of hearts and tongues— "For," said he, "when I have drunken plentifully of it, my heart is a thousand strong, and I can talk, too, with astonishing freedom and rapidity." ‡

Honor.—A chief of the Five Nations, who fought on the side of the English in the French wars, chanced to meet in battle his own father, who was fighting on the side of the French. Just as he was about to deal a deadly blow upon his head, he discovered who he was, and said to him, "You have once given me life, and now I give it to you. Let me meet you no more; for I have paid the debt I owed you." §

Recklessness.—In Connecticut River, about "200 miles from Long Island Sound, is a narrow of 5 yards only, formed by two shelving mountains of solid rock. Through this chasm are compelled to pass all the waters which in the time of the floods bury the northern country." It is a frightful passage of about 400 yards in length. No boat, or, as my author expresses it, "no living creature, was ever known to pass through this narrow, except an Indian woman." This woman had undertaken to cross the river just above, and although she had the god Bacchus by her side, yet Neptune prevailed in spite of their united efforts, and the canoe was hurried down the frightful gulf. While this Indian woman was thus hurrying to certain destruction, as she had every reason to expect, she seized upon her bottle of rum, and did not take it from her mouth until the last drop was quaffed. She was marvellously preserved, and was actually picked up several miles below, floating in the canoe, still quite drunk. When it was known what she had done, and being asked how she dared to drink so much rum with the prospect of certain death before her, she answered that she knew it was too much for one time, but she was unwilling that any of it should be lost. ‖

* Lectures on Zoology, &c. 464, 465. ed. 8vo. Salem, 1828.

† *A Memoir on the Antiquities of the Western Parts of the State of N. York,* pages 9, 10 8vo. Albany, 1818.

‡ Universal Museum for 1763. § Ibid. ‖ *Peters's* Hist. Connecticut

Justice.—A missionary residing among a certain tribe of Indians, was one day, after he had been preaching to them, invited by their chief to visit his wigwam. After having been kindly entertained, and being about to depart, the chief took him by the hand and said, "I have very bad squaw. She had two little children. One she loved well, the other she hated. In a cold night, when I was gone hunting in the woods, she shut it out of the wigwam, and it froze to death. What must be done with her?" The missionary replied, "She must be hanged." "Ah!" said the chief, "go, then, and hang your God, whom you make just like her."

Magnanimity.—A hunter, in his wanderings for game, fell among the back settlements of Virginia, and by reason of the inclemency of the weather, was induced to seek refuge at the house of a planter, whom he met at his door. Admission was refused him. Being both hungry and thirsty, he asked for a morsel of bread and a cup of water, but was answered in every case, "No! you shall have nothing here! *Get you gone, you Indian dog!*" It happened, in process of time, that this same planter lost himself in the woods, and, after a fatiguing day's travel, he came to an Indian's cabin, into which he was welcomed. On inquiring the way, and the distance to the white settlements, being told by the Indian that he could not go in the night, and being kindly offered lodging and victuals, he gladly refreshed and reposed himself in the Indian's cabin. In the morning, he conducted him through the wilderness, agreeably to his promise the night before, until they came in sight of the habitations of the whites. As he was about to take his leave of the planter, he looked him full in the face, and asked him if he did not know him. Horror-struck at finding himself thus in the power of a man he had so inhumanly treated, and dumb with shame on thinking of the manner it was requited, he began at length to make excuses, and beg a thousand pardons, when the Indian interrupted him, and said, "When you see poor Indians fainting for a cup of cold water, don't say again, 'Get you gone, you Indian dog!'" He then dismissed him to return to his friends. My author adds, "It is not difficult to say, which of these two had the best claim to the name of Christian."*

Deception.—The captain of a vessel, having a desire to make a present to a lady of some fine oranges which he had just brought from "the sugar islands," gave them to an Indian in his employ to carry to her. Lest he should not perform the office punctually, he wrote a letter to her, to be taken along with the present, that she might detect the bearer, if he should fail to deliver the whole of what he was intrusted with. The Indian, during the journey, reflected how he should refresh himself with the oranges, and not be found out. Not having any apprehension of the manner of communication by writing, he concluded that it was only necessary to keep his design secret from the letter itself, supposing that would tell of him if he did not; he therefore laid it upon the ground, and rolled a large stone upon it, and retired to some distance, where he regaled himself with several of the oranges, and then proceeded on his journey. On delivering the remainder and the letter to the lady, she asked him where the rest of the oranges were; he said he had delivered all; she told him that the letter said there were several more sent to which he answered that the letter lied, and she must not believe it. But he was soon confronted in his falsehood, and, begging forgiveness of the offence, was pardoned.†

Shrewdness.—As Governor Joseph *Dudley* of Massachusetts was superintending some of his workmen, he took notice of an able-bodied Indian, who, half-naked, would come and look on, as a pastime, to see his men work. The governor took occasion one day to ask him *why he did not work and get some clothes, wherewith to cover himself.* The Indian answered by asking him *why he did not work.* The governor, pointing with his finger to his head, said, "*I work head work*, and so have no need to work with my hands as you should." The Indian then said he would work if any one would employ him. The

* *Carey's* Museum, vi. 40.

† *Uring's* Voyage to N. England in 1709, 8vo. London, 1726

governor told him he wanted a calf killed, and that, if he would go and do it he would give him a shilling. He accepted the offer, and went immediately and killed the calf, and then went sauntering about as before. The governor, on observing what he had done, asked him why he did not dress the calf before he left it. The Indian answered, "*No, no, Coponoh;* that was not in the bargain: I was to have a shilling for killing him. *Am he no dead, Coponoh?*" [governor.] The governor, seeing himself thus outwitted, told him to dress it, and he would give him another shilling

This done, and in possession of two shillings, the Indian goes directly to a grog-shop for rum. After a short stay, he returned to the governor, and told him he had given him a bad shilling-piece, and presented a brass one to be exchanged. The governor, thinking possibly it might have been the case, gave him another. It was not long before he returned a second time with another brass shilling to be exchanged; the governor was now convinced of his knavery, but, not caring to make words at the time, gave him another and thus the fellow got four shillings for one.

The governor determined to have the rogue corrected for his abuse, and, meeting with him soon after, told him he must take a letter to Boston for him [and gave him a half a crown for the service.] * The letter was directed to the keeper of bridewell, ordering him to give the bearer so many lashes; but, mistrusting that all was not exactly agreeable, and meeting a servant of the governor on the road, ordered him, in the name of his master, to carry the letter immediately as he was in haste to return. The consequence was, this servant got egregiously whipped. When the governor learned what had taken place, he felt no little chagrin at being thus twice outwitted by the Indian.

He did not see the fellow for some time after this, but at length, falling in with him, asked him by what means he had cheated and deceived him so many times. Taking the governor again in his own play, he answered, pointing with his finger to his head, "*Head work, Coponoh, head work!*" The governor was now so well-pleased that he forgave the whole offence.†

Equality.—An Indian chief, on being asked whether his people were free, answered, "Why not, since I myself am free, although their king?" ‡

Matrimony.—"An aged Indian, who for many years had spent much time among the white people, both in Pennsylvania and New Jersey, one day, about the year 1770, observed that the Indians had not only a much easier way of getting a wife than the whites, but also a more certain way of getting a good one. 'For,' said he in broken English, 'white man court—court—may be one whole year!—may be two years before he marry! Well—may be then he get very good wife—but may be not—may be very cross! Well now suppose cross! scold so soon as get awake in the morning! scold all day!—scold until sleep!—all one—he must keep him!—White people have law forbidding throw away wife he be ever so cross—must keep him always! Well, how does Indian do? Indian, when he see industrious squaw, he go to him, place his two fore-fingers close aside each other make two like one—then look squaw in the face—see him smile—this is all one he say yes!—so he take him home—no danger he be cross! No, no—squaw know too well what Indian do if he cross! throw him away and take another!—Squaw love to eat meat—no husband no meat. Squaw do every thing to please husband, he do every thing to please squaw—live happy.'" §

Toleration.—In the year 1791, two Creek chiefs accompanied an American to England, where, as usual, they attracted great attention, and many flocked around them, as well to learn their ideas of certain things as to behold "the savages." Being asked their opinion of religion, or of what religion they were, one made answer, that they had no priests in their country, or established religion, for they thought, that, upon a subject where there was no possibility of people's agreeing in opinion, and as it was altogether matter of *mere*

* A sentence added in a version of this anecdote in *Carey's* Museum, vi. 204.
† *Uring, ut supra.* 120.
‡ *Carey's* Museum, vi. 482.
§ *Heckewelder's* Hist. Ind. Nations.

opinion, "it was best that every one should paddle his canoe his own way." Here is a volume of instruction in a short answer of a savage!

Justice.—A white trader sold a quantity of powder to an Indian, and imposed upon him by making him believe it was a grain which grew like wheat, by sowing it upon the ground. He was greatly elated by the prospect, not only of raising his own powder, but of being able to supply others, and thereby becoming immensely rich. Having prepared his ground with great care, he sowed his powder with the utmost exactness in the spring. Month after month passed away, but his powder did not even sprout, and winter came before he was satisfied that he had been deceived. He said nothing; but some time after, when the trader had forgotten the trick, the same Indian succeeded in getting credit of him to a large amount. The time set for payment having expired, he sought out the Indian at his residence, and demanded payment for his goods. The Indian heard his demand with great complaisance; then, looking him shrewdly in the eye, said, "*Me pay you when my powder grow.*" This was enough. The guilty white man quickly retraced his steps, satisfied, we apprehend, to balance his account with the chagrin he had received.

Hunting.—The Indians had methods to catch game which served them extremely well. The same month in which the Mayflower brought over the forefathers, November, 1620, to the shores of Plimouth, several of them ranged about the woods near by to learn what the country contained. Having wandered farther than they were apprized, in their endeavor to return, they say, "We were shrewdly puzzled, and lost our way. As we wandered, we came to a tree, where a young sprit was bowed down over a bow, and some acorns strewed underneath. *Stephen Hopkins* said, it had been to catch some deer. So, as we were looking at it, *William Bradford* being in the rear, when he came looking also upon it, and as he went about, it gave a sudden jerk up, and he was immediately caught up by the legs. It was (they continue) a very pretty device, made with a rope of their own making, [of bark or some kind of roots probably,] and having a noose as artificially made as any roper in England can make, and as like ours as can be; which we brought away with us."*

Preaching against Practice.—JOHN SIMON was a Sogkonate, who, about the year 1700, was a settled minister to that tribe. He was a man of strong mind, generally temperate, but sometimes remiss in the latter particular. The following anecdote is told as characteristic of his notions of justice. *Simon*, on account of his deportment, was created justice of the peace, and when difficulties occurred involving any of his people, he sat with the English justice to aid in making up judgment. It happened that *Simon's* squaw, with some others, had committed some offence. Justice *Almy* and *Simon*, in making up their minds, estimated the amount of the offence differently; *Almy* thought each should receive *eight* or *ten* stripes, but *Simon* said, "No, *four or five are enough—Poor Indians are ignorant, and it is not Christian-like to punish so hardly those who are ignorant, as those who have knowledge.*" *Simon's* judgment prevailed. When Mr. *Almy* asked *John* how many his wife should receive, he said, "*Double, because she had knowledge to have done better;*" but Colonel *Almy*, out of regard to *John's* feelings, wholly remitted his wife's punishment. *John* looked very serious, and made no reply while in presence of the court, but, on the first fit opportunity, remonstrated very severely against his judgment, and said to him, "*To what purpose do we preach a religion of justice, if we do unrighteousness in judgment?*

Sam Hide.—There are few, we imagine, who have not heard of this personage; but, notwithstanding his great notoriety, we might not be though serious in the rest of our work, were we to enter seriously into his biography for the reason, that from his day to this, his name has been a by-word in all New England, and means as much as to say the *greatest of liars*. It is on account of the following anecdote that he is noticed.

* Mourt's Relation

Sam Hide was a notorious cider-drinker as well as liar, and used to travel the country to and fro begging it from door to door. At one time he happened in a region of country where cider was very hard to be procured, either from its scarcity, or from *Sam's* frequent visits. However, cider he was determined to have, if lying, in any shape or color, would gain it. Being not far from the house of an acquaintance, who he knew had cider, but he knew, or was well satisfied, that, in the ordinary way of begging, he could not get it, he set his wits at work to lay a plan to insure it. This did not occupy him long. On arriving at the house of the gentleman, instead of asking for cider, he inquired for the man of the house, whom, on appearing, *Sam* requested to go aside with him, as he had something of importance to communicate to him. When they were by themselves, *Sam* told him he had that morning shot a fine deer, and that, if he would give him a crown, he would tell him where it was. The gentleman did not incline to do this, but offered half a crown. Finally, *Sam* said, as he had walked a great distance that morning, and was very dry, for a half a crown and a mug of cider he would tell him. This was agreed upon, and the price paid. Now *Sam* was required to point out the spot where the deer was to be found, which he did in this manner. He said to his friend, *You know of such a meadow,* describing it—Yes—*You know a big ash tree, with a big top by the little brook*—Yes—*Well, under that tree lies the deer.* This was satisfactory, and *Sam* departed. It is unnecessary to mention that the meadow was found, and the tree by the brook, but no deer. The duped man could hardly contain himself on considering what he had been doing. To look after *Sam* for satisfaction would be worse than looking after the deer, so the farmer concluded to go home contented. Some years after, he happened to fall in with the Indian; and he immediately began to rally him for deceiving him so, and demanded back his money and pay for his cider and trouble. *Why,* said *Sam, would you find fault if Indian told truth half the time?*—No—*Well,* says *Sam, you find him meadow?*—Yes—*You find him tree?*—Yes—*What for then you find fault* Sam Hide, *when he told you two truth to one lie?* The affair ended here. *Sam* heard no more from the farmer.

This is but one of the numerous anecdotes of *Sam Hide*, which, could they be collected, would fill many pages. He died in Dedham, 5 January, 1732 at the great age of 105 years. He was a great jester, and passed for an uncommon wit. In all the wars against the Indians during his lifetime, he served the English faithfully, and had the name of a brave soldier. He had himself killed 19 of the enemy, and tried hard to make up the 20th, but was unable.

Characters contrasted.—"An Indian of the Kennebeck tribe, remarkable for his good conduct, received a grant of land from the state, and fixed himself in a new township where a number of families were settled. Though not ill treated, yet the common prejudice against Indians prevented any sympathy with him. This was shown at the death of his only child, when none of the people came near him. Shortly afterwards he went to some of the inhabitants and said to them, *When white man's child die, Indian man he sorry—he help bury him.—When my child die, no one speak to me—I make his grave alone. I can no live here.* He gave up his farm, dug up the body of his child, and carried it with him 200 miles through the forests, to join the Canada Indians!"*

A ludicrous Error.—There was published in London, in 1762, "THE AMERICAN GAZETTEER," &c.† in which is the following account of BRISTOL, R. I. "A county and town in N. England. The capital is remarkable for the *King of Spain's having a palace in it, and being killed there;* and also for *Crown* the poet's begging it of *Charles* II." The blunder did not rest here, but is found in "THE N. AMERICAN and the WEST INDIAN GAZETTEER,"‡ &c. Thus *Philip* of Spain seems to have had the *misfortune* of being mistaken for *Philip* of the Wampanoags, alias *Pometacom* of Pokanoket.

---

* Tudor's Letters on the Eastern States, 294.

† 3 vols. 12mo without name.

‡ 2d edition, 12mo, London, 1788, also anonymous

Origin or Meaning of the Name Canada.—It is said, that Canada was discovered by the Spaniards, before the time of Cartier, and that the Bay of Chaleurs was discovered by them, and is the same as the *Baye des Espagnoles;* and that the Spaniards, not meeting with any appearances of mines of the precious metals, said to one another, *aca nada*, which in their language signified, *nothing here*, and forthwith departed from the country. The Indians, having heard these words, retained them in their memories, and, when the French came among them, made use of them, probably by way of salutation, not understanding their import; and they were supposed by the voyagers to be the name of the country. It was only necessary to drop the first letter, and use the two words as two syllables, and the word *Canada* was complete.*

But as long ago as when Father *Charlevoix* wrote his admirable HISTORY OF *New France*, he added a note upon the derivation of the name *Canada*, in which he said some derived it from an Iroquois word meaning an assemblage of nouses.† Doctor *J. R. Forster* has a learned note upon it also, in his valuable account of *Voyages and Discoveries in the North.* He objects to the *Aca Nada* origin, because, in Spanish, the word for *here* is not *aca*, but *aqui*, and that to form *Canada* from *Aquinada* would be forced and unnatural. Yet he says, "In ancient maps we often find *Ca: da Nada*," that is, Cape Nothing. "But from a Canadian [Indian] vocabulary, annexed to the original edition of the second voyage of *Jaques Cartier*, Paris, 1545, it appears, that an assemblage of houses, or habitations, i. e. a *town*, was by the natives called *Canada. Cartier* says, *Ilz appellent une Ville—Canada.*" Mr. *Heckewelder* is of much the same opinion as *Charlevoix* and *Forster.* He says, that in a prayer-book in the Mohawk language, he read "*Ne* KANADA-*gongh Konwayatsk Nazareth,*" which was a translation of "in a CITY called Nazareth."

Origin of the Name Yankee.—ANBURY, an author who did not respect the Americans, any more than many others who have been led captive by them, has the following paragraph upon this word‡—"The lower class of these *Yankees*—apropos, it may not be amiss here just to observe to you the etymology of this term: it is derived from a Cherokee word, *eankke*, which signifies coward and slave. This epithet of *yankee* was bestowed upon the inhabitants of N. England by the Virginians, for not assisting them in a war with the Cherokees, and they have always been held in derision by it. But the name has been more prevalent since [1775] the commencement of hostilities; the soldiery at Boston used it as a term of reproach; but after the affair at Bunker's Hill, the Americans gloried in it. *Yankee-doodle* is now their pœan, a favorite of favorites, played in their army, esteemed as warlike as the grenadier's march—it is the lover's spell, the nurse's lullaby. After our rapid successes, we held the yankees in great contempt; but it was not a little morti fying to hear them play this tune, when their army marched down to our surrender." §

But Mr. *Heckewelder* thinks that the Indians, in endeavoring to pronounce the name *English*, could get that sound no nearer than these letters give it, *yengees.* This was perhaps the true origin of *Yankee.*

A singular Stratagem to escape Torture.—"Some years ago the Shawano Indians, being obliged to remove from their habitations, in their way took a Muskohge warrior, known by the name of old *Scrany*, prisoner; they bastinadoed him severely, and condemned him to the fiery torture. He under-

* The authors who have adopted this opinion, are Doctor *Mather*, [Magnalia, B. viii. 71;] *Harris*, [Voyages, ii. 349;] *Moll*, [Geog. ii. 194;] *J. Long*, [Voyages and Travels, 2;] *Bozman*, [Maryland, 35;] *Moulton*, [N. York, i. 131;] *Martin*, [Louisiana, i. 7.]
Josselyn and *Jeffrys* seem to be without company as well as authorities for their derivations The former [N. England Rarities, 5] says, Canada was "so called from Monsieur *Cane.*" The latter [Hist. America, 1] says, "*Canada*, in the Indian language, signifies the *Mouth of the Country*, from *can*, mouth, and *ada*, the country."

† Quelques-unes dérivent ce nom du mot Iroquois *Kannata*, qui se prononce *canada*, et signifie un amas de cabannes. *Hist. Nouv. France*, i. 9.

‡ *Travels through the Interior Parts of North America*, 1776, &c. vol. ii. 46, 47. *Anbury* was an officer in General *Burgoyne's* army, and was among the captives surrendered at Saratoga.

§ This derivation is almost as ludicrous as that given by *Irving* in his Knickerbocker.

went a great deal without showing any concern; his countenance and behavior were as if he suffered not the least pain. He told his persecutors with a bold voice, that he was a warrior; that he had gained most of his martial reputation at the expense of their nation, and was desirous of showing them, in the act of dying, that he was still as much their superior, as when he headed his gallant countrymen: that although he had fallen into their hands, and forfeited the protection of the divine power by some impurity or other, when carrying the holy ark of war against his devoted enemies, yet he had so much remaining virtue as would enable him to punish himself more exquisitely than all their despicable, ignorant crowd possibly could; and that he would do so, if they gave him liberty by untying him, and handing him one of the red-hot gun-barrels out of the fire. The proposal, and his method of address, appeared so exceedingly bold and uncommon, that his request was granted. Then suddenly seizing one end of the red-hot barrel, and brandishing it from side to side, leaped down a prodigious steep and high bank into a branch of the river, dived through it, ran over a small island, and passed the other branch, amidst a shower of bullets; and though numbers of his enemies were in close pursuit of him, he got into a bramble-swamp, through which, though naked and in a mangled condition, he reached his own country."

An unparalleled Case of Suffering.—"The Shawano Indians captured a warrior of the Anantoocah nation, and put him to the stake, according to their usual cruel solemnities: having unconcernedly suffered much torture, he told them, with scorn, they did not know how to punish a noted enemy; therefore he was willing to teach them, and would confirm the truth of his assertion if they allowed him the opportunity. Accordingly he requested of them a pipe and some tobacco, which was given him; as soon as he had lighted it, he sat down, naked as he was, on the women's burning torches, that were within his circle, and continued smoking his pipe without the least discomposure: On this a head warrior leaped up, and said, they saw plain enough that he was a warrior, and not afraid of dying, nor should he have died, only that he was both spoiled by the fire, and devoted to it by their laws; however, though he was a very dangerous enemy, and his nation a treacherous people, it should be seen that they paid a regard to bravery, even in one who was marked with war streaks at the cost of many of the lives of their beloved kindred; and then by way of favor, he with his friendly tomahawk instantly put an end to all his pains."*

Ignorance the Offspring of absurd Opinions.—The resolution and courage of the Indians, says Colonel *Rogers*, "under sickness and pain, is truly surprising. A young woman will be in labor a whole day without uttering one groan or cry; should she betray such a weakness, they would immediately say, that she was unworthy to be a mother, and that her offspring could not fail of being cowards."†

A Northern Custom.—When Mr. *Hearne* was on the Coppermine River, in 1771, some of the Copper Indians in his company killed a number of Esquimaux, by which act they considered themselves unclean; and all concerned in the murder were not allowed to cook any provisions, either for themselves or others. They were, however, allowed to eat of others' cooking, but not until they had painted, with a kind of red earth, all the space between their nose and chin, as well as a greater part of their cheeks, almost to their ears. Neither would they use any other dish or pipe, than their own.‡

Another Pocahontas.—While *Lewis* and *Clarke* were on the shore of the Pacific Ocean, in 1805, one of their men went one evening into a village of the Killamuk Indians, alone, a small distance from his party, and on the opposite side of a creek from that of the encampment. A strange Indian happened to be there also, who expressed great respect and love for the white

* The two preceding relations are from *Long's Voyages and Travels*, 72 and 73, a book of small pretensions, but one of the best on Indian history. Its author lived among the Indians of the North-West, as an Indian trader, about 19 years.

† *Concise Account of N. America*, 212. ‡ *Journey to the Northern Ocean*, 205.

man; but in reality he meant to murder him for the articles he had about him This happened to come to the knowledge of a Chinnook woman, and she determined at once to save his life: therefore, when the white man was about to return to his companions, the Indian was going to accompany him, and kill him in the way. As they were about to set out, the woman caught the white man by the clothes, to prevent his going with the Indian. He, not understanding her intention, pulled away from her; but as a last resort, she ran out and shrieked, which raised the men in every direction; and the Indian became alarmed for his own safety, and made his escape before the white man knew he had been in danger.

Self-command in Time of Danger.—There was in Carolina a noted chief of the Yamoisees, who, in the year 1702, with about 600 of his countrymen, went with Colonel *Daniel* and Colonel *Moore* against the Spaniards in Florida. His name was *Arratommakaw.* When the English were obliged to abandon their undertaking, and as they were retreating to their boats, they became alarmed, supposing the Spaniards were upon them. *Arratommakaw,* having arrived at the boats, was reposing himself upon his oars, and was fast asleep. The soldiers rallied him for being so slow in his retreat, and ordered him to make more haste: "But he replied, 'No—THOUGH YOUR GOVERNOR LEAVES YOU, I WILL NOT STIR TILL I HAVE SEEN ALL MY MEN BEFORE ME.'"

Indifference.—*Archihau* was a sachem of Maryland, whose residence was upon the Potomack, when that country was settled by the English in 1633–4. The place of his residence was named, like the river, Potomack. As usual with the Indians, he received the English under Governor *Calvert* with great attention. It should be noted, that *Archihau* was not head sachem of the Potomacks, but governed instead of his nephew, who was a child, and who, like the head men of Virginia, was called *werowance.* From this place the colonists sailed 20 leagues farther up the river, to a place called Piscattaway. Here a werowance went on board the governor's pinnace, to treat with him. On being asked whether he was willing the English should settle in his country, in case they found a place convenient for them, he made answer, "*I will not bid you go, neither will I bid you stay, but you may use your own discretion.*" *

Their Notions of the Learning of the Whites.—At the congress at Lancaster, in 1744, between the government of Virginia and the Five Nations, the Indians were told that, if they would send some of their young men to Virginia, the English would give them an education at their college. An orator replied to this offer as follows:—"We know that you highly esteem the kind of learning taught in those colleges, and that the maintenance of our young men, while with you, would be very expensive to you. We are convinced, therefore, that you mean to do us good by your proposal, and we thank you heartily. But you who are wise must know, that different nations have different conceptions of things; and you will therefore not take it amiss, if our ideas of this kind of education happen not to be the same with yours. We have had some experience of it: several of our young people were formerly brought up at the colleges of the northern provinces; they were instructed in all your sciences; but when they came back to us, they were bad runners; ignorant of every means of living in the woods; unable to bear either cold or hunger; knew neither how to build a cabin, take a deer, or kill an enemy; spoke our language imperfectly; were therefore neither fit for hunters, warriors, or counsellors; they were totally good for nothing. We are, however, not the less obliged by your kind offer, though we decline accepting it: and to show our grateful sense of it, if the gentlemen of Virginia will send us a dozen of their sons, we will take great care of their education, instruct them in all we know, and make *men* of them." †

Success of a Missionary.—Those who have attempted to Christianize the Indians complain that they are too silent, and that their taciturnity was the greatest difficulty with which they have to contend. Their notions of pro

* *Oldmixon,* [Hist. Maryland.] † *Franklin's* Essays

priety upon matters of conversation are so nice, that they deem it improper, in the highest degree, even to deny or contradict any thing that is said, at the time; and hence the difficulty of knowing what effect any thing has upon their minds at the time of delivery. In this they have a proper advantage; for how often does it happen that people would answer very differently upon a matter, were they to consider upon it but a short time! The Indians seldom answer a matter of importance the same day, lest, in so doing, they should be thought to have treated it as though it was of small consequence. *We* oftener repent of a hasty decision, than that we have lost time in maturing our judgments. Now for the anecdote: and as it is from the Essays of Dr. *Franklin*, it shall be told in his own way.

"A Swedish minister, having assembled the chiefs of the Susquehannah Indians, made a sermon to them, acquainting them with the principal historical facts on which our religion is founded; such as the fall of our first parents by eating an apple; the coming of *Christ* to repair the mischief; his miracles and sufferings, &c.—When he had finished, an Indian orator stood up to thank him. '*What you have told us,*' said he, '*is all very good. It is indeed bad to eat apples. It is better to make them all into cider. We are much obliged by your kindness in coming so far to tell us those things, which you have heard from your mothers.*'

"When the Indian had told the missionary one of the legends of his nation, now they had been supplied with maize or corn, beans, and tobacco,* he treated it with contempt, and said, 'What I delivered to you were sacred truths; but what you tell me is mere fable, fiction, and falsehood.' The Indian felt indignant, and replied, '*My brother, it seems your friends have not done you justice in your education; they have not well instructed you in the rules of common civility. You see that we, who understand and practise those rules, believe all your stories: why do you refuse to believe ours?*'"

Curiosity.—"When any of the Indians come into our towns, our people are apt to crowd round them, gaze upon them, and incommode them where they desire to be private; this they esteem great rudeness, and the effect of the want of instruction in the rules of civility and good manners. '*We have,*' say they, '*as much curiosity as you, and when you come into our towns, we wish for opportunities of looking at you; but for this purpose we hide ourselves behind bushes where you are to pass, and never intrude ourselves into your company.*'"

Rules of Conversation.—"The business of the women is to take exact notice of what passes, imprint it in their memories, (for they have no writing,) and communicate it to their children. They are the records of the council, and they preserve tradition of the stipulations in treaties a hundred years back, which, when we compare with our writings, we always find exact. He that would speak rises. The rest observe a profound silence. When he has finished, and sits down, they leave him five or six minutes to recollect, that, if he has omitted any thing he intended to say, or has any thing to add, he may rise again, and deliver it. To interrupt another, even in common conversation, is reckoned highly indecent. How different this is from the conduct of a polite British House of Commons, where scarce a day passes without some confusion, that makes the speaker hoarse in calling *to order;* and how different from the mode of conversation in many polite companies of Europe, where, if you do not deliver your sentence with great rapidity, you are cut off in the middle of it by the impatient loquacity of those you converse with, and never suffered to finish it!"—Instead of being better since the days of *Franklin*, we apprehend it has grown worse. The modest and unassuming often find it exceeding difficult to gain a hearing at all. Ladies, and many who consider themselves examples of good manners, transgress to an insufferable degree, in breaking in upon the conversations of others. Some of these, like a ship

* The story of the beautiful woman, who descended to the earth, and was fed by the Indians, *Black-Hawk* is made to tell, in his life, page 78. It is the same often told, and alluded to by *Franklin*, in the text. To reward the Indians for their kindness, she caused corn to grow where her right hand touched the earth, beans where the left rested, and tobacco where she was seated

driven by a north-wester, bearing down the small craft in her course, come upon us by surprise, and if we attempt to proceed by raising our voices a little, we are sure to be drowned by a much greater elevation on their part. It is a want of good breeding, which, it is hoped, every young person whose eye this may meet, will not be guilty of through life. There is great opportunity for many of mature years to profit by it.

Lost Confidence.—An Indian runner, arriving in a village of his countrymen, requested the immediate attendance of its inhabitants in council, as he wanted their answer to important information. The people accordingly assembled, but when the messenger had with great anxiety delivered his message, and waited for an answer, none was given, and he soon observed that he was likely to be left alone in his place. A stranger present asked a principal chief the meaning of this strange proceeding, who gave this answer, "*He once told us a lie.*"

Comic.—An Indian having been found frozen to death, an inquest of his countrymen was convened to determine by what means he came to such a death Their verdict was, "Death from the freezing of a great quantity of water inside of him, which they were of opinion he had drunken for rum."

A serious Question.—About 1794, an officer presented a western chief with a medal, on one side of which President *Washington* was represented as armed with a sword, and on the other an Indian was seen in the act of burying the hatchet. The chief at once saw the wrong done his countrymen, and very wisely asked, "*Why does not the President bury his sword too?*" *

Self-esteem.—A white man, meeting an Indian, accosted him as brother. The red man, with a great expression of meaning in his countenance, inquired how they came to be brothers; the white man replied, O, by way of Adam, I suppose. The Indian added, "*Me thank him Great Spirit we no nearer brothers.*"

A Preacher taken at his Word.—A certain clergyman had for his text on a time, "*Vow and pay unto the Lord thy vows.*" An Indian happened to be present, who stepped up to the priest as soon as he had finished, and said to him, "Now me *vow* me go home with you, Mr. Minister." The priest, having no language of evasion at command, said, "You must go then." When he had arrived at the home of the minister, the Indian vowed again, saying, "Now me *vow* me have supper." When this was finished he said, "Me *vow* me stay all night." The priest, by this time, thinking himself sufficiently taxed, replied, "It may be so, but I *vow* you shall go in the morning." The Indian, judging from the tone of his host, that more *vows* would be useless. departed in the morning *sans cérémonie.*

A case of signal Barbarity.—It is related by BLACK HAWK, in his life, that some time before the war of 1812, one of the Indians had killed a Frenchman at Prairie des Chiens. "The British soon after took him prisoner, and said they would shoot him next day! His family were encamped a short distance below the mouth of the Ouisconsin. He begged permission to go and see them that night, as he was *to die the next day!* They permitted him to go after promising to return the next morning by sunrise. He visited his family, which consisted of a wife and six children. I cannot describe their meeting and parting, to be understood by the whites; as it appears that their feelings are acted upon by certain rules laid down by their *preachers!*—whilst ours are governed only by the monitor within us. He parted from his wife and children, hurried through the prairie to the fort, and arrived in time! The soldiers were ready, and immediately *marched out and shot him down!!*"—If this were not cold-blooded, deliberate murder, on the part of the whites, I have no conception of what constitutes that crime. What were the circumstances of the murder we are not informed; but whatever they may have been, they cannot excuse a still greater barbarity. I would not by any means be understood to advocate the cause of a murderer; but I will ask, whether crime is to be prevented *by crime:* murder for murder is only a brutal retaliation, except where the safety of a community requires the sacrifice.

* Eliot's Works 178.

Mourning much in a short Time.—"A young widow, whose husband had been dead about eight days, was hastening to finish her grief, in order that she might be married to a young warrior: she was determined, therefore, to grieve much in a short time; to this end she tore her hair, drank spirits, and beat her breast, to make the tears flow abundantly, by which means, on the evening of the eighth day, she was ready again to marry, having grieved sufficiently." *

How to evade a hard Question.—"When Mr. *Gist* went over the Alleganies, in Feb. 1751, on a tour of discovery for the Ohio Company, 'an Indian, who spoke good English, came to him, and said that their great man, the *Beaver*,† and Captain *Oppamyluah*, (two chiefs of the Delawares,) desired to know where the Indians' land lay; for the French claimed all the land on one side of the Ohio River, and the English on the other.' This question Mr. *Gist* found it hard to answer, and he evaded it by saying, that the Indians and white men were all subjects to the same king, and all had an equal privilege of taking up and possessing the land in conformity with the conditions prescribed by the king." ‡

Credulity its own Punishment.—The traveller *Wansey*, according to his own account, would not enter into conversation with an eminent chief, because he had heard that it had been said of him, that he had, in his time, "shed blood enough to swim in." He had a great desire to become acquainted with the Indian character, but his credulity debarred him effectually from the gratification. The chief was a Creek, named FLAMINGO, who, in company with another called *Double-head*, visited Philadelphia as ambassadors, in the summer of 1794. Few travellers discover such scrupulousness, especially those who come to America. That *Flamingo* was more bloody than other Indian warriors, is in no wise probable; but a mere report of his being a great shedder of blood kept Mr. *Wansey* from saying any more about him.

Just Indignation.—HATUAY, a powerful chief of Hispaniola, having fled from thence to avoid slavery or death when that island was ravaged by the Spaniards, was taken in 1511, when they conquered Cuba, and burnt at the stake. After being bound to the stake, a Franciscan friar labored to convert him to the Catholic faith, by promises of immediate and eternal bliss in the world to come if he would believe; and that, if he would not, eternal torments were his only portion. The cazique, with seeming composure, asked if there were any Spaniards in those regions of bliss. On being answered that there were, he replied, "*Then I will not go to a place where I may meet with one of that accursed race.*"

Harmless Deception.—In a time of Indian troubles, an Indian visited the house of Governor *Jenks*, of Rhode Island, when the governor took occasion to request him, that, if any strange Indian should come to his wigwam, to let him know it, which the Indian promised to do; but to secure his fidelity, the governor told him that when he should give him such information, he would give him a mug of flip. Some time after the Indian came again: "Well, Mr. Gubenor, strange Indian come my house last night!" "Ah," says the governor, "and what did he say?" "He no speak," replied the Indian. "What, no speak at all?" added the governor. "No, he no speak at all." "That certainly looks suspicious," said his excellency, and inquired if he were still there, and being told that he was, ordered the promised mug of flip. When this was disposed of, and the Indian was about to depart, he mildly said, "Mr. Gubenor, my squaw have child last night;" and thus the governor's alarm was suddenly changed into disappointment, and the strange Indian into a new-born pappoose.

Mammoth Bones.—The following very interesting tradition concerning these bones, among the Indians, will always be read with interest. The animal to which they once belonged, they called the *Big Buffalo*; and on the

* Account of the United States by Mr. *Isaac Holmes*, 36.
† Probably the same we have noticed in Book V. as *King Beaver*
‡ *Sparks's* Washington, ii, 15.

early maps of the country of the Ohio, we see marked, "Elepnants' bones said to be found here." They were, for some time, by many supposed to have been the bones of that animal; but they are pretty generally now believed to have belonged to a species of animal long since extinct. They have been found in various parts of the country; but in the greatest abundance about the salt licks or springs in Kentucky and Ohio. There has never been an entire skeleton found, although the one in *Peale's* museum, in Philadelphia, was so near perfect, that, by a little ingenuity in supplying its defects with wood-work, it passes extremely well for such.

The tradition of the Indians concerning this animal is, that he was carnivorous, and existed, as late as 1780, in the northern parts of America. Some Delawares, in the time of the revolutionary war, visited the governor of Virginia on business, which having been finished, some questions were put to them concerning their country, and especially what they knew or had heard respecting the animals whose bones had been found about the salt licks on the Ohio River. "The chief speaker," continues our author, Mr. *Jefferson*, "immediately put himself into an attitude of oratory, and, with a pomp suited to what he conceived the elevation of his subject," began and repeated as follows:—"*In ancient times, a herd of these tremendous animals came to the Big-bone Licks, and began an universal destruction of the bear, deer, elks, buffaloes, and other animals, which had been created for the use of the Indians: the great man above, looking down and seeing this, was so enraged, that he seized his lightning, descended to the earth, and seated himself on a neighboring mountain, on a rock of which his seat and the print of his feet are still to be seen, and hurled his bolts among them till the whole were slaughtered, except the big bull, who, presenting his forehead to the shafts, shook them off as they fell; but missing one at length, it wounded him in the side; whereon, springing round, he bounded over the Ohio, over the Wabash, the Illinois, and, finally, over the great lakes, where he is living at this day.*"

Such, say the Indians, is the account handed down to them from their ancestors, and they could furnish no other information.

Narrative of the Captivity and bold Exploit of Hannah Duston.—The relation of this affair forms the XXV. article in the Decennium Luctuosum of the Magnalia Christi Americana, by Dr. Cotton Mather, and is one of the best-written articles of all we have read from his pen. At its head is this significant sentence—Dux Fœmina Facti.

On the 15 March, 1697, a band of about 20 Indians came unexpectedly upon Haverhill, in Massachusetts; and, as their numbers were small, they made their attack with the swiftness of the whirlwind, and as suddenly disappeared. The war, of which this irruption was a part, had continued nearly ten years, and soon afterwards it came to a close. The house which this party of Indians had singled out as their object of attack, belonged to one Mr. *Thomas* * *Duston* or *Dunstan*, † in the outskirts of the town. ‡ Mr. *Duston* was at work, at some distance from his house, at the time, and whether he was alarmed for the safety of his family by the shouts of the Indians, or other cause, we are not informed; but he seems to have arrived there time enough before the arrival of the Indians, to make some arrangements for the preservation of his children; but his wife, who, but about a week before, had been confined by a child, was unable to rise from her bed, to the distraction of her agonized husband. No time was to be lost; Mr. *Duston* had only time to direct his children's flight, (seven in number,) the extremes of whose ages were two and seventeen, and the Indians were upon them. With his gun, the distressed father mounted his horse, and rode away in the direction of the children, whom he overtook but about 40 rods from the house. His first intention was to take up one, if possible, and escape with it. He had no sooner overtaken them, than this resolution was destroyed; for to rescue either to the exclusion of the rest, was worse than death itself to him. He therefore faced about and met the enemy, who had closely pursued him; each fired

* Mr. *Myrick's* Hist. Haverhill, 86. † *Hutchinson.*

‡ Eight houses were destroyed at this time, 27 persons killed, and 13 carried away captive In Mr. *B. L. Myrick's* History of Haverhill are the names of the slain &c

upon the other, and it is almost a miracle that none of the little retreating party were hurt. The Indians did not pursue long, from fear of raising the neighboring English before they could complete their object, and hence this part of the family escaped to a place of safety.

We are now to enter fully into the relation of this very tragedy. There was living in the house of Mr. *Duston*, as nurse, Mrs. *Mary Neff*,* a widow, whose heroic conduct in sharing the fate of her mistress, when escape was in her power, will always be viewed with admiration. The Indians were now in the undisturbed possession of the house, and having driven the sick woman from her bed, compelled her to sit quietly in the corner of the fire-place, while they completed the pillage of the house. This business being finished, it was set on fire, and Mrs. *Duston*, who before considered herself unable to walk, was, at the approach of night, obliged to march into the wilderness, and take her bed upon the cold ground. Mrs. *Neff* too late attempted to escape with the infant child, but was intercepted, the child taken from her, and its brains beat out against a neighboring apple-tree, while its nurse was compelled to accompany her new and frightful masters also The captives amounted in all to 13, some of whom, as they became unable to travel, were murdered, and left exposed upon the way. Although it was near night when they quitted Haverhill, they travelled, as they judged, 12 miles before encamping; "and then," says Dr. *Mather*, "kept up with their new masters in a long travel of an hundred and fifty miles, more or less, within a few days ensuing." †

After journeying awhile, according to their custom, the Indians divided their prisoners. Mrs. *Duston*, Mrs. *Neff*, and a boy named *Samuel Leonardson*, ‡ who had been captivated at Worcester, about 18 months before, fell to the lot of an Indian family, consisting of twelve persons,—two men, three women, and seven children. These, so far as our accounts go, were very kind to their prisoners, but told them there was one ceremony which they could not avoid, and to which they would be subjected when they should arrive at their place of destination, which was to run the gantlet. The place where this was to be performed, was at an Indian village, 250 miles from Haverhill, according to the reckoning of the Indians. In their meandering course, they at length arrived at an island in the mouth of Contookook River, about six miles above Concord, in New Hampshire. Here one of the Indian men resided. It had been determined by the captives, before their arrival, that an effort should be made to free themselves from their wretched captivity; and not only to gain their liberty, but, as we shall presently see, something by way of remuneration from those who held them in bondage. The heroine, *Duston*, had resolved, upon the first opportunity that offered any chance of success, to kill her captors and scalp them, and to return home with such trophies as would clearly establish her reputation for heroism, as well as insure her a bounty from the public. She therefore communicated her design to Mrs. *Neff* and the English boy, who, it would seem, readily enough agreed to it. To the art of killing and scalping she was a stranger; and, that there should be no failure in the business, Mrs. *Duston* instructed the boy, who, from his long residence with them, had become as one of the Indians, to inquire of one of the men how it was done. He did so, and the Indian showed him, without mistrusting the origin of the inquiry. It was now March the 31, and in the dead of the night following this bloody tragedy was acted. When the Indians were in the most sound sleep, these three captives arose, and softly arming themselves with the tomahawks of their masters, allotted the number each should kill; and so truly did they direct their blows, that but one escaped that they designed to kill. This was a woman, whom they badly wounded, and one boy, for some reason they did not wish to harm, and accordingly he was allowed to escape unhurt. Mrs. *Duston* killed her master, and *Leonardson* killed the man who had so freely told him, but one day before, where to deal a deadly blow, and how to take off a scalp.

---

* She was a daughter of *George Corliss*, and married *William Neff*, who went after the army, and died at Pemmaquid, Feb. 1688. *Myrick*, Hist. Havl. 87.

† Their course was probably very indirect, to elude pursuit.

‡ Hist. Haverhill, 89

All was over before the dawn of day, and all things were got ready for leaving this place of blood. All the boats but one were scuttled, to prevent being pursued, and, with what provisions and arms the Indian camp afforded, they embarked on board the other, and slowly and silently took the course of the Merrimack River for their homes, where they all soon after arrived without accident.

The whole country was astonished at the relation of the affair, the truth of which was never for a moment doubted. The ten scalps, and the arms of the Indians, were evidences not to be questioned; and the general court gave them fifty pounds as a reward, and numerous other gratuities were showered upon them. Colonel *Nicholson*, governor of Maryland, hearing of the transaction, sent them a generous present also.

Eight other houses were attacked besides *Duston's*, the owners of which, says the historian of that town, Mr. *Myrick*, in every case, were slain while defending them, and the blood of each stained his own door-sill.

*Narrative of the Destruction of Schenectady.**—This was an event of great distress to the whole country, at the time it happened, and we are able to give some new facts in relation to it from a manuscript, which, we believe, has never before been published. These facts are contained in a letter from Governor *Bradstreet*, of Massachusetts, to Governor *Hinckley*, of Plimouth, dated about a month after the affair. They are as follow:—"Tho' you cannot but have heard of the horrid massacre committed by the French and Indians at Senectada, a fortified and well compacted town 20 miles above Albany (which we had an account of by an express,) yet we think we have not discharged our duty till you hear of it from us. 'Twas upon the *Eighth of February* [1689-90] at midnight when those poor secure wretches were surprised by the enemy. Their gates were open, no watch kept, and hardly any order observed in giving and obeying commands. *Sixty* of them were butchered in the place; of whom Lieut. *Talmage* and four more were of Capt. *Bull's* company, besides five of said company carried captive. By this action the French have given us to understand what we may expect from them as to the frontier towns and seaports of New England. We are not so well acquainted what number of convenient Havens you have in your colony, besides those of Plimouth and Bristol. We hope your prudence and vigilance will lead you to take such measures as to prevent the landing of the enemy at either of those or any such like place." †

We now proceed to give such other facts as can be gathered from the numerous printed accounts. It appears that the government of Canada had planned several expeditions, previous to the setting out of this, against various important points of the English frontier,—as much to gain the warriors of the Five Nations to their interest, as to distress the English. Governor *De Nonville* had sent over several chief sachems of the Iroquois to France, where, as usual upon such embassies, great pains were taken to cause them to entertain the highest opinions of the glory and greatness of the French nation. Among them was *Taweraket*, a renowned warrior, and two others. It appears that, during their absence in France, the great war between their countrymen and the French had ended in the destruction of Montreal, and other places, as will be seen detailed in our Fifth Book. Hence, when Count *Frontenac* arrived in Canada, in the fall of 1689, instead of finding the Iroquois ready to join him and his forces which he had brought from France for the conquest of New York, he found himself obliged to set about a reconciliation of them. He therefore wisely despatched *Taweraket*, and the two others, upon that design. The Five Nations, on being called upon by these chiefs, would take no step without first notifying the English at Albany that a council was to be called. The blows which had been so lately given the French of Canada, had lulled the English into a fatal security, and they let this council pass with too little attention to its proceedings. On the other hand, the French were

* This was the German name of a *pine barren*, such as stretches itself between Albany and Schenectady, over which is now a rail-road.

† French ships, with land forces and munitions, had, but a short time before, hovered upon the coast.

fully and ably represented; and the result was, the existing breach was set in a fair way to be closed up. This great council was begun 22 January, 1690 and consisted of eighty sachems. It was opened by *Sadekanaghtie*,* a great Oneida chief.

Meanwhile, to give employment to the Indians who yet remained their friends, the expedition was begun which ended in the destruction of Schenectady. Chief Justice *Smith*† wrote his account of that affair from a manuscript letter left by Colonel *Schuyler*, at that time mayor of Albany; and it is the most particular of any account yet published. It is as follows, and bears date 15 February, 1689:—

After two-and-twenty days' march, the enemy fell in with Schenectady, February 8. There were about 200 French, and perhaps 50 Caughnewaga Mohawks, and they at first intended to have surprised Albany; but their march had been so long and tedious, occasioned by the deepness of the snow and coldness of the weather, that, instead of attempting any thing offensive, they had nearly decided to surrender themselves to the first English they should meet, such was their distressed situation, in a camp of snow, but a few miles from the devoted settlement. The Indians, however, saved them from the disgrace. They had sent out a small scout from their party, who entered Schenectady without even exciting suspicion of their errand. When they had staid as long as the nature of their business required, they withdrew to their fellows.

Seeing that Schenectady offered such an easy prey, it put new courage into the French, and they came upon it as above related. The bloody tragedy commenced between 11 and 12 o'clock, on Saturday night; and, that every house might be surprised at nearly the same time, the enemy divided themselves into parties of six or seven men each. Although the town was impaled, no one thought it necessary to close the gates, even at night, presuming the severity of the season was a sufficient security; hence the first news of the approach of the enemy was at every door of every house, which doors were broken as soon as the profound slumbers of those they were intended to guard The same inhuman barbarities now followed, that were afterwards perpetrated upon the wretched inhabitants of Montreal.‡ "No tongue," said Colonel *Schuyler*, "can express the cruelties that were committed." Sixty-three houses, and the church,§ were immediately in a blaze. *Enciente* women, in their expiring agonies, saw their infants cast into the flames, being first delivered by the knife of the midnight assassin! Sixty-three ‖ persons were put to death, and twenty-seven were carried into captivity.

A few persons fled towards Albany, with no other covering but their night-clothes; the horror of whose condition was greatly enhanced by a great fall of snow; 25 of whom lost their limbs from the severity of the frost. With these poor fugitives came the intelligence to Albany, and that place was in dismal confusion, having, as usual upon such occasions, supposed the enemy to have been seven times more numerous than they really were. About noon, the next day, the enemy set off from Schenectady, taking all the plunder they could carry with them, among which were forty of the best horses. The rest, with all the cattle and other domestic animals, lay slaughtered in the streets.

One of the most considerable men of Schenectady, at this time, was Captain *Alexander Glen.*¶ He lived on the opposite side of the river, and was suffered to escape, because he had delivered many French prisoners from torture and slavery, who had been taken by the Indians in the former wars. They had passed his house in the night, and, during the massacre, he had taken the alarm, and in the morning he was found ready to defend himself. Before leaving the village, a French officer summoned him to a council, upon the shore of the river, with the tender of personal safety. He at length adventured down, and had the great satisfaction of having all his captured friends and relatives delivered to him; and the enemy departed, keeping good their promise that no injury should be done him.‖

* *Sadageenaghtie* in Pownal on the Colonies, I. 398.
† Hist. N. York
‡ See Book V.
§ *Spafford.*
‖ *Colden*, 115.
¶ *Charlevoix* calls him *The Sieur Coudre.*

The great Mohawk castle was about 17 miles from Schenectady, and they did not hear of the massacre until two days after, owing to the state of travelling. On receiving the news, they immediately joined a party of men from Albany, and pursued the enemy. After a tedious pursuit, they fell upon their rear, killed and took 25 of them, and did them some other damage. Several chief sachems soon assembled at Albany, to condole with the people, and animate them against leaving the place, which, it seems, they were about to do. From a speech of one of the chiefs on this occasion, the following extract is preserved:—

"Brethren, we do not think that what the French have done can be called a victory; it is only a further proof of their cruel deceit. The governor of Canada sent to Onondago, and talks to us of peace with our whole house; but war was in his heart, as you now see by woful experience. He did the same formerly at Cadaracqui,* and in the Senecas' country. This is the third time he has acted so deceitfully. He has broken open our house at both ends; formerly in he Senecas' country, and now here. We hope to be revenged on them."

Accordingly, when messengers came to renew and conclude the treaty which had been begun by *Taweraket*, before mentioned, they were seized and handed over to the English. They also kept out scouts, and harassed the French in every direction.

We will now proceed to draw from *Charlevoix*' account of this affair, which is very minute, as it respects the operations of the French and Indians. Notwithstanding its great importance in a correct history of the sacking of Schenectady, none of our historians seem to have given themselves the trouble of laying it before their readers.

Governor *Frontenac*, having determined upon an expedition, gave notice to *M. de la Durantaye*, who then commanded at Michilimakinak, that he might assure the Hurons and Ottawas, that in a short time they would see a great change in affairs for the better. He prepared at the same time a large convoy to reinforce that post, and he took measures also to raise three war parties, who should enter by three different routes the country of the English. The first assembled at Montreal, and consisted of about 110 men, French and Indians, and was put under the command of *MM. d'Aillebout de Mantet*, and *le Moine de St. Helene*, two lieutenants, under whom *MM. de Repentigny*, *d'Iberville*, DE BONREPOS, DE LA BROSSE, and DE MONTIGNI, requested permission to serve as volunteers.

This party marched out before they had determined against what part of the English frontier they would carry their arms, though some part of New York was understood. Count *Frontenac* had left that to the two commanders. After they had marched five or six days, they called a council to determine upon what place they would attempt. In this council, it was debated, on the part of the French, that Albany would be the smallest place they ought to undertake; but the Indians would not agree to it. They contended that, with their small force, an attack upon Albany would be attended with extreme hazard. The French being strenuous, the debate grew warm, and an Indian chief asked them "how long it was since they had so much courage." To this severe rebuke it was answered, that, if by some past actions they had discovered cowardice, they should see that now they would retrieve their character; they would take Albany or die in the attempt. The Indians, however, would not consent, and the council broke up without agreeing upon any thing but to proceed on.

They continued their march until they came to a place where their path divided into two; one of which led to Albany, and the other to Schenectady: here *Mantet* gave up his design upon Albany, and they marched on harmoniously for the former village. The weather was very severe, and for the nine following days the little army suffered incredible hardships. The men were often obliged to wade through water up to their knees, breaking its ice at every step.

---

* See Book V.

At 4 o'clock in the morning, the beginning of February, they arrived within two leagues of Schenectady. Here they halted, and the *Great Agnier*, chief of the Iroquois of the Falls of St. Louis, made a speech to them. He exhorted every one to forget the hardships they had endured, in the hope of avenging the wrongs they had for a long time suffered from the perfidious English, who were the authors of them; and in the close added, that they could not doubt of the assistance of Heaven against the enemies of God, in a cause so just.

Hardly had they taken up their line of march, when they met 40 Indian women, who gave them all the necessary information for approaching the place in safety. A Canadian, named *Giguiere*, was detached immediately with nine Indians upon discovery, who acquitted himself to the entire satisfaction of his officers. He reconnoitred Schenectady at his leisure, and then rejoined his comrades.

It had been determined by the party to put off the attack one day longer; but on the arrival of the scout under *Giguiere*, it was resolved to proceed without delay.

Schenectady was then in form like that of a long square, and entered by two gates, one at each end. One opened towards Albany, the other upon the great road leading into the back country, and which was now possessed by the French and Indians. *Mantet* and *St. Helene* charged at the second gate, which the Indian women before mentioned had assured them was always open, and they found it so. *D'Iberville* and *Repentigni* passed to the left, in order to enter by the other gate, but, after losing some time in vainly endeavoring to find it, were obliged to return and enter with their comrades.

The gate was not only open but unguarded, and the whole party entered without being discovered. Dividing themselves into several parties, they waylaid every portal, and then the war-whoop was raised. *Mantet* formed and attacked a garrison, where the only resistance of any account was made. The gate of it was soon forced, and all of the English fell by the sword, and the garrison was burned. *Montigni* was wounded, in forcing a house, in his arm and body by two blows of a halberd, which put him *hors du combat;* but *St. Helene* being come to his assistance, the house was taken, and the wounds of *Montigni* revenged by the death of all who had shut themselves up in it.

Nothing was now to be seen but massacre and pillage in every place. At the end of about two hours, the chiefs, believing it due to their safety, posted bodies of guards at all the avenues, to prevent surprise, and the rest of the night was spent in refreshing themselves.

Mantet had given orders that the minister of the place should be spared, whom he had intended for his own prisoner; but he was found among the promiscuous dead, and no one knew when he was killed, and all his papers were burned.

After the place was destroyed, the chiefs ordered all the casks of intoxicating liquors to be staved, to prevent their men from getting drunk. They next set all the houses on fire, excepting that of a widow, into which *Montigni* had been carried, and another belonging to Major *Coudre:* they were in number about 40, all well built and furnished; no booty but that which could be easily transported was saved. The lives of about 60 persons were spared, chiefly women, children, and old men, who had escaped the fury of the onset, and 30 Indians who happened to be then in the place. The lives of the Indians were spared that they might carry the news of what had happened to their countrymen, whom they were requested to inform, that it was not against them that they intended any harm, but to the English only, whom they had now despoiled of property to the amount of four hundred thousand pounds.

They were too near Albany to remain long among the ruins, and they decamped about noon. The plunder—*Montigni*, whom it was necessary to carry—the prisoners, who were to the number of 40—and the want of provisions, with which they had in their hurry neglected to provide themselves—retarded much their retreat. Many would have even died of famine, had they not had 50 horses, of which there remained but six when they arrived at Montreal, upon the 27 March following.* Their want of provisions obliged them to separate, and in an attack which was made upon one party, three Indians and six Frenchmen were killed or taken; an attack, which, for want of proper caution, cost the army more lives than the capture of Schenectady; in which they lost but two men, a Frenchman and an Indian.

Murder of Miss Jane McCrea.—This young lady "was the second daughter of *James McCrea*, minister of Lamington, New Jersey, who died before the revolution. After his death, she resided with her brother, Colonel *John McCrea* of Albany, who removed in 1773 to the neighborhood of Fort Edward. His house was in what is now Northumberland, on the west side of the Hudson, three miles north of Fort Miller Falls. In July or August, 1777, being on a visit to the family of Mrs. *McNeil*, near Fort Edward, at the close of the week, she was asked to remain until Monday. On Sunday morning, when the Indians came to the house, she concealed herself in the cellar; but they dragged her out by the hair, and, placing her on a horse, proceeded on the road towards Sandy Hill. They soon met another party of Indians, returning from Argyle, where they had killed the family of Mr. *Bains;* these Indians disapproved the purpose of taking the captive to the British camp, and one of them struck her with a tomahawk and tore off her scalp. This is the account given by her nephew. The account of Mrs. *McNeil* is, that her lover, anxious for her safety, employed two Indians, with the promise of a barrel of rum, to bring her to him; and that, in consequence of their dispute for the right of conducting her, one of them murdered her. Gen. *Gates*, in his letter to Gen. *Burgoyne* of 2 September, says, 'she was dressed to receive her promised husband.'

"Her brother, on hearing of her fate, sent his family the next day to Albany, and, repairing to the American camp, buried his sister, with one Lieutenant *Van Vechten*, three miles south of Fort Edward. She was 23 years old, of an amiable and virtuous character, and highly esteemed by all her acquaintance. It is said, and was believed, that she was engaged in marriage to Captain *David Jones*, of the British army, a loyalist, who survived her only a few years, and died, as was supposed, of grief for her loss. Her nephew, Colonel *James McCrea*, lived at Saratoga, in 1823."†

Under the name of *Lucinda*, *Barlow* has dwelt upon this murder in a strain that may be imitated, but not surpassed. We select from him as follows:—

"One deed shall tell what fame great Albion draws
From these auxiliars in her barb'rous cause,—
Lucinda's fate. The tale, ye nations, hear;
Eternal ages, trace it with a tear."

The poet then makes *Lucinda*, during a battle, wander from her home to watch her lover, whom he calls *Heartly*. She distinguishes him in the conflict, and, when his squadron is routed by the Americans, she proceeds to the contested ground, fancying she had seen him fall at a certain point. But

"He hurries to his tent;—oh, rage! despair!
No glimpse, no tidings, of the frantic fair;
Save that some carmen, as a-camp they drove,
Had seen her coursing for the western grove.
Faint with fatigue, and choked with burning thirst,
Forth from his friends, with bounding leap, he burst,
Vaults o'er the palisade, with eyes on flame,
And fills the welkin with *Lucinda's* name."
"The fair one, too, of every aid forlorn,
Had raved and wandered, till officious morn
Awaked the Mohawks from their short repose,
To glean the plunder ere their comrades rose.
Two Mohawks met the maid——historian, hold!"—
"She starts—with eyes upturned and fleeting breath,
In their raised axes views her instant death.
Her hair, half lost along the shrubs she passed,
Rolls, in loose tangles, round her lovely waist;
Her kerchief torn betrays the globes of snow,
That heave responsive to her weight of woe.

* There is no doubt but that they were obliged to subsist chiefly upon their horses.
† President *Allen's* American Biographical Dictionary, 574.

With calculating pause and demon grin
They seize her hands, and, through her face divine,
Drive the descending axe!—the shriek she sent
Attained her lover's ear; he thither bent
With all the speed his wearied limbs could yield,
Whirled his keen blade, and stretched upon the field
The yelling fiends, who there disputing stood
Her gory scalp, their horrid prize of blood!
He sunk, delirious, on her lifeless clay,
And passed, in starts of sense, the dreadful day."

In a note to the above passages, Mr. *Barlow* says this tragical story of Miss *McCrea* is detailed almost literally.

"*Extraordinary instance of female heroism, extracted from a letter written by Col.* James Perry *to the Rev.* Jordan Dodge, *dated Nelson Co., Ky.*, 20 *April*, 1788."—"On the first of April inst., a number of Indians surrounded the house of one *John Merril*, which was discovered by the barking of a dog. *Merril* stepped to the door to see what he could discover, and received three musket-balls, which caused him to fall back into the house with a broken leg and arm. The Indians rushed on to the door; but it being instantly fastened by his wife, who, with a girl of about 15 years of age, stood against it, the savages could not immediately enter. They broke one part of the door, and one of them crowded partly through. The heroic mother, in the midst of her screaming children and groaning husband, seized an axe, and gave a fatal blow to the savage; and he falling headlong into the house, the others, supposing they had gained their end, rushed after him, until four of them fell in like manner before they discovered their mistake. The rest retreated, which gave opportunity again to secure the door. The conquerors rejoiced in their victory, hoping they had killed the whole company; but their expectations were soon dashed, by finding the door again attacked, which the bold mother endeavored once more to secure, with the assistance of the young woman. Their fears now came on them like a flood; and they soon heard a noise on the top of the house, and then found the Indians were coming down the chimney. All hopes of deliverance seemed now at an end; but the wounded man ordered his little child to tumble a couch, that was filled with hair and feathers, on the fire, which made such a smoke that two stout Indians came tumbling down into it. The wounded man, at this critical moment, seized a billet of wood, wounded as he was, and with it succeeded in despatching the half-smothered Indians. At the same moment, the door was attempted by another; but the heroine's arm had become too enfeebled by her over-exertions to deal a deadly blow. She however caused him to retreat wounded. They then again set to work to make their house more secure, not knowing but another attack would be made; but they were not further disturbed. This affair happened in the evening, and the victors carefully watched with their new family until morning. A prisoner, that escaped immediately after, said the Indian last mentioned was the only one that escaped. He, on returning to his friends, was asked, 'What news?' said, 'Plaguy bad news, for the squaws fight worse than the long-knives.' This affair happened at Newbardstown, about 15 miles from Sandy Creek, and may be depended upon, as I had the pleasure to assist in tumbling them into a hole, after they were stripped of their head-dresses, and about 20 dollars' worth of silver furniture."

Welsh or White Indians.

"*Narrative of Capt.* Isaac Stuart, *of the Provincial Cavalry of South Carolina, taken from his own mouth, by* I. C., Esq., *March*, 1782.

"I was taken prisoner, about 50 miles to the westward of Fort Pitt, about 18 years ago, by the Indians, and carried to the Wabash, with other white men. They were executed, with circumstances of horrid barbarity; but it was my good fortune to call forth the sympathy of a good woman of the village, who was permitted to redeem me from those who held me prisoner, by giving them a horse as a ransom. After remaining two years in bondage, a Spaniard came to the nation, having been sent from Mexico on discoveries

He made application to the chiefs of the Indians for hiring me, and another white man who was in the like situation, a native of Wales, and named *John Davey*, which was complied with. We took our departure and travelled to the westward, crossing the Mississippi near Red River, up which we travelled upwards of 700 miles. Here we came to a nation of Indians remarkably white, and whose hair was of a reddish color, at least, mostly so. They lived on a small river which emptied itself into Red River, which they called the River Post; and in the morning, the day after our arrival, the Welshman informed me that he was determined to remain with the nation of Indians, giving as a reason that he understood their language, it being very little different from the Welsh. My curiosity was excited very much by this information, and I went with my companion to the chief men of the town, who informed him, in a language that I had no knowledge of, and which had no affinity with that of any other Indian tongue that I ever heard, that the forefathers of this nation came from a foreign country, and landed on the east side of the Mississippi (describing particularly the country now called West Florida); and that, on the Spaniards taking possession of the country, they fled to their then abode; and, as a proof of what they advanced, they brought out rolls of parchment wrote with blue ink, at least it had a bluish cast. The characters I did not understand, and the Welshman being unacquainted with letters of any language, I was not able to know what the meaning of the writing was. They were a bold, hardy, intrepid people, very warlike, and their women were beautiful, compared with other Indians."

Thus we have given so much of Captain *Stuart's* narrative as relates to the WHITE INDIANS. The remainder of it is taken up in details of several excursions, of many hundred miles, in the interior of the continent, without any extraordinary occurrence, except the finding of a gold mine. He returned by way of the Mississippi, and was considered a man of veracity by the late Lieutenant-colonel *Cruger*, of South Carolina, who recommended him to the gentleman who communicated his narrative.

I had determined formerly to devote a chapter to the examination of the subject of the White Indians; but, on reference to all the sources of information in my possession, I found that the whole rested upon no other authority than such as we have given above, and therefore concluded to give the most interesting parts of the accounts without comment, and let the reader draw his own conclusions. There seem to have been a good many accounts concerning the White Indians in circulation about the same period, and the next we shall notice is found in Mr. *Charles Beatty's* journal, the substance of which is as follows: —

At the foot of the Alleghany Mountains, in Pennsylvania, Mr. *Beatty* stopped at the house of a Mr. *John Miller*, where he "met with one *Benjamin Sutton*, who had been taken captive by the Indians, and had been in different nations, and lived many years among them. When he was with the Choctaws, at the Mississippi River, he went to an Indian town, a very considerable distance from New Orleans, whose inhabitants were of different complexions, not so tawny as those of the other Indians, and who spoke Welsh. He saw a book among them, which he supposed was a Welsh Bible, which they carefully kept wrapped up in a skin, but they could not read it; and he heard some of those Indians afterwards, in the lower Shawanee town, speak Welsh with one *Lewis*, a Welshman, captive there. This Welsh tribe now live on the west side of the Mississippi, a great way above New Orleans."

At Tuscarora valley he met with another man, named *Levi Hicks*, who had been a captive from his youth with the Indians. He said he was once attending an embassy at an Indian town, on the west side of the Mississippi, where the inhabitants spoke Welsh, as he was told, for he did not understand them himself. An Indian, named *Joseph Peepy*, Mr. *Beatty's* interpreter, said he once saw some Indians, whom he supposed to be of the same tribe, who talked Welsh. He was sure they talked Welsh, for he had been acquainted with Welsh people, and knew some words they used.

To the above Mr. *Beatty* adds: "I have been informed, that many years ago, a clergyman went from Britain to Virginia, and having lived some time there, went from thence to S. Carolina; but after some time, for some reason, he resolved to return to Virginia, and accordingly set out by land, accompanied with some other persons. In travelling through the back parts of the country, which was then very thinly inhabited, he fell in with a party of Indian warriors, going to attack the inhabitants of Virginia. Upon examining the clergyman, and finding he was going to Virginia, they looked upon him and his companions as belonging to that province, and took them all prisoners, and told them they must die. The clergyman, in preparation for another world, went to prayer, and, being a Welshman, prayed in the Welsh language. One or more of the Indians was much surprised to hear him pray in their own language. Upon this they spoke to him, and finding he could understand them, got the sentence of death reversed, and his life was saved. They took him with them into their country, where he found a tribe whose native language was Welsh, though the dialect was a little different from his own, which he soon came to understand. They showed him a book, which he found to be the Bible, but which they could not read; and on his reading and explaining it, their regard for him was much heightened." After some time, the minister proposed to these people to return to his own country, and promised to return again to them with others of his friends, who would instruct them in Christianity; but not long after his return to England, he died, which put an end to his design.

It is very natural to inquire how these Indians, though descended from the Welsh, came by books; for it is well known that the period at which the Welsh must have come to America, was long before printing was discovered, or that any writings assumed the form of books as we now have them. It should be here noted that Mr. *Beatty* travelled in the autumn of 1766.

Major *Rogers*, in his "Concise Account of North America," published in 1765, notices the White Indians; but the geography of their country he leaves any where on the west of the Mississippi; probably never having visited them himself, although he tells us he had travelled very extensively in the interior. "This fruitful country," he says, "is at present inhabited by a nation of Indians, called by the others the White Indians, on account of their complexion; they being much the fairest Indians on the continent. They have, however, Indian eyes, and a certain guilty Jewish cast with them. This nation is very numerous, being able to raise between 20 and 30,000 fighting men. They have no weapons but bows and arrows, tomahawks, and a kind of wooden pikes, for which reason they often suffer greatly from the eastern Indians, who have the use of fire-arms, and frequently visit the White Indians on the banks of the easterly branch, [of Muddy River?] and kill or captivate them in great numbers. Such as fall alive into their hands, they generally sell for slaves. These Indians live in large towns, and have commodious houses; they raise corn, tame the wild cows, and use both their milk and flesh; they keep great numbers of dogs, and are very dexterous in hunting; they have little or no commerce with any nation that we at present are acquainted with."

In the account of Kentucky, written in 1784, by an excellent writer, Mr. *John Filson*, we find as follows:—After noticing the voyage of *Madoc*, who with his ten ships with emigrants sailed west about 1170, and who were, according to the Welsh historians, never heard of after, he proceeds:—"This account has at several times drawn the attention of the world; but as no vestiges of them had then been found, it was concluded, perhaps too rashly, to be a fable, or at least that no remains of the colony existed. Of late years, however, the western settlers have received frequent accounts of a nation, inhabiting at a great distance up the Missouri, in manners and appearance resembling the other Indians, but speaking Welsh, and retaining some ceremonies of the Christian worship; and at length this is universally believed there to be a fact. Capt. *Abraham Chaplain*, of Kentucky, a gentleman whose veracity may be entirely depended upon, assured the author that in the late war [revolution] being with his company in garrison, at Kaskaskia, some Indians came there, and, speaking the Welsh dialect, were perfectly understood and conversed with by two Welshmen in his company, and that they informed them of the situation of their nation as mentioned above."

Henry Ker, who travelled among 13 tribes of Indians in 1810, &c., names one near a great mountain which he calls Mnacedeus. He said Dr. *Sibley* had told him, when at Natchitoches, that a number of travellers had assured him, that there was a strong similarity between the Indian language and many words of the Welsh. Mr. *Ker* found nothing among any of the Indians to indicate a Welsh origin until he arrived among the Mnacedeus. Here he found many customs which were Welsh, or common to that people, and he adds; "I did not understand the Welsh language, or I should have been enabled to have thrown more light upon so interesting a subject," as they had "printed books among them which were preserved with great care, they having a tradition that they were brought there by their forefathers." Upon this, in another place, he observes, "The books appeared very old, and were evidently printed at a time when there had been very little improvement made in the casting of types. I obtained a few leaves from one of the chiefs, sufficient to have thrown light on the subject; but in my subsequent disputes with the Indians, I lost them, and all my endeavors to obtain more were ineffectual."

How or at what time these Indians obtained "printed books," Mr. *Ker* does not give us his opinion; although he says much more about them.

There are a great number of others who have noticed those Indians; but after an examination of them all, I am unable to add much to the above stock of information concerning them. Upon the whole, we think it may be pretty safely said, that the existence of a race of Welsh about the regions of the Missouri does not rest on so good authority as that which has been adduced to establish the existence of the sea-serpent. Should any one, however, choose to investigate the subject further, he will find pretty ample references to authors in which the subject has been noticed, in a note to the life of Madokawando, in our third book. In addition to which, he may consult the authorities of *Moulton*, as pointed out in his history of New York

CHAPTER IV.

AMERICAN ANTIQUITIES—*Few Indian Antiquities—Of Mounds and their contents—Account of those in Cincinnati—In the Miami country—Works supposed to have been built for defences or fortifications—Some at Piqua—Near Hamilton—Milford—Deerfield—Six miles above Lebanon—On Paint Creek—At Marietta—At Circleville—Their age uncertain—Works on Licking River Ancient excavations or wells near Newark—Various other works.*

To describe the antiquities of America would not require a very great amount of time or space, if we consider only those which are in reality such. And as to Indian antiquities, they consist in nothing like monuments, says Mr. *Jefferson;* "for," he observes, "I would not honor with that name, arrow-points, stone hatchets, stone pipes, and half-shapen images. Of labor on the large scale, I think there is no remain as respectable as would be a common ditch for the draining of lands, unless indeed it would be the Barrows, of which many are to be found all over in this country. These are of different sizes, some of them constructed of earth, and some of loose stones. That they were repositories of the dead, has been obvious to all; but on what particular occasion constructed, was a matter of doubt. Some have thought they covered the bones of those who have fallen in battles fought on the spot of interment. Some ascribe them to the custom, said to prevail among the Indians, of collecting at certain periods the bones of all their dead, wheresoever deposited at the time of death. Others again suppose them the general sepulchres for towns, conjectured to have been on or near these grounds; and this opinion was supported by the quality of the lands in which they are found, (those constructed of earth being generally in the softest and most fertile meadow-grounds on river sides,) and by a tradition, said to be handed down from the aboriginal Indians, that when they settled in a town, the first person who died was placed erect, and earth put about him, so as to cover and support him; and that when another died, a narrow passage was dug to the first, the second reclined against him, and the cover of earth replaced, and so on. There being one of these in my neighborhood, I wished to satisfy myself whether any, and which of these opinions were just. For this purpose, I determined to open and examine it thoroughly. It was situated on the low grounds of the Rivanna, about two miles above its principal fork, and opposite to some hills, on which had been an Indian town. It was of a spheroidal form, of about 40 feet diameter at the base, and had been of about 12 feet altitude, though now reduced by the plough to seven and a half, having been under cultivation about a dozen years. Before this it was covered with trees of 12 inches diameter, and round the base was an excavation of five feet depth and width, from whence the earth had been taken of which the hillock was formed."

In this mound my author found abundance of human bones, which, from their position, it was evident had been thrown or piled promiscuously there together; bones of the head and feet being in contact; "some vertical, some oblique, some horizontal, and directed to every point of the compass." These bones, when exposed to the air, crumbled to dust. Some of the skulls, jawbones, and teeth, were taken out nearly in a perfect state, but would fall to pieces on being examined. It was evident that this assemblage of bones was made up from persons of all ages, and at different periods of time. The mound was composed of alternate strata of bones, stones, and earth. Hence it would seem that barrows, or mounds, as they are most usually called, were formed by the Indians, whose custom it was to collect the bones of their deceased friends at certain periods, and deposit them together in this manner. "But," Mr. *Jefferson* observes, "on whatever occasion they may have been made, they are of considerable notoriety among the Indians: for a party passing, about 30 years ago, through the part of the country where this barrow is, went through the woods directly to it, without any instructions or inquiry, and having staid about it some time, with expressions which were construed to be those of sorrow, they returned to the high road, which they had left about half a dozen miles to pay this visit, and pursued their journey."

In these tumuli are usually found, with the bones, such instruments only as appear to have been used for superstitious purposes, ornaments or war. Of the latter kind, no more formidable weapons have been discovered than tomahawks, spears and arrow-heads, which can be supposed to have been deposited before the arrival of Europeans in America. What Mr. *Jefferson* found in the barrow he dissected besides bones, or whether any thing, he does not inform us. In several of these depositories in the city of Cincinnati, which Dr. *Daniel Drake* examined, numerous utensils were found. He has given a most accurate account of them, in which he has shown himself no less a philosopher than antiquary. He divides them into two classes, ancient and modern, or ancient and more ancient. "Among the latter," he says, "there is not a single edifice, nor any ruins which prove the existence, in former ages, of a building composed of imperishable materials. No fragment of a column, no bricks, nor a single hewn stone large enough to have been incorporated into a wall, has been discovered."

There were several of these mounds or tumuli, 20 years ago, within a short space in and about Cincinnati; but it is a remarkable fact, that the plains on the opposite side of the River Ohio have no vestiges of the kind. The largest of those in Cincinnati was, in 1794, about 35 feet in height; but at this time it was cut down to 27 by order of General *Wayne*, to make it serve as a watch-tower for a sentinel. It was about 440 feet in circumference.

Almost every traveller of late years has said something upon the mounds, or fortifications, scattered over the south and west, from Florida to the lakes, and from the Hudson to Mexico and the Pacific Ocean. By some they are reckoned at several thousands. Mr. *Brackenridge* supposes there may be 3000; but it would not outrage probability, I presume, to set them down at twice that number. Indeed no one can form any just estimate in respect to the number of mounds and fortifications which have been built, any more than of the period of time which has passed since they were originally erected, for several obvious reasons; one or two of which may be mentioned: — the plough, excavations and levellings for towns, roads, and various other works, have entirely destroyed hundreds of them, which had never been described and whose sites cannot now be ascertained. Another great destruction of them has been effected by the changing of the course of rivers.

There are various opinions about the uses for which these ancient remains were constructed: while some of them are too much like modern fortifications to admit of a doubt of their having been used for defences, others, nearly similar in design, from their situation entirely exclude the adoption of such an opinion. Hence we find four kinds of remains formed of earth: two kinds of mounds or barrows, and two which have been viewed as fortifications The barrows or burial piles are distinguished by such as contain articles which were inhumed with the dead, and those which do not contain them. From what cause they differ in this respect it is difficult to determine. Some have supposed the former to contain bones only of warriors, but in such mounds the bones of infants are found, and hence that hypothesis is overthrown; and indeed an hypothesis can scarcely be raised upon any one matter concerning them without almost a positive assurance that it has been created to be destroyed.

As a specimen of the contents of the mounds generally, the following may be taken; being such as Dr. *Drake* found in those he examined:—1. Cylindrical stones, such as jasper, rock-crystal, and granite; with a groove near one end. 2. A circular piece of cannel coal, with a large opening in the centre, as though made for the reception of an axis; and a deep groove in the circumference, suitable for a band. 3. A smaller article of the same shape, but composed of polished argillaceous earth. 4. A bone, ornamented with several carved lines, supposed by some to be hieroglyphics. 5. A sculptural representation of the head and beak of some rapacious bird. 6. Lumps of lead ore. 7. Isinglass (mica membranacea). This article is very common in mounds, and seems to have been held in high estimation among the people that constructed them; but we know not that modern Indians have any particular attachment to it. A superior article, though much like it, was also in great esteem among the ancient Mexicans. 8. Small pieces of sheet copper, with perforations. 9. Larger oblong pieces of the same metal, with longitudinal grooves and ridges. 10. Beads, or sections of small hollow cylinders, apparently of bone or shell. 11. Teeth of carnivorous animals. 12. Large marine shells, belonging, perhaps, to the genus buccinum; cut in such a manner as to serve for domestic utensils. These, and also the teeth of animals, are generally found almost entirely decomposed, or in a state resembling chalk. 13. Earthern ware. This seems to have been made of the same material as that employed by the Indians of Louisiana within our recollection, viz. pounded muscle and other river shells, and earth. Some perfect articles have been found, but they are rare. Pieces, or fragments, are very common. Upon most of them, confused lines are traced, which doubtless had some meaning; but no specimen has yet been found having glazing upon it like modern pottery. Some entire vases, of most uncouth appearance, have been found. Mr. *Atwater* of Ohio, who has pretty fully described the western antiquities, gives an account of a vessel, which seems to have been used as a jug. It was found in an ancient work on Cany Fork of Cumberland River, about four feet below the surface. The body of the vessel is made by three heads, all joined together at their backs. From these places of contact a neck is formed, which rises about three inches above the heads. The orifice of this neck is near two inches in diameter, and the three necks of the heads form the legs of the vessel on which it stands when upright. The heads are all of a size, being about four inches from the top to the chin. The faces at the eyes are about three inches broad, which increase in breadth all the way to the chin.

Of the works called fortifications, though already mentioned in general terms, their importance demands a further consideration.

At Piqua, on the western side of the Great Miami, there is a circular wall of earth inclosing a space of about 100 feet in diameter, with an opening on the side most remote from the river. "The adjacent hill, at the distance of half a mile, and at the greater elevation of about 100 feet, is the site of a stone wall, nearly circular, and inclosing perhaps 20 acres. The valley of the river on one side, and a deep ravine on the other, render the access to three fourths of this fortification extremely difficult. The wall was carried generally along the brow of the hill, in one place descending a short distance so as to include a spring. The silicious limestone of which it was built, must have been transported from the bed of the river, which, for two miles opposite these works, does not at present afford one of 10 pounds weight. They exhibit no marks of the hammer, or any other tool. The wall was laid up without mortar, and is now in ruins.

"Lower down the same river, near the mouth of Hole's Creek, on the plain, there are remains of great extent. The principal wall or bank, which is of earth, incloses about 160 acres, and is in some parts nearly 12 feet high. Also below Hamilton, there is a fortification upon the top of a high hill, out of view from the river, of very difficult approach. This incloses about 50 acres. Adjacent to this work is a mound 25 feet in diameter at its base, and about seven feet perpendicular altitude.

"On the elevated point of land above the confluence of the Great Miami and Ohio, there are extensive and complicated traces, which, in the opinion of military men, eminently qualified to judge, are the remains of very strong defensive works."

In the vicinity of Milford, on the Little Miami, are fortifications, the largest of which are upon the top of the first hill above the confluence of the East Fork with the Miami. "On the opposite side of the Miami River, above Round Bottom, are similar antiquities of considerable extent. On the East Fork, at its head waters, other remains have been discovered, of which the principal bears a striking resemblance to those above mentioned; but within, it differs from any which have yet been examined in this quarter, in having nine parallel banks or long parapets united at one end, exhibiting very exactly the figure of a gridiron.

"Further up the Little Miami, at Deerfield, are other interesting remains; but those which have attracted more attention than any others in the Miami country, are situated six miles from Lebanon, above the mouth of Todd's Fork, an eastern branch of the Miami. On the summit of a ridge at least 200 feet above the valley of the river, there are two irregular trapezoidal figures, connected at a point where the ridge is very much narrowed by a ravine. The wall, which is entirely of earth, is generally eight or ten feet high; but in one place, where it is conducted over level ground for a short distance, it rises to 18. Its situation is accurately adjusted to the brow of the hill; and as there is, in addition to the Miami on the west, deep ravines on the north, the south-east, and south, it is a position of great strength. The angles in this wall, both retreating and salient, are numerous, and generally acute. The openings or gateways are not less than 80! They are rarely at equal distances, and are sometimes within two or three rods of one another. They are not opposite to, or connected with any existing artificial objects or topographical peculiarities, and present, therefore, a paradox of some difficulty." These works inclose almost 100 acres, and one of the state roads from Cincinnati to Chillicothe passes over its northern part.

On Paint Creek, 10 miles from Chillicothe, are also very extensive as well as wonderful works. "The wall, which had been conducted along the verge of the hill, is by estimation about a mile and a half in length. It was formed entirely of undressed freestone, brought chiefly from the streams 250 feet below, and laid up without mortar or cement of any sort. It is now, like all the walls of a similar kind which have been discovered in the western country, in a state of ruins. It exhibits the appearance of having been shaken down by an earthquake, not a single stone being found upon another in such a manner as to indicate that to have been its situation in the wall. In several places there are openings, immediately opposite which, inside, lie piles of stone."

Dr. *Harris*, in 1803, very accurately described the remains at Marietta, at the confluence of the Muskingum and Ohio Rivers. "The largest SQUARE FORT," he observes, "by some called *the town*, contains 40 acres, encompassed by a wall of earth from 6 to 10 feet high, and from 25 to 36 in breadth at the base. On each side are three openings at equal distances, resembling 12 gateways. The entrances at the middle are the largest, particularly that on the side next the Muskingum. From this outlet is a COVERT WAY, formed of two parallel walls of earth, 231 feet distant from each other, measuring from centre to centre. The walls at the most elevated part on the inside are 21 feet in height, and 42 in breadth at the base, but on the outside average only of five feet high. This forms a passage of about 360 feet in length, leading by a gradual descent to the low grounds, where it, probably, at the time of its construction, reached the margin of the river. Its walls commence at 60 feet from the ramparts of the fort, and increase in elevation as the way descends tawards the river; and the bottom is crowned in the centre, in the manner of a well-formed turnpike road. Within the walls of the fort, at the north-west corner, is an oblong, elevated square, 188 feet long, 132 broad, and nine feet high; level on the summit, and nearly perpendicular at the sides. At the centre of each of the sides the earth is projected, forming gradual ascents to the top, equally regular, and about six feet in width. Near the south wall is another elevated square, 150 feet by 120, and eight feet high. At the south-east corner is the third elevated square, 108 by 54 feet, with ascents at the ends. At the south-east corner of the fort is a semicircular parapet, crowned with a mound, which guards the opening in the wall. Towards the south-east is A SIMILAR FORT, containing 20 acres, with a gateway in the centre of each side and at each corner. These openings are defended with circular mounds."

There are also other works at Marietta, but a mere description of them cannot interest, as there is so much of sameness about them. And to describe all that may be met with would fill a volume of no moderate size: for Dr. *Harris* says, "You cannot ride 20 miles in any direction without finding some of the mounds, or vestiges of the ramparts." We shall, therefore, only notice the most prominent.

Of first importance are doubtless the works upon the Scioto. The most magnificent is situated 26 miles south from Columbus, and consists of two nearly exact figures, a circle and a square, which are contiguous to each other. A town, having been built within the former, appropriately received the name of Circleville from that circumstance. According to Mr. *Atwater*, who has surveyed these works with great exactness and attention, the circle was originally 1138½ feet in diameter, from external parallel tangents, and the square was 907½ feet upon a side; giving an area to the latter of 3025 square rods, and to the circle 3739 nearly; both making almost 44 acres. The rampart of the circular fort consists of two parallel walls, and were, at least in the opinion of my author, 20 feet in height, measuring from the bottom of the ditch between the circumvallations, before the town of Circleville was built. "The inner wall was of clay, taken up probably in the northern part of the fort, where was a low place, and is still considerably lower than any other part of the work. The outside wall was taken from the ditch which is between these walls, and is alluvial, consisting of pebbles worn smooth in water and sand, to a very considerable depth, more than 50 feet at least." At the time Mr. *Atwater* wrote his account, (about 1819,) the outside of the walls was but about five or six feet high, and the ditch not more than 15 feet deep. The walls of the square fort were, at the same time, about 10 feet high. This fort had eight gateways or openings, about 20 feet broad, each of which was defended by a mound four or five feet high, all within the fort, arranged in the most exact manner; equidistant and parallel. The circular fort had but one gateway, which was at its south-east point, and at the place of contact with the square. In the centre of the square was a remarkable mound, with a semicircular pavement adjacent to its eastern half, and nearly facing the passage way into the square fort. Just without the square fort, upon the north side, and to the east of the centre gateway, rises a large mound. In the opposite point of the compass, without the circular one, is another. These, probably, were the places of burial. As the walls of the square fort lie pretty nearly in a line with the cardinal points of the horizon, some have supposed they were originally projected in strict regard to them; their variation not being more than that of the compass; but a single fact of this kind can establish nothing, as mere accident may have given them such direction. "What surprised me," says my authority, "on measuring these forts, was the exact manner in which they had laid down their circle and square; so that after every effort, by the most careful survey, to detect some error in their measurement, we found that it was impossible."

As it is not my design to waste time in conjectures upon the authors of these antiquities, or the remoteness of the period in which they were constructed, I will continue my account of them, after an observation upon a single circumstance. I refer to the fact of the immense trees found growing upon the mounds and other ancient works. Their having existed for a thousand years, or at least some of them, can scarcely be questioned, when we know from unerring data that trees have been cut upon them of the age of near 500 years; and from the vegetable mould out of which they spring, there is every appearance of several generations of decayed trees of the same kind; and no forest trees of the present day appear older than those upon the very works under consideration.

There are in the Forks of Licking River, above Newark, in the county of Licking, very remarkable remains of antiquity, said by many to be as much so as any in the west. Here, as at Circleville, the same singular fact is observable, respecting the openings into the forts; the square ones having several, but the round ones only one, with a single exception.

Not far below Newark, on the south side of the Licking, are found numerous wells or holes in the earth. "There are," says Mr. *Atwater*, "at least a thousand of them, many of which are now more than 20 feet deep." Though called wells, my author says they were not dug for that purpose. They have the appearance of being of the same age as the mounds, and were doubtless made by the same people; but for what purpose they could have been made, few seem willing to hazard a conjecture.

Four or five miles to the north-west of Somerset, in the county of Perry, and southwardly from the works on the Licking, is a stone fort, inclosing about 40 acres. Its shape is that of a heart, though bounded by straight lines. In or near its centre is a circular stone mound, which rises like a sugar-loaf from 12 to 15 feet. Near this large work is another small fort, whose walls are of earth, inclosing but about half an acre. I give these the name of forts, although Mr. *Atwater* says he does not believe they were ever constructed for defence.

There are curious remains on both sides of the Ohio, above and opposite the mouth of the Scioto. Those on the north side, at Portsmouth, are the most extensive, and those on the other side, directly opposite Alexandria, are the most regular. They are not more remarkable than many already described.

What the true height of these ruined works originally was, cannot be very well ascertained, as it is almost impossible to know the rate of their diminution, even were the space of time given; but there can be no doubt that most of them are much diminished from the action of tempests which have swept over them for ages. That they were the works of a different race from the present Indians, has been pretty confidently asserted; but as yet, proof is entirely wanting to support such conclusion. In a few instances, some European articles have been found deposited in or about some of the works; but few persons of intelligence pronounce them older than others of the same kind belonging to the period of the French wars.

As it respects inscriptions upon stones, about which much has been said and written, I am of the opinion, that such are purely Indian, if they were not made by some white maniac, as some of them most unquestionably have been, or other persons who deserve to be classed among such; but I would not be understood to include those of South America, for there the inhabitants evidently had a hieroglyphic language. Among the inscriptions upon stone in New England, the "Inscribed Rock," as it is called, at Dighton, Mass., is doubtless the most remarkable. It is in Taunton River, about six miles below the town of Taunton, and is partly immersed by the tide. If this inscription was made by the Indians, it doubtless had some meaning to it; but I doubt whether any of them, except such as happened to know what it was done for, knew any thing of its import. The divers faces, figures of half-formed animals, and zigzag lines, occupy a space of about 20 square feet. The whimsical conjectures of many persons about the origin of the inscription might amuse, but could not instruct; and it would be a waste of time to give an account of them.

A stone, once thought to contain some marvellous inscription, was deposited a few years since in the Antiquarian Hall, at Worcester, Mass.; and it was with some surprise, that, on examining it, I found nothing but a few lines of quartz upon one of its surfaces. The stone was singular in no respect beyond what may be found in half the farmers' fields and stone fences in New England.

In a cave on the bank of the Ohio River, about 20 miles below the mouth of the Wabash, called Wilson's or Murderer's Cave, are figures engraven upon stone, which have attracted great attention. It was very early possessed by one *Wilson*, who lived in it with his family. He at length turned robber, and, collecting about 40 other wretches like himself about him, took all the boats which passed on the river with any valuable goods in them, and murdered the crews. He was himself murdered by one of his own gang, to get the reward which was offered for his apprehension. Never having had any drawings of the hieroglyphics in this cave, we cannot form any very conclusive opinion upon them. As a proof of their antiquity, it has been mentioned, that among those unknown characters are many figures of animals not known now to be in existence; but in my opinion, this is in no wise a conclusive argument of their antiquity; for the same may be said of the uncouth figures of the Indian manitos of the present day, as well as those of the days of *Powhatan*.

At Harmony, on the Mississippi, are to be seen the prints of two feet imbedded in hard limestone. The celebrated *Rappe* conveyed the stone containing them from St. Louis, and kept it upon his premises to show to travellers. They are about the size of those made by a common man of our times, unaccustomed to shoes. Some conclude them to be remains of high antiquity. They may, or may not be: there are arguments for and against such conclusion; but on which side the weight of argument lies is a matter not easily to be settled. If these impressions of feet were made in the soft earth before it was changed into fossil stone, we should not expect to find *impressions*, but a formation filling them of another kind of stone (called organic) from that in which the impressions were made; for thus do organic remains discover themselves, and not by their absence.

A review of the theories and opinions concerning the race or races anterior to the present race of Indians would perhaps be interesting to many, and it would be a pleasing subject to write upon: but, as I have elsewhere intimated, my only object is to present facts as I find them, without wasting time in commentaries; unless where deductions cannot well be avoided without leaving the subject more obscure than it would evidently be without them.

Every conjecture is attended with objections when they are hazarded upon a subject that cannot be settled. It is time enough to argue a subject of the nature of this we are upon when all the facts are collected. To write volumes about Shem, Ham, and Japhet, in connection with a few isolated facts, is a most ludicrous and worse than useless business. Some have said, it is an argument that the first population came from the north, because the works of which we have been speaking increase in importance as we proceed south; but why they should not begin until the people who constructed them had arrived within 40° of the equator, (for this seems to be their boundary north,) it is not stated. Perhaps this people came in by way of the St. Lawrence, and did not need any works to defend them before arriving at the 40° of north latitude. The reader will readily enough ask, perhaps, For what purpose could fortifications have been built by the first people? To defend themselves from wild beasts, or from one another? With this matter, however, we have nothing to do, but were led to these remarks, preparatory to a comparison between the antiquities of the north with those of the south.

On the other hand, it is said the original people of North America must have come from the south, and that their progress northward is evident from the same works; with this difference, that as the people advanced, they dwindled into insignificance; and hence the remains which they left are proportionate to their ability to make them. But there is nothing artificial among the ancient ruins of North America that will compare with the artificial mountain of Anahuac, called Cholula, or Chlolula, which to this day is about 164 feet in perpendicular height, whose base occupies a square, the sides of which measure 1450 feet. Upon this the Mexicans had an immense wooden temple when *Cortez* overrun their empire. A city now bears the name of Cholula, in Puebla, 60 miles east of Mexico. Yet it appears from Dr. *Beck's* Gazetteer of Illinois, that there is standing between Belleville and St. Louis, a mound 600 yards in circumference at its base, and 90 feet in height. Mount Joliet, so named from the Sieur *Joliet*, a Frenchman, who travelled upon the Mississippi in 1673, is a most distinguished mound. It is on a plain about 600 yards west of the River Des Plaines, and 150 miles above Fort Clark. Mr. *Schoolcraft* computed its height at 60 feet, its length about 450 yards, and its width 75. Its sides are so steep that they are ascended with difficulty. Its top is a beautiful plain, from which a most delightful prospect is had of the surrounding country. It seems to have been composed of the earth of the plain on which it stands. Lake Joliet is situated in front of it; being a small body of water about a mile in length.

Although the remains of the ancient inhabitants of South America differ considerably from those of North America, yet I have no doubt but that the people are of the same race. The condition even of savages changes. No nation remains stationary. The western Indians in the neighborhood of the lakes do not make pottery at the present day, but earthen utensils are still in use among the remote tribes of the west, which is similar to that dug up in Ohio, and both are similar to that found in South America.

In speaking of ancient pottery, Mr. *Schoolcraft* observes, "It is common, in digging at these salt mines, [in Illinois,] to find fragments of antique pottery, and even entire pots of a coarse earthenware, at great depths below the surface. One of these pots, which was, until a very recent period, preserved by a gentleman at Shawaneetown, was disinterred at a depth of 80 feet, and was of a capacity to contain eight or ten gallons."

We see announced from time to time, in the various newspapers and other periodicals, discoveries of wonderful things in various places; but on examination it is generally found that they fall far short of what we are led to expect from the descriptions given of them. We hear of the ruins of cities in the banks of the Mississippi; copper and iron utensils found at great depths below the surface, and in situations indicating that they must have been deposited there for three, four, or five hundred years! Dr. *McMurtrie* relates, in his "Sketches of Louisville," that an iron hatchet was found beneath the roots of a tree at Shippingsport, upwards of 200 years old. He said he had no doubt that the tree had grown over the hatchet after it was deposited there, because "no human power could have placed it in the particular position in which it was found."

Upon some other matters about which we have already remarked, the same author says, "That walls, constructed of bricks and hewn stones, have been discovered in the western country, is a fact as clear as that the sun shines when he is in his meridian splendor; the dogmatical assertion of writers to the contrary notwithstanding." My author, however, had not seen such remains himself, but was well assured of their existence by a gentleman of undoubted veracity. Unfortunately for the case he relates, the persons who discovered the ruins came upon them in digging, at about 18 feet below the surface of the ground, and when about to make investigation, water broke in upon them, and they were obliged to make a hasty retreat.

"A fortified town of considerable extent, near the River St. Francis," upon the Mississippi, was said to have been discovered by a Mr. *Savage*, of Louisville. He found its walls standing in some places, and "part of the walls of a *citadel, built of bricks, cemented by mortar.*" Upon some of these ruins were trees growing whose annual rings numbered 300. Some of the bricks, says Dr. *McMurtrie*, were at Louisville when he wrote his Sketches; and they were "composed of clay, mixed with chopped and twisted straw, of regular figures, hardened by the action of fire or the sun."

Mr. *Priest*, in his "American Antiquities," mentions the ruins of two cities within a few miles of each other, nearly opposite St. Louis; but from what he says of them I am unable to determine what those ruins are composed of. After pointing out the sight of them, he continues, "Here is situated one of those pyramids, which is 150 rods in circumference at its base, and 100 feet high." He speaks of "cities," but describes pyramids and mounds. If there be any thing like the works of men, at the places he points out, different from what is common in the west, it is very singular that they should not have attracted the notice of some one of the many thousands of people who have for 50 years passed by them. Mr. *Brackenridge* speaks of the antiquities at this place, but does not say any thing about cities. He observes, "The most remarkable appearances are two groups of mounds or pyramids, the one about 10 miles above Cahokia, the other nearly the same distance below it, which, in all, exceed 150, of various sizes. The western side also contains a considerable number.

"A more minute description of those about Cahokia, which I visited in the fall of 1811, will give a tolerable idea of them all. I crossed the Mississippi at St. Louis, and after passing through the wood which borders the river, about half a mile in width, entered an extensive open plain. In 15 minutes I found myself in the midst of a group of mounds, mostly of a circular shape, and at a distance resembling enormous haystacks scattered through a meadow. One of the largest which I ascended was about 200 paces in circumference at the bottom, the form nearly square, though it had evidently undergone considerable alteration from the washing of the rains. The top was level, with an area sufficient to contain several hundred men."

When Mr. *Bartram* travelled into South Carolina, Georgia and Florida, be tween the years 1773 and 1776, he saw many interesting antiquities. At the Cherokee town of Cowe, on the Tennessee River, which then contained about 100 houses, he noticed that "The council or town-house was a large rotunda, capable of accommodating several hundred people: it stands on the top of an ancient artificial mount of earth, of about 20 feet perpendicular, and the rotunda on the top of it being about 30 feet more, gives the whole fabric an elevation of about 60 feet from the common surface of the ground. But," Mr. *Bartram* continues, "it may be proper to observe, that this mount, on which the rotunda stands, is of a much ancienter date than the building, and perhaps was raised for another purpose. The Cherokees themselves are as ignorant as we are, by what people or for what purpose these artificial hills were raised; they have various stories concerning them, the best of which amount to no more than mere conjecture, and leave us entirely in the dark; but they have a tradition common with the other nations of Indians, that they found them in much the same condition as they now appear, when their forefathers arrived from the west and possessed themselves of the country, after vanquishing the nations of red men who then inhabited it, who themselves found these mounts when they took possession of the country, the former possessors delivering the same story concerning them."

Hence it is to be observed that the mounds in the south are not only the same as those in the north, but Indian traditions concerning them are the same also.

At Ottasse, an important town of the Cherokees, the same traveller saw a most singular column. It stood adjacent to the town, in the centre of an oblong square, and was about 40 feet high, and only from two to three feet thick at its base, and tapered gradually from the ground to its top. What is very remarkable about this pillar is, that, notwithstanding it is formed of a single stick of pine timber, the Indians or white traders could give no account for what purpose it was erected; and to the inquiries which Mr. *Bartram* made of the Indians concerning it, the same answer was given as when questioned about the mounds; viz., that their ancestors found it there, and the people that those ancestors dispossessed knew nothing of its origin. This is not singular when reference is had to mounds of earth, but when the same account is given concerning perishable material, the shade, at least, of a suspicion is seen lurking in the back ground. As another singular circumstance, it is observed that no trees of the kind of which this column was made (*pin. palustris*) were to be found at that time nearer than 12 or 15 miles.

In the great council-houses at Ottasse were observed, upon the pillars and walls, various paintings and sculptures, supposed to be hieroglyphics of historical legends, and political and sacerdotal affairs. "They are," observes Mr. *Bartram*, "extremely picturesque or caricature, as men in a variety of attitudes, some ludicrous enough, others having the head of some kind of animal, as those of a duck, turkey, bear, fox, wolf, buck, &c., and again those kind of creatures are represented having the human head. These designs are not ill executed; the outlines bold, free and well proportioned. The pillars supporting the front or piazza of the council-house of the square are ingeniously formed in the likeness of vast speckled serpents, ascending upwards; the Ottasses being of the Snake tribe."

In the fourth book of this work mention has been made of the great highways in Florida. Mr. *Bartram* mentions them, but not in a very particular manner, upon the St. John's River. As his sentiments seem to be those of a man of intelligence, I will offer here his concluding remarks upon the Indian antiquities of the country he visited. "I deem it necessary to observe, as my opinion, that none of them that I have seen discover the least signs of the arts, sciences, or architecture of the Europeans or other inhabitants of the old world, yet evidently betray every sign or mark of the most distant antiquity."

The above remark is cited to show how different different people make up their minds upon the same subject; it shows how futile it is for us to spend time in speculating upon such matters. And, as I have before observed, it is time enough to build theories after facts have been collected. It can add nothing to our stock of knowledge respecting our antiquities, to talk or write forever about Nebuchadnezzar and the lost tribes of Jews; but if the time which has been spent in this manner had been devoted to some useful pursuit, *some* useful object would have been attained. As the matter now stands, *one* object, nevertheless, is clearly attained, namely, that of misleading or confounding the understandings of many uninformed people. I am led to make these observations to put the unwary upon their guard.

In the preceding chapter I have given various accounts of, or accounts from various authors, who imagine that a colony of Welsh came to America 7 or 800 years ago. It is as truly astonishing as any thing we meet with to observe how many persons had found proofs of the existence of tribes of Welsh Indians, about the same period. As a case exactly in point with that mentioned at the beginning of the last paragraph, I offer what Mr. *Brackenridge* says upon this matter. "That no Welsh nation exists," he observes, "at present, on this continent, is beyond a doubt. Dr. *Barton* has taken great pains to ascertain the languages spoken by those tribes east of the Mississippi, and the Welsh finds no place amongst them; since the cession of Louisiana, the tribes west of the Mississippi have been sufficiently known; we have had intercourse with them all, but no Welsh are yet found. In the year 1798, a young Welshman of the name of *Evans* ascended the Missouri, in company with *Makey*, and remained two years in that country; he spoke both the ancient and modern Welsh, and addressed himself to every nation between that river and New Spain, but found no Welshmen." This, it would seem, is conclusive enough.

Mr. *Peck*, in his "Gazetteer of Illinois," has aimed so happy a stroke at the writers on our antiquity, that, had I met with his rod before I had made the previous remarks, I should most certainly have made use of it. I shall nevertheless use it. After saying something upon the antiquities of Illinois, he proceeds: "Of one thing the writer is satisfied, that very imperfect and incorrect data have been relied upon, and very erroneous conclusions drawn, upon western antiquities. Whoever has time and patience, and is in other respects qualified to explore this field of science, and will use his spade and eyes together, and restrain his imagination from running riot amongst mounds, fortifications, horseshoes, medals, and whole cabinets of relics of the 'olden time,' will find very little more than the indications of rude savages, the ancestors of the present race of Indians."

END OF BOOK FIRST.

BIOGRAPHY AND HISTORY

OF THE

INDIANS OF NORTH AMERICA.

BOOK II.

BOOK II.

BIOGRAPHY AND HISTORY OF THE NORTHERN OR NEW ENGLAND INDIANS.

"'Tis good to muse on nations passed away
Forever from the land we call our own."
YAMOYDEN

CHAPTER I.

Conduct of the early voyagers towards the Indians—Some account of the individuals Donacona—Agona—Tasquantum, or Squanto—Dehamda—Skettwarroes—Assacumet—Manida—Pechmo—Monopet—Pekenimne—Sakaweston—Epanow—Manawet—Wanape—Coneconam.

THE first voyagers to a country were anxious to confirm the truth of their accounts, and therefore took from their newly-discovered lands whatever seemed best suited to that object. The inhabitants of America carried off by Europeans were not, perhaps, in any instance, taken away by voyagers merely for this object, but that they might, in time, learn from them the value of the country from whence they took them. Besides those forcibly carried away, there were many, doubtless, who went through overpersuasion, and ignorance both of the distance and usage they should meet with in a land of strangers; which was not always as it should have been, and hence such as were ill used, if they ever returned to their own country, were prepared to be revenged on any strangers of the same color, that chanced to come among them.

In the first voyage of *Columbus* to America, he took along with him, on his return to Spain, a considerable number of Indians; how many we do not know; but several died on their passage, and seven were presented to the king. *Vincente Yañez Pinzon*, a captain under *Columbus*, kidnapped four natives, whom he intended to sell in Spain for slaves; but *Columbus* took them from him, and restored them to their friends. In this first voyage to the islands of the new world, the blood of several Indians was shed by the hostile arms of the Spaniards.*

There were three natives presented to Henry VII. by *Sebastian Cabot*, in 1502, which he had taken from Newfoundland. What were their names, or what became of them, we are not informed; but from the notice of historians, we learn that, when found, "they were clothed with the skins of beasts, and lived on raw flesh; but after two years, [residence in England,] were seen in the king's court clothed like Englishmen, and could not be discerned from Englishmen." † These were the first Indians ever seen in England.‡ They

---

* My present concern not being with the Indians of South America, I beg leave to refer the reader to a little work lately published, entitled THE OLD INDIAN CHRONICLE, in which all the prominent facts concerning the atrocities of the Spaniards towards them will be found stated.

† Rapin's *Hist. England*, i. 685. ed. fol. See also *Purchas*, 738.

‡ This is upon the authority of *Berkely*. Instead of *England*, however, he says *Europe*; but, by saying the *six*, which *Columbus* had before taken from St. Salvador, made their escape, he shows his superficial knowledge of those affairs. Hear *Herrera*:—

"*En suitte de cela,* [*that is, after Columbus had replied to the king's letter about a second voyage,*] *il* [*Columbus*] *partit pour aller à Barcelone auec sept Indiens, parce que les autres estoient morts en chemin. Il fit porter aueque luy des perroquets verds, et de* were brought to the English court "in their country habit," and "spoke a language never heard before out of their own country." *

The French discovered the river St. Lawrence in 1508, and the captain of the ship who made the discovery, carried several natives to Paris, which were the first ever seen in France. What were their names, or even how many they were in number, is not set down in the accounts of this voyage. The name of this captain was *Thomas Aubert.*†

John Verazzini, in the service of Francis I., in 1524, sailed along the American coast, and landed in several places. At one place, which we judge to be some part of the coast of Connecticut, "20 of his men landed, and went about two leagues up into the country. The inhabitants fled before them, but they caught an old woman who had hid herself in the high grass, with a young woman about 18 years of age. The old woman carried a child on her back, and had, besides, two little boys with her. The young woman, too, carried three children of her own sex. Seeing themselves discovered, they began to shriek, and the old one gave them to understand, by signs, that the men were fled to the woods. They offered her something to eat, which she accepted, but the maiden refused it. This girl, who was tall and well shaped, they were desirous of taking along with them, but as she made a violent outcry, they contented themselves with taking a boy away with them." ‡ The name of New France was given to North America in this voyage. In another voyage here, *Verazzini* was killed, and, as some say, eaten by the Indians.

In the year 1576, Capt. *Martin*, afterwards Sir *Martin*, *Frobisher* sailed from England for the discovery of a north-west passage; "the only thing of the world," says a writer of his voyage, "that was left yet vndone." After the usual vicissitudes attending such an undertaking, at this early period of English navigation, he discovered a strait which has ever since borne his name. About 60 miles within that strait, he went on shore to make discovery of the country, and was suddenly attacked by the natives, "who had stolen secretly behinde the rockes;" and though he "bent himselfe to his halberd," he narrowly escaped with his life.

Hence there was a well-grounded suspicion in all future communications with the Indians in this region; yet, after considerable intercourse, *Frobisher's* men became less wary, and five of them, going on shore from a boat, were surprised and carried off, and never heard of again. After this "the subtile traitours were so wary, as they would after that never come within our men's danger." Notwithstanding, *Frobisher* found means to entice some of them alongside of his ship, and after considerable manuœvering, one of them had his fears so far overcome by the alluring sound of a cow-bell, that he came so near in his canoe, to obtain one of them, that "the captain, being ready provided, let the bell fall, and caught the man fast, and plucked him with maine force, boat and all," into his ship. Whereupon this savage finding himself in captivity, "for very choler and disdaine he bit his tongue in twaine within his mouth: notwithstanding he died not thereof, but liued vntil he came in England, and then he died of cold which he had taken at sea."

The next year (1577) *Frobisher* made another voyage to the same coasts of America, and on some excursion on land he was attacked and wounded by the Indians. In York Sound he attacked a party, and killed five or six of them, and shortly after took two women prisoners.

Such were the impressions given and received between the Europeans and Indians in that early day of American history.

This was indeed a comparatively barbarous age. Few of the early voyagers were better than demi-savages; for they measured the conduct of the Indians by their own scale of justice; in which might was too often taken for right. But we of this age — what will be said of us by generations to come, — by

---

rouges, et d'autres choses dignes d'admiration qui n'auoient iamais esté veuës en Espagne." Hist. des Indes Occident. i. 102. Ed. 1660, 3 tomes, 4to. See also *Harris, Voyages*, ii. 15. ed. 1764. 2 v. fol.; *Robertson, America*, i. 94. ed. 1778, 4to.

* Berkely's *Naval Hist. Brit.* 268. ed. 1756, fol. and Harris, *Voyages*, ii. 191.

† Forster, 432. ‡ Ibid. 434, 435.

the enlightened of distant ages, — when they inquire for the causes and reasons for our conduct in our wars with the Indians in our own times?

The next early voyager we shall notice is Capt. *Hendrick Hudson.* From *Robert Juet's* journal of his voyage it appears that *Hudson* discovered the river which bears his name, Sept. 6. 1609, and explored it probably as high up at least as the present site of *West Point,* before he left it. During his stay in the river *Manna-hata,* as it was called by the natives, the conduct of his men towards those people was most unjust, savage, and cruel. We are told that their first interviews with the natives were friendly, but we are not told how they became immediately otherwise. The same day Hudson entered the river, he sent out *John Colman* to make soundings, in which service he was shot in his throat with an arrow and killed; and the next day he was buried on a point of land which has ever since borne his name. What provocation, if any, led to this misfortune, is not mentioned, nor does it appear that there was any suspension of intercourse, though a few days after several Indians were taken captive by the ship's crew as they came to trade, and were confined on board. They escaped soon after, however, by jumping overboard.

By the 15th of September, Hudson had reached considerably above West Point, and on the 1st of October he began to descend, but came to an anchor "seven miles below the mountains." An Indian in a canoe, while many others were around the ship, came under the stern, climbed up by the rudder, entered the cabin window, which had been left open, and stole some trifling articles. Being discovered, he was pursued and killed by the mate, "by a shot through his breast." By this rash act several were so frightened that they jumped into the river. As a boat from the ship was pursuing them, one in the water caught hold of the side of the boat; whereupon the cook cut off his hands with a sword, and he was drowned. The next day two canoes approached the ship, and shot at it with their bows and arrows; "in recompense whereof," says *Juet,* "we discharged six muskets, and killed two or three of them." Soon after, about 100 Indians appeared on a point of land, "to shoot at us;" then "I shot a falcon at them," says this author, whom I take to have been the gunner of the ship, "and killed two of them. Yet they manned off another canoe with nine or ten men, which came to meet us; so I shot at it also a falcon, and shot it through, and killed one of them. Then our men with their muskets killed three or four more of them."

This must truly ever be looked upon as a sad beginning of an acquaintance between the Indians and white people on the southern boundary of New England. The former could not view the latter in any other light than a race far more barbarous than themselves; inasmuch as they had seen a score of their people, one after another, sacrificed, while they had killed but a single white man, probably in a quarrel. We now turn to the northern boundary for another example or two of early intercourse.

Donacona, a chief upon the River St. Croix, was met with, in 1535, by the voyager *James Cartier,* who was well received and kindly treated by him and his people; to repay which, *Cartier,* "partly by stratagem and partly by force." carried him to France, where he soon after died.* Notwithstanding, *Cartier* was in the country five years after, where he found *Agona,* the successor of *Donacona,* and exchanged presents with him, probably reconciling him by some plausible account of the absence of *Donacona.*

Tasquantum, or *Tisquantum,* was one of the five natives carried from the coast of New England, in 1605, by Capt. *George Waymouth,* who had been sent out to discover a north-west passage. This Indian was known afterwards to the settlers of Plimouth, by whom he was generally called *'Squanto,* or *'Squantum,* by abbreviation. The names of the other four were *Manida, Skettwarroes, Dehamda* and *Assacumet.*

Although *Gorges* does not say *Dehamda* was one brought over at this time, it is evident that he was, because, so far as we can discover, there were no other natives at that time in England, but these five.

Sir *Ferdinando Gorges* says, *Waymouth,* "falling short of his course, [in seeking the N. W. passage,] happened into a river on the coast of America, called *Pemmaquid,* from whence he brought five of the natives." "And it so pleased

* Foster, 440—443.

our great God that" *Waymouth*, on his return to England, "came into the harbor of Plymouth, where I then commanded." Three* of whose natives, namely, *Manida*, *Skettwarroes* and *Tasquantum*, "I seized upon. They were all of one nation, but of several parts, and several families. This accident must be acknowledged the means, under God, of putting on foot and giving life to all our plantations."

Paying great attention to these natives, he soon understood enough by them about the country from whence they came to establish a belief that it was of great value; not perhaps making due allowance for its being their *home*. And Sir *Ferdinando* adds, "After I had those people sometimes in my custody, I observed in them an inclination to follow the example of the better sort; and in all their carriages, manifest shows of great civility, far from the rudeness of our common people. And the longer I conversed with them, the better hope they gave me of those parts where they did inhabit, as proper for our uses; especially when I found what goodly rivers, stately islands. and safe harbors, those parts abounded with, being the special marks I leveled at as the only want our nation met with in all their navigations along that coast. And having kept them full three years, I made them able to set me down what great rivers run up into the land, what men of note were seated on them, what power they were of, how allied, what enemies they had," &c.

Thus having gained a knowledge of the country, Sir *Ferdinando* got ready "a ship furnished with men and all necessaries" for a voyage to America, and sent as her captain Mr. *Henry Challoung*,† with whom he also sent two of his Indians. The names of these were *Assacumet* and *Manida*. *Chalons*, having been taken sick in the beginning of the voyage, altered his course, and lost some time in the West Indies. After being able to proceed northward, he departed from Porto Rico, and was soon after taken by a Spanish fleet, and carried into Spain, "where their ship and goods were confiscate, themselves made prisoners, the voyage overthrown, and both my natives lost." One, however, *Assacumet*, was afterwards recovered, if not the other. This voyage of *Chalons* was in 1606.

It appears that the Lord Chief Justice *Popham*‡ had agreed to send a vessel to the aid of *Chalons*, which was accordingly done before the news of his being taken was known in England. For Sir *Ferdinando Gorges* says, "It pleased the lord chief justice, according to his promise, to despatch Capt. [*Martin*] *Prin* from Bristol, with hope to have found Capt. *Challounge*;" "but not hearing by any means what became of him, after he had made a perfect discovery of all those rivers and harbors," "brings with him the most exact discovery of that coast that ever came to my hands since, and, indeed, he was the best able to perform it of any I met withal to this present [time,] which, with his relation of the country, wrought such an impression in the lord chief justice, and us all that were his associates, that (notwithstanding our first disaster) we set up our resolutions to follow it with effect."

Dehamda and *Skettwarroes* were with *Prin*§ in this voyage, and were, without doubt, his most efficient aids in surveying the coast. It appears from *Gorges*, that *Dehamda* was sent by the chief justice, who we suppose had considered him his property,‖ and *Skettwarroes* by himself. They returned again to England with *Prin*.

---

* It seems, from this part of his narrative, that he had but three of them, but from subsequent passages, it appears he had them all. See also *America painted to the Life.*

† *Challons*, by some. *Gorges* has sometimes, *Chalowns*, *Chalon*, &c

‡ The same who presided at the trial of Sir *W. Ralegh* and his associates, in 1603. See *Prince's Worthies of Devon*, 672, 673. *Fuller*, in his *Worthies of England*, ii. 284, says, "Travelers owed their safety to this judge's severity many years after his death, which happened Anno Domini 16**," thinking, no doubt, he had much enlightened his reader by definitely stating that Sir *John Popham* died some time within a *hundred* years. The severity referred to has reference to his importuning King *James* not to pardon so many robbers and thieves, which, he said, tended to render the judges contemptible, and "which made him more sparing afterward."

§ *Gorges*, one of the main springs of these transactions, who wrote the account we give, makes no mention of any other captain accompanying him; yet Dr. *Holmes's* authorities, *Annals*, i. 125, led him to record *Thomas Hanam* as the performer of this voyage. And a writer of 1622 says, *Hanam*, or, as he calls him, *Haman*, went commander, and *Prinne* master. See 2 *Col. Mass. Hist. Soc.* ix. 3. This agrees with the account of *Gorges* the younger.

‖ He had probably been given to him by Sir *Ferdinando*.

The next year, 1607, these two natives piloted the first New England colony to the mouth of Sagadahock River, since the Kennebeck. They left England 30 May, and did not arrive here until 8 August following. "As soon as the president had taken notice of the place, and given order for landing the provisions, he despatched away Captain *Gilbert*, with *Skitwarres* his guide, for the thorough discovery of the rivers and habitations of the natives, by whom he was brought to several of them, where he found civil entertainment, and kind respects, far from brutish or savage natures, so as they suddenly became familiar friends, especially by the means of *Dehamda* and *Skitwarrers*." "So as the president was earnestly intreated by *Sassenow*, *Aberemet*, and others, the principal Sagamores, (as they call their great lords,) to go to the Bashabas, who it seems was their king." They were prevented, however, by adverse weather, from that journey, and thus the promise to do so was unintentionally broken, "much to the grief of those Sagamores that were to attend him. The Bashebas, notwithstanding, hearing of his misfortune, sent his own son to visit him, and to beat a trade with him for furs."

Several sad and melancholy accidents conspired to put an end to this first colony of New England. The first was the loss of their store-house, containing most of their supplies, by fire, in the winter following, and another was the death of Lord *Popham*. It consisted of 100 men, and its beginning was auspicious; but these calamities, together with the death of their president, broke down their resolutions. So many discouragements, notwithstanding a ship with supplies had arrived, determined them to abandon the country, which they did in the spring.* What became of *Dehamda* and *Skettwarroes* there is no mention, but they probably remained in the country with their friends, unless the passage which we shall hereafter extract be construed to mean differently.†

To return to *Tisquantum*. There is some disagreement in the narratives of the contemporary writers in respect to this chief, which shows, either that some of them are in error, or that there were two of the same name—one carried away by *Waymouth*, and the other by *Hunt*. From a critical examination of the accounts, it is believed there was but one, and that he was carried away by *Waymouth*, as Sir *Ferdinando Gorges* relates, whose account we have given above.‡ It is impossible that Sir *Ferdinando* should have been mistaken in the names of those he received from *Waymouth*. The names of those carried off by *Hunt* are not given, or but few of them, nor were they kidnapped until nine years after *Waymouth's* voyage. It is, therefore, possible that *Squantum*, having returned home from the service of *Gorges*, went again to England with some other person, or perhaps even with *Hunt*. But we are inclined to think there was but one of the name, and his being carried away an error of inadvertence.

Patuxet, afterward called *Plimouth*, was the place of residence of *Squantum*, who, it is said, was the only person that escaped the great plague of which we shall particularly speak in the life of *Massasoit*; where, at the same time, we shall take up again the life of *Squantum*, whose history is so intimately connected with it.

It was in 1611 that Captain *Edward Harlow*§ was sent "to discover an Ile supposed about Cape Cod," who "falling with Monahigan, they found onely Cape Cod no Ile but the maine; there [at Monhigon Island] they detained three Saluages aboord them, called *Pechmo*, *Monopet* and *Pekenimne*, but *Pechmo* leapt ouerboard, and got away; and not long after, with his consorts, cut their Boat from their sterne, got her on shore, and so filled her with sand and guarded her with bowes and arrowes, the English lost her."‖

This exploit of *Pechmo* is as truly brave as it was daring. To have got

---

* They had "seated themselves in a peninsula, which is at the mouth of this river, [Sagadahock,] where they built a fortress to defend themselves from their enemies, which they named *St. George*." *America Painted to the Life*, by *Ferd. Gorges, Esq.* p. 19.

† See life *Massasoit*.

‡ It is plain, from *Prince Chron.* 134, that his authors had confounded the names of these Indians one with another.

§ Sir *Fred. Gorges* is probably wrong in calling him *Henry Harley*.

‖ Capt. Smith's *Gen. Hist. N. Eng.*, ii. 174.

under the stern of a ship, in the face of armed men, and at the same time to have succeeded in his design of cutting away and carrying off the boat, was an act as bold and daring, to say the least, as that performed in the harbor of Tripoli by our countryman *Decatur*.

From Monhigon *Harlow*, proceeding southward, fell in with an island called then by the Indians *Nohono*. From this place "they tooke *Sakaweston*, that after he had lived many years in England, went a soldier to the wars of Bohemia."* Whether he ever returned we are not told. From this island they proceeded to Capawick, since called *Capoge*, [Martha's Vineyard.] Here "they tooke *Coneconam* and *Epenow*," and "so, with fiue Saluages, they returned for England."

Epenow, or, as some wrote, *Epanow*, seems to have been much such a character as *Pechmo* — artful, cunning, bold and daring. Sir *Ferdinando Gorges* is evidently erroneous in part of his statement about this native, in as far as it relates to his having been brought away by *Hunt*. For *Harlow's* voyage was in 1611, and *Epanow* was sent over to Cape Cod with Captain *Hobson*, in 1614, some months before *Hunt* left.

As it is peculiarly gratifying to the writer to hear such old venerable writers as *Smith*, *Gorges*, &c. speak, the reader perhaps would not pardon him were he to withhold what the intimate acquaintance of the interesting *Epanow* says of him. Hear, then, Sir *Ferdinando*: —

"While I was laboring by what means I might best continue life in my languishing hopes, there comes one *Henry Harley*† unto me, bringing with him a native of the Island of Capawick, a place seated to the southward of Cape Cod, whose name was *Epenewe*, a person of goodly stature, strong and well proportioned. This man was taken upon the main, [by force] with some 29‡ others by a ship of London that endeavored to sell them for slaves in Spaine, out being understood that they were Americans, and being found to be unapt for their uses, they would not meddle with them, this being one of them they refused, wherein they exprest more worth than those that brought them to the market, who could not but known that our nation was at that time in travel for setling of Christian colonies upon that continent, it being an act much tending to our prejudice, when we came into that part of the countries, as it shall further appear. How Capt. *Harley* came to be possessed of this savage, I know not, but I understood by others how he had been shown in London for a wonder. It is true, (as I have said) he was a goodly man, of a brave aspect, stout and sober in his demeanor, and had learned so much English as to bid those that wondered at him, Welcome, welcome; this being the last and best use they could make of him, that was now grown out of the people's wonder. The captain, falling further into his familiarity, found him to be of acquaintance and friendship with those subject to the Bashaba, whom the captain well knew, being himself one of the plantation, sent over by the lord chief justice, [*Popham*,] and by that means understood much of his language, found out the place of his birth," &c.

Before proceeding with the history of *Epanow*, the account of Capt. *Thomas Hunt's* voyage should be related; because it is said that it was chiefly owing to his perfidy that the Indians of New England were become so hostile to the voyagers. Nevertheless, it is plain, that (as we have already said) *Hunt* did not commit his depredations until after *Epanow* had escaped out of the hands of the English. Capt. *John Smith* was in company with *Hunt*, and we will hear him relate the whole transaction. After stating that they arrived at Monhigon in April, 1614,§ spent a long time in trying to catch whales without success; and as "for gold, it was rather the master's device to get a voyage, that projected it;" that for trifles they got "near 11000 beaver skins, 100

---

* Capt. Smith's *Gen. Hist. N. Eng.* ii. 174.

† Perhaps not the Capt. *Harlow* before mentioned, though *Prince* thinks *Gorges* means him.

‡ If in this he refers to those taken by *Hunt*, as I suppose, he sets the number higher than others. His grandson, *F. Gorges*, in *America Painted*, &c., says 24 was the number seized by *Hunt*.

§ Smith had an Indian named *Tantum* with him in this voyage, whom he set on shore at Cape Cod.

martin, and as many otters, the most of them within the distance of 20 leagues," and his own departure for Europe, Capt. *Smith* proceeds: —

"The other ship staid to fit herself for Spain with the dry fish, which was sold at Malaga at 4 rials the quintal, each hundred weight two quintals and a half.—But one *Thomas Hunt*, the master of this ship, (when I was gone,) thinking to prevent that intent I had to make there a plantation, thereby to keep this abounding country still in obscurity, that only he and some few merchants more might enjoy wholly the benefit of the trade, and profit of this country, betrayed four and twenty of those poor salvages aboard his ship, and most dishonestly and inhumanly, for their kind usage of me and all our men, carried them with him to Malaga; and there, for a little private gain, sold these silly salvages for rials of eight; but this vile act kept him ever after from any more employment to those parts."

F. Gorges, the younger, is rather confused in his account of *Hunt's* voyage, as well as the elder. But the former intimates that it was on account of *Hunt's* selling the Indians he took as slaves, the news of which having got into England before *Epanow* was sent out, caused this Indian to make his escape, and consequently the overthrow of the vogage; whereas the latter, Sir *Ferdinando*, does not attribute it to that. We will now hear him again upon this interesting subject: —

"*The reasons of my undertaking the employment for the island of Capawick.*

"At the time this new savage [*Epanow*] came unto me, I had recovered *Assacumet*, one of the natives I sent with Capt. *Chalownes* in his unhappy employment, with whom I lodged *Epenaw*, who at the first hardly understood one the other's speech, till after a while; I perceived the difference was no more than that as ours is between the northern and southern people, so that I was a little eased in the use I made of my old servant, whom I engaged to give account of what he learned by conference between themselves, and he as faithfully performed it."

There seems but little doubt that *Epanow* and *Assacumet* had contrived a plan of escape before they left England, and also, by finding out what the English most valued, and assuring them that it was in abundance to be had at a certain place in their own country, prevailed upon them, or by this pretended discovery were the means of the voyage being undertaken, of which we are now to speak. Still, as will be seen, Sir *Ferdinando* does not speak as though he had been quite so handsomely duped by his cunning man of the woods. Gold, it has been said, was the valuable commodity to which *Epanow* was to pilot the English. *Gorges* proceeds: —

"They [Capt. *Hobson* and those who accompanied him] set sail in June, in Anno 1614, being fully instructed how to demean themselves in every kind, carrying with them *Epenow*, *Assacomet*, and *Wanape*,* another native of those parts sent me out of the Isle of Wight,† for my better information in the parts of the country of his knowledge: when as it pleased God that they were arrived upon the coast, they were piloted from place to place, by the natives themselves, as well as their hearts could desire. And coming to the harbor where *Epenow* was to make good his undertaking, [to point out the gold mine, no doubt,] the principal inhabitants of the place came aboard; some of them being his brothers, others his near cousins, [or relatives,] who, after they had communed together, and were kindly entertained by the captain, departed in their canoes, promising the next morning to come aboard again, and bring some trade with them. But *Epenow* privately (as it appeared) had contracted with his friends, how he might make his escape without performing what he had undertaken, being in truth no more than he had told me he was to do though with loss of his life. For otherwise, if it were found that he had dis-

* Doubtless the same called by others *Manawet*, who, it would seem from Mr. *Hubbard*, (*Hist. N. Eng.* 39,) died before *Epanow* escaped, "soon after the ship's arrival."

† How he came there, we are at a loss to determine, unless natives were carried off, of whom no mention is made. This was unquestionably the case, for when it came to be a common thing for vessels to bring home Indians, no mention, of course, would be made of them, especially if they went voluntarily, as, no doubt, many did.

covered the secrets of his country,* he was sure to have his brains knockt out as soon as he came ashore;† for that cause I gave the captain strict charge to endeavor by all means to prevent his escaping from them. And for the more surety, I gave order to have three gentlemen of my own kindred to be ever at hand with him; clothing him with long garments, fitly to be laid hold on, if occasion should require. Notwithstanding all this, his friends being all come at the time appointed with twenty canoes, and lying at a certain distance with their bows ready, the captain calls to them to come aboard; but they not moving, he speaks to *Epenow* to come unto him, where he was in the forecastle of the ship, he being then in the waste of the ship, between the two gentlemen that had him in guard; starts suddenly from them, and coming to the captain, calls to his friends in English to come aboard, in the interim slips himself overboard: And although he were taken hold of by one of the company, yet, being a strong and heavy man, could not be stayed, and was no sooner in the water, but the natives, [his friends in the boats,] sent such a shower of arrows, and came withal desperately so near the ship, that they carried him away in despight of all the musquetteers aboard, who were, for the number, as good as our nation did afford. And thus were my hopes of that particular [voyage] made void and frustrate."

From the whole of this narration it is evident that *Epanow* was forcibly retained, if not forcibly carried off, by English. And some relate‡ that he attacked Capt. *Dermer* and his men, supposing they had come to seize and carry him back to England. It is more probable, we think, that he meant to be revenged for his late captivity, and, according to real Indian custom, resolved that the first whites should atone for it, either with their life or liberty. *Gorges* does not tell us what his brave "musquetteers" did when *Epanow* escaped, but from other sources we learn that they fired upon his liberators, killing and wounding some, but how many, they could only conjecture. But there is no room for conjecture about the damage sustained on the part of the ship's crew, for it is distinctly stated that when they received the "shower of arrows," Capt. *Hobson* and many of his men were wounded.§ And *Smith*‖ says, "So well he had contrived his businesse, as many reported he intended to have surprised the ship; but seeing it could not be effected to his liking, before them all he leaped ouer boord."

We next meet with *Epanow* in 1619. Capt. *Thomas Dormer*, or *Dermer*, in the employ of Sir *F. Gorges*, met with him at Capoge, the place where, five years before, he made his escape from Capt. *Hobson*. *Gorges* writes, "This savage, speaking some English, laughed at his owne escape, and reported the story of it. Mr. *Dormer* told him he came from me, and was one of my servants, and that I was much grieved he had been so ill used as to be forced to steal away. This savage was so cunning, that, after he had questioned him about me, and all he knew belonged unto me, conceived he was come on purpose to betray him; and [so] conspired with some of his fellows to take the captain; thereupon they laid hands upon him. But he being a brave, stout gentleman, drew his sword and freed himself, but not without 14 wounds. This disaster forced him to make all possible haste to Virginia to be cured of his wounds. At the second return [he having just come from there] he had the misfortune to fall sick and die, of the infirmity many of our nation are subject unto at their first coming into those parts."

The ship's crew being at the same time on shore, a fight ensued, in which some of *Epanow's* company were slain. "This is the last time," says a writer in the Historical Collections, "that the soil of Martha's Vineyard was stained with human blood; for from that day to the present [1807] no Indian has been killed by a white man, nor white man by an Indian."

In relation to the fight which Dermer and his men had with the Indians at the Vineyard, *Morton*¶ relates that the English went on shore to trade with them, when they were assaulted and all the men slain but one that kept the

* The *secrets* of the sandy island Capoge, or the neighboring shores of Cape Cod, whatever they are now, existed only in faith of such sanguine minds as Sir *Ferdinando* and his adherents.

† We need no better display of the craft of *Epanow*, or proof of his cunning in deep plots. ‡ *Belknap*, Amer. Biog. i. 362. § *Smith's* N. England, ii. 178.

‖ Ibid. ¶ N. Eng. Memorial, 58, 59.

boat. "But the [captain] himself got on board very sore wounded, and they had cut off his head upon the cuddy of the boat, had not his man rescued him with a sword, and so they got him away." *Squanto* was with Capt. *Dermer* at this time, as will be seen in the life of *Massasoit*.

CHAPTER II.

*Arrival and first Proceedings of the English who settle at Plimouth—Their first discovery of Indians—Their first battle with them—Samoset—Squanto—*MASSASOIT—*Iyanough—Aspinet—Cauneconam—*CAUNBITANT—WITTUWAMET—PEKSUOT—HOBOMOK—*Tokamahamon—Obbatinewat—*NANEPASHAMET—*Squaw-Sachem* of Massachusetts—*Webcowet.*

IN 1620 some determined white people, with the most astonishing and invincible firmness, undertook to wander 3000 miles from the land of their birth, and, in the most hazardous manner, to take up a permanent abode upon the borders of a boundless wilderness, — a wilderness as great, or far greater, for aught they knew, than the expanse of ocean which they were to pass. But all dangers and difficulties, there to be encountered, weighed nothing in comparison with the liberty of conscience which they might enjoy when once beyond the control of their bigoted persecutors.

These singular people had *liberty* from their oppressor, *James* I., to go and settle in this wilderness, and to possess themselves of some of the lands of the Indians, provided they *paid him* or *some of his friends* for them. No one seems then to have questioned how this king came by the right and title to lands here, any more than how he came by his crown. They were less scrupulous, perhaps, in this matter, as the king told them, in a charter* which he granted them, *though not till after they had sailed* for America, "THAT HE HAD BEEN GIVEN CERTAINLY TO KNOWE, THAT WITHIN THESE LATE YEARES THERE HATH, BY GOD'S VISITATION, RAIGNED A WONDERFUL PLAGUE, TOGETHER WITH MANY HORRIBLE SLAUGHTERS AND MURTHERS, COMMITTED AMOUNGST THE SAUAGES AND BRUTISH PEOPLE THERE HEERTOFORE INHABITING, IN A MANNER TO THE UTTER DESTRUCTION, DEVASTACION AND DEPOPULACION OF THAT WHOLE TERRITORYE, SO THAT THERE IS NOT LEFT, FOR MANY LEAGUES TOGETHER IN A MANNER, ANY THAT DOE CLAIME OR CHALLENGE ANY KIND OF INTERESTS THEREIN."† This was, doubtless, as wel. known, if not better, to the *Pilgrims* (as they were aptly called) as to King *James*

After numerous delays and disappointments, the Pilgrims, to the number of 41, with their wives,‡ children, and servants, sailed from Plimouth, in England, in one small ship, called the Mayflower, on Wednesday, the 6th of September. Their passage was attended with great peril; but they safely arrived at Cape Cod, 9 Nov. following, without the loss of any of their number. They now proceeded to make the necessary discoveries to seat themselves on the barren coast. One of the first things they found necessary to do, to preserve order among themselves, was, to form a kind of constitution, or general outline of government. Having done this, it was signed by the 41, two days after their arrival, viz. 11 Nov. The same day, 15 or 16 of their number, covered with armor, proceeded to the land, and commenced discoveries. The Indians did not show themselves to the English until the 15th, and then they would have nothing to say to them. About 5 or 6 at first only appeared, who fled into the woods as soon as they had discovered themselves. The Englishmen followed them many miles, but could not overtake them.

First Battle with the Indians.—This was upon 8 Dec. 1620, and we will give the account of it in the language of one that was an actor in it. "We went ranging up and down till the sun began to draw low, and then we hasted out

* This charter bears date 3 Nov. 1620. *Chalmers*, Polit. Annals, 81.

† *Hazard's* Hist. Collections, I, 105, where the entire charter may be seen. It was afterwards called THE GRAND PLIMOUTH PATENT. *Chalmers*, ib

‡ There were, in all, 28 females.

of the woods that we might come to our shallop. By that time we had done, and our shallop come to us, it was within night [7 Dec.], and we betook us to our rest, after we had set our watch.

"About midnight we heard a great and hideous cry, and our Sentinell called *Arm, arm.* So we bestirred ourselues, and shot off a couple of Muskets, and [the] noyse ceased. We concluded that it was a company of Wolues and Foxes, for one [of our company] told vs he had heard such a noyse in *New-found-land.* About fiue a clocke in the morning [8 Dec.] wee began to be stirring. Vpon a sudden we heard a great and strange cry, which we knew to be the same voyces, though they varied their notes. One of our company, being abroad, came running in and cryed, *They are men, Indians, Indians;* and withall their arrowes came flying amongst vs. Our men ran out with all speed to recover their armes. The cry of our enemies was dreadfull, especially when our men ran out to recover their Armes. Their note was after this manner, *Woath, woach, ha ha hach woach.* Our men were no sooner come to their Armes, but the enemy was ready to assault them. There was a lusty man, and no whit lesse valiant, who was thought to bee their Captain, stood behind a tree, within half a musket shot of vs, and there let his arrawes fly at vs. Hee stood three shots of a musket. At length one of vs, as he said, taking full ayme at him, he gave an extraordinary cry, and away they went all."

It is not certain that any blood was shed in this battle; but it was pretty strongly presumed that the big captain of the Indians was wounded. The Indians having retreated, the conquerors were left in possession of the battle-ground, and they proceeded to gather together the trophies of this their first victory. They picked up 18 arrows, which they sent to their friends in England by the return of the Mayflower. Some of these were curiously "headed with brasse, some with Harts' horne, and others with Eagles' clawes." *

It appeared afterwards that this attack was made by the Nauset Indians, whose chief's name was *Aspinet.* Whether he was the leader in this fight, is not known; but he probably was. The place where the affair happened was called by the Indians *Namskeket;* but the English now called it *The First Encounter.*

The ELEVENTH OF DECEMBER, ever memorable in the history of New England, was now come, and this was the day of the LANDING OF THE PILGRIMS. A place upon the inhospitable shore had been fixed upon, and was this day taken possession of, and never again deserted. The ship until then had been their permanent abode, which now they gladly exchanged for the sandy shore of the bay of Cape Cod.

Welcome, Englishmen! Welcome, Englishmen! are words so inseparably associated with the name of *Samoset,* that we can never hear the one without the pleasing recollection of the other. These were the first accents our pilgrim fathers heard, on the American strand, from any native. We mean intelligible accents, for when they were attacked at Namskeket, on their first arrival, they heard only the frightful war-whoop.

The first time Indians were seen by the pilgrims, was upon 15th Nov. 1620. "They espied fiue or sixe people, with a Dogge, coming towards them, who were Savages; who, when they saw them, ran into the Wood, and whistled the Dogge after them." † And though the English ran towards them, when the Indians perceived it "they ran away might and main," and the English "could not come near them." Soon after this, *Morton* says the Indians "got all the powaws in the country, who, for three days together, in a horid and devilish manner did curse and execrate them with their conjurations, which assembly

* *Mourt's Relation,* in 1 *Mass. Hist. Col.* VIII, 218, 219; or, original ed. p. 19 & 20.

† *Relation or Journal of a Plantation settled at Plymouth, in N. E.* usually cited *Mourt's Relation.* It was, no doubt, written by several of the company, or the writer was assisted by several. *Mourt* seems to have been the publisher. He appears not to have written any part of it but the "To the Reader," and I am inclined to believe that this G. Mourt, being zealous in the cause of the Pilgrims, may have published the work his own expense. He published, at least, one other kindred work. I have no scruple but that *Richard Gardner* was the principal author. About the early settlement of any country, there never was a more important document. It was printed in 1622, and is now reprinted in the *Mass. Hist. Col.,* and we hope soon to see it printed in a volume by itself in a style worthy of its importance. As it stands in the Hist. Collections, it is very difficult to consult, a part of it being contained in one volume, and the remainder in another.

and service they held in a dark and dismal swamp. Behold how Satan labored to hinder the gospel from coming into New England!"

It was on Friday, 16th March, 1621, that *Samoset* suddenly appeared at Plimouth, and, says *Mourt*, "He very boldly came all alone, and along the houses, strait to the rendezvous, where we intercepted him, not suffering him to go in, as undoubtedly he would, out of his boldness." He was naked, "only a leather about his waist, with a fringe about a span long." The weather was very cold, and this author adds, "We cast a horseman's coat about him." To reward them for their hospitality, *Samoset* gave them whatever information they desired. "He had, say they, learned some broken English amongst the Englishmen that came to fish at Monhiggon, and knew by name the most of the captains, commanders, and masters, that usually come [there]. He was a man free in speech, so far as he could express his mind, and of seemly carriage. We questioned him of many things: he was the first savage we could meet withal. He said he was not of those parts, but of Moratiggon, and one of the sagamores or lords thereof: had been 8 months in these parts, it lying hence [to the eastward] a day's sail with a great wind, and five days by land. He discoursed of the whole country, and of every province, and of their sagamores, and their number of men, and strength." "He had a bow and two arrows, the one headed, and the other unheaded. He was a tall, strait man; the hair of his head black, long behind, only short before; none on his face at all. He asked some beer, but we gave him strong water, and biscuit, and butter, and cheese, and pudding, and a piece of a mallard; all which he liked well." "He told us the place where we now live is called Patuxet, and that about 4 years ago all the inhabitants died of an extraordinary plague, and there is neither man, woman, nor child remaining, as indeed we have found none; so as there is none to hinder our possession, or lay claim unto it. All the afternoon we spent in communication with him. We would gladly been rid of him at night, but he was not willing to go this night. Then we thought to carry him on ship-board, wherewith he was well content, and went into the shallop; but the wind was high and water scant, that it could not return back. We lodged [with him] that night at *Stephen Hopkins'* house, and watched him."

Thus, through the means of this innocent Indian, was a correspondence happily begun. He left Plimouth the next morning to return to *Massasoit*, who, he said, was a sachem having under him 60 men. The English having left some tools exposed in the woods, on finding that they were missing, rightly judged the Indians had taken them. They complained of this to *Samoset* in rather a threatening air. "We willed him (say they) that they should be brought again, otherwise we would right ourselves." When he left them "he promised within a night or two to come again," and bring some of *Massasoit's* men to trade with them in beaver skins. As good as his word, *Samoset* came the next Sunday, "and brought with him 5 other tall, proper men. They had every man a deer's skin on him; and the principal of them had a wild cat's skin, or such like, on one arm. They had most of them long hosen up to their groins, close made; and aboue their groins, to their waist, another leather they were altogether like the Irish trousers. They are of complexion like our English gipsies; no hair, or very little, on their faces; on their heads long hair to their shoulders, only cut before; some trussed up before with a feather broadwise like a fan; another a fox-tail hanging out." The English had charged *Samoset* not to let any who came with him bring their arms; these, therefore, left "their bows and arrows a quarter of a mile from our town. We gave them entertainment as we thought was fitting them. They did eat liberally of our English victuals," and appeared very friendly; "sang and danced after their manner, like anticks." "Some of them had their faces painted black, from the forehead to the chin, four or five fingers broad: others after other fashions, as they liked. They brought three or four skins, but we would not truck with them all that day, but wished them to bring more, and we would truck for all; which they promised within a night or two, and would leave these behind them, though we were not willing they should; and they brought all our tools again, which were taken in the woods, in our absence. So, because of the day [Sunday], we dismissed them so soon as we could. But *Samoset*, our first acquaintance, either was sick, or feigned himself so, and would not go with them, and stayed with us till Wednesday morning. Then we sent him to them, to know the reason they came not according to their words; and we gave him a hat, a pair of stockings and shoes, a shirt, and a piece of cloth to tie about his waist."

Samoset returned again, the next day, bringing with him *Squanto*, mentioned in the last chapter. He was "the only native (says Mourt's Relation) of Patuxet, where we now inhabit, who was one of the 20 [or 24] captives, that by *Hunt* were carried away, and had been in England, and dwelt in Cornhill with master *John Slaine*, a merchant, and could speak a little English, with three others." They brought a few articles for trade, but the more important news "that their great sagamore, Massasoyt, was hard by," whose introduction to them accordingly followed.

In June, 1621, a boy, *John Billington*, having been lost in the woods, several English, with *Squanto* and *Tokamahamon*, undertook a voyage to Nauset in search for him. *Squanto* was their interpreter; "the other, *Tokamahamon*, a special friend." The weather was fair when they set out, "but ere they had been long at sea, there arose a storm of wind and rain, with much lightning and thunder, insomuch that a [water] spout arose not far from them." However, they escaped danger, and arrived at night at Cummaquid. Here they met with some Indians, who informed them that the boy was at Nauset. These Indians treated them with great kindness, inviting them on shore to eat with them.

Iyanough was sachem of this place, and these were his men. "They brought us to their sachim (says *Mourt*) or governor, whom they call *Iyanough*," who then appeared about 26 years of age, "but very personable, gentle, courteous, and fair-conditioned, indeed, not like a savage, save for his attire. His entertainment was answerable to his parts, and his cheer plentiful and various." Thus is portrayed the amiable character, *Iyanough*, by those who knew him. We can add but little of him except his wretched fate. The severity executed upon *Wittuwamet* and *Peksuot* caused such consternation and dread of the English among many, that they forsook their wonted habitations, fled into swamps, and lived in unhealthy places, in a state of starvation, until many died with diseases which they had thus contracted. Among such victims were *Iyanough*, *Aspinet*, *Coneconam*, and many more. Hence the English supposed they were in *Peksuot's* conspiracy, as will be more particularly related hereafter.

While the English were with *Iyanough*, at Cummaquid, they relate that there was an old woman, whom they judged to be no less than 100 years old, who came to see them, because she had never seen English; "yet (say they) [she] could not behold us without breaking forth into great passion, weeping and crying excessively." They inquired the reason of it, and were told that she had three sons, "who, when master *Hunt* was in these parts, went aboard his ship to trade with him, and he carried them captives into Spain." *Squanto* being present, who was carried away at the same time, was acquainted with the circumstances, and thus the English became knowing to her distress, and told her they were sorry, that *Hunt* was a bad man, but that all the other English were well disposed, and would never injure her. They then gave her a few trinkets, which considerably appeased her.

Our voyagers now proceed to Nauset, accompanied by *Iyanough* and two of his men. *Aspinet* was the sachem of this place, to whom *Squanto* was sent, *Iyanough* and his men having gone before. *Squanto* having informed *Aspinet* that his English friends had come for the boy, he "came (they relate) with a great train, and brought the boy with him," one carrying him through the water. This being at or near the place where an attack was made on the English, on their first arrival in the country, as has been related, caused them to be on their guard at this time.

At this time, *Aspinet* had in his company "not less than an hundred;" half of whom attended the boy to the boat, and the rest "stood aloof," with their bows and arrows, looking on. *Aspinet* delivered up the boy in a formal manner, "behung with beads, and made peace with us; we bestowing a knife on him, and likewise on another, that first entertained the boy, and brought him thither."

Iyanough did not accompany the expedition in their return from Nauset, but went home by land, and was ready to entertain the company on their return. From contrary winds and a want of fresh water, the voyagers were obliged to touch again at Cummaquid. "There (say they) we met again with *Iyanough*, and the most of his town." "He, being still willing to gratify us, took a rundet, and led our men in the dark a great way for water, but could find none good, yet brought such as there was on his neck with them. In the meantime the women joined hand in hand, singing and dancing before the shallop;* the men also showing all the kindness they could, *Iyanough* himself taking a bracelet from about his neck, and hanging it about one of us."

They were not able to get out of the harbor of Cummaquid from baffling winds and tides, which *Iyanough* seeing, the next morning he ran along the shore after them, and they took him into their shallop, and returned with him to his town, where he entertained them in a manner not inferior to what he had done before. They now succeeded in getting water, and shortly after returned home in safety.

While at Nauset, the English heard that *Massasoit* had been attacked and carried off by the Narragansets, which led to the expedition of *Standish* and *Allerton* against *Caunbitant*, as will be found related in his life.

About this time, six sachems of the neighboring country had their fidelity tested, by being called upon to sign a treaty subjecting themselves to King *James*, as will be found, also, in that life. But to return again to *Aspinet*, and other sachems of Cape Cod.

By the improvidence of a company settled at Wessaguscus, under the direction of Mr. *Thomas Weston*, in 1622, they had been brought to the very brink of starvation in the winter of that year. In fact, the Plimouth people were but very little better off; and but for the kindness of the Indians, the worst of consequences might have ensued to both these infant colonies.

As the winter progressed, the two colonies entered into articles of agreement to go on a trading voyage among the Indians of Cape Cod to buy corn, and whatever else might conduce to their livelihood. *Squanto* was pilot in this expedition; but he died before it was accomplished, and the record of his death stands thus in WINSLOW'S RELATION:—

"But here [at Manamoyk, since Chatham], though they had determined to make a second essay [to pass within the shoals of Cape Cod]; yet God had otherwise disposed, who struck *Tisquantum* with sickness, insomuch as he there died, which crossed their southward trading, and the more, because the master's sufficiency was much doubted, and the season very tempestuous, and not fit to go upon discovery, having no guide to direct them." His disorder, according to *Prince*, was a fever, "bleeding much at the nose, which the Indians reckon a fatal symptom." He desired the governor would pray for him, that he might go to the Englishmen's God, "bequeathing his things to sundry of his English friends, as remembrances of his love; of whom we have a great loss."

Thus died the famous *Squanto*, or *Tasquantum*, in December, 1622. To him the pilgrims were greatly indebted, although he often, through extreme folly and shortsightedness, gave them, as well as himself and others, a great deal of trouble, as in the life of *Massasoit* and *Hobomok* will appear.

Thus, at the commencement of the voyage, the pilot was taken away by death, and the expedition came near being abandoned. However, before *Squanto* died, he succeeded in introducing his friends to the sachem of Manamoick and his people, where they were received and entertained in a manner that would do honor to any people in any age. It is the more worthy of remark, as none of the English had ever been there before, and were utter strangers to them. After they had refreshed them "with store of venison and other victuals, which they brought them in great abundance," they sold them "8 *hogsheads of corn and beans, though the people were but few.*"

From Manamoick they proceeded to Massachusetts, but could do nothing

* It was a custom with most Indian nations to dance when strangers came among them. Baron *Lahontan* says it was the manner of the Iroquois to dance "*lorsque les étrangers parent dans leur païs, ou que leurs ennemis envoient des ambassadeurs pour faire des propositions de paix.*"—*Memoires de L'Amerique*, ii. 110.

there, as Mr. *Weston's* men had ruined the market by giving "as much for a quart of corn, as we used to do for a beaver's skin." Therefore they returned again to Cape Cod, to Nauset, "where the sachem *Aspinet* used the governor very kindly, and where they bought 8 or 10 hogsheads of corn and beans. also at a place called *Mattachiest*, where they had like kind entertainment and corn also." While here, a violent storm drove on shore and so damaged their pinnace, that they could not get their corn on board the ship: so they made a stack of it, and secured it from the weather, by covering it with mats and sedge. *Aspinet* was desired to watch and keep wild animals from destroying it, until they could send for it; also, not to suffer their boat to be concerned with. All this he faithfully did, and the governor returned home by land, "receiving great kindness from the Indians by the way." At this time there was a great sickness among the Massachusetts Indians, "not unlike the plague, if not the same;" but no particulars of it are recorded.

Some time after, *Standish* went to bring the corn left at Nauset, and, as usual, gets himself into difficulty with the Indians. One of *Aspinet's* men happening to come to one of *Standish's* boats, which being left entirely without guard, he took out a few trinkets, such as "beads, scissors, and other trifles," which when the English captain found out, "he took certain of his company with him, and went to the sachem, telling him what had happened, and requiring the same again, or the party that stole them," "*or else he would revenge it on them before his departure*," and so departed for the night, "*refusing whatsoever kindness they offered*." However, the next morning, *Aspinet*, attended by many of his men, went to the English, "in a stately manner," and restored all the "trifles;" for the exposing of which the English deserved ten times as much reprehension as the man for taking them.

Squanto being the only person that escaped the great sickness at Patuxet, inquirers for an account of that calamity will very reasonably expect to find it in a history of his life. We therefore will relate all that is known of it, not elsewhere to be noticed in our progress. The extent of its ravages, as near as we can judge, was from Narraganset Bay to Kennebeck, or perhaps Penobscot, and was supposed to have commenced about 1617, and the length of its duration seems to have been between two and three years, as it was nearly abated in 1619. The Indians gave a frightful account of it, saying that they died so fast "that the living were not able to bury the dead." When the English arrived in the country, their bones were thick upon the ground in many places. This they looked upon as a great providence, inasmuch as it had destroyed "multitudes of the barbarous heathen to make way for the chosen people of God."

> "Some had expired in fight,—the brands
> Still rusted in their bony hands,—
> In plague and famine some."—CAMPBELL

All wars and disasters, in those days, were thought to be preceded by some strange natural appearance, or, as appeared to them, unnatural appearance or phenomenon; hence the appearance of a comet, in 1618, was considered by some the precursor of this pestilence.*

We will give here, from a curious work,† in the language of the author, an interesting passage, relating to this melancholy period of the history of the people of *Massasoit*, in which he refers to *Squanto*. After relating the fate of a French ship's crew among the Wampanoags, as extracted in the life of *Massasoit*, in continuation of the account, he proceeds thus: "But contrary wise, [the Indians having said "they were so many that God could not kill them," when one of the Frenchmen rebuked them for their "wickedness," telling them God would destroy them,] in short time after, the hand of God fell heavily upon them, with such a mortall stroake, that they died on heaps, as they lay in their houses, and the living, that were able to shift for themselves, would runne away and let them dy, and let their carkases ly above the ground

* The year 1618 seems to have been very fruitful in comets, "as therein no less than four were observed." *I. Mather's Discourse concerning Comets*, 108. Boston, 12mo. 1683. There may be seen a curious passage concerning the comet of 1618 in *Rushworth's Hist. Col.* of that year.

† New English Canaan, 23, by *Thomas Morton*, 4to. Amsterdam, 1637.

without buriall. For in a place where many inhabited, there hath been but one left alive to tell what became of the rest; the living being (as it seems) not able to bury the dead. They were left for crowes, kites, and vermine to pray upon. And the bones and skulls, upon the severall places of their habitations, made such a spectacle, after my comming into those parts,* that, as I travailed in that forrest nere the Massachussets, it seemed to me a new-found Golgotha."

Sir *Ferdinando Gorges*, as we have seen, was well acquainted with the coast of New England. After his design failed at Sagadahock, he tells us that he sent over a ship upon his own account, which was to leave a company under one *Vines*,† to remain and trade in the country. These were his own servants, and he ordered "them to leave the ship and ship's company, for to follow their business in the usual place, (for, he says, I knew they would not be drawn to seek by any means,) by these, and the help of those natives formerly sent over, I come to be truly informed of so much as gave me assurance that in time I should want no undertakers, though as yet I was forced to hire men to stay there the winter quarter, at extreme rates, and not without danger, for that the war‡ had consumed the Bashaba, and the most of the great sagamores, with such men of action as followed them, and those that remained were sore afflicted with the plague; for that the country was in a manner left void of inhabitants. Notwithstanding, *Vines*, and the rest with him that lay in the cabins with those people that died, some more, some less, mightily, (blessed be God for it) not one of them ever felt their heads to ache while they stayed there." Here, although we are put in possession of several of the most important facts, yet our venerable author is deficient in one of the main particulars—I mean that of dates. Therefore we gain no further data as to the time or continuance of this plague among the Indians; for Sir *Ferdinando* adds to the above, "and this course I held some years together, but nothing to my private profit," &c.

In Capt. *Smith's* account of New England, published in 1631, he has a passage about the plague, which is much like that we have given above from *Morton*. The ship cast away, he says, was a fishing vessel, and the man that they kept a prisoner, on telling them he feared his God would destroy them, their king made him stand on the top of a hill, and collected his people about it that the man might see how numerous they were. When he had done this, he demanded of the Frenchman whether his God, that he told so much about, had so many men, and whether they could kill all those. On his assuring the king that he could, they derided him as before. Soon after, the plague carried off all of the Massachusetts, 5 or 600, leaving only 30, of whom 28 were killed by their neighbors, the other two escaping until the English came, to whom they gave their country. The English told the Indians that the disease was the plague. Capt. *Smith* says this account is second hand to him, and therefore begs to be excused if it be not true in all its particulars.

We have now come to one of the most interesting characters in Indian history.

MASSASOIT, chief of the Wampanoags, resided at a place called Pokanoket or Pawkunnawkut, by the Indians, which is now included in the town of Bristol, Rhode Island. He was a chief renowned more in peace than war, and was, as long as he lived, a friend to the English, notwithstanding they committed repeated usurpations upon his lands and liberties.

This chief's name has been written with great variation, as *Woosamequin*, *Asuhmequin*, *Oosamequen*, *Osamekin*, *Owsamequin*, *Owsamequine*, *Ussamequen*, *Wasamegin*, &c.; but the name by which he is generally known in history, is that with which we commence his life.§ Mr. *Prince*, in his Annals, says of that name,

* Mr. *Morton* first came over in 1622. He settled near Weymouth. After great trouble and losses from those of a different religion, he was banished out of the country, and had his property sequestered, but soon after returned. He died in York, Me., 1646. If it be pretended that *Morton had no religion*, we say, "Judge not." He professed to have.

† Mr. *Richard Vines*. *America painted to the Life*, by *Ferd. Gorges*, Esq. 4to. Lond. 165.

‡ A great war among the Indians at this time is mentioned by most of the first writers, but the particulars of it cannot be known. It seems to have been between the Tarratines and tribes to the west of Pascataqua.

§ Some have derived the name of *Massachusetts* from this chief, but that conjecture is not to be heeded. If any man knew, we may be allowed to suppose that *Roger Williams* did.

"the printed accounts generally spell him *Massasoit; Gov. Bradford* writes him *Massasoyt*, and *Massasoyet;* but I find the ancient people, from their fathers in Plimouth colony, pronounced his name *Ma-sas-so-it.*" Still we find no inclination to change a letter in a name so venerable, and which has been so long established; for if a writer suffer the spirit of innovation in himself, he knows not where to stop, and we pronounce him no *antiquary.*

It has often been thought strange, that so mild a sachem as *Massasoit* should have possessed so great a country, and our wonder has been increased when we consider, that Indian possessions are generally obtained by prowess and great personal courage. We know of none who could boast of such extensive dominions, where all were contented to consider themselves his friends and children. *Powhatan, Pontiac, Little-turtle, Tecumseh,* and many more that we could name, have swayed many tribes, but theirs was a temporary union, in an emergency of war. That *Massasoit* should be able to hold so many tribes together, without constant war, required qualities belonging only to few. That he was not a warrior no one will allow, when the testimony of *Annawon* is so direct to the point. For that great chief gave Capt. *Church* "an account of what mighty success he had had formerly, in the wars against many nations of Indians, when he served *Asuhmequin, Philip's* father."

The limits of his country towards the Nipmuks, or inland Indians, are not precise, but upon the east and west we are sure. It is evident, however, from the following extract, that, in 1647, the Nipmuks were rather uncertain about their sachem, and probably belonged at one time to *Massasoit,* and at another to the Narragansets, or others, as circumstances impelled. "The Nopnat (Nipnet, or Nipmuk) Indians having noe sachem of their own are at liberty; part of them, by their own choice, doe appertaine to the Narraganset sachem, and parte to the Mohegens."* And certainly, in 1660, those of Quabaog belonged to *Massasoit* or *Wassamegin,* as he was then called (if he be the same), as will be evident from facts, to be found in the life of *Uncas.* He owned Cape Cod, and all that part of Massachusetts and Rhode Island between Narraganset and Massachusetts bays; extending inland between Pawtucket and Charles rivers, a distance not satisfactorily ascertained, as was said before, together with all the contiguous islands. It was filled with many tribes or nations, and all looking up to him, to sanction all their expeditions, and settle all their difficulties. And we may remark, further, with regard to the Nipmuks, that at one time they were his tributaries. And this seems the more probable, for in *Philip's* war there was a constant intercourse between them, and when any of his men made an escape, their course was directly into the country of the Nipmuks. No such intercourse subsisted between the Narragansets and either of these. But, on the contrary, when a messenger from the Narragansets arrived in the country of the Nipmuks, with the heads of some of the English, to show that they had joined in the war, he was at first fired upon, though afterwards, when two additional heads were brought, he was received with them.

Massasoit had several places of residence, but the principal was Mount Hope, or Pokanoket. The English early gave it the name of Mount Hope, but from what circumstance we have not learned. Some suppose the words *Mount Hope* corrupted from the Indian words *Mon-top,*† but with what reason we are not informed. Since we have thus early noticed the seat of the ancient chiefs, before proceeding with the life of the first of the Wampanoags, we will give a description of it. It appears to the best advantage from the village of Fall River, in the town of Troy, Massachusetts, from which it is distant about four miles. From this place, its top very much resembles the dome of the state-

He learned from the Indian themselves, *"that the Massachusetts were called so from the Blue Hills."* In the vocabulary of Indian words, by Rev. *John Cotton,* the definition of *Massachusett* is, *"an hill in the form of an arrow's head."*

* Records of the U. Col. in *Hazard,* ii. 92.

† *Alden's* Collection of Epitaphs, iv. 685. President *Stiles,* in his notes to the second edition of CHURCH'S HIST. PHILIP'S WAR, p. 7, spells it *Mont-haup;* but it is not so in the text of either edition. Moreover, we have not been able to discover that *Mon-top* is derived from Indian word or words, and do not hesitate to pronounce it a corruption of the two English words commonly used in naming it.

house in Boston, as seen from many places in the vicinity, at four or five miles distance. Its height by admeasurement is said to be about 200 feet.* It is very steep on the side towards Pocasset, and its appearance is very regular To its natural appearance a gentleman of Bristol has contributed to add materially, by placing upon its summit a circular summer-house, and this is a principal reason why it so much resembles the Massachusetts state-house. This mount, therefore, since some time previous to 1824, does not appear as in the days of *Massasoit*, and as it did to his early friends and visitors, *Winslow* and *Hamden*. It was sufficiently picturesque without such addition, as an immense stone originally formed its summit, and completed its domelike appearance. The octagonal summer-house being placed upon this, completes the cupola or turret. From this the view of Providence, Warren, Bristol, and, indeed, the whole surrounding country, is very beautiful.

This eminence was known among the Narragansets by the name *Pokanoket*, which signified in their language *the wood or land on the other side of the water*, and to the Wampanoags by the name *Sowwams*. And it is worthy remark here that *Kúequenáku* was the name of the place where Philadelphia now stands. Mr. *Heckewelder* says, it signified *the grove of the long pine trees*. There was a place in Middleborough, and another in Raynham, where he spent some part of particular seasons, perhaps the summer. The place in Raynham was near Fowling Pond, and he no doubt had many others.

Sir *Francis Drake* is the first, of whom we have any account, that set foot upon the shores of New England. This was in 1586, about seven years after he had taken possession, and named the same country New England or New Albion, upon the western side of the continent. It is an error of long standing, that Prince *Charles* named the country New England, and it even now so stands upon the pages of history. But it is very clear that Sir *Francis* is justly entitled to the credit of it. American historians seem to have looked no further than *Prince* and *Robertson*, and hence assert that Capt. *Smith* named the country New England. We will now hear *Smith*† on this matter. "New England is that part of America, in the Ocean sea, opposite to *Noua Albion*, in the South Sea, discovered by the most memorable Sir *Francis Drake*, in his voyage about the world, *in regard whereof*, this is stiled New England."

Capt. *Smith*, in 1614, made a survey of the coast of what is now New England, and because the country was already named New England, or, which is the same, New Albion, upon its western coast, he thought it most proper to stamp it anew upon the eastern. Therefore Capt. *Smith* neither takes to himself the honor of naming New England, as some writers of authority assert, nor does he give it to King *Charles*, as Dr. *Robertson* and many others, copying him, have done.

The noble and generous minded *Smith*, unlike *Americus*, would not permit or suffer his respected friend and cotemporary to be deprived of any honor due to him in his day ; and to which we may attribute the revival of the name New England in 1614.

It was upon some part of Cape Cod that the great circumnavigator landed. He was visited by the "king of the country," who submitted his territories to him, as *Hioh* had done on the western coast. After several days of mutual trade, and exchange of kindnesses, during which time the natives became greatly attached to Sir *Francis*, he departed for England. Whether the "king of the country" here mentioned were *Massasoit*, we have not the means of knowing, as our accounts do not give any name ; but it was upon his dominions that this first landing was made, and we have therefore thought it proper to be thus particular, and which, we venture to predict, will not be unacceptable to our readers.‡

---

* Yamoyden, 259.

† See his "*Description of N. England*," and the error may henceforth be dispensed with.

‡ The first authority which we found for these interesting facts, (interesting to *every* son of New England,) is a work entitled "Naval Biography," &c. of Great Britain, 2 vols. 8vo. London, 1805, and is in these words :—"The first attempt towards a regular colonization of N England, occurs in the year 1606. It will easily be recollected, that this part of the American continent was first distinguished by the captains *Barlow* and *Amidas ;* that Sir *Francis Drake*, when he touched here on his return from the West Indies, in 1586, was the first Englishman who landed in these parts, and to whom one of the Indian kings submitted his territory ;

Smith landed in many places upon the shores of *Massasoit's* dominions, one of which places he named *Plimouth*, which happened to be the same which now bears that name.

Our accounts make Capt. *Bartholomew Gosnold* the next visitor to the shores of *Massasoit*, after Sir *Francis Drake*. His voyage was in 1602, and he was the first who came in a direct course from Old to New England. He landed in the same place where Sir *Francis* did 16 years before. The route had hitherto been by the Canaries and West India Islands, and a voyage to and from New England took up nearly a year.

We can know nothing of the early times of *Massasoit*. Our next visitor to his country, that we shall here notice, was Capt. *Thomas Dermer*. This was in May, 1619. He sailed for Monhigon; thence, in that month, for Virginia, in an open pinnace; consequently was obliged to keep close in shore. He found places which had been inhabited, but at that time contained no people; and farther onward nearly all were dead, of a great sickness, which was then prevailing, but nearly abated. When he came to Plimouth, all were dead. From thence he traveled a day's journey into the country westward, to Namasket, now Middleborough. From this place he sent a messenger to visit *Massasoit*. In this expedition, he redeemed two Frenchmen from *Massasoit's* people, who had been cast away on the coast three years before.

But to be more particular with Capt. *Dermer*, we will hear him in his own manner, which is by a letter he wrote to *Samuel Purchas*, the compiler of the Pilgrimage, dated 27 Dec. 1619.

"When I arrived at my savage's [*Squanto's*] native country, (finding all dead,) I travelled alongst a day's journey, to a place called *Nummastaquyt*, where finding inhabitants, I despatched a messenger, a day's journey farther west, to Pocanokit, which bordereth on the sea; whence came to see me two kings, attended with a guard of 50 armed men, who being well satisfied with that my savage and I discoursed unto them, (being desirous of novelty,) gave me content in whatsoever I demanded; where I found that former relations were true. Here I redeemed a Frenchman, and afterwards another at Massta-

and that Capt. *Gosnoll*, who made a little stay in the same place, gave such a report of N. England as to attract the attention of his adventurous countrymen, some of whom immediately procured a charter," &c.—Vol. I. p. 337, 338. If we could know from whence the above was taken (that is, the authority the writer of that work made use of), it might at once, perhaps, settle the question. *Oldmixon*, I. 25, has the same fact, though not quite so circumstantially related. Mr. *Bancroft*, in his I. Vol. of the Hist. United States, supposes *Oldmixon*, through carelessness, mistakes *Drake's* landing in California, in 1579, for that in N. England, in 1586, because, as we suppose, he had not seen the fact elsewhere stated. But *Drake* was 40 days from Virginia to Plymouth, which would give him time enough to have visited N. England. See "The Life and Dangerous Voyages of Sir *Francis Drake*," &c., small 12mo., London, (without date), page 133. See also *Stith's* Virginia, p. 16.

What is said in *Blome's* account of America, p. 210, is not very conclusive. His words are, "The year following (1585), Sir *Richard Greenvile* conveyed an English colony thither [this author mistakes the situation of the places he describes, in a wretched manner], under the government of Mr. *Ralph Lane*, who continued there [yet he is speaking of N. Eng.] till the next year (1586), but, upon some extraordinary occasion, returned, with Sir *Francis Drake*, into England, being accounted by some the first discoverer thereof." *Blome's* work was printed in 1687, and may have been *Oldmixon's* authority. In the Gent. Mag., Vol. XXV., p. 291, it is said, "Sir *Francis Drake*, who made a discent on the coast, continued there but a very short time, so that whatever had been known of this country was so much forgotten in 1602, that *Gosnold* fell in with the coast by accident, as he was pursuing another design." *Forster's* error about Sir *Francis's* being on the coast in 1585, is surprising; but it is still more surprising that any one, pretending to be an historian, should copy it. See *Forster*, 295, and *Anspach*, Newfoundland, 74. In *Prince's Worthies of Devon*, an account of Sir *Bernard Drake's* expedition to the New England seas, in 1585, may be seen; also in *Purchase*, v. 1882. Queen *Elizabeth* sent over Sir *Bernard*, with a naval force, to dispossess any Portuguese, or others, that he might find fishing there. He found many vessels employed in that business, some of which he captured, and dispersed the rest, and returned to England with several Portuguese prizes. Now it is not at all improbable that *Elizabeth* had instructed Sir *Francis* to coast up into these seas, when he had finished his designs in South America and Virginia, to see if there were any vessels of other nations usurping the rights of her citizens; and hence inattentive writers have confounded the names of Sir *Bernard* and Sir *Francis*, they being both distinguished admirals at that time, and both having the same surname, and originally of the same family. The expedition of Sir *Bernard* was the year before that of Sir *Francis*, and hence arose the anachronism. Several English navigators had been on this coast before 1600. Capt *George Drake* made a voyage to the river St. Lawrence in 1593; but whether any of them landed in what is now New England, is at present unknown.

chusit, who three years since escaped shipwreck at the north-east of Cape Cod."

We have mentioned his interview with *Massasoit*, whom we suppose was one of the kings mentioned in the letter, and *Quadequina* was no doubt the other.

In another letter, Mr. *Dermer* says the Indians would have killed him at Namasket, had not *Squanto* entreated hard for him. "Their desire of revenge (he adds) was occasioned by an Englishman, who, having many of them on board, made great slaughter of them with their murderers and small shot, when (as they say) they offered no injury on their parts."

Mr. *Thomas Morton*,* the author who made himself so merry at the expense of the Pilgrims of Plimouth, has the following passage concerning these Frenchmen:—"It fortuned some few yeares before the English came to inhabit at new Plimmouth in New England, that, upon some distast given in the Massachussets Bay, by Frenchmen, then trading there with the natives for beaver, they set upon the men, at such advantage, that they killed manie of them, burned their shipp, then riding at anchor by an island there, now called *Peddock's Island*, in memory of *Leonard Peddock* that landed there, (where many wilde anckies† haunted that time, which hee thought had bin tame,) distributing them unto five sachems which were lords of the severall territories adjoyning, they did keep them so long as they lived, only to sport themselves at them, and made these five Frenchmen fetch them wood and water, which is the generall worke they require of a servant. One of these five men outliving the rest, had learned so much of their language, as to rebuke them for their bloudy deede: saying that God would be angry with them for it; and that he would in his displeasure destroy them; but the salvages (it seems, boasting of their strength) replyed, and said, that they were so many that God could not kill them." This seems to be the same story, only differently told from that related above from *Smith*.

Dec. 11, O. S.,‡ 1620, the pilgrims had arrived at Plimouth, and possessed themselves of a portion of *Massasoit's* country. With the nature of their proceedings, he was at first unacquainted, and sent occasionally some of his men to observe their strange motions. Very few of these Indians, however, were seen by the pilgrims. At length he sent one of his men, who had been some time with the English fishing vessels about the country of the Kennebeck, and had learned a little of their language, to observe more strictly what was progressing among the strangers at his place of Patuxet, which these intruders now called Plimouth. This was in March, 1621.

---

* In his "*New Canaan*," 22, 23.

† Modern naturalists do not seem to have been acquainted with this animal!

‡ The length of a year was fixed by *Julius Cæsar* at 365 days and 6 hours, or 365¼ days. This ¼ of a day being omitted for 4 years amounted to a whole day, and was then added to the 365 in the month of *February*, which 4th year was called *leap year*, because it leaped forward one day. But by this supputation it was perceived that the year was too long, and consequently the seasons were getting out of place. *Pope Gregory* found, in 1582, that the vernal equinox, which at the time of the Nicene council, A. D. 325, fell on 21 March, fell now 10 days beyond it; therefore he ordered 10 days to be struck out of October, 1582; and to prevent the recurrence of the difficulty in future, decreed that 3 days should be abated in every 400 years, by restoring leap years to common years at the end of 3 successive centuries, and making leap year again at the close of every 4th century. Thus 1700, 1800, 1900, 2100, &c. though divisible by 4, are common years, but 2000, 2400, 2800, &c. are leap years. This method of keeping the year is called NEW STYLE, and that before the reformation by Gregory, OLD STYLE. Even this correction does not set the year exactly right; but the error is so small that it amounts to scarce a day and a half in 5000 years, and we need not trouble ourselves about a nearer approximation.

Because this correction had a Catholic or Popish origin, Protestants would not for a long time adopt it. At length, in the year 1751, the English Parliament enacted, that the 3d of Sept. of that year should be called the 14th, thereby striking out 11 days, which their calendar at that late period required, to reduce it to the Gregorian. And hence the reason of our calling the 11 Dec. O. S., the 22 N. S. The reason also of our adding 11 days instead of 10 is obvious, because, in adopting the Catholic method 170 years after it had been introduced by Gregory, another day was gained, and therefore 10+1=11.

We have, in speaking of *Samoset* and *Squanto*, observed that it was through the agency of the former that a knowledge was gained by the pilgrims of *Massasoit*. It was upon 22 March, 1621, that they brought the welcome news to Plimouth, that their chief was near at hand;* "and they brought with them (say the Pilgrims) some few skins to truck, and some red herrings, newly taken and dried, but not salted; and signified unto us, that their great sagamore, *Massasoit*, was hard by, with *Quadequina*, his brother. They could not well express in English what they would; but after an hour the king came to the top of an hill [supposed to be that now called *Watson's*, on the south side of Town-brook] over against us, and had in his train 60 men, that we could well behold them, and they us. We were not willing to send our governor to them, and they unwilling to come to us: so *Squanto* went again unto him, who brought word that we should send one to parley with him, which we did, which was *Edward Winslow*, to know his mind, and to signify the mind and will of our governor, which was to have trading and peace with him. We sent to the king a pair of knives, and a copper chain, with a jewel in it. To *Quadequina* we sent likewise a knife, and a jewel to hang in his ear, and withal a pot of strong water, a good quantity of biscuit, and some butter, which were all willingly accepted."

The Englishman then made a speech to him about his king's love and goodness to him and his people, and that he accepted of him as his friend and ally "He liked well of the speech, (say the English,) and heard it attentively, though the interpreters did not well express it. After he had eaten and drunk himself, and given the rest to his company, he looked upon our messenger's sword and armor, which he had on, with intimation of his desire to buy it; but, on the other side, our messenger showed his unwillingness to part with it. In the end he left him in the custody of *Quadequina*, his brother, and came over the brook, and some 20 men following him. We kept six or seven as hostages for our messenger."

As *Massasoit* proceeded to meet the English, they met him with six soldiers, who saluted each other. Several of his men were with him, but all left their bows and arrows behind. They were conducted to a new house which was partly finished, and a green rug was spread upon the floor, and several cushions for *Massasoit* and his chiefs to sit down upon. Then came the English governor, followed by a drummer and trumpeter and a few soldiers, and after kissing one another, all sat down. Some strong water being brought, the governor drank to *Massasoit*, who in his turn "drank a great draught, that made him sweat all the while after."

They now proceeded to make a treaty, which stipulated, that neither *Massasoit* nor any of his people should do hurt to the English, and that if they did they should be given up to be punished by them; and that if the English did any harm to him or any of his people, they (the *English*) would do the like to them. That if any did unjustly war against him, the English were to aid him, and he was to do the same in his turn, and by so doing King *James* would esteem him his friend and ally.

"All which (they say) the king seemed to like well, and it was applauded of his followers." And they add, "All the while he sat by the governor, he trembled for fear."

At this time he is described as "a very lusty man, in his best years, an able body, grave of countenance, and spare of speech; in his attire little or nothing differing from the rest of his followers, only in a great chain of white bone beads about his neck; and at it, behind his neck, hangs a little bag of tobacco, which he drank, and gave us to drink.† His face was painted with a sad red

---

* *Mourt's* narrative is here continued from the last extract in p. 10, without any omission.

† I presume that by "drinking tobacco," smoking is meant. The pilgrims were probably not acquainted with the practice of smoking at all, and hence this sort of misnomer is not strange, though it may be thought a little odd. How long *smoking* went by the name of *drinking* at Plimouth I do not learn; but in 1646 this entry is found in the Plimouth records: —"*Anthony Thacher* and *George Pole* were chosen a committee to draw up an order concerning disorderly drinking of Tobacco."

Roger Williams says, in his Key, "Generally all the men throughout the country have a tobacco-bag, with a pipe in it, hanging at their back."

Dr. *Thacher* says, that an aged man in Plimouth, who was a great smoker, used to term like murrey, and oiled both head and face, that he looked greasily. All his followers likewise were, in their faces, in part or in whole, painted, some black, some red, some yellow, and some white; some with crosses and other antic works; some had skins on them, and some naked; all strong, tall men in appearance. The king had in his bosom, hanging in a string, a great long knife. He marvelled much at our trumpet, and some of his men would sound it as well as they could. *Samoset* and *Squanto* stayed all night with us." *Massasoit* retired into the woods, about half a mile from the English, and there encamped at night with his men, women and children. Thus ended March 22d, 1621.

During his first visit to the English, he expressed great signs of fear, and during the treaty could not refrain from trembling.* Thus it is easy to see how much hand he had in making it, but *would that there had never been worse ones made.*

It was agreed that some of his people should come and plant near by, in a few days, and live there all summer. "That night we kept good watch, but there was no appearance of danger. The next morning divers of their people came over to us, hoping to get some victuals, as we imagined. Some of them told us the king would have some of us come to see him. Capt. *Standish* and *Isaac Alderton* went venterously, who were welcomed of him after their manner. He gave them three or four ground nuts and some tobacco. We cannot yet conceive, (they continue,) but that he is willing to have peace with us; for they have seen our people sometimes alone two or three in the woods at work and fowling, when as they offered them no harm, as they might easily have done; and especially because he hath a potent adversary, the Narrohigansets,† that are at war with him, against whom he thinks we may be some strength to him; for our pieces are terrible unto them. This morning they stayed till 10 or 11 of the clock; and our governor bid them send the king's kettle, and filled it with peas, which pleased them well; and so they went their way." Thus ended the first visit of *Massasoit* to the pilgrims. We should here note that he ever after treated the English with kindness, and the peace now concluded was undisturbed for nearly 40 years. Not that any writing or articles of a treaty, of which he never had any adequate idea, was the cause of his friendly behavior, but it was the natural goodness of his heart.

The pilgrims report, that at this time he was at war with the Narragansets. But if this were the case, it could have been nothing more than some small skirmishing.

Meanwhile *Squanto* and *Samoset* remained with the English, instructing them how to live in their country; equal in all respects to *Robinson Crusoe's man Friday*, and had *De Foe* lived in that age he might have made as good a story from their history as he did from that of *Alexander Selkirk.*—"*Squanto* went to fish [a day or two after *Massasoit* left] for eels. At night he came home with as many as he could lift in one hand, which our people were glad of. They were fat and sweet. He trod them out with his feet, and so caught them with his hands, without any other instrument."

---

it *drinking tobacco. Hist. Plim.* 34. This we infer was within the recollection of the author.

The notion that *tobacco* is so called from the island Tobago, is erroneously entertained by many. When Sir *Francis Drake* discovered the country to the north of California, in 1579, the writer of the account of his voyage says, the Indians presented the admiral with a small basket made of rushes, filled with an herb they called *tabah*. From another passage it appears, that the Indians of that region, like those of New England, had bags in which tobacco was carried. *Burney's Voyages*, I. 344–7.

* And, with this fact before him, the author of "*Tales of the Indians*" says, the treaty was made with *deliberation* and *cheerfulness* on the part of *Massasoit!*

† Few Indian names have been spelt more ways than this. From the nature of the Indian language, it is evident that no *r* should be used in it. Nahigonsik and Nantigansick, *R. Williams.*—Nechegansitt, *Gookin.*—Nantyggansiks, *Callender.*—Nanohigganset, *Winslow's Good News from N. Eng.*—Nanhyganset, *Judge Johnson's Life of Gen. Greene.*—These are but few of the permutations without the *r*, and those with it are still more numerous.

The meaning of the name is still uncertain. Madam *Knight*, in her Journal, 22 and 23, says, at a place where she happened to put up for a night in that country, she heard some of the "town topers" disputing about the origin of the word *Narraganset*. "One said it was so named by Indians, because there grew a brier there of a prodigious height and bigness, who quoted an Indian of so barbarous a name for his author that she could not write it." Another said it meant a celebrated spring, which was very cold in summer, and "as hot as could be imagined in the winter."

This *Squanto* became afterwards an important personage in Indian politics, and some of his manœuvres remind us of some managing politicians of our own times. In 1622, he forfeited his life by plotting to destroy that of *Massasoit*, as will be found related in the life of *Hobomok*. On that occasion, *Massasoit* went himself to Plimouth, "being much offended and enraged against *Tisquantum;*" but the governor succeeded in allaying his wrath for that time. Soon after, he sent a messenger to entreat the governor to consent to his being put to death; the governor said he deserved death, but as he knew not how to get along without him in his intercourse with the Indians, he would spare him.

Determined in his purpose, *Massasoit* soon sent the same messenger again, accompanied by many others, who offered many beaver skins that *Tisquantum* might be given up to them. They demanded him in the name of *Massasoit*, as being one of his subjects, whom, (says *Winslow*,) by our first articles of peace, we could not retain. But out of respect to the English, they would not seize him without their consent. *Massasoit* had sent his own knife to be used in cutting off his head and hands, which were to be brought to him.

Meantime *Squanto* came and delivered himself up to the governor, charging *Hobomok* with his overthrow, and telling him to deliver him or not to the messengers of *Massasoit*, as he thought fit. It seems from the narrative that, as the governor was about to do it, they grew impatient at the delay, and went off in a rage. The delay was occasioned by the appearance of a boat in the harbor, which the governor pretended might be that of an enemy, as there had been a rumor that the French had meditated breaking up the settlement of the English in this region. This, however, was doubtless only a pretence, and employed to wear out the patience of his unwelcome visitors. Hence that *Massasoit* should for some time after "seem to frown" on the English, as they complain, is certainly no wonder.

The next summer, in June or July, *Massasoit* was visited by several of the English, among whom was Mr. *Edward Winslow*, Mr. *Stephen Hopkins*, and *Squanto* as their interpreter. Their object was to find out his place of residence, in case they should have to call upon him for assistance; to keep good the friendly correspondence commenced at Plimouth; and especially to cause him to prevent his men from hanging about them, and living upon them, which was then considered very burdensome, as they had begun to grow short of provisions. That their visit might be acceptable, they took along, for a present, a trooper's red coat, with some lace upon it, and a copper chain; with these *Massasoit* was exceedingly well pleased. The chain, they told him, he must send as a signal, when any of his men wished to visit them, so that they might not be imposed upon by strangers.

When the English arrived at Pokanoket, *Massasoit* was absent, but was immediately sent for. Being informed that he was coming, the English began to prepare to shoot off their guns; this so frightened the women and children, that they ran away, and would not return until the interpreter assured them that they need not fear; and when *Massasoit* arrived, they saluted him by a discharge, at which he was very much elated; and "who, after their manner, (says one of the company,) kindly welcomed us, and took us into his house, and set us down by him, where, having delivered our message and presents, and having put the coat on his back, and the chain about his neck, he was not a little proud to behold himself, and his men also, to see their king so bravely attired."* A new treaty was now held with him, and he very good-naturedly assented to all that was desired. He then made a speech to his men, many of them being assembled to see the English, which, as near as they could learn its meaning, acquainted them with what course they might pursue in regard to the English. Among other things, he said, "*Am I not Massasoit, commander of the country about us? Is not such and such places mine, and the people of them? They shall take their skins to the English.*" This his people applauded. In his speech, "he named at least thirty places," over which he had control. "This being ended, he lighted tobacco for us, and fell to discoursing of England and of the king's majesty, marvelling that he should live without a wife.' He seems to have been embittered against the French, and wished "us not to suffer them to come to Narraganset, for it was King *James's* country, and he

* *Mourt's Relation,* in *Col. Mass. Hist. Soc*

was King *James's* man." He had no victuals at this time to give to the English, and night coming on, they retired to rest supperless. He had but one bed, if so it might be called, "being only planks laid a foot from the ground, and a thin mat upon them."* "He laid us on the bed with himself and his wife, they at the one end, and we at the other. Two more of his men, for want of room, pressed by and upon us; so that we were worse weary of our lodging than of our journey."

"The next day, many of their sachims or petty governors came to see us, and many of their men also. There they went to their manner of games for skins and knives." It is amusing to learn that the English tried to get a chance in this gambling affair. They say, "There we challenged them to shoot with them for skins," but they were too cunning for them, "only they desired to see one of us shoot at a mark; who shooting with hail shot, they wondered to see the mark so full of holes."

The next day, about one o'clock, *Massasoit* brought two large fishes and boiled them; but the pilgrims still thought their chance for refreshment very small, as "there were at least forty looking for a share in them;" but scanty as it was, it came very timely, as they had fasted two nights and a day. The English now left him, at which he was very sorrowful.

"Very importunate he was (says our author) to have us stay with them longer. But we desired to keep the sabbath at home, and feared we should either be light-headed for want of sleep; for what with bad lodging, the savages' barbarous singing, (for they used to sing themselves asleep,) lice and fleas within doors, and musketoes without, we could hardly sleep all the time of our being there; we much fearing, that if we should stay any longer, we should not be able to recover home for want of strength. So that, on Friday morning, before sunrising, we took our leave, and departed, *Massasoyt* being both grieved and ashamed, that he could no better entertain us. And retaining *Tisquantum* to send from place to place to procure truck for us, and appointing another, called *Tokamahamon*, in his place, whom we had found faithful before and after upon all occasions."

This faithful servant, *Tokamahamon*, was in the famous "voyage to the kingdom of Nauset," and was conspicuous for his courage in the expedition against *Caunbitant*.

In 1623, *Massasoit* sent to his friends in Plimouth to inform them that he was very dangerously sick. Desiring to render him aid if possible, the governor despatched Mr. *Winslow* again, with some medicines and cordials, and *Hobbomok* as interpreter; "having one Master *John Hamden*, a gentleman of London, who then wintered with us, and desired much to see the country, for my consort."† In their way they found many of his subjects were gone to Pokanoket, it being their custom for all friends to attend on such occasions. "When we came thither (says Mr. *Winslow*) we found the house so full of men, as we could scarce get in, though they used their best diligence to make way for us. There were they in the midst of their charms for him, making such a hellish noise, as it distempered us that were well, and, therefore, unlike to ease him that was sick. About him were six or eight women, who chafed his arms, legs and thighs, to keep heat in him. When they had made an end of their charming, one told him that his friends, the English, were come to see him. Having understanding left, but his sight was wholly gone, he asked, *who was come*. They told him *Winsnow*, (for they cannot pronounce the letter *l*,

* *La Salle* says (Expedition in America, p. 11.) of the Indians' beds in general, that "they are made up with some pieces of wood, upon which they lay skins full of wool or straw, but, for their covering, they use the finest sort of skins, or else mats finely wrought."

† *Winslow's Relation*. The Mr. *Hamden* mentioned, is supposed, by some, to be the celebrated *John Hamden*, famous in the time of *Charles* I., and who died of a wound received in an attempt to intercept Prince *Rupert*, near Oxford, while supporting the cause of the parliament. See *Rapin's* England, ii. 477, and *Kennet*, iii. 137.

It would be highly gratifying, could the certainty of this matter be known; but, as yet, we must acknowledge that all is mere speculation. Nevertheless, we are pleased to meet with the names of such valued martyrs of liberty upon any page, and even though they should sometimes seem rather *mal apropos* to the case in hand. We cannot learn that any of *Hamden's* biographers have discovered that he visited America. Still there is a presumption that he was

"The village *Hampden*, that, with dauntless breast,
The little tyrant of his fields withstood"—GRAY'S ELEGY

but ordinarily *n* in the place thereof.)* He desired to speak with me. When I came to him, and they told him of it, he put forth his hand to me, which I took. Then he said twice, though very inwardly, *Keen Winsnow?* which is to say, *Art thou Winslow?* I answered, *Ahhe*, that is, *Yes.* Then he doubled these words: *Matta neen wonckanet namen, Winsnow!*—that is to say, *O Winslow, I shall never see thee again!*" But contrary to his own expectations, as well as all his friends, by the kind exertions of Mr. *Winslow*, he in a short time entirely recovered. This being a passage of great interest in the life of the great *Massasoit*, we will here go more into detail concerning it. When he had become able to speak, he desired Mr. *Winslow* to provide him a broth from some kind of fowl: "so (says he) I took a man with me, and made a shot at a couple of ducks, some sixscore paces off, and killed one, at which he wondered: so we returned forthwith, and dressed it, making more broth therewith, which he much desired; never did I see a man so low brought, recover in that measure in so short a time. The fowl being extraordinary fat, I told *Hobbamock* I must take off the top thereof, saying it would make him very sick again if he did eat it; this he acquainted *Massassowat* therewith, who would not be persuaded to it, though I pressed it very much, showing the strength thereof, and the weakness of his stomach, which could not possibly bear it. Notwithstanding, he made a gross meal of it, and ate as much as would well have satisfied a man in health." As *Winslow* had said, it made him very sick, and he vomited with such violence that it made the blood stream from his nose. This bleeding caused them great alarm, as it continued for four hours. When his nose ceased bleeding, he fell asleep, and did not awake for 6 or 8 hours more. After he awoke, Mr. *Winslow* washed his face "and supplied his beard and nose with a linnen cloth," when taking a quantity of water into his nose, by fiercely ejecting it, the blood began again to flow, and again his attendants thought he could not recover, but, to their great satisfaction, it soon stopped, and he gained strength rapidly.

For this attention of the English he was very grateful, and always believed that his preservation at this time was owing to the benefit he received from Mr. *Winslow.* In his way on his visit to *Massasoit*, Mr. *Winslow* broke a bottle containing some preparation, and, deeming it necessary to the sachem's recovery, wrote a letter to the governor of Plimouth for another, and some chickens in which he gave him an account of his success thus far. The intention was no sooner made known to *Massasoit*, than one of his men was sent off, at two o'clock at night, for Plimouth, who returned again with astonishing quickness. The chickens being alive, *Massasoit* was so pleased with them, and, being better would not suffer them to be killed, and kept them with the idea of raising more. While at *Massasoit's* residence, and just as they were about to depart, the sachem told *Hobomok* of a plot laid by some of his subordinate chiefs for the purpose of cutting off the two English plantations, which he charged him to acquaint the English with, which he did. *Massasoit* stated that he had been urged to join in it, or give his consent thereunto, but had always refused, and used his endeavors to prevent it. The particulars of the evils which that plot brought upon its authors will be found in the history of *Wittuwamet.*

At this time the English became more sensible of the real virtues of *Massasoit* than ever before. His great anxiety for the welfare of his people was manifested by his desiring Mr. *Winslow*, or, as *Winslow* himself expresses it, "He caused me to go from one to another, [in his village,] requesting me to wash their mouths also, [many of his people being sick at that time,] and give to each of them some of the same I gave him, saying they were good folk"

* Every people, and consequently every language, have their peculiarities. Baron *Lahontan*, *Memoires de la Amerique*, ii. 236, 237, says, "*Je dirai de la langue des Hurons et des Iroquois une chose assez curieuse, qui est qu'il ne s'y trouve point de lettres labiales; c'est a dire, de* b, f, m, p. *Cependant, cette langue des Hurons paroît être fort belle et de un son tout a fait beau; quoi qu'ils ne ferment jamais leurs lévres en parlant.*" And "*J'ai passé quatre jours à vouloir faire prononcer à des Hurons les lettres labiales, mais je n'ai pû y réüssir, et je crois qu'en dix ans ils ne pourrout dire ces mots*, bon, fils, Monsieur, Pontchartrain; *car au lieu de dire* bon, *ils diroient* ouon, *au lieu de* fils, *ils prononceroient* rils; *au lieu de* monsieur, caounsieur, au lieu de Pontchartrain, Conchartrain." Hence it seems their languages are analogous.

An account of his character as given by *Hobomok* will be found in the life of that chief or paniese.

"Many whilst we were there (says *Winslow*) came to see him; some, by their report, from a place not less than 100 miles from thence."

In 1632, a short war was carried on between *Massasoit* and *Canonicus*, the sachem of the Narragansets, but the English interfering with a force under the spirited Captain *Standish*, ended it with very little bloodshed. *Massasoit* expected a serious contest; and, as usual on such occasions, changed his name, and was ever after known by the name of *Owsamequin*, or *Ousamequin*. Our historical records furnish no particulars of his war with the Narragansets, further than we have stated.

We may infer from a letter written by *Roger Williams*, that some of Plimouth instigated *Massasoit*, or *Ousamequin*, as we should now call him, to lay claim to Providence, which gave that good man some trouble, because, in that case, his lands were considered as belonging to Plimouth, in whose jurisdiction he was not suffered to reside; and, moreover, he had bought and paid for all he possessed, of the Narraganset sachems. It was in 1635 that Mr. *Williams* fled to that country, to avoid being seized and sent to England. He found that *Canonicus* and *Miantunnomoh* were at bitter enmity with *Ousamequin*, but by his great exertions he restored peace, without which he could not have been secure, in a border of the dominion of either. *Ousamequin* was well acquainted with Mr. *Williams*, whom he had often seen during his two years' residence at Plimouth, and was a great friend to him, and therefore he listened readily to his benevolent instructions; giving up the land in dispute between himself and the Narraganset sachems, which was the island now called Rhode Island, Prudence Island, and perhaps some others, together with Providence. "And (says Mr. *Williams*) I never denied him, nor *Meantinomy*, whatever they desired of me." Hence their love and attachment for him, for this is their own mode of living.

It appears that, before *Miantunnomoh's* reverses of fortune, he had, by some means or other, got possession of some of the dominions of *Ousamequin*. For at the meeting of the Commissioners of the United Colonies, in the autumn of 1643, they order, "That Plymouth labor by all due means to restore *Woosamequin* to his full liberties, in respect of any encroachments by the Nanohiggansetts, or any other natives; that so the properties of the Indians may be preserved to themselves, and that no one sagamore encroach upon the rest as of late: and that *Woosamequin* be reduced to those former terms and agreements between Plymouth and him." *

Under date 1638, Gov. *Winthrop* says, "*Owsamekin*, the sachem of Acoomemeck, on this side Connecticut, came to [him] the governor, and brought a present of 18 skins of beaver from himself and the sachems of Mohegan beyond Connecticut and Pakontuckett." They having heard that the English were about to make war upon them was the cause of their sending this present. The governor accepted it, and told *Ousamequin*, that if they had not wronged the English, nor assisted their enemies, they had nothing to fear; and, giving him a letter to the governor of Connecticut, dismissed him well satisfied.†

In 1649, *Ousamequin* sold to *Miles Standish*, and the other inhabitants of Duxbury, "a tract of land usually called *Saughtucket*," seven miles square. This was Bridgewater. It had been before granted to them, only, however, in preëmption. They agreed to pay *Ousamequin* seven coats, of a yard and a half each, nine hatchets, eight hoes, twenty knives, four moose skins, and ten and a half yards of cotton cloth.

By a deed bearing date 9th March, 1653, *Ousemaquin* and his son *Wamsitto*, [*Wamsutta*,] afterwards called *Alexander*, sold to the English of Plimouth "all those severall parcells of land lyeing on the south-easterly side of Sinkunke, alias Rehoboth, bounded by a little brooke of water called Moskituash westerly, and soe runing by a dead swamp eastward, and soe by marked trees as *Ousamequin* and *Wamsitto* directed, unto the great riuer, and all the meadow about

* Records of the U. Colonies. † *Journal*, i. 264.

the sides of both, and about the neck called Chachacust, also Papasquash neck, also the meadow from the bay to Keecomewett," &c. For this the consideration was "£35 sterling."

By a writing bearing date "this twenty-one of September, 1657," *Ousamequin* says, "I *Vssamequen* do by these presents ratify and allow the sale of a certain island called Chesewanocke, or Hogg Island, which my son *Wamsitta* sold to *Richard Smith*, of Portsmouth in R. I., with my consent, which deed of sale or bargain made the 7th of February in the year 1653, I do ratify, own and confirm."

In 1656, *Roger Williams* says that *Ousamequin*, by one of his sachems, "was at daily feud with *Pumham* about the title and lordship of Warwick;" and that hostility was daily expected. But we are not informed that any thing serious took place.

This is the year in which it has been generally supposed that *Ousamequin* died, but it is an error of *Hutchinson's* transplanting from Mr. *Hubbard's* work into his own. That an error should flourish in so good a soil as that of the "History of the Colony of Massachusetts Bay," is no wonder; but it is a wonder that the "accurate *Hutchinson*" should set down that date, from that passage of the Indian Wars, which was evidently made without reflection. It being at that time thought a circumstance of no consequence.

That the sachem of Pokanoket should be scarcely known to our records between 1657 and 1661, a space of only about three years, as we have shown, is not very surprising, when we reflect that he was entirely subservient to the English, and nearly or quite all of his lands being before disposed of, or given up to them. This, therefore, is a plain reason why we do not meet with his name to deeds and other instruments. And, besides this consideration, another sachem was known to be associated with him at the former period, who seems to have acted as *Ousamequin's* representative.

He was alive in 1661, and as late in that year as September.* Several months previous to this, *Oneko*, with about seventy men, fell upon a defenceless town within the dominions of *Ousamequin*, killing three persons, and carrying away six others captive. He complained to the General Court of Massachusetts, which interfered in his behalf, and the matter was soon settled.†

From the "Relation" of Dr. *I. Mather*, it is clear that he lived until 1662. His words are, "*Alexander* being dead, [having died in 1662,] his brother *Philip*, of late cursed memory, rose up in his stead, and he was no sooner styled sachem, but immediately, in the year 1662, there were vehement suspicions of his bloody treachery against the English."‡

Hence, as we do not hear of *Alexander* as sachem until 1662, which is also the year of his death, it is fair to conclude that he could not have been long in office at the time of his death; nor could he have been styled "chief sachem" until after the death of his father.

Whether *Massasoit* had more than two sons, is not certain, although it is confidently believed that he had. It is probable that his family was large. A company of soldiers from Bridgewater, in a skirmish with *Philip*, took his sister, and killed a brother of *Ousamequin*, whose name was *Unkompoen*, § or *Akkompoin*. ‖ That he had another brother, called *Quadequina*, has been mentioned.

Gov. *Winthrop* gives the following anecdote of *Ousamequin*. As Mr. *Edward Winslow* was returning from a trading voyage southward, having left his vessel, he traveled home by land, and in the way stopped with his old friend *Massasoit*, who agreed to accompany him the rest of the way. In the mean time, *Ousamequin* sent one of his men forward to Plimouth, to surprise the people with the news of Mr. *Winslow's* death. By his manner of relating it, and the particular circumstances attending, no one doubted of its truth, and every one was grieved and mourned exceedingly at their great loss. But

* Some records which Mr. *Daggett* consulted in preparing his *History* of Attleborough, led him to conclude that *Massasoit* died previous to June, 1660.

† Original *manuscript* documents. The particulars of these matters will be given at large when we come to treat of the *life* of *Uncas*.

‡ Relation, 72. § *I. Mather*, 44. ‖ *Church*, 38, edit 4to.

presently they were as much surprised at seeing him coming in company with *Ousamequin.* When it was known among the people that the sachem had sent this news to them, they demanded why he should thus deceive them. He replied that it was to make him the more welcome when he *did* return, and that this was a custom of his people.

One of the most renowned captains within the dominions of *Massasoit* was CAUNBITANT,* whose residence was at a place called *Mettapoiset,* in the present town of Swansey. His character was much the same as that of the famous *Metacomet.* The English were always viewed by him as intruders and enemies of his race, and there is little doubt but he intended to wrest the country out of their hands on the first opportunity.

In August, 1621, *Caunbitant* was supposed to be in the interest of the Narragansets, and plotting with them to overthrow *Massasoit;* and, being at Namasket seeking, say the Pilgrims, "to draw the hearts of *Massasoyt's* subjects from him; speaking also disdainfully of us, storming at the peace between Nauset, Cummaquid and us, and at *Tisquantum,* the worker of it; also at *Tokamahamon,* and one *Hobomok,* (two Indians or Lemes, one of which he would treacherously have murdered a little before, being a special and trusty man of *Massasoyt's,*) *Tokamahamon* went to him, but the other two would not; yet put their lives in their hands, privately went to see if they could hear of their king, and, lodging at Namaschet, were dicovered to *Coubatant,* who set a guard to beset the house, and took *Tisquantum,* (for he had said, if he were dead, the English had lost their tongue.) *Hobbamok* seeing that *Tisquantum* was taken, and *Coubatant* held [holding] a knife at his breast, being a strong and stout man, brake from them, and came to New Plimouth, full of fear and sorrow for *Tisquantum,* whom he thought to be slain."

Upon this the Plimouth people sent an expedition, under *Standish,* of 14 men,† "and *Hobbamok* for their guide, to revenge the supposed death of *Tisquantum* on *Coubatant* our bitter enemy, and to retain *Nepeof,* another sachem, or governor, who was of this confederacy, till we heard what was become of our friend *Massasoyt.*"

After much toil, the little army arrived near the place they expected to find *Caunbitant.* "Before we came to the town (says the narrator) we sat down and eat such as our knapsacks afforded; that being done, we threw them aside, and all such things as might hinder us, and so went on and beset the house, according to our last resolution. Those that entered, demanded if *Coubatant* were not there; but fear had bereft the savages of speech. We charged them not to stir, for if *Coubatant* were not there, we would not meddle with them; if he were, we came principally for him, to be avenged on him for the supposed death of *Tisquantum,* and other matters: but howsoever, we would not at all hurt their women or children. Notwithstanding, some of them pressed out at a private door, and escaped, but with some wounds. At length perceiving our principal ends, they told us *Coubatant* was returned [home] with all his train, and that *Tisquantum* was yet living, and in the town; [then] offering some tobacco, [and] other, such as they had to eat."

In this hurley hurley, (as they call it,) two guns were fired "at random," to the great terror of all but *Squanto* and *Tokamahamon,* "who, though they knew not our end in coming, yet assured them [so frightened] of our honesty, [and] that we would not hurt them." The Indian boys, seeing the squaws protected, cried out, *Neensquaes! Neensquaes!* that is, *I am a squaw! I am a squaw!* and the women tried to screen themselves in *Hobomok's* presence, reminding him that he was their friend.

This attack upon a defenceless house was made at midnight, and must have been terrible, in an inconceivable degree, to its inmates, especially the sound of the English guns, which few, if any of them, had ever heard before. The relator proceeds: "But to be short, we kept them we had, and made them make a fire that we might see to search the house; in the meantime,

---

* *Corbitant, Coubatant,* and *Conbitant,* were ways of writing his name also, by his contemporaries.

† Ten, says the Relation.

Hobbamok gat on the top of the house, and called *Tisquantum* and *Tokamahamon.*" They soon came, with some others with them, some armed and others naked. The English took away the bows and arrows from those that were armed, but promised to return them as soon as it was day, which they probably did.

They kept possession of the captured wigwam until daylight, when they released their prisoners, and marched into the town (as they call it) of the Namaskets. Here, it appears, *Squanto* had a house, to which they went, and took breakfast, and held a court afterward, from which they issued forth the following decree against *Caunbitant*:—

"Thither came all whose hearts were upright towards us, but all *Coubatant's* faction were fled away. There in the midst of them we manifested again our intendment, assuring them, that, although *Coubitant* had now escaped us, yet there was no place should secure him and his from us, if he continued his threatening us, and provoking others against us, who had kindly entertained him, and never intended evil towards him till he now so justly deserved it. Moreover, if *Massasoyt* did not return in safety from Narrohigganset, or if hereafter he should make any insurrection against him, or offer violence to *Tisquantum*, *Hobomok*, or any of *Massasoyt's* subjects, we would revenge it upon him, to the overthrow of him and his. As for those [who] were wounded, [how many is not mentioned,] we were sorry for it, though themselves procured it in not staying in the house at our command: yet, if they would return home with us, our surgeon should heal them. At this offer one man and a woman that were wounded went home with us, *Tisquantum* and many other known friends accompanying us, and offering all help that might be by carriage of any thing we had to ease us. So that by God's good providence we safely returned home the morrow night after we set forth."*

Notwithstanding these rough passages, *Caunbitant* became in appearance reconciled to the English, and on the 13th Sept. following (1621) went to Plimouth and signed a treaty of amity. It was through the intercession of *Massasoit* that he became again reconciled, but the English always doubted his sincerity, as most probably they had reason to. The treaty or submission was in these words:—

"Know all men by these presents, that we whose names are underwritten, do acknowledge ourselves to be the royal subjects of King *James*, king of Great Britain, France and Ireland, defender of the faith, &c. In witness whereof, and as a testimonial of the same, we have subscribed our names, or marks, as followeth:—

OHQUAMEHUD,	NATTAWAHUNT,	QUADAQUINA,
CAWNACOME,	CAUNBATANT,	HUTTMOIDEN,
OBBATINNUA,	CHIKKATABAK,	APANNOW."

Of some of these sachems nothing is known beyond this transaction, and of others very little.

Obbatinua is supposed to have been sachem of Shawmut, where Boston now stands.

Cawnacome and *Apannow* may be the same before spoken of as *Coneconam* and *Epanow*, though I am rather of opinion that *Apannow* means *Aspinet* of Nauset.† *Nattawahunt* we shall again meet with, under the name *Nashoonon*. *Coneconam* was sachem of *Manomet*, on Cape Cod.

When, in the winter of 1623, the English traversed the country to trade with the Indians for corn, they visited him among other chiefs; who, they say, "it seemed was of good respect, and authority, amongst the Indians. For whilst the governor was there, within night, in bitter cold weather, came two men from Manamoyck, before spoken of, and having set aside their bows

* From *Mourt, ut supra*, and signed only with the capital letter *A*, which is supposed to stand for *Isaac Allerton*, who accompanied *Standish* perhaps. From the use of the pronoun in the first person, the writer, whoever he was, must have been present

† See chapter i. of b. ii.

and quivers, according to their manner, sat down by the fire, and took a pipe of tobacco, not using any words in that time, nor any other to them, but all remained silent, expecting when they would speak. At length they looked toward *Canacum;* and one of them made a short speech, and delivered a present to him, from his sachim, which was a basket of tobacco, and many beads, which the other received thankfully. After which he made a long speech to him," the meaning of which *Hobomok* said was, that two of their men fell out in a game, "for they use gaming as much as any where, and will play away all, even their skin from their backs, yea their wive's skins also," and one killed the other. That the murderer was a powow, "one of special note amongst them," and one whom they did not like to part with; yet they were threatened with war, if they did not kill the murderer. That, therefore, their sachem deferred acting until the advice of *Coneconam* was first obtained.

After consulting with this chief, and some of his head men, these messengers desired *Hobomok's* judgment upon the matter. With some deference he replied, that "he thought it was better that one should die than many, since he had deserved it;" "whereupon he passed the sentence of death upon him."

We shall have occasion again to notice this chief, at whose house the first act of a tragic scene was acted, which in its course brought ruin upon its projectors.

When Mr. *Edward Winslow* and Mr. *John Hamden* went to visit *Massasoit* in his sickness, in 1623, they heard by some Indians, when near *Caunbitant's* residence, that *Massasoit* was really dead: they, therefore, though with much hesitation, ventured to his house, hoping they might treat with him, he being then thought the successor of *Massasoit.* But he was not at home. The squaw sachem, his wife, treated them with great kindness, and learning here that *Massasoit* was still alive, they made all haste to Pokanoket. When they returned, they staid all night with *Caunbitant*, at his house, who accompanied them there from *Massasoit's.*

Mr. *Winslow* gives the account in these words:—"That night, through the earnest request of *Conbatant*, who, till now, remained at Sowaams, or Puckanokick, we lodged with him at Mattapuyst. By the way, I had much conference with him, so likewise at his house, he being a notable politician, yet full of merry jests and squibs, and never better pleased than when the like are returned again upon him. Amongst other things he asked me, if in case *he* were thus dangerously sick, as *Massasoit* had been, and should send word thereof to Patuxet, for *maskiest*,* [that is, physic,] whether their master governor would send it; and if he would, whether I would come therewith to him. To both which I answered, yea; whereat he gave me many joyful thanks." He then expressed his surprise that two Englishmen should adventure so far alone into their country, and asked them if they were not afraid. Mr. *Winslow* said, "where was true love, there was no fear." "But," said *Caunbitant*, "*if your love be such, and it bring forth such fruits, how cometh it to pass, that when we come to Patuxet, you stand upon your guard, with the mouth of your pieces presented towards us?*" Mr. *Winslow* told him that was a mark of respect, and that they received their best friends in that manner: but to this he shook his head, and answered, that he did not like such salutations.†

When *Caunbitant* saw his visiters crave a blessing before eating, and return thanks afterwards, he desired to know what it meant. "Hereupon I took occasion (says our author) to tell them of God's works of creation and preservation, of the laws and ordinances, especially of the ten commandments." They found no particular fault with the commandments, except the seventh, but said there were many inconveniences in that a man should be tied to one woman. About which they reasoned a good while.

When Mr. *Winslow* explained the goodness of God in bestowing on them all their comforts, and that for this reason they thanked and blessed him,

---

* In Williams's Key, *Maskit* is translated, "Give me some physic."

† Good News from N. England, *Coll. Mass Hist. Soc.*

"this all of them concluded to be very well; and said they believed almost all the same things, and that the same power that we call God they called *Kichtan*." "Here we remained only that night, but never had better entertainment amongst any of them."

What became of this chief is unknown. His name appearing no more in our records, leads us to suppose that he either fled his country on the murder of *Wittuwamet*, *Peksuot*, and others, or that he died about that time.

Wittuwamet was a Massachusetts chief, as was his companion *Peksuot*, but their particular residence has not been assigned. *Wittuwamet* was a desperate and bold fellow, and, like most other warriors, delighted in shedding the blood of his enemies. It is not improbable but that he became exasperated against the English from the many abuses some of them had practised upon his countrymen. This will account, perhaps, for all the severity and malignity portrayed by the forefathers in his character. He was one of those, they say, who murdered some of the crew of the French ship, cast away upon Cape Cod, as we have before mentioned.

That *Wittuwamet*, *Peksuot*, and some other chiefs, intended to have freed their country of intruders in the year 1623, there can be no doubt, and in relating the rise, progress and termination of their league to effect this object, we shall, to avoid the charge of partiality, adhere closely to the record.

We have before, in speaking of *Caunecum*, or *Coneconam*, mentioned the voyage of the governor of Plimouth to that sachem's country to trade for corn; that was in January, 1623. Not being able to bring away all he obtained, Captain *Miles Standish* was sent the next month to take it to Plimouth, also to purchase more at the same place, but he did not meet with very good reception, which led him to apprehend there was mischief at hand. And immediately after, while at *Coneconam's* house with two or three of his company, "in came two of the Massachusetts men. The chief of them was called *Wittuwamat*, a notable insulting villain, one who had formerly imbrued his hands in the blood of English and French, and had oft boasted of his own valor, and derided their weakness, especially because, as he said, they died crying, making sour faces, more like children than men. This villain took a dagger from about his neck, which he had gotten of Master *Weston's* people, and presented it to the sachem, [*Coneconam*,] and after made a long speech in an audacious manner, framing it in such sort as the captain, though he be the best linguist among us, could not gather any thing from it. The end of it was afterwards discovered to be as followeth. The Massachuseucks formerly concluded to ruinate Mr. *Weston's* colony; and thought themselves, being about 30 or 40 men, strong enough to execute the same: yet they durst not attempt it, till such time as they had gathered more strength to themselves, to make their party good against us at Plimouth; concluding that if we remained, though they had no other arguments to use against us, yet we would never leave the death of our countrymen unrevenged; and therefore their safety could not be without the overthrow of both plantations. To this end they had formerly solicited this sachem, as also the other, called *Ianough*, and many others, to assist them; and now again came to prosecute the same; and since there was so fair an opportunity offered by the captain's presence, they thought best to make sure of him and his company."

Coneconam, after this speech, treated *Standish* with neglect, and was very partial to *Wittuwamet*, which much increased the jealousy of the former. These Indians meantime contrived to kill *Standish*, having employed a "lusty Indian of Paomet" to execute the plan. The weather was severely cold, and *Standish* lodged on shore at night, and this was the time he was to have been killed. But the extreme coldness of the night kept him from sleeping, and thus he avoided assassination.

We have had occasion, in the life of *Massasoit*, to mention that that chief had been solicited to engage in this confederacy, and of his charging *Hobomok* to warn the English of it. The people of the places named at that time by *Massasoit*, as in the plot, were Nauset, Paomet, Succonet, Mattachiest, Manomet, Agowaywam, and the Island of Capawack. "Therefore, (says Mr *Winslow* in his Relation,) as we respected the lives of our countrymen and our own safety, he advised us to kill the men of Massachuset, who were the authors of this intended mischief. And whereas we were wont to say, we would not strike a stroke till they first began, If, said he, [*Massasoit* to *Hobomok*,] upon this intelligence, they make that answer, te.l them, when their countrymen at Wichaguscusset are killed, they not being able to defend themselves, that then it will be too late to recover their lives," and it would be with difficulty that they preserved their own; "and therefore he counselled, without delay, to take away the principals, and then the plot would cease."

Meanwhile *Weston's* men had fallen into a miserable and wretched condition; some, to procure a daily sustenance, became servants to the Indians, "fetching them wood and water, &c., and all for a meal's meat." Those who were thus degraded, were, of course, only a few who had abandoned themselves to riot and dissipation, but whose conduct had affected the well being of the whole, notwithstanding. Some of these wretches, in their extremities, had stolen corn from the Indians, on whose complaint they had been put in the stocks and whipped. This not giving the Indians satisfaction, one was hanged. This was in February, 1623.

About this capital punishment much has been written; some doubting the fact that any one was hanged, others that it was the real offender, &c. But in our opinion the facts are incontestable that one was hanged; but whether the one really guilty or not, is not quite so easily settled. The fact that one was hanged for another appears to have been of common notoriety, both in Old and New England, from shortly after the affair until the beginning of the next century.*

Mr. *Hubbard*† has this passage upon the affair:—"Certain it is, they [the Indians] were so provoked with their filching and stealing, that they threatened them, as the Philistines did *Samson's* father-in-law, after the loss of their corn; insomuch that the company, as some report, pretended, in way of satisfaction, to punish him that did the theft, but, in his stead, hanged a poor, decrepit old man, that was unserviceable to the company, [an old bed-rid weaver,‡] and burdensome to keep alive, which was the ground of the story with which the merry gentleman, that wrote the poem called Hudibras, did, in his poetical fancy, make so much sport." And from the same author it appears that the circumstance was well known at Plimouth, but they pretended that the right person was hanged, or, in our author's own words, "as if the person hanged was really guilty of stealing, as may be were many of the rest, and if they were driven by necessity to content the Indians, at that time, to do justice, there being some of Mr. *Weston's* company living, it is possible it might be executed not on him that most deserved, but on him that could be best spared, or who was not like to live long if he had been let alone."

It will now be expected that we produce the passage of Hudibras. Here it is:—

"Though nice and dark the point appear,
(Quoth Ralph,) it may hold up, and clear.
That *Sinners* may supply the place
Of suffering *Saints*, is a plain *Case*.
Justice gives Sentence, many times,
On one Man for another's crimes.
Our Brethren of New England use
Choice Malefactors to excuse.
And *hang* the Guiltless in their stead,
Of whom the *Churches* have less need:
As lately 't happened: In a town
There lived a *Cobbler*, and but one,
That out of Doctrine could cut *Use*,
And mend Men's *Lives*, as well as *Shoes*.
This precious Brother having slain,
In times of *Peace*, an Indian,
(Not out of Malice, but mere Zeal,
Because he was an infidel,)
The mighty *Tottipottymoy*,
Sent to our *Elders* an *Envoy*,
Complaining sorely of the Breach
Of League, held forth by Brother *Patch*,
Against the *Articles* in force,
Between both churches, his and ours,
For which he craved the *Saints* to render
Into his Hands, or hang th' *Offender*:
But they, maturely having weighed,
They had no more but him o' th' Trade,
(A Man that served them in a double
Capacity, to *Teach* and *Cobble*,)
Resolved to spare him; yet to do
The *Indian Hoghan Moghgan*, too,
Impartial Justice, in his stead, did
Hang an old Weaver that was Bed-rid.
Then wherefore may not you be skipp'd,
And in your Room another Whipp'd?"

---

* See Col. N. H. Hist. Soc. iii. 148. and b. i. chap. iii. *ante*.

† Hist. N. Eng. 77.

‡ Col. N. H. Hist. Soc. iii. 148

The following note was early printed to this passage:—"The history of the cobbler had been attested by persons of good credit, who were upon the place when it was done." Mr. *Butler* wrote this part of his Hudibras before 1663.

Thomas Morton, who was one of the company, though perhaps absent at the time, pretends that there was no plot of the Indians, and insinuates that the Plimoutheans caused all the trouble, and that their rashness caused the Indians to massacre some of their men, as we shall presently relate from a book which Mr. *Morton* published.*

"Master *Weston's* plantation being settled at Wessaguscus, his servants, many of them lazy persons, that would use no endeavor to take the benefit of the country, some of them fell sick and died.

"One amongst the rest, an able-bodied man, that ranged the woods, to see what it would afford, lighted by accident on an Indian barn, and from thence did take a cap full of corn. The salvage owner of it, finding by the foot [track] some English had been there, came to the plantation, and made complaint after this manner. The chief commander of the company, on this occasion, called a Parliament of all his people, but those that were sick and ill at ease.† And wisely now they must consult, upon this huge complaint, that a privy [paltry] knife or string of beads would well enough have qualified: And Edward Iohnson was a special judge of this business. The fact was there in repetition, construction made, that it was fellony, and by the laws of England punished with death, and this in execution must be put for an example, and likewise to appease the salvage; when straightways one arose, moved as it were with some compassion, and said he could not well gainsay the former sentence; yet he had conceived, within the compass of his brain, an embrio, that was of special consequence to be delivered, and cherished, he said; that it would most aptly serve to pacify the salvage's complaint, and save the life of one that might (if need should be) stand them in some good stead; being young and strong, fit for resistance against an enemy, which might come unexpectedly, for any thing they knew.

"The oration made was liked of every one, and he intreated to show the means how this may be performed. Says he, you all agree that one must die, and one shall die. This young man's clothes we will take off, and put upon one that is old and impotent, a sickly person that cannot escape death; such is the disease on him confirmed, that die he must. Put the young man's clothes on this man, and let the sick person be hanged in the other's stead. Amen, says one, and so says many more. And this had like to have proved their final sentence; and being there confirmed by act of Parliament to after ages for a precedent. But that one, with a ravenous voice, begun to croak and bellow for revenge, and put by that conclusive motion; alleging such deceits might be a means hereafter to exasperate the minds of the complaining salvages, and that, by his death, the salvages should see their zeal to justice, and, therefore, he should die. This was concluded; yet, nevertheless, a scruple was made; now to countermand this act did represent itself unto their minds, which was how they should do to get the man's good will: this was indeed a special obstacle: for without that (they all agreed) it would be dangerous, for any man to attempt the execution of it, lest mischief should befall them every man. He was a person that, in his wrath, did seem to be a second *Sampson*, able to beat out their brains with the jawbone of an ass: therefore they called the man, and by persuasion got him fast bound in jest, and then hanged him up hard by in good earnest, who with a weapon, and at liberty, would have put all these wise judges of this Parliament to a pittiful *non plus*, (as it hath been credibly reported,) and made the chief judge of them all buckle to him."

This is an entire chapter of the New Canaan, which, on account of its great rarity, we have given in full. In his next chapter Mr. *Morton* proceeds to narrate the circumstances of the "massacre" of *Wittuwamet*, *Peksuot*, and other Massachusetts Indians, and the consequences of it. But we shall now

---

* Entitled New English Canaan, 4to. Amsterdam, 1637.

† Against this sentence, in the margin, is—"*A poor complaint.*"

draw from the Plimouth historian, and afterwards use *Morton's* chapter as we find occasion.

Mr. *Winslow* says that Mr. *Weston's* men "knew not of this conspiracy of the Indians before his [*John Sanders*, their 'overseer'] going; neither was it known to any of us till our return from Sowaams, or Puckanokick: at which time also another sachim, called *Wassapinewat*, brother to *Obtakiest*, the sachim of the Massachusets, who had formerly smarted for partaking with *Conbatant*, and fearing the like again, to purge himself, revealed the same thing," [as *Massasoit* had done.]

It was now the 23d March, 1623, "a yearly court day" at Plimouth, on which war was proclaimed, "in public court," against the Massachusetts Indians. "We came to this conclusion, (says *Winslow*,) that Captain *Standish* should take so many men, as he thought sufficient to make his party good against all the Indians in the Massachusetts Bay; and as because, as all men know that have to do with them in that kind, it is impossible to deal with them upon open defiance, but to take them in such traps as they lay for others; therefore he should pretend trade as at other times: but first go to the English, [at Wessaguscus,] and acquaint them with the plot, and the end of their own coming, that, comparing it with their own carriages towards them, he might better judge of the certainty of it, and more fitly take opportunity to revenge the same: but should forbare, if it were possible, till such time as he could make sure *Wittuwamat*, that bloody and bold villain before spoken of; whose head he had order to bring with him, that he might be a warning and terror to all that disposition."

We will now hear a word of what Mr. *Morton* has to say upon this transaction. "After the end of that Parliament, [which ended in the hanging of one,*] some of the plantation there, about three persons, went to live with *Checatawback* and his company, and had very good quarter, for all the former quarrel with the Plimouth planters.† They are not like *Will Sommers*,‡ to take one for another. There they purposed to stay until Master *Weston's* arrival: but the Plimouth men intending no good to him, (as appeared by the consequence,) came in the mean time to Wessaguscus, and there pretended to feast the salvages of those parts, bringing with them pork, and things for the purpose, which they set before the salvages. They eat thereof without suspicion of any mischief, [and] who were taken upon a watchword given, and with their own knives (hanging about their necks) were, by the Plimouth planters, stabbed and slain. One of which was hanged up there, after the slaughter."§ When this came to the knowledge of *Chikataubut's* people, they murdered the three English who had taken up their residence with them, as they lay asleep, in revenge for the murder of their countrymen.‖

After *Standish* was ready to proceed against *Wittuwamet*, but before he set out, one arrived from Wessaguscus almost famished,¶ and gave the people of Plimouth a lamentable account of the situation of his fellows; that not the least of their calamities was their being insulted by the Indians, 'whose boldness increased abundantly; insomuch as the victuals they got,

* As mentioned in our last extract from this author.

† Referring, it is supposed, to the quarrel with *Caunbitant*.

‡ The person who proposed hanging a sick man instead of the real offender.

§ New English Canaan, 111. ‖ Ibid.

¶ His name was *Phinehas Prat*. An Indian followed him to kill him, but, by losing the direct path, the Indian missed him. In 1662, the general court of Massachusetts, in answer to a petition of *Phinehas Prat*, then of Charlestown, which was accompanied "with a narrative of the straights and hardships that the first planters of this colony underwent in their endeavors to plant themselves at Plimouth, and since, whereof he was one, the court judgeth it meet to grant him 300 acres of land, where it is to be had, not hindering a plantation." *MS. among the files in our state-house.*

I have not been able to discover the narrative of *Prat*, after long search. Mr. *Hubbard* probably used it in compiling his Hist. of New England.

At the court, 3 May, 1665, land was ordered to be laid out for *Prat*, "in the wilderness on the east of the Merrimack River, near the upper end of Nacook Brook, on the south-east of it." *Court Files, ut supra.*

Prat married, in Plimouth, a daughter of *Cuthbert Cuthbertson*, in 1630. See 2 *Col. Hist. Soc* vii. 122.

they [the Indians] would take it out of their pots, and eat [it] before their faces," and that if they tried to prevent them, they would hold a knife at their breasts: and to satisfy them, they had hanged one of their company: "That they had sold their clothes for corn, and were ready to starve both with cold and hunger also, because they could not endure to get victuals by reason of their nakedness."

This truly was a wretched picture of this second colony of Massachusetts, the knowledge of which (says *Winslow*) "gave us good encouragement to proceed in our intendments." Accordingly, the next day, *Standish*, with *Hobomok* and eight Englishmen, set out upon the expedition. His taking so few men shows how a few English guns were yet feared by the Indians. Nevertheless, the historians would have us understand that *Standish* would take no more, because he would not have the Indians mistrust that he came to fight them; and they would insinuate that it was owing to his great valor.

When *Standish* arrived at Wessaguscus, he found the people scattered about, apprehending no danger whatever, engaged in their ordinary affairs. When he told them of the danger they were in from the Indians, they said "they feared not the Indians, but lived, and suffered them to lodge with them, not having sword or gun, or needing the same." *Standish* now informed them of the plot, which was the first intimation, it appears, they had of it. He ordered them to call in their men, and enjoined secrecy of his intended massacre. But it seems from *Winslow's* Relation, that the Indians got word of it, or mistrusted his design; probably some of the Wessaguscus men warned them of it, who did not believe there was any plot.

Meantime, an Indian came to trade, and afterwards went away in friendship. *Standish*, more sagacious than the rest, said he saw treachery in his eye, and suspected his end in coming there was discovered. Shortly after, *Peksuot*, "who was a paniese,* being a man of a notable spirit," came to *Hobomok*, and told him, *He understood the captain was come to kill him and the rest of the Indians there.* "Tell him, (said *Peksuot*,) we know it, but fear him not, neither will we shun him; but let him begin when he dare [s], he will not take us unawares."

The Indians now, as we might expect, began to prepare to meet the danger, and the English say many of them came divers times into their presence, and "would whet and sharpen the point of their knives," "and use many other insulting gestures and speeches. Amongst the rest, *Wittuwamat* bragged of the excellency of his knife. On the end of the handle there was pictured a woman's face; but, said he, *I have another at home, wherewith I have killed both French and English, and that hath a man's face on it; and by and by these two must marry.*" To this he added, HINNAIM NAMEN, HINNAIM MICHEN, MATTA CUTS: that is, *By and by it should see, and by and by it should eat, but not speak.* "Also *Pecksuot*, (continues *Winslow*,) being a man of greater stature than the captain, told him though he were a great captain, yet he was but a little man: *and*, said he, *though I be no sachem, yet I am a man of great strength and courage.* These things the captain observed, yet bare with patience for the present."

It will be seen, in what we have related, as well as what we are about to add, that *Thomas Morton's* account, in some of the main facts, agrees with that of *Winslow*. From the latter it appears that *Standish*, after considerable manœuvering, could get advantage over but few of the Indians. At length naving got *Peksuot* and *Wittuwamat* "both together, with another man, and a youth of some eighteen years of age, which was brother to *Wittuwamat*, and, villain like, trod in his steps, daily putting many tricks upon the weaker sort of men, and having about as many of his own company in a room with them, gave the word to his men, and, the door being fast shut, began himself with *Pecksuot*, and, *snatching his own knife from his neck*, though with much

* "The Panieses are men of great courage and wisedome, and to these also the Deuill appeareth more familiarly than to others, and as wee conceiue, maketh couenant with them to preserue them from death by wounds with arrows, knives, hatchets, &c." *Winslow's Relation.* In speaking of the origin of *calumet*, *Charlevoix* says, some Indians told him that it was given by the sun to *Panis*, a nation upon the Missouri. *Voyage dans l'Amerique.*

struggling, *and killed him therewith*—the point whereof he had made as sharp as a needle, and ground the back also to an edge. *Wittuwamet* and the other man *the rest killed, and took the youth, whom the* captain caused to be hanged."

We could now wish this bloody tale were finished, but we have promised to keep close to the record. Mr. *Winslow* continues, "*But it is incredible how many wounds these two panieses received before they died, not making any fearful noise, but catching at their weapons, and striving to the last.*

"*Hobbamock* stood by all this time,* and meddled not, observing how our men demeaned themselves in this action." After the affray was ended, he said to *Standish*, "Yesterday *Pecksuot* bragged of his own strength and stature, said, though you were a great captain, yet you were but a little man but to-day I see you are big enough to lay him on the ground."

Standish was now sent to a company of *Weston's* men, who ordered them to kill the Indians that were among them. *They killed two*. Himself with some of his men *killed another*, at another place. As they were pursuing this business, intending to kill all they could lay hands upon, "through the negligence of one man, an Indian escaped, who discovered [disclosed] and crossed their proceedings."

Joined by some of Mr. *Weston's* men, *Standish* discovered a few Indians, and pursued them. *Standish* gained a hill which the Indians also strove to occupy, and who, after shooting a few arrows, fled. "Whereupon *Hobbamock* cast off his coat, and being a known paniese, theirs being now killed, chased them so fast, as our people were not able to hold way with him." One who made a stand to shoot *Standish* had his arm broken by a shot, which is all the advantage claimed by the English. The Indians got into a swamp, and after some bravadoing on both sides, the parties separated. After assisting the settlers of Wessaguscus to leave the place, the English returned to Plimouth, taking along the head of *Wittuwamet*, which they set up in their fort.

Meanwhile the Indian that followed *Prat* from Wessaguscus, as he returned from Manomet, called at Plimouth in a friendly manner, and was there seized and put in irons. Being asked if he knew the head of *Wittuwamet*, said he did, and "looked piteously" upon it. "Then he confessed the plot," and said his sachem, *Obtakiest*, had been drawn into it by the importunity of all the people. He denied any hand in it himself, and begged his life might be spared. Said he was not a Massachuset, but only resided as a stranger among them. *Hobomok* "also gave a good report of him, and besought for him; but was bribed so to do it." They finally concluded to spare him, "the rather, because we desired he might carry a message to *Obtakiest*." The message they charged him with was this, that they had never intended to deal so with him, until they were forced to it by their treachery, and, therefore, they might thank themselves for their own overthrow; and as he had now began, if he persisted in his course, "his country should not hold him:" that he should forthwith send to Plimouth "the three Englishmen he had, and not kill them." †

The English heard nothing from *Obtakiest* for a long time; at length he sent a woman to them, (probably no man would venture,) to tell them he was sorry that the English were killed, before he heard from them, also that he wished for peace, but none of his men durst come to treat about it. The English learned from this woman, that he was in great consternation, "having forsaken his dwelling, and daily removed from place to place, expecting when we would take further vengeance on him." The terror was now general among them, and many, as we have elsewhere said, died through fear and want. To this dismal narrative Mr. *Winslow* adds, "And certainly

* This, we suppose, is the affair to which President *Allen* alludes, in his American Biography, (2d ed.) when he says, "he [*Hobomok*] *fought bravely* by his [*Standish's*] side, in 1623." If standing and looking on be fighting, then did *Hobomok fight bravely* on this occasion.

† *Morton*, in his *New Canaan*, 111, says, these three men went to reside with *Chikataubut* hence *Morton* very reasonably suggests, that if the Plimouth people intended the men of Wessaguscus any good, why did they not first see that all of them were out of danger, before beginning war?

it is strange to hear how many of late have, and still daily die amongst them; neither is there any likelihood it will easily cease; because through fear they set little or no corn, which is the staff of life, and without which they cannot long preserve health and strength."

These affairs call for no commentary, that must accompany every mind through every step of the relation. It would be weakness, as appears to us, to attempt a vindication of the rash conduct of the English. Amid their sufferings, some poor Indians resolved to attempt to appease the wrath of the English governor by presents. Four set out by water in a boat for Plimouth, but by accident were overset, and three of them were drowned; the other returned back.

When Mr. *Robinson*, the father of the Plimouth church, heard how his people had conducted in this affair with the Indians, he wrote to them, to consider of the disposition of Captain *Standish*, "who was of a warm temper," but he hoped the Lord had sent him among them for a good end, if they used him as they ought. "He doubted," he said, "whether there was not wanting that tenderness of the life of man, made after God's image," which was so necessary; and above all, that "it would have been happy if they had converted some before they had killed any."

The reader has now passed through a period of Indian history of much interest, wherein he will doubtless have found much to admire, and more that he could have wished otherwise. Our business, however, we will here remind him, is that of a dealer in facts altogether, and he must take them, dry as they are, without any labored commentaries from us. Although we have had occasion to introduce *Hobomok* several times, yet there remain transactions of considerable interest in his life yet to be noticed.

Hobomok, or *Hobbamock*, was a great paniese or war captain among the Wampanoags, as we have already had occasion to observe. He came to Plimouth about the end of July, 1621, and continued with the English as long as he lived. He was a principal means of the lasting friendship of *Massasoit*, which *Morton* says, he "much furthered; and that he was a proper lusty young man, and one that was in account among the Indians in those parts for his valor." He was of the greatest service in learning them how to cultivate such fruits as were peculiar to the country, such as corn, beans, &c. The account of his mission to *Massasoit*, to learn the truth of a report that the Narragansets had made war upon him, and his interruption and trouble from *Caunbitant* are already related.

Being a favorite of *Massasoit*, and one of his chief captains, the pilgrims found that they need not apprehend any treachery on his part, as *Hobomok* was so completely in their interest, and also in that of the great sachem, that he would advise them if any thing evil were on foot against them. What strengthened them in this opinion was the following circumstance. The Massachusetts Indians had for some time been inviting the English into their country to trade for furs. When, in March, 1622, they began to make ready for the voyage, *Hobomok* "told us, (says *Winslow*,) that he feared the Massachusetts, or Massachuseuks, for they so called the people of that place, were joined in confederacy with the Nanohigganneuks, a people of Nanohigganset, and that they, therefore, would take this opportunity to cut off Capt. *Standish* and his company abroad; but howsoever, in the meantime, it was to be feared, [he said,] that the Nanohigganeuks would assault the town at home; giving many reasons for his jealousy; as also that *Tisquantum* was in the confederacy, who, [he said,] we should find, would use many persuasions to draw us from our shallops to the Indians' houses for their better advantage."

Nevertheless, they proceeded on their voyage, and when they had turned the point called the *Gurnet's Nose*, a false messenger came running into Plimouth town, apparently in a great fright, out of breath, and bleeding from a wound in his face. He told them that *Caunbitant*, with many of the Narragansets, and he believed *Massasoit* with them, were coming to destroy the English. No one doubted of his sincerity, and the first thought of the people was to bring back their military leader, who had just gone in the boat with *Hobomok*. A piece of cannon was immediately discharged which, to their great joy, soon caused the boat to return, not having got out of hearing. They had no sooner arrived, than *Hobomok* told them there was no truth in the report, and said it was a plot of *Squanto*, who was then with them, and even one of those in the boat; that he knew *Massasoit* would not undertake such an enterprise without consulting him. *Hobomok* was confident, because he was himself a great chief, and one of *Massasoit's* counsellors. *Squanto* denied all knowledge of any plot, and thus ended the affair The English, however, seemed well satisfied that *Squanto* had laid this shallow plot to set them against *Massasoit*, thinking they would destroy him, by which means he expected to become chief sachem himself; and this seems the more probable, as *Massasoit* was for some time irreconcilable because they withheld him from *him*, when he had forfeited his life, as in our narration has been set forth. But entirely to satisfy the English, *Hobomok* sent his wife to Pokanoket privately to gain exact intelligence, and her return only verified what her husband had said.

"Thus by degrees (continues *Winslow*) we began to discover *Tisquantum*, whose ends were only to make himself great in the eyes of his countrymen, by means of his nearness and favor with us; not caring who fell, so he stood. In general, his course was, to persuade them he could lead us to peace or war at his pleasure; and would oft threaten the Indians, sending them word, in a private manner, we were intended shortly to kill them, that thereby he might get gifts to himself, to work their peace, insomuch as they had him in greater esteem than many of their sachems, yea, they themselves sought to him, who promised them peace in respect of us; yea, and protection also, so as they would resort to him. So that whereas divers were wont to rely on *Massassowat* for protection, and resort to his abode, now they began to leave him, and seek after *Tisquantum*. But when we understood his dealings, we certified all the Indians of our ignorance and innocency therein; assuring them, till they begun with us, they should have no cause to fear: and if any hereafter should raise any such reports, they should punish them as liars, and seekers of their and our disturbance; which gave the Indians good satisfaction on all sides." "For these and the like abuses, the governor sharply reproved him, yet was he so necessary and profitable an instrument, as at that time we could not miss him."

To the end that he might possess his countrymen with great fear of the English, *Tisquantum* told them the English kept the plague buried in their store-house, and that they could send it, at any time, and to any place, to destroy whatever persons or people they would, though they themselves stirred not out of doors. Among the rest, he had made *Hobomok* believe this tale, who asked the English if it were true, and being informed that it was not, it exploded like his other impostures.

There is but little doubt that *Squanto* was in the interest of *Caunbitant*, and lived among the English as a spy, while *Hobomok* was honestly, as he pretended, a strong friend to them; but for some time it was nearly impossible for them to know which was their best friend, as each seemed emulous to outvie the other in good offices. They were, however, at this time satisfied; for, *Hobomok's* wife having told *Massasoit* what had happened, and that it was one of *Squanto's* men that gave the alarm, satisfied him that that sagamore had caused it, and he therefore demanded him of the English, that he might put him to death, according to their law, as has been related. But the English, regarding the benefit resulting to them from saving his life, more than keeping inviolate the treaty before made with *Massasoit*, evaded the demand, and thus *Squanto* was permitted to escape.

Hobomok was greatly beloved by *Massasoit*, notwithstanding he became a professed Christian, and *Massasoit* was always opposed to the English religion himself. It has been told in the life of the great *Massasoit*, how valuable was the agency of *Hobomok*, in faithfully revealing the mischievous plot of *Caunbitant*, which terminated in the death of *Wittuwamet* and *Peksuot*. He was the pilot of the English when they visited *Massasoit* in his sickness, whom before their arrival they considered dead, which caused great manifestations of grief in *Hobomok*. He often exclaimed, as they were on their way, "*Neen womasu Sagimus, neen womasu Sagimus*," &c., which is,

"My loving Sachem, my loving Sachem! many have I known, but never any like thee." Then, turning to Mr. *Winslow*, said, "While you live you will never see his like among the Indians; that he was no liar, nor bloody and cruel like other Indians. In anger and passion he was soon reclaimed; easy to be reconciled towards such as had offended him; that his reason was such as to cause him to receive advice of mean men; and that he governed his people better with few blows, than others did with many."

In the division of the land at Plimouth among the inhabitants, *Hobomok* received a lot as his share, on which he resided after the English manner and died a Christian among them. The year of his death does not appear but was previous to 1642.

It has already been mentioned that the pilgrims made a voyage to Massachusetts in the autumn of 1621. It was in this voyage that they became acquainted with the fame of *Nanepashemet.* The English had heard that the Indians in the Massachusetts had threatened them, and they went (says *Mourt*) "partly to see the country, partly to make peace with them, and partly to procure their truck."

Squanto was pilot in this voyage. They went ashore in the bottom of the bay, and landed under a cliff which some * have supposed was what has been since called Copp's Hill, † now the north part of Boston. This was on 20th Sept. 1621. They saw no Indians until some time after they went ashore, but found a parcel of lobsters which they had collected, with which they refreshed themselves. Soon after, as they were proceeding on an excursion, "they met a woman coming for her lobsters." They told her what they had done, and paid her for them. She told them where to find Indians, and *Squanto* went to them to prepare them for meeting with the English.

Obbatinewat now received the voyagers. This sachem (if he be the same) had made peace with the English at Plimouth only seven days previous, as we have had occasion to notice. He told them he was sachem of the place, and was subject to *Massasoit;* and that he dared not remain long in any place, from fear of the Tarratines, who were "wont to come at harvest and take away their corn, and many times kill them." Also that *Squaw-Sachem* of Massachusetts was his enemy. This *Squaw-Sachem,* ‡ as we believe, was chief of those inland Indians since denominated the Nipnets, or Nipmucks, and lived at this time near Wachuset Mountain. The English intended § to have visited her at this time, but found the distance too great to proceed. They received the greatest kindness from all the Indians they met with, and mentioned that of *Obbatinewat* in particular. And they say, "We told him of divers sachims that had acknowledged themselves to be King *James* his men, *and if he also would submit himself,* ‖ we would be his safeguard from his enemies, which he did."

At another place, "having gone three miles, in arms, up in the country, we came (say they) to a place where corn had been newly gathered, a house pulled down, and the people gone. A mile from hence, *Nanepashemet,* their king, in his life-time had lived.¶ His house was not like others, but a scaffold was largely built, with poles and planks, some six foot from [the] ground, and the house upon that, being situated on the top of a hill. Not far from hence, in a bottom, we came to a fort," built by *Nanepashemet.* It

* Dr. *Belknap* appears to have been the first who suggested this. See his Biog. ii. 224.

† We had supposed this eminence to have been so called from a copse or clump of trees, which for a long time remained upon it, after it became known to the whites; but *Shaw, Descrip. Boston,* 67, says it was named from one *Copp,* a shoemaker. And *Snow, Hist. Boston,* 105, says *William Copp* was the proprietor of "a *portion* of the hill."

‡ "Sachems or sagamores,—which are but one and the same title,—the first more usual with the southward, the other with the northward Indians, to express the title of him that hath the chief command of a place or people." *Hist. N. E.* 60.

§ *Shattuck* (Hist. Concord, 2) says she was visited at this time by these voyagers, but I am not able to arrive at any such conclusion from any source of information in my possession.

‖ It does not seem from this that he is the same who before had submitted at Plimouth, as Mr. Prince *supposes.*

¶ Mr. *Shattuck* in his *Hist. Concord,* says, this "was in Medford, near Mystic Pond" was made with "poles some 30 or 40 foot long, stuck in the ground, as thick as they could be set one by another, and with these they enclosed a ring some 40 or 50 foot over. A trench, breast high, was digged on each side.* One way there was to get into it with a bridge. In the midst of this palisado stood the frame of an house, wherein, being dead, he lay buried. About a mile from hence, we came to such another, but seated on the top of an hill. Here *Nanepashemet* was killed, none dwelling in it since the time of his death."

According to Mr. *Lewis*, *Nanepashemet* was killed about the year 1619, and his widow, who was *Squaw-Sachem* before named, continued the government.† He left five children,‡ four of whose names we gather from the interesting History of Lynn; viz. 1. *Montowampate*, called by the English *Sagamore James*. He was sachem of Saugus. 2. *Abigail*, a daughter. 3. *Wonohaquaham*, called *Sagamore John*, sachem of Winnesimet. 4. *Winnepurkitt*, called *Sagamore George*, or *George Rumneymarsh*, the successor of *Montowampate* at Saugus. Of most of these we shall speak in detail hereafter.

Squaw-Sachem, according to the authority last mentioned, was the spouse of *Wappacowet*,§ or *Webcowit*, in 1635. She and her husband, four years after, 1639, deeded to *Jotham Gibbones* "the reversion of all that parcel of land which lies against the ponds of Mystic, together with the said ponds, all which we reserved from Charlestown and Cambridge, late called Newtown, after the death of me, the said *Squaw-Sachem*." The consideration was, "the many kindnesses and benefits we have received from the hands of Captain *Edward Gibbones*, of Boston."

The SQUA-SACHEM'S *mark* ~
WEBCOWIT'S *mark* ⊥⊥

Webcowit was a powwow priest, or magical physician, and was considered next in importance to *Nanepashemet* among the subjects of that chief, after his death; as a matter of course, his widow took him to her bed. It does not appear, that he was either much respected or thought much of; especially by his wife, as in the above extract from their deed, no provision seems to have been made for him after her death, if he outlived her. At all events, we may conclude, without hazard we think, that if breeches had been in fashion among Indians, the wife of *Webcowit* would have been accountable for the article in this case.

In 1643, Massachusetts covenanted with "*Wassamequin, Nashoonon, Kutchamaquin, Massaconomet*, and *Squaw-Sachem*,"‖ to the end that mutual benefit might accrue to each party. The sachems put themselves under the government of the English, agreeing to observe their laws, in as far as they should be made to understand them. For this confidence and concession of their persons and lands into their hands, the English on their part agreed to extend the same protection to them and their people as to their English subjects.¶

What had become of *Webcowit* at this time does not appear; perhaps he was off powwowing, or at home, doing the ordinary labor of the household. We hear of him, however, four years after, (1647,) "taking an active part" in the endeavors made by the English to Christianize his countrymen. "He asked the English why some of them had been 27 years in the land, and never taught them to know God till then. Had you done it sooner, (said he,) we might have known much of God by this time, and much sin might have been prevented, but now some of us are grown [too] old in sin."

---

* Might not, then, the western mounds have been formed by Indians?

† Hist. Lynn, 16.

‡ *Shattuck*, ib. who fixes her residence at Concord; she, doubtless, had several places of residence.

§ His name is spelt *Webcowits* to MS. deed in my possession, and in Mr. *Shattuck's* MSS *Wibbacowitts*, as appears from his History.

‖ In the *History of the Narraganset Country*, these names are written *Wassamegun, Nashawanon, Cutshamacke, Massanomell*, and *Squa-Sachem*. See 3 *Col. Mass. Hist. Soc* i. 212.

¶ See Gookin's *MS. Hist. Praying Indians*.

The English said they repented of their neglect; but recollecting themselves answered, "You were not willing to heare till now," and that God had not turned their hearts till then.*

Of the sachems who made the covenant above named, the first we suppose to have been *Massasoit*, on the part of the Wampanoags, who at this time was, perhaps, among the Nipmuks; *Nashoonon*, a Nipmuk chief, with whom *Massasoit* now resided. His residence was near what was since Magus Hill, in Worcester county. He was probably at Plimouth, 13 Sept., 1621, where he signed a treaty with eight others, as we have set down in the life of *Caunbitant*. His name is there spelt *Nattawahunt*. In *Winthrop's* Journal, it is *Nashacowam*, and we suppose he was father of *Nassowanno*, mentioned by *Whitney*.† *Kutchamaquin* was sachem of Dorchester and vicinity, and *Massaconomet* was *Mascononomo*.

CHAPTER III.

Some account of the Massachusetts—Geography of their country—CHIKATAUBUT—WAMPATUCK—*his war with the Mohawks*—MASCONONOMO—CANONICUS—MONTOWAMPATE—*Small-pox distresses the Indians*—WONOHAQUAHAM—WINNEPURKIT—MANATAHQUA—SCITTERYGUSSET—NATTAHATTAWANTS—WAHGUMACUT—JACK-STRAW—JAMES.

NOT long before the settlement of Plimouth, the Massachusetts had been a numerous people, but were greatly reduced at this time; partly from the great plague, of which we have already spoken, and subsequently from their wars with the Tarratines. Of this war none but the scanty records of the first settlers are to be had, and in them few particulars are preserved;‡ therefore it will not be expected that ever a complete account of the territories and power of the Massachusetts can be given; broken down as they were at the time they became known to the Europeans; for we have seen that their sachems, when first visited by the Plimouth people, were shifting for their lives—not daring to lodge a second night in the same place, from their fear of the Tarratines. Hence, if these Indians had existed as an independent tribe, their history was long since swept away "in gloomy tempests," and obscured in "a night of clouds," and nothing but a meagre tradition remained. For some time after the country was settled, they would fly for protection from the Tarratines to the houses of the English.

It is said, by Mr. *Gookin*, that "their chief sachem held dominion over many other petty governors; as those of Weechagaskas, Neponsitt, Punkapaog, Nonantum, Nashaway, some of the Nipmuck people, as far as Pokomtakuke, as the old men of Massachusetts affirmed. This people could, in former times, arm for war about 3000 men, as the old Indians declare. They were in hostility very often with the Narragansitts; but held amity, for the most part, with the Pawkunnawkutts."§ Near the mouth of Charles River "used to be the general rendezvous of all the Indians, both on the south and north side of the country."‖ *Hutchinson* ¶ says, "That circle which now makes the harbors of Boston and Charlestown, round by Malden, Chelsea, Nantasket, Hingham, Weymouth, Braintree, and Dorchester, was the capital of a great sachem,** much revered by all the plantations round about. The tradition is, that this sachem had his principal seat upon a small hill, or rising upland, in the midst of a body of salt marsh in the township of Dorchester, near to a place called Squantum."†† Hence it will

* Hist. Concord, 25. † Hist. Worcester Co. 174.

‡ This war was caused, says Mr. *Hubbard*, "upon the account of some treachery" on the part of the western tribes, i. e. the tribes west of the Merrimack. *Hist. New. Eng.* 30.

§ 1 Coll. Mass. Hist. Soc. i. 148. ‖ Hist. N. Eng. 32.

¶ From *Neal's Hist. N. Eng.*, probably, which see.

** It will be a good while before the present possessors of the country can boast of such a capital.

†† Hist. Mass. i. 460. And here it was, I suppose, that the Plimouth people landed in their

be observed, that among the accounts of the earliest writers, the dominions of the different sachems were considered as comprehended within very different limits; a kind of general idea, therefore, can only be had of the extent of their possessions. It is evident that the Massachusetts were either subject to the Narragansetts, or in alliance with them; for when the latter were at war with the Pequots, *Chikataubut* and Sagamore *John* both went with many men to aid *Canonicus*, who had sent for them. This war began in 1632, and ended in 1635, to the advantage of the Pequots.

We shall now proceed to speak of the chiefs agreeably to our plan.

Chikataubut, or *Chikkatabak*,—in English, a *house-a-fire*,—was a sachem of considerable note, and generally supposed to have had dominion over the Massachusetts Indians. *Thomas Morton* mentions him in his NEW CANAAN, as sachem of Passonagesit, (about Weymouth,) and says his mother was buried there. I need make no comments upon the authority, or warn the reader concerning the stories of *Morton*, as this is done in almost every book, early and late, about New England; but shall relate the following from him.

In the first settling of Plimouth, some of the company, in wandering about upon discovery, came upon an Indian grave, which was that of the mother of *Chikataubut*. Over the body a stake was set in the ground, and two bear-skins, sewed together, spread over it; these the English took away. When this came to the knowledge of *Chikataubut*, he complained to his people, and demanded immediate vengeance. When they were assembled, he thus harangued them: "When last the glorious light of all the sky was underneath this globe, and birds grew silent, I began to settle, as my custom is, to take repose. Before mine eyes were fast closed, me tho't I saw a vision, at which my spirit was much troubled, and trembling at that doleful sight, a spirit cried aloud, 'Behold! my son, whom I have cherished; see the paps that gave thee suck, the hands that clasped thee warm, and fed thee oft; canst thou forget to take revenge of those wild people, that hath my monument defaced in a despiteful manner; disdaining our ancient antiquities, and honorable customs. See now the sachem's grave lies like unto the common people, of ignoble race defaced. Thy mother doth complain, implores thy aid against this thievish people new come hither; if this be suffered, I shall not rest in quiet within my everlasting habitation.'"*

Battle was the unanimous resolve, and the English were watched, and followed from place to place, until at length, as some were going ashore in a boat, they fell upon them, but gained no advantage. After maintaining the fight for some time, and being driven from tree to tree, the chief captain was wounded in the arm, and the whole took to flight. This action caused the natives about Plimouth to look upon the English as invincible, and this was the reason why peace was so long maintained between them. Of the time and circumstances of this battle or fight we have detailed at length in a previous chapter.

Mourt's Relation goes far to establish the main facts in the above account. It says, "We brought sundry of the prettiest things away with us, and covered the corpse up again," and, "there was variety of opinions amongst us about the embalmed person," but no mention of the bear-skins.

From a comparison of the different accounts, there is but little doubt, that the English were attacked at Namskekit, in consequence of their depredations upon the graves, corn, &c. of the Indians.

In 1621, *Chikataubut*, with eight other sachems, acknowledged, by a written instrument, which we have already given, themselves the subjects of King *James*. Ten years after this, 23 March, 1631, he visited Governor *Winthrop* at Boston, and presented him with a hogshead of corn. Many of "his sannops and squaws" came with him, but were most of them sent away, "after they had all dined," although it thundered and rained, and the governor urged their stay; *Chikataubut* probably feared they would be

voyage to Massachusetts before spoken of, and from *Squanto* who was with them it probably received its name.

* If this be fiction, a modern compiler has deceived some of his readers. The article in the *Analectic Magazine* may have been his source of information, but the original may be seen in *Morton's New Canaan*, 106 and 107.

burdensome. At this time he wore English clothes, and sat at the governor's table, "where he behaved himself as soberly, &c. as an Englishman." Not long after, he called on Governor *Winthrop*, and desired to buy clothes for himself; the governor informed him that "English sagamores did not use to truck;* but he called his tailor, and gave him order to make him a suit of clothes; whereupon he gave the governor two large skins of coat beaver." In a few days his clothes were ready, and the governor "put him into a very good new suit from head to foot, and after, he set meat before them; but he would not eat till the governor had given thanks, and after meat he desired him to do the like, and so departed."

June 14, 1631, at a court, *Chikataubut* was ordered to pay a small skin of beaver, to satisfy for one of his men's having killed a pig,—which he complied with. A man by the name of *Plastowe*, and some others, having stolen corn from him, the same year, the court, Sept. 27, ordered that *Plastowe* should restore "two-fold," and lose his title of gentleman, and pay £5. This I suppose they deemed equivalent to four-fold. His accomplices were whipped, *to the same amount*. The next year we find him engaged with other sachems in an expedition against the Pequots. The same year two of his men were convicted of assaulting some persons of Dorchester in their houses. "They were put in the bilboes," and himself required to beat them, which he did.†

The small-pox was very prevalent among the Indians in 1633, in which year, some time in November, *Chikataubut* died.

The residence of the family of *Chikataubut* was at Tehticut, now included in Middleborough. He was in obedience to *Massasoit*, and, like other chiefs, had various places of resort, to suit the different seasons of the year; sometimes at Wessaguscusset, sometimes at Neponset, and especially upon that part of Namasket‡ called Tehticut. This was truly a river of sagamores. Its abundant stores of fish, in the spring, drew them from all parts of the realm of the chief sachem.

In deeds, given by the Indians, the place of their residence is generally mentioned, and from what we shall recite in the progress of this article, it will be seen that the same chief has different residences assigned to him.

August 5, 1665, Quincy, then Braintree, was deeded by a son of *Chikataubut*, in these terms:—

§ "To all Indian people to whom these presents shall come; *Wampatuck*, alias *Josiah Sagamore*, of Massathusetts, in Newengland, the son of *Chikataubut* deceased, sendeth greeting. Know yoo that the said *Wampatuck*, being of full age and power, according to the order and custom of the natives, hath, with the consent of his wise men, viz. *Squamog*, his brother *Daniel*, and *Old Hahatun*, and *William Mananiomott*, *Job Nassott*, *Manuntago William Nahanton*‖" "For divers goods and valuable reasons therunto; and in special for" £21 10*s.* in hand. It was subscribed and witnessed thus:—

JOSIAH, *alias* WAMPATUCK, *his* IO *marke.*
DANIEL SQUAMOG, *and a mark.*
OLD NAHATUN, *and a mark.*
WILLIAM MANUNION, *and a mark.*
JOB NOISTENNS.
ROBERT, *alias* MAMUNTAGO, *and a mark.*
WILLIAM HAHATUN.

In presence of
THOMAS KEYAHGUNSSON, *and a mark* O.
JOSEPH MANUNION, *his* I— *mark.*
THOMAS WEYMOUS, *his* O *mark.*

* However true this might have been of the governor, at least, we think, he should not have used the plural.

† "The most usual custom amongst them in exercising punishments, is, for the sachem either to beat, or whip, or put to death with his own hand, to which the common sort most quietly submit." *Williams.*

‡ Namaüasuck signified in their language *fishes*, and some early wrote Namascheuck.

§ History of Quincy, by Rev. Mr. *Whitney*, taken from the original in the possession of the Hon. *J. Q. Adams.*

‖ *Nahaton*, or *Ahaton*, and the same sometimes written *Nehoiden*. See *Worthington Hist. Dedham*, 21. He sold lands upon Charles River in 1680. *ib.*

There is a quit-claim deed from "*Charles Josias*, alias *Josias Wampatuck*, grandson of *Chikataubut*, dated 19 Mar. 1695, of Boston and the adjacent country, and the islands in the harbor, to the "proprietated inhabitants of the town of Boston," to be seen among the Suffolk records.* *Wampatuck* says, or some one *for* him, "Forasmuch as I am informed, and well assured from several ancient Indians, as well those of my council as others, that, upon the first coming of the English to sit down and settle in those parts of New England, my above-named grandfather, *Chikataubut*, by and with the advice of his council, for encouragement thereof moving, did give, grant, sell, alienate, and confirm unto the English planters," the lands above named.

Besides *Josias*, there signed this deed with him, *Ahawton*, sen., *William Hahaton*, and *Robert Momentauge*.

Josias, or *Josiah Wampatuck*, was sachem of Mattakeesett,† and, from the deeds which he gave, must have been the owner of much of the lands southward of Boston. In 1653, he sold to *Timothy Hatherly*, *James Cudworth*, *Joseph Tilden*, *Humphrey Turner*, *William Hatch*, *John Hoare*, and *James Torrey*, a large tract of land in the vicinity of Accord Pond and North River.

In 1662, he sold Pachage Neck, [now called *Ptchade*,] "lying between Namassakett riuer and a brook falling into Teticutt riuer, viz. the most westerly of the three small brookes that do fall into the said riuer;" likewise all the meadow upon said three brooks, for £21. Also, another tract bounded by Plimouth and Duxbury on one side, and Bridgewater on the other, extending to the great pond Mattakeeset; provided it included not the 1000 acres given to his son and *George Wampey*, about those ponds. This deed was witnessed by *George Wampey* and *John Wampowes*.

After the death of his father, *Josias* was often called *Josias Chikataubut*. In the PLIMOUTH RECORDS we find this notice, but without date: "Memorandum, that *Josias Chickabutt* and his wife doe owne the whole necke of Punkateesett to beloing vnto Plymouth men," &c.

In 1668, "*Josias Chickatabutt*, sachem of Namassakeesett," sold to *Robert Studson* of Scituate, a tract of land called *Nanumackeuitt*, for a "valuable consideration," as the deed expresses it. This tract was bounded on the east by Scituate.

Josias had a son *Jeremy*; and "*Charles Josiah*, son of *Jeremy*, was the last of the race."‡ Of *Josiah*, Mr. *Gookin* gives us important information.

War between the Massachusett Indians and Mohawks. In the year 1669, "the war having now continued between the Maquas and our Indians, about six years, divers Indians, our neighbors, united their forces together, and made an army of about 6 or 700 men, and marched into the Maquas' country, to take revenge of them. This enterprise was contrived and undertaken without the privity, and contrary to the advice of their English friends. Mr. *Eliot* and myself, in particular, dissuaded them, and gave them several reasons against it, but they would not hear us." Five of the Christian Indians went out with them, and but one only returned alive. "The chiefest general in this expedition was the principal sachem of Massachusetts, named *Josiah*, alias *Chekatabutt*, a wise and stout man, of middle age, but a very vicious person. He had considerable knowledge in the Christian religion; and sometime, when he was younger, seemed to profess it for a time;—for he was bred up by his uncle, *Kuchamakin*, who was the first sachem and his people to whom Mr. *Eliot* preached."§

Of those who went out with *Wampatuk* from other tribes we have no record; but there were many, probably, as usual upon such expeditions.

This army arrived at the Mohawk fort after a journey of about 200 miles when, upon besieging it some time, and having some of their men killed in sallies, and sundry others sick, they gave up the siege and retreated. Meanwhile the Mohawks pursued them, got in their front, and, from an ambush,

---

* Printed at length in *Snow's Hist. Boston*, 389, et cet.

† *Deane's Hist. Scituate*, 144.

‡ Ibid. *Squamaug* was a brother of *Josiah*, and ruled "as sachem during the minority" of *Jeremy*. Dr. *Harris*, *Hist. Dorchester*, 16, 17.

§ 1 Coll. Mass. Hist. Soc. i. 166.

attacked them in a defile, and a great fight ensued. Finally the Mohawks were put to flight by the extraordinary bravery and prowess of *Chikataubut* and his captains. But what was most calamitous in this disastrous expedition, was, the loss of the great chief *Chikataubut*, who, after performing prodigies of valor, was killed in repelling the Mohawks in their last attack, with almost all his captains, in number about 50, as was supposed.* This was a severe stroke to these Indians, and they suffered much from chagrin on their return home. The Mohawks considered themselves their masters, and although a peace was brought about between them, by the mediation of the English and Dutch on each side, yet the Massachusetts and others often suffered from their incursions.

A chief of much the same importance as *Chikataubut* and his sons, was *Masconnonomo*, or *Masconomo*, sachem of Agawam, since called *Ipswich*. When the fleet which brought over the colony that settled Boston, in 1630, anchored near Cape Ann, he welcomed them to his shores, and spent some time on board one of the ships.†

On the 28th June, 1638, *Masconnonomet* ‡ executed a deed of "all his lands in Ipswich," to *John Winthrop*, jr., for the sum of £20.§

At a court in July, 1631, it was ordered, that "the sagamore of Agawam is banished from coming into any Englishman's house for a year, under penalty of ten beaver-skins." ‖ This was probably done in retaliation for his having committed acts of violence on the Tarratines, who soon after came out with great force against *Masconnonomo;* he having, "as was usually said, treacherously killed some of those Tarratine families."¶ It would seem that he expected an attack, and had therefore called to his aid some of the sachems near Boston; for it so happened that *Montowampate* and *Wonohaquaham* were at Agawam when the Tarratines made an attack, but whether by concert or accident is not clear.

To the number of 100 men, in three canoes, the Tarratines came out on this enterprise, on the 8 August following. They attacked *Masconnonomo* and his guests in his wigwam in the night, killed seven men, wounded *Masconnonomo* himself, and *Montowampate*, and *Wonohaquaham*, and several others who afterwards died. They took the wife of *Montowampate* captive, but it so happened that *Abraham Shurd* of Pemmaquid ransomed her, and sent her home, where she arrived on the 17 September the same autumn.** From Mr. *Cobbet's* account, it appears that they came against the English, who, but for an Indian, named *Robin*, would have been cut off, as the able men at this time, belonging to Ipswich, did not exceed 30; and most of these were from home on the day the attack was to have been made. *Robin*, having by some means found out their intentions, went to *John Perkins*,†† and told him that on such a day four Tarratines would come and invite the English to trade, "and draw them down the hill to the water side," when 40 canoes full of armed Indians would be ready, under "the brow of the hill," to fall upon them. It turned out as *Robin* had reported; but the Indians were frightened off by a false show of numbers, an old drum, and a few guns, without effecting their object.‡‡

We hear no more of him until 1644, March 8, when, at a court held in Boston, "*Cutshamekin* and *Squaw-Sachem*, *Masconomo*, *Nashacowam* and *Wassamagin*, two sachems near the great hill to the west, called *Wachusett*, came into the court, and, according to their former tender to the governor, desired to be received under our protection§§ and government, upon the same terms

---

* 1 Coll. Mass. Hist. Soc. i. 167.

† Hist. N. England.

‡ This is doubtless the most correct spelling of his name. It is scarce spelt twice alike in the MS. records.

§ Records of Gen. Court, v. 381

‖ Prince, 357

¶ *Hubbard's* N. E. 145.

** *Winthrop's* Jour.—*Lewis's* Hist. Lynn, 39, 40.—*Felt's* Hist. Ipswich, 3.

†† Quarter-master, "living then in a little hut upon his father's island on this side of Jeofry's Neck." *MS. Narrative.*

‡‡ *Cobbet's* MS. Narrative.

§§ They desired this from their great fear of the Mohawks, it is said.

that *Pumham* and *Sacononoco* were. So we causing them to understand the articles, and all the ten commandments of God, and they freely assenting to all,* they were solemnly received, and then presented the court with twenty-six fathom of wampum, and the court gave each of them a coat of two yards of cloth, and their dinner; and to them and their men, every one of them, a cup of sac at their departure; so they took leave, and went away very joyful."†

In the Town Records of Ipswich, under date 18 June 1658, a grant is made to the widow of *Masconomo*, of "that parcel of land which her husband had fenced in," so long as she should remain a widow. Her husband was the last of the sachems of Agawam, and with him, says Mr. *Felt*, descended "his feble and broken scepter to the grave." He died on the 6 March, 1658, and was buried on Sagamore Hill, now within the bounds of Hamilton. His gun and other valuable implements were interred with him. "Idle curiosity, wanton, sacrilegious sport, prompted an individual to dig up the remains of this chief, and to carry his scull on a pole through Ipswich streets. Such an act of barbarity was severely frowned upon, and speedily visited with retributive civil justice."‡

MONTOWAMPATE, sagamore of Lynn and Marblehead, was known more generally among the whites as *Sagamore James*. He was son of *Nanepashemet*, and brother of *Wonohaquaham* and *Winnepurkitt*.§ He died in 1633, of the small-pox, "with most of his people. It is said that these two promised, if ever they recovered, to live with the English, and serve their God."‖ *Montowampate*, having been defrauded of 20 beaver-skins, by a man named *Watts*, who had since gone to England, he went to Gov. *Winthrop* on the 26 March, 1631, to know how he should obtain recompense. The governor gave him a letter to *Emanuel Downing*, Esq. of London, from which circumstance it would seem that the chief determined to go there; and it is said that he actually visited England and received his due.¶ The histories of those times give a melancholy picture of the distresses caused by the small-pox among the "wretched natives." "There are," says *Mather*, "some old planters surviving to this day, who helped to bury the dead Indians; even whole families of them all dead at once. In one of the wigwams they found a poor infant sucking at the breast of the dead mother."** The same author observes that, before the disease began, the Indians had begun to quarrel with the English about the bounds of their lands, "but God ended the controversy by sending the small-pox among the Indians at Saugus, who were before that time exceedingly numerous."

We have mentioned another of the family of *Nanepashemet*, also a sachem. This was *Wonohaquaham*, called by the English *Sagamore John*, of Winisimet. His residence was at what was then called *Rumneymarsh*, part of which is now in Chelsea and part in Saugus.§ As early as 1631, he had cause to complain that some of the English settlers had burnt two of his wigwams. "Which wigwams," says Governor *Dudley*,†† "were not inhabited, but stood in a place convenient for their shelter, when, upon occasion, they should travel that way." The court, upon examination, found that a servant of Sir *R. Saltonstall* had been the means of the mischief, whose master was ordered to make satisfaction, "which he did by seven yards of cloth, and that his servant pay him, at the end of his time, fifty shillings sterling."‡‡ *Sagamore John* died at Winisimet, in 1633, of the small-pox.§§ He desired to become acquainted with the Englishmen's God, in his sickness, and requested them to take his two sons and instruct them in Christianity, which they did.‖‖

Winnepurkitt,¶¶ who married a daughter of *Passaconaway*, makes considerable figure also in our Indian annals. He was born about 1616, and succeeded *Montowampate* at his death, in 1633. The English called him *George Rumney*

* The articles which they subscribed, will be seen at large when the *Manuscript Hist. of the Praying Indians, by Daniel Gookin*, shall be published. They do not read precisely as rendered by *Winthrop*.

† *Winthrop's* Journal. ‡ Hist. Ipswich, 5. § *Lewis's* Hist. Lynn, 16, 17.

‖ Hist. of New England, 195. ¶ History of Lynn, 38. ** Relation, &c. 23.

†† Letter to the Countess of Lincoln, 25, edition 1696.

‡‡ *Prince's* Chronology. §§ History of New England, 195, 650.

‖‖ Wonder-working Providence. ¶¶ Spelt also *Winnaperket*

marsh, and at one time he was proprietor of Deer Island, in Boston harbor In the latter part of his life, he went to Barbadoes. It is supposed that he was carried there with the prisoners who were sold for slaves, at the end of *Philip's* war. He died soon after his return, in 1684, at the house of *Muminquash*, aged 68 years." *Ahawayetsquaine*, daughter of *Poquanum*, is also mentioned as his wife, by whom he had several children.*

Manatahqua, called also *Black-william*, was a sachem, and proprietor of Nahant, when the adjacent country was settled by the whites. His father lived at Swampscot, and was also a sagamore, but probably was dead before the English settled in the country.† A traveller in this then‡ wilderness world, thus notices *William*, and his possessing Nahant. "One *Black-william*, an *Indian Duke*, out of his generosity gave this place in general to the plantation of Saugus, so that no other can appropriate it to himself." He was a great friend to the whites, but his friendship was repaid, as was that of many others of that and even much later times. There was a man by the name of *Walter Bagnall*, nicknamed *Great Wot*, "a wicked fellow," who had much wronged the Indians,§ killed near the mouth of Saco River, probably by some of those whom he had defrauded. This was in October, 1631. As some vessels were upon the eastern coast in search of pirates, in January, 1633, they put in at Richmond's Island, where they fell in with *Black-william*. This was the place where *Bagnall* had been killed about two years before; but whether he had any thing to do with it, does not appear, nor do I find that any one, even his murderers, pretended he was any way implicated; but, out of revenge for *Bagnall's* death, these pirate-hunters hanged *Black-william*. On the contrary, it was particularly mentioned ‖ that *Bagnall* was killed by *Squidrayset* and his men, some Indians belonging to that part of the country.

This *Squidrayset*, or *Scitterygusset*, for whose act *Manatahqua* suffered, was the first sachem who deeded land in Falmouth, Maine. A creek near the mouth of Presumpscot River perpetuates his name to this day. Mr. *Willis* supposes he was sachem of the Aucocisco tribe, who inhabited between the Androscoggin and Saco rivers; and that from Aucocisco comes Casco.¶ There can be but little doubt that *Bagnall* deserved his fate,** if any deserve such; but the other was the act of white men, and we leave the reader to draw the parallel between the two: perhaps he will inquire, *Were the murderers of* MANATAHQUA *brought to justice?* All we can answer is, *The records are silent.* Perhaps it was considered an *offset* to the murder of *Bagnall*.

Nattahattawants, in the year 1642, sold to *Simon Willard*, in behalf of "Mr. *Winthrop*, Mr. *Dudley*, Mr. *Nowell*, and Mr. *Alden*," a large tract of land upon both sides Concord River. "Mr. *Winthrop*, our present governor, 1260 acres, Mr. *Dudley*, 1500 acres, on the S. E. side of the river, Mr. *Nowell*, 500 acres, and Mr. *Allen*, 500 acres, on the N. E. side of the river, and in consideration hereof the said *Simon* giueth to the said *Nattahattawants* six fadom of waompampege, one wastcoat, and one breeches, and the said *Nattahattawants* doth covenant and bind himself, that hee nor any other Indians shall set traps within this ground, so as any cattle might recieve hurt thereby, and what cattle shall receive hurt by this meanes, hee shall be lyable to make it good." [In the deed, *Nattahattawants* is called sachem of that land.]

Witnessed by three whites.

The mark of ● NATAHATTAWANTS.
The mark of ● WINNIPIN, *an Indian that traded for him.*††

The name of this chief, as appears from documents copied by Mr. *Shattuck*,‡‡ was understood *Tahattawan*, *Tahattawants*, *Attawan*, *Attawanee*, and *Ahatawanee*. He was sachem of Musketaquid, since Concord, and a supporter and

* Hist. Lynn.
† Hist. N. Eng.
‡ 1633. *William Wood*, author of *New Eng. Prospect.*
§ *Winthrop's* Journal, i. 62, 63.
‖ *Winthrop*, ib.
¶ Col. Maine Hist. Soc. i. 68.
** He had, in about three years, by extortion, as we infer from *Winthrop*, accumulated about £400 from among the Indians. See Journal *ut supra.*
†† Suffolk Records of Deeds, vol. i. No. 34.
‡‡ Hist. Concord, Mass. *passim* chap. i.

propagator of Christianity among his people, and an honest and upright man. The celebrated *Waban* married his eldest daughter. *John Tahattawan* was his son, who lived at Nashoba, where he was chief ruler of the praying Indians—a deserving Indian. He died about 1670. His widow was daughter of *John*, sagamore of Patucket, upon the Merrimack, who married *Oonamog*, another ruler of the praying Indians, of Marlborough. Her only son by *Tahattawan** was killed by some white ruffians, who came upon them while in their wig wams, and his mother was badly wounded at the same time. Of this affair we shall have occasion elsewhere to be more particular. *Naanashquaw*, another daughter, married *Naanishcow*, called *John Thomas*, who died at Natick, aged 110 years.

We know very little of a sachem of the name of *Wahgumacut*,† except that he lived upon Connecticut River, and came to Boston in 1631, with a request to the governor "to have some English to plant in his country;" and as an inducement, said he would "find them corn, and give them, yearly, 80 skins of beaver." The governor, however, dismissed him without giving him any encouragement; doubting, it seems, the reality of his friendship. But it is more probable that he was sincere, as he was at this time in great fear of the Pequots, and judged that if some of the English would reside with him, he should be able to maintain his country.

There accompanied *Wahgumacut* to Boston an Indian named *Jackstraw*,‡ who was his interpreter, and Sagamore *John*. We have labored to find some further particulars of him, but all that we can ascertain with certainty, is, that he had lived some time in England with Sir *Walter Ralegh*.§ How Sir *Walter*

---

* Mr. *Gookin* writes this name *Tohatooner*, that of the father *Tahattawarre*. *MS. Hist. Praying Indians*, 105.

† *Wahginnacut*, according to Mr. *Savage's* reading of *Winthrop*. Our text is according to *Prince*, who also used *Winthrop* in MS. It is truly diverting to see how the author of *Tales of the Indians* has displayed his invention upon the passage in *Winthrop's* Journal bringing to our knowledge this chief. We will give the passage of *Winthrop*, that the reader may judge whether great ignorance, or misrepresentation "of set purpose" be chargeable to him. "He [Gov. *Winthrop*] discovered after [*Wahginnacut* was gone], that the said sagamore is a very treacherous man, and at war with the *Pekoath* (a far greater sagamore.") Now, every child that has read about the Indians, it seems to us, ought to know that the meaning of *Pekoath* was mistaken by the governor, and no more meant a chief than the *Massasoits* meant what the Plimouth people first supposed it to mean. In the one case, the name of a tribe was mistaken for that of a chief, and in the other the chief for the tribe. Mistakes of this kind were not uncommon before our fathers became acquainted with the country. *Winthrop* says, too, the Mohawks was a great sachem. Now, who ever thought there was a chief of that name?

‡ Probably so named from the Maidstone minister, who flourished in *Wat Tyler's* rebellion, and whose real name was *John Ball*, but afterwards nick-named *Jack Straw*. He became chaplain to *Wat's* army, they having let him out of prison. A text which he made great use of in preaching to his liberators was this:—

When Adam dalfe and Eve span,
Who was then a gentleman?

This we apprehend was construed, *Down with the nobility!* See *Rapin's Eng.* i. 457. In *Kennet*, i. 247, *John Wraw* is called *Jack Straw*. He was beheaded.

§ "The imputation of the first bringing in of *tobacco* into England lies on this heroic knight." *Winstanley's Worthies*, 259. "Besides the consumption of the purse, and impairing of our inward parts, the immoderate, vain and phantastical abuse of the hellish weed, corrupteth the natural sweetness of the breath, stupifieth the brain; and indeed is so prejudicial to the general esteem of our country." *Ibid.* 211. Whether *Jack-straw* were the servant who acted a part in the often-told anecdote of Sir *Walter Ralegh's* smoking tobacco, on its first being taken to England, we shall not presume to assert; but, for the sake of the anecdote, we will admit the fact; it is variously related, but is said to be, in substance, as follows. At one time, it was so very unpopular to use tobacco in any way in England, that many who had got attached to it, used it only privately. Sir *Walter* was smoking in his study, at a certain time, and, being thirsty, called to his servant to bring him a tankard of beer. *Jack* hastily obeyed the summons, and Sir *Walter*, forgetting to cease smoking, was in the act of spouting a volume of smoke from his mouth when his servant entered. *Jack*, seeing his master smoking prodigiously at the mouth, thought no other but he was all on fire inside, having never seen such a phenomenon in all England before; dashed the quart of liquor at once in his face, and ran out screaming, "Massa's a fire! Massa's a fire!"

Having dismissed the servant, every one might reasonably expect a few words concerning his master. Sir *Walter Ralegh* may truly be said to have lived in an age fruitful in great and worthy characters. Captain *John Smith* comes to our notice through his agency, and the came by him, does not satisfactorily appear. Captains *Amidas* and *Barlow* sailed to America in his employ, and on their return carried over two natives from Virginia, whose names were *Wanchese* and *Manteo*.* It is barely possible that one of these was afterwards *Jack-straw*.

A Nipmuck Indian, of no small note in his time, it may in the next place be proper to notice

James Printer, or *James-the-printer*, was the son of *Naoas*, brother of *Tukawewillin* † and *Anaweakin*. When a child, he was instructed at the Indian charity school, at Cambridge. In 1659, he was put apprentice to *Samuel Green*, to learn the printer's business; ‡ and he is spoken of as having run away from his master in 1675. If, after an apprenticeship of 16 years, one could not leave his master without the charge of absconding, at least, both the master and apprentice should be pitied. In relation to this matter, Mr. *Hub-*

renowned first English circumnavigator was his contemporary. He, like the last named, was born in the county of Devonshire, in 1552, in the parish of Budley. Sir *Humphrey Gilbert*, so well known in our annals, was his half-brother, his father having married Sir *Humphrey's* mother, a widow*, by whom he had *Walter*, a fourth son.† The great successes and discoveries of the celebrated admiral Sir *Francis Drake* gave a new impetus to the English nation in maritime affairs, and consequent thereupon was the settlement of North America; as great an era, to say the least, as was ever recorded in history. No one shone more conspicuous in those undertakings than Sir *Walter Ralegh*. After persevering a long time, he established a colony in Virginia, in 1607. He was a man of great valor and address, and a favorite with the great Queen *Elizabeth*, the promoter of his undertakings, one of whose "maids of honor" he married. In this affair some charge him with having first dishonored that lady, and was for a time under the queen's displeasure in consequence, but marrying her restored him to favor. The city of Ralegh in Virginia was so named by his direction. He was conspicuous with *Drake* and *Howard* in the destruction of the Spanish armada in 1588. On the death of the queen, he was imprisoned almost 13 years in the tower of London, upon the charge of treason. It was during his imprisonment that he wrote his great and learned work, *the History of the World*. The alleged crime of treason has long since been viewed by all the world as without foundation, and the punishment of *Ralegh* reflects all its blackness upon the character of *James* I. The ground of the charge was, that *Ralegh* and others were in a conspiracy against the *king*, and were designing to place on the throne *Arabella Stewart*.‡ He was never pardoned, although the king set him at liberty, and permitted him to go on an expedition to South America in search of a gold mine of which he had gained some intimations in a previous visit to those countries. His attempt to find gold failed, but he took the town of St. Thomas, and established in it a garrison. This was a depredation, as Spain and England were then at peace, but *Ralegh* had the king's commission. The Spanish ambassador complained loudly against the transaction, and the miserable *James*, to extricate himself, and appease the Spanish king, ordered *Ralegh* to be seized on his return, who, upon the old charge of treason, was sentenced to be beheaded, which was executed upon him 29th Oct. 1618.§ "I shall only hint," says Dr. *Polwhele*,‖ "that the execution of this great man, whom *James* was advised to sacrifice to the advancement of the peace with Spain, hath left an indelible stain on the memory of that misguided monarch." It appears from another account ¶ that Sir *Walter*, on arriving at the mouth of the Oronoko, was taken "desperately sick," and sent forward a company under one of his captains in search of the gold mine. That they were met by the Spaniards, who attacked them, and that this was the cause of their assaulting St. Thomas, and being obliged to descend the river without effecting the object they were upon.

The following circumstance respecting the celebrated History of the World, not being generally known, cannot but be acceptable to the reader. The first volume (which is what we have of it) was published before he was imprisoned the last time. Just before his execution, he sent for the publisher of it. When he came, Sir *Walter* took him by the hand, and, "after some discourse, askt him how that work of his sold. Mr. *Burre* [the name of the publisher] returned this answer, that it had sold so slowly that it had undone him. At which words of his, Sir *Walter Ralegh*, stepping to his desk, reaches his other part of his history to Mr. *Burre*, which he had brought down to the times he lived in; clapping his hand on his breast, he took the other unprinted part of his works into his hand, with a sigh, saying, 'Ah, my friend, hath the first part undone thee, the second volume shall undo no more; this ungrateful world is unworthy of it.' When, immediately going to the fire-side, threw it in and set his foot on it till it was consumed."**

* See *Cayley's* Life Sir *W. Ralegh*, i. 70. ed. Lond. 1816, 2 vols. 8vo.

† Some author of Indian tales might delight himself for a long time in ringing changes on this Indian preacher's name, without inventing any new ones; for it is not, as I remember spelt twice alike in our authorities.

‡ Thomas, Hist. Printing

* "Of *Otho Gilbert*, of Compton, Esq." *Polwhele's Hist. Devon*, ii. 219.

† *Stith*, Hist. Virginia, 7. Second son, says Mr. *Polwhele*, Devon, ii. 219.

‡ *Rapin's* Eng. ii. 161.

§ Tindal's notes in Rapin, ii. 195.

‖ Hist. Devonshire, i. 259.

¶ Winstanley, Worthies, 256.

** Winstanley, Worthies, 257.

bard says,* "He had attained some skill in printing, and might have attained more, had he not, like a false villain, ran away from his master before his time was out." And the same author observes that the name *printer* was superadded to distinguish him from others named *James*.

Dr. *I. Mather* † has this record of *James-printer*. "July 8, [1676.] Whereas the council at Boston had lately emitted a declaration, signifying, that such Indians as did, within 14 days, come in to the English, might hope for mercy, divers of them did this day return from among the Nipmucks. Among others, *James*, an Indian, who could not only read and write, but had learned the art of printing, notwithstanding his apostasy, did venture himself upon the mercy and truth of the English declaration, which he had seen and read, promising for the future to venture his life against the common enemy. He and the other now come in, affirm that very many of the Indians are dead since this war began and that more have died by the hand of God, in respect of diseases, fluxes and fevers, which have been amongst them, than have been killed with the sword."

Mr. *Thomas* says,‡ it was owing to the *amor patriæ* of *James-printer* that he left his master and joined in *Philip's* war. But how much *amor patriæ* he must have had to have kept him an apprentice 16 years is not mentioned.

It was in 1685 that the second edition of the famous Indian Bible was completed. From the following testimony of Mr. *Eliot* will be seen how much the success of that undertaking was considered to depend on *James-the-printer*. In 1683, in writing to the Hon. *Robert Boyle* at London, Mr. *Eliot* says, "I desire to see it done before I die, and I am so deep in years, that I cannot expect to live long; besides, we have but *one man*, viz. the *Indian Printer*, that is able to compose the sheets, and correct the press with understanding." In another, from the same to the same, dated a year after, he says, "Our slow progress needeth an apology. We have been much hindered by the sickness the last year. Our workmen have been all sick, and we have but few hands, (at printing,) one Englishman, and a boy, and one Indian," &c.

This Indian was undoubtedly *James-the-printer*. And Mr. *Thomas* adds, "Some of *James's* descendants were not long since living in Grafton; they bore the surname of *Printer*."§

There was an Indian named *Job Nesutan*, who was also concerned in the *first* edition of the Indian Bible. He was a valiant soldier, and went with the English of Massachusetts, in the first expedition to Mount Hope, where he was slain in battle. "He was a very good linguist in the English tongue, and was Mr. *Eliot's* assistant and interpreter in his translation of the Bible and other books in the Indian language."‖

In a letter of the commissioners of the U. C. of New England, to the corporation in England, we find this postscript.—"Two of the Indian youths formerly brought up to read and write, are put apprentice; the one to a carpenter, the other to Mr. *Green* the printer, who take their trades and follow their business very well." *James-the-printer* was probably one of these. *Nesutan*, we presume, was only an interpreter. The above-mentioned letter was dated 10th Sept. 1660.

In 1698, *James* was teacher to five Indian families at Hassinammisco.¶ In 1709, he seems to have got through with his apprenticeship, and to have had some interest in carrying on the printing business. For, in the title pages of the Indian and English Psalter, printed in that year, is this imprint "BOSTON, N. E. *Upprinthomunne au* B. GREEN, & J. PRINTER, *wutche guhtiantamwe Chapanukke ut New England*, &c. 1709."

We shall now pass to notice a Massachusetts sachem, who, like too many others, does not appear to the best advantage; nevertheless, we doubt not but as much so as he deserves, as by the sequel will be seen. We mean

Kutchmakin, known also by several other names, or variations of the same name; as, *Kutshamaquin*, *Cutshamoquen*, *Cutchamokin*, and many more, as, in

---

* Narrative, 96. † Brief Hist. 89. ‡ Hist. Printing, i. 290.
§ Hist. Printing, i. 292, 293. ‖ Gookin, *Hist. Praying Indians.*
¶ Information from Mr. *E. Tuckerman*, Jr.—Hassinammisco, Hassanamesit, &c. signified a *place of stones*. Thomas, *ut supra.*

different parts of our work, extracts will necessarily show. He was one of those sachems who, in 1643—4, signed a submission to the English, as has been mentioned in a preceding chapter.

In 1636, *Kutshamakin* sold to the people of Dorchester, Uncataquisset, being the part of that town since called Milton. This, it appears, was at some period his residence. Though he was a sachem under *Woosamequin*, yet, like *Caunbitant*, he was opposed to the settlement of the English in his country. He soon, however, became reconciled to it, and became a Christian. When Mr. *Eliot* desired to know why he was opposed to his people's becoming Christians, he said, then they would pay him no tribute.

When the English of Massachusetts sent to *Canonicus*, to inquire into the cause of the murder of *John Oldham*, *Kutshamakin* accompanied them as interpreter, fighter, or whatever was required of him.

As no satisfaction could be had of the Pequots, for the murder of Mr. *Oldham*, it was resolved, in 1636, to send an army into their country "to fight with them," if what, in the opinion of the English, as a recompense, were not to be obtained without. The armament consisted of about 90 men. These first went to Block Island, where they saw a few Indians before they landed, who, after shooting a few arrows, which wounded two of the English, fled. The Indians had here "two plantations, three miles in sunder, and about 60 wigwams, some very large and fair, and above 200 acres of corn." This the English destroyed, "staved seven canoes," and after two days spent in this business, and hunting for Indians without success, sailed to the main land, where *Kutshamakin* performed his part in hastening on the Pequot calamity. Having waylaid one of that nation, he shot and scalped him. The scalp he sent to *Canonicus*, who sent it about among all his sachem friends; thus expressing his approbation of the murder, and willingness to engage his friends to fight for the English. As a further proof of his approval of the act, he not only thanked the English, but gave *Kutshamakin* four fathom of wampum.

Capt. *Lion Gardener* gives us some particulars of this affair, which are very valuable for the light they throw on this part of our early transactions with the Pequots. The affair we have just mentioned happened immediately after *Endicott*, *Turner*, and *Underhill* arrived at Saybrook, from Block Island. Capt. *Gardener* then commanded the fort, who spoke to them as follows of their undertaking: "You come hither to raise these wasps about my ears, and then you will take wing and flee away." It so came to pass; and although he was much opposed to their going, yet they went, agreeably to their instructions. *Gardener* instructed them how to proceed, to avoid being surprised; but the Indians played them a Yankee trick, as in the sequel will appear.

On coming to the Pequot town, they inquired for the sachem,* wishing to parley with him: his people said "he was from home, but within three hours he would come; and so from three to six, and thence to nine, there came none." But the Indians came fearlessly, in great numbers, and spoke to them, through the interpreter, *Kutshamakin*, for some time. This delay was a stratagem which succeeded well; for they rightly guessed that the English had come to injure them in their persons, or property, or both. Therefore, while some were entertaining the English with words, others carried off their effects and hid them. When they had done this, a signal was given, and all the Indians ran away. The English then fell to burning and destroying every thing they could meet with. *Gardener* had sent some of his men with the others, who were unaccountably left on shore when the others reëmbarked, and were pursued, and two of them wounded by the Indians.

"The Bay-men killed not a man, save that one, *Kichomiquim*, an Indian sachem of the Bay, killed a Pequit; and thus began the war between the Indians and us, in these parts."† The Pequots henceforth used every means to kill the English, and many were taken by them, and some tortured in their manner. "Thus far," adds *Gardener*, "I had written in a book, that all men

---

* *Sassacus*, says *Winthrop* (i. 194.); but being told he was gone to Long Island the general demanded to see "the other sachem, &c." which was doubtless *Mononotto*.

† 3 *Coll. Hist. Soc.* iii. 141, &c.

and posterity might know how and why so many honest men had their blood shed, yea, and some flayed alive, others cut in pieces, and some roasted alive, only because *Kichamokin*, a Bay Indian, killed one Pequot."

To say the least of our author, he had the best possible means *to be correctly informed* of these matters, and we know not that he had any motive to misrepresent them.

Governor *Winthrop* mentions, under date 1646, that Mr. *Eliot* lectured constantly "one week at the wigwam of one *Wabon*, a new sachem near Watertown mill, and the other the next week in the wigwam of *Cutshamekin*, near Dorchester mill." We shall have occasion in another chapter to speak of *Kutshamakin*.

In 1648, *Cutchamekin*, as he was then called, and *Jojeuny* appear as witnesses to a deed made by another Indian called *Cato*, alias *Goodman*. *Lane* and *Griffin* were the grantees "in behalf of the rest of the people of Sudbury." The tract of land sold adjoined Sudbury, and was five miles square; for which *Cato* received five pounds. *Jojeuny* was brother to *Cato*.*

CHAPTER IV.

*Of the great nation of the Narragansets—Geography of their country—*CANONICUS*—*MIANTUNNOMOH*—His relations—Aids the English in destroying the Pequots—Sells Rhode Island—His difficulties with the English—Visits Boston—His magnanimity and independence—Charged with a conspiracy against the whites—Ably repels it—*WAIANDANCE *becomes his secret enemy—His speech to Waiandance and his people—His war with Uncas—His capture and death—Circumstances of his execution—Participation of the whites therein—Impartial view of that affair—Traditions—*NINIGRET—MEXAM, *alias* MEXANO*—Affair of Cuttaquin and Uncas—Character of Ascassassotick—Ninigret visits the Dutch—Accused by the English of plotting with them—Ably defends himself—Notices of various other Indians—War between Ninigret and Ascassassotick—Present condition of his descendants—Further account of Pessacus—Killed by the Mohawks.*

THE bounds of Narraganset were, as described in the times of the sachems,† "Pautuckit River, Quenebage[Quinebauge]and Nipmuck,"northerly; "westerly by a brook called Wequapaug, not far‡ from Paquatuck River; southerly by the sea, or main ocean; and easterly by the Nanhiganset Bay, wherein lieth many islands, by deeds bought of the Nanhiganset sachems." Coweesett and Niantick, though sometimes applied to this country, were names only of places within it. According to Mr. *Gookin*, "the territory of their sachem extended about 30 or 40 miles from Sekunk River and Narragansitt Bay, including Rhode Island and other islands in that bay." Pawcatuck River separated them from the Pequots. This nation, under *Canonicus*, had, in 1642, arrived at the zenith of its greatness, and was supposed to have contained a population of *thirty thousand*. This estimate was by *Richard Smith*, jr., who, with his father, lived in their country.

In 1766, or about that year, Mr. *Samuel Drake* made a catalogue of the Narraganset Indians. This catalogue contained the names of about 315 persons. Mr. *Drake* spent 14 years among them, chiefly in the capacity of a schoolmaster. He wrote an account of them, but whether it was ever published I cannot learn. §

A census of those calling themselves a remnant of the Narragansets, taken Feb. 1832, was 315; only seven of whom were unmixed. The Indians themselves make their number 364. ‖

Of the early times of this nation, some of the first English inhabitants learned from the old Indians, that they had, previous to their arrival, a sachem named *Tashtassuck*, and their encomiums upon his wisdom and valor were

---

* Suffolk Reg. Deeds. There is no name signed to the deed, but in the place thereof, is the picture of some four-legged animal drawn on his back.

† See 3 Coll. Mass. Hist. Soc. i. 210

‡ Four or five miles, says *Gookin*.

§ See *Beatty's* Journal, 106

‖ MS. letter of Rev. Mr. *Ely*.

much the same as the Delawares reported of their great chief *Tamany*, that since, there had not been his equal, &c. *Tashtassuck* had but two children, a son and daughter; these he joined in marriage, because he could find none worthy of them out of his family. The product of this marriage was four sons, of whom *Canonicus* was the oldest.*

Canonicus,† the great sachem of the Narragansets, was contemporary with *Miantunnomoh*, who was his nephew. We know not the time of his birth, but a son of his was at Boston in 1631, the next year after it was settled. But the time of his death is minutely recorded by Governor *Winthrop*, in his "Journal," thus: "June 4, 1647. *Canonicus*, the great sachem of Narraganset, died, a very old man." He is generally supposed to have been about 85 years of age when he died.

The Wampanoags were in great fear of the Narragansets about the time the English came to Plimouth, and at one time war actually existed, and *Massasoit* fled before *Canonicus*, and applied to the English for protection.

Edward Winslow relates, in his Good News from New England, that, in Feb. 1622, *Canonicus* sent into Plimouth, by one of his men, a bundle of arrows, bound with a rattlesnake's skin, and there left them, and retired. The Narragansets, who were reported at this time "many thousand strong," hearing of the weakness of the English, "began, (says the above-named author,) to breath forth many threats against us," although they had the last summer "desired and obtained peace with us."—"Insomuch as the common talk of our neighbor Indians on all sides was of the preparation they made to come against us." They were now imboldened from the circumstance that the English had just added to their numbers, but not to their arms nor provisions. The ship Fortune had, not long before, landed 35 persons at Plimouth, and the Narragansets seem to have been well informed of all the circumstances. This, (says Mr. *Winslow*,) "occasioned them to slight and brave us with so many threats as they did. At length came one of them to us, who was sent by *Conaucus*, their chief sachem or king, accompanied with one *Tokamahamon*, a friendly Indian. This messenger inquired for *Tisquantum*, our interpreter, who not being at home, seemed rather to be glad than sorry; and leaving for him a bundle of new arrows, lapped in a rattlesnake's skin, desired to depart with all expedition."

When *Squanto* was made acquainted with the circumstance, he told the English that it was a challenge for war. Governor *Bradford* took the rattlesnake's skin, and filled it with powder and shot, and returned it to *Canonicus;* at the same time instructing the messenger to bid him defiance, and invite him to a trial of strength. The messenger, and his insulting carriage, had the desired effect upon *Canonicus*, for he would not receive the skin, and it was cast out of every community of the Indians, until it at last was returned to Plimouth, and all its contents. This was a demonstration that he was awed into silence and respect of the English, by the decided stand and hostile attitude they assumed.

In 1621, soon after the war with *Caunbitant* was over, among those who sought the friendship of the English, was *Canonicus* himself, notwithstanding he was now courting war again so soon. He had doubtless nearly got rid of the fear that the news of *Standish's* conduct first inspired, and had taken up again his old resolution of fighting the strangers at Plimouth.

He is mentioned with great respect by Rev. *Roger Williams*,‡ in the year 1654. After observing that *many hundreds* of the English were witnesses to the friendly disposition of the Narragansets, he says, "Their late famous long-lived *Caunonicus* so lived and died, and in the same most honorable manner and solemnity, (in *their* way,) as *you* laid to sleep *your* prudent peace-maker, Mr. *Winthrop*, did they honor this their prudent and peaceable prince; yea,

---

* Hutchinson, i. 458, who met with this account in MS.; but we do not give implicit credit to it, as, at best, it is tradition.

† This spelling does not convey the true pronunciation of the name; other spellings will be noticed in the course of his biography. Its sound approached so near the Latin word *canonicus*, that it became confounded with it. *Qunnoune* was early written.

‡ Manuscript letter to the governor of Massachusetts.

through all their towns and countries how frequently do many, and oft times, our Englishmen travel alone with safety and loving kindness?"

The following statement of *Roger Williams* is in a deposition, dated Narraganset, 18 June, 1682, and, although varying a little from the above, contains facts very pertinent to our purpose. He says, "I testify that it was the general and constant declaration, that *Canonicus* his father had three sons, whereof *Canonicus* was the heir, and his youngest brother's son *Meantinomy* (because of his youth) was his marshal and executioner, and did nothing without his uncle *Canonicus'* consent. And therefore I declare to posterity, that were it not for the favor that God gave me with *Canonicus*, none of these parts, no, not Rhode Island, had been purchased or obtained; for I never got any thing of *Canonicus* but by gift."

When Mr. *John Oldham* was killed near Block Island, and an investigation set on foot by the English to ascertain the murderers, they were fully satisfied that *Canonicus* and *Miantunnomoh* had no hand in the affair, but that "the six other Narraganset sachems had." No wonder he took great offence at the conduct of the English concerning the death of *Miantunnomoh*. The Warwick settlers considered it a great piece of injustice, and Mr. *Samuel Gorton* wrote a letter for *Canonicus* to the government of Massachusetts, notifying them that he had resolved to be revenged upon the Mohegans. Upon this the English despatched messengers to Narraganset to inquire of *Canonicus* whether he authorized the letter. He treated them with great coldness, and would not admit them into his wigwam for the space of two hours after their arrival, although it was exceedingly rainy. When they were admitted, he frowned upon them, and gave them answers foreign to the purpose, and referred them to *Pessacus*. This was a very cold reception, compared with that which the messengers received when sent to him for information respecting the death of Mr. *Oldham*. "They returned with acceptance and good success of their business; observing in the sachem much state, great command of his men, and marvellous wisdom in his answers; and in the carriage of the whole treaty, clearing himself and his neighbors of the murder, and offering revenge of it, yet upon very safe and wary conditions."

This sachem is said to have governed in great harmony with his nephew. "The chiefest government in the country is divided between a younger sachem, *Miantunnomu*, and an elder sachem, *Caunaunacus*, of about fourscore years old,* this young man's uncle; and their agreement in the government is remarkable. The old sachem will not be offended at what the young sachem doth; and the young sachem will not do what he conceives will displease his uncle."† With this passage before him, Mr. *Durfee* versifies as follows, in his poem called *Whatcheer*:—

> "Two mighty chiefs, one cautious, wise, and old,
> One young, and strong, and terrible in fight,
> All Narraganset and Coweset hold;
> One lodge they build—one counsel fire they light."

"At a meeting of the commissioners of the United Colonies at Boston, vij Sept., 1643," it was agreed that Massachusetts, in behalf of the other colonies, "give *Conoonacus* and the Nanohiggunsets to understand, that from time to time" they have taken notice of their violation of the covenant between them, notwithstanding the great manifestations of their love to them by the English; that they had concurred with *Miantunnomoh* in his late mischievous plots, by which he had intended "to root out the body of the English" from the country, by gifts and allurements to other Indians; and that he had invaded *Uncas*, contrary to the "tripartie covenant" between himself, *Uncas*, and Connecticut. Therefore, knowing "how peaceable *Conanacus* and *Mascus*, the late father of *Myantenomo*, governed that great people," they ascribed the late "tumults and outbreakings" to the malicious, rash and ambitious spirit of *Miantunnomoh*, more than to "any affected way of their own."

Notwithstanding, *Miantunnomoh* being now put to death, the English and their confederate Indian sachems, namely, "*Vncus*, sagamore of the Mohegins,

---

* This was written about 1643

† Col. R. I. Hist. Soc. vol. i.

and his people, *Woosamequine* and his people, *Sacanocoe* and his people, *Pumham* and his people, were disposed, they said, still to have peace with the Narragansets; but should expect a more faithful observance of their agreement than they had shown hitherto." This determination was to be immediately laid before them, and a prompt answer demanded.

In a grave assembly, upon a certain occasion, *Canonicus* thus addressed *Roger Williams:* "I have never suffered any wrong to be offered to the English since they landed, nor never will;" and often repeated the word *Wunnaunewayean.* "If the Englishman speak true, if he mean truly, then shall I go to my grave in peace, and hope that the English and my posterity shall live in love and peace together."

When Mr. *Williams* said he hoped he had no cause to question the Englishmen's *wunnaumwaúonck,* that is, faithfulness, having long been acquainted with it, *Canonicus* took a stick, and, breaking it into ten pieces, related ten instances wherein they had proved false; laying down a piece at each instance. Mr. *Williams* satisfied him that he was mistaken in some of them, and as to others he agreed to intercede with the governor, who, he doubted not, would make satisfaction for them.

In 1635, Rev. *Roger Williams* found *Canonicus* and *Miantunnomoh* carrying on a bloody war against the Wampanoags. By his intercession an end was put to it, and he grew much in favor with all the sachems; especially *Canonicus* whose "heart (he says) was stirred up to love me as his son to his last gasp." He sold the Island of Rhode Island to *William Coddington, Roger Williams,* and others. A son of *Canonicus,* named *Mriksah,* is named by *Williams* as inheriting his father's spirit. This son is also called *Meika,* who, after his father's death, was chief sachem of the Narragansets, and was said to have been his eldest son. Many particulars of him will be found in our progress onward.

At the time of the Pequot war, much pains was taken to secure the friendship of *Canonicus* more firmly. Mr. *Williams* wrote to Governor *Winthrop* concerning him as follows: "Sir, if any thing be sent to the princes, I find *Canounicus* would gladly accept of a box of eight or ten pounds of sugar, and indeed he told me he would thank Mr. Governor for a box full." In another letter which Mr. *Williams* sent to the same by *Miantunnomoh* himself, he says, "I am bold to request a word of advice of you concerning a proposition made by *Caunounicus* and *Miantunnomu* to me some half year since. *Caunounicus* gave an island in this bay to Mr. *Oldham,* by name *Chibachuwese,* upon condition, as it should seem, that he would dwell there near unto them." The death of Mr. *Oldham,* it appears, prevented his accepting it, and they offered it to Mr. *Williams* upon the same conditions; but he first desired to know whether, in so doing, it would be perfectly agreeable to Massachusetts, and that he had no idea of accepting, without paying the chiefs for it; said he told them "once and again, that for the present he mind not to remove; but if he had it, would give them satisfaction for it, and build a little house and put in some swine, as understanding the place to have store of fish and good feeding for swine." When *Miantunnomoh* heard that some of the Massachusetts men thought of occupying some of the islands, *Canonicus,* he says, desired he would accept of half of it, "it being spectacle-wise, and between a mile or two in circuit;" but Mr. *Williams* wrote to inform them that, if he had any he desired the whole. This was not long before the Pequot war, which probably put a stop to further negotiation upon the subject.

There was another chief of the same name in *Philip's* war, which Mr. *Hubbard* denominates "the great sachem of the Narragansets," and who, "distrusting the proffers of the English, was slain in the woods by the Mohawks, his squaw surrendering herself: by this means her life was spared." He was probably a younger son of *Canonicus,* or an immediate descendant.

In 1632, a war broke out between the Narragansets and the Pequots, on account of disputed right to the lands between Paucatuck River and Wecapaug Brook.* It was a tract of considerable consequence, being about ten miles

* "The natives are very exact and punctual in the bounds of their lands, belonging to this

wide, and fifteen or twenty long. *Canonicus* drew along with him, besides his own men, several of the Massachusetts sagamores. This was maintained with ferocity and various success, until 1635, when the Pequots were driven from it, but who, it would seem, considered themselves but little worsted; for *Canonicus*, doubting his ability to hold possession long, and ashamed to have it retaken from him, made a present of it to one of his captains, who had fought heroically in conquering it; but he never held possession: however, after the Pequots were subdued by the English, these lands were possessed by the Narragansets again.

The name of this Pequot captain was SOKOSO, sometimes called *Soso*, *Sosoa*, &c. He had killed one of his countrymen and fled to the Narragansets, who protected him. This tract of country was afterwards in dispute between the English. *Sokoso* having deeded it to some of them, (9 June, 1660,) an Englishman afterwards testified, that *Sokoso* had acknowledged, that, although he had received money for it, he never owned it. But, according to the testimony of *Wawaloam*, the wife of *Miantunnomoh*, there was doubtless some false swearing about it. It was reckoned to contain 20,000 acres, and the following is attested concerning it:—"I, *Wawaloam*, do affirm it to be *Socho's* or his assigns', and further, whereas my uncle *Nenegrad* sayeth that it is his land, I do utterly deny it before all men; for it was conquered by my husband *Miantonomy*, and my uncle *Canonicus*, long before the English had any wars with the Pequots; and my uncle *Ninegrad* had no hand in the war. This land was given and past over to the valiant Captain *Socho*, for service done for us before the English had any wars with the Pequots." *

It is said that, in the war between *Uncas* and *Miantunnomoh*, two of the sons of *Canonicus* fought on the side of *Miantunnomoh*, and were wounded when he was taken prisoner at Sachem's Plain.

Canonicus has been the subject of a poem which was published at Boston, in 1803.† Among the tolerable passages are the following:—

"A mighty prince, of venerable age,
A peerless warrior, but of peace the friend;
His breast a treasury of maxims sage—
His arm, a host—to punish or defend."

Canonicus, at the age of 84 years, is made to announce his approaching dissolution to his people thus:—

"I die.—My friends, you have no cause to grieve:
To abler hands my regal power I leave.
Our god commands—to fertile realms I haste,
Compared with which your gardens are a waste.
There in full bloom eternal spring abides,
And swarming fishes glide through azure tides;
Continual sunshine gilds the cloudless skies,
No mists conceal Keesuckquand from our eyes."

About 1642, a son of *Canonicus* died, at which his grief was very great; insomuch that, "having buried his son, he burned his own palace, and all his goods in it, to a great value, in solemn remembrance of his son."

Like other men ignorant of science, *Canonicus* was superstitious, and was greatly in fear of the English, chiefly, perhaps, from a belief in their ability to hurt him by enchantment, which belief, very probably, was occasioned by the story that *Squanto* circulated, of which, in a previous chapter, we have spoken. When *Roger Williams* fled into his country, he at first viewed him with distrust, and would only frown upon him; at length he accused him, as well as the other English, of sending the plague among the Indians; but, as we have said before, he soon became reconciled to him, gave him lands, and even protected him. They became mutual helps to each other, and, but for animosities among the English themselves, it may be fair to conclude, friendship would have continued with the Narragansets through several generations.

or that prince or people, even to a river, brook, &c. And I have known them make bargain and sale amongst themselves, for a small piece, or quantity of ground; notwithstanding a sinful opinion amongst many, that Christians have right to heathen's lands." *R. Williams.*

* See *Potter's* History of Narraganset, in Col. R. I. His Soc. iii. 248.

† By *John Lathrop*, A. M. in 8vo.

Miantunnomoh * was the son of a chief called *Mascus*, nephew of *Canonicus*, brother or brother-in-law to *Ninigret*,† and brother of *Otash*. And, from a manuscript ‡ among the papers of the late Dr. *Trumbull*, it appears that *Mossup*, or *Mosipe*,§ and *Canjanaquond*,‖ were also his brothers.

"This *Miantonimo*," says Mr. *Hubbard*, "was a very good personage, [that is, well made,] of tall stature, subtil and cunning in his contrivements, as well as haughty in his designs."¶

As early as 3 Aug. 1632, this chief came with his wife to Boston, where he staid two nights. He was then known by the name of *Mecumeh*. While here he went to church with the English, and in the mean while, some of his men, twelve of whom had accompanied him, it seems, broke into a house, and committed a theft, on 5 March. Complaint was made to the English governor, who "told the sachem of it, and with some difficulty caused him to make one of his sannaps ** beat them." The authors of the mischief were immediately sent out of town, but *Miantunnomoh* and the others, the governor took to his house, "and made much of them."††

The English seem always to have been more favorably inclined towards other tribes than to the Narragansets, as appears from the stand they took in the wars between them and their enemies. And so long as other tribes succeeded against them, the English were idle spectators; but whenever the scale turned in their favor, they were not slow to intercede.

In the Life of *Canonicus*, the part *Miantunnomoh* exercised in the government of the great nation of the Narragansets is related.

In 1634, Captains *Stone* and *Norton* were killed by the Pequots, and in 1636, Mr. *John Oldham*, by the Indians "near Block Island." *Miantunnomoh* did all in his power to assist in apprehending the murderers, and was at much pains and trouble in furnishing the English with facts relative thereto, from time to time. And when it was told at Boston that there was a cessation of hostilities between the Narragansets and Pequots, *Miantunnomoh* was immediately ordered to appear there, which he did without delay, and agreed to assist them in a war against the Pequots; without whose aid and concurrence, the English would hardly have dared to engage in a war against them at that time.

Early in 1637, (March 21,) to show the governor of Massachusetts that he kept his promise of warring against the Pequots, *Miantunnomoh* sent him, by 26 of his men, a Pequot's hand and 40 fathom of wampom. The war with them now commenced, and though of short duration, destroyed them to such a degree, that they appeared no more as a nation. One hundred of the Narragansets joined themselves with the English in its accomplishment, and received a part of the prisoners as slaves for their services.‡‡ When the war was over, *Miantunnomoh* still adhered to the English, and seized upon such of the Pequots as had made their escape from bondage, and returned them to their English masters; gave up to them his claim of Block Island, and other places where the English had found Pequots, and which they considered as belonging to them by right of conquest.

About the same time, or in the course of the year 1638, troubles had grown to an alarming height between the Narragansets and Mohegans, and, as usual,

---

* This spelling is according to *Winthrop:* we prefer *Williams's* method, as more correct, which is *Miantunnomu;* but, having employed the former in our first edition, it is retained in this. It is, however, oftener written *Myantonimo* now, which only shows another pronunciation. The accent is usually upon the penultimate syllable. See *Callender's Cent. Discourse*, page 1.

† MSS. of *R. Williams*.

‡ Now published in the *Coll. Mass. Hist. Soc.*

§ Called also *Cussusquench*, or *Sucquaneh*, and *Paticus;* that is, *Pessacus*. He "was killed by the Moqui, [Mohawks,] in the wilderness, about 20 miles above Pisataqua, in his travel eastward, in the time of the Indian wars, and other Indians with him, and were buried by order of Major *Waldron*." 3 *Coll. Mass. Hist. Soc.*

‖ "Receaued this First of Iuly, 1659, of Maj[r]. *Humfrey Aderton*, [*Atherton*,] and the rest of his friends, the sume of 75 pounds in Wampam peag wth seueral other things as gratuity for certaine lands giuen y[e] said Maj[r]. *Aderton* and his friends, as may appeare by two seuerall deeds of gift. I say receaued by me.

Coginaquan — *his mark*."

[*MS. Documents*.

¶ *Hist. New Eng.* 446.

** A name the sachems gave their attendants.

†† *Winthrop's* Journal.

‡‡ *Miantunnomoh* received eighty. *Mather's Relation*, 39.

Roger Williams exercised all his skill to restore tranquillity. Many of the Pequots who had escaped the sword of the war of 1637, were among the Mohegans, and seem to have taken part with them against *Miantunnomoh.* They did this, no doubt, that the Mohegans might screen them from the English, who were still seizing on all of that nation against whom they could find any cause of suspicion of having been engaged in murdering the English, or in arms against them.

Miantunnomoh, it is probable, had been ordered before the magistrates of Connecticut, to give some account of the Pequot refugees in the hands of the Mohegans, as well as of those in his nation; which may have been a main cause of the war they had now waged against him. For, when he set out for Hartford, he had a guard of "upwards of 150 men, and many sachems, and his wife and children." Mr. *Williams* was with him, and strongly urged him not to venture upon the journey, even with this force, because of the hostility of the Mohegans; but the sachem would not be dissuaded, although he had no doubt that the Mohegans and their Pequots were in great force not far off. And while they were on their march, "about 660" of them fell upon the Wunnashowatuckoogs, a tribe under *Canonicus,* where they committed extensive robberies, and destroyed "about 23 fields of corn."

Notwithstanding this great Mohegan army had prepared an ambush to intercept and cut off *Miantunnomoh,* and gave out a threat *that they would boil him in a kettle,* yet he went to, and returned safe from, Connecticut.*

On this occasion he discovers great bravery, if it border not too closely upon temerity; for, when *Williams* urged him to retreat, they had performed half their journey, or about 50 miles; and *Miantunnomoh's* answer was, after holding a council with his chiefs, "that no man should turn back, resolving rather all to die."

The Mohegan sachem, *Uncas,* was at the same time ordered to appear at Hartford, to give an account of the Pequot warriors, or murderers, as the English called them, in his keeping, as well as to effect a reconciliation of differences between him and *Miantunnomoh;* but, instead of appearing, he sent a messenger, with word that he was lame and could not come. The governor of Connecticut, Mr. *Haynes,* at once saw through the artifice, and observed that it was a *lame* excuse, and immediately sent for him to come without delay.

Whether cured of his *lameness* or not before coming, we are not informed; but, in a few days after, the subtle sachem appeared, not daring to forfeit the friendship of the English, which, it seems, he preferred to hiding longer his guilty face from the presence of the magnanimous *Miantunnomoh.*

Now before the English, *Uncas* was charged with the depredations, some of which were too well attested to admit of a denial, and others were disowned in part. The inquiry seems to have ended after the parties were tired of it, without any advantage to the injured Narragansets, and we hear of no measures taken for their relief.

The next thing in order was a call upon *Uncas* for an account of the Pequots which he was sheltering, which resulted only in a new series of falsehoods from him. When he was requested to give their names, he said *he knew none of them,* and that there were but 20 in his dominions. Whereupon witnesses were called, whose testimonies proved, in his presence, that his statement was false. "Then he acknowledged that he had 30." At length Mr. *Haynes* dismissed him, with orders to bring in their names in 10 days, or he would take those Indians by force out of his country. But, when *Miantunnomoh* was called upon for the names of those with him, nothing was withheld.

At this time, at the request of the English, *Miantunnomoh* consented to lay aside all animosities, and take *Uncas* by the hand. When he had done this, he urged *Uncas* to dine with him; but the guilty sachem would not, though pressed by the English for some time to do so; and thus all efforts to bring about a peace vanished. †

---

* Coll. R. I. Hist. Soc. iii. 145. † Ibid. iii. 146, 147.

Rev. *Samuel Gorton* and his associates purchased Shaomet, afterwards called Warwick, from the Earl of Warwick, of *Miantunnomoh;* but, as *Gorton* could do nothing right in the eyes of the Puritans of Massachusetts, *Pumham* was instigated to claim said tract of country; and, although a sachem under *Miantunnomoh*,* did not hesitate, when supported by the English, to assert his claim as chief sachem. And the government of Massachusetts, to give to their interference the appearance of disinterestedness, which it would seem, from their own vindication, they thought there was a chance to doubt, "Send for the foresaid sachems, [who had complained of Mr. *Gorton* and others, through the instigation of the English,] and upon examination find, both by English and Indian testimony, that *Miantonomo* was only a usurper, and had no title to the foresaid lands." † This is against the testimony of every record, and could no more have been believed *then*, than that *Philip* was not sachem of Pokanoket. In all cases of purchase, in those times, the chief sachem's grant was valid, and maintained, in almost every instance, by the purchaser or grantee. It was customary, generally, to make the inferior sachems, and sometimes all their men, presents, but it was by no means a law. The chief sachems often permitted those under them to dispose of lands also, without being called to account. This was precisely the situation of things in the Warwick controversy, of which we shall have occasion again to speak, when we come to the life of *Pumham*.

In March, 1638, *Miantunnomoh*, with four other sachems, sold to *William Coddington* and others, the island now called Rhode Island, also most of the others in Narraganset bay, "for the full payment of 40 fathom of white peag, to be equally divided" between them. Hence *Miantunnomoh* received eight fathom. He was to "have ten coats and twenty hoes to give to the present inhabitants, that they shall remove themselves from the island before next winter."

The deed of this purchase, a copy of which is in my possession, is dated 24th March, and runs thus: "We, *Canonicas* and *Meantinomie*, the two chief sachems of Naragansets, by virtue of our general command of this Bay, as also the particular subjecting of the dead sachems of Aquednick, Kitackamucknut, themselves and lands unto us, have sold unto Mr. *Coddington* and his friends * * the great Island of Aquidnick, lying from hence [Providence] eastward * * also the marshes, grass upon Qunnonigat and the rest of the islands in the bay, excepting Chabatewece, formerly sold unto Mr. *Winthrop*, the now Gov. of Mass. and Mr. *Williams* of Providence, also the grass upon the rivers and coves about Kitackamuckqut, and from thence to Paupasquat."

"*The mark of* CONONICUS.
The mark of YOTNESH, [OTASH, *brother of* MIANTUNNOMOH.]
The mark of MEANTINOMIE.
The mark of ASOTAMNET.
The mark of MEIHAMMOH, CANONICUS *his son*.

"This witnesseth that I, *Wanamatanamet*, the present sachem of the island, have received five fathom of wampum and consent to the contents.

The mark of WANAMATANAMET.

"Memorandum. I, *Osemequon*, freely consent" that they may "make use of any grass or trees on the main land on Pocasicke side," having receiued five fathom of wampum also.

The mark of △ OSAMEQUEN.

As late as 21 Sept. 1638, the hand of *Miantunnomoh* is set to an instrument, with that of *Uncas*. Said instrument was a treaty of peace, a bond for the settling of difficulties between these two sachems and their men and an

* "The law of the Indians in all America is, that the inferior sachems and subjects shall plant and remove at the pleasure of the highest and supreme sachems." *Roger Williams* This is authority, and we need no other commentary on the arbitrary proceedings of the court of Massachusetts.

† In *manuscript* on file, at the state-house, Boston.

obligation from both to appeal to the English when any difficulty should arise between them. This treaty was done at Hartford, the substance of which follows:

1st. Peace and friendship is established between *Miantunnomoh* on the part of the Narragansets, and *Poquim*, as *Uncas* was then sometimes called, on the part of the Mohegans. And all former injuries and wrongs to be forgiven, and never to be renewed.

2d. Each of the sachems agree, "that if there fall out injuries" from either side, they will not revenge them, but that they will appeal to the English, whose decision shall stand; and if either party refuse to submit, "it shall be lawful for the English to compel him."

3d. The sachems further covenant with the English, that they nor none of their people shall harbor any Indians who shall be enemies to them, or shall have murdered any white people. They further agree that they will, "as soon as they can, either bring the chief sachem of our late enemies the Peaquots, that had the chief hand in killing the English, to the sd English, or take of" his head. As to the "murders that are now agreed upon amongst us that are living, they shall, as soon as they can possibly, take off their heads."

4th. And whereas it is agreed that there are now among the Narragansets and Mohegans, 200 Pequot men, besides squaws and papooses; this article is to provide, that the Narragansets have enough of them to make up 80, with the 11 they have already, "and *Poquime* his number, and that after they, the Peaquots, shall be divided as above, shall no more be called Peaquots, but Narragansets and Mohegans." They agree to pay for every sanop one fathom of wampom, and for every youth half as much—"and for every sanop papoose one hand to be paid at killing-time of corn at Connecticut yearly, and shall not suffer them for to live in the country that was formerly theirs, but is now the English's. Neither shall the Narragansets or Mohegans possess any part of the Pequot country without leaue of them."

JOHN HAINES,	MIANTINOMMY, •,
ROG'R LUDLOW,	POQUIAM, *alias* UNKAS. +"
EDW'RD HOPKINS.	

The wife of *Miantunnomoh*, named WAWALOAM, was alive as late as 1661, as appears by an information which she gave, dated 25 June, concerning the right of *Sokoso* to sell the lands adjacent to Wecapaug.

On a time previous to 1643, *Roger Williams* delivered a discourse to some Indians at their residence, as he was passing through their country. *Miantunnomoh* was present, and seemed inclined to believe in Christianity. Mr. *Williams*, being much fatigued, retired to rest, while *Miantunnomoh* and others remained to converse upon what they had heard. One said to the chief, "Our fathers have told us that our souls go to the south-west;" *Miantunnomoh* rejoined, "How do you know your souls go to the south-west? did you ever see a soul go that way?" (Still he was rather inclined to believe, as Mr. *Williams* had just said, that they went up to heaven or down to hell.) The other added, "When did he (meaning *Williams*) ever see a soul go up to heaven or down to hell?"

We have given the above anecdote, which is thought a good illustration of the mind of man under the influence of a superstitious or prejudiced education.

When it was reported, in 1640, that *Miantunnomoh* was plotting to cut off the English, as will be found mentioned in the account of *Ninigret*, and several English were sent to him in July, to know the truth of the matter, he would not talk with them through a Pequot interpreter, because he was then at war with that nation. In other respects he complied with their wishes, and treated them respectfully, agreeing to come to Boston, for the gratification of the government, if they would allow Mr. *Williams* to accompany him. This they would not consent to, and yet he came, agreeably to their desires. We shall presently see who acted best the part of civilized men in this affair

He had refused to use a Pequot interpreter for good reasons, but when he was at Boston, and surrounded by armed men, he was obliged to submit. "The governor being as resolute as he, refused to use any other interpreter, thinking it a dishonor to us to give so much way to them!" The great wisdom of the government now displayed itself in the person of Governor *Thomas Dudley.* It is not to be expected but that *Miantunnomoh* should resent their proceedings; for to the above insult they added others; "would show him no countenance, nor admit him to dine at our table, as formerly he had done, till he had acknowledged his failing, &c., which he readily did."* By their own folly, the English had made themselves jealous of a powerful chief, and they appear ever ready afterwards to credit evil reports of him.

That an independent chief should be obliged to conform to transitory notions upon such an occasion, is absolutely ridiculous; and the justness of the following remark from him was enough to have shamed good men into their senses. He said, "*When your people come to me, they are permitted to use their own fashions, and I expect the same liberty when I come to you.*"

In 1642, Connecticut became very suspicious of *Miantunnomoh,* and urged Massachusetts to join them in a war against him. Their fears no doubt grew out of the consideration of the probable issue of a war with *Uncas* in his favor, which was now on the point of breaking out. Even Massachusetts did not think their suspicions well founded; yet, according to their request, they sent to *Miantunnomoh,* who, as usual, gave them satisfactory answers, and, agreeably to their request, came again to Boston. Two days were employed by the court of Massachusetts in deliberating with him, and we are astonished at the wisdom of the great chief, even as reported by his enemies.

That a simple man of nature, who never knew courts or law, should cause such acknowledgments as follow, from the *civilized* and *wise,* will always be contemplated with intense admiration. "When he came," says *Winthrop,* "the court was assembled, and before his admission, we considered how to treat with him, for we knew him to be a very subtle man." When he was admitted, "he was set down at the lower end of the table, over against the governor," but would not at any time speak upon business, unless some of his counsellors were present; saying, "he would have them present, that they might bear witness with him, at his return home, of all his sayings." The same author further says, "In all his answers he was very deliberate, and showed good understanding in the principles of justice and equity, and ingenuity withal."

He now asked for his accusers, urging, that if they could not establish their allegations, they ought to suffer what he expected to, if they did; but the court said *they knew of none;* that is, they knew not whom they were, and therefore gave no credit to the reports until they had advised him according to a former agreement. He then said, "If you did not give credit to it, why then did you disarm the Indians?" Massachusetts having just then disarmed some of the Merrimacks under some pretence. "He gave divers reasons," says Governor *Winthrop,*† "why we should hold him free of any such conspiracy, and why we should conceive it was a report raised by *Uncas,* &c. and therefore offered to meet *Uncas,* and would prove to his face his treachery against the English, &c., and told us he would come to us at any time," although he said some had tried to dissuade him, saying that the English would put him to death, yet he feared nothing, as he was innocent of the charges against him.‡

The punishment due to those who had raised the accusations, bore heavily upon his breast, and "he put it to our consideration what damage it had been to him, in that he was forced to keep his men at home, and not suffer them to go forth on hunting, &c., till he had given the English satisfaction." After two days spent in talk, the council issued to the satisfaction of the English.

During the council, a table was set by itself for the Indians, which *Mian-*

* *Winthrop's* Journal.

† See book iii. chap. vii.

‡ Here, the reader may with propriety exclaim, was another *Michael Servetus:*—"*Pourquoy, Messeigneurs, je demande que mon faulx accusateur soit* puni pœna talionis," &c. Roscoe's *Leo* X. iv. 457.

tunnomoh appears not to have liked, and "would not eat, until some food had been sent him from that of the governor's."

That wisdom seems to have dictated to Massachusetts, in her answer to Connecticut; must be acknowledged; but, as justice to *Miantunnomoh* abundantly demanded such decision, credit in this case is due only to them, as to him who does a good act because it was his interest so to do. They urged Connecticut not to commence war alone, "alleging how dishonorable it would be to us all, that, while we were upon treaty with the Indians, they should make war upon them; for they would account their act as our own, seeing we had formerly professed to the Indians, that we were all as one; and in our last message to *Miantunnomoh*, had remembered him again of the same, and he had answered that he did so account us. Upon receipt of this our answer, they forbare to enter into a war, but (it seemed) unwillingly, and as not well pleased with us." The main consideration which caused Massachusetts to decide against war was, "That all those informations [furnished by Connecticut] might arise from a false ground, and out of the enmity which was between the Narraganset and Mohigan" sachems. This was no doubt one of the real causes; and, had *Miantunnomoh* overcome *Uncas*, the English would, from policy, as gladly have leagued with him as with the latter; for it was constantly pleaded in those days, that their safety must depend on a union with some of the most powerful tribes.

There can be no doubt, on fairly examining the case, that *Uncas* used many arts, to influence the English in his favor, and against his enemy. In the progress of the war between the two great chiefs, the English acted precisely as the Indians have been always said to do—stood aloof, and watched the scale of victory, determined to join the conquerors: and we will here digress for a moment, to introduce a character, more fully to illustrate the cause of the operations of the English against the chief of the Narragansets.

Miantunnomoh had a wretched enemy in *Waiandance*, a Long Island sachem, who had assisted in the destruction of the Pequots, at their last retreat. He revealed the plots and plans of *Miantunnomoh;* and, says *Lion Gardener*, "he told me many years ago," as all the plots of the Narragansets had been discovered, they now concluded to let the English alone until they had destroyed *Uncas* and himself, then, with the assistance of the Mohawks, "and Indians beyond the Dutch, and all the northern and eastern Indians, would easily destroy us, man and mother's son."

Mr. *Gardener* next relates that he met with *Miantunnomoh* at Meanticut, *Waiandance's* country, on the east end of Long Island. That *Miantunnomoh* was there, as *Waiandance* said, to break up the intercourse with those Indians. There were others with *Miantunnomoh*, and what they said to *Waiandance* was as follows:—

"*You must give no more wampum to the English, for they are no sachems, nor none of their children shall be in their place if they die. They have no tribute given them. There is but one king in England, who is over them all, and if you should send him* 100,000 *fathom of wampum, he would not give you a knife for it, nor thank you.*" Then said *Waiandance*, "They will come and kill us all, as they did the Pequits;" but replied the Narragansets, "*No, the Pequots gave them wampum and beaver, which they loved so well, but they sent it them again, and killed them because they had killed an Englishman; but you have killed none, therefore give them nothing.*"

Some time after, *Miantunnomoh* went again, "with a troop of men, to the same place, and, instead of receiving presents as formerly, he gave presents to *Waiandance* and his people, and made the following speech:—

"Brothers, we must be one as the English are, or we shall soon all be destroyed. You know our fathers had plenty of deer and skins, and our plains were full of deer and of turkeys, and our coves and rivers were full of fish. But, brothers, since these English have seized upon our country, they cut down the grass with scythes, and the trees with axes. Their cows and horses eat up the grass, and their hogs spoil our beds of clams; and finally we shall starve to death! Therefore, stand not in your own light, I beseech you, but resolve with us to act like men. All the sachems both to the east and west have joined with us, and we are all resolved to fall upon them, at a day appointed, and therefore I have come secretly to you, because you can persuade the Indians to do what you will. Brothers, I will send over 50 Indians to Manisses, and 30 to you from thence, and take an 100 of Southampton Indians, with an 100 of your own here. And, when you see the three fires that will be made at the end of 40 days hence, in a clear night, then act as we act, and the next day fall on and kill men, women and children, but no cows; they must be killed as we need them for provisions, till the deer come again."

To this speech all the old men said, "*Wurregen*," i. e. "IT IS WELL." But this great plot, if the account given by *Waiandance* be true, was by him brought to the knowledge of the English, and so failed. "And the plotter," says *Gardener*, "next spring after, did as *Ahab* did at Ramoth-Gilead.—So he to Mohegan,* and there had his fall."†

Capture and death of Miantunnomoh.—The war brought on between *Uncas* and *Miantunnomoh* was not within the jurisdiction of the English, nor is it to be expected that they could with certainty determine the justness of its cause. The broil had long existed, but the open rupture was brought on by *Uncas'* making war upon *Sequasson*, one of the sachems under *Miantunnomoh*. The English accounts say, (and we have no other,) that about 1000 warriors were raised by *Miantunnomoh*, who came upon *Uncas* unprepared, having only about 400 men; yet, after an obstinate battle, in which many were killed on both sides, the Narragansets were put to flight, and *Miantunnomoh* taken prisoner; that he endeavored to save himself by flight, but, having on a coat of mail, was known from the rest, and seized by two‡ of his own men, who hoped by their treachery to save their own lives. Whereupon they immediately delivered him up to the conqueror. *Uncas* slew them both instantly; probably with his own hand. This specimen of his *bravery* must have had a salutary effect on all such as afterwards chanced to think of acting the part of traitors in their wars, at least among the Narragansets.

The English of Rhode Island rather favored the cause of the Narragansets, nor could a different course be expected of them, satisfied as they were, that that nation were greatly wronged; while, on the other hand, Connecticut and Massachusetts rather favored the Mohegans. That *Miantunnomoh* should not suffer in his person, in battles which, it was now seen, were inevitable, *Samuel Gorton* furnished him with a heavy old English armor, or coat of mail; and this, instead of being beneficial, as it was intended, proved the destruction of his friend. For, when a retreat became necessary, not being used to this kind of caparison, it both obstructed his efforts at resistance and his means of flight. About 30 of his men were killed, and many more were wounded.

Being brought before *Uncas*, he remained without speaking a word, until *Uncas* spoke to him, and said, "*If you had taken me, I would have besought you for my life.*" He then took his prisoner to Hartford, and at his request left him a prisoner with the English, until the mind of the United Colonies should be known as to what disposition should be made of him.

The sorrowful part of the tale is yet to be told. The commissioners of the United Colonies, having convened at Boston, "taking into serious consideration, they say, what was safest and best to be done, were all of opinion that it would not be safe to set him at liberty, neither had we sufficient ground for us to put him to death."§ The awful design of putting to death *their friend* they had not yet fixed upon; but, calling to their aid in council "*five of the most judicious elders*," "*they* all agreed that *he ought to be put to death.*" This was the final decision; and, to complete the deed of darkness, secrecy was enjoined upon all. And their determination was to be made known to *Uncas*

* This goes to show that *Miantunnomoh* was not killed above Hartford, as *Winthrop* states; for the country at some distance from the mouth of Pequot River was called *Mohegan*. It probably included Windsor.

† 3 *Coll. Mass. Hist. Soc.* iii. 155.

‡ In the records, (*Hazard*, ii. 48,) but one person is mentioned as having taken *Miantunnomoh*, whose name was *Tantoqueson;* and there he is called a Mohegan captain. That therefore the Narragansets tried to kill him; came upon him once in the night, and dangerously wounded him, as he lay in his wigwam asleep. See *note* in the *Life of Ninigret.*

§ *Winthrop*, ii. 131

privately, with direction that he should execute him within his own jurisdiction, and without torture.

From their own account of this affair, the English (of the United Colonies) stand condemned in the trial of time at the bar of history. It is allowed that *Uncas* had made war upon *Sequasson*, in July, 1643, and done him much injury;* and that, according to a previous agreement with the English, *Miantunnomoh* had complained to the governor of Massachusetts of the conduct of *Uncas*, and had received answer from him, "that, if *Uncas* had done him or his friends wrong, and would not give satisfaction, he was left to take his own course." No account is given that *Sequasson* had injured *Uncas*, but that *Uncas* "set upon *Sequasson*, and killed 7 or 8 of his men, wounded 13, burnt his wigwams, and carried away the booty."*

We will now go to the record, which will enable us to judge of the justness of this matter. When the English had determined that *Uncas* should execute *Miantunnomoh*, *Uncas* was ordered to be sent for to Hartford, "with some considerable number of his best and trustiest men," to take him to a place for execution, "carrying him into the next part of his own government, and there put him to death: provided that some discreet and faithful persons of the English accompany them, and see the execution, for our more full satisfaction; and that the English meddle not with the head or body at all."†

The commissioners at the same time ordered, "that Hartford furnish *Uncas* with a competent strength of English to defend him against any present fury or assault, of the Nanohiggunsetts or any other." And "that in case *Uncas* shall refuse to execute justice upon *Myantenomo*, that then *Myantenomo* be sent by sea to the Massachusetts, there to be kept in safe durance till the commissioners may consider further how to dispose of him."†

Here, then, we see fully developed the real state of the case. The Mohegans had, by accident, captured *Miantunnomoh*, after which event, they were more in fear of his nation than before; which proves, beyond doubt, that they would never have dared to put him to death, had they not been promised the protection of the English

No one can read this account without being reminded of the fate of *Napoleon*. We do not say that the English of New England dreaded the power of *Miantunnomoh* as *much* as those of Old England did that of *Napoleon* afterwards; but that both were sacrificed in consequence of the fears of those into whose power the fortune of wars cast them, will not, we presume, be denied.

When the determination of the commissioners and *elders* was made known to *Uncas*, he "readily undertook the execution, and taking *Miantunnomoh* along with him, in the way between Hartford and Windsor, (where *Uncas* hath some men dwell,) *Uncas*' brother, following after *Miantunnomoh*, clave his head with an hatchet."‡ *Mather* says, they "very fairly cut off his head."§

Dr. *Trumbull*‖ records an account of cannibalism, at this time, which we ought to caution the reader against receiving as true history, as it no doubt rests on the authority of tradition, which is wont to transfer even the transactions of one continent to another, which is this:—"*Uncas* cut out a large piece of his shoulder, and ate it in savage triumph;" saying, "'it was the sweetest meat he ever ate; it made his heart strong.'"¶

---

* *Hubbard*, N. E. 450. † Records of the U. Colonies.

‡ *Winthrop's* Journal, ii. 134. As to the place of *Miantunnomoh's* execution, *Winthrop* seems to have been in a mistake. It is not very likely that he was taken in the opposite direction, from *Uncas's* own country, as Windsor was from Hartford. It is also unlikely that *Uncas* had *men dwell* so far from his country upon the Thames.

A gentleman who lately visited his sepulchre, says the wandering Indians have made a heap of stones upon his grave. It is a well-known custom of the race, to add to a monumental pile of the dead whenever they pass by it. See 3 *Coll. Mass. Hist. Soc.* iii. 135. and *Jefferson's Notes.* ☞ Some wretchedly ignorant neighbors to this sacred pile (whites, of course) have, not long since, taken stones from it to make wall! but enough remain to mark the spot. It is in the east part of Norwich. *Colls. Ibid.*

§ Magnalia. ‖ History of Connecticut, i. 135.

¶ That this is tradition, may be inferred from the circumstance of an *eminently* obscure writer's publishing nearly the same story, which he says, in his book, took place upon the

We are now certain that what Dr. *Trumbull* has given us as unquestionable history, from a "manuscript of Mr. *Hyde*," is only tradition. Having been put in possession of a copy of that manuscript,* we deem it highly important that it should be laid before the world, that its true weight may be considered by all who would be correctly informed in this important transaction.

By way of preliminary to his communication, Mr. *Hyde* says, "The following facts being communicated to me from some of the ancient fathers of this town, who were contemporary with *Uncas*," &c. "That before the settlement of Norwich, the sachem of the Narraganset tribe [*Miantunnomoh*] had a personal quarrel with *Uncas*, and proclaimed war with the Moheg[an]s: and marched with an army of 900 fighting men, equipped with bows and arrows and hatchets. *Uncas* be[ing] informed by spies of their march towards his seat, *Uncas* called his warriors together, about 600, stout, hard men, light of foot, and skilled in the use of the bow; and, upon a conference, *Uncas* told his men that it would not do to let y[e] Narragansets come to their town, but they must go and meet them. Accordingly, they marched, and about three miles, on a large plain, the armies met, and both halted within bow-shot. A parley was sounded, and gallant *Uncas* proposed a conference with the Narraganset sachem, who agreed. And being met, *Uncas* saith to his enemy word[s] to this effect: '*You have got a number of brave men with you, and so have I. A'nt it a pity that such brave men should be killed for a quarrel between you and I? Only come like a man, as you pretend to be, and we will fight it out. If you kill me, my men shall be yours; but if I kill you, your men shall be mine.*' Upon which the Narraganset sachem replied: '*My men came to fight, and they shall fight.*'

"*Uncas* having before told his men, that if his enemy should refuse to fight him, he would fall down, and then they were to discharge their artillery [arrows] on them, and fall right on them as fast as they could;" this was done, and the Mohegans rushed upon *Miantunnomoh's* army "like lions," put them to flight, and killed "a number on the spot." They "pursued the rest, driving some down ledges of rocks." The foremost of *Uncas's* men got ahead of *Miantunnomoh*, and impeded his flight, drawing him back as they passed him, "to give *Uncas* opportunity to take him himself."

"In the pursuit, at a place now called *Sachem's Plain*, *Uncas* took him by the shoulder. He then set down, knowing *Uncas*. *Uncas* then gave a whoop, and his men returned to him; and in a council then held, 'twas concluded by them, that *Uncas*, with a guard, should carry said sachem to Hartford, to the governor and magistrates, (it being before the charter,) to advise what they should do with him." "*Uncas* was told by them, as there was no war with the English and Narragansets, it was not proper for them to intermeddle, in the affair, and advised him to take his own way. Accordingly, they brought said Narraganset sachem back to the same spot of ground where he was took: where *Uncas* killed him, and cut out a large piece of his shoulder, roasted, and eat it; and said, '*It was the sweetest meel*† *he ever eat; it made him have strong hart.*' There they bury him, and made a pillar, which I have seen but a few years since."

This communication was in the form of a letter, and dated at Norwich, 9 Oct. 1769, and signed *Richard Hide*. The just remark of Mr. *Ely* upon it I cannot withhold, in justice to my subject.

"The above '*Manuscript of Mr. Hyde*,' as a *tradition*, is a valuable paper, and worthy of preservation; yet, being written 125 years after the event which it describes, it is surprising that Dr. *Trumbull* should have inserted it in his History of Connecticut, in its principal particulars, as matter of fact."‡

In the proceedings of the commissioners of the United Colonies, the main

---

death of *Philip*. *Oneko*, he says, cut out a pound of *Philip's* bleeding body and ate it. The book is by *one Henry Trumbull*, and purports to be a history of the discovery of America, the Indian wars, &c. The reader will find it about stalls by the street-side, but rarely in a respectable book-store. It has been forced through many editions, but there is scarce a word of true history in it.

* By Rev. *Wm. Ely*, of Connecticut.

† *Trumbull* says *meat*, but the MS. is plain, and means *meal*.

‡ Manuscript letter, 1 Mar 1833.

facts in reference to the death of *Miantunnomoh*, contained in the above account, are corroborated. The records of the commissioners say, that *Uncas*, before the battle, told *Miantunnomoh*, that he had many ways sought his life, and now, if he dared, he would fight him in single combat; but that *Miantunnomoh*, "presuming upon his numbers of men, would have nothing but a battle." *

It does not appear from these records, that *Uncas* had any idea of putting *Miantunnomoh* to death, but to extort a great price from his countrymen, for his ransom. That a large amount in wampum was collected for this purpose, appears certain; but, before it was paid, *Uncas* received the decision of the English, and then pretended that he had made no such agreement, or that the quantity or quality was not as agreed upon, as will more at length be seen in the life of *Uncas*.

NINIGRET was often called *Ninicraft*, and sometimes *Nenekunat*, † *Niniglud*, *Nenegelett*; and his name was written almost as many other ways as times mentioned, by some early writers. *Janemo* ‡ was the first name by which he was known to the English. He was generally styled sachem of the Nianticks, a tribe of the Narragansets, whose principal residence was at Wekapaug, now Westerly, in Rhode Island. He was cousin to *Miantunnomoh*, § and is commonly mentioned in history as the chief sachem of the Nianticks, which always made a part of the great nation of the Narragansets. *Ninigret* married a sister of *Cashawashett*, otherwise called *Harmon Garret*, who was his uncle.

The relation in which the Nianticks stood to the Narragansets is plain, from the representation given by *Miantunnomoh* to the government of Massachusetts in 1642. In treating with him, at that time, Governor *Winthrop* says, "Some difficulty we had, to bring him to desert the Nianticks, if we had just cause of war with them. They were," he said, "as his own flesh, being allied by continual intermarriages, &c. But at last he condescended, that if they should do us wrong, as he could not draw them to give us satisfaction for, nor himself could satisfy, as if it were for blood, &c. then he would leave them to us."

On the 12 July, 1637, *Ayanemo*, as his name was written by Governor *Winthrop* at this time, came to Boston with 17 men. The objects of his visit being stated to the governor, he promised him an answer the next day; but the governor, understanding meanwhile, that he had received many of the Pequots, who had taken refuge in his country after their defeat at Mystic, first demanded their delivery to the English. *Ninigret* was very loath to comply with the demand; but, finding he could get no answer to his propositions without, he consented to give up the Pequots, after a day's consideration. The governor shortly after dismissed him, with instructions to treat with the English captains then in the Pequot country.

On the 9 Mar. 1638, "*Miantunnomoh* came to Boston. The governor, deputy and treasurer treated with him, and they parted upon fair terms." "We gave him leave to right himself for the wrongs which *Janemoh* and *Wequash Cook* had done him; and, for the wrong they had done us, we would right ourselves, in our own time." ‖ Hence, it appears that, at this period, they were not so closely allied as they were afterwards.

The next year, *Janemo* was complained of by the Long Island Indians, who paid tribute to the English, that he had committed some robberies upon them. Captain *Mason* was sent from Connecticut with seven men to require satisfaction. *Janemo* went immediately to the English, and the matter was amicably settled. ¶

When it was rumored that *Miantunnomoh* was plotting to cut off the

* See *Hazard's* Historical Collections, ii. 7, 10.

† So written by *Roger Williams*.

‡ Mr. *Prince*, in his edition of *Hubbard's* Narrative, probably mistook *Winthrop's* MS., and wrote *Aganemo* instead of *Ayanemo*. See the edition 1775, of Nar. p. 40, and *Winthrop*, Jour. i. 232.

§ *Prince* says he was *uncle* to *Miantunnomoh*, (*Chronology*, ii. 59.) but that could not have been.

‖ *Winthrop's* Journal, i. 243. ¶ Ibid. i. 267.

English, and using his endeavors to unite other tribes in the enterprise, the English sent deputies to him, to learn the truth of the report, as will be found elsewhere fully stated. The deputies were well satisfied with the carriage of *Miantunnomoh;* but, they say, "*Janemoh*, the Niantick sachem, carried himself proudly, and refused to come to us, or to yield to any thing; only, he said, he would not harm us, except we invaded him." * Thus we cannot but form an exalted opinion of *Ninigret*, in the person of *Janemo*.

A Dutch and Indian war raged at this time, and was conducted with unrelenting barbarity by the former party. It grew out of a single murder, an Indian having killed a Dutchman in a drunken frolic. The murderer was immediately demanded, but could not be obtained; and the governor was urged to retaliate, and often called upon to take revenge. He waived the subject, foreseeing, no doubt, that retaliation was a bad course to pursue for satisfaction, especially with Indians. However, it soon happened that the Mohawks fell upon those Indians, killed about 30 of them, and the rest fled their country; many of whom sought protection from the Dutch themselves. Some evil-minded persons now thought to revenge themselves on these Indians, without the danger of suffering from resistance. It is reported that an inhuman monster, named *Marine*, a Dutch captain, obtained the consent of the governor to kill as many of them as he pleased; and, acting under that authority, surprised and murdered 70 or 80 of them, men, women, and children. No sooner was this blow of assassination struck, than the Indians flew to their arms, and began hostilities of the same kind; and, with such fury was their onset made, that they cut off 20 persons or more, before the alarm could spread; and they were soon masters of their settlements, and the Dutch were confined to their fort. By employing Captain *Underhill*, however, an experienced English officer in the Indian wars, and some others of the English, the Dutch were enabled to maintain their ground; and, fortunately, soon after, *Roger Williams* accidentally arrived there, through whose mediation a peace was effected, and an end was put to a bloody war. This *Marine*, who was the principal cause of it, quarrelled with the governor, on account of his employing *Underhill* instead of him, and even attempted his life on the account of it. He presented a pistol at his breast, which, being turned aside by a bystander, the governor's life was preserved. A servant of *Marine's* then discharged a gun at the governor, but missing him, one of the governor's guard shot the servant dead, and *Marine* was made prisoner, and forthwith sent into Holland. *Williams*, having been denied a passage through N. England by the *law* of banishment, was forced to take passage for England at N. York in a Dutch ship, by way of Holland; and this was the reason of his being there in the time of this war.

Before this war was brought to a close, Captain *Underhill*, with his company of Dutch and English, killed about 300 Indians on the main, and 120 more on Long Island. The Dutch governor's employing the English was charged upon him as a "plot" to engage the English in his quarrel with the Indians; "which," says *Winthrop*, † "we had wholly declined, as doubting of the justice of the cause."

It was about the beginning of this war, Sept. 1643, that "the Indians killed and drove away all the English" on the coast, from Manhattan to Stamford, the extent of the Dutch claim to the eastward. They then passed over "to Long Island, and there assaulted the Lady *Moodey* in her house divers times;" but she, having about 40 men at her place at that time, was able to defend herself. "These Indians at the same time," continues *Winthrop*, ‡ "set upon the Dutch with an implacable fury, and killed all they could come by, and burnt their houses, and killed their cattle without any resistance, so as the governor and such as escaped, betook themselves to their fort at Monhaton, and there lived and eat up their cattle."

Among the English people who were murdered when this war began, was a Mrs. *Ann Hutchinson*, from whom was descended the historian of Massachusetts. She, having given offence to the Puritans of the Bay state, (as Massachusetts was then called,) by her peculiar religious notions, to avoid

* *Winthrop's* Journal, ii. 8. † Ibid. ii. 157. ‡ Ibid. ii. 136.

persecution, fled first to Rhode Island, and afterwards to the Dutch possessions, not far beyond Stamford. This was in 1642. When the Indians broke up the settlements there, in Sept. 1643, they fell upon the family of this woman, killed her, a Mr. *Collins*, her son-in-law, and all her family except one daughter eight years old, whom they carried into captivity, and such of two other families, *Throckmorton* and *Cornhill's*, as were at home; in all 16 persons. They then collected their cattle into the houses and set them on fire and burned them alive! A greater slaughter would have been made at this time and place, but for the arrival of a boat while the tragedy was acting, into which several women and children escaped. But two of the boat's crew were killed in their humane exertions to save these distressed people. The daughter of Mrs. *Hutchinson* remained a prisoner four years, when she was delivered to the Dutch governor at New York, who restored her to her friends. She had forgotten her native language, and was unwilling to be taken from the Indians. This governor, with a kindness not to be forgotten, sent a vessel into Connecticut River, where its captain contrived to get several Pequots on board, whom he secured as prisoners. He then informed their friends, that they would not be set at liberty until the captive girl was delivered to him. This had the desired effect, and she was accordingly rescued.

Notwithstanding a peace was brought about in the manner before stated, yet it was of short duration, and the sparks of war which had for a short time laid hid in its own embers, was by sordid spirits fanned again into a flame. The series of murderous acts which followed, are nowhere recorded within my researches, but an end was not put to it until 1646. It ended in a sanguinary battle at Strickland's Plain, near what is since Horse Neck in New York, about 37 miles from the city. The numbers engaged on each side are not known, nor the numbers slain, but their graves are still pointed out to the curious traveller.

To return to our more immediate subject.

We hear little of *Ninigret* until after the death of *Miantunnomoh*. In 1644, the Narragansets and Nianticks united against the Mohegans, and for some time obliged *Uncas* to confine himself and men to his fort.

This affair probably took place early in the spring, and we have elsewhere given all the particulars of it, both authentic and traditionary. It appears, by a letter from *Tho. Peters*, addressed to Governor *Winthrop*, written about the time, that there had been some hard fighting; and that the Mohegans had been severely beaten by the Narragansets. Mr. *Peters* writes:—

"I, with your son, [*John Winthrop* of Con.,] were at *Uncas*' fort, where I dressed seventeen men, and left plasters to dress seventeen more, who were wounded in *Uncas*' brother's wigwam before we came. Two captains and one common soldier were buried, and since we came thence two captains and one common man more, are dead also, most of which are wounded with bullets. *Uncas* and his brother told me, the Narragansets had 30 guns which won them the day, else would not care a rush for them. They drew *Uncas*' forces out by a wile, of 40 appearing only, but a thousand [lay hid] in ambush, who pursued *Uncas*' men into their own land, where the battle was fought *vario marte*, till God put fresh spirit into the Moheagues, and so drave the Narragansets back again." So it seems that *Uncas* had been taken in his own play. The letter goes on:—"'Twould pity your hearts to see them [*Uncas*' men] lie, like so many new circumcised Sechemites, in their blood. Sir, whatever information you have, I dare boldly say, the Narragansets first brake the contract they made with the English last year, for I helped to cure one *Tantiquieson*, a Moheague captain, who first fingered [laid hands on] *Miantinomio*. Some cunning squaws of Narraganset led two of them to *Tantiquieson's* wigwam, where, in the night, they struck him on the breast through the coat with an hatchet, and had he not fenced it with his arm, no hope could be had of his life," &c.*

"The English thought it their concern," says Dr. *I. Mather*,† "not to suffer him to be swallowed up by those adversaries, since he had, (though for his

* *Winthrop's* Jour. ii. 380, 381. † Relation, 58.

own ends,) approved himself faithful to the English from time to time." An army was accordingly raised for the relief of *Uncas*. "But as they were just marching out of Boston, many of the principal Narraganset Indians, viz. *Pessecus*, *Mexano*,* and *Witawash*, sagamores, and *Awasequin*, deputy for the Nianticks; these, with a large train, came to Boston, suing for peace, being willing to submit to what terms the English should see cause to impose upon them. It was demanded of them, that they should defray the charges they had put the English to,† and that the sachems should send their sons to be kept as hostages in the hands of the English, until such time as the money should be paid." After remarking that from this time the Narragansets harbored venom in their hearts against the English, Mr. *Mather* proceeds:—"In the first place, they endeavored to play *legerdemain* in their sending hostages; for, instead of sachems' children, they thought to send some other, and to make the English believe that those base *papooses* were of a royal progeny; but they had those to deal with, who were too wise to be so eluded. After the expected hostages were in the hands of the English, the Narragansets, notwithstanding that, were slow in the performance of what they stood engaged for. And when, upon an impartial discharge of the debt, their hostages were restored to them, they became more backward than formerly, until they were, by hostile preparations, again and again terrified into better obedience. At last, Capt. *Atherton*, of Dorchester, was sent with a small party‡ of 20 English soldiers to demand what was due. He at first entered into the wigwam, where old *Ninigret* resided, with only two or three soldiers, appointing the rest by degrees to follow him, two or three dropping in at once; when his small company were come about him, the Indians in the mean time supposing that there had been many more behind, he caught the sachem by the hair of his head, and setting a pistol to his breast, protesting whoever escaped he should surely die, if he did not forthwith comply with what was required. Hereupon a great trembling and consternation surprised the Indians; albeit, multitudes of them were then present, with spiked arrows at their bow-strings ready to let fly. The event was, the Indians submitted, and not one drop of blood was shed."§ This, it must be confessed, was a high-handed proceeding.

"Some space after that, *Ninigret* was raising new trouble against us, amongst his Nianticks and other Indians; but upon the speedy sending up of Capt. *Davis*, with a party of horse to reduce him to the former peace, who, upon the news of the captain's approach, was put into such a panic fear, that he durst not come out of his wigwam to treat with the captain, till secured of his life by him, which he was, if he quietly yielded to his message, about which he was sent from the Bay. To which he freely consenting, that storm was graciously blown over."‖

Thus having, through these extracts, summarily glanced at some prominent passages in the life of *Ninigret*, we will now go more into particulars.

The case of the Narragansets, at the period of the treaty before spoken of, had become rather desperate; two years having passed since they agreed to pay 2000 fathom of "good white wampum," as a remuneration for the trouble and damage they had caused the English and Mohegans, and they were now pressed to fulfil their engagements. *Ninigret*, then called *Janemo*, was not at Boston at that time, but *Aumsaaquen* was his deputy, and signed the treaty then made, with *Pessacus* and others. At their meeting, in July, 1647, *Pessacus* and others, chiefs of the Narragansets and Nianticks, were

* The editor of *Johnson's* Wonder-working Providence, in *Coll. Mass. Hist. Soc.* makes a great mistake in noting this chief as *Miantunnomoh*. *Mriksah*, *Mixanno*, *Meika*, &c., are names of the same person, who was the eldest son of *Canonicus*. After the death of his father, he was chief sachem of the Narragansets. He married a sister of *Ninigret*, who was "a woman of great power," and no other than the famous *Quaiapen*, at one time called *Matantuck*, from which, probably, was derived *Magnus*. By some writers mistaking him for *Miantunnomoh*, an error has spread, that has occasioned much confusion in accounts of their genealogy.

† A yearly tribute in wampum was agreed upon. *Manuscript* Narrative of the Rev. I. *Cobbet*, which places the affair in 1645.

‡ MS. document among our *state papers*.

§ Relation of the Troubles, &c., 4to, 1677.

‖ *Cobbet's* MS. Narrative

sent to by the English commissioners, as will be found in the life of *Pessacus*. Being warned to come to Boston, *Pessacus*, not being willing to get any further into trouble by being obliged to sign whatever articles the English might draw up, feigned himself sick, and told the messengers he had agreed to leave all the business to *Ninigret*. This seems to have been well understood, and we shall next see with what grace *Ninigret* acted his part with the commissioners, at Boston. Their record runs thus:—

"August 3d, [1647,] *Ninegratt*, with some of the Nyantick Indians and two of *Pessack's* men, came to Boston, and desiring Mr. *John Winthrop*, that came from Pequatt plantation, might be present, they were admitted. The commissioners asked *Ninegratt* for whom he came, whither as a publick person on the behalf of *Pessack's* and the rest of the Narragansets' confederates, or only for himself as a particular sagamore? He at first answered that he had spoke with *Pessack*, but had no such commission from him;" and said there had not been so good an understanding between them as he desired; but, from Mr. *Winthrop's* testimony, and the answer *Thos. Stanton* and *Benedict Arnold* brought from *Pessacus*, and also the testimony of *Pessacus*' two men, "it appeared to the commissioners that whatever formality might be wanting in *Pessack's* expressions to *Ninegratt*, yet *Pessack* had fully engaged himself to stand to whatsoever *Ninegratt* should conclude." Therefore they proceeded to demand of him why the wampum had not been paid, and why the covenant had not been observed in other particulars. *Ninigret* pretended he did not know what covenants had been made. He was then reminded that his deputy executed the covenant, and that a copy was carried into his country, and his ignorance of it was no excuse for him, for Mr. *Williams* was at all times ready to explain it, if he had taken the pains to request it of him. "There could, therefore, be no truth in his answere."

Ninigret next demanded, "*For what are the Narragansets to pay so much wampum? I know not that they are indebted to the English!*" The commissioners then repeated the old charges—the breach of covenant, ill treating messengers, and what he had said himself to the English messengers, namely, that he knew the English would try to bring about a peace at their meeting at Hartford, but he was resolved on war, nor would *he* inquire who began it—that if the English did not withdraw their men from assisting *Uncas*, he would kill them and their cattle, &c. According to the records of the commissioners, *Ninigret* did not deny these charges with a very good face. He said, however, their messengers provoked him to say what he did.

In order to waive the criminating discourse, *Ninigret* called for documents; or wished the English to make a statement of their account against him, that he might know "how the reckoninge stood." The English answered, that they had received of *Pessacus*, 170 *fathom of wampum* at one time:—Afterwards *some kettles* and about 15 *fathom more*, "which beinge a *contemptible some*, was refused." As to the kettles, they said, "The Narraganset messengers had sould them to Mr. *Shrimpton*,* a brasier in Boston," for a shilling a pound. Their weight was 285 *lbs*., (not altogether so *contemptible* as one might be led to imagine,) which came to 14£. 5*s*., and the wampum to 4£. 4*s*. 6*d*.† Of the amount in Mr. *Shrimpton's* hands, the messengers took up 1£. probably to defray their necessary expenses while at Boston. The remainder an Englishman attached to satisfy "for goods stollen from him by a Narraganset Indian."

Ninigret said the attachment was not valid, "for that neither the kettles nor wampum did belonge to *Pessacks* himself, nor to the Indian that had stollen the goods," and therefore must be deducted from the amount now due. "The commissioners thought it not fit to press the attachment," but reckoned the kettles and wampum at 70 fathom, and acknowledged the receipt of 240 fathom, [in all,] besides a parcel sent by *Ninigret* himself to the governor and though this was sent as a present, yet, as it was not accepted by the governor, they left it to *Ninigret* to say whether it should be now so con-

* *Samuel Shrimpton*, probably, who bought a house and lands of *Ephraim Turner* brasier, situated in Boston, in 1671.

† Hence 4£. 4*s*. 6*d*. $\div$ 15 = 5*s*. 7$\frac{3}{5}$*d*. = value of a fathom of wampum in 1647.

sidered, or whether it should be taken in payment of the debt. *Ninigret* said the governor should do as he pleased about it. It was then inquired how much he had sent; (it being deposited in *Cutshamokin's* hands, as we have elsewhere stated;) he said he had sent 30 fathom of black, and 45 of white, in value together 105 fathom. *Cutshamokin* was sent for to state what he had received in trust. He had produced two girdles, "with a string of wampum, all which himself rated at 45 fathom, affirming he had received no more, except 8*s.* which he had used, and would repay." He was brought before *Ninigret* and questioned, as there appeared a great difference in their accounts. "He at first persisted," says our record, "and added to his lyes, but was at last convinced [confronted] by *Ninigret*, and his messengers who then brought the present, and besides *Cutshamokin* had sent him at the same time 10 fathom as a present also." It still remained to be settled, whether this wampum should be received as a part of the debt, or as a present; and *Ninigret* was urged to say how it should be. With great magnanimity he answered:—

"*My tongue shall not belie my heart. Whether the debt be paid or not, I intended it as a present to the governor.*"

It is unpleasant to contrast the characters of the two chiefs, *Cutshamokin* and *Ninigret*, because the former had long had the *advantage* of a civilized neighborhood, and the latter was from the depths of the forest, where he saw an Englishman but seldom. We could say much upon it; but, as it is thought by many that such disquisitions are unprofitable, we decline going into them here.

What we have related seems to have finished the business of the day, and doubtless the shades of night were very welcome to *Cutshamokin*. The next day, *Ninigret* came into court, with the deputies of *Pessacus*, and spoke to the following effect:—

"Before I came here I expected the burden had been thrown upon me, *Pessacus* not having done what he agreed to do. However, I have considered upon the treaty of 1645, and am resolved to give the English satisfaction in all things. I will send some of my men immediately to Narraganset and Niantick, to raise the wampum now due to them, and hope to hear what they will do in three days. In ten days I think the wampum will arrive, and I will stay here until it comes. I will tell this to the Narraganset confederates. But if there should not enough at this time be raised, I desire some forbearance as to time, as I assure you that the remainder shall be shortly paid, and you shall see me true to the English, henceforth."

This speech gave the commissioners great satisfaction, and they proceeded to other business.

The messengers sent out by *Ninigret* did not return so soon as was expected; but, on the 16 August, notice was given of their arrival; sadly, however, to the disappointment of the commissioners, for they brought only 200 fathom of wampum. The feelings of the court were somewhat changed, and they rather sternly demanded "what the reason was, that, so much being due, so little was brought, and from whom this 200 fathom came." *Ninigret* answered that *he* was disappointed that more had not been brought, but said, if he had been at home, more would have been obtained: that 100 fathom was sent by *Pessacus*, and the other 100 by his people.

The commissioners say, that, "not thinking it meet to begin a present war, if satisfaction, (though with a little forbearance, may be had otherwise,)" told *Ninigret*, that, since he had said the wampum would have been gathered and paid if he had been at home himself, they would now give him 20 days to go and get it in; and, if he could not procure enough by 500 fathom, still they would not molest him until "next spring planting time." That, as so much was still due, they would reckon the present before mentioned; but, if they did not bring 1000 fathom in twenty days, the commissioners would send no more messengers into his country, "but take course to right themselves." That, if they were "forced to seek satisfaction by arms, he and his confederates must not expect to make their peace, as lately they had done, by a little wampum. In the mean time, though for breach of covenants they might put their hostages to death, yet the commissioners would forthwith deliver the children to *Ninigret*,* expecting from him the more care to see engagements fully satisfied. And, if they find him real in his performance, they will charge all former neglects upon *Pessacus*," and "in such case they expect from *Ninigret* his best assistance, when he shall be required to recover the whole remainder from him. All which *Ninigret* cheerfully accepted, and promised to perform accordingly."

Notwithstanding all their promises, the Narragansets had not discharged their debt at the end of two years more, though in that time they had paid about 1100 fathom of wampum. At their meeting this year, 1649, at Boston, "the commissioners were minded of the continued complaint of *Uncas*" against the Narragansets, that they were "still vndermining his peace and seeking his ruine," and had lately endeavored "to bring in the Mowhaukes vppon him," which failing, they next tried to take away his life by witchcraft. A Narraganset Indian, named *Cuttaquin*, "in an English vessel, in Mohegan River, ran a sword into his breast, wherby hee receeved, to all appearance, a mortal wound, which murtherus acte the assalant then confessed hee was, for a considerable sum of wampum, by the Narragansett and Nianticke sachems, hired to attempt."

Meanwhile *Ninigret*, understanding what was to be urged against him, appeared suddenly at Boston before the commissioners. The old catalogue of delinquencies was read over to him, with several new ones appended. As it respected *Cuttaquin's* attempt upon the life of *Uncas*, *Ninigret* said that neither he nor *Pessacus* had any hand in it, but that "he [*Cuttaquin*] was drawn thereunto by torture from the Mohegans;" "but he was told, that the assailant, before he came into the hands of the Mohegans, presently after the fact was committed, layed the charge upon him, with the rest, which he confirmed, the day following, to Capt. *Mason*, in the presence of the English that were in the bark with him, and often reiterated it at Hartford, though since he hath denied it: that he was presented to *Uncas* under the notion of one appertaining to *Vssamequin*, whereby he was acknowledged as his friend, and no provocation given him." *Cuttaquin* had affirmed, it was said, that his desperate condition caused him to attempt the life of *Uncas*, "through his great engagement to the said sachems, having received a considerable quantity of wampum, which he had spent, who otherwise would have taken away his life."

The judgment of the court was, that the sachems were guilty, and we next find them engaged in settling the old account of wampum. *Ninigret* had got the commissioners debited more than they at first were willing to allow. They say that it appeared by the auditor's account, that no more than 1529½ fathom hath been credited, "nor could *Ninigret* by any evidence make any more to appear, only he alleged that about 600 fathom was paid by measure which he accounted by tale, wherein there was considerable difference. The commissioners, not willing to adhere to any strict terms in that particular, (and though by agreement it was to be paid by measure and not by tale,) were willing to allow 62 fathom and half in that respect, so that there remains due 408 fathom. But *Ninigret* persisting in his former affirmation, and not endeavoring to give any reasonable satisfaction to the commissioners in the premises, a small inconsiderable parcel of beaver being all that was tendered to them, though they understood he was better provided." They therefore gave him to understand that they were altogether dissatisfied, and that he might go his own way, as they were determined to protect *Uncas* according to their treaty with him.

The commissioners now expressed the opinion among themselves, that affairs looked rather turbulent, and advised that each colony should hold itself in readiness to act as circumstances might require, "which they the rather present to consideration, from an information they received since their sitting, of a marriage shortly intended betwixt *Ninigret's* daughter, and a brother or brother's son of *Sassaquas*, the malignant, furious Pequot, whereby probably

* Glad, no doubt, to rid themselves of the expense of keeping them; for it must be remembered, that the English took them upon the condition that they should support them at their own expense.

their aims are to gather together, and reunite the scattered conquered Pequates into one body, and set them up again as a distinct nation, which hath always been witnessed against by the English, and may hazard the peace of the colonies."

The four years next succeeding are full of events, but as they happened chiefly among the Indians themselves, it is very difficult to learn the particulars. *Ninigret* claimed dominion of the Indians of a part of Long Island, as did his predecessors; but those Indians, seeing the English domineering over the Narragansets, became altogether independent of them, and even waged wars upon them.

Ascassasotick was at this period the chief of those Indians, a warlike and courageous chief, but as treacherous and barbarous as he was brave. These islanders had, from the time of the Pequot troubles, been protected by the English, which much increased their insolence. Not only had *Ninigret*, and the rest of the Narragansets, suffered from his insults, but the Mohegans had also, as we shall more fully make appear hereafter.

When the English commissioners had met at Hartford in 1650, *Uncas* came with a complaint to them, "that the Mohansick sachem, in Long Island, had killed som of his men; bewitched diuers others and himself also," which was doubtless as true as were most of his charges against the Narragansets, "and desired the commissioners that hee might be righted therin. But because the said sachem of Long Island was not there to answer for himself," several Englishmen were appointed to examine into it, and if they found him guilty to let him know that they "will bring trouble upon themselves."

At the same meeting an order was passed, "that 20 men well armed be sent out of the jurisdiction of the Massachusetts to *Pessicus*, to demand the said wampum, [then in arrears,] which is 308 fathom;" but in case they could not get the wampum, they were ordered "to take the same, or the vallew therof, in the best and most suitable goods they can find." Or, if they could not find enough to satisfy all demands, they were ordered to seize and "bring away either *Pessacus* or his children, or such other considerable sachem or persons, as they prize, and may more probably bow them to reason."

From *Pessacus*, they were ordered to go to *Ninigret*, and inform him that the commissioners had heard "*that he had given his daughter in marriage to Sasecos his brother, who gathers Pequots under him, as if either he would become their sachem, or again possess the Pequot country*," which was contrary to "engagements," and what they would not allow, and he must inform them whether it were so. To inform him also that *Wequash Cook* "complains of sundry wrongs." And that, as to his hunting in the Pequot country, to inform him he had no right to do so, as that country belonged to the English. The termination of this expedition, in which *Ninigret* was taken "by the hair," has been previously mentioned in our extract from Dr. *Mather*.

We have in the life of *Miantunnomoh* given some account of the acts of a chief called *Waiandance*, especially relating to the disorganization of the plans of that great chief. We come, in this place, to a parallel act in relation to *Ninigret*. About a year after the death of *Miantunnomoh*, *Ninigret* undertook to organize a plan for expatriating the English; and sent a messenger to *Waiandance*, the Long Island sachem, to engage him in it. Instead of listening to his message, *Waiandance* seized upon *Ninigret's* messenger, bound him, and sent him to Captain *Gardener* at Saybrook fort. From thence he was sent, under a guard of 10 men, for Hartford. But they were windbound in their passage, and were obliged to put in to Shelter Island, where an old sachem lived, who was *Waiandance's* elder brother. Here they let *Ninigret's* ambassador escape, and thus he had knowledge that his plan was discovered and overthrown.

Since we have here introduced the sachem *Waiandance*, we will add the account of his last acts and death. One *William Hammond* being killed "by a giant-like Indian" near New York, about 1637, Captain *Gardener* told *Waiandance* that he must kill that Indian; but this being against the advice of the great sachem, his brother, he declined it, and told the captain that that

Indian was a mighty great man, and no man dared meddle with him, and that he had many friends. Some time after, he killed another, one *Thomas Farrington*, and in the mean time, *Waiandance's* brother having died, he undertook his execution, which he accomplished. This was his last act in the service of the English; "for in the time of a great mortality among them, he died, but it was by poison; also two-thirds of the Indians upon Long Island died, else the Narragansets had not made such havoc here as they have."

Ninigret passed the winter of 1652—3 among the Dutch of New York This caused the English great suspicion, especially as they were enemies to the Dutch at that time; and several sagamores who resided near the Dutch had reported that the Dutch governor was trying to hire them to cut off the English; consequently, there was a special meeting of the English commissioners at Boston, in April, 1653, occasioned by a rumor that the Narragansets had leagued with the Dutch to break up the English settlements. Whereupon a letter was sent by them to their agent at Narraganset, *Thomas Stanton*, containing "divers queries," by him to be interpreted "to *Ninegrett, Pessicus* and *Meeksam*, three of the chiefest Narraganset sachems," and their answers to be immediately obtained and reported to the commissioners.

The questions to be put to the sachems were, in substance, as follows:—1. Whether the Dutch had engaged them* to fight against the English.—2. Whether the Dutch governor did not endeavor such a conspiracy.—3. Whether they had not received arms and munitions of war from the Dutch.—4. What other Indians are engaged in the plot.—5. Whether, contrary to their engagement, they were resolved to fight against the English.—6. If they are so resolved, *what they think the English will do*.—7. Whether they had not better be true to the English.—8. Similar to the first.—9. What were their grounds of war against the English.—10. Whether they had not better come or send messengers to treat with the English.—11. Whether they had hired the Mohawks to help them.

"The answare of the sachems, viz. *Ninigrett, Pessecus* and *Mixam*, vnto the queries and letters sent by the messengers, Sarjeant *Waite* and Sarjeant *John Barrell*, the 18th of the second month, 1653."

Mexam seems to have been the first that answered; and of the first query he said:—

"I speak unfeignedly, from my heart, and say, without dissimulation, that I know of no such plot against the English, my friends; implicating either the Dutch governor or any other person. Though I be poor, it is not goods, guns, powder nor shot, that shall draw me to such a plot as this against the English, my friends.† If the Dutch governor had made known any such intention to me, I would have told it, without delay, to the English, my friends. With respect to your second question, I answer, *No*. What do the English sachems, my friends, think of us?—do they think we should prefer goods, guns, powder and shot, before our lives? our means of living? both of us and ours? As to the 4th query, I speak from my heart, and say, I know of no such plot by the Dutch governor. There may come false news and reports against us; let them say what they will, they are false. It is unnecessary to say more. But in answer to the 10th query I will say, It is just messengers should be sent to treat with the English sachems, but as for myself, I am old, and cannot travel two days together, but a man shall be sent to speak with the sachems. I have sent to Mr. *Smith*, and *Voll*‡ his man, to speak to Mr. *Brown*, and to say to him, that I love the English sachems, and all Englishmen in the Bay: And desire Mr. *Brown* to tell the sachems

* The third person singular, *he*, is used throughout, in the original, as it was supposed by the propounders that each chief would be questioned separately.

† Every one must be forcibly reminded of the answer given by one of our revolutionary worthies, *Joseph Reed*, Esq., to a British agent, on reading this answer of the chief *Mexam*, though not under circumstances exactly similar. Mr. *Reed* was promised a fortune if he would exert himself on the side of the king. Viewing it in the light of a bribe, he replied: "*I am not worth purchasing, but, such as I am, the king of Great Britain is not rich enough to do it.*" Dr. *Gordon's* America, iii. 172. ed. London, 4 vols. 8vo. 1788

‡ *Vallentine Whitman*, an interpreter, elsewhere named.

of the Bay, that the child that is now born, or that is to be born in time to come, shall see no war made by us against the English."

Pessacus spoke to this purpose:—

"I am very thankful to these two men that came from the Massachusetts, and to you *Thomas*, and to you *Poll*,* and to you Mr. *Smith*, you that are come so far as from the Bay to bring us this message, and to inform us of these things we knew not of before. As for the governor of the Dutch, we are loath to invent any falsehood of him, though we be far from him, to please the English, or any others that bring these reports. For what I speak with my mouth I speak from my heart. The Dutch governor did never propound any such thing unto us. Do you think we are mad? and that we have forgotten our writing that we had in the Bay, which doth bind us to the English, our friends, in a way of friendship? Shall we throw away that writing and ourselves too? Have we not reason in us? How can the Dutch shelter us, being so remote, against the power of the English, our friends—we living close by the doors of the English, our friends? We do profess, we abhor such things."

Lastly, we come to the chief actor in this affair, *Ninigret*. He takes up each query in order, and answers it; which, for brevity's sake, we will give in a little more condensed form, omitting nothing, however, that can in any degree add to our acquaintance with the great chief. He thus commences:—

"I utterly deny that there has been any agreement made between the Dutch governor and myself, to fight against the English. I did never hear the Dutchmen say they would go and fight against the English; neither did I hear the Indians say they would join with them. But, while I was there at the Indian wigwams, there came some Indians that told me there was a ship come in from Holland, which did report the English and Dutch were fighting together in their own country, and there were several other ships coming with ammunition to fight against the English here, and that there would be a great blow given to the English when they came. But this I had from the Indians, and how true it is I cannot tell. I know not of any wrong the English have done me, therefore WHY should I fight against them? Why do the English sachems ask me the same questions over and over again? Do they think we are mad—and would, for a few guns and swords, sell our lives, and the lives of our wives and children? As to their tenth question, it being indifferently spoken, whether I may go or send, though I know nothing myself, wherein I have wronged the English, to prevent MY going; yet, as I said before, it being left to my choice, that is, it being indifferent to the commissioners, whether I will send some one to speak with them, I will send."†

To the letters which the English messengers carried to the sachems, *Mexam* and *Pessacus* said, "*We desire there may be no mistake, but that we may be understood, and that there may be a true understanding on both sides. We desire to know where you had this news, that there was such a league made betwixt the Dutch and us, and also to know our accusers.*"

Ninigret, though of the most importance in this affair, is last mentioned in the records, and his answer to the letter brought him by the messengers is as follows:—

"You are kindly welcome to us, and I kindly thank the sachems of Massachusetts that they should think of me as one of the sachems worthy to be inquired of concerning this matter. Had any of the other sachems been at the Dutch, I should have feared their folly might have done some hurt, one way or other, but THEY have not been there. *I* am the man. I have been there myself. I alone am answerable for what I have done. And, as I have already declared, I do utterly deny and protest that I know of no such plot as has been apprehended. What is the story of these great rumors that I hear at Pocatocke—that I should be cut off, and that the English had a quarrel against

* So printed in *Hazard*, but probably means the same as *Voll; V*, in the latter case, having been taken for *P*. We have known such instances.

† The preceding sentence of our text, the author of *Tales of the Indians* thinks, "would puzzle the most *mystifying* politician of modern times." Indeed! What! a Philadelphia *lawyer?* Really, we cannot conceive that it ought in the least to puzzle even a *Boston lawyer*. If a *puzzle* exist any where, we apprehend it is in some *mystifying* word.

me? I know of no such cause at all for my part. Is it because I went hither to take physic for my health? or what is the cause? I found no such entertainment from the Dutch governor, when I was there, as to give me any encouragement to stir me up to such a league against the English, my friends. It was winter time, and I stood, a great part of a winter day, knocking at the governor's door, and he would neither open it, nor suffer others to open it, to let me in. I was not wont to find such carriage from the English, my friends."

Not long after the return of the English messengers, who brought the above relation of their mission, *Awashaw* arrived at Boston, as "messenger" of *Ninigret*, *Pessacus*, and *Mexam*, with "three or four" others. An inquisition was immediately held over him, and, from his *cross*-examination, we gather the following answers:—

"*Ninigret* told me that he went to the Dutch to be cured of his disease, hearing there was a Frenchman there that could cure him; and Mr. *John Winthrop* knew of his going. He carried 30 fathom of wampum, gave the doctor 10, and the Dutch governor 15, who, in lieu thereof, gave him coats with sleeves, but not one gun, though the Indians there gave him two guns. That, while *Ninigret* was there, he crossed Hudson's River, and there an Indian told him about the arrival of the Dutch ships. As to the corn sent to the Dutch by *Ninigret*, it was only to pay his passage, the Dutch having brought him home in a vessel. Five men went with *Ninigret*. Four came home with him in the vessel, and one came by land before. One of his company was a Mohegan, and one a Conecticott Indian, who lived on the other side of Hudson's River. A canoe was furnished with 60 fathom of wampum, after *Ninigret's* return from Monhatoes, to be sent there to pay for the two guns, but six fathom of it was to have been paid to the doctor, which was then due to him. There were in it, also, two raccoon coats, and two beaver skins, and seven Indians to go with it. They and the canoe were captured by *Uncas*."

An Indian named "*Newcom-Matuxes*, sometimes of Rhode Island," was one that accompanied *Awashaw*. "One *John Lightfoot*, of Boston," said *Matuxes* told him, in Dutch, (he had lived among them at Southhold, and learned their language,) that the Dutchmen would "cut off" the English of Long Island. "*Newcom* also confesseth [to him] that *Ninigret* said that he heard that some ships were to come from Holland to the Monhattoes to cut off the English." "That an Indian told him that the Dutch would come against the English, and cut them off, but they would save the women and children and guns, for themselves. But Capt. *Simkins* and the said *Lightfoot* do both affirm that the said *Newcom* told them that the Dutchmen *told him*, as before [stated,] though he now puts it off, and saith an *Indian* told him so." *Simkins* affirmed also that *Newcom* told him that if he would go and serve the Dutch, they would give him £100 a year.

On examining *Newcom*, the commissioners gave it as their opinion that he was guilty of perfidy, and that they should not have let him escape without punishment, but for his being considered as an ambassador. They, therefore, desired *Awashaw* to inform *Ninigret* of it, that he might send him to them again, "the better to clear himself." This we apprehend was not done. *Awashaw* next notified the court that he had not done with them, "whereupon he was sent for to speak what he had further to propound." He demanded how they came by their information "of all these things touching *Ninigret*." They said from several Indians, *particularly* "the Monheage Indian and the Narraganset Indian, which were both taken by *Uncas* his men, who had confessed the plot before Mr. *Haines* at Hartford." *Awashaw* also demanded restitution of the wampum taken by *Uncas*. The commissioners told him that they had not as yet understood of the truth of that action, but when they had thoroughly examined it, he should have an *answer*.

So, all this legislating was about *Ninigret's going* to the Dutch; for as to a plot there appears no evidence of any; but when *Uncas* had committed a great depredation upon *Ninigret*, why—"that altered the case"—they must inquire into it, which doubtless was all right so far; but if a like complaint had been preferred against *Ninigret* by *Uncas*, we have reason to think it would have been forthwith "inquired into," at least, without an *if*.

A story, it cannot be called evidence, told by *Uncas*, relating to *Ninigret's* visit to the Dutch, is recorded by the commissioners, and which, if it amount to any thing, goes to prove himself guilty, and is indeed an acknowledgment of his own perfidy in taking *Ninigret's* boat and goods, as charged by *Awashaw*. It is as follows:—

"*Uncas*, the Mohegan sachem, came lately to Mr. *Hains'* house at Hartford, and informed him that *Ninnigrett*, sachem of the Niantick Narragansetts went this winter to the Monhatoes" and made a league with the Dutch governor, and for a large present of wampum received 20 guns and a great box of powder and bullets. *Ninigret* told him of the great injuries he had sustained from *Uncas* and the English. That on the other side of Hudson's River, *Ninigret* had a conference with a great many Indian sagamores, and desired their aid to cut off the Mohegans and English. Also, that, about two years since, *Ninigret* "sent to the Monheage sachem, and gave him a present of wampum, pressing him to procure a man skilful in magic workings, and an artist in poisoning, and send unto him; and he should receive more one hundredth fathom of wampum, which was to have been conveyed to the Monheage sachem, and the powaugh at the return of him that was to bring the poison. *Uncas* having intelligence of these things, caused a narrow watch to be set, by sea and land, for the apprehending of those persons; and accordingly took them returning in a canoe to the number of seven: whereof four of them were Narragansets, two strangers and one Pequatt. This was done in his absence, while he was with Mr. *Haines*, at Conecticott, and carried by those of his men that took them to Mohegan. Being there examined, two of them, the [Wampeage*] sachem's brother, and one Narraganset freely confessed the whole plot formerly expressed, and that one of their company was that powaugh and prisoner, pointing out the man. Upon this, his men in a rage slew him, fearing, as he said, least he should make an escape, or otherwise do either mischief to *Uncas* or the English, in case they should carry him with the rest before them, to Conecticott to be further examined. And being brought to Conecticott before Mr. *Haines*, and examined, did assert these particulars."

An Indian squaw also informed "an inhabitant of Wethersfield, that the Dutch and Indians generally were" confederating to cut off the English, and that election day, [1654,] was the time set, "because then it is apprehended the plantations will be left naked and unable to defend themselves, the strength of the English colonies being gathered from the several towns. And the aforesaid squaw advised the said inhabitants to acquaint the rest of the English with it, desiring they would remember how dear their slighting of her former information of the Pequots coming upon the English cost them." †

It would seem, from a careful examination of the records, that something had been suggested either by the Dutch or Indians, about "cutting off the English," which justice to *Ninigret* requires us to state, might have been the case without *his* knowledge or participation. For, the testimony of the messengers of "nine Indian sagamores who live about the Monhatoes" no how implicates him, and, therefore, cannot be taken into account, any more than

---

* See declaration onward in the records. (*Haz.* ii. 222.)

† Referring to an affair of 1637, which Dr. *I. Mather* relates as follows: "In the interim, [while Capt. *Mason* was protecting Saybrook fort,] many of the Pequods went to a place now called *Wethersfield* on Connecticut River, and having confederated with the Indians of that place, (as it was generally thought,) they laid in ambush for the English people of that place, and divers of them going to their labor in a large field adjoining to the town, were set upon by the Indians. Nine of the English were slain upon the place, and some horses, and two young women were taken captive." *Relation of the Troubles*, &c. 26.—Dr. *Trumbull* says this happened in April. *Hist. Con.* i. 77.

The cause of this act of the Pequots, according to *Winthrop*, i. 260, was this. An Indian called *Sequin* had given the English lands at Wethersfield, that he might live by them and be protected from other Indians. But when he came there, and had set down his wigwam, the English drove him away by force. And hence it was supposed that he had plotted their destruction, as above related, with the Pequots.

what an Indian named *Ronnessoke* told *Nicholas Tanner*, as interpreted by another Indian called *Addam;* the latter, though relating to *Ninigret's* visit, was only a hearsay affair. *Ronnessoke* was a sagamore of Long Island.

Addam also interpreted the story of another Indian, called *Powanege*, "who saith he came from the Indians who dwell over the river, over against the Monhatoes, where the plot is a working, that was this: that the Dutchmen asked the Indians whether they would leave them at the last cast, or stand up with them. And told the Indians they should fear nothing, and not be discouraged because the plot was discovered," &c.

Addam the interpreter had also a story to tell. He said, "this spring [1653, O. S.] the Dutch governor went to Fort Aurania, [since Albany,] and first went to a place called *Ackicksack*, [Hackinsack,] a great place of Indians, from thence to Monnesick, [Minisink,] thence to Opingona, thence to Warranoke, thence to Fort Aurania: And so far he went in his own person. From thence he sent to Pocomtock, [Deerfield, on the Connecticut,] and he carried with him many note of sewan, that is, bags of wampum, and delivered them to the sagamores of the places, and they were to distribute them amongst their men; and withal he carried powder, shot, cloth, lead and guns; and told them he would get all the great Indians under him, and the English should have the scum of the Indians, and he would have those sagamores with their men to cut off the English, and to be at his command whenever he had use of them, and he was to find them powder and shot till he had need of them. Further he sent one Govert, a Dutchman, to Marsey, on Long Island, to *Nittanahom*, the sagamore, to assist him and to do for him what he would have [him] do: But the sagamore told him he would have nothing to [do] with it: whereupon Govert gave the sagamore a great kettle to be silent. *Nittanaham* told him he had but 20 men, and the English had never done him wrong, [and] he had no cause to fight against them. Further, he saith that *Ninnegrett*, the fiscal,* and the Dutch governor were up two days in a close room, with other sagamores; and there was no speaking with any of them except when they came for a coal of fire,† or the like. And much sewan was seen at that time in *Ninnegret's* hand, and he carried none away with him;" and that *Ronnesseoke* told him that the governor bid him fly for his life, for the plot was now discovered.

Nevertheless, as for any positive testimony that *Ninigret* was plotting against the English, there is none. That he was in a room to avoid company, while his physician was attending him, is very probable.

In a long letter, dated 26th May, 1653, which the governor of New Amsterdam, *Peter Stuyvesant*, wrote to the English, is the following passage:—"It is in part true, as your worships conclude, that, about January, there came a strange Indian from the north, called *Ninnigrett*, commander of the Narragansets. But he came hither with a pass from Mr. *John Winthrop*. Upon which pass, as we remember, the occasion of his coming was expressed, namely, to be cured and healed; and if, upon the other side of the river, there hath been any assembly or meeting of the Indians, or of their sagamores, we know not [of it.] We heard that he hath been upon Long Island, about Nayacke, where he hath been for the most part of the winter, and hath had several Indians with him, but what he hath negotiated with them remains to us unknown: only this we know, that what your worships lay unto our charge are false reports, and feigned informations."

The war with *Ascassasôtic*, of which we shall give all the particulars in our possession, was the next affair of any considerable moment in the life of *Ninigret*.

In 1654, the government of Rhode Island communicated to Massachusetts, that the last summer, *Ninigret*, without any cause, "that he doth so much as allege, fell upon the Long Island Indians, our friends and tributaries," and killed many of them, and took others prisoners, and would not restore them. "This summer he hath made two assaults upon them; in one whereof he killed a man and woman, that lived upon the land of the English, and within

---

* A Dutch officer, whose duty is similar to that of treasurer among the English.

† To light their pipes, doubtless—the Dutch agreeing well, in the particular of smoking, with the Indians.

one of their townships; and another Indian, that kept the cows of the English." He had drawn many of the foreign Indians down from Connecticut and Hudson Rivers, who rendezvoused upon Winthrop's Island, where they killed some of his cattle.* This war began in 1653, and continued "several years."†

The commissioners of the United Colonies seemed blind to all complaints against *Uncas;* but the Narragansets were watched and harassed without ceasing. Wherever we meet with an unpublished document of those times, the fact is very apparent. The chief of the writers of the history of that period copy from the records of the United Colonies, which accounts for their making out a good case for the English and Mohegans. The spirit which actuated the grave commissioners is easily discovered, and I need only refer my readers to the case of *Miantunnomoh.* Desperate errors require others, oftentimes still more desperate, until the first appear small compared with the magnitude of the last! It is all along discoverable, that those venerable records are made up from one kind of evidence, and that when a Narraganset appeared in his own defence, so many of his enemies stood ready to give him the lie, that his indignant spirit could not stoop to contradict or parley with them; and thus his assumed guilt passed on for history. The long-silenced and borne-down friend of the Indians of Moosehausic,‡ no longer sleeps. Amidst his toils and perils, he found time to raise his pen in their defence; and though his letters for a season slept with him, they are now awaking at the voice of day.

When the English had resolved, in 1654, to send a force against the Narragansets, because they had had difficulties and wars with *Ascassasôtic,* as we have related, Mr. *Williams* expressed his views of the matter in a letter to the governor of Massachusetts as follows:—"The cause and root of all the present mischiefs is the pride of two barbarians, *Ascassasôtick,* the Long Island sachem, and *Nenekunat* of the Narigenset. The former is proud and foolish, the latter is proud and fierce. I have not seen him these many years, yet, from their sober men, I hear he pleads, 1st. that *Ascassasôtick,* a very inferior sachem, (bearing himself upon the English,) hath slain three or four of his people, and since that sent him challenges and darings to fight and mend himself. 2d. He, *Nenekunat,* consulted by solemn messengers, with the chief of the English governors, Maj. *Endicot,* then governor of the Massachusetts, who sent him an implicit consent to right himself: upon which they all plead that the English have just occasion of displeasure. 3d. After he had taken revenge upon the Long Islanders, and brought away about 14 captives, (divers of them chief women,) yet he restored them all again, upon the mediation and desire of the English. 4th. After this peace [was] made, the Long Islanders pretending to visit *Nenekunat* at Block Island, slaughtered of his Narragansets near 30 persons, at midnight, two of them of great note, especially *Wepiteammock's* son, to whom *Nenekunat* was uncle. 5th. In the prosecution of this war, although he had drawn down the inlanders to his assistance, yet, upon protestation of the English against his proceedings, he retreated and dissolved his army.§

The great Indian apostle looked not so much into these particulars, being entirely engaged in the cause of the praying Indians: but yet we occasionally meet with him, and will here introduce him, as an evidence against the proceedings of *Uncas,* and his friends the commissioners:

"The case of the Nipmuk Indians, so far as by the best and most credible intelligence, I have understood, presented to the honored general court, [of Massachusetts,] 1. *Uncas* his men, at unawares, set upon an unarmed poor people, and slew eight persons, and carried captive twenty-four women and children. 2. Some of these were subjects to Massachusetts government, by being the subjects of *Josias.*‖ 3. They sued for relief to the worshipful governor and magistrates. 4. They were pleased to send, (by some Indians,) a commission to Capt. *Denison,* [of Stonington,] to demand these captives. 5. *Uncas* his

* *Manuscript documents.* † *Wood's* Hist. Long Island. ‡ Providence.
§ From the *original letter, in manuscript,* among the files in our state-house.
‖ Son of *Chikataubut*

answer was, (as I heard,) insolent. 6. They did not only abuse the women by filthiness, but have, since this demand, sold away (as I hear) some or all of those captives. 7. The poor bereaved Indians wait to see what you please to do. 8. You were pleased to tell them, you would present it to the free court, and they should expect their answer from them, which they now wait for. 9. *Nenecroft*, yea, all the Indians of the country, wait to see the issue of this matter." *

This memorial is dated 12th May, 1659, and signed by *John Eliot;* from which it is evident there had been great delay in relieving those distressed by the haughty *Uncas*. And yet, if he were caused to make remuneration in any way, we do not find any account of it.

In 1660, "the general court of Connecticut did, by their letters directed to the commissioners of the other colonies, this last summer, represent an intolerable affront done by the Narraganset Indians, and the same was now complained of by the English living at a new plantation at Mohegan, viz. that some Indians did, in the dead time of the night, shoot eight bullets into an English house, and fired the same; wherein five Englishmen were asleep. Of which insolency the Narraganset sachems have so far taken notice, as to send a slight excuse by Maj. *Atherton*, that they did neither consent to nor allow of such practices, but make no tender of satisfaction." † But they asked the privilege to meet the commissioners at their next session, at which time they gave them to understand that satisfaction should be made. This could not have been other than a reasonable request, but it was not granted; and messengers were forthwith ordered to "repair to *Ninigret*, *Pessicus*, *Woquacanoose*, and the rest of the Narraganset sachems," to demand "at least four of the chief of them that shot into the English house." And in case they should not be delivered, to demand five hundred fathoms of wampum. They were directed, in particular, to "charge *Ninigret* with breach of covenant, and high neglect of their order, sent them by Maj. *Willard*, six years since, not to invade the Long Island Indians; and [that they] do account the surprising the Long Island Indians at Gull Island, and murdering of them, to be an insolent carriage to the English, and a barbarous and inhuman act." These are only a few of the most prominent charges, and five hundred and ninety-five ‡ fathoms of wampum was the *price* demanded for them; and "the general court of Connecticut is desired and empowered to send a convenient company of men, under some discreet leader, to force satisfaction of the same above said, and the charges of recovering the same; and in case the persons be delivered, they shall be sent to Barbadoes," § and sold for slaves.

It appears that the force sent by Connecticut could not collect the wampum, nor secure the offenders; but for the payment, *condescended* to take a mortgage of all the Narraganset country, with the provision that it should be void, if it were paid in four months. *Quissoquus*, ‖ *Neneglud*, and *Scuttup*, ¶ signed the deed.

Ninigret did not engage with the other Narraganset chiefs, in *Philip's* war Dr. *Mather* ** calls him an "old crafty sachem, who had with some of his men withdrawn himself from the rest." He must at this time have been "an old sachem," for we meet with him as a chief, as early as 1632.

Although *Ninigret* was not personally engaged in *Philip's* war, still he must have suffered considerably from it; often being obliged to send his people to the English, to gratify some whim or caprice, and at other times to appear himself. On 10 Sept. 1675, eight of his men came as ambassadors to Boston, "having a certificate from Capt. *Smith*," †† who owned a large

* *Manuscript state paper.* † Record of the United Colonies, in *Hazard.*

‡ The additional ninety-five was for another offence, viz. "for the insolencies committed at Mr. *Brewster's*, in killing an Indian servant at Mrs. *Brewster's* feet, to her great affrightment, and stealing corn, &c., and other affronts." *Hazard*, ii. 433.

§ Records of the United Colonies, in *Hazard.*

‖ The same called *Quequegunent*, the son of *Magnus*. *Neucom* and *Awashars* were witnesses. The deed itself may be seen on file among our *State Papers*.

¶ Grandson of *Canonicus*, son of *Magnus*, and brother of *Quequegunent*.

** Brief History, 20.

†† Captain *Richard Smith*, probably, who settled quite early in that country. We find him there 15 years before this.

estate in Narraganset. After having finished their business, they received a pass from the authorities to return to their own country. This certificate or pass was fastened to a staff and carried by one in front of the rest. As they were going out of Boston "a back way," two men met them, and seized upon him that carried the pass. These men were brothers, who had *had* a brother killed by ***Philip's*** men some time before. This Indian they accused of killing him, and in court swore to his identity, and he was in a few days hanged.*

Notwithstanding these affairs, another embassy was soon after sent to Boston. On the 15 September "the authority of Boston sent a party" to order *Ninigret* to appear there in person, to give an account of his sheltering *Quaiapen*, the squaw-sachem of Narraganset. He sent word that he would come "provided he might be safely returned back." Mr. *Smith*, "living near him, offered himself, wife and children, and estate, as hostages" for his safe return, and the embassy forthwith departed for Boston. A son,† however, of *Ninigret*, was deputed prime minister, "he himself being very aged."

Captain *Smith* accompanied them, and when they came to Roxbury they were met by a company of English soldiers, whose martial appearance so frightened them, that, had it not been for the presence of Mr. *Smith*, they would have escaped as from an enemy.

They remained at Boston several days, until "by degrees they came to this agreement: That they were to deliver the squaw-sachem within so many days at Boston; and the league of peace was then by them confirmed, which was much to the general satisfaction; but many had hard thoughts of them, fearing they will at last prove treacherous."‡

Ninigret was opposed to Christianity; not perhaps so much from a disbelief of it, as from a dislike of the practices of those who professed it. When Mr. *Mayhew* desired *Ninigret* to allow him to preach to his people, the sagacious chief "bid him go and make the English good first, and chid Mr. *Mayhew* for hindering him from his business and labor."§

There were other Niantick sachems of this name, who succeeded *Ninigret*. According to the author of the "Memoir of the Mohegans,"‖ one would suppose he was alive in 1716, as that writer himself *supposed;* but if the anecdote there given be true, it related doubtless to *Charles Ninigret*, who, I suppose, was his son. He is mentioned by *Mason*, in his history of the Pequot war, as having received a part of the goods taken from Captain *Stone*, at the time he was killed by the Pequots, in 1634. The time of his death has not been ascertained.

The burying-places of the family of *Ninigret* are in Charlestown, R. I. It is said that the old chief was buried at a place called Burying Hill, "a mile from the street." A stone in one of the places of interment has this inscription:—

"*Here leth the Body of George, the son of Charles Ninigret, King of the Natives, and of Hannah his Wife. Died Decem^{r}. ye 22, 1732: aged 6 mo*"

"*George*, the last king, was brother of *Mary Sachem*, who is now, [1832,] sole heir to the crown. *Mary* does not know her age; but from data given by her husband, *John Harry*, she must be about 66. Her mother's father was *George Ninigret*. *Thomas* his son was the next king. *Esther*, sister of *Thomas*. *George*, the brother of *Mary* above named, and the last king crowned, died aged about 20 years. *George* was son of *Esther*. *Mary* has daughters, but no sons."¶

On a division of the captive Pequots, in 1637, *Ninigret* was to have twenty "when he should satisfy for a mare of *Eltweed*** *Pomroye's* killed by his men" This remained unsettled in 1659, a space of twenty-two years. This debt *certainly was outlawed! Poquin*, or *Poquoiam*, was the name of the man who killed the mare.†† He was a Pequot, and brother-in-law to *Miantunnomon*, and was among those captives assigned to him at their final dispersion when

* Old Indian Chronicle, 30.
† Probably *Catapazat*.
‡ Old Indian Chronicle, 32.
§ Douglas's Summary, ii 118.
‖ In 1 *Coll. Mass. Hist. Soc.* ix. 83.
¶ MS. communication of Rev. *Wm. Ely*
** Familiarly called *Elty*, probably from *Eltwood*.
†† Hazard, ii. 188, 189.

the Pequot war was ended; at which time *Pomeroy* states "all sorts of horses were at an high price." *Miantunnomoh* had agreed to pay the demand, but his death prevented him. *Ninigret* was called upon, as he inherited a considerable part of *Miantunnomoh's* estate, especially his part of the Pequots, of w.. m *Poquoiam* was one. He was afterwards called a Niantick and *brother* *igret.**

PESSA ften mentioned in the preceding pages, though under a variety of names, born about 1623, and, consequently, was about 20 years of age when his ..ier, *Miantunnomoh*, was killed.† The same arbitrary course, as we have seen already in the present chapter, was pursued towards him by the English, as had been before towards *Miantunnomoh*, and still continued towards *Ninigret*, and other Narraganset chiefs. Mr. *Cobbet*‡ makes this record of him: "In the year 1645, proud *Pessacus* with his Narragansets, with whom *Ninigret* and his Niantigs join; so as to provoke the English to a just war against them. And, accordingly, forces were sent from all the towns to meet at Boston, and did so, and had a party of fifty horse to go with them under Mr. *Leveret*, as the captain of the horse." *Edward Gibbons* was commander in chief, and Mr. *Thompson*, pastor of the church in Braintree, "was to sound the silver trumpet along with his army."§ But they were met by deputies from *Pessacus* and the other chiefs, and an accommodation took place, as mentioned in the account of *Ninigret*.

The commissioners, having met at New Haven in September 1646, expected, according to the treaty made at Boston with the Narragansets, as particularized in the life of *Uncas*, that they would now meet them here to settle the remaining difficulties with that chief. But the time having nearly expired, and none appearing, "the commissioners did seriously consider what course should be taken with them. They called to minde their breach of couenant in all the articles, that when aboue 1300 fadome of wampan was due they sent, as if they would put a scorne vpon the [English,] 20 fathome, and a few old kettles." The Narragansets said it was owing to the backwardness of the Nianticks that the wampum had not been paid, and the Nianticks laid it to the Narragansets. One hundred fathom had been sent to the governor of Massachusetts as a present by the Nianticks, they promising "to send what was due to the colonies uery speedily," but he would not accept of it. He told them they might leave it with *Cuchamakin*, and when they had performed the rest of their agreement, "he would consider of it." The commissioners had understood, that, in the mean time, the Narraganset sachems had raised wampum among their men, "and by good euidence it appeared, that by presents of wampum, they are practisinge with the Mohawkes, and with the Indyans in those parts, to engage them in some designe against the English and *Vncus*." Therefore, "the commissioners haue a cleare way open to right themselues, accordinge to iustice by war; yet to shew how highly they prize peace with all men, and particularly to manifest their forbearance and long sufferinge to these barbarians, it was agreede, that first the forementioned present should be returned," and then a declaration of war to follow.

At the same court, complaint was brought against the people of *Pessacus* by "Mr. *Pelham* on behalf of *Richard Woody* and Mr. *Pincham*," [*Pinchon*,] that they had committed sundry thefts. Mr. *Brown*, on behalf of *Wm. Smith* of Rehoboth, preferred a similar charge; but the Indians having no knowledge of the procedure, it was suspended.

Thus the Narragansets were suffered to remain unmolested until the next year, and we do not hear that the story about their hiring the Mohawks and others to assist them against *Uncas* and the English, turned out to be any thing else but a sort of bugbear, probably invented by the Mohegans. "One principall cause of the comissioners meetinge together at this time, [26 July, 1647,] being," say the records, "to consider what course should be held with the Narraganset Indyans;" the charges being at this time much the same as at the previous meeting. It was therefore ordered that *Thomas Stanton*,

* See *Hazard*, ii. 152.

† MS. letter, subscribed with the mark of the sachem *Pumham*, on the file at our capital, (Mass.)

‡ MS. Narrative.

§ *Mather's* Relation, and *Hazard*

Benedict Arnold, and Sergeant *Waite* should be sent to *Pessacks*, *Nenegratt* and *Webetamuk*, to know why they had not paid the wampum as they agreed, and why they did not come to New Haven; and that now they might meet *Uncas* at Boston: and therefore were advised to attend there without delay; but "yf they refuse or delay, they intend to send no more," and they must abide the consequences. When the English messengers had delivered their message to *Pessacus*, he spoke to them as follows:—

"The reason I did not meet the English sachems at New Haven last year, is, they did not notify me. It is true I have broken my covenant these two years, and that now is, and constantly has been, the grief of my spirit. And the reason I do not meet them now at Boston is because I am sick. If I were but pretty well I would go. I have sent my mind in full to *Ninigret*, and what he does I will abide by. I have sent *Powpynamett* and *Pomumsks* to go and hear, and testify that I have betrusted my full mind with *Nenegratt*. You know well, however, that when I made that covenant two years ago, I did it in fear of the army that I did see; and though the English kept their covenant with me, yet they were ready to go to Narraganset and kill me, and the commissioners said they would do it, if I did not sign what they had written."

Moyanno, another chief, said he had confided the business with *Ninigret* last spring, and would now abide by whatever he should do.

When the English messengers returned and made known what had been done, the commissioners said that *Pessacus'* speech contained "seuerall passages of vntruth and guile, and [they] were vnsatisfyed."

What measures the Whites took "to right themselues," or whether any immediately, is not very distinctly stated; but, the next year, 1648, there were some military movements of the English, and a company of soldiers was sent into Narraganset, occasioned by the non-payment of the tribute, and some other less important matters. *Pessacus*, having knowledge of their approach, fled to Rhode Island. "*Ninicraft* entertained them courteously, (there they staid the Lord's day,) and came back with them to Mr. *Williams'*, and then *Pessacus* and *Canonicus'* son, being delivered of their fear, came to them; and being demanded about hiring the Mohawks against *Uncas*, they solemnly denied it; only they confessed, that the Mohawks, being a great sachem, and their ancient friend, and being come so near them, they sent some 20 fathom of wampum for him to tread upon, as the manner of Indians is."* The matter seems to have rested here; *Pessacus*, as usual, having promised what was desired.

This chief was killed by the Mohawks, as we have stated in the life of *Canonicus*. His life was a scene of almost perpetual troubles. As late as September, 1668, his name stands first among others of his nation, in a complaint sent to them by Massachusetts. The messengers sent with it were, *Richd. Wayt*, Captain *W. Wright*, and Captain *Saml. Mosely*; and it was in terms thus:—

"Whereas Capt. *Wm. Hudson* and *John Viall* of Boston, in the name of themselves and others, proprietors of lands and farms in the Narraganset country, have complained unto us, [the court of Mass.,] of the great insolencies and injuries offered unto them and their people by several, as burning their hay, killing sundry horses, and in special manner, about one month since, forced some of their people from their labors in mowing grass upon their own land, and assaulted others in the high way, as they rode about their occasions; by throwing many stones at them and their horses, and beating their horses as they rode upon them," &c. The remonstrance then goes on warning them to desist, or otherwise they might expect severity. Had *Mosely* been as well known then among the Indians, as he was afterwards, his presence would doubtless have been enough to have caused quietness, as perhaps it did even at this time.

* *Winthrop's* Journal.

CHAPTER V.

UNCAS—*His character—Connections—Geography of the Mohegan country—General account of that nation—Uncas joins the English against the Pequots—Captures a chief at Sachem's Head—Visits Boston—His speech to Governor Winthrop—Specimen of the Mohegan language—Sequasson—The war between Uncas and Miantunnomoh—Examination of its cause—The Narragansets determine to avenge their sachem's death—Forces raised to protect Uncas—Pessacus—Great distress of Uncas—Timely relief from Connecticut—Treaty of* 1645—*Frequent complaints against Uncas—Wequash—Obechickwod*—NOWEQUA—*Woosamequin.*

UNCAS, called also *Poquin, Poquoiam, Poquim,* sachem of the Mohegans, of whom we have already had occasion to say considerable, has left no very favorable character upon record. His life is a series of changes, without any of those brilliant acts of magnanimity, which throw a veil over numerous errors. Mr. *Gookin* gives us this character of him in the year 1674: (Mr. *James Fitch* having been sent about this time to preach among the Mohegans:) "I am apt to fear," says he, "that a great obstruction unto his labors is in the sachem of those Indians, whose name is *Unkas;* an old and wicked, wilful man, a drunkard, and otherwise very vicious; who hath always been an opposer and underminer of praying to God." * Nevertheless, the charitable Mr. *Hubbard,* when he wrote his Narrative, seems to have had some hopes that he was a Christian, with about the same grounds, nay better, perhaps, than those on which Bishop *Warburton* declared *Pope* to be such.

Uncas lived to a great age. He was a sachem before the Pequot wars, and was alive in 1680. At this time, Mr. *Hubbard* makes this remark upon him: "He is alive and well, and may probably live to see all his enemies buried before him." †

From an epitaph on one of his sons, copied in the Historical Collections, we do not infer, as the writer there seems to have done, "that the race of *Uncas*" was "obnoxious in collonial history;" but rather attribute it to some waggish Englishman, who had no other design than that of making sport for himself and others of like humor. It is upon his tomb-stone, and is as follows:—

> "Here lies the body of *Sunseeto*
> Own son to *Uncas* grandson to *Oneko* ‡
> Who were the famous sachems of MOHEGAN
> But now they are all dead I think it is *werheegen.*" §

The connections of *Uncas* were somewhat numerous, and the names of several of them will be found as we proceed with his life, and elsewhere *Oneko,* a son, was the most noted of them.

In the beginning of August, 1675, *Uncas* was ordered to appear at Boston and to surrender his arms to the English, and give such other security for his neutrality or coöperation in the war now begun between the English and Wampanoags, as might be required of him. The messenger who was sent to make this requisition, soon returned to Boston, accompanied by three sons of *Uncas* and about 60 of his men, and a quantity of arms. The two younger sons were taken into custody as hostages, and sent to Cambridge, where they were remaining as late as the 10 November following. They are said to have been at this time not far from 30 years of age, but their names are not men-

* 1 *Coll. Mass. Hist. Soc.* i. 208. Moheek, since *Montville,* Connecticut, about 10 miles north of New London, is the place "where *Unkas,* and his sons, and *Wanuho,* are sachems." *Ibid.*

† Hist. New Eng. 464.—"Although he be a friend to the English, yet he and all his men continue pagans still," 1676. Dr. *I. Mather,* Brief Hist. 45.

‡ The writer or sculptor no doubt meant the contrary of this, if, indeed, he may be said to have meant any thing.

§ A genuine Indian word, and, as it is used here, means, simply, *well.* "Then they bid me stir my instep, to see if that were frozen: I did so. When they saw that, they said that was *wurregen.*" *Stockwell's Nar. of his Captivity among the Indians in* 1677.

tioned.* *Oneko* was employed with his 60 men, and proceeded on an expedition, as will be found stated elsewhere.

Uncas was originally a Pequot, and one of the 26 war captains of that famous, but ill-fated nation. Upon some intestine commotions, he revolted against his sachem, and set up for himself. This took place about the time that nation became known to the English, perhaps in 1634 or 5; or, as it would seem from some circumstances, in the beginning of the Pequot war. *Peters*,† an author of not much authority, says, that the "colonists declared him King of Mohegan, to reward him for deserting *Sassacus*." We are told, by the same author, that, after the death of *Uncas*, ONEKO would not deed any lands to the colony; upon which he was deposed, and his natural brother, *Abimileck*, was, by the English, advanced to the office of chief sachem. *Oneko*, not acknowledging the validity of this procedure, sold, in process of time, all his lands to two individuals, named *Mason* and *Harrison*. But, meantime, *Abimileck* sold the same lands to the colony. A lawsuit followed, and was, at first, decided in favor of the colony; but, on a second trial, *Mason* and *Harrison* got the case—*but not the property;* for, as *Peters* tells us, "the colony kept possession under *Abimileck*, their created King of Mohegan," and "found means to confound the claim of those competitors without establishing their own."

By the revolt of *Uncas*, the Pequot territories became divided, and that part called *Moheag*, or *Mohegan*, fell generally under his dominion, and extended from near the Connecticut River on the south, to a space of disputed country on the north, next the Narragansets. By a recurrence to our account of the dominions of the Pequots and Narragansets, a pretty clear idea may be had of all three.

This sachem seems early to have courted the favor of the English, which, it is reasonable to suppose, was occasioned by the fear he was in from his potent and warlike neighbors, both on the north and on the south. In May, 1637, he was prevailed upon to join the English in their war upon the Pequots. Knowing the relation in which he stood to them, the English at first were nearly as afraid of *Uncas* and his men, as they were of the Pequots. But when, on the 15 of the same month, they had arrived at Saybrook fort, a circumstance happened that tended much to remove their suspicions, and is related by Dr. *Mather* as follows: "Some of *Uncas* his men being then at Saybrook, in order to assisting the English against the Pequots, espied seven Indians, and slily encompassing them, slew five of them, and took one prisoner, and brought him to the English fort, which was great satisfaction and encouragement to the English; who, before that exploit, had many fears touching the fidelity of the Moheag Indians. He whom they took prisoner was a perfidious villain, one that could speak English well, having in times past lived in the fort, and knowing all the English there, had been at the slaughtering of all the English that were slaughtered thereabouts. He was a continual spy about the fort, informing *Sassacus* of what he could learn. When this bloody traitor was executed, his limbs were by violence pulled from one another, and burned to ashes. Some of the Indian executioners barbarously taking his flesh, they gave it to one another, and did eat it, withal singing about the fire."‡

Notwithstanding, both *Uncas* and *Miantunnomoh* were accused of harboring fugitive Pequots, after the Mystic fight, as our accounts will abundantly prove. It is true they had agreed not to harbor them, but perhaps the philanthropist will not judge them harder for erring on the score of mercy, than their English friends for their strictly religious perseverance in revenge.

A traditionary story of *Uncas* pursuing, overtaking, and executing a Pequot sachem, as given in the Historical Collections, may not be unqualifiedly true. It was after Mystic fight, and is as follows: Most of the English forces pursued the fugitives by water, westward, while some followed by land with *Uncas* and his Indians. At a point of land in Guilford, they came upon a great Pequot sachem, and a few of his men. Knowing they were pursued,

* Old Indian Chronicle, 15.

† In his Hist. of Connecticut.

‡ Relation of the Troubles, &c. 46.

they had gone into an adjacent peninsula, "hoping their pursuers would have passed by them. But *Uncas* knew Indian's craft, and ordered some of his men to search that point. The Pequots perceiving that they were pursued, swam over the mouth of the harbor, which is narrow. But they were waylaid, and taken as they landed. The sachem was sentenced to be shot to death. *Uncas* shot him with an arrow, cut off his head, and stuck it up in the crotch of a large oak-tree near the harbor, where the skull remained for a great many years."* This was the origin of SACHEM'S HEAD, by which name the harbor of Guilford is well-known to coasters.

Dr. *Mather* records the expedition of the English, but makes no mention of *Uncas*. He says, they set out from Saybrook fort, and "sailed westward in pursuit of the Pequots, who were fled that way. Sailing along to the westward of Mononowuttuck, the wind not answering their desires, they cast anchor." "Some scattering Pequots were then taken and slain, as also the Pequot sachem, before expressed,† had his head cut off, whence that place did bear the name of SACHEM'S HEAD."‡

Uncas's fear of the Pequots was doubtless the cause of his hostility to them; and when he saw them vanquished, he probably began to relent his unprovoked severity towards his countrymen, many of whom were his near relations; and this may account for his endeavors to screen some of them from their more vindictive enemies. The next spring after the war, 5 March, 1638, "*Unkus*, alias *Okoco*, the Monahegan sachem in the twist of Pequod River, came to Boston with 37 men. He came from Connecticut with Mr. *Haynes*, and tendered the governor a present of 20 fathom of wampum. This was at court, and it was thought fit by the council to refuse it, till he had given satisfaction about the Pequots he kept, &c. Upon this he was much dejected, and made account we would have killed him; but, two days after, having received good satisfaction of his innocency, &c. and he promising to submit to the order of the English, touching the Pequots he had, and the differences between the Narragansetts and him, we accepted his present. And about half an hour after, he came to the governor," and made the following speech. Laying his hand upon his breast, he said,

"*This heart is not mine, but yours. I have no men: they are all yours. Command me any difficult thing, I will do it. I will not believe any Indians' words against the English. If any man shall kill an Englishman, I will put him to death, were he never so dear to me.*"

"So the governor gave him a fair red coat, and defrayed his and his men's diet, and gave them corn to relieve them homeward, and a letter of protection to all men, &c. and he departed very joyful."§

For the gratification of the curious, we give, from Dr. *Edwards's* "Observations on the Muhkekaneew [Mohegan] Language," the Lord's prayer in that dialect. "*Nogh-nuh, ne spummuck oi-e-on, taugh mau-weh wneh wtu-ko-se-auk ne-an-ne an-nu-woi-e-on. Taugh ne aun-chu-wut-am-mun wa-weh-tu-seek ma-weh noh pum-meh. Ne ae-noi-hit-teeh mau-weh aw-au-neek noh hkey oie-cheek, ne aun-chu-wut-am-mun, ne au-noi-hit-teet neek spum-muk oie-cheek. Men-e nau-nuh noo-nooh wuh-ham-auk tquogh nuh uh-huy-u-tam-auk ngum-mau-weh Ohq-u-ut-a-mou-we-nau-nuh au-neh mu-ma-choi-e-au-keh he anneh ohq-u-ut-a-mou-woi-e-auk num-peh neek mu-ma-cheh an-neh-o-quau-keet. Cheen hqu-uk-quau-cheh-si-u-keh an-neh-e-henau-nuh. Pan-nee-weh htou-we-nau-nuh neen maum-teh-keh. Ke-ah ng-weh-cheh kwi-ou-wau-weh mau-weh noh pum-meh; kt-an-woi; es-tah aw-aun w-tin-noi-yu-wun ne au-noi-e-yon; han-wee-weh ne kt-in-noi-een.*"

Such was the language of the Mohegans, the Pequots, the Narragansets and Nipmucks; or so near did they approach one another, that each could understand the other through the united extent of their territories.

Uncas was said to have been engaged in all the wars against his countrymen, on the part of the English, during his life-time.‖ He shielded some of the infant settlements of Connecticut in times of troubles, especially Norwich

* Hist. *Guilford*, in 1 *Coll. Mass. Hist. Soc.* 100.

† His name is not mentioned.

‡ Relation, 49.

§ *Winthrop*, Jour. i. 265-6

‖ MS. communication of Rev. Mr. *Ely*.

To the inhabitants of this town the Mohegans seemed more particularly attached probably from the circumstance of some of its settlers having relieved them when besieged by *Ninigret*, as will be found related in the ensuing history. The remnant of the Mohegans, in 1768, was settled in the north-east corner of New London, about five miles south of Norwich; at which place they had a reservation.

The Mohegans had a burying-place called the Royal *burying-ground*, and this was set apart for the family of *Uncas*. It is close by the falls of the stream called Yantic River, in Norwich city; "a beautiful and romantic spot." The ground containing the grave of *Uncas* is at present owned by *C. Goddard*, Esq. of Norwich. This gentleman has, very laudably, caused an inclosure to be set about it.*

When the commissioners of the United Colonies had met in 1643, complaint was made to them by *Uncas*, that *Miantunnomoh* had employed a Pequot to kill him, and that this Pequot was one of his own subjects. He shot *Uncas* with an arrow, and, not doubting but that he had accomplished his purpose, "fled to the Nanohigganesets, or their confederates," and proclaimed that he had killed him. "But when it was known *Vncas* was not dead, though wounded, the traitor was taught to say that *Uncus* had cut through his own arm with a flint, and hired the Pequot to say he had shot and killed him. *Myantinomo* being sent for by the governor of the Massachusetts upon another occasion, brought the Pequot with him: but when this disguise would not serve, and that the English out of his [the Pequot's] own mouth found him guilty, and would have sent him to *Uncus* his sagamore to be proceeded against, *Myantinomo* desired he might not be taken out of his hands, promising [that] he would send [him] himself to *Vncus* to be examined and punished; but, contrary to his promise, and fearing, as it appears, his own treachery might be discouered, he within a day or two cut off the Peacott's head, that he might tell no tales. After this some attempts were made to poison *Vncus*, and, as is reported, to take away his life by sorcery. That being discovered, some of *Sequasson's* company, an Indian sagamore allied to, and an intimate confederate with *Myantinomo*, shot at *Uncus* as he was going down Conectacatt River with a arrow or two. *Vncus*, according to the foresaid agreement," which was, in case of difficulty between them, that the English should be applied to as umpires, complained to them. They endeavored to bring about a peace between *Uncas* and *Sequasson;* but *Sequasson* would hear to no overtures of the kind, and intimated that he should be borne out in his resolution by *Miantunnomoh*. The result was the war of which we have given an account in the life of *Miantunnomoh*. We have also spoken there of the agency of the English in the affair of *Miantunnomoh's* death; but that no light may be withheld which can in any way reflect upon that important as well as melancholy event, we will give all that the commissioners have recorded in their records concerning it. But firstly, we should notice, that, after *Miantunnomoh* was taken prisoner, the Indians affirmed, (the adherents of *Uncas* doubtless,) that *Miantunnomoh* had engaged the Mohawks to join him in his wars, and that they were then encamped only a day's journey from the frontiers, waiting for him to attain his liberty. The record then proceeds:—

"These things being duly weighed and considered, the commissioners apparently see that *Vncus* cannot be safe while *Myantenomo* lives; but that, either by secret treachery or open force, his life will be still in danger Wherefore they think he may justly put such a false and blood-thirsty enemy to death, but in his own jurisdiction, not in the English plantations. And advising that, in the manner of his death, all mercy and moderation be showed, contrary to the practice of the Indians who exercise tortures and cruelty. And *Vncus* having hitherto shown himself a friend to the English, and in this craving their advice; [therefore,] if the Nanohiggansitts Indians or others shall unjustly assault *Vncus* for this execution, upon notice and request the English promise to assist and protect him, as far as they may, against such violence."

We presume not to commentate upon this affair, but we would ask whether

---

* 3 Coll. Mass. Hist. Soc. iii. 135.

it does not appear as probable, that *Uncas* had concerted the plan with his Pequot subject for the destruction of *Miantunnomoh*, as that the latter had plotted for the destruction of the former. Else, why did *Miantunnomoh* put the Pequot to death? The commissioners do not say that the Pequot had by his confession any how implicated *Miantunnomoh*. Now, if this Pequot had been employed by him, it does not seem at all likely that he would have put him to death, especially as he had not accused him. And, on the other hand, if he had acknowledged himself guilty of attempting the life of his own sachem, that it might be charged upon others, it is to us a plain reason why *Miantunnomoh* should put him to death, being fully satisfied of his guilt upon his own confession. It may be concluded, therefore, that the plot against *Uncas* was of his own or his Pequot subject's planning. The Pequot's going over to *Miantunnomoh* for protection is no evidence of that chief's participation in his plot. And it is highly probable that, after they had left the English court, his crime was aggravated, in *Miantunnomoh's* view, by some new confession or discovery, which caused him to be forthwith executed.

As though well assured that the justness of their interference would be called in question, the commissioners shortly after added another clause to their records, as much in exoneration of their conduct as they could find words in which to express themselves. They argue that, "whereas *Uncas* was advised [by them] to take away the life of *Miantunnomoh* whose lawful captive he was, they [the Narragansets] may well understand that this is without violation of any covenant between them and us; for *Uncas* being in confederation with us, and one that hath diligently observed his covenants before mentioned, for aught we know, and requiring advice from us, upon serious consideration of the premises, viz. his treacherous and murderous disposition against *Uncas*, &c. and how great a disturber he hath been of the common peace of the whole country, we could not in respect of the justice of the case, safety of the country, and faithfulness of our friend, do otherwise than approve of the lawfulness of his death; which agreeing so well with the Indians' own manners, and concurring with the practice of other nations with whom we are acquainted; we persuaded ourselves, however his death may be grievous at present, yet the peaceable fruits of it will yield not only matter of safety to the Indians, but profit to all that inhabit this continent."

It is believed that the reader is now put in possession of every thing that the English could say for themselves, upon the execution of *Miantunnomoh*. He will therefore be able to decide, whether, as we have stated, their judgment was made up of one kind of evidence; and whether the Narragansets had any lawyers to advocate their cause before the commissioners.

After *Miantunnomoh* was executed, the Narragansets demanded satisfaction of *Uncas* for the money they had raised and paid for the redemption of their chief. This demand was through the English commissioners; who, when they were met, in Sept. 1644, deputed *Thomas Stanton* to notify both parties to appear before them, that they might decide upon the case according to the evidence which should be produced.

It appears that *Kienemo*,* the Niantick sachem, immediately deputed *Weetowisse*, a sachem, *Pawpiamet* and *Pummumshe*, captains, from the Narragansets, with two of their men, to maintain their action before the commissioners, and to complain of some insolences of *Uncas* besides.† On a full hearing, the commissioners say, that nothing was substantiated by them. "Though," they say, "several discourses had passed from *Uncas* and his men, that for such quantities of wampum and such parcels of other goods to a great value, there might have been some probability of sparing his life." Hence it appears that *Uncas* had actually entered upon a negotiation with the Narragansets, as in the life of *Miantunnomoh* has been stated; and it does not, it is thought, require but a slight acquaintance with the general drift of these affairs, to discern, that *Uncas* had encouraged the Narragansets to send

* The same afterwards called *Ninigret*. *Janemo* was doubtless the pronunciation, *J* being at that time pronounced *ji*; therefore *Jianemo* might have been sometimes understood *Kianemo*. *Winthrop* writes the name *Ayanemo* in one instance.

† The author of *Tales of the Indians* seems dismally confused in attempting to narrate these affairs, but see *Hazard*, ii. 25 and 26.

wampum, that is, their money, giving them to understand that he would not be hard with them; in so far, that they had trusted to his generosity, and sent him a considerable amount. The very face of it shows clearly, that it was a trick of *Uncas* to leave the amount indefinitely stated, which gave him the chance, (that a knave will always seize upon,) to act according to the caprice of his own mind on any pretence afterwards.

The commissioners say, that "no such parcels were brought," though, in a few lines after, in their records, we read: "And for that wampums and goods sent, [to *Uncas*,] as they were but *small parcels*, and scarce considerable for such a purpose," namely, the redemption of their chief: and still, they add; "But *Uncas* denieth, and the Narraganset deputies did not alledge, much less prove that any ransom was agreed, nor so much as any treaty begun to redeem their imprisoned sachem." Therefore it appears quite clear that *Uncas* had all the English in his favor, who, to preserve his friendship, caressed and called him their friend; while, on the other hand, the agents from the Narragansets were frowned upon, and no doubt labored under the disadvantage of not being personally known to the English.

As to the goods which *Uncas* had received, the commissioners say, "A part of them [were] disposed [of] by *Miantunnomoh* himself, to *Uncas*' counsellors and captains, for some favor, either past or hoped for, and part were given and sent to *Uncas*, and to his squaw for preserving his life so long, and using him courteously during his imprisonment."

Here ended this matter; but before the Narraganset deputies left the court, the English made them sign an agreement, that they would not make war upon *Uncas*, "vntill after the next planting of corn." And even then, that they should give 30 days' notice to the English before commencing hostilities. Also that if "any of the Nayantick Pecotts should make any assault upon *Uncas* or any of his, they would deliver them up to the English to be punished according to their demerits. And that they would not use any means to procure the Mawhakes to come against *Uncas* during this truce." At the same time the English took due care to notify the Narraganset commissioners, by way of awing them into terms, that if they did molest the Mohegans, all the English would be upon them.

The date of this agreement, if so we may call it, is, "Hartford, the xviijth of September, 1644," and was signed by four Indians; one besides those named above, called *Chimough*.

That no passage might be left open for excuse, in case of war, it was also mentioned, that "proof of the ransom charged" must be made satisfactory to the English before war was begun.

The power of *Pessacus* and *Ninigret* at this time was much feared by the English, and they were ready to believe any reports of the hostile doings of the Narragansets, who, since the subjection of the Pequots, had made themselves masters of all their neighbors, except the English, as the Pequots had done before them. The Mohegans were also in great fear of them, as well after as before the death of *Miantunnomoh*; but for whose misfortune in being made a prisoner by a stratagem of *Uncas*, or his captains, the English might have seen far greater troubles from them than they did, judging from the known abilities of that great chief.

There was "a meeting extraordinary" of the commissioners of the United Colonies, in July, 1645, at Boston, "concerning the French business, and the wars between *Pissicus* and *Vncus* being begun." Their first business was to despatch away messengers to request the appearance of the head men of the belligerents to appear themselves at Boston, or to send some of their chief men, that the difficulties between them might be settled.

These messengers, Sergeant *John Dames*, [*Davis*?] *Benedict Arnold*, and *Francis Smyth*, on their first arrival at Narraganset, were welcomed by the sachems, who offered them guides to conduct them to *Uncas*; but, either having understood their intentions, or judging from their appearance that the English messengers meant them no good, changed their deportment altogether, and in the mean time secretly despatched messengers to the Nianticks before them, giving them to understand what was going forward. After this, say the messengers, "there was nothing but proud and insolent passages [from *Ninigret.*] The Indian guides which they had brought with them from *Pumham* and *Sokakanoco* were, by frowns and threatening speeches, discouraged, and returned; no other guides could be obtained.' The sachems said they knew, by what was done at Hartford last year, that the English would urge peace, "*but they were resolved*, they said, *to have no peace without Uncas his head.*" As to who began the war, they cared not, but they were resolved to continue it; that if the English did not withdraw their soldiers from *Uncas*, they should consider it a breach of former covenants, and would procure as many Mohawks as the English had soldiers to bring against them. They reviled *Uncas* for having wounded himself, and then charging it upon them, and said he was no friend of the English, but would now, if he durst, kill the English messengers, and lay that to them. Therefore, not being able to proceed, the English messengers returned to the Narragansets, and acquainted *Pessacus* of what had passed, desiring he would furnish them with guides; "he, (in scorn, as they apprehended it,) offered them an old Peacott squaw."

The messengers now thought themselves in danger of being massacred; "three Indians with hatchets standing behind the interpreter in a suspicious manner, while he was speaking with *Pessacus*, and the rest, frowning and expressing much distemper in their countenance and carriage." So, without much loss of time, they began to retrace their steps. On leaving *Pessacus*, they told him they should lodge at an English trading house not far off that night, and if he wanted to send any word to the English, he might send to them. In the morning, he invited them to return, and said he would furnish them with guides to visit *Uncas*, but he would not suspend hostilities. Not daring to risk the journey, the messengers returned home. *Arnold*, the interpreter, testified that this was a true relation of what had passed, which is necessary to be borne in mind, as something may appear, as we proceed, impeaching the veracity of *Arnold.*

Meanwhile the commissioners set forth an armament to defend *Uncas*, at all hazards. To justify this movement, they declare, that, "considering the great provocations offered, and the necessity we should be put unto of making war upon the Narrohiggin, &c. and being also careful in a matter of so great weight and general concernment to see the way cleared and to give satisfaction to all the colonists, did think fit to advise with such of the magistrates and elders of the Massachusetts as were then at hand, and also with some of the chief military commanders there, who being assembled, it was then agreed: First, that our engagement bound us to aid and defend the Mohegan sachem. Secondly, that this aid could not be intended only to defend him and his, in his fort or habitation, but, (according to the common acceptation of such covenants or engagements considered with the ground or occasion thereof,) so to aid him as hee might be preserved in his liberty and estate. Thirdly, that this aid must be speedy, least he might be swallowed up in the mean time, and so come too late."

"According to the counsel and determination aforesaid, the commissioners, considering the present danger of *Uncas* the Mohegan sachem, (his fort having been divers times assaulted by a great army of the Narrohiggansets, &c.) agreed to have 40 soldiers sent with all expedition for his defense." Lieutenant *Atherton* and Sergeant *John Davis* led this company, conducted by two of "*Cutchamakin's*" Indians as guides. *Atherton* was ordered not to make an "attempt upon the town otherwise than in *Uncas'* defence." Captain *Mason* of Connecticut was to join him, and take the chief command. Forty men were ordered also from Connecticut, and 30 from New Haven under Lieutenant *Sealy*. In their instructions to *Mason*, the commissioners say, "We so now aim at the protection of the Mohegans, that we would have no opportunity neglected to weaken the Narragansets and their confederates, in their number of men, their cane canoes, wigwams, wampum and goods. We look upon the Nianticks as the chief incendiaries and causes of the war, and should be glad they might first feel the smart of it." The Nianticks, therefore, were particularly to be had in view by *Mason*, and he was informed at the same time that Massachusetts and Plimouth were forthwith to send "another army to invade the Narragansets."

The commissioners now proceeded to make choice of a commander in chief of the two armies. Major *Edward Gibbons* was unanimously elected. In his instructions is this passage: "Whereas the scope and cause of this expedition is not only to aid the Mohegans, but to offend the Narragansets, Nianticks, and other their confederates." He was directed also to conclude a peace with them, if they desired it, provided it were made with special reference to damages, &c. And they say, "But withal, according to our engagements, you are to provide for *Uncas'* future safety, that his plantations be not invaded, that his men and squaws may attend their planting and fishing and other occasions without fear or injury, and *Vssamequine, Pomham, Sokakonoco, Cutchamakin,* and other Indians, friends or subjects to the English, be not molested," &c.

Soon after the death of *Miantunnomoh,* which was in September, 1643, his brother *Pessacus,* "the new sachem of Narraganset," then "a young man about 20," sent to Governor *Winthrop* of Massachusetts, as a present, an *otter coat,* a girdle of wampum, and some of that article besides, in value about £15. The messenger, named *Washose,** also a sachem, told the governor that his chief desired to continue in peace with the English; but that he was about to make war upon *Uncas,* to avenge the death of his brother, and hoped they would not interfere, nor aid *Uncas.* The governor said they wished to be at peace with all Indians, and that all Indians would be at peace among themselves, and that they must agree to this, or they could not accept their present. *Washose* said he was instructed no further than to make known his mission and leave the present, which he did, and returned to his own country. This was in February, 1644, N. S. Within the same month, the same messenger appeared again at Boston; and "his errand was, (says Governor *Winthrop,*) that, seeing they, at our request, had set still this year, that now this next year we would grant their request, and suffer them to fight with *Onkus,* with many arguments." But he was answered, that the English would not allow such a proceeding, and if they persisted all the English would fall upon them.

Planting time, and 30 days besides, had passed before the English sent an army to invade the Narragansets. *Pessacus* and the other chiefs had done all they could do to cause the English to remain neutral, but now determined to wait no longer, and hostile acts were committed on both sides.

The traditionary account of *Uncas's* being besieged in his fort by the Narragansets will very properly be looked for in this connection, as it has not only adorned some *tales of the Indians,* but has been seriously urged as truth in more imposing forms. What we are about to give is contained in a letter, dated at New Haven, 19 September, 1796, by *Wm. Leffingwell,* and directed *Dr. Trumbull.*

"At the time the Mohegan tribe of Indians were besieged by the Narraganset tribe, in a fort near the River Thames, between Norwich and New London, the provisions of the besieged being nearly exhausted, *Uncas,* their sachem, found means to inform the settlers at Saybrook of their distress, and the danger they would be in from the Narragansets, if the Mohegan tribe were cut off. Ensign *Thomas Leffingwell,* one of the first settlers there, loaded a canoe with beef, corn and peas, and in the night time paddled from Saybrook into the Thames, and had the address to get the whole into the fort of the besieged;—received a deed from *Uncas* of the town of Norwich, and made his escape that very night. In consequence of which, the besiegers, finding *Uncas* had procured relief, raised the siege, and the Mohegan tribe were saved, and have ever proved strict friends to the N. England settlers." †

The above agrees very well with Mr. *Hyde's* account. "When *Uncas* and tribe were attacked by a potent enemy, and blocked up in their fort on a hill, by the side of the great river, and almost starved to death, Lieut. *Thos. Leffingwell,* Capt. *Benj. Brewster,* of said Norwich, and others, secretly carried

---

* Perhaps the same as *Awashers.*

† Copied from the original, for the author, by Rev. *Wm. Ely,* who thus remarks upon it: "This tradition, from a highly respectable source, *Trumbull* states as history; yet, in some minor points, at least, it would seem obvious that the tradition could not have been strictly preserved for 150 years." *MS. letter.*

their provision, in the night seasons, upon which the enemy raised the siege."* In consideration of which, "*Uncas* gave sundry donations of land," &c.†

At the congress of the commissioners at Boston, in 1645, above mentioned, it was ascertained that the present from *Pessacus* still remained among them, and therefore he might think it was probable that the English had complied with their desires, as they had not returned it. Lest this should be so understood, Captain *Harding*, Mr. *Welborne*, and *Benedict Arnold*, were ordered and commissioned to repair to the Narraganset country, and to see, if possible, "*Pissus, Canownacus, Janemo*," and other sachems, and to return the present before mentioned, and to inform them that the English were well aware of their beginning and prosecuting a war upon *Uncas*, and their "having wounded and slain divers of his men, seized many of his canoes, taken some prisoners, spoiled much of his corn," refused to treat with him, and threatened the English. Nevertheless, if they would come themselves forthwith to Boston, they should be heard and protected in their journey, but that none except themselves would be treated with, and if they refused to come, the English were prepared for war, and would proceed immediately against them.

Harding and *Welborne* proceeded to Providence, where *Arnold* was to join them. But he was not there, and they were informed that he dared not venture among the Narragansets. Whether he had been acting the *traitor* with them, or something quite as much to merit condemnation, we will leave the reader to judge from the relation. The two former, therefore, made use of Reverend Mr. *Williams* as interpreter in their business, but were reprimanded by the commissioners for it on their return. On going to the Narraganset sachems, and opening their business, it appeared that all they were ordered to charge them with was not true; or, at least, denied by them. These charges, it appears, had been preferred by *Arnold*, and sworn to upon oath. The chiefs said "that *Ianemo*, the Nyantick sachem, had been ill divers days, but had now sent six men to present his respects to the English, and to declare his assent and submission to what the Narrohiggenset sachems and the English should agree upon."

It was in the end agreed, that the chiefs, *Pessacus, Mexam*, and divers others, should proceed to Boston, agreeably to the desire of the English, which they did, in company with *Harding* and *Welborne*, who brought back the old present, and for which they also received the censure of the congress. They arrived at Boston just as the second levy of troops were marching out for their country, and thus the expedition was stayed until the result of a treaty should be made known.

It appeared, on a conference with the commissioners, that the sachems did not fully understand the nature of all the charges against them before leaving their country, and in justice to them it should be observed, that, so far as the record goes, their case appears to us the easiest to be defended of the three parties concerned. They told the commissioners of sundry charges they had against *Uncas*, but they said they could not hear them, for *Uncas* was not

---

* Some very beautiful verses appeared several years since in the Connecticut Mirror, to which it seems the above had given rise. They were prefaced with the following among other observations: "In the neighborhood of Mohegan is a rude recess, environed by rocks, which still retains the name of the 'chair of *Uncas*;' and that the people of *Uncas* were perishing with hunger when *Leffingwell* brought him relief. We give the following stanzas from it:—

"The monarch sat on his rocky throne,
Before him the waters lay;
His guards were shapeless columns of stone,
Their lofty helmets with moss o'ergrown,
And their spears of the bracken gray

"His lamps were the fickle stars, that beamed
Through the veil of their midnight shroud,
And the reddening flashes that fitfully gleamed
When the distant fires of the war-dance streamed
Where his foes in frantic revel screamed
'Neath their canopy of cloud," &c.

† MS letter to Dr. *Trumbull*, before cited, and life of *Miantunnomoh*.

14

there to speak for himself; and that they had hindered his being notified of their coming. As to a breach of covenant, they maintained, for some time, they had committed none, and that their treatment of the English had been misrepresented. "But, (says our record,) after a long debate and some priuate conferrence, they had with Serjeant *Cullicutt*, they acknowledged they had brooken promise or couenant in the afore menconed warrs, and offerred to make another truce with *Vncas*, either till next planting tyme, as they had done last yeare at Hartford, or for a yeare, or a yeare and a quarter."

They had been induced to make this admission, no doubt, by the persuasion of *Cullicut*, who, probably, was instructed to inform them that the safety of their country depended upon their compliance with the wishes of the English at this time. An army of soldiers was at that moment parading the streets, in all the pomposity of a modern training, which must have reminded them of the horrible destruction of their kindred at Mystic eight years before.

The proposition of a truce being objected to by the English, "one of the sachems offered a stick or a wand to the commissioners, expressing himself, that therewith they put the power and disposition of the war into their hands, and desired to know *what the English would require of them.*" They were answered that the expenses and trouble they had caused the English were very great, "besides the damage *Vncas* had sustained; yet to show *their moderacon*, they would require of them but *twoo thousand* fathome of white wampon for their owne satisfaccon," but that they should restore to *Uncas* all the captives and canoes taken from him, and make restitution for all the corn they had spoiled. As for the last-mentioned offence, the sachems asserted there had been none such; for *it was not the manner of the Indians to destroy corn.*

This most excellent and indirect reproof must have had no small effect on those who heard it, as no doubt some of the actors as well as the advisers of the destruction of the Indians' corn, previous to and during the Pequot war, were now present: Block Island, and the fertile fields upon the shores of the Connecticut, must have magnified before their imaginations.

Considering, therefore, that this charge was merely imaginary, and that *Uncas* had taken and killed some of their people, the English *consented* that *Uncas* "*might*" restore such captives and canoes as he had taken from them. Finally, they agreed to pay the wampum, "crauing onely some ease in the manner and tymes of payment," and on the evening of "*the* xxvij*th of the* 6 *month*, (August,) 1645," articles to the following effect were signed by the principal Indians present:—

1. That the Narragansets and Nianticks had made war upon the Mohegans contrary to former treaties; that the English had sent messengers to them without success, which had made them prepare for war.

2. That chiefs duly authorized were now at Boston, and having acknowledged their breach of treaties, having "thereby not only endamaged *Vncas*, but had brought much charge and trouble vpon all the English colonies, which they confest were just they should satisfy."

3. That the sachems agree for their nations to pay to the English 2000 fathom "of good white wampum, or a third part of good black wampempeage, in four payments, namely," 500 fathom in 20 days, 500 in four months, 500 at or before next planting time, and 500 in two years, which the English agree to accept as full "satisfaccon."

4. That each party of the Indians was to restore to the other all things taken, and where canoes were destroyed, others "in the roome of them, full as good," were to be given in return. The English obligated themselves for *Uncas.*

5. That as many matters cannot be treated of on account of the absence of *Uncas*, they are to be deferred until the next meeting of the commissioners at Hartford, in Sept. 1646, where both parties should be heard.

6. The Narraganset and Niantic sachems bind themselves to keep peace with the English and their successors, "and with *Vncas* the Mohegan sachem

and his men, with *Vssamequin,** *Pomham*, *Sokaknooco*, *Cutchamakin*, *Shoanan*,† *Passaconaway*, and all others. And that, in case difficulties occur, they are to apply to the English.

7. They promise to deliver up to the English all fugitives who shall at any time be found among them; to pay a yearly tribute, "a month before Indian harvest, every year after this, at Boston," "for all such Pecotts as live amongst them," according to the treaty of 1638;‡ "namely, one fathom of white wampum for each Pequot man, and half a fathom for each Peacott youth, and one hand length of wampum for each Peacott man-child; and if *Weckwash Cake* § refuse to pay this tribute for any Peacotts with him, the Narrohigganset sagamores promise to assist the English against him;" and to yield up to the English the whole Pequot country.

8. The sachems promise to deliver four of their children into the hands of the English, "vizt. *Pissacus* his eldest sonn, the sonn of *Tassaquanawitt*, brother to *Pissacus*, *Awashanoe* his sonn, and *Ewangeso's* sonn, a Nyantick, to be kept as pledges or hostages," until the wampum should be all paid, and they had met *Uncas* at Hartford, and *Janemo* and *Wypetock* ‖ had signed these articles. As the children were to be sent for, *Witowash*, *Pomamse*, *Jawassoe*, and *Waughwamino* offered their persons as security for their delivery, who were accepted.

9. Both the securities and hostages were to be supported at the charge of the English.

10. That if any hostilities were committed while this treaty was making, and before its provisions were known, such acts not to be considered a violation thereof.

11. They agree not to sell any of their lands without the consent of the commissioners.

12. If any Pequots should be found among them who had murdered English, they were to be delivered to the English. Here follow the names, with a mark to each.

PESSECUS,
AUMSAAQUEN, ¶ *deputy for the Niantícks*,
ABDAS,
POMMUSH,
CUTCHAMAKINS,
WEEKESANNO,
WITTOWASH.

We do not see *Mexam's* or *Mixanno's* name among the signers, although he is mentioned as being present, unless another name was then applied to him. There were four interpreters employed upon the occasion, namely, Sergeant *Cullicut* and his Indian man, *Cutchamakin* and *Josias*.**

From this time to the next meeting of the commissioners, the country seems not to have been much disturbed. In the mean time, however, *Uncas*, without any regard to the promise and obligations the English had laid themselves under for him, undertook to chastise a Narraganset sachem for some alleged offence. On opening their congress, at New Haven, letters from Mr. *Morton* and Mr. *Peters*, at Pequot, were read by the commissioners, giving accounts of *Uncas's* perfidy. The complainants were sent to, and informed that *Uncas* was shortly to be there, and that they should bring their proof in order to a trial.

Meanwhile *Uncas* came, who, after waiting a few days, and his accusers not appearing, was examined and dismissed. It appears that the English at Nameoke, since Saybrook, were the suffering party, as their neighborhood was the scene of *Uncas's* depredations. Of some of the charges he acknowledged himself guilty, especially of fighting *Neckwash* [Wequash] *Cooke* so near to the plantation at Pequot; although he alleged that some of the English there had encouraged *Wequash* to hunt upon his lands. He was informed

* *Ousamequin.* † Perhaps *Shoshanim*, or *Sholan*.
‡ See page 61, *ante*. § *Wequash Cook.* ‖ *Wepiteamock.*
¶ *Awasequin.* ** Son of *Chikataubut*, probably

that his brother had also been guilty of some offence, but neither the accuser nor the accused were present, and, therefore, it could not be acted upon. So, after a kind of *reprimand*, *Uncas* was dismissed, as we have just mentioned. But before he had left the town, Mr. *Wm. Morton* arrived at court, with three Indians, to maintain the action against him; he was, therefore, called in, and a hearing was had, "but the commissioners founde noe cause to alter the former writinge giuen him." This was as regarded the affair with *Wequash*. Mr. *Morton* then produced a Pequot powwow, named *Wampushet*, who, he said, had charged *Uncas* with having hired him to do violence to another Indian, or to procure it to be done, which accordingly was effected, the Indian being wounded with a hatchet. This crime was at first laid to the charge of *Wequash*, as *Uncas* had intended. "But after [wards,] the Pequat's powwow, troubled in conscience, could have no rest till he had discoured *Vncus* to be the author." He first related his guilt to *Robin*,* an Indian servant of Mr. *Winthrop*; but, to the surprise of the whole court, *Wampushet*, the only witness, on being questioned through Mr. *Stanton*, the interpreter, told a story diametrically the reverse of what he had before stated. "He cleared *Vncus*, and cast the plot and guilt vpon *Neckwash Cooke* and *Robin*;" "and though the other two Pequats, whereof the one was *Robin's* brother, seemed much offended," and said *Uncas* had hired him to alter his charge, "yet he persisted, and said *Neckwash Cooke* and *Robin* had giuen him a payre of breeches, and promised him 25 fadome of wampum, to cast the plot upon *Vncus*, and that the English plantacon and Pequats knew it. The commissioners abhorring this diuilish falshoode, and advisinge *Vncus*, if he expected any favoure and respect from the English, to haue no hand in any such designes or vniust wayes."

Hence it appears that the court did not doubt much of the villany of *Uncas*, but, for reasons not required here to be named, he was treated as a fond parent often treats a disobedient child; reminded of the end to which such crimes lead; and seem to threaten chastisement in their words, while their deportment holds out quite different language.

At the congress of the United Colonies, at Boston, in July, 1647, Mr. *John Winthrop* of Connecticut presented a petition, "in the name of many Pequatts," in the preamble of which *Casmamon* and *Obechiquod* are named, requesting that they might have liberty to dwell somewhere under the protection of the English, which they might appoint. They acknowledged that their sachems and people had done very ill against the English formerly, for which they had justly suffered and been rightfully conquered by the English; but that they had had no hand, by consent or otherwise, in shedding the blood of the English, and that it was by the advice of *Necquash* † that they fled from their country, being promised by him that the English would not hurt them, if they did not join against them. The names of 62 craving pardon and protection were at the same time communicated.

In answer the commissioners say, that while *Wequash* lived he had made no mention of "such innocent Pequats, or from any other person since;" and on "enquiry from *Thomas Stanton*, from *Foxon*, one of *Uncus* his men, and at last by confession of the Pequats present, found that some of the petitioners were in Mistick fort in fight against the English, and fled away in the smoke," and that others were at other times in arms against the English and Mohegans, and, therefore, the ground of their petition was false and deceitful.

It appears that they had taken refuge under *Uncas*, who had promised them good usage, which was probably on condition that they should pay him a tribute. They resided at this time at Namyok.

At the same court, *Obechiquod* complained that *Uncas* had forcibly taken away his wife, and criminally obliged her to live with him. "*Foxon* being present, as *Uncas's* deputy, was questioned about this base and unsufferable outrage; he denied that *Uncas* either took or kept away *Obechiquod's* wife by force, and affirmed that [on] *Obechiquod's* withdrawing, with other Pequots,

* His Indian name was *Casmamon*, perhaps the same as *Cassassinnamon*, or *Casasinemon*, &c.

† *Wequash*, the traitor. He became a noted praying Indian, after the Pequot war, and was supposed to have died by poison. Frequent mention will be found of him elsewhere in our work

from *Uncas*, his wife refused to go with him; and that, among the Indians, it is usual when a wife so deserts her husband, another may take her. *Obechiquod* affirmed that *Uncas* had dealt criminally before, and still kept her against her will."

Though not satisfied in point of proof, the commissioners said, "Yet abhoring that lustful adulterous carriage of *Uncas*, as it is acknowledged and mittigated by *Foxon*," and ordered that he should restore the wife, and that *Obechiquod* have liberty to settle under the protection of the English, where they should direct.*

Complaints at this time were as thick upon the head of *Uncas* as can well be conceived of, and still we do not imagine that half the crimes he was guilty of, are on record. Another Indian named *Sanaps*, at the same time, complained that he had dealt in like manner with the wife of another chief, since dead; that he had taken away his corn and beans, and attempted his life also. The court say they found no proof, "first or last, of these charges," still, as to the corn and beans, "*Foxon* conceives *Uncas* seized it because *Sannop*, with a Pequot, in a disorderly manner withdrew himself from *Uncas*." Hence it seems not much evidence was required, as *Uncas's* deputy uniformly pleaded guilty; and the court could do no less than order that, on investigation, he should make restitution. As to *Sannop*, who was "no Pequot," but a "Connecticut Indian," he had liberty to live under the protection of the English also.

To the charges of the Pequots against *Uncas*, of "his vnjustice and tyranny, drawinge wampam from them vpon new pretences," "they say they haue giuen him wampam 40 times since they came vnder him, and that they haue sent wampam by him to the English 25 times," and had no account that he ever delivered it; it was answered by *Foxon*, that *Uncas* had received wampum divers times as tribute, but denied that, in particular, any had been given him for the English, and that "he thinks the nomber of 25 times to be altogether false."

There were a long train of charges against *Uncas* for his oppression of the Pequots, which when the commissioners had heard through, they "ordered that *Vncus* be duly reproved, and seriously enformed that the English cannot owne or protect him in any vnlawful, much lesse trecherous and outrageous courses." And notwithstanding the commissioners seem not to doubt of the rascality of their ally, yet nothing seems to have been done to relieve the distressed Pequots, because that "after the [Pequot] warre they spared the liues of such as had noe hand in the bloude of the English." To say the least of which, it is a most extraordinary consideration, that because some innocent people had not been destroyed in war, they might be harassed according as the caprice of abandoned minds might dictate.

Mr. *John Winthrop* next prefers a complaint against *Uncas* from another quarter: the Nipmuks had been attacked, in 1646, by 130 Mohegans, under *Nowequa*, a brother of *Uncas*. It does not appear that he killed any of them, but robbed them of effects to a great amount; among which are enumerated 35 fathom of wampum, 10 copper kettles, 10 "great hempen baskets," many bear skins, deer skins, &c. Of this charge *Foxon* said *Uncas* was not guilty, for that he knew nothing of *Nowequa's* proceedings in it; that at the time of it [September] *Uncas*, with his chief counsellors, was at New Haven with the commissioners of the United Colonies; and that *Nowequa* had at the same time robbed some of *Uncas's* own people.

It was also urged by *Winthrop*, that not long before the meeting of the commissioners in September, 1647, this same *Nowequa* had been with 40 or 50 men to Fisher's Island, where he had broken up a canoe belonging to him, and greatly alarmed his man and an Indian who were there at that time. That *Nowequa* next "hovered against the English plantation, in a suspicious manner, with 40 or 50 of his men, many of them armed with gunns, to the affrightment not onely of the Indians on the shore (soe that some of them began to bring their goods to the English houses) but divers of the English themselues."

* This chief is the same, we believe, called in a later part of the records (Hazard, ii. 413) *Abbachickwood*. He was fined, with seven others, ten fathom of wampum for going to fight the Pocomptuck Indians with *Uncas*, in the summer of 1659.

These charges being admitted by *Foxon*, the commissioners "ordered that *Vncus* from them be fully informed, that he must either regulate and continue his brother in a righteous and peaceable frame for the future vnderstandinge, and providing that vpon due proof due restitution to be made to such as haue been wronged by him, or else wholy disert and leaue him, that the Narragensett and others may requere and recouer satisfaction as they can."

We pass now to the year 1651, omitting to notice some few events more or less connected with our subject, which, in another chapter, may properly pass under review.

Last year, *Thomas Stanton* had been ordered "to get an account of the number and names of the several Pequots living among the Narragansets, Nianticks, or Mohegan Indians, &c.; who, by an agreement made after the Pequot war, are justly tributaries to the English colonies, and to receive the tribute due for this last year." *Stanton* now appeared as interpreter, and with him came also *Uncas* and several of his men, *Wequash Cook* and some of "*Ninnacraft's*" men, "*Robert*, a Pequot, sometimes a servant to Mr. *Winthrop*, and some with him, and some Pequots living on Long Island." They at this time delivered 312 fathom of wampum. Of this *Uncas* brought 79, *Ninigret's* men 91, &c.

"This wampum being laid down, *Uncas* and others of the Pequots demanded why this tribute was required, how long it was to continue, and whether the children to be born hereafter were to pay it." They were answered that the tribute had been due yearly from the Pequots since 1638, on account of their murders, wars, &c. upon the English. "Wherefore the commissioners might have required both account and payment, as of a just debt, for time past, but are contented, if it be thankfully accepted, to remit what is past, accounting only from 1650, when *Thomas Stanton's* employment and salary began." Also that the tribute should end in ten years more, and that children hereafter born should be exempt. Hitherto all male children were taxed.

The next matter with which we shall proceed, has, in the life of *Ousamequin*, been merely glanced at, and reserved for this place, to which it more properly belongs.

We have now arrived to the year 1661, and it was in the spring of this year that a war broke out between *Uncas* and the old sachem before named. It seems very clear that the Wampanoags had been friendly to the Narragansets, for a long time previous; being separated from them, were not often involved in their troubles. They saw how *Uncas* was favored by the English, and were, therefore, careful to have nothing to do with the Mohegans, from whom they were still farther removed. Of the rise, progress and termination of their war upon the Quabaogs, a tribe of Nipmuks belonging to *Wasamagin*, the reader may gather the most important facts from some documents,* which we shall in the next place lay before him.

"Mercurius de Quabaconk, or a declaration of the dealings of *Uncas* and the Mohegin Indians, to certain Indians the inhabitants of Quabaconk, 21, 3d mo. 1661.

"About ten weeks since *Uncas'* son, accompanied with 70 Indians, set upon the Indians at Quabaconk, and slew three persons, and carried away six prisoners; among which were one squaw and her two children, whom when he had brought to the fort, *Uncas* dismissed the squaw, on conditions that she would go home and bring him £25 in peag, two guns and two blankets, for the release of herself and her children, which as yet she hath not done, being retained by the sagamore of Weshakeim, in hopes that their league with the English will free them.

"At the same time he carried away also, in stuff and money, to the value of £37, and at such time as *Uncas* received notice of the displeasure of the English in the Massachusetts by the worshipful Mr. *Winthrop*, he insolently laughed them to scorn, and professed that he would still go on as he had begun, and assay who dares to controll him. Moreover, four days since there came home a prisoner that escaped; two yet remaining, whom *Uncas*

* In manuscript, and never before published.

threatens, the one of them to kill, and the other to sell away as a slave, and still threatens to continue his war against them, notwithstanding any prohibition whatsoever; whose very threats are so terrible, that our Indians dare not wander far from the towns about the Indians for fear of surprise.

From the relation of
Pambassua,
and testimony of
Wasamagin,
Quaquequunset,
and others."

From this narrative it is very plain that *Uncas* cared very little for the displeasure of the English: it is plain, also, that he knew as well as they what kept them from dealing as severely with him as with the Narragansets, his neighbors. They must succumb to him, to keep him in a temper to aid in fighting their battles when called upon. Hence, when he had committed the grossest insults on other Indians, the wheels of justice often moved so slow, that they arrived not at their object until it had become quite another matter. It must, however, be considered, that the English were very peculiarly situated—upon the very margin of an unknown wilderness, inclosed but on one side by Indians, whose chief business was war. They had destroyed the Pequots, but this only added to their fears, for they knew that revenge lurked still in the breasts of many, who only were waiting for an opportunity to gratify it; therefore, so long as one of the most numerous tribes could possibly be kept on their side, the English considered themselves in safety. They had made many missteps in their proceedings with the Indians, owing sometimes to one cause and sometimes to another, for which now there was no remedy; and it is doubtful whether, even at this day, if any set of men were to go into an unknown region and settle among wild men, that they would get along with them so much better than our fathers did with the Indians here, as some may have imagined. These are considerations which must be taken into account in estimating the "wrongs of the Indians." They seem the more necessary in this place; for, in the biography of *Uncas*, there is as much, perhaps, to censure regarding the acts of the English, as in any other article of Indian history.

The narrative just recited, being sent in to the court of Massachusetts, was referred to a select committee, who, on the 1 June, reported,

That letters should be sent to *Uncas*, signifying how sensible the court was of the injuries he had done them, by his outrage upon the Indians of Quabaconk, who lived under their sagamore, *Wassamagin*, as set forth in the narrative. That, therefore, they now desired him to give up the captives and make restitution for all the goods taken from them, and to forbear for time to come all such unlawful acts. That, if *Wassamagin* or his subjects had or should do him or his subjects any wrong, the English would, upon due proof, cause recompense to be made. Also that *Uncas* be given to understand and assured, that if he refuse to comply with the request, they were then resolved to right the injuries upon him and his, and for all costs they might be put to in the service. "That for the encouragement and safety of the sayd *Wassamagin* and his subjects, there be by order of Major *Willard* three or four armed men, well accomodate in all respects, with a proporcon of powder, bulletts and match sent from Lancaster to Quabaconk vnto the sayd *Wassamagin*, there to stay a night or two, and to shoote of their musquets so often, and in such wise, as the major shall direct, to terrifie the enemies of *Wassamagin*, and so to return home again." To inform *Wassamagin* and his subjects, that the authorities of Massachusetts would esteem it an acknowledgment of their regard, if they would permit them to have the captives to be recovered from *Uncas*, to bring them up in a proper manner, that they might be serviceable to their friends, &c. Also, "aduice and require *Wassamagin* and his men to be verie carefull of iniuring or any ways prouoking of *Vncas*, or any of his men, as he will answer our displeasure therein, and incurr due punishment for the same." That if *Uncas* committed any other hostile acts, he must complain to them, &c.* Thus *Wassamegin* was as much threatened as *Uncas*.

Matters seem to have remained thus until the meeting of the commissioners in September following; when, in due course, the business was called up, and acted upon as follows:—

"Vpon complaint made to the comissionars of the Massachusetts against *Vnkas*, this following message was sent to him:—

"*Vncas*, wee haue receiued information and complaint from the generall court of the Massachusetts of youer hostile invading of *Wosamequin* and the Indians of Quabakutt, whoe are and longe haue bine subjects to the English, killing some and carrying away others; spoyling theire goods to the vallue of 33lb. as they allege." That he had done this contrary to his covenants, and had taken no notice of the demands of the Massachusetts, though some time since they had ordered him to deliver up the captives, make remuneration, &c. And to all he had returned no answer; "which," continues the letter, "seemes to bee an insolent and proud carriage of youers. We cannot but wonder att it, and must beare witness against it." He was, as before, required to return the captives, &c. and give reasons for his operations; and if he neglected to do so, the Massachusetts were at liberty to right themselves.

In the mean time, as we apprehend, a letter from *Uncas* was received, written by Captain *Mason*, which was as follows:—

"Whereas there was a warrant sent from the court of Boston, dated in my last to *Vncas*, sachem of Mohegen, wherin it was declared vpon the complaint of *Wesamequen*, † a sachem subject to the Massachusetts, that the said *Vncas* had offered great violence to theire subjects at Quabauk, killing some and taking others captiue; which warrant came not to *Uncas*, not aboue 20 daies before these presents, who, being summoned by Major *John Mason*, in full scope of the said warrant, wherein he was deeply charged if he did not return the captiues, and £33 damage, then the Massachusetts would recouer it by force of armes, which to him was uery grieuous: professing he was altogether ignorant that they were subjects belonging to the Massachusetts; and further said that they were none of *Wesamequen's* men, but belonging to *Onopequin*, his deadly enemie, whoe was there borne; one of the men then taken was his own cousin, who had formerly fought against him in his own person; and yett sett him att libertie; and further saith that all the captiues were sent home. Alsoe that *Wesamequin*['s] son ‡ and diuers of his men had fought against him diuers times. This he desired might bee returned as his answare to the comissioners.

"*Allexander* allis *Wamsutta*, sachem of Sowamsett, being now att Plymouth, hee challenged Quabauke Indians to belong to him; and further said that hee did warr against *Vncas* this summer on that account. §

Signed by

JOHN MASON."

---

* Here end our MSS. relating to this affair.

† By this it would seem that *Massasoit* had, for some time, resided among the Nipmucks. He had, probably, given up Pokanoket to his sons.

‡ There can scarce be a doubt that this refers to *Alexander*, and that the next paragraph confirms it; hence *Massasoit* was alive in May, 1661, as we have before stated. And the above letter of *Mason* was probably written in September, or while the commissioners were in session.

§ It seems always to have been uncertain to whom the Nipmucks belonged. *Roger Williams* says, in 1668, "That all the Neepmucks were unquestionably subject to the Nanhigonset sachems, and, in a special manner, to *Mejksah*, the son of *Caunounicus*, and late husband to this old *Squaw-Sachem*, now only surviving. I have abundant and daily proof of it," &c. *MS. letter.* See life *Massasoit*, b. ii. ch. ii.

At one time, *Kutshamakin* claimed some of the Nipmucks, or consented to be made a tool of by some of them, for some private end. But Mr. *Pynchon* said they would not own him as a sachem any longer "than the sun shined upon him." Had they belonged to him, Massachusetts must have owned them, which would have involved them in much difficulty in 1648 by reason of several murders among them.

The particulars of the issue of these troubles were not recorded, and the presumption is, that *Uncas* complied with the reasonable requests of the English, and the old, peaceable *Ousamequin*, being unwilling to get into difficulty, put up with the result without avenging his wrongs. His son, *Wamsutta*, as will be seen, about this time found himself involved in difficulties nearer home, which probably prevented him from continuing the war against *Uncas*, had he been otherwise disposed.

CHAPTER VI.

Of the Pequot nation—Geography of their country—SASSACUS, *their first chief, known to the English—Tassaquanott—War—The cause of it*—WEQUASH—*Canonicus and Miantunnomoh accused of harboring fugitive Pequots—Sassamon*—MONONOTTO—*Otash*—CASSASSINNAMON.

"But since I've mentioned *Sassacus*' great name,
That day so much a terror where it came;
Let me, in prosecution of my story,
Say something of his pride and kingdom's glory."—WOLCOTT

IT is said by Mr. *Hubbard*,* that the Pequots,† "being a more fierce, cruel, and warlike people than the rest of the Indians, came down out of the more inland parts of the continent, and by force seized upon one of the goodliest places near the sea, and became a terror to all their neighbors." The time of their emigration is unknown. They made all the other tribes "stand in awe, though fewer in number than the Narragansets, that bordered next upon them." ‡

Their country, according to Mr. *Gookin*, § "the English of Connecticut jurisdiction, doth now, [1674,] for the most part, possess." Their dominion, or that of their chief sachem, was, according to the same author, "over divers petty sagamores; as over part of Long Island, over the Mohegans, and over the sagamores of Quinapeake, [now New Haven,] yea, over all the people that dwelt upon Connecticut River, and over some of the most southerly inhabitants of the Nipmuck country, about Quinabaag." The principal seat of the sagamores was near the mouth of Pequot River, now called the Thames, where New London stands. "These Pequots, as old Indians relate, could, in former times, raise 4000 men fit for war." ‖ The first great chief of this nation, known to the English, was

SASSACUS, whose name was a terror to all the neighboring tribes of Indians. From the fruitful letters of the Reverend *Roger Williams*, we learn that he had a brother by the name of *Puppompoges*, whose residence was at Monahiganick, probably Mohegan. Although *Sassacus's* principal residence was upon the Thames, yet, in his highest prosperity, he had under him no less than 26 sachems, and his dominions were from Narraganset Bay to Hudson's River, in the direction of the sea-coast. Long Island was also under him, and his authority was undisputed far into the country.

A brother of *Sassacus*, named *Tassaquanott*, survived the Pequot war, and was one of those complained of by *Uncas* in 1647, for giving his countrymen "crooked counsell" about a present of wampum, which he had advised to be given to the English instead of him. It appears that on the death of a child of *Uncas*, the Pequots had presented him with 100 fathom of wampum,¶ which, when *Tassaquanott* knew, he disapproved of it, politicly urging, that if the English were conciliated by any means towards them, it mattered not much about *Uncas*.

* Narrative, i. 116.
† We believe this name meant *Gray foxes*, hence Gray-fox Indians, or Pequots.
‡ Hist. New England, 33.
§ See his *Collections* in 1 Coll. Mass. Hist. Soc. i. 147.
‖ Ibid.
¶ *Hazard*, Hist. Col. ii. 90.

We are informed,* that Connecticut was claimed by right of conquest at one time by the first white settlers, who found much of it cultivated and settled by its Indian inhabitants, although they endeavored that it should be understood otherwise. The numbers of the natives in that region were "thousands, who had three kings, viz. *Connecticote*, *Quinnipiog*, and SASSACUS." *Connecticote* was "emperor," or chief of chiefs, an elevation in which he and his ancestors had stood for about 400 years, according to their traditions.

About the time the English had determined on the subjugation of the Pequots, *Roger Williams* wrote to Governor *Winthrop* of Massachusetts, giving him important directions how they should proceed to advantage, and what was very important then, gave the following rude draft of their country:—

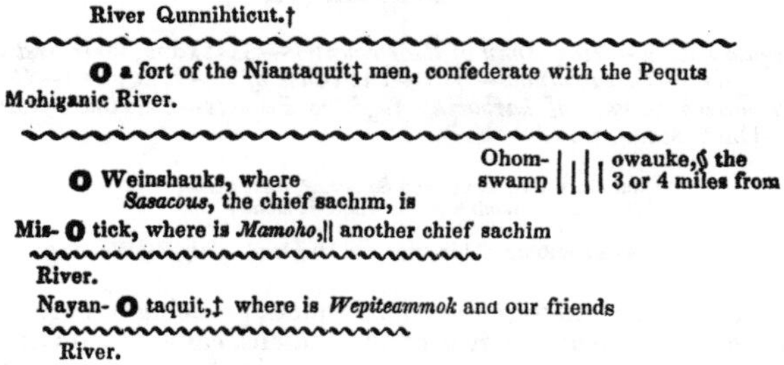

In the same letter, Mr. *Williams* urges the necessity of employing faithful guides for the English forces; "as shall be best liked of [to] be taken along to direct, especially two Pequts; viz. *Wequash*, [whose name signified a swan,] and *Wuttackquiackommin*, valiant men, especially the latter, who have lived these three or four years with the Nanhiggonticks, and know every pass and passage amongst them, who desire armor to enter their houses."

In 1634, as has been before incidentally mentioned, one Captain *Stone* was killed by the Pequots, while upon a trading expedition in Connecticut River. Without knowing the reason of their killing *Stone*, the English demanded the murderers soon after, and as *Sassacus* was involved in troubles with the Narragansets and all his neighbors, he thought it not best entirely to slight the demand of the English; he therefore sent messengers to Boston, where they arrived 6 November, with offers of peace, which, after considerable deliberation on the part of the English, were accepted, and a treaty was entered into on the 9th following.

A messenger had been sent, in October, upon the same errand, but was dismissed with orders to inform *Sassacus*, that he must send persons of greater quality, and then the English would treat with him. "He brought," says *Winthrop*, "two bundles of sticks, whereby he signified how many beaver and otter skins he would give us for that end, and great store of wampompeage, (about two bushels, by his description.)" He had a small present with him, which was accepted by the English, who gave him in return, "a moose coat of as good value."

The treaty entered into on the 9 November, 1634, between the Pequots and English, stipulated that the murderers of Captain *Stone* should be given up to the English, of whom there were at that time left but two, as attested by the ambassadors of *Sassacus*, who further observed in explanation, that the sachem in whose time the act was committed, was dead, having been slain in a war with the Dutch, and that all the men concerned in it, except two, had also died of the small-pox. This, together with the facts given in concerning the death of *Stone*, inclined the English to believe the account altogether; and, but for what happened afterwards, it is probable that the historians of that

---

* But with what truth I know not, for it rests upon the authority of *Peters*.
† Connecticut. ‡ Niantick. § A name signifying an *Owl's nest*. Same lette
‖ Probably *Mononotto*.

period would have relied more upon the Pequots' own account than the general rumor. Such are the events of time—a circumstance may change the fate, nay, the character of a nation, for a period, in the eyes of many generations! But

"O Time! the beautifier of the dead!
Adorner of the ruin!—comforter,
And only healer, when the heart hath bled!
Time, the correcter where our judgments err."

In the progress of the treaty, the Pequot ambassadors said, that if the two men then living who had been concerned in *Stone's* death, "were worthy of death, they would move their sachem to deliver them" to the English, but that as to themselves, they had no power to do so, and at once urged the justness of their act without qualification. *Stone*, they said, came into their river and seized upon two of their men, and bound them hand and foot, and, in that situation, obliged them to pilot him up the river. When he had gone up as far as he desired, himself and two other white men, and the two manacled Indians, went on shore. Meanwhile they had been watched by nine Indians, who, when they found the Englishmen asleep on the following night, fell upon them and massacred them.

Considering the state of the Indians, no blame could be attached to them for this act; two of their countrymen were in the hands of an unknown people, who, from every appearance, were about to put them to death, and it was by an act of pure benevolence and heroism that they delivered them out of the hands of an invading foe.

Therefore, being satisfied with the account, the English agreed to have peace with them, provided they would give up the two men when they should send for them; "to yeld up Connecticut;" to give 400 fathom of wampom, and 40 beaver and 30 otter skins; and that the English should immediately send a vessel with a cargo of cloth to trade with them.

The names of these ambassadors are not recorded; but one signed the treaty with the mark of a bow and arrow, and the other with that of a hand.

The same day about 2 or 300 Narragansets were discovered at Neponset, who had marched out for the purpose of killing these ambassadors. This discovery being made before the treaty was concluded, the English met them at Roxbury, and there negotiated a treaty between the Pequots and them. For the furtherance of which, the Pequots instructed the English to present them with a portion of the wampom which they were to give to them; but not as coming from them, because they disdained to purchase peace of that nation The Narragansets readily conceding to the wishes of the English, all parties retired satisfied.

Distrust soon grew again into antipathy; it having been reported that *Stone* and those with him were treacherously surprised by the Pequots who had gone on board his vessel in a friendly manner to trade; and seeing Captain *Stone* asleep in his cabin, they killed him, and the other men one after the other, except Captain *Norton*, who, it seems, was with him; he being a resolute man, defended himself for some time in the cook-room, but at length, some powder, which for the more ready use he had placed in an open vessel, took fire and exploded, by which he was so seriously injured, especially in his eyes, that he could hold out no longer, and he was forthwith despatched by them.

This matter at length having become fixed in the minds of the English according to the latter relation, they were the more ready to charge other circumstances of a like nature upon the Pequots. On the 20 July, 1636, as Mr. *John Oldham* was on his passage passing near Manisses, that is, Block Island, in a small pinnace, 14 Narraganset Indians attacked and killed him, and made his crew prisoners, which consisted only of two boys and two Narraganset Indians. The same day, as *John Gallop* was on his passage from Connecticut, in a bark of 20 tons, an adverse wind drove him near the same island. On seeing a vessel in possession of Indians, he bore down upon her, and immediately knew her to be Captain *Oldham's*. He hailed those on board, but received no answer, and soon saw a boat pass from the vessel to the shore full of men and goods. As *Gallop* neared the suspicious vessel, she slipped her fastening, and the wind being off the land drifted her towards Narraganset. Notwithstanding some of the Indians were armed with guns and swords, *Gallop*, being in a stouter vessel, resolved on running them down; he therefore made all sail, and immediately stemmed the pirate vessel on the quarter with such force as nearly to overset her, and in their fright six Indians jumped overboard and were drowned. The rest standing upon the defensive, and being yet far superior in numbers to *Gallop's* crew, which consisted of two little boys and one man, to board them was thought too hazardous; *Gallop* therefore stood off to repeat his broadside method of attack. Meanwhile he contrived to lash his anchor to his bows in such a manner, that when he came down upon the Indians a second time, the force was sufficient to drive the fluke of the anchor through their quarter; which, holding there, both vessels floated along together. The Indians had now become so terrified, that they stood not to the fight, but kept in the hold of the pinnace. *Gallop* fired in upon them sundry times, but without much execution, and meantime the vessels got loose from one another, and *Gallop* stood off again for a third attack. As soon as he was clear of them, four more of the Indians jumped overboard, and were also drowned. *Gallop* now ventured to board his prize. One of the remaining Indians came up and surrendered, and was bound; another came up and submitted, whom they also bound, but fearing to have both on board, this last was cast into the sea. Two out of the 14 now remained, who had got possession of the hold of the pinnace, and there successfully defended themselves with their swords against their enemy. Captain *Oldham* was found dead in the vessel, concealed under an old seine, and as his body was not entirely cold, it was evident that he had been killed about the time his pinnace was discovered by *Gallop*.

From the condition in which *Oldham's* body was found, it was quite uncertain whether he had fallen in an affray, or been murdered deliberately; but it is very probable that the former was the fact, because it was uncommon for the Indians to disfigure the slain, unless killed as enemies, and *Oldham's* body was shockingly mangled. But Captain *Oldham* had been killed by the Indians, and the cry of vengeance was up, and cool investigation must not be looked for. The murder had been committed by the Indians of Manisses, but Manisses was under the Narragansets; therefore it was believed that the Narragansets had contrived his death because he was carrying into effect the articles of the late treaty between the Pequots and English.

The two boys who were with Mr. *Oldham* were not injured, and were immediately given up and sent to Boston, where they arrived the 30th of the same month. As soon as *Miantunnomoh* heard of the affair of Captain *Oldham*, he ordered *Ninigret* to send for the boys and goods to Block Island. The boys he caused to be delivered to Mr. *Williams*, and the goods he held subject to the order of the English of Massachusetts.

Meanwhile, 26 July, the two Indians who were in Mr. *Oldham's* pinnace when she was taken, were sent by *Canonicus* to Governor *Vane*. They brought a letter from *Roger Williams*, which gave an account of the whole affair, and some circumstances led the English to believe these messengers were accessory to the death of *Oldham;* but we know not if any thing further were ever done about it. The same letter informed the governor that *Miantunnomoh* had gone, with 200 men in 17 canoes, "to take revenge, &c."

These events and transactions soon caused the convening of the governor and council of Massachusetts, who forthwith declared war against the Indians of Manisses. Accordingly 90 men were raised and put under the command of Captain *John Endecott*, who was general of the expedition. *John Underhill* and *Nathaniel Turner* were captains, and *Jenyson* and *Davenport* ensigns. *Endecott's* instructions were to put to death the men of Block Island, but to make captives of the women and children. This armament set forth in three pinnaces, with two Indians as guides, 25 September, 1636.

On arriving at Manisses they saw many Indians, but could not get near them. At Pequot harbor, a part of the armament seized a quantity of corn belonging to the Pequots, and were attacked and obliged to fly. However, the Narragansets reported that there were 13 Pequots killed during the expedition. The English were satisfied that they had harbored the murderers of *Oldham*, which occasioned their sailing to Pequot harbor. It being now late in the season, the expedition was given up, to be resumed early in the spring.

The Pequots, being now left to themselves, commenced depredations whenever they dared appear. About the beginning of October, as five men from Saybrook were collecting hay at a meadow four miles above that place, they were attacked, and one of them, named *Butterfield*, was taken and killed; from which circumstance the meadow still bears his name. About 14 days after, two men were taken in a cornfield two miles from Saybrook fort. There were six of the whites, and they were surrounded by 2 or 300 Indians, yet all escaped but two. Thus imboldened by success, they carried their depredations within bowshot of Saybrook fort, killing one cow and shooting arrows into sundry others.

On the 21 October, *Miantunnomoh*, fearing for the safety of his English friends, came to Boston, accompanied by two of *Canonicus's* sons, another sachem, and about 20 men. *Kutshamakin* had given notice of his coming, and a company of soldiers met him at Roxbury and escorted him into the town. Here he entered into a treaty with the English, by which it was mutually agreed that neither should make peace with the Pequots without the consent of the other; and to put to death or deliver up murderers.

About the same time, *John Tilley* was taken and killed, and tortured in a most barbarous manner. As he was sailing down Connecticut River in his bark, he landed about three miles above Saybrook fort, and having shot at some fowl, the report of his gun directed the Indians to the spot. They took him prisoner at first, and then cut off his hands and feet. He lived three days after his hands were cut off, and bore this torture without complaint, which gained him the reputation of being "a stout man" among his tormentors. These facts were reported by the Indians themselves. Another man who was with *Tilley* was at the same time killed.

On the 22 February, Lieutenant *Gardner* and nine men went out of Saybrook fort, and were drawn into an ambush, where four of them were killed, and the rest escaped with great difficulty.

On April 12, six men and three women were killed at Weathersfield. They at the same time killed 20 cows and a horse, and carried away two young women.

Alarm was now general throughout the English plantations. *Miantunnomoh* having sent a messenger to Boston to notify the English that the Pequots had sent away their women and children to an island, 40 men were immediately sent to Narraganset to join others raised by *Miantunnomoh*, with the intention of falling upon them by surprise.

In the mean time, Captain *Mason*, with a company of 90 men, had been raised by Connecticut and sent into the Pequot country. He was accompanied by *Uncas* and a large body of his warriors, who, in their march to Saybrook, 15 May, fell upon about 30 Pequots and killed 7 of them. One being taken alive, to their everlasting disgrace it will be remembered, that the English caused him to be tortured; and the heads of all the slain were cut off, and set up on the walls of the fort.*

Immediately after Captains *Mason* and *Underhill* set out to attack one of the forts of *Sassacus*. This fort was situated upon an eminence in the present town of Groton, Connecticut. The English arrived in its vicinity on the 25th of May; and on the 26th, before day, with about 500 Indians, encompassed it, and began a furious attack. The Mohegans and Narragansets discovered great fear on approaching the fort, and could not believe that the English would dare to attack it. When they came to the foot of the hill on which it was situated, Captain *Mason* was apprehensive of being abandoned by them, and, making a halt, sent for *Uncas*, who led the Mohegans, and *Wequash*, their pilot, who was a fugitive Pequot chief,† and urged them not to desert him, but to follow him at any distance they pleased. These Indians had all along told the English they dared not fight the Pequots, but boasted how *they* themselves would fight. *Mason* told them now they should see whether Englishmen

* *Winthrop's* Journal, and *Mason's* Hist. Pequot War.—Dr. *Mather's* account of this affair has been given in the life of *Uncas*.

† The same, it is believed, elsewhere called *Waquash Cook*; "which *Wequash* (says Dr. *I. Mather*) was by birth a sachem of that place [where *Sassacus* lived], but upon some disgust received, he went from the Pequots to the Narragansets, and became a chief captain under *Miantunnomoh*."—*Relation*, 47.

15

would fight or not. Notwithstanding their boastings, they could not overcome the terror which the name of *Sassacus* had inspired in them, and they kept at a safe distance until the fight was over; but assisted considerably in repelling the attacks of the Pequots, in the retreat from the fort;—for their warriors, on recovering from their consternation, collected in a considerable body, and fought the confederates for many miles.

The English had but 77 men, which were divided into two companies, one led by *Mason*, and the other by *Underhill*. The Indians were all within their fort, asleep in their wigwams, and the barking of a dog was the first notice they had of the approach of the enemy, yet very few knew the cause of the alarm, until met by the naked swords of the foe. The fort had two entrances at opposite points, into which each party of English were led, sword in hand. "*Wanux! Wanux!*"* was the cry of *Sassacus's* men; and such was their surprise, that they made very feeble resistance. Having only their own missile weapons, they could do nothing at hand to hand with the English rapiers. They were pursued from wigwam to wigwam, and slaughtered in every secret place. Women and children were cut to pieces, while endeavoring to hide themselves in and under their beds. At length fire was set in the mats that covered the wigwams, which furiously spread over the whole fort, and the dead and dying were together consumed. A part of the English had formed a circumference upon the outside, and shot such as attempted to fly. Many ascended the pickets to escape the flames, but were shot down by those stationed for that purpose. About 600 persons were supposed to have perished in this fight; or, perhaps I should say, massacre.† There were but two English killed, and but one of those by the enemy, and about 20 wounded. *Sassacus* himself was in another fort; and, being informed of the ravages of the English, destroyed his habitations, and, with about 80 others, fled to the Mohawks, who treacherously beheaded him, and sent his scalp to the English.

The author of the following lines in "Yamoyden," alludes to this melancholy event happily, though not truly:—

"And Sassacus, now no more,
Lord of a thousand bowmen, fled;
And all the chiefs, his boast before,
Were mingled with the unhonored dead.
Sannap and Sagamore were slain,
On Mystic's banks, in one red night:
The once far-dreaded king in vain
Sought safety in inglorious flight;
And reft of all his regal pride,
By the fierce Maqua's hand he died."

One of the most unfeeling passages flows from the pen of *Hubbard*, in his account of this war; which, together with the fact he records, forms a most distressing picture of depravity. We would gladly turn from it, but justice to the Indians demands it, and we give it in his own words:—

The Narragansets had surrounded "some hundreds" of the Pequots, and kept them until some of Captain *Stoughton's* soldiers "made an easy conquest of them." "The men among them to the number of 30, were presently turned into *Charon's* ferry-boat, under the command of Skipper *Gallop*, who dispatched them a little without the harbor!"

Thus were 30 Indians taken into a vessel, carried out to sea, murdered, and, in the agonies of death, thrown overboard, to be buried under the silent waves! Whereabouts they were captured, or "without" what "harbor" they perished, we are not informed; but, from the nature of the circumstances, it would seem that they were taken on the borders of the Narraganset country, and murdered at the mouth of some of the adjacent harbors.

That these poor wretches were thus revengefully sacrificed, should have been enough to allay the hatred in the human breast of all who knew it, especially the *historian!* But he must imagine that, in their passage to their grave, they did not go in a vessel of human contrivance, but in a boat belonging to a river of hell! thereby forestalling his reader's mind that they had been sent to that abode.

---

* *Allen's* History of the Pequot War. It signified, *Englishmen! Englishmen!* In *Mason's* history, it is written *Owanux*. *Allen* merely copied from *Mason*, with a few such variations.

† "It was supposed," says *Mather*, "that no less than 500 or 600 Pequot souls were brought down to hell that day." *Relation*, 47. We in charity suppose, that by hell the doctor only meant death

Notwithstanding the great slaughter at Mistick, there were great numbers of Pequots in the country, who were hunted from swamp to swamp, and their numbers thinned continually, until a remnant promised to appear no more as a nation.

The English, under Captain *Stoughton*, came into Pequot River about a fortnight after the Mistick fight, and assisted in the work of their extermination. After his arrival in the enemy's country, he wrote to the governor of Massachusetts, as follows: "By this pinnace, you shall receive 48 or 50 women and children, unless there stay any here to be helpful, &c. Concerning which, there is one, I formerly mentioned, that is the fairest and largest that I saw amongst them, to whom I have given a coate to cloathe her. It is my desire to have her for a servant, if it may stand with your good liking, else not. There is a little squaw that steward *Culacut* desireth, to whom he hath given a coate. Lieut. *Davenport* also desireth one, to wit, a small one, that hath three strokes upon her stomach, thus: — ||| +. He desireth her, if it will stand with your good liking. *Sosomon*, the Indian, desireth a young little squaw, which I know not.

"At present, Mr. *Haynes*, Mr. *Ludlo*, Captain *Mason*, and 30 men are with us in Pequot River, and we shall the next week joine in seeing what we can do against *Sassacus*, and another great sagamore, *Monowattuck*, [*Mononotto*.] Here is yet good work to be done, and how dear it will cost is unknown. *Sassacus* is resolved to sell his life, and so the other with their company, as dear as they can." *

Perhaps it will be judged that *Stoughton* was looking more after the profit arising from the sale of captives, than for warriors to fight with. Indeed, *Mason's* account does not give him much credit.

Speaking of the English employed in this expedition, *Wolcott* thus immortalizes them :—

> "These were the men, this was the little band,
> That durst the force of the new world withstand.
> These were the men that by their swords made way
> For peace and safety in America."
>
> VACANT HOURS, 44.

There was a manifest disposition on the part of *Uncas*, *Canonicus*, *Miantunnomoh* and *Ninigret*, and perhaps other chiefs, to screen the poor, denounced, and flying Pequots, who had escaped the flames and swords of the English in their war with them. Part of a correspondence about these sachems' harboring them, between *R. Williams* and the governor of Massachusetts, is preserved in the Collections of the Massachusetts Historical Society; from which it appears, that Massachusetts had requested Mr. *Williams* to explain to the chiefs the consequences to be depended upon, if they did not strictly observe their agreement in regard to the fugitive Pequots. *Otash* † carried to Mr. *Williams* a letter from the Massachusetts governor upon this subject. After he had obeyed its contents, as far as he was able, he answered, that he went with *Otash* "to the Nanhiggonticks, and having got *Canounicus* and *Miantunnomu*, with their council, together, I acquainted them faithfully with the contents of your letter, *both grievances and threatenings;* and to demonstrate, I produced the copy of the league, (which Mr. [Sir *Henry*] *Vane* sent me,) and, with breaking of a straw in two or three places, I showed them what they had done."

These chiefs gave Mr. *Williams* to understand, that, when Mr. Governor understood what they had to say, he would be satisfied with their conduct; that they did not wish to make trouble, but they "*could relate many particulars wherein the English had broken their promises*" since the war.

In regard to some squaws that had escaped from the English, *Canonicus* said he had not seen any, but heard of some, and immediately ordered them to be carried back again, and had not since heard of them, but would now have the country searched for them, to satisfy the governor.

Miantunnomoh said he had never heard of but six, nor saw but four of them

* Manuscript letter of Captain *Stoughton*, on file among our state papers.

† *Yotaash*, Mr. *Williams* writes his name.

which being brought to him, he was angry, and asked those who brought them why they did not carry them to Mr. *Williams*, that he might convey them to the English. They told him the squaws were lame, and could not go; upon which *Miantunnomoh* sent to Mr. *Williams* to come and take them. Mr. *Williams* could not attend to it, and in his turn ordered *Miantunnomoh* to do it, who said he was busy and could not; "as indeed he was (says *Williams*) in a strange kind of solemnity, wherein the sachims eat nothing but at night, and all the natives round about the country were feasted." In the mean time the squaws escaped.

Miantunnomoh said he was sorry that the governor should think he wanted these squaws, for he did not. Mr. *Williams* told him he knew of his sending for one. Of this charge he fairly cleared himself, saying, the one sent for was not for himself, but for *Sassamun*,* who was lying lame at his house; that *Sassamun* fell in there in his way to Pequt, whither he had been sent by the governor. The squaw he wanted was a sachem's daughter, who had been a particular friend of *Miantunnomoh* during his lifetime; therefore, in kindness to his dead friend, he wished to ransom her.

Moreover, *Miantunnomoh* said, he and his people were true "to the English in life or death," and but for which, he said, *Okase* [*Unkus*] and his Mohiganeucks had long since proved false, as he still feared they would. For, he said, they had never found a Pequot, and added, "*Chenock ejuse wetompatimucks?*" that is, "Did ever friends deal so with friends?" Mr. *Williams* requiring more particular explanation, *Miantunnomoh* proceeded:—

"My brother, *Yotaash*, had seized upon *Puttaquppuunck*, *Quame*, and 20 Pequots, and 60 squaws; they killed three and bound the rest, whom they watched all night. Then they sent for the English, and delivered them in the morning to them. I came by land, according to promise, with 200 men, killing 10 Pequots by the way. I desired to see the great sachem *Puttaquppuunck*, whom my brother had taken, who was now in the English houses, but the English thrust at me with a pike many times, that I durst not come near the door."

Mr. *Williams* told him they did not know him, else they would not; but *Miantunnomoh* answered, "All my company were disheartened, and they all, and *Cutshamoquene*, desired to be gone." Besides, he said, "two of my men, *Wagonckwhut*† and *Maunamoh* [*Meihamoh*] were their guides to Sesquankit, from the river's mouth." Upon which, Mr. *Williams* adds to the governor: "Sir, I dare not stir coals, but I saw them too much disregarded by many."

Mr. *Williams* told the sachems "they received Pequts and wampom without Mr. Governor's consent. *Cannounicus* replied, that although he and *Miantunnomu* had paid many hundred fathom of wampum to their soldiers, as Mr. Governor did, yet he had not received one yard of beads nor a Pequt. Nor, saith *Miantunnomu*, did I, but one small present from four women of Long Island, which were no Pequts, but of that isle, being afraid, desired to put themselves under my protection."

The Pequot war has generally been looked upon with regret, by all good men, since. To exterminate a people before they had any opportunity to become enlightened, that is, to be made acquainted with the reason of other usages towards their fellow beings than those in which they had been brought up, is a great cause of lamentation; and if it proves any thing, it proves that great ignorance and barbarism lurked in the hearts of their exterminators. We do not mean to exclude by this remark the great body of the present inhabitants of the earth from the charge of such barbarism.

In the records of the United Colonies for the year 1647, it is mentioned that "Mr. *John Winthrop* making claim to a great quantity of land at Niantic by purchase from the Indians, gave in to the commissioners a petition in those words:—'Whereas I had the land of Niantick by a deed of gift and purchase from the sachem [Sassacus] before the [Pequot] wars, I desire the commissioners will be pleased to confirm it unto me, and clear it from any claim of

* Probably the same mentioned afterwards. He might have been the famous *John Sassamon*, or his brother *Rowland*.

† Perhaps *Wahgumacut*, or *Wahginnacut*.

English and Indians, according to the equity of the case.'" *Winthrop* had no writing from *Sassacus*, and full ten years had elapsed since the transaction, but *Fromatush*, *Wamberquaske*, and *Antuppo* testified some time after, that "upon their knowledge before the wars were against the Pequots, *Sassacus* their sachem of Niantic did call them and all his men together, and told that he was resolved to give his country to the governor's son of the Massachusetts, who lived then at Pattaquassat alias Connecticut River's mouth, and all his men declared themselves willing therewith. Thereupon he went to him to Pattaquassets, and when he came back he told them he had granted all his country to him the said governor's son, and said he was his good friend, and he hoped he would send some English thither some time hereafter. Moreover, he told him he had received coats from him for it, which they saw him bring home." This was not said by those Indians themselves, but several English *said they heard them say so.* The commissioners, however, set aside his claim with considerable appearance of independence.

Dr. *Dwight* thus closes his poem upon the destruction of the Pequots:—

"Undaunted, on their foes they fiercely flew;
As fierce the dusky warriors crowd the fight;
Despair inspires; to combat's face they glue;
With groans and shouts, they rage, unknowing flight,
And close their sullen eyes, in shades of endless night.

Indulge, my native land, indulge the tear
That steals, impassioned, o'er a nation's doom.
To me, each twig from Adam's stock is near,
And sorrows fall upon an Indian's tomb."

And, O ye chiefs! in yonder starry home,
Accept the humble tribute of this rhyme.
Your gallant deeds, in Greece, or haughty Rome,
By Maro sung, or Homer's harp sublime,
Had charmed the world's wide round, and triumphed over time."

Another, already mentioned, and the next in consequence to *Sassacus* was MONONOTTO. *Hubbard* calls him a "noted Indian," whose wife and children fell into the hands of the English, and as "it was known to be by her mediation that two English maids (that were taken away from Weathersfield, upon Connecticut River) were saved from death, in requittal of whose pity and humanity, the life of herself and children was not only granted her, but she was in special recommended to the care of Gov. *Winthrop*, of Massachusetts." *Mononotto* fled with *Sassacus* to the Mohawks, for protection, with several more chiefs. He was not killed by them, as *Sassacus* was, but escaped from them wounded, and probably died by the hands of his English enemies. He is thus mentioned by Governor *Wolcott*, in his poem upon *Winthrop's* agency, &c.

"Prince *Mononotto* sees his squadrons fly,
And on our general having fixed his eye,
Rage and revenge his spirits quickening,
He set a mortal arrow in the string."

On the 5 August, 1637, Governor *Winthrop* makes the following entry in his journal:—"Mr. *Ludlow*, Mr. *Pincheon*, and about 12 more, came by land from Connecticut, and brought with them a part of the skin and lock of hair of *Sasacus* and his brother and 5 other Pequod sachems, who being fled to the Mohawks for shelter, with their wampom (being to the value of £500) were by them surprised and slain, with 20 of their best men. *Mononottoh* was also taken, but escaped wounded. They brought news also of divers other Pequods which had been slain by other Indians, and their heads brought to the English so that now there had been slain and taken between 8 and 900."

The first troubles with the Pequots have already been noticed. It was among the people of *Mononotto*, that the English caused the blood of a Pequot to flow. Some English had been killed, but there is no more to excuse the murder of a Pequot than an Englishman. The English had injured the Indians of Block Island all in their power, which, it seems, did not satisfy them, and they next undertook to make spoil upon them in their own country upon Connecticut River. "As they were sailing up the river, says Dr. *I. Mather*, many of the Pequots on both sides of the river called to them, desirous to know what was their end in coming thither." * They answered, that they desired to speak with *Sassacus;* being told that *Sassacus* had gone to Long Island, they then demanded that *Mononotto* should appear, and they pretended he was from home also. However, they went on shore and demanded the murderers of Captain *Stone*, and were told that if they would wait they would send for them, and that *Mononotto* would come immediately. But very wisely the Pequots, in the mean time, "transported their goods, women and children to another place." † One of them then told the English that *Mononotto* would not come. Then the English began to do what mischief they could to them, and a skirmish followed, wherein one Indian was killed, and an Englishman was wounded." ‡

The name of *Mononotto's* wife appears to have been Wincumbone. She should not be overlooked in speaking of *Mononotto*, as she was instrumental in saving the life of an Englishman, as disinterestedly as *Pocahontas* saved that of Captain *Smith*. Some English had gone to trade with the Pequots, and to recover some horses which they had stolen, or picked up on their lands. Two of the English went on shore, and one went into the sachem's wigwam and demanded the horses. The Indians within slyly absented themselves, and *Wincumbone*, knowing their intention, told him to fly, for the Indians were making preparations to kill him. He barely escaped to the boat, being followed by a crowd to the shore.

Cassassinnamon was a noted Pequot chief, of whom we have some account as early as 1659. In that year a difficulty arose about the limits of Southerton, since called Stonington, in Connecticut, and several English were sent to settle the difficulty, which was concerning the location of Wekapauge. "For to help us (they say) to understand where Wekapauge is, we desired some Poquatucke Indians to go with us." *Cassassinnamon* was one who assisted. They told the English that "*Cashawasset* (the governor of Wekapauge) did charge them that they should not go any further than the east side of a little swamp, near the east end of the first great pond, where they did pitch down a stake, and told us [the English] that *Cashawasset* said that that very place was Wekapauge; said that *he* said it and not them; and if they should say that Wekapauge did go any further, *Cashawasset* would be angry." *Cashawasset* after this had confirmed to him and those under him, 8000 acres of land in the Pequot country, with the provision that they continued subjects of Massachusetts, and should "not sell or alienate the said lands, or any part thereof, to any English man or men, without the court's approbation."

The neck of land called *Quinicuntauge* was claimed by both parties; but *Cassassinnamon* said that when a whale was some time before cast ashore there, no one disputed *Cashawasset's* claim to it, which, it is believed, settled the question: *Cashawasset* was known generally by the name of *Harmon Garrett*. §

We next meet with *Cassassinnamon* in Philip's war, in which he commanded a company of Pequots, and accompanied Captain *Denison* in his successful career, and was present at the capture of *Canonchet*. ‖

In November, 1651, *Cassassinnamon* and eight others executed a sort of an agreement "with the townsmen of Pequot," afterward called *New London*. What kind of *agreement* it was we are not told. His name was subscribed *Casesymamon*. Among the other names we see *Obbachickwood*, *Neesouweégun* alias *Daniel*, *Cutchámaquin* and *Mahmawámbam*. *Cassassinnamon*, it is said, signed "in his own behalf and the behalf of the rest of Nameeag Indians." ¶

---

* Relation, 44. † Ibid.

‡ Ibid. Captain *Lion Gardener*, who had some men in this affair, gives quite a different account. See life of *Kutshamoquin*, alias *Kutshamakin*.

§ Several manuscript documents. ‖ *Hubbard*.

¶ 1 *Coll. Mass. Hist. Soc.* x. 101.

CHAPTER VII.

Of the Praying or Christian Indians in New England—Difficult to Christianize them—Labors of John Eliot—WAUBAN *the first Christian sagamore—Indian laws*—Uncas *protests against the attempt to convert his people*—Ninigret *refuses to receive missionaries—The Indian Bible*—PIAMBOUHOU—SPEEN—PENNAHANNIT—TUKAPEWILLIN—OONAMOG—AHATAWANCE—WATTASSACOMPONUM—HIACOOMES—MIOHQSOO—OCCUM—TITUBA.

IT must be exceedingly difficult, as all experience has shown, to cause any people to abandon a belief or faith in a matter, unless it be one on which the reasoning powers of the mind can be brought to act. The most ignorant people must be convinced, that many effects which they witness are produced by obvious causes; but there are so many others for which they cannot discover a cause, that they hesitate not to deny any *natural* cause for them at once. And notwithstanding that, from day to day, causes are developing themselves, and showing them, that many results which they had viewed as proceeding from a *super* natural cause hitherto, was nothing but a natural one, and which, when discovered, appeared perfectly simple, too, yet, for the want of the means of investigation, they would be looked upon as miraculous. These facts have been more than enough, among the scientific world, to cause them to look upon the most latent causes, with a hope that, in due time, they would unfold themselves also; and, finally, leave nothing for any agent to perform but nature itself. When the Indian, therefore, is driven by reason, or the light of science, from his strong-hold of ignorance, or, in other words, superstition, he is extremely liable to fall into the opposite extreme, to which allusion has just been made, because he will unhesitatingly say, what once appeared past all discovery has been shown to be most plain, and therefore it is not only possible, but even probable, that others will be disclosed of a like character.

It so happens, that in attempting to substitute one faith for another, in the minds of Indians, that the one proposed admits of no better demonstration than the one already possessed by them; for their manner of transmitting things to be remembered, is the most impressive and sacred, as will be elsewhere observed in our work. That any thing false should be handed down from their aged matrons and sires, could not be for a moment believed; and hence, that the stories of a strange people should be credited, instead of what they had heard from day to day from their youth up, from those who could have no possible motive to deceive them, could not be expected; and therefore no one will wonder for a moment that the gospel has met with so few believers among the Indians. All this, aside from their dealers in mysteries, the powwows, conjurers or priests, as they are variously denominated, whose office is healing the sick, appeasing the wrath of the invisible spirits by charms and unintelligible mummery. These characters took upon themselves, also, the important affair of determining the happiness each was to enjoy after death; assuring the brave and the virtuous that they should go to a place of perpetual spring, where game in the greatest plenty abounded, and every thing that the most perfect happiness required. Now, as a belief in any other religion promised no more, is it strange that a new one should be slow in gaining credence?

Considerations of this nature inevitably press in upon us, and cause us not to wonder, as many have done, that, for the first thirty years after the settlement of New England, so little was effected by the gospel among the Indians. The great difficulty of communicating with them by interpreters must have been slow in the extreme; and it must be considered, also, that a great length of time must have been consumed before any of these could perform their office with any degree of accuracy; the Indian language being unlike every other, and bearing no analogy to any known tongue whatever; and then, the peculiar custom of the Indians must be considered; their long delays before they would answer to any proposition; but more than all, we have to con sider the natural distrust that must necessarily arise in the minds of every people, at the sudden influx of strangers among them. When any new theory was presented to their minds, the first questions that would present themselves, would most unquestionably be, What are the *real* motives of this new people?—Do they really *love* us, as they pretend?—Do they *really* love one another? or do they not live, many of them, upon one another?—Is not this new state of things, which they desire, to enable them to subsist by us, and in time to enslave us, or deprive us of our possessions?—Does it not appear that these strangers are full of selfishness, and, therefore, have every motive which that passion gives rise to for deceiving us?—Hence, we repeat, that it can hardly be thought strange that Christianity has made so slow progress among the Indians.

Notwithstanding one of the ostensible objects of nearly all the royal charters and patents issued for British North America was the Christianizing of the Indians, few could be found equal to the task on arriving here: where wants of every kind required nearly all their labors, few could be found willing to forego every comfort to engage in a work which presented so many difficulties. Adventurers were those, generally, who emigrated with a view to bettering their own condition, instead of that of others.

At length Mr. *John Eliot*, seeing that little or nothing could be effected through the medium of his own language, resolved to make himself master of the Indian, and then to devote himself to their service. Accordingly he hired * an old † Indian, named *Job Nesutan*, ‡ to live in his family, and to teach him his language. When he had accomplished this arduous task, which he did in "a few months,"§ he set out upon his first attempt; having given notice to some Indians at *Nonantum*,‖ since Newton,¶ of his intention. With three others he met the Indians for the first time, 28 October, 1646. *Waaubon*,** whose name signified *wind*,†† "a wise and grave man, though no Sachem, with five or six Indians met them at some distance from their wigwams, and bidding them welcome, conducted them into a large apartment, where a great number of the natives were gathered together, to hear this new doctrine."‡‡ After prayers, and an explanation of the ten commandments, Mr. *Eliot* informed them "of the dreadful curse of God that would fall upon all those that brake them: He then told them who *Jesus Christ* was, where he was now gone, and how he would one day come again to judge the world in flaming fire."

After about an hour spent in this manner, the Indians had liberty to ask any questions in relation to what had been said. Whereupon one stood up and asked, *How he could know Jesus Christ?*—Another, *Whether Englishmen were ever so ignorant of him as the Indians?*—A third, *Whether Jesus Christ could understand prayers in Indian?*—Another, *How there could be an image of God, since it was forbidden in the second commandment?*—Another, *Whether, according to the second commandment, the child must suffer, though he be good, for the sins of its parents?*—And lastly, *How all the world became full of people, if they were all once drowned in the flood?*

The second meeting was upon 11 November, following. Mr. *Eliot* met the Indians again, and after catechising the children, and preaching an hour to the congregation, heard and answered, among others, the following questions.—*How the English came to differ so much from the Indians in their knowledge of God and Jesus Christ, since they had all at first but one Father?*—Another desired to know, *How it came to pass that sea-water was salt and river water fresh?*—And another, *That if the water was higher than the earth, how it happened that it did not overflow it?*

The third meeting took place soon after, namely, on 26 of the same month,

* *Neal*, Hist. N. Eng. i. 222.
† N. Eng. Biog. Dictionary, *art.* Eliot.
‡ See p. 54 of this book, *ante.*
§ *Neal*, Hist. N. Eng. i. 123.
‖ "Near Watertown mill, upon the south side of Charles River, about four or five miles from his own house, [in Roxbury,] where lived at that time *Waban*, one of their principal men, and some Indians with him." *Gookin*, (Hist. Col.) 168.
¶ Nonantum, or Noonatomen, signified *a place of rejoicing*, or *rejoicing*. *Neal*, i. 216.
** Wauban, *Magnalia*, iii. 196.
†† Ibid.
‡‡ Day-breaking of the Gospel in N. Eng., in *Neal*, i. 223

but was not so well attended. The powwows and sachems had dissuaded some, and by threats deterred others from meeting upon such occasions. Still there were considerable numbers that got attached to Mr. *Eliot*, and in a few days after, *Wampas*, "a wise and sage Indian," and two others, with some of his children, came to the English. He desired that these might be educated in the Christian faith. At the next meeting all the Indians present "offered their children to be catechised and instructed by the English, who upon this motion resolved to set up a school among them."

Mr. *Eliot*, notwithstanding his zeal, seems well to have understood, that something beside preaching was necessary to reform the lives of the Indians; and that was, their civilization by education. It is said that one of his noted sayings was, *The Indians must be civilized as well as, if not in order to their being, Christianized.** Therefore, the request of the Indians at Nonantum was not carried into effect until a place could be fixed upon where a regular settlement should be made, and the catechumens had shown their zeal for the cause by assembling themselves there, and conforming to the English mode of living. In the end this was agreed upon, and Natick was fixed as the place for a town, and the following short code of laws was set up and agreed to:—I. If any man be idle a week, or at most a fortnight, he shall pay five shillings.—II. If any unmarried man shall lie with a young woman unmarried, he shall pay twenty shillings.—III. If any man shall beat his wife, his hands shall be tied behind him, and he shall be carried to the place of justice to be severely punished.—IV. Every young man, if not another's servant, and if unmarried, shall be compelled to set up a wigwam, and plant for himself, and not shift up and down in other wigwams.—V. If any woman shall not have her hair tied up, but hang loose, or be cut as men's hair, she shall pay five shillings.—VI. If any woman shall go with naked breasts, she shall pay two shillings.—VII. All men that wear long locks shall pay five shillings.—VIII. If any shall kill their lice between their teeth, they shall pay five shillings.

In January following another company of praying Indians was established at Concord; and there were soon several other places where meetings were held throughout the country, from Cape Cod to Narraganset.† Of these, Mr. *Eliot* visited as many and as often as he was able. From the following passage in a letter which he wrote to Mr. *Winslow* of Plimouth, some idea may be formed of the hardships he underwent in his pious labors. He says, "I have not been dry night nor day, from the third day of the week unto the sixth, but so travelled, and at night pull off my boots, wring my stockings, and on with them again, and so continue. But God steps in and helps."‡

The chiefs and powwows would not have suffered even so much ground to have been gained by the gospel, but for the awe they were in of the English power. "Nor is this to be wondered at," says the very good historian, Mr. *Neal*, "for if it be very difficult to civilize barbarous nations, 'tis much more so to make them Christians: All men have naturally a veneration for the religion of their ancestors, and the prejudices of education § are insuperable without the extraordinary grace of God."

"The Monhegin Indians were so jealous of the general court's obliging them to pray to God, that *Uncas*, their sachem, went to the court at Hartford to protest against it. *Cutshamoquin*, another sachem, came to the Indian lecture, and openly protested against their building a town, telling the English, that all the sachems in the country were against it. He was so honest as to tell Mr. *Eliot* the reason of it; for (says he) the Indians that pray to God do not pay me tribute, as formerly they did; which was in part true, for whereas before the sachem was absolute master of his subjects; their lives and fortunes being at his disposal; they gave him now no more than they thought reasonable; but to wipe off the reproach that *Cutshamoquin* had laid upon them, those few praying Indians present, told Mr. *Eliot* what they had

* *Hutchinson*, Hist. Mass. i. 163. † *Neal*, i. 226—230. ‡ *Magnalia*, iii. 196.

§ This word, when applied to the *education* of the Indians among themselves, is to be understood in an opposite sense from its common acceptation: thus, to instruct in superstitions and idolatry, is what is *not* meant by education among us.

done for their sachem the two last years, leaving him to judge whether their prince had any reason to complain." They said they had given him 26 bushels of corn at one time, and six at another; that, in hunting for him two days, they had killed him 15 deers; broke up for him two acres of land; made him a great wigwam; "made him 20 rods of fence with a ditch and two rails about it;" paid a debt for him of £3, 10s. "One of them gave him a skin of beaver of two pounds, besides many days works in planting corn altogether; yea, they said they would willingly do more if he would govern them justly by the word of God. But the sachem swelling with indignation, at this unmannerly discourse of his vassals, turned his back upon the company and went away in the greatest rage imaginable; though upon better consideration, himself turned Christian not long after."

Mr. *Experience Mayhew* met with similar occurrences many years after. Upon a visit to the Narragansets, he sent for *Ninigret*, the sachem, and desired of him leave to preach to his people; but the sachem told him to go and make the English good first; and observed, further, that some of the English kept Saturday, others Sunday, and others no day at all for worship; so that if his people should have a mind to turn Christians, they could not tell what religion to be of. *Ninigret* further added, that Mr. *Mayhew* might try his skill first with the Pequots and Mohegans, and if they submitted to the Christian religion, possibly he and his people might, but they would not be the first.*

In the meanwhile, Mr. *Eliot* had translated the whole Bible into Indian,† also Baxter's Call, Mr. *Shepherd's* Sincere Convert, and his Sound Believer,‡ besides some other performances, as a Grammar, Psalter, Primers, Catechisms, the Practice of Piety, &c.§

It is amusing to hear what our old valued friend, Dr. *C. Mather*, says of *Eliot's* Bible. "This Bible," he says, "was printed here at our Cambridge; and it is the only Bible that ever was printed in all America, from the very foundation of the world."‖ The same author observes, that "the whole translation was writ with but *one pen*, which pen had it not been lost, would have certainly deserved a richer case than was bestowed upon that pen, with which *Holland*¶ writ his translation of *Plutarch*"

It was long since inquired, "What benefit has all this toil and suffering produced?—Is there a vestige of it remaining?—Were the Indians in reality bettered by the great efforts of their friends?" "Mr. *Eliot*," says Dr. *Douglass*, "with immense labor translated and printed our Bible into Indian. It was done with a good, pious design, but it must be reconed among the *Otiosorum hominum negotia:* It was done in the Natick [Nipmuk] language. Of the Naticks, at present, there are not 20 families subsisting, and scarce any of these can read.—*Cui boni!*"**

By the accounts left us, it will be perceived, that for many years after the exertions of *Eliot, Gookin, Mayhew* and others, had been put in operation, there was no inconsiderable progress made in the great undertaking of Christianizing the Indians. Natick, the oldest praying town, contained, in 1674, 29 families, in which perhaps were about 145 persons. The name *Natick* signified *a place of hills. Waban* was the chief man here, "who," says Mr. *Gookin*, "is now about 70 years of age. He is a person of great prudence and piety: I do not know any Indian that excels him."

Pakemitt, or Punkapaog, ("which takes its name from a spring, that riseth out of red earth,") is the next town in order, and contained 12 families or

---

* *Neal's* N. England, i. 257

† See book ii. chap. iii. p. 57, *ante.*

‡ *Moore's* Life Eliot, 144.

§ *Magnalia*, b. iii. 197.

‖ Ibid.

¶ *Philemon Holland* was called the translator-general of his age; he wrote several of his translations with one pen, upon which he made the following verses:

With one sole pen I writ this book,
  Made of a grey goose quill;
A pen it was, when I it took,
  And a pen I leave it still.
      Fuller's Worthies of England.

** *Douglass*, Hist. America, i. 172, *note* See also *Halket*, Hist. Notes, 248, &c *Douglass* wrote about 1745 about 60 persons. It was 14 miles south of Boston, and is now included in Stoughton. The Indians here removed from the Neponset. Hassanamesit is the third town, and is now included in Grafton, and contained, like the second, 60 souls. Okommakamesit, now in Marlborough, contained about 50 people, and was the fourth town. Wamesit, since included in Tewksbury, the fifth town, was upon a neck of land in Merrimack River, and contained about 75 souls, of five to a family. Nashobah, now Littleton, was the sixth, and contained but about 50 inhabitants. Magunkaquog, now Hopkinton, signified *a place of great trees*. Here were about 55 persons, and this was the seventh town.

There were, besides these, seven other towns, which were called the new praying towns. These were among the Nipmuks. The first was Manchage, since Oxford, and contained about 60 inhabitants. The second was about six miles from the first, and its name was Chabanakongkomun, since Dudley, and contained about 45 persons. The third was Maanexit, in the north-east part of Woodstock, and contained about 100 souls. The fourth was Quantisset, also in Woodstock, and containing 100 persons likewise. Wabquissit, the fifth town, also in Woodstock, (but now included in Connecticut,) contained 150 souls. Pakachoog, a sixth town, partly in Worcester and partly in Ward, also contained 100 people. Weshakim, or Nashaway, a seventh, contained about 75 persons. Waeuntug was also a praying town, included now by Uxbridge; but the number of people there is not set down by Mr. *Gookin*, our chief authority.

Hence it seems there were now *supposed* to be about 1150 praying Indians in the places enumerated above. There is, however, not the least probability, that even one fourth of these were ever sincere believers in Christianity. This calculation, or rather supposition, was made the year before *Philip's* war began; and how many do we find who adhered to their profession through that war? That event not only shook the faith of the common sort, but many that had been at the head of the praying towns, the Indian ministers themselves, were found in arms against their white Christian neighbors.

At the close of *Philip's* war, in 1677, Mr. *Gookin* enumerates "seven places where they met to worship God and keep the sabbath, viz. at Nonatum, at Pakemit, or Punkapog; at Cowate, alias the Fall of Charles River, at Natik and Medfield, at Concord, at Namekeake, near Chelmsford." There were, at each of these places, he says, "a teacher, and schools for the youth." But, notwithstanding they had occupied seven towns in the spring of 1676, on their return from imprisonment upon the bleak islands in Boston harbor, they were too feeble long to maintain so many. The appearance of some straggling Mohawks greatly alarmed these Indians, and they were glad to come within the protection of the English; and so the remote towns soon became abandoned.

We have seen that 1150 praying Indians were claimed before the war, in the end of the year 1674, but not half this number could be found when it was proclaimed that all such must come out of their towns, and go by themselves to a place of safety. Mr. *Gookin* says, at one time there were *about* 500 upon the islands; but when some had been employed in the army, and other ways, (generally such as were indifferent to religion,) there were but about 300 remaining. Six years after that disastrous war, Mr. *Eliot* could claim but *four* towns! viz. "Natick, Punkapaog, Wamesit, and Chachaubunkkakowok."

Before we pass to notice other towns in Plimouth colony, we will give an account of some of the most noted of the praying Indians.

Wauban we have several times introduced, and will now close our account of him. He is supposed to have been originally of Concord; but, at the time Mr. *Eliot* began his labors, he resided at Nonantum, since Newton. At Natik, or Natick, he was one of the most efficient officers until his death.

When a kind of civil community was established at Natik, *Wauban* was made a ruler of fifty, and subsequently a justice of the peace. The following is said to be a copy of a warrant which he issued against some of the transgressors. "*You, you big constable, quick you catch um* Jeremiah Offscow *strong you hold um, safe you bring um, afore me,* Waban, *justice peace.*"*

A young justice asked *Wauban* what he would do when Indians got drunk and quarrelled; he replied, "*Tie um all up, and whip um plaintiff, and whip um fendant, and whip um witness.*"

We have not learned the precise time of *Wauban's* death,† but he was certainly alive in the end of the year 1676, and, we think, in 1677. For he was among those sent to Deer Island, 30 October, 1675, and was among the sick that returned in May, 1676; and it is particularly mentioned that he was one that recovered.

Piambouhou‡ was the next man to *Wauban*, and the next after him that received the gospel. At the second meeting at Nonantum, he brought a great many of his people. At Natik he was made ruler of ten. When the church at Hassanamesit was gathered, he was called to be a ruler in it. When that town was broken up in *Philip's* war, he returned again to Natik, where he died. He was one of those also confined to Deer Island; hence, he lived until after the war. The ruling elder of Hassanamesit, called by some *Piambow*, was the same person.

John Speen was another teacher, contemporary with *Piambo*, and, like him, was a "grave and pious man." In 1661, *Timothy Dwight*, of Dedham, sued *John Speen* and his brother, *Thomas*, for the recovery of a debt of *sixty* pounds, and Mr. *Eliot* bailed them. This he probably did with safety, as *John Speen* and "his kindred" owned nearly all the Natik lands, when the Christian commonwealth was established there. This valuable possession he gave up freely, to be used in common, in 1650. Notwithstanding "he was among the first that prayed to God" at Nonantum, and "was a diligent reader," yet he died a drunkard; having been some time before discarded from the church at Natik.

Pennahannit, called Captain *Josiah*, was "Marshal General" over all the praying towns. He used to attend the courts at Natik; but his residence was at Nashobah.

Tukapewillin was teacher at Hassanamesit, and his brother, *Anaweakin*, ruler. He was, according to Major *Gookin*, "a pious and able man, and apt to teach." He suffered exceedingly in *Philip's* war; himself and his congregation, together with those of the two praying towns, "Magunkog and Chobonekonhonom," having been enticed away by *Philip's* followers. His father, *Naoas*, was deacon of his church, and among the number. They, however, tried to make their escape to the English soon after, agreeably to a plan concerted with *Job Kattenanit*, when he was among *Philip's* people as a spy; but, as it happened, in the attempt, they fell in with an English scout, under Captain *Gibbs*, who treated them as prisoners, and with not a little barbarity; robbing them of every thing they had, even the minister of a pewter cup which he used at sacraments. At Marlborough, though under the protection of officers, they were so insulted and abused, "especially by women," that *Tukapewillin's* wife, from fear of being murdered, escaped into the woods, leaving a sucking child to be taken care of by its father. With her went also her son, 12 years old, and two others. The others, *Naoas* and *Tukapewillin*, with six or seven children, were, soon after, sent to Deer Island. *Naoas* was, at this time, about 80 years old.

Oonamog was ruler at Marlborough, and a sachem, who died in the summer of 1674. His death "was a great blow to the place. He was a pious and discreet man, and the very soul, as it were, of the place." The troubles of the war fell very heavily upon his family. A barn containing corn and hay was burnt at Chelmsford, by some of the war party, as it proved afterwards; but some of the violent English of that place determined to make the Wamesits suffer for it. Accordingly, about 14 men armed

---

* *Allen's* Biog. Dict. *art.* WABAN.

† Dr. *Homer*, Hist. Newton, says he died in 1674, but gives no authority. We have cited several authorities, showing that he was alive a year later, (see b. iii. pp. 10 and 79.)

‡ *Piam Boohan*, *Gookin's* Hist. Coll. 184.—*Piambow*, his Hist. Praying Indians.

themselves, and, under a pretence of scouting, went to the wigwams of the Wamesits, and ordered them to come out. They obeyed without hesitation, being chiefly helpless women and children, and not conceiving any harm could be intended them; but they were no sooner out than fired upon, when five were wounded and one killed. Whether the courage of the *brave* English now failed them, or whether they were satisfied with what blood was already shed, is not clear; but they did no more at this time. The one slain was a little son of *Tahatooner;* and *Oonamog's* widow was severely wounded, whose name was *Sarah,* "a woman of good report for religion." She was daughter of *Sagamore-John,* who lived and died at the same place, before the war, "a great friend to the English." *Sarah* had had two husbands: the first was *Oonamog,* the second *Tahatooner,* who was son of *Tahattawan,* sachem of Musketaquid. This affair took place on the 15 November, 1675.

Numphow was ruler of the praying Indians at Wamesit, and *Samuel,* his son, was teacher, "a young man of good parts," says Mr. *Gookin,* "and can speak, read and write English and Indian competently;" being one of those taught at the expense of the corporation. *Numphow* experienced wretched trials in the time of the war; he with his people having fled away from their homes immediately after the horrid barbarity of which we have just spoken, fearing to be murdered if they should continue there. However, after wandering a while up and down in the woods, in the dismal month of December, they returned to Wamesit, in a forlorn condition, and hoped the carriage of their neighbors would be such that they might continue there. It did not turn out so, for in February they again quitted their habitations, and went off towards Canada. Six or seven old persons remained behind, who were hindered from going by infirmity. These poor blind and lame Indians were all burnt to death in their wigwams. This act, had it occurred by accident, would have called forth the deepest pity from the breast of every human creature to whose knowledge it should come. But horror, anguish and indignation take the place of pity, at being told that the flames which consumed them were lighted by the savage hands of white men!! It was so—and whites are only left to remember in sorrow this act of those of their own color! But to return--

During the wanderings of *Numphow* and his friends, famine and sickness destroyed many of them. Himself and *Mistic George,* or *George Mistic,* a teacher, were numbered with the dead. The others, having joined *Wannalancet* to avoid falling in with war parties on both sides, at the close of the war, surrendered themselves to the English, at Dover, in August, 1676. New troubles now came upon them. Some English captives testified that some of them had been in arms against them, and such were either sold into slavery, or executed at Boston. Several shared the latter fate. *Numphow's* son *Samuel* barely escaped, and another son, named *Jonathan George,* was pardoned; also *Symon Betokam.*

Numphow was in some public business as early as 1656. On 8 June that year, he, *John Line* and *George Mistic,* were, upon the part of the "Indian court," employed to run the line from Chelmsford to Wamesit.* And 23 years after he accompanied Captain *Jonathan Danforth* of Billerica in renewing the bounds of *Brenton's* Farm, now Litchfield, N. H.†

Wannalancet, whose history will be found spoken upon at large in our next book, countenanced religion, and it was at his wigwam that Mr. *Eliot* and Mr. *Gookin* held a meeting on the 5 May, 1674. His house was near Pawtucket Falls, on the Merrimack. "He is," said Major *Gookin,* "a sober and grave person, and of years, between 50 and 60."

John Ahatawance was ruler of Nashobah, a pious man, who died previous to 1674. After his decease, *Pennahannit* was chief. *John Thomas* was their teacher. "His father was murdered by the Maquas in a secret manner, as he was fishing for eels at his wear, some years since, during the war" with them.

Wattasacompanum, called also Captain *Tom,* is thus spoken of by Mr. *Gookin,* who was with him at Pakachoog, 17 September, 1674. "My chief assistant was *Wattasacompanum,* ruler of the Nipmuk Indians, a grave and pious man, of the chief sachem's blood of the Nipmuk country He resides at Hassana-

* *Allen's* Hist. Chelmsford. † MS. letter of *John Farmer,* Esq.

mesit; but by former appointment, calleth here, together with some others." Captain *Tom* was among *Tukapewillin's* company, that went off with the enemy, as in speaking of him we have made mention. In that company there were about 200, men, women and children. The enemy, being about 300 strong, obliged the praying Indians to go off with, or be killed by them. There were, however, many who doubtless preferred their company to that of their friends on Deer Island. This was about the beginning of December, 1675. Captain *Tom* afterwards fell into the hands of the English, and, being tried and condemned as a rebel, was, on 26 June, 1676, executed at Boston; much to the grief of such excellent men as *Gookin* and *Eliot*.

Although something had been done towards Christianizing the Indians in Plimouth colony, about a year before Mr. *Eliot's* first visit to Nonantum, yet for some years after, Massachusetts was considerably in advance in this respect. Some of the principal congregations or praying towns follow:—

At Meeshawn, since Provincetown or Truro, and Punonakanit, since Billingsgate, were 72 persons; at Potanumaquut, or Nauset, in Eastham, 44; at Monamoyik, since Chatham, 71; at Sawkattukett, in Harwich; Nobsqassit, in Yarmouth; at Matakees, in Barnstable and Yarmouth; and Weequakut, in Barnstable, 122; at Satuit, Pawpoesit, Coatuit, in Barnstable, Mashpee, Wakoquet, near Mashpee, 95; at Codtanmut, in Mashpee, Ashimuit, on the west line of Mashpee, Weesquobs, in Sandwich, 22; Pispogutt, Wawayoutat, in Wareham, Sokones, in Falmouth, 36. In all these places were 462 souls; 142 of whom could read, and 72 write Indian, and 9 could read English. This account was furnished Major *Gookin* in 1674, by the Rev. *Richard Bourne* of Sandwich. *Philip's* war broke up many of these communities, but the work continued long after it dwindled to almost nothing in Massachusetts. In 1685 there were 1439 considered as Christian Indians in Plimouth colony.

Mr. *Thomas Mayhew* Jr. settled in Martha's Vineyard, called by the Indians *Nope*, in 1642. He was accompanied by a few English families, who made him their minister; but not being satisfied with so limited usefulness, he learned the Indian language, and began to preach to them. His first convert was

Hiacoomes, in 1643, a man of small repute among his own people, whose residence was at Great Harbor, near where the English first settled. He was regularly ordained 22 August, 1670, but he began to preach in 1646. *John Tokinosh* was at the same time ordained teacher. His residence was at Numpang, on the east end of the island. He died 22 January, 1684, and *Hiacoomes* preached his funeral sermon. For some years before his death *Hiacoomes* was unable to preach. He was supposed to have been about 80 years old at the time of his death, which happened about 1690.

Pahkehpunnassoo, sachem of Chappequiddik, was a great opposer of the gospel, and at one time beat *Hiacoomes* for professing a belief of it. Not long after, as himself and another were at work upon a chimney of their cabin, they were both knocked down by lightning, and the latter killed. *Pahkehpunnassoo* fell partly in the fire, and but for his friends would have perished. Whether this escape awakened him, is not mentioned; but he soon after became a Christian, and Mr. *Mayhew* aptly observes that "at last he was a *brand plucked out of the fire*."

Miohqsoo, or *Myoxeo*, was another noted Indian of Nope. He was a convert of *Hiacoomes*, whom he had sent for to inquire of him about his God. He asked *Hiacoomes* how many gods he had, and on being told but ONE, immediately reckoned up 37 of his, and desired to know whether he should throw them all away for one. On being told by *Hiacoomes* that he had thrown away all those and many more, and was better off by so doing, *Miohqsoo* said, he would forthwith throw away his, which he did, and became one of the most eminent of the Indian converts. One of his children, a son, sailed for England in 1657, with Mr. *Thomas Mayhew* Jr., in a ship commanded by Captain *James Garrett*, and was never heard of after. The time of the death of *Miohqsoo* is unknown, but he lived to a great age.

Among the Mohegans and Narragansets nothing of any account was effected, in the way of Christianizing them, for a long time. The chief sachems of those nations were determined and fixed against it, and though it was from time to time urged upon them, yet very little was ever done.

SAMPSON OCCUM, or, as his name is spelt in a sermon * of his, *Occom*, was a Mohegan, of the family of *Benoni Occum*, who resided near New London, in Connecticut. He was the first of that tribe who was conspicuous in religion, if not the only one. He was born in 1723, and becoming attached to the Rev. *Eleazar Wheelock*, the minister of Lebanon in Connecticut, in 1741 he became a Christian.† Possessing talents and great piety, Mr. *Wheelock* entertained sanguine hopes that he would be able to effect much among his countrymen as a preacher of the gospel. He went to England in 1765 to procure aid for the keeping up of a school for the instruction of Indian children, which was begun by Mr. *Wheelock*, and furthered by a Mr. *Moore*, by a donation of a school house and land, about 1763. While in England he was introduced to Lord *Dartmouth*, and other eminent persons. He preached there to crowds of people, and returned to America in September, 1768, having landed at Boston on his return.‡ It is said he was the first Indian that preached in England. He was ordained, in 1759, a preacher to the Montauks on L. Island. About this time he visited the Cherokees. He finally settled among the Oneida Indians, with many of his Mohegan brethren, about 1768; they having been invited by the Oneidas. He died in July, 1792, at N. Stockbridge, N. York, aged 69.

Tituba is noticed in the annals of New England, from her participation in the witch tragedies acted here in 1691. In a valuable work giving a history of that horrible delusion, § mention is thus made of her. "It was the latter end of February, 1691, when divers young persons belonging to [Rev.] Mr. *Parris'* ‖ family, and one more of the neighborhood, began to act after a strange and unusual manner, viz., as by getting into holes, and creeping under chairs and stools, and to use other sundry odd postures, and antic gestures, uttering foolish, ridiculous speeches, which neither they themselves nor any others could make sense of." "March the 11th, Mr. *Parris* invited several neighboring ministers to join with him in keeping a solemn day of prayer at his own house; the time of the exercise those persons were, for the most part, silent, but after any one prayer was ended, they would act and speak strangely, and ridiculously, yet were such as had been well educated and of good behavior, the one a girl of 11 or 12 years old, would sometimes seem to be in a convulsion fit, her limbs being twisted several ways, and very stiff, but presently her fit would be over. A few days before this solemn day of prayer, Mr. *Parris'* Indian man and woman, made a cake of rye meal, with the children's water, and baked it in the ashes, and, as it is said, gave to the dog; this was done as a means to discover witchcraft. Soon after which those ill-affected or afflicted persons named several that they said they saw, when in their fits, afflicting of them. The first complained of, was the said Indian woman, named *Tituba*. She confessed that the devil urged her to sign a book, which he presented to her, and also to work mischief to the children, &c. She was afterwards committed to prison, and lay there till sold for her fees. The account she since gives of it is, that her master did beat her, and otherwise abuse her, to make her confess and accuse (such as he called) her sister witches; and that whatsoever she said by way of confessing or accusing others, was the effect of such usage; her master refused to pay her fees, unless she would stand to what she had said."

We are able to add to our information of *Tituba* from another old and curious work,¶ as follows:—That when she was examined she "confessed the making a cake, as is above mentioned, and said her mistress in her own country was a witch, and had taught her some means to be used for the discovery of a witch and for the prevention of being bewitched, &c., but said "that she herself was not a witch." The children who accused her said "that she did pinch, prick, and grievously torment them; and that they saw her here

* At the execution of *Moses Paul*, for murder, at New Haven, 2 September, 1772. To his letter to Mr. *Keen*, his name is *Occum*.

† Life Dr. *Wheelock*, 16.

‡ His Letter to Mr. *Keen*, in Life *Wheelock*, 175.

§ Wonders of the Invisible World, by *R. Calef*, 90, 91, 4to. London, 1700.

‖ "*Samuel Paris*, pastor of the church in Salem-village." *Modest Enquiry into the Nature of Witchcraft*, by John Hale, *pastor of the church in Beverly*, p. 23, 16mo. Boston, 1702.

¶ *Modest Enquiry*, &c. 25.

and there, where nobody else could. Yea, they could tell where she was, and what she did, when out of their human sight." Whether the author was a witness to this he does not say; but probably he was not. Go through the whole of our early writers, and you will scarce find one who witnessed such matters: (Dr. *Cotton Mather* is nearest to an exception.) But they generally preface such marvellous accounts by observing, "I am slow to believe rumors of this nature, nevertheless, some things I have had certain information of." *

The Rev. Mr. *Felt* † gives the following extract from the "Quarterly Court Papers." "March 1st. *Sarah Osborn, Sarah* and *Dorothy Good, Tituba,* servant of Mr. *Parris, Martha Cory, Rebecca Nurse, Sarah Cloyce, John Proctor* and his wife *Elizabeth,* all of Salem village, are committed to Boston jail on charge of witchcraft."

The other servant of Mr. *Parris* was the husband of *Tituba,* whose name was *John.* It was a charge against them that they had tried means to discover witches. But there is little probability that these ignorant and simple Indians would ever have thought of "trying a project" for the detection of witches, had they not learned it from some more miserably superstitious white persons. We have the very record to justify this stricture. ‡ Take the words. "*Mary Sibly* having confessed, that she innocently counselled *John,* the Indian, to attempt a discovery of witches, is permitted to commune with Mr. *Parris'* church. She had been previously disciplined for such counsel and appeared well." We are not told *who disciplined* her for the examination. Was it Mr. *Parris?*

This is the only instance I have met with of Indians being implicated in *white* witchcraft.

* *I. Mather's* Brief Hist. Philip's War, 34.
† In his valuable *Annals of Salem,* 303.
‡ Danvers Records, published by the author last cited.

END OF BOOK SECOND.

BIOGRAPHY AND HISTORY

OF THE

INDIANS OF NORTH AMERICA.

BOOK III.

BOOK III.

BIOGRAPHY AND HISTORY OF THE NEW ENGLAND INDIANS CONTINUED.

CHAPTER I.

Life of ALEXANDER *alias* WAMSUTTA—*Events which led to the war with Philip*—WEETAMOO *his wife*—*Early events in her life*—PETANANUET, *her second husband*—*Weetamoo's latter career and death*—*Ninigret*—*Death of Alexander*—JOHN SASSAMON—*His country and connections*—*Becomes a christian*—*Schoolmaster*—*Minister*—*Settles at Assawomset*—FELIX *marries his daughter*—*Sassamon discovers the plots of Philip*—*Is murdered*—*Proceedings against the murderers*—*They are condemned and executed*

ALEXANDER was the English name of the elder son of *Massasoit*. His real name appears at first to have been *Mooanam*, and afterwards *Wamsutta*, and lastly *Alexander*. The name of *Mooanam* he bore as early as 1639; in 1641 we find him noticed under the name *Wamsutta*. About the year 1656, he and his younger brother, *Metacomet*, or rather *Pometacom*, were brought to the court of Plimouth, and being solicitous to receive English names, the governor called the elder *Alexander*, and the younger *Philip*, probably from the two Macedonian heroes, which, on being explained to them, might have flattered their vanities; and which was probably the intention of the governor.

Alexander appears pretty early to have set up for himself, as will be seen in the course of this chapter; occasioned, perhaps, by his marrying a female sachem of very considerable authority, and in great esteem among her neighbors.

NAMUMPUM, afterwards called *Weetamoo*, squaw-sachem of Pocasset, was the wife of *Alexander*; and who, as says an anonymous writer,* was more willing to join *Philip* when he began war upon the English, being persuaded by him that they had poisoned her husband. This author calls her "as potent a prince as any round about her, and hath as much corn, land, and men, at her command."

Alexander having, in 1653, sold a tract of the territory acquired by his wife, as has been related in the life of *Massasoit*, about six years after, *Weetamoo* came to Plimouth, and the following account of her business is contained in the records.

"I, *Namumpum*, of Pokeesett, hauing, in open court, June last, fifty-nine, [1659,] before the governour and majestrates, surrendered up all that right and title of such lands as *Woosamequin* and *Wamsetta* sould to the purchasers; as appeeres by deeds giuen vnder theire hands, as alsoe the said *Namumpum* promise to remoue the Indians of from those lands; and alsoe att the same court the said *Wamsutta* promised *Namumpum* the third part of the pay, as is

---

* Old Indian Chronicle, p. 6

expressed in the deed of which payment *Namumpum* haue receiued of *John Cooke*, this 6 of Oct. 1659: these particulars as followeth: item; 20 *yards bleu trading cloth*, 2 *yards red cotton*, 2 *paire of shooes*, 2 *paire stockings*, 6 *broade hoes and* 1 *axe;* And doe acknowledge receiued by me, Namumpum."

Witnessed by *Squabsen*, *Wahatunchquatt*, and two English

Thus this land affair seems to have been amicably settled; but the same year of *Alexander's* death, whether before or after we are not assured, *Namumpum* appeared at Plimouth, and complained that *Wamsutta* had sold some of her land without her consent. "The court agreed to doe what they could in conuenient time for her relief."

We apprehend there was some little difficulty between *Alexander* and his wife about this time, especially if her complaint were before his death, and we are rather of the opinion that it was, for it was June when her complaint was made, and we should assign a little later date for the death of her husband; and therefore all difficulty was settled in his death.

On the 8 April, 1661, *Wamsutta* deeded the tract of country since called Rehoboth to *Thomas Willet* "for a valuable consideration."* What that was the deed does not inform us; but we may venture to question the fact, for if the consideration had in truth been valuable, it would have appeared in the deed, and not have been kept out of sight.

What time *Namumpum* deeded land to *John Sanford* and *John Archer*, we are not informed, but it was probably about the beginning of 1662. It was a deed of gift, and appears to have been only deeded to them to prevent her husband's selling it; but these men, it seems, attempted to hold the land in violation of their promise; however, being a woman of perseverance, she so managed the matter, that, in the year 1668, she found witnesses who deposed to the true meaning of the deed, and thus was, we presume, restored to her rightful possessions.

Since we have been thus particular in acquainting the reader with the wife of *Wamsutta*, we will, before proceeding with our account of the husband, say all that we have to say of the interesting *Weetamoo*.

Soon after the death of *Alexander*, we find *Namumpum*, or *Weetamoo*, associated with another husband, named *Petonowowet*. He was well known to the English, and went by the familiar name of *Ben*. Now, unless *Peto-nowowet*, or *Pe-tan-a-nuet* has been corrupted into Peter Nunnuit, we must allow her to have had a third husband in 1675. We, however, are well satisfied that these two names are, as they appear to be, one and the same name.

This husband of *Weetamoo* does not appear to have been of so much importance as her first, *Wamsutta;* and as he only appears occasionally in the crowd, we are of opinion that she took good care in taking a second husband, and fixed upon one that she was better able to manage than she was the determined *Wamsutta*.

On the 8 May, 1673, *Tatamomock*, *Petonowowett*, and *William* alias *Ijasocke*, sold to *Nathaniel Paine* of Rehoboth, and *Hugh Cole* of Swansey, a lot of land in Swansey, near Mattapoiset, and Showamet neck, for £35 5*s*. *Weetamoo Philip* alias *Wagusoke*, and *Steven* alias *Nucano*, were the Indian witnesses.

About the same time, one *Piowant* was intruded upon by some others claiming his lands, or otherwise molesting him, and the business seems to have undergone a legal scrutiny; in this affair both *Weetamoo* and her husband appear upon our records. They testify that the tract of land bounded by a small river or brook called *Mastucksett*, which compasseth said tract to Assonett River, and so to Taunton River, [by trees, &c.] hath for many years been in the possession of *Piowant*. The place of the bounds on Taunton River was called *Chippascuitt*, which was a little south of Mastucksett. *Pantauset*, *Quanowin*, *Nescanoo*, and *Panowwin*, testified the same.

It does not appear that *Peta-nan-u-et* was at all concerned in *Philip's* war against the English, but, on the contrary, forsook his wife and joined them against her. Under such a leader as *Church*, he must have been employed against his countrymen with great advantage. At the time he came over to

* See the Hist. of Attleborough, by *John Daggett*, Esq., p. 6, where the deed is preserved.

the English, he no doubt expected his wife would do the same, as she gave *Church* to understand as much. After the war he was honored with a command over the prisoners, who were permitted to reside in the country between Sepecan and Dartmouth. *Numpus*, or *Nompash*, and *Isaac* were also in the same office.

After Mr. *Church* left *Awashonks'* council, a few days before the war broke out, he met with both *Weetamoo* and her husband at Pocasset. He first met with the husband, *Petananuet*, who had just arrived in a canoe from *Philip's* head quarters at Mount Hope. He told *Church* there would certainly be war, for that *Philip* had held a war dance of several weeks, and had entertained the young men from all parts of the country. He said, also, that *Philip* expected to be sent for to Plimouth, about *Sassamon's* death, knowing himself guilty of contriving that murder. *Petananuet* further said, that he saw Mr. *James Brown* of Swansey, and Mr. *Samuel Gorton*, who was an interpreter, and two other men that brought a letter from the governor of Plimouth to *Philip*. *Philip's* young warriors, he said, would have killed Mr. *Brown*, but *Philip* told them they must not, for his father had charged him to show kindness to him; but to satisfy them, told them, that on the next Sunday, when the English had gone to meeting, they might plunder their houses, and afterwards kill their cattle.

Meanwhile *Weetamoo* was at her camp just back from Pocasset shore, on the high hill a little to the north of what is now Howland's ferry, and *Petananuet* requested Mr. *Church* to go up and see her. He did so, and found her in rather a melancholy mood, all her men having left her and gone to *Philip's* war dance, much, she said, against her will.

Church, elated with his success at *Awashonks'* camp, and thinking both "queens" secured to the English interest, hastened to Plimouth to give the governor an account of his discoveries.—This was a day big to *Philip;* he immediately took measures to reclaim *Weetamoo*, and had nearly drawn off *Awashonks* with the vivid hopes of conquest and booty.

Weetamoo could no longer remain neutral; the idea still harrowed upon her mind, that the authorities of Plimouth had poisoned her former husband,* and was now sure that they had seduced her present one; therefore, from the power of such arguments, when urged by the artful *Philip*, there was no escape or resistance. Hence his fortune became her own, and she moved with him from place to place about her dominions, in the country of Pocasset, until the 30 July, when all the Wampanoags escaped out of a swamp, and retired into the country of the Nipmuks. From this time *Weetamoo's* operations become so blended with those of her allies, that the life of *Philip* takes up the narration.

When, by intestine divisions, the power of *Philip* was destroyed among the Nipmucks, *Weetamoo* seems to have been deserted by almost all her followers, and, like *Philip*, she sought refuge again in her own country. It was upon the 6 August, 1676, when she arrived upon the western bank of Tehticut River in Mettapoiset, where, as was then supposed, she was drowned by accident, in attempting to cross the river to Pocasset, at the same point she had crossed the year before in her flight with *Philip*.

Her company consisted now of no more than 26 men, whereas, in the beginning of the war, they amounted to 300; and she was considered by the English "next unto *Philip* in respect of the mischief that hath been done."† The English at Taunton were notified by a deserter of her situation, who offered to lead any that would go, in a way that they might easily surprise her and her company. Accordingly, 20 men volunteered upon this enterprise, and succeeded in capturing all but *Weetamoo*, "who," according to Mr. *Hubbard*‡ "intending to make an escape from the danger, attempted to get over a river or arm of the sea near by, upon a raft, or some pieces of broken wood; but whether tired and spent with swimming, or starved with cold and hunger she was found stark naked in Metapoiset, not far from the water side, which made some think she was first half drowned, and so ended her wretched life." "Her head being cut off and set upon a pole in Taunton, was known by some

* OLD INDIAN CHRONICLE, p. 8. † *I. Mather.* ‡ Narrative, 103 and 109.

Indians then prisoners [there,] which set them into a horrible lamentation."
Mr. *Mather* improves upon this passage, giving it in a style more to suit the taste of the times: "They made a most horid and diabolical lamentation, crying out that it was their queen's head."

The authors of Yamoyden thus represent *Philip* escaping from the cold grasp of the ghostly form of *Weetamoo*:—

"As from the water's depth she came,
With dripping locks and bloated frame,
Wild her discolored arms she threw
To grasp him; and, as swift he flew,
Her hollow scream he heard behind
Come mingling with the howling wind:
'Why fly from *Wetamoe?* she died
Bearing the war-axe on thy side.'"

Although *Weetamoo* doubtless escaped from Pocasset with *Philip*, yet it appears that instead of flying to the Nipmuks she soon went down into the Niantic country, and the English immediately had news of it, which occasioned their sending for *Ninigret* to answer for harboring their enemy, as in his life has been related.

In this connection it should be noted, that the time had expired, in which *Ninigret* by his deputies agreed to deliver up *Weetamoo*, some time previous to the great fight in Narraganset, and hence this was seized upon, as one pretext for invading the Narragansets. And moreover, it was said, that if she were taken by that formidable army of a 1000 men, "her lands would more than pay all the charge" the English had been at in the whole war.*

Weetamoo, it is presumed, left *Ninigret* and joined the hostile Narragansets and the Wampanoags in their strong fort, some time previous to the English expedition against it, in December. And it was about this time that she connected herself with the Narraganset chief *Quinnapin*, as will be found related in his life. She is mentioned by some writers as *Philip's* kinswoman, which seems to have been the case in a two-fold manner; first from her being sister to his wife, and secondly from her marrying *Alexander*, his brother. To return to *Wamsutta*.

A lasting and permanent interest will always be felt, and peculiar feelings associated with the name of this chief. Not on account of a career of battles, devastations or murders, for there were few of these,† but there is left for us to relate the melancholy account of his death. Mr. *Hubbard's* account of this event is in the hands of almost every reader, and cited by every writer upon our early history, and hence is too extensively known to be repeated here. Dr. *I. Mather* agrees very nearly in his account with Mr. *Hubbard*, but being more minute, and rarely to be met with, we give it entire:—

"In A. D. 1662, Plimouth colony was in some danger of being involved in trouble by the Wampanoag Indians. After *Massasoit* was dead, his two sons, called *Wamsutta* and *Metacomet*, came to the court at Plimouth, pretending high respect for the English, and, therefore, desired English names might be imposed on them, whereupon the court there named *Wamsutta*, the elder brother, *Alexander*, and *Metacomet*, the younger brother, *Philip*. This *Alexander*, *Philip's* immediate predecessor, was not so faithful and friendly to the English as his father had been. For some of Boston, having been occasionally at Narraganset, wrote to Mr. *Prince*, who was then governor of Plimouth, that *Alexander* was contriving mischief against the English, and that he had solicited the Narragansets to engage with him in his designed rebellion. Hereupon, Capt. *Willet*, who lived near to Mount Hope, the place where *Alexander* did reside, was appointed to speak with him, and to desire him to attend the next court in Plimouth, for their satisfaction, and his own vindication. He seemed to take the message in good part, professing that the Narragansets, whom, he said, were his enemies, had put an abuse upon him, and he readily promised to attend at the next court But when the day for his appearance was come, instead of that, he at that very time went over to the Narragansets, his pretended enemies, which, compared with other circumstances, caused the gentlemen at Plimouth to suspect there was more of truth in the infor-

* Old Indian Chronicle, p. 31, 32.

† In 1661, he was forced into a war with *Uncas*, the account of which, properly belonging to the life of that chief, will be found there related.

mation given, than at first they were aware of. Wherefore the governor and magistrates there ordered Major *Winslow*, (who is since, and at this day [1677] governor of that colony,) to take a party of men, and fetch down *Alexander*. The major considering that *semper nocuit deferre paratis*, he took but 10 armed men with him from Marshfield, intending to have taken more at the towns that lay nearer Mount Hope. But Divine Providence so ordered, as that when they were about the midway between Plimouth and Bridgewater,* observing an hunting house, they rode up to it, and there did they find *Alexander* and many of his men† well armed, but their guns standing together without the house. The major, with his small party, possessed themselves of the Indians' arms, and beset the house; then did he go in amongst them, acquainting the sachem with the reason of his coming in such a way; desiring *Alexander* with his interpreter to walk out with him, who did so a little distance from the house, and then understood what commission the major had received concerning him. The proud sachem fell into a raging passion at this surprise saying the governor had no reason to credit rumors, or to send for him in such a way, nor would he go to Plimouth, but when he saw cause. It was replied to him, that his breach of word touching appearance at Plimouth court, and, instead thereof, going at the same time to his pretended enemies, augmented jealousies concerning him. In fine, the major told him, that his order was to bring him to Plimouth, and that, by the help of God, he would do it, or else he would die on the place; also declaring to him that if he would submit, he might expect respective usage, but if he once more denied to go, he should never stir from the ground whereon he stood; and with a pistol at the sachem's breast, required that his next words should be a positive and clear answer to what was demanded. Hereupon his interpreter, a discreet Indian, brother to *John Sausaman*,‡ being sensible of *Alexander's* passionate disposition, entreated that he might speak a few words to the sachem before he gave his answer. The prudent discourse of this Indian prevailed so far as that *Alexander* yielded to go, only requesting that he might go like a sachem, with his men attending him, which, although there was some hazard in it, they being many, and the English but a few, was granted to him. The weather being hot, the major offered him an horse to ride on, but his squaw and divers Indian women being in company, he refused, saying he could go on foot as well as they, entreating only that there might be a complying with their pace, which was done. And resting several times by the way, *Alexander* and his Indians were refreshed by the English. No other discourse happening while they were upon their march, but what was pleasant and amicable. The major sent a man before, to entreat that as many of the magistrates of that colony as could would meet at Duxbury. Wherefore having there had some treaty with *Alexander*, not willing to commit him to prison, they entreated Major *Winslow* to receive him to his house, until the governor, who then lived at Eastham, could come up. Accordingly, he and his train were courteously entertained by the major. And albeit, not so much as an angry word passed between them whilst at Marshfield; yet proud *Alexander*, vexing and fretting in his spirit, that such a check was given him, he suddenly fell sick of a fever. He was then nursed as a choice friend. Mr. *Fuller*, the physician, coming providentially thither at that time, the sachem and his men earnestly desired that he would administer to him, which he was unwilling to do, but by their importunity was prevailed with to do the best he could to help him, and therefore gave him a portion of working physic, which the Indians thought did him good. But his distemper afterwards prevailing, they entreated§ to dismiss him, in order to a return home, which upon engagement

* Within six miles of the English towns. *Hubbard*, 10, (Edition, 1677.) *Massasoit*, and likewise *Philip*, used to have temporary residences in eligible places for fishing, at various sites between the two bays, Narraganset and Massachusetts, as at Raynham, Namasket, Titicut, [in Middleborough,] and Munponset Pond in Halifax. At which of these places he was, we cannot, with certainty, decide: that at Halifax would, perhaps, agree best with Mr. *Hubbard's* account.

† Eighty, says *Hubbard*, 6.

‡ He had a brother by the name of *Roland*.

§ "Entreating those that held him prisoner, that he might have liberty to return home, of appearance at the next court was granted to him. Soon after his being returned home he died." *

Thus ends Dr. *Mather's* "relation" of the short reign of *Alexander*. And although a document lately published by Judge *Davis* of Boston sets the conduct of the English in a very favorable light yet it is very difficult to conceive how *Mather* and *Hubbard* could have been altogether deceived in their information. We mean in respect to the treatment *Alexander* received at the hands of his captors. They both wrote at the same time, and at different places, and neither knew what the other had written. Of this we are confident, if, as we are assured, there was, at this time, rather a misunderstanding between these two reverend authors.

This affair caused much excitement, and, judging from the writers of that time, particularly *Hubbard*, some recrimination upon the conduct of the government of Plimouth, by some of the English, who were more in the habit of using or recommending mild measures towards Indians than the Plimouth people appear to have been, seems to have been indulged in. After thus premising, we will offer the document, which is a letter written by the Rev. *John Cotton*, of Plimouth, to Dr. *I. Mather*, and now printed by Judge *Davis*, in his edition of *Morton's* Memorial. There is no date to it, at least the editor gives none; but if it were written in answer to one from Mr. *Mather* to him, desiring information on that head, dated 21st April, 1677,† we may conclude it was about this time; but Mr. *Mather's* "Relation" would not lead us to suppose that he was in possession of such information, and, therefore, he either was not in possession of it when he published his account, or that he had other testimony which invalidated it.

The letter begins, "Major *Bradford*, [who was with Mr. *Winslow* when *Alexander* was surprised,] confidently assures me, that in the narrative *de Alexandro* ‡ there are many mistakes, and, fearing lest you should, through misinformation, print some mistakes on that subject, from his mouth I this write. Reports being here that *Alexander* was plotting or privy to plots, against the English, authority sent to him to come down. He came not. Whereupon Major *Winslow* was sent to fetch him. Major *Bradford*, with some others, went with him. At Munponset River, a place not many miles hence, they found *Alexander* with about eight men and sundry squaws. He was there about getting canoes. He and his men were at breakfast under their shelter, their guns being without. They saw the English coming, but continued eating; and Mr. *Winslow* telling their business, *Alexander*, freely and readily, without the least hesitancy, consented to go, giving his reason why he came not to the court before, viz., because he waited for Captain *Willet's* return from the Dutch, being desirous to speak with him first. They brought him to Mr. *Collier's* that day, and Governor *Prince* living remote at Eastham, those few magistrates who were at hand issued the matter peaceably, and immediately dismissed *Alexander* to return home, which he did part of the way; but, in two or three days after, he returned and went to Major *Winslow's* house, intending thence to travel into the *bay* and so home; but, at the major's house, he was taken very sick, and was, by water, conveyed to Major *Bradford's*, and thence carried upon the shoulders of his men to Tethquet River, and thence in canoes home, and, about two or three days after, died."

Thus it is evident that there is error somewhere, and it would be very satisfactory if we could erase it from our history; but, at present, we are able only to agitate it, and wait for the further discovery of documents before *Alexander's* true history can be given; and to suspend judgment, although

---

promising to return again if he recovered, and to send his son as hostage till he could so do. On that consideration, he was fairly dismissed, but died before he got half way home.' — *Hubbard*.

* It is a pity that such an able historian as *Grahame* should not have been in possession of other authorities upon this matter than those who have copied from the above. See his *Hist. N. America*, i. 401.

† See his Memorial, 288.

‡ A paper drawn up by the authorities of Plimouth, and now, I believe, among the MSS in the library of the *Hist. Soc. of Mass.* This was, probably, Mr. *Hubbard's* authority.

some may readily decide that the evidence is in favor of the old printed accounts. It is the business of a historian, where a point is in dispute, to exhibit existing evidence, and let the reader make up his own judgment.

We are able, from the first extract given upon this head, to limit the time of his sachemship to a portion of the year 1662.

It will have appeared already, that enough had transpired to inflame the minds of the Indians, and especially that of the sachem *Philip*, if, indeed, the evidence adduced be considered valid, regarding the blamableness of the English. Nevertheless, our next step onward will more fully develop the causes of *Philip's* deep-rooted animosities.

We come now to speak of JOHN SASSAMON, who deserves a particular notice; more especially as, from several manuscripts, we are able not only to correct some important errors in former histories, but to give a more minute account of a character which must always be noticed in entering upon the study of this part of our history. Not that he would otherwise demand more notice than many of his brethren almost silently passed over, but for his agency in bringing about a war, the interest of which increases in proportion as time carries us from its period.

John Sassamon was a subject of *Philip*, an unstable-minded fellow; and, living in the neighborhood* of the English, became a convert to Christianity, learned their language, and was able to read and write, and had translated some of the Bible into Indian. Being rather insinuating and artful, he was employed to teach his countrymen at Natick, in the capacity of a schoolmaster. How long before the war this was, is not mentioned, but must have been about 1660, as he was *Philip's* secretary, or interpreter, in 1662, and this was after he had become a Christian. He left the English, from some dislike, and went to reside with *Alexander*, and afterwards with *Philip*, who, it appears, employed him on account of his learning. Always restless, *Sassamon* did not remain long with *Philip* before he returned again to the English; "and he manifested such evident signs of repentance, as that he was, after his return from pagan *Philip*, reconciled to the praying Indians and baptized, and received, as a member, into one of the Indian churches; yea, and employed as an instructor amongst them every Lord's day."†

Previous to the war, we presume in the winter of 1672, *Sassamon* was sent to preach to the Namaskets,‡ and other Indians of Middleborough, who, at this time, were very numerous. The famous *Watuspaquin* was then the chief of this region and who appears to have been disposed to encourage the new religion taught by *Sassamon*. For, in 1674, he gave him a tract of land near his own residence, to induce him to remain among his people. The deed of gift of this land was, no doubt, drawn by *Sassamon*, and is in these words:—

"Know all men by these presents, that I, *Old Watuspaquin*, doe graunt vnto *John Sassamon*, allies *Wassasoman*, 27 acrees of land for a home lott at Assowamsett necke. This is my gift, giuen to him the said *John Sassamon*, by me the said *Watuspaquin*, in Anno 1673, [or 1674, if between 1 Jan. and 25 March.]

OLD WATUSPAQUIN ◎ *his marke.*
WILLIAM TUSPAQUIN □V *his marke.*

Witness, alsoe, NANEHEUNT § + *his marke.*"

As a further inducement for *Sassamon* to settle here, *Old Tuspaquin* and his son deeded to *Felix*, an Indian who married *Sassamon's* daughter, 58 and an half acres of land; as "a home lott," also. This deed was dated 11 March, 1673, O. S., which doubtless was done at the same time with the other.

---

* "This *Sassamon* was by birth a Massachusett, his father and mother living in Dorchester, and they both died Christians."—*I. Mather.*

† *Mather's* Relation, 74.

‡ The inhabitants of the place call it *Nemasket*. In the records, it is almost always written *Namassakett*.

§ Spelt also *Memeheutt*.

This daughter of *Sassamon* was called by the English name *Betty*,* but her original name was Assowetough. To his son-in-law, *Sassamon* gave his land, by a kind of will, which he wrote himself, not long before his death; probably about the time he became tired of his new situation, which we suppose was also about the time that he discovered the design of *Philip* and his captains to bring about their war of extermination.

Old Tuspaquin, as he called himself, and his son, not only confirmed *Sassamon's* will, but about the same time made a bequest themselves to his daughter, which, they say, was "with the consent of all the chieffe men of Assowamsett." This deed of gift from them was dated 23 Dec. 1673. It was of a neck of land at Assowamsett, called Nahteawamet. The names of some of the places which bounded this tract were Mashquomoh, a swamp, Sasonkusuett, a pond, and another large pond called Chupipoggut. *Tobias*, *Old Thomas*, *Pohonoho*, and *Kankunuki*, were upon this deed as witnesses.

Felix served the English in *Philip's* war, and was living in 1679, in which year Governor *Winslow* ordered, "that all such lands as were formerly *John Sassamon's* in our colonie, shall be settled on *Felix* his son-in-law," and to remain his and his heirs "foreuer." *Felix's* wife survived him, and willed her land to a daughter, named *Mercy*. This was in 1696, and *Isacke Wanno* witnessed said will. There was at a later period an Indian preacher at Titicut† named *Thomas Felix*, perhaps a son of the former.‡ But to return to the more immediate subject of our discourse.

There was a *Sassaman*, or, as my manuscript has it, *Sosomon*, known to the English as early as 1637; but as we have no means of knowing how old *John Sassamon* was when he was murdered, it cannot be decided with probability, whether or not it were he. This *Sosomon*, as will be seen in the life of *Sassacus*, went with the English to fight the Pequots.

Sassamon acted as interpreter, witness or scribe, as the case required, on many occasions. When *Philip* and *Wootonekanuske* his wife, sold, in 1664, Mattapoisett to *William Brenton*, *Sassamon* was a witness and interpreter. The same year he was *Philip's* agent "in settling the bounds of Acushenok, Coaksett, and places adjacent." Again, in 1665, he witnessed the receipt of £10 paid to *Philip* on account of settling the bounds the year before.

There was a *Rowland Sassamon*, who I suppose was the brother of *John*. His name appears but once in all the manuscript records I have met with, and then only as a witness, with his brother, to *Philip's* deed of Mattapoisett, above mentioned.

The name *Sassamon*, like most Indian names, is variously spelt, but the way it here appears is nearest as it was understood in his last years, judging from the records. But it was not so originally. *Woosansaman* was among the first modes of writing it.

This detail may appear dry to the general reader, but we must occasionally gratify our antiquarian friends. We now proceed in our narrative.

While living among the Namaskets, *Sassamon* learned what was going forward among his countrymen, and, when he was convinced that their design was war, went immediately to Plimouth, and communicated his discovery to the governor. "Nevertheless, his information," says Dr. *I. Mather*,§ "(because it had an Indian original, and one can hardly believe them when they do speak the truth,) was not at first much regarded."

It may be noticed here, that at this time if any Indian appeared friendly all Indians were so declaimed against, that scarcely any one among the English could be found that would allow that an Indian could be faithful or honest in any affair. And although some others besides *Sassamon* had intimated, and that rather strongly, that a "rising of the Indians" was at hand, still, as Dr. *Mather* observes, because Indians said so, little or no attention

---

* The English sometimes added her surname, and hence, in the account of Mr. *Bennet*, (1 *Col. Mass. Hist. Soc.* iii. 1.) *Betty Sasemore*. The noted place now called *Betty's Neck*, in Middleborough, was named from her. In 1793, there were eight families of Indians there.

† *Cotuhticut*, *Ketchiquut*, *Tehticut*, *Keketticut*, *Keticut*, *Teightaquid*, *T[illegible]* are spellings of this name in the various books and records I have consulted.

‡ *Backus's* Middleborough, in 1 *Col. Mass. Hist. Soc.* iii. 150.

§ *Relation of the Troubles*, &c., 74

was paid to their advice. Notwithstanding, Mr. *Gookin*, in his MS. history,* says, that, previous to the war, none of the Christian Indians had "been *justly* charged, either with unfaithfulness or treachery towards the English." "But, on the contrary, some of them had discovered the treachery, particularly *Walcut* the ruler, of *Philip* before he began any act of hostility." In another place the same author says, that, in April, 1675, *Wauban* "came to one of the magistrates on purpose, and informed him that he had ground to fear that sachem *Philip*, and other Indians his confederates, intended some mischief shortly." Again in May, about six weeks before the war, he came and said the same, adding that *Philip's* men were only waiting for the trees to get leaved out, that they might prosecute their design with more effect. To return to *Sassamon:*

In the mean time, some circumstances happened that gave further grounds of suspicion, that war was meditated, and it was intended that messengers should be sent to *Philip*, to gain, if possible, the real state of the case. But before this was effected, much of the winter of 1674 had passed away, and the Rev. *Sassamon* still resided with the Namaskets, and others of his countrymen in that neighborhood. And notwithstanding he had enjoined the strictest secrecy upon his English friends at Plimouth, of what he had revealed, assuring them that if it came to *Philip's* knowledge, he should be immediately murdered by him, yet it by some means got to the chief's knowledge, and *Sassamon* was considered a traitor and an outlaw; and, by the laws of the Indians, he had forfeited his life, and was doomed to suffer death. The manner of effecting it was of no consequence with them, so long as it was brought about, and it is probable that *Philip* had ordered any of his subjects who might meet with him, to kill him.

Early in the spring of 1675, *Sassamon* was missing, and, on search being made, his body was found in Assawomset Pond, in Middleborough.† Those that killed him not caring to be known to the English, left his hat and gun upon the ice, that it might be supposed that he had drowned himself; but from several marks upon his body, and the fact that his neck was broken, it was evident he had been murdered.‡ Several persons were suspected, and, upon the information of one called *Patuckson*, *Tobias* § one of *Philip's* counsellors, his son, and *Mattashinnamy*, were apprehended, tried by a jury, consisting of half Indians,‖ and in June, 1675, were all executed at Plimouth; "one of them before his execution confessing the murder," but the other two denied all knowledge of the act, to their last breath. The truth of their guilt may reasonably be called in question, if the circumstance of the bleeding of the dead body at the approach of the murderer, had any influence upon the jury. And we are fearful it was the case, for, if the most learned were misled by such hallucinations in those days, we are not to suppose that the more ignorant were free from them. Dr. *Increase Mather* wrote within two years of the affair, and he has this passage: "When *Tobias* (the suspected murderer) came near the dead body, it fell a bleeding on fresh, as if it had been newly slain; albeit, it was buried a considerable time before that."¶

Nothing of this part of the story is upon record among the manuscripts, as we can find, but still we do not question the authenticity of Dr. *Mather*, who, we believe, is the first that printed an account of it. Nor do the records of Plimouth notice *Sassamon* until some time after his death. The first record is in these words: "The court seeing cause to require the per-

---

* Not yet published, but is now, (April, 1836,) printing with notes by the author of this work, under the direction of the American Antiquarian Society. It will form a lasting monument of one of the best men of those days. The author was, as Mr. *Eliot* expresses himself, "a pillar in our Indian work." He died in 1687, aged 75.

† Some would like to know, perhaps, on what authority Mr. *Grahame* (*Hist. N. Amer.* i 402.) states that *Sassamon's* body *was found in a field.*

‡ *Gookin's* MS. Hist. of Christian Indians. This author says, "*Sassamand* was the first Christian martyr," and that "it is evident he suffered death upon the account of his Christian profession, and fidelity to the English."

§ His Indian name was *Poggapanossoo.*

‖ *Mather's* Relation, 74. Judge *Davis* retains the same account, (*Morton's* Memorial 289.) which we shall presently show to be erroneous.

¶ *Mather's* Relation 75

sonal appearance of an Indian called *Tobias* before the court, to make further answer to such interrogatories as shall be required of him, in reference to the sudden and violent death of an Indian called *John Sassamon*, late deceased." This was in March, 1674, O. S.

It appears that *Tobias* was present, although it is not so stated, from the fact that *Tuspaquin* and his son *William* entered into bonds of £100 for the appearance of *Tobias* at the next court in June following. A mortgage of land was taken as security for the £100.

June having arrived, three instead of one are arraigned as the murderers of *Sassamon*. There was no intimation of any one but *Tobias* being guilty at the previous court. Now, *Wampapaquan*, the son of *Tobias*, and *Mattashunannamo* * are arraigned with him, and the bill of indictment runs as follows: "For that being accused that they did with joynt consent vpon the 29 of January ann° 1674, [or 1675, N. S.] att a place called *Assowamsett Pond*, wilfully and of sett purpose, and of mallice fore thought, and by force and armes, murder *John Sassamon*, an other Indian, by laying violent hands on him, and striking him, or twisting his necke vntill hee was dead; and to hyde and conceale this theire said murder, att the tyme and place aforesaid, did cast his dead body through a hole of the iyce into the said pond."

To this they pleaded "not guilty," and put themselves on trial, say the records. The jury, however, were not long in finding them guilty, which they express in these words: "Wee of the jury one and all, both English and Indians doe joyntly and with one consent agree upon a verdict."

Upon this they were immediately remanded to prison, "and from thence [taken] to the place of execution and there to be hanged by the head † vntill theire bodies are dead." Accordingly, *Tobias* and *Mattashunannamo* were executed on the 8 June, 1675. "But the said *Wampapaquan*, on some considerations was reprieued until a month be expired." He was, however, shot within the month.

It is an error that the jury that found them guilty was composed of half Indians; there were but four, while there were twelve Englishmen. We will again hear the record:—

"Itt was judged very expedient by the court, that, together with this English jury aboue named, some of the most indifferentest, grauest and sage Indians should be admitted to be with the said jury, and to healp to consult and aduice with, of, and concerning the premises: there names are as followeth, viz. one called by an English name *Hope*, and *Maskippague*, *Wannoo*, *George Wampye* and *Acanootus;* these fully concurred with the jury in theire verdict."

The names of the jurymen were *William Sabine*, *William Crocker*, *Edward Sturgis*, *William Brookes*, *Nath*[l]. *Winslow*, *John Wadsworth*, *Andrew Ringe*, *Robert Vixon*, *John Done*, *Jon*[a]. *Bangs*, *Jon*[a]. *Shaw* and *Benj*[n]. *Higgins*.

That nothing which can throw light upon this important affair be passed over, we will here add, from a hitherto exceeding scarce tract, the following particulars, although some parts of them are evidently erroneous: "About five or six years since, there was brought up, amongst others, at the college at Cambridge, (Mass.) an Indian, named *Sosomon;* who, after some time he had spent in preaching the gospel to *Uncas*, a sagamore Christian in his territories, was, by the authority of New Plimouth, sent to preach in like manner to King *Philip*, and his Indians. But King *Philip*, (heathen-like,) instead of receiving the gospel, would immediately have killed this *Sosomon*, but by the persuasion of some about him, did not do it, but sent him by the hands of three men to prison; who, as he was going to prison, exhorted and taught them in the Christian religion. They, not liking his discourse, immediately murthered him after a most barbarous manner. They, returning to King *Philip*, acquainted him with what they had done. About two or three months after this murther, being discovered to the authority of

* The same called *Mattashinnamy*. His name in the records is spelt four ways.

† This old phraseology reminds us of the French mode of expression, *couper le cou*, that is, to cut off the neck instead of the head; but the French say, *il sera pendu par son cou*, and so do modern hangmen, alias *jurists*, of our times.

New Plimouth, *Josiah Winslow* being then governor of that colony, care was taken to find out the murtherers, who, upon search, were found and apprehended, and, after a fair trial, were all hanged. This so exasperated King *Philip*, that, from that day after, he studied to be revenged on the English—judging that the English authority had nothing to do to hang an Indian for killing another." *

CHAPTER II.

Life of KING PHILIP—*His real name—The name of his wife—Makes frequent sales of his lands—Account of them—His first treaty at Plimouth—Expedition to Nantucket—Events of* 1671—*Begins the* WAR *of* 1675—*First acts of hostility—Swamp Fight at Pocasset—Narrowly escapes out of his own country—is pursued by Oneko—Fight at Rehoboth Plain—Cuts off a company of English under Captain Beers—Incidents—Fight at Sugar-loaf Hill, and destruction of Captain Lathrop's company—Fights the English under Mosely—English raise* 1500 *men—Philip retires to Narraganset—Strongly fortifies himself in a great swamp—Description of his fortress—English march to attack him—The great Fight at Narraganset—Again flies his country—Visits the Mohawks—Ill-devised stratagem—Events of* 1676 *—Returns again to his country—Reduced to a wretched condition—Is hunted by Church —His chief counsellor, Akkompoin, killed, and his sister captured—His wife and son fall into the hands of Church—Flies to Pokanoket—Is surprised and slain.—Specimen of the Wampanoag Language—Other curious matter.*

IN regard to the native or Indian name of PHILIP, it seems a mistake has always prevailed, in printed accounts. POMETACOM gives as near its Indian sound as can be approached by our letters. The first syllable was dropped in familiar discourse, and hence, in a short time, no one imagined but what it had always been so; in nearly every original deed executed by him, which we have seen, and they are many, his name so appears. It is true that, in those of different years, it is spelt with some little variation, all which, however, conveyed very nearly the same sound. The variations are *Pumatacom, Pamatacom, Pometacome*, and *Pometacom*; the last of which prevails in the records.

We have another important discovery to communicate: † it is no other than the name of the wife of *Pometacom*—the innocent WOOTONEKANUSKE! This was the name of her who, with her little son, fell into the hands of Captain *Church*. No wonder that *Philip* was "now ready to die," as some of his traitorous men told *Church*, and that "his heart was now ready to break!" All that was dear to him was now swallowed up in the vortex! But they still lived, and this most harrowed his soul—lived for what? to serve as slaves in an unknown land! could it be otherwise than that madness should seize upon him, and despair torment him in every place? that in his sleep he should hear the anguishing cries and lamentations of *Wootonekanuske* and his son? But we must change the scene.

It seems as though, for many years before the war of 1675, *Pometacom*, and nearly all of his people sold off their lands as fast as purchasers presented themselves. They saw the prosperity of the English, and they were just such philosophers as are easily captivated by any show of ostentation. They were forsaking their manner of life, to which the proximity of the whites was a deadly poison, and were eager to obtain such things as their neighbors possessed; these were only to be obtained by parting with their lands. That the reader may form some idea of the rapidity with which the Indians' lands in Plimouth colony were disposed of, we add the following items:—

* *Present State of New England*, by a merchant of Boston, *in respect to the present Bloody Indian Wars*, page 3, folio, London, 1676. This, with four other tracts upon PHILIP'S WAR, (covering the whole period of it, with notes by myself, accompanied by a CHRONOLOGY of all Indian events in America from its discovery to the present time, (March 7th, 1836,) has just been published under the title of the OLD INDIAN CHRONICLE.

† The author feels a peculiar satisfaction that it has fallen to his lot to be the first to publish the real name of the great sachem of the Wampanoags, and also that of the sharer of his perils, *Wootonekanuske*

In a deed dated 23 June, 1664, "*William Brenton*, of Newport, R. I. merchant," "for a valuable consideration" paid by him, buys Matapoisett of *Philip* This deed begins, "I, *Pumatacom* alias *Philip*, chief sachem of Mount Hope, Cowsumpsit and of all territories thereunto belonging." *Philip* and his wife both signed this deed, and *Tockomock*, *Wecopauhim*,* *Nesetaquason*, *Pompaquase*, *Aperniniate*, *Taquanksicke*, *Paquonack*, *Watapatahue*, *Aquetaquish*, *John Sassamon* the interpreter, *Rowland Sassamon*, and two Englishmen, signed as witnesses.

In 1665, he sold the country about Acushena, [now New Bedford,] and Coaxet, [now in Compton.] *Philip's* father having previously sold some of the same, £10 was now given him to prevent any claim from him, and to pay for his marking out the same. *John Woosansman* [one of the names of *Sassamon*] witnessed this deed.

The same year the court of Plimouth presented *Philip* with a horse, but on what account we are not informed.

In 1662, Wrentham was purchased of *Philip* by the English of Dedham. It was then called *Wollomonopoag*, and, by the amount assessed, appears to have cost £24 10*s*., and was six miles square. For this tract of land the English had been endeavoring to negotiate five years.† "In Nov. 1669, upon notice of *Philip*, Sagamore of Mount Hope, now at Wollomonopoag, offering a treaty of his lands thereabouts, not yet purchased," the selectmen appoint five persons to negotiate with him "for his remaining right, provided he can show that he has any." ‡ Whether his right were questionable or not, it seems a purchase was made, at that time, of the tract called *Woollommonuppogue*, "within the town bounds [of Dedham] not yet purchased." What the full consideration was, our documents do not state, but from a manuscript order which he drew on Dedham afterwards, and the accompanying receipt, some estimate may be formed. The order requests them "*to pay to this bearer, for the use of* King Philip, £5, 5*s*. *in money*, and £5 *in trucking cloth at money price*." In a receipt signed by an agent of *Philip*, named *Peter*, the following amount is named: "*In reference to the payment of* King Philip *of* Mount Hope, *the full and just sum of* £5, 5*s*. *in money*, and 12 *yards of trucking cloth*, 3 *lbs. of powder, and as much lead as will make it up; which is in full satisfaction with* £10 *that he is to receive of Nathaniel Paine*." §

We next meet with a singular record of *Philip*, the authorship of which we attribute to *John Sassamon*, and which, besides extending our knowledge of *Philip* into his earlier times, serves to make us acquainted with *Sassamon's* acquirements in the language of the pilgrims.

"Know all men by these presents, that *Philip* haue giuen power vnto *Watuchpoo* ‖ and *Sampson* and theire brethren to hold and make sale of to whom they will by my consent, and they shall not haue itt without they be willing to lett it goe it shal be sol by my consent, but without my knowledge they cannot safely to: but with my consent there is none that can lay claime to that land which they haue marked out, it is theires foreuer, soe therefore none can safely purchase any otherwise but by *Watachpoo* and *Sampson* and their bretheren.

Philip 1666."

Whether the following letter were written earlier or later than this we have no means of knowing; it is plain, however, from its contents, that it was written at a time when he was strongly opposed to selling his lands, and that the people of Plimouth were endeavoring to get him to their court, where they had reason to believe they could succeed better in getting them than by a negotiation in his own country. The letter follows:—

"*To the much honored Governer, Mr.* Thomas Prince, *dwelling at Plimouth.*

"King Philip desire to let you understand that he could not come to the court, for *Tom*, his interpreter, has a pain in his back, that he could not travil

---

* Perhaps *Uncompoin*.

† *Worthington's* Hist. Dedham, 20—from which work it would seem that the negotiation had been carried on with *Philip*, but *Philip* was not sachem until this year.

‡ Ibid.

§ General Court Files.

‖ Sometimes *Tukpoo* by abbreviation. A further account of him will be found in the life of *Tatoson*.

so far, and *Philip* sister is very sick. *Philip* would intreat that favor of you, and any of the majestrats, if aney English or Engians speak about aney land, he pray you to giue them no ansewer at all. This last summer he maid that promis with you that he would not sell no land in 7 years time, for that he would have no English trouble him before that time, he has not forgot that you promis him. He will come a sune as posseble he can to speak with you, and so I rest,

your very loveing friend
PHILIP **P**
dwelling at mount hope nek." *

In 1667, *Philip* sells to *Constant Southworth*, and others, all the meadow lands from Dartmouth to Matapoisett, for which he had £15. Particular bounds to all tracts are mentioned in the deeds, but as they were generally or often stakes, trees, and heaps of stones, no one at this time can trace many of them.

The same year, for "£10 sterling," he sells to *Thos. Willet* and others, "all that tract of land lying between the Riuer Wanascottaquett and Cawatoquissett, being two miles long and one broad." *Pawsaquens*, one of *Philip's* counsel lors, and *Tom* alias *Sawsuett*, an interpreter, were witnesses to the sale.

In 1668, "*Philip Pometacom*, and *Tatamumaque* † alias *Cashewashed*, sachems," for a "valuable consideration," sell to sundry English a tract of some square miles. A part of it was adjacent to Pokanoket. In describing it, Memenuckquage and Towansett neck are mentioned, which we conclude to be in Swansey. Besides two Englishmen, *Sompointeen*, alias *Tom*, and *Nananuntnew*, son of *Thomas Piants*, were witnesses to this sale.

The next year, the same sachems sell 500 acres in Swansey for £20. *Wanueo*, a counsellor, and *Tom* the interpreter, were witnesses.

In 1668, *Philip* and *Uncompawen* laid claim to a part of New-meadows neck, alleging that it was not intended to be conveyed in a former deed, by *Ossamequin* and *Wamsutta*, to certain English, "although it appears, says the record, pretty clearly so expressed in said deed," "yet that peace and friendship may be continued," "Capt. *Willet*, Mr. *Brown* and *John Allen*, in the behalf of themselves and the rest," agree to give *Philip* and *Uncompawen* the sum of £11 in goods.

PHILIP NANUSKOOKE ‡ *his* ℔ *mark*,
VNCOMPAWEN *his* ✕ *mark*.

TOM SANSUWEST, *interpreter*,
And NIMROD.

The same year, we find the following record, which is doubly interesting, from the plan with which we are able to accompany it, drawn by *Philip* himself. He contracts or agrees, by the following writing under his hand, in these words: "this may inform the honoured court [of Plimouth,] that I *Philip* ame willing to sell the land within this draught; but the Indians that are vpon it may liue vpon it still; but the land that is [waste]§ may be sould, and *Wattachpoo* is of the same minde. I have sed downe all the principall names of the land wee are willing should bee sould."

"From Pacanaukett
the 24 of the 12 mo. 1668."

PHILLIP **P** *his marke*."

* 1 *Coll. Mass. Hist. Soc.* ii. 40. The original was owned by a Mr. White of Plimouth, about 30 years ago. It is probably another production of *John Sassamon*.

† Written in another deed, *Atunkamomake*. This deed was in the next year. It was of 500 acres of land, "more or lesse," in Swansey; and £20 the consideration. *Hugh Cole*, *Josias Winslow*, *John Coggeshall*, and *Constant Southworth* were the purchasers, and *Wanueo*, a counsellor, one of the witnesses.

‡ This double name, we suppose, was meant to stand for the signature of himself and wife

§ So in the records.

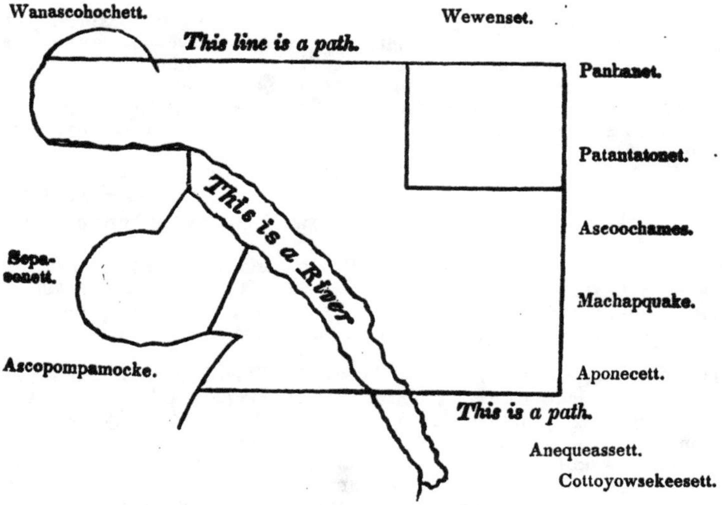

"*Osamequen*" having, "for valuable considerations," in the year 1641, sold to *John Brown* and *Edward Winslow* a tract of land eight miles square, situated on both sides of Palmer's River, *Philip*, on the 30 Mar. 1668, was required to sign a quit-claim of the same. This he did in presence of *Umptakisoke*, *Phillip*, and *Peebe*,* counsellors, *Sonconewhew*, *Phillip's* brother, and *Tom* the interpreter.† This tract includes the present town of Rehoboth.

Also in 1669, for £10 "and another valuable and sufficient gratuity," he sells to *John Cook* of Akusenag in Dartmouth,‡ "one whole island nere the towne," called Nokatay.

The same year, *Philip* and *Tuspaquin* sell a considerable tract of land in Middleborough, for £13. *Thomas* the interpreter, *William*, the son of *Tuspaquin*, and *Benjamin Church*, were witnesses.

In 1671, *Philip* and "*Monjokam* of Mattapoisett," for £5, sell to *Hugh Cole*, of Swansey, shipwright, land lying near a place called *Acashewah*, in Dartmouth.

In 1672, *Philip* sold to *William Brenton* and others, of Taunton, a tract to the southward of that town, containing twelve square miles, for £143; and, a few days after, adjoining it, four square miles more, to *Constant Southworth*. Others were concerned in the sale of the larger tract, as is judged by the deeds being signed by *Nunkampahoonett*, *Umnathum*, alias *Nimrod*, *Cheemaughton*, and Captain *Annawam*, besides one *Philip*. *Thomas*, alias *Sanksuit*, was among the witnesses. The sale of the last tract was witnessed by *Munashum*, alias *Nimrod*, *Woackompawhan*,§ and Captain *Annowan*.

These are but a part of the sales of land by *Pometacom:* many other chiefs sold very largely, particularly *Watuspaquin* and *Josias Wampatuck*.

At the court of Plimouth, 1673, "Mr. *Peter Talmon* of Rhode Iland complained against *Philip* allies *Wewasowanuett*, sachem of Mount Hope, brother or predecessor of *Pakanawkett* as heire adminnostrator or successor vnto his brother or predecessor *Wamsitta*, *Sopaquitt*,‖ or *Alexander* deceased, in an action on the case, to the damage of £800 forfeiture of a bond of such a value, bearing date, June the 28th, 1661, giuen to the said *Peter Talman*, obliging

* Called, in Mr. *Hubbard's* history, *Thebe;* he was afterwards killed at Swansey, in the beginning of the war. There is a pond in Narraganset of the same name.

† Mr. *Bliss*, in his History of Rehoboth, 64, 65, has printed this deed from the original.

‡ The place where *Cook* lived is now included in New Bedford.

§ Probably "*Philip's* old uncle *Akkompoin*."

‖ That is, nicknamed *Alexander*, according to the French mode of expression; *ou par sobriquet Alexander*, as I imagine. Mr. *Hubbard* says of *Philip*, (Narrative, 10,) that, "for his ambitious and haughty spirit, [he was] nicknamed *King Philip*."

nim the said *Wamsitta* allies *Alexander* to make good to him, his heirs and a deed of gift of a considerable track of land att Sapowett and places adjacent, as in the said deed is more particularly expressed; for want wherof the complainant is greatly damnifyéd."

Whether the conduct of the people of Plimouth towards *Wamsutta*, *Pometacom's* elder brother, and other neighboring Indians, made them always suspicious of the chief sachem, as it had their neighbors before in the case of *Miantunnomoh*, or whether *Philip* were in reality "contriving mischief," the same year of his coming in chief sachem, remains a question, to this day, with those best acquainted with the history of those times.

The old benevolent sachem *Massasoit*, alias *Woosamequin*, having died in the winter of 1661–2, as we believe, but few months after died also *Alexander*, *Philip's* elder brother and predecessor, when *Philip* himself, by the order of succession, came to be chief of the Wampanoags.

Philip having by letter complained to the court of Plimouth of some injuries, at their October term, 1668, they say, "In answer unto a letter from *Philip*, the sachem of Pokanokett, &c., by way of petition requesting the court for justice against *Francis Wast*, [*West*,] for wrong done by him to one of his men about a gun taken from him by the said *Wast;* as also for wrong done unto some swine of the said Indian's. The court have ordered the case to be heard and determined by the selectmen of Taunton; and in case it be not by them ended, that it be referred unto the next March court at Plimouth to be ended." How the case turned we have not found. But for an Indian to gain his point at an English court, unless his case were an exceeding strong one, was, we apprehend, a rare occurrence.

"He was no sooner styled sachem," says Dr. *I. Mather*,* "but immediately, in the year 1662, there were vehement suspicions of his bloody treachery against the English." This author wrote at the close of *Philip's* war, when very few could speak of Indians, without discovering great bitterness. Mr. *Morton*† is the first who mentions *Metacomet* in a printed work, which, being before any difficulty with him, is in a more becoming manner. "This year," (1662,) he observes, "upon occasion of some suspicion of some plot intended by the Indians against the English, *Philip*, the sachem of Pokanoket, otherwise called *Metacom*, made his appearance at the court held at Plimouth, August 6, did earnestly desire the continuance of that amity and friendship that hath formerly been between the governor of Plimouth and his deceased father and brother."

The court expressing their willingness to remain his friends, he signed the articles prepared by them, acknowledging himself a subject of the king of England, thus:—

" *The mark of* ꟸ PHILLIP, *sachem*
of Pocanakett,
The mark of ◁ VNCUMPOWETT,
vnkell to the aboue said sachem."

The following persons were present, and witnessed this act of *Philip*, and his great captain *Uncompoin:*—

"JOHN SASSAMON,
The mark ♏ *of* FRANCIS, *sachem of Nauset,*
The mark DI *of* NIMROD *alias* PUMPASA,
The mark ꝭ *of* PUNCKQUANECK,
The mark ⋦ *of* AQUETEQUESH."‡

Of the uneasiness and concern of the English at this period, from the hostile movements of *Philip*, Mr. *Hubbard*, we presume, was not informed; or so important an event would not have been omitted in his minute and valuable history. Mr. *Morton*, as we before stated, and Mr. *Mather* mention it, but neither of these, or any writer since, to this day, has made the matter appear in its true light, from their neglect to produce the names of those that appeared with the sachem.

* Relation, 72. † In his N. England's Memorial. ‡ From the records in *manuscript*.

For about nine years succeeding 1662, very little is recorded concerning *Philip*. During this time, he became more intimately acquainted with his English neighbors, learned their weakness and his own strength, which rather increased than diminished, until his fatal war of 1675. For, during this period, not only their additional numbers gained them power, but their arms were greatly strengthened by the English instruments of war put into their hands. *Roger Williams* had early brought the Narragansets into friendship with *Massasoit*, which alliance gained additional strength on the accession of the young *Metacomet*. And here we may look for a main cause of that war, although the death of *Alexander* is generally looked upon by the early historians, as almost the only one. The continual broils between the English and Narragansets, (we name the English first, as they were generally the aggressors,) could not be unknown to *Philip;* and if his countrymen were wronged he knew it. And what friend will see another abused, without feeling a glow of resentment in his breast? And who will wonder, if, when these abuses had followed each other, repetition upon repetition, for a series of years, that they should at last break out into open war? The Narraganset chiefs were not conspicuous at the period of which we speak; there were several of them, but no one appears to have had a general command or ascendency over the rest; and there can be little doubt but that they unanimously reposed their cause in the hands of *Philip*. *Ninigret* was at this time grown old, and though, for many years after the murder of *Miantunnomoh*, he seems to have had the chief authority, yet pusillanimity was always rather a predominant trait in his character. His age had probably caused his withdrawal from the others, on their resolution to second *Philip*. *Canonchet* was at this period the most conspicuous; *Pumham* next; *Potok*, *Magnus*, the squaw-sachem, whose husband, *Mriksah*, had been dead several years; and lastly *Mattatoag*.

Before proceeding with later events, the following short narrative, illustrative of a peculiar custom, may not be improperly introduced. *Philip*, as tradition reports, made an expedition to Nantucket in 1665, to punish an Indian who had profaned the name of *Massasoit*, his father; and, as it was an observance or law among them, that whoever should speak evil of the dead should be put to death, *Philip* went there with an armed force to execute this law upon *Gibbs*. He was, however, defeated in his design, for one of *Gibbs's* friends, understanding *Philip's* intention, ran to him and gave him notice of it, just in time for him to escape; not, however, without great exertions, for *Philip* came once in sight of him, after pursuing him some time among the English from house to house; but *Gibbs*, by leaping a bank, got out of sight, and so escaped. *Philip* would not leave the island until the English had ransomed *John* at the exorbitant price of nearly all the money upon the island.* *Gibbs* was a Christian Indian, and his Indian name was *Assasamoogh*. He was a preacher to his countrymen in 1674, at which time there were belonging to his church 30 members.

What grounds the English had, in the spring of the year 1671, for suspecting that a plot was going forward for their destruction, cannot satisfactorily be ascertained; but it is evident there were some warlike preparations made by the great chief, which very much alarmed the English, as in the life of *Awashonks* we shall have occasion again to notice. Their suspicions were further confirmed when they sent for him to come to Taunton and make known the causes for his operations; as he discovered "shyness," and a reluctance to comply. At length, on the 10th of April, this year, he came to a place about four miles from Taunton, accompanied with a band of his warriors, attired, armed and painted as for a warlike expedition. From this place he sent messengers to Taunton, to invite the English to come and treat with him. The governor either was afraid to meet the chief, or thought it beneath his dignity to comply with his request, and therefore sent several

* For some of what we have given above, see 1 *Coll. Mass. Hist. Soc.* iii. 159, furnished for that work by Mr. *Zaccheus Macy*, whose ancestor, it is said, assisted in secreting *Assasamoogh*.

In a late work, Hist. Nantuckett by *Obed Macy*, an account of the affair is given, but with some variation from the above.

persons, among whom was *Roger Williams*, to inform him of their determination, and their good disposition towards him, and to urge his attendance at Taunton. He agreed to go, and hostages were left in the hands of his warriors to warrant his safe return. On coming near the village with a few of his warriors, he made a stop, which appears to have been occasioned by the warlike parade of the English, many of whom were for immediately attacking him. These were the Plimouth people that recommended this rashness, but they were prevented by the commissioners from Massachusetts, who met here with the governor of Plimouth to confer with *Philip*.

In the end it was agreed that a council should be held in the meeting-house, one side of which should be occupied by the Indians, and the other by the English. *Philip* had alleged that the English injured the planted lands of his people, but this, the English say, was in no wise sustained. He said his warlike preparations were not against the English, but the Narragansets, which the English also say was proved to his face to be false; and that this so confounded him, that he confessed the whole plot, and "that it was the naughtiness of his own heart that put him upon that rebellion, and nothing of any provocation from the English." * Therefore, with four of his counsellors, whose names were *Tavoser*, Captain *Wispoke*, *Woonkaponehunt*. [*Unkomvoin*,] and *Nimrod*, he signed a submission, and an engagement of friendship, which also stipulated that he should give up all the arms among his people, into the hands of the governor of Plimouth, to be kept as long as the government should "see reason." †

The English of Massachusetts, having acted as umpires in this affair, were looked to, by both parties, on the next cause of complaint. *Philip* having delivered the arms which himself and men had with them at Taunton, ‡ promised to deliver the rest at Plimouth by a certain time. But they not being delivered according to agreement, and some other differences occurring, a messenger was sent to Boston from Plimouth, to make complaint; but *Philip*, perhaps, understanding what was intended, was quite as early at Boston in person; § and, by his address, did not fail to be well received, and a favorable report of him was returned to Plimouth; and, at the same time, proposals that commissioners from all the United Colonies should meet *Philip* at Plimouth, where all difficulties might be settled. This meeting took place the same year, September, 1671, and the issue of the meeting was very nearly the same as that at Taunton. "The conclusion was," says Mr. *Mather*, ‖ "*Philip* acknowledged his offence, and was appointed to give a sum of money to defray the charges which his insolent clamors had put the colony unto."

As usual, several articles were drawn up by the English, of what *Philip* was to submit to, to which we find the names of three only of his captains or counsellors, *Uncompaen*, who was his uncle, ¶ *Wotokom*, and *Samkama*.

Great stress in those days was laid on the Indians submitting themselves as "subjects to his majesty the king of England." This they did only to get rid of the importunity of the English, as their course immediately afterwards invariably showed.

The articles which the government of Plimouth drew up at this time, for *Philip* to sign, were not so illiberal as might be imagined, were we not to produce some of them. Article second reads,—

"I [*Philip*] am willing, and do promise to pay unto the government of Plimouth £100, in such things as I have; but I would entreat the favor that I might have three years to pay it in, forasmuch as I cannot do it at present." And in article third, he promises "to send unto the governor, or whom he shall appoint, five wolves' heads, *if he can get them*; or as many as he can procure,

---

* *Hubbard*, Indian Wars, 11, 1st edition.

† The articles of this treaty may be seen in *Hubbard*, *Mather*, and *Hutchinson's* histories they amount to little, and we therefore omit them.

‡ *Mather's* Relation, 73.

§ Perhaps this was the time Mr. *Josselyn* saw him there richly caparisoned, as will hereafter be mentioned. ‖ *Mather's* Relation, 73.

¶ Called by *Church*, *Akkompoin*. Hist. King *Philip's War*, 110 of my edition.

until they come to five wolves' heads yearly." These articles were dated * 29 Sept. 1671, and were signed by

The mark **P** *of* PHILLIP;
The mark **T** *of* WOHKOWPAHENITT;
The mark **V** *of* WUTTAKOOSEEIM;
The mark **T** *of* SONKANUHOO;
The mark **2** *of* WOONASHUM, *alias* NIMROD;
The mark **Y** *of* WOOSPASUCK, *alias* CAPTAIN.

On the 3 Nov. following, *Philip* accompanied *Takanumma* to Plimouth, to make his submission, which he did, and acknowledged, by a writing, that he would adhere to the articles signed by *Philip* and the others, the 29 Sept. before. *Tokamona* was brother to *Awashonks*, and, at this time, was sachem of Seconet, or Saconett. He was afterwards killed by the Narragansets.†

A general disarming of the neighboring Indians was undertaken during the spring and summer of 1671, and nothing but trouble could have been expected to follow.

That nothing may be omitted which can throw light upon this important era in the biography of *Philip*, we will lay before the reader all the unpublished information furnished by the records.‡ Having met in June, 1671, "The court [of Plimouth] determins all the guns in our hands, that did belong to *Philip*, are justly forfeit; and do at the present order the dividing of them, to be kept at the several towns, according to their equal proportions, until October court next, and then to be at the court's dispose, as reason may appear to them, and then to belong unto the towns, if not otherwise disposed of by the court.

"That which the court grounds their judgment upon is,—For that at the treaty at Taunton, *Philip* and his council did acknowledge that they had been in a preparation for war against us; and that not grounded upon any injury sustained from us, nor provocation given by us, but from their naughty hearts, and because he had formerly violated and broken solemn covenants made and renewed to us; he then freely tendered, (not being in a capacity to be kept faithful by any other bonds,) to resign up all his English arms, for our future security in that respect. He failed greatly in the performance thereof, by secret[ly] conveying away, and carrying home several guns, that might and should have been then delivered, and not giving them up since, according to his engagement; nor so far as is in his power; as appears in that many guns are known still to be amongst the Indians that live by him, and [he] not so much as giving order to some of his men, that are under his immediate command, about the bringing in of their arms.

"In his endeavoring, since the treaty [at Taunton,] to render us odious to our neighbor colony by false reports, complaints and suggestions; and his refusing or avoiding a treaty with us concerning those and other matters that are justly offensive to us, notwithstanding his late engagement, as well as former, to submit to the king's authority, and the authority of this colony.

"It was also ordered by the court that the arms of the Indians of Namassakett and Assowamsett, that were fetched in by Major *Winslow*, and those that were with him, are confiscated, and forfeit, from the said Indians, for the grounds above expressed; they being in a compliance with *Phillipe* in his late plot: And yet would neither by our governor's order, nor by *Phillipe's* desire, bring in their arms, as was engaged by the treaty; and the said guns are ordered by the court to the major and his company for their satisfaction, in that expedition.

"This court have agreed and voted" to send "some" forces to "Saconett to fetch in" the arms among the Indians there.

---

* There is no date, but the year, set to any printed copy of this treaty. Mr. *Hubbard* by mistake omitted it, and those who have since written, have not given themselves the pleasure of recurring to the records.

† See *Church*, 39. ‡ Plimouth Colony Records, in *manuscript*.

If then, therefore, these Indians had not already become hostile, no one would marvel had it now become the case. Bows and arrows were almost entirely out of use. Guns had so far superseded them, that undoubtedly many scarce could use them with effect, in procuring themselves game: Nor could it be expected otherwise, for the English had, by nearly 40 years' intercourse, rendered *their* arms far more necessary to the existence of the Indians than to their own: hence their unwillingness to part with them. *Philip*, it is said, directed the Middleborough Indians to give up their guns. His object in this was to pacify the English, judging that if war should begin, these Indians would join the English, or at least many of them; and, therefore, it affected his cause but little which party possessed them; but not so with his immediate followers, as we have just seen in the record.

A council of war having convened at Plimouth, 23 August, 1671, the following, besides the matters already expressed, they took into consideration: *Philip's* "entertaining of many strange Indians, which might portend danger towards us. In special by his entertaining of divers Saconett Indians, professed enemies to this colony, and this against good counsel given him by his friends. The premises considered [the council] do unanimously agree and conclude, that the said *Phillip* hath violated [the] covenant plighted with this colony at Taunton in April last.

"2. It is unanimously agreed and concluded by the said council, that we are necessarily called to cause the said sachem to make his personal appearance to make his purgation, in reference to the premises; which, in case of his refusal, the council, according to what at present appears, do determin it necessary to endeavor his reducement by force; inasmuch as the controversy which hath seemed to lie more immediately between him and us, doth concern all the English plantations. It is, therefore, determined to state the case to our neighbor colonies of the Massachusetts and Rhode Island; and if, by their weighty advice to the contrary, we are not diverted from our present determinations, to signify unto them, that if they look upon themselves concerned to engage in the case with us against a common enemy, it shall be well accepted as a neighborly kindness, which we shall hold ourselves obliged to repay, when Providence may so dispose that we have opportunity.

"Accordingly, letters were despatched and sent from the council, one unto the said *Phillip* the said sachem, to require his personal appearance at Plymouth, on the 13th day of September next, in reference to the particulars above mentioned against him. This letter was sent by Mr. *James Walker*, one of the council, and he was ordered to request the company of Mr. *Roger Williams* and Mr. *James Brown*, to go with him at the delivery of the said letter. And another letter was sent to the governor and council of the Massachusetts by the hands of Mr. *John Freeman*, one of our magistrates, and a third was directed to the governor and council of Rhode Island, and sent by Mr. *Thomas Hinckley* and Mr. *Constant Southworth*, two other of our magistrates, who are ordered by our council with the letter, to unfold our present state of matters relating to the premises, and to certify them, also, more certainly of the time of the meeting together, in reference to engagement with the Indians, if there be a going forth, which will be on the 20 of September next.

"It was further ordered by the council, that those formerly pressed shall remain under the same impressment, until the next meeting of the said council, on the 13 day of Sept. next, and so also until the intended expedition is issued, unless they shall see cause to alter them, or add or detract from them, as occasion may require: And that all other matters remain as they were, in way of preparation to the said expedition, until we shall see the mind of God further by the particulars forenamed, improved for that purpose.

"It was further ordered by the council, that all the towns within this jurisdiction shall, in the interim, be solicitously careful to provide for their safety, by convenient watches and wardings, and carrying their arms to the meetings on the Lord's days, in such manner, as will best stand with their particulars, and the common safety.

"And in particular they order, that a guard shall be provided for the safety of the governor's person, during the time of the above-named troubles and expeditions.

"And the council were summoned by the president, [the governor of Plimouth,] to make their personal appearance at Plymouth, on the 13th day of Sept. next, to attend such further business as shall be then presented by Providence, in reference to the premises. [Without any intermediate entry, the records proceed:]

"On the 13 Sept. 1671, the council of war appeared, according to their summons, but *Phillip* the sachem appeared not; but instead thereof repaired to the Massachusetts, and made complaint against us to divers of the gentlemen in place there; who wrote to our governor, by way of persuasion, to advise the council to a compliance with the said sachem, and tendered their help in the achieving thereof; declaring, in sum, that they resented not his offence so deeply as we did, and that they doubted whether the covenants and engagements that *Phillip* and his predecessors had plighted with us, would plainly import that he had subjected himself, and people, and country to us any further than as in a neighborly and friendly correspondency."

Thus, whether *Philip* had been able by misrepresentation to lead the court of Massachusetts into a conviction that his designs had not been fairly set forth by Plimouth, or whether it be more reasonable to conclude that that body were thoroughly acquainted with the whole grounds of complaint, and, therefore, considered Plimouth nearly as much in error as *Philip*, by assuming authority not belonging to them, is a case, we apprehend, not difficult to be settled by the reader. The record continues:—

"The council having deliberated upon the premises, despatched away letters, declaring their thankful acceptance of their kind proffer, and invited the commissioners of the Massachusetts and Connecticut, they [the latter] then being there in the Bay, [Boston,] and some other gentlemen to come to Plymouth and afford us their help: And, accordingly, on the 24 of Sept. 1671, Mr. *John Winthrop*, Gov. of Connecticut, Maj. Gen. *Leverett*, Mr. *Thos. Danforth*, Capt. *Wm. Davis*, with divers others, came to Plimouth, and had a fair and deliberate hearing of the controversy between our colony and the said sachem *Phillip*, he being personally present; there being also competent interpreters, both English and Indians. At which meeting it was proved by sufficient testimony to the conviction of the said *Phillip*, and satisfaction of all that audience, both [to] the said gentlemen and others, that he had broken his covenant made with our colony at Taunton in April last, in divers particulars: as also carried very unkindly unto us divers ways.

"1. In that he" had neglected to bring in his arms, although "competent time, yea his time enlarged" to do it in, as before stated. "2. That he had carried insolently and proudly towards us on several occasions, in refusing to come down to our court (when sent for) to have speech with him, to procure a right understanding of matters in difference betwixt us."

This, to say the least, was a wretchedly sorry complaint. That an independent chief should refuse to obey his neighbors whenever they had a mind to command him, of the justness of whose mandates he was not to inquire, surely calls for no comment of ours. Besides, did *Philip* not do as he agreed at Taunton?—which was, that in case of future troubles, both parties should lay their complaints before Massachusetts, and abide by their decision?

The 3d charge is only a repetition of what was stated by the council of war, namely, harboring and abetting divers Indians not his own men, but "vagabonds, our professed enemies, who leaving their own sachem were harbored by him."

The 4th has likewise been stated, which contains the complaint of his going to Massachusetts, "with several of his council, endeavoring to insinuate himself into the magistrates, and to misrepresent matters unto them," which amounts to little else but an accusation against Massachusetts, as, from what has been before stated, it seems that the "gentlemen in place there" had, at least in part, been convinced that *Philip* was not so much in fault as their friends of Plimouth had pretended.

"5. That he had shewed great incivility to divers of ours at several times; in special unto Mr. *James Brown*, who was sent by the court on special occasion, as a messenger unto him; and unto *Hugh Cole* at another time, &c.

"The gentlemen forenamed taking notice of the premises, having fully heard what the said *Phillip* could say for himself, having free liberty so to do without interruption, adjudged that he had done us a great deal of wrong and injury, (respecting the premises,) and also abused them by carrying lies and false stories to them, and so misrepresenting matters unto them, and they persuaded him to make an acknowledgment of his fault, and to seek for reconciliation, expressing themselves, that there is a great difference between what he asserted to the government in the Bay, and what he could now make out concerning his pretended wrongs; and such had been the wrong and damage that he had done and procured unto the colony, as ought not to be borne without competent reparation and satisfaction; yea, that he, by his insolencies, had (in probability) occasioned more mischief from the Indians amongst them, than had fallen out in many years before; they persuaded him, therefore, to humble himself unto the magistrates, and to amend his ways, if he expected peace; and that, if he went on in his refractory way, he must expect to smart for it."

The commissioners finally drew up the treaty of which we have before spoken, and *Philip* and his counsellors subscribed it; and thus ended the chief events of 1671.

A very short time before the war of 1675 commenced, the governor of Massachusetts sent an ambassador to *Philip*, to demand of him why he would make war upon the English, and requested him, at the same time, to enter into a treaty. The sachem made him this answer:—

"*Your governor is but a subject of King Charles* * *of England. I shall not treat with a subject. I shall treat of peace only with the king, my brother. When he comes, I am ready.*" †

This is literal, although we have changed the order of the words a little, and is worthy of a place upon the same page with the speech of the famous *Porus*, when taken captive by *Alexander*. ‡

We meet with nothing of importance until the death of *Sassamon*, in 1674, the occasion of which was charged upon *Philip*, and was the cause of bringing about the war with him a year sooner than he had expected. This event prematurely discovered his intentions, which occasioned the partial recantation of the Narragansets, who, it is reported, were to furnish 4000 men, to be ready to fall upon the English in 1676. Concert, therefore, was wanting; and although nearly all the Narragansets ultimately joined against the English, yet the powerful effect of a general simultaneous movement was lost to the Indians. *Philip's* own people, many of whom were so disconcerted at the unexpected beginning of the war, continued some time to waver, doubting which side to show themselves in favor of; and it was only from their being without the vicinity of the English, or unprotected by them, that determined their course, which was, in almost all cases, in favor of *Philip*. Even the praying Indians, had they been left to themselves, would, no doubt, many of them, have declared in his favor also, as a great many really did.

Until the execution of the three Indians, supposed to be the murderers of *Sassamon*, no hostility was committed by *Philip* or his warriors. About the time of their trial, he was said to be marching his men "up and down the country in arms," but when it was known that they were executed, he could no longer restrain many of his young men, who, having sent their wives and children to Narraganset, upon the 24th of June, provoked the people of Swansey, by killing their cattle, and other injuries,§ until they fired upon them and

---

* *Charles* II., whose reign was from 1660 to 1676.

† Old Indian Chronicle, 68.

‡ The conqueror asked him how he would be treated, who, in two words, replied, "Like a king." Being asked if he had no other request to make, he said, "No. Every thing is comprehended in that." (*Plutarch's Life of Alexander.*) We could wish, that the English conquerors had acted with as much magnanimity towards the Indians, as *Alexander* did towards those he overcame. *Porus* was treated as he had desired

§ "In the mean time King *Philip* mustered up about 500 of his men, and arms them compleat; and had gotten about 8 or 900 of his neighboring *Indians*, and likewise arms them compleat; (i. e. guns, powder and bullets;) but how many he hath engaged to be of his party, is unknown to any among us. The last spring, several *Indians* were seen in small parties, about *Rehoboth* and *Swansey*, which not a little affrighted the inhabitants. Who demanding the reason of them, wherefore it was so? Answer was made, That they were only on their own defence, for they understood that the *English* intended to cut them off. About the 20th

killed one, which was a signal to commence the war, and what they had desired; for the superstitious notion prevailed among the Indians, that the party who fired the first gun would be conquered.* They had probably been made to believe this by the English themselves.

It was upon a fast day that this great drama was opened. As the people were returning from meeting, they were fired upon by the Indians, when one was killed and two wounded. Two others, going for a surgeon, were killed on their way. In another part of the town, six others were killed the same day. Swansey was in the midst of *Philip's* country, and his men were as well acquainted with all the walks of the English as they were themselves.

It is not supposed that *Philip* directed this attack, but, on the other hand, it has been said that it was against his wishes. But there can be no doubt of his hostility and great desire to rid his country of the white intruders; for had he not reason to say,

> "Exarsere ignes animo; subit ira, cadentem
> Ulcisci patriam, et sceleratas sumere pœnas?"

The die was cast. No other alternative appeared, but to ravage, burn and destroy as fast as was in his power. There had been no considerable war for a long time, either among themselves or with the English, and, therefore, numerous young warriors from the neighboring tribes, entered into his cause with great ardor; eager to perform exploits, such as had been recounted to them by their sires, and such as they had long waited an opportunity to achieve. The time, they conceived, had now arrived, and their souls expanded in proportion to the greatness of the undertaking. To conquer the English! to lead captive their haughty lords! must have been to them thoughts of vast magnitude, and exhilarating in the highest degree.

Town after town fell before them, and when the English forces marched in one direction, they were burning and laying waste in another. A part of Taunton, Middleborough, and Dartmouth, in the vicinity of Pocasset, upon Narraganset Bay, soon followed the destruction of Swansey, which was burnt immediately after the 24th of June, on being abandoned by the inhabitants.

Though now in great consternation, the people of Swansey and its vicinity did not forget to make known their distressed situation by sending runners with the utmost despatch to Boston and Plimouth for assistance. "But," says our chronicler of that day, "before any came to them, they of both towns, Rehoboth and Swansey, were gathered together into three houses, men, women, and children, and there had all provisions in common, so that they who had nothing wanted nothing. Immediately after notice hereof came to Boston, drums beat up for volunteers, and in 3 hours time were mustered up about 110 men, Capt. *Samuel Mosely* being their commander. This Capt. *Mosely* hath been an old privateer at Jamaica, an excellent soldier, and an undaunted spirit, one whose memory will be honorable in New England for his many eminent services he hath done the public.

"There were also among these men, about 10 or 12 privateers, that had been there some time before. They carried with them several dogs, that proved serviceable to them, in finding out the enemy in their swamps; one whereof would, for several days together, go out and bring to them 6, 8 or 10 young pigs of King *Philip's* herds. There went out also amongst these men, one *Cornelius*, a Dutchman, who had lately been condemned to die for piracy, but afterwards received a pardon; he, willing to show his gratitude therefor, went out and did several good services abroad against the enemy."

All who have sought after truth in matters of this kind, are well aware of the

---

of *June* last, seven or eight of King *Philip's* men came to *Swansey* on the Lord's day, and would grind a hatchet at an inhabitant's house there; the master told them, it was the sabbath day, and their God would be very angry if he should let them do it. They returned this answer: They knew not who his God was, and that they would do it, for all him, or his God either. From thence they went to another house, and took away some victuals, but hurt no man. Immediately they met a man travelling on the road, kept him in custody a short time, then dismist him quietly; giving him this caution, that he should not work on his God's day, and that he should tell no lies." *Chronicle*, 8, 9.

* *Callendar's* Discourse on the Hist. of R. Island.

extreme difficulty of investigation. Twenty persons may write an account of an affair, to the passage of which all may have been witnesses, and no two of them agree in many of its particulars. The author of the tracts which we cite under the name of THE OLD INDIAN CHRONICLE, wrote his accounts in Boston, and we have no doubt of his intention to record every event with the strictest regard to truth; if he had erred, it is doubtless from his recording the first news of an event, which often varies in point of fact afterwards. *Hubbard* and *Mather*, two contemporary historians, had the advantage of a comparison of reports, and of revising their works in their passage through the press; whereas the author of the tracts wrote them as letters to a friend in London, where they were immediately printed. With allowances for these circumstances, as full credit should be given to his relation, as to either of the others. His accounts of the first events at Swansey are detailed in his own words in a previous note, and we here proceed with another portion of his narrative.

"By this time the Indians have killed several of our men, but the first that was killed was June 23, a man at Swansey; that he and his family had left his house amongst the rest of the inhabitants, and adventuring with his wife and son (about twenty years old) to go to his house to fetch them corn, and such like things: (he having just before sent his wife and son away) as he was going out of the house, was set on and shot by Indians. His wife being not far off, heard the guns go off, went back," and fell into their hands. Dishonored, and afterwards scalped by them, she immediately died, and her son was at the same time scalped. "They also the next day [24 June] killed six or seven men at Swansey, and two more at one of the garrisons; and as two men went out of one of the garrisons to draw a bucket of water, they were shot and carried away, and afterwards were found with their fingers and feet cut off, and the skin of their heads flayed off," that is, scalped.

"About 14 days after that they sent for more help; whereupon the authority of Boston made Capt. *Thomas Savage* the major general in that expedition, who, with 60 horse, and as many foot, went out of Boston; having pressed horses for the footmen, and six carts to carry provisions with them." "They traveled day and night till they came to their garrisons, and within three days after marched, horse and foot, leaving guards in the garrisons, towards Mount Hope, where King *Philip* and his wife was. They came on him at unawares, so that he was forced to rise from dinner, and he and all with him fled out of that land called Mount Hope, up further into the country. They pursued them as far as they could go for swamps, and killed 15 or 16 in that expedition, then returned and took what he had that was worth taking, and spoiled the rest; taking all his cattle and hogs that they could find, and also took possession of Mount Hope, which had then a thousand acres under corn, which is since cut down by the English, and disposed of according to their discretion. *Cornelius* [before mentioned] was in this exploit, and pursued *Philip* so hard, that he got his cap off his head, and now wears it."

It was June 26, that the English marched out of Boston for Swansey; and they arrived there two days after, namely, June 28, a little before night.* Twelve men immediately marched out to invade *Philip's* territories, who were attacked by about the same number of *Philip's* men. The invaders were repulsed, having one killed, and one wounded, and his horse killed under him. Of the Indians two were killed.

The next day, June 29, the Indians appeared boldly in view of the English, and by their shouts, it would seem, dared them to come out and fight. *Mosely* sallied out at the head of a company of volunteers, and rushed furiously upon them. They fled to their coverts, but even here made a stand only for a moment; for after one fire they all fled. One of the English, Ensign *Savage*, was wounded, the ball lodging in his thigh, and another passed through the brim of his hat.† *Mosely* pursued the Indians above a mile, and killed five or six of them, as they were making their retreat into a swamp. It was in this pursuit that the exploit of *Cornelius* took place, just related, and *Philip* was not seen at

* *Hubbard*, Narrative, 18.

† *Church*, who was in this action, says *Savage* was wounded by his own party: having divided themselves into two wings, in their confusion one fired upon the other.

Mount Hope again until the next year. The next day the English forces traversed Mount Hope Neck, found *Philip's* wigwam, but himself and all his people had made good their retreat. They found the heads of eight of the English that had been killed, set upon poles, at Keekamuit, which they took down and interred.

On the morning of July 1, as Lieutenant *Oakes* was returning to head-quarters at Swansey, having encamped at Rehoboth the preceding night, he discovered a company of Indians, and attacked them. How many were killed is not stated, but two of *Philip's* chief captains were among the number, one of whom was named Thebe, "a sachem of Mount Hope." Of the English one was killed. The scalps of three Indians that were killed were taken off by the English and sent to Boston, which were the first taken by them in this war.*

At the solicitation of Benjamin Church, a company of 36 men were put under him and Captain *Fuller*, who, on the 8 July, marched down into Pocasset Neck. *Church*, who was well acquainted with the Indians, had urged the officers of the army to pursue *Philip* on the Pocasset side, being fully persuaded that there were no Indians in Mount Hope Neck, the part of the country they were taking so much pains to guard and fortify; but they would not hear to his advice, and the consequence was, *Philip* burned and destroyed the towns towards Plimouth.—But to return to the force under Church and Fuller. This, though but small at first, was divided into two. *Church* had 19 men, and *Fuller* the remaining 17. The party under *Church* proceeded into a point of land called Punkateeset, now the southerly extremity of Tiverton, where they were attacked by a great body of Indians, 300, as *Church* learned afterwards, who nearly encompassed them; but after a few minutes fight, the English retreated to the sea shore, and thus saved themselves from immediate destruction. *Church* gave orders for a retreat the very moment he discovered that the object of the Indians was to surround them. This proved their safety although, as they were now situated, they could expect but little else than to sell their lives at the price of a greater number of their enemies. These Indians were well armed, "their bright guns glittering in the sun," which gave them a formidable appearance. Thus hemmed in, *Church* had a double duty to perform; that of preserving the spirits of his famished followers, many of whom were ready to give up all for lost, and erecting defences of stones to defend them. Many were the hair-breadth escapes of individuals in this little band on this trying occasion. In the language of *Church*, "they were beset with multitudes of Indians, who possessed themselves of every rock, and stump, tree or fence, that was in sight," from which they fired without ceasing.

Boats had been appointed to attend upon the English in this expedition, but they had grounded on the Rhode Island shore, and could not come to their assistance; at length, however, one got off, and came towards them, which gave them hopes of escape, but these were of short duration: the Indians fired into it, and prevented their landing. *Church* ordered those in it to ride off beyond musket shot, and to send a canoe ashore; but they dared not even to do this. When *Church* saw that, in a moment of vexation, he ordered the boat to be gone in an instant or he would fire upon it; she immediately left, and the peril of the English was greatly increased; for now the Indians were encouraged, and they fired "thicker and faster than before."

Night was now almost enshrouding them, their ammunition nearly spent, and the Indians had possessed themselves of a stone house that overlooked them, but as though preserved by a miracle, not one of the English in all this time was wounded. But fortune's sport was now nearly ended: a sloop was discovered bearing down towards them, and soon after, *Church* announced that relief was coming, for that the vessel was commanded by "Capt. Golding, whom he knew to be a man for business." True, it was *Golding*. He sent his canoe ashore, but it was so small that it would take but two at a time to the vessel. The embarkation immediately commenced, and meantime the Indians plied their shot with such effect that the colors, sails, and stern of the sloop were full of bullet-holes. *Church* was the last man to embark,

* I deduce the facts in this sentence from a comparison of *Hubbard*, 20, with the Chronicle, 13.

who, as he was retreating backward to the boat, a ball grazed the hair of his head, two others struck the canoe as he entered it, and a fourth lodged in a stake, which accidentally stood just before "the middle of his breast!"

Thus this little band, after a fight of about six hours, escaped. The party under Captain *Fuller* met with similar fortune; they were attacked by great numbers, but escaped by getting possession of an old house close upon the water's edge and were early taken off by boats. But two of the party were wounded. Some of the Indians were killed and wounded this day, but how many is not known.

The same day this fight took place, a boat's crew went from Rhode Island to Pocasset to look after some cattle, and were fired upon by the Indians, and one of their number, a servant of Captain *Church*, was severely wounded.

Some of the acts of the English, in retrospect, do not discover that judgment the circumstances seem to have elicited, especially that in relation to the Narragansets. They had now driven *Philip* out of Mount Hope Neck, and, not knowing exactly where to find him, the forces in that quarter remained doubting what next to do. At this juncture Captain *Hutchinson* arrived from Boston with orders from the government there, "for them to pass into Narraganset, to treat with the sachems, and if it might be, to prevent their joining with *Philip*." Accordingly they marched into that country, but all the chief men and warriors fled on their approach. The historical conclusion is, therefore, that this act was viewed by them as a declaration of war, and it is rational that they should have so considered it; because the army assumed a most hostile attitude, "resolving they would go to make peace with a sword in their hands." Having arrived in the Narraganset country, three or four days were spent in finding Indians with whom to treat; (for they could find none to fight;) at length, four men were found, whom the English styled sachems, and a treaty was drawn up at great length and signed by the parties. To ensure its observance the following hostages were taken into custody by the army: JOHN WOBEQUOB, WEOWTHIM,* PEWKES, and WEENEW, "four of the sachems near kinsmen and choice friends." Among the stipulations of the treaty we find these:

The said sachems shall carefully seize all and every of *Philip's* subjects, and deliver them up to the English, alive or dead; that they shall use all acts of hostility against *Philip* and his subjects, to kill them wherever they can be found; that if they seize *Philip*, and deliver him alive to the English, they shall receive 40 trucking cloth coats; and for his head alone, 20 of said coats; and for every subject of said sachem 2 coats, if alive, and one if dead. This treaty is dated *Petaquanscot*, 15 *July*, 1675;

In presence of	*and signed by the marks of*
Daniel Henchman,	TAWAGESON,
Thomas Prentice,	TAYTSON,
Nicholas Paige,	AGAMAUG,
Joseph Stanton, Interpreter.	WAMPSH, *alias*
Henry Hawlaws, } [Indians,	CORMAN.
Pecoe Bucow, } probably.]	
Job Neff.	

Philip commanded in person upon Pocasset, where, upon the 18th of July, he was discovered in a "dismal swamp." He had retired to this place, which is adjacent to Taunton River, with most of his Wampanoags, and such others as had joined him, to avoid falling in with the English army, which was now pursuing him. From their numbers, the English were nearly able to encompass the swamp, and the fate of *Philip* they now thought sealed. On arriving at its edge, a few of *Philip's* warriors showed themselves, and the English rushed in upon them with ardor, and by this feint were drawn far into an ambush, and "about 15 were slain." The leaves upon the trees were so thick, and the hour of the day so late, that a friend could not be distinguished from a foe, "whereby 'tis verily feared," says Dr. *Mather*, "that [the English themselves] did sometimes unhappily shoot Eng-

* Probably the same called in another place NOWEQUA.

lishmen instead of Indians." A retreat was now ordered, and, considering *Philip's* escape impossible, the most of the forces left the place, a few only remaining, "to starve out the enemy." That *Philip's* force was great at this time is certain, from the fact that a hundred wigwams were found near the edge of the swamp, newly constructed of green bark. In one of those the English found an old man, who informed them that *Philip* was there. He lost but few men in the encounter, though, it is said, he had a brother killed.*

The idle notion of building a fort here to starve out *Philip*, was sufficiently censured by the historians of that day. For, as Captain *Church* expresses it, *to build a fort for nothing to cover the people from nobody*,† was rather a ridiculous idea. This observation he made upon a fort's being built upon Mount Hope Neck, some time after every Indian had left that side of the country, and who, in fact, were laying waste the towns before mentioned.

The swamp where *Philip* was now confined, was upon a piece of country which projected into Taunton River, and was nearly seven miles in extent. After being guarded here 13 days, which, in the end, was greatly to his advantage, and afforded him sufficient time to provide canoes in which to make his escape, he passed the river with most of his men, and made good his retreat into the country upon Connecticut River. In effecting this retreat, an accident happened which deprived him of some of his choicest and bravest captains, as we shall proceed to relate.

About the 26 July, 1675, *Oneko*, with two of his brothers, and about 50 men, came to Boston, by direction of *Uncas*, his father, and declared their desire to assist the English against the Wampanoags. A few English and three Naticks were added to their company, and immediately despatched, by way of Plimouth, to the enemy's country. This circuitous route was taken, perhaps, that they might have their instructions immediately from the governor of that colony; Massachusetts, at that time, probably, supposing the war might be ended without their direct interference. This measure, as it proved, was very detrimental to the end in view; for if they had proceeded directly to Seekonk, they would have been there in season to have met *Philip* in his retreat from Pocasset; and this force, being joined with the other English forces, then in the vicinity, they in all probability might have finished the war by a single fight with him. At least, his chance of escape would have been small, as he had to cross a large extent of clear and open country, where many of his men must have been cut down in flight, or fought man to man with their pursuers. Whereas *Oneko* was encamped at some distance, having arrived late the night before, and some time was lost in rallying‡ after Philip was discovered. They overtook him, however, about 10 o'clock in the morning of the 1st of August, and a smart fight ensued. *Philip* having brought his best men into the rear, many of them were slain; among these was *Nimrod*, alias *Woonashum*, a great captain and counsellor, who had signed the treaty at Taunton, four years before.

From what cause the fight was suspended is unknown, though it would seem from some relations, that it was owing to *Oneko's* men, who, seeing themselves in possession of considerable plunder, fell to loading themselves with it, and thus gave *Philip* time to escape. From this view of the case, it would appear that the Mohegans were the chief actors in the offensive. It is said that the Naticks urged immediate and further pursuit, which did not take place, in consequence of the extreme heat of the weather; and thus the main body were permitted to escape.

Mr. *Newman*, of Rehoboth, gave an account of the affair in a letter, in which he said that "14 of the enemy's principal men were slain." He also mentioned, in terms of great praise, the Naticks and Mohegans under *Oneko*.

Philip having now taken a position to annoy the back settlements of

---

* This is upon the authority of the anonymous author of the "*Present State*," &c., of which we shall elsewhere have occasion to take notice. That author seems to have confounded the fight between *Thebe* and Lieut. *Oakes* with that of Rehoboth Plain.

† Hist. Philip's War, p. 6. ed. 4to.

‡ *Gookin's* MS. Hist. Praying Indians.

Massachusetts, his warriors fell vigorously to the work. On 14 July, five people are killed at Mendon, in Mass., which is the first blood shed in the colony in this war. Those that were killed were about their work in the field, and knew not their murderers; and whether they were killed by Philip's men is unknown.

Soon after the war began, Massachusetts, fearing the Nipmuks might join with *Philip*, sent messengers to treat with them. The young Indians were found "surly," but the old men were for a renewal of friendship; but the person or persons sent upon this business did not acquit themselves in a manner that gave satisfaction; and *Philip*, being now in the country of the Nipmuks, it was concluded by the authorities of Massachusetts to make a further test of their intentions. Accordingly, on the 28 July, Captains *Hutchinson* and *Wheeler*, with a company of 20 mounted men, and 3 Christian Indians as pilots and interpreters, viz. *Memecho*, *Joseph*, and *Sampson*, went with some of the inhabitants of Brookfield, agreeably to appointment, to meet the Nipmuk sachems. It had been agreed by these sachems to meet the English in a treaty at a certain tree at Quabaog on the 2 August, on a plain 3 miles from Brookfield village. Having arrived here according to agreement, the English found no Indians to treat with. It was now a question with all but the Brookfield men, whether or not they should proceed to a certain place where they believed the Indians to be; at length the confidence of the Brookfield people in the pacific disposition of the Indians, prevailed, and they marched on. The way was so bad that they could march only in single file, as they approached the place where they expected to find the Indians, and when they came near Wikabaug Pond, between a swamp on the left and a very abrupt and high hill on the right,* suddenly 2 or 300 Indians rose up, encompassed, and fired upon them. Eight were killed outright, and three fell mortally wounded. Of the latter number was Captain *Hutchinson*, who, though carried off by the survivors, died on the 19 August following. Captain *Wheeler* had his horse shot under him, and himself was shot through the body; but his life was saved through the bravery and presence of mind of a son then with him. This son, though his own arm was broken by a bullet, seeing the peril of his father, dismounted from his horse, and succeeded in mounting his father upon it. A retreat now began, and, by cutting their way through the Indians, the small remnant of English got back to Brookfield.†

The three Christian Indians of whom we have spoken, rendered most eminent service on this day; for had they not been there, there had been no possibility of one Englishman's escaping. One of them, *George Memecho*, fell into the hands of the Indians: the other two, by skill and bravery, led the English, by an unknown route, in safety to Brookfield. Yet these Indians were afterwards so badly treated by the English, that they were forced to fly to *Philip* for protection. *Sampson* was afterwards killed in a fight by the English Indians, and *Joseph* was taken in Plimouth colony, and sold for a slave, and sent to Jamaica. He afterwards was suffered to return, at the intercession of Mr. *Eliot*. *Memecho* escaped from his captors, and brought beneficial intelligence to the English of the state of *Philip's* affairs.‡

The English having now arrived at Brookfield, as just related, the Indians pursued them, and arrived almost as soon; fortunately, however, there was barely time to alarm the inhabitants, who, to the number of about 80, flocked into a garrison house, where, through persevering efforts, they were enabled to maintain themselves until a force under Major *Willard* came to their relief, August 4. He was in the vicinity of Lancaster, with 48 dragoons and four friendly Indians, when he received the intelligence of the perilous condition of Brookfield, and had just taken up his line of march to surprise a lodge of Indians not far from that place. He now quickly

* According to all tradition this place is at the north end of Wickaboag pond, and the hill was a cemetery for the Indians; for when cultivated afterwards by the whites, numerous bones were exhumed. *Foot's* Hist. Brookfield, 30.

† Narrative of the affair by Captain *Wheeler* himself, p. 1 to 5.

‡ GOOKIN'S MS. History of the Praying Indians.—*Joseph* and *Sampson* were brothers sons of "old ROBIN PETUHANIT, deceased, a good man." Ib.

changed his course for Brookfield, distant about 30 miles, which, by a forced march, he reached in safety the night following. That he was not attacked as he approached the distressed garrison, is most extraordinary, for the hostile Indians are said to have guarded every passage to it; and there are different reasons stated for that neglect: one is, that the guard through which the English passed, suffered them to proceed, expecting another guard stationed still nearer the garrison would attack them in front while they should fall on them in the rear; another is, that they were deceived as to the numbers of the English, thinking them many more than they really were, and dared not attack them. It would seem, however, more probable, that the Indians had no guard at all at the point in which they approached at the time they arrived; for a drove of cattle, which had been frightened from Brookfield into the woods, followed the rear of *Willard's* company to the garrison, and were not attacked, which would not have been the case, in all probability, had the Indians been aware of their approach.

No sooner was it known to the besiegers that relief was come, but they fell with more fury, if possible, upon the devoted garrison than before; shooting continually from all quarters upon it, which shows that they had accidentally let the reinforcement get into the garrison. Thus to a most fortunate circumstance did this assemblage of English owe their safety.

At the very time *Willard* arrived at Brookfield the Indians were contriving some machinery to set the garrison on fire; and this may account for their remissness in suffering him to come in unmolested. They first endeavored by fire arrows, and rags dipped in brimstone tied to long poles spliced together, to fire the garrison, but not succeeding, those within firing upon them often with such deadly effect, they next, in the language of Mr *Hubbard*, "used this devilish stratagem, to fill a cart with hemp, flax, and other combustible matter, and so thrusting it backward with poles together spliced a great length, after they had kindled it; but as soon as it had begun to take fire, a storm of rain, unexpectedly falling, put it out.' *

During this siege several of the whites were wounded, though but one was killed. Of the Indians 80 were supposed to have been killed,† but this was doubtless setting the number much too high, although they exposed themselves beyond what was common on similar occasions. On the 5 August they quitted the place, satisfied they could not take it, and joined *Philip*, who was now about 6 miles from the place where *Hutchinson* was ambushed.

After *George Memecho's* return to the English, he gave the following information: "Upon Friday, August 5, *Philip* and his company came to us at a swamp, 6 miles from the swamp where they killed our men. *Philip* brought with him about 48 men, but women and children many more. *Philip's* men were, about 30 of them, armed with guns, the rest had bows and arrows. He observed there were about 10 of *Philip's* men wounded. *Philip* was conducted to the swamp by two Indians, one of them [was] CALEB of Tatumasket, beyond Mendon. The Indians told *Philip*, at his first coming, what they had done to the English at Quabaog; then he presented and gave to three Sagamores, viz. JOHN, *alias* APEQUINASH, QUANANSIT, and MAWTAMPS, to each of them about a peck of unstrung wompom, which they accepted. *Philip*, as I understood, told Quabaog and Nipmuck Indians, that when he first came towards the Nipmuck country, and left his own, he had in his company about 250 men, besides women and children, including the Squaw-Sachem [*Weetamoo*] and her company but now they had left him, and some of them were killed and he was reduced to 40 men. I heard also that *Philip* said if the English had charged upon him and his people at the swamp in his own country [18 July] one or two days more, they had been all taken, for their powder was almost spent. He also said,

* Captain *Wheeler* does not mention the rain, but says they succeeded in setting the house on fire, which was extinguished at great peril by those within, who had two of their men wounded.

† *Hoyt's* Indian Wars, 101.

that if the English had pursued him closely," as he retreated to the Nipmuck country, "he must needs have been taken." *

A considerable number of partly christianized Indians belonged to the neighborhood of Hadley, near which they had a wooden fort to protect them from any hostile Indians. On the breaking out of the calamities in that region, these, with all other Indians, were watched, and suspected of conniving with *Philip*, and an intention of joining with him. To test their pretensions, Captains *Lothrop* and *Beers*, who, with a force of 180 men, were now at Hadley, ordered them to surrender their arms to them. They hesitated to do so then, but intimated that they would immediately; yet on the following night, 25 August, they left their fort and fled up the river towards *Pecomptuk*, since Deerfield, to join *Philip*. The next day *Lothrop* and Beers pursued and overtook them near a swamp a short distance to the south of Sugarloaf Hill, opposite to the present town of Sunderland. The Indians bravely stood their ground, and a sharp and bloody contest ensued. They were finally routed, having 26 of their number slain, while the whites are reported to have lost but 10 in killed, and their number wounded is not mentioned. †

A garrison being established at Northfield, Captain *Richard Beers*, of Watertown, ‡ with 36 men, was attacked while on their way to reinforce it, Sept. 3, and 20 of the 36 were killed. *Robert Pepper*, of Roxbury, was taken captive, and the others effected their escape. *Philip's* men had the advantage of attacking them in a place of their own choosing, and their first fire was very destructive. *Beers* retreated with his men to a small eminence, and maintained the unequal fight until their ammunition was spent, at which time a cart containing ammunition fell into the hands of the Indians, and, the captain being killed, all who were able took to flight. The hill to which the English fled, at the beginning of the fight, was known afterwards by the name of *Beers's Mountain*. "Here," says Mr. *Hubbard*, "the barbarous villains showed their insolent rage and cruelty, more than ever before; cutting off the heads of some of the slain, and fixing them upon poles near the highway, and not only so, but one, if not more, was found with a chain hooked into his under-jaw, and so hung up on the bough of a tree, ('tis feared he was hung up alive,) by which means they thought to daunt and discourage any that might come to their relief."

The place where this fight occurred was within about two miles of the garrison at Squakkeag, (Northfield,) and the plain on which it began is called *Beers's Plain*. Meanwhile the garrison was reduced to the brink of ruin, and, like that at Brookfield, was saved by the arrival of a company of soldiers. Two days after Captain *Beers* was cut off, Major *Treat* arrived there with 100 men, and conveyed the garrison safe to Hadley.

Philip probably conducted both affairs; this of Captain *Beers*, and that of Captain *Thomas Lothrop*, about to be related, although it is not positively known to be the fact.

Some time in the month of August, "King *Philip's* men had taken a young lad alive, about 14 years old, and bound him to a tree two nights and two days, intending to be merry with him the next day, and that they would roast him alive to make sport with him; but God, over night, touched the heart of one Indian, so that he came and loosed him, and bid him *run grande*, (i. e. run apace,) and by that means he escaped." §

About this time, some English found a single Indian, an old man, near Quabaog, whom they captured. As he would not give them any information respecting his countrymen, or, perhaps, such as they desired, they pronounced him worthy of death; so "they laid him down, *Cornelius*, the Dutchman, lifting up his sword to cut off his head, the Indian lifted up his hand between, so that his hand was first cut off, and partly his head, and the second blow finished the execution." ‖

* Hutchinson's Hist. Mass. I, 293—4. n.
† *Hubbard*, Nar. 36, 37.—Chronicle, 28.—*Hoyt*, 102, 103.
‡ Manuscript documents.
§ Chronicle, 25.
‖ Manuscript in library of Mass. Hist. Soc.

It was about this time, as the author of the "Present State" relates, that "King *Philip*, now beginning to want money, having a coat made all of wampampeag, (i. e. Indian money,) cuts his coat to pieces and distributes it plentifully among the Nipmoog sachems and others, as well as to the east-ward as southward, and all round about."*

On the 18 Sept. Captain *Lothrop*, of Beverly, was sent from Hadley with about 88 men, to bring away the corn, grain, and other valuable articles, from Deerfield. Having loaded their teams and commenced their march homeward, they were attacked at a place called *Sugarloaf Hill*, where almost every man was slain. This company consisted of "choice young men, the very flower of Essex county, 'none of whom were ashamed to speak with the enemy in the gate.'"† Eighteen of the men belonged to Deerfield.‡ Captain *Mosely*, being not far off, upon a scout, was drawn to the scene of action by the report of the guns, and, having with him 70 men, charged the Indians with great resolution although he computed their numbers at 1000. He had two of his men killed and eleven wounded. The Indians dared him to begin the fight, and exultingly said to him, "*Come, Mosely, come, you seek Indians, you want Indians; here is Indians enough for you.*"§ On this occasion the conduct of *Mosely's* lieutenants, *Savage* and *Pickering*, are mentioned in high terms of praise, "as deserving no little part of the honor of that day's service." After continuing a fight with them, from eleven o' clock until almost night, he was obliged to retreat.‖ The Indians cut open the bags of wheat and the feather-beds, and scattered their contents to the winds.§ After *Mosely* had commenced a retreat, Major *Treat*, with 100 English and 60 Mohegans, came to his assistance. Their united forces obliged the Indians to retreat in their turn.¶ The Indians were said to have lost, in the various encounters, 96 men. It was a great oversight, that Captain *Lothrop* should have suffered his men to stroll about, while passing a dangerous defile. 'Many of the soldiers having been so foolish and secure, as to put their arms in the carts, and step aside to gather grapes, which proved dear and deadly *grapes* to them."** The same author observes, "This was a black and fatal day, wherein there were eight persons made widows, and six-and-twenty children made fatherless, all in one little plantation and in one day; and above sixty persons buried in one dreadful grave!"

The place of this fight and ambush is in the southerly part of Deerfield, on which is now the village called Bloody Brook, so named from this memorable tragedy. A brook which passes through the village is crossed by the road not far from the centre of it, and it was at the point of crossing that it happened.††

Until this period the Indians near Springfield remained friendly, and refused the solicitations of *Philip*, to undertake in his cause. But, now that Northfield and Deerfield had fallen into his hands, they were watched closer by the whites, whose cause these great successes of *Philip* had occasioned them to look upon as rather precarious. They therefore, about 40 in number, on the night of the 4 Oct., admitted about 300 of *Philip's* men into their fort, which was situated at a place called *Longhill*, about a mile below the village of Springfield, and a plan was concerted for the destruction of that place. But, as in many cases afterwards, one of their number betrayed them. Toto,‡‡

---

* Old Ind. Chronicle. If this were the case, *Philip* must have had an immense big coat—yea, even bigger than Dr. *Johnson's great* coat, as represented by *Boswell;* the side pockets of which, he said, were large enough each to contain one of the huge volumes of his folio dictionary!

† *Hubbard's* Narrative, 38.

‡ These were the teamsters.

§ Manuscript letter, written at the time.

‖ "Whereupon, after having killed several of the Indians, he was forced to retreat, and continued fighting for all the time that he and his men were retreating nine miles. Capt. *Mosely* lost out of his company 9, and 13 wounded."—Old. Ind. Chron. 29. This author has blended the two accounts of *Beers* and *Lothrop* together, and relates them as one

¶ *I. Mather's* History of the War, 12.

** Ibid.

†† Last year, (1835), a splendid celebration was held at Bloody Brook, in commemoration of the event, and an oration was pronounced by our Prince of Orators, the present governor of this commonwealth, His Excellency Edward Everett, LL. D

‡‡ *Hubbard.*—Top, *Hutchinson.*

an Indian at Windsor, revealed the plot, and the people of Springfield had time only to escape into their garrisons. The whole force of the Indians came like a torrent upon the place the next day, and burnt the deserted houses and barns, in all 57 buildings. In this business, however, some of their number were killed* by the people in the garrisons; but it is not known how many. They would have succeeded against the lives of the English as well as against their property, had not a force arrived about the same time for their relief.

Animated by his successes, *Philip* aimed his next blow at the head-quarters of the whites in this region. With 7 or 800 of his men he fell upon Hatfield on the 19 Oct., which, had it not been well provided with men, would have shared the fate of Springfield; but Captain *Mosely* and Captain *Poole*, with their companies, were in the place, and Captain *Samuel Appleton* was at Hadley on the opposite side of the river; and against such commanders they could hardly have expected success. However, they made a bold attempt on all sides at once; but their greatest force fell on the point where Captain *Appleton* commanded. His sergeant was mortally wounded by his side, and a bullet passed through the hair of his own head; "by that whisper telling him," says *Hubbard*, "that death was very near, but did him no other harm. Night coming on, it could not be discerned what loss the enemy sustained; divers were seen to fall, some run through a small river, [now called *Mill River*,] others cast their guns into the water, (it being their manner to venture as much to recover the dead bodies of their friends, as to defend them when alive.)" And thus they were driven from the place, after killing but three, and wounding 10 of the whites, and burning a small number of buildings. They had, before their attack on the town, killed three belonging to some scouts, and seven others of Captain *Mosely's* men. This was among their last important efforts on the Connecticut River before retiring to the country of the Narragansets.

The Nipmuck sachems had well contrived their attack on Hatfield; having made fires in the woods about seven miles from it, to draw out the soldiers, for whom they had prepared ambushes; but only ten of *Mosely's* men were sent out to learn the cause of the fires. These were all cut off except one, according to the CHRONICLE, but according to *Hubbard*, seven only were killed. The Indians probably supposed the main body was cut off, and therefore proceeded directly to the assault of the town, where a new force had just arrived; and hence they met with a brave resistance and final defeat.†

The Narragansets had not yet heartily engaged in the war, though there is no doubt but they stood pledged so to do. Therefore, having done all that could be expected upon the western frontier of Massachusetts, and concluding that his presence among his allies, the Narragansets, was necessary to keep them from abandoning his cause, *Philip* was next known to be in their country.

An army of 1500 English was raised by the three colonies, Massachusetts, Plimouth, and Connecticut, for the purpose of breaking down the power of *Philip* among the Narragansets. They determined upon this course, as they had been assured that, the next spring, that nation would come with all their force upon them. It was not known that *Philip* was among them when this resolution was taken, and it was but a rumor that they had taken part with him. It was true, that they had promised to deliver up all the Wampanoags, who should flee to them, either alive or dead; but it is also true, that those who made this promise, had it not in their power to do it; being persons, chiefly in subordinate stations, who had no right or authority to bind any but themselves. And, therefore, as doubtless was foreseen by many, none of *Philip's* people were delivered up, although many were known to have been among them. Thus, in few words, have we exhibited the main grounds of the mighty expedition against the Narragansets in the winter of 1675.

* A pewter platter is still exhibited in Springfield with a hole through the middle of it, made by a ball from the garrison at this time. An Indian had taken it from one of the deserted houses, and wore it before his breast as a shield. Thus shielded, he ventured towards the garrison, and was shot. *Hoyt*, 110.

† OLD INDIAN CHRONICLE, 36, 37.

Upon a small island, in an immense swamp, in South Kingston, Rhode Island, *Philip* had fortified himself, in a manner superior to what was common among his countrymen. Here he intended to pass the winter, with the chief of his friends. They had erected about 500 wigwams of a superior construction, in which was deposited a great store of provisions. Baskets and tubs of corn * were piled one upon another, about the inside of them, which rendered them bullet proof. It was supposed that about 3000 persons had here taken up their residence.

But, to be more particular upon the situation of "the scene of the destruction of the Narragansets," we will add as follows from the notes of a gentleman lately upon the spot, for the express purpose of gaining information. "What was called *The Island* is now an upland meadow, a few feet higher than the low meadow with which it is surrounded. The island, by my estimate, contains from three to four acres. One fourth of a mile west, is the Usquepaug; a small stream also at a short distance on the east." The celebrated island on which the fort was built is now in the farm of *J. G. Clark*, Esq. a descendant of *John Clark*, of R. I. and about 30 rods west of the line of the "Pettyswamscot Purchase." Water still surrounds it in wet seasons. It was cleared by the father of the present possessor about 1780, and, although improved from that time to the present, charred corn and Indian implements are yet ploughed up.†

President *Stiles*, in his edition of Church's History of Philip's War, states that the Narraganset fort is seven miles nearly due west from the South Ferry. This agrees with data furnished by Mr. *Ely*, in stating the returning march of the English army. Pine and cedar were said to have been the former growth.‡ An oak 300 years old, standing upon the island, was cut down in 1782, two feet in diameter, 11 feet from the ground. From another, a bullet was cut out, surrounded by about 100 *annuli*, at the same time. The bullet was lodged there, no doubt, at the time of the fight. We will now return to our narrative of the expedition to this place in December, 1675.

After nearly a month from their setting out, the English army arrived in the Narraganset country, and made their head-quarters about 18 miles from *Philip's* fort. They had been so long upon their march, that the Indians were well enough apprized of their approach, and had made the best arrangements in their power to withstand them. The army had already suffered much from the severity of the season, being obliged to encamp in the open field, and without tents to cover them!

The 19th of December, 1675, is a memorable day in the annals of New England. Cold, in the extreme,—the air filled with snow,—the English were obliged, from the low state of their provisions, to march to attack *Philip* in his fort. Treachery hastened his ruin. One of his men, by hope of reward, betrayed his country into their hands. This man had, probably, lived among the English, as he had an English name. He was called *Peter*,§ and it was by accident that himself, with thirty-five others, had just before fallen into the hands of the fortunate Captain *Mosely*. No Englishman was acquainted with the situation of *Philip's* fort; and, but for their pilot, *Peter*, there is very little probability that they could have even found, much less effected any thing against it. For it was one o'clock on that short day of the year, before they arrived within the vicinity of the swamp. There was but one point where it could be assailed with the least probability of success; and this was fortified by a kind of block-house, directly in front of the entrance, and had also flankers to cover a cross fire. Besides high palisades, an immense hedge of fallen trees, of nearly a rod in thickness,

* 500 bushels, says Dr. *I. Mather*. Hollow trees, cut off about the length of a barrel, were used by the Indians for tubs. In such they secured their corn and other grains.

† MS. communication of Reverend Mr. *Ely*, accompanied by a drawing of the island. Its shape is very similar to the shell of an oyster. Average rectangular lines through it measure one 35 rods, another 20.

‡ Holmes's Annals, i. 376.

§ The name of *Peter* among the Indians was so common, that it is perhaps past determination *who* this one was. Mr. *Hubbard* calls him a fugitive from the Narragansets.

surrounded it, encompassing an area of about five acres. Between the fort and the main land was a body of water, over which a great tree had been felled, on which all must pass and repass, to and from it. On coming to this place, the English soldiers, as many as could pass upon the tree, which would not admit two abreast, rushed forward upon it, but were swept off in a moment by the fire of *Philip's* men. Still, the English soldiers, led by their captains, supplied the places of the slain. But again and again were they swept from the fatal avenue. Six captains and a great many men had fallen, and a partial, but momentary, recoil from the face of death took place

Meanwhile, a handful, under the fortunate *Mosely*, had, as miraculous as it may seem, got within the fort. These were contending hand to hand with the Indians, and at fearful odds, when the cry of "*They run! they run!*" brought to their assistance a considerable body of their fellow-soldiers. They were now enabled to drive the Indians from their main breastwork, and their slaughter became immense. Flying from wigwam to wigwam—men, women and children, indiscriminately, were hewn down, and lay in heaps upon the snow. Being now masters of the fort, at the recommendation of Mr. *Church*, who led the second party that entered the fort, General *Winslow* was about to quarter the army in it for the present, which offered comfortable habitations to the sick and wounded, besides a plentiful supply of provisions. But one of the captains * and a surgeon opposed the measure; probably from the apprehension that the woods was full of Indians, who would continue their attacks upon them, and drive them out in their turn. There was, doubtless, some reason for this, which was strengthened from the fact that many English were killed after they had possessed themselves of the fort, by those whom they had just dispossessed of it. Notwithstanding, had *Church's* advice been followed, perhaps many of the lives of the wounded would have been saved; for he was seldom out in his judgment, as his continued successes proved afterwards.

After fighting three hours, the English were obliged to march 18 miles, before the wounded could be dressed, and in a most dismal and boisterous night. Eighty English were killed in the fight, and 150 wounded, many of whom died afterwards. The shattered army left the ground in considerable haste, leaving eight of their dead in the fort.

Philip, and such of his warriors as escaped unhurt, fled into a place of safety, until the enemy had retired; when they returned again to the fort. The English, no doubt, apprehended a pursuit, but *Philip*, not knowing their distressed situation, and, perhaps, judging of their loss from the few dead which they left behind, made no attempt to harass them in their retreat. Before the fight was over, many of the wigwams were set on fire. Into these, hundreds of innocent women and children had crowded themselves, and perished in the general conflagration! And, as a writer of that day expresses himself, "no man knoweth how many." The English learned afterwards, from some that fell into their hands, that in all about 700 perished.†

The sufferings of the English, after the fight, are almost without a parallel in history. The horrors of Moscow will not longer be remembered. The myriads of modern Europe, assembled there, bear but small propor-

---

* Probably *Mosely*, who seems always to have had a large share in the direction of all affairs when present.

† There is printed in *Hutchinson's* Hist. Mass. i. 300. a letter which gives the particulars of the Narraganset fight. I have compared it with the original, and find it correct in the main particulars. He mistakes in ascribing it to Major *Bradford*, for it is signed by *James Oliver*, a Massachusetts captain. *Hutchinson* copied from a copy, which was without signature. He omits a passage concerning *Tift*, or *Tiffe*, who, *Oliver* says, confirmed his narrative. That man had "married an Indian, a Wompanoag—and, says *Oliver*, he shot 20 times at us in the swamp—was taken at Providence, [by Captain *Fenner*,] Jan. 14th—brought to us the 16th—executed the 18th; a sad wretch. He never heard a sermon but once this 14 years; he never heard of the name of *Jesus Christ*. His father going to recall him, lost his head, and lies unburied." *Hubbard* says, (Narrative, 59,) that "he was condemned to die the death of a traitor," and traitors of those days were quartered. "As to his religion, he was found as ignorant as an heathen, which, no doubt, caused the fewer tears to be shed at his funeral. A sorrowful record!

tion to the number of their countrymen, compared with that of the army of New England and theirs, at the fight in Narraganset.

Colonel *Church*, then only a volunteer, was in this fight, and we will hear a few of his observations. "By this time, the English people in the fort had begun to set fire to the wigwams and houses, which Mr. *Church* labored hard to prevent; they told him they had orders from the general to burn them; he begged them to forbear until he had discoursed the general." Then, hastening to him, he urged, that "the wigwams were musket-proof being all lined with baskets and tubs of grain, and other provisions, sufficient to supply the whole army until the spring of the year; and every wounded man might have a good warm house to lodge in; which, otherwise, would necessarily perish with the storms and cold. And, moreover, that the army had no other provision to trust unto or depend upon; that he knew that Plymouth forces had not so much as one biscuit left." The general was for acceding to *Church's* proposition, but a captain and a doctor prevented it, as we have before observed; the former threatening to shoot the general's horse under him, if he attempted to march in, and the latter said, *Church* should bleed to death like a dog, (he having been badly wounded on entering the fort,) before he would dress his wounds, if he gave such advice. *Church* then proceeds: "And, burning up all the houses and provisions in the fort, the army returned the same night in the storm and cold. And, I suppose, every one that is acquainted with the circumstances of that night's march, deeply laments the miseries that attended them; especially the wounded and dying men. But it mercifully came to pass that Capt. *Andrew Belcher* arrived at Mr. *Smith's*, [in Narraganset,] that very night from Boston, with a vessel loaden with provisions for the army, who must otherwise have perished for want." *

After the English army had gone into quarters at Wickford, the Connecticut troops returned home, which was considered very detrimental to the service by the other colonies; and soon after a reinforcement of 1000 men was assembled at Boston and ordered to the assistance of their countrymen. In their march to Narraganset in the beginning of Jan. 1676, they suffered intolerably from the cold; no less than 11 men were frozen to death, and many others were taken sick by reason of their exposure in that severe season.

Meanwhile the Indians had sent deputies to the commander-in-chief to treat of peace; but it was judged that they were insincere in their overtures, and no terms were settled. While matters were thus progressing, *Philip* removed his provisions, women and children to a strong place protected by rocks, in a swamp, about 20 miles from the late battle-ground in Narraganset, into the country of the Nipmuks. At length, the weather having become mild, and the Connecticut forces returned, together with a body of Mohegans under *Uncas*, it was resolved to suprise *Philip* in his rocky fortress. Accordingly the army, consisting now of 1600 men, marched out on this enterprise. On its approach, the Indians abandoned their position and fled farther northward. They were pursued a small distance, and about 60 or 70 of them killed and taken, (probably women and children.) The army soon after returned home, and was chiefly disbanded.

On 27 Jan., while the army was pursuing the main body of the Indians, a party of about 300 attacked Mr. *William Carpenter's* plantation, and attempted to burn his house, which they set on fire, but those within succeeded in putting it out. In the skirmish, one of their number was killed, and two of the whites were wounded. The assaulting party collected and drove off from this place 180 sheep, 50 large cattle, and 15 horses, and from a Mr *Harris* another drove of cattle, and killed his negro servant.†

Soon after this, *Philip*, with many of his followers, left that part of the

* "Our wounded men, (in number about 150,) being dressed, were sent into Rhode Island, as the best place for their accommodation; where, accordingly, they were kindly received by the governor and others, only some churlish Quakers were not free to entertain them, until compelled by the governor. Of so inhumane, peevish and untoward a disposition are these *Nabals*, as not to vouchsafe civility to those that had ventured their lives, and received dangerous wounds in their defence." *Old Ind. Chronicle*, 74.

† Old Indian Chronicle, 58, 59.—*Hubbard*, 59.

country, and resided in different places upon Connecticut River. Some report that he took up his residence near Albany, and that he solicited the Mohawks to aid him against the English, but without success.

The story of the foul stratagem said to have been resorted to by *Philip* for this object, is, if true, the deepest stain upon his character. According to one of the historians * of the war, it was reported at Boston, in the end of June, or beginning of July, 1676, that "those Indians who are known by the name of Mauquawogs, (or Mohawks, i. e. man-eaters,) had lately fallen upon *Philip*, and killed 40 of his men. And if the variance between *Philip* and the Mauquawogs came to pass, as is commonly reported and apprehended, there was a marvellous finger of God in it. For we hear that *Philip*, being this winter entertained in the Mohawks' country, made it his design to breed a quarrel between the English and them; to effect which, divers of our returned captives do report, that he resolved to kill some scattering Mohawks, and then to say that the English had done it; but one of these, whom he thought to have killed, was only wounded, and got away to his countrymen, giving them to understand that not the English, but *Philip*, had killed the men that were murdered; so that, instead of bringing the Mohawks upon the English, he brought them upon himself."

The author of the anonymous "LETTERS TO LONDON" has this passage † concerning *Philip's* visit to the Mohawks. "King *Philip*, and some of these northern Indians, being wandered up towards Albany, the Mohucks marched out very strong, in a warlike posture, upon them, putting them to flight, and pursuing them as far as Hassicke River, which is about two days' march from the east side of Hudson's River to the north-east, killing divers, and bringing away some prisoners with great pride and triumph, which ill success on that side, where they did not expect any enemy, having lately endeavored to make up the ancient animosities, did very much daunt and discourage the said northern Indians, so that some hundreds came in and submitted themselves to the English at Plimouth colony, and *Philip* himself is run skulking away into some swamp, with not above ten men attending him."

Although *Philip* was supposed to be beyond the frontier by some, and by others to be "snugly stowed away in some swamp," yet his warriors, whether directed by him in person or not, is immaterial, as every thing was done against the English that could well be under such broken circumstances as he now labored. On the 10 Feb. 1676, they surprised Lancaster with complete success, the particulars of which we shall fully narrate in our next chapter. Eleven days after, (21 Feb.) about 300 Indians attacked Medfield, and in spite of 200 soldiers stationed there to guard it, burnt about 50 houses, killed 18 of its inhabitants, and wounded 20 others. Among the slain were Lieutenant *Adams* and his wife: the latter was killed accidentally by Captain *Jacob*. She was in bed in a chamber, under which was a room occupied by the soldiers; as Captain *Jacob* was about to leave the house, his gun went off, the ball from which passed through the chamber floor and killed her.

The Indians managed this attack with their usual skill; having placed some of their number prepared with fire implements in various parts of the town, they set the houses on fire, "as it were," says Major *Gookin*, "in one instant of time." And as the people issued out of them, parties lay ready and shot them down. As soon as the whites were mustered to oppose them, they retired over the bridge towards Sherburne, and set it on fire, so that the soldiers could not pursue them. In the pride of their success, they now wrote a letter to the whites, and stuck it up on a post of the bridge. It reads,

"*Know by this paper, that the Indians that thou hast provoked to wrath and anger will war this* 21 *years if you will. There are many Indians yet. We come* 300 *at this time. You must consider the Indians lose nothing but their life. You must lose your fair houses and cattle.*"‡

On the 13 March, the entire town of Groton, consisting of 40 houses, was burnt, except one garrison,§ by shots from which several Indians were said to have been killed.

* Dr. *I. Mather*, Brief Hist. 38. † Chronicle, 99.

‡ *Gookin's* MS. Hist. Praying Indians.—The above letter was doubtless written by some of the Christian Indians who had joined *Philip*.

§ In our *Chronicle*, 80, it is said that Groton was burnt on the 14th; that Major *Willard's*

Philip had for some time directed matters with such address that his enemies could not tell where or how to meet him, or whether he actually were in the vicinity of the frontiers or not. But there can be little doubt of his special agency and direction in all the important enterprises. On the 18 March, Northampton was assaulted, but not with quite as good success as was anticipated by the besiegers; for they lost eleven men, while the whites had but three killed and six wounded.

On the 27 March, a large body of 300 Indians, as was supposed, were discovered encamped not far from Marlborough, which they had burnt the day before. A company of men belonging to that town, attached themselves to a number of soldiers under one Lieutenant *Jacobs*, who, falling upon them in the night while they were asleep in their wigwams, killed and wounded about 40 of them, without any loss to themselves.

The Indians seem to have resolved that this midnight assassination should not go long unrequited, and events so determined, as what we are about to relate will fully exemplify. On the morning of the 20 April, the largest body of Indians which had at any time appeared, attacked Sudbury, and before resistance could be made, set fire to several buildings, which were consumed. The inhabitants, however, made a brave stand, and were soon joined by some soldiers from Watertown, under Captain *Hugh Mason;* and the Indians retreated over the bridge, and were prevented from doing any further mischief during the day, against Sudbury.

Some of the people of Concord hearing of the distress at Sudbury, sallied forth for its protection. As they approached a garrison house, they discovered a few Indians, and pursued them. These, as it proved, were a decoy, and they soon found themselves ambushed on every side. They fought with desperation, but were all, except one, cut off, being eleven in number. This affair took place immediately after Captain *Wadsworth* had marched from Sudbury with 70 men to strengthen the garrison at Marlborough; and the news of the situation of the place he had just left reached his destination as soon as he did; and although he had marched all the day and night before, and his men almost exhausted with fatigue, yet, taking Captain *Brocklebank* and about ten men from the garrison at Marlborough, he marched directly back for Sudbury. On the morning of the 21st, they arrived within about a mile and a half of the town, near where a body of about 500 Indians had prepared an ambush behind the hills. From thence they sent out two or three of their party, who crossed the march of the English, and, being discovered by them, affected to fly through fear, to decoy them into a pursuit. This stratagem succeeded, and with great boldness the Indians began the attack. For some time the English maintained good order, and, having retreated to an adjacent hill, lost but five men for near four hours. Meantime the Indians had lost a great number, which so increased their rage that they resolved to put in practice another stratagem, which it seems they had not before thought of. They immediately set the woods on fire to windward of the English, which spread with great rapidity, owing to an exceeding high wind and the dryness of the grass and other combustibles. This stratagem likewise succeeded, even better than the first; that, although it served to bring on the attack, was near proving fatal to its originators, but this was crowned with complete success. The fury of the flames soon drove the English from their advantageous position, which gave the Indians an opportunity to fall upon them with their tomahawks! Many were now able to fall upon one, and resistance fast diminished. All but about twenty were killed or fell into the hands of the conquerors; among the former were the two captains; some of those that escaped took shelter in a mill not far off, and were saved by the arrival of a few men under Captain *Prentice*, and a company under Captain *Crowell*. Both of these officers and their men very narrowly escaped the fate of *Wadsworth*.* As the former was about to fall into a fatal

house was burnt first, and that "afterwards they destroyed 65 more there, leaving but six houses standing in the whole town."

* "So insolent were the Indians grown upon their first success against Captain *Wadsworth*, that they sent us word, to provide store of good cheer; for they intended to dine with us [at Boston] on the election day." *Chronicle*, 95.

snare, he was rescued by a company from a garrison; and as the latter approached Sudbury, he saved himself by pursuing an unexpected route; and, though attacked, he succeeded in fighting his way through the Indians with a loss only of six or seven of his men. Captain *Crowell's* arrival at this time was accidental, though fortunate; being on his return from Quabaog, whither he had been sent to reinforce that garrison.* With this great achievement ended the chief operations in Massachusetts; and we have now to return towards Plimouth.

When success no longer attended *Philip* in Massachusetts, those of his allies whom he had seduced into the war, upbraided and accused him of bringing all their misfortunes upon them; that they had no cause of war against the English, and had not engaged in it but for his solicitations; and many of the tribes scattered themselves in different directions. With all that would follow him, as a last retreat, *Philip* returned to Pokanoket. The Pecomptuck or Deerfield Indians were among the first who abandoned his cause, and many of the other Nipmucks and Narragansets soon followed their example.

On the 11th of July, he attempted to surprise Taunton, but was repulsed†. His camp was now at Matapoiset. The English came upon him here, under Captain *Church*, who captured many of his people, but he escaped over Taunton River, as he had done a year before, but in the opposite direction, and screened himself once more in the woods of Pocasset. He used many stratagems to cut off Captain *Church*, and seems to have watched and followed him from place to place, until the end of this month; but he was continually losing one company of his men after another. Some scouts ascertained that he, and many of his men, were at a certain place upon Taunton River, and, from appearances, were about to repass it. His camp was now at this place, and the chief of his warriors with him. Some soldiers from Bridgewater fell upon them here, on Sunday, July 30, and killed ten warriors; but *Philip*, having disguised himself, escaped.‡ His uncle, *Akkompoin*, was among the slain, and his own sister taken prisoner.

The late attempt by *Philip* upon Taunton had caused the people of Bridgewater to be more watchful, and some were continually on the scout. Some time in the day, Saturday, 29 July, four men, as they were ranging the woods, discovered one Indian, and, rightly judging there were more at hand, made all haste to inform the other inhabitants of Bridgewater of their discovery *Comfort Willis* and *Joseph Edson* were "pressed" to go "post" to the governor of Plimouth, at Marshfield, who "went to Plimouth with them, the next day, [30 July,] to send Captain *Church* with his company. And Captain *Church* came with them to Monponset on the sabbath, and came no further that day, he told them he would meet them the next day." Here *Willis* and *Edson* left him, and arrived at home in the evening. Upon hearing of the arrival of *Church* in their neighborhood, 21 men "went out on Monday, supposing to meet with Captain *Church;* but they came upon the enemy and fought with them, and took 17 of them alive, and also much plunder. And they all returned, and not one of them fell by the enemy; and received no help from *Church*." This account is given from an old manuscript, but who its author was is not certain.§ *Church's* account differs considerably from it. He says, that on the evening of the same day he and his company marched from Plimouth, "they heard a smart firing at a distance from them, but it

---

* Old Indian Chronicle 79, 92, 93.—*Hubbard*, 80.—*Gookin's* MS. Hist.—A son of Captain *Wadsworth* caused a monument to be erected upon the place of this fight, with an inscription upon it, which time has discovered to be erroneous in some of its historical particulars. It was recently standing to the west of Sudbury causeway, about a quarter of a mile from the great road that leads from Boston to Worcester. *Hoyt*, 122. *Holmes*, i. 380.

† A captive negro made his escape from *Philip's* men, and gave notice of their intention; "whereupon the inhabitants stood upon their guard, and souldiers were timously sent in to them for their relief and defence." *Prevalency of Prayer*, 8.

‡ "'Tis said that he had newly cut off his hair, that he might not be known." *Hubbard, Nar.* 101.

§ It is published by Mr. *Mitchell*, in his valuable account of Bridgewater, and supposed to have been written by *Comfort Willis*, named above. See 2 Coll. Mass. Hist. Soc. vii. 157.

being near night, and the firing of short continuance, they missed the place, and went into Bridgewater town."

On the 1 August, the intrepid *Church* came upon *Philip's* head-quarters, killed and took about 130 of his people, *Philip* himself very narrowly escaping. Such was his precipitation, that he left all his wampum behind, and his wife and son fell into the hands of *Church.*

No sooner had the story of the destruction of the Indians begun to attract attention, (which, however, was not until a long time after they had been destroyed,) much inquiry was made concerning the fate of this son of the famous *Metacomet;* and it was not until considerable time had elapsed, that it was discovered that he was sold into slavery! It is gratifying to learn what did become of him, although the knowledge of the fact must cause pain in every humane breast; not more for the lot of young *Metacomet,* than for the wretched depravity of the minds of those who advised and executed the decree of slavery upon him.

Great numbers of *Philip's* people were sold for slaves in foreign countries. In the beginning of the war Captain *Mosely* captured 80, who were confined at Plimouth. In September following, 178 were put on board a vessel commanded by Captain *Sprague,* who sailed from Plimouth with them for Spain.

*Church** relates the attack of Aug. 1 upon the flying chief as follows:—"Next morning, [after the skirmish in which *Akkompoin* was killed,] Capt. *Church* moved very early with his company, which was increased by many of Bridgewater that listed under him for that expedition, and, by their piloting, he soon came, very still, to the top of the great tree which the enemy had fallen across the river; and the captain spied an Indian sitting upon the stump of it, on the other side of the river, and he clapped his gun up, and had doubtless despatched him, but that one of his own Indians called hastily to him not to fire, for he believed it was one of his own men: upon which the Indian upon the stump looked about, and Capt. *Church's* Indian, seeing his face, perceived his mistake, for he knew him to be *Philip;* clapped up his gun and fired, but it was too late; for *Philip* immediately threw himself off the stump, leaped down a bank on the side of the river, and made his escape. Capt. *Church,* as soon as possible, got over the river, and scattered in quest of *Philip* and his company, but the enemy scattered and fled every way; but he picked up a considerable many of their women and children, among which were *Philip's* wife and son of about nine years old." The remainder of the day was spent in pursuing the flying *Philip,* who, with his Narragansets, was still formidable. They picked up many prisoners, from whom they learned the force of those of whom they were in pursuit. At night, *Church* was under obligation to return to his men he had left, but commissioned *Lightfoot,* captain, to lead a party on discovery. *Lightfoot* returned in the morning with good success, having made an important discovery, and taken 13 prisoners. *Church* immediately set out to follow up their advantage He soon came where they had made fires, and shortly after overtook their women and children, who "were faint and tired," and who informed them "that *Philip,* with a great number of the enemy, were a little before." It was almost sunset when they came near enough to observe them, and "*Philip* soon came to a stop, and fell to breaking and chopping wood, to make fires; and a great noise they made." *Church,* concentrating his followers, formed them into a circle, and set down "without any noise or fire." Their prisoners showed great signs of fear, but were easily put in confidence by the conciliatory conduct of *Church.* Thus stood matters in *Church's* camp through the night of the 2 August, 1676. At dawn of day, he told his prisoners they must remain still where they were, until the fight was over, (for he now had every reason to expect a severe one shortly to follow,) "or, as soon as the firing ceased, they must follow the tracks of his company, and come to them. (An Indian is next to a bloodhound to follow a track.)"†

It being now light enough to make the onset, *Church* sent forward two soldiers to learn *Philip's* position. *Philip,* no less wary, had, at the same time, sent out two spies, to see if any were in pursuit of him. The re-

* Hist. *Philip's* War, 38, ed. 4to. † Ibid. 39.

spective spies of the two famous chiefs gave the alarm to both camps at the same time; but, unhappily for *Philip*, his antagonist was prepared for the event, while he was not. "All fled at the first tidings, [of the spies,] left their kettles boiling, and meat roasting upon their wooden spits, and run into a swamp with no other breakfast, than what Capt. *Church* afterwards treated them with." *Church* sent his lieutenant, Mr. *Isaac Howland*, on one side of the swamp, while himself ran upon the other, each with a small party, hoping, as the swamp was small, to prevent the escape of any. Expecting that when *Philip* should discover the English at the farther extremity of the swamp, he would turn back in his own track, and so escape at the same place he entered, *Church* had, therefore, stationed an ambush to entrap him in such an event. But the wariness of *Philip* disappointed him. He, thinking that the English would pursue him into the swamp, had formed an ambush for them also, but was, in like manner, disappointed. He had, at the same time, sent forward a band of his warriors, who fell into the hands of *Church* and *Howland*. They, at first, attempted to fly, and then offered resistance; but *Church* ordered *Matthias* * to tell them the impracticability of such a step. He accordingly called to them, and said, "*If they fired one gun they were all dead men.*" This threat, with the presence of the English and Indians, so amazed them, that they suffered "the English to come and take the guns out of their hands, when they were both charged and cocked." Having secured these with a guard, armed with the guns just taken from them, *Church* presses through the swamp in search of *Philip*, towards the end at which that chief had entered. Having waited until he had no hopes of ensnaring Captain *Church*, *Philip* now moved on after the company he had sent forward, and thus the two parties met. The English had the advantage of the first discovery, and, covered by trees, made the first fire. *Philip* stood his ground for a time, and maintained a desperate fight; but, a main body of his warriors having been captured, which, by this time, he began to apprehend, as they did not come to his aid, he, therefore, fled back to the point where he entered the swamp, and thus fell into a second ambush. Here the English were worsted, having one of their number slain, viz. *Thomas Lucas*, † of Plimouth: thus escaped, for a few days, *Philip* and some of his best captains: such were *Tuspaquin* and *Tatoson*. This was August the 3d, and *Philip's* numbers had decreased, since the 1st, 173, by the exertions of *Church*. ‡

Philip, having now but few followers left, was driven from place to place, and lastly to his ancient seat near Pokanoket. The English, for a long time, had endeavored to kill him, but could not find him off his guard; for he was always the first who was apprized of their approach. He having put to death one of his own men for advising him to make peace, this man's brother, whose name was *Alderman*, fearing the same fate, deserted him, and gave Captain *Church* an account of his situation, and offered to lead him to his camp. Early on Saturday morning, 12 Aug., *Church* came to the swamp where *Philip* was encamped, and, before he was discovered, had placed a guard about it, so as to encompass it, except a small place. He then ordered Captain *Golding* § to rush into the swamp, and fall upon *Philip* in his camp; which he immediately did—but was discovered as he approached, and, as usual, *Philip* was the first to fly. Having but just awaked from sleep, and having on but a part of his clothes, he fled with all his might. Coming directly upon an Englishman and an Indian, who composed a part of the ambush at the edge of the swamp, the Englishman's gun missed fire, but *Alderman*, the Indian, whose gun was loaded with two balls, "sent

---

* One of *Church's* Indian soldiers, but of whom *he* makes no mention.

† An improvident fellow, given to intoxication, and, from *Church's* expression about his being killed, "not being so careful as he might have been," it leaves room to doubt whether he were not, at this time, under the effects of liquor. He had been often fined, and once whipped, for getting drunk, beating his wife and children, defaming the character of deceased magistrates, and other misdemeanors.

‡ *Church*, 41. In the account of *Tatoson*, *Church's* narrative is continued.

§ Captain *Roger Goulden*, of R. I. Plimouth granted him 100 acres of land on Pocasset, in 1676, for his eminent services. *Plim. Records.*

one through his heart, and another not above two inches from it. He fell upon his face in the mud and water, with his gun under him."

"Cold, with the beast he slew, he sleeps;
O'er him no filial spirit weeps;
* * * * * * * *
Even that he lived, is for his conqueror's tongue;
By foes alone his death-song must be sung;
No chronicles but theirs shall tell
His mournful doom to future times;
May these upon his virtues dwell,
And in his fate forget his crimes."—Sprague.

The name of the man stationed with *Alderman* was *Caleb Cook*,* who had shared in many of *Church's* hazardous expeditions before the present. Seeing that he could not have the honor of killing *Philip*, he was desirous, if possible, of having a memento of the mighty exploit. He therefore prevailed upon *Alderman* to exchange guns with him. This gun was kept in the family until the present century, when the late *Isaac Lothrop*, Esq. of Plimouth obtained the lock of it from Mr. *Sylvanus Cook*, late of Kingston. *Sylvanus* was great-grandson of *Caleb*.† The stock and barrel of the gun are still retained by the descendants of the name of *Cook*.‡ There is a gun-lock shown in the library of the Mass. Hist. Soc. said to be the same which *Alderman* used in shooting *Philip*. This *Alderman* was a subject of *Weetamoo*, who, in the commencement of this war, went to the governor of Plimouth, and desired to remain in peace with the English, and immediately took up his residence upon an island, remote from the tribes engaged in it. But, after *Philip* had returned to his own country, *Alderman*, upon some occasion, visited him. It was at this time that he learned the fate of his brother before spoken of; or he may have been killed in his presence. This caused his flight to the English, which he thought, probably, the last resort for vengeance. He "came down from thence, says *Church;* (where *Philip's* camp now was,) on to Sand Point over against *Trips*, and hollow'd, and made signs to be fetch'd over" to the island. He was immediately brought over, and gave the information desired. Captain *Church* had but just arrived upon Rhode Island, and was about eight miles from the upper end, where *Alderman* landed. He had been at home but a few minutes, when "they spy'd two horsemen coming a great pace," and, as he prophesied, "they came with tydings." Major *Sanford* and Capt. *Golding* were the horsemen, "who immediately ask'd Capt. *Church what he would give to hear some news of Philip.* He reply'd, *That was what he wanted.*" The expedition was at once entered upon, and *Alderman* went as their pilot. But to return to the fall of *Philip*:—

"By this time," continues *Church*, "the enemy perceived they were waylaid on the east side of the swamp, tacked short about," and were led out of their dangerous situation by the great Captain *Annawon*. "The man that had shot down *Philip* ran with all speed to Capt. *Church*, and informed him of his exploit, who commanded him to be silent about it, and let no man more know it until they had drove the swamp clean; but when they had drove the swamp through, and found the enemy had escaped, or at least the most of them, and the sun now up, and the dew so gone that they could not easily track them, the whole company met together at the place where the enemy's night shelter was, and then Capt. *Church* gave them the news of *Philip's* death. Upon which the whole army§ gave three loud huzzas. Capt. *Church* ordered his body to be pulled out of the mire on to the upland. So some of Capt. *Church's* Indians took hold of him by his stockings, and

* *Baylies*, in his N. Plymouth, ii. 168, says his name was *Francis;* but as he gives no authority, we adhere to older authority.

† This *Caleb Cook* was son of *Jacob*, of Plimouth, and was born there 29 Mar. 1651. He had two or more brothers; *Jacob*, born 14 May, 1653, and *Francis*, 5 Jan. 1663—4. Hence it is not probable that *Francis* was a soldier at this time, as he was only in his 13th year.

‡ *Col. Mass. Hist. Soc.* iv. 63.

§ Eighteen English and twenty-two Indians constituted his army a week before; but we know not how many were at the taking of *Philip*, though we may suppose about the same number. Hence this expedition cost the colony £9.

some by his small breeches, being otherwise naked, and drew him through the mud into the upland; and a doleful, great, naked dirty beast, he looked like." Captain *Church* then said, "*Forasmuch as he has caused many an Englishman's body to lie unburied and rot above ground, not one of his bones shall be buried!*"

With the great chief, fell five of his most trusty followers, one of whom was his chief captain's son,* and the very Indian who fired the first gun at the commencement of the war.

"*Philip* having one very remarkable hand, being much scarred, occasioned by the splitting of a pistol in it formerly, Capt. *Church* gave the head and that hand to *Alderman*, the Indian who shot him, to show to such gentlemen as would bestow gratuities upon him; and accordingly he got many a penny by it."†

The barbarous usage of beheading and quartering traitors was now executed upon the fallen *Philip*. *Church*, "calling his old Indian executioner, bid him behead and quarter him. Accordingly, he came with his hatchet, and stood over him, but before he struck, he made a small speech, directing it to *Philip*," saying, "*You have been a very great man, and have made many a man afraid of you; but so big as you be I will now chop your ass for you.*" He then proceeded to the execution of his orders.

His head was sent to Plimouth, where it was exposed upon a gibbet for 20 years, and one of his hands to Boston, where it was exhibited in savage triumph, and his mangled body was denied the right of sepulture. It having been quartered, was hung upon four trees, and there left as a monument of shocking barbarity.

Church and his company returned to the island the same day, and arrived with the prisoners at Plimouth two days after, namely, Tuesday, August 15, "ranging through all the woods in their way." They now "received their premium, which was 30 *shillings* per head," for all enemies killed or taken, "instead of all wages, and *Philip's* head went at the same price." *This amounted to only four and sixpence a-piece*, "which was all the reward they had, except the honor of killing *Philip*."

Having in the year 1824 visited the memorable retreat of the Wampanoag sachems, we can give the reader some idea of its situation. There is a natural angular excavation, in an almost perpendicular rock, about 6 or 7 feet from its base, where it is said *Philip* and some of his chief men were surprised on the morning of the 12 August. We have in the Life of *Massasoit* described Mount Hope, and it is at the north part of it that the nigh rock is situated; variously estimated from 30 to 50 feet in height, and is nearly 2 miles from the village of Bristol. From the seat, or throne of KING PHILIP as some have called it, a fine view of Mount Hope Bay opens upon us. Near the foot of the rock is a fine spring of water, known to this day by the name of *Philip's Spring*.

Mr. *Alden*, the curious collector of epitaphs, says "the late Lieut. Gov. *Bradford*, [who died at Bristol in 1808,] in early life, knew an aged squaw, who was one of *Philip's* tribe, was well acquainted with this sagamore in her youthful days, and had often been in his wigwam. The information, through her, is, therefore, very direct, as to the identical spot, where he fixed his abode. It was a few steps south of Capt. *James De Wolfe's* summer house, near the brow of a hill, but no vestige of the wigwam remains. The eastern side of this hill is very steep, vastly more so than that at Horse Neck, down which the intrepid *Putnam* trotted his sure-footed steed, in a manner worthy of a knight of the tenth century." "When *Church's* men were about to rush upon *Philip*, he is said to have evaded them by springing from his wigwam as they were entering it, and rolling, like a hogshead, down the precipice, which looks towards the bay. Having reached the lower part of this frightful ledge of rocks, without breaking his bones, he got upon his feet, and ran along the shore in a north-eastern direction, about 100 rods, and endeavored to screen himself in a swamp, then a quagmire, but now terra firma."

* Very probably a son of *Uncompoin*, or *Woonashum*. † *Philip's* War.

How much of the above is apocryphal is uncertain, but that a part of it is I have no doubt. That *Philip's* camp was near the top of Mount Hope at the time he was surprised, is contrary to rational conclusion, but seems rather to have been fixed there by the imagination of some one, for the pleasure it might afford them in contemplating the manner of the chief's escape by rolling down a rugged precipice.

During the bloody contest, the pious fathers wrestled long and often with their God, in prayer, that he would prosper their arms and deliver their enemies into their hands; and when, upon stated days of prayer, the Indians gained advantage, it was looked upon as a rebuke of Providence, and animated them to greater sincerity and fervor; and on the contrary, when their arms prevailed upon such days, it was viewed as an immediate interposition in their favor. The philosophic mind will be shocked at the expressions of some, very eminent in that day for piety and excellence of moral life. Dr. *Increase Mather*,* in speaking of the efficacy of prayer, in bringing about the destruction of the Indians, says, "Nor could they [the English] cease crying to the Lord against *Philip*, until they had prayed the bullet into his heart." And in speaking of the slaughter of *Philip's* people, at Narraganset, he says, "We have heard of two-and-twenty Indian captains, slain all of them, and brought down to hell in one day." Again, in speaking of a chief who had sneered at the English religion, and who had, "withal, added a most hideous blasphemy, immediately upon which a bullet took him in the head, and dashed out his brains, sending his cursed soul in a moment amongst the devils, and blasphemers, in hell forever." †

The low and vulgar epithets ‡ sneeringly cast upon the Indians by their English contemporaries are not to be attributed to a single individual, but to the English in general.§ It is too obvious that the early historians viewed the Indians as inferior beings, and some went so far as hardly to allow them *to be* human.

Like *Massasoit*, *Philip* always opposed the introduction of Christianity among his people. When Mr. *Eliot* urged upon him its great importance, he said he cared no more for the gospel than he did for a button upon his coat. ‖ This does not very well agree with the account of Mr. *Gookin*, respecting *Philip's* feelings upon religious matters; at least, it shows that there was a time when he was willing to listen to such men as the excellent and benevolent *Gookin*. In speaking of the Wampanoags, he says, "There are some that have hopes of their greatest and chiefest sachem, named *Philip*, living at Pawkunnawkutt. Some of his chief men, as I hear, stand well inclined to hear the gospel: and himself is a person of good understanding and knowledge in the best things. I have heard him speak very good words, arguing that his conscience is convicted: but yet, though his will is bowed to embrace *Jesus Christ*, his sensual and carnal lusts are strong bands to hold him fast under *Satan's* dominions." ¶ And Dr. *Mather* adds, "It was not long, before the hand which now writes, [1700,] upon a certain occasion took off the jaw from the exposed *skull* of that blasphemous *leviathan;* and the renowned *Samuel Lee* hath since been a pastor to an English congregation, sounding and showing the praises of heaven, upon that very spot of ground, where *Philip* and his Indians were lately worshipping of the devil." **

The error that *Philip* was grandson to *Massasoit*, is so well known to be such, that it would hardly seem to have required notice, but to inform the

* In his "Prevalency of Prayer," page 10. † Ibid. page 7.

‡ Such as *dogs, wolves, blood-hounds, demons, devils-incarnate, caitiffs, hell-hounds, fiends monsters, beasts*, &c. Occasional quotations will show what authors have used these.

§ The author of "*Indian Tales*" has fathered all he could think of upon Mr. *Hubbard*. He *may be* called upon to point out the passage in that valuable author's works where he has called one or *any* of the Indians "*hell-hounds.*" Such loose, gratuitous expressions will not do at the bar of history.

‖ Magnalia.

¶ 1 *Coll. Mass. Hist. Soc.* i. 200.

** Mr. *Lee* was taken by the French in a voyage to England, and carried into their country, where he died, in 1691. This event, it was thought, hastened his end. Perhaps the surviving natives did not attribute the disaster to his usurping their territory, and teaching a religion they could not believe; but might they not with equal propriety?

reader of its origin. The following passage from *John Josselyn's* work * will, besides proving him to be the author of the error, at least the first writer that so denominates him, furnish some valuable information. Speaking of the Indians in general, he says, "Their beads are their money; of these, there are two sorts, blue beads and white beads; the first is their gold, the last their silver. These they work out of certain shells, so cunningly, that neither *Jew* nor *Devil* can counterfeit.† They drill them and string them, and make many curious works with them, to adorn the persons of their sagamores and principal men, and young women, as belts, girdles, tablets, borders for their women's hair, bracelets, necklaces, and links to hang in their ears. Prince *Philip*, a little before I came for England, [1671,] coming to Boston, had a coat on and buskins set thick with these beads, in pleasant wild works, and a broad belt of the same; his accoutrements were valued at £20. The English merchant giveth them 10*s*. a fathom for their white, and as much more, or near upon, for their blue beads." "The roytelet now of the Pocanakets is prince *Philip*, alias *Metacon*, the grandson of *Massasoit*." ‡

While Mrs. *Rowlandson* was a captive in the wilderness with the allies of *Philip*, she mentions meeting with him; and although she speaks often with bitterness of the Indians in general, yet of him nothing of that nature appears in her journal. The party she was with visited *Philip* on the west side of the Connecticut, about five miles above Northfield, then called *Squakeag*. Having arrived at the point of crossing, Mrs. *Rowlandson* says, "We must go over the river to *Philip's* crew. When I was in the canoe, I could not but be amazed at the numerous crew of pagans that were on the bank on the other side." She was much afraid they meant to kill her here, but, being assured to the contrary, become more resigned to her fate. "Then came one of them, (she says,) and gave me two spoonfuls of meal (to comfort me,) and another gave me half a pint of peas, which was worth more than many bushels at another time. Then I went to see King *Philip;* he bade me come in and sit down; and asked me whether I would smoke it; (a usual compliment now a days, among the saints and sinners;) but this no ways suited me." §

"During my abode in this place, *Philip* spake to me to make a shirt for his boy, which I did; for which he gave me a shilling." "Afterward he asked me to make a cap for his boy, for which he invited me to dinner, I went, and he gave me a pancake, about as big as two fingers; it was made of parched wheat, beaten and fried in bears' grease; but I thought I never tasted pleasanter meat in my life." ‖

It is extremely gratifying to hear any testimony in favor of the humanity of a chief who in his time was so much execrated. To say the least of *Philip's* humanity, it was as great towards captives, so far as we have any knowledge, as was that of *any* of the English to the captive Indians.

As the Indians were returning from their recesses upon the Connecticut, (in what is now New Hampshire and Vermont,) towards Wachuset, "having indeed my life, (says Mrs. *Rowandson*,) but little spirit, *Philip*, who was in the company, came up, and took me by the hand, and said, '*Two weeks more and you shall be mistress again.*' I asked him if he spoke true: he said, '*Yes, and quickly you shall come to your master* ¶ *again*,' who had been gone from us three weeks." **

In bringing our account of this truly great man towards a close, we must not forget to present the reader with a specimen of the language in which he spoke. The following is the Lord's prayer in Wampanoag:—

Noo-shun kes-uk-qut, qut-tian-at-am-unch koo-we-su-onk, kuk-ket-as-soo-tam-oonk pey-au-moo-utch, kut-te-nan-tam-oo-onk ne nai, ne-ya-ne ke-suk-qut

---

* Account of two Voyages to New England, 142, 143.

† Of this he was misinformed. There was much spurious wampum, which became a subject of legislation. See *Hazard's Hist. Col.* vol. ii.

‡ Account of two Voyages to New England, 146. He is also called grandson of *Massasoit*, in the work entitled *Present State of New England, in respect to the Indian War*, fol London, 1676; the author of that work doubtless copied from *Josselyn*.

§ *Narrative of her Captivity*, 38, 39.

‖ Ibid. 40

¶ *Quinnapin*. See his Life

** Narrative of Mrs. *Rowlandson*, 63

kah oh-ke-it. ***As-sa-ma-i-in-ne-an*** *ko-ko-ke-suk-o-da-e nut-as-e-suk-ok-ke pe-****tuk-qun-neg.*** *Kah* ***ah-quo-an-tam-a-i-in-ne-an*** *num-match-e-se-ong-an-on-ash,* ***ne-wutch-e ne-na-wun wonk*** *nut-ah-quo-an-tam-au-o-un-non-og nish-noh pasuk* ***noo-na-mon-tuk-quoh-who-nan,*** *kah ahque sag-kom-pa-gin-ne-an en qutch-e-het-tu-ong-a-nit, qut poh-qua-wus-sin-ne-an wutch match-i-tut.**

Since we are upon curiosities, the following may very properly be added. There is to be seen in the library of the Mass. Hist. Society a large skimmer, which some have mistaken for a bowl, cut out of the root of ash, that will hold about two quarts. On this article is this historical inscription, in gilt letters: "*A trophy from the wigwam of* King Philip; *when he was slain in* 1676, *by* Richard; *presented by* Ebenezer Richard, *his grandson.*" †

CHAPTER III.

LIVES OF PHILIP'S CHIEF CAPTAINS.

Nanuntenoo—*Reasons for his aiding Philip—His former name—Meets the English and Indians under Captain Peirse—Fights and destroys his whole company at Pawtucket—Incidents relating to that fight—Notice of Captain Peirse—Nanuntenoo surprised and taken—His magnanimity—Speech to his captors—Is executed and his body burnt — Cassassinnamon — Catapazet — Monopoide —* Annawon — *His escape from the swamp when Philip was killed—Captain Church sent out to capture him—Discovers his retreat—Takes him prisoner—His magnanimous behavior—His speech to Church—Presents him with Philip's ornaments—Description of them—Church takes Annawon to Plimouth, where he is put to death—*Quinnapin—*His connections and marriage—At the capture of Lancaster—Account of his wives—Weetamoo—He is taken and shot—*Tuspaquin—*His sales of lands—His operations in Philip's War—Surrenders himself, and is put to death—Reflections upon his executioners—*Tatoson—*Early notices of— Captures a garrison in Plimouth—Trial and execution of Keweenam—Totoson dies of a broken heart—*Barrow *cruelly murdered—*Tyasks.

NANUNTENOO, son of *Miantunnomoh,* "was chief sachem of all the Narragansets, and heir of all his father's pride and insolency, as well as of his malice against the English." ‡ Notwithstanding this branding character, drawn by a contemporary, we need only look into the life of *Miantunnomoh,* to find excuse for "malice and insolency" tenfold more than was contained in the breast of *Nanuntenoo.*

The English had cut to pieces the women and children of his tribe, burned them to death in their wigwams, and left their mangled bodies bleaching in the wintry blast! The swamp fight of the 19 Dec. 1675, could not be forgotten! *Nanuntenoo* escaped from this scene, but we cannot doubt that he acquitted himself agreeably to the character we have of him.

The first name by which he was known to the English was *Canonchet,* though, like others, his name was written with many variations. In 1674, he was styled "chief surviving sachem of Narraganset," and in a deed in which he was so styled his name is written "*Nawnawnoantonnew* alias *Quananchit,* eldest son now living of *Miantomomio.*" § He had been in Boston the October before the war, upon a treaty, at which time he received, among other presents, a silver-laced coat. Dr. *Mather* says, speaking of the Narragansets, "their great sachem called *Quanonchet,* was a principal ringleader in the Narraganset war, and had as great an interest and influence, as can be said of

---

* *Eliot's* Indian Bible, Luke xi. 2—4.

† No mention is made to whom, or when it was presented. It does not appear to us to be of such antiquity as its inscription pretends; and the truth of which may very reasonably be questioned, in this particular, when the more glaring error of the name of the person said to have killed *Philip,* is staring us in the face.

‡ *Hubbard,* 67.—Mr. *Oldmixon* calls him "the mighty sachem of Narraganset."—*Brit. Empire.*

§ *Potter's* Hist. Narraganset, *Coll. R. Hist. Soc.* iii. 172.

any among the Indians;"* and that, "when *he* was taken and slain, it was an amazing stroke to the enemy."†

The name of *Canonchet* stands first to the treaty, to which we have just alluded, which was entered into at Boston, 18 Oct. 1675. By that treaty, the Narragansets agreed to deliver to the English in 10 days, "all and euery one of the said Indians, whether belonging vnto *Philip*, the Pocasset Sqva, or the Saconett Indians, Quabaug, Hadley, or any other sachems or people that haue bin or are in hostillitie with the English, or any of their allies or abettors."‡ The names to the treaty are as follows:

"QUANANCHETT'S ✓ *mark*, *sachem in behalf of himself and* Conanacus *and the* Old Queen *and* Pomham *and* Quaunapeen, (seal)
MANATANNOO *counceller his* + *mark, and* Cannonacus *in his behalf*, (seal)
AHANMANPOWETT'S + *mark*, *counceller and his* (seal)
CORNMAN, *cheiffe counceller to* Ninnegrett, *in his behalfe, and a seal* (S.)"

Witnesses.
RICHARD SMITH,
JAMES BROWNE,
SAMUEL GORTON, *Jr.*
Interpreters.
JOHN NOWHENETT'S × *mark*,
Indian interpreter.

The Indians having carried their whirlwind of war to the very doors of Plimouth, caused the sending out of Captain *Peirce*, (or as his name is uniformly in the records, *Peirse*,) to divert them from these ravages, and destroy as many of them as he was able. He had a large company, consisting of 70 men, 20 of whom were friendly Indians. With these, no doubt, *Peirse* thought himself safe against any power of the Indians in that region.

Meanwhile this most valiant chief captain of the Narragansets, *Nanuntenoo*,§ learning, we presume, by his spies, the direction the English were taking assembled his warriors at a crossing place on Pawtucket River, at a point adjacent to a place since called *Attleborough-Gore*, and not far distant from Pawtucket falls. It is judged that *Nanuntenoo* was upon an expedition to attack Plimouth, or some of the adjacent towns, for his force was estimated at upwards of 300 men.

On arriving at this fatal place, some of *Nanuntenoo's* men showed themselves retiring, on the opposite side of the river. This stratagem succeeded,—*Peirse* followed.‖ No sooner was he upon the western side, than the warriors of *Nanuntenoo*, like an avalanche from a mountain, rushed down upon him; nor striving for coverts from which to fight, more than their foes, fought them face to face with the most determined bravery.

A part of *Nanuntenoo's* force remained on the east side of the river, to prevent the retreat of the English, which they most effectually did, as in the event will appear. When Captain *Peirse* saw himself hemmed in by numbers on every side, he drew up his men upon the margin of the river, in two ranks, back to back,¶ and in this manner fought until nearly all of them were slain. *Peirse* had timely sent a messenger to Providence for assistance, and although the distance could not have been more than six or eight miles, from some inexplicable cause, no succor arrived; and Mr. *Hubbard*** adds, "As Solomon saith, a faithful messenger is as snow in harvest."

This dreadful fight was on Sunday, 26 March, 1676, when, as Dr. *Mather* says, "Capt. *Peirse* was slain and forty and nine English with him, and eight, (or more,) Indians, who did assist the English." The Rev. Mr. *Newman* of Rehoboth wrote a letter to Plimouth, dated the day after the slaughter, in

* *Brief Hist.* 26. † *Prevalency of Prayer*, 11.

‡ It may be seen at large in *Hazard's Collections*, i. 536, 537.

§ That *Nanuntenoo* commanded in person in the fight with the force under Capt. *Peirse* has been a question; indeed, our only authority is not very explicit upon the matter, (*Hubbard*, Postscript 7.) who observes that when *Denison* surprised him, he "was, at that moment, divertizing himself with the recital of Capt. *Peirse's* slaughter, surprized by his men a few days before."

‖ Dr. *Mather* (Brief Hist. 24.) says, "a small number of the enemy who in desperate subtlety ran away from them, and they went limping to make the English believe they were lame," and thus effected their object.

¶ *Deane's* Hist. Scituate, 121 ** Narrative, 64.

which he says, "52 of our English, and 11 Indians," were slain.* The company was, no doubt, increased by some who volunteered as they marched through the country, or by such as were taken for pilots.

Nanuntenoo's victory was complete, but, as usual on such occasions, the English consoled themselves by making the loss of the Indians appear as large as possible. Dr. *Mather* says, that some Indians that were afterwards taken confessed they lost 140, which, no doubt, is not far from the truth.†

An Englishman, and perhaps the only one who escaped from this disastrous fight, was saved by one of the friendly Indians in this manner: The friendly Indian being taken for a Narraganset, as he was pursuing with an uplifted tomahawk the English soldier, no one interfered, seeing him pursue an unarmed Englishman at such great advantage. In this manner, covering themselves in the woods, they escaped.

A friendly Indian, being pursued by one of *Nanuntenoo's* men, got behind the roots of a fallen tree. Thus screened by the earth raised upon them, the Indian that pursued waited for him to run from his natural fort, knowing he would not dare to maintain it long. The other soon thought of an expedient, which was to make a port-hole in his breast-work, which he easily did by digging through the dirt. When he had done this, he put his gun through, and shot his pursuer, then fled in perfect safety.

Another escaped in a manner very similar. In his flight he got behind a arge rock. This afforded him a good shelter, but in the end he saw nothing but certain death, and the longer he held out the more misery he must suffer. In this deplorable situation, he bethought himself to try the following device. Putting his cap upon his gun, he raised it very gradually above the rock, as though to discover the position of his enemy: it had the desired effect—he fired upon it. The one behind the rock now rushed upon him, before he could reload his gun, and despatched him. Thus, as Mr. *Hubbard* says, "it is worth the noting, what faithfulness and courage some of the Christian Indians showed in this fight." That this most excellent author did not approve of the severity exercised towards those who appeared friendly, is abundantly proved by his writings. In another place he says, "Possibly if some of the English had not been too shy in making use of such of them as were well affected to their interest, they never need have suffered so much from their enemies."

A notice may be reasonably expected of the unfortunate Captain *Michael Peirse*, of Scituate. He was one of those adventurous spirits "who never knew fear," and who sought rather than shrunk from dangers. He was, like his great antagonist, in the Narraganset fight; and in 1673, when the government of Plimouth raised a force to go against the Dutch, who had encroached upon them in Connecticut, he was appointed ensign in one of the companies. He resided in several places before going to Plimouth. Mr. *Deane*, in his *History of Scituate*, gives a genealogical account of his family, from which we learn that he had a second wife, and several sons and daughters. Of what family he was, there is no mention.‡ He possessed considerable estate, and made his will on engaging in the war with the Indians.

The "sore defeat" of Captain *Peirse*, and the tide of the Indians' successes about this time, caused the United Colonies to send out almost their whole strength.

Nanuntenoo came down from the country upon Connecticut River, early in March, for the purpose of collecting seed corn to plant such ground as the English had been driven from, and to effect any other object he might meet with. Whether he had effected the first-named object before falling in with *Peirse*, we are not able to state; but certain it is, that he was but few days after encamped very near the ground where the fight had been, and was there fallen

---

* See the letter giving the names of the company in *Deane's* Scituate, 122, 123.

† Mr. *Hubbard's* account is *the same.*

‡ In the *Records of Plimouth*, under date March, 1669, there is this entry:—"*Miche. Peirse* of Scittuate" was presented at the court for vnseemly carriages towards *Sarah Nichols* of Scittuate," and "forasmuch as there appeared but one testimony to the p'sentment, and that the testimony was written and not read vnto the deponant, the court saw cause to remit the said p'sentment."

upon at unawares, when but a few of his men were present, and there taken prisoner.

Nanuntenoo was nearly as much dreaded as *Philip* himself, and consequently his capture caused great rejoicing among his enemies, and requires to be particularly related.

Four volunteer companies from Connecticut began their march into the enemy's country the next day after Pawtucket fight. Among the captains of these companies, *George Denison* of Southerton was the most conspicuous. The others were commanded by *James Avery*, *John Staunton*, and Major *Palmer*, who also had the chief command. With these were three companies of Indians; one led by *Oneko*, composed of Mohegans; one of Pequots, by *Cassasinnamon;* and the other of Nianticks, by *Catapazet;* in all about 80.

When this formidable army came near to *Nanuntenoo's* camp, on the first week in April, 1676, "they met with a stout Indian of the enemie's, whom they presently slew, and two old squaws," who informed them of the situation of *Nanuntenoo.* At the same time, their own scouts brought the same intelligence. The news of the enemy's approach reached the chief in his tent when but seven of his men were about him; the rest were probably in the neighborhood attending to their ordinary affairs. And although he had stationed two sentinels upon an adjacent hill, to give him timely notice if any appeared, their surprise was so great, at the sudden approach of the English, that, in their fright, they ran by their sachem's wigwam, "as if they wanted time to tell what they saw." Seeing this, the sachem sent a third, to learn the cause of the flight of the two first, but he fled in the same manner; and lastly he sent two more, one of which, "either endued with more courage, or a better sense of his duty, informed him in great haste that all the English army was upon him: whereupon, having no time to consult, and but little to attempt an escape, and no means to defend himself, he began"* to fly with all speed. Running with great swiftness around the hill, to get out of sight upon the opposite side, he was distinguished by his wary pursuers, and they immediately followed him with that eagerness their important object was calculated to inspire.

The pursuers of the flying chief were *Catapazet* and his Nianticks, "and a few of the English lightest of foot." Seeing these were gaining upon him, he first cast off his blanket, then his silver-laced coat, and lastly his belt of peag. On seeing these, a doubt no longer remained of its being *Nanuntenoo*, which rged them, if possible, faster in the chase. There was in the company of *Catapazet*, one *Monopoide*, a Pequot, who outran all his companions, and who, gaining upon *Nanuntenoo*, as he fled upon the side of the river, obliged him to attempt to cross it sooner than he intended. Nevertheless, but for an accident in his passage, he would doubtless have effected his escape. As he was wading through the river, his foot slipped upon a stone, which brought his gun under water. Thus losing some time in recovering himself, and also the use of his gun, it probably made him despair of escaping; for *Monopoide* came up and seized upon him, "within 30 rods of the river side."

Nanuntenoo, having made up his mind to surrender, made no resistance, although he was a man of great physical strength, of superior stature, and acknowledged bravery; and the one who seized upon him very ordinary in that respect. One of the first Englishmen that came up was *Robert Staunton*, a young man, who presumed to ask the captured chief some questions. He appeared at first to regard the young man with silent indignity, but at length, casting a disdainful look upon his youthful face, "this manly sachem," said, in broken English, "YOU MUCH CHILD! NO UNDERSTAND MATTERS OF WAR! LET YOUR BROTHER OR CHIEF COME, HIM I WILL ANSWER." And, adds Mr. *Hubbard*, he "was as good as his word: acting herein, as if, by a *Pythagorean* metempsychosis, some old Roman ghost had possessed the body of this western pagan. And, like *Attilius Regulus*,† he

* This elegant passage of Mr. *Hubbard* brings to our mind that inimitable one of *Clavigero*, in his account of the woful days of the Mexicans: "They had neither arms to repel the multitude and fury of their enemies, strength to defend themselves, nor space to fight upon; the ground of the city was covered with dead bodies, and the water of every ditch and canal purpled with blood. *Hist. Mexico*, iii. 73.

† *Marcus Attilius Regulus*, a Roman consul and general, taken prisoner by the Cartha

would not accept of his own life, when it was tendered him." This tender of life to *Nanuntenoo* was, no doubt, upon the condition of his obtaining the submission of his nation. He met the idea with indignation; and when the English told him that he should be put to death if he did not comply, in the most composed manner he replied, that killing him would not end the war. Some of his captors endeavored to reflect upon him, by telling him, that he had said *he would burn the English in their houses*, and that he had boasted, in defiance of his promise last made to the English, which was to deliver the Wampanoags to them, that *he would not deliver up a Wampanoag or the paring of a Wampanoag's nail.* To this he only replied, "OTHERS WERE AS FORWARD FOR THE WAR AS MYSELF, AND I DESIRE TO HEAR NO MORE ABOUT IT."

Had the English not burned his people in *their* houses? Did they ever deliver up any that had committed depredations upon the Narragansets? No! —Who, then, will ask for an excuse for the magnanimous *Nanuntenoo?* So indignant was he at their conduct, that he would hear nothing about peace; "refusing to send an old counsellor of his to make any motion that way," on a promise of life if he would do so.

Under the eye of *Denison*, *Nanuntenoo* was taken to Stonington, where, by the "advice of the English commanders, he was shot." His head was cut off and carried to Hartford, and his body consumed by fire. The English prevailed upon some of each tribe of their allies, viz. Pequots, Mohegans and Nianticks, to be his executioners, "thereby the more firmly to engage the said Indians against the treacherous Narragansets." * "Herein," says another writer † of that day, "the English dealt wisely, for by this means the three Indian nations are become abominable to the other Indians." And a respectable writer ‡ of our own times says, "It may be pleasing to the reader to be informed" of the fate of *Nanuntenoo!*

When it was announced to the noble chief that he must be put to death, he was not in the least daunted, and all he is reported to have said is this:—

"I LIKE IT WELL; I SHALL DIE BEFORE MY HEART IS SOFT, OR HAVE SAID ANY THING UNWORTHY OF MYSELF." With *Nanuntenoo*, fell into the hands of the English 43 others. §

The author of the anonymous "*Letters to London*" ‖ says the Indians were "commanded by that famous but very bloudy and cruel sachem, *Quononshot*, otherwise called *Myantonomy*," whose "carriage was strangely proud and lofty after he was taken; being examined why he did foment that war, which would certainly be the destruction of him and all the heathen Indians in the country, &c., he would make no other reply to any interrogatories, but this: that he was born a prince, and if princes came to speak with him he would answer, but none present being such, he thought himself obliged, in honor, to hold his tongue;" and that he said he would rather die than remain a prisoner, and requested that *Oneko* might put him to death, as he was of equal rank. "Yet withall threatened, he had 2000 men, [who] would revenge his death severely. Wherefore our forces, fearing an escape, put the stoutest men to the sword, but preserved *Myantonomy* till they returned to Stoneington; where our Indian friends, and most of the English soldiers declaring to the commanders their fear that the English should, upon conditions, release him, and that then he would, (though the English might

---

ginians, 251 years B. C. They sent him to Rome to use his endeavors to effect a peace, by his solemn promise to return within a given period. The most excruciating tortures awaited him, should he not execute his mission according to his instructions. When arrived at Rome he exhorted his countrymen to hold out, and maintain the war against the Carthaginians stating their situation, and the great advantages that would accrue. He knew what would be his fate on returning to Carthage, and many a noble Roman besought him not to return, and thus sacrifice his life; but he would not break his promise, even with his barbarous enemies. This is what is meant by not accepting his own life when tendered him. He returned. and, if history be true, no Indian nation ever tortured a prisoner, beyond what the Carthaginians inflicted upon *Marcus Attilius Regulus*. See *Echard's Roman Hist.* i. 188—9.

* *Hubbard.* † *I. Mather.* ‡ *Deane*, Hist. Scituate, 124.

§ Manuscript letter in Hist. Library. Both *Hubbard* and *Mather* say 44; perhaps they included *Nanuntenoo.*

‖ Elsewhere cited as *The Old Indian Chronicle.*

have peace with him,) be very pernicious to those Indians that now assisted us, the said Indians, (on these considerations, and the mischiefs and murthers he had done during this war,) permitted to put him to death.* And that all might share in the glory of destroying so great a prince, and come under the obligation of fidelity, each to other, the Pequods shot him, the Mohegins cut off his head and quartered his body, and the *Ninnuocks* men made the fire and burned his quarters, and, as a token of their love and fidelity to the English, presented his head to the council at Hartford!

ANNAWON was a Wampanoag, and one of *Philip's* most famous counsellors and captains. He was his fast friend, and resisted as long as there was a beam of hope; and when at last every chance of success had failed, he gave himself up in the most heroic manner, as will appear in the following account.

At the swamp, when *Philip* was killed, he escaped with most of his men, as has been related, by his thoroughly understanding the situation of his enemies. "Perceiving (says *Church*) they were waylaid on the east side of the swamp, tacked short about. One of the enemy, who seemed to be a great surly old fellow, hallooed with a loud voice, and often called out, *I-oo-tash, I-oo-tash.* Captain *Church* called to his Indian *Peter*,† and asked him who that was that called so. He answered that it was old *Annawon, Philip's* great captain, calling on his soldiers to stand to it, and fight stoutly."

"Captain *Church* had been but little while at Plimouth, [after the death of *Philip*,] before a post from Rehoboth came to inform the governor that old *Annawon, Philip's* chief captain, was with his company ranging about their woods, and was very offensive and pernicious to Rehoboth and Swansey. Captain *Church* was immediately sent for again, and treated with to engage in one expedition more. He told them their encouragement was so poor, he feared his soldiers would be dull about going again. But being a hearty friend to the cause, he rallies again, goes to Mr. *Jabez Howland*, his old lieutenant, and some of his soldiers that used to go out with him, told them how the case was circumstanced, and that he had intelligence of old *Annawon's* walk and haunt, and wanted hands to hunt him. They did not want much entreating, but told him they would go with him as long as there was an Indian left in the woods He moved and ranged through the woods to Pocasset."

In the early part of this expedition, some of Captain *Church's* Indian scouts captured a number of *Annawon's* company, but from whom they could learn nothing of the old chief, only that he did not lodge "twice in a place."

"Now a certain Indian soldier, that Captain *Church* had gained over to be on his side, prayed that he might have liberty to go and fetch in his father, who, he said, was about four miles from that place, in a swamp, with no other than a young squaw. Captain *Church* inclined to go with him, thinking it might be in his way to gain some intelligence of *Annawon;* and so taking one Englishman and a few Indians with him, leaving the rest there, he went with his new soldier to look his father. When he came to the swamp, he bid the Indian go and see if he could find his father. He was no sooner gone, but Captain *Church* discovered a track coming down out of the woods, upon which he and his little company lay close, some on one side of the track, and some on the other. They heard the Indian soldier making a howling for his father, and at length somebody answered him; but while they were listening, they thought they heard somebody coming towards them. Presently they saw an old man coming up, with a gun on his shoulder, and a young woman following in the track which they lay by. They let them come between them, and then started up and laid hold of them both. Captain *Church* immediately examined them apart, telling them what they must trust to if they told false stories. He asked the young woman what company they came from last. She said from Captain *Annawon's.* He asked her how many were in company with him when she left

* This seems to us the most probable account of the affair of all we have seen.

† The son of *Awashonks*, it is supposed.

him. She said 'fifty or sixty' He asked her how many miles it was to the place where she left him. She said she did not understand miles, but he was up in Squannaconk swamp. The old man, who had been one of *Philip's* council, upon examination, gave exactly the same account." On being asked whether they could get there that night, answered, "If we go presently, and travel stoutly, we may get there by sunset." The old man said he was of *Annawon's* company, and that *Annawon* had sent him down to find some Indians that were gone down into Mount Hope neck to kill provisions. Captain *Church* let him know that that company were all his prisoners.

The Indian who had been permitted to go after his father, now returned with him and another man. Captain *Church* was now at great loss what he should do. He was unwilling to miss of so good an opportunity of giving a finishing blow to the Indian power. He had, as himself says, but "half a dozen men beside himself," and yet was under the necessity of sending some one back to give Lieutenant *Howland*, whom he left at the old fort in Pocasset, notice, if he should proceed. But, without wasting time in pondering upon what course to pursue, he put the question to his men, "whether they would willingly go with him and give *Annawon* a visit." All answered in the affirmative, but reminded him "that they knew this Captain *Annawon* was a great soldier; that he had been a valiant captain under *Asuhmequin*, [*Woosamequin*,] *Philip's* father; and that he had been *Philip's* chieftain all this war." And they further told Captain *Church*, (and these men knew him well,) that he was "a very subtle man, of great resolution, and had often said that he would never be taken alive by the English."

They also reminded him that those with *Annawon* were "resolute fellows, some of *Philip's* chief soldiers," and very much feared that to make the attempt with such a handful of soldiers, would be hazardous in the extreme. But nothing could shake the resolution of Captain *Church*, who remarked to them, "that he had a long time sought for *Annawon*, but in vain," and doubted not in the least but Providence would protect them. All with one consent now desired to proceed.

A man by the name of *Cook*,* belonging to Plimouth, was the only Englishman in the company, except the captain. Captain *Church* asked Mr. *Cook* what his opinion of the undertaking was. He made no other reply than this: "I am never afraid of going any where when you are with me." The Indian who brought in his father informed Captain *Church*, that it was impossible for him to take his horse with him, which he had brought thus far. He therefore sent him and his father, with the horse, back to Lieutenant *Howland*, and ordered them to tell him to take his prisoners immediately to Taunton, and then to come out the next morning in the Rehoboth road where, if alive, he hoped to meet him.

Things being thus settled, all were ready for the journey. Captain *Church* turned to the old man, whom he took with the young woman, and asked him whether he would be their pilot. He said, "You having given me my life, I am under obligations to serve you." They now marched for Squannaconk. In leading the way, this old man would travel so much faster than the rest, as sometimes to be nearly out of sight, and consequently might have escaped without fear of being recaptured, but he was true to his word, and would stop until his wearied followers came up.

Having travelled through swamps and thickets until the sun was setting, the pilot ordered a stop. The captain asked him if he had made any discovery. He said, "About that hour of the day, *Annawon* usually sent out his scouts to see if the coast was clear, and as soon as it began to grow dark the scouts returned, and then we may move securely." When it was sufficiently dark, and they were about to proceed, Captain *Church* asked the old man if he would take a gun and fight for him. He bowed very low, and said, "I pray you not to impose such a thing upon me as to fight against Captain *Annawon*, my old friend, but I will go along with you, and be helpful to you, and will lay hands on any man that shall offer to hurt you." They

* *Caleb*, doubtless, who was present at the time *Philip* was killed

had proceeded but a short space, when they heard a noise, which they concluded to be the pounding of a mortar. This warned them that they were in the vicinity of *Annawon's* retreat. And here it will be very proper to give a description of it. It is situated in the south-easterly corner of Rehoboth, about eight miles from Taunton Green, a few rods from the road which leads to Providence, and on the south-easterly side of it. If a straight line were drawn from Taunton to Providence, it would pass very nearly over this place. Within the limits of an immense swamp of nearly 1000 acres, there is a small piece of upland, separated from the main only by a brook, which in some seasons is dry. This island, as we may call it, is nearly covered with an enormous rock, which to this day is called *Annawon's Rock*. Its south-east side presents an almost perpendicular precipice, and rises to the height of 25 or 30 feet. The north-west side is very sloping, and easy of ascent, being at an angle of not more than 35 or 40°. A more gloomy and hidden recess, even now, although the forest tree no longer waves over it, could hardly be found by any inhabitant of the wilderness.

When they arrived near the foot of the rock, Captain *Church*, with two of his Indian soldiers, crept to the top of it, from whence they could see distinctly the situation of the whole company, by the light of their fires. They were divided into three bodies, and lodged a short distance from one another. *Annawon's* camp was formed by felling a tree against the rock, with bushes set up on each side.

> " He passed, in the heart of that ancient wood—
> * * * * * * * *
> Nor paused, till the rock where a vaulted bed
> Had been hewn of old for the kingly dead
> Arose on his midnight way "—HEMANS.

With him lodged his son, and others of his principal men. Their guns were discovered standing and leaning against a stick resting on two crotches, safely covered from the weather by a mat. Over their fires were pots and kettles boiling, and meat roasting upon their spits. Captain *Church* was now at some loss how to proceed, seeing no possibility of getting down the rock without discovery, which would have been fatal. He therefore creeps silently back again to the foot of the rock, and asked the old man, their pilot, if there was no other way of coming at them. He answered, "No;" and said that himself and all others belonging to the company were ordered to come that way, and none could come any other without danger of being shot.

The fruitful mind of *Church* was no longer at loss, and the following stratagem was put in successful practice. He ordered the old man and the young woman to go forward, and lead the way, with their baskets upon their backs, and when *Annawon* should discover them, he would take no alarm, knowing them to be those he had lately sent forth upon discovery. "Captain *Church* and his handful of soldiers crept down also, under the shadow of those two and their baskets. The captain himself crept close behind the old man, with his hatchet in his hand, and stepped over the young man's head to the arms. The young *Annawon* discovering him, whipped his blanket over his head, and shrunk up in a heap. The old Captain *Annawon* started up on his breech, and cried out '*Howoh!*' which signified, 'Welcom.'"* All hope of escape was now fled forever, and he made no effort, but laid himself down again in perfect silence, while his captors secured the rest of the company. For he supposed the English were far more numerous than they were, and before he was undeceived, his company were all secured.

---

* It is a curious fact, that among the tribes of the west, the same word is used to signify approbation: thus, when a speech had been made to some in that region, which pleased them, at the end of each paragraph they would exclaim, "*Hoah! Hoah!*"—*Weld's Travels in America.*

The fact becomes still more curious when we find the same word used yet farther west—even on the North-west Coast, and with very nearly the same signification. See *Dixon's Voyage*, 189, 4to. London, 1789. In this work it is spelt *Whoah*. See, also, *Burney's* Voyages, i. 346, and *Colden's* Five Nations, ii. 95.

One circumstance much facilitated this daring project. It has been before mentioned, that they heard the pounding of a mortar, on their approach. This continued during their descent down the rock. A squaw was pounding green dried corn for their supper, and when she ceased pounding, to turn the corn, they ceased to proceed, and when she pounded again, they moved. This was the reason they were not heard as they lowered themselves down, from crag to crag, supported by small bushes that grew from the seams of the rock. The pounded corn served afterwards for a supper to the captors.

Annawon would not have been taken at this time but for the treachery of those of his own company. And well may *their Lucan* exclaim, as did the *Roman*,

> "A race renowned, the world's victorious lords,
> Turned on themselves with their own hostile swords."—*Rowe's Trans.*

The two companies situated at a short distance from the rock knew not the fate of their captain, until those sent by *Church* announced it to them. And, to prevent their making resistance, they were told, that Captain *Church* had encompassed them with his army, and that to make resistance would be immediate death; but if they all submitted peaceably, they should have good quarter. "Now they being old acquaintance, and many of them relations," readily consented: delivering up their guns and hatchets, they were all conducted to head-quarters.

"Things being thus far settled, Captain *Church* asked *Annawon* what he had for supper, 'for,' said he, 'I am come to sup with you.'" *Annawon* replied, "*Taubut*," with a "big voice," and, looking around upon his women, ordered them to hasten and provide Captain *Church* and his company some supper. He asked Captain *Church* "whether he would eat cow beef or horse beef." *Church* said he would prefer cow beef. It was soon ready, and, by the aid of some salt he had in his pocket, he made a good meal. And here it should be told, that a small bag of salt (which he carried in his pocket) was the only provision he took with him upon this expedition.

When supper was over, Captain *Church* set his men to watch, telling them if they would let him sleep two hours, they should sleep all the rest of the night, he not having slept any for 36 hours before; but after laying a half hour, and feeling no disposition to sleep, from the momentous cares upon his mind,—for, as Dr. *Young* says in the Revenge,

> "The dead alone, in such a night, can rest,—"

he looked to see if his watch were at their posts, but they were all fast asleep. *Annawon* felt no more like sleeping than *Church*, and they lay for some time looking one upon the other. *Church* spoke not to *Annawon*, because he could not speak Indian, and thought *Annawon* could not speak English, but it now appeared that he could, from a conversation they held together. *Church* had laid down with *Annawon* to prevent his escape, of which, however, he did not seem much afraid, for after they had laid a considerable time, *Annawon* got up and walked away out of sight, which *Church* considered was on a common occasion; but being gone some time, "he began to suspect some ill design." He therefore gathered all the guns close to himself, and lay as close as he possibly could under young *Annawon's* side, that if a shot should be made at him, it must endanger the life of young *Annawon* also. After laying a while in great suspense, he saw, by the light of the moon, *Annawon* coming with something in his hands. When he had got to Captain *Church*, he knelt down before him, and, after presenting him what he had brought, spoke in English as follows:—"*Great captain, you have killed* Philip, *and conquered his country. For I believe that I and my company are the last that war against the English, so suppose the war is ended by your means, and therefore these things belong unto you.*" He then took out of his pack a beautifully wrought belt, which belonged to *Philip*. It was nine inches in breadth, and of such length, as when put about the shoulders of Captain *Church*, it reached to his ankles. This was considered, at that time, of great value, being embroidered all over with money, that is, wampumpeag,* of various colors, curiously wrought into figures of birds, beasts and flowers. A second belt, of no less exquisite workmanship, was next presented, which belonged also to *Philip*. This, that chief used to ornament his head with; from the back part of which flowed two flags, which decorated his back. A third was a smaller one, with a star upon the end of it, which he wore upon his breast. All three were edged with red hair, which, *Annawon* said, was got in the country of the Mohawks. These belts, or some of them, it is believed, remain, at this day, the property of a family in Swansey. He next took from his pack two horns of glazed powder, and a red cloth blanket. These, it appears, were all that remained of the effects of the great chief. He told Captain *Church* that those were *Philip's* royalties, which he was wont to adorn himself with, when he sat in state, and he thought himself happy in having an opportunity to present them to him.

The remainder of the night they spent in discourse, in which *Annawon* "gave an account of what mighty success he had had formerly in wars against many nations of Indians, when he served *Asuhmequin, Philip's* father."

Morning being come, they took up their march for Taunton. In the way they met Lieutenant *Howland*, according to appointment, at his no small surprise. They lodged at Taunton that night. The next day "Capt. *Church* took old *Annawon*, and half a dozen Indian soldiers, and his own men, and went to Rhode Island; the rest were sent to Plimouth, under Lieutenant *Howland*.

Annawon, it is said, had confessed "that he had put to death several of the English, that had been taken alive; ten in one day, and could not deny but that some of them had been tortured;"† and therefore no mercy was to be expected from those into whose hands he had now fallen. His captor, Captain *Church*, did not mean that he should have been put to death, and had entreated hard for him; but in his absence from Plimouth, not long after, he was remorselessly executed. We shall again have occasion to advert to the execution of *Annawon*, and shall now pass to consider the events in the life of a sachem of nearly equal interest.

QUINNAPIN was by birth a noble Narraganset, being the son of *Coginaquan*, otherwise *Conjanaquond*, who was nephew to *Canonicus*. Therefore *Miantunnomoh* was uncle to *Quinnapin*, and *Canonicus* was his great uncle.

We find his name spelled in almost every possible way, and for the amusement of the reader will offer a few of them—*Quanopin, Quonopin, Qunnapin, Quannopin, Quenoquin, Panoquin, Sowagonish*, and *Quanepin*. His name has also been confounded with that of *Quaiapen*, the "old queen" of Narraganset.

In 1672, *Quinnapin* confirmed, by a writing, the sale of a tract of land previously granted by *Coginaquan*, his father.

This sachem took part with the Wampanoags in *Philip's* war, and from the punishment which the English executed upon him, on his falling into their hands, we may suppose he acted well his part in that war, although but little is recorded of him by the historians of that period. From Mrs. *Rowlandson's* account of him, we must conclude he was not wanting in attentions to the fair sex, as he had certainly three wives, one of whom was a sister of *Wootonekanuske*; consequently he was, according to the English method of calculating relationships, brother-in-law to the famous *Metacomet* himself.

Quinnapin was one of the chiefs who directed the attack on Lancaster, the 10 Feb. 1675, O. S., and he purchased Mrs. *Rowlandson* from a Naraganset Indian who had seized her when she came out of the garrison, among the captives of that place. And it was this circumstance which caused her to notice him in her Narrative.‡ *Wettimore*, whom she mentions in the following extract, as his wife, we have said, was *Weetamoo*, the "queen of Pocasset."

In the winter of 1676, when the Narragansets were at such "great straits," from the loss of their provisions, in the great swamp fight, ("corn being two

* An Iroquois word signifying *a muscle*. *Gordon's Hist.* Pennsylvania, page 598.
† *Hubbard, Nar.* 108. ‡ Mr. *Willard's* edition of it, (p. 25.) Lancaster, 1828.

shillings a pint with them,") the English tried to bring about a peace with them; but their terms were too hard, or some other cause prevented. "*Canonchet* and *Panoquin* said they would fight it out, to the last man, rather than they would become servants to the English."* A truly noble resolution, and well worthy of the character we have of *Canonchet*.

"My master (says Mrs. *Rowlandson*) had three squaws, living sometimes with one and sometimes with another. *Onux*, this old squaw at whose wigwam I was, and with whom my master [*Quinnapin*] had been these three weeks. Another was *Wettimore*, with whom I had lived and served all this while. A severe and proud dame she was; bestowing every day in dressing herself near as much time as any of the gentry of the land—powdering her hair and painting her face, going with her necklaces, with jewels in her ears, and bracelets upon her hands. When she had dressed herself, her work was to make girdles of wampum and beads. The third squaw [or wife] was a young one, by whom he had two papooses."†

While the Narragansets and Nipmucks were encamped at a place on Connecticut River at considerable distance above Northampton, perhaps near as far as Bellows Falls, Mrs. *Rowlandson* says, "My master's maid came home: she had been gone three weeks into the Narraganset country to fetch corn, where they had stored up some in the ground. *She brought home about a peck and a half of corn*"!

We shall relate, in the Life of *Nepanet*, the mission of Mr. *Hoar* to *Philip's* quarters for the redemption of Mrs. *Rowlandson*. This was not long after Sudbury fight, and the Indians were preparing to commemorate it by a great dance, "which was carried on by eight of them, (as Mrs. *R.* relates,) four men and four squaws; my master and mistress [*Quinnapin* and *Weetamoo*] being two. He was dressed in his Holland shirt, with great stockings, his garters hung round with *shillings*, and had girdles of *wampom* upon his head and shoulders. She had a kearsey coat, covered with girdles of *wampom* from the loins upward. Her arms, from her elbows to her hands, were covered with bracelets; there were handfuls of necklaces about her neck, and several sorts of jewels in her ears. She had fine red stockings, and white shoes, her hair powdered, and her face painted red, that was always before black. And all the dancers were after the same manner. There were two others singing and knocking on a kettle for their music. They kept hopping up and down one after another, with a kettle of water in the midst, standing warm upon some embers, to drink of when they were dry. They held on till almost night, throwing out their *wampom* to the standers-by. At night I asked them again, if I should go home: they all as one said, No, except my husband would come for me. When we were lain down, my master went out of the wigwam, and by and by sent in an Indian called *James-the-printer*, who told Mr. *Hoar*, that my master would let me go home to-morrow, if he would let him have one pint of liquor. Then Mr. *Hoar* called his own Indians, *Tom* and *Peter*, and bid them all go and see if he would promise it before them three; and if he would he should have it, which he did, and had it. *Philip* smelling the business, called me to him, and asked me what I would give him, to tell me some good news, and to speak a good word for me, that I might go home to-morrow? I told him I could not tell what to give him, I would any thing I had, and asked him what he would have. He said two coats and 20 shillings in money, half a bushel of seed corn, and some tobacco. I thanked him for his love, but I knew that good news as well as that crafty fox. My master, after he had his drink, quickly came ranting into the wigwam again, and called for Mr. *Hoar*, drinking to him and saying *he was a good man*; and then again he would say, *Hang him a rogue*. Being almost drunk, he would drink to him, and yet presently say he should be hanged. Then he called for me; I trembled to hear him, and yet I was fain to go to him, and he drank to me, shewing no incivility. He was the first Indian I saw drunk, all the time I was among them. At last his squaw ran out, and he after her, round the wigwam, with his money jingling at his

* *Hubbard*. † Narrative, 63, 64.

knees, but she escaped him; but having an old squaw, he ran to her,"* and troubled the others no more that night.

A day or two after, the sagamores had a council, or *general court*, as they called it, in which the giving up of Mrs. *R.* was debated. All seemed to consent for her to go, except *Philip*, who would not come to the council. However, she was soon dismissed, and some who were at first opposed to her going, seemed now to rejoice at it. They shook her by the hand, and asked her to send them some tobacco, and some one thing and some another.

When the extensive system of war carried on by *Philip* was broken in the west by intestine bickerings, *Quinnapin* returned with *Philip* to his country of the Wampanoags. About the end of July, 1676, Captain *Church* learned by a captive squaw that *Quinnapin* and *Philip* were in a "great cedar swamp" near Aponaganset with "abundance of Indians." This news, together with a discovery the captain soon after made, induced him to leave that country without disturbing so formidable an enemy. Soon after, *Quinnapin* escaped from a company of Bridgewater men, who killed *Akkompoin*, as he and *Philip's* company were crossing Taunton River. The next day, *Church* pursued him, but he effected his escape.

Not long after this, he was taken, and, immediately after the war, 25 August, was shot at Newport in R. Island. It appears that *Quinnapin* had had some difficulty with the R. Island people, who, some time before the war, had cast him into prison; but that by some means he had escaped, and become active in the war. He was reported "a young lusty sachem, and a very rogue."† A court-martial was held at Newport, R. I., on the 24 August, 1676, by the governor and assistants of that colony, for the trial of *Quinnapin*, or *Sowagonish*, as he was sometimes called, and several others. He was charged with adhering to *Philip* in the war, which he confessed, and owned he was in the Narraganset Swamp fight of December, 1675, and next in command to *Canonchet;* whereupon he was sentenced to be shot the next day. A brother of his, who had but one eye, named *Sunkeejunasuc*, had the same sentence passed upon him. *Ashamattan*, another brother, was tried, but at that time received no sentence.‡

TUSPAQUIN, whose biography we shall next pursue, was one of *Philip's* most faithful captains, and sachem of Assawomset, as we have before had occasion to notice, in speaking of *John Sassamon*. His name in printed accounts differs but little, and is abbreviated from *Watuspaquin*. Also in our life of *Tatoson* it was necessary to speak of this chief. From a survey of the deeds which he executed of various large tracts of land, it is evident his sachemdom was very extensive. It will be necessary to glance at some of the conveyances of *Watuspaquin* for several reasons, the principal of which is, that the part he acted in the great drama of 1675 and 1676 may not be underrated. His conveyances to the Reverend *John Sassamon* and his family are already related.

On 9 August, 1667, "*Tuspequin*, otherwise called the *Black-sachem*," for £4, sells to *Henry Wood* of Plimouth his right and title to the land on the east side of "Namassakett" River,§ bounded "on one end" by the pond called *Black-sachem's Pond*, or, in Indian, *Wanpawcutt;* on the other end, by a little pond called *Asnemscutt*. How much was included in the given bounds, is not mentioned, nor could we now by the description possibly tell how far said tract extended back from the river. With *Tuspaquin*, his wife, *Amey*, signed this deed, and it was witnessed only by two Englishmen.

On 17 July, 1669, *Tuspaquin* and his son *William* sell for £10 a tract or parcel of land near "Assowampsett," half a mile wide, and "in length from said ponds to Dartmouth path." Besides two English, *Samuel Henry*, *Daniel* and *Old Harry* were witnesses. *Experience Mitchell*, *Henry Sampson*, of Duxborough, *Thomas Little*, of Marshfield, and *Thomas Paine*, of Eastham, were the purchasers.

* Narrative, 73—75.

† Captain *More's* account of "The Warr in N. E. visibly ended," &c. in our INDIAN CHRONICLE.

‡ *Potter's* Narraganset. 98.

§ He, however, reserved the right "to gett ceder barke in the swamps."

June 10, 1670, *Tuspaquin* and his son *William* sold for £6, to *Edward Gray*, "in the behalf of the court of Plimouth," "all that our meddow that lyeth in or neare the town of Middleberry," on the west side of a tract belonging to *John Alden* and *Constant Southworth*, "and is between Assowamsett Pond and Taunton path, being in three parsells vpon three brookes;" also another parcel on the other side of Taunton path. Witnessed by "*Amie*," the wife of *Tuspaquin*, and two English

30 June, 1672, *Tuspaquin*, "sachem of Namassakett, and *Mantowapuct* alias *William* his son," sell to *Edward Gray* and *Josias Winslow*, lands on he easterly side of Assowamsett, to begin where Namasket River falleth out of the pond, and so south by the pond; thence by perishable bounds to *Tuspaquin's* Pond, and so home to the lands formerly sold to *Henry Wood*.

3 July, 1673, *Tuspaquin* and his son *William* sell to *Benjamin Church* of Duxborough, house carpenter, and *John Tompson* of Barnstable, lands about Middleborough, for which they paid him £15. It is described as "lying att and neare the township of Middleberry," bounded westerly by a river called *Monhuggen*, which runs into a pond called *Quisquasett*, and so by a cedar swamp to *Tuspaquin's* Pond; thence by *Henry Wood's* land to a place called *Pochaboquett*. Nahudset River is named as a northern boundary; and the two "places" called *Tuscomanest* and *Massapanoh* are also named, likewise a pond called *Sniptuett*, and a "river's mouth called *Tuppatuett* which runneth into a pond called *Quittuwashett*." Two English, *Sam Harry*, and *Joseph* of Namasket, were witnesses.

1 November 1673, *William Watuspaquin*, *Assaweta*, *Tobias* and *Bewat*, for £10 sell to three English of Barnstable a tract of land bounded by Quetaquash Pond northerly, by Quetaquash River easterly, Snepetuitt Pond, &c.

14 May, 1675, the two *Tuspaquins*, father and son, "make over to *John Tompson*, *Constant Southworth*" and others, of Middleborough, "all that tract of land which we now have in possession, called commonly *Assowamset* neck or necks, and places adjacent," as a security against the claims of others, &c. of other lands deeded at the same time; if, therefore, they are not disturbed in the possession of the former lands deeded, then they "are not to be outed of Assawamsett neck." *Pottawo*, alias *Daniel*, *Poyman*, *Pagatt*,* alias *Joseph*, were witnesses.

For the land deeded they received £33, "sterling." It consisted of uplands and meadows about the pond called *Ninipoket*, *Quiticus*,† &c., and, judging from the price paid, was, no doubt, a very large tract.

Thus are a few of the acts of *Watuspaquin* sketched previous to the war. We are now to trace his operations in quite another sphere. In our opinion, Mr. *Hubbard* was right in styling him "the next noted captain to *Philip*," but erroneously calls *Old Tuspaquin* "the Black-sachem's son." He does not appear to have known of the son *William*. Indeed, we hear nothing of him in the war, but it is probable he shared the fate of his father.

In the spring of 1676, *Tuspaquin* was marching from place to place with about 300 men, and was doubtless in high expectation of humbling the pride of his enemies, and, but for *Philip's* western disasters, occasioned by the disaffection of his Pocomptucks and others, his expectations might have been realized. It was doubtless under his direction that 19 buildings in Scituate were burnt on 20 April; and on the 8 May, had not a shower prevented, most, if not all, the houses in Bridgewater would have shared the same fate. *Tuspaquin* was known to have led his men in this attack.‡ The inhabitants exerted themselves to repel the Indians, but, conscious of their strength, they maintained their ground until the next day, when they retreated. Notwithstanding the rain, they succeeded in burning 17 buildings before they decamped.

On 11 May, 1676, there were eleven houses and five barns burnt in Plimouth, and a few weeks after, seven houses more and two barns. These

* Two names, probably; but in the MS. there is no comma between, as is often the case.

† *Titicut*, probably, now.

‡ Mr. *Hubbard* says, (Nar. 71.) the Indians were led by one *Tusguogen*, but we are satisfied *Tuspaquin* is meant.

were probably such as were at a considerable distance from the village, and had chiefly been deserted. This "mischief" was attributed to *Tuspaquin* and his men.

About this time, *Benjamin Church* was commissioned by the government of Plimouth to lead parties in different directions over the colony; and from the time he commenced operations, the Indians found but few opportunities to do mischief in Plimouth colony.

Tuspaquin still kept his ground in the Assawomset country, and for a long time baffled all the skill Captain *Church* was master of in his endeavors to take him prisoner. *Church* received his commission 24 July, 1676, and the same night set out on an expedition against *Tuspaquin.* His Indian scouts brought him before day upon a company of his people in Middleborough, every one of whom fell into his hands. How many there were, *Church* does not say. He took them directly to Plimouth, "and disposed of them all," except "one *Jeffery*, who, proving very ingenious and faithful to him in informing where other parcels of the Indians harbored, Capt. *Church* promised him, that if he continued to be faithful to him, he should not be sold out of the country, but should be his waiting man, to take care of his horse, &c., and accordingly he served him faithfully as long as he lived." *

Thus strengthened by *Tuspaquin's* own men, *Church* pursued his successes with manifold advantage. There was a small tribe residing near Munponset Pond, which was next captured without loss on either side, and there was henceforth scarcely a week passed wherein he did not capture some of these people.

Not long after this, it was found that *Tuspaquin* had encamped about Assawomset, and *Church* set out on an expedition there; but finding *Old Tuspaquin* was ready for him at the neck between the two great ponds, † he was glad to make the best of his way on towards Acushnet and Dartmouth. As he was crossing Assawomset neck, a scout from *Tuspaquin's* camp fired upon him, but did him no injury.

Meanwhile the great *Annawon* having been surprised by the indefatigable *Church*, *Tuspaquin* saw no chance of holding out long; he therefore appears afterwards only intent upon keeping out of the way of the English. This could not be long reasonably expected, as their scouts were ranging in every direction.

On 4 Sept. 1676, according to *Church's* account, *Tuspaquin's* company were encamped near Sippican, doing "great damage to the English in killing their cattle, horses and swine." The next day, *Church* and his rangers were in their neighborhood, and, after observing their situation, which was "sitting round their fires in a thick place of bruch,"‡ in seeming safety, the captain "ordered every man to creep as he did; and surrounded them by creeping as near as they could, till they should be discovered, and then to run on upon them, and take them alive, if possible, (for their prisoners were their pay.) They did so, taking every one that was at the fires, not one escaping. Upon examination, they agreed in their story, that they belonged to *Tispaquin*, who was gone with *John Bump* and one more to Agawom and Sipican to kill horses, and were not expected back in two or three days."§ *Church* proceeds: "This same *Tispaquin* had been a great captain, and the Indians reported that he was such a great pouwau, [priest or conjurer,] that no bullet could enter him. Capt. *Church* said he would not have him killed, for there was a war broke out in the eastern part of the country, and he would have him saved to go with them to fight the eastern Indians. Agreeably, he left two old squaws of the prisoners, and bid them tarry there until their Captain *Tispaquin* returned, and to tell him, that *Church* had been there, and had taken his wife, children and company, and carried them down to Plymouth; and would spare all their lives, and his too, if he would

* *Church*, Narrative, 31.

† Just below where *Sampson's* tavern now stands.

‡ I suspect Mr. *Hubbard* mistakes the situation of this place, in saying it was "in Lakenham, upon Pocasset neck." *Church* is so unregarding of all geography, that it is quite uncertain where it was. If it were near Sippican, it was a long way from any part of Pocasset.

§ By this it seems the place might have been as far off as Pocasset.

come down to them and bring the other two that were with him, and they should be his soldiers, &c. Capt. *Church* then returned to Plymouth, leaving the old squaws well provided for, and bisket for *Tispaquin* when he returned."

This *Church* called laying a trap for *Tuspaquin*, and it turned out as he expected. We shall now see with what faith the English acted on this occasion. *Church* had assured him that, if he gave himself up, he should not be killed, but he was not at Plimouth when *Tuspaquin* came in, having gone to Boston on business for a few days; "but when he returned he found, to his grief, the heads of *Annawon, Tispaquin*, &c. cut off, which were the last of *Philip's* friends"!

It is true that those who were known to have been personally engaged in killing the English were, in the time of the greatest danger, cut off from pardon by a law; that time had now passed away, and, like many other laws of exigency, it should then have been considered a dead letter; leaving out of the case the faith and promise of their best servant, *Church*. View it, therefore, in any light, and nothing can be found to justify this flagrant inroad upon that promise. To give to the conduct of the Plimouth government a pretext for this murder, (a milder expression I cannot use,) Mr. *Hubbard* says, *Tuspaquin* having pretended that a bullet could not penetrate him, trial of his invulnerableness was resolved upon. So he was placed as a mark to shoot at, and "he fell down at the first shot"!

This was doubtless the end of numerous others, as we infer from the following passage in Dr. *Mather's* PREVALENCY OF PRAYER. He asks, "Where are the six Narraganset sachems, with all their captains and counsellors? Where are the Nipmuck sachems, with their captains and counsellors? Where is *Philip* and *Squaw-sachem* of Pocasset, with all their captains and counsellors? God do so to all the implacable enemies of Christ, and of his people in N. England"!! The next of *Philip's* captains, in our arrangement, is

TATOSON, also a great captain in the war of 1675. It seems rather uncertain whether he were a Narraganset or Wampanoag. He (or one bearing the same name) signed the treaty made with the Narragansets in the beginning of the war. It is quite certain that his residence afterwards was in Sandwich, since Rochester;* and when he signed the treaty just named, it is probable he was only among the Narragansets upon a mission or visit. He was a son of the "noted Sam Barrow," but of his own family, or whether he had any, we are not informed.

We first meet with *Tatoson*,† or, as his name is commonly printed, *Totoson*, in 1666, in the respectable company of Mr. Secretary *Morton* of Plimouth, and *Acanootus, Wannoo*, two "graue and sage Indians," and a number more, of whose characters we are not so well prepared to speak. Among this assemblage he is only conspicuous, however, as a witness to a deed of the lands upon *Weequancett* neck. Mr. *Morton's* name follows *Tatoson's*, on this instrument.

There was a general disarming of the Indians in 1671, as will elsewhere be mentioned. Among a great number ordered to appear at Plimouth the same year, to bind themselves more strongly in allegiance to the English, we find the name of *Tatoson*, or, as his name was then written, *Tautozen*. Also *Toby*, alias *Nauhnocomwit*,‡ and *Will*, alias *Washawanna*.

On the 12th of June, 1676, several Indians, who had been sent in by *Bradford* and *Church*, were "convented before the councell" at Plimouth; being "such of them as were accused of working vnsufferable mischeiffe vpon some of ours." Among them was one named WATUKPOO, or, as he

---

* On the right of the main road, as you pass from Matapoiset to Rochester village, and about two miles from the former, at a small distance from the road, is a kind of island in a miry swamp. Upon this, it is said, was *Tatoson's* camp. This island is connected by an isthmus to the main land.

† So almost always in the MSS.

‡ Sometimes called *Toby Cole*. The same, we conclude, who joined *Philip* afterwards and fell into the hands of Captain *Church*, as did his mother, and many more at the same time.

was often called, *Tukpoo.** Against him, several charges were brought, such as his going off to the enemy, and trying to deceive the governor about the prospect of war; telling him that *Philip's* men had deserted him, and that he had only a few old men and boys remaining. At this time were present three other Indians, whose names were *Woodcock, Quanapawhan* and *John-num.* The two first were accused by a squaw of destroying *Clark's* garrison at Eel River in Plimouth, and murdering the inhabitants. This had been done on the 12 March previous, and with such secrecy and effect, that the English knew not whom to accuse of it. Many supposed that *Watuspaquin* conducted the affair, and Mr. *Hubbard* charges it upon him without hesitation, but it is now quite certain that he had nothing to do with it, as in the sequel we shall show.

The two just mentioned, finding themselves detected, accused their fellow prisoner, *John-num.* It appears that *Num* not only owned himself guilty of this charge, but acknowledged, also, that he was concerned in the murder of "*Jacob Mitchel* and his wife, and *John Pope,* † and soe centance of death was pronounced against them, which accordingly emediately was executed."

Before these were executed, they implicated a fourth, whose name was KEWEENAM. Although *Tatoson* commanded the company that put to death the people at *Clark's* garrison, yet *Keweenam* set the expedition on foot. He lived at Sandwich, and was probably one of *Tatoson's* men. However, on Saturday, the 11 March, he was at Mr. *William Clark's,* and observed how every part of the garrison was conditioned. He then went to his chief, *Tatoson,* and told him that it could be easily taken, as it was but slightly fortified; and that the next day, being Sunday, would be the proper time to execute their plan, as the residents would mostly be gone to meeting; "and in case they left a man at home, or so, they might soon dispatch him."

This intelligence was pleasing to *Tatoson,* and he found himself at the head of ten warriors the same day. Their names were as follows: *Woonashenah, Musquash, Wapanpowett, Tom,* "the son of *Tatoson's* brother," *Uttsooweest,* and *Tom Piant;* which, with the three before named, made up the whole company. Commencing their march before night, they arrived in the borders of Plimouth, where they lay concealed until the people had gone to public worship. About 10 o'clock in the morning, they came upon the garrison, which fell easily into their hands. After killing all they met with, they took what plunder they could carry, and burned the buildings; then again dispersed into the woods.

There were some of two other families in this garrison, mostly women and children. Three only were of Mr. *Clark's* family, but there were eight others belonging to the other two. Mrs. *Elizabeth Clark,* ‡ one of the heads of the family, was among the slain. §

---

* This Indian, whom we shall have occasion several times to mention, was not one of those sent in by *Bradford,* as appears from *Mather,* (Brief Hist. 40.) but they "informed that a bloudy Indian called *Tuckpoo,* (who the last summer murdered a man of Boston, at Namasket,) with about 20 Indians more, was at a place within 16 miles of Plimouth." Eight English and fourteen Indians succeeded in taking them all, and *Tuckpoo* was immediately executed.

† The murder of these people is supposed to be referred to by Mr. *Hubbard* in his "Table." The passage follows: "In June, 1676, [1675?] a man and a woman were slain by the Indians; another woman was wounded and taken; but because she had kept an Indian child before, so much kindness was showed her, as that she was sent back, after they had dressed her wound; the Indians guarded her till she came within sight of the English." Mr. *Mitchel* informs us that the name of the wounded woman was *Dorothy Haywood* See 2 *Coll. Mass. Hist. Soc.* vii. 159.

‡ "Who was the daughter of a godly father and mother, that came to N. England on the account of religion." "They also killed her sucking child, and knocked another child (who was about eight years old) in the head, supposing they had killed him, but afterwards he came to himself.". *I. Mather,* Brief Hist. 24.

§ We relate all that is to be found in the MS. records, but the author of the *Present State, &c.* furnishes the following valuable facts: "About this time, [his last date mentioned being 14 March,] one Mr. *Clarke's* wife, children, and all his family, at his farm-house, two miles from Plimouth, were surprised and killed, except one boy, who was knockt down, and left for dead, but afterwards taken up and revived. The house they plundered of provision and goods to a great value; eight complete arms, 30*l.* [*lb.*] of powder, with an answerable quan

Keweenam was beheaded, but how the other three were disposed of, we are not informed; it is very probable that the whole number suffered in due time. At the trial of *Keweenam* and the other three, some of them pleaded that the governor's proclamation was now their protection; from which it would seem that they had surrendered themselves. But there was none to plead their case, except their accusers, and they explained things in their own way. The court said, "Forasmuch as the council had before this engaged to several Indians desirous to come in and tender themselves to mercy, that they should find favor in so doing: it was fully made known to such Indians as were then present, that the said engagement *was to be understood with exception* against such as by murder as above said had so acted, and not against such as killed his enemie in the field in a souldierlike way."

This kind of argument would answer among duelists, but when did the Indians agree to fight the English according to *their* rules of war? The former might with equal propriety demand that the English should conform to their manner, and not depend on their numbers, forts, and superior weapons.

Although the murder at *Clark's* garrison was one of those horrible acts in Indian warfare, which would justify the most rigid retaliation, still, as the English began the war, they had no right to expect but that it would be prosecuted by the Indians in all the ways at their command. On this ground the philanthropist will ever condemn the severity of the English.

When Captain *Church* came upon *Philip* and a great number of his people, the 3d of August, 1676, "*Tispaquin, Totoson,* &c." prevented the entire destruction of some of them, by combating the English while their chief and others extricated themselves from a small swamp into which they had fled. "In this swamp skirmish Capt. *Church* with his two men which always ran by his side as his guard, met with three of the enemy, two of which surrendered themselves, and the captain's guard seized them; but the other, being a great stout surly fellow, with his two locks ty'd up with red, and a great rattlesnake's skin hanging to the back part of his head, (whom Capt. *Church* concluded to be *Totoson*,) ran from them into the swamp. Capt. *Church* in person pursued him close, till, coming pretty near up with him, presented his gun between his shoulders, but it missing fire, the Indian perceiving it, turned and presented at Capt. *Church*, and missing fire also, (their guns taking wet with the fog and dew of the morning,) but the Indian turning short for another run, his foot trip'd in a small grape-vine, and he fell flat on his face. Capt. *Church* was by this time up with him and struck the muzzle of his gun an inch and an half into the back part of his head, which dispatched him without another blow. But Capt. *Church* looking behind him saw *Totoson*, the Indian whom he tho't he had killed, come flying at him like a dragon; but this happened to be fair in sight of the guard that were set to keep the prisoners, who spying *Totoson* and others that were following him, in the very seasonable juncture made a shot upon them, and rescued their captain, though he was in no small danger from his friends' bullets, for some came so near him that he thought he felt the wind of them."* The celebrated *Church*, in the skirmishes he had in these two days, August 1 and 2, took and killed 173 Indians.

Little more than a month after the fall of *Philip*, *Church* surprised *Tatoson's* whole company, about 50 persons. He was the last that was left of the family of *Barrow;* and, says *Church*, "the wretch reflecting upon the miserable condition he had brought himself into, his heart became a stone within him, and he died. The old squaw [that *Church* had employed to persuade him to submit] flung a few leaves and brush over him—came into Sandwich, and gave this account of his death; and offered to show them where she left his body, but never had an opportunity, for she immediately fell sick and died also."

The fate of the father of *Tatoson* does not so much excite sympathy, as

---

tity of lead for bullets, and 150*l.* in ready money; the said Mr. *Clark* himself narrowly escaping their cruelty, by being at that instant at a meeting."

* Hist. *Philip's* War, 41.

does that of the son, but is one of those cases more calculated to arouse the fiercer passions. The old chief fell into the hands of Captain *Church*, in one of his successful expeditions in the vicinity of Cape Cod. *Church* says, in his history, that he was "as noted a rogue as any among the enemy." Captain *Church* told him that the government would not permit him to grant him quarter, "because of his inhuman murders and barbarities," and therefore ordered him to prepare for execution. "*Barrow* replied, that the sentence of death against him was just, and that indeed he was ashamed to live any longer, and desired no more favor, than to smoke a whiff of tobacco before his execution. When he had taken a few whiffs, he said, 'I am ready;' upon which one of Captain *Church's* Indians sunk his hatchet into his brains."

TIASHQ,* or *TYASKS*† "was the next man to *Philip*," says *Church*; there were others also said to be "next to him," and it may be all reconciled by supposing these chiefs as having the chief command over particular tribes. Mr. *Hubbard*‡ says only this of the famous *Tiashq*: "In June last, [1676,] one *Tiashq*, a great captain of *Philip's*, his wife and child, or children, being taken, though he escaped himself at first, yet came since and surrendered himself." Dr. *I. Mather*, writing under date of 22 July, 1676, says it was "this week" that Captain *Church* and his Indian soldiers fell upon *Tiashq* and his company. It appears therefore that Mr. *Hubbard* is in error, as the account given by *Church* corroborates that of *Mather*, who speaks thus of his operations: "It having been his manner when he taketh any Indians by a promise of favor to them, in case they acquit themselves well, to set them an hunting after more of these wolves, whereby the worst of them sometimes do singular good service in finding out the rest of their bloody fellows. In one of these skirmishes, *Tiashq*, *Philip's* chief captain, ran away leaving his gun behind him, and his squaw, who was taken." § These Indian soldiers, who performed this exploit, were forced upon it by *Church*. They had been seeking Indians about Aponaganset River, and discovered that a large company of them had just been gathering the apples at a deserted settlement on the east side of it. The English and Indians immediately pursued in their track.‖ "Traveling three miles or more, they came into the country road, where the track parted: one parcel steered towards the west end of the great cedar swamp, and the other to the east end. The captain halted and told his Indian souldiers that they had heard as well as he what some men had said at Plymouth about them,¶ &c., that now was a good opportunity for each party to prove themselves. The track being divided, they should follow one, and the English the other, being equal in number. The Indians declined the motion, and were not willing to move any where without him: said *they should not think themselves safe without him.* But the captain insisting upon it, they submitted. He gave the Indians their choice to follow which track they pleased. They replied, *They were light and able to travel, therefore if he pleased they would take the west track.* And appointing the ruins of *John Cook's* house at Cushnet** for the place to meet at, each company set out briskly to try their fortunes."†† When the parties met, "they very remarkably found that the number that each company had taken and slain was equal. The Indians had killed three of the enemy, and taken 63 prisoners, as the English had done before them."‡‡ Both parties were much rejoiced at their successes, but the Indians, told Captain *Church* "that they had missed a brave opportunity by parting. They came upon a great town of the enemy, viz: Captain *Tyasks'* company. (*Tyasks* was the next man to

* *Hubbard, Mather.* † *Church.* ‡ Narrative, 106.

§ Brief Hist. 42. ‖ *Church*, 33.

¶ The detestation in which the Indians were held by "some men," in many other places as well as in Plimouth, will often appear in this work. Such people could know nothing of human nature, and many would not have believed the Indians capable of good actions, though *one from the dead* had assured them they were.

** Abbreviated from Acushnet. See *Douglass*, Summary, i. 403, who writes it *Accushnot* Thus many Indian names are changed. Instead of Aponaganset, we hear *Ponaganset*, and for Asonet, *Sonet*, &c. Cushnet is the river on which New Bedford and Fairhaven stand.

†† *Church*, 34. ‡‡ Ibid. 36

Philip.) They fired upon the enemy before they were discovered, and ran upon them with a shout. The men ran and left their wives and children and many of them their guns. They took *Tyasks'* wife and son, and thought that if their captain and the English company had been with them they might have taken some hundreds of them, and now they determined not to part any more." * This transaction, in the opinion of Captain *Church*, was a "remarkable providence," inasmuch, perhaps, as the equality of their successes prevented either party from boasting, or claiming superiority over the other. Nevertheless, *Church* adds,—"But the Indians had the fortune to take more arms than the English." It would add not a little, perhaps, to the gratification of the reader, could he know the name of the Indian captain in this far-famed exploit, or even that of one of his men; but at present they are hid alike from us and from him.

CHAPTER IV.

Chief women conspicuous in Philip's war—MAGNUS—*Her country and relations*—*Her capture and death*—AWASHONKS—*Is greatly annoyed in the events of* 1671—*Her men disarmed*—*Philip's endeavors to engage her against the English*—*Church prevents her*—*Is finally in the power of Philip*—*Reclaimed by Church*—*Some particulars of her family.*

ALTHOUGH, before we had finished the life of *Weetamoo*, we deemed it proper to have deferred it to this chapter, but as we had been led rather imperceptibly into many particulars concerning her in that place,† we could not break off our narrative without a greater impropriety than an omission here would have been, and shall therefore begin here with one of her contemporaries, the bare facts in whose life are sufficient to maintain a high interest, we believe, in the mind of every reader.

MAGNUS was squaw-sachem of some part of the extensive country of the Narragansets, and was known by several names at different and the same times; as *Old Queen, Sunk Squaw,*‡ *Quaiapen*, and *Matantuck.* She married *Mriksah*, or *Mexam*, a son of *Canonicus*, and was sister to *Ninigret.* She had two sons, *Scuttup* and *Quequaquenuct* otherwise *Quequegunent*, called by the English *Gideon*, and a daughter named *Quinemiquet.* These two died young. *Gideon* was alive as late as 1661; *Scuttup*, and a sister also, in 1664. She was, in 1675, one "of the six present sachems of the whole Narraganset country."

In the beginning of *Philip's* war, the English army, to cause the Narragansets to fight for them, whom they had always abused and treated with contempt, since before the cutting off of *Miantunnomoh's* head, marched into their country, but could not meet with a single sachem of the nation. They fell in with a few of their people, who could not well secrete themselves, and who concluded a long treaty of mere verbosity, the import of which they could know but little, and doubtless cared less; for when the army left their country, they joined again in the war.

We hear no more of her until the next year, when herself and a large company of her men were discovered by Major *Talcot*, on the 2 July, in Narraganset. The English scouts discovered them from a hill, having pitched their tents in a valley in the vicinity of a swamp, as was usually their custom. About 300 of the English, mounted upon fleet horses, divided into two squadrons, and fell upon them before they were aware of their approach, and made a great slaughter of them. The Mohegans and Pequots came upon them in the centre, while the horsemen beset them on each side and

* *Church*, 36. † Book iii. chap. 1.

‡ *Trumbull*, i. 347. from *Hubbard*, I suppose, i. 51. Female chiefs were called *saunks* by the Indians, which signified wife of the sachem; but writers, being ignorant of that fact thought it a proper name of a particular person, and hence the appellations of *Snuke, Sunke, Snake*, &c. applied to *Magnus.*

thus prevented many from escaping into the swamp. When all were killed and taken within the encampment, Captain *Newbury*, who commanded the horsemen, dismounted, and with his men rushed into the swamp, where, without resistance, they killed a hundred, and made many prisoners. In all, they killed and took 171* in this swamp fight, or rather massacre. Not an Englishman was hurt in the affair, and but one Mohegan killed, and one wounded, which we can hardly suppose was done by *Magnus's* people, as they made no resistance, but rather by themselves, in their fury mistaking one another. Ninety of the captives were put to death! among whom was *Magnus*.† The swamp where this affair took place is near the present town of Warwick, in Rhode Island; and thus ends our short history of *Magnus*.

AWASHONKS, squaw-sachem of Sogkonate,‡ was the wife of an Indian called TOLONY, but of him we learn very little. From her important standing among the Indians, few deserve a more particular attention; and we shall, therefore, go as minutely into her history as our documents will enable us.

The first notice we have of *Awashonks* is in 1671, when she entered into articles of agreement with the court of Plimouth as follows:—"In admitting that the court are in some measure satisfied with your voluntary coming in now at last, and submission of herself unto us; yet this *we expect* that she give some meet satisfaction for the charge and trouble she has put us upon by her too long standing out against the many tenders of peace we have made to her and her people. And that we yet see an intention to endeavor the reducement of such as have been the incendiaries of the trouble and disturbance of her people and ours. And as many of her people as shall give themselves and arms unto us, at the time appointed, shall receive no damage or hurt from us, which time appointed is ten days from the date hereof. Thus we may the better keep off such from her lands as may hereafter bring upon her and us the like trouble, and to regulate such as will not be governed by her, she having submitted her lands to the authority of the government. And that, if the lands and estates of such as we are necessitated to take arms against, will not defray the charge of the expedition, that she shall bear some due proportion of the charge. In witness whereof, and in testimony of the sachem, her agreement hereunto, she hath subscribed her hand in presence of *Samuel Barker* and *John Almey*.

Mark × *of the squaw-sachem* AWASUNCKS;
the mark × *of* TOTATOMET, *and* SOMAGAONET."

Witnessed at the same time by "TATTACOMMETT,
SAMPONCUT, *and*
TAMOUEESAM, *alias* JEFFERY

Plimouth, 24 *July*, 1671."

The last-named witness appeared again, in the same capacity, 4 September following, when "between 40 and 50 Indians, living near or in the town of Dartmouth, made a like submission." *Ashawanomuth*, *Noman*, *Marhorkum*, *James*, and *John*, were other witnesses.

Awashonks was at Plimouth when the former articles were executed, from which it appears there was considerable alarm in Plimouth colony. There were about this time many other submissions of the Indians in different places. This step was taken to draw them from *Philip*, or at least to give a check to their joining with him, as he was now on the point of attacking the English settlements, under a pretence of injury done him in his planting lands.

Not only the chiefs of tribes or clans subscribed articles, but all their men, that could be prevailed with, did the same. The August following, 42 of *Awashonks's* men signed a paper, approving what she had done, and binding

---

* Trumbull. 200 says *Cobbet's manuscript*; 240, Hubbard.

† Hubbard, Ind. Wars, i. 97, 98. I. Mather's Brief Hist. 39. Trumbull's Hist. Connecticut, i. 347.

‡ The point of land below Pocasset, and now chiefly included in the town of Compton Rhode Island, and commonly called *Seconet*.

themselves in like manner. Out of 42, we can give names of three only—*Totatomet*, *Tunuokum* and *Sausaman*.

It appears from the following letter from *Awashonks* to Governor *Prince*, that those who submitted themselves, delivered up their arms to the English:—

"August 11, 1671, Honored sir, I have received a very great favor from your honor, in yours of the 7th instant, and as you are pleased to signify, that if I continue faithful to the agreement made with yourselves at Plimouth, I may expect all just favors from your honor. I am fully resolved, while I live, with all fidelity to stand to my engagement, and in a peaceable submission to your commands, according to the best of my poor ability. It is true, and I am very sensible thereof, that there are some Indians who do seek an advantage against me, for my submitting to his majesty's authority in your jurisdiction, but being conscious to myself of my integrity and real intentions of peace, I doubt not but you will afford me all due encouragement and protection. I had resolved to send in all my guns, being six in number, according to the intimation of my letter; but two of them were so large, the messengers were not able to carry them. I since proffered to leave them with Mr. *Barker*, but he not having any order to receive them, told me he conceived I might do well to send them to Mr. *Almy*, who is a person concerned in the jurisdiction, which I resolved to do; but since then an Indian, known by the name of *Broad-faced-will*, stole one of them out of the wigwam in the night, and is run away with it to Mount Hope; the other I think to send to Mr. *Almy*. A list of those that are obedient to me, and, I hope, and am persuaded, faithful to you, is here enclosed. Honored sir, I shall not trouble you further, but desiring your peace and prosperity, in which I look at my own to be included, I remain, your unfeigned servant,

× Awasuncks."

This letter was very probably written by Mr. *Barker*, named in it.

October 20, 1671, Governor *Prince* wrote to *Awashonks*, that he had received the list of names of her men and husband, that freely submitted themselves to his majesty's authority; and assured her that the English would befriend her on all just occasions; but intimates her disappointment and his own, that she had succeeded no better in procuring the submission of her subjects. "Though," he continued, "I fault not you, with any failing to endeavor, only to notice your good persuasions of them outwent their deserts, for aught yet appeareth. I could have wished they had been wiser for themselves, especially your two sons, that may probably succeed you in your government, and your brother also, who is so nearly tied unto you by nature. Do they think themselves so great as to disregard and affront his majesty's interest and authority here; and the amity of the English? Certainly, if they do, I think they did much disservice, and wish they would yet show themselves wiser, before it be too late." He closed by recommending her to send some of hers to the next court, to desire their arms, that her people might have the use of them in the approaching season. Desires her to let him hear from her and her husband.

On the 20 June, 1672, the following writing appears on record: Whereas *Awashunckes*, squa-sachem, stand indebted vnto Mr. *John Almey* the sume of £25 to be paid in porke att three pence a pound, or peage att 16 peney, and 20 pole of stone wall att £4, which stone wall, or £4, is to be vnderstood to be prte of the fiue and twenty pound," therefore *Awashonks*, having failed to pay agreeably to her promise, agrees to set off land on the north side of "the Indian field," next Punkateesett, on the east line till it meets with "a great runing brooke," thence northerly to a fresh meadow, thence bounded to the river by a salt cove:—this "is morgaged vnto the court of Plymouth" for the payment of said debt, which debt is to be paid 10 of February, 1672, O. S.

"*The mark* × *of* Awashunkes."

To illustrate the connections and genealogy of the family of *Awashonks* we give from the Records of Plimouth the following exceedingly valuable facts:—

July 14, 1673. "Whereas *Mamaneway* [a son of *Awashonks*] hath by full and clear testimony proved to this court, in behalf of himself and brethren, the sons of *Toloney*, and a kinsman of theirs called *Anumpash*, [commonly written *Numposh*,] son to *Pokattawagg*, that they are the chief proprietors and sachems of Saconett, or places commonly so called; and yet it being also probable that *Tatuckamna* * *Awashunckes* and those of that kindred who are of the same stock, the more remote may have some right to lands there, as they are relations to the above said *Mamaneway*, &c. and have been long inhabitants of that place. This court adviseth that convenient proportions of land be settled on the above said *Tatacamana Awashanks*, &c. at Saconett aforesaid; concerning which, the above said *Mamaneway* and his brethren and kinsman who have proved their right to those lands do not or cannot agree, this court do appoint that some meet persons, by order of this court, shall repair to the place, and make settlement of the said lands by certain and known boundaries to intent that peace may be continued among the said Indians, and they may all be accommodated for their subsisting and payment of their debts in an orderly way."

The same year, we hear again of *Tokamona*, or, as he is then called, *Totomonna*, who, with his brother *Squamatt*, having endeavored to hinder the English from possessing some lands in Dartmouth, was, from some consideration, not named, induced to relinquish his right to them. And the next year, 1674, *Mamanawachy*, or, as his name was before written, *Mamaneway*, surrendered his right also. The rights of these Indians, it is said, had been sold by others.

We hear no more of *Awashonks* until about the commencement of *Philip's* war. The year before this war, Mr. *Benjamin Church*, afterwards the famous and well-known Colonel *Church* † settled upon the peninsula of Sogkonate, in the midst of *Awashonks's* people. This peninsula is on the north-east side of Narraganset Bay, against the south-east end of the island of Rhode Island. Here he lived in the greatest friendship with these Indians, until the spring of the year 1675, when suddenly a war was talked of, and messengers were sent by *Philip* to *Awashonks*, to engage her in it. She so far listened to their persuasions, as to call her principal people together, and make a great dance; and because she respected Mr. *Church*, she sent privately for him also. *Church* took with him a man that well understood Indian, and went directly to the place appointed. Here they found hundreds of Indians gathered together from all parts of her dominions. *Awashonks* herself, in a foaming sweat, was leading the dance; but when it was announced that Mr. *Church* was come, she stopped short, and sat down; ordered her chiefs into her presence, and then invited Mr. *Church*. All being seated, she informed him that *Metacomet*, that is, *Philip*, had sent six of his men to urge her to join with him in prosecuting a war against the English. She said these messengers informed her that the *Umpames*, ‡ that is, Plimouth men, were gathering a great army to invade his country, and wished to know of him if this were truly the case. He told her that it was entirely without foundation, for he had but just come from Plimouth, and no preparations of any kind were making, nor did he believe any thoughts of war were entertained by any of the head men there. "He asked her whether she thought he would have brought up his goods to settle in that place," if he in the least apprehended a war; at which she seemed somewhat convinced. *Awashonks* then ordered the six Pokanokets into their presence. These made an imposing appearance, having their faces painted, and their hair so cut as to represent a cock's comb; it being all shaved from each side of the head, left only a tuft upon the crown, which extended from the forehead to the occiput. They had powder-horns and shot-bags at their

* Or *Tokamona*, killed by the Narragansets, not long after, probably in 1674.

† After an active life, spent chiefly in his country's service, he died suddenly at his residence in Compton, then called Little Compton, 17 Jan. 1718, in the 78 year of his age. He had become corpulent, and seemed impressed with the idea that he should not live long. The morning before his death, he rode 2 miles to visit an only sister. On leaving her, he bid her "a last farewell." As he was returning home, his horse stumbled and threw him. In the fall a blood-vessel was ruptured, and he died in about 12 hours.

‡ *Umpame* and *Apaum* were Indian names of Plimouth.

backs, which denoted warlike messengers of their nation. She now informed them of what Captain *Church* had said. Upon which they discovered dissatisfaction, and a warm talk followed, but *Awashonks* soon put an end to it; after which she told Mr. *Church* that *Philip* had told his messengers to tell her, that, unless she joined with him, he would send over some of his warriors, privately, to kill the cattle and burn the houses of the English, which they would think to be done by her men, and consequently would fall upon her.*

Mr. *Church* asked the Mount Hopes what they were going to do with the bullets in their possession, to which they scoffingly answered, ' to shoot pigeons with." *Church* then told *Awashonks* that, if *Philip* were resolved on war, " her best way would be to knock those six Mount Hopes on the head, and shelter herself under the protection of the English." When they understood this, they were very silent, and it is to be lamented that so worthy a man as *Church* should be the first to recommend murder, and a lasting remembrance is due to the wisdom of *Awashonks*, that his unadvised counsel was not put in execution.

These six Pokanokets came over to Sogkonate with two of *Awashonks's* men, who seemed very favorably inclined to the measures of *Philip*. They expressed themselves with great indignation, at the rash advice of *Church*. Another of her men, called *Little-eyes*, one of her council, was so enraged, that he would then have taken *Church's* life, if he had not been prevented. His design was to get Mr. *Church* aside from the rest, under a pretence of private talk, and to have assassinated him when he was off his guard. But some of his friends, seeing through the artifice, prevented it.

The advice of *Church* was adopted, or that part which directed that *Awashonks* should immediately put herself under the protection of the English, and she desired him to go immediately to Plimouth and make the arrangement, to which he agreed. After kindly thanking him for his information and advice, she sent two of her men with him to his house, to guard him. These urged him to secure his goods, lest, in his absence, the enemy should come and destroy them; but he would not, because such a step might be thought a kind of preparation for hostilities; but told them, that in case hostilities were begun, they might convey his effects to a place of safety. He then proceeded to Plimouth, where he arrived 7 June, 1675.

In his way to Plimouth, he met, at Pocasset, the husband of *Weetamoo*. He was just returned from the neighborhood of Mount Hope, and confirmed all that had been said about *Philip's* intentions to begin a war. But before Mr. *Church* could return again to *Awashonks*, the war commenced, and all communication was at an end. This he very much regretted, and the benevolent *Awashonks* was carried away in the tide of *Philip's* successes, which, as she was circumstanced, was her only alternative.

Mr. *Church* was wounded at the great swamp fight, 19 December following, and remained upon Rhode Island until about the middle of May 1676. He now resolved to engage again in the war, and, taking passage in a sloop bound to Barnstable, arrived at Plimouth the first Tuesday in June. The governor and other officers of government were highly pleased to see him, and desired him to take the command of a company of men to be immediately sent out, to which he consented. We thus notice *Church's* proceeding, because it led to important matters connected with the history of *Awashonks*. Before he set out with the soldiers raised at Plimouth, it was agreed that he should first return to Rhode Island, for the purpose of raising other forces to be joined with them. In his return to the island, as he passed from Sogkonesset, now called *Wood's Hole*, to the island, and when he came against Sogkonate Point, some of the enemy were seen fishing upon the rocks. He was now in an open canoe, which he had hired at Sogkonesset, and two Indians to paddle it. He ordered them to go so near the rocks that he might speak with those upon them; being persuaded that if he could have an opportunity, he might still gain over the Sogkonates to the side of the English,

* This may strengthen the belief that *Philip* put in practice a similar expedient to gain the Mohawks to his cause, as we have seen in his life.

for he knew they never had any real attachment to *Philip*, and were now in his interest only from necessity. They accordingly paddled towards them, who made signs for them to approach; but when they had got pretty near, they skulked away among the rocks, and could not be seen. The canoe then paddled off again, lest they should be fired upon; which when those among the rocks observed, they showed themselves again, and called to them to come ashore; and said they wished to speak with them. The Indians in the canoe answered them, but those on shore informed them that the waves dashed so upon the rocks that they could not understand a word they said. *Church* now made signs for two of them to go along upon the shore to a beach, where one could see a good space round, whether any others were near. Immediately two ran to the place, one without any arms, but the other had a lance. Knowing *Church* to be in the boat, they urged him to come on shore, and said they wanted to discourse with him. He told him that had the lance, that if he would carry it away at considerable distance, and leave it, he would. This he readily did. Mr. *Church* then went ashore, left one of his Indians to guard the canoe, and the other he stationed upon the beach to give notice if any should approach. He was surprised to find that *George* was one of them, a very good man, and the last Sogkonate he had spoken with, being one of those sent to guard him to his house, and to whom he had given charge of his goods when he undertook his mission to Plimouth. On being asked what he wanted that he called him ashore, answered, "that he took him for *Church*, as soon as he heard his voice in the canoe, and that he was glad to see him alive." He also told him that *Awashonks* was in a swamp about three miles off, and that she had left *Philip* and did not intend to return to him any more; and wished Mr. *Church* to stay while he should go and call her. This *Church* did not think prudent, but said he would come again and speak with *Awashonks*, and some other Indians that he should name. He therefore told *George* to notify *Awashonks*, her son *Peter*, their chief captain, and one *Nompash*, to meet him two days after at a certain rock, "at the lower end of Capt. *Richmond's* farm, which was a very noted place." It was provided that if that day should prove stormy, the next pleasant day should be improved. They parted with cordiality, *George* to carry the news to *Awashonks*, and *Church* for Newport.

On being made acquainted with *Church's* intention to visit those Indians, the government of Rhode Island marvelled much at his presumption, and would not give him any permit under their hands; assuring him that the Indians would kill him. They said also that it was madness on his part, after such signal services as he had done, to throw away his life in such a manner. Neither could any entreaties of friends alter his resolution, and he made ready for his departure. It was his intention to have taken with him one *Daniel Wilcox*,* a man who well understood the Indian language, but the government utterly refused him; so that his whole retinue, in this important embassy, consisted only of himself, his own man, and the two Indians who conducted him from Sogkonesset. As an important item in his outfit, must be mentioned a *bottle of rum*, and a *roll of tobacco*.

The day appointed having arrived, after paddling about three miles, they came to the appointed rock, where the Indians were ready to receive them, and gave him their hands in token of friendship. They went back from the shore about fifty yards, for a convenient place for consultation, when all at once rose up from the high grass, a great many Indians, so that they were entirely encompassed. They were all armed with guns, spears and hatchets faces painted and hair trimmed, in complete warlike array. If ever a man knew fear, we should apprehend it would discover itself upon an occasion like this. But, judging from his conduct, we should say he was one of those "who never felt fear."

As soon as he could be heard, Mr. *Church* told *Awashonks* that *George* had said that she desired to see him, about making peace with the English. She

* 1667, "*Daniel Willcockes* tooke the oath off fidelitie this court." *Plim. Rec.*
In 1642, one *Wilcox* set up a trading house in the Narraganset country. See *Callender' Cent. Discourse*, 38. If he were the same, it will well account for his being an interpreter

said, 'Yes." Then, said Mr. *Church*, "it is customary when people meet to treat of peace, to lay aside their arms, and not to appear in such hostile form as your people do" At this there was much murmuring among them, and *Awashonks* asked him what arms they should lay aside. Seeing their displeasure, he said, only their guns, for form's sake. With one consent they then laid away their guns, and came and sat down. He then drew out his bottle of rum, and asked *Awashonks* whether she had lived so long up at Wachusett * as to forget to drink *occapeches*. Then, drinking to her, he observed she watched him very narrowly to see whether he swallowed, and, on offering it to her, she wished him to drink again. He then told her there was no poison in it, and, pouring some into the palm of his hand, sipped it up. After he had taken a second hearty dram, *Awashonks* ventured to do likewise; then she passed it among her attendants. The tobacco was next passed round, and they began to talk. *Awashonks* wanted to know why he had not come, as he promised, the year before, observing that, if he had, she and her people had not joined with *Philip*. He told her he was prevented by the breaking out of the war, and mentioned that he made an attempt, notwithstanding, soon after he left her, and got as far as Punkatesse, when a multitude of enemies set upon him, and obliged him to retreat. A great murmur now arose among the warriors, and one, a fierce and gigantic fellow, raised his war club, with intention to have killed Mr. *Church*, but some laid hold on him and prevented him. They informed him that this fellow's brother was killed in the fight at *Punkateese*, and that he said it was *Church* that killed him, and he would now have his blood. *Church* told them to tell him that his brother began first, and that if he had done as he had directed him, he would not have been hurt. The chief captain now ordered silence, telling them they should talk no more about old matters, which put an end to the tumult, and an agreement was soon concluded. *Awashonks* agreed to serve the English "in what way she was able," provided "Plimouth would firmly engage to her that she and all of her people, and their wives and children should have their lives spared, and none of them transported out of the country." This, *Church* told her he did not doubt in the least but Plimouth would consent to.

Things being thus matured, the chief captain stood up, and, after expressing the great respect he had for Mr. *Church*, said, "Sir, if you will please accept of me and my men, and will head us, we will fight for you, and will help you to *Philip's* head before the Indian corn be ripe." We do not expect that this chief pretended to possess the spirit of prophecy, but certainly he was a truer prophet than many who have made the pretension.

Mr. *Church* would have taken a few of the men with him, and gone directly through the woods to Plimouth; but *Awashonks* insisted that it would be very hazardous. He therefore agreed to return to the island and proceed by water, and so would take in some of their company at Sogkonate Point, which was accordingly brought about. And here it should be mentioned that the friendship, now renewed by the industry of Mr. *Church*, was never afterward broken. Many of these Indians always accompanied *Church* in his memorable expeditions, and rendered great service to the English. When *Philip's* war was over, *Church* went to reside again among them, and the greatest harmony always prevailed. But to return to the thread of our narrative:—

On returning to the island. Mr. *Church* "was at great pains and charge to get a vessel, but with unaccountable disappointments; sometimes by the falseness, and sometimes by the faint-heartedness of men that he bargained with, and sometimes by wind and weather, &c." he was hindered a long time. At length, Mr. *Anthony Low*, of Swansey, happening to put into the harbor, and although bound to the westward, on being made acquainted with Mr. *Church's* case, said he would run the venture of his vessel and cargo to wait upon him. But when they arrived at Sogkonate Point, although the Indians were there according to agreement waiting upon the rocks, they met

* She had passed the preceding winter, it would seem, with *Philip's* people on the frontiers of Massachusetts

with a contrary wind, and so rough a sea, that none but *Peter Awashonks* could get on board. This he did at great peril, having only an old broken canoe to get off in. The wind and rain now forced them up into Pocasset Sound, and they were obliged to bear away, and return round the north end of the island, to Newport.

Church now dismissed Mr. *Low*, as he viewed their effort against the will of Providence. He next drew up an account of what had passed, and despatched *Peter*, on the 9 July, by way of Sogkonate, to Plimouth.

Major *Bradford** having now arrived with an army at Pocasset, Mr. *Church* repaired to him, and told him of his transactions and engagements with *Awashonks*. *Bradford* directed him to go and inform her of his arrival, which he did. *Awashonks* doubtless now discovered much uneasiness and anxiety, but Mr. *Church* told her "that if she would be advised and observe order, she nor her people need not fear being hurt." He directed her to get all her people together, "lest, if they should be found straggling about, mischief might light on them;" and that the next day the army would march down into the neck to receive her. After begging him to consider the short time she had to collect them together, she promised to do the best she could, and he left her.

Accordingly, two days after, she met the army at Punkateese. *Awashonks* was now unnecessarily perplexed by the stern carriage of Major *Bradford*. For she expected her men would have been employed in the army; but instead of that he "presently gave forth orders for *Awashonks*, and all her subjects, both men, women and children, to repair to Sandwich, and to be there upon peril, in six days." *Church* was also quite disconcerted by this unexpected order, but all reasoning or remonstrance was of no avail with the commander in chief. He told Mr. *Church* he would employ him if he chose, but as for the Indians, "he would not be concerned with them," and accordingly sent them off with a flag of truce, under the direction of *Jack Havens*, an Indian who had never been engaged in the war. Mr. *Church* told *Awashonks* not to be concerned, but it was best to obey orders, and he would shortly meet her at Sandwich.

According to promise, *Church* went by way of Plimouth to meet the Sogkonates. The governor of Plimouth was highly pleased at the account *Church* gave him of the Indians, and so much was he now satisfied of his superior abilities and skill, that he desired him to be commissioned in the country's service. He left Plimouth the same day with six attendants, among whom were Mr. *Jabez Howland*, and Mr. *Nathanied Southworth*. They slept at Sandwich the first night, and here taking a few more men, agreeably to the governor's orders, proceeded to *Agawam*, a small river of Rochester, where they expected to meet the Indians. Some of his company now became discouraged, presuming, perhaps, the Indians were treacherous, and half of them returned home. When they came to Sippican River, which empties into Buzzard's Bay in Rochester, Mr. *Howland* was so fatigued that they were obliged to leave him, he being in years, and somewhat corpulent. *Church* left two more with him as a reserve, in case he should be obliged to retreat. They soon came to the shore of Buzzard's Bay, and, hearing a great noise at considerable distance from them, upon the bank, were pres-

* Out of a curious book we take the following note, as, besides giving us an interesting fact concerning the major, it contains others of value. It was written in 1697. At that time, some pretended that the age of people was much shorter in America than in Europe; which gave rise to what we are about to extract.—*Mary Brown* was the first-born of Newbury, Mass., who married a *Godfry*; and, says our book, she "is yet alive, and is become the mother and grandmother of many children." "The mention of *Mary Brown* brings to our mind an idle whimsey, as if persons born in New England would be short-lived; whereas, the natives live long. And a judgment concerning Englishmen cannot well be made till 20 or 30 years hence. Capt. *Peregrine White*, born [on board the *Mayflower*] Nov. 1620, is yet alive, and like to live. [He died 7 years after, in 1704.] Major *William Bradford* is more than 73 years old, and hath worn a bullet in his flesh above 20 of them, [which he doubtless received in *Philip's* war. He died aged 79.] *Elizabeth Alden*, (now *Paybody*, whose granddaughter is a mother,) Capt. *John Alden*, her brother, *Alex^r. Standish*, and *John Howland*, have lived more than 70 years." S. Sewall's *New Heaven upon the New Earth*, 59, 60.

ently in sight of a "vast company of Indians, of all ages and sexes, some on horseback, running races, some at foot-ball, some catching eels and flat fish in the water, some clamming, &c." They now had to find out what Indians these were, before they dared make themselves known to them. *Church* therefore halloed, and two Indians that were at a distance from the rest, rode up to him, to find out what the noise meant. They were very much surprised when they found themselves so near Englishmen, and turned their horses to run, but, *Church* making himself known to them, they gave him the desired information. He sent for *Jack Havens*, who immediately came. And when he had confirmed what the others had related, there arrived a large number of them on horseback, well armed. These treated the English very respectfully. *Church* then sent *Jack* to *Awashonks*, to inform her that he would sup with her that night, and lodge in her tent. In the mean time, the English returned with their friends they had left at Sippican. When they came to the Indian company, they "were immediately conducted to a shelter, open on one side, whither *Awashonks* and her chiefs soon came and paid their respects." When this had taken place, there were great shouts made by the "multitudes," which "made the heavens to ring." About sunset, "the *Netops* * came running from all quarters, laden with the tops of dry pines, and the like combustible matter, making a huge pile thereof, near Mr. *Church's* shelter, on the open side thereof. But by this time supper was brought in, in three dishes, viz. a curious young bass in one dish, eels and flat fish in a second, and shell fish in a third;" but salt was wanting. When the supper was finished, "the mighty pile of pine knots and tops &c. was fired, and all the Indians, great and small, gathered in a ring around it. *Awashonks*, with the eldest of her people, men and women mixed, kneeling down, made the first ring next the fire, and all the lusty stout men standing up made the next; and then all the rabble, in a confused crew, surrounded on the outside. Then the chief captain stepped in between the rings and the fire, with a spear in one hand, and a hatchet in the other, danced round the fire, and began to fight with it, making mention of all the several nations and companies of Indians in the country that were enemies to the English. And at naming of every particular tribe of Indians, he would draw out and fight a new fire-brand, and at his finishing his fight with each particular fire-brand, would bow to Mr. *Church* and thank him." When he had named over all the tribes at war with the English, he stuck his spear and hatchet in the ground, and left the ring, and then another stepped in, and acted over the same farce; trying to act with more fury than the first. After about a half a dozen had gone through with the performance, their chief captain stepped to Mr. *Church*, and told him "they were making soldiers for him, and what they had been doing was all one swearing of them." *Awashonks* and her chiefs next came and told him "that now they were all engaged to fight for the English." At this time *Awashonks* presented to Mr. *Church* a very fine gun. The next day, July 22, he selected a number of her men, and proceeded to Plimouth. A commission was given him, and, being joined with a number of English, volunteers, commenced a successful series of exploits, in which these Sogkonates bore a conspicuous part, but have never, since the days of *Church*, been any where noticed as they deserved.

It is said † that *Awashonks* had two sons; the youngest was *William Mommynewit*, who was put to a grammar school, and learned the Latin language, and was intended for college, but was prevented by being seized with the palsy. We have been able to extend the interesting memoir of the family of *Awashonks* in the early part of this article much beyond any before printed account; of *Tokamona* we have no printed notice, except what *Church* ‡ incidentally mentions. Some of his Indian soldiers requested liberty to pursue the Narragansets and other enemy Indians, immediately

* Signifying *friends*, in Indian. † *Coll. Mass Hist. Soc.*

‡ Hist. Philip's War, 39. It is usual to cite Captain *Church* as the author or recorder of his own actions; it is so, although his son *Thomas* appears as the writer of the history. The truth is, the father dictated to the son, and corrected what appeared erroneous after the work was written

after they had captured *Philip's* wife and son. "They said the Narragansets were great rogues, and they wanted to be revenged on them, for killing some of their relations; named *Tokkamona*, (*Awashonk's* brother,) and some others."

About 130 years ago, i. e. 1700, there were 100 Indian men of the Sogkonate tribe, and the general assembly appointed *Numpaus* their captain, who lived to be an old man, and died about 1748, after the taking of Cape Breton, 1745. At the commencement of the eighteenth century, they made quite a respectable religious congregation; had a meeting-house of their own, in which they were instructed by Rev. Mr. *Billings*, once a month, on Sundays. They had a steady preacher among themselves, whose name was *John Simon*, a man of a strong mind.

About 17[illegible]0, a very distressing fever carried off many of this tribe, and in 1803 there were not above ten in Compton, their principal residence.

CHAPTER V

A further account of chiefs conspicuous in Philip's war—PUMHAM—*Taken and slain*—*His son* QUAQUALH—CHICKON—SOCONONOCO—POTOCK—*His residence*—*Complaint against Wildbow's encroachments*—*Delivers himself up*—*Put to death*—STONE-WALL-JOHN—*A great captain*—*A mason*—*His men greatly annoy the English army in Narraganset*—*Kills several of them*—*They burn a garrison, and kill fifteen persons*—*A traffic in Indian prisoners*—*The burning of Rehoboth and Providence*—*John's discourse with Roger Williams*—*Is killed*—SAGAMORE JOHN—*Fate of* MATOONAS—*Put to death on Boston Common*—*His son hanged for murder*—MONOCO—*David*—*Andrew*—*James-the-printer*— OLD-JETHERO—SAGAMORESAM, *alias* SHOSHANIM—*Visited by Eliot in 1652*—*Anecdote*—PETER-JETHERO

PUMHAM, it may be truly said, "was a mighty man of valor." Our history has several times heretofore brought him before us, and we shall now proceed to relate such facts concerning him as we have been able to collect. He was sachem of Shawomet, the country where the old squaw-sachem *Magnus* was taken and slain, as in her life we have shown.

As in almost every other case, we can only learn how to estimate the consequence of a chief from the story of his enemies. It is peculiarly so in the biography of *Pumham*. When it was reported that he was slain, every chronicler seems to have stood ready, with the ink of exultation in his pen, to record all the particulars of his fall; and to make it appear the greater, it is to be feared, they have sometimes raised many to a height to which they were not entitled, for that object. But it was not so in the case of *Pumham*. When it was reported at Boston that he was killed, an author in our *Chronicle* said, "If it is so, the glory of that nation is sunk with him forever."

This chief was brought into considerable difficulty by the English as early as 1645. In 1642, the Rev. *Samuel Gorton* took refuge in his country, and was kindly treated by him; and in January the next year, *Miantunnomoh* and *Canonicus* deeded to him Mishawomet, or Shaomet, which he afterward called *Warwick*, after the earl of that name. This settlement was grievous to the Puritan fathers of Massachusetts, as they soon showed by their resentment to *Miantunnomoh;* and here we cannot but discover the germ of all the subsequent disasters of that sachem. Mr. *Gorton* was kindly treated by him, as well as *Pumham*, until the latter was urged by Mr. *Gorton's* enemies to lay claim to the lands he had purchased of *Miantunnomoh*, whom the court of Massachusetts declared an usurper,* as in his life has been told.

By the letters of the unimpeachable *Roger Williams*, the above conclusions will appear evident. In 1656, he wrote to Massachusetts, showing them the wretched state Warwick was in from their difficulties with the Indians, as follows:—"Your wisdoms know the inhuman insultations of these wild creatures, and you may be pleased also to imagine, that they have not been sparing of your name as the patron of all their wickedness against

* MS *state paper.*

our English men, women and children, and cattle, to the yearly damage of 60, 80 and 100£. The remedy is, (under God,) only your pleasure that *Pumham* shall come to an agreement with the town or colony."* Now it should be remembered, that when Warwick was purchased, *Pumham* and some other inferior sachems received presents for their particular interests in what was sold, agreeably to the laws and usages of the Indians.

The Plimouth people had their share in the Warwick controversy, having caused *Ousamaquin* to lay claim to the same place, or a sachem who lived with him, named *Nawwashawsuck;* between whom and *Pumham* the quarrel ran so high that the former stabbed the latter.

The affairs of Warwick had been under consideration by the commissioners of the United Colonies for several years before this, and in 1649, they say, "Vppon a question betwixt the two collonies of the Massachusets and Plymouth, formerly propounded, and now again renewed by the commissioners of the Massachusetts, concerning a tract of land now or lately belonging to *Pamham* and *Saconoco*, two Indian sagamores who had submitted themselves and their people to the Massachusetts goverment, vppon part of which land som English, (besides the said Indians,) in anno 1643, were planted and settled." The decision was, that though the said tract of land fall within Plimouth bounds, it should henceforth belong to Massachusetts.

About 1646, we find the following record† of these chiefs:—"*Pomihom* and *Saconanoco* complaining to us [the court of Mass.] that many Indians dwelling 20 miles beyond them, (being friends and helpers to the Narragansetts in their present wars with *Uncas*,) are come upon their lands, and planted upon the same against their wills, they not being able of themselves to remove them, and therefore desire our counsel and help. We shall therefore advise them, if the deputies agree thereunto, to send a messenger to the sachem of those intruders to come to us to give an account of such his intention; and if he come to us, then to offer him protection upon the same terms that *Pumham* hath it, provided they satisfy *Uncas* for any injury they have done him. If he refuse to come, then we would have our messenger charge them to depart from *Pomham* and *Soconanocho* their lands, which also if they refuse, then we shall account them our enemies."

Though, by the aid of the English, *Pumham* had been able to maintain a kind of independence for some years after the death of the chief sachem, yet he was among the first who espoused the cause of *Philip* in his war, as it would seem from his not attending at the treaty in June, immediately after hostilities commenced. The army who went to make that treaty passed through his country in their march, and, as Mr. *Hubbard* states, "They found the Indians in *Pomham's* country (next adjoining to *Philip's* borders) all fled, and their wigwams without any people in them." The English army also marched through his country, in their return from the attack on *Philip* and his confederates in Narraganset, in December, 1675. At this time a small fight took place between some of the English and a number of *Pumham's* men, under a chief whose name was QUAQUALH, who gained some advantage of the English, wounding four of their men. The whites, however, report that they killed five of the Indians. *Quaqualh* himself was wounded in the knee. At the same time they burnt *Pumham's* town,‡ which contained near 100 wigwams. The English were commanded by Captain *Prentice.* §

Pumham was not the chief captain in the fight at the great falls in the Connecticut, which took place 19 May, 1676, although we presume, from the known character of him, that he was the most conspicuous in it on the side of the Indians; being a man of vast physical powers and of extraordinary bravery. In this affair the English acted a most cowardly part, having every advantage of their enemy, who acquired credit upon the occasion, even at the time, from the historian. The English came upon them before day, while none were awake to give the alarm, and, "finding them secure indeed, yea, all asleep, without having any scouts abroad, so that our soldiers came

* *Hutchinson's* papers, and *Hazard.*
† In *manuscript*, among the papers on file in the secretary's office, Mass. without date.
‡ *Old Indian Chron.* 58. This author has his name *Bumham.* There were many instances, at this time, of the use of *B.* for *P.* § *Hubbard*, Nar. 57.

and put their guns into their wigwams, before the Indians were aware of them, and made a great and notable slaughter amongst them." * Many in their fright ran into the river, and were hurled down the falls,† some of whom, doubtless, were drowned. As soon as the English, who were led by Captains *Turner* and *Holioke*, had murdered the unresisting, and the Indians having begun to rally to oppose them, they fled in the greatest confusion, although they had "about an hundred and four score" men, ‡ of whom but one was wounded when the flight began. This enhances the valor of the Indians, in our mind, especially as we read the following passage, in Mr. *Mather's* Brief History:—"In the mean while, a party of Indians from an island, (whose coming on shore might easily have been prevented, and the soldiers, before they set out from Hadley, were earnestly admonished to take care about that matter,) assaulted our men; yea, to the great dishonor of the English, a few Indians pursued our soldiers four or five miles, who were in number near twice as many as the enemy." In this flight Captain *Turner* was killed, as he was crossing Green River. *Holioke* exerted himself with great valor, and seems well calculated to oppose such a chief as *Pumham*. We hear of no other bravery among the English in this massacre, but the following passage concerning *Holioke*, which we are sorry is so sadly eclipsed. During the fight, some old persons, (whether men or women is not mentioned,) and children, had hid themselves under the bank of the river. Captain *Holioke* discovered them, and with his own hands put five of them, "young and old," to death. § This English captain did not long survive his antagonist, for, by his great exertions in this fight, a fever was brought upon him, of which he died in September following, "about Boston."‖

It would seem from the several accounts, that, although the English were sadly distressed in this fight, the Indians could never have repaired their loss; which, says the author of the PRESENT STATE, "was almost as much, nay, in some respects more considerable, than their lives." He continues, "We destroyed all their ammunition and provision, which we think they can hardly be so soon and easily recruited with, as possibly they may be with men. We likewise here demolished two forges they had to mend their arms, took away all their materials and tools, and drove many of them into the river, where they were drowned, and threw two great pigs of lead of theirs, (intended for making of bullets,) into the said river." ¶—"As our men were returning to Hadley, in a dangerous pass, which they were not sufficiently aware of, the skulking Indians, (out of the woods,) killed, at one volley, the said captain, and eight-and-thirty of his men, but immediately after they had discharged, they fled."

In relating the capture and death of *Pumham*, Mr. *Hubbard* says,** "He was one of the stoutest and most valiant sachems that belonged to the Narragansets; whose courage and strength was so great that, after he had been mortally wounded in the fight, so as himself could not stand; yet catching hold of an Englishman that by accident came near him, had done him mischief, if he had not been presently rescued by one of his fellows" This was on 25 July, 1676. *Pumham*, with a few followers, had for some time secreted themselves in Dedham woods, where it was supposed they were "almost starved for want of victuals." In this sad condition, they were fallen upon by the English under Captain *Hunting*, who killed fifteen

---

* *I. Mather*, 30.

† We cannot agree with our friend Gen. *Hoyt*, that these falls should be named *Turner's Falls*, although we once thought it well enough. We would rather call them the *Massacre Falls*, IF, indeed, their Indian name cannot be recovered. A beautiful view of these celebrated falls is given by Professor *Hitchcock*, in the volume of plates accompanying his Geology of Mass.

‡ *I. Mather*, 30. § *Hubbard*, Nar. 88. ‖ Ibid.

¶ Many of the Indians learned trades of the English, and in the wars turned their knowledge to good account. They had a forge in their fort at Narraganset, and the Indian blacksmith was killed when that was taken. The author of the *Present State*, &c. says, he was the only man amongst them that fitted their guns and arrow-heads; that among other houses they burnt his, demolished his forge, and carried away his tools.

** Narrative, 100. 4to. edition.

and took thirty-five of them without resistance.* They found here considerable plunder; "besides kettles, there was about half a bushel of wampumpeag, which the enemy lost, and twelve pounds of powder, which the captives say they had received from Albany but two days before." † A son of *Pumham* was among the captives, "a very likely youth," says *Hubbard*, ‡ "and one whose countenance would have bespoke favor for him, had he not belonged to so bloody and barbarous an Indian as his father was." It would seem from this unfeeling account that he was put to death. Dr. *Mather* says he was carried prisoner to Boston. From the same author we must add to the revolting picture of the father's death. "This *Pumham*, after he was wounded so as that he could not stand upon his legs, and was thought to have been dead, made a shift, (as the soldiers were pursuing others,) to crawl a little out of the way, but was found again, and when an Englishman drew near to him, though he could not stand, he did, (like a beast,) in rage and revenge, get hold on the soldier's head, and had like to have killed him, had not another come in to his help, and rescued him out of the enraged dying hands of that bloody *barbarian*." †

That it may be seen how the same story, recorded at the same time, at the same place, and by different individuals, varies on comparison, we give here the account of the fight in which *Pumham* was slain, from an author in the Chronicle; in which it will be observed that a different date is given to the event. "Upon the 27 of July it was, that about 20 Indians were slain, and 30 taken prisoners. We had 5 and 20 English, and 20 of our Indian friends in this exploit. One of these that were slain was *Pomham*. After he had received a deadly shot in his back, he withdrew himself from his men, (for they were all his relations and subjects that were slain and taken at this time,) and thought to hide himself in a bushy hole, but was found out by an Englishman, who, as he went to apprehend him, found that the stout sachem was unwilling to fall into the hands of the English, for he gave him a stunning blow with his hatchet, which he had reserved of all his weapons, and perhaps had slain the Englishman, but God ordered it so that he had a sudden revival, and took courage and grappled with him, [*Pumham*,] and threw him under him, and others coming in to his assistance, *Pumham* was soon despatched. There was about £20 of Indian money found in their baskets," which the English gave to their Indian friends, and their guns they took to themselves.

A short time before this, a grandson of this chief was killed by a party under *Denison*, § "who was also a sachem, and another sachem called *Chickon*."

POTOK, a Narraganset chief, we may properly, in the next place, notice. None of his acts in *Philip's* war are recorded, at least none have come to our knowledge, but they could not have been inconsiderable, in the opinion of his enemies, as his life atoned for them. We find him first mentioned, on account of his opposition to the introduction of Christianity into his nation. When, in the beginning of *Philip's* war, the English army marched into the Narraganset country, to treat or fight with that nation, as they might be found inclined, *Potok* appeared as the principal chief. In the treaty which was concluded at that time, a condition was urged by him, "that the English should not send any among them to preach the gospel or call upon them to pray to God." But the English would not admit such an article; but if an article of this character had been urged on the other hand, we doubt whether there would have been any objection urged by the Indians. On this policy of the English *Roger Williams* should be heard, as, at this day even, we need no better commentary on the matter in hand. It is contained in a letter ‖ to the governor of Massachusetts, and is as follows:—'At my last departure for England, I was importuned by ye Narraganset sachems, and especially by *Nenecunat*, to present their petition to the high

* MS. Narrative of Rev. *T. Cobbet*.

† Mather's Brief Hist. 43

‡ Narrative, *ut supra*.

§ Many write *Dennison*, but his own signature, in my possession, is as in the text.

‖ In MS. dated Providence, 5: 8: 1654.

sachems of England, that they might not be forced from their religion; and, for not changing their religion, be invaded by war. For they said they were daily visited with threatenings by Indians, that came from about the Massachusetts; that if they would not pray, they should be destroyed by war." And again, in the same letter: "Are not all the English of this land, (generally,) a persecuted people from their native soil? and hath not the God of peace and Father of mercies made the natives more friendly in this than our native countrymen in our own land to us? have they not entered leagues of love, and to this day continued peaceable commerce with us? are not our families grown up in peace amongst them? Upon which I humbly ask how it can suit with Christian ingenuity, to take hold of some seeming occasions for their destruction."

We are able to fix the place of his residence in the vicinity of Point Judith. In the year 1661, *Potok*, with several other chiefs, complained to the court of Massachusetts, that "*Samuel Wildbow*, and others of his companie," claimed jurisdiction at Point Judith, in their country, and lands adjacent. They came on and possessed themselves forcibly, bringing their cattle and other effects with them.* What order the court took upon it does not appear. About the close of *Philip's* war, *Potok* came voluntarily to Rhode Island, no doubt with the view of making friends again with his enemies; but was sent to Boston, where, after answering all their inquiries, he was put to death without ceremony.

It is related by an author in the OLD INDIAN CHRONICLE, that *Potok* was captured by the forces under Major *Talcot*, in June, 1676, at or near the same time *Stone-Layer-John* was. In closing his account of the capture of *John*, he adds, "Likewise *Potucke*, the great Indian counsellor, a man considering his education of wonderful subtlety, was brought prisoner into Rhode Island."

In the account carried to London by Captain *More*, mentioned in the last chapter, is this notice of *Potok*:—"There is one *Potuck*, a mischievous Engine, and a Counsellour, taken formerly, said to be in Goal at Rhode Island, is now sent to Boston, and there shot to death."†

In the detail of the great Narraganset expedition of 1675, we have omitted to notice a by-no-means-unimportant Indian captain.

Stone-wall-John, *Stone-layer-John*, and sometimes simply *Stone-wall*, were names by which his English friends knew him, and we have not discovered what was his Indian name. One writer of his time observes that he was called the *Stone-layer*, "for that, being an active, ingenious fellow, he had learned the mason's trade, and was of great use to the Indians in building their forts, &c." Hence we may hazard but little in the conjecture that he was the chief engineer in the erection of the great Narraganset fort, which has been described in the life of *Philip*. Although but little is known of him, he was doubtless one of the most distinguished Narraganset captains.

The first notice of *Stone-layer-John*, which we now remember, is contained in a letter of Captain *Oliver*,‡ which he wrote while on his march with the English army to attack the fort, which we have just mentioned. He says, "Dec. 15 ca[me in] *John* a rogue, with a pretence of peace, and was dismissed with [this] errand: That we might speak with sachems. That evening, he not being gone a quarter of an hour, his company, that lay hid behind a hill of our quarters, killed two Salem men, and wounded a th'r'l within a mile of us, that he is dead. And at a house three miles off, where I had ten men, they killed two of them. Instantly Capt. *Mosely*, myself and Capt. *Gardner* were sent to fetch in Major *Appleton's* company, that kept three miles and a half off, and coming, they lay behind a stone wall, and fired on us in sight of the garrison, we killed the captain that killed one of the Salem men, and had his cap." Mr. *Hubbard* says, "A few desperate Indians, creeping under a stone-wall, fired twenty or thirty guns at *Mosely* in particular, a commander well known amongst them, but the rest of the com-

* MS. State Papers.
† Old Indian Chronicle, 111.
‡ In *manuscript*. See an account of it in a note to the life of *Philip*.

pany running down upon them, killed one of them and scattered the rest." Thus did the scouts from the main body of the Indians, under such captains as the *Stone-layer*, annoy the English in their march into their country. Immediately after these skirmishes, "they burnt *Jerry Bull's** house, and killed seventeen [persons.] † Dec. 16, came that news. Dec. 17, came news that Connecticut forces were at Petaquamscut; killed four Indians and took six prisoners. That day we sold Capt. *Davenport* 47 Indians, young and old, for £80 in money." ‡

How much *John* had to do in the devastations which had been perpetrated the previous season, is unknown, but we are told that he had no small agency in "the sacking of Providence," § and Rehoboth also, without doubt. In the former about 30 houses ‖ were burned, and in the latter place "near upon 40" houses and 30 barns.

Stone-wall-John was doubtless one who conversed with the Reverend Mr. *Williams* at the time Providence was burned. The substance of that conversation is related by our anonymous author, already cited, in these words:— "But indeed the reason that the inhabitants of the towns of Seaconick and Providence generally escaped with their lives, is not to be attributed to any compassion or good nature of the Indians, (whose very mercies are inhumane cruelties,) but, [the author soon contradicts himself, as will be seen,] next to God's providence to their own prudence in avoiding their fury, when they found themselves too weak, and unable to resist it, by a timely flight into Rhode Island, which now became the common *Zoar*, or place of refuge for the distressed; yet some remained till their coming to destroy the said towns; as in particular Mr. *Williams* at Providence, who, knowing several of the chief Indians that came to fire that town, discoursed with them a considerable time, who pretended, their greatest quarrel was against Plimouth; and as for what they attempted against the other colonies, they were constrained to it, by the spoil that was done them at Narraganset.¶ They told him, that when Capt. *Pierce* engaged them near Mr. *Blackstone's*, they were bound for Plimouth. They gloried much in their success, promising themselves the conquest of the whole country, and rooting out of all the English. Mr. *Williams* reproved their confidence, minded them of their cruelties, and told them, that the Bay, viz. Boston, could yet spare 10,000 men; and, if they should destroy all them, yet it was not to be doubted, but our king would send as many every year from Old England, rather than they should share the country.** They answered proudly, that they should be ready for them, or to that effect, but told Mr. *Williams* that he was a good man, and had been kind to them formerly, and therefore they would not hurt him."

This agrees well with Mr. *Hubbard's* account of the carriage of *John* at the time he went to the English army to talk about peace, already mentioned. His words are, "yet could the messenger, [*John*,] hardly forbear threatening, vaporing of their numbers and strength, adding, withal, that the English durst not fight them."

We have now to close the career of this Indian captain, for which it requires but a word, as he was killed on the 2 July, 1676, at the same time the old squaw-sachem *Quaiapen* and most of her people were fallen upon by Major *Talcot*, as we have related in a former chapter.

Many Indians bore the name of *John*, but when they were any ways conspicuous, some distinguishing prefix or affix was generally added, as we have seen in several instances in the preceding chapters. We have already

---

* *Jerah* was probably his name.

† Ten men and five women and children. *Hubbard*, 50. "About 14." *I. Mather*, 20. "Eighteen, men, women and children." *Chronicle*, 46.

‡ Captain *Oliver's* MS. letter.

§ Old Indian Chronicle, 98.

‖ The building containing the records of R. I. was consumed at this time, and part of its contents. Some of them were saved by being thrown out of a window into some water. They bear to this time the marks of their immersion.—Oral information of *W. R. Staples*, Esq. of Providence.

¶ And who could ask for a better reason?

** This was rather gasconading for so reverend a man! Had he lived since the revolutionary war, he would hardly have *meant* so, whatever he might have *said*.

given the [illegible] one *Sagamore-John*, but another of that name, still more conspicuous for his treachery to his own nation,) here presents himself. This *Sagamore-John* was a Nipmuk sachem, and a traitor to his country On the 27th of July, 1676, doubtless from a conviction of the hopelessness of his cause, he came to Boston, and threw himself on the mercy of the English. They pardoned him, as he enticed along with him about 180 others. And, that he might have a stronger claim on their clemency, he seized *Matoonas*, and his son, against whom he knew the English to be greatly enraged, and delivered them up at the same time. On death's being immediately assigned as the lot of *Matoonas*, *Sagamore-John* requested that he might execute him with his own hands. To render still more horrid this story of blood, his request was granted; and he took *Matoonas* into the common, bound him to a tree, and there "shot him to death." To the above Dr. *Mather* adds,* "Thus did the Lord retaliate upon him the innocent blood which he had shed; as he had done, so God requited him."

Although much had been alleged against *John*, before he came in, afterwards the most favorable construction was put upon his conduct. Mr. *Hubbard* says, he "affirmed that he had never intended any mischief to the English at Brookfield, the last year, (near which village it seems his place was,) but that *Philip*, coming over night amongst them, he was forced, for fear of his own life, to join with them against the English." †

MATOONAS was also a Nipmuk chief. A son of his was said to have murdered an Englishman in 1671, when "traveling along the road," which Mr. *Hubbard* says was "out of mere malice and spite," because he was "vexed in his mind that the design against the English, intended to begin in that year, did not take place." This son of *Matoonas* was hanged, and afterwards beheaded, and his head set upon a pole, where it was to be seen six years after. The name of the murdered Englishman was *Zachary Smith*, a young man, who, as he was passing through Dedham, in the month of April, put up at the house of Mr. *Caleb Church*. About half an hour after he was gone, the next morning, three Indians passed the same way; who, as they passed by *Church's* house, behaved in a very insolent manner. They had been employed as laborers in Dorchester, and said they belonged to *Philip*; they left their masters under a suspicious pretence. The body of the murdered man was soon after found near the saw-mill in Dedham, and these Indians were apprehended, and one put to death, as is stated above. ‡

Mr. *Hubbard* supposes that the father, "an old malicious villain," bore "an old grudge against them," on the account of the execution of his son. And the first mischief that was done in Massachusetts colony was charged to him; which was the killing of four or five persons at *Mendon*, a town upon Pawtucket River; and, says *I. Mather*, "had we *amended* our ways as we should have done, this misery would have been prevented." §

When *Matoonas* was brought before the council of Massachusetts, he "confessed that he had rightly deserved death, and could expect no other." "He had often seemed to favor the praying Indians, and the Christian religion, but, like *Simon Magus*, by his after practice, discovered quickly that he had no part nor portion in that matter." ‖

The following is the statement of this affair in the OLD INDIAN CHRONICLE. *John* "declared himself sorry that he had fought against the English, and promised to give some testimonial to them soon of his fidelity; and at his return now with his men, women and children, he brought down, bound with cords, old *Mattoonus* and his son prisoners. This *Mattoonus'* eldest son had been tried at Boston, and executed, 5 or 6 years ago, for an execrable murder by him committed on a young maid ¶ of the English near Woburn, and his head was

---

* Brief History of the War, 43.

† Narrative, 101. 4to edition. If this be true, *Philip* had the chief direction in the ambushing of *Hutchinson* and *Wheeler* at Wickabaug, as related in the life of *Philip*; but in our opinion not much credit should be given to any thing coming from a traitor.

‡ Manuscript among the files in the office of the secretary of the state of Massachusetts.

§ Brief Hist. 5.

‖ *Hubbard*, 101.

¶ This author is evidently in error about the Woburn murder. Dr. *I. Mather* says, Relation, 75, "Some few private murthers there have been, as namely those at Nantucket, and that by *Matoonas* his son, and that at Woburn." No other particulars are given by *Mather*

fastened to a pole at one end of the gallows. This old *Mattoonus* father had given it out that he would be avenged of us for his son's death, which coming to the knowledge of the council, he was sent for and examined about it; and having denied it, and there not being sufficient evidence of it, he was dismissed, having only confessed this, that *considering the death of his son, he found his heart so big hot within him, but that he resolved to abide a faithful friend to the English*, and so that accusation ended. But after sachem *Philip* had begun his murders in Plimouth colony, this savage first appeared an enemy to us, and slew the two first men that were killed within the limits of our colony (to wit, at Mendham) and in that cruel and outrageous attempt at Quabaog this old *Mattoonus* was the principal ringleader. Being now brought a prisoner to Boston, he was by the council the same day, [28 July,] adjudged, to be shot to death, which was executed in Boston common, by three Indians. His head was cut off and placed upon a pole on the gallows, opposite to his son's that was there formerly hanged. His son, brought along with him, remains still a prisoner."

While *Matoonas* belonged to the Christian Indians, his residence was at Pakachoog. Here he was made constable of the town.* On joining in the war, he led parties which committed several depredations. He joined the main body of the Nipmuks in the winter of 1675, when *James Quanapohit* was among them as a spy, who saw him arrive there with a train of followers, and take the lead in the war dances.† Doubtless *Quanapohit's* evidence drew forth the confessions which he made, and added to the severity exercised at his execution.‡

A Nipmuk captain we will in the next place notice, who makes a sudden inroad upon the frontier of Massachusetts, and who as suddenly disappears.

NETUS, on the 1 February, 1676, with about 10 followers, attacked the house of one *Thomas Eames*, 4 or 5 miles beyond Sudbury, and took his and his son's families prisoners. They then destroyed every thing upon his farm, burnt up his house and his barns with the cattle and corn in them, and withdrew beyond the reach of the English, as *Totoson* had done at Eel River. When this onset was made, *Eames* himself was absent at Boston to procure ammunition. In all, seven § persons were killed or fell into the hands of this party of Indians. About three months afterwards, one of the children taken at this time escaped, and after wandering 30 miles alone through the wilderness, under extreme sufferings, arrived among the English settlements. On the 27 March following, *Netus* was killed near Marlborough, by a party of English under Lieutenant *Jacobs*, with about 40 others.‖

We have yet to notice a distinguished Nipmuk sachem, called

MONOCO by his countrymen, but, by the English, generally, *One-eyed-John*; as though deficient in the organs of vision, which probably was the case. He was, says an early writer, "a notable fellow," who, when *Philip's* war began, lived near Lancaster, and consequently was acquainted with every part of the town, which knowledge he improved to his advantage, on two occasions, in that war. On Sunday, 22 August, 1675, a man, his wife

---

but *Hubbard*, in the preface to his Narrative, edition of 1677, says, "a murther was committed at Farmington, another at Woburn, by some Indians in their drunken humors upon a maid servant or two, who denied them drink."

* *Shattuck's* Hist. Concord, 31. † 1 *Coll. Mass. Hist. Soc.* vi. 206.

‡ The Nipmuks were at this time chiefly under five sachems, which, Mr. *Hubbard* says, were "four too many to govern so small a people." The same author says, "The Nipnets were under the command of the sachem of Mount Hope," which fact is verified by numerous passages of our history. The names of the five principal sachems were MONOCO, MAUTAMP, SHOSHANIM, MATOONAS, and SAGAMORE JOHN.

§ According to the *Cotton* MSS. seven were killed and two children only taken. This agrees with our CHRONICLE, 77, where it is said "they killed seven people in a barbarous manner, and carried some away captive." *Hubbard*, 84 and Table, says *Eames'* wife was killed, and his son's wife died the next day, but says nothing of the number killed or taken.

‖ Compare *Hubbard*, 79 and 84.—This was the affair which he says was done "when it was so dark that an Indian could hardly be discerned from a better man." See BOOK III. CHAP. II. On 21 Sept. following, three Indians were hanged as concerned in the murder of *Eames's* family and two children were killed at that place.* At this time the Hassanamesit praying Indians were placed at Marlborough by authority. No sooner was it known that a murder was committed at Lancaster, than not a few were wanting to charge it upon the Hassanamesits. Captain *Mosely*, who it seems was in the neighborhood, sent to their quarters, and found "much suspicion against *eleven* of them, for singing and dancing, and having bullets and slugs, and much powder hid in their baskets." For this *offence*, these eleven were sent to Boston 30 August, on suspicion, and there *tried*. "But upon trial, the said prisoners were all of them acquitted from the fact, and were either released, or else were, with others of that fort, sent for better security, and for preventing future trouble in the like kind, to some of the islands below Boston, towards Nantasket." Fifteen was the number brought down to Boston, but *eleven* only were suspected of the alleged offence. The others, among whom were *Abram Speen* and *John Choo*, were taken along and imprisoned, for no other reason but their being accidentally, at that time, at Marlborough, or the *crime* of being Indians. It appears some time had elapsed after the murder was committed, before they were sent down for trial, or more probably they were suffered to return home before being sent to Deer Island. For *Ephraim Turner* and *William Kent* were not sent up to find out where "they all were," and what answers they could get from those they should meet, until the beginning of October; at which time these eleven Indians were scattered in various directions, about their daily callings. And all the information *Turner* and *Kent* handed into court was, that they were thus dispersed. *Waban* and Mr. *John Watson*, who had been appointed to reside among those Indians, were the only persons questioned. What steps the court took upon this information, we are not informed, but they were about this time sent to Deer Island.

The names of these Indians, concerning whom more particular inquiry may hereafter be made by the benevolent antiquary, it is thought should be given; especially as they may not elsewhere be preserved. They were,

Old-jethro and two sons, *James-the-printer*, *James Acompanet*, *Daniel Munups*, *John Cquasquaconet*, *John Asquenet*, *George Nonsequesewit*, *Thomas Mamuxonqua*, and *Joseph Watapacoson*, alias *Joseph Spoonant*.

After a trial of great vexation to these innocent Indians, *David*, the main witness against them, acknowledged he had perfidiously accused them; and at the same time, a prisoner was brought in, who testified that he *knew One-eyed-john* had committed the murder at Lancaster, and a short time after another was taken, who confirmed his testimony.

These Indians brought all these troubles upon themselves by reason of their attachment to the English. It was in their service that they discovered and captured *Andrew*, a brother of *David*, who, on being delivered to the soldiery, was shot by them with ferocious precipitancy. Therefore, when the Lancaster murder happened, Captain *Mosely*, having already sundry charges against *David*, held an inquisition upon him to make him confess relative to the Lancaster affair. The method taken to *make* him confess, (agreeably to the desire of his inquisitors,) was this: they bound him to a tree, and levelled guns at his breast. In this situation, to avert immediate death, as well as to be revenged for the death of his brother, he proceeded to accuse the eleven Indians before named. For thus falsely accusing his countrymen, and shooting at a boy who was looking after sheep at Marlborough, *David* was condemned to slavery, and accordingly sold, as was one of the eleven named *Watapacoson*. This last act being entirely to calm the clamors of the multitude; after he had been once acquitted, a new trial was got up, and a new jury for this particular end.†

Andrew's history is as follows: He had been gone for some time before the war, on a hunting voyage towards the lakes; and on his return homeward, he fell in among *Philip's* men about Quabaog. This was about a month

* The above is Mr. *Hubbard's* account. Mr. *Willard*, in his excellent history of Lancaster, gives us the names of six, and says eight were killed. But in his enumeration I count *nine*; and *Gookin* says seven. Our text is according to *Hubbard*, Nar. 30.

† *Gookin*, Manuscript Hist. Praying Indians.

before the affair at Lancaster. The reason he staid among the hostile Indians is very obvious: he was afraid to venture into the vicinity of the whites, lest they should treat him as an enemy. But as his ill fortune fell out, he was found in the woods, by his countrymen of Marlborough, who conducted him to the English, by whom he was shot, as we have just related. The officer who presided over and directed this affair, would, no doubt, at any other time, have received a reward proportionate to the malignity of the offence; but in this horrid storm of war, many were suffered to transgress the laws with impunity.

From one account of this affair,* it would seem that one of the Indians seized by *Mosely* at this time was actually executed; "for," says the writer to whom we refer, "the commonalty were so enraged against Mr. *Eliot*, and Capt. *Guggins* especially, that Capt. *Guggins* said on the bench, [he being a judge,] that he was afraid to go along the streets; the answer was made, you may thank yourself; however an order was issued out for the execution of that one (notorious above the rest) Indian, and accordingly he was led by a rope about his neck to the gallows. When he came there, the executioners (for there were many) flung one end over the post, and so hoisted him up like a dog, three or four times, he being yet half alive, and half dead; then came an Indian, a friend of his, and with his knife made a hole in his breast to his heart, and sucked out his heart-blood. Being asked his reason therefor, his answer [was] *Umh, Umh nu*, me stronger as I was before; me be so strong as me and he too; he be ver strong man fore he die. Thus with the dog-like death (good enough) of one poor heathen, was the people rage laid, in some measure."

We have yet to add a word concerning *Monoco*. When *Quanapohit* was out as a spy, *Monoco* kindly entertained him, on account of former acquaintance not knowing his character. They had served together in their wars against the Mohawks. On 10 Feb. 1676, about 600 Indians fell upon Lancaster, and, after burning the town, carried the inhabitants into captivity. Among them was the family of Reverend Mr. *Rowlandson*. Mrs. *Rowlandson*, after her redemption, published an amusing account of the affair. *Monoco*, or *One-eyed-john*, it is said, was among the actors of this tragedy. On 13 March following, Groton was surprised. In this affair, too, *John Monoco* was principal; and on his own word we set him down as the destroyer of Medfield. After he had burned Groton, except one garrison house, he called to the captain in it, and told him he would burn in succession Chelmsford, Concord, Watertown, Cambridge, Charlestown, Roxbury and Boston. He boasted much of the men at his command; said he had 480 warriors; and added—"*What me will me do.*" The report of this very much enraged the English, and occasioned his being entitled a "bragadocio" by the historian. At the close of *Philip's* war, with others, he gave himself up to Major *Waldron* at Cochecho; or, having come in there, at the request of *Peter-jethro*, to make peace, was seized and sent to Boston, where, in the language of Mr. *Hubbard*, he, "with a few more bragadocios like himself, *Sagamore-sam*, *Old-jethro*, and the sachem of Quabaog, [*Mautamp*,†] were taken by the English, and was seen, (not long before the writing of this,) marching towards the gallows, (through Boston streets, which he threatened to burn at his pleasure,) with a halter about his neck, with which he was hanged at the town's end, Sept. 26, in this present year, 1676."‡

On the 24 July, 1675, five of the principal Nipmuk sachems signed an agreement to meet the governor of Massachusetts to treat of peace soon after, but not appearing according to agreement Captain *Hutchinson* was sent out

* In the INDIAN CHRONICLE, 26, 27.

† Compare *Hubbard*, 35 and 75.—The same, probably, called *Mattawamppe*, who, in 1665, witnessed the sale of Brookfield, Mass., deeded at that time by a chief named *Shattookquis*. *Mautamp* claimed an interest in said lands, and received part of the pay.—Rev. Mr. *Foot's Hist. Brookfield*.

‡ This, so far as it goes, agrees with an entry in *Sewall's* MS. Diary, cited in *Shattuck's* Concord, 63—"*Sagamore Sam* goes, *One-ey'd John, Maliompe* [*Mautamp*] Sagamore of Quabaog, General at Lancaster, &c. *Jethro* (the father) walked to the gallows. *One ey'd John* accuses *Sagamore John* to have fired the first gun at Quabaog and killed Capt. *Hutchinson*."

to ascertain the cause, and was ambushed by them, as we have in the life of *Philip* related. At this time, "SAM, sachem of Weshacum," and NETAUMP, are particularly mentioned as having been hanged at Boston.

It was reported, (no doubt by the Indians, to vex their enemies,) that Mrs. *Rowlandson* had married *Monoco*. "But," the author of the PRESENT STATE, &c. says, "it was soon contradicted," and, "that she appeared and behaved herself amongst them with so much courage and majestic gravity, that none durst offer any violence to her, but on the contrary (in their rude manner) seemed to show her great respect."

In the above quotation from Mr. *Hubbard*, we have shown at what time several of the Nipmuck chiefs were put to death beside *Monoco*.

OLD-JETHRO was little less noted, though of quite a different character. His Indian name was *Tantamous*. He was present at the sale of Concord (Mass.) to the English, about which time he lived at Natick. In 1674, he was appointed a missionary to the Nipmuks living at Weshakim, since Sterling, but his stay there was short.* He and his family (of about 12 persons) were among those ordered to Deer Island, on the breaking out of the war the next year. Their residence then was at Nobscut Hill, near Sudbury His spirit could not brook the indignity offered by those English who were sent to conduct the praying Indians to Boston, and in the night he escaped, with all his family, into his native wilds. His son *Peter* had been so long under the instruction of the English, that he had become almost one of them. He deserted his father's cause, and was the means of his being executed with the other Nipmuk sachems already mentioned. This occasioned Dr. *I. Mather* to say of him, "That abominable Indian, *Peter-jethro*, betrayed *his own father*, and other Indians of his special acquaintance, unto death." It seems he had been employed by the English for this purpose.

About a month before the fall of *Philip*, the Nipmucks became fully aware of their wretched condition, who, on the 6 July, 1676, sent an Indian messenger to the English with a white flag. He came, says our Chronicle, "from *Sagamore Sam* of Nassoway (a proud Salvage, who two months since insulted over the English, and said, if the English would first begge Peace of him, he would let them have Peace, but that he would never ask it of them;) This Indian was sent from him with Letters, desiring Peace of us, and expressely praying us in the name of *Jesus Christ*, and for his sake to grant it whose holy name they have so much blasphemed. Thus doth the Lord Jesus make them to bow before him, and to lick the dust. And having made mention of his letter it will not be unacceptable to transcribe some copies of the Letters sent by him, and others on this subject, which take as followeth. The reader must bear with their barbarisms, and excuse the omission of some expressions in them, that can hardly admit of good English."

"*The first Letter, July the 6th*, 1676.†

"Mr. *John Leverett*, my Lord, Mr. *Waban*, and all the chief men our Brethren, Praying to God: [*This Mr.* Waban *is a Praying Indian, faithful, and a Ruler amonst them; by their Brethren praying to God, they mean those of the same Nation.*] We beseech you all to help us; my wife she is but one, but there be more Prisoners, which we pray you keep well: Mattamuck his wife, we entreat you for her, and not onely that man, but it is the Request of two Sachems, *Sam* Sachem of *Weshakum*, and the *Pakashoag* Sachem.

"And that further you will consider about the making Peace We have spoken to the People of Nashobah (viz. *Tom Dubler* and *Peter*,) that we would agree with you, and make a Covenant of Peace with you. We have been destroyed by your Souldiers, but still we Remember it now, to sit still; do

---

* Mr. *Shattuck's* Hist. Concord, 30.

† The tenor of the following letters, is very different from those in April previous, which I had discovered in MS. and printed in the former editions of the Book of the Indians. These were then unknown to me

you consider it again; we do earnestly entreat you, that it may be so by *Jesus Christ*, O! let it be so! *Amen, Amen.**

It was signed

MATTAMUCK, *his Mark* N
SAM SACHEM, *his Mark* Ψ.
SIMON POTTOQUAM, *Scribe.*|
UPPANIPPAQUEM, *his* — C.
PAKASKOKAG *his Mark* Ψ."

"*Superscribed*," "*To all* Englishmen *and* Indians, *all of you hear* Mr. Waban, Mr. Eliott."

"*Second Letter.*

"My Lord, Mr. *Leveret* at *Boston*, Mr. *Waban*, Mr. *Eliott*, Mr. *Gookin*, and Council, hear yea. I went to Connecticot about the Captives, that I might bring them into your hands, and when we were almost there, the *English* had destroyed those *Indians*: when I heard it, I returned back again; then when I came home, we were also destroyed; after we were destroy'd, then *Philip* and *Quanipun* went away into their own Countrey againe; and I knew they were much afraid, because of our offer to joyn with the *English*, and therefore they went back into their own Countrey, and I know they will make no Warre; therefore because when some *English* men came to us, *Philip* and *Quanapun* sent to kill them; but I said, if any kill them, I'll kill them.‡

SAM SACHEM.

Written by Simon Boshokum Scribe." §

Third Letter

"For Mr. *Eliot*, Mr. *Gookin*, and Mr. *Waban*.

Consider of this I entreat you, consider of this great businesse that is done and my wonder concerning *Philip*; but his name is ——— *Wewesawannit*,‖ he engageth all the people that were none of his subjects: Then when I was at *Penakook*, *Numpho John*, *Alline*,¶ *Sam Numpho*, and others who were angry, and *Numpho* very much angry that *Philip* did engage so many people to him; and *Numpho* said it were a very good deed that I should go and kill him that

---

* This surpasseth any thing, in supplication, that we have, from the poor Indians. They were truly sensible of their deplorable condition! Little to subsist upon—the northern and western wilderness so full of their native enemies, that a retreat upon those hunting-grounds was cut off—all the fishing places near and upon the coast watched by their successful enemy—hence nothing now remained but to try the effect of an offer of unconditional submission!—This letter, however, must not be regarded as the language of the warriors, it was the language of the Christian Indians, in behalf of them and themselves.

† The name of this sachem approaching nearly in sound to that of the place since called Worcester, of which *Sagamore-John* was chief, almost induces the belief that he is the same. A sachem of the name having deeded Worcester to the whites in 1671, is additional proof. See the elaborate history of that town by *Wm. Lincoln*, Esq., now in course of publication.

‡ This letter will be regarded as an admirable specimen of Indian sentiment, and its value is much enhanced, as it unfolds truths of great value—truths that lay open the situation of things at this period that will be gladly received. *Sam* was a magnanimous sachem. So was *Monoco*. We doubt if any thing can in truth be brought against either, that would not comport with a warrior of their time, but they did not come within the limits of a pardon offered in the Proclamation! When messengers were sent to treat with the Indians for the redemption of prisoners, to prevent the evil such negotiation was calculated to produce, and which *Philip*, doubtless, foresaw, he ordered such to be summarily dealt with. *Quanapohit* was suspected for a spy, and *Philip* had ordered him to be killed, but *Monoco* said, "I will kill whomsoever shall kill *Quanapohit*." *Shoshanim* afterwards said the same when visited by Mr. *Hoar* and *Nepanet*, who were sent to treat for the ransom of Mr. *Rowlandson's* family. "If any kill *them*, I will kill them," that is, he would kill the murderer. But these kind offices were forgotten in the days of terror!

§ The same person, whose name to the last letter is spelt *Pettoquam*, and in Book ii. Chap. vii., *Betokam*

‖ This stands in the MS. records, *Wewasowanuett*. See Book iii. Chap. ii.

¶ There is some error concerning this person's name. *John U. Line* means the same person, I think, in *Gookin's* MS. history. See Book ii. Chap. vii.; an account of several others here mentioned may there also be found.

joyned so many to himself without cause: In like manner I said so too. Then had you formerly said be at peace, and if the Council had sent word to kill *Philip* we should have done it: then let us clearly speak, what you and we shall do. O let it be so speedily, and answer us clearly.

PUMKAMUN,
PONNAKPUKUN,
or, JACOB MUTTAMAKOOG."

"The answer the Council made them, was, 'That treacherous persons who began the war and those that have been barbarously bloody, must not expect to have their lives spared, but others that have been drawn into the war, and acting only as Souldiers submitting to be without arms, and to live quietly and peaceably for the future shall have their lives spared.'"

Sagamore Sam was one of those that sacked Lancaster, 10 February, 1676. His Indian name was at one time *Shoshanim*, but in *Philip's* war it appears to have been changed to *Uskatuhgun;* at least, if he be the same, it was so subscribed by *Peter-jethro*, when the letter was sent by the Indians to the English about the exchange of Mrs. *Rowlandson* and others, as will be found in the life of *Nepanet*. He was hanged, as has been before noted. *Shoshanim* was successor to *Matthew*, who succeeded *Sholan*.

This last-mentioned sachem is probably referred to by the author quoted in Mr. *Thorowgood's* curious book. In the summer of 1652, Reverend *John Eliot* intended to visit the Nashuas, in his evangelical capacity, but understanding there was war in that direction among the Indians,* delayed his journey for a time. The sachem of Nashua, hearing of Mr. *Eliot's* intention, "took 20 men, armed after their manner," as his guard, with many others, and conducted him to his country. And my author adds, "this was a long journey into the wilderness of 60 miles: it proved very wet and tedious, so that he was not dry three or four days together, night nor day." † One of the Indians at this time asked Mr. *Eliot* why those who prayed to God among the English loved the Indians that prayed to God "more than their own brethren." The good man seemed some at a loss for an answer, and waived the subject by several scriptural quotations.

We may be incorrect in the supposition that the sachem who conducted Mr. *Eliot* on this occasion was *Sholan*, as perhaps *Passaconaway* would suit the time as well.

CHAPTER VI.

Friendly Indians—CAPTAIN AMOS—*Pursues Tatoson and Penachason—Escapes the slaughter at Pawtucket—Commands a company in the eastern war*—CAPTAIN LIGHTFOOT—*His services in Philip's war—In the eastern war*—KETTENANIT—*His services*—QUANNAPOHIT—*His important services as a spy*—MAUTAMP—*Monoco*—NEPANET—*Employed to treat with the enemy—Brings letters from them—Effects an exchange of prisoners*—PETER CONWAY—PETER EPHRAIM.

AMOS, commonly called *Captain Amos*, was a Wampanoag, whose residence was about Cape Cod. We have no notice of him until *Philip's* war, at which time he was entirely devoted to the service of the English. After the Plimouth people had found that *Tatoson* was concerned in the destruction of *Clark's* garrison, they sought for some friendly Indians who would under take to deliver him and his abettors into their hands. Captain *Amos* tendered his services, and was duly commissioned to prosecute the enterprise,

* In 1647, three Indians were killed between Quabaog and Springfield, by other Indians. The next year, five others were killed about midway between Quabaog and Lancaster.—*Winthrop's Journal*, (*Savage's* ed.) Such instances were common among the Indians.

† Sure Arguments to prove that the Jews inhabit now in America.—By *Thomas Thorowgood*, 4to. London, 1652. Sir *Roger L'Estrange* answered this book by another, entitled THE AMERICANS NO JEWS.

and to take into that service any of his friends. Meantime, *Tatoson* had fled to Elizabeth Island, in company with *Penachason*, another chief who was also to be taken, if he could be found. This *Penachason* was probably *Tatoson's* brother's son, sometimes called *Tom*, who, if the same, was also at the destroying of *Clark's* garrison. Yet the wily chiefs eluded the vigilance of Captain *Amos*, by flying from that region into the Nipmuks' country, where they joined *Philip*.

To encourage greater exertion on the part of the friendly Indians, to execute their commission, it was ordered, that in case they captured and brought in either *Tatoson* or *Penachason*, "they may expect for their reward, for each of them four coats, and a coat apiece for every other Indian that shall prove merchantable."

We have mentioned in a former chapter the horrid catastrophe of Captain *Peirse* and his men at Pawtucket. Captain *Amos* escaped that dreadful slaughter. He fought there with 20 of his warriors, and when Captain *Peirse* was shot down by a ball which wounded him in the thigh, he stood by his side, and defended him as long as there was a gleam of hope. At length, seeing nearly all his friends slain, with admirable presence of mind he made his escape, by the following subtle stratagem:—

Nanuntenoo's warriors had blackened their faces, which Captain *Amos* had observed, and by means of powder contrived to discolor his own unobserved by them. When he had done this, he managed, by a dextrous manœuvre to pass among the enemy for one of them, and by these means escaped.

What were Captain *Amos's* other acts in this war, if any, we have not learned; nor do we meet again with him until 1689. In that year, he went with Col. *Church* against the eastern Indians and French, in which expedition he also had the command of a company. *Church* arrived with his forces in Sept. at Casco, now Portland, and, having landed secretly under cover of the night, surprised, on the following morning, about four hundred Indians, who had come to destroy the place. Although the Indians did not receive much damage, yet, Governor *Sullivan* says,* the whole eastern country was saved by the timely arrival of this expedition. In the fight at Casco, 21 September, eight of the English were killed and many wounded. Two of Captain *Amos's* men were badly wounded, and *Sam Moses*, another friendly Indian, was killed. There was another Indian company in this expedition, commanded by Captain *Daniel*, out of which one man was killed, who was of Yarmouth on Cape Cod.†

LIGHTFOOT, of the tribe of the Sogkonates, distinguished in *Philip's* war, was also in the service under *Church* at Casco; a memorable expedition, on more than one account. One circumstance we will name, as it well nigh proved the ruin of the undertaking. When, on the following morning, after the arrival of the forces, the attack was begun, it was, to the inexpressible surprise of the English, found, that the bullets were much larger than the calibre of their guns. This was a most extraordinary and unaccountable occurrence, and great blame was chargeable somewhere. In this wretched dilemma, the fight having already begun, *Church* set some at work making the bullets into slugs, by which resort he was able to continue the fight. It being high water at the time, an estuary separated the battle-ground from the town. The bullets were to be carried to the army engaged, in buckets, after being hammered. When the first recruit of slugs was made up, Colonel *Church* ran with it to the water's edge, and, not caring to venture himself to wade across, called to those on the other side to send some one to take it over to the army. None appeared but *Lightfoot*. This Indian dextrously repassed the estuary, with a quantity of powder upon his head, and a "kettle" of bullets in each hand, and thus the fight was maintained, and the enemy put to flight.

In *Philip's* war, *Lightfoot's* exploits were doubtless very numerous, but few of them have come down to us. He volunteered to fight for the English, at *Awashonk's* great dance at Buzzard's Bay, already mentioned. When *Little-eyes* was taken at Cushnet, in 1676, *Lightfoot* was sent with him to what is

* Hist. *District of Maine*, 102. † MS. letter of Captain *Basset* of the expedition.

now called *Palmer's Island*, near the mouth of Cushnet River, where he held him in guard until he could be safely conducted to Plimouth. About the time *Akkompoin* was killed, and *Philip's* wife and son were taken, *Church* gave him a captain's commission, after which he made several successful expeditions.—We now pass to characters hitherto less known, though perhaps of more interest.

Very little was known of certain important characters among the friendly Indians of Massachusetts, which should have by no means been overlooked until the discovery of Mr. *Gookin's* manuscript history of the praying Indians, not long since, and to which we have often referred already. We shall, therefore, devote the remainder of the present chapter to their history

JOB KATTENANIT seems first to demand attention. He was a Christian Indian, and lived some time at Natick, but was at one time a preacher at Magunkog, and belonged originally, we believe, to Hassanamesit. However that may have been, it is certain he lived there in the beginning of *Philip's* war, when that chief's men made a descent upon the place, with the intention of carrying away those Christian Indians prisoners. *Job* made his escape from them at this time, and came in to the English at Mendon. He had still three children in the enemy's hands, and he was willing to run any venture to release them. He therefore applied for and obtained a pass, assuring him safety, provided that, in his return, he should fall into the hands of the English scouts. Besides liberating his children, considerable hopes were entertained, that he might be enabled to furnish information of the enemy. It unfortunately happened, that, before he had passed the frontier, he fell in with some English soldiers, who treated him as a prisoner, and an enemy, even taking from him his clothes and gun, sending him to the governor of Boston; "who, more to satisfy the clamors of the people than for any offence committed," assigned him to the common jail, where he suffered exceedingly; himself and many others being crowded into a narrow and filthy place. After about three weeks, he was taken out and sent to Deer Island. The clamors of the people were indeed high at this time, and many accused Major *Gookin*, who gave him the pass, of being guilty of furnishing the enemy with intelligence.

After the Narraganset fight, 19 December, 1675, the English were very anxious to gain information relative to the position of the enemy, and accordingly instructed Major *Gookin* to use his endeavors to employ some friendly Indian spies; who, after considerable negotiation among those at Deer Island, engaged *Job* again, and *James Quannapohit*, alias *Quanapaug*. Their reward was to be *five* pounds apiece! They departed upon this service before day, the 30th of December, and, during their mission, behaved with great prudence, and brought valuable information to the English on their return; but which, from intestine bickerings among the English, turned to small account.

James Quannapohit returned 24th of January following, nearly worn out and famished; having travelled about 80 miles in that cold season, upon snowshoes, the snow being very deep. The information which he gave was written down by Major *Gookin*.* Among other matters, he stated that the enemy had taken up their quarters in different places, probably near Scattacook; and many others, including the Nipmuks, about Menumesse. The Narragansets had not yet joined *Philip* openly, but while *James* and *Job* were among the Nipmuks, messengers arrived from Narraganset which gave them much joy, for they expressed an ardent desire to join them and *Philip* in prosecuting the war. They said their loss in the great swamp fight was small. In three weeks, *James* learned, they would assault Lancaster, which accordingly came to pass, upon the very day which he said they intended it. He learned and thus divulged their plans to a great extent. A circumstance now occurred which obliged him to make his escape, which was this: He found a friend and protector in *Mautamp*,† one of the Nipmuk chiefs, who, it seems,

* The same published in *Coll. Mass. Hist. Soc.* 1. vi. 205—208.

† The same, probably, called *Netaump*, who was afterwards executed at Boston, at the same time with *Sagamore-sam*. See *Hubbard*, 35.

intended shortly to visit *Philip;* and insisted that *Quannapohit* should accompany him, and it was with no small difficulty he was able to elude the vigilant eye of *Mautamp*, and make his escape, which, however, was effected only by a cunning stratagem, as follows:—He told *Mautamp* that he had fought against *Philip* in the commencement of the war, and that *Philip* knew him, and that, unless he could go to him with some important trophy, *Philip* would not believe him, and would immediately kill him. And moreover, *Tukapewillin* had privately told him that *Philip* had given out word that certain praying Indians should be sought after, and, if possible, seized and brought to him; for he wanted to put them to death in a cruel manner, with his own hands, and that *he* was one of them. He therefore told *Mautamp* that he would go, in the first place, and kill some English, and take their heads along with him, and then he should consider himself safe. This being consented to, he lost no time in retracing his steps to the frontiers of the English.

He mentions *Monoco*, or *One-eyed-john*, as a great captain among the enemy, who also treated him kindly, and entertained him in his wigwam during his stay there; they being old acquaintance, having served together in their wars against the Mohawks, ten years before.*

And here also Mr. *Gookin* gives a favorable account of *Monoco. Philip* had ordered that the persons above named should be brought to him, if taken alive, "that he might put them to some tormenting death, *which had hitherto* been prevented by the care and kindness of a great captain among them, named *John-with-one-eye*, belonging to Nashua,† who had civilly treated and protected *James*, and entertained him at his wigwam, all the time of his being there." ‡

Job was requested to come away with *Quanapohit*, but saw no way of getting away his children, which was a main object with him. He knew, too, that *James* could give all the information they both possessed at that period, and not considering himself in imminent danger, preferred to tarry longer.

At Wanexit, or Manexit, they fell in with seven Indians, who took them and conveyed them about twenty miles, across the path leading to Connecticut, northward from Quabaog. These were some of the Quahmsits and Segunesits. At this place were three towns which contained about 300 warriors well armed. Here they were threatened with death, their mission being truly guessed. But going to the wigwam of *One-eyed-john*, "Sagamore of Nashua," or *Monoco*, he charged his gun and said, "I will kill whomsoever shall kill *Quanapohit.*" § Some said he had killed one of *Philip's* counsellors ‖ at Mount Hope, and *Philip* had hired some to kill him; also *James Speen*, *Andrew Pitimy*, Captain *Hunter*, *Thomas Quanapohit*, and *Peter Ephraim.* On being ordered to visit *Philip*, "*Job* and he pretended to go out a hunting, killed three dear quickly, and perceiving they were dogged by some other Indians, went over a pond and lay in a swamp till before day, and when they had prayed together he ran away." *Job* was to return to the enemy, and tell them that *James* ran away because they had threatened to kill him. *Job*, not being particularly obnoxious to them, concluded to remain longer for the end of ransoming his children, as we have said. He returned to the English in the night of the 9th of February, and said, as *James* had before, that on the next day Lancaster would be attacked, for he knew about four hundred of the enemy were already on their march, and it so resulted. He further informed the English, that the enemy would shortly attack Medfield, Groton, Marlborough, and other places, and that the Narragansets had joined *Philip* and the Nipmuks.

While *James* was there, "a Narraganset brought to them one English head: they shot at him, and said the Narragansets were the English friends all last

---

* Of this war we have given an account in Book II. chap. III.

† Called sagamore of Nashua, in the *Cotton manuscripts.*

‡ Hist. Praying Indians.

§ Cotton Manuscripts.

‖ Referring probably, to Thebe. See Book III. chap. II.

summer. Afterwards two messengers came with twelve heads, craving their assistance, they then accepted them." *

Before he left the enemy, he appointed a place of safety for his children, and sundry others of his friends, captured at Hassanamesit, where he would afterwards meet and conduct them to the English. He therefore petitioned the council for liberty to meet them, which was granted. But he now had new difficulties to encounter, owing to "the rude temper of those times," as one of the wise men of that age expressed it.† Although both these men had acquitted themselves to the entire satisfaction of the authorities who sent them forth, yet the populace accused them of giving information to the enemy, and that they were secretly their advisers, or else they had not returned in safety; to appease which they were confined again to the island. This so interfered with the time set by *Job* to meet his children and friends, that great sufferings overtook them, as well as himself; and he knew not that ever he should have an opportunity to see his children again. But it much sooner happened, no doubt, than he expected, although in an indirect way. About the time he was sent to the island, a vote passed in the general court of Massachusetts, to raise an army of six hundred men, and Major *Thomas Savage* was applied to, to conduct them in the war. He refused, unless he could have some of the friendly Indians from the island for assistants. On a messenger being sent among them, six of their principal and bravest men volunteered in that service, among whom was *Job Kattenanit.* The army marched about the first of March, 1675, O. S. But when at Marlborough, *Job* got liberty of Major *Savage* and Major-general *Denison,* to attempt the finding of his friends and children, whom he had appointed to meet near Hassanamesit. When it was known to Captain *Mosely,* he behaved himself very unbecoming towards the commanding officer, and nothing but his popularity with the army saved his reputation. Indeed, his conduct seems quite as reprehensible as that of a more modern Indian hunter in the Floridas, which all friends of humanity joined to condemn. *Mosely,* it appears, would place no confidence in any Indian, and doubtless thought he was acting for the best interests of the country. He urged that it was a most impolitic measure to suffer any Indian to go away at this time, knowing their natural treacherousness; and he doubted not but *Job* (although a tried friend) would inform the enemy of the approach of the army, which would frustrate all their designs. The great ascendency which this officer held in the army can best be understood by a simple statement of the fact, that Major *Savage* and General *Denison* were obliged to send after *Job* before the soldiery would cease their clamors. Captain *Wadsworth* and Captain *Syll,* accompanied by *James Quannapohit,* went in pursuit with the utmost speed. But they did not overtake him, and he soon returned to the army without finding his friends; they, from fear of discovery, having changed their place, the time having been much longer than was set, and their consequent sufferings were indescribable.

We shall only add here concerning them, that they afterwards fell into the hands of a party of English, who treated them in a savage manner, taking every thing from them. But when they were brought to Major *Savage,* he treated them kindly, and had them sent to Boston, all except four, who ran away from Marlborough, where they stopped for the night, from the fear of being murdered, some of the people so abused and insulted them. About two months after that, they were found and brought in by *Nepanet* Finally, *Job* recovered all his children, and, marrying again, lived happily. His wife was one of those whom he had managed to deliver out of the hands of the enemy at such hazard and pains. She had, during their wanderings, nursed and kept alive his children, one, especially, which was very young.

When the Hassanamesits went off with the enemy, *James Quannapohit* was in the neighborhood with the English forces. Captain *Syll* sent out a scout, and *James* and *Elizer Pegin* accompanied. Seven of the enemy were

* Cotton Manuscripts.
† Major *Daniel Gookin,* who was at least a hundred years in advance of that age.

soon discovered, one of whom was leading an English prisoner. They discovered the English scout, and fled. *James* and *Elizer* pursued them, and recovered the prisoner, whose name was *Christopher Muchin*, who had been taken from Marlborough. *James* also took one of the enemy's guns.*

The English having, by means of spies, as in the preceding life we have stated, learned the state of feeling among their enemies, felt themselves prepared, as the spring of 1676 advanced, to make overtures to them for peace, or an exchange of prisoners, or both, as they might be found inclined.

TOM NEPANET was fixed upon as plenipotentiary in this business. And, although unjustly suffering with many of his brethren upon a bleak island in Boston harbor, consented, at the imminent risk of his life, to proceed to meet the Indians in the western wilderness, in the service, and for the benefit, of those who had caused his sufferings.

Nepanet set out, 3 April, 1676, to make overtures to the enemy for the release of prisoners, especially the family of Mr. *Rowlandson*, which was taken at Lancaster, returned on the 12 following, with a written answer from the enemy, saying, "*We nou give answer by this one man, but if you like my answer sent one more man besides this one* Tom Nepanet, *and send with all true heart and with all your mind by two men; because you know and we know your heart great sorrowful with crying for your lost many many hundred man and all your house and all your land and woman child and cattle as all your thing that you have lost and on your backside stand.*

Signed by SAM, *Sachem*,
KUTQUEN, *and*
QUANOHIT, *Sagamores.*
Peter Jethro, scribe.

At the same time, and I conclude in the same letter, they wrote a few words to others, as follows: "*Mr.* Rowlandson, *your wife and all your child is well but one dye. Your sister is well and her 3 child.* John Kittell, *your wife and all your child is all well, and all them prisoners taken at Nashua is all well.*——

Mr. Rowlandson, *se your loving sister his hand* O Hanah.
And old Kettel *wif his hand.* +
Brother Rowlandson, *pray send thre pound of Tobacco for me, if you can my loving husband pray send thre pound of tobacco for me.*

"*This writing by your enemies*—Samuel Uskattuhgun *and* Gunrashit, *two Indian sagamores.*"

Mrs. *Rowlandson*, in her account of "The Sixteenth Remove," relates, that when they had waded over Baquaug † River, "Quickly there came up to us an Indian who informed them that I must go to Wachuset to my master, for there was a letter come from the council to the saggamores about redeeming the captives, and that there would be another in 14 days, and that I must be there ready." ‡ This was doubtless after the letter just recorded had been sent to the English. "About two days after," Mrs. *R.* continues, "came a company of Indians to us, near 30, all on horseback. My heart skipt within me, thinking they had been Englishmen, at the first sight of them: For they were dressed in English apparel, with hats, white neck-cloths, and sashes about their waists, and ribbons upon their shoulders. But when they came near, there was a vast difference between the lovely faces of Christians, and the foul looks of those heathen, which much damped my spirits again." §

Having, after great distress, arrived at Wachuset, our authoress adds, "Then came *Tom* and *Peter* with the second letter from the council, about the captives." "I asked them how my husband did, and all my friends and

* *Gookin's* MS. Hist. Christian Indians.

† Or Payquage, now Miller's River. Its confluence with the Connecticut is between Northfield and Montague.

‡ Narrative of her Captivity, 59.

§ Ibid. 60. The regimentals in which they were now tricked out, were probably taken from the English whom they had killed in battle.

acquaintance. They said they were well, but very melancholy." They brought her two biscuits and a pound of tobacco. The tobacco she gave to the Indians, and, when it was all gone, one threatened her because she had no more to give; probably not believing her. She told him when her husband came, she would give him some. "Hang him, rogue, says he, I will knock out his brains, if he comes here." "Again, at the same breath, they would say, if there should come an hundred without guns they would do them no hurt. So unstable and like madmen they were." * There had been something talked about Mr. *Rowlandson's* going himself to ransom his wife, but she says she dared not send for him, "for there was little more trust to them than to the master they served." *

Nepanet learned by the enemy that they lost in the fight when Capt. *Peirse* was killed, "scores of their men that sabbath day." †

As they refused to treat with *Tom Nepanet* alone, *Peter Conway* was joined with him on a second expedition, as we have seen, which led to several others, to which some English ventured to add themselves, which resulted in the redemption of Mrs. *Rowlandson* and several others.

"When the letter was come, (says Mrs. *R.*), the saggamores met to consult about the captives, and called me to them, to inquire how much my husband would give to redeem me: When I came and sat down among them, as I was wont to do, as their manner is: Then they bid me stand up, *and said they were the general court.* They bid me speak what I thought he would give. Now knowing that all that we had was destroyed by the Indians, I was in a great strait." ‡ She ventured, however, to say £20, and *Tom* and *Peter* bore the offer to Boston.

Of their return the same writer proceeds: "On a sabbath day, the sun being about an hour high in the afternoon, came Mr *John Hoar*, (the council permitting him, and his own forward spirit inclining him,) together with the two fore-mentioned Indians, *Tom* and *Peter*, with the third letter from the council. When they came near, I was abroad; they presently called me in, and bid me sit down, and not stir. Then they catched up their guns and away they ran, as if an enemy had been at hand, and the guns went off apace. I manifested some great trouble, and asked them what was the matter. I told them I thought they had killed the Englishman; (for they had in the mean time told me that an Englishman had come;) they said, *No, they shot over his horse, and under, and before his horse, and they pushed him this way and that way, at their pleasure,* SHOWING HIM WHAT THEY COULD DO." §

They would not at first suffer her to see Mr. *Hoar*, but when they had gratified their tantalizing whim sufficiently, she was permitted to see him. He brought her a pound of tobacco, which *she sold for nine shillings.* "The next morning, Mr. *Hoar* invited the saggamores to dinner; but when we went to get it ready, we found they had stolen the greatest part of the provisions Mr. *Hoar* had brought. And we may see the wonderful power of God, in that one passage, in that, when there was such a number of them together, and so greedy of a little good food, and no English there but Mr. *Hoar* and myself, that there they did not knock us on the head, and take what we had; there being not only some provision, but also trading cloth, a part of the 20 pounds agreed upon: But instead of doing us any mischief, they seemed to be ashamed of the fact, and said it was the *matchit* [bad] Indians that did it." ‖

It is now certain that this negotiation was the immediate cause of their final overthrow. For before this time the Pokanokets and Narragansetts went hand in hand against their common enemy, and they were the most powerful tribes. This parleying with the English was so detestable to *Philip*, that a separation took place among these tribes in consequence, and he and the Narragansets separated themselves from the Nipmuks, and other inland tribes, and went off to their own country. This was the reason they were so easily subdued after the separation took place.

---

* Narrative of her Captivity, 64, 65. † Manuscripts of Rev. *J. Cotton.*
‡ Narrative, *ut supra*, 65. § Ibid. 71, 72. ‖ Ibid. 72, 73.

It was through *Nepanet's* means that a party of English, under Captain *Henchman*, were enabled to surprise a body of his countrymen at Weshakom* Ponds near Lancaster, 30 May, 1676. Following in a track pointed out by *Nepanet*, the Indians were fallen upon while fishing, and, being entirely unprepared, seven were killed, and 29 taken, chiefly women and children.

PETER-EPHRAIM and ANDREW-PITYME were also two other considerably distinguished Nipmuk Indians. They rendered much service to the English in *Philip's* war. They went out in January, 1676, and brought in many of the Nipnets, who had endeavored to shelter themselves under *Uncas*. But, Mr. *Hubbard* observes, that *Uncas*, having "shabbed" them off, "they were, in the beginning of the winter, [1676,] brought in to Boston, many of them, by *Peter-ephraim* and *Andrew-pityme*." *Ephraim* commanded an Indian company, and had a commission from government. The news that many of the enemy were doing mischief about Rehoboth caused a party of English of Medfield to march out to their relief; *Ephraim* went with them, with his company, which consisted of 29. The snow being deep, the English soon grew discouraged, and returned, but Captain *Ephraim* continued the march, and came upon a body of them, encamped, in the night. Early the next morning, he successfully surrounded them, and offered them quarter. "Eight resolute fellows refused, who were presently shot;" the others yielded, and were brought in, being in number 42. Other minor exploits of this Indian captain are recorded.

THOMAS QUANAPOHIT, called also *Rumney-marsh*, was a brother of *James*, and was also a Christian Indian. In the beginning of hostilities against *Philip*, Major *Gookin* received orders to raise a company of praying Indians to be employed against him. This company was immediately raised, and consisted of 52 men, who were conducted to Mount Hope by Captain *Isaac Johnson*. *Quanapohit* was one of these. The officers under whom they served testified to their credit as faithful soldiers; yet many of the army, officers and men, tried all in their power to bring them into disrepute with the country. Such proceedings, we should naturally conclude, would tend much to dishearten those friendly Indians; but, on the contrary, they used every exertion to win the affections of their oppressors. *Quanapohit*, with the other two, received from government a reward for the scalps which they brought in. Though not exactly in order, yet it must be mentioned, that when *Thomas* was out, at or near Swansey, in the beginning of the war, he by accident had one of his hands shot off. He was one of the troopers, and carried a gun of remarkable length. The weather being excessively hot, his horse was very uneasy, being disturbed by flies, and struck the lock of the gun as the breech rested upon the ground, and caused it to go off, which horribly mangled the hand that held it; and, notwithstanding it was a long time in getting well, yet he rendered great service in the war afterward. The account of one signal exploit having been preserved, shall here be related. While Captain *Henchman* was in the enemy's country, he made an excursion from Hassanamesit to Packachoog, which lies about ten miles north-west from it. Meeting here with no enemy, he marched again for Hassanamesit; and having got a few miles on his way, discovered that he had lost a tin case, which contained his commission, and other instructions. He therefore despatched *Thomas* and two Englishmen in search of it. They made no discovery of the lost article until they came in sight of an old wigwam at Packachoog, where, to their no small surprise, they discovered some of the enemy in possession of it. They were but a few rods from them, and being so few in number, that to have given them battle would have been desperate in the extreme, as neither of them was armed for such an occasion stratagem, therefore, could only save them. The wigwam was situated upon an eminence; and some were standing in the door, when they approached, who discovered them as soon as they came in sight. One presented his gun, but, the weather being stormy, it did not go off. At this moment our chief, looking back, called, and made many gestures, as though he were disposing of a large force to encompass them. At this manœuvre they all fled

* *Roger Williams* sets down *sea* as the definition of *Wechêcum*.

being six in number, leaving our heroes to pursue their object. Thus their preservation was due to *Quanapohit;* and is the more to be admired, as they were in so far destitute of the means of defence. Captain *Quanapohit* had himself only a pistol, and one of his men a gun without a flint, and the other no gun at all.*

It was about the time these events occurred, that Captain *Tom*, of whom we have spoken, his daughter, and two children, were taken by a scout sent out by Captain *Henchman*, about 10 miles south-east of Marlborough. They appear to have been taken on the 11 June, and on the 26 of the same month Captain *Tom* was executed.

CHAPTER VII.

*Of the Indians in New Hampshire and Maine previous to their wars with the whites—Dominions of the bashaba—Perishes in war—*PASSACONAWAY*—His dominions—His last speech to his people—His life—His daughter marries Winnapurket—Petitions the court of Massachusetts—Lands allotted to him—English send a force to disarm him—Their fears of his enmity unfounded—they seize and illtreat his son—He escapes—Passaconaway delivers his arms, and makes peace with the English—Traditions concerning—Life of* WANNALANCET*—His situation in Philip's war—Messengers and letters sent him by the English—Leaves his residence—His humanity—Fate of* JOSIAH NOUEL*—Wannalancet returns to his country—His lands seized in his absence—He again retires into the wilderness—Mosely destroys his village, &c.—Imprisoned for debt—Favors Christianity—A speech—*WEHANOWNOWIT*, sachem of New Hampshire—*ROBINHOOD*—His sales of land in Maine—*MONQUINE KENNEBIS*—*ASSIMINASQUA*—*ABBIGADASSET*—Their residences and sales of land Melancholy fate of* CHOCORUA.

SOME knowledge of the Indians eastward of the Massachusetts was very early obtained by Captain *John Smith*, which, however, was very general; as that they were divided into several tribes, each of which had their own sachem, or, as these more northern Indians pronounced that word, *sachemo*, which the English understood *sagamore;* and yet all the sachemos acknowledged subjection to one still greater, which they called *bashaba.*

Of the dominions of the bashaba, writers differ much in respect to their extent. Some suppose that his authority did not extend this side the Pascataqua, but it is evident that it did, from Captain *Smith's* account.† Wars and pestilence had greatly wasted the eastern Indians but a short time before the English settled in the country; and it was then difficult to determine the relation the tribes had stood in one to the other. As to the bashaba of Penobscot, tradition states that he was killed by the Tarratines, who lived still farther east, in a war which was at its height in 1615.

PASSACONAWAY seems to have been a bashaba. He lived upon the Merrimack River, at a place called *Pennakook*, and his dominions, at the period of the English settlements, were very extensive, even over the sachems living upon the Pascataqua and its branches. The Abenaques inhabited between the Pascataqua and Penobscot, and the residence of the chief sachem was upon Indian Island.‡ *Fluellen* and Captain *Sunday* were early known as chiefs among the Abenaques, and *Squando* at a later period; but

* *Gookin's* MS. Hist. Praying Indians.

† "The principal habitations I saw at northward, was Penobscot, who are in wars with the Terentines, their next northerly neighbors. Southerly up the rivers, and along the coast, we found Mecadacut, Segocket, Pemmaquid, Nusconcus, Sagadahock, Satquin, Aumaughcawgen and Kenabeca. To those belong the countries and people of Segotago, Pauhunlanuck, Pocopassum, Taughtanakagnet, Wabigganus, Nassaque, Masherosqueck, Wawrigwick, Moshoquen, Waccogo, Pasharanack, &c. To those are allied in confederacy, the countries of Aucocisco, Accominticus, Passataquak, Augawoam and Naemkeek, all these, for any thing I could perceive, differ little in language or any thing; though most of them be sagamos and lords of themselves, yet they hold the bashabes of Penobscot the chief and greatest amongst them." 3 *Coll. Mass. Hist. Soc.* iii. 21, 22.

‡ *Williamson's* Hist. Maine, ii. 4.

of these we shall be more particular hereafter: the first sachem we should notice is *Passaconaway*. He "lived to a very great age; for," says the author of my manuscript, "I saw him alive at Pawtucket, when he was about a hundred and twenty years old."* Before his death, he delivered the following speech to his children and friends: "*I am now going the way of all flesh, or ready to die, and not likely to see you ever meet together any more. I will now leave this word of counsel with you, that you may take heed how you quarrel with the English, for though you may do them much mischief, yet assuredly you will all be destroyed, and rooted off the earth if you do; for, I was as much an enemy to the English, at their first coming into these parts, as any one whatsoever, and did try all ways and means possible, to have destroyed them, at least to have prevented them settling down here, but I could no way effect it; therefore I advise you never to contend with the English, nor make war with them.*" And Mr. *Hubbard* adds, "it is to be noted, that this *Passaconawa* was the most noted powow and sorcerer of all the country."

A story of the marriage of a daughter of *Passaconaway*, in 1629, is thus related. *Winnepurket*, commonly called *George*, sachem of Saugus, made known to the chief of Pennakook, that he desired to marry his daughter, which, being agreeable to all parties, was soon consummated, at the residence of *Passaconaway*, and the hilarity was closed with a great feast. According to the usages of the chiefs, *Passaconaway* ordered a select number of his men to accompany the new-married couple to the dwelling of the husband. When they had arrived there, several days of feasting followed, for the entertainment of his friends, who could not be present at the consummation at the bride's father's, as well as for the escort; who, when this was ended, returned to Pennakook.

Some time after, the wife of *Winnepurket*, expressing a desire to visit her father's house and friends, was permitted to go, and a choice company conducted her. When she wished to return to her husband, her father, instead of conveying her as before, sent to the young sachem to come and take her away. He took this in high dudgeon, and sent his father-in-law this answer: "When she departed from me, I caused my men to escort her to your dwelling, as became a chief. She now having an intention to return to me, I did expect the same." The elder sachem was now in his turn angry, and returned an answer which only increased the difference; and it is believed that thus terminated the connection of the new husband and wife.†

This same year, [1662,] we find the general court acting upon a petition of *Passaconaway*, or, as his name is spelt in the records themselves, *Papisseconeway*. The petition we have not met with, but from the answer given to it, we learn its nature. The court say: "In answer to the petition of *Papisseconeway*, this court judgeth it meete to graunt to the said *Papisseconeway* and his men or associates about Naticot,‡ above Mr. *Brenton's* lands, where it is free, a mile and a half on either side Merremack Riuer in breadth, three miles on either side in length: provided he nor they do not alienate any part of this grant without leave and license from this court, first obtained."

Governor *Winthrop* mentions this chief as early as 1632. One of his men, having gone with a white man into the country to trade, was killed by another Indian "dwelling near the Mohawks country, who fled away with his goods;" but it seems from the same account, that *Passaconaway* pursued and took the murderer. In 1642, there was great alarm throughout the English settlements, from the belief that all the Indians in the country were about to make a general massacre of the whites. The government of Massachusetts took prompt measures "to strike a terror into the Indians." They therefore "sent men to *Cutshamekin*, at Braintree, to fetch him and his guns,

* *Gookin's Hist. of Praying Indians.* This history was drawn up during the year 1677, and how long before this the author saw him, is unknown; but there can be no doubt but he was dead some years before *Philip's* war. Nevertheless, with Mr. *Hubbard* and our text before him, the author of *Tales of the Indians* has made *Passaconaway* appear in the person of *Aspinquid*, in 1682, at Agamentacus in Maine.

† Deduced from facts in *Morton's N. Canaan.*

‡ Another version of *Nahum-keag*.

bows, &c., which was done; and he came willingly: And being late in the night when they came to Boston, he was put into the prison; but the next morning, finding, upon examination of him and divers of his men, no ground of suspicion of his partaking in any such conspiracy, he was dismissed. Upon the warrant which went to Ipswich, Rowley and Newbury, to disarm *Passaconamy*, who lived by Merrimack, they sent forth 40 men armed the next day." These English were hindered from visiting the wigwam of *Passaconaway*, by rainy weather, "but they came to his son's and took him." This son we presume was *Wannalancet*. This they had orders to do; but for taking a squaw and her child, they had none, and were ordered to send them back again immediately. Fearing *Wannalancet's* escape, they "led him in a line, but he taking an opportunity, slipped his line and escaped from them, but one very indiscreetly made a shot at him, and missed him narrowly." These were called, then, "unwarranted proceedings," as we should say they very well might have been. The English now had some actual reason to fear that *Passaconaway* would resent this outrage, and therefore "sent *Cutshamekin* to him to let him know that what was done to his son and squaw was without order," and to invite him to a parley at Boston; also, "to show him the occassion whereupon we had sent to disarm all the Indians, and that when we should find that they were innocent of any such conspiracy, we would restore all their arms again." *Passaconaway* said when he should have his son and squaw returned safe, he would go and speak with them. The squaw was so much frightened, that she ran away into the woods, and was absent ten days. It seems that *Wannalancet* was soon liberated, as he within a short time went to the English, "and delivered up his guns, &c." * These were the circumstances to which *Miantunnomoh* alluded so happily afterwards.

At a court in Massachusetts in 1644, it is said, "*Passaconaway*, the Merrimack sachem, came in and submitted to our government, as *Pumham*, &c. had done before;" and the next year the same entry occurs again, with the addition of his son's submission also, "together with their lands and people." †

This chief is supposed to have died about the same time with *Massasoit*, a sachem whom in many respects he seems to have much resembled. ‡ He was often styled *the great sachem*, and, according to Mr. *Hubbard*, was considered a great powwow or sorcerer among his people, and his fame in this respect was very extensive; and we know not that there was any thing that they thought him not able to perform: that he could cause a green leaf to grow in winter, trees to dance, and water to burn, seem to have been feats of common notoriety in his time.

WANNALANCET, or *Wonolancet*, in obedience to the advice of his father, always kept peace with the English. He resided at an ancient seat of the sagamores, upon the Merrimack, called at that time *Naamkeke*, but from whence he withdrew, in the time of the war with *Philip*, and took up his quarters among the Pennakooks, who were also his people.

About the beginning of September, 1675, Captain *Mosely*, with about 100 men, was ordered to march up into the country of the Merrimack to ascertain the state of affairs under *Wannalancet*. These men scouted in warlike array as far as Pennakook, now Concord, N. H. They could not find an Indian, but came upon their wigwams, and burned them, and also a quantity of dried fish and other articles. Although this was a most wanton and unwarrantable, not to say unnecessary act of these whites, yet no retaliation took place on the part of the Indians. And whether to attribute their forbearance to cowardice, or to the great respect in which the dying advice of *Passaconaway* was

---

* *Winthrop's Journal.* † Ibid.

‡ Among other stanzas in *Farmer* and *Moore's Collections*, the following very happily introduces *Passaconaway*:—

"Once did my throbbing bosom deep receive
The *sketch*, which one of *Passaconaway* drew
Well may the muse his memory retrieve
From dark oblivion, and, with pencil true,
Retouch that picture strange, with tints and honors due."

held, is not certain; for *Wanalancet* and his men had notice of the approach of *Mosely*, and lay concealed while he was destroying their effects; and might have cut off his company, which the young warriors advised, but *Wannalancet* would not permit a gun to be fired.

Having abundant reason now to fear the resentment of the Pawtuckett and Pennakook Indians, the council of Massachusetts, 7 September, 1675, ordered that Lieutenant *Thomas Henchman*, of Chelmsford, should send some messengers to find him, and persuade him of their friendship, and urge his return to his place of residence. With this order, a letter was sent to *Wannalancet* at the same time. They are as follows: "It is ordered by the council that Lieut. *Thos. Henchman* do forthwith endeavor to procure by hire, one or two suitable Indians of Wamesit, to travel and seek to find out and speak with *Wannalancet* the sachem, and carry with them a writing from the council, being a safe conduct unto the said sachem, or any other principal men belonging to Natahook, Penagooge, or other people of those northern Indians, giving (not exceeding six persons) free liberty to come into the house of the said *Henchman*, where the council will appoint Capt. *Gookin* and Mr. *Eliot* to treat with them about terms of amity and peace between them and the English; and in case agreements and conclusions be not made to mutual satisfaction, then the said sachem and all others that accompany him shall have free liberty to return back again; and this offer the council are induced to make, because the said *Wannalancet* sachem, as they are informed, hath declared himself that the English never did any wrong to him, or his father *Passaconaway*, but always lived in amity, and that his father charged him so to do, and that said *Wannalancet* will not begin to do any wrong to the English." The following is the letter to *Wannalancet*:—

"This our writing or safe conduct doth declare, that the governor and council of Massachusetts do give you and every of you, provided you exceed not six persons, free liberty of coming unto and returning in safety from the house of Lieut. *T. Henchman* at Naamkeake, and there to treat with Capt. *Daniel Gookin* and Mr. *John Eliot*, whom you know, and [whom] we will fully empower to treat and conclude with you, upon such meet terms and articles of friendship, amity and subjection, as were formerly made and concluded between the English and old *Passaconaway*, your father, and his sons and people; and for this end we have sent these messengers [*blank in the MS.*] to convey these unto you, and to bring your answer, whom we desire you to treat kindly, and speedily to despatch them back to us with your answer. Dated in Boston, 1 Oct. 1675. Signed by order of the council. John Leverett, Govr.

Edwd. Rawson, Secr."

The messengers who went out with this letter, to find *Wannalancet*, could not meet with him, but employed another to find him, and returned; and whether he ever received it is not distinctly stated. However, with a few followers, he retired into the wilderness near the source of the Connecticut, and there passed the winter. The next summer he was joined by parties of Nipmuks under *Sagamore sam*, *One-eyed-john*, and others, who, coming in with him, were in hopes of receiving pardon, but their fate has been stated.

Major *Waldron* of Cochecho had many Indians in his interest during the war with *Philip*. Some of these were employed to entice men from the enemy's ranks, and they succeeded to a great extent. And by the beginning of September, 1676, about 400 Indians, from various clans far and near, had been induced to come into Dover. Among these was *Wannalancet* and his company. They came without hesitation, as they had never been engaged in the war; and many who had been engaged in hostility came along with them, presuming they might be overlooked in the crowd, and so escape the vengeance of their enemies; but they were all made prisoners on the 6 September by a stratagem devised by several officers, who with their men happened then to be at Dover with *Waldron*, and somewhat more than half of the whole were sold into foreign slavery or executed at Boston: about 200 were of the former number.

The stratagem made use of to trepan those Indians was as follows: It was proposed by the English that they should join with the Indians in a training, and have sham-fights. While performing their evolutions, a movement was made by the whites, which entirely surrounded the Indians, and they were all secured without violence or bloodshed.

On the 3 May, 1676, *Thomas Kimbal* of Bradford was killed, and his wife and five children carried into the wilderness. From the circumstance that *Wannalancet* caused them to be sent home to their friends again, it would seem that they were taken by some of the enemy within his sachemdom, or by some over whom he had some control. From a manuscript written about the time,* we are able to make the following extract, which goes to show that *Wannalancet* was ever the friend of the English, and also his disposition to humane actions. Mr. *Cobbet* says, "though she [Mrs. *Kimbal*,] and her sucking child were twice condemned by the Indians, and the fires ready made to burn them, yet, both times, saved by the request of one of their own grandees; and afterwards by the intercession of the sachem of Pennicook, stirred up thereunto by Major *Waldron*, was she and her five children, together with *Philip Eastman* of Haverhill, taken captive when she and her children were, set at liberty, without ransom."

The 400 Indians surprised at Cochecho, by *Hathorne*, *Frost*, *Sill*, and *Waldron*, included *Wannalancet* with his people, who did not probably exceed 100. This chief, then, with a few of his people, being set at liberty, was persuaded to return to his former residence at Naamkeke, but he never felt reconciled here afterwards, for it had become almost as another place: some lawless whites had seized upon his lands, and looked upon him with envious eyes, as though he had been an intruder and had no right there. He, however, continued for about a year afterwards, when, upon the 19 September, 1677, he was visited by a party of Indians from Canada, who urged him to accompany them to their country. He finally consented, and with all of his people, except two, in number about 50, of whom not above eight were men, departed for Canada, and was not heard of after.†

It was on this very same day, viz. 19 September, that a party of Indians fell upon Hatfield, the particulars of which irruption, though in one view of the case does not strictly belong to the life of *Wannalancet*, we give here in the words of Mr. *Hubbard*.‡ "About Sept. 19th, 40 or 50 River Indians § fell suddenly upon the town of Hatfield, whose inhabitants were a little too secure, and too ready to say the bitterness of death was past, because they had neither seen nor heard of an enemy in those parts for half a year before. But at this time, as a considerable number of the inhabitants of that small village were employed in raising the frame of an house without the palisadoes, that defended their houses from any sudden incursions of the enemy, they were violently and suddenly assaulted by 40 or 50 Indians, whom they were in no capacity to resist or defend themselves, so as several were shot down from the top of the house which they were raising, and sundry were carried away captive, to the number of 20 or more, which was made up 24 with them they carried away the same or the next day from Deerfield, whither some of the inhabitants had unadvisedly too soon returned. One of the company escaped out of their hands two or three days after, who informed that they had passed with their poor captives two or three times over the Connecticut to prevent being pursued."

At first this attack was supposed to have been made by a party of Mohawks, according to *Gookin*, because it took place the next day after some of the nation had passed through the place with some Christian Indians prisoners, and a scalp, which was afterwards found to have been taken from the head of an Indian named *Josiah Nouel*,‖ near Sudbury. But one of the captives

* By Rev. *T. Cobbet* of Ipswich.

† GOOKIN'S MS. Hist. Praying Indians.

‡ Hist. N. England, 636.

§ They inhabited chiefly in New York along the Hudson; a few in the N. W. corner of Connecticut, and a few on the Housatunnuk River. HOPKIN'S *Memoir of the Housatunnuk Indians*, p. 1.—"The Wabinga, sometimes called River Indians, sometimes Mohicanders, and who had their dwellings between the west branch of Delaware and Hudson's River, from the Kittatinney ridge down to the Rariton." *Jefferson's Notes*, 308.

‖ By his death four small children were left fatherless. *Nouel* and *James Speen* had been

24 *

taken at Hatfield escaped, and returned soon after, and reported that the company of Indians that attacked Hatfield consisted of 23 men and four women, and were some of those who had belonged to *Philip's* party, but had taken up their residence in Canada, from whence they made this expedition.* Another party left Canada at the same time, who, after separating from the former, directed their course towards Merrimack, and this was the company who persuaded or compelled *Wannalancet* to go with them. That he went not by compulsion is very probable; for the party with whom he went off "were his kindred and relations, one of them was his wife's brother, and his eldest son also lived with the French" in Canada.†

While at Pawtucket, and not long before his final departure, *Wannalancet* went to the Reverend Mr. *Fiske* of Chelmsford, and inquired of him concerning the welfare of his former acquaintances, and whether the place had suffered much during the war. Mr. *Fiske* answered that they had been highly favored in that respect, and for which he thanked God. "Me next," said the chief, thereby intimating that he was conscious of having prevented mischief from falling upon them.‡

In 1659, *Wannalansit* was thrown into prison for a debt of about £45. His people, who owned an island in Merrimack River, three miles above Pawtuckett Falls, containing 60 acres, half of which was under cultivation, relinquished it, to obtain his release. About 1670, he removed to Pawtuckett Falls, where, upon an eminence, he built a fort, and resided until *Philip's* war. He was about 55 years of age in 1674; always friendly to the English, but unwilling to be importuned about adopting their religion. When he had got to be very old, however, he submitted to their desires in that respect. Upon that occasion he is reported to have said, "*I must acknowledge I have all my days been used to pass in an old canoe, and now you exhort me to change and leave my old canoe and embark in a new one, to which I have hitherto been unwilling, but now I yield up myself to your advice, and enter into a new canoe, and do engage to pray to God hereafter.*"

Reverend *John Eliot* thus writes to the Honorable *Robert Boyle* § in England,

---

together but half an hour before the former was killed, and by appointment were to have met again. But when *Speen* came to the place, he could find nothing of his friend. They were brothers-in-law.

* It seems from the narrative of *Quintin Stockwell*, that the party who committed this depredation was led by a great and magnanimous sachem called ASHPELON, of whom, further than the events of this famous expedition, I have learned nothing. "Sept. 19, 1677, about sunset," says *Stockwell*, "I and another man being together, the Indians with great shouting and shooting came upon us, [at Deerfield,] and some other of the English hard by, at which we ran to a swamp for refuge; which they perceiving, made after us, and shot at us, three guns being discharged upon me. The swamp being miry I slipt in and fell down; whereupon an Indian stept to me, with his hatchet lifted up to knock me on the head, supposing I was wounded, and unfit for travel. It happened I had a pistol in my pocket, which though uncharged, I presented to him, who presently stept back, and told me, if I would yield I should have no hurt; boasted that they had destroyed all Hatfield, and that the woods were full of Indians; whereupon I yielded myself." He was then taken back to Deerfield, where he was pinioned, and with other captives marched into the wilderness. Their sufferings, as usual in Indian captivity, were most cruel and severe; for many nights together they were "staked down" to the cold ground, in this manner: The captive being laid upon his back, his arms and feet were extended, and with cords or withes lashed to stakes driven into the ground for that purpose. Besides lashing the arms and legs, the neck and body were also secured in the same way, and often so tight as to cause swellings and the most excruciating pains. While on their march, the captives had frequent opportunities of escaping singly, but would not, for fear of endangering the lives of the rest; but at length *Benjamin Stebbins*, in a journey with his Indian master to Wachuset hill, made his escape. When the rest knew this, they were for burning the remaining captives, but some being opposed to the measure, they agreed to have a *court* and debate the subject. *Ashpelon* told the English not to fear, for he would speak last, and would frustrate the design of burning, for he would show that it was not *Stebbins's* fault for running away, but the fault of the Indian who had him in charge; and he brought it to pass, as he had promised. Having at length arrived among the French, *Stockwell* was pawned to one of them, and in the end sold for 21 beaver skins, and some time the next year got home again. *Remarkable Providences. Blome's America*, 221

† *Gookin's* MS. History. ‡ *Allen's* Hist. Chelmsford, 157.

§ For many years at the head of the Society for Propagating the Gospel among the Indians. He was a great benefactor of N. England, and one of the founders of the Royal Society of London. He was by birth an Irishman, but settled finally at Oxford, England. He died in Lon in 1677:—"We had a sachem of the greatest blood in the country submitted to pray to God, a little before the wars: his name is *Wanalauncet:* in the time of the wars he fled, by reason of the wicked actings of some English youth, who causelessly and basely killed and wounded some of them. He was persuaded to come in again. But the English having plowed and sown with rye all their lands, they had but little corn to subsist by. A party of French Indians, (of whom some were of the kindred of this sachem's wife,) very lately fell upon this people, being but few and unarmed, and partly by persuasion, partly by force, carried them away. One, with his wife, child and kinswoman, who were of our praying Indians, made their escape, came in to the English, and discovered what was done. These things keep some in a continual disgust and jealousy of all the Indians." *

It may be proper to add a word upon the name of the place which we have often mentioned in this life, as the same word, differently pronounced, was applied to a great many places by the Indians, and is the same word which Dr. *I. Mather* and some others made many believe was made up of two Hebrew words, to prove that the Indians were really the descendants of the dispersed Jews; but for which purpose, if we are not misinformed, any other Indian word would answer the same purpose. The doctor writes the name *Nahumkeik*, and adds that *Nahum* signifies *consolation*, and *keik* a *bosom*, or *heaven;* and hence the settlers of places bearing this name were seated in the bosom of consolation.† He points out this etymological analogy in speaking of the settlement of Salem, which was called by the Indians *Naumkeag*, *Namkeg*, *Naamhok*, *Naumkuk*, or something *a little* somewhat like it. *A sad bosome of consolation*, did it prove in the days of *Tituba*, (to say nothing of some more modern events,) and even in Dr. *Mather's* own days. [Though a digression, we shall, I doubt not, be pardoned for inserting here Dr. *C. Mather's* account of a curiosity at Amoskeag Falls, which he gave in a letter to London, and which afterwards appeared in the Philosophical Transactions: ‡ "At a place called Amnuskeag, a little above the hideous § falls of Merimack River, there is a huge rock in the midst of the stream, on the top of which are a great number of pits, made exactly round, like barrels or hogsheads of different capacities, some so large as to hold several tuns. The natives know nothing of the time they were made; but the neighboring Indians have been wont to hide their provisions in them, in their wars with the Maquas; affirming, God had cut them out for that use for them. They seem plainly to be artificial." It could certainly have required no great sagacity to have supposed that one stone placed upon another in the water, so as to have been constantly rolled from side to side by the current, would, in time, occasion such cavities. One quite as remarkable we have seen near the source of this river, in its descent from the Franconia Mountains; also upon the Mohawk, a short distance below Little Falls. They may be seen as you pass upon the canal.

Early purchases of lands bring to our notice a host of Indians, many of

---

don, 1691, aged 64 years. The following lines are no less well conceived by the poet than deserved by this benevolent philosopher:

> How much to BOYLE the learned world does owe,
> The learned world does only know.
> He traced great nature's secret springs;
> The causes and the seeds of things;
> What strange elastic power the air contains,
> What mother earth secures within her secret veins.
>
> *Athenian Oracle*, i. 67.

* *Coll. Mass. Hist. Soc.* iii. 179.

† *Relation of the Troubles*, &c. 20. Dr. *Increase Mather* was the author of a great many works, chiefly sermons, many of which have become curious for their singularity, and some others valuable for the facts they contain. His sermons, like many others of that day, had very little meaning in them, and consequently are now forgotten. He was son of *Richard Mather*, preached in Boston above 60 years, died in 1723, aged 84 years. See *his life*, by his son, Dr. *Cotton Mather*, who was born 12 Feb. 1662—3, died 13 Feb. 1727—8, aged 65. See his life by *Samuel Mather*.

‡ Vol. v. of Jones's Abridgement, part ii. 164.

§ We cannot say what they were in those days, but should expect to be laughed at if we should call them *hideous* at the present time.

whom, though sachems, but for such circumstances of trade, would never have come to our knowledge. There are some, however, of whom we shall in this chapter take notice, as such notices assist in enabling us to judge how the natives regarded their lands, and the territories of their neighboring countrymen.

WEHANOWNOWIT was a New Hampshire sachem, whose name has been considerably handled within a few years, from its being found to the much-talked-of deed conveying lands in New Hampshire to the Reverend *John Wheelwright*, and others, 3 April, 1638. If *Wehanownowit* were sachem of the tract said to have been by him conveyed, his "kingdom" was larger than some can boast of at this day who call themselves kings. It was to contain 30 miles square, and its boundaries were thus described: "lying and situate within three miles on the northerne side of ye River Meremoke, extending thirty miles along by the river from the sea side, and from the sayd river side to Pisscataqua Patents, 30 miles up into the countrey north-west, and so from the falls of Piscataqua to Oyster River, 30 miles square every way." The original is in possession of Mr. *John Farmer*, of Concord, N. H.[*] TUMMADOCKYON was a son of *Wehanownowit*, and his name is also to the deed above mentioned; and another Indian, belonging to that tract of country, named *Watchenowet:* these both relinquished their title to, or concurred in the sale of said tract.

ROBINHOOD[†] was the father of a more noted chief, whose Indian name was *Wohawa*, but commonly known among the English as *Hopehood.* His territories, as will appear, were upon the Kennebeck River in the first settlement of N. England.

Our first notice of *Robinhood* runs as follows: "Be it known"—"that I, *Ramegin,*[‡] soe called by my Indian name, or *Robinhood*, soe called by English name, sagamore of Negusset, [or Neguasseag,] doe freely sell vnto *James Smith,*"—"part of my land, beginning att Merry-meeting Cove, and soe downward the maine riuer vnto a rocke, called *Winslowe's Rocke*, in the longe reach, and in breadth eastward ouer the little riuer, runinge through the great mersh, with the priuilidges [reserved to me] as hunting, fowlinge, fishing, and other games." *Smith* was to pay him or his heirs, on the 1 November annually, "one peck of Indian corn." This deed bears date 8 May, 1648, and is signed and witnessed as follows:—[§]

NEGWINIS *his* ⊤ *mark.*
SONGREEHOOD *his* ⊢ *mark*
and two English.

ROBINHOOD ♑ *his mark.*
Mr. THOMAS △ *his mark.*
PEWAZEGSAKE ♌ *his mark.*
The mark ∽ *of* ROBIN.

The next year, 1649, he sold the island of Jeremysquam, on the east side of the Kennebeck, and in 1654 we find him selling his place of residence, which was in what is now Woolwich, to *Edward Bateman* and *John Brown.* In 1663, *Robinhood* is mentioned as one of the principal chiefs among the eastern Indians.[‖]

In 1667, the inhabitants upon Connecticut River, about Hadley, sustained some injury from Indians, in their lands and domestic animals, and satisfaction therefor was demanded of *Robinhood;* at the same time threatening him with the utmost severity, if the like should be repeated. But whether his people were the perpetrators we are not told; but from the following facts it may be thought otherwise. "To promote amity with them, license was at length given to the traders in fur and in peltries, to sell unto *Indian friends*

---

[*] MS. communication of that gentleman.

[†] This name was adopted, I have no doubt, as it came something near the sound of his Indian name, as was the case in several instances which we have already recorded: the old English robber of that name, or fables concerning him, are among the first in the nursery. Even at this day, the curious adult will dispense with Mr. *Ritson's* collections of legends concerning him with peculiar regret.

[‡] The same, I suppose, called in *Sullivan's* Hist. *Rogomok.*

[§] From a *manuscript* copy of the original deed.

[‖] B *Josselyn,* who visited the country at this time. See his *Voyages.*

guns and ammunition."* Hence these *friends* could see no reason, afterwards, why arms were prohibited them, as we shall again have occasion to notice.

On the breaking out of *Philip's* war, *Robinhood* was in no wise inclined to join in it, and when a party of English was sent at that time to learn the feelings of his people in that respect, he made a great dance, and by songs and shouts expressed his satisfaction that the English were disposed to maintain peace.

MONQUINE, "alias *Natahanada*, the son of old *Natawormett*, sagamore of Kennebeck River," sold to *William Bradford* and others, all the land on both sides of said river, "from Cussenocke upwards to Wesserunsicke." This sale bore date 8 August, 1648. The signature is "*Monquine*, alias *Dumhanada*." Then follows: "We, *Agodoademago*, the sonne of *Wasshemett*, and *Tassucke*, the brother of *Natahanada*,† do consent freely unto the sale to *Bradford*, *Paddy*, and others."‡

KENNEBIS was a sachem from whom it has been supposed that the Kennebeck River derived its name. But whether there were a line of sagamores of this name, from whom the river was so called, or whether sachems were so called from their living at a certain place upon it, is uncertain. It is certain, however, that there was one of this name residing there, contemporaneously with *Robinhood*, who, besides several others, deeded and redeeded the lands up and down in the country. He was sometimes associated in his sales with *Abbigadasset*, and sometimes with others. In 1649, he sold to *Christopher Lawson* all the land on the Kennebeck River up as high as Taconnet falls, now Winslow, which was the residence of the great chief *Essiminasqua*, or *Assiminasqua*, elsewhere mentioned. About the same time, he sold the same tract, or a part of it, to *Spencer* and *Clark*. The residence of *Kennebis* was upon Swan Island, "in a delightful situation, and that of *Abbigadasset* between a river of his name and the Kennebeck, upon the northern borders of Merry-meeting Bay."§ Swan Island was purchased of *Abbigadasset* in 1667, by *Humphry Davie*, and afterwards claimed by Sir *John Davy*, a serjeant at law.‖

We shall proceed to notice here one, of another age, whose melancholy fate has long since commanded the attention of writers.

Some time previous to the settlement of Burton, N. H., that is, previous to 1766, there resided in that region a small tribe of Indians, among whom was one named

CHOCORUA, and he was the last of the primitives of those romantic scenes. This region was attracting to them on account of the beaver which were found in its pellucid waters, and its cragged cliffs afforded safe retreats to a plentiful game. It is handed to us by tradition, that *Chocorua* was the last of this region, and that he was murdered by a miserable white hunter, who, with others of his complexion, had wandered here in quest of game. This solitary man had retired to a neighboring mountain, and was there discovered and shot. The eminence to which it is said this Indian had retired, is the highest mountain in Burton, and commands a beautiful view of a great extent of surrounding country. One of the most superb engravings that has appeared in all our annuals, is that representing *Chocorua* in his last retreat.

It is a fact well known in all the neighboring parts of the country, that cattle cannot long survive in Burton, although there appears abundance of all that is necessary for their support. They lose their appetite, pine and

---

* *Williamson's Maine*, i. 428, from 3 *Mass. Rec.*

† It appears from the "*Answer to the Remarks of the Plymouth Company*," that ESSEMENOSQUE was also one that consented to the sale. He is the same whom we shall notice as *Assiminasqua* in our next chapter.

‡ People of Plimouth.—*William Paddy* died at Boston. His gravestone was dug out of the rubbish under the old state-house in 1830

§ *Williamson*, i. 467.

‖ *Williamson*, i. 331. Dr. *Holmes*, in his Annals, places the sale of Swan Island under 1668.

die. It is said that *Chocorua* cursed the English before he expired, and the superstitious, to this day, attribute the disease of cattle to the curse of *Chocorua*. But a much more rational one, we apprehend, will be found in the affection of the waters by minerals.

CHAPTER VIII.

Squando, *sachem of Saco—Attacks the town of Saco—Singular account of him by a contemporary—The ill treatment of his wife a cause of war—His humanity in restoring a captive*—Madokawando—*Causes of his hostility*—Assiminasqua—*His speech—Speech of* Tarumkin—Mugg—*Is carried to Boston to execute a treaty—Is Madokawando's ambassador—Release of Thomas Cobbet—Madokawando's kindness to prisoners*—Moxus *attacks Wells and is beaten off—Attacked the next year by the Indians under Madokawando and a company of Frenchmen—Are repulsed with great loss—Incidents of the siege—Mons. Casteins—A further account of Moxus*—Wanungonet—Assacombuit—*Further account of Mugg—His death*—Symon, Andrew, Jeoffrey, Peter *and* Joseph—*Account of their depredations—Life of* Kankamagus—*Treated with neglect—Flies his country—Becomes an enemy—Surprise of Dover and murder of Maj. Waldron*—Masandowet—Worombo—*His fort captured by Church—Kankamagus's wife and children taken*—Hopehood—*Conspicuous in the massacre at Salmon Falls—His death*—Mattahando—Megunneway.

The first chief which will here be properly noticed is *Squando*, a Tarratine, sachem of the Socokis, commonly called sagamore of Saco. He is mentioned with a good deal of singularity by the writers of his times. And we will here, by way of exordium, extract what Mr. *Mather*, in his Brief History, &c., says of him. "After this, [the burning of Casco,] they [the Indians] set upon Saco, where they slew 13 men, and at last burnt the town. A principal actor in the destruction of Saco was a strange *enthusiastical sagamore* called *Squando*, who, some years before, pretended that God appeared to him in the form of a tall man, in black clothes, declaring to him that he was God, and commanded him to leave his drinking of strong liquors, and to pray, and to keep sabbaths, and to go to hear the word preached; all which things the Indian did for some years, with great seeming devotion and conscience, observe. But the God which appeared to him said nothing to him about *Jesus Christ;* and therefore it is not to be marvelled at, that at last he discovered himself to be no otherwise than a child of him that was a murderer and a liar from the beginning." Mr. *Hubbard* says that he was "the chief actor or rather the beginner" of the eastern war of 1675—6; but rather contradicts the statement, as we apprehend, in the same paragraph, by attributing the *same cause* to the "rude and indiscrete act of some English seamen," who either for mischief overset a canoe in which was *Squando's* wife and child, or to see if young Indians could swim naturally like animals of the brute creation, as some had reported.* The child went to the bottom, but was saved from drowning by the mother's diving down and bringing it up, yet "within a while after the said child died." "The said *Squando*, father of the child, hath been so provoked thereat, that he hath ever since set himself to do all the mischief he can to the English." The whites did not believe that the death of the child was owing to its immersion; still we must allow the Indians to know as well as they. As the most memorable exploit in which *Squando* was engaged was the burning of Saco, it will be proper to enter here more in detail into it. The two principal inhabitants of the place were Captain *Bonithon* and Major *Phillips*, whose dwellings were situated on opposite sides of Saco River; the former on the east and the latter on the west. On 18 September, 1675, Captain *Bonithon's* house was discovered to be on fire, but himself and family had just

* "They can swim naturally, striking their paws under their throat like a dog, and not spreading their arms as we do." *Josselyn's Voyage* to *N. E.* 142.

before escaped across the river to Major Phillip's, and thus fortunately defeated a part of the design of their enemies. For this fortunate escape, however, they were under deep obligation to a friendly Indian who lived near by; he having been some how made acquainted with the design of *Squanto*, immediately imparted his information to the English.

The fire of Bonithon's house, says Mr. *Hubbard*, "was to them [at *Phillips's* garrison,] as the firing of a beacon," which gave them "time to look to themselves." A sentinel in the chamber soon gave notice that he saw an Indian near at hand, and Major *Phillips* going into the top of the house to make further discovery, received a shot in the shoulder; but it proved to be only a flesh wound. Knowing *Phillips*, and supposing him to be slain, the Indians raised a great shout, and instantly discovered themselves on all sides of the garrison; but the English, being well prepared, fired upon them from all quarters of their works, killing some and wounding others. Among the latter was a chief who died in his retreat, three or four miles from the place. He advised his fellows to desist from the enterprise, but they refused, and after continuing the siege for about an hour longer, they began to devise some means to set the garrison on fire. But in order to draw out the men from it in the first place, they set a house on fire near it, and also a saw and grist mill; that not having the desired effect, they called to them in an exulting tone, and said, "*You cowardly English dogs, come out and put out the fire!*"

The attack had begun about 11 o'clock in the day, and though the night partially put an end to it, yet the English were alarmed every half hour, until about four or five o'clock in the morning, when the work of the preceding night discovered itself. A noise of axes and other tools had been heard in the neighborhood of the saw-mill, and it was expected the Indians were preparing some engine with which to accomplish their object, and it proved true. A cart with four wheels had been constructed, and on one end they had erected a breastwork, while the body of the cart was filled with birch, straw, powder, and such like matters for the ready consummation of their stratagem. The approach of this formidable machine dismayed some of the Englishmen in the garrison; but being encouraged by their officers, they stood to their quarters, and awaited its approach. Their orders were not to fire until it came within pistol shot. When it had got within about that distance, one of the wheels stuck fast in a gutter, which its impellers not observing in season, they forced the other wheels onward, and brought themselves into a position to be effectually raked by the right flank of the garrison. This mistake of the enemy was improved to great advantage by the English. They poured in a sudden fire upon them, killing six and wounding 15 more. This sudden and unexpected reverse decided the fate of the garrison. The Indians immediately retreated, and the garrison received no further molestation.

As was generally the case in sieges of this kind, the English learned what damage they did their enemy, their numbers, &c., some time after the affair happened. In this case, however, nothing more is related concerning the loss of the Indians than we have given, and their numbers Mr. Hubbard does not expressly state, but says the people in the garrison "espied 40 of them marching away the next morning at sunrise, but how many more were in their company they could not tell." * There were 50 persons in the garrison, though but 15 of them were able to act in its defence.

But few days before the affair at Saco, viz. on 12 † September, the family of *Thomas Wakely* at Presumpscot River were massacred in a revolting manner The "old man," his son, and his daughter-in-law, then *enceinte*, with three grandchildren, were all murdered, and when discovered by their neighbors, partly burned in the ruins of their habitation, to which the Indians had set fire on leaving the place. One of the family was taken captive, a girl about 11 years old, who, after having passed through all the tribes from the Sokokis to the Narragansets, was restored to the English at Dover by *Squando*. But

* Mr. *Folsom*, Hist. Saco and Biddeford, 155, says they were computed at 100.
† Williamson's Hist. Maine, i. 520.

it does not appear whether this chief had any thing further to do in the matter, although it may be inferred, that he had some control or command over those that held her prisoner. From the circumstance that this child was shown to the hostile tribes through the country, it would seem that the eastern Indians were in concert with those to the west; and it is probable that this captive was thus exhibited to prove that they had taken up the hatchet. Upon her being returned, Mr. *Hubbard* remarks, "She having been carried up and down the country, some hundreds of miles, as far as Narraganset fort, was, this last June, returned back to Major *Waldron's* by one *Squando*, the sagamore of Saco; a strange mixture of mercy and cruelty!" And the historian of Maine observes, that his "conduct exhibited at different times such traits of cruelty and compassion, as rendered his character difficult to be portrayed."

He was a great powwow, and acted in concert with *Madokawando*. These two chiefs "are said to be, by them that know them, a strange kind of moralized savages; grave and serious in their speech and carriage, and not without some show of a kind of religion, which no doubt but they have learned from the prince of darkness." In another place, Mr. *Hubbard* calls him an "enthusiastical, or rather diabolical miscreant." His abilities in war gained him this epithet.

Madokawando, of whom we have just made mention, was chief of the Penobscot tribe. He was the adopted son of a chief by the name of *Assiminasqua.* Some mischief had been done by the Androscoggin Indians in *Philip's* war, and the English, following the example of those whom they so much reprobated, retaliated on any Indians that fell in their way.

Madokawando was not an enemy, nor do we learn that his people had committed any depredations, until after some English spoiled his corn, and otherwise did him damage.

Many of the eastern Indians had been kidnapped and sold for slaves, about the time *Philip's* war commenced. This, it will not be questioned, was enough to cause a war, without *Philip's* instigation, or the affront offered to the wife and child of *Squando*. The English had prohibited the sale of arms and ammunition to them, as they had before to the western tribes, as a means of lessening their power, provided they should declare themselves hostile; thus properly regarding their own safety, and totally disregarding whatever evils might accrue from the measure to the Indians. Knowing enough had been done to excite their resentment, agents were sent to parley with them, in the spring and summer of 1676, to hinder, if possible, their taking offence at these proceedings.

Meanwhile the Indians had complained to some friendly English of the outrage upon their friends, who were unacquainted with the circumstance, and hardly believed it; still, told the Indians, that if it were so, those kidnapped should be restored, and the perpetrators punished. But knowing the circumstance to be as they had represented, it is rather marvellous, that *Indians*, instead of at once retaliating, should hearken to unsatisfactory parleyings, as will appear; for when the English agents went to treat with them, or rather to excuse themselves for what they could not, or pretended they could not, amend, the Indians, in the course of the interview, said, "*We were driven from our corn last year by the people about Kennebeck, and many of us died. We had no powder and shot to kill venison and fowl with to prevent it. If you English were our friends, as you pretend you are, you would not suffer us to starve as we did.*" "However," says Mr. *Hubbard*, "the said agent, *making the best he could of a bad cause*, used all means to *pacify the complainants.*" The great "*all means*" was, that they should try to get the Androscoggin Indians *to come and hold a treaty!* so that if the English could effect a treaty with them, then there would be a general peace with the eastern Indians. This talk, it was said, they received with joy. "Yet," adds the same author, still by one fatal accident or other, jealousies still seemed to increase in their minds, or else the former injuries began to boil afresh in their spirits, as not being easily digested," &c.

A meeting had been agreed upon at Totononnock, or Taconnet, and immediately after the meeting just mentioned a runner was sent down from thence, with word that *Squando* would be there with "divers Amonoscoggan sachems," *Mugg* having been sent as a messenger to him. Accordingly the English proceeded to Taconnet. On their arrival, they were honored with a salute, and conducted into the council house, where they found *Madokawando, Assiminasqua, Tarumkin, Hopehood, Mugg*, and many attendants. *Madokawando* was prime negotiator, and *Assiminasqua* chief speaker, who soon after proceeded to make a speech, and among other things said,—

"*It is not our custom when messengers come to treat of peace, to seize upon their persons, as sometimes the Mohawks do; yea, as the* English have done, *seizing upon fourteen Indians, our men, who went to treat with you—setting a guard over them, and taking away their guns. This is not all, but a second time you required our guns, and demanded us to come down unto you, or else you would kill us. This was the cause of our leaving both our fort and our corn, to our great loss.*"

This speech caused considerable embarrassment to the English, "yet," says *Hubbard*, "to put the best construction might be, on such irregular actions, which could not well be justified, they told them, the persons who had so done * were not within the limits of their government, and therefore, though they could not call them to an account for so acting, yet they did utterly disallow thereof." † And to be as expeditious as possible, the English commissioners told these chiefs that they came to treat with the Androscoggins, and were sorry that *Squando* was not there. And it appears that, though the English reported a peace with the Penobscots, yet *Madokawando* and his coadjutors scarcely understood as much; and it is also evident that the business was hurried over as fast as possible by the English commissioners.

ASSIMINASQUA, it will be proper here to observe, was a Kanibas sachem, whose residence was at or near the place where the treaty was held.

What had been said by *Assiminasqua* in the morning was merely preliminary, and it was his intention in the afternoon to enter more particularly into details; but the English cut the matter short, and proceeded to treat with such of the Androscoggins as were present. *Tarumkin* was their orator, and he spoke to this effect:—

"*I have been to the westward, where I have found many Indians unwilling to make peace; but for my own part, I am willing,*" which he confirmed by taking the English by the hand, as did seven or eight of his men, among whom were *Mugg* and *Robinhood's* son. The English had now, as *they* supposed, got matters into a regular train; but *Madokawando*, it appears, was not willing to leave things in quite so loose a manner, as it regarded his people. He therefore interrupted:—

"*What are we to do for powder and shot, when our corn is consumed? what shall we do for a winter's supply? Must we perish, or must we abandon our country, and fly to the French for protection?*"

The English replied that they would do what they could with the governor; "*some might be allowed them for necessity.*" *Madokawando* added: "*We have waited a great while already, and now we expect you will say yes or no.*" The English rejoined: "You say yourselves that many of the western Indians would not have peace, and, therefore, if we sell you powder, and you give it to the western men, what do we *but cut our own throats?* It is not in our power, *without leave*, if you should wait *ten years more*, to let you have powder." Here, as might reasonably have been expected, ended the negotiation, and massacres and bloodshed soon after desolated that part of the country.

At the close of the war of 1675 and 6, this sachem's people had among them about 60 English captives. When it was known to him that the English desired to treat about peace, he sent *Mugg*, one of his chiefs, to Pascataqua, to receive proposals; and, that he might meet with good acceptance, sent along with him a captive to his home. General *Gendal*, of Massachusetts, being there, forced *Mugg* on board his vessel, and carried him to Boston, for which treacherous act an excuse was pleaded, that he was not vested with sufficient authority to treat with him. *Madokawando's* ambassador, being now in the power of the English, was obliged to agree to such terms

* That is, those who had kidnapped their friends.

† *Hubbard*, part ii. 38

as the English dictated.* It is no wonder, therefore, if the great chief soon appears again their enemy. Still, when *Mugg* was sent home, *Madokawando* agreed to the treaty, more readily, perhaps, as two armed vessels of the English conveyed him.

A son of Reverend *Thomas Cobbet* had been taken, and was among the Indians at Mount Desert. It so happened that his master had at that time sent him down to *Castein's* trading-house, to buy powder for him. *Mugg* took him by the hand, and told him he had been at his father's house, and had promised to send him home. *Madokawando* demanded a ransom, probably to satisfy the owner of the captive, "*fearing*," he said "*to be killed by him, if he yielded him up without he were there to consent; for he was a desperate man, if crossed, and had* crambd † *two or three in that way.*" Being on board one of the vessels, and treated to some liquor, "he walked awhile," says *Cobbet*, "to and again on the deck, and on a sudden made a stand, and said to Captain *Moore*, 'Well captain, since it is so, take this man: I freely give him up to you; carry him home to his friends.'" ‡ A red coat was given to *Madokawando*, which gave him great satisfaction.

The historians of the war have all observed that the prisoners under *Madokawando* were remarkably well treated.

In February, 1677, Major *Waldron*, and Captain *Frost*, with a body of men, were sent into the eastern coast to observe the motions of the Indians, who still remained hostile. At Pemmaquid, they were invited on shore to hold a treaty, but the English finding some weapons concealed among them, thought it a sufficient umbrage to treat them as enemies, and a considerable fight ensued, in which many of the Indians were killed, and several taken prisoners; among whom was a sister of *Madokawando*. He had no knowledge of the affair, having been gone for several months at a great distance into the country, on a hunting voyage.

We hear no more of *Madokawando* until 1691. It will be found mentioned in the account of *Egeremet*, that in that year a treaty was made with him and other eastern chiefs. This was in November, and it was agreed by them, that, on the first of May following, they would deliver all the captives in their possession, at Wells. "But," says Dr. *Mather*,§ "as it was not upon the *firm land*, but in their *canoes* upon the *water*, that they signed and sealed this instrument; so, reader, we will be jealous that it will prove but a fluctuating and unstable sort of business; and that the Indians will *do a lie* as they used to do."

Meanwhile *Madokawando*, among other important expeditions which he planned, attempted one upon York, in which he succeeded nearly to his wishes, if not beyond his expectations. Such was his manner of attack, that the English scarce knew their enemy; from whence they came, or their numbers. But it was afterwards found by the Indians' own confession, and some captives they had liberated, that *Madokawando* was the leader in the business. Whether he had during the winter been to Canada, and got the assistance of some Frenchmen, or whether *Castiens*, his son-in-law, and some other Frenchmen who then resided among his people at Penobscot, were with him, we cannot take it upon us to state; but certain it is, some French were in his company, but how many is also uncertain, but the number of Indians was stated at about 250. It was on Monday, February 5, in the year 1692, early in the morning, that York was laid in ashes, all except three or four garrisoned houses, and about 75 of its inhabitants killed, and 85 taken captive.

Such only escaped as reached the garrisons, and these were summoned to surrender, but the besiegers dared not to continue long enough to make any effectual assault upon them, and thus they escaped. The wretched captives

* A treaty was signed 9th of Dec. 1676. *Manuscript Nar. of Rev. T. Cobbet* It may be seen in *Hubbard's* Narrative.

† The Indian word for *killed*. *Wood's N. E. Prospect*.

‡ Manuscript Narrative, before cited. Perhaps this was the same Captain *Moore* who carried the news of *Philip's* defeat and death to London afterwards. See OLD INDIAN CHRONICLE, 105.

§ Magnalia, vii. 76.

were hurried into the wilderness, and many suffered and died by the way. The Reverend *Shubael Dummer*, minister of the place, a man in high estimation for his virtues, was about the first victim; he was shot as he was mounting his horse at his own door; his wife was among the captives, and died in captivity. York was at this time one of the most important towns in the country.*

Circumstances having thus transpired, the English had very little reason to expect an observance of the articles of the treaty before alluded to, yet persons were sent to Wells to receive the captives, provided they should be offered. They took care to be provided with an armed force, and to have the place of meeting at a strong place, which was *Storer's* garrison-house. But, as the author just cited observes, "The Indians being poor *musicians* for *keeping of time*, came not according to their articles." The reason of this we cannot explain, unless the warlike appearance of the English deterred them. After waiting a while, Captain *Converse* surprised some of them, and brought them in by force, and having reason to believe the Indians provoked by this time, immediately added 35 men to his force. These, says *Mather*, "were not come half an hour to *Storer's* house, on the 9th of June, 1691, nor had they got their *Indian weed* fairly lighted, into their mouths, before fierce *Moxus*, with 200 Indians, made an attack upon the garrison," † but were repulsed and soon drew off. *Madokawando* was not here in person, but when he knew of the disaster of his chief captain, he said, "*My brother Moxus has missed it now, but I will go myself the next year, and have the dog* Converse *out of his hole.*"

The old chief was as good as his word, and appeared before the garrison 22 June, 1692. He was joined by *Portneuf* and *Labrocre*, two French officers, with a body of their soldiers, and their united strength was estimated at about 500 men. They were so confident of success, that they agreed before the attack, how the prisoners and property should be divided. *Converse* had but 15 men, but fortunately there arrived two sloops with about as many more, and supplies, the day before the battle.

Madokawando's men had unwisely given notice of their approach, by firing upon some cattle they met in the woods, which running in wounded, gave the inhabitants time to fly to the garrison. The Indians were not only seconded by the two French officers and a company of their men, as before observed, but *Moxus*, *Egeremet* and *Worombo* were also among them.

They began the attack before day, with great fierceness, but after continuing it for some time without success, they fell upon the vessels in the river; and here, although the river was not above twenty or thirty feet broad, yet they met with no better success than at the garrison. They tried many stratagems, and succeeded in setting fire to the sloops several times, by means of fire arrows, but it was extinguished without great damage. Tired of thus exposing themselves and throwing away their ammunition, they returned again to the garrison, resolving to practise a stratagem upon that, and thus ended the first day of the attack. They tried to persuade the English to surrender, but finding they could not prevail, made several desperate charges, in which they lost many. Beginning now to grow discouraged, they sent a flag to the garrison to effect a capitulation, but *Converse*, being a man of great resolution, replied, "that he wanted nothing but men to come and fight him." To which the bearer of the flag said, "*Being you are so stout, why don't you come and fight in the open field like a man, and not fight in a garrison like a squaw?*" This attempt proving ineffectual also, they cast out many threats, one of which was, "*We will cut you as small as tobbaco, before to-morrow morning.*" The captain ordered them "to come on, for he wanted work."

Having nearly spent their ammunition, and General *Labrocre* being slain, they retired in the night, after two days' siege, leaving several of their dead behind; among whom was the general just named, who was shot through the head. They took one Englishman, named *John Diamond*, who had ven-

* *Magnalia*, vii. 77.—*Williamson*, Hist. Maine i. 628—9.

† Magnalia, vii. 76.

tured out of the garrison on some occasion, whom they tortured in a most barbarous manner. About the time of their retreating, they fired upon the sloops, and killed the only man lost by the vessels during the assault. In the attack upon the vessels, among other stratagems, they prepared a breastwork upon wheels, which, notwithstanding their previous experience in this kind of engine, at Brookfield and Saco, they again resolved to try, and therefore endeavored to bring it close to the edge of the river. When they had got it pretty near, one wheel sunk in the ground, and a French soldier, endeavoring to lift it out with his shoulder, was shot down; a second was also killed in the like attempt, and it was abandoned. They also built a raft in the creek above the vessels, and placed on it an immense pile of combustibles, and, setting them on fire, floated it down towards them. But when within a few rods of the sloops, the wind drove it on shore, and thus they were delivered from the most dangerous artifice of the whole. For it was said that, had it come down against them, they could not have saved themselves from the fury of its flames.

As late as 1736 an attempt was made to prove that *Madokawando* was not chief sachem of the Penobscots, which it seems no one in his lifetime thought of questioning. Nor had the fact at this time been questioned but from mercenary motives. A claim having been set up to lands upon St. George's River, in opposition to that of the heirs of Governor *Leverett*, that falsehood was resorted to, to maintain it. The foundation of Leverett's claim was in a deed dated Pemmaquid, 9 May, 1694, by which *Madokawando* conveyed to Sir *William Phips* the tract of land on both sides of St. George's River, bounded east by Wessamesskek River, west by Hatthett's Cove Island, thence by a line to the upper falls of St. George's River; also Mastomquoog Island in the mouth of said river, and St. George's Islands. A valuable consideration is said to have been paid, but what it was does not appear from the deed. The deponents called upon afterwards to prove *Madokawando's* power to sell that tract, state the consideration variously, though none of them definitely; some said Sir *William Phips* gave a large amount in money,* and one that he gave a *hatfull*.† To this deed were the following signatures:—

Signed, sealed and delivered in presence of
The mark ♃ *of* Edgar Emit, *Sagamore of Kennebek.*
The mark ⌗ *of* Wenemouet, *cozin to Madokawando.*
The mark ⋇ *of* John Saugmore, *of Sheepsgut River*, interpreter.
Also 6 or 7 whites.

The mark of Madokawando, *Sagamore of Penobscot*, ⁂ *and a seal.*

From an examination of the various affidavits before mentioned we derive the following interesting historical facts in the life of *Madokawando*; viz. that he died in 1698, and was succeeded by *Wenamouet*, or, as his name is sometimes spelled, *Wenoggonet*. This appears from the deposition of Captain *Cyprian Southack*, who further says "that he was with *Madokawando*, when a present of 10 barrels of gunpowder, a quantity of fire-arms, and some clothes, were delivered him by Governor *Willebone*, which was a present sent him by the King of France." "And that Monsieur *Castain* married the said *Madokawando's* daughter."

Joseph Bane deposed, "that, in 1691, he was with *Theodore Atkinson*, late of Newcastle, in N. Hampshire, Esq., said *Atkinson's* wife, and Mrs. *Elizabeth Alcock* of Portsmouth, widow, and many others at the house of *Joseph Moulton* of York in the county of York, when they were taken captive by a large number of Indians," that *Madokawando* was then commander of said Indians, and was then reputed chief sachem of Penobscot. *Bane* farther relates that he was sold to an Amaroscoggen Indian, with whom he lived till 1699, and that he was present when *Madokawando* ordered *Theodore*

* Deposition of *John Phillips*, 2 July, 1736.—*Waldo's* Defence, 3. † Ibid. 35.

Atkinson, who was his captive, to write to the governor of Massachusetts to send a vessel to Sagadahok with goods to redeem the captives; that it was accordingly sent there, and *Atkinson*, his wife, and about 40 others were redeemed.

John Longley was taken prisoner at Groton in July, 1694, and was servant to *Madokawando* two years and a half.

The inhabitants of Black Point gave, yearly, a peck of corn each to *Madokawando*, as an acknowledgment that he was sachem of Penobscot.

In 1690 *Tobias Oakman* was taken by the Indians at Black Point. At which time he says he "personally knew *Edgar Emet* who was then chief sachem of Kenebeck and *Squando* who was then chief sachem of Saco, and *Moxus* who was then chief sachem of Noridgawock, and *Shepcot John* who was then chief sachem of Shepscot and with *Oorumby*, who was then chief sachem of Pejemscot." *Oakman* was taken prisoner by 30 Indians in 3 parties under 3 chiefs; one from Penobscot, one from Norridgewok and the other from Pejepscot; *Madokawando*, *Moxus* and *Oorumby* being the respective sachems; hence *Madokawando* was sachem of Penobscot at that time.

In the treaty which the eastern chiefs made with Sir. *William Phips* at Pemmaquid, 11 August, 1693, the following hostages were delivered to the English to ensure its observance. "AHASSAMHAMET, brother to *Edger Emet*; WENOMOUETT, cousin to *Madokawando*; BAGATAWAWONGON, and SHEEPSCOTT JOHN." *

A daughter of *Madokawando*, as we have seen, married the Baron *De Casteins*, by whom he had several children.

In all of our former editions we gave *Lahontan's* account of *Casteins* in a note, and in the French language; but it having been suggested by friends, that it should not only occupy a place in the text, but be rendered in English, I improve the opportunity to make the change.

The Baron *De St. Casteins*, a gentleman of Oleron in Bearn, having for about 20 years resided among the Abenakis, gained so much of their esteem, that they regarded him as their tutelar deity. He had been an officer of the Carignan regiment in Canada; but when that regiment was disbanded, he cast himself among the savages, of whom he learned their language. He took from them a wife after their manner, preferring the forests of Acadie, to the Pyrenean mountains, which environ his native country. He lived, during the first years of his abode with the Indians, in such a manner as to gain a respect from them, above what can be imagined. They made him great chief, which is the same as sovereign of the nation, and by little and little he has worked up a fortune, which any other man would have turned to good account, and withdrawn from the country with two or three hundred thousand crowns of gold in his coffers. However, he only uses it to buy merchandise, with which to make presents to his Indian brethren, who, when they return from their hunting excursions, reimburse him for his presents with a triple amount in beaver.† The governors of Canada direct him, and those of New England fear him. He has several daughters, all of whom are advantageously married to Frenchmen, with each a rich dowry. He has never changed his wife,‡ showing the Indians by his example that God is not pleased with inconstant men. It is said that he has endeavored to convert these poor people, but that his words produce no good fruit, and hence it is of no use for the Jesuits to preach the truths of Christianity to them; yet these fathers relax not their labors, and consider that to confer baptism upon a dying infant repays them ten fold for the sufferings and privations they experience in living among that people.§

---

* *Waldo's* Defence, 39.—The names of these hostages differ materially from those in the *Magnalia*, vii. 85.

† We should think that to a man of a sordid mind, this was "turning a fortune to good account."

‡ That this amounts to a denial, as Mr. *Halket* reads it, (*Notes on the American Indians*, 230,) that *Casteins* had but one wife, we do not agree. His not changing his wife, (*Il n'a je nais changé de femme*,) might be true, if, as some assert, he had several at the same time.

§ *Memoires de l'Amerique*, ii. 29, 30.

The town now called *Castine*, on the Penobscot River, was the place of the residence of the French baron, and a son of his succeeded him in the sachemdom of the Penobscots. He was with *Iberville* at the capture of Pemmaquid in 1696, in which expedition he led 200 Indians. Captain *Chubb* of whom we have spoken before, commanded the fort, which was well manned and supplied, having 15 pieces of cannon and 90 men, but surrendered it in a cowardly manner. He helped defend Port Royal in 1706, in defence of which he was wounded in 1707. He finally retired to his native country, where he ended his days. In 1688, Governor *Andros*, with an armament, took possession of *Castain's* village, plundered his house, and committed other depredations, but himself escaped. In 1721, his son was seized by the English, and carried to Boston; but they not long after set him at liberty.

Some have endeavored to ground an argument upon the similarity of the name of this chief to that of *Madock* the Welshman, that the eastern Indians were descended from a Welsh colony, who, in 1170, left that country, and were never heard of after. The *story* of some white Indians speaking Welsh, on the Missouri River, has gained supporters in former and latter periods.*

Moxus, or, as he was sometimes called, *Agamagus*, was also a noted chief. We can add little concerning him, to what has already been said. After *Madokawando* was dead, and the war between the French and English nations had ceased, the eastern chiefs were ready to submit to terms. *Moxus* seems the successor of *Madokawando*, and when delegates were sent into the eastern country to make peace with the Indians, in 1699, his name stood first among the signers of the treaty.† He concluded another treaty with Governor *Dudley*, in 1702. The next year, in company with *Wanungonet*, *Assacambuit*, and a number of French, he invested Captain *March* in the fort at *Casco*. After using every endeavor to take it by assault, they had recourse to the following stratagem. They began at the water's edge to undermine it by digging, but were prevented by the timely arrival of an armed vessel under Captain *Southack*. They had taken a vessel and a great quantity of plunder. About 200 canoes were destroyed, and the vessel retaken. From which circumstance it may be inferred that their number was great.

Moxus was at Casco in 1713, to treat with the English, and at Georgetown, upon Arowsike Island, in 1717. There were seven other chiefs who attended also at the time and place last mentioned.

Mugg was a chief among the Androscoggins, and very conspicuous in the eastern war of 1676–7, into which he seems to have been brought by the same cause as *Madokawando*, already stated. He had been very friendly to the English, and had lived some time with them.

On the 12 October, 1676, he made an assault upon Black Point, now in Scarborough, with about 100 warriors. All the inhabitants being gathered into one fortified place upon that point, a few hands might have defended it against all the Indians on that side of the country.‡ While the captain of the garrison was gone out to hold a talk with *Mugg*, the people fled from the garrison and took all their effects along with them. A few of his own servants, however, remained, who fell into the hands of the chief, who treated them kindly. When *Francis Card* was a prisoner among his men, he told him "*that he had found out the way to burn Boston,*" and laughed much about the English; saying he would have all their vessels, fishing islands, and whole country and bragged about his great numbers. He was killed at Black Point, on 16 May, the same place where, the year before, he had had such good success. He had besieged the garrison three days, killed three men, and taken one captive The celebrated *Symon*, who had done so much mischief in many places, was with him here. Lieutenant *Tippin*, who commanded the garrison, "made a

* See Janson's *Stranger in America*, 270, ed. 4to. London, 1807; *Universal Magazine*, vol. xciii. 21; Dr. Southey's *Preface to his Madock*; Bouquet's *Exped. against Ohio Indians*, 69. ed. 4to. London, 1766; Ker's *Travels in America*, 167—172; Burk, *Hist. Virginia*, ii. 84 Beatty, *Jour.* 24; Moulton's *New-York*, i. 45.; Barton's *Physical Jour.* i. pt. ii. 79 *Columb. Mag.* for 1787.

† Magnalia, vii. 94. It is dated 7 Jan. 1698—9.

‡ Hubbard, *Ind. Wars*, ii. 46.

successful shot upon an Indian, that was observed to be very busy and bold in the assault, who at that time was deemed to be *Symon*, the arch villain and incendiary of all the eastward Indians, but proved to be one almost as good as himself, who was called *Mogg*." *

SYMON, just named, was a troublesome fellow, who continued to create considerable alarm to the inhabitants upon the Merrimack River, in the vicinity of Newbury and Amesbury, about which part seems to have been his residence, as late as the month of July, 1677. On the 9th of July, six Indians were seen to go into the bushes not far from the garrison at Amesbury; two days before, several men had been killed in the neighborhood, and one woman wounded, whose name was *Quimby*. *Symon* was the alleged leader of the party which committed the depredation. Mrs. *Quimby* was sure that it was he who "knocked her on the head," and she knew the names of many of the rest with him, and named *Andrew*, *Geoffrey*, and *Joseph*. She begged of *Symon* not to kill her. He replied, "*Why, goodwife Quimby, do you think that I will kill you?*" She said she was afraid he would, because he killed all the English. *Symon* then said, "I will give quarter to never an English dog of you all," and then gave her a blow on the head, which did not happen to hurt her much; at which, being a woman of great courage, she threw a stone at him; he then turned upon her, and "struck her two more blows," at which she fell, and he left her for dead. Before he gave her the last blows, she called to the garrison for help. He told her she need not do that, for, said he, "I will have that too, by and by." *Symon* was well known to many of the inhabitants, and especially to Mrs. *Quimby*, as he had formerly lived with her father, *William Osgood*.† In April, 1677, *Symon* and his companions burnt the house of *Edward Weymouth* at Sturgeon Creek, and plundered the house of one *Crawley*, but did not kill him, because he had shown kindness to *Symon's* grandmother.‡

Symon was one of the Christian Indians, as were *Andrew*, *Geoffrey*, *Peter*, and several others of the same company, a circumstance which, with many, much aggravated their offences. The irruption just mentioned is thus related by Mr. *Hubbard*: § "*Symon* and *Andrew*, the two brethren in iniquity, with a few more, adventured to come over Pascataqua River on Portsmouth side, when they burnt one house within four or five miles of the town, and took a maid and a young woman captive; one of them having a young child in her arms, with which not willing to be troubled, they gave leave to her that held it, to leave it with an old woman, whom the Indian *Symon* spared because he said she had been kind to his grandmother; yet one of the two captives escaped from their hands two days after, as did the other, April 22, who gave notice of the Indians, (being not so narrowly looked to as they used to do others.")

It was on 3 May, 1676, that *Symon*, *Andrew* and *Peter* fell upon the house of *Thomas Kimbal*, of Bradford, killed him, and carried off his wife and five children into the wilderness.‖ Having on the whole concluded to make peace with the English while they could, did, before the end of six weeks, restore the captives. Instead of improving the opportunity of securing their friendship, the English seized *Symon* and *Andrew*, and confined them in the jail at Dover. This treatment they considered, as very naturally they should, only a precursor of something of a different character; and therefore found means to break jail, and make good their escape. They joined their eastern friends, and hence followed many other cruelties, some of which we have already related. About the first depredation which followed their flight from Dover, was committed at Greenland. One *John Keniston* was killed, and his house burned. A writer of that day, after observing that the perpetrators of the outrage were *Symon*, *Andrew*, and *Peter*, observes that they were the "three we had in prison, and should have killed," and closes with this exclamation,

* *Hist. N. England.* † MS. Documents. ‡ Belknap's *N. Hampshire.*

§ *Hist. N. England*, 631.

‖ See the very creditable History of Haverhill, (p. 53.) by Mr *Myrick*, for other interesting particulars respecting this affair

"The good Lord pardon us." * Thus some considered they had need of *pardon* for not dealing with more rigor towards the Indians!

One of the most important actions in which *Symon* was engaged remains to be related. Mr. *Anthony Brackett*, who lived at Back Cove, upon a large estate now owned in part by Mr. *Deering* of Portland, had been visited by *Symon*, occasionally, who, like *Totoson*, in the case of *Clarke* at Eel River, in Plimouth, had made himself well acquainted with the situation of his house and family. On the 9th of August, 1676, some Indians had killed one of *Brackett's* cows. *Brackett* immediately complained to *Symon* of the outrage, who promised to bring to him the perpetrators. Meanwhile a complaint was despatched to Major *Waldron* at Dover, which might have been the cause of the course *Symon* immediately after pursued; for, if, when he had promised to aid in adjusting the affair, he learned that, at the same time, a force had been secretly applied for, it is a sufficient reason, in this ruffled state of things, that he should show himself an enemy, as he did, on the morning of the 11th, two days after the injury was done. Friday was the 11 August, and it was early in the morning that *Symon* appeared at the head of a party, at the house of Captain *Anthony Brackett*. "These are the Indians," said he, "that killed the cow." No sooner was this said, than the house was entered, and the guns seized upon belonging to the family. *Brackett* then asked what was the meaning of their carriage, and *Symon* replied, "So it must be," and demanded of him whether he would go with them, as a captive, or be killed; to which he answered, that if the case were so, he preferred to serve as a captive; *Symon* then said they must be bound, and, accordingly, Mr. *Brackett*, his wife, (who was a daughter of *Michael Mitton*,) and a negro, were bound. Mrs. *Brackett's* brother *Nathaniel*, only son of *M. Mitton*, was of the family, and made some resistance when they were about to bind him, and was killed upon the spot. The rest, *Brackett*, his wife and five children were carried away prisoners. They continued in captivity until the November following, when some of them found means to effect an escape; which was singularly fortunate, and worth relating. In their wanderings, those who held them captive, came to the north side of Casco Bay. Here news reached the Indians that Arowsike Island had been captured by their brethren, and they at once determined to share in the booty; so, in their hurry, their eagerness for the spoil of Arowsike outweighed their fears of losing their prisoners. Therefore they promised Captain *Brackett* and the rest, that if they would come after them, they should have a share in the good things which had been taken; and accordingly set off and left them. Mrs. *Brackett*, taking advantage of their good feeling, just before they left, asked them for some meat, which was readily granted; she found an old birchen canoe, which had been probably abandoned by the Indians, by reason of its being nearly broken up, but in which it was resolved to attempt an escape; and with the help of a needle which Mrs. *Brackett* also found in an old house at that place, she was enabled so to mend the canoe, that it wafted herself and child, her husband and the negro man to the opposite shore of the bay, a distance of eight or nine miles, in safety. They hardly could have expected but what, on landing near Black Point, they would have been in the very presence of Indians, yet it so happened that although they had but just destroyed the settlements there, they had all left the place. And a vessel, which happened very fortunately in that neighborhood, took them in safety to Portsmouth.

The wife of Captain *Anthony Brackett* should not be overlooked in enumerating the heroines of our country. Her name was *Ann*. She died after this war, but the time is not ascertained. Her husband married again, a daughter of *Abraham Drake*, Senior, of Hampton, whose name was *Susannah*,† by whom he had several children. When Colonel *Church* had the memorable fight with the Indians at Casco, 21 September, 1689, Captain *Brackett* was killed. After this his wife and children went to her father's at Hampton, but finally returned to their possessions.

We are now to commence upon the recital of one of the most horrid massacres any where recorded—the sacking of Dover by the famous chiefs *Kan*

* *Hist. N. England*, i. 158 † *Hubbard's* Nar. and *Willis's* Portland, i. 143—155.

kamagus and *Massandowet*, and the barbarous murder of Major *Waldron* and many of his people.

KANKAMAGUS, commonly in the histories called *Hogkins, Hawkins*, or *Hakins*, was a Pennakook sachem, and an artful, persevering, faithful man, as long as he could depend upon the English for protection. But when Governor *Cranfield*, of New Hampshire, used his endeavors to bring down the Mohawks to destroy the eastern Indians, in 1684, who were constantly stirred up by the French to commit depredations upon the English, *Kankamagus*, knowing the Mohawks made no distinction where they came, fled to the eastward, and joined the Androscoggins. He had a fort upon that river, where his family and that of another sachem, called *Worombos*, or *Worombo*, lived. But before he fled his country, he addressed several letters to the governor, which discover his fidelity as well as his fears; and from which there is no doubt but he would always gladly have lived in his own country, and on the most intimate and friendly terms with the English, to whom he had become attached, and had adopted much of their manner, and could read and write, but for the reasons just stated. The following letters fully explain the situation of his mind and his feelings, at the time he expected the Mohawks would ravage his country:—

"*May* 15*th*, 1685. *Honor governor my friend. You my friend I desire your worship and your power, because I hope you can do som great matters this one. I am poor and naked, and have no men at my place because I afraid allways Mohogs he will kill me every day and night. If your worship when please pray help me you no let Mohogs kill me at my place at Malamake River called Panukkog and Natukkog, I will submit your worship and your power. And now I want pouder and such alminishon, shatt and guns, because I have forth at my hom, and I plant theare.*"

This all Indian hand, but pray you do consider your humble servant.

SIMON DETOGKOM,*	JOHN HOGKINS,
JOSEPH × TRASK,	PETER ꝺ ROBIN,
KING ☿ HARRY,	MR. JORGE × RODUNNONUKGUS,
SAM ☊ LINIS,	MR. HOPE × HOTH,†
WAPEGUANAT ♍ SAGUACHUWASHAT,	JOHN TONEH,
OLD ⋇ ROBIN,	JOHN ∞ CANOWA,
MAMANOSGUES ⸸ ANDRA.	JOHN × OWAMOSIMMIN,
	NATONILL ⁑ INDIAN.

The same day, as appears by the date of it, *Hogkns* wrote the following letter, which bears the same signature as the above:—

"*Honor Mr. Governor,—Now this day I com your house, I vant se you, and I bring my hand at before you I want shake hand to you if your worship when please, then receive my hand then shake your hand and my hand. You my friend because I remember at old time when live my grant father and grant mother then Englishmen com this country, then my grant father and Englishmen they make a good government, they friend allwayes, my grant father living at place called Malamake-rever, other name chef Natukko and Panukkog, that one rever great many names and I bring you this few skins at this first time I will giue my friend.*

"*This all Indian hand.*"

The two following are from the same.

"*Please your worship,—I will intreat you matther you my friend now* [ ] *this if my Indian he do you long pray you no put your law, because som my Indians fool, som men much love drunk then he no know what he do, may be he do mischief when he drunk if so pray you must let me know what he done because I will ponis*

* The same called *Betokom* in *Gookin*, probably.—See *ante*, Book ii. Chap. vii.

† Perhaps *Hopehood*

him about what he haue done, you, you my friend if you desire my business, then sent me I will help you if I can. John Hogkins."

"*Mr. Mason,—Pray I want speak you a few words if your worship when please because I com parfas I will speake this governor but he go away so he say at last night, and so far I understand this governor his power that your power now, so he speak his own mouth. Pray if you take what I want pray com to me because I want go hom at this day. Your humble servant,*

"*May* 16, 1685. John Hogkins, *Indian sagmor.*"

About the time these letters were written, persons were sent among the Indians to ascertain whether, as was reported, they were assuming a warlike attitude. Those to whom the inquiry was intrusted, on their return reported, "that four Indians came from fort Albany to the fort at Penacook, and informed them [the Indians there] that all the Mohawks did declare they would kill all Indians from *Uncas* at Mount Hope to the eastward as far as Pegypscot.

"The reason of *Natombamat*, sagamore of Saco, departed his place was, because the same news was brought there, as himself declared, upon reading my orders at Penacook. *Natombamat* is gone to carry the Indians down to the same place, where they were before departed from us on Sunday morning, and desired Captain *Hooke* to meet him at Saco five days after. Both sagamores of Penacook, viz. *Wonalanset* and *Mesandowit*, the latter of which is come down, did then declare they had no intention of war, neither indeed are they in any posture for war, being about 24 men, besides squaws and papooses. The reason, they said, why they did not come among the English as formerly, was, their fear, that if the Mohawks came and fought them, and they should fly for succor to the English, that then the Mohawks would kill all the English for harboring them."

Notwithstanding this state of affairs, commissioners met the Indians on the 8 September, 1685, and a peace was concluded "between the subjects of his Majesty King *James* II, inhabiting N. Hampshire and Maine, and the Indians inhabiting the said provinces." The articles were subscribed on the part of the Indians by

The mark △ of Mesandowit.
" ✕ of Wahowah, *alias* Hopehood
" ⅃ of Tecamorisick, *alias* Josias.
The mark ⊂ of John Nomony, *alias* Upsawah.
" ⊟ of *Umbesnowah*, *alias* Robin.

The following signers agree to comply with the terms of the treaty "as their neighbors have done."

The mark ♑ of Netambomet.
" of Wahowah, *alias* Hopehood.
" C of Ned Higgon
" ɔ of Newcome

KANCAMAGUS, *alias* John Hawkins, *sagamore, signed this instrument*, 19th 7ber, 1685, *his* ▭ *mark.*

Bagesson, *alias* Joseph Traske, *his* ⚟ *mark.* And agreed to all within written.

Whether *Hogkins* were among the Penakooks seized by Major *Waldron* about ten years before, is not certain, or, if he were, it is not probable any resentment remained in his breast against him on that account, as the Pennakooks were all permitted to return home; but it is certain that he was the director and leader in the dreadful calamity which fell upon *Waldron* not long afterward, and which is as much chargeable upon the maltreatment they received from the English, at least, as upon any agency of the French. It may be true that many belonging to the eastward, who were seized with the Pennakooks, and sold or left in foreign countries, had found their way back among their friends again, and were glad of the first opportunity of revenging themselves upon the author of their unjust expatriation.

Major *Waldron* lived at Dover, then called by its Indian name, *Quochecho*, in New Hampshire, in a strong garrison-house, at which place were also four others. *Kankamagus* had artfully contrived a stratagem to effect the surprise of the place, and had others beside the Pennakooks from different places ready in great numbers, to prosecute the undertaking. The plan was this. Two squaws were sent to each garrison-house to get liberty to stay for the night, and when all should be asleep, they were to open the gates to the warriors. *Masandowet*, who was next to *Kankamagus*, went to Major *Waldron's*, and informed him that the Indians would come the next day and trade with him. While at supper with the major, *Masandowet* said to him, with an air of familiarity, "Brother *Waldron*, what would you do if the strange Indians should come?" To which he vauntingly replied, "that he could assemble an hundred men by lifting up his finger." In this security the gates were opened at midnight, and the work of death raged in all its fury. One garrison only escaped, who would not admit the squaws. They rushed into *Waldron's* house in great numbers, and while some guarded the door, others commenced the slaughter of all who resisted. *Waldron* was now 80 years of age, yet, seizing his sword, defended himself with great resolution, and at first drove the Indians before him from room to room, until one getting behind him, knocked him down with his hatchet. They now seized upon, and dragged him into the great room, and placed him in an armed chair upon a table. While they were thus dealing with the master of the house, they obliged the family to provide them a supper, which when they had eaten, they took off his clothes, and proceeded to torture him in the most dreadful manner. Some gashed his breast with knives, saying, "*I cross out my account;*" others cut off joints of his fingers, and said to him, "*Now will your fist weigh a pound?*"

After cutting off his nose and ears, and forcing them into his mouth, he became faint from loss of blood; and some holding his own sword on end upon the floor, let him fall upon it, and thus ended his misery.

The Indians had been greatly abused and wronged in their trading with the whites, and it is a tradition to this day all over that part of the country, that Major *Waldron* took great advantage of them in trade, and did not cross out their accounts when they had paid him; and that, in buying beaver, his fist was accounted to weigh a pound. Although he may have taken no more advantage of the Indians than the majority of Indian traders, yet, at this distant day, extenuation will not be looked for in impartial accounts of the transactions of our ancestors with the Indians.

To enumerate the villanies practised upon this devoted people, would be to expose to everlasting odium the majority of frontier traders from the earliest to the present time; but true history, now-a-days, is but little read, and little indeed where the facts militate against the pride of ancestry. A history of wrongs and sufferings preserved only to be read by those who have committed them, must be an unwelcome record! It was, and to this day is, in many places, a uniform practice among speculators or land-jobbers, to get the Indians drunk, and then make their bargains with them! In the time of *Philip's* war, an Androscoggin Indian said "that he had given an *hundred pound* for water drawn out of Mr. P. [Purchas] his well."* But to return to our narrative.

Several were killed at each of the garrison-houses that fell into their hands. They kept the place until the next morning, when, after collecting all the plunder they could carry, took up their march, with 29 captives, into the wilderness towards Canada; where the chief of them were bought by the French, and in time got home to their country again. Twenty-three were killed before they left the place. This affair took place on the night of the 27th of June, 1689. Several friendly Indians informed the English at Chelmsford of the certainty of an attack upon Dover, and they caused a letter to be de-

---

* *Hubbard*, ii. 77.—*Thomas Purchase's* house at Pegypscot was among the first that fell a prey to the eastern Indians in *Philip's* war. In the beginning of September, about 20 of them went there, and at first offered to trade, but Mr. *Purchase* and his son being from home, they took what they liked without even asking the price of it killed a few sheep and calves, and departed. Ibid, 14, 15.

spatched in season to have notified the people, but on account of some delay at Newbury ferry, the benefit of that information was lost.

Four years after, Colonel *Church* took *Worombo's* fort, in which were *Kankamagus's* wife and children. This fort was upon the Androscoggin, about 25 or 30 miles from its mouth. In another place, we have given a history of *Church's* expedition to this fort. The prisoners taken here informed *Church* that there had been lately a great council held there by the Indians, in which "many were for peace and many against it;" but they finally agreed to go with 300 warriors to Wells with a flag of truce, and to offer the English peace, which if not accepted, they would then fall upon them. "If they could not take Wells, then they resolved to attack Piscataqua. The which, says *Church*, when we were well informed of, we left two old squaws that were not able to march, gaue them victuals enough for one week of their own corn, boiled, and a little of our pruisions, and buried their dead, and left them clothes enough to keep them warme, and left the wigwams for them to lye in: gaue them orders to tell their friends how kind we were to them, biding them doe the like to ours. Also if they were for peace to come to goodman *Small's*, att Barwick, within 14 days, who would attend to discourse them; then we came away with our own five captiues, [English that they had delivered,] and nine of theirs." *

In the same letter we are informed that among these prisoners were *Kankamagus's* wife and four children. His brother-in-law was taken, but he "ran away from them." Among the slain was *Kankamagus's* own sister. A girl was brought away whose father and mother had been slain before her eyes. Two of the children of *Worombo* were also among the prisoners, all of whom were carried to Plimouth. This expedition upon the Androscoggin was on Sunday, 14 September, 1690.

A few days after this, *Church* landed at Casco, where the Indians fell upon him by surprise, and were not beaten off for some time, and then only by hard fighting. This was on the 21 September. *Church* had seven men killed and 24 wounded, two of whom died in a day or two after. The Indians who made this attack were probably led by *Kankamagus* and *Worombo*.

Hopehood was a chief nearly as celebrated, and as much detested in his time, as the chiefs of whom we have just spoken. He was chief of the tribe of the Kennebecks generally known as the Nerigwoks. He was the son of *Robinhood*, a sachem of whom we have spoken in a former chapter. According to some writers *Hopehood* was also known by the name *Wohawa*.† The career of his warlike exploits was long and bloody. Our first notice of him is in *Philip's* war, at the attack of a house at Newichewannok, since Berwick, in Maine. Fifteen persons, all women and children, were in the house, and *Hopehood*, with one only beside himself, *Andrew* of Saco, whom we have before mentioned as an accomplice with *Symon*, thought to surprise them, and but for the timely discovery of their approach by a young woman within, would have effected their purpose. She fastened and held the door, while all the others escaped unobserved. *Hopehood* and his companion hewed down the door, and knocked the girl on the head, and, otherwise wounding her, left her for dead. They took two children, which a fence had kept from escaping. One they killed, the other they carried off alive. The young woman recovered, and was entirely well afterwards.

One of the most important actions in which *Hopehood* was engaged was that against Salmon Falls in New Hampshire, which is minutely detailed by *Charlevoix*, from whose history we translate as follows. Three expeditions had been set on foot by Governor *Frontenac*, the troops for which had been raised at three places, Montreal, Three Rivers, and Quebeck. Those raised at Three Rivers were ordered against New England; and such was the insignificance of that place, that but 52 men could be raised, including 5 Algonquins and 20 Sokokis: these Indians had lately returned from an eastern expedition. They had at their head one of the officers of the colony, to

* Manuscript letter written at the time by *Church*, and sent to Governor *Hinckley* of Plimouth.

† *Harris*, in his Voyages, ii. 302, who says he was a Huron; but as he cites no authorities, we know not how he came by his information.

whom could be intrusted the execution of an enterprise of such a nature, with the greatest confidence; such is the testimony which Count *Frontenac* gave in a letter which he wrote at the time to *M. de Seignelay.* That officer was the Sieur *Hertel.* In the small company which he commanded, he had three of his sons and two of his nephews; viz. The Sieur *Crevier*, Lord of S. *François*, and the Sieur *Gatineau.*

He left Three Rivers the 28 January 1690, proceeding directly south into the country, leaving Lake Champlain to his left, then turning to the east, and after a long and rugged march he arrived on the 27 * March, near Salmon Falls,† which he had reconnoitred by his spies. He then divided his men into three companies; the first, composed of 15 men, was ordered to attack a large fortified house. The second, consisting of 11 men, was ordered to seize upon a fort, defended by four bastions. The third, which *Hertel* commanded in person, marched to attack a still greater fort, which was defended by cannon. All was executed with a conduct and bravery which astonished the English, who made at first stout resistance; but they could not withstand the fire of the assailants: the bravest were cut to pieces,‡ and the rest, to the number of 54, were made prisoners of war. It cost the victors but one Frenchman, who had his thigh broken, and who died the next day: 27 houses were reduced to ashes, and 2000 § domestic animals perished in the barns, which had been set on fire.

Salmon Falls was but six leagues from a great town called Pascataqua,‖ from whence men enough might be sent to swallow up *Hertel*, and cut off his retreat. In fact, upon the evening of the same day two savages gave notice that 200 ¶ English were advancing to attack them. *Hertel* expected it, and had taken his measures to frustrate those of his enemy. He drew up his men in order of battle upon the edge of a river,** over which there was a very narrow bridge, one extremity of which he had secured, and it was impossible for the English to come upon him at any other point. They, however, attempted it, despising the small numbers of the French, whom they engaged with great confidence. *Hertel* suffered them to advance without firing a gun, and all at once fell upon them, sword in hand; 8 were killed and 10 wounded in the first shock, and the rest fled with precipitation.†† He lost in this encounter the brave *Crevier*, his nephew, and one of the Sokokis. *La Fresniere*, his elder son, was shot in the knee; the scar of which wound he bore for 50 years.‡‡

As *Hertel* §§ was returning to Canada, he fell in with another party of his countrymen, which proved to be that raised at Quebec, before mentioned, under *M. de Portneuf*, ‖‖ and with him agreed upon an expedition against

---

* *Belknap*, Hist. N. H. i. 132, following *Mather*, Magnalia, vii. 68, dates this affair 18 March: there is in reality no error, allowing for the difference of style, (except one day;) the English not yet having adopted the Gregorian method, which the French had.—See BOOK II CAP. II.

† Prés d'une bourgade Angloise, appellée *Sementels.*

‡ About 30 were killed, according to *Belknap*, Hist. N. H. i. 132.

§ *Charlevoix* has been misconstrued by some authors, and made to say 2000 head of cattle were burned.—See *Williamson*, Hist. Maine, i. 619, who probably did not refer to the text of *Charlevoix*, or perhaps used an exceptionable translation. "*Deux mille pièces de bétail perirent dans les etables, où l'on avoit mis le feu.*" *Nouvelle France*, ii. 51.

‖ Sementels n'étoit qu'à six lieues d'une assez grosse bourgade de la Nouvelle Angleterre, nommée *Pescadouët. Nouvelle France*, ii. 51.

¶ "About 140 men." *Belknap*, ii. 132.

** Wooster's River, in Berwick. *Ibid.*

†† The English advanced with great intrepidity, and a warm engagement ensued, which lasted till night, when they retired with the loss of four or five killed. *Ibid.*

‡‡ The English, although warned by the fate of Schenectaday, "dreamt," says *Mather*, "that while the deep snow of the winter continued, they were safe enough; but this proved as vain as a *dream of a dry summer*. On March 18, the French and Indians, being half one, half t'other, half Indianised French, and half Frenchified Indians, commanded by Monsieur *Artel* and *Hoop-Hood*, fell suddenly upon Salmon-falls," &c. *Magnalia*, vii. 68.

§§ The English called him *Artel*, as his name was pronounced. See *Magnalia*, ibid.

‖‖ The French wrote English names queer enough, but really I should be sadly puzzled to tell which should laugh at the other: however, modern writers should not copy old errors of ignorance. It is easy to see how we come by the name of *Burneffe* in our Histories of *New England*.—See *Hist. Maine*, i. 621.

Casco. As *Portneuf* marched through the country of the Abenakis, many of them joined him, and he came into the neighborhood of Casco, according to the French account, on the 25 May. On the following night, he prepared an ambush, and towards morning an Englishman fell into it and was killed. The Indians then raised the war-whoop, and about noon 50 English marched out from the garrison to learn what was the occasion of it; they made no discovery until they were within a few paces of the ambush, when they were fired upon; and before they could resist were fallen upon by the French and Indians with their swords and tomahawks with great slaughter: but four escaped, and these were badly wounded.

The English seeing now they must stand a siege, abandoned four garrisons, and all retired into one, which was provided with cannon. Before these were abandoned, an attack was made upon one of them, in which the French were repulsed, with the loss of one Indian killed and one Frenchman wounded. *Portneuf* began now to doubt of his ability to take Casco, fearing the issue; for his commission only ordered him to lay waste the English settlements, and not to attempt fortified places; but in this dilemma *Hertel* and HOPEHOOD arrived.* It was now determined to press the siege. In the deserted forts they found all the necessary tools for carrying on the work, and they began a mine within 50 feet of the fort, under a steep bank, which entirely protected them from its guns. The English became discouraged, and on the 28 † May surrendered themselves prisoners of war. There were 70 men, and probably a much greater number of women and children. All of whom, except Captain *Davis*, who commanded the garrison, and three or four others, were given up to the Indians, who murdered most of them in their cruel manner; and if the accounts be true, *Hopehood* excelled all other savages in acts of cruelty. In the course of the same month, with a small party he fell upon Fox Point, in New Hampshire, killed about fourteen persons, and carried away six, after burning several houses. This was as easily done, says *Cotton Mather*, ‡ "as to have spoiled an ordinary *hen-roost*." Two companies of English soon collected and pursued them; came up with them, killed some, and recovered considerable plunder. In this action *Hopehood* was wounded, and lost his gun. §

Many were the horrid acts of barbarity inflicted on the prisoners taken at this time. Not long after this, *Hopehood* went to the westward, "with a design, says *Mather*, to bewitch another crew at Aquadocta into his assistance." The Indians of Canada and the Five Nations were then at war, and he being in their country, was met by some of the Canada Indians, who, taking him to be of the Iroquois nation, slew him and many of his companions. He had been once a captive to the English, and served a time in Boston as a slave. There appears to have been another Nerigwok chief of the same name, who treated with Governor *Dudley* at Casco, in 1703. ‡

We have, in narrating the events in the life of *Madokawando*, noticed the voyage of Major *Waldron* to the eastern coast of Maine, which was at the close of *Philip's* war. How much treachery was manifested at that time by the Indians, which caused the English to massacre many of them, we shall not take upon us to declare; yet this we should bear in mind, that we have only the account of those who performed the tragedy, and not that of those who suffered in it.

Captain *Charles Frost*, of Kittery, was with *Waldron* upon that expedition, and, next to him, a principal actor in it; and, like him, was killed by the Indians afterwards. ‖ Mr. *Hubbard* gives this account of his taking a noted warrior as follows:—"Capt. *Frost* seized an Indian called *Megunneway*, a notorious rogue, that had been in arms at Connecticut last June, at the falls,

* *Madokawando* was also at the taking of Casco, as were the *Doneys* and the *Higuers* [Higgins] Captain *Davis's* Nar. in 3 Coll. Mas. Hist. Soc. 104, 5.—*Hopehood* had been taken prisoner, and held as a hostage, with about a dozen others, and was set at liberty by *Andros* some time before. *Ibid.*

† This agrees with the English accounts, abating 10 days, as observed in a note on the last page.

‡ Magnalia Christ. Americana, b. vii. 73.

§ "An heathen Indian would rather part with his head than with his gun." *Loskiel*, ii. 214.

‖ At his native place, 4 July, 1697. *MS. letter of John Farmer, Esq.*

and saw that brave and resolute Capt. *Turner*, when he was slain about Green River; and helped to kill *Thomas Bracket* * at Casco, [11th] August last, [1676.] And with the help of Lieut. *Nutter*, according to the major's order, carried him aboard" their vessel. "By this time," the same author continues, "some of the soldiers were got ashore, and instantly, according to their major's command, pursued the enemy towards their canoes. In the chase, several of the enemy were slain, whose bodies these [soldiers] found at their return, to the number of seven; amongst whom was *Mattakando* the sagamore, with an old powow, to whom the *Devil* had revealed, as sometimes he did to *Saul*, that on the same day he should be with him; for he had a little before told the Indians, that within two days the English would come and kill them all, which was at the very same time verified upon himself." Here we must acknowledge, notwithstanding our great respect for this author, that his commentary upon that passage was rather gratuitous. He might have considered that *Sauls* among the English would not be wanting of whom parallels might be made. Indeed, the historian of *Kankamagus* might say the *Devil* was less deceitful with this powwow than he was afterwards in the case of Major *Waldron.*

The English took much plunder from the Indians at this time, among which were about 1000 lbs. of dried beef, and various other commodities. *Megunneway*, after having fallen into their hands as we have stated, was shot without ceremony.

CHAPTER IX.

BOMAZEEN—*Treuchery of the whites towards him—Is imprisoned at Boston—Saves the life of a female captive—Captures Saco—Is killed*—ARRUHAWIKWABEMT—*His capture and death*—EGEREMET—*Seized at Pemmaquid—Barbarously murdered—Treachery of Chubb—Its requital*—*Captain* TOM—*Surprises Hampton*—DONY—*His fort captured by Colonel Church—Events of Church's expedition—Captain* SIMMO—*Treats with the English at Casco—His speech*—WATTANUMMON—*Captain* SAMUEL—*His fight at Damaris Cove*—HEGAN—*One of the name barbarously destroyed by the whites*—MOGG—*Westbrook burns Nerigwok—Some account of the Jesuit Rasle—Moulton's expedition to Nerigwok—Death of Mogg—Death of Father Rasle—Notice of Moulton—Charlevoix's account of this affair*—PAUGUS—*Bounty offered for indian scalps—Captain John Lovewell's first expedition—His second hunt for Indians—Falls in with* PAUGUS—*Fights him, and is slain—Particulars of the affair—Incidents—Songs composed on the event.*

WE will continue here our catalogue of eminent chiefs of the east, which, though a remote section, has no less claim than any other; and the first of them which we shall introduce was called, by the whites,

BOMAZEEN, who was a sachem of a tribe of the Canibas, or Kennebecks, whose residence was at an ancient seat of sagamores, upon a river bearing their name, at a place called *Norridgewock.* † Whether *Bomazeen* were the leader in the attack upon Oyster River in New Hampshire, Groton in Massachusetts, and many other places, about the year 1694, we cannot determine, but *Hutchinson* says he was "a principal actor in the carnage upon the

* He was brother to *Anthony*, and was killed the 11 August, as we have mentioned in our account of *Symon.* These Indians, or some of their party [that captured *Anthony Bracket*] went over upon the neck, where they shot *John Munjoy* and *Isaac Wakely.* Three men, who were going to reap at *Anthony Bracket's*, having heard from *Munjoy* and *Wakely* of the transaction there, left them to return, when, hearing the guns, they turned towards *Thomas Bracket's*, who lived near Clark's Point, where they had left their canoe, having probably crossed over from Purpooduck. Here they saw *Thomas Bracket* shot down, and his wife and children taken; they then made their escape to *Munjoy's* garrison, at the lower end of the neck, which had become a place of refuge. *Willis's* Hist. Portland, i. 144.—This was an extensive depredation, 34 persons having been killed and carried into captivity.

† *Nerigwok* is believed to be the most proper way of spelling the name of this place, as agreeing best with its orthoepy; at least, with that heard at and in the vicinity of it, at this day, as pronounced by the oldest inhabitants. It is a delightful place, and will be found elsewhere described.

English," after the treaty which he had made with Governor *Phips*, in 1693. In 1694, he came to the fort at Pemmaquid with a flag of truce, and was treacherously seized by those who commanded, and sent prisoner to Boston, where he remained some months, in a loathsome prison. In 1706, new barbarities were committed. Chelmsford, Sudbury, Groton, Exeter, Dover, and many other places, suffered more or less.* Many captives were taken and carried to Canada, and many killed on the way. A poor woman, one *Rebecca Taylor*, who had arrived at the River St. Lawrence, was about to be hanged by her master, an "overgrown Indian," named *Sampson*. The limb of the tree on which he was executing his purpose gave way, and, while he was making a second attempt, *Bomazeen* happened to be passing, and rescued her.

We hear of him just after the death of *Arruhawikwabemt*, in October 1710, when he fell upon Saco with 60 or 70 men, and killed several people, and carried away some captives. He is mentioned as a "notorious fellow," and yet but few of his acts are upon record. Some time after the peace of 1701, it seemed to be confirmed by the appearance of *Bomazeen*, and another principal chief, who said the French friars were urging them to break their union with the English, "*but that they had made no impression on them, for they were as firm as the mountains, and should continue so as long as the sun and moon endured.*" On peace being made known to the Indians, as having taken place between the French and English nations, they came into Casco, with a flag of truce, and soon after concluded a treaty at Portsmouth, N. H., dated 13 July, 1713. *Bomazeen's* name and mark are to this treaty.

When Captain *Moulton* was sent up to Nerigwok, in 1724, they fell in with *Bomazeen* about Taconnet, where they shot him as he was escaping through the river. Near the town of Nerigwok, his wife and daughter were, in a barbarous manner, fired upon, the daughter killed, and the mother taken.

We purposely omit Dr. *C. Mather's* account of *Bomazeen's* conversation with a minister of Boston, while a prisoner there, which amounts to little else than his recounting some of the extravagant notions which the French of Canada had made many Indians believe, to their great detriment, as he said; as that *Jesus Christ* was a French man, and the Virgin *Mary* a French woman; that the French gave them poison to drink, to inflame them against the English, which made them run mad. We hear of others, who, to excite them against the English, endeavored to make them believe, among other absurdities, that they put *Jesus Christ* to death in London.

Arruhawikwabemt, just mentioned, was a sachem of the same tribe, and was said to be of Norridgewock also. We can find but very few particulars of him, but, from the fate he met with, it is presumed he had been very instrumental in continuing or bringing about the eastern war of 1710. In that year, Colonel *Walton* made an expedition to the eastern coast of Maine with 170 men. As they were encamped upon an island, the smoke of their fires decoyed some of the Indians into their hands, among whom was *Arruhawikwabemt*. *Penhallow* says, he was "an active, bold fellow, and one of an undaunted spirit; for when they asked him several questions, he made them no reply, and when they threatened him with death, *he laughed at it with contempt!* At which they delivered him up unto our friendly Indians, who soon became his executioners. But when the squaw saw the destiny of her husband, she became more flexible, and freely discovered where each party of them encamped." The savage perpetrators of this act called themselves Christian warriors! and it must be acknowledged that civilization gains nothing in contrasting the conduct of the whites, under *Walton*, and that of *Bomazeen* towards a captive, just related.

Egeremet, as we have seen, was chief sachem of Kennebeck in 1690, and his principal residence appears to have been at Machias. This chief, and Honquid, with three or four others, having been invited to a conference at Pemmaquid, were treacherously murdered there, 16 February, 1696. Their seizure and murder could not have been outdone, by the greatest barbarians,

* *Bomazeen* was supposed to have led the party that attacked the south part of Oyster River, now Durham, in which 10 persons were killed. This was on 27 April

for faithlessness; and we shall learn that its author paid for it in due time with his life. We are not disposed to add to transactions which are in themselves sufficiently horrible, but we will venture to give the account as we find it in Dr. *C. Mather's decennium luctuosum*:—*

"Let us, before the year be quite gone, see some vengeance taken upon the *heads in the house of the wicked.* Know then, reader, that Capt. *March* petitioning to be dismissed from his command of the fort at Pemmaquid, one *Chub* succeeded him. This *Chub* found an opportunity, in a pretty *chubbed* manner, to kill the famous *Edgeremet* and *Abenquid*, a couple of principal sagamores, with one or two other Indians, on a Lord's day. Some that well enough liked the *thing* which was now done, did not altogether like the *manner* of doing it, because there was a pretence of *treaty* between *Chub* and the sagamores, whereof he took his advantage to lay violent hands on them."

Thus the *manner* is seen in which this horrid and cold-blooded act is related!! Few are the instances that we meet with in history, where *Indian treachery*, as it is termed, can go before this. The reverend author adds, "If there were any unfair dealing (which I know not) in this action of *Chub*, there will be another *February* not far off, wherein the *avengers of blood* will take their *satisfaction*." By this innuendo, what befell Captain *Chubb* afterwards is understood, and of which we shall presently give an account.

The point of land called *Trott's Neck*, in Woolwich, in the state of Maine, was sold, in 1685, by *Egeremet* and several other sachems. In 1693, on the 11 August, with 12 other chiefs, he made a treaty† with Sir *William Phips*, at Pemmaquid, to which their names stood as follows, and without marks in the printed account.

EDGEREMETT.
MADOCKAWANDO.
WASSAMBOMET *of Noridgwock.*
WENOBSON *of Teconnet*, in *behalf of* MOXUS.
KETTERRAMOGIS *of Narridgwock.*
AHANQUID *of Penobscot.*
BOMASEEN.
NITAMEMET.
WEBENES.
AWANSOMECK.
ROBIN DONEY.
MADAUMBIS.
PAQUAHARET, *alias* NATHANIEL.
John Hornybrook.
John Bagatawawongo, *alias* Sheepscott John.
Phill. Dunsakis, *Squaw*, interpreters.

Before this, in 1691, "New England being quite out of breath," says Dr. *C. Mather*, a treaty, or truce, was entered into between the eastern sachems and Messrs. *Hutchinson* and *Townsend*, of Boston, and others of the eastern coast, at Sagadahock. Here ten captives were given up by them, and the English gave up eight captive Indians. One was a woman by the name of *Hull*, who had been of great service to them, having written letters on various occasions, such as their affairs required, and with whom they regretted much to part. Another was *Nathaniel White*, who had been bound and tortured in a wretched manner. His ears were cut off, and, instead of food, he was forced to eat them, after which, but for this time y treaty, the sentence of burning would have been executed upon him. This truce stipulated that no hurt should be done the English until May, 1692, and that, on the first of that mouth, they would deliver, at Wells, all English captives in their hands, and, in the mean time, would inform of any plots that they might know of the French against the English. *Egeremet* being the chief sachem, and most forward in this business, Dr. *Mather* utters his contempt for him by saying, "To this instrument were set the *paws* of *Egeremet*, and five more of their sagamores and noblemen."‡

This treaty may be seen at length in the Collections of the Mass. Hist. Soc., but is dated one year earlier than it is in the Magnalia. The fact that it was made upon the water, as Dr. *C. Mather* says, and as we have quoted in the life of *Madokawando*, appears from the last paragraph of that instrument,

* Magnalia, b. vii. 89.
† It may be seen in the *Magnalia*, vii. 85
‡ Magnalia Christ. Americana, book vii. art. xxviii. p. 94.

which is in these words:—"Signed and sealed interchangeably, upon the water, in canoes, at Sackatehock, *when the wind blew.*" It was headed, "At a treaty of peace with the eastward Indian enemy sagamores." The other five sachems, beside *Egeremet*, were *Toquelmut, Watombomt, Watombamet, Walumbe*, [*Worombos*,] and *John Hawkins*, [or *Kankamagus*.] The places for which they stipulated are, according to the treaty, "Pennecook, Winnepisseockeege, Ossepe, Pigwocket, Amoscongen, Pechepscut, Kennebeck River, and all other places adjacent, within the territory and dominions of the above-named sagamores." The witnesses were, *Dewando*, [the same called *Adiwando*, by *Penhallow* probably,] *Ned Higon, John Alden*, jr., and *Nathaniel Alden*.

The next year, *Egeremet* was with *Madokawando, Moxus*, and a body of French under *Labrocre*, and made the notable attack upon the garrison at Wells, which will be found recorded in the last chapter.

We will now inform the reader of the wretched fate of Captain *Pasco Chub*. It was not long after he committed the bloody deed of killing the Indian sagamores, before he and the fort were taken by the French and Indians. He was exchanged, and returned to Boston, where he suffered much disgrace for his treachery with the Indians.* He lived at Andover in Massachusetts, where about 30 Indians made an attack in 1698, on 22 February, in which he, with others, was killed, and five were captivated. It was not thought that they expected to find him there; but when they found they had killed him it gave them as much joy, says *Hutchinson*, "as the destruction of a whole town, because they had taken their beloved vengeance of him for his perfidy and barbarity to their countrymen." They shot him through several times after he was dead.

In his characteristic style, Mr. *Oldmixon* speaks of this event.† He says, "Nor must we forget *Chub*, the false wretch who surrendered Pemmaquid Fort. The governor kept him under examination some time at Boston, and then dismissed him. As he was going to his house, at Andover, the Indians surprised him and his wife, and massacred them; a just reward of his treason." The author, we think, should have added, according to the jurisprudence of savages.

The most favorable account given of the conduct of *Chub*, and indeed the only one, follows: "An Indian sagamore's son appeared with a flag of truce, and Capt. *Chub* went out to them without arms, man for man. An Indian asked for rum and tobacco: the captain said, '*No; it is Sabbath day.*' They said, '*We will have rum, or we will have rum and you too.*' Two Indians laid hold on the captain. Then he called to his men, to fall on, for God's sake. Then he made signs to his men, to come from the fort. One of the English had a hatchet under his coat, took it out and killed an Indian; and then ours killed two more Indians, and took another alive, and wounded another, supposed mortally. Then many of the enemy came near to the English, who retreated all safe to the fort."‡

There was another sagamore of the same name, noticed in the following wars with the eastern Indians, who was friendly to the whites; it was probably he who sometimes bore the name of *Moxus*.

---

* *Harris's* Voyages, ii. 305, (ed. 1764,) says *Chub* was arrested by Colonel *Gedney*, who was sent east with three ships of war, on hearing of the surrender of the fort, and that no French or Indians could be found; that after he strengthened the garrison, he returned home.

"Col. *Gedney* had been by land with 500 men, to secure the eastern frontiers. Finding the enemy gone, he strengthened the garrisons, which were not taken. He also arrested *Pasco Chubb*, for surrendering Pemaquid Fort, while under his command in July, and had him brought to Boston. Here Captain *Chubb* was confined, till it was decided that he should lose his commission, and not be eligible for any other. This unfortunate man, with his wife Hannah, and three others, were killed by the Indians at Andover, Feb. 22, 1698." *Rev. Mr. Felt's Annals of Salem.*

A naval force was sent at the same time; hence the accounts are not altogether irreconcilable. Three men-of-war were sent out in pursuit of the French, "but meeting with contrary winds, they could never get sight of them." *Neal*, His. N. Eng. ii. 551.

† British Empire in America, i. 77, 78.

‡ Manuscript letter in library Mass. Hist. Soc. written in the following month. As it was written at a great distance from the place, and from a report of the day, little reliance can be placed upon it. It may have been *Chub's* report of the case.

In the Indian war of 1703, there was a great Indian captain who resided somewhere to the east of Pascataqua River, who made his name dreaded among the settlements in that region, by some bloody expeditions which he conducted. He was called, by the English,

CAPTAIN TOM. On 17 August of this year, this daring war-captain, with about 30 others, surprised a part of Hampton, killed five persons, whereof one was a widow *Hussey*, "who was a remarkable speaking Quaker, and much lamented by her sect." After sacking two houses near the garrison, they drew off.*

Many Indians bore the name of *Tom*. Indian Hill, in Newbury, was owned by *Great Tom*. He is supposed to have been the last Indian proprietor of lands in that town. In written instruments, he styles himself, "*I Great Tom Indian.*" †

We come, in the next place, to an interesting portion of our eastern history. It has been generally supposed that the name *Dony*, or *Doney*, was the name of an Indian chief, but it is now quite certain that he was a Frenchman, who took up his residence among the Indians, as Baron de St. *Casteins* did. There appears in our history, in 1645, a "Monsieur *Dony*," who had some difficulty with Lord *de la Tour*, about their eastern possessions, and he was, doubtless, the same of whom we have an account afterwards, in the war of 1690, with the eastern Indians. At this time, there were two of the name in Maine, father and son. The son, perhaps, like *Casteins* the younger, was half Indian, but of this we are not sure; nevertheless, to preserve our narrative of the events of Colonel *Church's* expedition of 1690, we shall notice them among others.

Church landed at Maquait, 12 September, before day, and, after a wet, fatiguing march into the woods of about two days, on the south-west side of the Androscoggin, came into the neighborhood of a fort. They came upon an Indian and his wife who were leading two captives; and immediately pursuing and firing upon them, killed the Indian woman, who proved to be the wife of *Young Doney*.‡ We can only hope it was not their design thus to have killed an innocent woman. Which party it was that fired upon them (for they divided themselves into three) is unknown, and we in charity must suppose that, at considerable distance, and in much confusion, it was difficult to know an Indian man from a woman.

As *Church* expected, *Doney* ran into one gate of the fort, and out at the other, giving the alarm so effectually, that nearly all within it escaped. They found and took prisoners "but two men and a lad of about 18, with some women and children. Five ran into the river, three or four of which were killed. The lad of 18 made his escape up the river." The whole number killed in this action was "six or seven." The English had but one wounded. They took here, at this time,§ a considerable quantity of corn, guns, and ammunition, and liberated Mrs. *Huckings*, widow of Lieutenant *Robert Huckings*, taken at Oyster River, Mrs. *Barnard*, wife of *Benjamin Barnard*, of Salmon Falls, *Anne Heard*, of Cocheco, a young woman, daughter of one *Willis*, of Oyster River, and a boy belonging to Exeter. These captives, says *Church*, "were in a miserable condition." They learned by them that most of their men were gone to Winter Harbor to get provisions for the Bay of Fundy Indians. This information was given by a prisoner taken in the fort, who also said that the Bay of Fundy Indians were to join them against the English, in the spring. "The soldiers, being very rude, would hardly spare the Indian's life, while in examination; intending, when he had done, that he should be executed. But Capt. *Hucking's* wife, and another woman, down on their knees and begged for him, saying, that he had been a means of saving their lives, and a great many more; and had helped several to opportunities to run away and make their escape; and that never, since he came amongst them, had fought against the English, but being related to *Hakin's* ‖ wife, kept at the

* *Penhallow*, Ind. Wars, 8; *Farmer's Belknap*, i. 167.

† Manuscript Hist. Newbury, by *J. Coffin*.

‡ And the same called in the Magnalia *Robin Doney*.

§ Says my record, which is a manuscript letter from *Church*, written at that time.

‖ The same called *Kankamagus*.

fort with them, having been there two years; but his living was to the westward of Boston. So upon their request, his life was spared."

Two old squaws were left in the fort, provided with provisions, and instructed to tell those who returned who they were, and what they were determined to do. They then put *four* or *five* to death, and decamped. Those, we must suppose, were chiefly women and children! "*Knocked on the head for an example.*" We know not that any excuse can be given for this criminal act; and it is degrading to consider that the civilized must be supposed to imagine that they can prevent barbarities by being wretchedly barbarous themselves.

Old Doney, as he is called, was next to be hunted. As they were embarking at Maquait, Mr. *Anthony Bracket* * came to the shore and called to them to take him on board, which they did. He learning that an English army was thereabout, made his escape from the Indians, with whom he had been some time a prisoner. The fleet now proceeded to Winter Harbor, from whence they despatched a detachment of 60 men to Saco Falls. When they came near, they discovered *Doney's* company on the opposite side of the river, who chiefly made their escape. A canoe, with three Indians, was observed coming over the river; they did not see the English, and were fired upon, and "all three perished." This gave the first alarm to *Doney's* company. They did not, however, leave their ground without returning the fire of the English, by which Lieutenant *Hunnewell* was shot through the thigh.† When the parties fired upon each other, *Old Doney*, with an English captive, was higher up the river, who, hearing the firing, came down to see what it meant; and thus he discovered the English time enough to escape. *Doney* fled from the canoe, leaving his captive, who came to the English. His name was *Thomas Baker*, who had lived before at Scarborough.

There were many other movements of the English after this, in which they got much plunder, and which tended to cause an uneasiness among them, and their final determination to return home. *Church* urged a longer continuance, but was outvoted in a council of officers, and thus ended the expedition. Many in the country reproached *Church* with cowardice, and almost every thing but what we should have looked for. If putting to death captives had been the charge, many might have accorded *Amen!* But we do not find that urged against him.

Two years after this, in 1693, *Robin Doney* became reconciled to the English, and signed a treaty with them at Pemmaquid. But within a year after he became suspected, whether with or without reason, we know not, and coming to the fort at Saco, probably to settle the difficulty, was seized by the English. What his fate was is rather uncertain, but the days of forgiveness and mercy were not yet.

Among the chiefs which we shall next proceed to notice, there were several of nearly equal notoriety.

Captain Simmo's name should, perhaps, stand most conspicuous. We shall, therefore, go on to narrate the events in his life, after a few preliminary observations.

Whenever war commenced between the English and French in Europe, their colonies in America were involved in its calamities, to an unknown and fearful extent. This was the aspect which affairs wore in 1703. With the first news, therefore, of its flame, the New Englanders' thoughts were turned towards the Indians. Governor *Dudley* immediately despatched messengers to most of the eastern tribes, inviting them to meet him in council upon the peninsula in Falmouth, on the 20 June. His object was so to attach them to the English, that, in the event of hostilities between the rival powers on this side of the Atlantic, they would not take arms against them. Agreeably to the wishes of the English, a vast multitude assembled at the time appointed the chiefs *Adiwando* and *Hegan* for the Pennakooks, *Wattanummon* for the Pequakets, *Mesambomett* and *Wexar* for the Androscoggins, *Moxus* and *Hopehood* (perhaps son of him killed by the Mohawks) for the Nerigwoks, *Bomazeen* and Captain *Samuel* for the Kennebecks, and *Warrungunt* and *Wanadu*

* Son of *Anthony*, who was killed by the Indians, as we have related, *ante*.
† Official letter in MS. from the expedition.

gunbuent for the Penobscots. After a short speech to them, in which the governor expressed brotherly affection, and a desire to settle every difficulty "which had happened since the last treaty," Captain *Simmo* replied as follows:—

"*We thank you, good brother, for coming so far to talk with us. It is a great favor. The clouds fly and darken—but we still sing with love the songs of peace. Believe my words.*—SO FAR AS THE SUN IS ABOVE THE EARTH ARE OUR THOUGHTS FROM WAR, OR THE LEAST RUPTURE BETWEEN US." *

The governor was then presented with a belt of wampum, was to confirm the truth of what had been said. At a previous treaty, two heaps of small stones had been thrown together, near by the treaty ground, and called the *Two-brothers*, to signify that the Indians and English were brothers, and were considered by the parties in the light of seals to their treaties. They now repaired to these heaps of stones, and each increased their magnitude, by the addition of other stones. Thus was happily terminated this famous treaty. Some parade and rejoicing now commenced, and a circumstance transpired which threw the English into great fear, and, perhaps, greater suspicion. A grand salute was to be fired upon each side, at parting, and the English, advisedly, and very warily, it must be confessed, but in appearance complimentary, expressed their desire that the Indians would fire first. The Indians received the compliment, and discharged their guns; to their great surprise, the English found they had been loaded with bullets. They had before doubted of their sincerity, but, owing to this discovery, considered their treachery certain, and marvelled at their escape. However, it can only be presumed, that, according to the maxim of the whites, the Indians had come prepared to treat or fight, as the case might require; for no doubt their guns were charged when they came to the treaty, otherwise why did they not fire upon the English when they saluted them?

What became of Captain *Simmo* we have as yet no account. Several of the other chiefs who attended this council were, perhaps, equally conspicuous.

WATTANUMMON being absent when the council first met on the 20 June, no business was entered upon for several days. However, the English afterwards said it was confirmed that it was not on that account that they delayed the conference, but that they expected daily a reinforcement of 200 French and Indians, and then they were to seize upon the English, and ravage the country. Whether this were merely a rumor, or the real state of the case, we have no means of knowing. *Wattanummon* was supposed to have been once a Pennakook, as an eminence still bears his name about a mile from the state-house in New Hampshire.†

Captain SAMUEL was an Indian of great bravery, and one of the most forward in endeavoring to lull the fears of the English at the great council just mentioned. What gave his pretensions the air of sincerity was his coming with *Bomazeen*, and giving some information about the designs of the French. They said,

"*Although several missionaries have come among us, sent by the French friars to break the peace between the English and us, yet their words have made no impression upon us.* WE ARE AS FIRM AS THE MOUNTAINS, AND WILL SO CONTINUE, AS LONG AS THE SUN AND MOON ENDURES."

Notwithstanding these strong expressions of friendship, "within six weeks after," says *Penhallow*, "the whole eastern country was in a conflagration, no house standing nor garrison unattacked." The Indians were no doubt induced to commit this depredation from the influence of the French, many of whom assisted them in the work. And it is not probable that those Indians who had just entered into the treaty were idle spectators of the scene; but who of them, or whether all were engaged in the affair, we know not. A hundred and thirty people were said to have been killed and taken, within that time.

Captain *Samuel* was either alive 20 years after these transactions, or another

* This is Mr. *Williamson's* version of the speech, Hist. Maine, ii. 36.

† MS. communication of *J. Farmer*, Esq.

of the name made himself conspicuous. In June, 1722, this warrior chief, at the head of five others, boarded Lieutenant *Tilton*, as he lay at anchor a fishing, near Damaris Cove. They pinioned him and his brother, and beat them very sorely; but, at last, one got clear and released the other, who then fell with great fury upon the Indians, threw one overboard, and mortally wounded two more.* Whether Captain *Samuel* were among those killed is not mentioned.

There was a Captain *Sam* in the wars of 1745. In the vicinity of St. George's, Lieutenant *Proctor*, at the head of 19 militia, had a skirmish with the Indians, 5 Sept., in which two of their leaders were killed, viz. Colonel *Morris* and Captain *Sam*, and one Colonel *Job* was taken captive; the latter being sent to Boston, he died in prison. To quiet the resentment of his relatives, the government made his widow a valuable present after the peace.†

We should not, perhaps, omit to speak separately of another chief, who was present at the famous treaty mentioned above; we refer to

Hegan. His name is also spelt *Hegon* and *Heigon*. There were several of the name. One, called *Moggheigon*, son of *Walter*, was a sachem at Saco, in 1664. This chief, in that year, sold to *Wm. Phillips*, "a tract of land, being bounded with Saco River on the N. E. side, and Kennebunk River on the S. W. side." To extend from the sea up Saco River to Salmon Falls, and up the Kennebunk to a point opposite the former. No amount is mentioned for which the land was sold, but merely "a certain sum in goods."‡ One *Sampson Hegon* attended the treaty of Pemmaquid, in 1698; *John*, that at Casco, in 1727; *Ned* was a Pennakook; *Walter*, brother of *Mogg*;§ The fate of one of the name of *Hegon* is remembered among the inhabitants of some parts of Maine to this day. He was tied upon a horse with spurs on his heels, in such a manner that the spurs continually goaded the animal. When the horse was set at liberty, he ran furiously through an orchard, and the craggy limbs of the trees tore him to pieces. *Mather*, in his Decennium Luctuosum,‖ seems to confirm something of the kind, which took place at Casco, in 1694, where the Indians, having taken some horses, made a bridle of the mane and tail of one, on which "a son of the famous *Hegon* was ambitious to mount." "But being a pitiful horseman, he ordered them, for fear of his falling, to tie his legs fast under the horse's belly. No sooner was this *beggar set on horseback*, and the spark, in his own opinion, thoroughly equipped, but the nettlesome *horse* furiously and presently ran with him out of sight. Neither *horse* nor *man* was ever seen any more. The astonished tawnies howled after one of their nobility, disappearing by such an unexpected accident. A few days after, they found one of his *legs*, (and that was all,) which they buried in Capt. *Bracket's* cellar, with abundance of lamentation."

Here we cannot but too plainly discover the same spirit in the narrator, which must have actuated the authors of the deed. He who laughs at crime is a participator in it.—From these, we pass to affairs of far greater notoriety in our eastern history; and shall close this chapter with two of the most memorable events in its Indian warfare.

Mogg, the chief sachem of Norridgewok in 1724, may very appropriately stand at the head of the history of the first event. How long he had been sachem at that period, we have not discovered, but he is mentioned by the English historians, as the old chief of Norridgewok at that time. Notwithstanding *Mogg* was the chief Indian of the village of Nerigwok, or, as Father *Charlevoix* writes it, Narantsoak, there was a French priest settled here, to whom the Indians were all devotedness; and it is believed that they undertook no enterprise without his knowledge and consent. The name of this man, according to our English authors, was *Rallé*, but according to his own historian, *Charlevoix*, it was *Rasle*.¶ The depredations of the Abénaquis, as these Indians were called by those who lived among them,

---

* *Penhallow's* Ind. Wars, 86.
† *Williamson's* Hist. Me. ii. 241.
‡ MS. among the files in our state-house.
§ MS. letter of *John Farmer*, Esq
‖ Magnalia, vii. 87.
¶ Hist. Gen. de la Nouv. Fr. ii. 380, *et suiv.*

were, therefore, directly charged by the English upon Father *Rasle;* hence their first step was to offer a reward for his head.* The object of the expedition of Colonel *Westbrook*, in 1722, was ostensibly to seize upon him, but he found the village deserted, and nothing was effected by the expedition but the burning of the place. Father *Rasle* was the last that left it, which he did at the same time it was entered by the enemy; having first secured the sacred vases of his temple and the ornaments of its altar. The English made search for the fugitives, but without success, although, at one time, they were within about eight feet of the very tree that screened the object for which they sought. Thus the French considered that it was by a remarkable interposition of Providence, or, as *Charlevoix* expresses it, *par une main invisible*, that Father *Rasle* did not fall into their hands.

Determined on destroying this assemblage of Indians, which was the head-quarters of the whole eastern country, at this time, the English, two years after, 1724, sent out a force, consisting of 208 men and three Mohawk Indians, under Captains *Moulton, Harman*, and *Bourne*, to humble them. They came upon the village, the 23 August, when there was not a man in arms to oppose them. They had left 40 of their men at Teconet Falls, which is now within the town of Winslow, upon the Kennebeck, and about two miles below Waterville college, upon the opposite side of the river The English had divided themselves into three squadrons: 80, under *Harman*, proceeded by a circuitous route, thinking to surprise some in their corn-fields, while *Moulton*, with 80 more, proceeded directly for the village, which, being surrounded by trees, could not be seen until they were close upon it. All were in their wigwams, and the English advanced slowly and in perfect silence. When pretty near, an Indian came out of his wigwam, and, accidently discovering the English, ran in and seized his gun, and giving the war-whoop, in a few minutes the warriors were all in arms, and advancing to meet them. *Moulton* ordered his men not to fire until the Indians had made the first discharge. This order was obeyed, and, as he expected, they overshot the English, who then fired upon them, in their turn, and did great execution. When the Indians had given another volley, they fled with great precipitation to the river, whither the chief of their women and children had also fled during the fight. Some of the English pursued and killed many of them in the river, and others fell to pillaging and burning the village. *Mogg* disdained to fly with the rest, but kept possession of a wigwam, from which he fired upon the pillagers. In one of his discharges he killed a Mohawk, whose brother observing it, rushed upon and killed him; and thus ended the strife. There were about 60 warriors in the place, about one half of whom were killed.

The famous *Rasle* shut himself up in his house, from which he fired upon the English; and, having wounded one, Lieutenant *Jaques*,† of Newbury,‡ burst open the door, and shot him through the head; although *Moulton* had given orders that none should kill him. He had an English boy with him, about 14 years old, who had been taken some time before from the frontiers, and whom the English reported *Rasle* was about to kill. Great brutality and ferocity are chargeable to the English in this affair, according to their own account; such as killing women and children, and scalping and mangling the body of Father *Rasle.*

There was here a handsome church, with a bell, on which the English committed a double sacrilege, first robbing it, then setting it on fire; herein surpassing the act of the first English circumnavigator, in his depredations upon the Spaniards in South America; for he only took away the gold and

* "*Après plusieurs tentatives, d'abord pour engager ces sauvages par les offres et les promesses les plus séduisantes à le livrer aux Anglois, ou du moins à le renvoyer à Quebec, et à prendre en sa place un de leurs ministres; ensuite pour le surpendre et pour l'enlever, les Anglois résolus de s'en défaire, quoiqu'il leur en dût coûter, mirent sa tête à prix, et promirent mille livres sterling à celui, qui la leur porteroit.*" *Charlevoix*, ut supra.

† Who, I conclude, was a volunteer, as I do not find his name upon the return made by *Moulton*, which is upon file in the garret, west wing of our state-house.

‡ Manuscript History of Newbury, by *Joshua Coffin*, S. H. S., which, should the world ever be so fortunate as to see in print, we will insure them not only great gratification, but a fund of amusement.

silver vessels of a church, and its crucifix, because it was of massy gold, set about with diamonds, and that, too, upon the advice of his chaplain. "This might pass," says a reverend author, "for sea divinity, but justice is quite another thing." Perhaps it will be as well not to inquire here what kind of *divinity* would authorize the acts recorded in these wars, or indeed any wars.

Upon this memorable event in our early annals, Father *Charlevoix* should be heard. There were not, says he, at the time the attack was made, above 50 warriors at Neridgewok; these seized their arms, and run in disorder, not to defend the place against an enemy, who was already in it, but to favor the flight of the women, the old men and the children, and to give them time to gain the side of the river, which was not yet in possession of the English. Father RASLE, warned by the clamors and tumult, and the danger in which he found his proselytes, ran to present himself to the assailants, hoping to draw all their fury upon him, that thereby he might prove the salvation of his flock. His hope was vain; for hardly had he discovered himself when the English raised a great shout, which was followed by a shower of shot, by which he fell dead near to the cross which he had erected in the centre of the village: seven Indians who attended him, and who endeavored to shield him with their own bodies, fell dead at his side. Thus died this charitable pastor, giving his life for his sheep, after 37 years of painful labors.

Although the English shot near 2000 muskets, they killed but 30 and wounded 40. They spared not the church, which, after they had indignantly profaned its sacred vases, and the adorable body of Jesus Christ, they set on fire. They then retired with precipitation,* having been seized with a sudden panic. The Indians returned immediately into the village; and their first care, while the women sought plants and herbs proper to heal the wounded, was to shed tears upon the body of their holy missionary. They found him pierced with a thousand shot, his scalp taken off, his skull fractured with hatchets, his mouth and eyes filled with dirt, the bones of his legs broken, and all his members mutilated in a hundred different ways.†

Such is the account of the fall of *Rasle*, by a brother of the faith; a deplorable picture, by whomsoever related! Of the truth of its main particulars there can be no doubt, as will be seen by a comparison of the above translation with the account preceding it. There were, besides *Mogg*, other chief Indians, who fell that day; "BOMAZEEN, MOGG, WISSEMEMET, JOB, CARABESETT, and BOMAZEEN'S son-in-law, all famous warriors." The inhumanity of the English on this occasion, especially to the women and children, cannot be excused. It greatly eclipses the lustre of the victory.

Harman was the general in the expedition,‡ and, for a time, had the honor of it; but *Moulton*, according to Governor *Hutchinson*, achieved the victory, and it was afterward acknowledged by the country. He was a prisoner, when a mall boy, among the eastern Indians, being among those taken at the destruction of York, in 1692. He died at York, 20 July, 1765, aged 77. The township of Moultonborough, in New Hampshire, was named from him, and many of his posterity reside there at the present day.

Under the head *Paugus*, we shall proceed to narrate our last event in the present chapter, than which, may be, few, if any, are oftener mentioned in New England story.

PAUGUS, slain in the memorable battle with the English under Captain *Lovewell*, in 1725, was chief of the Pequawkets. Fryeburg, in Maine, now includes the principal place of their former residence, and the place where the battle was fought. It was near a considerable body of water, called *Saco Pond*, which is the source of the river of the same name. The cruel and barbarous murders almost daily committed by the Indians upon the defenceless frontier inhabitants, caused the general court of Massachusetts to offer a bounty of £100 for every Indian's scalp. Among the excursions

* They encamped the following night in the Indian wigwams, under a guard of only 40 men. *Hutchinson*, ii. 312.

† Histoire Generale de Nouvelle France, ii. 382—4.

‡ He did not arrive at the village till near night, when the action was over *Hutchinson*, ii. 313

performed by *Lovewell*, previous to that in which he was killed, the most important was that to the head of Salmon-fall River, now Wakefield, in New Hampshire.* With 40 men, he came upon a small company of ten Indians, who were asleep by their fires, and, by stationing his men advantageously, killed all of them. This bloody deed was performed near the shore of a pond, which has ever since borne the name of *Lovewell's Pond*. After taking off their scalps, these 40 warriors marched to Boston in great triumph, with the ten scalps extended upon hoops, displayed in the Indian manner, and for which they received £1000. This exploit was the more lauded, as it was supposed that these ten Indians were upon an expedition against the English upon the frontiers; having new guns, much ammunition, and spare blankets and moccasons, to accommodate captives. This, however, was mere conjecture; and whether they had killed friends or enemies, was not quite so certain as that they had killed Indians.

It is said that PAUGUS was well known to many of the English, and personally to many of *Lovewell's* men. That his name was a terror to the frontiers, we have no doubt; and that his appearance at Pequawket, when met by *Lovewell*, was enough to have struck terror into all that beheld him, may not be questioned, we will let the poet† describe him.

1. 'Twas *Paugus* led the Pequ'k't tribe:
As runs the fox, would *Paugus* run;
As howls the wild wolf, would he howl;
A huge bear-skin had *Paugus* on.

2. But *Chamberlain*, of Dunstable,
One whom a savage ne'er shall slay,
Met *Paugus* by the water-side,
And shot him dead upon that day.

The second in command among the Indians on that memorable day was named WAHWA, but of him we have no particulars. Captain *Lovewell* marched out from Dunstable with 46 men, about the 16 April, 1725, of which event the poet thus speaks:—

3. What time the noble *Lovewell* came,
With fifty men from Dunstable,
The cruel Pequ'k't tribe to tame,
With arms and bloodshed terrible.

4. With *Lovewell* brave *John Harwood* came;
From wife and babes' twas hard to part;
Young *Harwood* took her by the hand,
And bound the weeper to his heart.

5. "Repress that tear, my Mary, dear,
Said Harwood to his loving wife;
It tries me hard to leave thee here,
And seek in distant woods the strife.

6. "When gone, my Mary, think of me,
And pray to God that I may be
Such as one ought that lives for thee,
And come at last in victory."

7. Thus left young *Harwood*, babe and wife;
With accent wild she bade adieu:
It grieved those lovers much to part,
So fond and fair, so kind and true.

8. *John Harwood* died all bathed in blood,
When he had fought till set of day;
And many more we may not name,
Fell in that bloody battle fray

9. When news did come to *Harwood's* wife
That he with *Lovewell* fought and died;
Far in the wilds had given his life
Nor more would in this home abide;

10. Such grief did seize upon her mind,
Such sorrow filled her faithful breast,
On earth she ne'er found peace again,
But followed *Harwood* to his rest.

They arrived near the place where they expected to find Indians, on the 7 May; and, early the next morning, while at prayers, heard a gun, which they rightly suspected to be fired by some of *Paugus's* men, and immediately prepared for an encounter. Divesting themselves of their packs, they marched forward to discover the enemy. But not knowing in what direction to proceed, they marched in an opposite direction from the Indians. This gave *Paugus* great advantage; who, following their tracks, soon fell in with their packs, from which he learned their strength. Being encouraged by his superior numbers, *Paugus* courted the conflict, and pursued the English with ardor. His number of men was said to have been

* In December of the previous year, (1724,) with a few followers, he made an expedition to the north-east of Winnipisiogee Lake, in which he killed one and took another prisoner. For these he received the bounty offered by government.

† The editors or publishers of the N. H. collections have inserted the above lines, in imitation of the ancient Chevy Chase; but whence they were obtained, or who was their author, they do not inform us; perhaps, like that of which they are an imitation, the author remains unknown. We give it entire.

80, while that of the English consisted of no more than 34, having left ten in a fort, which they built at Ossipee; and one, an Indian named *Toby*, had before returned home, on account of lameness. The fort at Ossipee was for a retreat in case of emergency, and to serve as a deposit of part of their provisions, of which they disencumbered themselves before leaving it.

After marching a considerable distance from the place of their encampment on the morning of the 8 * May, Ensign *Wyman* discovered an Indian, who was out hunting, having in one hand some fowls he had just killed, and in the other, two guns. There can be no probability that he thought of meeting an enemy, but no sooner was he discovered by the English, than several guns were fired at him, but missed him. Seeing that sure death was his lot, this valiant Indian resolved to defend himself to his last breath; and the action was as speedy as the thought: his gun was levelled at the English, and *Lovewell* was mortally wounded. Ensign *Wyman*, taking deliberate aim, killed the poor hunter; which action our poet describes in glowing terms as follows:

11. *Seth Wyman*, who in Woburn lived,
A marksman he of courage true,
Shot the first Indian whom they saw;
Sheer through his heart the bullet flew.

12. The savage had been seeking game;
Two guns, and eke a knife, he bore,
And two black ducks were in his hand;
He shrieked, and fell to rise no more.

He was scalped by the chaplain and another, and then they marched again by the way they came, to recover their packs. This movement was expected by the wily PAUGUS, and he accordingly prepared an ambush to cut them off, or to take them prisoners, as fortune should will.

13. Anon, there eighty Indians rose,
Who'd hid themselves in ambush dread;
Their knives they shook, their guns they aimed,
The famous *Paugus* at their head.

14. *John Lovewell*, captain of the band,
His sword he waved, that glittered bright,
For the last time he cheered his men,
And led them onward to the fight.

When the Indians rose from their coverts, they nearly encircled the English, but seemed loath to begin the fight; and were, no doubt, in hopes that the English, seeing their numbers, would yield without a battle; and, therefore, made towards them with their guns presented, and threw away their first fire. They then held up ropes which they had provided for securing captives, and asked them if they would have quarter. This only encouraged the English, who answered "only at the muzzles of their guns;" and they rushed toward the Indians, fired as they pressed on, and, killing many, drove them several rods. But they soon rallied and fired vigorously in their turn, and obliged the English to retreat, leaving nine dead and three wounded, where the battle began. *Lovewell*, though mortally wounded before, had led his men until this time, but fell before the retreat.

Although we transpose the verses in the song, to accommodate them to the circumstances of the fight, yet we cannot avoid entirely their irregularity in reference to it. By the next that follow, it would seem, that *Lovewell* received a second wound before he fell.

15. "Fight on, fight on," brave *Lovewell* said;
"Fight on, while Heaven shall give you breath!"
An Indian ball then pierced him through,
And *Lovewell* closed his eyes in death.

16. Good heavens! is this a time for prayer?
Is this a time to worship God;
When *Lovewell's* men are dying fast,
And *Paugus'* tribe hath felt the rod?

In this 16th verse the poet, perhaps, had reference to the morning prayer, which Mr. *Frye*, the chaplain, made before marching, on the day of the battle; or, perhaps, more probably, to the ejaculations he made on the field after he was mortally wounded. In the morning he prayed thus patriotically: "We came out to meet the enemy; we have all along prayed God we might find them; we had rather trust Providence with our lives; yea, die for our country, than try to return without seeing them, if we might; and be called cowards for our pains." †

---

* This was O. S. and corresponds to May 19, N. S.—See *note* in last chapter.

† Address of *C. S. Davis*, (p. 17,) delivered at Fryeburg, 100 years after the fight.

17. The chaplain's name was *Jonathan Frye;*
In Andover his father dwelt,
And oft with *Lovewell's* men he'd prayed,
Before the mortal wound he felt.

18. A man was he of comely form,
Polished and brave, well learnt and kind;
Old Harvard's learned halls he left,
Far in the wilds a grave to find.

19. Ah! now his blood-red arm he lifts,
His closing lids he tries to raise;
And speak once more before he dies,
In supplication and in praise.

20. He prays kind Heaven to grant success,
Brave *Lovewell's* men to guide and bless,
And when they've shed their hearts'-blood true,
To raise them all to happiness.

21. "Come hither, *Farwell*," said young *Frye*,
"You see that I'm about to die;
Now for the love I bear to you,
When cold in death my bones shall lie;

22. "Go thou and see my parents dear,
And tell them you stood by me here;
Console them when they cry, Alas!
And wipe away the falling tear."

23. Lieutenant *Farwell* took his hand,
His arm around his neck he threw,
And said, "Brave chaplain, I could wish
That Heaven had made me die for you."

24. The chaplain on kind *Farwell's* breast
Bloody, and languishing, he fell;
Nor after that, said more but this,
'I love thee, soldier; fare thee well!"

"The fight continued," says the Reverend Mr. *Symmes*, "very furious and obstinate till towards night. The Indians roaring and yelling and howling like wolves, barking like dogs, and making all sorts of hideous noises: the English frequently shouting and huzzaing, as they did after the first round. At one time Captain *Wyman* is confident they were got to Powawing, by their striking on the ground, and other odd motions; but at length *Wyman* crept up towards them, and, firing amongst them, shot the chief Powaw, and broke up their meeting." *

25. Good heavens! they dance the powow dance,
What horrid yells the forest fill!
The grim bear crouches in his den,
The eagle seeks the distant hill.

26. "What means this dance, this powow dance?"
Stern *Wyman* said; with wondrous art,
He crept full near, his rifle aimed,
And shot the leader through the heart

The first of the following stanzas is very happily conceived, and although not in the order of the poet, is as appropriate here, as where it originally stood.

27. Then did the crimson streams, that flow'd,
Seem like the waters of the brook,
That brightly shine, that loudly dash,
Far down the cliffs of Agiochook. †

28. Ah! many a wife shall rend her hair,
And many a child cry, "Woe is me,"
When messengers the news shall bear,
Of *Lovewell's* dear-bought victory.

---

* Narrative of the fight at Piggwacket, vii.

† The Indian name of the White Mountains, or, as the people of New Hampshire would say, White Hills. The natives believed the summits of these mountains to be inhabited by invisible beings, but whether good or evil we are not informed. Nor is it of much importance, since they reverenced the one as much as the other.

It is always highly gratifying to the curious to observe how people primitively viewed objects which have become familiar to them. We will here present the reader with Mr. *Josselyn's* description of the White Mountains, not for its *accuracy*, but for its curious extravagance. "Four score miles, (upon a direct line,) to the N. W. of Scarborow, a ridge of mountains run N. W. and N. E. an hundred leagues, known by the name of the White Mountains, upon which lieth snow all the year, and is a landmark twenty miles off at sea. It is a rising ground from the sea shore to these hills, and they are inaccessible but by the gullies which the dissolved snow hath made. In these gullies grow saven bushes, which being taken hold of, are a good help to the climbing discoverer. Upon the top of the highest of these mountains, is a large level, or plain, of a day's journey over, whereon nothing grows but moss. At the farther end of this plain is another hill called the *Sugar-loaf*, to outward appearance a rude heap of massie stones piled one upon another, and you may, as you ascend, step from one stone to another, as if you were going up a pair of stairs, but winding still about the hill, till you come to the top, which will require half a day's time, and yet it is not above a mile, where there is also a level of about an acre of ground, with a pond of clear water in the midst of it, which you may hear run down, but how it ascends is a mystery. From this rocky hill you may see the whole country round about; it is far above the lower clouds, and from hence we beheld a vapor, (like a great pillar,) drawn up by the sun-beams out of a great lake, or pond, into the air, where it was formed into a cloud. The country beyond these hills, northward, is daunting terrible, being full of rocky hills, as thick as mole-hills in a meadow, and cloathed with infinite thick woods." *New England's Rarities*, 3, 4. Sad recollections are associated with the name of these mountains. The destruction of lives,

29 With footsteps slow shall travellers go,
Where *Lovewell's* pond shines clear and bright,
And mark the place where those are laid,
Who fell in *Lovewell's* bloody fight.

30. Old men shall shake their heads, and say
"Sad was the hour and terrible,
When *Lovewell*, brave, 'gainst *Paugus* went,
With fifty men from Dunstable."

If miracles had not then ceased in the land, we should be induced to pass to their credit the extraordinary escape of several of the wounded Englishmen. *Solomon Keyes*, having received three wounds, said he would hide himself, and die in a secret place, where the Indians could not find him to get his scalp. As he crawled upon the shore of the pond, at some distance from the scene of action, he found a canoe, into which he rolled himself, and was drifted away by the wind. To his great astonishment, he was cast ashore at no great distance from the fort at Ossipee, which he found means to recover, and there met several of his companions; and, gaining strength, returned home with them.

Those who escaped did not leave the battle-ground until near midnight. When they arrived at the fort, they expected to have found refreshment, and those they had left as a reserve; but a fellow, whose name is not mentioned, who deserted the rest when the battle began, and fled there, so frightened them, that they fled in great confusion and dismay to their homes.

The place where this fight took place was 50 miles from any white inhabitants; and that any should have survived the famine which now stared them in the face, is almost as miraculous as that they should have escaped death at the hands of the courageous warriors of *Paugus;* yet 14 lived to return to their friends.

Fifty men, from New Hampshire, afterwards marched to the scene of action, where they found and buried the dead. They found but three Indians, one of whom was *Paugus.* The rest were supposed to have been taken away when they retreated from the battle.

Thus progressed and terminated the expedition against the Pequawkets. And although the whites could scarcely claim the victory, yet, as in the case of the Narragansets, the Northern Indians received a blow from which they never recovered. With the Androscoggins, the Pequawkets soon after retired towards the sources of the Connecticut River. After remaining in those regions about two years, they separated, and the Androscoggins removed to Canada, where they were afterwards known as the St. Francis tribe. The Pequawkets remained upon the Connecticut, who, in the time of the revolutionary war, were under a chief named Philip. In 1728, a tract of country, since Pembroke, N. H., was granted to the men that went out with *Lovewell,* and it for some time bore the name of *Lovewell's Town.*

We had here nearly concluded to close our account of this affair, but cannot relieve ourself easily of the recollection of the following song, without inserting it, although we, and others, have elsewhere published it. It is said to have been composed the same year of the fight, and for several years afterwards was the most beloved song in all New England:

1. Of worthy Captain *Lovewell* I purpose now to sing,
How valiantly he served his country and his king;
He and his valiant soldiers did range the woods full wide,
And hardships they endured to quell the Indian's pride.

2. 'Twas nigh unto Pigwacket, on the eighth day of May,
They spied a rebel Indian soon after break of day;
He on a bank was walking, upon a neck of land,
Which leads into a pond, as we're made to understand.

3. Our men resolved to have him, and travelled two miles round,
Until they met the Indian, who boldly stood his ground;
Then speaks up Captain *Lovewell,* "Take you good heed," says he;
"This rogue is to decoy us, I very plainly see.

---

occasioned by an avalanche at the celebrated Notch, in 1826, will not soon be forgotten Mr. *Moore,* of Concord, has published an interesting account of it in the Coll N. H. Hist. Soc vol iii

4. "The Indians lie in ambush, in some place nigh at hand,
In order to surround us upon this neck of land;
Therefore we'll march in order, and each man leave his pack,
That we may briskly fight them when they shall us attack."

5. They came unto this Indian, who did them thus defy;
As soon as they came nigh him, two guns he did let fly,
Which wounded Captain *Lovewell*, and likewise one man more;
But when this rogue was running, they laid him in his gore.

6. Then having scalped the Indian, they went back to the spot,
Where they had laid their packs down, but there they found them not;
For the Indians having spied them, when they them down did lay,
Did seize them for their plunder, and carry them away.

7. These rebels lay in ambush, this very place hard by,
So that an English soldier did one of them espy,
And cried out, "Here's an Indian!" with that they started out,
As fiercely as old lions, and hideously did shout.

8. With that our valiant English all gave a loud huzza,
To shew the rebel Indians they feared them not a straw;
So now the fight began, as fiercely as could be,
The Indians ran up to them, but soon were forced to flee.

9. Then spake up Captain *Lovewell*, when first the fight began,
"Fight on, my valiant heroes! you see they fall like rain."
For, as we are informed, the Indians were so thick,
A man could scarcely fire a gun and not some of them hit.

10. Then did the rebels try their best our soldiers to surround
But they could not accomplish it, because there was a pond,
To which our men retreated, and covered all the rear;
The rogues were forced to flee them, although they skulked for fear.

11. Two logs there were behind them that close together lay,
Without being discovered, they could not get away;
Therefore our valiant English they travelled in a row,
And at a handsome distance as they were wont to go.

12. 'Twas ten o'clock in the morning when first the fight begun,
And fiercely did continue till the setting of the sun,
Excepting that the Indians, some hours before, twas night.
Drew off into the bushes and ceased a while to fight.

13. But soon again returned in fierce and furious mood,
Shouting as in the morning, but yet not half so loud,
For, as we are informed, so thick and fast they fell,
Scarce twenty of their number, at night did get home well.

14. And that our valiant English, till midnight there did stay,
To see whether the rebels would have another fray;
But they no more returning, they made off towards their home,
And brought away their wounded as far as they could come.

15. Of all our valiant English, there were but thirty-four,
And of the rebel Indians, there were about four score,
And sixteen of our English did safely home return;
The rest were killed and wounded, for which we all must mourn.

16. Our worthy Captain *Lovewell* among them there did die;
They killed Lieutenant *Robbins*, and wounded good young *Frye*,
Who was our English chaplain; he many Indians slew,
And some of them he scalped when bullets round him flew.

17 Young *Fullam* too I'll mention, because he fought so well;
Endeavoring to save a man, a sacrifice he fell,
And yet our valiant Englishmen in fight were ne'er dismayed,
But still they kept their motion, and *Wyman* captain made;

18. Who shot the old chief PAUGUS, which did the foe defeat,
Then set his men in order, and brought off the retreat;
And braving many dangers and hardships in the way,
They safe arrived at Dunstable, the thirteenth day of May

CHAPTER X.

The St. Francis Indians—Rogers' *expedition against them*—PHILIP—SABATIS—Arnold's *expedition*—NATANIS—*The modern Penobscots*—AITTEON—NEPTUNE—CAPTAIN FRANCIS—SUSUP *murders an Englishman*—*Specimen of the Penobscot language.*—ROWLES—*his prophecy*—BLIND WILL—*Killed by the Mohawks*—ASSACAMBUIT—*Visits France and is knighted by the king*—*Attacks and burns Haverhill*—*His death.*

TOWARDS the close of the last chapter, mention was made of the St. Francis Indians, and, as they were, a part of them, the remnant of the once respectable Androscoggins,* their history will here be resumed. We have already related some of their hardships and sufferings, both in *Philip's* war and the French wars afterwards, when they had to contend with the old experienced chief, Colonel *Church*; and also their severe disaster in opposing *Lovewell*.

After their arrival upon the Lake St. Francis, from which their village took its name, they were under the influence and guidance of French ecclesiastics. Their village, in 1755, consisted of about 40 wigwams and a church, and a friar resided among them. What time the Androscoggins joined the St. Francis tribe has not been discovered; but whenever war existed between France and England, they generally had some participation in it, the frequent occurrence of which at length ended in their almost total destruction, in 1759.

Before the capture of Quebec, in that year, and while the English army under General *Amherst* lay at Crown Point, an expedition against St. Fran-- was ordered by him; being so "exasperated," says Colonel *Rogers*, "at the treatment Capt. *Kennedy* had received from those Indians, to whom he had been sent with a flag of truce, and proposals of peace, who had been by them made prisoner with his party, that he determined to bestow upon them a signal chastisement." This does not appear, however, to be all that was charged against them, for Major *Rogers* continues, "They had, within my own knowledge, during the six years past, killed and carried away more than 600 persons." Accordingly Major *Rogers* was despatched upon this enterprise with 142 effective men, including officers, and a few Indians of the Pequawket tribe, under *Philip*, their chief. It was a most perilous undertaking; near 300 miles of wild country to be passed, late in October, 1759. When they came in sight of the town, towards evening, on the 5 October, the inhabitants were dancing about in great glee, celebrating a wedding. Half an hour before sunrise the next morning, the English fell suddenly upon them, in three divisions, and completely surprised them, killing 200 Indians, and capturing a few women and children.† With such secrecy and promptitude did the English act on this occasion, says our author, "that the enemy had no time to recover themselves, or take arms in their own defence, until they were mostly destroyed." Some few ran down to the river to escape by swimming or in their canoes, but were pursued and destroyed. Their village, except three houses, was burnt, and many persons in it. By seven o'clock the butchery was ended, and a retreat was immediately commenced. Two Indian boys were brought away prisoners, one of whom was

---

* "At St. Français, from some of *Zanghe'darankiac*, or *people from the mouth of this river*, I learned, that they call it, or rather its banks, *Amilcungantiquoke*, or *banks of the river abounding in dried meat.*" *Kendal's* Travels, iii. 143.

† I lately received a letter from a gentleman who subscribed himself "*Joseph Alex. Mastа*, an Indian of the St. Francis tribe," complaining of the inaccurate account given by Major *Rogers* of the destruction of that tribe; but as the author of the letter does not give an account himself, nor direct me where I can obtain one, better than I have used, I am constrained to reprint my account without much emendation. The only facts which I can gather from his letter, are, that, "before this event [Rogers's Expedition] took place, the St. Francis tribe numbered from 1800 to 2000 inhabitants; but since, this number has made rapid decline, and at present on the point of total dissolution." *Letter, dated Vincennes, Vt. 25 April, 1836.*

named *Sebatis.* The English commander says, " We found 600 scalps hanging upon poles over the doors of their wigwams."

Although the English had made such havoc among the Indians, yet a wretched calamity awaited them in their homeward march. They had but one of their number killed, who was an Indian, and six wounded, during the massacre, but on their return many were lost in the wilderness, starved and frozen to death. The scenes of individual suffering, could they be known, would probably exceed those which followed *Lovewell's* fight. Having mistaken the Upper for the Lower Coos, some set off by point of compass, and were never heard of after, and the enemy followed and cut off others. But *Philip*, at the head of his company, made good his retreat without losing a man in the way.

Besides this expedition, in which *Philip* was one of "Rogers' rangers," he was at the capture of Louisburgh, under General *Amherst*, and was the first man that took possession of the fortress.*

In the winter of 1757, when the English and French armies had gone into winter quarters, Colonel *Rogers* was left in command of Fort Edward, and had several severe battles with the French and Indians in scouting expeditions. In one of these, he fell in with a superior force to his own, near Ticonderoga, and lost many of his men, in killed and prisoners. This was on 21 January. The chief, *Philip*, was in that affair, and acted as sergeant. Concerning this chief, it is further said that he was but "half Indian," and that in the revolution, he joined the Americans, saying "he was a whig Indian."

Mention has been made of an Indian of the name of SEBATIS or SABATIS. There were several of the name, and doubtless it was peculiar to the Abenaquies; and hence that *Sabatis*, captured at St. Francis, was descended from an Abenaquis family, who had settled there. It is possible also, that he may be the same who afterwards resided, near the head waters of the Kennebeck, with a brother named *Natanis*, who is brought to our notice in the accounts † of General *Arnold's* expedition through that region in the fall of 1775; but this is conjecture. However, what is known of these two brothers follows.

General *Arnold* having, on his arrival in the Kennebeck River, ordered a small band to proceed in advance of the army, to discover and mark out a route for it, gave strict orders that *Natanis* should be captured or killed. This order had been given, because the general had been informed that he had been fixed there by the English of Canada, as a spy, to give information if an enemy should approach in that direction. But this, as it proved, was false information, and *Natanis* was the friend of the Americans, as also was his brother *Sabatis*, who lived about seven miles higher up the river, above him.

The residence of *Natanis* was a lonesome place, upon the bank of the river; his cabin, situated in the centre of a green, the border of which was beyond musket shot from it, was a discovery which added to the suspicions of the party, who, having arrived in the neighborhood, 4 October, surrounded it at every point, and run in upon it with great eagerness; expecting, without doubt, to have taken him prisoner. In this they were disappointed, for it appeared that the place had been deserted a week. Near by, at the shore of the river, a map drawn upon birch bark, was found in the top of a stake, very accurately delineating the courses of the rivers towards Canada, and lines denoting places of crossing from one to another. This greatly surprised them, but they profited much by it. Nothing was seen of any Indians during the excursion of the exploring party, who, after about 22 days, in which they suffered every thing but death, rejoined the army.

When the army had arrived within the bounds of Canada, which was on the 4 November, "we for the first time," says Mr. *Henry*, "had the pleasure of seeing the worthy and respectable Indian, *Natanis*, and his brother, *Saba-*

---

* *Rogers'* Reminiscences, Appendix to new edition.

† See that of Judge *John J. Henry*, 32, to 36, and 74, &c. See also *Shallu's* Tables, n 509, and Col. Maine Hist. Soc. i. 394.

tis, with some others of their tribe." *Natanis* went to each of the companies of spies, and shook them by the hand, as though he had been formerly acquainted with them. He explained himself by telling them, that he had kept close to them all the time they were making their discovery beyond his residence, and until they returned, but did not dare to make himself known, for fear they would kill him—a wise resolution.

Natanis and Sabatis, with 17 others of their tribe, joined the army on the River Chaudiere, and marched with it to Canada. When the attack on Quebec was made, 31 December, 1775, *Natanis* was wounded by a shot through the wrist, and fell into the hands of the British general, *Carleton*, who immediately set him at liberty. These were the first Indians employed in the revolutionary contest by the Americans.*

We cannot pass over the momentous undertaking of *Arnold*, without requesting the reader to notice how many men of note and eminence survived its ruins—General *Daniel Morgan* of Virginia, then a captain—General *Henry Dearborn* of Massachusetts, of like rank—*Timothy Bigelow* of Massachusetts, a major—*Return J. Meigs*, father of the late postmaster-general, of the same rank—*Samuel Spring*, D. D. of Newburyport, a chaplain—*Aaron Burr* of New Jersey, and General *Benedict Arnold* of Connecticut.† Numerous others deserve equal notice; but it is not our province to enumerate them here. And from this digression we return to notice another chief nearly similar in name to the last.

At the treaty of Georgetown, on Arrowsik Island, held by the eastern tribes with the English, 9 August, 1717, *Sabbadis*, as his name was then written, appeared for the Androscoggins. Also at the treaty of Casco, dated 25 July, 1727, we find among the signers *Sabatists* of Arresagontacook.‡ What part *Sabatis* acted in the tragedies from 1722 to 1725, does not appear. In the History of Maine§ we find the following passage concerning *Sabbatist*, as he is there called. "In 1730, a chaplain was allowed at Fort George; and it was in this place, where *Sabbatist*, the Anasagunticook sagamore, requested government to keep some supplies: for, said he, in '*cold winters and deep snows, my Indians, unable to go to Fort Richmond, sometimes suffer.*' "

We now pass to our own times to notice some modern Indians in the state of Maine. In 1816, the Penobscot tribe at Old Town,‖ having lost its sachem, entered upon the election of another. It was some months before they could agree upon a successor, although it is their custom to elect a near relation of the deceased. At length party spirit having run unreasonably high, their priest, who is a Roman Catholic, interfered, and they forsook the rival candidates, and elected *John Aitteon*. This man, it is said, was a descendant of Baron de *Saint Castiens*. The induction into office took place 19 September, 1816. At the same time *John Neptune* was constituted his lieutenant, and Captain *Francis* and another were confirmed as chief captains.

A specimen of modern oratory among these Indians is given by Mr. Williamson, who heard it, in his History of Maine. It was made in a court, by *John Neptune*, in extenuation of the murder of one *Knight*, by *Peol Susup*. The case was nearly as follows: In the evening of 28 June, 1816, this Indian was intoxicated, and at the tavern of said *Knight* at Bangor, (whether he had procured liquor there with which to intoxicate himself, we are not informed,) and being noisy and turbulent, *Knight* endeavored to expel him from his house. Having thrust him out of door, he endeavored to drive him away and in the attempt was stabbed, and immediately died. On his arrest, *Susup* acknowledged his guilt, but said he was in liquor, and that *Knight* abused

* Judge *Henry*, 75.

† *Henry*, our authority before mentioned, was a private, aged but 16, who ran away from his father, and joined the army clandestinely; he died in 1810, aged 52. *Morgan* died in 1802, æt. 65; *Dearborn* in 1829, æt. 78; *Meigs* in 1823; *Spring* in 1819, æt. 73; *Arnold* in 1801, at London, æt. 61; *Burr* died in New York, in 1836.

‡ Coll. N. H. Hist. Soc. ii. 242. 260.

§ *Williamson*, ii. 159.

‖ In 1811, this tribe consisted of but 57 families, and 241 persons. In 1820 there were 277 souls. Their increase, says Dr. *Morse*, Appendix to Indian Report, 65, is owing to an obligation of the chiefs imposed upon their young men to marry early.

him, or he had not done it. Being brought to trial in June the next year at Castine, by advice of counsel, he pleaded *not guilty;* and after a day spent in his trial, a verdict was rendered, according to the defence set up, *manslaughter. Susup* had a wife and several children; four of whom, with their mother, were present, as were many other Indians from St. Johns and Passamaquoddy, besides a great crowd of whites.

After sentence was declared, *Susup* was asked by the court if he had any thing to say for himself; to which he replied, "JOHN NEPTUNE *will speak for me.*" NEPTUNE rose up, and, having advanced towards the judges, deliberately said, in English,

"*You know your people do my Indians great deal wrong. They abuse them very much—yes they murder them; then they walk right off—nobody touches them. This makes my heart burn. Well, then my Indians say, we will go kill your very bad and wicked men. No, I tell'em never do that thing, we are brothers. Some time ago a very bad man* about Boston, shot an Indian dead. Your people said surely he should die, but it was not so. In the great prison house he eats and lives to this day. Certainly he never dies for killing Indian. My brothers say let that bloody man go free—*Peol Susup *too. So we wish. Hope fills the hearts of us all—Peace is good. These, my Indians, love it well. They smile under its shade. The white men and red men must be always friends. The Great Spirit is our father.—I speak what I feel.*"

"*Susup* was sentenced to another year's imprisonment, and required to find sureties for keeping the peace two years, in the penal sum of 500 dollars; when *John Neptune, Squire Jo Merry Neptune,* of his own tribe, Capt. *Solmond,* from Passamaquoddy, and Capt. *Jo Tomer,* from the River St. Johns, became his sureties in the cognizance." †

Captain *Francis,* the first captain of the tribe, has been mentioned, and who, according to the historian of Maine, is a man of good understanding. If the information he has given concerning the eastern Indians be correct,—and we see no cause to doubt it,—it is of much value, and no less interest. He assured Mr. *Williamson,* "that all the tribes between the Saco and the St. Johns, both inclusive, are brothers; that the eldest lived on the Saco; that each tribe is younger as we pass eastward, like the sons of the same father though the one at Passamaquoddy ‡ is the youngest of all, proceeding from those upon the River St. Johns and Penobscot.§ '*Always,*' he affirms, '*I could understand all these brothers very well when they speak; but when the Mickmaks or the Algonquins, or Canada Indians talk, I cannot tell all what they say.*' "

Before dismissing the interesting Tarratines, it may be proper to present a specimen of their language.

Metunk'senah, ouwa'ne, spum'keag-aio, kee'nuck de we-seh, keah'-dabel'-dock now-dō'-sch, keah'-olct-haut'ta-mon-a, numah-zee, mse tah'-mah, t'hah-lah-wee' keunah, spum'-keag-aio, me-lea'neh, neo'nah, ne-qum-pe-bem-gees'o'coque, maje' me, gees'-cool, ar'bon, nus-see-a'tos'see, neo'nah, commont'en-esk-sock, 't-hah-lah wee-keunah, num-e-se-comele'ent, tah-hah-la-we-u keah-ma-che-ke'-cheek, a-que-he a-que-ah-lah-ke-me-sah'coque, n'gah'ne, numa-se', nea-nah, neo je, saw'-gor

---

* "He alluded to one *Livermore,* who had received sentence of death for killing an Indian, which was commuted to hard labor for life in the state's prison." *Williamson.*

An Indian named CREVAY, a Penobscot of the tribe of St. Francis, to avoid being distressed by the war on the frontiers of Canada, with his wife wandered down into Massachusetts, and erected a wigwam on the shore of Spot Pond, in the town of Stoneham, where they lived. At length some abominable white ruffians, on the night of the 23 November, 1813, shot him while he was asleep, and badly wounded his squaw. Not being killed outright, this Indian crawled from his wigwam, and was found the next day almost lifeless and in great agony, and he expired in a few days after. The names of the murderers I will not give, for I abhor to sully my page with them. Four were guilty. One fled from justice, two were tried and condemned to be hanged, December 25th, following. *Report of the Trial.*

† Ibid.

‡ The Indians said, *Pascodum-oquon-keag.* Pascodum meant *pollock;* oquon, *catch a great many;* eag, *land* or *place.*

§ Penops, *rocks;* keag, a *place of*

*woo-saw'me, keah-dabeld'-ock, ego-mah, keeloah', nu u'chee, done-ah'le, sazoos neah'lets, quos'-que.**

In speaking of the New Hampshire sachems, it was not intended that so conspicuous a chief as *Rowls* should have been silently passed over, and therefore we will give him a place here. This chief has of late years become noted, from the circumstance of his name's being found to the celebrated *Wheelwright* deed of 1629. That deed, it may be proper to remark, purported to have been given by *Passaconaway, Runaawitt, Wehanownowit*, and *Rowls.* The tract of country conveyed was included between the Pascataqua and Merrimack Rivers, and bounded inland by a line from "Pawtucket" Falls in the latter, and Newichawannok in the former. It is pretty certain, now that these sachems gave no such deed at the time specified.

ROWLS was sachem of the Newichawannoks, and his dwelling-place was upon the north side of the Pascataqua, not far from Quampeagan Falls, in Berwick, then Kittery. "In 1643, he conveyed the lands of his vicinity to *Humphrey Chadbourn;* and others afterwards, to *Spencer;* the former being the earliest Indian deed found upon our records. It is certain that all the Indians upon the river to its mouth, were his subjects, though he was under Passaconaway."† Mr. *Hubbard* ‡ says, "There was within the compass of the seven years now current, [about 1670,] a sagamore about Kittary, called *Rouls* or *Rolles:* who laying very sick, and bedrid, (being an old man,) he expected some of the English, that seized upon his land, should have shown him that civility, as to have given him a visit in his aged infirmities and sickness. It matters not much whether it was totally neglected or not; to be sure at the last, he sent for the *chiefs* of the town and desired a favor of them, viz. that though he might, as he said, challenge [claim] all the plantation for his own, where they dwelt, that yet they would please to sell or give him a small tract of land, possibly an hundred or two of acres, and withall desired it might be recorded in the town book, as a public act, that so his children, which he left behind, might not be turned out, like vagabonds, as destitute of an habitation amongst, or near the English, adding this as a reason: That he knew there would shortly fall out a war between the Indians and the English, all over the country, and that the Indians at the first should prevail, and do much mischief to the English, and kill many of them: But after the third year, or after three years, all the Indians which so did, should be rooted out, and utterly destroyed." This account, the same author says, "is reported by Maj. *Waldron*, Mr. *Joshua Moody*, Capt. *Frost*, that live upon, or near the place."

A chief named *Blind-will* was successor to *Rolls*, and in *Philip's* war served the English. Why the word *blind* was prefixed to his name is not mentioned, but probably he had lost an eye.

In 1677, the wretched expedient was resorted to by the whites, of employing the Mohawks against the Tarratines, and two messengers, Majors *Pinchon* and *Richards*, were despatched to their country. They were kindly received by them, and promised their assistance. "Accordingly some parties of them came down the country, about the middle of March, and the first alarm was given at Amuskeeg Falls; where the son of *Wonolanset* being hunting, discovered 15 Indians on the other side, who called to him in a language which he did not understand; upon which he fled, and they fired near 30 guns at him without effect. Presently after this they were discovered in the woods near Cochecho. Major *Waldron* sent out eight of his Indians, whereof *Blind-will* was one, to make further discovery. They were all surprised together by a company of the Mohawks; two or three escaped, the others were either killed or taken. *Will* was dragged away by his hair; and being wounded, perished in the woods, on a neck of land, formed by the confluence of Cochecho and Ising-glass Rivers, which still bears the name of *Blind-will's* Neck."§ Such were the exploits of the allies of the English

* *Williamson's* Maine, i. 513. † *Williamson*, i. 460. ‡ Indian Wars, ii. 8?
§ *Belknap*, Hist. N. H. i. 125.

at this time; nor do we find that any others were performed of a different character. Notwithstanding, the same miserable policy was talked of again about nine years after; but we do not learn that it was carried into practice.

It was, perhaps, at the time of which we have been speaking, that the Narraganset chief *Pessacus* was murdered, as has been mentioned.*

We had not thus long delayed our notice of one of the most renowned chiefs, but from the untoward circumstance of having mislaid a valuable communication concerning him.† The sachem of whom we are now to speak was known among the French by the name of *Nescambioüit*, but among the English he was called

ASSACAMBUIT,‡ and *Assacombuit*.‡ This chief was as faithful to the French as one of their own nation; and our account of him begins in 1696, when, with *Iberville* and the famous *Montigny*, he rendered important service in the reduction of the English Fort St. Johns, 30 November, of that year. Being apprized of the approach of the French and Indians, the English sent out 88 men to oppose them, who, on the 28, were met and attacked by a part of *Iberville's* army, under *Montigny* and *Nescambioüit*, and defeated with the loss of 55 men. On the night before St. Johns capitulated, *Iberville*, with *Nescambioüit* as his second, at the head of 30 men, made a sally to burn one part of the town, while *D'Muys* and *Montigny*, with 60 others, were ordered to fire it at another point. Both parties succeeded. §

In 1699, he is noticed for some cruelty, which, it was said, he inflicted upon a child, named *Thomasin Rouse*. He having ordered it to carry something to the water side, it cried; he took a stick and struck her down, and she lay for dead. He then threw her into the water, but she was saved by another Indian. She was an English captive, and was soon after restored. This account was handed Dr. *Mather*, by one who had just returned from Casco Bay, where he had been to hold a treaty with the Indians. The account closes in these words: "This *Assacombuit* hath killed and taken this war, (they tell me,) 150 men, women and children. A bloody Devil." ||

It is said that *Mauxis*, *Wanungonet*, and *Assacombuit*, were "three of the most valiant and puissant sachems" of the east.¶ Their attack upon the fort at Casco, in August, 1703, has been mentioned.** In 1704, some of the Abenaquis, having established themselves in Newfoundland, were attacked by the English, and some of them killed. Whereupon they applied to Governor *Vaudreuil* for assistance to repel them, and he sent *Montigny* with a few Canadians, who joined themselves with about 50 Abenaquis under *Nescambioüit*, and attacked the English with great success. They pillaged and burnt one fort, and took many prisoners. ††

In 1705, *M. Subercase*, having succeeded *M. Brouillon* in the government of Newfoundland, endeavored to make thorough work with the remaining English there. Their success was nearly complete, and here again *Nescambioüit* is noticed as acting a conspicuous part. *Subercase's* army consisted of 400 men,‡‡ in all, and they set out from Placentia 15 January, upon snowshoes, with 20 days' provisions. They suffered much from the rigor of the weather, and did not fall upon the English until the 26, which was at a place called Rebou. They next took Petit Havre. At St. Johns they found some resistance, where the English now had two forts, which were supplied with cannon and mortars, and, after losing five men in killed and wounded, were obliged to raise the siege, in consequence of want of powder; having damaged much of what they brought with them in wading rivers. They next attacked Forrillon and took it. §§ This was 5 March. Here was also a fort,

---

* See B. II. p. 58. note §.

† From Rev. Mr. *Felt*, of Hamilton.

‡ *Penhallow*.

§ *Charlevoix*, ii. 193.

|| Magnalia, vii. 95.

¶ *Penhallow*, 6.

** Page 104, lib. iii.

†† *Charlevoix*, ii. 294.

‡‡ This is according to *Charlevoix*, but *Penhallow* says 500, and *Anspack*, (Hist. Newfoundland, 123.) *about* 500. *Charlevoix* is, doubtless, nearest the truth.

§§ *Le Bourg fut brûlé, après quoi* MONTIGNY, *qui avoit amené à cette expédition son fidèle* NESCAMBIOUIT, *fut détaché avec les sauvages, et une partie des Canadiens, peur aller du côté de Carbonniere, et de Bonneriste, avec order de brûler et de détruire toute le côté, ce qu'il exécuta sans perdre un seul homme, tant la terreur étoit grande parmi les Anglois.* N France, ii. 300.

into which the inhabitants at first retired, and endeavored to defend themselves, but soon surrendered prisoners of war.*

Not long after these services *Nescambioüit* sailed for France, and in 1706 visited his majesty, King Louis XIV, at Versailles. Here, among other eminent personages, he became known to the historian Charlevoix.† The king having presented him an elegant sword, he is reported to have said, holding up his hand, "*This hand has slain one hundred and forty of your majesty's enemies in New England;*"‡ and that whereupon, the king forthwith knighted him, and ordered that henceforth a pension of eight livres a day be allowed him for life.

Nescambioüit returned to America in 1707, and the next year accompanied Rouville to attack Haverhill in Massachusetts. The French had intended a much more formidable conquest, and had engaged bands of Indians from four nations to coöperate with them, and all were to rendezvous at Lake Nikisipique, as they called Winnipesauke or Winnipisiogee. But all except the Algonquins and Abenaquis under *Nescambioüit*, having failed and deserted them, they were on the point of abandoning their enterprise altogether. Having made known their situation to Governor *Vaudreuil*, and requested his orders, he directed, that though all the Indians deserted them, they should not give over the expedition. *Des Chaillons* having communicated this intelligence to the Indians, they entreated him to lead them forward, and said they would follow him wherever he chose to go.

From Nikisipique they marched, at last, with 200 men, fell upon Haverhill,§ and sacked it. The attack was made, sun about an hour high, 29 August, 1708. The contest was short as the opposition was feeble. The English lost about 100 persons by this irruption, 40 or 50 of whom were killed at Haverhill. *Nescambioüit*, in this affair, fought by the side of the commander-in-chief, and performed prodigies of valor with the sword which he brought from France.

Having burned the fort and many of the buildings in the village,‖ they began to retrace their steps, with precipitation. The English, having rallied, formed an ambush in the edge of the woods, about a mile and a half from the town, attacked them vigorously, killing and wounding many of them. In the ambush were 60 or 70 English, who, after hanging upon their flanks for near an hour, retreated. In this last affair the French suffered most. In both encounters, 18 men were wounded, three Indians and five Frenchmen killed. In the ambush fell *Hertel* of Chambly, and *Vercheres*, both officers of experience; and the renowned *Assacambuit*, as though, elsewhere, like *Achilles*, invulnerable, was wounded by a shot in the foot. This last attack had the happy effect of immediately restoring many of the prisoners.

From 1708 to 1727, we hear nothing of *Assacambuit*. In June of the latter year, his death is recorded, accompanied with a short account of him, in a newspaper of that time. Mention is made, among other things, that, like Hercules, he had a "famous club" which he always carried with him, on which were 98 notches, denoting the number of "English" he had killed; that he was knighted while in France, the insignia of which, on his return home, he wore upon his breast in large letters. In this newspaper communication he is styled "Old *Escambuit*," "formerly the principal sagamore of (the now dispersed) tribe of the Saco or Pigwacket Indians." He probably went to reside among the St. Francis tribe about 1700. He was restless when there was no war, and our account says, "when there was something of a prospect of settled peace, about 30 years ago, [1700,] he marched off the

* *Anspach*, 124.

† Hist. Gen. de la Nouv. France, ii. 326.

‡ *Penhallow*, 40. This must be, we think, a great misrepresentation of his *real* speech as subsequent details will lead one to suppose. Perhaps he might have said *forty*.

§ "*Ils prirent alors le parti de marcher contre un village appellé* Hawreuil, *composé de vintcinq à trente maisons bien bâtis, avec un fort, où logeoit le gouverneur. Ce fort avoit une garrison de trente soldats, et il y en avoit au moins dix dans chaque maison.*"

‖ *Charlevoix* says, "*Toutes les maisons se défendirent aussi très-bien, et eureut le même sort. Il'y eut environ cent Anglois de tués dans ces différentes attaques; plusieurs autres, qui attendirent trop tard à sortir du fort et des maisons,* y furent brûlés." None of the English accounts mention this, and it was doubtless supposition, without foundation in fact.

ground as a disbanded officer, left his brethren and travelled towards the Mississippi, where he was constantly engaged in wars, and never heard of till the last fall he returned to those [eastern] parts." This was probably the report among the English of New England; but in truth he was with the French in Canada, as we have seen. Had PENHALLOW published his INDIAN WARS one year later, he would not, probably, have closed his account as he did concerning him. He says that, at his return from France, he was so exalted that he treated his countrymen in the most haughty and arrogant manner, "murdering one and stabbing another, which so exasperated those of their relations, that they sought revenge, and would have instantly executed it, but that he fled his country, and never returned after."

CHAPTER XI.

Destruction of Deerfield, and captivity of Reverend John Williams and family, in 1704.

SOMETIMES in a volume, and sometimes in a pamphlet, the narrative of this affair had often been given to the world previous to 1774, by one of the principal actors in it, whose name is at the beginning of this chapter, and which is doubtless familiar to every reader of New England legends. The edition of Mr. *Williams's* work, out of which I take this, was prepared by the renowned New England annalist, the Reverend *Thomas Prince*, and was the 5th, printed at Boston "by *John Boyle*, next door to the *Three Doves* in Marlborough Street, 1774." It was a closely printed 8vo. pamphlet of 70 pages.

It will be necessary to relate some important facts of historical value before proceeding with the narrative. As at several other times, the plan was laid early in 1703, in Canada, for laying waste the whole English frontier, but like former and later plans, laid in that region, this but partially succeeded. Though the eastern settlements from Casco to Wells were destroyed, and 130 people killed and captivated, the summer before, yet the towns on the Connecticut had neglected their precautionary duty. And although Governor *Dudley* of Massachusetts had but little while before been notified of the design of the French, yet it was impossible to guard the eastern coast against the attack. Deerfield had been palisaded and 20 soldiers placed in it, but had been quartered about in different houses, and, entirely forgetting their duty as soldiers, were surprised with the rest of the town. The snow was deep, which gave the enemy an easy entrance over the pickets. The French were commanded by *Hertel de Rouville*, but the commanders of the Indians remain unknown.

Mr. *Williams* thus begins his narrative: "On Tuesday the 29th of February, 1703–4, not long before break of day, the enemy came in like a flood upon us; our watch being unfaithful: an evil, whose awful effects, in a surprizal of our fort, should bespeak all watchmen to avoid, as they would not bring the charge of blood upon themselves. They came to my house in the beginning of the onset, and by their violent endeavors to break open doors and windows, with axes and hatchets, awakened me out of sleep; on which I leaped out of bed, and running towards the door, perceived the enemy making their entrance into the house. I called to awaken two soldiers in the chamber; and returning toward my bedside for my arms, the enemy immediately brake into my room, I judge to the number of 20, with painted faces, and hideous acclamations. I reached up my hands to the bed-tester, for my pistol, uttering a short petition to God, expecting a present passage through the valley of the shadow of death." "Taking down my pistol, I cocked it, and put it to the breast of the first Indian who came up; but my pistol missing fire, I was seized by 3 Indians who disarmed me, and bound me naked, as I was, in my shirt, and so I stood for near the space of an hour." Meanwhile the work of destruction and pillage was carried on with great fury. One of the three who captured Mr. *Williams* was a captain against whom, says our captive, "the judgment of God did not long slumber for by sun-rising he received a mortal shot from my next neighbor's house." This, though not a garrison, and containing but seven men, withstood the efforts of the 300 French and Indians which now beset them. That house remains to this day, bearing upon its front door the marks of the hatchet.*

After about two hours the enemy took up their march from the town, having plundered and burnt it, and put 47 persons to death, including those killed in making defence. Mrs. *Williams* having lately lain in, was feeble, which, without the scene now acting before her, rendered her case hopeless; but to this was added the most shocking murders in her presence—two of her children were taken to the door and killed, also a black woman belonging to the family.

"About sun an hour high," continues the redeemed captive, "we were all carried out of the house for a march, and saw many of the houses of my neighbors in flames, perceiving the whole fort, one house excepted, to be taken!" "We were carried over the river, to the foot of the mountain, about a mile from my house, where we found a great number of our christian neighbors, men, women, and children, to the number of 100; nineteen of whom were afterward murdered by the way, and two starved to death near Coos, in a time of great scarcity, or famine, the savages underwent there. When we came to the foot of our mountain, they took away our shoes, and gave us Indian shoes, to prepare us for our journey." The army had left their packs at this place, and while they were getting ready to decamp, the few English that had escaped at the town, and a few from Hatfield, who had been notified of the fate of Deerfield by one or two, who had escaped there, pursued, and in a meadow between the town and the main body, met a party of the enemy, and a sharp fight ensued. The small band of Englishmen did not retreat until the main body under *Rouville* were about to encircle them, and then they left nine of their number slain. Such was the success of the English in the beginning of the fight, that, fearing a defeat, *Rouville* had ordered the captives to be put to death; but, fortunately, the bearer of the fatal message was killed by the way.

Three hundred miles of a trackless wilderness was now to be traversed, and that too at a season of all others the most to be dreaded; boughs of trees formed the beds of *enceinte* women and little children for 40 days, which was the time taken for the journey. The first day's journey was but about four miles, and although one child was killed, in general the children were treated well; probably, the historians say, that by delivering them at Canada, the Indians would receive a valuable ransom for them. Mr. *Williams* proceeds: "God made the heathen so to pity our children, that though they had several wounded persons of their own to carry upon their shoulders, for 30 miles before they came to the river, [the Connecticut 30 miles above Deerfield,] yet they carried our children, uncapable of traveling, in their arms, and upon their shouldiers."

At the first encampment some of the Indians got drunk with liquor they found at Deerfield, and in their rage killed Mr. *Williams's* negro man, and caused the escape of a Mr. *Alexander*. In the morning Mr. *Williams* was ordered before the commander-in-chief, (he considering him the principal of the captives,) and ordered to inform the other captives, that if any more attempted to escape, the rest should be put to death. In the second day's march occurred the death of Mrs. *Williams*, the affecting account of which we will give nearly in the language of her husband. At the upper part of Deerfield meadow it became necessary to cross Green River. The Indian that captured Mr. *Williams* was unwilling that he should speak to the other captives; but on the morning of the second day, that Indian captain being appointed to command in the rear, he had another master put over him, who not only allowed him to speak to others, but to walk with his wife, and assist her along. This was their last meeting, and she very calmly told him that her strength was failing fast, and that he would soon lose her. She spoke no discoura-

* See Col. *Hoyt's* Ant. Resear. which, we are glad to observe, is the best volume of New England Indian wars that has yet appeared.

ging words, or complained of the hardness of her fortune. The company soon came to a halt, and Mr. *Williams's* old master resumed his former station, and ordered him into the van, and his wife was obliged to travel unaided. They had now arrived at Green River, as we have related. This they passed by wading, although the current was very rapid, (which was the cause, no doubt, of its not being frozen over,) and about two feet in depth. After passing this river, they had to ascend a steep mountain. "No sooner," says Mr. *Williams*, "had I overcome the difficulty of that ascent, but I was permitted to sit down, and be unburthened of my pack. I sat pitying those who were behind, and intreated my master to let me go down and help my wife, but he refused. I asked each of the prisoners, as they passed by me, after her, and heard, that passing through the above said river, she fell down and was plunged all over in the water; after which she travelled not far, for at the foot of that mountain, the cruel and bloodthirsty savage who took her slew her with his hatchet at one stroke." The historians have left us no record of the character of this lady, but from the account left us by her husband, she was a most amiable companion. She was the only daughter of Reverend *Eleazer Mather*, minister of Northampton, by his wife Esther, daughter of Reverend *John Warham*, who came from England in 1630.

The second night was spent at an encampment in the northerly part of what is now Bernardstown, and in the course of the preceding day a young woman and child were killed and scalped. At this camp a council was held upon the propriety of putting Mr. *Williams* to death, but his master prevailed on the rest to save his life; for the reason, no doubt, that he should receive a high price for his ransom. The fourth day brought them to Connecticut River, about 30 miles above Deerfield. Here the wounded, children and baggage were put into a kind of sleigh, and passed with facility upon the river. Every day ended the suffering and captivity of one or more of the prisoners. The case of a young woman named *Mary Brooks*, was one to excite excessive pity, and it is believed, that had the Indians been the sole directors of the captives, such cases could hardly have occurred. This young woman, being *enceinte*, and walking upon the ice in the river, often fell down upon it, probably with a burthen upon her; which caused premature labor the following night. Being now unfitted for the journey, her master deliberately told her she must be put to death. With great composure she got liberty of him to go and take leave of her minister. She told him she was not afraid of death, and after some consoling conversation, she returned and was executed! This was March 8.

At the mouth of a river since known as *Williams's* River, upon a Sunday, the captives were permitted to assemble around their minister, and he preached a sermon to them from Lam. i. 18. At the mouth of White River *Rouville* divided his force into several parties, and they took different routes to the St. Lawrence.

In a few instances the captives were purchased of the Indians, by the French, and the others were at the different lodges of the Indians.

During his captivity, Mr. *Williams* visited various places on the St. Lawrence. At Montreal he was humanely treated by Governor *Vaudreuil*. In his interviews with the French Jesuits he uniformly found them using every endeavor to convert him and others to their religion. However, most of the captives remained steady in the Protestant faith. And in 170€, fifty-seven of them were by a flag-ship conveyed to Boston. A considerable number remained in Canada, and never returned, among whom was *Eunice Williams*, daughter of the minister. She became a firm catholic, married an Indian, by whom she had several children, and spent her days in a wigwam. She visited Deerfield with her Indian husband, dressed in Indian style, and was kindly received by her friends. All attempts to regain her were ineffectual. Reverend *Eleazer Williams*, late a missionary to the Greenbay Indians, is a descendant. He was educated by the friends of missions in New England.

In the History of Canada by *Charlevoix*, the incursions undertaken by the French and Indians are generally minutely recorded; but this against Deerfield he has unaccountably summed up in a dozen lines of his work. The following is the whole passage:

In the end of autumn, 1703, the English, despairing of securing the Indians, made several excursions into their country, and massacred all such as they could surprise. Upon this, the chiefs demanded aid of M. *de Vaudreuil*, and he sent them during the winter 250 men under the command of the Sieur *Hertel de Rouville*, a reformed lieutenant, who took the place of his already renowned father, whose age and infirmities prevented his undertaking such great expeditions. Four others of his children accompanied *Rouville*, who in their tour surprised the English, killed many of them, and made 140 of them prisoners. The French lost but three soldiers, and some savages, but *Rouville* was himself wounded.*

CHAPTER XII.

Various incidents in the history of the New England Indians, embracing several important events, with a sequel to some previous memoirs.

He felt his life's blood freezing fast;
He grasped his bow, his lance, and steel;
He was of Wampanoag's last.
To die were easy—not to yield.
His eyes were fixed upon the sky;
He gasped as on the ground he fell;
None but his foes to see him die—
None but his foes his death to tell.

The performances of one *Cornelius*, "the Dutchman," in Philip's war, are very obscurely noticed in the histories of the times, none of them giving us even his surname; and we have, in a former chapter, given the amount of what has before been published. I am now able to add concerning him, that his name was *Cornelius Consert;* that the last time he went out against the Indians, he served about six weeks; was captain of the forlorn hope in the Quabaog expedition, in the autumn of the first year of Philip's war; marched also to Groton and Chelmsford, and was discharged from service, "being ready to depart the country," October 13, 1675. It was probably in his Quabaog expedition that he committed the barbarous exploit upon "an old Indian," the account of which has been given; it was doubtless during the same expedition, which appears to have terminated in September, that "he brought round five Indians to Boston," who, being cast into prison, were afterwards "delivered to Mr. *Samuel Shrimpton*, to be under his employ on Noddle's Island," subject "to the order of the council." I shall here pass to some further account of the money of the Indians.

We have quoted the comical account of the money of the Indians of New England, by John Josselyn, and will now quote the graphic and sensible one given by the unfortunate *John Lawson*, in his account of Carolina, of the money in use among the southern Indians. "Their money," he says, "is of different sorts, but all made of shells, which are found on the coast of Carolina, being very large and hard, and difficult to cut. Some English smiths have tried to drill this sort of shell money, and thereby thought to get an advantage, but it proved so hard that nothing could be gained;" and *Morton*, in his New English Canaan, says that, although some of the English in New England have tried "by example to make the like, yet none hath ever attained to any perfection in the composure of them, so but that the salvages have found a great difference to be in the one and the other; and have known the counterfeit beads from those of their own making; and have, and doe slight them." Hence the conclusion of *Josselyn*, before extracted, namely, that "neither Jew nor devil could counterfeit the money of the Indians." Mr. *Lawson* continues: "The Indians often make, of the same kind of shells as those of which their money is made, a sort of gorget, which they wear abou

* Histoire Generale de la Nouv. France, ii. 290.

their necks in a string; so it hangs on their collar, whereon sometimes is engraven a cross, or some odd sort of figure which comes next in their fancy There are other sorts valued at a doeskin, yet the gorgets will sometimes sell for three or four buckskins ready dressed. There be others, that eight of them go readily for a doeskin; but the general and current species of all the Indians in Carolina, and I believe, all over the continent, as far as the bay of Mexico, is that which we call *Peak*, and *Ronoak*, but *Peak* more especially. This is that which at New York they call *Wampum*, and have used it as current money amongst the inhabitants for a great many years. Five cubits of this purchase a dressed doeskin, and seven or eight buy a dressed buckskin. To make this *Peak* it cost the English five or ten times as much as they could get for it, whereas it cost the Indians nothing, because they set no value upon their time, and therefore have no competition to fear, or that others will take its manufacture out of their hands. It is made by grinding the pieces of shell upon stone, and is smaller than the small end of a tobacco-pipe, or large wheat-straw. Four or five of these make an inch, and every one is to be drilled through and made as smooth as glass, and so strung, as beads are. A cubit, of the Indian measure, contains as much in length as will reach from the elbow to the end of the little finger. They never stand to question, whether it be a tall man or a short one that measures it. If this wampum-peak be black or purple, as some part of that shell is, then it is twice the value. The drilling is the most difficult and tedious part of the manufacture. It is done by sticking a nail in a cane or reed, which they roll upon their thighs with their right hand, while with their left they apply the bit of shell to the iron point. But especially in making their *ronoak*, four of which will scarce make one length of wampum. Such is the money of the Indians, with which you may buy all they have. It is their mammon, (as our money is to us,) that entices and persuades them to do any thing, part with their captives or slaves, and, sometimes, even their wives' and daughters' chastity. With it they buy off murderers; and whatever a man can do that is ill, this wampum will quit him of, and make him, in their opinion, good and virtuous, though never so black before." To return to the chiefs.

Of the Narraganset Indian *Corman* very little had been found when he was noticed before, and it is but little that we can now add concerning the "cheiffe counceller" of the "old crafty sachem" of Niantik. It appears that in the month of September, 1675, *Corman* was in Boston, whither he had been sent as an ambassador by the Narraganset sachems, and especially by Ninigret; and although Ninigret was a peace-maker, and had not been any how implicated in the war then going on, yet, such was the rage of the populace against all Indians, that it was not deemed safe for even a friend from among them to walk alone in the streets of the town. On the evening of the 28th of September, as *Corman*, now an old man, was walking through one of the streets, guarded by persons on each side of him, a certain miscreant, named *William Smith*, ran furiously against him, and thus separating him from those about him, did, by another motion, strike his feet from under him in such a manner that his head and shoulders came in violent contact with the ground, very seriously injuring him. Complaint having been made to the governor and council, they had both *Smith* and *Corman* brought before them the next day, and the charge against the former being established by the evidence of Mrs. *Sarah Pickering*, who saw the fact committed, "the court, in hearing of the case, judged it meet to bear due testimony against such abuse, and sentence the said *Smith* to pay, as a fine to the country, the sum of forty shillings, or be whipt with ten stripes; also to pay the said *Corman* for his damage the sum of ten shillings in money." It is very difficult to understand the grounds of the decision of the honorable court, unless they seriously thought that the *ground* on which poor old *Corman* fell was hurt four times as much as he was! If this was not its reason, why should forty shillings be paid to *the country* and only *ten* to CORMAN?

As new local and other histories appear, and the decaying manuscripts are put in a situation and condition to be conveniently consulted, new lights are daily reflected on the dark passages of our history. The presence of *Nanuntenoo* at the battle of Pawtucket, or, as it is more commonly called, *Peirse* fight, has been questioned by a very excellent local historian, Mr. Bliss, in his history of Rehoboth, but, as I apprehend, from a misconstruction of some passages in Hubbard's Narrative, especially from that passage where it is said that Nanuntenoo, when surprised by Denison's men, "was divertising himself with the recital of Captain *Peirse's* slaughter, surprised by his men a few days before." It is true that this sentence will admit of two constructions, either that the chief was diverting himself by recounting to his men his particular acts in that tragedy, or by a general account of its progress, or that they were diverting him; the former would be by no means improbable, especially if some of those about him had not been in the action, which would not be at all strange, as numbers of them were, doubtless, strolling upon hunting and other expeditions when the battle was fought. That Nanuntenoo did not leave the Connecticut River until the "first week in April" cannot be true, nor by that loosely stated date does Hubbard refer to his leaving the Connecticut, but to "about the time" of his capture. If he refers to the time of his leaving the river, he refers to his men also, who, he says, did not leave until after he did; but it was his men that defeated Peirse. These are all the lights we are able to throw on that great event, and must here leave it in the same doubt we found it, and which is ever, most likely, to shroud it.

It would be highly gratifying to be able to give sketches of some of the prominent English captains, or others, who were conspicuous in Indian history, but our design and limits both preclude such digressions, and we cannot indulge in but a few. In a recent ramble in the Hill burying-ground, in Middleborough, I discovered the grave of a Lieutenant Nathaniel Southworth, upon the head-stone of which it is inscribed that he died January 14, 1710, in his 62d year; he was therefore about 28 in the time of Philip's war, and is, very probably, the same who distinguished himself on many occasions under Captain Church. He lies among a group of graves of his family connections. We did not intentionally omit to notice the death of his commander in another chapter. Colonel Church died on the 17 of January, 1718, in the 78th year of his age, and lies buried at Compton in Massachusetts. He was born at Plymouth in 1639, and not long after removed to Duxbury with his father.* He was a housewright by trade, as were his father and one or two of his brothers. How many he had I am not sure, but Caleb and Joseph are mentioned, and a sister who married an Irish, and lived in Compton. In 1674 he bought land of the government and removed to Sogkonate, the then Indian name of the tract of country since Compton. Here he was prosperously making a farm when Philip's war broke out, and was obliged to quit his improvements. Possessing a remarkably active mind, vigorous body, and glowing patriotism, he was not long an idle spectator of the war, engaging in it without reward as a volunteer; and our previous pages have shown that he raised himself to the chief military place in the country, and several civil offices of honor. After Philip's war Colonel Church resided at Bristol, then at Fall River, and, lastly, again at Sogkonate; in each of which places he left a good estate. In his latter years he had become very corpulent, and burdensome to himself. The morning before his death he visited his sister, Mrs. Irish, about two miles from his residence, on horseback; returning home, his horse stumbled, and threw him with such force upon the ground that a blood-vessel was broken, and he died in about 12 hours after. He married Mrs. Alice Southworth, by whom he had five sons and one daughter. One of his sons, Thomas, published "The Entertaining History of Philip's War," which has been published in 4to., 8vo., 12mo., and is authority in all matters where Church was himself concerned.

We have next to recur to the subject of the Indian letters, pending the redemption of Mrs. Rowlandson. Those given in the third chapter of this book were copied from a transcript made at the time they were received from the Indians, but a recurrence to the originals has supplied the following additions. *Nepanet*, when sent out on the 3 April, 1676, as noted on page 90, had with him the following letter from Governor Leverett:

* His biographers have said that he was born at Duxbury; but Judge Davis informed me that he was born at Plymouth and that some records he had seen there were his authority

"*For the Indian Sagamores and people that are in warre against us.*—Intelligence is come to us that you have some English, especially women and children, in captivity among you. We have therefore sent the messenger offering to redeem them, either for payment in goods or wampom, or by exchange of prisoners. We desire your answer by this our messenger, what price you demand for every man, woman, and child, or if you will exchange for Indians. If you have any among you that can write your answer to this our message, we desire it in writing; and to that end have sent paper, pen and incke by the messenger. If you lett our messenger have free accesse to you, freedome of a safe returne, wee are willing to doe the like by any messenger of yours, provided he come unarmed, and carry a white flag upon a staffe, visible to be seene, which we take as a flagge of truce, and is used by civilized nations in time of warre, when any messengers are sent in a way of treaty, which we have done by our messenger. In testimony whereof I have set to my hand and seal.

JOHN LEVERETT, *Gov'r.*

Boston, 31 *March*, 1676. Passed by the council.

EDWARD RAWSON, *Secretary.*"

The answer returned to this letter is that printed on page 90, which does not differ essentially from the original; and the English at Boston immediately complied with the request of the Indians, by sending two messengers to renew the negotiation. By these messengers an answer was returned, written by *James the Printer*, as follows:

"*For the Governor and Council at Boston:*—The Indians, *Tom Nepenomp* and *Peter Tatatiqunca*, hath brought us letter from you about the English captives, especially for Mrs. *Rolanson*. The answer is, I am sorrow that I have don much wrong to you: and yet, I say, the fault is lay upon you; for when we begun to quarrell at first with Plimouth men, I did not think that you should have so much trouble as now is: therefore I am willing to heare your desire about the captives. Therefore we desire you to sent Mr. Rolonson and goodman Kettle (for their wives) and these Indians, Tom and Peter, to redeeme their wives: They shall come and go very safely: Whereupon, wee ask Mrs. Rolonson, how much your husband willing to give for you? Shee give on answer, 20 pound in goods: but John Kettel's wife could not tel. And the rest, captives, may be spoken of hereafter."

When this letter was taken to Boston, the governor immediately despatched another. "*To the Indian Sachems about Wachuset.*—We received your letter by *Tom* and *Peter*, which doth not answer ours to you; neither is it subscribed by the sachems; nor hath it any date, which we know your scribe, *James Printer*, doth well understand should be. We have sent the said *Tom* and *Peter* againe to you, expecting you will, speedily, by them, give us a plaine and direct answer to our last letter, and if you have any thing more to propound to us, wee desire to have it from you under your hands, by these our messengers, and you shall have a speedy answer. Dated at Boston, 28 April, 1676." Such are all the additions we are able to make to that memorable negotiation, which was one of the immediate causes of Philip's reverses and final overthrow.

Of a chief so prominent as *Madokawando*, we are glad to be able at any time to extend our memoir, for, in our opinion, few leaders of any country appear to better advantage. Taking nothing but what his enemies have said of him, we have much to admire. No warrior was ever more humane to prisoners than Madokawando, where he commanded in person. He entered into the war against the English with the greatest reluctance, but when he had once "stepped in," they found him no common foe. Repeated depredations from the whites at length brought him into the field; the desolation of York followed; its inhabitants were nearly all killed or led into captivity, the particulars of which we have already related. Before Wells he was not so successful, but for that failure he is not accountable, as the expedition against it was under the direction of two prominent French officers. His preservation and liberation of Thomas Cobbet were acts of pure humanity.

Whether the expedition against Groton was under the immediate direction of Madokawando, or not, we are not informed, but it was, without doubt, executed under the command of one of his chief captains, the noted *Moxus*, or, as he was sometimes called, *Toxus*. That place was laid waste on the 27th of July, 1694; 22 people were killed, and 13 led into captivity. The scalps of the unfortunate slain were said to have been presented to Governor *Frontenac* by *Madokawando* himself.

At the destruction of York was taken the family of the Rev. Mr. *Dummer* and our authority made us say that Mrs. Dummer died in captivity, but we are now assured, by other testimony,* that she lived to return out of captivity, having been redeemed. For such termination of a wretched fate she was, no doubt, indebted to *Madokawando*.

This chief seems to have had unlimited control over the country upon the Penobscot River, as has been seen from what we have already before stated; judging from the amount of property paid him, from time to time, for sundry tracts of his country. Yet, though we are satisfied that the amounts he received were large, still they are expressed in such vague terms that it is impossible to arrive at any thing like a tolerable notion of their extent. One testifies that, for a certain tract of land, Madokawando "received a large amount of money;" another, that he received a *hatful;* and a third states it to have been "a *hatful* of *pieces of eight*."†

We have said that the great sachem was succeeded at his death by *Wenamovet*, and at the same time "*Moxus* seemed his successor." We find nothing yet to vary this statement, but in explanation we would note that *Wenamovet* appears not to have been a war chief, or in any other way very conspicuous, except as a counsellor; and though in name the successor of *Madokawando*, yet was willing to let "fierce *Moxus*" bear his well-earned title of chief in all matters of war.

One of the most signal exploits of *Moxus* was the capture of Pemmaquid, on the 2d of August, 1689. From this place his men led 16 of the English into a most miserable captivity, whence but very few ever returned. A considerable number were killed before the fort was taken, among whom was the worthy Captain *Gyles;* three other captains were also slain, and the fort capitulated the second day, and all within it were suffered to leave it and return to the English settlements in safety.‡

We have seen that the chief *Bomazeen* was intrapped and thrown into prison in Boston, in 1694. He was also a prisoner there four years after, having probably been retained all this time to restrain acts of barbarity on white captives; and it was rumored that he had been the leader at Groton, which probably had some influence in lengthening his captivity, but it is not now a question who the leader was in that sanguinary exploit. Mr. *John Gyles* returned out of a ten years' captivity in 1698, and on the 14th of October of that year, he says he was sent for by Lieutenant-Governor *Stoughton*, to interpret a conference with *Bomazeen* and other Indians then in jail. This same Mr. *Gyles*, afterwards captain of Fort George, went as interpreter with Captain Southack in the province galley to the eastern shores, for the ransom and exchange of captives. Our chief was at this time exchanged, and the galley returned to Boston in December, 1698.

Whether, upon mere suspicion, injury was added to crime in the case of *Bomazeen*, we cannot, upon our slender evidence, aver; but if it were a parallel case to that of the seizure and death of *Egeremet* and *Honquid*, or, as others write his name, *Ahanquid*, *Abenquid*, &c., it could scarcely be surpassed in atrocity. There are no facts to show that *Abenquid* had been an enemy to the English, or, if an enemy, that he had been engaged in any depredations.

Notwithstanding it is a custom among some tribes of Indians to obliterate all remembrance of the dead, their near connections, it was by no means common among all tribes, for we have had occasion to mention many instances where the name of a noted chief has been perpetuated, both

---

* *Greenleaf's* Ecclesiastical Sketches of Maine, p. 10.

† The printed treaty of 1742, and authorities *ut supra*.

‡ Narrative of *John Gyles*, as published in our "Indian Captivities."

among the western as well as among the eastern Indians. *Abenquid* was killed by Captain *Chubb* in 1696, and in 1725 there was another chief of the same name, of equal distinction. And he deserves some notice in this place, as do many others. While Captain *Lovewell* was on his march against the Pequawkets, measures were being devised in Boston for a peace with the eastern Indians. There were, at the same time, several Indians there, some as prisoners and others as hostages, and the English concluded to send some of them out to invite their countrymen to come to Boston to settle difficulties; accordingly *Saquarexis* and *Nebine*, one a hostage and the other a captive, were despatched upon that business. They, "after some time," returned and reported, "that the Indians were generally disposed to a peace, for that the losses they met with, and the daily terror they were under, made their lives miserable. After this they went out again," and meeting with several others of their countrymen, received further assurances of a general desire for peace. Whereupon commissioners were sent with those two Indians to Fort St. George, to procure a meeting of chiefs and to make a treaty. They arrived there on the 2d July, and on the 14th thirteen chiefs had assembled, not at the fort, but at a safe distance therefrom, fearing treachery from their white brethren on a more extended scale than they had experienced not many days before.* However, after considerable parleying, in which the Indians made the English swear by their God, in the most solemn manner, that their intentions were of a tenor with their pretensions, the parties came together.

The battle of Pequawket was recent, and it was evident that the Indians had become conscious of their weakness, and did not urge their wrongs at this meeting, although, as it were, in their own country, but seemed determined to have peace on any terms. They did indeed, to the demand of the English, "Why they had made war upon them?" reply, that it was because they had taken up their land, even to Cape Newagen; and not only seized upon their lands to that place westward, but that they had there beaten two of their men to death. To this the English commissioners answered: "The lands are ours, and we can show you they were fairly bought of your fathers; and if your men were beaten to death by the English, it was your business to complain to our government, and not to make war." This seems to have silenced the poor Indians, and we hear nothing further from them at this time but an earnest desire that peace might be concluded, or that a cessation of arms might take place. The commissioners informed them that they had not power to grant a cessation of arms, but said that, probably, if a deputation of their chiefs would go to Boston, it might be granted by their government. It was finally agreed that the two chiefs, *Loron*, or, as he was sometimes called, *Saguaaram*, now an old and venerable chief, and *Ahanquid*, should return with the English to Boston, and see what could be done towards a general peace.

LORON and AHANQUID having come to Boston, it was soon after settled that these two chiefs should go into their country, and return in 40 days with a sufficient number of chiefs, with whom a proper treaty might be made. Meanwhile several depredations having been committed on both sides, the time of the return of the Indians was considerably protracted in consequence; and, as we have in a previous chapter mentioned, the forty days had nearly twice expired before their reappearance; but, in the beginning of November, the faithful *Loron* and *Ahanquid* returned to Boston, bringing with them *Arexus*, *Francis Xavier*, and *Meganumba*, representatives from the eastern Indians, clothed with full power to negotiate of peace. More than a month was passed by these chiefs in Boston before a treaty was signed. This was done on the 15 December, 1725, and peace was thereby restored to the eastern frontiers.

* "And indeed they had cause of being so, for that about 10 days before, [20 June, says Williamson, ii. 144,] under a flag of truce, some of the English treacherously attempted to lay violent hands upon them, but lost one in the skirmish and had another wounded, which was the occasion of the like unhappy disaster that afterwards happened unto Captain *Saunders* in Penobscot Bay." *Penhallow*, 120.

In our notice of Captain *Tom* in a previous chapter, and his depredation at Hampton, it should have been stated that he had abundant excuse for retaliations of the nature there described. Length of time, to whatever number of years extended, is no guaranty that an injury will not be repaid by an Indian, with Indian interest; and *Hannibal* did not more strictly observe his vow to war against the Romans, than the savage of America adhered to his resolution of revenging an insult, even though its origin were removed several generations from him. In the chapter already referred to, we have detailed the expedition of Colonel *Church* upon the Androscoggin, and his capture and destruction of a fort some 30 or 40 miles up that river.* This fort was the residence of Agamcus, more generally known among the English as *Great Tom*. This chief, according to my authority, was taken captive at the time of the assault by Church, "but he slipt away from the hands of his too careless keepers, which was a disaster they much complained of. But if this piece of carelessness did any harm, there was another which did some good; for *Great Tom* having terribly scared a part of his men with the tidings of what had happened, and an English lad in their hands also telling them some truth, they betook themselves to such a *flight* in their *fright*, as gave Mr. *Anthony Bracket*, then a prisoner with them, an opportunity to fly four score miles another way." But we have recorded the escape of poor *Anthony Bracket*, who, says Dr. Mather, "if he had not found one of Church's vessels *aground* at Maquait, would have been miserably *aground* himself," after all his severe travel and sufferings to effect an escape.† And now we have arrived at the extent of our information concerning *Agamcus*.

Wahwa shall here receive additional notice. He may be the same spoken of before,‡ though there the name, if it be the same, has another syllable in it. He was the renowned *Hopehood*, doubly celebrated by the stroke of oblivion aimed at his head by the classic *Magnalian*. But *Wahwa* could hardly have been *Hopehood* of 1675, § as he would have been very old at *Lovewell's* fight, in 1725; yet it is not impossible, notwithstanding he is made to die,‖ by the hand of the Mohawks, not long after the capture of Salmon Falls, in 1690, "while on his way westward to bewitch another crew at Aquadocta." His name of *Hopehood* had, very probably, been manufactured out of an Indian name approaching it in sound, as are many others we possess.

He did not leave the scenes of his exploits until the summer of 1690, as we have seen;¶ he was the leader at Fox Point, in Newington, in May of that year; and he very probably had the direction of the party, if he did not lead it, who, on the 4th of July, killed eight people as they were mowing in a field near Lamprey River, and took a boy captive. On the 5th they attacked Captain *Hilton's* garrison at Exeter, but Lieutenant *Bancroft*, arriving to its relief, beat off the Indians "with the loss of a few of his men." One man they were forced to leave without scalping, and though shot in 9 places, was still alive. To these desperate wounds they had added two blows with the tomahawk at his neck, endeavoring to sever his head from his body; "which blows, you may be sure," says Mather, "added more enormous wounds unto the *port-holes* of death already opened, and from which his life was running out as fast as it could." When discovered by his friends he was looked upon as dead, but on being stirred was observed to gasp; "whereupon an Irish fellow then present, advised them to give him another dab with a hatchet, and so bury him with the rest." Yet this man recovered, and was afterwards well. His name was *Simon Stone*. There are daily occurrences, which in those days would have been viewed as miracles, or as retaliations of the Creator upon miserable wretches for thoughtless acts or expressions. Upon all such as came to the knowledge of *Cotton Mather* he laid his potent hand with manifest satisfaction. Doubtless the poor Irishman thought it would have been a favor to the wounded man, who could not live, to put him out of his misery; but this weighed nothing in the mind of the

---

* Fort "*Amonoscoggin*," according to the Magnalia, about 40 miles up the river.

† *Magnalia*, ib. ‡ Page 105, 114, 124, ante § Page 116. ‖ By *Mather*, Magnalia

¶ Page 118.

historian. "Teague," he says, "as he was foolishly pulling a canoe ashore, about this time, with the cock of his gun, it went off, breaking his arm with a fearful wound, by which he was made a cripple ever after."

By a council of war held at Portsmouth, occasioned by these depredations of "that memorable tiger *Hopehood*," it was decided that Captain *Wiswall* should go out in search of him with a large scouting party. Several other prominent men, being emulous of the service, offering to join him in command with another party, it by lot fell on Captain *Floyd*. Having rendezvoused at Dover to the number of about one hundred men, they marched into the woods on the since memorable day, July 4th, 1690. On the 6th, having sent out their scouts "before breakfast" in the morning, they "immediately returned with tidings of *breakfast* enough for those who had their stomachs sharp set for fighting." The parties immediately met at a place called Wheelwright's Pond, in Lee, and an obstinate battle ensued, which lasted from two to three hours. Owing, however, to the Indian mode of fighting, adopted by the English, comparatively but few were killed. Neither party could boast of a victory, for, as at Pequawket, each was glad to retreat from the other. Of the whites above 30 were killed and wounded, of which 15 were of the former number. Among these were included Captain *Wiswall*, his lieutenant, *Flagg*, and Sergeant *Walker*. Captain *Floyd* maintained the fight until most of his men had retreated, which obliged him to retreat also. "For this *some* blamed him, who, probably, would not have continued it as long as he did." Captain *Converse* visited the battle ground the next morning, and brought off seven wounded still alive, but the Indians had removed all of theirs, and it could never be known how many of them were killed. There was no doubt about the precipitancy of their retreat, as they left much of their plunder upon the field.

The same week "these rovers made their descent as far as Amesbury, where Captain *Foot* being ensnared by them, they tortured him to death. This so alarmed the other inhabitants, that they flew from their beds to their garrisons, otherwise before the next morning they had found their beds their graves. However, they killed three persons, burnt three houses, and many cattle. In fine, from the first mischief done at Lamprey-eel River, (on July 4th,) to this last at Amesbury, all belonging to one Indian expedition, forty English people were cut off."

Thus *Hopehood* is considered the leader in all these transactions, although our chroniclers of that day do not mention him, excepting where we have done so, nor do they mention the names of any other Indians. He was the commander of his countrymen at the taking of Casco, on which event the garrisons of Purpooduck, Spurwink, Black Point, and Blue Point, drew off to Saco, and in a few days from Saco they retreated to Wells, "twenty miles within the said Saco, and about half Wells drew off as far as Lieutenant *Storer's*. But the arrival of orders and soldiers from government stopped them from retiring any farther; and *Hopehood*, with a party that staid for farther mischief, meeting with some resistance here, turned about, and having first had a skirmish with Captain *Sherburn*, they appeared the next Lord's-day at Newichawannok or Berwick, where they burnt some houses and slew a man." This last event was three days previous to the massacre at Fox Point, before related.

We now are to speak again of *Wahwa*, and as we have before considered him a different chief from *Hopehood Wahowah*, we shall still do so, yet the character of his exploits agrees well with those of that chief; but that argues nothing as to his identity, for numerous other chiefs correspond equally as well.

On the 27th of October, 1726, a band of seven Indians surprised the family of *Philip Durell* at Kennebunk, capturing ten persons, eight women and two children, and carried them off. The attack was made late in the afternoon, while Mr *Durell* was absent. On his return he found his house in flames, chairs piled on the fire, trunks split to pieces, but no traces of his wife and children. The Indians had been watching for an opportunity to attack when Mr. *Durell* should be absent, fearing, it was thought, his powerful arm, if made when he was at home. Twenty-three years before Mrs. *Durill* had been a captive,* but unlike most of her sex in like circumstances, she foreboded no evil of a like kind from the Indians, but looked upon her former capture by them as we do upon a malady that never attacks a second time; but in this case it was otherwise.

The perpetrators were pursued with vigor the next morning, which caused the Indians to put most of their captives to death, by which means they were able to make good their flight.

It was for some time doubtful what Indians, or how many, had committed this horrid act, but it was finally ascertained that the bloody "*Wahwa, Paucaunaumpoijte*, formerly a Mohegan, *Acteon*, afterwards known as Captain *Moses*, an Arisaguntacook, *Omborowees, Manneenhowhau, Pier, Sungebaugundo*, probably of the same tribe, though one or more was of Wowenok, but then residing among the St. Francis Indians. Yet five-and-twenty years or more afterwards, Colonel *Job*, a noted orator and chief speaker at Governor *Shirley's* treaty in 1754, denied that *Acteon* was an Arisaguntacook, and said he was an Albany Indian; but as *Job* was accused of telling lies in his talk at the treaty by one of his own party, not much dependence can be given to what he did say.† But it appears that he was a Norridgewok, but having taken an Arisaguntacook woman for a wife, became one of them. He was the same chief who, on the 28 April, 1752, with a party of 10 or 12 of that tribe, fell upon four men on a branch of Contoocook River, shot one of them dead, one escaped, and the other two were taken and carried to Canada; but this affair we shall notice more at large presently.

We hear of but one that ever returned of those taken at Kennebunk. His name was *John Durell*, son of *Philip*, whose family were destroyed; and he, though he was redeemed in about two years, was, according to the historian of Kennebunk, "ever after more of an Indian than a white man."* He was alive when Governor *Sullivan* wrote his history, and resided there. It was not long after *Wahwa's* depredation, that two friendly Indians, *Quinoise*, of Wowenok, and *Ogicsand*, were sent by the governor of Massachusetts to learn the fate of the captives, as well as what Indians had done the mischief these ambassadors, from causes not explained, though doubtless no uncommon ones on such undertakings, were not heard of for nearly a year after, and then could give no satisfactory account in the business they undertook. At the treaty of Casco, in 1727, *Auyaummowett*, chief speaker of the Arisaguntacooks, said he had learned that a boy taken at that time was among the French. This was probably *John Durell*.

After peace was made, and intercourse commenced again between the Indians and the settlers, it seems *Wahwa* used frequently to visit Kennebunk, and often talked familiarly with the friends of those he had massacred. Like most other Indians, he would get drunk when he could get liquor. On one occasion, as he lay drunk at the house of a Mr. *Baxter*, whose wife was among the murdered in the exploit above related, some of *Baxter's* acquaintances advised him to tumble him into the well,‡ but he had too much humanity to wish to *immortalize* his name by an act so dastardly. And *Wahwa* remained a monument of his own cruelty, but not a more despised one than the advisers of his death; while the injured man, deprived of his nearest friends, remained a monument of humanity.

We now return to *Acteon*, and his expedition to Contoocook. A small company of young men, four in number only, went out early in the spring of the year 1752, to hunt in the north-western part of New Hampshire. Their names were, *Amos Eastman*, of Concord, *John* and *William Stark*, of Dunbarton, and *David Stinson*, of Londonderry. What we are about to relate will be of more interest to the reader, doubtless, if he is told that *John Stark*, of this party of hunters, was the same who afterwards defeated Colonel *Baum* at Bennington, in the early part of the revolutionary war. These young men, wandering far beyond the confines of civilization, were, on the 28th of April,

* Bradbury's History of Kennebunk Port, 120, 121.

† He was a fearless, bold fellow; accused Governor *Shirley* of "letting his young men act the *Devil's* part by doing mischief to the Indians," notwithstanding his protestations of justice to them.

‡ History of Kennebunk Port, 121.

pursuing their arduous employment on a branch of the Pemigewaset, called Baker's River, in what is since Rumney, when suddenly they were surprised by ten Indians under the famous *Acteon*, who at this time was known by the name of Captain *Moses*. The whites had, but little while before, discovered traces of Indians, and had become alarmed, and were determined to leave their position. Accordingly, *John Stark* went out very early in the morning to collect their traps, and while thus separated from his companions, was made prisoner. As soon as he was secured, he was ordered to direct them to his friends. This he undertook to do, but purposely led them two miles farther from them, hoping that, by some means, they might take the alarm and escape; but it was not to be ended so. They seem not to have imagined that *John* was taken by Indians, and soon began to shoot off their guns to direct him where they were. This also directed the Indians, and they immediately proceeded down the river, beyond the whites, and taking a station, waylaid them as they came down. All that had now passed had not taken up much time, for about sunrise the party appeared, two in a boat, *William Stark* and *Stinson*, and *Eastman* on the shore, who next fell into the Indians' hands. They now ordered *John* to hail his friends in the boat, to decoy them to the shore; but, with a boldness characteristic of great minds, he called to them, and instead of requesting them to land, told them he was taken, and ordered them to save themselves by pulling to the opposite shore. They pulled accordingly, and were quickly fired upon by four of the Indians, whose guns were loaded. Like a truly heroic spirit, without regarding the risk he ran, at the moment of the shot *John* knocked up two of the Indians' guns, and repeated the manœuvre when the rest of the party fired a second volley. He then hallooed to his brother in the boat to fly with all his might, for all the guns were discharged. He did so successfully; regained the shore and escaped. Poor *Stinson* was killed, and the boat and oars were pierced with bullets. *John* was sorely beaten and ill used at first, for the liberties he had taken in giving their shots a false direction; but they afterwards used him kindly.

The whites had collected a considerable quantity of furs, of which the Indians possessed themselves, and commenced their retreat. They made a stop at Lower Coos, about the present vicinity of Haverhill, N. H., where they had left two of their party to prepare provisions against their return. After one night's stay here they proceeded to Upper Coos. From this place Captain *Moses* despatched three of his men with *Eastman* to St. Francis, while the rest of the company hunted on a small stream in that neighborhood. *Stark* was meantime closely watched, and every night confined. They allowed him to hunt, and he, having shot one beaver and caught another in a trap, was approbated by a present of their skins.

At length, on the 9 of July, Captain *Moses* returned with his prisoner to St Francis. Here the two captives were compelled to run the gantlet. *Eastman* fared hard in that business; but *Stark*, understanding Indian play better seized a club from an Indian at the head of one of the ranks through which he was to run, and laid it about him with such force, that running the gantlet was wholly on the part of the Indians; for they were glad to escape and leave the ground to him, much to the delight of the old Indians, who were seated at a distance to witness the sport.

Fortunately, *Stark* and *Eastman's* captivity was not a long one. In about six weeks from *Stark's* arrival at St. Francis, there arrived Captain *Stevens*, of No. Four, and Mr. *Wheelwright*, of Boston, in search of some captives, who had been taken from Massachusetts, and not finding any, redeemed *Stark* and *Eastman*, who arrived home, by way of Albany, in August following The same Indians accompanied them to Albany, where they sold the furs they had taken from them, to the amount of £560, old tenor. *Stark* paid for his ransom 103 dollars, and *Eastman* 60 dollars. The names of two others of the Indians who did this mischief, were *Francis Titigaw*, and *Peer*, a young chief, each of whom has been mentioned as chief in the capture; but it is not material.

At the treaty of 1727, which the preceding relation required us to notice, mention was made by the chiefs, at that treaty, of a great many Indians, and among others, of one of considerable note, of whom we have before* said something, if, indeed, he be the same, namely, *Sabatis*. This Indian had previously, though perhaps not long before that treaty, with others, taken many captives in their depredations on the English frontiers. At this time he was living at St. Francis in Canada, and had two captives with him; but their names we cannot learn. He was of a bloody disposition, and the act which terminated his career was by a hand not less bloody, though, perhaps, more necessarily so. We have, on another occasion, and in another work,† related the circumstances of it, and shall therefore pass it over here. He was killed in 1753, and we have before expressed the opinion that he was the father of him brought away a captive from St. Francis by Captain *Rogers* in 1759, and who in 1775 followed the fortunes of Arnold's expedition against Quebec.

As noted an exploit as we have passed over in our history is that which was enacted at Walpole, N. H., in the year 1755. If Philip, the leader of the Indians on that occasion, be the same that we have before given some account of, his patriotism as well as his courage must have undergone an important change; but as we cannot settle that matter to the satisfaction of the critical antiquary without spending more time than we shall get credit for, we will relate the affair at Walpole as we have heard it.

One *John Kilburn* had settled at that place in 1749, and though far beyond any other settlement, and frequently watched, and sometimes annoyed by the Indians, yet no hostile act was attempted upon him until 1755. When it became certain that war would soon begin between England and France, measures were taken by General *Shirley* to warn the settlers along the extensive frontier of New England of the approaching calamity. But the Indians seem to have known or expected it sooner than the English, for before the latter had received word from General *Shirley*, the cunning *Philip*, in the capacity of a spy, had visited every principal settlement, under the pretence of trading for flints and other hunting munitions, all along the Connecticut River; and it was not until two Indians, employed by General *Shirley*, had informed the settlers that 400 or 500 Indians were preparing in Canada to make a descent upon them, that *Philip's* expedition for trade was understood in its real character.

Kilburn lived in a good garrison-house, and on the day *Philip* appeared against it with some 300 Indians, he, with three other men, were at work some distance from it; but keeping a good watch, the Indians were discovered in time to afford them sufficient opportunity to regain the garrison without molestation. The timely discovery was made about mid-day, August 17, and in less than half an hour after, they were surrounded by 197 fierce warriors, flushed with confidence of an easy and speedy victory; the remainder of the Indians forming an ambush of reserve at the mouth of Cold River about half a mile from the garrison.

Meanwhile *Philip* had endeavored to cut off Colonel *Bellows*, who, with 30 men, was milling about a mile east of *Kilburn's;* but in this he was foiled by a masterly manœuvre of the colonel. His men were returning from the mill, each with a bag of meal upon his back, when his dogs by their growling gave timely notice of the neighborhood of an enemy, and the thoughts of an ambush at the same moment passed through his mind: he as soon knew what to do. He ordered his men to throw off their bags, advance to a certain eminence over which their path lay, and about which he doubted not the Indians were prepared for him. The ground contiguous was covered with high sweet fern. Up to these *Bellows* and his men crawled, into the very presence of the enemy. They now, agreeably to the plan proposed at the discovery, sprung upon their feet, and giving a tremendous whoop, after the manner of their adversary, dropped down again the same instant. The Indians at the very moment rose up, forming a thick front across the path in a semicircle. Each of *Bellows's* men had now an Indian in his power; and such was the effect of the first fire of these 30 men, that *Philip* and his whole party precipitately retreated, and the victors, without waiting for a further

* Ante, page 135, 136 of this Book.

† In the Appendix to my edition of *Church's Philip's War*, &c., page 337.

display of tactics, regained their garrison, not having one of their number killed or wounded. Of the loss of the Indians no mention is made.

Finding so warm a reception from Colonel *Bellows*, *Philip*, it would seem, as well as the colonel, had no notion of taking a second hand at the same game, and, as we have said, immediately appeared before *Kilburn's* garrison, where he hoped for better success. *Philip* was an old acquaintance here, and approaching the house as near as he could find a tree for shelter, called out to *Kilburn*, "*Old John, young John, come out here. We give you good quarter.*" *Philip* is represented as of great stature, and proportionate strength and *Kilburn* was not his inferior. He answered the warrior "with a voice of thunder," that flowed over the adjacent hills, "Quarter! you black rascals. begone, or we'll *quarter* you."

Thus stood the affair which was shortly to decide the fate of Walpole between six English, four men and two women, and about 400 Indians, at the commencement of the siege. *Philip* returned to his men, and, after a short pause, the silence was broken by yells and whoops of the whole body of Indians, which appeared, as we have heard the old people express it, "*as though all the devils in hell had broke loose.*" A furious onset was now begun, and in a few minutes the roof of the house was perforated like a sieve. As usual in their attacks on garrisons, they employed stratagems, but when the whole afternoon was spent, they found they had made no impression, but were greatly weakened themselves, and at night drew off, thus ending their inglorious expedition.

Such deeds could a few men, well provided, perform, well knowing it was not numbers that could save them in times of peril, while many others, relying upon their numbers, neglecting their duties, have fallen an easy prey to an enemy not half equal to themselves. *Kilburn* had extra guns in his house, and his wife and daughter cast bullets, and performed every other service in their power. When one of the men's guns became too much heated to be used with safety, a woman exchanged it for another, so that every man was every moment at his place. When their lead began to grow short, blankets were suspended in the roof, to catch the balls of the enemy, with good success; and thus many of the Indians fell by their own bullets! To use their powder without loss of time, they poured it into hats, which were placed close at hand; by such means an incessant fire was kept up, which probably deceived the Indians in regard to their numbers. They found time, before drawing off, to kill all the cattle, burn and destroy all the hay and grain belonging to the settlement; but this was looked upon as nothing, scarcely to be considered towards the price of their deliverance. We do not learn as it was ever known to the English what the loss of the Indians was;* but the garrison lost Mr. *Peak*, who, exposing himself too much before a port-hole, was shot in the hip. The wound would probably have been cured if good surgical aid could have been had; but it proved mortal in five days after the battle. Each of these men, *Kilburn* and *Peak*, had a son with them in the garrison; and such was the force opposed to that army of Indians! JOHN KILBURN lived to be 85 years of age, and died on the 8 April, 1789, and lies buried in the Walpole burying-ground. The son (*John*) attained the same age, and died at his residence, in Shrewsbury, Vt., in 1822.†

Only two days after the battle of Bunker's Hill, there arrived at Cambridge, the head quarters of the Americans, a deputation from the Penobscot Indians, of whom the celebrated ORONO was chief. An order was passed for their entertainment while there, and "for their return home." They came to tender their services to the Americans in the war now begun, which was done by *Orono*, in a speech to a committee of the provincial congress, on the 21 June, 1775. "In behalf of the whole Penobscot tribe," the chief said, if the grievances under which his people labored were removed, they would aid with their whole force to defend the country. Those grievances were briefly stated, and consisted chiefly of trespasses by the whites upon their timber

* *Kilburn*, during the engagement, had a deliberate shot at a large Indian, whom he saw fall, and he believed it was *Philip* himself.

† Chiefly from the *Cols. N. Hist. Soc.* ii. 52—58.

lands, cheating them in trade, &c. The committee returned an affectionate address; and although the groans of the dying, from the late terrible field of battle, were sounding in their ears, they say nothing about engaging the Indians in the war, but assured them that "as soon as they could take breath from their present fight," their complaints should receive attention. Some of the Penobscots did eventually engage in the war, but we have no particulars of them.

We have said before,* upon authority which will generally be received, that *Natanis* and *Sabatis* were the first Indians employed by the Americans in the revolution, and we see no reason yet to form a different opinion, although our attention has been called again to the subject,† and some facts stated for our consideration, which have elicited further investigations and comparisons, of which the following is the result.‡ Of a chief named *Swausen*, or *Swashan*, well known on the borders of New Hampshire in the latter French wars, we have before given some notice;§ at that time, or about the close of those wars, he retired to St. Francis. When the revolution began, he seems to have decided on taking the part of the Americans; and with a few followers marched to Kennebeck, and with some of the Norridgewoks rendezvoused at Cobbossee, now Gardiner, at the mouth of the Cobbosseeconta River. Over the Norridgewoks, or Pequawkets, or some of both, was a chief, named *Paul Higgins*, who, though a white man, had lived so long among Indians, that to all intents he was one of them. He was born at Berwick, but had been taken captive when quite young, and spent most of his days with them. This company set out for Cambridge, the head quarters of General *Washington*, about the beginning of August, 1775, under the direction of one *Reuben Coburn*. There were 20 or 30 of them, "and they were rowed down in canoes to Merrymeeting Bay by their squaws;" here they left them, and proceeded to Cambridge on foot, where they arrived about the 13 August.‖ They tendered their services to the general, who gave them all the encouragement he could, consistently, but evidently advised them to remain neutral.¶ *Swashan* said half of his tribe was ready to join the Americans, and that four or five other tribes stood ready, if wanted, and that the Canadians were in favor of the Americans also; and this was the general opinion, and corresponds with accounts given by intelligent settlers on the frontiers. They say, "We have had positive accounts from many of the Indian tribes, who have been applied to by Governor *Carleton* to distress the settlements; but they say they have no offence from the people, and will not make war on them. The French, too, say it is a war of our own raising, and they will have no part in it."** We hear no more of *Swashan*.

Of Assacambuit, an extended account has been given,†† and we should not again recur to him, but to correct the statement, that "nothing was heard of him from 1708 to the time of his death." We have since found that in 1714, he was at Portsmouth, upon a friendly visit with several other Indians. On the 10 May of that year, as the Indians were about to leave the place, "the council of N. H. ordered their treasurer to furnish him and his companions with necessary provisions and liquors to carry them to their several habitations."

---

* Page 136, ante, of this Book.

† In a polite and obliging manner, by Rev. Wm. S. Bartlett, of Little Falls, N. Y.

‡ As early as May 19th, 1775, the provincial congress of Massachusetts "*Voted*, That Captain John Lane have enlisting papers delivered to him, for raising a company of Indians at the eastward."

§ Cols. N. H. Soc iii. 76 7.

‖ MS. communication of Rev. W. S. Bartlett.

¶ *Botta*, i. 228.

** *Almon's* Remembrancer, i. 147—149

†† Book III. p. 139—141.

BIOGRAPHY AND HISTORY

OF THE

INDIANS OF NORTH AMERICA

BOOK IV.

BOOK IV.

BIOGRAPHY AND HISTORY OF THE SOUTHERN INDIANS.

"I will go to my tent, and lie down in despair;
I will paint me with black, and will sever my hair;
I will sit on the shore where the hurricane blows,
And reveal to the God of the tempest my woes;
I will weep for a season, on bitterness fed,
For my kindred are gone to the mounds of the dead;
But they died not by hunger, or wasting decay:
The steel of the white man hath swept them away."

ANONYMOUS.

CHAPTER I.

Preliminary observations respecting the country of the southern Indians—WINGINA, *the first Virginia chief known to the English—Destroys the first colony settled there*—MENATONON—SKIKO—ENSENORE—*Second colony abandons the country—Tobacco first carried to England by them—Curious account of prejudices against it*—GRANGANEMEO—*His kindnesses—His family—His death*—POWHATAN—*Boundaries of his country—Surprises the Payankatanks—Captain Smith fights his people—Opekankanough takes Smith prisoner—The particulars of that affair—He marches him about the country—Takes him, at length, to Powhatan, who condemns him to be put to death—Smith's life saved at the intercession of Pocahontas—Insolence of Powhatan increased by Newport's folly—Smith brings him to terms—A crown sent over to him from England—Is crowned emperor—Speech—Uses every stratagem to kill Smith—Is baffled in every attempt—Smith visits him—Speeches—Pocahontas again saves Smith and his comrades from being murdered by her father*—TOMOCOMO.

THE difficulty of rightly partitioning between the southern nations and the Iroquois, or Five Nations, can easily be seen by all such as have but very partially taken a survey of them, and considered their wandering habits. Therefore, should we, in this book, not always assign a sachem to his original family or nation, we can only plead in excuse, that we have gone according to our best information. But we have endeavored to draw a kind of natural boundary between the above-mentioned nations, distinguishing those people beyond the Chesapeake and some of its tributaries, as the southern Indians, and those between that boundary and the Hudson, by the name Iroquois. To their respective territories inland, we shall not, nor is it necessary to, fix bounds, in our present business. We are aware that some writers suppose that all the Indians, from the Mississippi to the vicinity of the Hudson, and even to the Connecticut, were originally of the same stock. If this were the case, the period is so remote when they spread themselves over the country, that these great natural divisions had long since caused quite a difference in the inhabitants which they separated; and hence the propriety of noticing them according to our plan.

It is said that the territory from the sea-coast to the River Alleghany, and from the most southern waters of James River up to Patuxent, in the state of Maryland, was inhabited by three different nations, and that the language of each differed essentially from the others. The English called these nations by the names *Powhatans*, *Manahoacs*, and *Monacans;* these were the Tuscaroras. The Powhatans were the most powerful, and consisted of several tribes, or communities, who possessed the country from the sea-coast to the falls of the rivers.*

To give a tolerable catalogue of the names of the various nations of Virginia, the Carolinas, and thence to the Mississippi, would far exceed our plan. We shall, therefore, pass to notice the chiefs of such of those nations as are distinguished in history, pointing out, by the way, their localities, and whatever shall appear necessary in way of elucidation, as we pass, and as we have done in the preceding books.

WINGINA was first known to the English voyagers *Amidas* and *Barlow*, who landed in Virginia in the summer of 1584, upon an island called, by the Indians, *Wokokon*. They saw none of the natives until the third day, when three were observed in a canoe. One of them got on shore, and the English went to him. He showed no signs of fear, "but spoke much to them," then went boldly on board the vessels. After they had given him a shirt, hat, wine, and some meat, "he went away, and in half an hour he had loaded his canoe with fish," which he immediately brought, and gave to the English.

Wingina, at this time, was confined to his cabin from wounds he had lately received in battle, probably in his war with *Piamacum*, a desperate and bloody chief.

Upon the death of *Granganemeo*, in 1585, *Wingina* changed his name to *Pemissapan*. He never had much faith in the good intentions of the English, and to him was mainly attributed the breaking up of the first colony which settled in Virginia

It was upon the return to England of the Captains *Amidas* and *Barlow*, from the country of *Wingina*, that Queen *Elizabeth*, from the wonderful accounts of that fruitful and delightful place, named it, out of respect to herself, *Virginia;* she being called the virgin queen, from her living unmarried. But, with more honor to her, some have said, "Because it still seemed to retain the virgin purity and plenty of the first creation, and the people their primitive innocency of life and manners."† *Waller* referred to this country when he wrote this:—

"So sweet the air, so moderate the clime,
None sickly lives, or dies before his time.
Heav'n sure has kept this spot of earth uncurst,
To show how all things were created first."

Sir *Richard Greenvil*, stimulated by the love of gain, next intruded himself upon the shores of *Wingina*. It was he who committed the first outrage upon the natives, which occasioned the breaking up of the colony which he left behind him. He made but one short excursion into the country, during which, by foolishly exposing his commodities, some native took from him a silver cup, to *revenge* the loss of which, a town was burned. He left 108 men, who seated themselves upon the island of Roanoke. *Ralph Lane*, a military character of note, was governor, and Captain *Philip Amidas*, lieutenant-governor of this colony. They made various excursions about the country, in hopes of discovering mines of precious metals; in which they were a long time duped by the Indians, for their ill conduct towards them, in compelling them to pilot them about. *Wingina* bore, as well as he could, the provocations of the intruders, until the death of the old chief *Ensenore*, his father. Under pretence of honoring his funeral, he assembled 1800 of his people, with the intention, as the English say, of destroying them. They, therefore, upon the information of *Skiko*, son of the chief MENATONON,‡ fell upon them, and, after killing five or six, the rest made their escape into the woods. This

* From a communication of Secretary *Thompson* to Mr. *Jefferson*, and appended to the Notes on Virginia, ed. of 1801.

† *Stith*, 11.

‡ *Smith* calls him the "lame king of Moratos."

was done upon the island where *Wingina* lived, and the English first seized upon the boats of his visitants, to prevent their escape from the island, with the intention, no doubt, of murdering them all. Not long after, "*Wingina* was entrapped by the English, and slain, with eight of his chief men."

MENATONON was king of the Chawonocks, and OKISKO of the Weopomeokes, "a powerful nation, possessing all that country from Albemarle Sound and Chowan River, quite to the Chesapeakes and our bay."* At this time, *Menatonon* was lame, and is mentioned as the most sensible and understanding Indian with whom the English were at first acquainted. It was he that made *Lane* and his followers believe in the existence of the mine already mentioned. "So eager were they," says Mr. *Stith*, "and resolutely bent upon this golden discovery, that they could not be persuaded to return, as long as they had one pint of corn a man left, and two mastiff dogs, which, being boiled with sassafras leaves, might afford them some sustenance in their way back." After great sufferings, they arrived upon the coast again.

The reason why *Menatonon* deceived the English, was because they made him a prisoner for the purpose of assisting them in making discoveries. After he was set at liberty, he was very kind to them. Two years after, when Governor *White* was in the country, they mention his wife and child as belonging to Croatan, but nothing of him.

White and his company landed at Roanoke, 22 July, 1587, and sent 20 men to Croatan, on Point Lookout, with a friendly native called MANTEO, to see if any intelligence could be had of a former colony of 50 men left there by Sir *Richard Greenvil*. They learned, from some natives whom they met, that the people of Dassamonpeak, on what is now Alligator River, had attacked them, killed one, and driven the others away, but whither they had gone none could tell. One of their present company, a principal man of their government, had also been killed by the same Indians. This tribe and several others had agreed to come to Roanoke, and submit themselves to the English; but not coming according to appointment, gave the English an opportunity to take revenge for former injuries. Therefore, Captain *Stafford* and 24 men, with *Manteo* as a guide, set out upon that business. On coming to their village, "where seeing them sit by the fire, we assaulted them. The miserable soules amazed, fled into the reeds, where one was shot through, and we thought to have been fully revenged, but we were deceived, for they were our friends come from Croatan to gather their corn!" "Being thus disappointed of our purpose, we gathered the fruit we found ripe, left the rest unspoiled, and took *Menatonon*, his wife with her child, and the rest with us to Roanoak."† But to return to *Wingina*.

While the English were upon the errand we have been speaking of, *Wingina* pretended to be their friend, but deceived them on every opportunity, by giving notice to his countrymen of their course and purpose, and urging them to cut them off. He thought, at one time, that the English were destroyed, and thereupon scoffed and mocked at such a God as theirs, who would suffer it. This caused his father, *Ensenore*, to join their enemies, but on their return he was their friend again. He, and many of his people, now believed, say the voyagers, that "we could do them more hurt being dead, than liuing, and that, being an hundred myles from them, shot, and struck them sick to death, and that when we die it is but for a time, then we return again." Many of the chiefs now came and submitted themselves to the English, and, among others, *Ensenore* was persuaded again to become their friend, who, when they were in great straits for provisions, came and planted their fields, and made wears in the streams to catch fish, which were of infinite benefit to them. This was in the spring of 1586, and, says *Lane*, "we not having one corn till the next harvest to sustain us." What added greatly to their distresses, was the death of their excellent friend *Ensenore*, who died 20th of April following. The Indians began anew their conspiracies, and the colony availed themselves of the first opportunity of returning to England,

* *Stith's* Virginia, 14. By "our bay" is meant *James River Bay*

† *Smith's* Hist. Virginia.

which was in the fleet of Sir *Francis Drake*, which touched there in its way from an expedition against the Spaniards in the West Indies.*

The conduct of *Lane* and his company in this fruitless attempt to establish themselves in Virginia, was, in the highest degree, reprehensible. They put to death some of the natives on the most frivolous charges, and no wonder they were driven out of the country, as they ought to have been.† While they were there, they became acquainted with the use of *tobacco*, and, taking it to England, its introduction into general use soon rendered it a great article of commerce. And here it will not be improper to notice how many different persons have had the credit, or, perhaps, I should say *discredit*, of introducing this "Indian weed" into England; as, Sir *Francis Drake*, Sir *Walter Ralegh*, *Ralph Lane*, and some others. Now, as some writer observes, the reader may father it upon whom he pleases, as it is evident Sir *Francis Drake* took *Ralph Lane* and tobacco both together into England; and no one will dispute the agency of the gallant knight, Sir *Walter Ralegh*, for he sent out *Lane* in his employ. Mr. *John Josselyn*, in his "Two Voyages to N. England," has this passage: "Others will have tobacco to be first brought into England from Peru, by Sir *Francis Drake's* mariners."

There were many who affected a violent disgust towards the use of tobacco; the most conspicuous was King *James*, whose mind seems to have been just weak enough to fight windmills. He even wrote a book denouncing its use in the severest terms he could command. It grew spontaneously in Wingandacoa, (Virginia,) and the natives called it *Uppowoc*. It is generally supposed to be called *tobacco* from the island *Tobago*, but this derivation is much questioned.‡

Granganemeo was a chief very favorably spoken of. As soon as the arrival of the English was made known to him, he visited them with about 40 of his men, who were very civil, and of a remarkably robust and fine appearance. When they had left their boat, and came upon the shore near the ship, *Granganemeo* spread a mat and sat down upon it. The English went to him armed, but he discovered no fear, and invited them to sit down; after which he performed some tokens of friendship; then making a speech to them, they presented him with some toys. None but four of his people spoke a word, or sat down, but maintained the most perfect silence. On being shown a pewter dish, he was much pleased with it, and purchased it with 20 deer-skins, which were worth, in England, one hundred shillings sterling!! The dish he used as an ornament, making a hole through it, and wearing it about his neck. While here, the English entertained him, with his wife and children, on board their ship. His wife had in her ears bracelets of pearl, which reached to her middle. Shortly after, many of the people came out of the country to trade, "but when *Granganemeo* was present, none durst trade but himself, and them that wore red copper on their heads as he did." He was remarkably exact in keeping his promise, "for oft we trusted him, and he would come within his day to keep his word." And these voyagers further report, that "commonly he sent them every day a brace of bucks, conies, hares, and fish, and sometimes melons, walnuts, cucumbers, pease, and divers roots."

In their wanderings, Captain *Amidas* and seven others visited the island of Roanoake, where they found the family of *Granganemeo* living in great comfort and plenty, in a little town of nine houses. The chief was not at home, "but his wife entertained them with wonderful courtesy and kindness. She made some of her people draw their boat up, to prevent its being injured by the beating of the surge; some she ordered to bring them ashore on their backs, and others to carry their oars to the house, for fear of being stole. When they came into the house, she took off their cloathes and stockings, and washed them, as likewise their feet in warm water. When their dinner was ready, they were conducted into an inner room, (for there were five in

* Relation of *Lane*, printed in *Smith's* Virginia.
† *Herriot's* Observations, (one of *Lane's* company,) printed in *Smith*.
‡ *Stith's* Hist. Virginia, 19.—See Book ii. Chap. ii.

the house, divided by mats,) where they found hominy,* boiled venison, and roasted fish; and, as a desert, melons, boiled roots, and fruits of various sorts. While they were at meat, two or three of her men came in with their bows and arrows, which made the English take to their arms. But she, perceiving their distrust, ordered their bows and arrows to be broken, and themselves to be beaten out of the gate. In the evening, the English returned to their boat; and, putting a little off from shore, lay at anchor; at which she was much concerned, and brought their supper, half boiled, pots and all to the shore; and, seeing their jealousy, she ordered several men, and 30 women, to sit all night upon the shore, as a guard; and sent five mats to cover them from the weather."† Well hath the poet demanded, "Call ye them savage?" If the wife of *Granganemeo* was savage, in the common acceptation of the term, where shall we look for civilization?

Sir *R. Greenvil*, having arrived on the coast in 1585, anchored off the island Wokokon, 26 May, and, by means of *Manteo*, had some intercourse with the inhabitants. At Hatteras, where they staid a short time, soon after, *Granganemeo*, with *Manteo*, went on board their ships. This was the last visit he made to the English, for he died very soon after.

This must close our account of the excellent family of *Granganemeo*, and would that the *account* of the English would balance as well,—but they exhibit their own,—and one item more from it, and we close the comparison. For a small kettle they took 50 skins, worth in England £12 10s. sterling.‡ We have now arrived at the most interesting article in Virginia history. POWHATAN was, of all the chiefs of his age, the most famous in the regions of Virginia. The English supposed, at first, that his was the name of the country; a common error, as we have seen in several cases in the previous books of our biography, but, in this case, unlike the others, the error prevailed, and a part of his people, ever after the settlement of the English, were called the *Powhatans*. A great river, since called the *James*, and a bay received his name also.§ He had three brothers, *Opitchepan*, *Opekankanough*, and *Catatanugh*, and two sisters. His principal residence was at a place called *Werowocomoco*, when the English came into the country; which was upon the north side of what is now York River, in the county of Gloucester, nearly opposite the mouth of Queen's Creek, and about 25 miles below the fork of the river.|| He lived here until the English began to intrude themselves into his vicinity, when he took up his residence at Orakakes.

Powhatan was not his Indian name, or rather original name; that was *Wahunsonacock*. He is described as tall and well-proportioned—bearing an aspect of sadness—exceedingly vigorous, and possessing a body capable of sustaining great hardships. He was, in 1607, about 60 years of age, and his hair was considerably gray, which gave him a majestic appearance. At his residence, he had a kind of wooden form to sit upon, and his ornamental robe was of raccoon skins, and his head-dress was composed of many feathers wrought into a kind of crown. He swayed many nations upon the great rivers and bays, the chief of whom he had conquered. He originally claimed only the places called Powhatan, (since named Haddihaddocks,) Arrohattock, (now Appomattox,) Youghtanund, Pamunky, Mattapony, Werowocomoco, and Kiskiak; at which time, his chief seat was at Powhatan, near the falls of James River. But when he had extended his conquests a great way north, he removed to Werowocomoco, as a more commodious situation.

At the termination of his warlike career, the country upon James River from its mouth to the falls, and all its branches, was the boundary of his country, southerly—and so across the country, "nearly as high as the falls of all the great rivers, over Potowmack, even to Patuxent, in Maryland," and

---

* "A food made of Indian corn, or maize, beaten and carefully husked, something like furmety in England; and is an excellent dish various ways."

† *Stith's* Hist. Virginia, 10, 11. ‡ *Smith's* Hist. Virginia.

§ These, according to *Heckewelder*, Philos. Trans. 31, should have been called *Powhathan* "which would signify the river of progeny, fruitfulness, the fruitful river."

|| About two miles below where Richmond now stands. The farm of a gentleman of the name of *Mayo* included the site of a part of his town, in 1813.—*Campbell's* Virginia

some of the nations on the north shore of the Chesapeake. His dominions, according to his law of succession, did not fall to his children, but to his brothers, and then to his sisters, (the oldest first,) thence to the heirs of the oldest; but never to the heirs of the males.

He usually kept a guard of 40 or 50 of the most resolute and well-formed men about him, especially when he slept; but, after the English came into his country, he increased them to about 200. He had as many, and such women as he pleased; and, when he slept, one sat at his head and another at his feet. When he was tired of any of his wives, he bestowed them upon such of his men as most pleased him. Like the New England chiefs, he had many places where he passed certain seasons of the year; at some of which he had very spacious wigwams, 30 or 40 yards in extent, where he had victuals provided against his coming.

In 1608, he surprised the people of Payankatank, who were his neighbors and subjects. Captain *Smith*, in the account, "*writ with his own hand*," says, "the occasion was to vs vnknowne, but the manner was thus." He sent several of his men to lodge with them the night on which he meant to fall upon them; then, secretly surrounding them in their wigwams, commenced a horrid slaughter. They killed 24 men, took off their scalps, and, with the women and children prisoners, returned to the sachem's village. The scalps they exhibited upon a line between two trees, as a trophy, and the *werowance* (their name of a chief) and his wife *Powhatan* made his servants.

Up to the year 1607, every attempt to settle a colony in Virginia had failed; and, at this time, would have failed also, but for the unexampled perseverance of one man. I need but pronounce the name of Captain John Smith. The colony with which he came did not arrive until the planting season was over; and, in a short time, they found themselves in a suffering condition, from want of suitable provisions. *Smith*, therefore, undertook to gain a supply by trafficking with the Indians back in the country, who, being acquainted with his situation, insulted him and his men wherever they came; offering him but a handful of corn, or a piece of bread, for a gun or a sword. "But seeing by trade and courtesie there was nothing to be had, he made bold to try such conclusions as necessitie inforced, though contrary to his commission." So he fired upon them, and drove them into the woods. He then marched to their village. There they found corn in abundance, which, after some manœuvring, he succeeded in trading for, and returned with a supply to Jamestown.

Smith, soon after, proceeded to discover the source of the Chikahamania. When he had passed up as far as it was navigable for his barge, he left it in a wide place, at a safe distance from the shore, and ordered his men not to go on shore on any condition. Taking two of his own men and two Indians, he proceeded to complete his discovery. As soon as he was gone, his men went on shore; one was killed, and the rest hardly escaped. *Smith* was now 20 miles into the wilderness. *Opekankanough*, with 300 warriors, having learned, from the men they had just taken, which way he was gone, followed after him, and came upon the two Englishmen belonging to his company, and killed them both while asleep, he being absent to shoot some fowls for provisions; they then continued their pursuit after him. He was not far from his canoe, and endeavored to retreat to it, but, being hard pressed, made a shield of one of his Indians, and, in this manner, fought upon the retreat, until he had killed three, and wounded divers others. Being obliged to give all his attention to his pursuers, he accidentally fell into a creek, where the mud was so deep that he could not extricate himself. Even now, none dared to lay hands upon him, and those whom their own numbers forced nearest to him, were observed to tremble with fear. The Indian he had bound to his arm with his garters, doubtless saved him from being killed by their arrows, from which, owing to his Indian shield, he received but very little hurt, except a wound in his thigh, though his clothes were shot full of them.

When he could stand no longer in the mire, without perishing with cold, he threw away his arms, and suffered them to come and take him. After pulling him out of the mire, they took him to the place where his men had just been killed, where there was a fire. They now showed him kindness, rubbing his benumbed limbs, and warming him by the fire. He asked for their chief, and *Opekankanough* appeared, to whom he gave a small compass. This amused them exceedingly. "Much they marvelled at the playing of the fly and needle, which they could see so plainly, and yet not touch it, because of the glass that covered them. But when he demonstrated, by that globe-like iewell, the roundnesse of the earth, and skies, the spheare of the sunne, and moone, and starres, and how the sunne did chase the night round about the world, continually—the greatnesse of the land and sea, the diversity of the nations, varietie of complexions, and how we were to them antipodes, and many other such like matters, they all stood as amazed with admiration!" Yet, notwithstanding he had such success in explaining to them his knowledge of geography and astronomy, (how much of it they understood we will not undertake to say,) within an hour after, they tied him to a tree, and a multitude of them seemed prepared to shoot him. But when their bows were bent, *Opekankanough* held up his compass, and they all laid down their weapons. They now led him to Orapakas, or Orakakes, a temporary seat of *Powhatan*, on the north side of Chikahominy swamp, in what is now Gloucester county on York river.* Here they feasted him, and treated him well.

When they marched him, they drew themselves up in a row, with their chief in the midst, before whom the guns and swords they had taken from the English were borne. *Smith* came next, led by three great men hold of each arm, and on each side six more, with their arrows notched, and ready, if he should attempt to escape. At the town, they danced and sung about him, and then put him into a large house, or wigwam. Here they kept him so well, that he thought they were fatting him to kill and eat. They took him to a sick man to cure him; but he told them he could not, unless they would let him go to Jamestown, and get something with which he could do it. This they would not consent to.

The taking of Jamestown was now resolved upon, and they made great preparations for it. To this end, they endeavored to get *Smith's* assistance, by making large promises of land and women; but he told them it could not be done, and described to them the great difficulty of the undertaking in such a manner that they were greatly terrified. With the idea of procuring something curious, *Smith* prevailed upon some of them to go to Jamestown; which journey they performed in the most severe frosty and snowy weather. By this means, he gave the people there to understand what his situation was, and what was intended against them, by sending a leaf from his pocket-book, with a few words written upon it. He wrote, also, for a few articles to be sent, which were duly brought by the messengers. Nothing had caused such astonishment as their bringing the very articles *Smith* had promised them. That he could talk to his friends, at so great a distance, was utterly incomprehensible to them.

Being obliged to give up the idea of destroying Jamestown, they amused themselves by taking their captive from place to place, in great pomp and triumph, and showing him to the different nations of the dominions of *Powhatan*. They took him to Youghtannund, since called *Pamunkey River*, the country over which *Opekankanough* was chief, whose principal residence was where the town of Pamunkey since was; thence to the Mattaponies, Piankatanks, the Nautaughtacunds, on Rappahanock, the Nominies, on the Patowmack River; thence, in a circuitous course, through several other nations, back again to the residence of *Opekankanough*. Here they practised conjurations upon him for three successive days; to ascertain, as they said, whether he intended them good or evil. This proves they viewed him as a kind of god. A bag of gunpowder having fallen into their hands they preserved it with great care, thinking it to be a grain, intending, in the spring, to plant it, as they did corn. He was here again feasted, and none could eat until he had done.

Being now satisfied, having gone through all the manœuvres and pranks with him they could think of, they proceeded to *Powhatan*. "Here more than 200 of those grim courtiers stood wondering at him, as he had been a monster

* *Bancroft's* Hist. U. States, i. 146.

till *Powhatan* and his trayne had put themselves in their greatest braveries. He was seated before a fire, upon a seat like a bedstead, having on a robe of raccoon skins, "and all the tayles hanging by." On each side of him sat a young woman; and upon each side of the house two rows of men, and with as many women behind them. These last had their heads and shoulders painted red—some of whose heads were adorned with white down; and about their necks white beads. On *Smith's* being brought into the presence of *Powhatan*, all present joined in a great shout. "The queen of Apamatuck was appointed to bring him water to wash his hands, and another brought him a bunch of feathers, instead of a towel, to dry them." Then, having feasted him again, "after their best barbarous manner they could, a long consultation was held, but the conclusion was, two great stones were brought before *Powhatan* —then as many as could lay hands on him, dragged him to them and thereon laid his head, and being ready, with their clubs, to beat out his brains, *Pocahontas*, the king's dearest daughter, when no entreaty could prevail, got his head in her armes, and laid her own upon his, to save him from death."

Powhatan was unable to resist the extraordinary solicitations and sympathetic entreaties of his kind-hearted little daughter, and thus was saved the life of Captain *Smith;* a character, who, without this astonishing deliverance, was sufficiently renowned for escapes and adventures.

The old sachem, having set the sentence of death aside, made up his mind to employ *Smith* as an artisan; to make, for himself, robes, shoes, bows, arrows, and pots; and, for *Pocahontas*, bells, beads, and copper trinkets. *Powhatan's* son, named *Nantaquaus*, was very friendly to *Smith*, and rendered him many important services, as well after as during his captivity.

"Two days after, *Powhatan*, having disguised himself in the most fearfullest manner he could, caused Captain *Smith* to be brought forth to a great house in the woods, and there, upon a mat by the fire, to be left alone. Not long after, from behinde a mat that divided the house, was made the most dolefullest noyse he ever heard; then *Powhatan*, more like a Devill than a man, with some 200 more, as black as himselfe, came unto him, and told him, now they were friends; and presently he should go to Jamestowne, to send him two great gunnes, and a gryndestone, for which he would give him the country of Capahowosick [Capahowsick], and forever esteem him his sonne, *Nantuquond*. So to Jamestowne, with 12 guides, *Powhatan* sent him. That night they quartered in the woods, he still expecting, (as he had done all this long time of his imprisonment,) every hour to be put to one death or another." Early the next morning, they came to the fort at Jamestown. Here he treated his guides with the greatest attention and kindness, and offered *Rawhunt*, in a jesting manner, and for the sake of a little sport, a huge mill-stone, and two demi-culverins, or nine pound cannons, to take to *Powhatan*, his master; thus *fulfilling* his engagement to send him a grindstone and two guns. This *Rawhunt* was a sachem under *Powhatan*, and one of his most faithful captains, and who, it seems, accompanied *Smith* in his return out of captivity.

"They found them somewhat too heavie, but when they did see him discharge them, being loaded with stones, among the boughs of a great tree loaded with isickles, the yce and branches came so tumbling down, that the poore salvages ran away half dead with fear. But, at last, we regained some conference with them, and gave them such toyes, and sent to *Powhatan*, his women, and children, such presents, and gave them in generall full content." *

Powhatan was now completely in the English interest, and almost every other day sent his daughter, *Pocahontas*, with victuals, to Jamestown, of which they were greatly in need. *Smith* had told *Powhatan* that a great chief, which was Captain *Newport*, would arrive from England about that time, which coming to pass as he had said, greatly increased his admiration of the wisdom of the English, and he was ready to do as they desired in every thing, and, but for the vanity and ostentation of *Newport*, matters would have gone on well, and trade flourished greatly to their advantage. But he lavished so many presents upon *Powhatan*, that he was in no way inclined to trade, and soon

* This is Captain *Smith's* own account, which I shall follow minutely; adding occasionally from *Stith*, to illustrate the geography of the country.

began to show his haughtiness, by demanding five times the value of an article, or his contempt for what was offered.

By *Newport's* imprudence and folly, what had cost *Smith* so much toil and pains to achieve, was blown away by a single breath of vanity. Nevertheless, his great mind, continually exercised in difficult matters, brought the subtle chief again to his own terms. Himself, with *Newport*, and about 20 others, went to *Powhatan's* residence to trade with him. "Wherein *Powhatan* carried himself so proudly, yet discreetly, (in his salvage manner,) as made us all to admire his natural gifts." He pretended that it was far beneath *his* dignity to *trade* as his men did. Thus his craft to obtain from *Newport* his goods for whatever he pleased to give in return. *Smith* saw through *Powhatan's* craft, and told *Newport* how it would turn out, but being determined to show himself as dignified as the Indian chief, repented of his folly, like too many others, when it was too late. *Smith* was the interpreter in the business, and *Newport* the chief. *Powhatan* made a speech to him, when they were about to enter upon trading. He said, "Captain *Newport*, it is not agreeable to my greatness, in this peddling manner, to trade for trifles; and I esteem you also a great werowance. Therefore, lay me down all your commodities together; what I like I will take, and in recompense give you what I think fitting their value." Accordingly, *Newport* gave him all his goods, and received in return only about three bushels of corn; whereas they expected to have obtained twenty hogsheads. This transaction created some hard thoughts between *Smith* and *Newport*.

If it add to raise *Powhatan* in our admiration, it can detract nothing from the character of *Smith*, to say, that he was as wily as the great Indian chief. For, with a few blue beads, which he pretended that he had shown him only by accident, and which he would hardly part with, as he pretended, because they were of great price, and worn only by great kings, he completely got his end, at this time, answered. Tantalization had the desired effect, and *Powhatan* was so infatuated with the lure, that he was almost beside himself, and was ready to give all he had to possess them. "So that, ere we departed," says my relation, "for a pound or two of blew beades, he brought over my king for 2 or 300 bushells of corne."

An English boy was left with *Powhatan*, by Captain *Newport*, to learn the language, manners, customs and geography of his country; and, in return, *Powhatan* gave him *Namontack*, one of his servants, of a shrewd and subtle capacity, whom he afterwards carried to England. *Powhatan* became offended with Captain *Smith*, when *Newport* left the country, in 1608; at whose departure he sent him 20 turkeys, and demanded, in return, 20 swords, which were granted. Shortly after, he sent the same number to *Smith*, expecting the like return; but, being disappointed, ordered his men to seize the English wherever they could find them. This caused difficulty—many of the English being robbed of their swords, in the vicinity of their forts. They continued their depredations until *Smith* surprised a number of them, from whom he learned that *Powhatan* was endeavoring to get all the arms in his power, to be able to massacre the English. When he found that his plot was discovered, he sent *Pocahontas*, with presents, to excuse himself, and pretended that the mischief was done by some of his ungovernable chiefs. He directed her to endeavor to effect the release of his men that were prisoners, which *Smith* consented to, wholly, as he pretended, on her account; and thus peace was restored, which had been continually interrupted for a considerable time before.

On the 10th of September, 1608, *Smith* was elected governor of Virginia. *Newport*, going often to England, had a large share in directing the affairs of the colony, from his interest with the proprietors. He arrived about this time, and, among other baubles brought over a crown for *Powhatan*, with directions for his coronation; which had the ill effect to make him value himself more than ever. *Newport* was instructed to discover the country of the Monacans, a nation with whom *Powhatan* was at war, and whom they would assist him against, if he would aid in the business. Captain *Smith* was sent to him to invite him to Jamestown to receive presents, and to trade for corn. On arriving at Werowocomoco, and delivering his message to the old chief, he replied, "If your king have sent me presents, I also am a king, and this is my land.

Eight days I will stay to receive them. Your father [meaning *Newport*] is to come to me, not I to him, nor yet to your fort—neither will I bite at such a bate. As for the Monacans, I can revenge my own injuries; and as for *Atquanachuck*, where you say your brother was slain, it is a contrary way from those parts you suppose it; but, for any salt water beyond the mountains, the relations you have had from my people are false." Some of the Indians had made the English believe that the South Sea, now called the Pacific Ocean, was but a short distance back. To show *Smith* the absurdity of the story, he drew a map of the country, upon the ground. *Smith* returned as wise as he went.

A house was built for *Powhatan*, about this time, by some Germans, who came over with *Newport*. These men, thinking that the English could not subsist in the country, wantonly betrayed all the secrets of their condition to *Powhatan*, which was again the source of much trouble. They even urged him to put all the English to death, agreeing to live with him, and assist him in the execution of the horrible project. *Powhatan* was pleased at the proposition, and thought, by their assistance, to effect what he had formerly hoped to do by engaging *Smith* in such an enterprise. Their first object was to kill Captain *Smith;* by which act, the chief obstacle to success would be removed; and, accordingly, they took every means in their power to effect it.

In the first place, he invited him to come and trade for corn, hoping an opportunity, in that business, would offer. That his design might not be mistrusted, *Powhatan* promised to load his ship with corn, if he would bring him a grindstone, 50 swords, some muskets, a cock and a hen, and a quantity of copper and beads. *Smith* went accordingly, but guarded, as though sure of meeting an enemy.

In their way, the English stopped at Warrasqueake, and were informed, by the sachem of that place, of *Powhatan's* intentions. That sachem kindly entertained them, and, when they departed, furnished them with guides. On account of extreme bad weather, they were obliged to spend near a week at Kicquotan. This obliged them to keep their Christmas among the Indians, and, according to our authorities, a merry Christmas it was; having been "never more merry in their lives, lodged by better fires, or fed with greater plenty of good bread, oysters, fish, flesh, and wild fowl."

Having arrived at Werowocomoco, after much hardship, they sent to *Powhatan* for provisions, being in great want, not having taken but three or four days' supply along with them. The old chief sent them immediately a supply of bread, turkeys, and venison, and soon after made a feast for them, according to custom.

Meanwhile, *Powhatan* pretended he had not sent for the English; telling them he had no corn, "and his people much less," * and, therefore, intimated that he wished they would go off again. But *Smith* produced the messenger that he had sent, and so confronted him; *Powhatan* then laughed heartily, and thus it passed for a joke. He then asked for their commodities, "but he liked nothing, except guns and swords, and valued a basket of corn higher than a basket of copper; saying, he could rate his corn, but not the copper." Captain *Smith* then made a speech to him, in which he endeavored to work upon his feelings and sense of honor; said he had sent his men to build him a house while his own was neglected; that, because of his promising to supply him with corn, he had neglected to supply himself with provisions when he might have done it. Finally, *Smith* reproached him of divers negligences, deceptions, and prevarications; but the main cause of *Powhatan's* refusing to trade seems to have been because the English did not bring the articles he most wanted.

When *Smith* had done, *Powhatan* answered him as follows:—"We have but little corn, but what we can spare shall be brought two days hence. As to your coming here, I have some doubt about the reason of it. I am told, by my men, that you came, not to trade, but to invade my people, and to possess my country. This makes me less ready to relieve you, and frightens my

* The reader may wonder how this could be, but it is so in the old history, by *Stith*, 86.

people from bringing in their corn. And, therefore, to relieve them of their fear, leave your arms aboard your boats, since they are needless here, where we are all friends, and forever Powhatans."

In these, and other speeches of like amount, they spent the first day. "But whilst they expected the coming in of the country, they wrangled *Powhatan* out of 80 bushels of corn, for a copper kettle; which the president seeing him much affect, [value,] he told him it was of much greater value; yet, in regard of his scarcity, he would accept that quantity at present; provided he should have as much more the next year, or the Manakin country," were that condition not complied with.

This transaction will equal any thing of the kind in the history of New England, but we will leave the reader to make his own comment.

At the same time, *Powhatan* made another speech, in which were some very singular passages, as reported by *Smith*. One was, that he had seen the death of all his people three times; and that none of those three generations was then living, except himself. This was evidently only to make the English think him something more than human. The old chief then went on and said,

"I am now grown old, and must soon die; and the succession must descend, in order, to my brothers, *Opitchapan*, *Opekankanough*, and *Catataugh*,* and then to my two sisters, and their two daughters. I wish their experience was equal to mine; and that your love to us might not be less than ours to you. Why should you take by force that from us which you can have by love? Why should you destroy us, who have provided you with food? What can you get by war? We can hide our provisions, and fly into the woods; and then you must consequently famish by wronging your friends. What is the cause of your jealousy? You see us unarmed, and willing to supply your wants, if you will come in a friendly manner, and not with swords and guns, as to invade an enemy. I am not so simple, as not to know it is better to eat good meat, lie well, and sleep quietly with my women and children; to laugh and be merry with the English; and, being their friend, to have copper, hatchets, and whatever else I want, than to fly from all, to lie cold in the woods, feed upon acorns, roots, and such trash, and to be so hunted, that I cannot rest, eat, or sleep. In such circumstances, my men must watch, and if a twig should but break, all would cry out, '*Here comes Capt. Smith;*' and so, in this miserable manner, to end my miserable life; and, Capt. *Smith*, this *might* be soon your fate too, through your rashness and unadvisedness. I, therefore, exhort you to peaceable councils; and, above all, I insist that the guns and swords, the cause of all our jealousy and uneasiness, be removed and sent away."

Smith interpreted this speech to mean directly contrary to what it expressed, and it rather confirmed, than lessened, his former suspicions. He, however, made a speech to *Powhatan*, in his turn, in which he endeavored to convince him that the English intended him no hurt; urging, that, if they had, how easily they might have effected it long before; and that, as to their perishing with want, he would have him to understand that the English had ways to supply themselves unknown to the Indians; that as to his sending away the arms, there was no reason in that, since the Indians were always allowed to bring theirs to Jamestown and to keep them in their hands. Seeing *Smith's* inflexibility, and despairing of accomplishing his intended massacre, he spoke again to *Smith* as follows:—

"Capt. *Smith*, I never use any werowance so kindly as yourself; yet from you I receive the least kindness of any. Capt. *Newport* gave me swords, copper, clothes, or whatever else I desired, ever accepting what I offered him; and would send away his guns when requested. No one refuses to lie at my feet, or do what I demand, but you only. Of you I can have nothing, but what you value not; and yet, you will have whatsoever you please. Capt. *Newport* you call father, and so you call me; but I see, in spite of us both, you will do what you will, and we must both study to humor and content you. But if you intend so friendly, as you say, send away your arms; for you see

* Catanaugh, *Stith*.

my undesigning simplicity and friendship cause me thus nakedly to forget myself."

Smith now was out of all patience, seeing *Powhatan* only trifled away the time, that he might, by some means, accomplish his design. The boats of the English were kept at a distance from the shore, by reason of ice *Smith*, therefore, resorted to deception; he got the Indians to break the ice, that his men might come in and take on board the corn they had bought, and, at the same time, gave orders to them to seize *Powhatan; Smith*, in the mean time, was to amuse him with false promises. But *Smith's* talk was too full of flattery not to be seen through by the sagacious sachem; and, before it was too late, he conveyed himself, his women, children, and effects, into the woods; having succeeded in his deception better than *Smith;* for two or three squaws amused him while *Powhatan* and the rest escaped. Unwilling, however, to renounce his purpose, *Powhatan* sent *Smith*, soon after, a valuable bracelet, as a present, by an old orator of his, who tried to excuse the conduct of his sachem; he said *Powhatan* ran off because he was afraid of the English arms, and said, if they could be laid aside, he would come with his people, and bring corn in abundance. At length, finding all artifices vain, *Powhatan* resolved to fall upon the English, in their cabins, on the following night. But here, again, *Pocahontas* saved the life of *Smith* and his attendants. She came alone, in a dismal night, through the woods, and informed *Smith* of her father's design. For this most signal favor, he offered her such articles as he thought would please her; but she would accept of nothing, and, with tears standing in her eyes, said if her father should see her with any thing, he would mistrust what she had done, and instant death would be her reward; and she retired by herself into the woods, as she came.

Powhatan was so exasperated at the failure of his plots, that he threatened death to his men if they did not kill *Smith* by some means or other. Not long after, a circumstance occurred, which gave him security the rest of his administration. One of *Powhatan's* men, having, by some means, got a quantity of powder, pretended that he could manage it like the English. Several came about him, to witness his exploits with the strange commodity, when, by some means, it took fire, "and blew him, with one or two more, to death." This struck such a dread into the Indians, and so amazed and frightened *Powhatan*, that his people came from all directions, and desired peace;* many of whom returned stolen articles that the English had never before missed. *Powhatan* would now send to Jamestown such of his men as had injured the English, that they might be dealt with as they deserved. The same year, 1609, he sent them nearly half his crop of corn, knowing them to be in great want.

Captain *Smith*, having, by accident, been shockingly burned by his powder-bags taking fire, for want of surgical aid, was obliged to leave the country and go to England, from whence he never returned. He published the account of the first voyages to Virginia, and his own adventures, which is almost the only authority for the early history of that country. He died in London, in 1631,† in the 52d year of his age.

The Dutchmen of whom we have spoken, and who had been so assiduous to bring ruin upon the colony, came to a miserable end. One of them died in wretchedness, and two others had their brains beat out by order of *Powhatan*, for their deception.

After *Smith* had left Virginia, the Indians were made to believe that he was dead. *Powhatan* doubted the report, and, some time after, ordered one of his counsellors, named *Uttamatomakin*,‡ or *Tomocomo*,§ whom he sent to England, to find out, if possible, where he was. He instructed him, also, to note the number of the people, to learn the state of the country, and, if he found *Smith*, to make him show him the God of the English, and the king and queen. When he arrived at Plimouth, he took a long stick, and began to perform a part of his mission by cutting a notch for every person he should see. But

* Did not the English of New England owe their safety to *Massasoit* and *Miantunnomoh's* fear of the same article?

† *Josselyn*, N. Eng. Rarities, 106. ‡ Or *Uttamaccomack*, Smith. § Purchas.

he soon gave up that business. And, when he returned to his own country, his chief asked him, among other things, to give him an account of the number of the inhabitants in England. His answer to that inquiry, we hazard not much in saying, is nearly as extensively known as the golden rule of *Confucius*. It was as follows: "*Count the stars in the sky, the leaves on the trees, and the sand upon the sea-shore,—for such is the number of the people of England.*"

TOMOCOMO had married a sister of *Pocahontas*, and, probably, accompanied her to England.* While there, the famous antiquary, *Samuel Purchas*, had an interview with him, and from whom he collected many facts relating to the manners and customs of his countrymen; the result of which he afterwards published in his Pilgrims.†

The difficulties were almost perpetual between *Powhatan* and the English very little time passed, while he lived, but what was full of broils and dissatisfaction, on the one part or the other. Few Indian chiefs have fallen under our notice, possessing such extraordinary characteristics as *Powhatan*. He died at peace with the English, in April, 1618, and was succeeded by *Opitchavan*, his second brother, who was known afterwards by the name *Itopatin*.

Our readers will be compelled to acknowledge that Captain *Smith* was barbarous enough towards the Indians, but we have not met with any thing quite so horrible, in the course of his proceedings, as was exhibited by his successor, Lord *De La War*. This *gentleman*, instead of taking a mean course between the practices of *Smith* and *Newport*, went into the worst extreme. Finding *Powhatan* insolent, on his arrival in the country, he determined, by severity, to bring him to unconditional submission. Having, therefore, got into his hands an Indian prisoner, his lordship caused his right hand to be cut off. In this maimed and horrid condition, he sent him to *Powhatan;* at the same time giving the sachem to understand, that all his subjects would be served in this manner, if he refused obedience any longer; telling him, also, that all the corn in the country should be immediately destroyed, which was just then ripe.‡ This wretched act increased, as reasonably it should, the indignation of *Powhatan*, and his acts were governed accordingly.

CHAPTER II.

Reflection upon the character of Powhatan—POCAHONTAS—*She singularly entertains Captain Smith—Disaster of a boat's crew—Smith's attempt to surprise Powhatan frustrated in consequence—Pocahontas saves the life of Wyffin—Betrayed into the hands of the English*—JAPAZAWS—*Mr. Rolfe marries Pocahontas*—OPACHISCO—*Pocahontas visits England—Her interview with Smith—Dies at Gravesend—Her son*—OPEKANKANOUGH—*Made prisoner by Smith—Is set at liberty*—NEMATTANOW—*Murders an Englishman—Is murdered in his turn—His singular conduct at his death—Conducts the massacre of 1622—Plots the extirpation of the English—Conducts the horrid massacre of 1644—Is taken prisoner—His conduct upon the occasion—Barbarously wounded by the guard—Last speech, and magnanimity in death—Reflections*—NICKOTAWANCE—TOTOPOTOMOI—*Joins the English against the Rechahecrians—Is defeated and slain.*

IT is impossible to say what would have been the conduct of the great *Powhatan* towards the English, had he been treated by them as he ought to have been. The uncommonly amiable, virtuous, and feeling disposition of his daughter, will always be brought to mind in reading his history; and, notwithstanding he is described by the historians as possessing a sour, morose, and savage disposition, full of treachery, deceit and cunning—and whose word was never to be depended upon—yet, on the very page that he is thus

* Mr. *Oldmixon* (Brit. Empire, i. 285.) says, "That when the princess *Pocahontas* came for England, a coucarousa, or lord of her own nation, attended her; his name was *Uttamaccomack.*"

† Vol. v. b. viii. chap. vi. page 955.

‡ *Harris*, Voyages, ii. 226.

represented, we shall find the same faults set him as examples by the English themselves.

The first and most memorable events in the life of *Pocahontas* have necessarily been detailed in the account of her father; therefore we shall, under her own name, give those which are more disconnected with his.

POCAHONTAS was born about the year 1594 or 5, and hence was no more than 12 or 13 years old when she saved the life of Captain *Smith*, in 1607 Every particular of that most extraordinary scene has been exhibited. The name *Pocohántes* or *Pockohántês*, says Heckewelder, means a run between two hills. It has been mentioned, that, at the suggestion of Captain *Newport*, *Smith* went with a few men to Werowocomoco, to invite *Powhatan* to Jamestown to receive presents, hoping thereby to influence him to open a trade in corn with them.

When he arrived at that place, *Powhatan* was not at home, but was at the distance of 30 miles off. *Pocahontas* and her women received him, and while he waited for her father, they thus entertained him:—"In a fayre plaine field, (says *Smith*,) they made a fire, before which, he sitting upon a mat, suddainly amongst the woods was heard such a hydeous noise and shrecking, that the English betooke themselves to their arms, and seized on two or three old men by them, supposing *Powhatan*, with all his power, was come to surprise them. But presently *Pocahontas* came, willing him to kill her if any hurt were intended; and the beholders, which were men, women and children, satisfied the captain there was no such matter. Then presently they were presented with this anticke; 30 young women came naked out of the woods, onely covered behind and before with a few greene leaues, their bodies all painted, some of one color, some of another, but all differing. Their leader had a fayre payre of buck's hornes on her head, and an otter-skinne at her girdle, and another at her arme, a quiver of arrowes at her backe, a bow and arrows in her hand. The next had in her hand a sword, and another a club, another a pot-sticke, all horned alike; the rest every one with their seuerall devises. These fiends, with most hellish shouts and cryes, rushing from among the trees, cast themselves in a ring about the fire, singing and dancing with most excellent ill varietie, oft falling into their infernall passions, and solemnly again to sing and daunce. Having spent neare an houre in this mascarado, as they entred, in like manner they departed." After a short time, they came and took the English to their wigwams. Here they were more tormented than before, "with crowding, pressing, hanging about them, most tediously crying, 'Love you not me? love you not me?'" When they had finished their caresses, they set before them the best victuals their country afforded, and then showed them to their lodgings.

While Captain *Smith* was upon an expedition into the country, with an intention of surprising *Powhatan*, there happened a melancholy accident at home, to a boat's crew, which had been sent out in very severe weather, by one who was impatient to have the direction of matters. In the boat were Captain *Waldo*, Master *Scrivener*, the projector of the expedition, Mr. *Anthony Gosnold*, brother of the well-known *Bartholomew Gosnold*,* and eight others. By the sinking of the boat, these all perished, and none knew what had become of them, until their bodies were found by the Indians. The very men on whom *Smith* depended to remain at the fort for his succor, in case he sent for them, were among the number. Therefore, to prevent the failure of this expedition, somebody must be sent to apprize *Smith* of the catastrophe. None volunteered for the hazardous service, but Mr. *Richard Wyffin*, who was obliged to undertake it alone. This was a time when *Powhatan* was very insolent, and urged daily the killing of *Smith* upon his men. Nevertheless, after many difficulties, he arrived at Werowocomoco. Here he found himself amidst preparations for war, and in still greater danger than he had yet been But *Pocahontas* appeared as his savior. Knowing the intention of the warriors to kill him, she first secreted him in the woods, and then directed those who sought him in an opposite direction from that he had gone; so, by this

* Who had miserably perished by disease and famine at Jamestown, 22 Aug., 1607 See *Bancroft*, U. States, i. 144.

means, he escaped, and got safe to *Smith* at Pamunkey. This was in the winter of 1609.

We next hear of her saving the life of *Henry Spilman*, who was one of 31 that went to trade, upon the confidence of *Powhatan*, but who were all, except *Spilman*, killed by his people.

Such was the wretched state to which the colony of Virginia was now reduced, that scarce a parallel in the annals of the world can be found. No sooner had *Smith* left the country, but all was in confusion. Officers spent their time in riotings, while the men seem to have taken no means for defence or preservation; so that the Indians made constant spoil upon their domestic animals, and whatever else had been provided for their support. Insomuch, that when Captain *Smith* had been gone six months, the colony was reduced from above 500 to about 60 persons. Herbs and roots were eaten to sustain life, in the early part of their distresses; but as the famine increased, the skins of horses were eagerly devoured, and an Indian, who had been some time dead, was disinterred and eaten by these miserable creatures. In one instance, a wretched man killed his own wife, and preserved the body by salt, which enormity was not discovered until it had been chiefly devoured.*

It was during this season of horror that Captain *Ratcliff* went out with 30 men, who were trepanned as we have related. This was in the beginning of the year 1610. *Spilman* lived many years afterwards among the Patowamack Indians, by the care of *Pocahontas*.†

From 1609, the time *Smith* left the country, until 1611, *Pocahontas* was not seen at Jamestown. In the latter year, she was treacherously taken prisoner by Captain *Argal*, and kept by the English to prevent *Powhatan* from doing them injury, and to extort a great ransom from him, and such terms of peace as they should dictate. At the time she was betrayed into the hands of Captain *Argal*, she was in the neighborhood of the chief of Potomack, whose name was *Japazaws*, a particular friend of the English, and an old acquaintance of Captain *Smith*. Whether she had taken up her residence here, or whether she was here only upon a visit, we are not informed. But some have conjectured, that she retired here soon after *Smith's* departure, that she might not witness the frequent murders of the ill-governed English, at Jamestown. Captain *Argal* was in the Potomack River, for the purpose of trade, with his ship, when he learned that *Pocahontas* was in the neighborhood. Whether *Japazaws* had acquired his treachery from his intercourse with the English, or whether it were natural to his disposition, we will not undertake to decide here; but certain it is, that he was ready to practise it, at the instigation of *Argal*. And for a copper kettle for himself, and a few toys for his squaw, he enticed the innocent girl on board *Argal's* ship, and betrayed her into his hands. It was effected, however, without compulsion, by the aid of his squaw. The captain had previously promised that no hurt should befall her, and that she should be treated with all tenderness. This circumstance should go as far as it may to excuse *Japazaws*. The plot to get her on board was well contrived. Knowing that she had no curiosity to see a ship, having before seen many, *Japazaws'* wife pretended a great anxiety to see one, but would not go on board unless *Pocahontas* would accompany her. To this she consented, but with some hesitation. The attention with which they were received on board soon dissipated all fears, and *Pocahontas* soon strayed from her betrayers into the gun-room. The captain, watching his opportunity, told her she was a prisoner. When her confinement was known to *Japazaws* and his wife, they feigned more lamentation than she did, to keep her in ignorance of the plot; and, after receiving the price of their perfidy, were sent ashore, and *Argal*, with his pearl of great price, sailed for Jamestown. On being informed of the reason why she was thus captivated, her grief, by degrees, subsided.

The first step of the English was to inform *Powhatan* of the captivity of his daughter, and to demand of him their men, guns and tools, which he and his people had, from time to time, taken and stolen from them. This unexpected news threw the old, stern, calculating chief into a great dilemma, and what course to take he knew not; and it was three months before he returned any

* *Keith's* Hist. Virginia, 121.

† *Stith*, Hist. Virginia, 116.

answer. At the end of this time, by the advice of his council, he sent back seven Englishmen, with each a gun which had been spoiled, and this answer that when they should return his daughter, he would make full satisfaction and give them 500 bushels of corn, and be their friend forever; that he had no more guns to return, the rest being lost. They sent him word, that they would not restore her, until he had complied with their demand; and that, as for the guns, they did not believe they were lost. Seeing the determination of the English, or his inability to satisfy them, was, we apprehend, why they "heard no more from him for a long time after."

In the spring of the year 1613, Sir *Thomas Dale* took *Pocahontas*, and went, with a ship, up *Powhatan's* River to Werowocomoco, the residence of her father, in hopes to effect an exchange, and bring about a peace. *Powhatan* was not at home, and they met with nothing but bravadoes, and a disposition to fight from all the Indians they saw. After burning many of their habitations, and giving out threats, some of the Indians came and made peace, as they called it, which opened the way for two of *Pocahontas's* brothers to come on board the ship. Their joy at seeing their sister may be imagined.

A particular friendship had some time existed between *Pocahontas* and a worthy young Englishman, by the name of *John Rolfe;* which, at length, growing into a sincere attachment, and being mutual between them, he made known his desire to take her for his companion. This being highly approved of by Sir *Thomas Dale*, and other gentlemen of high standing and authority, a consummation was soon agreed upon. Acquainting her brother with her determination, it soon came to the knowledge of her father also; who, as highly approving of it as the English, immediately sent *Opachisco*, her uncle, and two of his sons, to witness the performance, and to act as her servants upon the occasion; and, in the beginning of April, 1613, the marriage was solemnized according to appointment. *Powhatan* was now their friend in reality; and a friendly intercourse commenced, which was, without much interruption, continued until his death.

Pocahontas lived happily with her husband, and became a believer in the English religion, and expressed no desire to live again among those of her own nation. When Sir *Thomas Dale* returned to England, in 1616, *Pocahontas* accompanied him, with her husband, and several other young natives. They arrived at Plimouth on the 12th of June of that year. She met with much attention in that country, being taken to court by the Lord and Lady *Delaware*, and others of distinction. She was, at this time, called the Lady *Rebecca.* Her meeting with Captain *Smith* was affecting; more especially as she thought herself, and very justly, no doubt, too slightly noticed by him, which caused her much grief. Owing to the barbarous nonsense of the times, *Smith* did not wish her to call him father, being afraid of giving offence to royalty, by assuming to be the father of a king's daughter. Yet he did not intend any cause of offence, and did all in his power to make her happy. At their first interview, after remaining silent some time, she said to him, "*You promised my father, that what was yours should be his; and that you and he would be all one. Being a stranger in our country, you called* Powhatan *father; and I, for the same reason, will now call you so. You were not afraid to come into my father's country, and strike fear into every body but myself; and are you here afraid to let me call you father? I tell you, then, I will call you father, and you shall call me child; and so I will forever be of your kindred and country. They always told us that you were dead, and I knew not otherwise, till I came to Plimouth. But* Powhatan *commanded* Tomocomo *to seek you out, and know the truth, because your countrymen are much given to lying.*"

The useful and worthy young *Pocahontas*, being about to embark for her native country, in the beginning of the year 1617, fell sick at Gravesend, and died; having attained only the age of 22 years. She left one son, whose name was *Thomas Rolfe*, very young; and whom Sir *Lewis Steukly*,* of Plimouth,

* "As to the infamous Sir *Lewis Stucley*, who had betrayed *Ralegh*, he was taken soon after [*Ralegh* was beheaded] in Whitehall, clipping the very gold which was the produce of his infamy, and tried and condemned for it; and having stripped himself to his shirt to raise money to purchase his pardon, he banished himself to the Island of Sundy, where he died, both mad and a beggar, in less than two years after Sir *Walter Raleigh*."—*Prince's Worthies of Devon*, 677.—*Harding's Naval Biography*, i. 330.

desired to be left with him, that he might direct his education. But, from the unmanly part this gentleman took against the unfortunate *Ralegh*, he was brought into such merited disrepute, that he found himself obliged to turn all his attention to his own preservation; and the son of *Pocahontas* was taken to London, and there educated by his uncle, Mr. *Henry Rolfe*. He afterwards came to America, to the native country of his mother, where he became a gentleman of great distinction, and possessed an ample fortune. He left an only daughter, who married Colonel *Robert Bolling*, and died, leaving an only son, Major *John Bolling*, who was the father of Colonel *John Bolling*, and several daughters; one of whom married Colonel *Richard Randolph*, from whom are descended the distinguished JOHN RANDOLPH, and those bearing that name in Virginia, at this day.*

Barlow thus notices *Pocahontas*:—

"Blest *Pocahontas!* fear no lurking guile;
Thy hero's love shall well reward thy smile.
Ah, soothe the wanderer in his desperate plight,
Hide him by day, and calm his cares by night;
Tho' savage nations, with thy vengeful sire,
Pursue their victim with unceasing ire—
And tho' their threats thy startled ear assail,
Let virtue's voice o'er filial fears prevail."—COLUMBIAD

OPEKANKANOUGH has already received our notice. He was a very conspicuous character in his time, and was styled, by the Virginians, King of the Pamunkies. The dreadful massacre, of which he was author, brings to mind his name oftener than almost any other chief of his times.

There seems to be some contradiction, or difference of opinion, with regard to the origin of this chief. Some of the Indians reported that he came from the west, and was not a brother of *Powhatan;* but that story, we judge, is merely a fable, invented and told by his enemies, to influence the English against him, that they might destroy him.

Opekankanough seems to have borne the name of *Mangopeomen* in 1621,† a circumstance unnoticed by most historians, and, therefore, we conclude that it prevailed only among his own tribe, and, perhaps, even among them fell into disuse soon after.

OPITCHAPAN, called also *Oetan*, and lastly *Sasauopeomen*,‡ was the successor of *Powhatan*, but he seems never to have been otherwise noted. "The defects of the new emperor," says Mr. *Burk*, "were aggravated in the minds of the Indians, by a comparison with the accomplished *Opekankanough*, who, in the council and the field, was the most conspicuous warrior amongst the Powhatans; and who, during the lifetime of the late emperor, had procured from the free tribe of the Chickahominies, the title of their king." The same author calls *Opitchapan* a "feble and decrepid" chief, who "was little calculated to secure respect, or enforce obedience." §

In 1608, the Indians had become universally at variance with the English, and insulted them whenever they appeared abroad; knowing their miserable, half-starved condition. Insult followed insult, upon both sides, and, but for the never-tiring perseverance of *Smith*, this colony, like the first, would have been soon destroyed. The Indians would promise to trade with them, but when they went to them for that purpose, they only "laughed at their calamities;" sometimes putting jokes upon them, and at others, running away into the woods.

In this extremity of their circumstances, though in the depth of winter, *Smith* resolved to make himself master of some of the Indians' store of provisions, by some means or other. He, therefore, proceeded to Pamunkey, the residence

* JOHN RANDOLPH, *of Roanoke*, died in Philadelphia, 24 May, 1834. He had come there in very low health, intending to embark for Europe in a few days. Having met with some perplexity in procuring lodgings on his arrival in Philadelphia, being taken from the steam-boat to one hotel after another, in a bad hack, in bad weather, he was much irritated, and, from his frequent allusions to it in his sickness, it was supposed to have hastened his end. He was about 60 years of age at his death.

† *Burk's* Va. i. 228. ‡ Ibid. § Hist. Virginia i. 233

of *Opekankanough*, with 15 men, where he tried to trade with him for corn but, not succeeding, he, in a desperate manner, seized upon the chief by his hair, in the midst of his men, "with his pistoll readie bent against his breast. Thus he led the trembling king, neare dead with fear, amongst all his people." * *Smith* told him that he had attempted to murder him, which was the cause of his treating him thus. No one can doubt, on reading the history of those affairs, that the Indians all wished *Smith* dead, but whether they all wanted to kill him, is not quite so plain.

One great end of *Smith's* design was now answered; for *Opekankanough's* people came in loaded with presents to ransom their chief, until his boats were completely filled. News being brought of a disaster at Jamestown, he was set at liberty.

Nemattanow, a renowned warrior, we have to introduce here, as well on account of his supposed agency in bringing about the great massacre of 1622 as for the object of exhibiting a trait of character equally to be admired and lamented. We are not certain that he belonged to the people of *Opekankanough*, but it is storied that a jealousy existed between them, and that the chief had informed Sir *George Yeardley* that he wished *Nemattanow's* throat were cut, some time before the massacre took place, to which we have alluded. However, *Opekankanough* denied it afterwards, and affected great indignation at his murder, and the Indians said the massacre was begun by him, to revenge *Nemattanow's* death. But our present object is to portray the character of *Nemattanow*, who was both eccentric and vain, and "who was wont, out of bravery and parade, to dress himself up, in a strange, antic, and barbaric fashion, with feathers, which, therefore, obtained him the name of *Jack-of-the-feather*." He was even more popular among his countrymen than *Opekankanough*, which, doubtless, was the ground of that chief's jealousy; especially as he was one of the greatest war-captains of his times. He had been in many fights and encounters with the English, always exposing himself to the greatest danger, and yet was never wounded in any of them. This circumstance caused the Indians to believe in his invulnerability, and hence he was by them considered superhuman. Only about 14 days before the massacre, *Jack-of-the-feather* went to the house of one *Morgan*, where he saw many such articles exhibited as were calculated to excite admiration in such people. *Jack*, perhaps, had not the means to purchase, but, it seems, he was resolved, some how or other, to possess them. He, therefore, told *Morgan*, that if he would take his commodities to Pamunkey, the Indians would give him a great price for them. Not in the least mistrusting the design of *Nemattanow*, the simple Englishman set out for Pamunkey, in company with this Indian. This was the last the English heard of *Morgan*. However, strange as it may seem, *Jack's* ill-directing fate sent him to the same place again, and, what was still more strange, he had the cap of the murdered *Morgan* upon his head. *Morgan's* servants asked him where their master was, who very deliberately answered, that he was dead. This satisfied them that he had murdered him. They, therefore, seized him, in order to take him before a magistrate at Berkeley; but he made a good deal of resistance, which caused one of his captors to shoot him down. The singular part of the tragedy is yet to be related. Though mortally wounded, *Nemattanow* was not killed outright, and his captors, which were two stout young men, got him into a boat to proceed to Mr. *Thorp's*, the magistrate. As they were going, the warrior became satisfied that he must die, and, with the most extraordinary earnestness, besought that two things might be granted him. One was, that it should never be told to his countrymen that he was killed by a bullet; and the other, that he should be buried among the English, so that it should never be discovered that he had died, or was subject to death like other men. Such was the pride and vanity exhibited by an Indian at his death. The following inference, therefore, is naturally to be drawn; that a desire to be renowned, and held in veneration by posterity, is not confined to the civilized and learned of any age or nation.

* Perhaps the New Englanders followed *Smith's* example, afterwards, in the case of *Alexander*, *Ninigret*, and others.

Meanwhile, *Opekankanough*, the better to increase the rage of his warriors, affected great grief at *Nemattanow's* death, which had the effect he intended owing, especially, to the favor in which that warrior had stood among the Indians. But the English were satisfied that this was only pretence, as we have before observed; because they were informed of his trying to engage some of his neighbors against them, and otherwise acted suspiciously, some time before *Nemattanow's* death; of the justice of which, however, the English tried arguments at first, and threats afterwards, to convince them. By his dissimulation, *Opekankanough* completely deceived them, and, just before the massacre, treated a messenger that was sent to him with much kindness and civility; and assured him that the peace, which had been some time before concluded, was held so firm by him that the sky should fall sooner than it should be violated on his part. And such was the concert and secrecy among all the Indians, that, only two days before the fatal 22 March, some kindly conducted the English through the woods, and sent one of their youth to live with the English, and learn their language. Moreover, on the morning of that very day, they came unarmed among them, and traded as usual, and even sat down to breakfast with their victims, in several instances. Never, perhaps, was a massacre so well contrived and conducted, to ensure success, as was this of *Opekankanough*. The English were lulled into a fatal security and even unknowingly assisted the Indians in their design; lending them their boats to communicate with distant tribes, and furnishing them with various utensils, which were converted at once into weapons of death.

The 22 March, 1622, having come, and the appointed hour of that memorable day arrived, with a simultaneousness unparalleled on any former occasion, the Indians rose from their ambushes, and, with the swiftness of the tiger, appeared, in a moment, amidst the English settlements. Age, sex, nor condition, shielded no one; their greatest benefactors were among their first victims. Thus, in the space of about one hour, fell *three hundred and forty-seven* men, women, and children. By this horrid calamity, out of 80 plantations, six only were left uninjured. And these were saved by the timely information of a Christian Indian called *Chanco*.

The ensuing summer was spent, by the surviving English, in strengthening themselves against further attacks, and preparations for taking vengeance on the Indians; wholly neglecting all improvements, works of utility, and even their planting. Every thing was lost sight of in their beloved project of revenge; and the English, in their turn, showed themselves more treacherous, if not more barbarous, than their enemy. For, under pretence of making peace again with them, they fell upon them at unawares, and murdered many without mercy. This crime was vastly aggravated, in that, to induce the Indians to come forward and make peace, the English had not only solemnly assured them forgiveness, but likewise security and safety in their persons.

It was, for some time, supposed that *Opekankanough* was among the slain, but, if Mr. *Beverly* was not misinformed, the same sachem, 22 years afterwards, executed a still greater massacre upon the English, as, in the next place, we shall relate.

How long *Opekankanough* had been secretly plotting to cut off the intruders of his soil cannot be known; but, in 1644, all the Indians, over a space of country of 600 miles in extent, were leagued in the enterprise. The old chief, at this time, was supposed to be near 100 years of age, and, though unable to walk, would be present in the execution of his beloved project. It was upon the 18 April, when *Opekankanough*, borne in a litter, led his warriors forward, and commenced the bloody work. They began at the frontiers, with a determination to slay all before them, to the sea. After continuing the massacre two days, in which time about 500* persons were murdered, Sir *William Berkeley*, at the head of an armed force, checked their progress. The destruction of the inhabitants was the greatest upon York and Pamunkey Rivers, where *Opekankanough* commanded in person. The Indians now, in their turn, were driven to great extremity, and their old chief was taken prisoner

* This is the number generally set down in the histories, but the probably just scrutiny of Mr. *Bancroft*, Hist. U. S. i. 224, caused him to fix upon the number 300.

and carried in triumph to Jamestown. How long after the massacre this happened, we are not informed; but it is said that the fatigues he had previously undergone had wasted away his flesh, and destroyed the elasticity of his muscles to that degree, that he was no longer able to raise the eyelids from his eyes; and it was in this forlorn condition, that he fell into the hands of his enemies. A soldier, who had been appointed to guard him, barbarously fired upon him, and inflicted a mortal wound. He was supposed to have been prompted to the bloody deed, from a recollection of the old chief's agency in the massacre. Just before he expired, hearing a great bustle and crowd about him, he ordered an attendant to lift up his eyelids; when he discovered a multitude pressing around, to gratify the untimely curiosity of beholding a dying sachem. Undaunted in death, and roused, as it were, from sleep at the conduct of the confused multitude, he deigned not to observe them; but, raising himself from the ground, with the expiring breath of authority, commanded that the governor should be called to him. When the governor came, *Opekankanough* said, with indignation, "*Had it been my fortune to have taken Sir* Wm. Berkeley *prisoner, I would not meanly have exposed him as a show to my people;*" * and soon after expired.

It is said, and we have no reason to doubt the fact, that it was owing to the encroachments upon his lands, that caused *Opekankanough* to determine upon a massacre of the whites. These intrusions were, nevertheless, conformable to the grants of the proprietors. He could hardly have expected entire conquest, as his people had already begun to waste away, and English villages were springing up over an extent of country of more than 500 miles, with a populousness beyond any preceding example; still, he was determined upon the vast undertaking, and sacrificed himself with as much *honor*, it will, perhaps, be acknowledged, as did *Leonidas* at Thermopylæ.

Sir *William Berkeley* intended to have sent him, as a present, to the king of England; but assassination deprived him of the wretched satisfaction, and saved the chief from the mortification.†

None of the Virginia historians seem to have been informed of the true date of this last war of *Opekankanough;* the ancient records of Virginia, says Mr. *Burk*, are silent even upon the events of it, (an extraordinary omission.) Mr. *Beverly* thinks it began in 1639, and, although Mr. *Burk* is satisfied that it took place after 1641, yet he relates it under the date 1640. And we are not certain that the real date would ever have been fixed, but for the inestimable treasury of New England history, *Winthrop's* Journal.‡

That it took place subsequent to 1641, Mr. *Burk* assures us, upon the evidence of the MS. records; for they relate that, in 1640, one *John Burton* had been convicted of the murder of an Indian, and that his punishment was remitted, "at the intercession of *Opekankanough*, and his great men." And that, in the end of the year 1641, *Thomas Rolfe*, the son of *Pocahontas*, petitioned the governor for permission to visit his kinsman, *Opekankanough*, and *Cleopatre*, the sister of his mother. That, therefore, these events happened previous to the war, and death of *Opekankanough*. §

Nickotawance succeeded *Opekankanough*, as a tributary to the English In 1648, he came to Jamestown, with five other chiefs, and brought 20 beaver skins to be sent to King *Charles*. He made a long oration, which he concluded with the protestation, "that the sun and moon should first loose their glorious lights, and shining, before he, or his people, should ever more hereafter wrong the English."

Totopotomoi probably succeeded *Nickotawance*, as he was king of Pamunkey in 1656. In that year, a large body of strange Indians, called *Rechahecrians*, came down from the inland mountainous country, and forcibly

* *Beverly*, Hist. Virg. 51. † See British Empire in America, i. 240, 1.

‡ Whether it be preserved in *Hening's* Statutes, I have not learned, but presumed it, from the inference of *Bancroft*.

§ Like most of the early writers, the author of *A New Description of Virginia*, (2 Coll. Mass. Hist. Soc. ix. 111.) speaks of the Indians in terms dictated by indignation. "Their great king," he says, "*Opechankenow*, that bloody monster upon a hundred years old, was taken by Sir *William Berkely*." This tract was published in 1659, but no date is given to the massacre.

possessed themselves of the country about the falls of James River. The legislature of Virginia was in session, when the news of their coming was received. What cause the English had to send out an army against them, our scanty records do not satisfactorily show;* but, at all events, they determined at once to dispossess them. To that end, an army of about 100 men was raised, and put under the direction of Colonel *Edward Hill*, who was joined by *Totopotomoi*, with 100 of his warriors. They did not find the Rechahecrians unprepared, but of the particulars of the meeting of the adverse parties we are not informed. The event, however, was, to the allies, most disastrous. *Totopotomoi*, with the most of his men, was slain, and the English suffered a total defeat, owing, it is said, to the criminal management of Colonel *Hill*. This officer lost his commission, and his property was taken to defray the losses sustained by the country. A peace seems to have been concluded with the Indians soon after.

CHAPTER III.

*Of the Creek Indians—Muskogees—Prohibit the use of ardent spirits—Their rise and importance—Their origin—Catawbas—Chikasaus—Cherokees—A mode of flattening their heads—Complexion lighter than other Indians—Seminoles—Ruins at Oakmulgee Fields—Expedition of Soto—Kills 2000 Indians—Laudonniere—Gourges expedition—Grijalva—*MOYTOY *made emperor of the Cherokees—Sir Alexander Cumming—His travels among the Cherokees—Seven chiefs accompany him to England—Attakullakulla—*SKIJAGUSTAH*—His speech to the king—His death.*

IN the preceding chapters of this book, much has been narrated of the southern nations in general; and, in particular, of many prominent individuals and events. It is designed, in the present chapter, to speak more particularly upon the events of the great nation of Creek Indians.

It will be proper, in the first place, to give some general account of the nation, whose men of eminence have been, and are to be, noticed; for there are some facts that will not necessarily fall in otherwise; but, in such digression, if so it should be termed, our chief axiom is not overturned, which is, that to write the history of the men of a country, is to write the history of such country. The reader, however, should be reminded, that a general history of a people at one period, will not exactly apply to them at another. This observation is not only true with regard to their political and civil history, but also in regard to the manners and customs of the same nations: these facts are true, both as they regard people called civilized, as well as those called savage. Hence, descriptions of tribes or nations by one observer, at one time, differ from those of another at a different period; and yet both may be true in the main particulars. Students, therefore, not aware of this fact, may be disposed to discredit writers for such disagreements, which, in fact, are altogether imaginary. But it is time to commence upon the immediate business of the present chapter.

The Creek Indians take their name from that of the country in which they live; that is, the English gave them the name of Creeks, because their country is full of creeks.

* By the following preamble and resolve of the legislature, all we possess, touching this matter, is to be gathered:—"Whereas information hath been received, that many western or inland Indians are drawn from the mountains, and lately set down near the falls of James River, to the number of 6 or 700, whereby, upon many several considerations being had, it is conceived great danger might ensue to this colony. This assembly, therefore, do think fit and resolve, that these new come Indians be in no sort suffered to seat themselves there, or any place near us, it having cost so much blood to expel and extirpate those perfidious and treacherous Indians, which were there formerly. It being so apt a place to invade us, and within the limits, which, in a just war, were formerly conquered by us, and by us reserved, at the conclusion of peace, with the Indians." *Burk*, Hist. Virginia, ii. 105.

The nation of most importance among the Creeks was, in 1775 the Muskogees. That community, or nation, like the Iroquois, was more politic than their neighbors, and vastly increased their strength and importance by encouraging small declining tribes to incorporate themselves with them. At one time, another most wise resolution was adopted among them, which, above all others, should be mentioned; that was a prohibition of the importation of all kinds of ardent spirits into their country. How long this resolution was maintained, or at what period, cannot, at this time, be stated. It was very probably at the period of their greatest prosperity, which was just before the breaking out of the revolutionary war. The Muskogees had another excellent regulation, namely, the men assisted their women in their planting before setting out on their warlike and other expeditions. This was called the Creek nation, which, in what was called its best days, about 1786, contained 17,000 souls;* but they were reckoned, in 1829, at 20,000.

Some have, latterly, given the name of Creeks only to a part of the nations of which we have begun to treat; but it is here intended to include under that head all the tribes between the Savannah on the east, the Mississippi on the west, and the country bordering on the Ohio on the north.

The following is a specimen of their language, which will answer tolerably well as a specimen of all the southern languages, from Carolina to the Mississippi:—

Isti tsukhvlhpi laksakat Tshihofv inhomitsi tomis; momais fvtsv opunahoyan im afvlski tomis.† In English, *Lying lips are an abomination to the Lord; but they that deal truly are his delight.*

The following is Choktau reckoning: Achvfa, 1, Tuklo, 2, Tuchina, 3, Ushta, 4, Tahlapi, 5, Hanali, 6, Untuklo, 7, Untuchina, 8, Chakali, 9, Pokoli, 10. By prefixing *auh* to the names of the digits, they arrive at 20; then, by prefixing *Pokoli* (10) to the series of digits, they arrive at 30, and so on.‡

The Cherokees have now a written language, and, before the late troubles with Georgia, were making good advancement in all the useful arts. One of the most remarkable discoveries of modern times has been made by a Cherokee Indian, named George Guess. His invention was that of a syllabic alphabet of the language of his nation, which he applied to writing with unparalleled success. Young Cherokees learned by it to write letters to their friends in three days' time; and although the inventor used a part of the English alphabet in making up his own, yet he was acquainted with no other language but the Cherokee. This invention was brought to maturity in 1826. Two years after, a newspaper, called the Cherokee Phœnix, was established in the Cherokee nation, printed chiefly in Cherokee, with an English translation.§ Being considered an independent nation, they instituted a form of government similar to that of the United States.

It was some time after the Natchez massacred the French, that the principal nation of Creeks, the Muskogees, began to rise into importance. For a time after that memorable event, the country of the Natchez was desolate; but when some years had elapsed, a tribe seated themselves there, and it became the seat of a powerful nation; and this was the Muskogees. That nation, like the ancient Romans, had, in about 30 years, extended their dominions over a fertile country near 200 miles square; had 3500 bow-men, and 50 considerable towns. They had dominion also over one town of the Shawanese. Their chief places were upon the branches of the Alabama and the Apalachicola rivers; the people upon the latter being called the *lower* Creeks. This, as well as the other nations whom we call Creeks, are generally supposed to have originally come from the south or south-west; but the Indians themselves believe, or pretend to believe, that they came from the east, or place of the sun's rising; concerning which opinion we may observe once for all, that it most probably had the same origin among all ignorant people, which arose from no other than a desire that others should think them descended from the

* It is common to reckon a third warriors.

† This specimen I take from a little volume, called the "Muskogee (Creek) Assistant" published in Boston, 1835, by the Am. Board of Com. for Foreign Missions.

‡ Choktau Arithmetic, printed as above.

§ *Hist. Missions* ii, 354.—*Missionary Herald*

sun; that being the most glorious and noble origin of which they could conceive. Indeed, such is not altogether unnatural; for that luminary quickens and enlivens every thing that has life, whether animal or vegetable.

Beside the Muskogees, the Kataubahs, or Catawbas, Cherokees, Choktaus, and Chikasaus, were other numerous tribes spread over the great country of which we have spoken.

The Kataubahs and the Chikasaus were very warlike; but their vicinity to Europeans was as detrimental to them, and even more so, than their own exterminating wars; for, as in other cases, as soon as an intercourse commenced, degradation and ruin followed.

The Cherokees have withstood the deletery effects of civilization much beyond what can be said of any other tribe of Indians. Their country is chiefly in Alabama, Mississippi, and Tennessee; but they occupy also the western part of the state of Georgia. Before the war of 1812, their country covered 24,000 square miles.* Numbers of this tribe have emigrated to Arkansaw.

The Choktaus possessed a country not so filled with creeks and rivers as the Muskogees. This circumstance, it is said, was a great hinderance to their prosperity; for in their wars with their neighbors, they suffered greatly from their ignorance of swimming. There were Upper and Lower Choktau towns; the former were situated about 160 miles from the Chikasaus, and the latter about 200 above New Orleans. The people of this nation flattened their heads by wearing bags of sand on them,† and, according to Father *Hennepin*,‡ the heads of all the Indians upon the Mississippi are flatter than those of Canada. It is said also that they are of a lighter complexion; but this has reference only to the Muskogees, according to somê writers. The Choktaus principally inhabit Mississippi. They were, in 1820, set down at 25,000 souls, and are rather increasing.

The Chikasaus are supposed to have come from the west of the Mississippi, and as it was a custom among the Creeks for their unoccupied lands to be taken by any that came among them, as emigrants, the Chikasaus found no obstacles in the way of establishing themselves on this side the Mississippi. Where they first established themselves is unknown, but in 1770 they were a powerful and warlike nation, and were seated upon the western branches of the Mobile. The tribe of Yazoos belonged to this nation. The Chikasaus reside in Mississippi, Kentucky, and Tennessee. They do not exceed 4900 in number.

The Seminoles were a nation made up similar to many others, and chiefly of Muskogees. The Creeks called them Seminoles, which signified *wild*, because they had estranged themselves from their former country. This nation was principally seated, 40 years ago, upon the rivers Apalachicola and Flint, and had a large town on Calos Bay, on the west side of East Florida. They now reside in Florida, a scattered remnant of about 1200.

The names alone of the different clans or tribes of these nations would fill several pages, and it is not necessary here to enumerate them; we shall therefore, after some general observations, pass to the consideration of those chiefs who have been conspicuous.

There are upon the east bank of the Oakmulge, near its confluence with the Ocone, beautiful fields, extensively known as the Oakmulge fields; they are upon the rich low lands of the river, and upon the elevated part of them are yet visible remains of a town. These fields extend 20 miles along the river. The Creek Indians give this account of them, namely, that here was the place where they first set down after crossing the Mississippi; that their journey from the west had been attended with incredible suffering, and that they were opposed at every step by various hostile bands of Indians, and that on reach-

* Dr. *Morse's* Report.

† *Adair.*—"As soon as the child is born, the nurse provides a cradle or wooden case, hollowed and fashioned, to receive the infant, lying prostrate on its back, that part of the case where the head reposes, being fashioned like a brick-mould. In this portable machine the little boy is fixed, a bag of sand being laid on his forehead."—*Bartram.* 515

‡ New Discovery, 176.

ing this place they fortified themselves, and could proceed no furtner, and at length gained ground and became conquerors in their turn.

There are few greater curiosities in the south, than the great highways or roads, which, 50 years ago, struck the traveller with surprise. In West Florida they are still easily traced for near 50 miles in a straight line upon the Oklokoney River. All history is silent about them; and it is a singular fact that the Indians will make no use of them, but studiously make their paths in any other direction.*

The country of the southern Indians has suffered in some respects as much as some parts of South America; it having been traversed and overrun from time to time by bands of mercenary whites. In the year 1538, *Ferdinand de Soto*, with a commission from the Emperor *Charles* V., sailed with a considerable fleet for America. He was a Portuguese gentleman, and had been with *Pizarro* in the conquest (as it is called) of Peru. His commission constituted him governor of Cuba and general of Florida.† Although he sailed from St. Lucar in 1538, he did not land in Florida‡ until May, 1539. With about 1000 men, 213 of whom were provided with horses, he undertook the conquest of Florida and countries adjacent. After cutting their way in various directions through numerous tribes of Indians, traversing nearly 1000 miles of country, losing a great part of their army, their general died upon the banks of the Mississippi, and the survivors were obliged to build vessels in which to descend the river; which, when they had done, they sailed for Mexico. This expedition was five years in coming to nothing, and bringing ruin upon its performers. A populous Indian town at this time stood at or near the mouth of the Mobile, of which *Soto's* army had possessed themselves. Their intercourse with the Indians was at first friendly, but at length a chief was insulted, which brought on hostilities. A battle was fought, in which, it is said, 2000 Indians were killed, and 83 Spaniards.

We shall not attempt here to go more into detail concerning the band of marauding Spaniards under *Soto*, as it will answer the present purpose to observe, that what has just been related, is but one of the many butcheries committed by that band; and, moreover, our accounts are rather indistinct upon the whole affair, and savor much of exaggeration.

The French, under *René de Laudonniere*, settled in Florida in 1564, near where Pensacola was since built. The Spaniards claimed the country, and hence the bloody wars which followed. This first settlement of the French, projected by Admiral *Coligni*, was soon broken up by the Spaniards: they, in the basest and most savage manner, murdered the whole colony. A religious war at this period distracted the French nation, and this outrage would have remained unrevenged, but for the indignation of an individual. In 1567, *Dominique de Gourges* sailed to Florida, took three forts from the Spaniards, put the men to the sword, and hanged all the other settlers he could find.§ A French garrison was again established, but, being left without protection, was soon retaken by the Spaniards, who remained masters of the country for more than a hundred years.‖

From these transactions of antiquity, we must descend to times nearer our own. In the year 1730, Sir *Alexander Cumming* travelled among the southern Indians, and from whose account we are able to give several interesting particulars. At this period, he relates that the Cherokee nation was governed by seven Mother Towns, each of which chose a king to preside over them and their dependants. He was elected out of certain families, and the descent

---

* *Williams's* W. Florida, 32.

† *Chaudon de Delandine*, Nouveau Dict. Historique, art. Soto.

‡ "So called, because it was first discovered by the Spaniards on Palme-Sunday, or, as the most interpret, Easter-day, which they call *Pasqua Florida*, and not, as *Theuet* writeth, for the flourishing verdure thereof." *Purchas*, 769. Modern writers of discoveries would do better were they to look more to the sources of information.

§ See an animated account of these bloody affairs in *Johnson's* Life of General *Greene*, i. 480, &c.

‖ Dupratz, i. 1—3. *Juan de Grijalva* discovered the country upon the Gulf of Mexico in 1518, (*Herrera*, ii. 199,) and some report that he carried off Indians as slaves. (See *Williams's* Florida, 90.) But we are not aware that the fact is elsewhere recorded. *Herrera*, though very minute, does not name it. *Purchas* (812) agrees with him was regarded only on the mother's side. These *mother towns* were, according to Sir *Alexander*, Tannassie, Kettooah, Ustenary, Telliquo, Estootowie, Keyowee, and Noeyeoee. Four of these towns were without kings at this time, they having died. Some towns had princes, as our author called them; namely, Tomasso, one; Settecho, one; Tassettchee, one; Iwassee, one; Telliquo, two; Tannassie, two; Cannostee, one; Cowee, one.

The chief *Moytoy* was called emperor, and presided over the seven towns, in 1730. His residence was at Telliquo. On the 3 April, this year, deputies from all parts of the nation met at Nequassie, and in presence of Sir *Alexander Cumming* and 12 other Englishmen, declared *Moytoy* emperor, he having been nominated by Sir *Alexander*.* The nation consented to receive *Moytoy* as their king, provided he was held accountable to Sir *Alexander*. At the ceremony of declaring *Moytoy* king or emperor, by whose order Sir *Alexander* was placed in a chair, himself and the conjurers standing about him, and a throng of warriors "stroked him with 13 eagles' tails, and their singers sung from morning till night." After this was done with, he made a speech to the great concourse of Indians; in which, among a good deal besides, he displayed the power and goodness of the king beyond the great water; and "required *Moytoy* and all the head warriors to acknowledge themselves dutiful subjects and sons to King *George*," "all which they did on their knees, calling upon every thing that was terrible to them to destroy them, and that they might become no people, if they violated their promise and obedience."

The next day, 4 April, "the crown was brought from great Tannassie, which, with five eagles' tails and four scalps of their enemies, *Moytoy* presented to Sir *Alexander*, impowering him to lay the same at his majesty's feet." The conjurers were well pleased with the English baron, and told him they would follow all his directions. "That when he left them they would still consider him as present in the person of *Moytoy* of Telliquo, who would punctually do what he had bid." Sir *Alexander* was now at Tannassie, 400 miles from Charleston, according to his reckoning, and had but 15 days to arrive there in, to go for England in the Fox man-of war, which was then to sail. He therefore asked *Moytoy* if the Indians could travel there in so short a time on foot. The chief said it might be done, and that he would have accompanied him, but for the dangerous illness of his wife, and requested him to choose such as he desired from among his people, to go with him.†

Accordingly, Sir *Alexander* chose, as evidences of what had happened, *Skijagusta*,‡ the head warrior of Tassetchie, "a man of great power and interest, who had a right to be a king," *Attakullakulla*, and *Otassite*, or *Outacite*, a third warrior, *Collannah*, a fourth; "and from Tannassie, the remotest town of the country, he took *Clogoittah* and *Oukanaekah*,§ warriors." About 23 miles from Charleston they met with the warrior *Ounakannowine*, a friend of these chiefs, "who had just come from the Kattarbe nation, and desired to go along with his countrymen, to which Sir *Alexander* consented."

They went on board the Fox, a man-of-war, and sailed from Charleston Bay 4 May, and arrived at Dover 5 June; thus performing a passage across the Atlantic in a month and a day, in 1730, not much inferior to what is done now-a-days. At Dover Sir *Alexander* "took post to London, with the crown

---

* This part of the sentence is upon the authority of a good writer, (*Hewatt*, Hist. Carolina, ii. 5,) but Sir *Alexander* does not say quite as much in his account.

† *Moytoy* was a bitter enemy afterwards. In 1758 he went with his warriors to a place called Statiquo, and killed several whites, without, as was said, *any* provocation *Hewatt*, ii. 220.

‡ Or *Kitagusta*. This chief was one of the *seven*, as will appear immediately onward, although Sir *Alexander*, in his communication, does not name him. Neither does he name *Attakullakulla*, or *Outassite*; yet it is certain they were both in England, and we believe at this time: they make up the number *seven*, with those named in his own narrative. That *Attakullakulla* was, see *Hewatt*, ii. 221, and *Wynne*, ii. 280, *n*. We can only account for the blanks in the narrative, by supposing that Sir *Alexander's* amanuensis did not understand him, (for he did not write himself,) and the enumeration of the chiefs which he took with him, is very blundering. Thus, after naming one only, it is set down, "and ———— a third warrior," &c.

§ Perhaps *Ockonostota*, who was called the great warrior of the Cherokee nation. *Hewatt* ii. 217.

of the Cherokee nation, leaving the Indians behind to come up with the man-of-war. He let the secretary of state immediately know that he had full power from that nation to lay their crown at his majesty's feet, and that he had brought over seven Indian chiefs, as an evidence of the truth. His majesty was graciously pleased to order Sir *Alexander* to bring in his people to the installation, the 18th of June, where they were extremely surprised at the magnificence of every thing about them: they compared the king and queen to the sun, the princes to the stars, and themselves to nothing. On the 22d of June, Sir *Alexander* was introduced to his majesty, and upon his knee, in presence of the court, declared the full power he had received, the Indian chiefs all kneeling at the same time, as a testimony of their submission and approbation. Sir *Alexander* laid the crown of the Cherokee nation at his majesty's feet, with the five eagles' tails, as an emblem of his majesty's sovereignty, and four scalps of Indian enemies; all which his majesty was graciously pleased to accept of."

While in England, they made a treaty with the king, every article of which was accompanied, on his part, with presents of some sort or other: such as cloth, guns, vermilion, hatchets, knives, &c. This treaty was dated at Whitehall, 7 September, 1730, and from it we get the names of the seven chiefs. It begins, "Whereas you, SCAYAGUSTA OUKAH, chief of the town of Tasseta; you, SCALILOSKEN KETAGUSTA; you, TETHTOWE; you, CLOGOITTAH; you, COLANNAH; you, UNNACONOY; you, OUCOUNACOU, have been deputed by the whole nation of the Cherokee Indians, to come to Great Britain," * &c. After the treaty was finished, a certified copy was presented to the chiefs by Sir *Alexander Cumming*; upon which *Skijagustah*, in the name of the whole, made the following speech:—

"We are come hither from a mountainous place, where nothing but darkness is to be found; but we are now in a place where there is light. There was a person in our country, he gave us a yellow token of warlike honor, which is left with *Moytoy* of Telliquo, and as warriors we received it. He came to us like a warrior from you. A man he is; his talk is upright, and the token he left preserves his memory among us. We look upon you as if the great king were present; we love you as representing the great king. We shall die in the same way of thinking. The crown of our nation is different from that which the great King GEORGE wears, and from that we saw in the tower. But to us it is all one. The chain of friendship shall be carried to our people. We look upon the great King *George* as the sun, and as our father, and upon ourselves as his children. For though we are red, and you are white, yet our hands and hearts are joined together. When we shall have acquainted our people with what we have seen, our children from generation to generation will always remember it. In war we shall always be one with you. The enemies of the great king shall be our enemies. His people and ours shall be one, and shall die together. We came hither naked and poor as the worms of the earth, but you have every thing, and we that have nothing must love you, and will never break the chain of friendship which is between us. Here stands the governor of Carolina, whom we know.† This small rope‡ we show you is all that we have to bind our slaves with, and it may be broken. But have iron chains for yours. However if we catch your slaves, we will bind them as well as we can, and deliver them to our friends, and take no pay for it. We have looked round for the person that was in our country —he is not here: However, we must say he talked uprightly to us, and we shall never forget him. Your white people may very safely build houses near us. We shall hurt nothing that belongs to them, for we are children of one father, the great king, and shall live and die together."

When *Skijagustah* had proceeded thus far, he laid his feathers upon a table, and closed as follows:—

* Report of the Commissioners (1736) on the Affairs of Georgia, p. 53.—If *Attakullakulla* were among these chiefs, he went under another name, as did also *Outacite*. See a few pages forward.

† There was at this time no governor, though *Robert Johnson* was nominally such. In 1729 the government of Carolina was delivered to the crown of England, for about £17,000. *Johnson* was reappointed in 1731.

‡ String of wampum, probably

"This is our way of talking, which is the same thing to us as your letters in the book are to you, and to you, beloved men, we deliver these feathers in confirmation of all we have said."

In October, the Indians embarked at Portsmouth with Mr. *Johnson*, the governor of Carolina, for their own country, and in the same ship in which they went over.

Skijagustah, or, as he was sometimes called, *Kittagusta*, "was brother of *Oucconnostota*, or the great warrior, and also chief of Chote. He lived to be very old, and died in May, 1768.

CHAPTER IV.

Settlement of Carolina and Georgia—TOMOCHICHI *receives the English*—*Goes to England with* General Oglethorpe—*Makes a speech to the King*—*His death*—*War with the Spaniards*—OUTACITIE—MALACHTY—ATTAKULLAKULLA—*Indians murdered*—ATTAKULLAKULLA *prevents retaliation upon whites in his power*—*Cherokee War begins*—Governor Littleton's *expedition*—*Imprisons their Ambassadors*—*They are massacred*—Colonel Montgomery *sent against them*—*Battle near Keowee*—*Cherokees take Fort London*—SILOUCE—*Saves the life of* Colonel Byrd—Colonel Grant *subdues the Cherokees, and they make peace with the whites*—CHLUCCO.

THE presumption is pretty strongly supported, that Sir *Walter Ralegh* visited the southern shores of North America. When General *Oglethorpe* landed in Georgia, in 1732,* O. S., and communicated to the Indians the contents of a journal of Sir *Walter's*, they seemed to have a tradition of him, which they had fondly cherished; although, if the person they met were *Ralegh*, a hundred years had elapsed since he was there. They pointed out to Mr. *Oglethorpe* a place near Yamacraw bluff, since Charleston, on which was a large mound, in which was buried, they said, a chief who had talked with Sir *Walter Ralegh* upon that spot. The chief had requested his people to bury him there, that the place might be kept in veneration.

TOMOCHICHI was the principal chief, or Mico, as chiefs were called, of a small band of Creeks and Yamasees, who, having in some way offended their countrymen, fled their country, and "wandered about in the woods some time, until about 1732, when they begged leave of this government to sit down on the high land of Yamacraw, on the south side of Savannah river, at or near the place where the new town of Savannah, in Georgia, is now situated."† They consisted of but 17 or 18 families, and their first chief appears to have been called BOCACHEE. Several chief men, of various tribes, came to welcome the English, immediately after their arrival. "They were as follows: From the tribe of Coweeta, *Yahan-lakee*, their king, or mico; *Essaboo*, their warrior, the son of *Old-brim*, lately dead, whom the Spaniards called emperor of the Creeks, with eight men and two women attendants. From the tribe of Cussetas, *Cusseta*, their mico; *Tatchiquatchi*, their head warrior, with four attendants. From the tribe of Owseecheys, *Ogeese*, the mico, or war king; *Neathlouthko* and *Ougachi*, two chief men, with three attendants. From the tribe of Cheechaws, *Outhleteboa*, their mico, *Thlautho-thlukee*, *Figeer*, *Sootamilla*, war captains, with three attendants. From the tribe of Echetas, *Chutabeeche* and *Robin*, two war captains, (the latter was bred among the English,) with four attendants. From the tribe of Polachucolas, *Gillattee*, their head warrior, and five attendants. From the tribe of Oconas, *Oueekachumpa*, called by the English *Long-king*, *Koowoo*, a warrior. From the tribe of Eufaule, *Tomaumi*, head warrior, and three attendants.

* Many gentlemen in England contributed, in various ways, this year, for the advancement of the colony; some in cattle, some in labor, some in provisions, and others as soldiers. The contribution of one gentleman, for its singularity, shall be mentioned. "Mr. *Hume* gave a silver boat and spoon for the first child born in Georgia, which being born of Mrs. *Close*, were given accordingly."—*Commissioners' Report on Georgia Affairs*, p. 119.

† Report of the Commissioners, *ut supra*, 11, 116, 117.

"The Indians being all seated, *Oueekachumpa*, a very tall old man, stood, and made a speech, which was interpreted by Mr. *Wiggan* and Mr. *Musgrove*,* in which he said all the lands to the southward of Savannah River belonged to the Creeks. He said, the Indians were poor, but the same Power that gave the English breath, gave them breath also. That that Power had given the English the most wisdom. That as they had come to instruct them, they should have all the lands which they did not use themselves. That this was not only his mind, but the minds of the eight towns of Creeks, who had, after consulting together, sent some of their chief men with skins, which was their wealth. At this period of *Oueekachumpa's* speech, some of the chiefs of the eight towns brought each a bundle of buck's skins, and laid them down before Mr. *Oglethorpe*. Then the chief said, "*These are the best things we possess, but we give them with a good heart. I thank you for your kindness to* Tomochichi, *and his people. He is my kinsman, and, though he was banished from his nation, he is a good man and a great warrior. It was on account of his wisdom and justice, that the banished men chose him their king. I hear that the Cherokees have killed some Englishmen. If you* [addressing Mr. Oglethorpe] *will command us, we will go against them with all our force, kill their people, and destroy their living.*"

When *Oueekachumpa* had done speaking, *Tomochichi* drew near with his men, and, after making a low bow, said,—"*I was a banished man, and I came here poor and helpless to look for good land near the tombs of my ancestors, and when you came to this place, I feared you would drive us away; for we were weak and wanted corn. But you confirmed our land to us, and gave us food.*" The other chiefs spoke in the same manner as *Oueekachumpa* had, and then agreed upon and executed an amicable treaty.

By the assistance of his interpreter, *Mary Musgrove*, General *Oglethorpe* had been able to draw together, at one time, 50 chiefs from the upper and lower Creek towns, and, by his conciliatory conduct, had secured their friendship. He next resolved to take a deputation of them to England, hoping what they might witness and experience there, would result in lasting benefits to both their nations and the English. Accordingly, measures having been taken for the furtherance of this project, the general and the Indian chiefs embarked for England, in the Aldborough man-of-war, and arrived at St. Hellens, in the Isle of Wight, 16 June, 1734. The names of the Indians were Tomochichi, Senawki, his consort, and Toonakowi, the prince, his nephew; also Hillispilli, a war captain, and Apakowtski, Stimalechi, Sintouchi, Hinguithi, and Umphychi, five other chiefs, with their interpreter.

Immediately after their arrival, orders were given for preparing proper habits for them, in order to their being introduced at court. This having been done, Sir *Clement Cotterel*, knight, master of the ceremonies, was sent, August 1, with three of the king's coaches, drawn by six horses each, to the Georgia office, where the chiefs, all except one, were taken in and carried to Kensington, where their introduction to his majesty, King *George* II., took place. The one left at the Georgia office was sick with the small-pox, of which he died the next day. Tomochichi, after presenting the king with several eagle's feathers, which were considered, by his nation, the most respectful present they could send, delivered the following speech to his majesty:—

"This day I see the majesty of your face, the greatness of your house, and the number of your people. I am come for the good of the whole nation of the Creeks, to renew the peace they had long ago made with the English. I am come over in my old days; and, though I cannot live to see any advantage to myself, I am come for the good of the children of all the nations of the Upper and Lower Creeks, that they may be instructed in the knowledge of the English. These are the feathers of the eagle, which is the swiftest of birds, and who flieth all round our nations. These feathers are a sign of peace in our land, and we have brought them over to leave them with you, great king, as a sign of everlasting peace. O! great king, whatsoever words

* His wife was the interpreter, according to *M'Call*, i. 35, who was a half breed named *Mary*. *Oglethorpe* first purchased her friendship with presents, and afterwards allowed her a hundred pounds a year for her services.—*Commissioners' Report on Georgia Affairs.*

you shall say unto me, I will tell them faithfully to all the kings of the Creek nations." The king's answer, though short, was, in the highest degree, conciliatory, and what was termed gracious.*

When the chiefs were introduced at court, his majesty received them upon his throne, in the presence chamber, attended by the officers of state, and a numerous court. They were introduced by the Duke of *Grafton*, chamberlain of his majesty's household; and, after the ceremonies, they returned to their apartments, at the Georgia office.

Their first care, after returning from court, was to inter their deceased companion, which was accordingly done with great ceremony, in the burial-ground of St. John the Evangelist, Westminster, according to the custom of the "Cherokee Creeks," which was in the following manner:—"The deceased being sewed up in two blankets, with one deal board under and another over him, and tied down with a cord, was placed upon a bier, and carried to the place of interment. There were only present at the time of his being put into the grave, King *Tomo*, and some of the chiefs, the upper church warden of the parish, and the grave digger. When the corpse was laid in the earth, the clothes of the deceased were thrown into the grave; after this a quantity of glass beads were cast in, and then some pieces of silver; the custom of those Indians being to bury all the deceased's effects with him."

Although we have the names of all the chiefs given us that went over with Mr. *Oglethorpe*, we have not the means of knowing which it was that died. Indians often died on their visits to Europe. One of the five Iroquois chiefs died in England,† in 1710, and of his name too we are ignorant.

Mr. *Oglethorpe's* chiefs, after having been showed the chief curiosities in and about London, were taken to Spithead, where the English fleet lay, that they might go on board and view the tremendous ship *Britannia*, and some others of great magnitude. On the 30 October, 1734, a little past noon, they embarked at Gravesend, on board the Prince of Wales, for Georgia.

Of *Tomochichi*, who was the most prominent character among them, we have yet a little to add. He lived until he had attained his 97th year, and died 15 October, 1739, five years, wanting 15 days, after he sailed from England. He resided, at the time of his death, about four miles from Savannah. He was highly beloved by the English, having always been their particular friend, fought for them in war, and aided them by his counsel in peace. He was aware of the approach of death, and expressed but little desire to live longer, as he should be unable to aid his allies any more against the Spaniards. For General *Oglethorpe* he expressed the greatest tenderness, and entreated the Indians to bear in remembrance the kindnesses with which the king of England had treated him, and hoped they would always remain his subjects. Having expressed a wish that his body might be buried among the English in Savannah, accordingly, his corpse was there interred in Percival Square, with military parade, and General *Oglethorpe* ordered a pyramid to be erected over it, with an appropriate inscription.‡

Thus are traced the first steps in the history of Georgia, and thus did every thing promise a continuance of that friendship so well begun by General *Oglethorpe*. Nothing was left undone, while the Creek chiefs were in England, to impress upon their minds exalted ideas of the power and greatness of the English nation. The nobility were not only curious to see them, but entertained them at their tables in the most magnificent style. Multitudes flocked around them, conferring gifts and marks of respect upon them. The king allowed them £20 sterling a week, during their stay, and it was computed that, at their return to America, they brought presents to the amount of £400 sterling. After remaining in England four months, they embarked at Gravesend for Georgia. They were conveyed to the place of embarkation in his majesty's carriages.§

In the invasion of Georgia by the Spaniards, in 1743, many Indians were drawn into the controversy, on both sides. *Toeanoeowi*,‖ or *Tooanohowi*, a nephew of *Tomochichi*, was shot through the right arm, in an encounter with

* *Harris*, Voyages.
† *Kalm's* Travels in America, i. 210.
‡ *M'Call*, Hist. Georgia, i. 196, 197
§ Ib. i. 45.
‖ *Harris*

the Spaniards, by a Spanish captain. *Tooanohowi* drew his pistol with his left hand, and shot the captain through the head.

Thus, with the Spaniards upon one hand, and the English upon the other and the French in the midst of them, the Creeks and Cherokees became subject to every possible evil to which the caprice of those several nations gave rise. In 1723, a chief, whose name we find in writers of that day, *Wootassitaw*, *Woosatasate*, *Wootassitau*, *Wrosetasatow*,* &c. is styled "Governor of the Lower and Middle Settlements of the Charikees." He is presumed to be the same with *Otacite*, or *Otassite*, one of the prisoners above enumerated, and from what we are about to relate of him, his eminence will be apparent. In 1721, *Francis Nicholson* went over as governor of S. Carolina, who was said to have been very successful in managing affairs with the Indians. Soon after his arrival, the Cherokees despatched messengers to Charleston to adjust some difficulties which had for some time existed; and, not long after, another more full and complete deputation arrived. Governor *Nicholson* opened the council by a long speech to "*Wootassite*, King, and to the heads of the Lower and Middle Settlements of the Charokee Nations."

In the course of his speech, he observes, that, when they delivered their acknowledgments and paid their submission to the government, "the other day," they had made mention of 37 towns that had sent down their chiefs for that purpose, and wished to be satisfied that these towns were represented, that his words might be carried to all their inhabitants. After laying much stress on their submission and respect to the king of England, he speaks thus sensibly upon their trading with the whites, which at the same time discovers to us the origin of former troubles.

After ordering that if either party injured the other, restitution should be made by the aggressor, he says, "Frequent complaints have been made that your people have often broke open the stores belonging to our traders, and carry'd away their goods; and also pillaged several of their packs, when employ'd and entrusted to carry them up; and restitution has never been made, which are great faults: We therefore recommend to you, to take all possible precautions to prevent such ill practices for the future," &c. "And to prevent any injury or misunderstanding, we have pass'd a law, which appoints commissioners that are to go twice a year to the Congaree, or Savana garrison, to hear and redress all grievances."

"*Woosatasate* being a man in great esteem amongst you, having given frequent testimonies of his affection and firm adherence to this government, and being appointed king over you by the former governor† of this province; so I, who am sent immediately from his majesty, having the same regard to so deserving a man, and in compliance with your own request, that I would constitute proper commanders over you, do now declare the said *Woosatasate*, your leader and commander in chief over all the lower settlements of the Cherrokees, and give him a commission for that office, under the broad seal of this his Majesty's province," &c. "I expect that you, *Woosatasate*, do, within a month after your return, call together all the chief men in your district, and that you make them thoroughly acquainted with what I now say to you, and require of you, and shall give directions, that all the Englishmen amongst you shall be at that meeting. That your ancient government may be restored, I recommend to you to keep your young men in that due decorum they us'd to be," &c. This treaty was held 3 February, 1721, O. S., or this is the date to Governor *Nicholson's* speech; but it appears by our account that it was the middle of March before the Indian deputies left Charleston.

Although there were events, in every year, of importance, yet, in this place we shall take up the period rendered more memorable by the distinguished chiefs

---

* *Hewatt*, I. 298.

† *James Moore*, who, according to *Hewatt* (I. 276), was put into office in opposition to the regular course, by a kind of revolutionary spirit. See *Oldmixon*, who is far more particular, I. 348.—*Moore* was elected in 1701. The author of "The British Dominions," (142,) says the Indians were cruelly treated during his administration. There were several other governors before *Nicholson*, beside *Moore*.

ATTAKULLAKULLA and OCKONOSTOTA * The fame of Carolina had, in 1753, drawn a multitude of Europeans to her shores. The same year on the 26 May, MALACHTY, attended by the *Wolf-king* and the Ottasee chief, with about 20 others, and above a hundred of their people, came to Charleston. They were met, on their way, by a troop of horsemen, who conducted them to the town, by the governor's order, in great state. This was to induce them to make peace and remain their allies, and, to this end, the governor, *Glenn*, made a very pacific speech, in the Indian manner. *Malachty*, who, at this time, seems to have been the head chief among the Creeks, presented the governor with a quantity of skins, and readily consented to a peace with the English; but, in regard to a peace with the Cherokees, he said, that was a matter of great moment, and he must deliberate with his people, before he could give an answer. The Cherokees were already under the protection of the English, and some of them had, not long before, been killed by the Creeks, in the very neighborhood of Charleston. The party which committed this outrage was led by *Malachty*. Notwithstanding, a cessation of hostilities seems to have taken place, for numbers of each nation joined the English immediately after the capture of Oswego, by the French, in 1756. The Cherokees are particularly named, as having rendered essential service in the expedition against Fort Duquesne; but a circumstance happened, while those warriors were returning home from that expedition, which involved them in an immediate war with the English, in whose service they had been engaged. Having lost their horses, and being worn out with toil and fatigue, on coming to the frontiers of Virginia, they picked up several of those animals, which belonged to the inhabitants of the places through which they travelled. This, Dr. *Ramsay* † says, was the cause of the massacre which they suffered at that time. But Mr. *Adair*, ‡ who lived then among the Indians in those parts, says, —"Several companies of the Cheerake, who joined our forces under Gen. *Stanwix*, at the unfortunate Ohio, affirmed that their alienation from us was because they were confined to our martial arrangement, by unjust suspicion of them—were very much contemned,—and half starved at the main camp: their hearts told them, therefore, to return home, as freemen and injured allies, though without a supply of provisions. This they did, and pinching hunger forced them to take as much as barely supported nature, when returning to their own country. In their journey, the German inhabitants, without any provocation, killed, in cool blood, about 40 of their warriors, in different places —though each party was under the command of a British subject." It must be remembered that, upon *Braddock's* defeat, Virginia had offered a reward for the scalps of hostile Indians. Here, then, was an inducement for remorseless villains to murder, and it was impossible, in many cases, to know whether a scalp were taken from a friend or an enemy. Out of this, then, we have no hesitation in saying, grew the excessive calamities, which soon after distressed the southern provinces. Forty innocent men, and friends, too, murdered in cold blood by the backwoodsmen of Virginia, brought on a war, which caused as much distress and misery among the parties engaged, as any since that region of country was planted by the whites.

At one place, a monster entertained a party of Indians, and treated them kindly, while, at the same time, he caused a gang of his kindred ruffians to lie in ambush where they were to pass, and, when they arrived, barbarously shot them down to a man! The news was forthwith carried to the Cherokee nation, and the effect of it upon the minds of the warriors, was like that of electricity. They seized their tomahawks and war clubs, and, but for the wisdom of *Attakullakulla*, would have murdered several Englishmen, then in their country upon some matters respecting a treaty. As *Attakullakulla* was a chief sachem, he was among the first apprized of the murders, and the design

---

* Ouconnostotah, Ouconnostota, Ouconnostata, *Wynne*.—Occonostota, *Ramsay*.—*Attakullakulla* was generally called the *Little-carpenter*.

† Hist. South Carolina, i. 169.

‡ Hist. Amer. Indians, 245. That the Indians' taking horses was no pretext for the murders, even at the time, appears evident. "As (says Captain *M'Call*, i. 257.) the horses in those parts ran wild in the woods, it was customary, both among the Indians and white people on the frontiers, to catch them and appropriate them to their own use."

of vengeance. He therefore goes immediately to them, and informed them of their danger, and assisted them to secrete themselves; then, without loss of time, he assembled his warriors, and made a speech to them, in which he inveighed, with great bitterness, against the murderous English, and urged immediate war against them; "*and never* (said he) *shall the hatchet be buried until the blood of our countrymen be atoned for. Let us not* (he continued) *violate our faith, or the laws of hospitality, by imbruing our hands in the blood of those who are now in our power. They came to us in the confidence of friendship, with belts of wampum to cement a perpetual alliance with us. Let us carry them back to their own settlements; conduct them safely within their confines, and then take up the hatchet, and endeavor to exterminate the whole race of them.*" This counsel was adopted. Before commencing hostilities, however, the murderers were demanded, but were blindly refused them, and we have related the consequences.

The French, it was said, used their influence to enrage the Indians; but if that were the case, we should not deem it worth naming, as it appears to us that nothing more could be necessary to inflame them than the horrid outrages of which we have spoken.

It appears from another source,* that Governor *Littleton* was met at Charleston by a deputation of 32 Cherokee chiefs, among whom was *Ockonostota*, who, on hearing of the warlike movements at that place, had set out to visit the English, and if possible to prevent a war with them. For although some of their young warriors had committed several acts of violence, yet the great body of the nation were friendly towards the English, and desired peace. But instead of seizing on this opportunity of treating with the chiefs, he insultingly told them, "That he would soon be in their country, where he would let them know his demands." *Ockonostota* began to speak in reply, "but the governor being determined that nothing should prevent his military expedition, declared he would hear no talk he had to make, neither in vindication of his nation, nor any proposals with regard to peace." The Lieutenant-Governor Bull saw the bad policy of this step, and urged the necessity of hearing what *Ockonostota*, the *Great Warrior*, as he was called, had to say, and settling their difficulties; but this good advice had no effect on *Littleton*, and he marched from Charleston in October, a few days after At a place of rendezvous, about 140 miles from that place, his force amounted to about 1400 men. The chiefs, by order of the governor, had marched with the army to this place, and, although burning with resentment at their treatment, yet they discovered no signs of discontent. When the army was about to march from Congarees, (this being their place of rendezvous,) the chiefs were all made prisoners, and under guard were marched to Fort Prince George.†

Their resentment now showed itself; "stung to the heart by such base treatment," they cringed in sullen silence, and we may suppose that "they spent their time in concerting plots for obtaining their liberty, and satisfaction for the injuries done them."‡

Being now at Fort Prince George with his army, *Littleton* found himself in about the same repute with his own men as with the injured Indians; he therefore concluded not to carry his *conquests* any further at present, but to make a treaty, and retain captive Indians enough as hostages to insure its observance. He therefore sent a messenger to *Attakullakulla*, who was reckoned the wisest man in the nation, or the best friend to the English, requesting him to come to Fort George. He immediately came; and to show the English he was their friend, produced a French prisoner whom he had just taken in an expedition against that nation, and whom he presented to Governor *Littleton*. A "congress" was now (about 18 December, 1759) held with *Attakullakulla*, in which a long speech, in which all the grievances he could think of were enumerated by the governor; after which the chief made another, in which he promised to do all he could to persuade his countrymen to give the governor the satisfaction he demanded; yet he said, "it

---

* *Hewatt*, Hist. Carolina, ii. 216.
† This fort was upon the Savannah River, near the Cherokee town called Keowee.
‡ *Hewatt*, Hist. Carolina, ii. 18.

neither would nor could be complied with, as they had no coercive authority, one over another." He desired that some of the chiefs then confined might be liberated to aid him in restoring tranquillity; and accordingly *Ockonostota*, *Fiftoe*, chief of Keowee, and the head warrior of Estatoe, were given up, and two Indians were taken in exchange and put in irons. The other Cherokees present, observing what was going forward, withdrew into the woods, and *Attakullakulla*, presuming the business must end here, withdrew also. It had been premised, or rather demanded, in the governor's speech, that 24 Indians, who were known to have killed white people, should be given into his hands to be put to death, or otherwise disposed of. Two only had been delivered, and 22 yet remained of the number of the murderers, in their own native forests.

As soon as *Littleton* knew of *Attakullakulla's* departure, he sent for him, and he immediately returned, and the business of a treaty was renewed, and on the 26 December, 1759, it was signed by

ATTAKULLAKULLA,	OTASSITE,	OCONNOECA, and
OUCONNOSTOTA,	KITAGUSTA,	KILLCANNOKEA.

By article III. of the treaty,* it was agreed that 22 chiefs, (those who had been treacherously seized,) should remain as hostages, to ensure the delivery of the like number of murderers to the English. There seems, however, to have been but 21 retained, whose names we are able to give below, and who, under the name of hostages, were thrown into a dismal, close prison, scarce large enough for six men, where they remained about two months, and were then masacred, as in the sequel we shall show:—

Chenohe, *Ousanatanah*, *Tallichama*, *Tallitahe*, *Quarrasattahe*, *Connasaratah*, *Kataetoi*, *Otassite* of Watogo, *Ousanoletah* of Jore, *Kataeletah* of Cowetche, *Chisquatalone*, *Skiagusta* of Sticoe, *Tanaesto*, *Wohatche*, *Wyejah*, *Oucahchistanah*, *Nicolche*, *Tony*, *Toatiahoi*, *Shallisloske*, and *Chistie*.†

Things having been thus settled, Mr. *Littleton* returned to Charleston, where he was received like a conqueror, although what he had done, it will appear, was worse than if he had done nothing.

Ockonostota, for good reason, no doubt, entertained a deep-rooted hatred against Captain *Cotymore*, an officer of the garrison, and the army had but just left the country, when it was found that he was hovering about the garrison with a large number of warriors. But it was uncertain, for some time, whether they intended to attack the fort, or whether they wished to continue near their friends, who were imprisoned in it. However, it is said, that, by some means, a plan was concerted between the Indians without and those confined within the fort, for surprising it. Be this as it may, *Ockonostota*, on the 16 February, 1760, practised the following wile to effect the object. Having placed a party of his warriors in a dark cane-brake near at hand, he sent a squaw to the garrison to invite the commander to come out, for he had something of importance to communicate to him. Captain *Cotymore* imprudently went out, accompanied by two of his officers, and *Ockonostota* appeared upon the opposite bank of the Savannah, with a bridle in his hand, the better to conceal his intentions. He told the captain he was going to Charleston to effect the release of the hostages, and requested that a white man might accompany him; and that, as the distance was great, he would go and try to catch a horse. The captain promised him a guard, and hoped he would succeed in finding a horse. *Ockonostota* then quickly turned himself about, and swinging his bridle thrice over his head, which was the signal to his men, and they promptly obeying it, about 30 guns were discharged upon the officers at the same moment. Captain *Cotymore* received a shot in his left breast, from which he died in two or three days after, and both the others were wounded.‡ On recovering the fort, an attempt was made to put the

---

* It is printed at length in the BRITISH EMPIRE, by *Huddlestone Wynne*, Esq. ii. 273—277; an author of no inconsiderable merit on our affairs.

† Several of these 22 were of the number who had been in England in 1730, and executed a treaty with the king, as has been before stated, and as will be seen by comparing the names above with those named in the treaty.

‡ "Two Indian women appeared at Keowee, on the other side of the river. Mr. *Doherty* went out, and accosting them, asked what news? *Ockonostota* joined them, pretending some

hostages in irons. An Englishman, who laid hold on one of them for that purpose, was stabbed and slain; and, in the scuffle, two or three more were wounded, and driven out of the place of confinement. The tragedy in the fort had now only commenced; the miserable prisoners had repelled their assassins for the moment, and, doubtless, hoped for deliverance from their friends without, who had now closely besieged the place. But, unfortunately for these poor wretches, the fort was too strong to be carried by their arts of war, and the dastardly whites found time and means to murder their victims, one by one, in a manner too horrible to relate.* There were few persons among the Cherokees who did not lose a friend or relation by this massacre; and, as one man, the nation took up the hatchet, and desolations quickly followed.

Meanwhile, singular as it may appear, *Attakullakulla* remained the fast friend of the whites, and used all his arts to induce his countrymen to make peace. But it was in vain he urged them to consider that they had more than revenged themselves; they were determined to carry all before them. *Attakullakulla* was now an old man, and had become much attached to the English, from several causes. On the other hand, *Ockonostota* was a stern warrior, in the vigor of manhood, and, like the renowned *Pontiac*, was determined to rid his country of his barbarous enemies.

The leaders in every town seized the hatchet, telling their followers that the spirits of murdered brothers were flying around them, and calling out for vengeance. All sung the war-song, and, burning with impatience to imbrue their hands in the blood of their enemies, rushed down among innocent and defenceless families on the frontiers of Carolina, where men, women, and children, without distinction, fell a sacrifice to their merciless fury. Such of the whites as fled to the woods, and escaped the scalping-knife, perished with hunger. Every day brought fresh accounts to the capital of their ravages and desolations. But, while the back settlers impatiently looked to their governor for relief, the small-pox raged to such a degree in town, that few of the militia could be prevailed on to leave their distressed families to serve the public. In this extremity, an express was sent to General *Amherst*, the commander-in-chief in America, for assistance, in terms too pressing to be denied. Accordingly, he ordered a battalion of Highlanders, and four companies of Royal Scots,† under the command of Colonel *Montgomery*, afterwards Earl *Eglinton*, to embark at New York for Carolina. In the mean time, *Littleton*, having been appointed governor of Jamaica, *William Bull* succeeded him; a change much to the advantage of the province.

Colonel *Montgomery* arrived in Carolina towards the end of April, to the great joy of the people, who had taken measures to coöperate with him to the best advantage; but, as the conquest of Canada was the grand object now, General *Amherst* had ordered Colonel *Montgomery* to strike a sudden blow for the relief of the Carolinians, and then to return to head-quarters at Albany, without loss of time; and we have scarce an example in military history, where an officer fulfilled his commission with greater promptitude. He soon after rendezvoused at the Congarees; and, being joined by many gentlemen of distinction as volunteers, besides the principal strength of the country, he marched for the heart of the Cherokee country. After reaching a place called Twelve Mile River, he encamped upon advantageous ground, and marched with a party to surprise Estatoe, about 20 miles from his camp. In the way, he took Little Keowee, and put every man to the sword. Estatoe he found abandoned, except by a few that could not escape, and it was reduced to ashes, as was Sugar Town, and every other settlement in the lower nation. About 60 Indians were killed, and 40 taken prisoners; but the

matters of business; he drew from the fort several of the officers to converse with them."—*Haywood's* Hist. Tennessee, 30.

* "A bottle of poison was found with one of the dead hostages, probably intended to be dropped into the well; and several tomahawks were found buried in the earth." *Haywood*, Hist. Tennessee, 30.—Any stories would gain credence among the whites, which went to make the Indians as bad as themselves. Whether the bottle spoken of contained poison, may be questioned; and, if it did, it may be reasonably doubted whether the Indians knew any thing about it.

† I am following *Hewatt*, but the *Annual Register*, iii. 62, says, "a regiment of Highlanders, a battalion of Royal Americans, a body of grenadiers," &c.

warriors had generally escaped to the mountains and deserts. Thus far, the campaign had been prosperous with the whites, but three or four men having been killed; but it had no other effect upon the Indians than to increase their rage.

Meanwhile, Fort Prince George had been closely invested, and Colonel *Montgomery* marched to its relief. From this place, two friendly chiefs were despatched to the middle settlements, to offer peace to the people there, and orders were sent to those in command at Fort Loudon, to use means to bring about an accommodation with the Upper Towns; but the Indians would not hear to any terms, and Colonel *Montgomery* was constrained to march again to find the enemy. He had now the most difficult part of his service to perform. The country through which he had to march was covered by dark thickets, numerous deep ravines, and high river banks; where a small number of men might distress and wear out the best appointed army.

Having arrived within five miles of Etchoe, the nearest town of the middle settlements, the army was attacked on the 27 June, in a most advantageous place for the attacking party. It was a low valley, in which the bushes were so thick, that the soldiers could see scarcely three yards before them; and in the bottom of this valley flowed a muddy river, with steep clay banks. Through this place the army must march. Rightly judging the enemy had not omitted so important a pass, Colonel *Montgomery* ordered out a company of rangers, under Captain *Morrison*, to enter the ravine and make discovery No sooner had he entered it, but the fierce war-whoop was raised, and the Indians darted from covert to covert, at the same time firing upon the whites Captain *Morrison* was immediately shot down, and his men closely engaged but, being without delay supported by the infantry and grenadiers, they were able to maintain their ground, and the battle became obstinate; nor could the Indians be dislodged, until near an hour of hard fighting. In the mean time, the Royal Scots took possession of a place between the Indians and a rising ground on their right, while the Highlanders sustained the light infantry and grenadiers on the left. As the left became too warm for them, and not well understanding the position of the Royal Scots, the Indians, in their retreat, fell in with them, and were sharply encountered; but they soon effected their retreat to a hill, and could no more be brought to action. In this fight, 96 of the whites were killed and wounded, of whom 20 were of the former number. Of the Cherokees, 40 were said to have been killed.

The Indians had now been driven from one ravine, with a small loss; but Colonel *Montgomery* was in no condition to pursue his advantage farther, and he therefore, after destroying so much of his provisions as would afford horses for the wounded, began his retreat out of the Indian country, and, in obedience to his commission, soon after returned to New York; not, however, without leaving 400 men for the security of the province. But it was soon seen, that what had yet been done only increased the rage of the Indians, and their depredation continued at the very heels of the retreating army. They immediately cut off all communication with Fort Loudon, which was garrisoned with 200 men.* *Ockonostota*, with his numerous warriors, kept strict watch, insomuch that there was no means of escape. At length, the garrison having miserably subsisted, for some time, upon poor famished horses, dogs, &c., many of them became resolved to throw themselves into the power of the Indians, wishing rather to die by their hands, than miserably to perish within their fortress. Captain *Steuart*, an officer among them, was well known to the Indians, and possessed great address and sagacity. He resolved, at this crisis, to repair to Chote, the residence of *Ockonostota*, and make overtures for the surrender of the garrison. He accordingly, effected his object, and returned with articles of capitulation agreed upon. Besides the names of *Ockonostota* and *Paul Demere*, the commander of the garrison, the name of another chief was to the articles, called *Cunigacatgoae*. The articles stipulated, that the garrison should march

* The Cherokees were now supposed to number 3000 warriors, and it was daily expected that the Chocktaws were about to join them.

out with their arms and drums, each soldier having as much powder and bal as his officers should think necessary, and that they should march for Virginia unmolested.

Accordingly, on 7 August, 1760, the English took up their march for Fort Prince George. They had proceeded but about 15 miles, when they encamped, for the night, upon a small plain near Taliquo. They were accompanied thus far by *Ockonostota* in person, and many others, in a friendly manner, but at night they withdrew without giving any notice. The army was not molested during the night, but, at dawn of day, a sentinel came running into camp with the information that a host of Indians were creeping up to surround them. Captain *Demere* had scarce time to rally, before the Indians broke into his camp with great fury. The poor emaciated soldiers made but feeble resistance. Thirty of their number fell in the first onset, among whom was their captain. Those that were able, endeavored to save themselves by flight, and others surrendered themselves upon the place. This massacre, it will not be forgotten, was in retaliation for that of the hostages already related. Among the prisoners was Captain *Steuart.* They were conducted to Fort Loudon, which now became *Ockonostota's* head-quarters.

Attakullakulla, learning that his friend *Steuart* was among the captives, proceeded immediately to Fort Loudon, where he ransomed him at the expense of all the property he could command, and took care of him with the greatest tenderness and affection.

The restless *Ockonostota* next resolved to invest Fort Prince George. He was induced to undertake that project, as fortune had thrown in his way some of the means for such an undertaking, hitherto beyond his reach. Before abdicating Fort Loudon, the English had hid in the ground several bags of powder. This his men had found. Several cannon had also been left behind, and he designed to force his English prisoners to get them through the woods, and manage them in the attack upon Fort Prince George. But *Attakullakulla* defeated these operations, by assisting Captain *Steuart* to escape. He even accompanied him to the English settlements, and returned loaded with presents.

The French were said to have had their emissaries busily employed in spiriting on the Indians. One, named *Lewis Latinac*, an officer, is particularly mentioned. He persuaded them that the English had nothing less in view than their total extermination, and, furnishing them with arms and ammunition, urged them to war. At a great council of the nation, after brandishing his hatchet, he struck it into a log of wood, calling out, "*Who is the man that will take this up for the king of France?*"

SALOUE or SILÒUEE, a young warrior of Estatoe, instantly laid hold of it, and cried out, "*I am for war. The spirits of our brothers* who have been slain, still call upon us to avenge their death. He is no better than a woman that refuses to follow me." Others were not wanting to follow his example, and the war continued.

Silòuee was a Cherokee chief, and was introduced by Mr. *Jefferson*, to illustrate the observation in his Notes on Virginia, that the Indian "is affectionate to his children, careful of them, and indulgent in the extreme; that his affections comprehend his other connections, weakening, as with us, from circle to circle, as they recede from the centre; that his friendships are strong and faithful to the uttermost extremity." "A remarkable instance of this appeared in the case of the late Col. *Byrd*,* who was sent to the Cherokee nation to transact some business with them. It happened that some of our disorderly people had just killed one or two of that nation. It was therefore proposed in the council of the Cherokees, that Col. *Byrd* should be put to death, in revenge for the loss of their countrymen. Among them was a chief called *Silòuee*, who, on some former occasion, had contracted an acquaintance and friendship with Col. *Byrd*. He came to him every night in his tent, and told him not to be afraid, they should not kill him. After many days' deliberation,

* Perhaps the same mentioned by *Oldmixon*, (i. 283,) who, in speaking of the Indian powwows, says, "one very lately conjured a shower of rain for Col. *Byrd's* plantation in time of drouth, for two bottles of rum;" and our author says he should not have believed, had he not found it in an author who was on the spot!

however, the determination was, contrary to *Silòuee's* expectation, that *Byrd* should be put to death, and some warriors were despatched as executioners. *Silòuee* attended them; and when they entered the tent, he threw himself between them and *Byrd*, and said to the warriors, '*This man is my friend. before you get at him you must kill me!*' On which they returned, and the council respected the principle so much, as to recede from their determination."

A more impolitic and barbarous measure, perhaps, never entered the heart of man, than that of offering a reward for human scalps. This was done by Virginia, as we have before related. It is true the government of Virginia was not alone in this criminal business, but that betters not her case. The door of enormity being thus opened, it was easy to have foreseen, that many men upon the frontiers, "of bad lives and worse principles," says an intelligent writer,* stood ready to step in. As the event proved, many friendly Indians were *murdered*, and the government *defrauded*. It was at the news of a murder of this description that Colonel *Byrd* was seized.

Such was the condition of the country, that a second application was made to General *Amherst* for aid, and he promptly afforded it. Colonel *James Grant* arrived there early in 1761, and not long after took the field with a force of English and Indians, amounting to about 2600 men.† He traversed the Cherokee country, and subdued that people in a hard-fought battle, near the same place where Colonel *Montgomery* was attacked the year before. It lasted about three hours, in which about 60 whites were killed and wounded. The loss of the Indians was unknown. Colonel *Grant* ordered his dead to be sunk in the river, that the Indians might not find them, to practise upon them their barbarities. He then proceeded to the destruction of their towns, 15 in number, which he accomplished without molestation.‡ Peace was at last effected by the mediation of *Attakullakulla*. This chief's residence was upon the Tennessee or Cherokee River, at what was called the *Overhill Towns*. In 1773, when the learned traveller, *Bartram*, travelled into the Cherokee country, he met the old chief on his way to Charleston; of which circumstance he speaks thus in his Travels:—"Soon after crossing this large branch of the Tanase, I observed descending the heights, at some distance, a company of Indians, all well mounted on horseback. They came rapidly forward; on their nearer approach, I observed a chief at the head of the caravan, and apprehending him to be the *Little-carpenter*, emperor or grand chief of the Cherokees, as they came up, I turned off from the path to make way, in token of respect, which compliment was accepted, and gratefully and magnanimously returned; for his highness, with a gracious and cheerful smile, came up to me, and clapping his hand on his breast, offered it to me, saying, I am *Ata-cul-culla*, and heartily shook hands with me, and asked me if I knew it; I answered, that the good spirit who goes before me spoke to me, and said, that is the great *Ata-cul-culla*." Mr. *Bartram* added, that he was of Pennsylvania, and though that was a great way off, yet the name of *Attakullakulla* was dear to his white brothers of Pennsylvania. The chief then asked him if he came directly from Charleston, and if his friend "*John Stewart* were well." Mr. *Bartram* said he saw him lately, and that he was well. This was, probably, the same person whom *Attakullakulla* had assisted to make an escape, as we have just related.

In carrying out the history of the two chiefs, *Attakullakulla* and *Ockonostota*, we have omitted to notice *Chlucco*, better known by the name of the *Long-warrior*, king or mico of the Seminoles. He went out with Colonel *Montgomery*, and rendered him essential service in his unsuccessful expedition, of which we have spoken. A large band of Creeks accompanied him, and there is but little doubt, if it had not been for him and his warriors, few of the English would have returned to their friends. But, as usual, the English leader, in his time, had all the honor of successfully encountering many difficulties, and returning with his own life and many of his men's. It was by the aid of *Chlucco*, that the army escaped ambush after ambush, destroyed many of the Cherokee villages, and finally his warriors covered its retreat out of one of the most dangerous countries through which an army could pass. *Long-warrior* was what the New England Indians termed a great powwow. That he was

* Doctor *Burnaby*. † *Hewatt*. ‡ *Annual Register*, iv. 58; *Hewatt*, ii. 248—51.

a man possessing a good mind, may fairly be inferred from his ability to withstand the temptation of intoxicating liquors. He had been known to remain sober, when all his tribe, and many whites among them, had all been wallowing in the mire of drunkenness together. In the year 1773, at the head of about 40 warriors, he marched against the Chocktaws of West Florida. What was the issue of this expedition we have not learned. We may have again occasion to notice *Chlucco.*

CHAPTER V.

MONCACHTAPE, *the Yazoo—Narrative of his adventures to the Pacific Ocean*—GRAND-SUN, *chief of the Natchez—Receives great injustice from the French—Concerts their destruction—700 French are cut off—War with them—The Natchez destroyed in their turn*—GREAT-MORTAR—M'GILLIVRAY—*His birth and education—Visits New York —Troubles of his nation—His death*—TAME-KING—MAD-DOG.

MONCACHTAPE was a Yazoo, whose name signified, in the language of that nation, *killer of pain and fatigue.* How well he deserved this name, the sequel will unfold. He was well known to the historian *Du Pratz,* about 1760, and it was owing to his singular good intelligence, that that traveller was able to add much valuable information to his work. "This man (says *Du Pratz* *) was remarkable for his solid understanding and elevation of sentiment; and I may justly compare him to those first Greeks, who travelled chiefly into the east, to examine the manners and customs of different nations, and to communicate to their fellow citizens, upon their return, the knowledge which they had acquired." He was known to the French by the name of the *Interpreter,* as he could communicate with several other nations, having gained a knowledge of their languages. Monsieur *Du Pratz* used great endeavors among the nations upon the Mississippi, to learn their origin, or from whence they came; and observes concerning it, "All that I could learn from them was, that they came from between the north and the sun-setting; and this account they uniformly adhere to, whenever they give any account of their origin." This was unsatisfactory to him, and in his exertions to find some one that could inform him better, he met with *Moncachtape.* The following is the result of his communications in his own words:—

"I had lost my wife, and all the children whom I had by her, when I undertook my journey towards the sun-rising. I set out from my village contrary to the inclination of all my relations, and went first to the Chicasaws, our friends and neighbors. I continued among them several days, to inform myself whether they knew whence we all came, or, at least, whence they themselves came; they, who were our elders; since from them came the language of the country. As they could not inform me, I proceeded on my journey. I reached the country of the Chaouanous, and afterwards went up the Wabash, or Ohio, near to its source, which is in the country of the Iroquois, or Five Nations. I left them, however, towards the north; and, during the winter, which, in that country, is very severe and very long, I lived in a village of the Albenaquis, where I contracted an acquaintance with a man somewhat older than myself, who promised to conduct me, the following spring, to the great water. Accordingly, when the snows were melted, and the weather was settled, we proceeded eastward, and, after several days' journey, I at length saw the great water, which filled me with such joy and admiration, that I could not speak. Night drawing on, we took up our lodging on a high bank above the water, which was sorely vexed by the wind, and made so great a noise that I could not sleep. Next day, the ebbing and flowing of the water filled me with great apprehension; but my companion quieted my fears, by assuring me that the water observed certain bounds, both in advancing and

* Hist. Louisiana, ii. 121

retiring. Having satisfied our curiosity in viewing the great water, we returned to the village of the Abenaquis, where I continued the following winter; and, after the snows were melted, my companion and I went and viewed the great fall of the River St. Lawrence, at Niagara, which was distant from the village severa days' journey. The view of this great fall, at first, made my hair stand on end, and my heart almost leap out of its place; but afterwards, before I left it, I had the courage to walk under it. Next day, we took the shortest road to the Ohio, and my companion and I, cutting down a tree on the banks of the river we formed it into a pettiaugre, which served to conduct me down the Ohio and the Mississippi, after which, with much difficulty, I went up our small river, and at length arrived safe among my relations, who were rejoiced to see me in good health.—This journey, instead of satisfying, only served to excite my curiosity. Our old men, for several years, had told me that the ancient speech informed them that the red men of the north came originally much higher and much farther than the source of the River Missouri; and, as I had longed to see, with my own eyes, the land from whence our first fathers came, I took my precautions for my journey westwards. Having provided a small quantity of corn, I proceeded up along the eastern bank of the River Mississippi, till I came to the Ohio. I went up along the bank of this last river, about the fourth part of a day's journey, that I might be able to cross it without being carried into the Mississippi. There I formed a cajeux, or raft of canes, by the assistance of which I passed over the river; and next day meeting with a herd of buffaloes in the meadows, I killed a fat one, and took from it the fillets, the bunch, and the tongue. Soon after, I arrived among the Tamaroas, a village of the nation of the Illinois, where I rested several days, and then proceeded northwards to the mouth of the Missouri, which, after it enters the great river, runs for a considerable time without intermixing its muddy waters with the clear stream of the other. Having crossed the Mississippi, I went up the Missouri, along its northern bank, and, after several days' journey, I arrived at the nation of the Missouris, where I staid a long time to learn the language that is spoken beyond them. In going along the Missouri, I passed through meadows a whole day's journey in length, which were quite covered with buffaloes.

"When the cold was past, and the snows were melted, I continued my journey up along the Missouri, till I came to the nation of the west, or the Canzas. Afterwards, in consequence of directions from them, I proceeded in the same course near 30 days, and at length I met with some of the nation of the Otters, who were hunting in that neighborhood, and were surprised to see me alone. I continued with the hunters two or three days, and then accompanied one of them and his wife, who was near her time of lying in, to their village, which lay far off betwixt the north and west. We continued our journey along the Missouri for nine days, and then we marched directly northwards for five days more, when we came to the fine river, which runs westward in a direction contrary to that of the Missouri. We proceeded down this river a whole day, and then arrived at the village of the Otters, who received me with as much kindness as if I had been of their own nation. A few days after, I joined a party of the Otters, who were going to carry a calumet of peace to a nation beyond them, and we embarked in a pettiaugre, and went down the river for 18 days, landing now and then to supply ourselves with provisions. When I arrived at the nation who were at peace with the Otters, I staid with them till the cold was passed, that I might learn their language, which was common to most of the nations that lived beyond them.

"The cold was hardly gone, when I again embarked on the fine river, and in my course I met with several nations, with whom I generally staid but one night, till I arrived at the nation that is but one day's journey from the great water on the west. This nation live in the woods about the distance of a league from the river, from their apprehension of bearded men, who come upon their coasts in floating villages, and carry off their children to make slaves of them. These men were described to be white, with long black beards that came down to their breast; they were thick and short, had large heads, which were covered with cloth; they were always dressed even in the greatest heats; their clothes fell down to the middle of their legs, which, with their feet, were covered with red or yellow stuff. Their arms made a great fire and a great noise; and when they saw themselves outnumbered by red men, they retired on board their large pettiaugre, their number sometimes amounting to thirty, but never more.

"Those strangers came from the sun-setting, in search of a yellow stinking wood, which dyes a fine yellow color; but the people of this nation, that they might not be tempted to visit them, had destroyed all those kind of trees. Two other nations in their neighborhood, however, having no other wood, could not destroy the trees, and were still visited by the strangers; and being greatly incommoded by them, had invited their allies to assist them in making an attack upon them, the next time they should return. The following summer I accordingly joined in this expedition, and, after travelling five long days' journey, we came to the place where the bearded men usually landed, where we waited seventeen days for their arrival. The red men, by my advice, placed themselves in ambuscade to surprise the strangers, and accordingly when they landed to cut the wood, we were so successful as to kill eleven of them, the rest immediately escaping on board two large pettiaugres, and flying westward upon the great water.

"Upon examining those whom we had killed, we found them much smaller than ourselves, and very white; they had a large head, and in the middle of the crown the hair was very long; their head was wrapt in a great many folds of stuff, and their clothes seemed to be made neither of wool nor silk; they were very soft, and of different colors. Two only, of the eleven who were slain, had fire-arms, with powder and ball. I tried their pieces, and found that they were much heavier than yours, and did not kill at so great a distance.

"After this expedition, I thought of nothing but proceeding on my journey, and, with that design, I let the red men return home, and joined myself to those who inhabited more westward on the coast, with whom I travelled along the shore of the great water, which bends directly betwixt the north and the sun-setting. When I arrived at the villages of my fellow-travellers, where I found the days very long, and the nights very short, I was advised by the old men to give over all thoughts of continuing my journey. They told me that the land extended still a long way in a direction between the north and sun-setting, after which it ran directly west, and at length was cut by the great water from north to south. One of them added, that, when he was young, he knew a very old man who had seen that distant land before it was eat away by the great water, and that when the great water was low, many rocks still appeared in those parts. Finding it, therefore, impracticable to proceed much further, on account of the severity of the climate, and the want of game, I returned by the same route by which I had set out; and, reducing my whole travels westward to days' journeys, I compute that they would have employed me 36 moons; but, on account of my frequent delays, it was five years before I returned to my relations among the Yazoos."

Thus ends the narrative of the famous traveller *Moncachtape*, which seems to have satisfied *Du Pratz*, that the Indians came from the continent of Asia, by way of *Behring's* Straits. And he soon after left him, and returned to his own country. It would have been gratifying, could we have known more of the history of this very intelligent man. The same author brings also to our knowledge a chief called

GRAND-SUN, chief of the Natchez. Although *Sun* was a common name for all chiefs of that nation, this chief was particularly distinguished in the first war with the French, which exhibits the compass of our information concerning him, and which we purpose here to sketch. He was brother to the great warrior, known to the French by the name of Stung-serpent, and like him was a friend to the whites, until the haughty, overbearing disposition of one man brought destruction and ruin on their whole colony. This affair took place in the year 1729. The residence of the *Grand-sun* was near the French post of Natchez, where he had a beautiful village called the *White Apple*. M. *de Chopart* had been reinstated in the command of the post, whence he was for a time removed by reason of misconduct, and his abominable injustice to the Indians became more conspicuous afterwards than before. To gratify his pride and avarice, he had projected the building of an elegant village, and none appeared to suit his purpose so well as the White Apple of the *Grand-sun.* He sent for the chief to his fort, and unhesitatingly told him that his village must be immediately given up to him, for he had resolved to erect one a league square upon the same ground, and that he must remove elsewhere The great chief stifled his surprise, and modestly replied, "That his ancestors had lived in that village for as many years as there were hairs in his double cue, and, therefore, it was good that they should continue there still." When this was interpreted to the commandant, he showed himself in a rage, and threatened the chief, that, unless he moved from his village speedily, he would have cause of repentance. *Grand-sun* left the fort, and said he would assemble his counsellors, and hold a talk upon it.

In this council, which actually assembled, it was proposed to lay before the commandant their hard situation, if they should be obliged to abandon their corn, which then was just beginning to shoot from the ground, and many other articles on which they were to depend for subsistence. But, on urging these strong reasons, they met only with abuse, and a more peremptory order to remove immediately. This the *Grand-sun* reported to the council, and they saw all was lost, unless, by some stratagem, they should rid themselves of the tyrant *Chopart,* which was their final decision. The secret was confided to none but the old men. To gain time, an offer was to be made to the avaricious commandant, of tribute, in case he would permit them to remain on their land until their harvest. The offer was accepted, and the Indians set about maturing their plan with the greatest avidity. Bundles of sticks were sent to the suns of the neighboring tribes, and their import explained to them by the faithful messengers. Each bundle contained as many sticks as days which were to pass before the massacre of all the French in the Natchez. And that no mistake should arise in regard to the fixed day, every morning a stick was drawn from the bundle and broken in pieces, and the day of the last stick was that of the execution.

The security of the wicked, in the midst of their wickedness, and their deafness to repeated warnings, though a standing example before them upon the pages of all history, yet we know of but few instances where they have profited by it. I need cite no examples; our pages are full of them.

The breast of women, whether civilized or uncivilized, cannot bear the thoughts of revenge and death to prey upon them for so great a length of time as men. And, as in the last case, I need not produce examples; on our pages will be found many.

A female sun having, by accident, understood the secret design of her people, partly out of resentment for their keeping it from her, and partly from her attachment to the French, resolved to make it known to them. But so fatally secure was the commandant, that he would not hearken to her messengers, and threatened others of his own people with chastisement, if they continued such intimations. But the great council of so many suns, and other motions of their wise men, justly alarmed many, and their complaints to the commandant were urged, until seven of his own people were put in irons, to dispel their fears. And that he might the more vaunt himself upon their fears he sent his interpreter to demand of the *Grand-sun,* whether he was about to fall upon the French with his warriors. To dissemble, in such a case, was only to be expected from the chief, and the interpreter reported to the commandant as he desired, which caused him to value himself upon his former contempt of his people's fears.

The 30th of November, 1729, at length came, and with it the massacre of near 700 people, being all the French of Natchez. Not a man escaped. It being upon the eve of St. *Andrew's* day, facilitated the execution of the horrid design. In such contempt was M. *Chopart* held, that the suns would allow no warrior to kill him, but one whom they considered a mean person. He was armed only with a wooden tomahawk, and with such a contemptible weapon. wielded by as contemptible a person, was M. *Chopart* pursued from his house into his garden, and there met his death.

The design of the *Grand-sun* and his allies was, to have followed up their success until all the French were driven out of Louisiana. But some tribes would not aid in it, and the governor of Louisiana, promptly seconded by the people of New Orleans, shortly after nearly annihilated the whole tribe of the Natchez. The Choctaws offered themselves, to the number of 15 or 1600 men, and, in the following February, advanced into the country of the Natchez, and were shortly after joined by the French, and encamped near the old fort, then in possession of the *Grand-sun*. Here flags passed between them and terms of peace were agreed upon, which were very honorable to the Indians; but, in the following night, they decamped, taking all their prisoners and baggage, leaving nothing but the cannons of the fort and balls behind them. Some time now passed before the French could ascertain the retreat of the Natchez. At length, they learned that they had crossed the Mississippi, and settled upon the west side, near 180 miles above the mouth of Red River Here they built a fort, and remained quietly until the next year.

The weakness of the colony caused the inhabitants to resign themselves into the hands of the king, who soon sent over a sufficient force, added to those still in the country, to humble the Natchez. They were accordingly invested in their fort, and, struck with consternation at the sudden approach of the French, seem to have lost their former prudence. They made a desperate sally upon the camp of the enemy, but were repulsed with great loss. They then attempted to gain time by negotiation, as they had the year before, but could not escape from the vigilance of the French officer; yet the attempt was made, and many were killed, very few escaped, and the greater number driven within their fort. Mortars were used by their enemies in this siege, and the third bomb, falling in the centre of the fort, made great havoc, but still greater consternation. Drowned by the cries of the women and children, *Grand-sun* caused the sign of capitulation to be given. Himself, with the rest of his company, were carried prisoners to New Orleans, and thrown into prison. An increasing infection caused the women and children to be taken out and employed as slaves on the king's plantations; among whom was the woman who had used every endeavor to notify the commandant, *Chopart*, of the intended massacre, and from whom the particulars of the affair were learned. Her name was *Stung-arm*. These slaves were shortly after embarked for St. Domingo, entirely to rid the country of the Natchez.* The men, it is probable, were all put to death.

GREAT-MORTAR, or *Yah-yah-tustanage*, was a very celebrated Muskogee chief, who, before the revolutionary war, was in the French interest, and received his supplies from their garrison at Alabama, which was not far distant from his place of abode, called *Okchai*. There was a time when he inclined to the English, and but for the very haughty and imprudent conduct of the superintendent of Indian affairs, among them, might have been reclaimed, and the dismal period of massacres which ensued averted. At a great council, appointed by the superintendent, for the object of regaining their favor, the pipe of peace, when passing around, was refused to *Great-mortar*, because he had favored the French. This, with much other ungenerous treatment, caused him ever after to hate the English name. As the superintendent was making a speech, which doubtless contained severe and hard sayings against his red hearers, another chief, called the *Tobacco-eater*, sprung upon his feet, and darting his tomahawk at him, it fortunately missed him, but stuck in a plank just above his head. Yet he would have been immediately killed, but for the interposition of a friendly warrior. Had this first blow been effectual, every Englishman present would have been immediately put to death. Soon after, *Great-mortar* caused his people to fall upon the English traders, and they murdered ten. Fourteen of the inhabitants of Longcane, a settlement near Ninety-six,† next were his victims. He now received a commission from the French, and the better to enlist the Cherokees and others in his cause, removed with his family far into the heart of the country, upon a river, by which he could receive supplies from the fort at Alabama. Neither the French nor *Great-mortar* were deceived in the advantage of their newly-chosen position for young warriors joined him there in great numbers, and it was fast becoming

* Mons. *Du Pratz*, Hist. de Louisiana, tome i. ch. xii.

† So called because it was 96 miles from the Cherokee. *Adair*.

a general rendezvous for all the Mississippi Indians. Fortunately, however for the English, the Chickasaws in their interest plucked up this *Bohon upas* before its branches were yet extended. They fell upon them by surprise, killed the brother of *Great-mortar*, and completely destroyed the design. He fled, not to his native place, but to one from whence he could best annoy the English settlements, and commenced anew the work of death. Augusta, in Georgia, and many scattering settlements were destroyed* Those ravages were continued until their united forces were defeated by the Americans under General *Grant*, in 1761, as we have narrated.

We have next to notice a chief, king, or emperor as he was at different times entitled, whose omission, in a biographical work upon the Indians, would incur as much criminality, on the part of the biographer, as an omission of *Buokongehelas, White-eyes, Pipe*, or *Ockonostota*; yea, even more. We mean

ALEXANDER M'GILLIVRAY, who was, perhaps, one of the most conspicuous, if not one of the greatest, chiefs that has ever borne that title among the Creeks; at least, since they have been known to the Europeans. He flourished during half of the last century, and such was the exalted opinion entertained of him by his countrymen, that they styled him "king of kings." His mother was his predecessor, and the governess of the nation, and he had several sisters, who married leading men. On the death of his mother, he came in chief sachem by the usages of his ancestors, but such was his disinterested patriotism, that he left it to the nation to say whether he should succeed to the sachemship. The people elected him "emperor." He was at the head of the Creeks during the revolutionary war, and was in the British interest. After the peace, he became reconciled to the Americans, and expressed a desire to renounce his public life, and reside in the U. States, but was hindered by the earnest solicitations of his countrymen, to remain among them, and direct their affairs.

His residence, according to General *Milfort*,† who married his sister, was near Tallahassee, about half a league from what was formerly Fort Toulouse. He lived in a handsome house, and owned 60 negroes, each of whom he provided with a separate habitation, which gave his estate the appearance of a little town.‡

M'Gillivray was a son of an Englishman of that name who married a Creek woman, and hence was what is called a half breed. He was born about 1739, and, at the age of ten, was sent by his father to school in Charleston, where he was in the care of Mr. *Farquhar M'Gillivray*, who was a relation of his father His tutor was a Mr. *Sheed*. He learned the Latin language under the tuition of Mr. *William Henderson*, afterwards somewhat eminent among the critics in London. When young *M'Gillivray* was 17, he was put into a counting-house in Savannah, but mercantile affairs had not so many charms as books, and he spent all the time he could get, in reading histories and other works of usefulness. After a short time, his father took him home, where his superior talents soon began to develop themselves, and his promotion followed. He was often styled general, which commission, it is said, he actually held under *Charles* III., king of Spain. This was, probably, before he was elected emperor.

To be a little more particular with this distinguished man, I will hazard a repetition of some facts, for the sake of giving an account of him as recorded by one§ who resided long with him, and consequently knew him well. He was the son of a Creek woman, of the family of the Wind, whose father was an officer in the French service, stationed at Fort Toulouse, near the nation of the Alabamas. This officer, in trading with the Indians, became acquainted with the mother of our chief, whom he married. They had five children, two boys and three girls. Only one of the boys lived to grow up. As among other tribes, so among the Creeks, the children belong to the mother; and when *M'Gillivray's* father desired to send him to Charleston to get an education, he was obliged first to get the mother's consent. This, it seems, was easily obtained, and young *M'Gillivray* was put there, where he acquired a good

* *Adair's* Hist. N. American Indians, 254, &c.

† Memoire ou coup-d'œil rapide sur mes différens voyages et mon séjour dans la nation Creek. p. 27. ‡ Ibid. § General *Milfort*.

education. He did not return for some time to his nation, which was at the commencement of the revolutionary war; and he then went, commissioned by the royalists, to invite his countrymen to a treaty upon the frontiers, and to unite them against the rebels.* He generally spoke the English language, which was not pleasing to his mother, who would not speak it.†

After the war he became attached to the Americans, and although the borderers caused frequent troubles, yet he made and renewed treaties with them. In 1790, he came to New York with 29 of his chiefs. Owing to some misunderstanding, he had refused to treat at Rock Landing a short time before, where commissioners from the U. States had attended; and the government, justly fearing a rupture, unless a speedy reconciliation should take place, despatched Colonel *Marinus Willet* into the Creek country, with a pacific letter to General *M'Gillivray*. He succeeded in his mission, and the chiefs arrived in New York 23 July, 1790.‡ They were conducted to the residence of the secretary of war, General *Knox*, who conducted them to the house of the president of the U. States, and introduced them to him. President *Washington* received them "in a very handsome manner, congratulated them on their safe arrival, and expressed a hope that the interview would prove beneficial both to the U. States and to the Creek nation." They next visited the governor of the state, from whom they received a most cordial welcome. They then proceeded to the City Tavern, where they dined in company with General *Knox*, and other officers of government. A correspondence between Governor *Telfair*, of Georgia, and "*Alexander M'Gillvary*, Esq." probably opened the way for a negotiation, which terminated in a settlement of difficulties. From the following extract from *M'Gillivray's* letter, a very just idea may be formed of the state of the affairs of his nation previous to his visit to New York. "In answer to yours, I have to observe, that, as a peace was not concluded on between us at the Rock-landing meeting, your demand for property taken by our warriors from off the disputed lands cannot be admitted. We, also, have had our losses, by captures made by your people. We are willing to conclude a peace with you, but you must not expect extraordinary concessions from us. In order to spare the further effusion of human blood, and to finally determine the war, I am willing to concede, in some measure, if you are disposed to treat on the ground of mutual concession. It will save trouble and expense, if the negotiations are managed in the nation. Any person from you can be assured of personal safety and friendly treatment in this country." It was dated at Little Tellassee, 30 March, 1790, and directed to "His Excellency *Edward Telfair*, Esq." and signed "*Alex. M'Gillivray*."

This chief seems afterwards to have met with the censure of his people, at least some of them, in a manner similar to that of *M'Intosh* recently; and was doubtless overcome by the persuasions of designing whites, to treat for the disposal of his lands, against the general voice of his nation. One *Bowles*, a white man, led the councils in opposition to his proceedings, and, for a time, *M'Gillivray* absented himself from his own tribe. In 1792, his party took *Bowles* prisoner, and sent him out of the country, and solicited the general to return.§ To this he consented, and they became more attached to him than ever. He now endeavored to better their condition by the introduction of teachers among them. In an advertisement for a teacher, in the summer of 1792, he styles himself emperor of the Creek nation. His quiet was soon disturbed, and the famous *John Watts*, the same summer, with 500 warriors, Creeks, and five towns of the Chickamawagas, committed many depredations. The Spaniards were supposed to be the movers of the hostile party. *M'Gillivray* died at Pensacola, February 17, 1793,‖ and is thus noticed in the Pennsylvania Gazette:—"This idolized chief of the Creeks styled himself king of kings. But, alas he could neither restrain the meanest fellow of his

---

* *Milfort*, 323, 324. † See *Holmes*, Amer. Annals, ii. 384.

‡ Colonel *Willet's* Narrative, 112. "They were received with great splendor by the Tammany Society, in the dress of their order," on their landing. *Ib.*

§ In 1791, this *Bowles*, with five chiefs, was in England, and we find this notice of him in the European Magazine of that year, vol. 19, p. 268:—"The ambassadors consisted of two Creeks, and of Mr. *Bowles*, (a native of Maryland, who is a Creek by adoption, and the present general of that nation,) and three Cherokees.

‖ *Milfort*, 325

nation from the commission of a crime, nor punish him after he had committed it! He might persuade or advise, all the good an Indian king or chief can do." This is, generally speaking, a tolerably correct estimate of the extent of the power of chiefs; but it should be remembered that the chiefs of different tribes exercise very different sway over their people, according as such chief is endowed with the spirit of government, by nature or circumstance. There is great absurdity in applying the name or title of king to Indian chiefs, as that title is commonly understood. The first Europeans conferred the title upon those who appeared most prominent, in their first discoveries, for want of another more appropriate; or, perhaps, they had another reason, namely, that of magnifying their own exploits on their return to their own countries, by reporting their interviews with, or conquests over, "many kings of an unknown country."

Contemporary with General *M'Gillivray* was a chief called the

TAME-KING, whose residence was among the Upper Creeks, in 1791; and he is noticed in our public documents of that year, as a conspicuous chief in matters connected with establishing the southern boundary. At this time one *Bowles*, an English trader, had great influence among the Lower Creeks, and used great endeavors, by putting himself forward as their chief, to enlist all the nations in opposition to the Americans. He had made large promises to the Upper Creeks, to induce them not to hear to the American commissioners They so far listened to him, as to consent to receive his talk, and accordingly the chiefs of the upper and lower towns met at a place called the *Half-way-house*, where they expected *Bowles* in person, or some letters containing definite statements. When the chiefs had assembled, *Tame-king* and *Mad-dog*, of the upper towns, asked the chiefs of the lower, "whether *they* had taken *Bowles's* talks, and where the letters were which this *great man* had sent them, and where the white man was, to read them." An Indian in *Bowles's* employ said, "he was to give them the talk." They laughed at this, and said, "they could hear his mouth every day; that they had come there to see those letters and hear them read." Most of the chiefs of the upper towns now left the council, which was about the termination of *Bowles's* successes. He was shortly afterwards obliged to abdicate, as we have already declared in the life of *M'Gillivray*. He returned again, however, after visiting Spain and England, and spending some time in prison.*

Mr. *Ellicott* observes,† that, at the close of a conference with sundry tribes, held 15 August, 1799, in which objects were discussed concerning his passage through their country, that "the business appeared to terminate as favorably as could be expected, and the Indians declared themselves perfectly satisfied; but I nevertheless had my doubts of their sincerity, from the depredations they were constantly making upon our horses, which began upon the Coeneuck, and had continued ever since; and added to their insolence, from their stealing every article in our camp they could lay their hands on." Mr. *Ellicott* excepts the Upper Creeks, generally, from participating in these robberies, all but *Tame-king* and his people.

Though we have named *Tame-king* first, yet *Mad-dog* was quite as conspicuous at this time. His son fought for the Americans in the last war, and was mentioned by General *Jackson* as an active and valuable chief in his expeditions. His real name we have not learned, and the general mentions him only as *Mad-dog's* son.

In the case of the boundary already mentioned, the surveyors met with frequent difficulties from the various tribes of Indians, some of whom were influenced by the Spanish governor, *Folch*, of Louisiana. *Mad-dog* appeared their friend, and undeceived them respecting the governor's pretensions. A conference was to be held about the 4 May, between the Indians, Governor *Folch*, and the American commissioners. The place of meeting was to be upon Coenecuh River, near the southern estuary of the bay of Pensacola. When

* He was confined in the Moro castle in the Havana, with three Cherokees that accompanied him. This was in 1792. It was said that this inveterate enemy of the United States, *Bowles*, was with the Indians, at St. Clair's defeat.—*Carey's Museum*, xi. 40 †.

† In his Journal, 214.

the Americans arrived there, *Mad-dog* met them, and informed Colonel *Hawkins*, the Indian agent, that two Indians had just gone to the Tallessees with bad talks from the governor. The colonel told him it could not be possible. Shortly after, *Mad-dog* asked Colonel *Hawkins* and Mr. *Ellicott*, the commissioner, if they supposed that Governor *Folch* would attend at the treaty; they said, "Most assuredly." "*No*," returned *Mad-dog*, "*he will not attend, he knows what I shall say to him about his crooked talks. His tongue is forked, and, as you are here, he will be ashamed to show it. If he stands to what he has told us, you will be offended, and if he tells us that the line ought to be marked, he will contradict himself: but he will do neither; he will not come.*" It turned out as *Mad-dog* declared. When it was found that the governor would not attend, the chief went to Colonel *Hawkins* and Mr. *Ellicott*, and, by way of pleasantry, said, "*Well, the governor has not come. I told you so. A man with two tongues can only speak to one at a time.*" This observation has reference to the governor's duplicity, in holding out to the Indians his determination not to suffer a survey of the boundary, while, at the same time, he pretended to the Americans that he would facilitate it.*

Mad-dog was an upper town Creek, of the Tuckaabatchees tribe.

CHAPTER VI.

WEATHERFORD—*His character and country—The corner-stone of the Creek confederacy—Favors the designs of Tecumseh—Captures Fort Mimms—Dreadful massacre—Subjection of the Creeks—Weatherford surrenders himself—His speeches—* M'INTOSH—*Aids the Americans—Battle of Autossee—Great slaughter of the Indians—Battle of the Horse-shoe-bend—Late troubles in the Creek nation—M'Intosh makes illegal sale of lands—Executed for breaking the laws of his country—*MENAWWAY—TUSTENUGGE—HAWKINS—CHILLY M'INTOSH, *son of William—Marriage of his sister—*LOVETT.

WEATHERFORD, one of the most conspicuous war chiefs of the Creek nation, demands an early attention, in the biographical history of the late war. Mr. *Claiborne*, in his NOTES ON THE WAR IN THE SOUTH, informs us that, "among the first who entered into the views of the British commissioners was the since celebrated *Weatherford;*" that he was born in the Creek nation, and whose "father was an itinerant pedler, sordid, treacherous, and revengeful; his mother a full-blooded savage, of the tribe of the Seminoles. He partook (says the same author) of all the bad qualities of both his parents,† and engrafted, on the stock he inherited from others, many that were peculiarly his own. With avarice, treachery, and a thirst for blood, he combines lust, gluttony, and a devotion to every species of criminal carousal. (Fortune, in her freaks, sometimes gives to the most profligate an elevation of mind, which she denies to men whose propensities are the most vicious.) On *Weatherford* she bestowed genius, eloquence, and courage. The first of these qualities enabled him to conceive great designs, the last to execute them; while eloquence, bold, impressive, and figurative, furnished him with a passport to the favor of his countrymen and followers. Silent and reserved, unless when excited by some great occasion, and superior to the weakness of rendering himself cheap by the frequency of his addresses, he delivered his opinions but seldom in council; but when he did so, he was listened to with delight and approbation. His judgment and eloquence had secured the respect of the old; his vices made him the idol of the young and the unprincipled." "In his person, tall, straight, and well proportioned; his eye black, lively, and penetrating, and indicative of courage and enterprise; his nose prominent, thin, and elegant in its formation; while all the features of his

* *Ellicott's* Journal, 203, &c.

† The reader should be early apprized that this was written at a time when *some* prejudice *might* have infected the mind of the writer.

face, harmoniously arranged, speak an active and disciplined mind. Passionately devoted to wealth, he had appropriated to himself a fine tract of land, improved and settled it; and from the profits of his father's pack, had decorated and embellished it. To it he retired occasionally, and, relaxing from the cares of state, he indulged in pleasures which are but rarely found to afford satisfaction to the devotees of ambition and fame. Such were the opposite and sometimes disgusting traits of character in the celebrated *Weatherford*, the key and corner-stone of the Creek confederacy!"

It is said that this chief had entered fully into the views of *Tecumseh*, and that, if he had entered upon his designs without delay, he would have been amply able to have overrun the whole Mississippi territory. But this fortunate moment was lost, and, in the end, his plans came to ruin. Not long before the wretched butchery at Fort Mimms, General *Claiborne* visited that post, and very particularly warned its possessors against a surprise. After giving orders for the construction of two additional block-houses, he concluded the order with these words:—"To respect an enemy, and prepare in the best possible way to meet him, is the certain means to ensure success." It was expected that *Weatherford* would soon attack some of the forts, and General *Claiborne* marched to Fort Early, as that was the farthest advanced into the enemy's country. On his way, he wrote to Major *Beasley*, the commander of Mimms, informing him of the danger of an attack; and, strange as it may appear, the next day after the letter was received, (30 August, 1813,) *Weatherford*, at the head of about 1500 warriors, entered the fort at noon-day, when a shocking carnage ensued. The gate had been left open and unguarded; but, before many of the warriors had entered, they were met by Major *Beasley*, at the head of his men, and for some time the contest was bloody and doubtful; each striving for the mastery of the entrance. Here, man to man, the fight continued for a quarter of an hour, with tomahawks, knives, swords and bayonets: a scene there presented itself almost without a parallel in the annals of Indian warfare! The garrison consisted of 275: of these only 160 were soldiers; the rest were old men, women and children, who had here taken refuge. It is worthy of very emphatical remark, that every officer expired fighting at the gate. A lieutenant, having been badly wounded, was carried by two women to a block-house, but when he was a little revived, he insisted on being carried back to the fatal scene, which was done by the same heroines, who placed him by the side of a dead companion, where he was soon despatched.

The defenders of the garrison being now nearly all slain, the women and children shut themselves up in the block-houses, and, seizing upon what weapons they could find, began, in that perilous and hopeless situation, to defend themselves. But the Indians soon succeeded in setting these houses on fire, and all such as refused to meet death without, perished in the flames within!! Seventeen only escaped of all the garrison, and many of those were desperately wounded. It was judged that, during the contest at the gate, near 400 of *Weatherford's* warriors were wounded and slain.

The horrid calamity at Fort Mimms, in the Tensau settlement, as it is called, was not the commencement of the bloody war with the Creek Indians. The motions of the Shawanee *Prophet* had been scrutinized by people upon the frontiers of several states, and memorials from Indiana and Illinois had been sent to the president of the United States by some of their principal inhabitants, in 1811, calling on him to send out an armed force for their security.

In the summer of 1812, some families were cut off near the mouth of the Ohio, and soon after, upon the border of Tennessee, two other families, consisting of women and children, were butchered in a manner too shocking for description! Georgia was also a sufferer in the same kind.

In respect to the bloody affair at Fort Mimms, a different aspect has been thrown around it from that generally given in the histories of the war. The severe, though probably just reflections of Judge *Martin* upon the conduct of the unfortunate *Beasley*, has passed without contradiction. Not only had that officer been warned by General *Claiborne* of his danger, as already stated, but a Creek Indian informed him in a friendly manner that he must expect an attack in less than two days. When he had made his communication, he left the place, "and was hardly out of sight, when 20 or 30 of his countrymen came in view, and forcibly entered the fort. In the attempt to shut the gate, *Beasley* was killed: the garrison revenged his death by that of all the assailants. This first party was, however, soon followed by a body of about 800: the garrison was overpowered, the fort taken, and every man, woman and child in it, slaughtered, with the exception of four privates, who, though severely wounded, effected their escape, and reached Fort Stoddard."* *Beasley* himself was carried into the kitchen of one of the houses within the fort, and was there, with many others, consumed in the burning ruins!†

When the news of this affair was circulated through the country, many cried aloud for vengeance, and two powerful armies were soon upon their march into the Indian country, and the complete destruction of the Indian power soon followed. The Indians seeing all resistance was at an end, great numbers of them came forward and made their submission. *Weatherford*, however, and many who were known to be desperate, still stood out; perhaps from fear. General *Jackson* determined to test the fidelity of those chiefs who had submitted, and, therefore, ordered them to deliver, without delay, *Weatherford*, bound, into his hands, that he might be dealt with as he deserved. When they had made known to the sachem what was required of them, his noble spirit would not submit to such degradation; and, to hold them harmless, he resolved to give himself up without compulsion. Accordingly, he proceeded to the American camp, unknown, until he appeared before the commanding general, to whose presence, under some pretence, he gained admission. General *Jackson* was greatly surprised, when the chief said, "*I am Weatherford, the chief who commanded at the capture of Fort Mimms. I desire peace for my people, and have come to ask it.*" *Jackson* had, doubtless, determined upon his execution when he should be brought bound, as he had directed; but his sudden and unexpected appearance, in this manner, saved him. The general said he was astonished that he should venture to appear in his presence, as he was not ignorant of his having been at Fort Mimms, nor of his inhuman conduct there, for which he so well deserved to die. "I ordered," continued the general, "that you should be brought to me bound; and, had you been brought in that manner, I should have known how to have treated you." In answer to this, *Weatherford* made the following famous speech:—

"*I am in your power—do with me as you please—I am a soldier. I have done the whites all the harm I could. I have fought them, and fought them bravely. If I had an army, I would yet fight—I would contend to the last: but I have none. My people are all gone. I can only weep over the misfortunes of my nation.*"

General *Jackson* was pleased with his boldness, and told him that though he was in his power, yet he would take no advantage; that he might yet join the war party, and contend against the Americans, if he chose, but to depend upon no quarter if taken afterward; and that unconditional submission was his and his people's only safety. *Weatherford* rejoined, in a tone as dignified as it was indignant,—"*You can safely address me in such terms now. There was a time when I could have answered you—there was a time when I had a choice—I have none now. I have not even a hope. I could once animate my warriors to battle—but I cannot animate the dead. My warriors can no longer hear my voice. Their bones are at Talladega, Tallushatches, Emuckfaw and Tohopeka. I have not surrendered myself without thought. While there was a single chance of success, I never left my post, nor supplicated peace. But my people are gone, and I now ask it for my nation, not for myself. I look back with deep sorrow, and wish to avert still greater calamities. If I had been left to contend with the Georgia army, I would have raised my corn on one bank of the river, and fought them on the other. But your people have destroyed my nation. You are a brave man. I rely upon your generosity. You will exact no terms of a conquered people, but such as they should accede to. Whatever they may be, it would now be madness and folly to oppose them. If they are opposed, you shall find me*

* *Martin's* Hist. Louisiana, ii. 316. † *Perkins's* Late War, 19[illegible]

amongst the sternest enforcers of obedience. Those who would still hold out, can be influenced only by a mean spirit of revenge. To this they must not, and shall not sacrifice the last remnant of their country. You have told our nation where we might go and be safe. This is good talk, and they ought to listen to it. They shall listen to it." And here we must close our present account of *Weatherford*, and enter upon that of a character opposed to him in the field, and, if we can believe the writers of their times, opposite in almost all the affairs of life. This was the celebrated and truly unfortunate

General WILLLIAM M'INTOSH, a Creek chief of the tribe of Cowetaw. He was, like *M'Gillivray*, a half-breed, whom he considerably resembled in several particulars, as by his history will appear. He was a prominent leader of such of his countrymen as joined the Americans in the war of 1812, 13, and 14, and is first mentioned by General *Floyd*,* in his account of the *battle*, as he called it, of Autossee, where he assisted in the brutal destruction of 200 of his nation. There was nothing like fighting on the part of the people of the place, as we can learn, being surprised in their wigwams, and hewn to pieces. "The Cowetaws," says the general, "under *M'Intosh*, and Tookaubatchians,† under *Mad-dog's-son*, fell in on our flanks, and fought with an intrepidity worthy of any troops." And after relating the burning of the place, he thus proceeds:—"It is difficult to determine the strength of the enemy, but from the information of some of the chiefs, which it is said can be relied on, there were assembled at Autossee, warriors from eight towns, for its defence; it being their beloved ground, on which they proclaimed no white man could approach without inevitable destruction. It is difficult to give a precise account of the loss of the enemy; but from the number which were lying scattered over the field, together with those destroyed in the towns, and the many slain on the bank of the river, which respectable officers affirm that they saw lying in heaps at the water's edge, where they had been precipitated by their surviving friends, [!!] their loss in killed, independent of their wounded, must have been at least 200, (among whom were the Autossee and Tallassee kings,) and from the circumstance of their making no efforts to molest our return, probably greater. The number of buildings burnt, some of a superior order for the dwellings of savages, and filled with valuable articles, is supposed to be 400." This was on the 29 November, 1813.

M'Intosh was also very conspicuous in the memorable battle of the Horse-shoe-bend, in the Tallapoosie River. At this place the disconsolate tribes of the south had made a last great stand, and had a tolerably regular fortified camp. It was said that they were 1000 strong. They had constructed their works with such ingenuity, that little could be effected against them but by storm. "Determined to exterminate them," says General *Jackson*, "I detached General *Coffee* with the mounted, and nearly the whole of the Indian force, early on the morning of yesterday, [March 27, 1814,] to cross the river about two miles below their encampment, and to surround the bend, in such a manner, as that none of them should escape by attempting to cross the river." "*Bean's* company of spies, who had accompanied Gen. *Coffee*, crossed over in canoes to the extremity of the bend, and set fire to a few of the buildings which were there situated; they then advanced with great gallantry towards the breast-work, and commenced a spirited fire upon the enemy behind it." This force not being able to effect their object, many others of the army showed great ardor to participate in the assault. "The spirit which animated them was a sure augury of the success which was to follow." "The regulars, led on by their intrepid and skilful commander, Col. *Williams*, and by the gallant Maj. *Montgomery*, soon gained possession of the works in the midst of a most tremendous fire from behind them, and the militia of the venerable Gen. *Doherty's* brigade accompanied them in the charge with a vivacity and firmness which would have done honor to regulars. The enemy was completely routed. *Five hundred and fifty seven* ‡ were left dead on the peninsula, and a great number were killed by the horsemen in attempting to cross the river. It is believed that not more than *twenty* have escaped.

"The fighting continued with some severity about five hours; but we con-

* *Brannan's* official letters. † Tuckabatche *Bartram*, 447

‡ These are the general's italics; at least, *Brannan* so prints his official letter.

tinued to destroy many of them, who had concealed themselves under the banks of the river, until we were prevented by the night. This morning we killed 16 who had been concealed. We took about 250 prisoners, all women and children, except two or three. Our loss is 106 wounded, and 25 killed. Major *M'Intosh*, the Cowetau, who joined my army with a part of his tribe, greatly distinguished himself."* Truly, this was a war of extermination! The friend of humanity may inquire whether all those poor wretches who had secreted themselves here and there in the "caves and reeds," had deserved death?

The most melancholy part of the life of the unfortunate *M'Intosh* remains to be recorded. The late troubles of the Creek nation have drawn forth many a sympathetic tear from the eye of the philanthropist. These troubles were only the consequences of those of a higher date. Those of 1825, we thought, completed the climax of their affliction, but 1832 must sully her annals with records of their oppression also. It is the former period with which our article brings us in collision in closing this account. In that year, the government of the U. States, by its agents, seemed determined on possessing a large tract of their country, to satisfy the state of Georgia. *M'Intosh*, and a small part of the nation, were for conceding to their wishes, but a large majority of his countrymen would not hear to the proposal. The commissioners employed were satisfied of the fact, and communicated to the president the result of a meeting they had had for the purpose. He was well satisfied, also, that *M'Intosh* could not convey the lands, as he represented but a small part of his nation, but still the negotiation was ordered to be renewed. A council was called by the commissioners, (who were Georgians,) which assembled at a place called *Indian-spring*. Here the chief of the Tuckaubatcheese spoke to them as follows: "We met you at Broken Arrow, and then told you we had no land to sell. I then heard of no claims against the nation, nor have I since. We have met you here at a very short notice, and do not think that the chiefs who are here have any authority to treat. General *M'Intosh* knows that we are bound by our laws, and that what is not done in the public square, in the general council, is not binding on the nation. I am, therefore, under the necessity of repeating the same answer as given at Broken Arrow, that we have no land to sell. I know that there are but few here from the upper towns, and many are absent from the lower towns. Gen. *M'Intosh* knows that no part of the land can be sold without a full council, and with the consent of all the nation, and if a part of the nation choose to leave the country, they cannot sell the land they have, but it belongs to the nation." "This is the only talk I have for you, and I shall return home immediately." He did so. The ill-advised commissioners informed *M'Intosh* and his party, that the Creek nation was sufficiently represented by them, and that the United States would bear them out in a treaty of sale. The idea of receiving the whole of the pay for the lands among themselves, was doubtless the cause of the concession of *M'Intosh* and his party. "Thirteen only of the signers of the treaty were chiefs. The rest were such as had been degraded from that rank, and unknown persons; 36 chiefs present refused to sign. The whole party of *M'Intosh* amounted to about 300, not the tenth part of the nation." Still they executed the articles, in direct violation to the laws of their nation, which themselves had helped to form. It must be remembered that the Creeks had made no inconsiderable advances in what is termed civilization. They had towns, and even printed laws by which they were to be governed, similar to those of the United States.

The treaty of *Indian-spring*, dated 8 January, 1821, gave universal uneasiness; and, from that day, *M'Intosh* lost popularity. It was generally believed that he had been tampered with by the whites to convey to them the inheritance of his nation! and the following letter pretty clearly proves such suspicions had been justly grounded. It is dated

"Newtown, 21*st October*, 1823.

"My Friend: *I am going to inform you a few lines, as a friend. I want you to give me your opinion about the treaty;*† *whether the chiefs will be willing or not*

---

* *Brannan, ut supra*

† That at Indian-spring, 8 January, 1821.

If the chiefs feel disposed to let the United States have the land, part of it, I want you to let me know; I will make the U. States commissioners give you 2000 dollars, A. M'Coy *the same, and* CHARLES HICKS 3000 *dollars, for present, and nobody shall know it; and if you think the land* woulden [*should'nt ?*] *sold, I will be satisned. If the land should be sold, I will get you the amount before the treaty sign* [*is signed :*] *and if you get any friend you want him to* received, *they shall receive. Nothing more to inform you at present.*

"*I remain your affectionate friend,* WM. McINTOSH.

"JOHN ROSS.*

"*An answer return.*

"N. B. *The whole amount is* $12,000, *you can divide among your friends, exclusive,* $7,000."

Hence there can be no question as to the guilty conscience of *M'Intosh*, although some parts of the above letter are scarcely intelligible. He had mistaken his friend; *Ross* was not to be bought; for three days after the letter was written, viz. 24 October, a council was held, and *M'Intosh* was present; the letter was read, and he was publicly exposed.

Notwithstanding what had been done at Indian-Spring, it appears, from the above letter, that another attempt at selling land was made in 1823, but could not be carried into effect, the villany of *M'Intosh* was so apparent; and it appears that it could not be brought about until 12 February, 1825, which is the date of the last treaty made by *M'Intosh.*

"*M'Intosh* was aware, that, after signing the treaty, his life was forfeited. He, and others of his coadjutors, repaired to Milledgeville, stated their fears, and claimed the protection of Georgia, which was promised by Gov. *Troup.*" It must be observed that the greater part of the purchased territory was within the claimed limits of Georgia;† and that the Georgians had no small share in the whole transaction. It is not stranger that the people of Georgia should conduct as they have, than that the United States' government should place it in her power so to act. To take, therefore, into account the whole merits of the case, it must be remembered, that, by a compact between the two parties in 1802, the former, in consideration of the latter's relinquishing her claim to the Mississippi territory, agreed to extinguish, at the national expense, the Indian title to the lands occupied by them, in Georgia, *whenever it could be done, upon reasonable terms.*‡ Who was to decide *when* the practicable time had arrived, we believe was not mentioned. However, previous to 1825, the United States had succeeded in extinguishing the aboriginal title of 15,000,000 acres, and there were yet about 10,000,000 to be bought off.§ The change of life from wandering to stationary, which the arts of civilization had effected among the Indians, made them prize their possessions far more highly than heretofore, and hence their reluctance and opposition to relinquish them.

Thus much it seemed necessary to premise, that the true cause of the fate of *M'Intosh* should be understood. It appears that when the whole of the nation saw that the treaty which he and his party had made could not be abrogated, forty-nine fiftieths of them were violent against them; and therefore resolved that the sentence of the law should be executed upon him. The execution, and circumstances attending it, are thus related:‖ "About two hours before day, on Sunday morning, 1 May,¶ the house of Gen. *M'Intosh* was surrounded by *Menaw-way*, and about 100 Oakfuskee warriors. *M'Intosh* was within, as likewise were his women and children, and some white men. *Menaw-way* directed an interpreter to request the whites, and the women and children, to come out, as the warriors did not wish to harm them; that Gen. *M'Intosh* had broken the law that he himself had long since made, and they had come to execute him accordingly. They came out of the house, leaving *M'Intosh* and *Etomi-tustenugge*, one of his adherents,

---

* Then President of the National Council of the Creeks.

† *Perkins*, Hist. U. States, a work, by the way, of great value, and which we are surprised should have issued from the press with little or no notice.

‡ Amer. An. Regr. i. § Ibid. ‖ In the Annual Register, *ut supra.*

¶ 30 April is mentioned, in another part of the same work, as the date of the execution, and so it is set down by Mr. *Perkins*, in his Hist. U. S.

therein. The warriors then set fire to the house; and as *M'Intosh* and his comrade [*Tustenugge*] attempted to come out at the door, they shot them both down. The same day, about 12 o'clock, they hung *Sam Hawkins*, a half breed, in the Huckhosseliga Square. On Monday, the 2 May, a party of Halibee Indians fired on and wounded *Ben Hawkins*, another half breed, very badly. The chiefs stated, at the time, that no danger whatever was to be apprehended by persons travelling through the nation; that they were friends to the whites, and wished them not to be alarmed by this execution, which was only a compliance with the laws that the great chiefs of the nation made at Polecat Spring. *Chilly M'Intosh* escaped from the house with the whites, and was not fired at or wounded." He is now chief among the western Creeks, and some time since increased his notoriety by beating a member of Congress, in Washington.

The great agitation which the execution of the head chiefs of the *M'Intosh* party caused was allayed only by the interference of the United States' government. Governor *Troup* of Georgia declared vengeance against the Creek nation, denouncing the execution of the chiefs as an act of murder; however, he, by some means, learned that his judgment was gratuitous, and, by *advice* of President *Adams*, desisted from acts of hostility, the survey of the disputed lands, &c.

We have not learned much of the family of *M'Intosh*. His principal residence was on the Chattahoochie, where he had two wives, *Susannah* and *Peggy*, one a Creek, the other a Cherokee woman, and this is the place where he was killed. About 50 miles from this place, on the western branch of the Tallapoosa, he had a plantation; here lived another of his wives, named *Eliza*. She was the daughter of *Stephen Hawkins*, and sister to *Samuel* and *Benjamin Hawkins*,* whose fate we have just related. On 14 August, 1818, *Jenny*, his eldest daughter, was married to *William S. Mitchel*, Esq., assistant Indian agent of the Creek nation. They were married at a place called *Theacatckkah* near Fort Mitchel, in that nation.†

General *M'Intosh* participated in the Seminole campaigns, as did another chief of the name of *Lovett*, with about 2000 of their warriors. They joined the American army at Fort Scott in the spring of 1818.‡

CHAPTER VII.

Creek war continued—View of the Creek country—General Jackson *ordered out against them—Relieves* CHINNABY—SHELOKTA—PATH-KILLER—*Capture of Litta futche—The Tallushatches destroyed by General* Coffee—*Battle of Talladega—Anecdote—Massacre of the Hallibees—Further account of Autossee battle—Battle of Camp Defiance*—TIMPOOCHIE—*Battle of Eckanakaka*—PUSHAMATA—*Weatherford*—JIM FIFE—*Battle of Emukfau—A second battle—Fife's intrepidity—Battle of Enotochopko—Tohopeka—End of the Creek war—Death of three Prophets*—MONOHOE—M'QUEEN—COLBERT, *alias* PIOMINGO—*His exploits—Anecdote—Murder of* John Morris—MUSHALATUBEC—PUSHAMATA—*Speech of Mushalatubec and of Pushamata to Lafayette at Washington—Pushamata dies there*—HILLISHAGO *visits England—Excites the Seminoles to war—A modern Pocahontas*—HORNOTLIMED—*Massacres a boat's crew in Apalachicola River—Is captured with* HILLISHAGO, *and hanged*—NEAMATHLA—*Removal of the Florida Indians—Their wretched condition*—M'QUEEN—*Rich in lands and slaves—Flies to Florida, and loses his effects.*

AT this period the Creek Indians occupied a country containing about 900 square miles; bounded on the north by Tennessee, east by Georgia, south by the Floridas, and west by the Mississippi; the soil and climate of which could not be considered inferior to any in the United States. These Indians, consisting of Creeks, properly so called, Chikasaws, Choktaws, and Chero-

* Report of the Select Committee of the House of Representatives, U. S., 578, &c.
† *Niles's* Register, 14, 407
‡ N. Y. Monthly Mag. iii 74.

kees, had for a long time been on amicable terms with their white neighbors, exchanging their furs and other articles with them for such others as their wants required. This state of things, but for the breaking out of the war in Canada, might, and would, in reason, have continued, and the great Creek nation would have increased, and at this day have gained vastly in population and importance, instead of being dismembered, its inhabitants sent into banishment, and finally ruined. Intermarriages between Indians and whites had become frequent, from which a race of half-breeds were springing up, and instead of slavery, the Indian women were taking their proper places in society, and the men were cultivating the fields. And notwithstanding the *Prophet* and *Tecumseh* had used all their eloquence to engage them in an early quarrel, it was not until they heard of the success of the British at Malden, that they decided on taking up the hatchet, generally. Such was the alacrity among the northern Indians on the capture of General *Hull*, on the 16 August, 1812, that runners arrived from among them to the Creeks some time before it was known to their white neighbors.

For the horrid butchery at Tensau, the followers of *Weatherford*, *Monohoe*, and *M'Quin*, or *M'Queen*, were shortly to atone, in the most summary manner. There was a great encampment of Creeks under *Weatherford*, at the Tallahasse, or Tallushatches towns, on the Coosa River, a northern branch of the Alabama. The eyes of the south seemed to centre upon General *Jackson* to execute vengeance on the Indians, and notwithstanding he was confined to his room, from a wound in the arm, which he had lately received in a private quarrel, when the news of the massacre arrived in Tennessee, the governor of that state issued an order to him to raise 2000 men with all possible despatch, and rendezvous at Fayetteville. Colonel *Coffee* was already in the field. *Jackson's* march into the enemy's country was hastened by a false alarm, and when he had got into the Indian country, he found himself almost destitute of provisions for his army, which caused considerable delay. At a place on the Tennessee River, called Ditto's Landing, General *Jackson* met with Colonel *Coffee's* regiment. Here he remained several days, but despatched *Coffee* with 700 men to scour the Black Warrior River. At Ten Islands, on the Coosa, was a band of friendly Creeks, at whose head was a chief named *Chinnaby*. This chief had a kind of fort there, and was now blockaded in it by the war party. *Chinnaby*, hearing of *Jackson's* position, sent his son, SHELOKTA, also a principal chief, to the general's camp, for relief, who, without loss of time, marched up the river, but was obliged to encamp at the distance of 24 miles from *Ditto's*, from the failure of his supplies. While here, PATH-KILLER,* a Cherokee chief, sent two runners to him, confirming the former news, and that without immediate relief, they said, they should be immediately cut off, for the hostile Indians were assembling in great force from nine towns. *Jackson* now resolved to move on, and told the messengers of *Path-killer* to speak thus to their chief from him:—

"*The hostile Creeks will not attack you until they have had a brush with me, and that, I think, will put them out of the notion of fighting for some time.*"

When the army had arrived within a few miles of the Ten Islands, it was met by *Chinnaby*. This old chief had succeeded in capturing two hostile Creeks, which he gave up to General *Jackson*. The army was yet about 16 miles from the Indian encampment, and in a lamentable condition for want of provisions; insomuch, that almost any one but *Jackson* would have despaired, and given up the campaign; but his resolution was not to be shaken, and he happily diffused his spirit into his men. He said, in a letter to Governor *Blount*, that *whilst they could procure an ear of corn apiece*, they would not give up the expedition.

* We would here observe that *Path-killer* was, in 1822, a Christian chief, and governed in the same tribe with the famous Mr. *Charles Hicks*; and his residence was in that year 25 miles from Turkeytown. The missionary, Mr. *Butrick*, notes in his Journal, that *Path-killer* was "the *king* or *first beloved man*, of the Cherokee nation," and that Mr. *Hicks* was "the *second beloved man*." *Path killer* had had a son murdered by some white man, before this visit, and complained of the outrage, and said he had written twice to the president of the United States about it. Both these chiefs died in the winter of 1826

On the 28 October, Colonel *Dyer* returned from the capture of a town called Littafutche, on the head of Canoe Creek, which empties into the Coosa from the west. His force consisted of 200 cavalry, and they brought in 29 prisoners, chiefly women and children.

The Indians were now drawn off from Ten Islands, and had taken post at Tallushatches, on the south side of the Coosa. *Coffee* was immediately despatched with 900 men to attack them. This he did on the 3 November, sun about an hour high in the morning. A number of men in advance of the main body, sent forward for the purpose, drew out the warriors from their cabins, who made a fierce attack upon them. The Americans gave way by falling back upon the main body, agreeably to their preconcerted plan, which had the good effect of bringing the Indians at once into their power. Having fired upon them, they made a successful charge, and soon obliged them to shelter themselves in their wigwams. Colonel *Coffee* says, "The enemy retreated firing, until they got around, and in their buildings, where they made all the resistance that an overpowered soldier could do—they fought as long as one existed, but their destruction was very soon completed. Our men rushed up to the doors of the houses, and in a few minutes killed the last warrior of them. The enemy fought with savage fury, and met death with all its horrors, without shrinking or complaining—not one asked to be spared, but fought as long as they could stand or sit. In consequence of their flying to their houses, and mixing with the families, our men, in killing the males, without intention killed and wounded a few of the squaws and children." In this sanguinary affair, 186 Indians were killed; and the commander thought, that there were enough others killed in the woods, which they could not find, to make up in all 200. *This calculation*, he observed, he thought *a reasonable one.* They took captive 84 women and children, and "not one of the warriors escaped to carry the news; a circumstance unknown heretofore!" The whites had 5 killed and 41 wounded; "none mortally, the greater part slightly, a number with arrows: this appears to form a very principal part of the enemy's arms for warfare; every man having a bow with a bundle of arrows, which is used after the first fire with the gun, until a leisure time for loading offers."

The destruction at Tallushatches was rendered the more complete by their being entirely surrounded on every side by the troops. Some have said that even the women united with the warriors, and contended in the battle with fearless bravery. This may account for many that were killed; but General *Coffee* does not mention it.

Meanwhile General *White* had been detached to Turkeytown, for the relief of *Path-killer*, and he was now ordered to join the main army, with as much expedition as he was able. This request was transmitted on the 4, and renewed on the 7 November, 1813; and on the evening of the same day, an Indian brought news to the general, that Talladega was besieged by a great body of the enemy, and would certainly be destroyed, unless immediately relieved. Talladega was a fort occupied by friendly Creeks, about 30 miles below Ten Islands.

Without loss of time, General *Jackson* marched to relieve Talladega. His operations were conducted with such promptitude, that by midnight following the same day, he was within six miles of his enemy. Here he encamped until about daylight. Then moving on, at sunrise he came within half a mile of the Indian encampment, which was only about 80 rods from Fort Talladega. The general, having formed his line of battle like the Spanish Armada, moved on to the attack. The Indians were not taken by surprise, but rushed upon their adversaries with such impetuosity that they made considerable impression in one part of the line; insomuch, that a considerable body of militia gave way. Their places being immediately supplied by the mounted men, the Indians fought but a short time, before they were obliged to fly for the mountains, about three miles distant. In their flight they were hard pressed by the right wing of the Americans, and great numbers were cut down. In the whole affair, 299 were killed, that were found, of the Indians; and the whites lost 15 in killed, and 85 were wounded, several of whom afterwards died. Over 1080 Indians were said to have been engaged, and some of them afterwards said their loss at the battle of Talladega was 600.

It was expected that a supply of provisions would arrive at Camp Strother at Ten Islands, before the army should return there; but on its arrival, a total failure was experienced by the hungry soldiers; even what had been left behind of the general's private stores had been distributed—it was a melancholy time, indeed, and reminds us of the sufferings of captives in the old Indian wars, who were obliged to subsist upon berries and roots. It was during this campaign that a circumstance occurred which has been variously related; and, as it is an excellent anecdote, we will lay it before our readers.

One morning, a soldier, with a doleful countenance, approached General *Jackson*, and told him he was almost famished, and knew not what to do. The general was seated at the foot of a tree, and was observed by the poor half-starved soldier to be eating something. This no doubt caused him to make his complaint, thinking it a favorable time to have his wants relieved. The general observed, that it was never his custom to turn away a hungry person, when he had it in his power to relieve him; then, putting his hand into his pocket, took out a handful of acorns, and, offering them to his astonished guest, observed, that such was his fare, and all he had, but to that he was welcome. The soldier went away contented, and told his companions they ought no more to complain, so long as their general was obliged to subsist upon nothing but acorns. Out of this grew the story, that the general having invited his officers to dine with him, set nothing before them but a tray of acorns and some water.

Meanwhile mutiny after mutiny took place in General *Jackson's* army, and the campaign came near being abandoned. A circumstance, too, occurred about this time, ever to be lamented. General *Cocke*, of East Tennessee, considering himself possessed of a command independent of *Jackson*, gave his orders to some brigadiers, at the same time that General *Jackson* did. General *White* chose to act under General *Cocke's* orders, and this occasioned some confusion, and, in the end, the lamentable affair to which we have just alluded, and of which we now proceed to give an account.

The Hallibee Indians, who had been the principal sufferers at Talladega, had despatched ambassadors for General *Jackson's* camp, to sue for peace, which they would accept on any terms he might please to grant them. At the same time these proposals were out, General *White* marched against their towns, and on the 18 November completely surprised them; killed 60 warriors, took 256 prisoners, and made good his retreat without the loss of a man.

The Indians thought they had been attacked by General *Jackson's* army, and that therefore they were now to expect nothing but extermination; and this was thought to be the reason why they fought with such desperation afterwards. And truly they had reason for their fears: they knew none but *Jackson*, and supposed now that nothing short of their total destruction would satisfy him. as their conduct exemplified on every occasion. They knew they had asked peace on any terms, and their immediate answer was the sword and bayonet. A company of Cherokees aided not a little in this affair.

We have given the chief features of the battle of Autossee, when drawing a sketch of the life of *M'Intosh*. Here may be added some other matters of history, for the better understanding the events of the memorable Creek war.

Autossee is situated on the south bank of the Tallapoosie, 18 miles from the Hickory Ground, and 20 above the junction of that river with the Coosa. With General *Floyd's* white troops were four companies of friendly Indians. *M'Intosh* led the Cowetaus, and *Mad-dogs-son* the Tookaubatchians, or Tukabatchies. The names of the other leaders are not set down, but there were doubtless several of them, as there were about 350 warriors who accompanied the expedition. That sure work was intended, will not be doubted, when it is known that the force, exclusive of Indians, was 950 men. When the army arrived near the place where it was expected Indians would be found, and having discovered one small town before it was light in the morning, the general was surprised immediately after by the discovery of another. This was filled with men who had been apprized of his approach, and were prepared for battle. The order of battle was immediately changed, and the army proceeded in two divisions to attack both towns at once. The besiegers, being provided with artillery, soon accomplished their work, and all the resistance the Indians seem to have made, was in endeavoring to effect a retreat into caves and other hiding-places. Nevertheless, the Georgians had 11 killed outright, and 54 wounded. Among the latter was General *Floyd* himself severely, and Adjutant-General *Newman* slightly.

M'Intosh and *Mad-dogs-son's* loss was considerable, but was not thought of importance enough to be communicated by their allies, who were greatly indebted to them, if, indeed, destroying their own countrymen made them so. They did not, however, do so much butchering as they intended, or, rather, as they agreed to do; for the day before the massacre, they agreed to post themselves on the opposite side of the river, and to kill all who should attempt an escape. Had they done this, very few would have escaped.

After resting a few days, General *Floyd* marched to Camp Defiance, 50 miles directly into the Indian country, and westward of Autossee. Here, early in the morning of 2 January, the hostile Indians killed his sentinels before they were discovered, and then with great fury attacked his camp, and for a quarter of an hour continued to fight with bravery. By this time the army had got formed in order of battle, and soon obliged the Indians to fly. One company of whites, under Captain *Broadnax*, had its retreat cut off by the assailants, and escaped only by cutting its way through them.

In this fight, TIMPOOCHIE-BARNUEL, or *Barnard*, a half-breed, chief of the Uchies, commanded a company of them, and, in the language of the general, "greatly distinguished himself." It was owing to his promptness, that Captain *Broadnax* was enabled to effect a retreat. The enemy, in that manœuvre, had advanced within 50 yards of the artillery. All the other part of the Indian army took shelter within the lines, and looked on during the contest.

After this battle, 37 Indians were found dead on the field, as the whites reported; and of their own number 17 were killed, and 130 wounded. At the first onset, General *Newman* had three balls shot into him, which prevented his further service; and several of the principal officers had their horses shot under them. How the Indians under *Timpoochie* fared in these particulars, we have not yet learned.

Weatherford, *Francis*, *Sinquisturs-son*, with some Shawanese, had established themselves on the Alabama, above the mouth of the Cahaba, and there built a town, which they called Eckanakaka. Its name signified that it was built upon *holy ground*; and hence the prophets told their followers that they had nothing to fear, as no polluted and murderous whites could ever enter there. However, General *Claiborne*, at the head of a small army, accompanied by a band of Choktaws under *Pushamata*, their chief, resolved to make a trial of the virtue of the Indian prophets' pretensions.

Weatherford and his followers, being apprized of the approach of the army, had put themselves into an attitude of defence. On 23 December, 1813, as the army approached, they were met by the Indians, and a short engagement followed. As usual, the Indians gave way, and were pursued; but as their town was surrounded by fastnesses, few were killed in the pursuit. Thirty were found dead of the enemy Indians, and of the army, two or three were killed, and as many wounded. This was quite an Indian depot, the captors having found here "a large quantity of provisions, and immense property of various kinds." It was all destroyed with the town, which consisted of 200 houses: the women and children had only time to escape across the Alabama. The next day, another town was destroyed, eight miles above, consisting of 60 houses. We will now proceed with General *Jackson*, until he puts an end to the Creek war.

On the 17 January, 1814, General *Jackson* marched, at the head of 930 men, from near Fort Strother, for the heart of the enemy's country. In his route lay Talladega, the residence of *Fife*, a noted warrior, and friend of the whites; and here he joined the army with 200 of his men. The Indians were supposed to be assembled in great numbers, at the Great Bend of the Tallapoosie, from 14 or 15 of their towns upon that river; and it was daily expected that they would attack Fort Armstrong, in their vicinity, which was in no state to meet them. It was the news of its situation, that caused *Jackson* to march to its immediate relief. When he had arrived at Hallibee Creek, the general, from the accounts of his spies, supposed he must be in the immediate vicinity of the enemy, and he soon after encamped at a small Hallibee village, called Enotochopko. Here he discovered that he was 12 miles from the enemy, who were upon an island in the Tallapoosie, near the mouth of a creek called Emukfau. The next day the army encamped very near Emukfau, and had every sign of being hard by the adverse Indians. The order of encampment was that of battle, and every precaution was taken to guard against surprise About 6 in the morning of the 22d, the warriors from Emukfau fell with great force upon *Jackson's* left flank, and the left of his rear; and although the attack was made in full confidence that they should rout their adversaries, yet they were disappointed, and no ground was gained by the onset. The assailants fought with a determined bravery, and it was near half an hour before they could be made to retire. The Americans, having encamped in a hollow square, met the attack at advantage, but it was only at the point of the bayonet, that the Indians were put to flight. *Fife*, at the head of his warriors, joined in the pursuit, which continued about two miles, with considerable havoc.

Matters did not end here; for, in a short time, the Indians returned again to the attack, and with greater success than before. They attacked a picket at advantage, at a small distance from the main body, and General *Coffee*, in his turn, attacked the left flank of the attacking party. As his number of men was small, he soon found himself in imminent danger of being entirely cut off. General *Jackson*, seeing this, ordered *Fife* to advance to his rescue, which he did with the utmost promptitude. This attack of the enemy was upon the right flank, and was, as it turned out, only a feint to weaken the left by drawing the force from that quarter to its support; but the general was not to be outwitted by such a manœuvre. He kept the left flank firm, and the alarm gun soon gave notice, that that part was assailed. The general here met the enemy in person, seconded by Colonel *Carroll*, who ordered the charge, and led on the pursuers. The friendly Indians were successful at this time also, slaying many of their countrymen as they fled.

Meanwhile General *Coffee* had got deeper into difficulty, and was contending at fearful odds with a brave band of warriors, and was again relieved by the Indians under Captain *Fife*. This, *Fife* was enabled to do, only by charging them with the bayonet. The enemy seemed determined to wrest their country from the invaders, and retired slowly, at first, as men driven from their country will always do. *Fife* and his comrades pursued them about three miles, killing 45 of them, which they found afterwards. The reason of *Coffee's* great peril, was this, *Fife* having been ordered to his rescue before the attack on the left was made the second time; and now, hearing the firing in that direction, supposed his aid was more needed in that quarter; and thus *Coffee* was left without support. He was severely wounded, and his aid-de-camp, Colonel *A. Donaldson*, and three others, were slain.

General *Jackson*, not having provisions for a longer stay, and being considerably crippled, began a retreat to Fort Strother. The most memorable part of this expedition is yet to be related. The Indians now supposed the Americans were beaten, or they would not retreat. They therefore resolved to pursue and harass them. *Jackson* expected this, and marched, in order of battle, through one dangerous defile after another. At length, on the morning of the 24, after having nearly passed one of the most dangerous places, at Enotochopko Creek, his rear was attacked in a spirited manner; and although it was not at all unexpected, yet the columns gave way, and a good deal of confusion and slaughter ensued. At length, a six-pounder was, with great difficulty, dragged up a small eminence which commanded the battle-ground, and being charged with grape-shot, did great execution, and was a principal means of putting the enemy to flight.

The getting the cannon up the hill was done at the greatest peril; the men who undertook it being sure marks for the enemy, having nothing to screen them in the least. By the time they had discharged it once, Lieutenant *Armstrong*, Captain *Hamilton*, of East Tennessee, Captains *Bradford* and *M'Gavock*, had all fallen. *Bradford* exclaimed, as he lay, "*My brave fellows, some of you may fall, but you must save the cannon.*"

The army having, meantime, recovered from their panic, attacked in their turn, and the Indians were every where put to flight, and pursued about two miles. The Indians' loss in this battle was 189, that were found. The Americans had, in both days' fights, 24 killed, and 71 wounded. It was evident now, that the Indians were satisfied that they were not victors, for in their flight they threw away their packs and arms in abundance, and the army met with no further molestation during their return march.

We have now arrived to the termination of the Creek war. It ended in the battle of the Great Bend of the Tallapoosie, as we have related in the life of *M'Intosh.* This bend, usually called the Horse-Shoe, by the whites, was called by the Indians Tohopeka, which, in their language, it is said, signified a *horse-shoe:* therefore the battle of Tohopeka, the Great Bend, and the Horse-Shoe, are one and the same.

Nothing could be more disastrous to the deluded Creeks than this battle. The loss of their great prophets was, however, the least. Three of them, and the last upon the Tallapoosie, fell among those whom they had made believe that no wounds could be inflicted upon them by the whites; and incredible as it may seem, that although they had witnessed a total failure of all their prophecies hitherto, such was the influence those miserable impostors held over the minds of the warriors, that they still believed in their soothsayings, and that their incantations would at last save them, and that they should finally root out the whites and possess their country. Such are the errors of delusions in all ages—it is visible in all history, and will continue to be so until a knowledge of the nature of things shall diffuse itself, and the relation of cause and effect be more extensively known.

Monohoe was one, and we believe the son of *Sinquistur* was another, who fell in the great battle at Tohopeka. In one of his accounts of the battle, General *Jackson* observes: "Among the dead was found their famous prophet, *Monohooe*, shot in the mouth by a grape shot, as if Heaven designed to chastise his impostures by an appropriate punishment." The manner in which he was killed, required but little aid from the whites to satisfy the Indians that he was a false prophet, and it was soon generally believed among them.

These prophets were decorated, says Colonel *Eaton*, "in the most fantastic manner—the plumage of various birds about their heads and shoulders; with savage grimaces, and horrid contortions of the body, they danced and howled their cantations." *Monohoe*, in the very act of divination, muttering to the sun, with eyes almost strained from their sockets, and his limbs distorted in every possible unnatural direction, received his death wound. The faith of the warriors in such abominable fooleries must now have been shaken, but the Hallibee massacre was alone sufficient to account for their desperation—as we have seen, their most submissive offers of peace had been met by the sword—all confidence therefore in the humanity and integrity of the whites, had, in their minds, been forfeited. From every appearance it was evident that they had determined to conquer at Tohopeka, or never to survive a defeat; for they did not, as on former occasions, send away their women and children: about 300 of these were taken.

Whether the famous prophet *Hillishago*, or *Francis*, were in this battle, is not known. On 18 April, 1814, General *Jackson* wrote from his camp, at the junction of the Coosa and Tallapoosie, saying, "Peter *M'Quin* has been taken, but escaped; he must be taken again. *Hillishagee*, their great prophet, has also absconded; but he will be found." In this, however, as will be seen, the general was no prophet; for *Francis* and *M'Queen* were both alive in 1817.

The friendly Indians rendered the Americans most efficient aid in this battle, and their loss in killed and wounded was greater in proportion to their numbers than that of the whites. In all 23 were killed, and many more were wounded.

It was supposed by General *Floyd*, that in the battle of Autossee he had killed the famous prophet and king of Tallassee, but it turned out not to be so, for he fell into the hands of the Americans afterwards. He was supposed to be a hundred years old, his head being entirely white, and bowed almost to the ground. His name, we believe, was *Eneah-thlukkohopoiee.* He was taken about the time of *Weatherford's* surrender; and but for the protection afforded him by the whites, their friends, the Creeks, would have put him to death without mercy But *Weatherford* had nothing to fear from them: they carefully avoided meeting, and when any by accident or necessity came into his presence, they were observed to tremble with fear. Such is the difference in the carriage and aspect of men.

We will close the present chapter by detailing some particulars in the lives of several distinguished chiefs.

It was very seldom that the names of any chiefs appeared in the accounts of the late war, but they were many, especially in the south, and deserved as much notice, and often more than many that did receive it. When the war was over, some of them occasionally visited Washington, and the novelty of their appearance sometimes caused them to receive such notices as follows: "On the 8th ultimo, [Feb. 1816,] arrived Col. *Return J. Meigs*, the agent of the U. States in the Cherokee nation, with a deputation from the nation, consisting of Col. *Lowry*, Maj. *Walker*, Maj. *Ridge*, Capt. *Taylor*, Adjt. *Ross*, and *Kunnesee*. These Indians are men of cultivated understandings, were nearly all officers of the Cherokee forces which served under General *Jackson* during the late war, and have distinguished themselves as well by their bravery as by their attachment to the U. States."

In June following, another deputation visited the capital of the United States, of whom it was said, their appearance was such as entitled them to the highest respect. The delegates were from the Chickasaws, and consisted of General *William Colbert*, the great war chief of that nation, Major *James Colburt*, interpreter; *Ettissue; Mingo*, the great warrior; *Appasantubbee*, a chief; *Chastauny* and *Colleetchee*, warriors. Most of these fought for the whites in the south. General *Colbert* was now aged, having fought with the Americans in *St. Clair's* army, with seven others of his countrymen; one of whose names was *Piomingo*, or the *Mountain-lader*, of whom we shall presently speak.

In the late war, while his men were preparing to join the Americans, *Colbert*, impatient to be unemployed, joined the third regiment of the United States infantry. When he had served with them nine months, he returned to his nation, collected his warriors, and marched to Fort Montgomery on the Alabama, from thence against Pensacola, crossed the Esanibia, and pursued the hostile Creeks almost to Apalachicola, killing many of them, and returning to Fort Montgomery with 85 prisoners. He and his comrades were now at Washington, to obtain a settlement of the boundaries of their country. Accordingly commissioners were sent into their country, and on the 20 September following, [1816,] a treaty was entered into. In this treaty *Colbert* is styled Major-General, and by the sixth article of it he was allowed an annuity of 100 dollars during life. His name is not to the treaty of Hopewell, made 10 January, 1786, but that of *Piomingo* is. To that of Chikasaw Bluffs, 24 October, 1801, instead of his mark, we find W. C., which shows that he had been paying some attention to learning; but in subsequent treaties his mark again appears.

From the circumstance that the name of *Piomingo* is not seen to any of the treaties after that of *Colbert* appears, induces the belief that he is the same person, and that, from his attachment to the whites, he took one of their names.

Piomingo is thus mentioned by General *St. Clair*, on his arrival at his quarters. "Oct. 27. *Payamingo* arrived in camp with his warriors. I was so unwell, could only see him and bid him welcome." "Oct. 29. *Payamingo* and his people, accompanied by Captain *Sparks*, and four good riflemen, going on a scout; they do not propose to return under 10 days." We have no account of the success of the excursion, but they did not join the army again until after the defeat, which took place six days after. As they were proceeding to Fort Jefferson, one of the enemy mistook them for his companions, and was captured before he discovered his mistake. *Piomingo* accosted him with harsh language, saying, "*Rascal, you have been killing white men!*" He then ordered two of his men to extend his arms, and a third to shoot him. When this was done, and his scalp taken, they proceeded to join the army.

We learn the name of one other who was with *St. Clair*. He was called

James Anderson, and was brother to the chief *John Morris*, who, 23 June, 1793, was murdered not above 600 paces from Governor *Blount's* house, in Knoxville. He was shot by some unknown persons. The governor ordered him to be buried in the burying-ground of the white people, with military honors. A procession was formed, headed by himself, and he was interred with great respect.

In 1793, the Spaniards of Louisiana made large offers to the Chikasaws, to induce them to forsake the Americans; but their offers were treated with contempt, especially by *Piomingo*.

MUSHALATUBEE was a Chikasaw chief, with whom General *Lafayette* became acquainted in his last visit to this country. His first knowledge of him, as will appear from the following extracts out of *M. Levasseur's* work, "LAFAYETTE EN AMERIQUE," &c., was at the residence of the "sage of Monticello."

Mushalatubee, and *Pushamata*, a Chocktaw chief, already mentioned, were at Washington when the general arrived there, in December, 1824, being there at the meeting of congress, according to custom, with many other chiefs, to brighten the chain of friendship, receive presents, and make known the wants of their countrymen. At this time *Mushalatubee* made the following agreeable speech to General *Lafayette*.

"You are one of our fathers. You have fought by the side of the great *Washington*. We will receive here your hand as that of a friend and father. We have always walked in the pure feelings of peace, and it is this feeling which has caused us to visit you here. We present you pure hands—hands that have never been stained with the blood of Americans. We live in a country far from this, where the sun darts his perpendicular rays upon us. We have had the French, the Spaniards and the English for neighbors; but now we have only the Americans; in the midst and with whom we live as friends and brothers."

Then PUSHAMATA, the first of their chiefs, began a speech in his turn, and expressed himself in these words: "There has passed nearly 50 snows since you drew the sword as a companion of *Washington*. With him you have combated the enemies of America. Thou hast generously mingled thy blood with that of the enemy, and hast proved thy devotedness to the cause which thou defendedst. After thou hadst finished that war, thou hadst returned into thy country, and now thou comest to revisit that land where thou art honored and beloved in the remembrance of a numerous and powerful people. Thou seest every where the children of those for whom thou hast defended liberty, crowd around thee, and press thy hands with filial affection. We have heard related all these things in the depths of the distant forests, and our hearts have been ravished with a desire to behold thee. We are come, we have pressed thy hand, and we are satisfied. This is the first time that we have seen thee,* and it will probably be the last. We have no more to add. The earth will part us forever."

"In pronouncing these last words, the old Indian had in his manner and voice something very solemn. He seemed agitated by some sad presentiments. We heard of his death a few days after; he was taken sick, and died before he could set out to return to his own people. When satisfied that his end was approaching, he caused all his companions to be assembled, and he desired them to raise him up, and to put upon him all his ornaments, and bring to him his arms, that his death should be that of a man's. He manifested a desire that at his interment the Americans would do him military honors, and that they would discharge cannon over his grave. They promised him that it should be done; he then talked freely with his friends and expired without a groan in the midst of conversation." His monument occupies a place among the great men in the cemetery at Washington. Upon one side is this inscription:—

* They might not have been introduced to the general when he saw them at Mr. *Jefferson's*. *M. Levasseur* says, in speaking of the Indian deputation, "*A leur tête étaient deux chefs que nous avions vous s'asseoir un jour à la table de M. Jefferson, pendant notre séjour à Monticello. Je les reconnus à leurs oreilles decoupées en longues lanières, garnies de longues lames de plomb.*"

"PUSH-MA-TAHA, A CHOCTAW CHIEF, LIES HERE. THIS MONUMENT TO HIS MEMORY IS ERECTED BY HIS BROTHER CHIEFS, WHO WERE ASSOCIATED WITH HIM IN A DELEGATION FROM THEIR NATION IN THE YEAR 1824, TO THE GENERAL GOVERNMENT OF THE UNITED STATES."

And on the other:

"PUSH-MA-TAHA WAS A WARRIOR OF GREAT DISTINCTION. HE WAS WISE IN COUNCIL, ELOQUENT IN AN EXTRAORDINARY DEGREE; AND ON ALL OCCASIONS, AND UNDER ALL CIRCUMSTANCES, THE WHITE MAN'S FRIEND. HE DIED IN WASHINGTON, ON THE 24TH OF DECEMBER, 1824, OF THE CRAMP, IN THE 60TH YEAR OF HIS AGE."

That *Pushamata*, or *Pushmataha*, was a warrior, has been said. In the late war with England, he assisted in subduing his countrymen at the south. In General *Claiborne's* army he distinguished himself, particularly in the battle of the Holy Ground, (called by the Indians Eccanachaca,) upon the Alabama River, 80 miles from Fort Claiborne. Here the celebrated *Weatherford* resided, also *Hillishago* the prophet.

In the treaty which the chiefs and warriors of the Choktaus held with the U. S. commissioners, 18 October, 1820, "at the treaty ground, in said nation, near Doak's Stand, on the Natches Road," the following passage occurs: "Whereas the father of the beloved chief *Mushulatubee*, of the lower towns, for and during his life, did receive from the United States the sum of 150 dollars, annually; it is hereby stipulated, that his son and successor, *Mushulatubee*, shall annually be paid the same amount during his natural life." Hence it would lead us to suppose, without further investigation, that both the father and son had rendered the country very important services.

As has been the case in all former Indian wars, so in the present, every neighboring Indian is viewed with distrust. No sooner had the present existing Seminole war begun, than, by report at least, hundreds of the Creeks were leaving their country for Florida, to join their hostile neighbors. Early this spring, 1836, it was reported far and wide that the Chocktaws had taken up the hatchet. This occasioned a national council to be called, which assembled on the 12 May. The venerable chief MUSHULATUBEE was present, and, among other things, said, "*It makes my heart bleed to be accused of this treachery, when it is well known I and my tribe have fought side by side with* Gen. Wayne, Jackson, *and others, against the Seminoles, Creeks and British.*"

HILLISHAGO, or HILLIS HADJO, it appears, survived General *Jackson's* campaigns, and, not long after, went to England, still hoping to gain assistance from that nation to enable him to operate with effect against the Americans. He was, upon his return, the immediate instigator and cause of the Seminole war, having taken up his residence among that nation, unable to stay longer in his own country. The belief was imposed upon him by some abandoned English traders, that there was a provision in the treaty of Ghent for the restoration of their country. He received much attention while in England, and some encouragement, but nothing absolute. An English journal thus mentions his arrival:—"The sound of trumpets announced the approach of the patriot *Francis*, who fought so gloriously in our cause in America during the late war. Being drest in a most splendid suit of red and gold, and wearing a tomahawk set with gold, gave him a highly imposing appearance."

He received large presents from the king's stores, but, it is said, that of these he was chiefly defrauded afterwards by the notorious *Woodbine*, who, it seems, accompanied him in his travels.*

About the end of November, or beginning of December, 1817, a war party of Seminoles captured an American, and conveyed him immediately to their principal village, called Mikasauky. Here it appears dwelt *Francis* and his family. The American, whose name was *M'Krimmon*, was ordered to be immediately burnt to death. The stake was set, *M'Krimmon*, with his head

* Seminole War Documents D. 23, published by order of congress.

shaved, was bound to it, and wood was piled up about him. When the Indians had finished their dance, and the fire was about to be kindled, a daughter of the chief, named *Milly*, who had been witnessing the preparations with a sad countenance, flew to her father, and, upon her knees, begged that he would spare the prisoner's life; and it was not until, like the celebrated *Pocahontas*, she showed a determination to perish with him, that her father consented to prolong his life for the present. It was still his intention, if he could not sell the victim for a certain sum, to have carried his former purpose into effect; but on offering him to the Spaniards, at St. Marks, the demanded sum, 7½ gallons of rum, was paid for him, and thus his liberation was effected.

After *Francis* fell into the hands of the Americans and was hanged, his family, consisting of a wife and several daughters, surrendered themselves to the Americans at St. Mark's. The youngest daughter, *Milly*, about fourteen years of age, was treated with great attention by all the officers for having saved the life of *M'Krimmon*. She was said to have been very handsome. When *M'Krimmon* heard of her being among the captives, he went and offered himself to her as a partner. She would not, however, receive him, until satisfied that he was prompted to offer himself from other motives than a sense of the supposed obligation of his life having been saved by her.

Mikasauky was the chief rendezvous of the war party, and had been known at least a century by the name of Bâton Rouge. This name was given it by the French, and the Anglo-Americans called it the Red Sticks, to avoid the use of the same name in French. Hence the Indians who made this their quarters, were called Red Sticks. At this period they had revived the practice of setting up poles or *sticks*, and striping them with red paint, which was only when they intended war. The Americans, not knowing their practice, supposed these poles were painted with red stripes in derision of their liberty poles. Mikasauky, now Red Sticks, was upon a border of Mikasauky Lake.

HORNOTLIMED, or as General *Jackson* called him, "HOMATTLEMICO, an old Red Stick," was another principal Seminole chief, whose residence was at Foul Town in the beginning of the war; but, being driven from thence, he repaired to Mikasauky. Three vessels having arrived at the mouth of the Apalachicola on the 30 November, 1817, with military stores for the supply of the garrison, were, from contrary winds, unable to ascend. Lieutenant *Scott* was despatched for their assistance, in a boat with forty men. The old chief *Hornotlimed*, who had just before been driven from Foul Town, by a detachment of General *Gaines's* army, with a band of his warriors, had concealed themselves in the bank of the river; and when Lieutenant *Scott* and his men returned, they fired upon them, and all except six soldiers, who jumped overboard and swam to the opposite shore, were killed. Twenty of the soldiers had been left for the aid of the ascending vessels, and about the same number of women and sick were in their places. These fell into the hands of *Hornotlimed* and his warriors, who dashed out their brains upon the sides of the boat, took off their scalps, and carried them to Mikasauky, where they exhibited them upon their red pole, in memory of their victory. This chief and his companion, *Hillishago*, were doomed shortly to expiate with their lives for this massacre.

The Mikasauky town was soon after visited by the army, but the Indians had all fled, their red pole was left standing, and the scalps upon it; many of which were recognized as having been taken from Lieutenant *Scott's* men. At length a vessel cruising near the mouth of Apalachicola River, to prevent the escape of the Indians in that direction, with English colors displayed, decoyed on board the famous chiefs, *Hornotlimed*, and the prophet *Francis*. These the Americans hanged without trial or delay.

NEAMATHLA was a warrior of note and renown, before the war of 1812 with Great Britain. He was a Seminole chief; but where his residence was previous to that war we have not heard; but after the Seminole war, he lived upon a good estate, at Tallahassee, of which estate a mile square was under improvement. This, in 1823, *Neamathla*, at the head of the chiefs of his nation, gave up, with other lands, for the benefit of the United States, by a treaty which they made with its agents at Moultrie Creek, in Florida, on the 18 September of that year.

In an additional article of said treaty, we read—"Whereas *Nea Mathla*, *John Blount*, *Tuski Hajo*, *Mullato King*, *Emathlochee*, and *Econchatimico*, six of the principal chiefs of the Florida Indians, and parties to the treaty to which this article has been annexed, have warmly appealed to the commissioners for permission to remain in the district of country now inhabited by them, and in consideration of their friendly disposition, and past services to the U. States," it was agreed that *Neamathla* and his followers should have four square miles, embracing Tuphulga village, on Rocky Comfort Creek; *Blount* and *Hajo* a tract on Apalachicola River; *Mullato King* and *Emathlochee* upon the same river; and *Econchatimico* on the Chatahoochie. With *Neamathla* there settled 30 men; with *Blount*, 43; *Mullato King*, 30; with *Emathlochee*, 28; with *Econchatimico*, 38: the other Florida Indians, by the same treaty, were to remove to the Amazura, or Ouithlacooche river, upon the peninsula of Florida.

But whether "the other Florida Indians" had any hand in making this treaty, does not appear, though from after circumstances, there is no probability that they had. Hence two facts are duly to be considered concerning this transaction, as they have led to fatal mistakes: one is, as it concerns the number of the Seminoles; and it will be asked, Were their numbers greatly underrated, that it might seem that those who made the treaty were the most important part of the nation? If this problem come out affirmative, then, I say, *this* mistake, or imposition upon the inhabitants of the United States, has been a *fatal* one. The other fact or circumstance resolves itself into another problem, but not more difficult of solution than the other. It may be thus stated: Had these few chiefs *any* authority to stipulate for, or bind any others but themselves? If not, where is the obligation for them to leave their country and habitations? But I forbear to pursue this subject further in this place, and will return to *Neamathla*.

The United States agreed by the same treaty to award 500 dollars to *Neamathla*, as a compensation for the improvements abandoned by him, as well as to meet the expenses of his removal.

A word more of the countrymen of *Neamathla*, who emigrated to the western coast of the peninsula, before we proceed to other subjects. "The land," says Mr. *Williams*,* to which they are "*legally banished*, consists of dry sand ridges and interminable swamps, almost wholly unfit for cultivation; where it has cost the U. States more than their land was worth to support them. They are now in a starving condition; they have killed the stock of the American settlers, in every part of the territory, to support themselves, already; and there is no present prospect of their situation becoming improved." What is calculated to add to their miserable condition, is the limits within which they are restricted; they are not allowed to go nearer than within 15 miles of the sea. A garrison was established at Tampa to supply them with necessaries, and keep them in order. Recent events, however, had considerably changed their condition before the commencement of the present distressing war, and they are found much more numerous, and far better off, as to resources, than was supposed they could be.

A chief, whom the whites called *Peter M'Queen*, has been incidentally mentioned, in our account of the Creek war. His Indian name was TALMUCHES HATCHO, and he belonged to the tribe of Tukabatchie. In 1814 he fled before the Americans under General *Jackson*, and took up his residence in Florida, and was among others declared an outlaw. In 1817 he was chief of the Tallapoosies, and resided upon the Oklokne or Okoloknee River, and was styled "an old Red Stick." He was one of the 12 Creek chiefs who gave Mr. *Alexander Arbuthnott* power of attorney to manage their affairs. This was done on the 17 June, 1817. He was a chief of consequence, possessed a valuable property, in lands and negroes. His effects were seized upon as lawful booty, about the time of his escape from Tukabatchie. A half-breed, by the name of *Barney*, shared 10 negroes that had belonged to him, and a chief called

* Account of Florida, 72, 73.

Auchi hatche, alias *Colonel*, had 20 more. To the persons who had made plunder of his slaves, he protested, they could have no claim upon him, and that he had never injured them. He therefore applied to Mr. *R. Arbuthnott*, to intercede with the officer at the United States military post, Fort Gaines, for some relief; this he did in a very respectful letter, but with what success, we are as yet unprepared to speak.

KING-PAINE was a chief who might have demanded early attention, but who, not having been very conspicuous but in a single affair, has been deferred to this place. Early in 1812, at the head of sundry bands of Seminoles and negroes, who had run away from their American masters, *King-paine* issued forth in quest of blood and plunder. There were several other chiefs at the same time, (among whom *Bow-legs* * was conspicuous,) who assisted in making war on the frontiers of Georgia. Whether either or both of the above-named chiefs commanded the daring party, who, on 11 September, 1812, attacked and defeated a small force under Captain *Williams*, we are not certain; but it is certain that they commanded a large force soon after, when General *Newman* marched against them, and fought him with desperation. Captain *Williams*, with about 20 men, was convoying some loaded wagons towards Davis Creek, and when within about 10 miles of their destination, they were attacked by a party of Indians and negroes, supposed to be 50 in number. Although the whites were few, they protracted the fight until all their ammunition was expended, their captain mortally wounded, and six others slightly. They then effected a retreat, leaving their wagons in the hands of their enemies. Two of the Americans were killed, and, it was supposed, a much greater number of the enemy.

Expecting a force would be soon sent against them, *King-paine*, with *Bow-legs* as his lieutenant, marched out from the Lotchway towns, at the head of 150 warriors, as was supposed. They were not disappointed with regard to a force being sent against them, for in the mean time General *Newman*, † of the Georgia volunteers, marched with 117 men to destroy the Lotchway towns. When he had arrived within about six miles, he fell in with the Indians, all of whom were mounted. It appears the parties met unexpectedly, and no time was lost on either side in preparing for battle. Having dismounted, the Indians advanced a few paces, hoping thereby to intimidate their adversaries; but *Newman*, at the same time, ordered his men to charge, which being promptly obeyed, the Indians were put to flight. The battle-ground, being skirted with swamps upon three sides, was advantageous for the operations of the Indians; nevertheless, before gaining these coverts, a well-directed fire stopped the flight of many, among whom was *King-paine* himself, and *Bow-legs* was severely wounded; but this was only the commencement of the fight; for no sooner was the fall of the great chief known among his men, than they returned and charged in their turn, but were again forced to fly, leaving the body of their leader in the hands of the whites. This, more than any, or all considerations together, wrought up their minds to desperation, and they determined on its recovery, or to sacrifice themselves in the attempt; and they accordingly returned again to the charge, which, it is said, was met with firmness by the whites, who, after encountering several shocks, again succeeded in routing them; but they immediately returned again, with greater fury than before, and with greater success; for they obliged the Americans to give ground in their turn, and after some time spent in this most desperate work, they succeeded in recovering the body of *King-paine*, and carried it off. Their loss in the several charges was unknown, but supposed by the whites to have been about 30; while, on their own side, they report but one killed and nine wounded. This fight was on the 26 September, and lasted about four hours.

---

* To a document exhibited in the trial of *Arbuthnott* and *Ambrister*, his name is signed BOLECK. This was probably his real name, which required but a slight corruption to change it into *Bow-legs*.

† *Thomson* (Hist. War, 51) writes this officer's name *Newnan*; but *Brannan*, *Perkins*, and *Brackenridge*, all write it as in the text. There is a town in Florida called *Newnansville* where a newspaper is printed.

The whites were greatly distressed after this fight, for the Indians were reinforced, and harassed them until the 4 October, when they gave up the business and retired. General *Newman*, having thrown up a slight work, was able to prevent being entirely cut off, and at length retreated out of the country. The Indians did not give up the siege until they had been pretty severely cut up. The whites, by concealing themselves on the night of the 3d, made them believe they had abandoned their fort; and they came up to it in a body without apprehending danger; when on a sudden they received a most deadly fire, and immediately fled.

We shall close this chapter with some revolutionary and other matters. The Cherokees had engaged not to operate with the British, towards the close of the war; and what is very singular, all the time that the greatest successes attended the British arms, they strictly adhered to their engagement; and it was not until the fortune of war had changed, and the Americans had become masters of nearly all the country, that many of the ill-fated Indians, instigated, no doubt, by abandoned white desperadoes, fell upon the settlement called Ninety Six, killing many persons, and burning several houses. Upon this, General *Pickens* took the field, at the head of a band of mounted men, and in about five weeks following the 10 September, 1781,* finished this Cherokee war, in which 40 Indians were killed, 13 towns destroyed, and a great number of men, women and children taken prisoners.† A white man by the name of *Waters* was supposed to have been the prime mover of the Indians, who with a few of them fled through the Creek country into Florida, and made good their escape.

On 17 October, 12 chiefs and 200 warriors met General *Pickens* at Long Swamp Creek, and a treaty was concluded, by which Georgia acquired a large accession of territory.‡

We have next to relate the bold exploits of a Creek warrior, of the name *Guristersigo.*§ The British held possession of Savannah, in June, 1782, and General *Wayne* was sent there to watch their motions. On the 21 May, Colonel *Brown* marched out of Savannah to meet, according to appointment, a band of Indians under *Emistessigo*, or *Guristersigo*. But some difficulty among the Indians had delayed their march, and the movement of *Brown* was disastrous in the extreme. General *Wayne*, by a bold manœuvre, cut off his retreat, fell upon him at midnight, killed 40 of his men, took 20 prisoners, and the rest escaped only under cover of darkness. In this fight *Wayne* would not permit a gun to be fired, and the execution was effected wholly with the sword and bayonet; the flints having been previously taken from the soldiers' guns.

Meanwhile, *Emistessigo* was traversing the whole transverse extent of Georgia, (strange as it may seem,) without being discovered, except by two boys, who were taken and killed. It was the 24 June, however, before he arrived in the neighborhood of General *Wayne*, who was encamped about five miles from Savannah. *Wayne* did not expect an attack, especially by Indians, and consequently was completely surprised. But being well seconded by his officers, and happily resorting to his favorite plan of fighting, extricated himself from imminent danger, and put the Indians to flight, after a hard-fought battle.

The plan adopted by the Indian chief, though simple, was wise; but in its execution he lost some time, which was fatal to him. He captured two of *Wayne's* cannon, and while endeavoring to turn them upon the Americans, they had time to rally. And, as the sword and bayonet were only used by them, no chance was left the Indians to take advantage of position from the flashes of the guns of their adversaries. If *Wayne* merited censure for being taken thus unprepared, he deserved it quite as much for exposing himself in the fight beyond what prudence required; but more than all, for putting to death 12 prisoners who had been decoyed into his power, after the fight.

The severest part of the action was fought at the cannons. *Emistessigo* was loath to relinquish such valuable trophies, and he did it only with his life.

* *Johnson's* Life of *Green*, ii. 347.

† *Lee's* Memoirs, 382, 383.

‡ *Johnson's* Life of *Green*, ii. 348.

§ *Lee*. Dr. *Holmes* writes *Emistessigo*. Annals, ii. 340.

Seventeen of his warriors fell by his side, besides his white guides. He received a spear and two bayonets in his body before he fell, and encouraged his warriors to the last. When he began to faint, he retired a few steps, and calmly laying himself down, breathed his last without a groan or struggle.

This chief was six feet three inches high, weighing about 220 pounds, bearing a manly and expressive countenance, and 30 years of age; and General *Lee* adds, "*Guristersigo* died, as he had lived, the renowned warrior of the Overhill Creeks." In this singular affair but 12 Americans were killed and wounded. Among the plunder taken from the Indians were 117 packhorses, laden with peltry. Exertions were made to capture those warriors that escaped from the attack on *Wayne's* camp, but so well did they understand the country, that not one of them was taken.

Although not in the order of time, we will introduce here one of the earliest advocates for temperance that we have met with among the Indians. This person, though a Creek, was a descendant, by his own account, of the renowned *Grangula*. His name was *Onughkallydawwy-grangulakopak*. All we know of his history, can be told in a few words, and but for one speech of his which happened to be preserved, even his name we had never perhaps heard. That he lived in 1748, and was eminent for his good morals, except the speech, before mentioned, is all we know of him. As to the speech, which is so highly extolled, it has, like numerous others, we are of opinion, passed through too many hands to be considered by all who may meet with it as genuine; nevertheless, throwing aside all the unmeaning verbiage with which it is encumbered, an Indian speech might remain that would be read with pleasure. As it stands in the work before us,* its length excludes it from our pages, and we shall select but few sentences. It was delivered in a great council of the Creek nation, and taken down in short hand by some white present, and about four years after came into the hands of an agent of Sir *William Johnson*, thence into the hands of sundry others.

"FATHERS, BRETHREN, AND COUNTRYMEN.—We are met to deliberate. Upon what?—Upon no less a subject, than whether we shall, or shall not be a people!" "I do not stand up, O countrymen! to propose the plans of war or to direct the sage experience of this assembly in the regulation of our alliances: your wisdom renders this unnecessary for me."—"The traitor, or rather the tyrant, I arraign before you, O Creeks! is no native of our soil; but rather a lurking miscreant, an emissary of the evil principle of darkness. 'Tis that pernicious liquid, which our pretended WHITE FRIENDS artfully introduced, and so plentifully pour in among us!"—"O, ye Creeks! when I thunder in your ears this denunciation; that if this cup of perdition continues to rule among us, with sway so intemperate, YE will cease to be a nation! Ye will have neither heads to direct, nor hands to protect you.—While this diabolical juice undermines all the powers of your bodies and minds, with inoffensive zeal, the warrior's enfeebled arm will draw the bow, or launch the spear in the day of battle. In the day of council, when national safety stands suspended on the lips of the hoary sachem, he will shake his head with uncollected spirits, and drivel the babblings of a second childhood."

The above, though not a third of the speech, contains chief of all that was intended to be conveyed in several pages. A true Indian speech need not here be presented to show the difference of style between them; but as we have a very good one, by the famous Creek chief, BIG-WARRIOR, not elsewhere noticed, it shall be laid before the reader. It was delivered at the time General *Jackson* was treating with the Creeks, about the close of the last war with England, and was in reference, as will be seen, to the conditions demanded of the vanquished. And, although *Big-warrior* was the friend of the Americans, yet he now felt for his countrymen, and after saying many other things, concluded as follows:—

"The president, our father, advises us to honesty and fairness, and promises

* Sermons, &c., by Reverend *William Smith*

that justice shall be done: I hope and trust it will be! I made this war, which has proved so fatal to my country, that the treaty entered into a long time ago, with father Washington, might not be broken. To his friendly arm I hold fast. I will never break that bright chain of friendship we made together, and which bound us to stand to the U. States. He was a father to the Muscogee people; and not only to them, but to all the people beneath the sun. His talk I now hold in my hand. There sits the agent he sent among us. Never has he broken the treaty. He has lived with us a long time. He has seen our children born, who now have children. By his direction, cloth was wove, and clothes were made, and spread through our country; but the Red Sticks came, and destroyed all;—we have none now. Hard is our situation; and you ought to consider it. I state what all the nation knows: nothing will I keep secret.—There stands the little warrior. While we were seeking to give satisfaction for the murders that had been committed, he proved a mischief-maker; he went to the British on the lakes; he came back, and brought a package to the frontiers, which increased the murders here. This conduct has already made the war party to suffer greatly; but, although almost destroyed, they will not yet open their eyes, but are still led away by the British at Pensacola. Not so with us. We were rational, and had our senses. We yet are so. In the war of the revolution, our father beyond the waters encouraged us to join him, and we did so. We had no sense then. The promises he made were never kept. We were young and foolish, and fought with him. The British can no more persuade us to do wrong. They have deceived us once, and can do it no more. You are two great people. If you go to war, we will have no concern in it; for we are not able to fight. We wish to be at peace with every nation. If they offer me arms, I will say to them, You put me in danger, to war against a people born in our own land. They shall never force us into danger. You shall never see that our chiefs are boys in council, who will be forced to do any thing. I talk thus, knowing that father Washington advised us never to interfere in wars. He told us that those in peace were the happiest people. He told us, that if an enemy attacked him, he had warriors enough, and did not wish his red children to help him. If the British advise us to any thing, I will tell you—not hide it from you. If they say we must fight, I will tell them, No."

He had previously spoken of the causes of the war, and of the sufferings it had brought upon them, but asked indulgence from compassion. The fine tract of country, now the state of Alabama, was argued for by *Shelokta*, another famous chief, who had large claims on the whites, but *Jackson* would not concede. This chief had rendered them the greatest services in the war, and appealed to *Jackson's* feelings, by portraying the dangers they had passed together, and his faithfulness to him in the most trying scenes; but all availed nothing.

Big Warrior was a conspicuous chief for many years. In 1821, one of his nation undertook to accompany a Mr. *Lucas* as a guide, and killed him by the way. Complaint was immediately made to *Big-warrior*, who ordered him to be executed without delay. In 1824 he was the most noted among the opposers of the missionaries. In this it was thought he was influenced by the Indian agents, which opinion was perhaps strengthened from the fact that a sub-agent, Captain *Walker*, had married his daughter. He was head chief of the nation when General *M'Intosh* forfeited his life by breaking the law of the nation in selling a part of the Creek country. The troubles of his nation having brought him to Washington, at the head of a delegation, he fell sick and died there, 8 March, 1825.* He was a man of colossal stature, and proportionate physical powers; and it is said "his mind was as colossal as his body," and that he had done much towards improving the condition of his countrymen. He had a son named *Tuskehenaha*.

* *Niles's* Register, xxviii. 48.—By a passage in the report of a committee of congress on the Creek affairs in 1827, it would seem that *Big-warrior* died as early as February.

CHAPTER VIII.

*Grounds of the Seminole War—Circumstances of those Indians misunderstood—Justness of the War—*Neamathla *deposed—Treaties—Of Moultrie Creek—Payne's Landing—Council at Camp King—Is broken up by* Osceola*—It is renewed, and a party agree to emigrate—*Osceola's *opposition—Is seized and put in irons—Feigns a submission and is released—Executes an agreement to comply with the demands of the whites—The physical condition of the Indians.*

Having, in a former chapter of this our fourth book, given many of the necessary particulars for a right understanding of the former Florida war, it will not be necessary here to repeat the same, and we shall, therefore, proceed at once to a notice of the grounds of the present war with the Indians in that region.

It has been formerly said, that nearly all the Indian wars have the same origin; and, on attentively examining the subject, it will be found that the remark has much of truth in it. The Seminoles of Florida have been found quite different from what they had been supposed. Every body had considered them a mere outcast remnant, too much enfeebled by their proximity to the whites, to be in the least dreaded in a war. Indeed, such conclusion was in perfect accordance with the accounts which were circulated among intelligent people; but the truth seems to be, people have always been misinformed on the subject, owing chiefly to the ignorance of their informers. Nor is it strange that misinformation should be circulated, when it is considered that the very agents who lived among them, and those who made treaties with them, could not give any satisfactory account as to their numbers or other circumstances. General *Jackson*, in 1817 and 18, made an easy matter of ravaging a part of Florida. His being opposed but by very few Indians, led to the belief that there were but few in the country. The war of 1814 was then too fresh in their recollections to suffer them to adventure too much, and the probability is, that but few could be prevailed upon to join in a war again so soon. Hence, one of two conclusions must now evidently be fixed upon,—either that the Seminole Indians were much more numerous, 20 years ago, than what was supposed, or that they have increased very considerably within that time. For my part, I am convinced that both conclusions are correct.

When we are told, that at such a time, and such a place, commissioners of the United States government met a delegation of the principal chiefs of the Southern Indians, and made a treaty, the articles of which were satisfactory to the Indians, two or three queries present themselves for solution; as, by what means have the chiefs been got together; what other chiefs and principal men are there belonging to such a nation, who *did not* participate in the business of the treaty. Anxious to effect their object, commissioners have sometimes practised unwarrantable means to obtain it; especially in encouraging sales of territory by a minority of chiefs, or gaining their consent to a removal by presents.

In the early part of the present war, the number of Seminole warriors was reckoned, by persons upon the spot, at 2000; but they have generally, since that period, been rated higher. But it is my opinion, that 2000 able men, led by such a chief as *Osceola* has proved himself to be, are amply sufficient to do all that has been done on the part of the Indians in Florida, in 1835 and 6.

There can be but one opinion, among discerning people, of the justness of the present war, as it appears to me; nevertheless, however unjustly created, on the part of the whites, the most efficient measures should have been taken. in its earliest stages, for its suppression; because, the sooner it is ended, the fewer will be the sacrifices of lives; to say nothing of the concomitant sufferings of individuals, and destructions of property. It has been frequently asked, what the executive and the congress of the nation have been about all this time! A few soldiers have been sent to Florida at a time; some have been cut off, and the services of others rendered abortive, by some childish bickerings among their officers about "precedency of rank." But whose fault it is that those officers should have been there under commissions o instructions of such a nature as to set them in such an awkward positi n in respect to each other, I will not take upon me to state, the facts being of sufficient notoriety.

A writer has given the following facts relative to the Seminoles recently, and, as they are suited to my course of remarks, I give them in his own words:—"Shortly after the cession, [of Florida to the U. S.] a treaty was made by which the Seminoles consented to relinquish by far the better part of their lands, and retire to the centre of the peninsula,—a quarter consisting for the most part of pine barrens of the worst description, and terminating towards the south in unexplored and impassable marshes. When the time came for the execution of the treaty, old *Neha Mathla*, the head of the tribe, thought it savored too much of the cunning and whiskey of the white man, and summoned his warriors to resist it. Gov. *Duval*, who succeeded Gen. *Jackson* in the chief magistracy of this territory, broke in upon his war council, deposed the war leaders, and elevated the peace party to the chieftaincies. The Seminoles retired peaceably to the territory assigned them, and old *Neha Mathla* retired to the Creeks, by whom he was raised to the dignity of a chief."

The next event of considerable moment in the history of the Seminoles, is the treaty of *Payne's Landing*. Of this affair I am able to speak in the language of the principal agent in it, on the part of the whites. The individual to whom I refer, General *Wiley Thompson*, will be particularly noticed hereafter, from the melancholy fate which he met in the progress of this war.

I have, in a previous chapter, spoken of the treaty at Moultrie Creek; but, before going into the particulars of that at Payne's Landing, it will be necessary to make a few additional observations. The Indians who consented to that treaty, by such consent agreed "to come under the protection of the U. States, to give up their possessions, and remove to certain restricted boundaries in the territory, the extreme point of which was not to be nearer than 15 miles to the sea coast of the Gulf of Mexico. For any losses to which they might be subjected by their removal, the government agreed to make liberal donations, also to provide implements of husbandry, schools, &c., and pay an annuity of 5000 dollars for 20 years; besides which there were presents of corn, meat, &c. &c. It was required of the Indians that they should prevent absconding slaves from taking refuge among them, and they were to use all proper exertions to apprehend and deliver the same to their proper owners."

Our account next goes on to state, that the harmony which existed at the conclusion of this treaty was very great, and that the Indians were so well satisfied with its provisions, "that they had a clause expressly inserted, by which the United States agent, Major *Gad. Humphreys*, and the interpreter, *Richards*, were to have each one mile square, in fee simple, as a mark of the confidence they reposed in these officers of the government."

Before this treaty was carried into effect, the Indians were intruded upon, and they gradually began to be rather slow in the delivery of the runaway negroes. Clamors were therefore loud against them, and difficulties followed, in quick succession, for several years. At length it was determined that the Seminoles should be, somehow or other, got out of Florida, and the treaty of Payne's Landing was got up for this object.

Accordingly, in 1832, on the 9th of May, a treaty was entered into "on Ocklawaha River, known by the name of the treaty of Payne's Landing, by which they stipulated to relinquish all their possessions in Florida, and emigrate to the country allotted to the Creeks, west of the Mississippi; in consideration of which the government was to pay 15,400 dollars, on their arrival at their new home, and give to each of the warriors, women and children one blanket and one homespun frock. The whole removal was stipulated to take place within three years after the ratification."

What object the government could have had in view by stipulating that the Indians should deliver into its hands all their cattle and horses, previous to their emigration, I know not, unless it was the intention of its agents to *speculate in stocks;* or perhaps the mode by which the Indians were to be transported would not admit of their being transported with them. Be this as it might, we shall see that this stock affair was among the beginning of the sparks of war.

It appears that between 1832 and 1834, it had become very apparent that no removal was intended by the Indians; and it was equally apparent that those who had engaged a removal for the nation, were not the first people in it,—and, consequently, a difficulty would ensue, let the matter be urged when it would. General *Thompson* was the government agent in Florida, and he (whether with advice or without, I am not informed) thought it best to have a talk with some of the real head men of the nation, upon the subject of removal, which he effected about a year before the time of removal expired, namely, in the fall of 1834.

Meanwhile, the chief who had been put in the place of *Neamathla*, by Governor *Duval*, had been executed, by some of the nation, for adhering to the whites, and advocating a removal beyond the Mississippi. The name of the chief executed upon this account was *Hicks*. To him succeeded one named *Charles*, or, as he is sometimes called, *Charles Omathla*, and he shared the same fate not long after. Nine warriors came into his council, and learning that he insisted upon a removal, shot nine bullets through his heart! No more doubtful characters were now raised to the chieftaincy, but a warrior, named *Louis*, well known for his hostility to the whites, was made chief.

In the council which General *Thompson* got together for the purpose of holding a talk, as has been remarked, appeared OSCEOLA, and several other distinguished chiefs. This council was held at Fort King, and was opened by General *Thompson* in a considerable speech, wherein he endeavored to convince the Indians of the necessity of a speedy removal; urging, at the same time, that their own safety, as well as that of their property, required it; and requested their answer to the subject of his discourse, which he presented in form of propositions. "The Indians retired to private council, to discuss the subject, when the present young and daring chief *Aceola* (*Powell*) [OSCEOLA] addressed the council, in an animated strain, against emigration, and said that any one who should dare to recommend it should be looked upon as an enemy, and held responsible to the nation. There was something in his manner so impressive and bold, that it alarmed the timid of the council; and it was agreed, in private talk, that the treaty should be resisted. When this was made known to the agent, he made them a long and eloquent harangue, setting forth the dangers that surrounded them if they were subjected to the laws of the *pale faces*, where a red man's word would not be taken; that the whites might make false charges against them, and deprive them of their negroes, horses, lands, &c. All this time *Aceola* was sitting by, begging the chiefs to remain firm." When this was finished, a chief, named

"HOLATEE MICO, said the great Spirit made them all—they had come from one woman—and he hoped they would not quarrel, but talk until they got through." The next chief who spoke was named

MICANOPEE. He was the king of the nation. All he is reported to have said was, that he had no intention to remove. "POWELL then told the agent he had the decision of the chiefs, and that the council was broken up. In a private talk, an old chief said he had heard much of his great father's regard for his red children. It had come upon his ears, but had gone through them; he wanted to see it with his eyes;—that he took land from other *red skins* to pay them for theirs, and by and by he would take that also. The *white skins* had forked tongues, and hawks' fingers; that *David Blount* told him the people in the great city made an Indian out of paint, and then sent after him and took his lands, (alluding to the likenesses of the chiefs, in the war department, at Washington.) He wanted, he said, to sleep in the same land with his fathers, and wished his children to sleep by his side."

The plea set up, that Spain ceded Florida to the United States in 1819, without any provision for those Indians, need only to be noticed to show its absurdity. It is worthy of remark, that when the right of the Seminoles to the lands of Florida was talked about, the idea was derided by many influential men; but when such persons desired to take possession of some of the territory, they seemed more inclined to acknowledge the Indians' rights by agreeing to pay them for them, than of exercising either their own *right*, or that of the United States, by taking unceremonious possession. This can be accounted for in the same way that we account for one's buying an article that he desires, because he dares not take it without.

When a removal was first urged upon the Seminole Indians, their chiefs said, "Let us see what kind of a country this is of which you talk, then if we like it, it is time enough to exchange ours for it." But it is said, the government agent had no authority to authorize a deputation of Indians to visit the promised land, and here the matter rested awhile.

How long after this it was, I shall not undertake to state, that the Indians made known their desire of exchanging their country; but this was said to have been the fact, and the result was the treaty of Payne's Landing, already described.

It appears that General *Thompson*, nothing discouraged at the result of the council which had been terminated by the wisdom of *Osceola*, without the slightest concurrence in any of his measures, by unceasing efforts had prevailed upon a considerable number of "chiefs and sub-chiefs to meet him afterwards and execute a writing, agreeing to comply with the treaty of 1832." This was evidently done without *Osceola's* consent, but its being done by some whom he had considered his partisans, irritated him exceedingly. He now saw that in spite of all he could do or say, the whites would get terms of agreement of some of the Indians; enough, at least, for a pretence for their designs of a removal.

In this state of things, *Osceola* remonstrated strongly with the agent for thus taking the advantage of a few of his people, who doubtless were under much greater obligation to him than to the people of the United States. Remonstrance soon grew into altercation, which ended in a *ruse de guerre*, by which *Osceola* was made prisoner by the agent, and put in irons, in which situation he was kept one night and part of two days.

Here then we see the origin of *Osceola's* strong hatred to General *Thompson*. While lying in chains he no doubt came to the fixed resolution to resist the whites to his utmost ability, and therefore, with perfect command over himself, dissembled his indignation, and deceived the agent by a pretended compliance with his demands. The better to blind the whites, he not only promised to sign the submission which he had so strongly objected to, but promised that his friends should do so, at a stated time; and his word was kept with the strictest accuracy. He came to Fort King with 79 of his people, men, women, and children, and then the signing took place. This punctuality, accompanied with the most perfect dissimulation, had the effect that the chief intended it should—the dissipation of all the fears of the whites. These transactions were in the end of May and beginning of June, 1835.

Thus we have arrived very near the period of open hostilities and bloodshed; but before proceeding in the details of these sanguinary events, it may not be improper to pause a moment in reviewing some of the matters already touched upon. The first to which the attention is naturally called, is so prominent as scarcely to need being presented, but I cannot refrain asking attention to a comparison between the number of "chiefs and sub-chiefs," (which was SIXTEEN) who on the 23 April, 1835, agreed to "acknowledge the validity of the treaty of 9 May, 1832," and the number of warriors and chiefs now in open hostility. These have not been rated below 2000 able men. Does any body suppose that those 16 "chiefs and sub-chiefs," (among whom was *not* the "king of the nation" nor *Osceola*,) had full power to act for 2000 warriors on so extraordinary an occasion? The question, in my mind, need only be stated; especially when it is considered how ignorant every body was of the actual force of these Indians.

It will doubtless be asked, how it happens that the Indians of Florida, who, a few years since, were kept from starving by an appropriation of congress, should now be able to maintain themselves so comfortably in their fastnesses. The truth undoubtedly is, that the "starving Indians" were those then lately forced down into the peninsula, who had not yet learned the resources of the country; for not much has been said about the "starving Indians of Florida" for several years past.

In addition to the great amount of cattle, hogs, corn, grain, &c. taken from the whites, from the commencement of the war to the present time, the Seminoles make flour of a certain root, called coonty, upon which they can subsist without inconvenience for a considerable length of time, which is of incalculable advantage to them in their war operations.

The strength of the Indians has been not a little augmented by the blacks. Some accounts say there are 800 among them, some of whom have joined them, on absconding from their white owners; but it is well known that the Florida Indians own many slaves. Old *Micanopy* is said to have 80.

CHAPTER IX.

The Indians prepare for war—Affair of Hogtown—A mail-carrier killed—Sales of the Indians' cattle and horses advertised by the Indian agent, but none takes place—Burnings and murders are committed—Settlement at New River destroyed—Remarkable preservation of a Mr. Godfrey's *family—Colonel* Warren's *defeat—Swamp fight—Destruction of New Smyrna—Defeat and death of Major* Dade, *with the destruction of nearly his whole party—Visit to his battle-ground.*

From April until harvest time, preparations had gone on among the Indians, and they only waited for the whites to begin to compel a removal, when the blow should be struck. The time allowed them over and above the three years, to prepare for their journey to the prairies of the Arkansaw, was spent in making ready to resist at the termination of it.

As early, however, as the 19 June, 1835, a serious affray took place between some whites and Indians, at a place called Hogtown, not far from Mickasauky in which the former were altogether the aggressors. The Indians, about seven in number, were discovered by a gang of whites, hunting "beyond their bounds," upon whom they undertook to inflict corporal punishment. Two of the Indians were absent when the whites came up to them, and they seized and disarmed them, and then began to whip them with cowhide whips. They had whipped four, and were in the act of whipping the fifth, when the other two Indians came up. On seeing what was going on, they raised the war-whoop and fired upon the whites, but whether they received any injury, we are not told; but they immediately returned the fire, and killed both the Indians. When General *Thompson* was made acquainted with the affair, he summoned the chiefs together, and stated the facts to them, and they disclaimed all knowledge of it, and, it is said, agreed to deliver the offenders into the hands of the whites, to be dealt with according to their laws. This must be taken as the story of the whites; for in this case *they*, and not the Indians, were the "offenders." It was altogether a singular report, that after the Indians had all been whipped and killed, they should be required to *give up the offenders;* but such was stated to be the fact, and I know not that it has been contradicted.

Frequent signs of uneasiness had been manifested during the summer among the Indians, some of whom could not be restrained from acts of violence by the chiefs, although, it is pretty evident, such acts were against their advice. A mail-carrier was killed and robbed between St. Augustine and Camp King, and two or three houses had from time to time been broken open in different places; but it is not impossible but that these acts might have been committed by other people than Indians. However, the Indians were mistrusted, and not only mistrusted, but reported as the perpetrators: and whether they were or not is but of small moment, as affairs turned out.

Things remained in this state until December following, when the Indian agent notified such of the Indians as he was able, that their time had expired, and that they must forthwith prepare for their journey over the Mississippi, and to that end must bring in their cattle and horses according to the terms of the treaty. And so confident was he that they would be brought in, that he had advertised them for sale, and the 1st and 15th of the month were the days in which the sales were to be made. The appointed days passed, and no Indians appeared; and it was immediately discovered that they had sent their women and children into the interior, and the warriors were marching from place to place with arms in their hands, ready to strike.

Consternation and dismay was depicted on the countenances of the bordering whites, and they began to fly from their dwellings, which were immediately destroyed by the Indians. One of the first places attacked was the plantation of Captain *Priest*, the buildings on which were burned. Small companies of whites were immediately organized for scouring the country. One of these was fired upon by some Indians in ambush, who wounded two, one supposed mortally, and a son of Captain *Priest* had his horse killed under him. Soon after, as 30 or 40 men were at work getting out ship-timber on Drayton's Island, in Lake George, they were fired upon and driven from the place. None were wounded, although the bullets passed through the clothes of some of them.

On the 5th of Jan. 1836, a small party, supposed to be about 30, of Indians struck a fatal blow on a poor family at New River, which is about 22 miles to the north of Cape Florida. It was the family of the light-house keeper of this place, named *Cooley*. And what renders the case peculiarly aggravating is, that this family, like that of *Clark*, at Eel River near Plimouth, in *Philip's* war, were, and had always been, on terms of great intimacy with the very Indians who destroyed them. Mr. *Cooley*, being absent when the attack was made, escaped the butchery. The number murdered was six, one of whom was a man named *Flinton*, from Cecil county, Maryland, who had been hired as a family teacher, his mother, wife, and three children. *Flinton* he found shockingly mutilated, apparently with an axe; his two older children were lying near him shot through the heart, with the books they were using at the time they were murdered by their sides; from which circumstance it is evident they met death at the same moment they knew of the vicinity of the foe. His wife, with the other child at her breast, he found about 100 yards from the others, both apparently killed by the same bullet. Mrs. *Cooley* had formerly been a captive among the Indians, understood their language, as did one of the children, a boy, and both were much liked by them.

Here the Indians found a rich booty. They carried off about 12 barrels of provisions, 30 hogs, 3 horses, 480 dollars in silver, one keg of powder, above 200 pounds of lead, and 700 dollars worth of dry goods.

A family of several persons in the neighborhood of *Cooley's*, witnessed the murder, and barely made their escape. Also another, that of the widow *Rigley*; herself, two daughters and a son; these escaped by flight to Cape Florida. Here were soon gathered about 60 persons, who had escaped from along the coast, and not being able to subsist long for want of provisions, made a signal of distress, and were soon discovered by a vessel, which took them to St. Augustine.

There was, among the families who fled to save their lives about this time, one, very remarkably preserved. The family of *Thomas Godfrey*, viz. his wife and four female children, having escaped to a swamp unobserved, were relieved by a negro, about the end of the fourth day. This man was drawn to the spot by the moans of one of the children, whose poor famished mother could no longer give it its usual support at the breast. This negro belonged to the hostile Indians, and came upon these sufferers with an uplifted axe; but when he saw the children in their distress, his arm was unnerved by the recollection that his own children were then in the power of the whites. He therefore came to the humane resolution of setting them at liberty, which could not be done, without great hazard, for the Indians were yet in possession of all the adjacent country; but he directed them to remain as quiet as possible until night, when he would bring them something to eat. This he did, and also brought them blankets to sleep upon. The next day a company of mounted whites dispersed the Indians, and the negro conveyed Mrs. *Godfrey* and her children in sight of them, and then made his escape. The husband of Mrs. *Godfrey* had some time before been ordered out in defence of the country.

Nothing but devastations of the most alarming and destructive character seem to have occurred in the region of East Florida, so long as there was a place left, which was not strong enough to withstand an attack.

About the 18 of December, Colonel *Warren*, at the head of a small detachment of his regiment, was ordered to convoy a train of wagons loaded with provisions and munitions from St. Augustine to the main body, which was encamped at Fort Croom, near *Micanopy's* town. While on their march they were attacked by a superior force of Indians, who killed 8 or 10 of them, and put the rest to flight, almost in sight of the force they were sent to relieve. All the wagons fell into the hands of the Indians, which, after taking from them what they desired, broke them up and burnt them.

On the 20 of December, as General *Call*, with the Middle Florida troops, was marching for Fort Draine, his advanced guard discovered a house on fire near Micanopy, and a trail of Indians was discovered leading to a pond, which was full of bushes and logs. This pond the whites nearly encircled, and although at first no Indians were seen, yet the flashes of their guns soon pointed out their hiding-places, and considerable firing ensued on both sides, but the fire of the Indians was soon silenced, and on searching the bog four Indians were found dead, but all the others, if there were any more, had effected their escape. In this swamp fight, three whites were badly wounded, and one killed.

On the 26 of December, a band of about 100 Indians, under a chief named Philip, and a number of Indian negroes, made an attack on New Smyrna, to the south of Mosquito Inlet, on the east side of the Peninsula, where they found nothing to obstruct their ravages. They began with the house of Mr. *Dunham*, which when they had plundered, "parties of them scattered about the neighboring plantations of *Cruger*, *Depeyster*, and *Hunter*. The Indian negro, *John Cæsar*, endeavored to decoy Mr. *Hunter* from his house, on pretence of selling him cattle and horses; he, however, having heard by his negroes that large numbers of Indians were about, and in the afternoon he crossed the river to Colonel *Dummet's*. The Indians held possession of *Dunham's* house all day, and about one the next morning set it on fire, together with all the out-buildings. In the course of the 27, they burned and destroyed all the buildings on *Cruger's* and *Depeyster's* plantations except a corn-house, and, on *Hunter's*, all except a corn-house. They now crossed over the river to Colonel *Dummet's* house, and after destroying every thing in it, set that on fire, but from some cause the fire did not burn it. They next burnt the house of Mr. *Ratcliff*, a little to the north of Colonel *Dummet's*, and broke and destroyed the lantern and every thing belonging to the light-house."

The war having now become serious, and the Indians no longer looked upon as a despicable foe, the most melancholy forebodings were entertained for the very existence of the strongest places in Florida, and the call for protection from that quarter had become loud and frequent; but notwithstanding war had been expected all the preceding autumn, no effectual measures had been taken by the proper authorities to check the Indians in such an event. There had, however, late in December, arrived at Fort Brooke a small number of United States' troops under Major *Dade*, of the 4th regiment of infantry, the official account of whose operations and defeat, I give as follows, in the language of Major *Belton*. It should be observed, that Major *Dade* was detached for the relief of General *Clinch* at Camp King, who was supposed to be in the most imminent danger from the Indians, and also in great want of supplies.

His despatch was dated at Fort Brooke, 1 January, 1836, and proceeds as follows:—"The schooner Motto arrived on the 21 December from Key West, with brevet Major *Dade* and his company, A infantry, 39 strong, with a small supply of musket-ball cartridges, after looking in at several points between the Key and this place. Being thus reinforced, I hesitated no longer to put *Gardiner's* company, C 2d artillery, and *Frazer's* company, B 3d infantry, in motion for Fort King, pursuant to General *Clinch's* orders; which movement had been ordered on the 16th, and suspended the same day, on account of intelligence I had received of the force of the Mickasukies, and their strong position, near the forks of the Wythlacoochee. I despatched the public schooner Motto on 23d, with Lieutenant *Duncan*, 2d artillery, to Key West for a battery of two twelve-pounders, and such stores as co d be serviceable and at 6 o'clock, on 24th, the companies, *Gardiner's* and *Frazier's*, made fifty bayonets each, by details from those companies remaining here, and with one of the two six-pounders of this post with four oxen, I had ordered to be purchased, one light wagon and ten days' provisions were put in march.

"The first halt of this command was at Little Hillsboro' River, seven miles from this post, the bridge of which I had reconnoitred by Indians of *Emathla's* band the day before. From this I heard from Maj. *Dade* pressing me to forward the six-pounder, by all means, it having been left by the failure of the team four miles out. I accordingly ordered the purchase of three horses and harness, and it joined the column at nine that night. On the night of the 24th, I heard that the transport with Maj. *Mountford* and company, long and anxiously expected, was in the bay. I sent at one o'clock a letter to him, (received at day-light) by an Indian express, urging him on. He landed with his strong company on the 25th about noon, and informed me that *Legate's* company, under Lieut. *Grayson*, nearly full, must be near at hand. Of this Maj. *Dade* was informed by a gallant volunteer, *Jewell*, C company, 2d artillery, who had left the detachment with the news of the burning of Big Hillsboro' bridge, near which Maj. *D.* had halted the second day, 25th. I also informed him that I was using every exertion to push on about thirteen hundred rations on pack-horses, with what ammunition could be spared. A duplicate of this was sent the next day by a young Indian, who became lame and could not overtake the column, and returned with his letters. Pr. *Jewell* joined Maj. *Dade* about 11 o'clock on the night of the 25th.

"In the chain of events, it is proper that I should mention, that three Tallahassee Indians came in on the evening of the 22d, and caused great excitement in *Itolase Emathla's* camp. They brought a talk of *Inicanopas* of a pacific or neutral character, or they affected it; but I believe not distinctly, until after I had made them prisoners, while in full council with *Emathla's* warriors, which step I considered imperative, if they were spies, and as much so if they were charged with any propositions likely to detach the chiefs from the treaty; or indeed by an act of self-devotion, to take the scalps of *Emathla*, *Black Dirt*, and *Big Warrior*, faithful chiefs, who have been hunted in this way since the scalping of *Charles Emathla*. In a council with *Emathla* that night, Maj. *Dade* expressed every confidence in Indian character; and particularly upon the salutary influence of *Abraham* upon *Micanopa*. On reflection I detained two of the imprisoned Tallahassees, as hostages, and sent the youngest and best runner with letters to General *Clinch*, and General *Thompson*, via *Inicanopa*, as I could do no better, and of course, through *Abraham's* lands.

"These letters of course involved many details; but numbers and other facts, to guard against treachery, were stated in French. The runner returned two days beyond his time, with a message from *Abraham* and *Broken Sticks*, stating my talk was good, and that I might expect him on the 30th. This we freely rendered that he would be at the attack fixed for Christmas week. A negro, his intimate, named *Harry*, controls the Pea Creek band of about a hundred warriors, forty miles south-east of us, who have done most of the mischief, and keep this post constantly observed, and communicate with the Mickasukians at Wythlacoochee by means of powerful bands of Eufollahs and Alafiers, under *Little Cloud*, and the *Alligator*. In tracing Maj. *Dade's* movements, I have every reason to believe that he made on the 26th six miles, 27th to Big Wythlacoochee; on the fifth day, 28th, to the battle-ground, sixty-five miles.

"Here it may be proper to state that Maj. *Mountford's* command was ready to move on the 26th, but the transport, in which was a company of the 2d artillery under Lieut. *Grayson*, unfortunately entered the wrong bay, and got into shoal water, and was not seen, or certainly heard of, till the morning of the 28th of December, when, by sending a party with a flag as a signal, Lieut. *Grayson* was put in possession of instructions, and landed his company at a point four miles west of us, on the east side of Tampa Bay (proper) and joined at sunset that evening; his transport did not get round to land his baggage till the 30th; so long an interval as to put all hope of junction out of the question, and Maj. *Mountford's* baggage was unladed.

"Now it becomes my melancholy duty to proceed to the catastrophe of this fated band, an elite of energy, patriotism, military skill, and courage. On the 29th, in the afternoon, a man of my company, *John Thomas*, and temporarily transferred to C company, second artillery, came in, and yesterday Pr. *Ransom Clark*, of same company, with four wounds very severe, and stated, that an action took place on the 28th, commencing about 10 o'clock, in which every officer fell, and nearly every man. The command entrenched every night, and about four miles from the halt, were attacked, and received at least fifteen rounds before an Indian was seen. Maj. *Dade* and his horse were both killed on the first onset, and the interpreter, '*Louis*.' Lieut. *Mudge*, third artillery, received his mortal wound the first fire, and afterwards received several other wounds. Lieut. *Basenger*, third artillery, was not wounded till after the second attack; and, at the latter part of that, he was wounded several times before he was tomahawked. Capt. *Gardiner*, second artillery, was not wounded until the second attack, and at the last part of it. Mr. *Basenger*, after Capt. *Gardiner* was killed, remarked, "I am the only officer left; and, boys, we will do the best we can." Lieut. *Keays*, third artillery, had both arms broken the first shot; was unable to act, and was tomahawked the latter part of the second attack, by a negro. Lieut. *Henderson* had his left arm broken the first fire, and after that, with a musket, fired at least thirty or forty shot. Dr. *Gatlin* was not killed until after the second attack, nor was he wounded; he placed himself behind the breastwork, and with two double-barrelled guns, said, "he had four barrels for them." Capt. *Frazier* fell early in the action with the advanced guard, as a man of his company, B third artillery, who came in this morning, wounded, reports.

"On the attack they were in column of route, and after receiving a heavy fire from the unseen enemy, they then rose up in such a swarm, that the ground, covered, as was thought, by light infantry extension, showed the Indians between the files. Muskets were clubbed, knives and bayonets used, and parties were clenched; in the second attack, our own men's muskets from the dead and wounded, were used against them; a cross-fire cut down a succession of artillerists at the fence, from which forty-nine rounds were fired; the gun-carriages were burnt, and the guns sunk in a pond; a war-dance was held on the ground. Many negroes were in the field, but no scalps were taken by the Indians; but the negroes, with hellish cruelty, pierced the throats of all, whose loud cries and groans showed the power of life to be yet strong. The survivors were preserved by imitating death, excepting *Thomas*, who was partly stifled, and bought his life for six dollars, and in his enemy recognized an Indian whose axe he had helved a few days before at this post. About one hundred Indians were well mounted, naked, and painted. The last man who came in brought a note from Capt. *Frazier*, addressed to Maj. *Mountford*, which was fastened in a cleft stick, and stuck in a creek, dated, as is supposed, on 27th, stating that they were beset every night, and pushing on.

F. S. Belton, *Capt. 2d Artillery*."

Such was the fate of Major *Dade* and his gallant companions. *Osceola* was present, as was the old chief *Micanopy*. Of the latter, it is said, he had, in the beginning of the troubles, avowed that *he would neither leave his country, nor would he fight;* but when the force under Major *Dade* approached his town, he altered his resolution, seized his rifle, and shot that officer.

The situation of affairs, at this period cannot better be described than in the language of a gentleman attached to Major *Mountford's* command, stationed at Fort Brooke, and is contained in a letter, dated on the first day of the year:—"We are," says he, "really in the theatre of war of the most horrible kind. We arrived here on Christmas day. and found the inhabitants flying in from all quarters to camp. Major *Dade*, with seven officers and 110 men, started, the day before we arrived, for Fort King. We were all prepared to overtake them the next day, and were upon the eve of departure, when an intervention of circumstances deferred it for one day; and, in the course of that day, three soldiers, horribly mangled, came into camp, and brought the melancholy tidings that Major *Dade* and every officer and man, except themselves, were murdered and terribly mangled. We are at work, night and day, entrenching ourselves in every possible manner. We expect every moment to be attacked, as the savages have sworn we should all be massacred before the 6th of January. We are only about 200 strong, with officers and men, and about 50 citizens, and 100 friendly Indians, under their chief, *Black Dirt*. The savages are said to number 4000."

After the arrival of General *Gaines* in Florida, he ordered a detachment, under Captain *Hitchcock*, to visit the battle-ground of Major *Dade*. And when he had performed his orders, he gave the following report of that distressing spectacle. His report is dated "Fort King, Florida, Feb. 22, 1836," and is addressed to General *Gaines*, as follows:—"Agreeably to your directions, I observed the battle-ground, six or seven miles north of the Ouithlecooche river, where Major *Dade* and his command were destroyed by the Seminole Indians, on the 28 Dec. last, and have the honor to submit the following report:—

"The force under your command, which arrived at this post to-day from Tampa Bay, encamped, on the night of the 19th inst., on the ground occupied by Major *Dade* on the night of the 27th of December. He and his party were destroyed on the morning of the 28th December, about four miles in advance of that position. He was advancing towards this post, and was attacked from the north, so that on the 20th instant we came on the rear of his battle-ground, about nine o'clock in the morning. Our advanced guard had passed the ground without halting, when the General and his staff came upon one of the most appalling scenes that can be imagined. We first saw some broken and scattered boxes; then a cart, the two oxen of which were lying dead, as if they had fallen asleep, their yokes still on them; a little to the right, one or two horses were seen. We then came to a small enclosure, made by felling trees in such a manner as to form a triangular breastwork for defence. Within the triangle, along the north and west faces of it, were about thirty bodies, mostly mere skeletons, although much of the clothing was left upon them. These were lying, almost every one of them, in precisely the position they must have occupied during the fight,—their heads next to the logs over which they had delivered their fire, and their bodies stretched, with striking regularity, parallel to each other. They had evidently been shot dead at their posts, and the Indians had not disturbed them, except by taking the scalps of most of them. Passing this little breastwork, we found other bodies along the road, and by the side of the road, generally behind trees, which had been resorted to for covers from the enemy's fire. Advancing about two hundred yards further, we found a cluster of bodies in the middle of the road. These were evidently the advanced guard, in the rear of which was the body of Major *Dade*, and, to the right, that of Capt. *Fraser*.

"These were all doubtless shot down on the first fire of the Indians, except, perhaps, Capt. *Fraser*, who must, however, have fallen very early in the fight. Those in the road, and by the trees, fell during the first attack. It was during a cessation of the fire, that the little band still remaining, about thirty in number, threw up the triangular breastwork, which, from the haste with which it was constructed, was necessarily defective, and could not protect the men in the second attack.

"We had with us many of the personal friends of the officers of Major *Dade's* command; and it is gratifying to be able to state, that every officer was identified by undoubted evidence. They were buried, and the cannon, a six-pounder, that the Indians had thrown into a swamp, was recovered, and placed vertically at the head of the grave, where, it is to be hoped, it will long remain. The bodies of the non-commissioned officers and privates were buried in two graves; and it was found that every man was accounted for. The command was composed of eight officers, and one hundred and two non-commissioned officers and privates. The bodies of eight officers and ninety-eight men were interred,—four men having escaped, three of whom reached Tampa Bay; the fourth was killed the day after the battle.

"It may be proper to observe, that the attack was not made from a hammock, but in a thinly-wooded country; the Indians being concealed by palmetto and grass, which has since been burned.

"The two companies were Capt. *Fraser's*, of the 3d artillery, and Capt. *Gardiner's*, of the 2d artillery. The officers were Major *Dade*, of the 4th infantry, Capts. *Frazer* and *Gardiner*, second Lieutenant *Basinger*, brevet second Lieut. *R. Henderson*, *Mudge* [late of Boston] and *Keais*, of the artillery, and Dr. *J. S. Gatlin*."

From a comparison of the above report with the official account before given, of Captain *Belton*, nearly every thing concerning this signally great disaster is learned; but from the report of the three men that had the singular fortune to escape, many incidents have, from time to time, been gathered, and communicated through the newspapers. In fact, until the late visit to the battle-ground, no other account, but such as could be gathered from the three poor half-murdered soldiers, *could* be obtained; and yet it appears that they gave the facts as they really were. They all came in separately, sorely wounded,—one of them with no less than eight wounds. He was supposed to be dead, and was thrown promiscuously into a heap of the slain, about which a dance was held by the Indians, before leaving the ground. This man crawled away in the following night, and thus effected his escape.

CHAPTER X.

Of the principal chiefs and war leaders of the Seminoles—Osceola—Micanopy—Jumper—*Massacre of* General Thompson *and others at Fort King*—Battle of the Ouithlecooche—*Fight near Wetumka*—*Great distress of the country*—*Action of Congress upon it*—*Battle at Musquito*—*Many Creeks join the Seminoles*—*Fight on the Suanee River*.

There has been occasion already pretty fully to sketch the character of the chief generally called *Powell* by the whites, but whose real name is Osceola, or *Oseola*. This chief has shown himself to be, thus far, equal to the desperate cause in which he is engaged. We, at a distance from the Indians, marvel that they should be so short-sighted as not to see that to wage a war is only to hasten their ruin; but, when we thus reflect, we do not consider the scanty information which the Indians have of the real strength of the whites. Our means of getting a knowledge of the Indians, is incalculably greater than theirs is of getting a knowledge of us. They cannot read, neither can they converse (or but very few of them) with intelligent white men; therefore, that they know much less of us than we do of them, must be very apparent. They know nothing of geography. If an Indian, in the interior of Florida, should be told that New England was a great place, without considerable trouble he could not be made to understand whether it were a great town, as large as a village of 50 wigwams in his own country, or as large as the whole of Florida. We learn every thing of this nature by comparison; and how shall the Indian comprehend our terms, but by comparing them with his own? Hence it is owing, mainly, to the unavoidable ignorance of the Indians of our actual condition, that induces them to hazard a war with us. I know, from the best authority, that the western Indians, previous to *Black Hawk's* war, were generally of the opinion that they were far more numerous than the whites; and when a trader told them they certainly were not, they laughed at him with scornful gestures. We have no reason to believe the Florida Indians any better informed; and, besides, they are cheated and baffled so often by knaves who go among them for that purpose, that they imagine all the whites to be of the same character, and they cannot tell whether a talk really comes from their great father, the president, or whether some impostor be cheating them with one of his own, to get their lands for his particular benefit.

With this view of the case before us, it will not appear altogether unaccountable that a daring chief, like *Osceola*, should engage in a war. He is said not to be a chief by birth, but has raised himself by his courage and peculiar abilities to that station. His father is said to have been an Englishman, and his mother a Creek woman. He belongs to the Red Stick tribe. In person he is slender, but well formed, muscular, and capable of enduring great fatigue; is an excellent tactician, and an admirer of order and discipline. He would frequently practise military manœuvres with the whites, and none of them, it was observed, could excel him. His complexion is rather light, deep restless eyes, clear and shrill voice, and not more than about 35 years of age. He is said to have conducted in person every important action from the time of *Warren's* defeat to the battle of the Ouithlecoochee. General *Thompson* imprisoned him, as we have before related, because he would not acknowledge his authority, and for asserting that the country was the Indians', "that they wanted no agent, and that he had better take care of himself."

Of old *Micanopy* as well as *Osceola* I have already had occasion to speak. He was said to have joined the latter with 500 men: he is a short, thick-set, "ugly-looking Indian, and much given to intoxication." JUMPER is *Micanopy's* chief counsellor, and a warrior of great perseverance, activity, and courage. We shall now take up the narrative of events in the order of their occurrence, and the next of importance was the massacre near Camp King, which happened on the same day, but at a later hour than the destruction of the detachment under Major *Dade*.

Osceola, it will be remembered, had been roughly treated at this place, not many months before, and had been by coercion obliged to comply with the demands of Mr. Agent *Thompson*, about a removal, &c. He was known afterwards to declare that *Thompson* should pay with his life for his conduct. Accordingly, with a small band of warriors, at noon day, on the 28 of December, he approached Camp King for this avowed purpose. *Thompson* resided here, and was in the employ of the United States' government, as agent for the removal of the Seminole Indians, and other affairs concerning them. He was a man of considerable consequence, and had formerly, it is believed, been a member of congress. Whether it was his usual custom to dine out of the fort, we are not informed, but on this fatal day, it seems, he, with nine other gentlemen, met at the store house of Mr. *Rogers*, which was but 250 yards from the fort, and while seated at dinner there, they were attacked by *Osceola*; and what was remarked, at the time, as very singular, was, that those people should be beset and slain, and all scalped, within reach of two six-pound cannon then mounted upon the fort, which was garrisoned with 50 men; but such are the facts upon record.

Mr. *Rogers* was sitting at the head of his table, and the first intimation of the presence of Indians was a volley of, as was judged, 100 guns. The door of the house being open, nothing prevented the deadly aim of the foe, who, after the first discharge, rushed upon the house with savage fury. Those who were not killed jumped out of the windows, on each side, and fled; five, who ran to the fort, escaped; the others, in running for a hammock near by, were shot down. The negro woman, a cook, ran behind the counter and hid behind a barrel. *Osceola*, at the head of his warriors, rushed into the house, but did not discover her, and immediately left it. The names of the five that were killed, were, General *Thompson*, Lieutenant *Constantine Smith*, *Erastus Rogers*, sutler, a Mr. *Suggs* and *Hitzler*. Fifteen bullets were found to have been shot through General *Thompson*, and 16 through Mr. *Rogers*. Their heads were scalped all over, as far as the hair extended.

Bloody events now followed each other in quick succession. We have seen that upon the same day happened the two massacres last related, and scarcely had the news of them ceased vibrating on the ear, when the battle of the Ouithlecoochee was announced. The movements of General *Clinch*, in the very end of the year 1835, brought about this event, which will presently be detailed in his own words. He was lying in garrison at Fort Drane, a stockade about 30 miles from Camp King. He had here a plantation, upon which was a large crop of corn; this he liberally dealt out to the soldiers; other supplies having failed. On the arrival of General *Call*, an expedition was immediately set on foot for the head-quarters of the Indians.

As the narrative of every transaction is of increased importance and value, in proportion to the means of knowledge and veracity of the narrator, we are always led to a desire to hear the history of such transactions from the very actors in them; because, from such sources, we seldom fail of arriving at the truth. A commander or leader in a battle or expedition, if he would wish to misrepresent a transaction, would, in scarce one time in a thousand, dare to do so; because all his followers, or at least all those wronged by a false statement, would rise in evidence against him. I need not, however, have prefaced General CLINCH's *official account* of the BATTLE of OUITHLECOOCHEE with these observations, for, from the very face of it, his aim at the strictest veracity is apparent. But it is proper that we know how to value the real sources of history; it was to this end that the above observations were made. I will now proceed with General *Clinch's* account of his battle with *Osceola*.

"*Head Quarters, Territory of Florida, Fort Drane, Jan.* 4, 1836.

"SIR—On the 24 ultimo, brigadier Gen. *Call*, commanding the volunteers called into service by his excellency, *G. R. Walker*, acting governor of Florida, formed a junction with the regular troops at this post, and informed me that his command had been raised to meet the crisis; that most of their terms of service would expire in a few days, which made it necessary to act promptly. Two large detachments were sent out on the 15th [Dec.] to scour the country on our right and left flank. Lieut. Col. *Fanning*, with three companies from Fort King, arrived on the 27th; and, on the 29th, the detachment having returned, the brigade of mounted volunteers, composed of the 1st and 2d regiments, commanded by Brig. Gen. *Call*, and a battalion of regular troops commanded by Lieut. Col. *Fanning*, took up the line of march for a point on the Ouithlecooche river, which was represented by our guides as being a good ford. About 4 o'clock on the morning of the 31st [of Dec.] after leaving all our baggage, provisions, &c., protected by a guard commanded by Lieut. *Dancy*, we pushed on with a view of carrying the ford, and of surprising the main body of the Indians, supposed to be concentrated on the west bank of the river; but on reaching it, about day-light, we found, instead of a good ford, a deep and rapid stream, and no means of crossing, except in an old and damaged canoe. Lieut. Col. *Fanning*, however, soon succeeded in crossing; the regular troops took a position in advance, whilst Brig. Gen. *Call* was actively engaged in crossing his brigade, and in having their horses swam over the river. But before one half had crossed, the battalion of regulars, consisting of about 200 men, were attacked by the enemy, who were strongly posted in the swamp and scrub, which extended from the river. This little band, however, aided by Col. *Warren*, Maj. *Cooper*, and Lieut. *Yeoman*, with 27 volunteers, met the attack of a savage enemy, nearly three times their number, headed by the chief OSEOLA, with Spartan valor. The action lasted nearly an hour, during which time the troops made three brilliant charges into the swamp and scrub, and drove the enemy in every direction. And after the third charge, although nearly one third of their number had been cut down, they were found sufficiently firm and steady to fortify the formation of a new line of battle, which gave entire protection to the flanks, as well as the position selected for recrossing the troops. Brig. Gen. *Call*, after using every effort to induce the volunteers remaining on the east bank, when the action commenced, to cross the river, and in arranging the troops still remaining on that bank, crossed over and rendered important service by his coolness and judgment in arranging part of his corps on the right of the regulars, which gave much strength and security to that flank. Col. *Fanning* displayed the greatest firmness throughout the action, and added much to the high reputation long since established. Captains *Drane* and *Mellon* exhibited great bravery and judgment, and likewise added to the character they acquired in the late war. Nor was Capt. *Gates* wanting in firmness. Capt. *Wm. M. Graham*, 4th infantry, was fearlessly brave, and although very severely wounded early in the engagement, continued to head his company in the most gallant manner, until he received another severe wound, when he was taken from the field. His brother, Lieut. *Campbell Graham*, commanding the adjacent company, was likewise severely wounded early in the fight, but continued with his men until another wound forced him, from loss of blood, to retire from the field. Lieut. *Maitland*, who commanded a company, contributed much, by his gallantry, to encourage his men.

Lieuts. *Talcot, Capron, John Graham, Ridgely,* (who was wounded early in the action,) and *Brooks*, all displayed good courage and coolness throughout the action. When almost every non-commissioned officer and private exhibited such firmness, it was almost impossible to discriminate between them; but the commanding-general cannot withhold his high approbation of judgment and courage displayed by sergeant *Johnson* of H company, third artillery, on whom the command of the company devolved, after Lieut. *Graham* was removed from the field; and who, although severely wounded, continued at the head of the company till the action was over. Also of sergeants *Kenton* and *Lofton*, and corporal *Paget*, 4th infantry. Sergeants *Scoffield* and *Potter* D company, 2d artillery; sergeant *Smith*, C company, first artillery, and corporal *Chapin*, C company, 3d artillery. Colonel *John Warner*, commandant 1st regiment volunteers, Maj. *Cooper*, and Lieut. *Yeoman* of same corps, who had formed on the left flank, were all severely wounded, while leading their little band to the charge, and all behaved with great bravery, as well as adjutant *Phillips*. Lieut. Col. *Mills* displayed great coolness and judgment during the action, and in recrossing the river with his command. Lieuts. *Stewart* and *Hunter* of the 2d regiment, with a few men of that regiment, were judiciously posted on the right, and, from their reputation for firmness, would have given a good account of the enemy, had he made his appearance in that quarter. Col. *Parkill*, of the F. volunteers, who performed the duties of adjutant-general, displayed much military skill and the utmost coolness and courage throughout the whole action; and his services were of the first importance. Col. *Reid*, inspector-general, displayed much firmness, but he had his horse shot, and received a slight wound early in the engagement, and was sent with orders to the volunteers. My volunteer aid, Maj. *Lytle*, and Maj. *Welford*, aid to Brig. Gen. *Call*, were near me throughout the action, and displayed the most intrepid courage and coolness. Col. *J. H. McIntosh*, one of my aids, and Maj. *Gamble*, aid to Gen. *Call*, both displayed much firmness and courage, and were actively employed on the left flank. I also feel it due to Lieut. Col. *Bailey*, Capt. *Scott*, and Lieut. *Cuthbert*, to say, that, although the action was nearly over before they could cross the river with a few of the 2d regiment, they took a judicious position, and showed much firmness. Capt. *Wyatt*, of the same corps, was entirely employed in erecting a temporary bridge, and manifested much firmness. Much credit is also due to the medical department, composed of Doctors *Wightman, Hamilton, Randolph*, and *Bradon*, for their activity and attention to the wounded.

"The time of service of the volunteers having expired, and most of them having expressed an unwillingness to remain longer in the service, it was considered best, after removing the dead and taking care of the wounded, to return to this post, which we reached on the 2d instant, without the least interruption, and, on the following day, the volunteers from Middle Florida took up the line of March for Tallahassee; and this morning those from East Florida proceeded to their respective homes, leaving me a very few men to guard this extensive frontier. I am now fully convinced that there has been a great defection among the Florida Indians, and that a great many Creeks have united with them, consequently it will require a strong force to put them down.

"I also have the honor to enclose you a list of the killed and wounded of the respective regiments and corps. I am, sir, with high respect, your most obedient,

D. L. CLINCH,

Brevet B. General U. S. Army, Commanding.

"R. Jones, *Adjutant-General U. S. Army.*"

"Return of the killed and wounded at the battle of the Ouithlecooche on the 31st day of December, 1835.—C company, 1st artillery, Capt. *Gates* commanding—one artificer killed; 1 corporal and 3 privates wounded. D company, 2d artillery, Capt. *G. Drane* commanding—1 private killed; 1 second Lieut., 1 corporal, and 12 privates wounded. F company, 2d artillery, bt. Capt. *Mellon* commanding—1 artificer killed. C company, 3d artillery, 1st Lieut. *Maitland* commanding—1 artificer killed, and 7 privates wounded. H company, 3d artillery, 1st Lieut. *C. Graham* commanding—1 private killed 1 first Lieut., 1 sergeant, 2 corporals, and 12 privates wounded.

"TOTAL—4 killed, and 52 wounded." How many of the wounded died after the return was made out, I cannot ascertain; but no doubt many did, as is always the case. The loss of the Indians is, as usual on such occasions, variously estimated. Some friendly Indians who came into Tallahassee, said that *Osceola* lost 104 men, and was himself twice wounded during the battle.

There were with General *Clinch*, as guides in his expedition, three or four Indians of the white party, relatives of the chief, *Charles Omathla*, who doubtless rendered eminent service.

Osceola was observed foremost of all his men in this battle, and was well known to General *Clinch* and many of his men. He wore a red belt, and three long feathers. Having taken his stand behind a tree, he would step boldly out, level his rifle, and bring down a man at every fire; nor was he dislodged until several volleys from whole platoons had been fired upon him. The tree behind which he stood was literally cut to pieces. It is almost a wonder that he had not now fulfilled the measure of his threat made on a former occasion, which was to kill General *Clinch*. He probably tried his best to do it, for the general received several shots through his clothes. General *Thompson*, *Charles Omathla*, and General *Clinch* were the three persons he had declared vengeance against.

An officer in General *Clinch's* army wrote the next day after the battle, to a friend in Washington, "You will see from Gen. *Clinch's* official letter, giving an account of the battle, that he says nothing of himself. I was in this battle, and allow me to say to you respecting him, what I saw and know to be true. Throughout the engagement he was in the hottest of the fight. His horse was shot under him in two places, neck and hip. A ball passed through his cap, entering the front, and passing out at the back part of the top. Another ball passed through the sleeve of the bridle-arm of his coat. This was my first battle, and I may not be the best judge, but I do not believe that any man ever displayed more intrepid courage than Gen. *Clinch* did on this occasion. At one moment a little confusion occurred among the troops, in consequence of some soldiers giving the word "*Retire!*" The general immediately threw himself in front of the men, and his horse staggering under him, he dismounted, advanced to the front, and, amidst a shower of bullets from the Indians, said, that before he would show his back to the enemy, he would die upon the field. The high and chivalric bearing of the general kindled among the men an enthusiasm, which, I believe, was never surpassed. A gallant charge followed, which routed and drove the enemy from the field, and they did not again show themselves. We kept the field about three hours, and then recrossed the river in good order, and without disturbance."

The next events which occurred were not of so much moment as those immediately preceding them; but it is our duty to notice all, which we will do in the order of time.

On the 12 January, "Col. *Parish*, at the head of 200 mounted volunteers, composed of the companies of Capt. *Alston*, *Bellamy*, and *Caswell*, had a sharp encounter with a large body of Indians near Wetumka, in Middle Florida. The attack commenced with the advanced guard under Capt. *Bellamy*, who had been allowed by the enemy to pass their main body. Col. *Parish* immediately hastened forward to his support, when suddenly he was attacked on both flanks by the enemy in ambush. The volunteers made an unsuccessful attempt to charge on horseback; they were then dismounted and formed in admirable order. They then charged the enemy in a manner worthy of veterans. In the mean time, Capt. *Bellamy*, having routed the attacking party opposed to him, fell back on the main body. The enemy were soon forced to take shelter in a thicket. By this time, night coming on, it was not thought prudent to follow them, where the localities of the place and the darkness would have given them great advantages. Our men rested on their arms in the open pine woods, prepared to renew the action at day-light; but during the night the savages effected their retreat. Their loss must have been considerable, as six dead bodies were counted in one part of the field of battle.

Two days after, Col. ***Parish*** marched for Fort King, and arrived there in safety. He then proceeded to ***Powell's*** [***Osceola's***] town, and destroyed it. The volunteers then returned to Fort Drane."

The best opinion can be formed of the distress of the people of Florida at this period, from the sufferers themselves, or those momentarily expecting to become such. On the 16 January, a newspaper published at Tallahassee contained as follows:—"Since the engagement on the Wythlacoochee, no intelligence has been had of the main body of the Indians. The situation of the inhabitants east of the St. John's and south of St. Augustine, is truly deplorable. New Smyrna has been burnt, and all the fine plantations in that neighborhood are broken up. Many of the negroes have been carried off, or have joined the savages. The Indians are dispersed in small parties, and when pursued they take refuge in the thickets, which abound every where, and fight with desperation, until they are dead, no matter by what numbers they are assailed. It is literally a war of extermination, and no hope is entertained of putting an end to it, but by the most vigorous measures. In the mean time, the number of the enemy is daily increasing by desperadoes from other tribes, and absconding slaves. The Mickasooky tribe is considered the leading [one] of the Seminoles. They have always been noted as the most ruthless and determined of the savage race."

But it must not be supposed, that the measure of the sufferings of the Floridians was yet full, at this date of our history, nor even at the very writing hereof, (20 July,) although the whole coast from St. Augustine to Cape Florida is in the hands of the Indians, and has remained so ever since the 11 February. Nevertheless, nothing seems yet to have occurred sufficiently alarming to awaken the sympathies of the heads of the nation. But on the 30 January, Mr. *White*, in the house of representatives, asked leave to introduce the following resolution:—

"Resolved by the senate and house of representatives of the United States of America, in Congress assembled, That the president of the U. States be authorized to cause rations to be delivered from the public stores to the unfortunate sufferers who have been driven from their homes by Indian depredations, until they can be re-established in their possessions, and enabled to procure provisions for the sustenance of themselves and families."

This resolution, after some debate, was passed, and became a law. The notice of this act of congress is in anticipation of the order of events; but one thing is certain, that if I have noticed congress a little prematurely, they have not committed the like *fault* in noticing the affairs of Florida.

Upon the 17 January, as *George W. Rockleff* and *Jerry Bowers*, pilots in the sloop Pilot, of Mosquito, were proceeding up Halifax River, and when nearly opposite Mrs. *Anderson's* plantation, they were fired upon by Indians, about 100 in number, as they judged, who continued their fire about a quarter of an hour. They overshot the men, but the sail and rigging of their vessel was much injured; 30 bullets having passed through the mainsail.

The next day, 18 January, Major ***Putman***, who was at the head of the independent company, styled the St. Augustine Guards, stationed at Mosquito, proceeded to Mrs. *Anderson's* plantation, at a place called Dun Lawton, about 50 miles south of St. Augustine, on the Halifax River, upon discovery. It will be remembered that the whole of the Mosquito country was destroyed on the 26 and 27 of December as we have before related, and the buildings of Mrs. *Anderson* were at that time burned. While there, this company, composed of the generous and spirited young men of St. Augustine, joined by a few from Mosquito, making about 40 men, was attacked by 150 Indians, as was supposed. Mr. *Geo. Anderson* and Mr. *Douglas Dummit*, standing on guard, saw two Indians approaching, upon whom they fired, killing one and wounding the other. *Dummit* ran to the fallen Indian, and as he was stooping over him, received a wound in the back of the neck. At the same moment the whole body of the Indians rushed out of a scrub, distant a little more than musket shot, and commenced a furious attack upon Major *Putman's* men, who, from behind the fragments and broken walls of the burnt buildings gave the Indians a warm reception; and although but 40 in number, having coverts from which to fight, and the Indians being in open space, they kept them at bay for about an hour During this time but one had been wounded. The Indians now charged them with such determined fury upon their flanks, that they were obliged to fly to their boats, which were at considerable distance from the shore, and were closely pursued by the Indians. In their hurry, the whites rendered all their guns, but one, useless, by wetting them, with this one, however, they fired as often as possible, and pushed off with energy; but the water being shallow for a great distance, they were in the most imminent danger of being boarded by the numerous Indians; in such event, every man must have perished. However, they escaped with 19 badly wounded, and several of these mortally. One boat fell into the hands of the Indians, in which were eight or ten men, who all jumped overboard and escaped, except one, a Mr. *Edward Gould*, who swam to Pelican Island, and was there left; nor was it in the power of the others to relieve him, they being pursued by the Indians in the boat which they had just taken. He was not heard of afterwards, and was supposed to have been drowned next day in endeavoring to swim from the island. A Mr. *Marks* swam to the opposite beach, and escaped to Bulowville; the others were taken into the boats again.

Great fears having, all along, been entertained that the Seminoles would be aided by the Creeks, it is now confidently affirmed that at least 1000 of them have gone down into Florida for that end.

About the 20 January, Captain *Hooder*, on the lower Suanee River, finding the opposite side in possession of the Indians, crossed over with nine men to attack them. As they landed, two of his men were shot down; one with nine balls, the other with five. With his remaining men he charged the Indians with great boldness. In the mean time his boat got adrift, and no other alternative was left but victory or death. After a close and deadly contest of some minutes, the Indians were routed with severe loss.

CHAPTER XI.

Congress *makes an appropriation for carrying on the war—Remarks in the Senate of the United States on the war with the Seminoles—Debate in the house of representatives on the bill for the relief of the inhabitants of Florida—Attack on some Creeks at Bryant's Ferry—General Gaines's campaign in Florida—Fights the Indians on the Ouithlacoochee—His conference with* Osceola*—Resigns his command, and leaves the country—Captain* Allison's *skirmish—The chief* Ouchee Billy *killed—Siege of Camp McLemore—Great sufferings of its garrison—Delivered by Captain* Read*—The chief* Mad Wolf *slain.*

Towards the close of the preceding chapter, notice was taken of the delay in congress, and by the executive of the nation, to agitate the subject of this war. At length Mr. *Webster* of the senate, from the committee on finance, reported, without amendment, a bill making further appropriation for suppressing hostilities with the Seminole Indians, and asked for its immediate consideration, as the state of the country required its passage with the utmost despatch. The amount of the appropriation was 500,000 dollars, and the bill was passed after some explanatory remarks; which remarks, as they not only set the affairs of the war forth as they were known in Washington at that period, but discover to us something by which we can judge who has been in fault there, shall here be laid before the reader.

"Mr. *Clay* said he should be glad to hear the communications from the departments read, in order to see whether they gave any account of the causes of this war. No doubt, he said, whatever may have been the causes, it was necessary to put an end to the war itself, by all the possible means within our power. But it was a condition, altogether without precedent, in which the country was now placed. A war was raging with the most rancorous violence within our borders; congress had been in session nearly two months, during which time this conflict was raging; yet of the causes of the war, how it was produced, if the fault was on one side or on both sides, in short, what had lighted up the torch, congress was altogether uninformed, and no inquiry on the subject had been made by either branch of the legislature. He should be glad, he said, if the chairman of the committee on finance, or of the committee on Indian affairs, or any one else, would tell him how this war had burst forth, and what were its causes, and to whom the blame of it was to be charged.

"Mr. *Webster* replied, that he could not give any answer to the senator from Kentucky. It was as much a matter of surprise to him, as to any one, that no official communication had been made to congress of the causes of the war. All he knew on the subject he had gathered from the gazettes. The communications from the departments spoke of the war, as a war growing out of the relations between the Indians and the government of the U. States, and gave no reason to suppose that it had its origin in any quarrel with the citizens. It probably grew out of the attempts to remove these Indians beyond the Mississippi. According to the latest accounts, the country between Tallahassee and St. Augustine was overrun by hostile Indians, and the communication between those places was interrupted. The view taken by the gentleman from Kentucky was undoubtedly the true one. But the war rages, the enemy is in force, and the accounts of their ravages are disastrous. The executive government has asked for the means of suppressing these hostilities, and it was entirely proper that the bill should pass.

"Mr. *White* expressed his regret that he could add nothing to the information given on this subject. He knew nothing of the cause of the war, if it commenced in any local quarrel or not. It was the object of the government to remove these Indians to the west side of the Mississippi, and he was apprehensive that the difficulty had arisen out of this measure. He had, however, no information, which was not in the possession of every other senator. He was for the bill.

"Mr. *Benton* said he was also ignorant of the causes of the war. Some years ago, he said, he was a member of the committee on Indian affairs. At that time these Indians in Florida were in a state of starvation; they would not work, and it was necessary that they should be fed by the U. States, or they must subsist on the plunder of our citizens. These Indians are a very bad tribe, as their very name signifies, the word *Seminole*, in Indian, being, '*wild runaway Indians*.' They were therefore considered a bad race. It was obviously the best policy to remove these Indians to a place where they would be able to obtain plenty."

When the bill for the relief of the distressed inhabitants of Florida was before the house of representatives, which was noticed in our last chapter, the following interesting debate arose upon it, which shall be laid before the reader, for the same reasons which caused the remarks in the senate to be given above.

"The resolution having been twice read, the house, on motion of Mr. *White*, agreed to consider it now.

"Mr. *W.* said that he would not occupy the time of the house further than to say, that in East Florida, five hundred families were driven from their homes, and had had their possessions destroyed in the progress of a war, which had commenced in consequence of relations between the Indians and this government, and with which the suffering inhabitants of that country have had nothing to do.

"Appropriations had frequently been made to succor Indians when in circumstances of distress, and he hoped that no member of the house would object to the adoption of the resolution for the succor of our own citizens.

"Mr. *Granger* of New York rose and said,—Mr. Speaker, in the little observation I have had of men and things, I have learned that precedent is often used to restrain our generous impulses, but seldom to impel us to generous action. In the little time I have been here, I have not been so much gratified with any thing that has occurred, as I have at the prompt manner in which this house has stepped forward to provide means for carrying on the war in Florida. Whilst we have been without any official information from the executive department of government—whilst the newspapers have been discussing the question, whether censure should rest upon one of the departments, or upon the commanding officer in Florida, this house and the other branch of the legislature have stepped forward to sustain this war, although no requisition has been made by the chief magistrate of the nation. Sir I rejoice that they have done so.

"Mr. *Cambreleng* rose to explain, and Mr. *Granger* yielded the floor.

"Mr. *Cambreleng* said, that great injustice had been done in the newspapers to the conduct pursued by the departments. The committee of ways and means had been furnished with the first communication on which they acted by the secretary of war. They next day received a second communication with all the documents relating to the Indian war, and which contained all the information that was requisite. The documents had not gone forth to the public—which was an extraordinary circumstance. They certainly were sent by the committee to this house, and ought to have accompanied the bill and been printed and sent to the senate. If they had, the erroneous impression as to the remissness of the department, or the executive, would not have gone into the newspapers. It was not the fault of the executive, or of the committee on ways and means, that this had not been done.

"Mr. *Granger* resumed. If the gentleman had listened to me a little longer, he would have discovered that I intended no censure on the executive; but as he has chosen to challenge me to speak, I do say that the history of this nation can present nothing like the silence which has existed on this subject. I do say that whilst this hall has been ringing with plaudits upon one administration, and whilst we have been called upon day after day to hunt up the bones of dead quarrels here—whilst your settlements have been laid waste and desolate, no communication has been made to this house as a branch of the government. Whatever information you have, even upon the gentleman's own showing, is a letter from the secretary of war to the chairman of the committee of ways and means.

"Mr. *Cambreleng*. That letter contained all that was necessary.

"Mr. *Granger* continued: Sir, I repeat that, with a war known to exist in this country, we have been occupied in hunting up the possibility, not only of a war which might take place hereafter with a foreign nation, but also to discover whether a war was last year likely to have existed.

"We have war enough upon our hands to take care of. The war-cry is up in the woods; the tomahawk glitters in the sunbeam; the scalping-knife is urged to its cruel duty; the flower of your chivalry is strewed along the plain, and yet every department of this administration is as dumb as the bleeding victims of this inglorious contest.

"In legislating for a suffering people, I want no precedent but that which my Creator has implanted in my bosom. I do not believe that we stand here with the sympathies of our nature chilled and frozen by the mere force of the oath which we have taken; I do not believe that our duty requires that we should be thus chilled and frozen. I believe that the existence of this government depends upon its extending its fostering hand to the unfortunate whenever it can be done within the limits of the constitution. Especially should this be the case, where the sufferers reside within a territory, and have no state government to which they can look for succor.

"Such is the true course to be pursued in this nation; and then our people will feel that they are indeed members of one common family, and that, whilst they bear equal burdens, they are the equal recipients of the bounty and protection of the government.

"On motion of Mr. *White*, the resolution was read a third time and passed.'

We have now to return to the recital of warlike operations. About the middle of January, great alarm spread through the confines of Georgia, that the Creek Indians were imbodying in various parts of their country, and the utmost consternation prevailed. On the 23 January, it being reported at Columbus, that the Indians were in force at Bryant's Ferry, 15 miles below that place, a company of whites, consisting of about 20 or 30 men, under Captain *Watson*, marched down upon discovery. They discovered 30 or 40 Indians, some of whom had rifles, but it does not appear that they had done, or intended, any mischief. However, the whites pursued them, and pretty soon a firing commenced, and, though of short duration, two were killed on each side, and the whites were driven from the ground, having several of their number wounded.

The next operations of importance were those between the forces under General *Gaines* and *Osceola*, and upon the memorable Ouithlecoochee. General *Gaines* was upon a tour of inspection and duty, when he first learned that serious disturbances had occurred between the whites and Seminoles. This was about the 15 January, and the general was arrived at New Orleans. His previous head-quarters had been at Memphis, in Tennessee. He therefore called on the governor of Louisiana, to have a body of volunteers in readiness for military service, and set out himself immediately for the scene of hostilities. At Pensacola he found some vessels of war, under Commodores *Dallas* and *Bolton*, and Captain *Webb*, who had already commenced operations in the neighborhood of Tampa Bay, and other adjacent inlets. Colonel *Twiggs* had been ordered to receive into service eight companies of volunteers, to be raised by the governor of Louisiana, and the regular force at Baton Rouge, New Orleans, and other stations in the immediate vicinity of New Orleans, and to hold himself in readiness for a movement towards Tampa. This force consisted of about 1100 men.

That no time should be lost, General *Gaines* returned immediately to New Orleans (about 26 January), and, on the 4 February, was under way again for Florida, with his forces organized. He arrived at Tampa, with his forces, in three steam-boats, on the 9th, and, on the 13th began to proceed into the Indian country. His first movement was to the east, on the Alafia River, having understood there had been a fight in that direction, near Fort Brooke, between the hostile and friendly Indians; but after two days, no enemy being discovered. the line of march was altered for Fort King. General *Gaines's* army had but ten days' rations; but, by advices, he was assured that there was plenty at Fort King.

On the 20 February, the army passed Major *Dade's* fatal field, on which was found 106 men, all of whom they decently interred. All the officers who fell in that disastrous fight were identified, and, what was very remarkable, every man was accounted for; but what struck every one with the greatest surprise, was, that the dead were in no instance pillaged; articles the most esteemed by savages were untouched; the officers' bosom-pins remained in their places; their watches were found in their pockets, and money, in silver and gold, was left to decay with its owner,—a lesson to all the world—a testimony that the Indians are not fighting for plunder!—nay, they are fighting for their rights, their country, their homes, their very existence! The arms and ammunition were all that had been taken, except the uniform coat of Major *Dade*.

On the 22 February, the army arrived at Fort King, much to the agreeable surprise of the garrison, which it had been reported was cut off by the Indians. Owing to the country's being in possession of the Indians, no supplies had arrived; and, the next day, a troop of horse was despatched to Fort Drane, (22 miles north-west,) in hopes to obtain further supplies. They returned the 24, but with only seven days' additional rations. To this they added two days' more at Fort King. The general scarcely knew what course next to take; but he finally concluded to move down the Ouithlecoochee, over General *Clinch's* battle-ground, and so to Tampa, thinking such a route might bring him in contact with the main body of the Indians. Accordingly the army moved, on the 26th, from Fort King, and, at two o'clock on the 27th, arrived at General *Clinch's* crossing-place. Here, while examining and sounding the river, the Indians fired upon them, and set up a fierce war-cry; but their numbers were not sufficient to make any material impression, although they continued the fight for about half an hour. The whites lost one killed, and eight wounded.

On the 28th, the army, having resumed its march, was again attacked, about two miles from its former position, and a fire was kept up about half of the day. At the commencement of the action, Lieutenant *Izard*, of the United States dragoons, fell, mortally wounded. In the course of the fight, another was killed, and two wounded. In the evening, express was sent to Fort Drane, with directions for the commanding officer to march down with a force upon the opposite side of the Ouithlecoochee and thus come upon the rear of the Indians which movement, should it succeed, it was hoped, would finish the war.

On the morning of the 29th, no Indians were to be seen; but the general did not relax his precautions. A party was preparing timber and canoes for crossing the river, when, about 9 o'clock, they were sharply fired upon, and, at the same time, the encampment was attacked upon every side, but that towards the river. The Indians now seemed in great force, (12 or 1500, as was supposed,) having been collecting, from all quarters, since the fight on the previous day. They continued the contest two hours, in which time one man was killed and 33 wounded. Among the latter was the general himself,—a rifle ball having passed through his lower lip, knocked out one tooth, and damaged two others. When it was found that the general was wounded, his companions expressed much regret; but he talked of it as a matter of small moment; said "it was very unkind in the rascals to take away a tooth which he valued so highly."

On reconnoitering the enemy's ground, after he had fled, *Gaines's* men found one of their dead, which had been dragged a considerable distance and left unburied, from which circumstance they conjectured he had fled in haste. His rifle had been taken away, but he was found to be well provided with ammunition, having plenty of powder and sixty bullets. The place of this attack *Gaines* called Camp *Izard*.

The flight of the Indians was no security for their not appearing again; for, on the 2d of March, they returned, and commenced pouring in their shot upon the whites, which, at intervals, they continued to do until the 5th. Meantime all of their provisions were exhausted, and they began the slaughter of their horses to sustain life. But it is said that, during all this time, no one was heard to murmur or complain.

On the night of the 5th, about 10 o'clock, a call was heard from the woods, and some one requested a parley. On the officer of the guard's demanding what was wanted, it was answered that the Indians were tired of fighting, and wished for peace. The general ordered the officer of the guard to answer, that if the Indians wished to treat, to send a messenger the next morning, with a white flag, and he should come and go in safety. He replied, "very well," and added that "he desired to have a friendly talk, and to shake hands." Accordingly, on the morning of the 6th, about 300 Indians filed out from the river, and took a position in the rear of the whites, about 500 yards off. They expected nothing now but a most bloody contest, supposing the main body of the Indians to be concealed in a neighboring hammock. Both parties remained a short time in suspense, each doubting what the other would do. At length, one or two advanced within hailing distance, and, being joined with others, repeated what had been said the night before. The general now sent out to them a staff officer, and they told him they did not wish to fight any more, but requested that the army should withdraw from the Ouithlecoochee. *Osceola* was at the head of the Indian deputation. When the officer who had met the Indians reported this talk to *Gaines*, he ordered him to return to *Osceola*, and to inform him, in the plainest terms, that they would be subdued, that a large force was on the way into their country, and that, unless they submitted, every Indian found in arms would be shot. When this was communicated to the Indians, they said they would go and hold a council, and would meet them again in the afternoon. The meeting in the afternoon, accordingly, took place, and the Indians urged what they had said in the morning, and added that they had lost many of their men by death and wounds, and were tired of the war; but as their governor (as they styled *Micanopy*) was not there, they must first consult him, and asked to have the war suspended until he could be consulted. They were told that if they would cease from acts of hostility, go south of the Ouithlacoochee, and attend a council when called upon by the United States commissioners, they should not be molested. This they agreed to, and, at the same moment, General *Clinch* came upon the main body of the Indians, and they all fled with the utmost precipitation, probably concluding this was a stratagem which the whites had prepared to cut them off. *Clinch* came with 500 men and supplies, which was doubtless more agreeable to the starving army, than even a treaty with *Osceola*.

The Indians seem to have been well acquainted with the condition of General *Gaines's* army; for, during the interview with *Osceola*, he asked how they were off for provisions, and when they told him they had enough, he shook his head, saying, "It is not so; you have nothing to eat; but, if you will come over the river, I will give you two beeves, and some brandy." It is therefore surprising that he should have been now asking for peace. It shows, however, that he was well aware of the hopelessness of his case; and, although he was able to deal with General *Gaines*, he early knew of the approach of General *Clinch*, and it was, probably, on his gaining that knowledge, that he concluded to see what kind of terms could be got of the whites, as the affairs of war then stood.

General *Gaines*, having transferred his command to General *Clinch*, left for New Orleans about the 9 March, and General *Clinch* proceeded with his united forces to Fort Drane. A negro spy, who had been sent among the hostile Indians, from Camp Izard, soon after returned, and confirmed the peaceable intentions of the chiefs: they told him, that in their various skirmishes with General *Gaines* on the Ouithlacooche they had lost 30 men. Of the whites but 5 were killed, and 60 wounded. It is rather uncommon that there should be so great a disproportion between the slain of the parties, when it is considered that the Indians almost always fought from coverts.

On the 9 March, Captain *Allison* of the Florida volunteers had a skirmish near his camp, not far from Fort Brooke. He routed the Indians, whom he judged to be a thousand strong, and took considerable plunder. Hence, notwithstanding the Indians were supposed to desire peace, skirmishes continued. And on the 23 March, a company of volunteers were attacked about six miles from Volusia, in which the whites lost three men killed, and six wounded, and the Indians five or six. Among the latter was their chief, called *Ouchee Billy*, or *Billy Hicks*. He was found the day after the fight, concealed in some brush.

About the 5 April, Major *McLemore*, by order of General *Scott*, took a position on the Ouithlacoochee, and erected a block-house, which was called Camp McLemore. Here, about 40 men, far removed into the heart of the Indian country, were to remain until relieved by the General, or Major *McLemore*, who, it appears, after establishing the post, immediately left it. This small force seems to have arrived here at a most fortunate time, for it was four days before they were discovered by the Indians, and during this period they had completed a block-house for their protection.

It is scarcely to be credited that this little company of men, sent here by the commander-in-chief of the army, should be left without the means of escape in extremity of circumstances, and no way kept open by which their situation from time to time might be known; such, however, was the case, and for about six weeks nothing was heard of them. They had not been provided with provisions for more than two weeks, and it was the general impression of every one that they had all perished by famine or the hands of the Indians.

The following account of the siege of Camp McLemore by Dr. *Lawrence*, surgeon there at the time, shall be given in his own words:—"We had just completed building the block-house, and dug out a spring near the edge of the fort, when, on the morning of the 9th of April, at a little before dawn of day, we were attacked by the Indians, who had encompassed us on three sides, and were in number about 150 or 200. The engagement lasted one hour and three quarters, when they found out, to their sorrow, that our reception was not only too warm, but that they had ventured too near us without due reflection. On the next day, we had one man killed on his post by an Indian rifle, fired from the opposite side of the river. On the 15 April, we were attacked by a body of the savages who had completely surrounded us, and whose number we computed at 4 to 500, though we have since heard that *Powell* had 1000 to 1500 of them. This was the hottest engagement we had during our stay on the Ouithlacoochee. They fired their guns by hundreds at the same moment at our block-house, and succeeded in taking our only means of escape, our boat—which they took down the river and destroyed after the battle. The engagement continued two hours and 45 minutes, and we had three men slightly wounded.

"On the 24th, we had a very severe battle, in which they displayed their ingenuity by shooting fire-arrows on fire upon the roof of the house, which destroyed the roof and left us exposed to the inclemency of the weather. This arrow-firing was performed by 26 of their men, whilst about 3 to 500 used their guns. We had, on this occasion, two or three of our men wounded. We probably killed 40 or 50 of the Indians. The night after the battle, we heard their chief hail us, and say, "that he was going away in the morning, and would trouble us no more." He kept his promise very well, though he did give us about 100 guns the next morning, ere he left. Our captain, *Holloman*, was killed on the 3 May, whilst endeavoring to fortify and strengthen our position. The Indians continued to give us a passing shot, from 50 to 100 guns, every five or six days, though he kept a spy upon us at other times. The officers were 21 days living on corn, without salt or meat, and the men about 28 days."

It appears that the great danger of ascending the Ouithlacoochee, together with the known circumstances of the garrison, had fixed in the minds of all those who were able to lend them aid, that they had been cut off; and therefore, to hazard any thing to clear up this extremely doubtful case, was considered next to crime itself. At length, the poor distressed handful at Camp McLemore, found among their number, three that would venture out for succor, and they arrived at Tallahassee in a canoe, about the 16 April. This circumstance, in all probability, proved the safety of their fellows, as well as themselves. A company was made up at St. Marks, and under Captain *Leigh Read*, proceeded in a steam-boat for the Ouithlacoochee on the 22 May, and on the 24 took off the garrison without the loss of a man.

While these affairs were being transacted on the Ouithlacoochee, a considerable force marched from Volusia to a point on the Oklawaha River, distant 30 miles, on their way to Fort Brooke. The river being higher than usual, the force was obliged to halt to build a bridge for the passage of their cannon and baggage wagons. On the opposite side of a lake, on the left of the detachment, two fires were soon discovered, which it was supposed were made as signals by two parties of Indians. Colonel *Butler* immediately proceeded to cross over the river with his battalion, and when he had marched about three miles, some Indians were discovered and pursued by the advanced guard. General *Joseph Shelton* was of *Butler's* party, who, being ahead of the advanced guard, charged upon one of the Indians, who was in the rear of the retreating party. At about 25 paces from him, the Indian turned, and they both levelled their rifles—*Shelton* fired first, and mortally wounded the Indian in the neck, who then endeavored to make his escape. *Shelton* dropped his gun, and rushed on him with his pistol, which missed fire at five or six paces from him. The Indian now turned and shot *Shelton* in the hip, and at the same moment another white came up and shot the Indian in the back, and he was immediately despatched. The ball which entered *Shelton's* hip passed round near the spine, and was cut out, and he was recovering.

I have been particular in detailing this affair, as the Indian who fell in it, proved to be a chief of distinction, known among the whites by the name of Mad Woff, which was the English signification of his name. In Indian it was Kohahajo. He was of *Micanopy's* tribe, and had under him 40 or 50 warriors, and was probably one of the leaders on the Ouithlacoochee, who beset General *Gaines* so long. His name was given in among them by *Black Dirt*, as *Coaharjo*. It is also to the treaty of Payne's Landing, and he was one of the Indian deputation who visited the country west of the Mississippi afterwards.

The next day after *Kohahajo* was killed, Colonel *Butler* and *Goodwin*, with a battalion of mounted men, were sent to reconnoitre Pilaklikaha, the residence of *Jumper* and *Micanopy*. When they had proceeded about six miles, their advanced guard received a sharp fire from a hammock on the left, but were soon dislodged by a charge from the main body. Two of the whites were badly wounded, one horse killed, and four wounded. After another considerable swamp-fight, in which several were wounded, the army proceeded to the Indian town, but it had been deserted for a long time. They burnt it, and then proceeded to Fort Brooke.

An officer in General *Scott's* army at Tampa wrote on the 15 April:—"Al the militia will leave us by the 20 May, and the regulars will go into summer quarters at this place, Key West, Volusia, Mosquito, and one or two more posts at the south. Without the greatest good luck nothing will be done this summer, and the war must be renewed in the autumn."

About the time General *Gaines* left Fort Draine, General *Scott* arrived there, with instructions to assume the chief command of the forces in Florida. Since that time the operations have been of not much importance. About the 20 March, Captain *Hitchcock* communicated the following valuable information respecting the hostile Indians, which was given him by the friendly chief, *Black Dirt*, whose Indian name is TUCK-ALUSTER HARJO. He says that in the fights with General *Gaines* were the following chiefs and warriors, viz.:—JUMPER with 30, ASSUHOLA [*Osceola*] with 7, ALLBURTUHARJO with 30, JARHARTO CHEE with 30, CARCHAR TOSKNUSK (*Mecosukee*) with 470, MECANOP (principal chief) with 80, ABRAM (*Negro*) with 80, WEEA FLOCKO MATTEZ with 70, YARHARHACJO with 160, TOSKIEUCAR with 50, ECHUA MATTEZ with 50, HAT HOW EMATTEZ with 30, CHARLES (a Negro) with 3, COAHARJO with 1, and TOPARLAGEE with 40.

There had been about 400 Seminoles collected at Tampa, chiefly women and children of *Black Dirt's* tribe, who were on the 12 April shipped off for "beyond the Mississippi" by General *Scott*.

CHAPTER XII.

CREEK WAR—*Murders and devastations begin—Eleven persons killed near Columbus—Mail routes in possession of the Indians—A steam-boat attacked and men killed—Chiefs of the war parties—Mail stages destroyed—The town of Roanoak burnt—Colonel* Lindsay's *Florida affair—Excessive dismay of the people of Georgia—Murder of families—Fight on the Chattahoochie—Capture of* JIM HENRY *and* NEAMATHLA—*Account of the chiefs—Surrender of the Indians.*

ADJUTANT-GENERAL *McIntosh* wrote from Fort Mitchel, Alabama, (on the Chattahoochie, 15 miles above Columbus,) 7 May last, as follows:—"It has just been reported to me, that Col. *Flournoy* was shot dead by the Indians on the 5th instant, about 15 miles below this post. I am also informed that a report is currently circulating among the Creeks, that the Seminole Indians have defeated the whites in Florida. This report will no doubt imbolden them to many acts of hostility that they would not otherwise dare commit. A constant communication must be kept up between them, as the Creeks are conversant with every transaction that occurs in Florida. *Marshal*, the half-breed, says he is apprehensive mischief will be done by the Indians before long. Other friendly Indians are of this opinion. *Opothleyohola*, principal of the upper Creeks, says he cannot keep his people together, or restrain them."

At the same time Colonel *Flournoy* was killed, ten others met a like fate, some of them within 12 miles of Columbus, at the Ochee Bridge on the Old Federal Road. "The Indians have entire possession of that road, and all the settlers have fled. A train consisting of 150 wagons, with about 150 fugitives, on their way to Columbus, were fired upon, on the 10 April."

Up to the 18 May, at Augusta, (Ga.) it was reported that all the southern mail routes were in possession of the Indians, except that to Mobile. The day before, all the mails were brought back. Colonel *Crowell's* plantation, and many others, had been burnt, and a stage agent and two drivers had been killed. The governor of Georgia had ordered two regiments of volunteers to take the field. About this time the steam-boat Hyperion was attacked on her passage up the Chattahoochie, and two pilots and one passenger were killed. She was then run on shore on the Georgia side, and after being abandoned, was taken and destroyed by the Indians.

The Creek towns and tribes which have declared themselves hostile are a part of the Ochees, the Hitchetas, the Pah-lo-cho-ko-los, the So-wok-ko-los, and a part of the Ufallays. The principal chiefs who have showed themselves as their leaders, are old NEAMATHLA, of whom we have already several times spoken, chief of the Hitchetas, JIM HENRY, and NEO MICO. Many friendly Indians immediately joined the whites, one of the principal leaders of whom is a chief called JIM BOY. The war party have discovered great boldness. About the 10 May a party came within 30 or 40 yards of Fort Mitchell, a strong and well-defended place, entered the hospital, and carried off what they pleased, and the garrison thought it not best to disturb them.

On the 14 following, the mail from Montgomery to Columbus was attacked about 20 miles from the latter place. A driver on that route was riding along the road on horseback, about 50 yards ahead of the stage, when he was fired upon by about 30 Indians, yet he unaccountably escaped injury. His horse took fright and threw him, and he escaped into a thicket. When he arrived at the next stage relay, the horses had got there, but without any carriage, but had about them some fragments of their harnesses. Mr. *Adams*, who was in the stage, made his escape by leaping into the woods when the stage upset. A driver and two others were killed. There were 19 horses belonging to the line in the company, of which but three were recovered, and these were wounded.

About this time the old steam-boat Georgian was burnt while lying at Roanoak, and all on board, except the engineer, perished. The town of Roanoak was at the same time laid in ashes, but the citizens escaped to a fort. Irwinton, a flourishing town on the Georgia side of the river, soon after shared the same fate.

Meanwhile some affairs of considerable moment were transpiring in Florida. Colonel *Lindsay* had been despatched, at the head of about 750 men, from Fort Brooke, with orders to proceed to Fort Alabama, to destroy it, and bring away the sick, wounded, and provisions. Having proceeded there, and effected their object, the forces marched again for Fort Brooke. Before leaving the fort, a mine was prepared, by leaving powder in the magazine, which should explode on its being opened. They had got but a mile or two, when the mine was sprung with a fearful noise, but what effect it had produced was not known. The whites had missed two of their number the day before, whom they found on their return march, about 12 miles from Fort Alabama, killed in the way, and one shockingly mangled. While the army was contemplating this spectacle, it was fired upon by 500 Indians, as was supposed, from a hammock, no more than 30 yards off. The whites immediately formed, and fired in their turn, and a regular fight ensued. The Indians could not be dislodged until several rounds of grape shot from the artillery had been poured in upon them. This was a bloody affray for them, but their loss was not fully known; several were found dead on the field, and numerous traces of others who had been dragged off dead or severely wounded were discovered. The whites had 3 killed and 22 wounded.

A letter addressed to the editor of the Richmond Enquirer gives a fearful picture of the affairs in the Creek country. It was written at Talbotton, (Ga.) 11 May, and is in these words:—"I wrote you yesterday, informing you of the hostile movements of the Creek Indians, and the commencement of their murderous career. We have full information here to-day of the distressing state of things among the whites who have settled over in that territory. The Indians are killing all—men, women, and children. Vast numbers have been butchered without doubt; and the whole country on this side of the Chattahoochie is in uproar and confusion. The population of the territory had become considerable, and they who have been fortunate enough to escape are come over in droves on the Georgia side; some with a part of their children some who have lost their children; some their husbands; and many children without father or mother; some are found as they were wandering about so young that they could give no account who their parents were. So perfect a mixture and confusion as never was witnessed before. Many have seen a part of their families murdered. One gentleman saw his father shot down near him, and his mother and sisters. Some of the dead have been brough over shockingly mangled. It is thought the whole nation is in hostile array;

their warriors are computed at 6 or 7000 st.ong. The general impression is, that a part of the Seminoles have come up among them. The town of Columbus is in great danger of an attack, as they have threatened it strongly. A company of 40 or 50 men left Columbus yesterday morning, and went over. On their return at night they brought in seven children, which they had found scattered about."

Such are the accounts which have been daily circulated for two months together and although they are distorted in many particulars, yet out of them we are at present to collect all that is known of this war. The Columbus Centinel of the 13 May contains the following facts, which are confirmed from other quarters:—"On Monday we received information that hostilities had commenced on the road between Columbus and Montgomery, at the Uchee bridge, and further on, and in the evening the bridge at this place, the streets leading from it were thronged with the unfortunate refugees, who were fleeing before their savage neighbors. The pitiable condition of many of them was past the power of description. Wives severed from their husbands, and parents from their children; all dismayed, all terror-stricken; presented a scene which we never again desire to see. An interesting-looking girl, just blooming into womanhood, was brought in on horseback, behind a benevolent stranger, who had found her in the nation, making her way, unattended, to this place. She started with her parents, but before they had proceeded far, they were brutally shot down before her eyes. She fled to the woods and escaped from her savage pursuers, and was found and brought to Columbus as above stated. A young man arrived at this place also witnessed the savage murder of his parents. Another young man, in the act of fleeing, perceived the Indians dragging away his sister. He returned, declaring he would rescue her or die in the attempt, and he has not been heard of. From this time their deeds of savage barbarity have been too numerous to particularize. A woman was brought in on Tuesday, wounded in the hand, whose husband had been shot the preceding evening at the Uchee bridge. Col. *A. B. Dawson's* negroes, who were taken by the Indians, and made their escape, state that they saw three corpses on the road near the Uchee bridge; a man, woman and child, who had all been murdered. We learn that about 150 friendly Indians have reported themselves at Fort Mitchell, and are ready to assist the whites. Accounts to the 17 May further state that the Indians had entered the house of one family, and murdered the whole—including husband, wife, and six children. All were scalped, and the children beheaded. The house of a Mr. Colton had been attacked, and himself killed."

Generals *Scott* and *Jesup* were at Fort Mitchell on the 3 June; the former left that place on that day with an escort of 150 men for Alabama, to take the command of the troops of that state. On the 4th, Capt. *Page* reported to General *Scott* that a party of Indians was about to cross the Chattahoochie in their way to Florida, and steps were immediately made to stop them. The day before a party was stopped by a company of Georgia militia, after a sharp skirmish, in which one white and several Indians were supposed to have been killed. Two chiefs were wounded, *Ealahayo* in the shoulder, and *Jim Henry* in the head. The action took place across the river, which being high and wide, little was effected. The Indians dared the whites to come over, called them dogs and cowards, and the most the whites could do was to retaliate in the same sort of language.

About the end of June, a party of whites, who were scouting on Flint River, accidentally found a young woman about three miles from Cambridge, who had been wounded by a shot in the breast. She stated that, on the 26 of June, about 300 Indians killed all the family to which she belonged, 13 in number, except herself, and her father, who made his escape. After being shot, she feigned death, and as the murdered were not scalped, she made her escape after the Indians left the scene of butchery.

Up to the 16 June, all the houses of the whites in the Creek country had been burned. On the 13th, in an attack on an Indian town by some whites, 24 persons were taken, among whom were three chiefs. These were held as hostages at Fort Mitchell, and word was sent to the hostile party, that if they did not come in and surrender they should be put to death. The next day

120 came in and declared themselves friendly. As late as the 28th of June, it was reported at Columbus, Ga., that the Creek war was probably at an end, "as far as fighting was concerned. *Jim Henry's* party have nearly all been taken. They were confined at Fort Mitchell, and all the smiths were at work making handcuffs for them." These will doubtless be sent beyond the Mississippi, "except the chiefs, five or six in number, who will be punished with death," as was supposed.

On the 1st of July, *Jim Henry* fell into the hands of a band of friendly Indians, under a chief named *Jim Boy*. For a few days previous he was supposed to have been on his way for the "promised land;" but he was found in the Creek nation, a few miles from Tuskegee. About the same time old *Neamathla* gave himself up to the whites, and was, on the day of the capture of *Jim Henry*, with about 1500 others, sent off for Arkansas. The circumstance of his falling in with the whites is said to be as follows:—General *Jessup* had left Tuskegee with about 700 men, intending to make a direct march for *Neamathla's* camp, which was on Hatchahubbee River. As *Jesup* marched along, his forces increased to 2700 men, of which 1500 were Indians, under the chiefs *Hopoithleyohola* and *Jim Boy*. When he had arrived within about seven miles of *Neamathla's* camp, he ordered a halt, to refresh his men and horses, at the expense of the beautiful oatfields of the Indians. While the army lay here, a scout discovered *Neamathla* on horseback. He had concluded to surrender, and had a white cloth tied about his head, and some white garment for a flag, extended upon a stick, and was approaching towards them. They ordered him to halt, but he gave no heed to them, until within a few paces. He was taken to Gen. *Jessup's* camp, and made prisoner. With him were his son and daughter, and a niece of *Nea Mico*. The two females were released, but his son was confined with him at Fort Mitchell. On being asked where he was going when he was taken, he said his life had been threatened by his own people, and he was hastening to Fort Mitchell, to give himself up.

Nea Mico had some days before given himself up. He was considered a great chief. *David Hardige*, a half-breed, was taken by surprise, with about a hundred of his men, with their women and children. By the 8th of June, there had been secured between 3 and 4000 Indians, which were despatched for the west as fast as circumstances would admit.

A party of about 60 warriors, who were endeavoring to escape into Florida, were overtaken by Col. *Beal*, in Chickasatchie Swamp, Baker county, Alabama, and a considerable skirmish ensued. Nine Indians were killed and 20 wounded. Of Col. *Beal's* men, two were killed and seven wounded. The Indians were left in possession of the swamp.

The following account was published in the Georgia Herald of the 28 June, at Columbus. It is headed, "Grand Entree into Fort Mitchell," and then proceeds:—"On the 22 June, we witnessed the *grand entree* of a drove of savages into the Fort [Mitchell] consisting of men, women and children, in all about 1000; among them 200 warriors; they were brought in by a battalion of Alabama cavalry, under the command of Maj. Gen. *Patterson*. The men were placed within the walls of the fort, while the women and children were encamped on the outside. It was an assemblage of human beings, such as we had never before witnessed, and the sight filled us with thoughts and feelings to which we shall not give vent at this time. They were of all ages, from a month old to a hundred years,—of all sizes, from the little papoose to the giant warrior. The old "*Blind King*," as he is called, rode in the centre of the throng, and although it has been many years since he beheld the light of day, yet has the feelings of hostility continued to rankle at his heart. The names of the hostile chiefs who have been taken and have come in, are *Nea E-Mathla, Octo Archo-Emathla*, [probably son of *Neamathla*,] *Miccocholey* or *Blind King, Tustee-Nuggee, Chopko-Yar-bar-Hadjo*."

CHAPTER XIII.

HISTORY OF THE EXPATRIATION OF THE CHEROKEES.

"Some entertain, that the history of these present times must not be written by any one alive; which, in my opinion, is disgraceful to an historian, and very prejudicial to posterity; as if they were to write at a distance, that obscurity might protect their mistakes from discovery. Others also say the truth is not ripe enough to be writ in the age we live in: So politicians would not have the historian to tread on the heels of the times, lest the times tread on his heels."

WINSTANLEY

"Still to the white man's wants there is no end:
He said, 'beyond those hills he would not come.'
But to the western seas his hands extend,
Ere yet his promise dies upon his tongue."—UNPUBLISHED POEM.

WHILE the war is progressing in Florida, we will proceed to lay open a few pages of Cherokee history, praying, in the mean time, for its speedy conclusion.

The situation of the Cherokee country is most delightful; it is every thing that heart could wish, whether actuated by the best or worst of motives. It lies in about thirty-five degrees of northern latitude, bounded north and west by Tennessee, on the south by Alabama, and easterly by Georgia and North Carolina, comprising about 8,000 square miles. In 1802 it contained 11,175; the difference having been sold to the United States for the use of Georgia.

That country is well watered by living springs, in every part, whose fountains are like reservoirs raised to a great height by the art of man; they having the superior advantage of being natural reservoirs, raised by springs in their lofty range of mountains which stretch across the whole nation. In the north it is hilly; but in the south are numerous fertile plains, in part covered with tall trees, through which beautiful streams of water glide. Here cattle, in vast herds, roam, and horses are plenty, and in all the ordinary uses among the Indians. Flocks of sheep, goats, and swine, live on the slopes of the hills. On their navigable rivers the Cherokees have vessels engaged in commerce. Their spring opens in great beauty; the soil is excellent for corn, cotton, tobacco, wheat, oats, indigo, sweet and Irish potatoes; and the people had, in 1825, begun to export cotton to New Orleans in their own vessels.

They have public roads, and taverns with good accommodations, and butter and cheese are common upon the ordinary tables of the Indian inhabitants. Neat and flourishing villages have already sprung into being. Cotton and woollen cloths are manufactured, and *by native Indian hands.* There is scarcely a family which does not raise cotton sufficient for its own use. Their trade is almost wholly carried on by native Cherokees. The mechanic arts are considerably cultivated, although agriculture chiefly engages the attention of the inhabitants.

In 1819, there were about 10,000 inhabitants, and in 1825 they had increased to 13,563, all natives; there were, in addition, 147 white men married in the nation, and 73 white women. Of slaves there were 1,277. Hence it is plain that the Cherokees do not decrease, but have, in about five years, increased over 3,500. This is equal, at least, to the increase of white population under similar circumstances.

By the laws of the nation, the whites are allowed the privileges of natives, except that of suffrage, together with their ineligibility to hold offices. Some of the Cherokees, following the example of their southern neighbors, have become slave-holders; buying their negroes of white men who bring them into the nation. And here the reflection naturally arises in the inquiry upon the relative barbarity of the white and red men. It was strongly urged by some southern *statesmen*, that the Indians were such barbarous wretches that they could not think of living beside them; and yet poor Africans are sold by them to these *barbarians!* But, unlike the whites in *one* particular, they will not mix with their slaves.

The nation was reorganized in 1820, and by a resolve of its national council, divided into eight districts, each of which had the privilege of sending four members to the legislature. The pay of members was established at one dollar per day; that of the speaker being fixed at one and a half dollars and the principal chiefs were to receive 150 dollars a year. Some of their principal laws and regulations were—a prohibition of spirituous liquors being brought into the nation by white men. If a white man took a Cherokee wife, he must marry her according to their laws; but her property was not affected by such union. No man was allowed but one wife. A judge, marshal, sheriff and deputy, and two constables, were commissioned in each district. Embezzlement, intercepting and opening sealed letters, was punished by a fine of 100 dollars, and 100 lashes on the bare back. No business was allowed on Sundays; and fences were regulated by statute. They also had a statute of limitations, which, however, did not affect notes or settled accounts. A will was valid, if found, on the decease of its maker, to have been written by him, and witnessed by two creditable persons. A man leaving no will, all his children shared equal, and his wife as one of them; if he left no children, then the widow to have a fourth part of all property; the other three fourths to go to his nearest relations. And so if the wife died, leaving property. Before the division of the nation into districts, and the appointment of the above-named civil officers, there was an organized company of light-horse, which executed the orders of the chiefs, searched out offenders, and brought them to justice. It was a fundamental law, that no land should be sold to the white people, without the authority of a majority of the nation. Transgressors of this law were punished with death.

The Cherokees were similarly situated to the Creeks, in respect to the United States. They had been treated with from the earliest days of the republic, as an independent nation, with only this difference—the United States regarding treaty stipulations with them without any regard to their weakness, or inability to defend themselves against unjust intrusions. And thus were they considered through the early administrations of this government; until political intrigue had become the order of the day, and to strengthen a party by the accession of a state, it was found necessary to disregard sacred treaties, not at first by an open denial of obligations, but by a perversion of language, authorizing "any means to encompass the end." And like the Creek nation, the Cherokees were tampered with, and eventually divided and ruined; thus verifying that remarkable passage of Scripture, namely, "a house divided against itself cannot stand."

The consequences which, by every thinking mind, were considered sure to follow, did follow; but not so immediately as had been anticipated, reasoning from the summary course which the Creeks had pursued in executing vengeance upon the heads of a similar faction, for a precisely similar outrage upon the will and the laws of that nation. But the day of retribution was at hand, and the heads of the Cherokee faction have met a like fate in the distant land to which they had forced their despairing executioners. The history of the fate of Ridge and his associates will go down upon the same page of history with that of Mackintosh; over which the philanthropist of succeeding ages will mourn, and the philosopher will frown with just indignation, as he contemplates the source of guilt whence the stream flowed.

But the bare recital of the events in the history of the Cherokees is sufficient to create the deepest feelings of commiseration in every breast, without any reflections from the historian.

Georgia, finding she could not drive the United States government into her measures for the forcible possession of the Cherokee country, resolved to do so on her own account; but not having the courage to go sword in hand, and do it at a blow, she resorted to the equally condemnable course of management, which was to seize upon the country under color of law. And those laws, made for the very occasion, were so exceedingly oppressive that the Indians could not live under them.

The laws alluded to were passed on the 20th of December, 1829, by the legislature of the state of Georgia, and were of this complexion: "It is hereby ordained that all the laws of Georgia are extended over the Cherokee country. That after the 1st day of June, 1830, all Indians then and at that time residing in said territory, shall be liable and subject to such laws and regulations as the legislature may hereafter prescribe. That all laws, usages, and customs, made and established, and enforced in the said territory, by the said Cherokee Indians, be, and the same are hereby, on and after the 1st day of June, 1830, declared null and void; and no Indian, or descendant of an Indian residing within the Creek or Cherokee nations of Indians, shall be deemed a competent witness, or party to any suit in any court, where a white man is a defendant." Such is a specimen of the laws alluded to; framed to throw the Indians into entire confusion, that they might be the more easily overcome, destroyed, or forced from the land of their nativity.

That the Cherokees could not live under the laws of Georgia is most manifest, and it is equally manifest that said laws were never made in expectation that they could be submitted to. Thus the constitution of the United States was trampled on with impunity, by an utter disregard of one of its express provisions, "That no state shall pass any law or laws going to impair the obligation of contracts." Now, how could a Cherokee compel a Georgian to perform a contract? Thus was the axe not only laid at the foot of the tree of Cherokee liberty, but it was shortly to be wielded by the strong arm of power with deadly effect.

Alarm now, as well it might, was seen perched upon the brow of every true Cherokee, and they began to revolve in their minds the nature of their condition, and to inquire of one another what they were to do. They remonstrated, but remonstrance was met with contumely, and all the haughtiness that characterizes the triumph of might over right.

Though conscious of the rectitude of their intentions, the Cherokees were determined not to persist in any course, however just it might appear to them, without first consulting some of the ablest jurists and best men, as well as the most devoted to the good of their country, among the eminent men of the United States. There was but one opinion among them. Chief Justice Marshall, Chancellor Kent, William Wirt, Mr. Justice M'Lane, Daniel Webster, and Henry Clay, are names carrying authority with them; an array of talent which other nations may equal, but not surpass.

Accordingly the Indians brought their case before the supreme court of the United States, where it was argued with fidelity and ability by Mr. Sargent and Mr. Wirt, and finally and clearly given in favor of the Cherokees. Mr. Wirt happily adverted, in his argument, to the past and present conduct of Georgia; reminded her that, with the other states, she had coöperated with the most Christian assiduity and perseverance to bring about a change in the intellectual and moral condition of that people; and having completely effected the purpose, she found in this very change a ground of quarrel with them, as well as with her sister states, her auxiliaries in the laudable work; accusing these of hypocrisy and an affected benevolence, by which they were violating Georgia's sovereignty in bringing up an independent government within her chartered limits; that so long as they were savages and barbarians, Georgia had no objection to their governing themselves, but having now become civilized, and consequently capable of governing themselves, their right of self-government must cease. "Hence we ask," says Mr. Wirt, "what can this unfortunate people do?"

"The existence of this remnant of a once great and mighty nation," added Mr. Wirt, "is at stake, and it is for this court to say whether they shall be blotted out from creation, in utter disregard of all our treaties. They are here in the last extremity, and with them must perish forever the honor of the American name. The faith of our nation is fatally linked with their existence, and the blow which destroys them quenches forever our own glory; for what glory can there be of which a patriot can be proud, after the good name of his country shall have departed? We may gather laurels on the field of battle, and trophies on the ocean, but they will never hide this foul blot upon our escutcheon. 'Remember the Cherokee nation,' will be answer enough to the proudest boasts that we can ever make. Such, it is possible, there may be who are willing to glory in their own shame, but thank Heaven, they are comparatively few. The great majority of the American people see this subject in its true light. And I cannot believe that this honorable court, possessing the power of preservation, will stand by and see these people stripped of their property and extirpated from the earth, while they are holding up to us their treaties and claiming the fulfilment of our engagements. If truth, and faith, and honor, and justice, have fled from every other part of our country, we shall find them here. If not, our sun has gone down in treachery, blood, and crime, in the face of the world; and instead of being proud of our country, we may well call upon the rocks and mountains to hide our shame from earth and heaven."

Such were the opinions of the great and good upon the Cherokee question; but how was he mistaken in respect to the virtue of a government, of which he was a pillar and chief supporter in all its just dealings! With what grief must he have seen, notwithstanding the sacrifices and efforts he had made to obtain justice, and the decision of the highest tribunal of his country, all disregarded, this decision set at naught, and that country's *sun go down in treachery, blood, and crime!* And it is with deep melancholy we add, that the great statesman and philanthropist saw the near approach to the horizon of the once glowing star of empire of a noble people! He saw, as his own lamp flickered on the eve of departure to another world, that deep stain fall upon the escutcheon of his country's honor, which he had so much feared. William Wirt descended to the tomb in the beginning of the year 1835.

The Cherokees, like the Creeks, had, by designing and avaricious men, been divided into two parties, which were distinguished from one another by very marked differences. The people composing the first were generally temperate, industrious, and frugal; had made great advancement in the arts of civilized life, and hence had become far more attached to their country than those of an opposite character. The other part of the nation consisted of a majority of indolent, intemperate, roving, and ignorant citizens; always restless, ever ready to hear to any new smooth-tongued miscreant, who might throw himself among them upon any design. Yet there were many among the second party whose character was good, and who were made seriously to think that it would be for their interest to sell out their possessions, and take up a new country beyond the Mississippi. But the talent and learning were not with them, and consequently they had not the ability to judge of such a project, according to the admonitions of the true policy of the nation.

At the period of Cherokee history now under consideration, that nation contained a population of 18,000 souls. How near it was divided in respect to numbers is not precisely known, but that part I have denominated the first was by far the most numerous, as well as the most respectable. These two parties had each its head or leader, and was known by his name. Mr. John Ross led the first, and Major Ridge the second. Mr. Ross had become an eminent citizen, and being possessed of a fine education, respectable talents, and extensive and enlarged views upon all subjects, soon became prominent without any efforts to make himself so. On the other hand Mr. Ridge, though greatly beloved by his own people, and highly respected among the whites, had not the moral courage to withstand tempations that a true patriot requires.

Such was the condition of things, when it was decided by the supreme court of the United States, that Georgia must not execute her pernicious laws in and over the Cherokee country. Yet, as has already been observed, she did proceed to execute them, and finding that many of the Indians would not at once be forced away by their cruel and oppressive execution, but continued to suffer under them, resort was had to buying up such of the chiefs and head men of the nation as money would succeed with. And, finally, a treaty was made with such men as bribery influenced, and on its strength, eventually, the Cherokees were forced beyond the Mississippi.

The engagement entered into with Georgia by the United States government in 1802, has, in a former chapter,* been noticed. In that compact there was no stipulation that the Cherokees should, at any time, be forced to sell their remaining lands; but when they were *willing*, if any such time should ever arrive, and the price should not be an objection, then the United States had the *power*, and not till then, to buy out the Cherokees.

* Book IV., page 53, ante.

But, in 1835, Georgia had become so clamorous, that "the government" thought best to make an attempt to treat with these Indians to go west, on some terms or other. Accordingly, the president appointed one Rev. J. F. Schermerhorn, of New York, to proceed to the Cherokee country for that purpose. He proceeded to the nation, and, with some trouble, got the chiefs together, and opened the nature of his mission before them. He was informed that they would not treat for the sale of their country on any con ditions, and the commissioner gave up the design and returned to Washington. But there is no safety to the innocent where the cupidity of designing knaves can be brought to bear upon them.

The plan immediately adopted by *Schermerhorn* was to seduce some of the chiefs by gratuities of money, and thereby to get together such as he could of the nation, and, if possible, make a treaty with them which should bind all the rest; but to the honor of the secretary at war, Gen. Cass, it will be remembered, that when such a project was made known to him, he rejected it with disdain. Whether this instrument of injustice was countenanced by men higher in office than the secretary at war, I leave to be determined; but however that might be, it is certain that Schermerhorn was found without loss of time pursuing that nefarious plan, which Gov. Cass had set his seal of unqualified disapprobation upon. He circulated notices of his design throughout the Cherokee nation, requesting them to meet him in council; and finally he got a number of the nation together, which he called *a council of the nation*, and made a treaty with them. By the stipulations of this treaty, (falsely so called,) the whole country was to be given up to the whites within two years from the time it should be ratified by the senate of the United States.

The great majority of the Cherokees, as has been observed, would have nothing to do with Schermerhorn, and consequently, whatever he did had nothing to do with them; and when its acknowledgment and acceptance were urged at Washington, it was rebutted with the astounding memorial, signed by near *fifteen thousand* of the nation, protesting in the strongest terms, that the instrument procured by Schermerhorn was utterly false, and unauthorized by the Cherokees. Yet after all that those 15,000 people could do, that *treaty* was, with some little variation, published to the world, at the city of Washington, on the 14th of March, 1836, as the act of that nation!

When the nation found that the party which had executed the treaty were going to Washington to further its ratification, the council of the nation immediately appointed a delegation of twenty of its best men to proceed there also, clothed with authority to represent their countrymen truly. It had become now apparent that if they would not sell their country *for what it was the pleasure of the government to give*, they would be driven from it without any thing; therefore, all that was left for them to do, was to get the best terms they could. And it was finally agreed by the authorized delegation, that they would abide by such an award as the senate should make for their lands, provided that when it was laid before the nation, it should be consented to by it; accordingly, a paper was signed by the Indians, agreeing to abide the action of the senate. Of that action, Mr. Ross, the principal chief, says, he would not have complained, if it had been "fully and fairly" obtained; but "a resolution was submitted at midnight, on the 3d of March, just as the senate were about to separate, premising, that, in its opinion, the president ought to allow a sum not exceeding 5,000,000 of dollars. This resolution, proposed in a hurry, was carried in as great a hurry, and, though *a mere opinion*, not pledging either the president or the senate to any consequent action, was represented to us as an '*award*,' and we were told we had engaged ourselves to be bound by it."

The delegation next proceeded to lay the matter before the nation; which having done, the "award" of the senate was unanimously rejected. But Gen Jackson had now taken the matter into his hands, and whatever might be said or done by an Indian council, would make no difference with his determination. And when he found that they were reluctant to submit to what they had never had any intention of agreeing to, he ordered Mr. Secretary Harris to inform them, "that no propositions for a treaty would hereafter be made, more favorable than those now offered. The sum of five millions of dollars was fixed upon by the senate, as an ample equivalent for the relinquishment of all their rights and possessions; that *most assuredly* the president would not sanction any expectation, that more favorable arrangements would hereafter be held out to them; that this was the *last proposition* the president would make them while *he was president*, and they might abide the consequences; that they need not expect either branch of the government would ever do any more, and that, therefore, they need not expect *another dollar*."*

Thus all further negotiation was cut off, and the Indians had nothing further to do, but to submit to what they had long foreseen would probably be their only alternative.

With regard to the treaty of December, 1835, procured by Schermerhorn, and since called by his name, as also "the treaty of New Echota," we have but a remark or two more to make; and, firstly, it will be inquired, who or what part of the Cherokee nation made that treaty? According to the account of Schermerhorn himself, the number which he got together to treat with, did not exceed 600 persons, men, women, and children; of which number but 70 were men, and of these, about 30 were Arkansas emigrants, or Cherokees enrolled for emigration, and consequently had no real interest in the nation, and had no right to act in matters affecting its affairs. The reader has only to compare this statement with the memorial before spoken of, signed by 15,000 persons, to enable him to decide on the magnitude of the injustice done that people. Secondly, of the course "this great and mighty government" has pursued to disinherit Indians in certain cases.

In May, 1839, Gen. Carroll was sent with instructions by our government, to induce the Cherokees to remove. Some passages in those instructions would never be believed, were they not past contradiction, and staring us by thousands in the face. They recite, that, whereas nothing could probably be effected *in open council*, by negotiation, "he must go to them, *not as a negotiator*, but *as a friend;* appeal to the chiefs and influential men, *not together, but apart;* make offers to them *of extensive reservations* in fee simple, and other rewards; *secure, even from the chiefs, your official character;* move upon them in the line of their *prejudices;* tell them, unless they remove, *their laws will be trodden under foot;* enlarge upon the *advantages of their condition in the west.*" Such is another specimen of another *state paper*, which emanated from this administration.

The case has changed. The whites have become powerful, and the red men have become weak. They are able to destroy, or drive them before them to another country, and how has it turned? The red men have gone. Who are the "cruel savages?" In the "great debate," as it was termed, on the "Indian bill," in 1830, some of its supporters pointed to the east, and cried out, "Savages! savages!" because the voice of humanity had been heard in that direction; but they might, with almost equal propriety, have pointed to the capital of the state of Georgia—even that, where those most oppressive laws originated, contained philanthropists too. The votes in that house stood but little more than equally divided, on the bill to take forcible possession of the Cherokee country. But the philanthropist is derided and scorned; and that people have only escaped the iron grasp of superstition's hand, to die by that of avarice. It used to be a proverb, that Justice had leaden feet, but yet was sure to overtake her enemies; but where her feet are clogged with *gold*, the proverb requires a new explication.

We have seen how the Schermerhorn treaty was disposed of in the senate of the United States. The house of representatives must vote the appropriation, or it could not be carried into effect. When it came up there for action, some gave as a reason for voting for it, that they had no choice, but were bound to do so, because the treaty had been ratified by the president and senate, and it was hence the law of the land. On the other hand, it was

* This certainly was a state paper worthy of "My government," "My currency," and above all, "My responsibility." Mr. Jackson had before told certain Indians that all the lands beyond the Mississippi *belonged to him* If the Cherokees believed he told the truth, no one will wonder they did not wish to go there!

argued that the action of the president and senate could never make that instrument a treaty which was false, and had not been agreed to by but one party; that this was true abundantly appeared by a protest then before the house, signed by almost the entire Cherokee nation. And besides this, the most zealous advocates for removal did not pretend that the treaty was fairly made by the nation, or by any body authorized by it; but they argued that the bill ought to pass from necessity, as it was to benefit the Indians more than any body else. And with this kind of argument the bill passed, 102 to 97.

Thus we are to be judges of what is best for our neighbor, and if he does not conform to our wishes, we will force him to do so. On the same principle we may say, that it is decreed by unerring fate that the red men must be swept from the face of the earth; but does it follow that we must hasten their ruin? With as much reason all mankind might commit suicide, because fate has decreed that we must all die, sooner or later.

As soon as congress had disposed of the Cherokee question, the executive of the nation, apprehensive that trouble would arise between Georgia and the Cherokees, ordered Gen. Scott to repair thither without delay. He was soon on the way, with about 2,000 men. This was early in the year 1838. Meanwhile Gov. Gilmer had threatened "collision," unless the work of expulsion was immediately begun. How much in fear Mr. Van Buren stood of this and other bravadoes, we do not undertake to say; but he pressed matters as fast as he could, more afraid, doubtless, of the *votes*, than the steel of Georgia.

But what did that excellent old general find on his arrival in the Cherokee country? Armed Indians behind every bush, prepared to shed the last drop of their blood in defence of their beloved country? No. Not a semblance of opposition was there; all was quietness; all were about their ordinary affairs, in their own fields, and by their own habitations. Having established his head quarters in the nation, he issued a proclamation, requesting them to assemble at certain points, from whence they would be sent to Arkansas. They obeyed the summons, and thus, in due time, the whole nation were removed.

CHAPTER XIV

EXPATRIATION OF THE CHEROKEES, CONTINUED

"Where is my home—my forest home? the proud land of my sires?
Where stands the wigwam of my pride? Where gleam the council fires
Where are my fathers' hallowed graves? my friends, so light and free?
Gone, gone,—forever from my view! Great Spirit! can it be?"—A. W. B.

IT has somehow or other happened that great changes have taken place in the minds of our rulers, or some of them, within a few years, in regard to what certain laws and treaties mean. As late as 1826, no question was raised about the rights of the Indians; nothing was attempted to be done, *by government*, on their lands, without their consent being first obtained; no one even dreamed of laying out a road through their lands without their permission. But, of a sudden, it is discovered that the government has been laboring under a great mistake all the time of its existence; that during the administration of *Andrew Jackson*, wisdom had shed her light so abundant, that numbers had risen up in her full armor, and unhesitatingly declared that the very men who formed our constitution knew very little about it; that under its provisions no valid treaty could be made with Indians; that neither WASHINGTON, JEFFERSON, nor JOHN ADAMS, could make the discovery; but it must be reserved to add lustre to the era of which we are speaking.

The compact between the general government and Georgia, in 1802, is the principal theme of their oppressors. Now every body knows that with that compact the Cherokees had nothing to do; they had no hand in forming it, nor never consented to it. A treaty is a compact of mutual concessions and agreements between nations. The Cherokees agreed that if they ever sold their lands, or any part of them, it should be to the United States. Now this was, as times have been, a very important concession on the part of the Indians; but if the faith of the United States had been kept inviolate, it would as yet have amounted to but little,—a small tract of land here and there,—but it has now amounted to an entire country. When the treaties were formed, it was supposed that against this concession the United States had put one of much greater moment, namely, that of *protection*. What have we seen? the whites in possession of all the lands of the Indians, the Indians protected? Not by the United States; for it has driven them where it cannot, from the nature of their situation, protect them. These conclusions inevitably follow, and we challenge proof in contradiction.

That we have given the Indians more than their lands were worth, has been urged as an argument that no wrong has been done them. That has nothing to do with the point at issue. Unenviable must the mind of that man be, who holds nothing above price, mere pecuniary compensation. What though the government did stipulate that it would buy out the Cherokees as soon as it could be done, (a very foolish bargain, by the way,) on reasonable and equitable terms; is it to be understood that they *must* sell their lands just when a demand is made for them? This argument is too fallacious to be thought of by rational men. Hence the only way left to dispossess a nation, too weak to defend themselves by force, is to declare they have no right where they are. And, to the astonishment of all the world, such were the grounds of argument, and such the arguments that succeeded in an American congress in ruining a nation. What though the nation were small, and consequently weak? So much the greater the crime. Are not laws made for the protection of the weak against the strong? as well in property as person? Shall the United States of enlightened America deal worse with their friends and allies than ancient despotic Rome? Even nations subdued by the Romans, and included in their dominions, were suffered "to live under their own laws, and be governed by their own magistrates."*

It has been urged as a reason for disinheriting the Cherokees, that it is absurd to allow a nation to exist under a separate government, within another government or state, and hence unconstitutional. Allowing all this to be true, (which we do not,) what has it to do with the Cherokees? Had not the Cherokees as good a right to say to a state which had undertaken to extend a line beyond them, "You have no authority to do this, and must instantly desist." Now there can be no question but that a state would be compelled to desist, if the party so included were able to defend itself against usurpation. This happening not to be the case with the Cherokees, a cordon is passed about them, at first, merely nominal; but, at length, like the coil of the serpent, it is drawn tighter and tighter, until they discover, too late, that a death-blow is aimed at their very existence. Who, or what is Georgia, that it should claim priority to the Cherokees? Were not the Cherokees a nation long before it was heard of? Which permitted the other to grow up by its side? How long is it since the Cherokees were able to drive that handful of white intruders beyond a more formidable boundary than the Mississippi? They did not attempt it. Their "avarice" was not strong enough to tempt them to so cruel an action. No. They took them by the hand at Yamacraw Bluff, and at Holston, and said, "Brothers, here is land enough for us and for you. Lie down upon our skins until you can make wigwams and mats for yourselves." How have these kindnesses been returned?

We will hear what Georgia herself said about the validity of Indian treaties, no longer ago than 1825. In that year a treaty was made with the Creeks, by which a cession of a portion of their territory in Georgia was made; and by an article in said treaty, it was provided, that the United States should protect the Indians against the encroachments and impositions of the whites, until their removal should take place. The governor of Georgia, *G. M. Troup*, issued his proclamation in accordance with the treaty, a passage of which is in these words:

---

* *Vattel*, "Law of Nations," B. I. ch. i. sec. 11

"I have thought proper to issue this, my proclamation, warning all persons, citizens of Georgia, or others, against trespassing or intruding upon lands occupied by the Indians within the limits of this state, either for the purpose of settlement or otherwise; as every such act will be in direct violation of the provisions of *the treaty*, aforesaid, and will expose the aggressors to the most certain and summary punishment by the authorities of the state, and of the United States. All good citizens, therefore, pursuing the dictates of *good faith*, will unite in enforcing the *obligations of the treaty* as the *supreme law*."

How does this accord with a resolve of the legislature of that state, but a few years afterwards, to take forcible possession of the country of the Cherokees? A comparative view of these enactments led a high-minded senator* to declare, "that treaties were *very lawful* when made for the *use* of Georgia."

In 1824, the Georgia delegation in congress, in an address to the president of the United States, complained, in no very moderate terms, of the injustice done to their state, by the delay of the government in not extinguishing the Cherokee title to lands within its limits; thereby acknowledging what they denied afterwards, namely, that the Cherokees had any title. They say, "If the Cherokees are unwilling to remove, the *causes* of that unwillingness are to be traced to the United States. If peaceable purchase cannot be made in the ordinary mode, nothing remains to be done but to order their removal to a designated territory beyond the limits of Georgia." And, in conclusion, they add, "Our duty is performed by *remonstrating* against the policy heretofore pursued, by which the interests of Georgia have been disregarded; and by *insisting*, as we do, most *earnestly*, upon an immediate fulfilment of the obligations of the articles of cession of 1802."

Such is a specimen of the language of two senators and six representatives of Georgia, to the president of the United States, upon this question. And we venture to assert that the autocrat of all the Russias is not more despotic in his decrees, than these gentlemen were on this occasion.

A few days after the address of the Georgia delegates, the secretary of war, the Hon. JOHN C. CALHOUN, issued his report on our Indian relations, in which he says, "The United States have ever been solicitous to fulfil, at the earliest period, the obligation of the convention, by the extinguishment of the Indian titles within the limits of Georgia; a most satisfactory proot of which may be found in the number of treaties which have been held for that purpose, the quantity of lands which has been acquired, and the price paid. In fact, such has been the solicitude of the government, that but little regard has been had to the price, *whenever it has been found possible to obtain a cession* of lands to the state. The price given has far exceeded that which has ever been given in other purchases from the Indians." Thus a mighty clashing of opinions is apparent on a comparison of these two extracts.

From certain other facts in Mr. *Calhoun's* report, it appears that, in 1802, the Cherokees owned 7,152,110 acres of land in the limits of Georgia. Since the late war with England, they had held two treaties with the United States, by which they had ceded 995,310 acres. Emigration had been uniformly encouraged, and many had voluntarily gone to Arkansas. To this course nobody objected. But in this way matters progressed too slow for greedy speculators, and it was urged that, as many Cherokees had emigrated, a proportionate quantity of the country should be set off for Georgia. An enumeration or census had been attempted, to ascertain what the proportion would be, and it was eventually concluded that one third of the nation had left the country, and a treaty was entered into at Washington, in 1819, by which that amount of territory was ceded. Between 1819 and 1824, two attempts to treat with them for further cessions of territory had been made, and both proved abortive. "It cannot be doubted," says Mr. Calhoun, "that much of the difficulty of acquiring additional cession from the Cherokees, and the other southern tribes, results from their growing civilization and knowledge, by which they have learned to place a higher value upon their lands than more rude and savage tribes. Many causes have contributed to place them

* Mr. *Frelinghuysen*, of New Jersey.

higher in the scale of civilization than other Indians within our limits — the genial nature of their climate, which enables them to pass more readily from the hunter to the herdsman state; and the fertility of their soil, and the value of their staple articles, particularly cotton. To these, however, must be added the humane and benevolent policy of the government, which has ever directed a fostering care to the Indians within our limits. This policy is as old as the government itself; and has been habitually and strongly extended to the Cherokee nation." Such, in 1824, were allowed to be the reasons why the Cherokees could not be prevailed upon to forsake their country. Now, if they had no right there, but that of sufferance, why is it that "this fostering policy, as old as the government," has been held forth and maintained towards them? The reason is obvious: no president before Gen. *Jackson*, could bring his mind——to do as he has done.

At some future day, ask some remnant of the Cherokees, of the Creeks, or of the Seminoles, if any should remain, why they should leave the lands of their fathers to become wanderers beyond the Mississippi, and their reply can be no other than this: "We were forced away by the white men. Some of our men were traitors; of them they bought our rights, *knowing them to be false.*"

• Compare the language held by Gen. Jackson, in 1821, with what he has since said and done. On the 18th of January of that year, he wrote from his head quarters at Nashville, to *Path Killer*, and other Cherokee chiefs, as follows: "Friends and brothers: I have never told a red brother a lie nor deceived him. The intruders [on your lands,] if they attempt to return, will be sent off. But your light-horse should not let them settle down on your land. You ought to drive the stock away from *your lands*, and deliver the intruders to the agent; but if you cannot keep intruders from *your land*, report it to the agent, and on his notice, I will drive them from *your land*."

On the 6th of June, 1830, he informs the Cherokees, "that, having no power to interfere and oppose the exercise of the sovereignty of any state, over and upon all who may be within the limits of any state, they will prepare themselves to abide the issue of such new relations, without any hope that he will interfere." It must be borne in mind, that the Indians had done nothing meanwhile to forfeit any one right, or the protection promised them by all the treaties, sanctioned by all the presidents, including Jackson himself!

In April, 1824, a deputation of Cherokees was at Washington, and on the 15th day of that month they laid before congress a memorial "on matters of vast importance" to them. In this memorial they refer to the oppressive stand taken by the governor of Georgia, as communicated by him in a letter to the secretary of war, and to the acrimonious and incongruous address of the Georgia delegation to the president, already noticed. Upon these the delegation remark: "We cannot but view the design of those letters as an attempt, bordering on a hostile disposition towards the Cherokee nation, to arrest from them, by arbitrary means, their just rights and liberties." And this is the harshest language they any where complain in, in answer to the grossest insults.

In regard to the cession of more land, they declare their sentiments in the following words: "In relation to the *disposition* and *determination* of the nation, *never again to cede another foot of land* is *positively the production* and *voice* of the *nation*, and what has been uttered by us, in the communications which we have made to the government, since our arrival in this city, is expressive of the *true sentiments of the nation*, agreeably to our instructions, and *not one word* of which has been put into *our mouths* by a *white man*. Any surmises or statements to the contrary are ill-founded and ungenerous." It should be remembered, that it had been basely insinuated by their enemies, in every public way, that the Indians were influenced by designing white men from the north, in all their opposition to the will of Georgia. This memorial was signed by JOHN ROSS, GEORGE LOWREY, the mark of MAJOR RIDGE, and ELIJAH HICKS.

Immediately after this, Gov. *Troup* writes from Milledgeville a very *conclusive* letter to Mr. *Calhoun*, secretary of war so far as sophistry and angry words *can be* conclusive on a subject. As a specimen of his logic, we will cite as follows from his communication. Forasmuch "as the Puritans of New England, and Quakers of Pennsylvania, had never repaired the wrongs done Indians, why is Georgia to be called upon to make propitiatory offerings?" And "if the principle of Penn's treaty was right, all others that have followed are wrong."

About the same time the Cherokee memorial was before the house of representatives, of which we have spoken, its authors, to counteract certain false reports of their traducers, published in the National Intelligencer a statement of their case, from which we note the following passages: "Not satisfied with wishing the executive of the United States violently to rupture the solemn bond of our rights to our lands, and to put at defiance the pledges which existing treaties contain, *guarantying* to us our lands, it is attempted to take from us the intellect which has directed us in conducting the several negotiations with commissioners appointed to treat with us for our lands, and with the executive government, by the unfounded charge, that '*the last letter of the Cherokees to the secretary at war contains internal evidence that it was never written or dictated by an Indian.*' Whilst we profess to be complimented on the one hand by this blow at our intelligence, we cannot, in justice, allow it to pass, upon the other, without a flat contradiction. That letter, and every other letter, was not only *written*, but *dictated* by an Indian."

We are not surprised that the Georgia statesmen are not willing to allow that they have insulted so much intellect and intelligence, aware, as they must have been, that in point of manner and matter, their own compositions, side by side with the Cherokees, would suffer in no inconsiderable degree by comparison. In closing they say, "It is not for us to vindicate, or attempt to vindicate, our great father the president; he does not need an Indian's aid, nor an Indian's eulogy; but, however we are bound to love him, yet it is due to justice to state, that we have been often pained, and especially of late, at the earnestness with which he has *pressed upon us* the subject of ceding our lands. Why he has acted thus we are at a loss to conceive. We are not ignorant of the nature of the convention of 1802. We know every one of its promises. If, however, these are to be violated, and the fell war-whoop should ever be raised against us, to dispossess us of our lands, we will gratify the delegation of Georgia, in their present earnestness to see us removed or destroyed, by adding additional fertility to our land, by a deposit of our body and our bones; *for we are resolved never to leave them but by parting from them and our lives together.*" Such was the resolution of the Cherokees at this period. But fifteen years' suffering overcame them, and they were compelled to submit to a fate they could not avert.

We have, in an earlier page,* stated the manner in which the Creeks had been divested of their country, and the fatal catastrophe that fell upon the heads of the chiefs, who, against the will of the nation, had bargained it away. The most prominent character in that work among the Creeks was Gen. WILLIAM M'INTOSH. We have, in the same place, stated the attempt made by that chief to bribe Mr. Ross to undermine his nation, in the same corrupt manner as himself had done in regard to his own; and the part enacted by the Cherokees, upon that occasion, is now necessary to be stated.

A meeting of the legislative council of the Cherokees was held in October, 1823, to hear what the agents of our government had to say to them, they having procured the meeting. The object, of course, was well understood, and the agents urged their case in every possible form; but they were answered in the most manly manner, that the nation would never part with another foot of land. Gen. M'Intosh was present at this conference, and with his son was treated with every kindness, and during the proceedings were seated by the side of Mr. Ross, as was customary with both nations at their councils, when any distinguished chiefs were present, to signify that good correspondence between them existed. At, or about this time, M'Intosh ventured to recommend a cession to some of the chief men in conversations, what feigned encouragement he met with, to draw out his real character, is not upon our records, but it is certain that a communication in writing was

* Of this Book, Chap. vi., p. 52.

thereupon made to Mr. Ross, who, without delay, laid it before the council, when it was decided that it should be read in M'Intosh's presence. He was accordingly called in, and his letter was read,* after which Mr. Ross made the following address:

"My friends: five years have elapsed since I have been called to preside over the national committee; and your approbation of my conduct in the discharge of my official duties, is manifested by the successive reappointments which you have bestowed on me. The trust which you have reposed in me has been sacredly maintained, and shall ever be preserved. A traitor, in all nations, is looked upon in the darkest color, and is more despicable than the meanest reptile that crawls upon the earth. An honorable and honest character is more valuable than the filthy lucre of the whole world. Therefore, I would prefer to live as poor as the worm that inhabits the earth, than to gain the world's wealth and have my reputation as an honest man tarnished by the acceptance of a pecuniary bribe, for self-aggrandizement. It has now become my painful duty to inform you that a gross contempt is offered to my character, as well as to that of the members of the general council. This letter which I hold in my hand will speak for itself. But, fortunately, the author of it has mistaken our character and sense of honor."

This took place on the 24 October, 1823, and was but the commencement of the denunciations M'Intosh was to receive. As chief speaker of the nation, the duty of severely reprimanding the traitor devolved on Major Ridge. This was an exceedingly painful duty to him, especially as they had been old friends and officers together; had fought under Jackson, side by side, at Taladega, Tohopeka, and in numerous other battles; they had been colaborers in the civil field; frequently called together to settle and adjust important matters between their respective nations; and they were, at this time, under an appointment as commissioners to run the boundary line between the two nations. But all these considerations and circumstances did not cause Major Ridge to shrink from his duty. He said that what he was about to say must not only be heard by the Cherokees, but by others, far and wide. He adverted to their acknowledged maxims in reference to the duties of those intrusted with their government, who, if once found astray from their duty, were never again to be trusted. M'Intosh, he said, had borne the character of high moral rectitude among his own people, the Creeks, but how stands his character now? "I cast him behind my back. He may depart in peace. I here publicly disgrace him. He now knows we are not to be bought with money. We will not exult over fallen greatness. He may go to his own nation, and in the bosom of his family mourn the loss of a good name." Such is the substance of the speech of Major Ridge, who himself fell into the same snare afterwards, and suffered the same fate, with the man he now so pointedly and justly condemned.

In 1829, a society was formed in New York, "for the emigration, preservation, and improvement, of the aborigines of America," an account of which was transmitted to the president of the United States, then at the Rip Raps, in Virginia. The president replied to a letter which accompanied the account, through Major Eaton, in a very conciliatory and gracious manner. One passage is especially worthy of notice, from its surprising contrast with what was afterwards avowed by the same *authors*. "I beg leave to assure you," says the general, "that nothing of a compulsory course, to effect the removal of this unfortunate race of people, has ever been thought of by the president; although it has been so asserted." Now, all the world knows what has since been said and done. In a sort of a reply which Mr. *Benton* made to Mr. *Clay* in the senate, in 1835, he said he rose not for the purpose of taking any part in the *little* discussion, [about Indians,] but of calling up a voice far more powerful than his own—that of Mr. *Jefferson*." But as he said nothing in his half hour's talk that he attributed to Mr. *Jefferson*, or that Mr. Jefferson ever thought of, except that good man's name, it is fair to presume that that was the extent of his argument. We are prepared to use something more than the name of *Jefferson* against the oppressors of the In-

* The same we have given, ante, page 52.

dians, and we here offer some of his sound and sober convictions. "I am of opinion," he says in a letter to Gen. *Knox*, of 10 August, 1791, "that government should firmly maintain this ground; that the Indians have a right to the occupation of their lands, *independent of the states within whose chartered limits they happen to be;* that, until they cede them by treaty, or other transaction equivalent to a treaty, no act of a state can give a right to such lands; that neither under the present constitution, nor the ancient confederation, had any state, or persons, a right to treat with the Indians without the consent of the general government; that that consent has never been given to any treaty for the cession of the lands in question; that the government is determined to exert *all its energy for the patronage and protection of the rights of the Indians*, and the preservation of peace between the United States and them; and that if any settlements are made on lands not ceded by them, without the previous consent of the United States, the government will think itself bound, not only to declare to the Indians that such settlements *are without the authority or protection of the United States, but to remove them also by the public force.*" Such was the "voice" Col. *Benton* said he was to "call up," to drown that of the friend of the Indians. But "how are the mighty fallen!" The helpless Indians have been forced to fly before the steel of the white man to inhospitable regions, leaving their fine fields and comfortable houses to their avaricious oppressors.

But after all that has happened, all the wrong that has been done the Indian, all the wrong that has been done to every countryman of Jefferson, we would not change our condition with a subject of Algiers, because we have well-grounded hopes that good men will ere long stand in the place where justice emanates; yet it fills the heart of the philanthropist with sorrow, that their coming cannot relieve the Cherokees.

The dey of Algiers holds out no pretensions to Christians that they may expect justice at his hands; but he says to them, "Do you not know that my people are a band of robbers, and that I am their captain?"* A president of the United States has said that he intended no harm to the Cherokees; but what has he done?

It is painful to be compelled to reproach the government of a beloved country with acts like these; but we have no alternative, excepting in a dereliction of duty. We would gladly have been spared this part of our undertaking; but Justice has claims upon us now as strong as she had upon our government, and we cannot so deliberately disregard them.

CHAPTER XV.

HISTORY OF THE CHEROKEES, CONTINUED.

"They have taken the realm which our ancestors gave;
They have thrown their chains o'er the land and the wave;
The forest is wasted with sword and with flame;
And what have we left but our once honored name?"—ALONZO LEWIS.

WE have seen how *Jefferson* viewed the rights of the Indians, as guarantied to them in the times of *Washington*; and what have the Cherokees since done, that they are to forfeit those rights? Have they forfeited them by adopting the manners and customs of a civilized people? or by fighting their battles? That a president of this day should say to them, when they are about to be grossly tyrannized over by a state, "that he has no power to interfere and to oppose the exercise of the sovereignty of any state, over or upon all who may be within the limits of any state; that, therefore, they must prepare themselves to abide the issue of such *new relations*, without any hope that he will interfere;"—thus did Gen. *Jackson* speak to the insulted Cherokees, on

* See Mr. *Blunt's* Brief Examination, &c., page 15.

the 6 June, 1830. He, at the same time, assured them "that he loves them; (!) that he is their friend; that he feels for them as a father feels for his children." With whatever truth this might have been spoken, we do not hesitate to presume that such was not the way the Cherokees felt "for their children." And in an address to the people of the United States, which they published on the 17 July of the same year, they say, "It would be impossible to describe the sorrow which affects their minds, on learning that the chief magistrate of the United States has come to this conclusion, that all his illustrious predecessors had held intercourse with them on erroneous principles; principles that could not be sustained; that they had made promises of vital importance to them, which could not be fulfilled—promises made hundreds of times, in almost every conceivable manner—often in the form of solemn treaties—sometimes in letters written by the chief magistrate with his own hand—very often in letters written by the secretary of war under his direction—these, all these, are now discovered to be upon false principles."

The Cherokees had now become capable of meeting the white people with the arguments of reason, and not with steel; and they were capable of judging between sincerity and mere pretension. This was well portrayed by the chief SPECKLED SNAKE, in a speech which he made in a council which had been summoned to hear a talk from President Jackson read to them. It was as follows:

"*Brothers!* We have heard the talk of our great father; it is very kind. He says he loves his red children. *Brothers!* When the white man first came to these shores, the Muscogees gave him land, and kindled him a fire to make him comfortable; and when the pale faces of the south* made war on him, their young men drew the tomahawk, and protected his head from the scalping knife. But when the white man had warmed himself before the Indian's fire, and filled himself with the Indian's hominy, he became very large; he stopped not for the mountain tops, and his feet covered the plains and the valleys. His hands grasped the eastern and the western sea. Then he became our great father. He loved his red children; but said, 'You must move a little farther, lest I should, by accident, tread on you.' With one foot he pushed the red man over the Oconee, and with the other he trampled down the graves of his fathers. But our great father still loved his red children, and he soon made them another talk. He said much; but it all meant nothing, but 'move a little farther; you are too near me.' I have heard a great many talks from our great father, and they all begun and ended the same. *Brothers!* When he made us a talk on a former occasion, he said, 'Get a little farther; go beyond the Oconee and the Oakmulgee; there is a pleasant country.' He also said, 'It shall be yours forever.' Now he says, 'The land you live on is not yours; go beyond the Mississippi; there is game; there you may remain while the grass grows or the water runs.' *Brothers!* Will not our great father come there also? He loves his red children, and his tongue is not forked."

The doctrine of a right inherent in the government of the United States to remove the Cherokees by force, is comparatively new. It was not thought or even dreamed of before 1808. In that year a deputation from that nation was encouraged to visit the seat of government, more for the renewal of friendship than any thing else perhaps, who, in a conference they had with President Jefferson, "*declared their anxious desire to engage in the pursuit of agriculture and civilized life, in the country they then occupied;*" but said, "as all their countrymen could not be induced to exchange the hunter's life for an agricultural one, they requested that their country might be divided by a line between the upper and lower towns, so as to include all the waters of the Highwassee River to the upper towns; that, by thus contracting their society within narrower limits, they might *begin the establishment of fixed laws and a regular government.* Those wishing to lead the hunter's life, owing to the scarcity of game in their country, requested liberty to go over the Mississippi, and occupy some vacant lands belonging to the United States. To these

* The Spaniards of Florida endeavored to break up the English settlement under Gen. Oglethorpe in Georgia.

propositions the president gave his entire and unqualified approbation. No objection is heard of against their erecting a government for themselves, or a wish to restrain them in any manner.

Eventually, some four or five thousand of the lower town Cherokees did emigrate to Arkansas, and there a wretched life many of them worried out many fell in wars with the Osages, some few got back to their own country, and sickness swept off many more. Such fruits of emigration tended to strengthen the upper towns in their resolution of cultivating the land; and when, in 1823, commissioners were appointed to treat with them for their country, and for their removal west, they directly refused, and showed how much better off they were for continuing in their own nation than those who had emigrated. And here ended for some years all attempts on the part of the United States to treat with them for a removal. The seeds of avarice, although sown, had not come to maturity, but, like a plant in an uncongenial soil, remained without seeming to flourish or decay; yet at length a prosperous cultivator being found in a president of the United States, its growth soon astonished all beholders, and its branches cast a deathlike shade over a prosperous nation, and withered it away.

We have before remarked upon the discovery made by the southern politicians, namely, that from the time of WASHINGTON, there had been no president (including that great man) who knew what laws and treaties meant; that all the time and money which had been spent in making treaties, had been thrown away; for it was now discovered that Indians were only tenants at will, and had no right on any lands within certain state boundaries, any longer than the charity of the good people near them would humanely permit. In fact, all these treaties were now found out to be *unconstitutional.* This doctrine was finally the hinge on which the whole business turned. But Georgia herself could condescend to treat with the Cherokees in 1783, and obtained from them a considerable tract of country. Did that state *condescend* then to acknowledge the Cherokees an independent nation to get from them by treaty that which she was not strong enough to take by force? I will not aver that it was so. One thing, however, there is, about which there can be no misconception; the Cherokees were then powerful; and though, in the war with England, which had just terminated, they fought against us, they now came forward and declared for us; and their alliance was considered of no small account, situated as we then were in relation to the Spaniards in Florida. And, besides, it must be considered that at the close of the revolution, our people desired peace with the Cherokees as much as they with us; and, in the language of Chief Justice Marshall,* "When the United States gave peace, did they not also receive it? Did the Cherokees come to us, to our seat of government, to solicit peace; or did our government send commissioners to them to ask it?" The result, however, was the treaty of Hopewell, "within the Cherokee nation," and not at New York, that that celebrated treaty was made.

The series of usurpations commenced upon the Cherokees and other Indians, has at length, in this present year, 1840, reached the climax of oppression contemplated by its originators. That people had long viewed further encroachments upon them as certain, inasmuch as such encroachments had never actually ceased from the day of their acquaintance with the white man; but the awful thunder which burst upon them in our day had never been thought of by the whites, much less by themselves, until within a few years. They had, indeed, as early as 1823, observed a dark cloud gathering in the north-east, but they rationally thought that the extent of country it must pass over, before it should reach them, would qualify its rage, and waste its deadly effects; happy for them had it proved as they had hoped, and as every friend of humanity and justice had hoped it would; but it came and swept away the Cherokees.

The monstrous project of a removal of all the Indians within our limits beyond the Mississippi, is not chargeable to any one of our chief magistrates, but Mr. Monroe is conspicuous among them. He proposed it with diffidence

* Opinion in the case, *Worcester* vs. *the State of Georgia*, p. 14.

in his opening message to congress, on the 7th of December, 1824; and here let us observe, that the suggestion was made upon the same month, and nearly the same day of the month, that our fathers came to these shores; and on the 27th of January, following, he strongly recommended the measure. He was induced to propose such a plan, he said, as the only one he could devise to relieve the country from the difficulty by which its executive was surrounded, and which every day thickened. Georgia was pressing with severe earnestness; alleging that the time had arrived when the Indian title to lands within its limits should be extinguished, and the new states were crowding on all sides with undue importunity, that their claim for Indians' lands was as good as their neighbors'. The president, therefore, like a bankrupt, who, to get rid of a difficult demand to-day, obligates himself to pay a greater one to-morrow, disregards the dictates of his own judgment It was under these circumstances that a removal was recommended

But with this recommendation of removal, Mr. Monroe, although he speaks of *force*, repudiates in the strongest terms its employment. And we cannot doubt his suggestion was dictated by the purest benevolence. He says, "The condition of the aborigines within our limits, and especially those who are within the limits of any of the states, merits peculiar attention. Experience has shown, that unless the tribes be civilized, they can never be incorporated into our system, in any form whatever. It has likewise shown, that in the regular augmentation of our population, with the extension of our settlements, their situation will become deplorable, if their extinction is not menaced. Some well-digested plan, which will rescue them from such calamities, is due to their rights, to the rights of humanity, and to the honor of the nation. Their civilization is indispensable to their safety, and this can be accomplished only by degrees. Difficulties of the most serious character present themselves to the attainment of this very desirable result, on the territory on which they now reside. To remove them from it *by force*, even with a view to their own security or happiness, would be revolting to humanity, and utterly unjustifiable."

And touching this matter we have a very clear view of the opinions of Mr. Monroe, regarding Indian rights, in another message, in which he expresses himself as follows: "I have no hesitation, however, to declare it as my opinion, that the Indian title was not affected in the slightest circumstance by the compact with Georgia, and that *there is no obligation on the United States to remove the Indians by force*. The express stipulation of the compact, that their title should be extinguished at the expense of the United States, when it may be done *peaceably*, and on *reasonable* conditions, is a full proof that it was the clear and distinct understanding of both parties to it, that the Indians had a right to the territory, in the disposal of which they were to be regarded as free agents. An attempt to remove them by force would, in my opinion, be unjust. In the future measures to be adopted in regard to the Indians within our limits, and, in consequence, within the limits of any state, the United States have duties to perform, and a character to sustain, to which they ought not to be indifferent." But what have the admonitions of all good men availed? And the more we meet with, the more we are astonished at the result of things, and the more severely do we deprecate and denounce the advocates of the course pursued.

The president evidently had not thought very seriously about the removal of the Indians at this time, and knew little of the history, or actual state of the Cherokees; they had then become considerably civilized, and instead of decreasing, were increasing. But about two months after, he again makes the Indian subject the object of a special message, in the outset of which he holds this language: "Being deeply impressed with the opinion, that the removal of the Indian tribes from the lands which they now occupy within the limits of the several states and territories, to the country lying westward and northward thereof, within our acknowledged boundaries, is of very high importance to our Union, and may be accomplished on conditions and in a manner to promote the interest and happiness of those tribes, the attention of government has been long drawn, with great solicitude, to the subject."

First a removal is barely thought about, then talked about, then proposed, then strongly recommended; so far there must be no compulsion, because it would be too barefaced an outrage on the common sense of the people; because the Indians *will* remove without force; they can be bought out. Time showed that they could not be obliged to sell their country; then the project of extending state laws over them is started, which, though unconstitutional, can be enforced in spite of the general government, to the incalculable mischief of the Indians; and besides, could it be supposed that the general government would resist state laws unto a drop of white blood in defence of the *rights of Indians?* A preposterous idea! A result which could not be allowed to happen in these days of light and reason in abundance. While the executive of the general government is pondering the matter, not only Indians, but citizens of the United States, among them as instructors, and by the direction and under the authority of the president himself, are seized by an armed force, dragged to a distant region, and thrown into prison! Months pass away, and the *government* is still *pondering* on what is to be done. In the mean time Georgia sends out an armed force to protect the Indians, and we will hear how this force performed the service, as set forth in a memorial to congress from some of the most respectable of the Cherokees, in 1831.

"In the name and authority of G. R. Gilmar, governor of Georgia, a bill was filed in chancery, in the superior court of Hall county, in July last, (1830,) against certain Cherokees, praying for an injunction to stop them from digging and searching for gold within the limits of their own nation; and the bill being sworn to before Judge Clayton, he awarded an injunction against the parties named in the bill as defendants, commanding them, forthwith, to desist from working on those mines, under the penalty of 20,000 dollars; at the same time and place there were unmolested several thousand intruders from Georgia and other states, engaged in robbing the nation of gold, for which the owners were ordered not to work by the said writ. Under the authority of this injunction, the sheriff of Hall county, with an armed force, invaded the nation, consisting of a colonel, a captain, and 30 or 40 of the militia of the state of Georgia, who arrested a number of Cherokees engaged in digging for gold, who were at first rescued by the troops of the United States, stationed near the place, and the sheriff and his party themselves made prisoners, and conducted fifteen miles to the military camp, when a council of examination was held, and the exhibition of their respective authorities made, which resulted in the release of the sheriff and his party, and a written order by the commanding officer of the United States troops, directing the Cherokees to submit to the authority of Georgia, and that no further protection could be extended to them at the gold mines, as he could no longer interfere with the laws of Georgia, but would afford aid in carrying them into execution. On the return of the sheriff and his party, they passed by the Cherokees who were still engaged in digging for gold, and ordered them to desist, under the penalty of being committed to jail, and proceeded to destroy their tools and machinery for cleaning gold, and after committing some further aggression, they returned. Shortly afterwards, the sheriff, with a guard of four men, and a process from the state of Georgia, arrested three Cherokees for disobeying the injunction, while peaceably engaged in their labors, and conducted them to Wadkinsville, a distance of 75 miles, before the same judge, A. S. Clayton, who then and there sentenced them to pay a fine of 93 dollars, costs, and to stand committed to prison until paid; and also compelled them to give their bond in the sum of 1,000 dollars, for their personal appearance before his next court, to answer the charges of violating the writ of injunction aforesaid. They were retained in custody five days, then paid the costs, and gave the required bond. They appeared agreeably to the bonds, and Judge Clayton dismissed them, on the ground that the governor of Georgia could not become a prosecutor in the case. For these unwarrantable outrages, committed on their persons and property, no apology was offered, nor to this day has any of their money been refunded."

If there are any blacker cases of outrage any where committed in a Christian country, we are not informed of them. Such would not be submitted to in Turkey or China. The manner in which affairs were managed in Georgia, under color of law, is a disgrace to the least civilized community. Gen. Macomb marched the troops of the United States into the Cherokee country, *he* said, to guard against the difficulties which it was apprehended would grow out of the conflicting operations of the Cherokees and *the lawless intruders* upon the mineral district, and having *fulfilled the instructions of the government*, the troops were directed to return for the winter to their respective quarters."

About the same time Gov. Gilmar wrote to the secretary of war, requesting the withdrawal of the troops, observing that Georgia could enforce her own laws. When this notice was received at Washington, the secretary wrote to Gilmar that he had "just ordered their withdrawal, because the object for which they had been sent was, *in a great measure*, accomplished!" Now, if the Cherokee country belonged to Georgia, it is difficult to see what business the general government had to send its troops into her territory, to remove gold diggers or any other kind of diggers, whether digging lawfully in their "own diggings," or unlawfully in those of another It was a new doctrine, but of a tenor with all the rest, that the United States must enforce the laws of Georgia. That is to say, she must enforce them for Georgia, if Georgia desired it, or if not, there would be no interference on the part of the general government.

CHAPTER XVI.

HISTORY OF THE CHEROKEES, CONCLUDED.

"Come, Lethe, come! thy tide oblivious roll
O'er all that proud complacency of soul,
That generous ardor, that enlivening flame,
That warmed my bosom, when I heard the name
Of my *once* honored country;—let thy wave,
Dark as Avernus, gloomy as the grave,
Drown every vestige of that country's fame,
And shade the light that bursts upon her shame!"—PIERPONT

To mark the progress of oppression, we here note as follows from the Cherokee Phœnix, under date, "*New Echota*, 19 February, 1831. This week we present to our readers but half a sheet. The reason is, one of our printers has left us; and we expect another, who is a white man, to quit us very soon, either to be dragged to the Georgia penitentiary for a term not less than four years, or for his personal safety to leave the nation, to let us shift for ourselves as well as we can. Thus is the liberty of the press guarantied by the constitution of Georgia. But we will not give up the ship while she is afloat. We have intelligent youths enough in the nation, and we hope before long to make up our loss. Let our patrons bear in mind that we are in the woods, and, as is said by many, in a *savage country*, where printers are not plenty; and therefore they must not expect to receive the Phœnix regular for a while, but we will do the best we can."

One month after, namely, March 19, the Phœnix says, "The law of Georgia, making it a high misdemeanor for a white man to reside in the Cherokee nation, without taking the oath of allegiance, and obtaining a permit from the governor of Georgia, or his agent, is now in a course of execution. On last Sabbath, after the usual time of divine service, the Georgia guard arrived, and arrested three of our citizens, viz., Rev. Samuel A. Worcester, Mr. J. F. Wheeler, one of our printers, and Mr. Thomas Gann, the two last being citizens, with Cherokee families. Mr. Isaac Proctor, assistant missionary at Carmel, had the evening before been taken, and came with the guard as a prisoner. On Monday they were marched to Etahwah, where, the same evening, were taken the Rev. John Thompson, and Mr. William Thompson." Upon this outrage the editor of the Phœnix meekly remarks, that his object was simply to give facts, and not indulge in any remarks upon their origin. William Thompson was thrown into jail, but afterwards discharged, it being ascertained that he did not live in the nation. The missionaries and two others were taken before Judge Clayton, on a writ of habeas corpus, and liberated by him on the ground that they were agents of the government; they, however, made no such plea. It was aptly said by the Cherokees, that if the missionaries were agents of the government, the public might rest assured that Gen. Jackson would reform them out.

They were true prophets; for it seems that Mr. Worcester, being postmaster at New Echota, was an agent of government, and was discharged to make room for a more certain process against him. The next thing to be done was to drive him from the post office, which Mr. Barry did without delay, and put another in his place, who, besides performing his duty of postmaster, performed another, of more profit to himself, probably, of selling liquors to the Indians, in violation of the laws of the United States, as well as those of the Cherokees.

We will produce another short narrative, exhibiting the progress of crime and oppression against the Cherokee nation, before passing to other details. It is contained in a letter from John Ridge to Elias Boudinot, and is in these words: "The Georgia guard, under Col. Nelson, are now here [at Ougillogy] with four prisoners, Mr. Elliott and Mr. Dennis, white men, citizens of this nation by marriage, and the Rev. Mr. Trott, also a white man, who are charged with a violation of the Georgia laws, in living in this nation by its allowance and laws. The other is Mr. John West, a young gentleman, a Cherokee, who is charged with the high crime of using insolent language to the guard. These four I saw last night under guard, *chained together in pairs*, and fastened together with locks. Mr. David Vann, a member of the Cherokee senate, and Thomas Woodward, are also arrested, but not chained, who are not allowed to know the reason of their arrest until they arrive at head quarters, 70 or 80 miles from their homes. The guard are still in pursuit of other men. They have a wagon along, in which they have a drum, on which they beat, and a fife, to make martial music."

The above was under date of June 1. On the 21 May, some of the principal Cherokee citizens assembled at New Echota, and issued an appeal to the people of the United States, which, though claiming nothing but justice, and asking for protection, time passed away, and none were found to step forward to relieve them. We have a heavy debt to pay, at some time and in some manner, which will, it is feared, be more difficult to discharge, than it would have been to have supported the Cherokees against an insignificant rabble of self-constituted, inflated contemners of law and justice.

In 1826, Georgia sent on commissioners to make a topographical survey through the Cherokee nation. *C. R. Hicks* was then principal chief, who forbids the proceeding in a friendly letter to Mr. W. Lumpkin, under whom the survey was to be prosecuted. No attention being paid to this notice, Mr. Hicks sent his son with two other Indians to remonstrate with the surveyor in more pointed terms. He was told, that unless he desisted, his instruments should be taken from him. Not thinking it proper to incur further displeasure, he accordingly desisted for that time. It was against the express will of the Cherokee council that any survey should be undertaken without an order from the secretary of war, because no state has any authority to go upon the lands of the Indians for any such purpose; and even the United States never take such liberty without a grant from them.

Affairs progressed, without much of interest until the next year. Meanwhile Georgia had been informed that she was transcending her powers, and that she would not be tolerated by the United States in her encroachments upon the Indians. Whereupon, Gov. Troup, not finding any object whereon to use his sword, if he had had one, seized that "mighty instrument of little men," his pen; and had we not known that steam is harmless when there is nothing to confine it, we should have apprehended "an awful explosion." Take, as a specimen, what he says to the Hon. JAMES BARBOUR, secretary at war: "Sir, you are sufficiently explicit as to the means by which you propose to carry your resolution into effect. Thus the military character of the menace is established, and I am only at liberty to give to it the defiance which it merits. From the first decisive act of hostility, you will be consid ered and treated as a public enemy; and with the less repugnance, because you, to whom we might constitutionally have appealed for our own defence against invasion, are yourselves invaders; and what is more, *the unblushing allies of the savages*, whose cause you have adopted."

Vapor is soon dissolved in air, and words from a southern furnace amount to no more in this case than echoes from an iceberg. In 1828, a long report was made by a committee of the house of representatives of Georgia, seconded by sundry resolutions of a character with former proceedings. It was resolved, that inasmuch as the United States had failed to procure the Cherokee lands "as early," and upon as "reasonable terms," as it might have done, they had thereby "*palpably violated their contract with Georgia*, and are now bound, at all hazards, and without regard to terms, to procure said lands for the use of Georgia; that all said lands belong to her absolutely, and that the Indians are tenants at her will." This, the committee said, was their *last appeal*.

The administration of Mr. Adams being at an end, Georgia had no longer any thing to fear, but practised its abuses with singular impunity. Parties from that state would go over the Cherokee line, steal and drive off their stock; and the Indians had not the least remedy left. Some despairingly said, "If they could get no redress, they could *feel deeply the injustice done them*."

Had the upright and consummate statesman, John Quincy Adams, been continued in the presidential chair, the fate of the Cherokees would have been different; at least, so long as his sage counsel had been followed, they would have been secure in their rights. In his message to congress on the 5 February, 1827, he said, "It is my duty to say, that if the legislative and executive authorities of the state of Georgia should persevere in acts of encroachment upon the territory, secured by a solemn treaty to the Indians, and the laws of the Union remain unaltered, a superadded obligation, even higher than that of human authority, will compel the executive of the United States to enforce the laws, and fulfil the duties of the nation, by all the force committed for that purpose to his charge." It was to such decisive language, held by the head of the government, that the Cherokees owed what little quiet they had, until 1829, when a new interpretation given to our laws changed order into anarchy.

On the 15 September, 1831, eleven persons were brought to trial at Lawrenceville, for the *crime* of living in the Cherokee nation, without taking an oath to obey the laws of Georgia. They were all brought in guilty by a jury, after being out fifteen minutes. Nine of the *convicts* were pardoned, on giving assurances that they would not offend again. The two missionaries, Worcester and Butler, having, as they averred, committed no crime, would accept no pardon, and were accordingly taken to the penitentiary. The governor (Gilmar) of Georgia, dreading the expression of public opinion, was in hopes to have got rid of the missionaries at a cheaper rate than was now promised, writes to the inspectors of the prison, requesting that they would "converse with each convict alone, and ascertain from them whether they are disposed to promise not again to offend the laws, if they should be pardoned." But this overture amounted to nothing, for they were determined in their course, and went accordingly to "hard labor" among felons! Prison clothes were put on them, bearing about their waists the initials of their names in large red letters.

In November following, Georgia was cited to appear before the supreme court of the United States, to show cause why the judgment of one of her courts should not be set aside in the case of Messrs. Butler and Worcester. Georgia, through her executive, raised the cry of state rights, and said that any attempt of the United States to interfere with her criminal jurisdiction, *would challenge the most determined resistance*, and, if persisted in, would *inevitably annihilate the Union*. When the case came on, there was no appearance on the part of Georgia; thus showing its contempt for that tribunal. And when it was decided that that state had no right to imprison any persons on the ground assumed, and a mandamus was served on the court which had tried the missionaries, for a habeas corpus, it was refused, and the mandamus disregarded. Thus stood matters in March, 1832, and nothing was expected to be done in favor of the prisoners for a year to come, owing to the delays consequent upon law proceedings. And here we will remark, that laws are excellent when they suit the views of avaricious men, but when they thwart their base propensities, they are exceedingly oppressive. In the time of Mr. Jefferson's administration, Pennsylvania attempted to resist a mandate of the supreme court, but in due time wisely yielded to her duty; and be it remembered, that Georgia was among the foremost to declare that Pennsylvania should be coerced into submission.

In September, 1830, a detachment of United States troops again scoured the gold mine country. At the upper mines they arrested upwards of one hundred persons, whites and Cherokees. The latter, after being kept under guard one night, were dismissed with the peremptory injunction, *not to dig any more.* Hence it follows, that if the Cherokees had potatoes in the ground, they had no right to dig them up, neither had they any right to plant them. In short, Georgia having carried her injustice as far as she could, the United States steps in and lends her a hand in extending it!

About the time of this *military* expedition, the principal men of Agnohee district met in council, and, in an affectionate and feeling manner, thanked all those citizens of the United States who had in any way come forward and raised their voices against their oppressors. They, at the same time, issued an address to us, which would do honor to the head or heart of any philanthropist that ever flourished upon the proudest page of history. And we doubt if there exists that nation under the sun, even in this enlightened age, which would have suffered as the Cherokees have done, without taking revenge on their inhuman oppressors. To what then are we to attribute their noble and philosophic forbearance: to their civilization or degradation?

As matters now stood, it seemed that serious difficulty must ensue between the United States and Georgia, if swaggering and high-sounding words had any meaning, when proceeding from governors, ex-governors, and others, hi[illegible] office in that state. But while the decision of the supreme court was sleeping, Georgia was sweeping onward in full triumph; she parcelled out the Cherokee country, and drove the honest owners out of doors, put her own citizens in their places from one corner to the other of their country; every white man who had moral courage enough to question these nefarious proceedings, was obliged, at the same time, to exercise discretion enough to keep himself at a safe distance from penitentiary jurisdiction.

Hence, in about a year from the time the missionaries were thrown into prison, Georgia had got full and undisturbed possession of all the country in question, and had nothing to fear from missionary or any other influence. It was therefore concluded that a sort of a drawn game might be played with the supreme court; thinking, probably, that it was not worth while to try their strength with it at this time, for if they should, it might establish a precedent which would prevent a profitable use of the same farce hereafter, when it might be convenient for them to usurp other powers.

It seemed now understood, that if Georgia would liberate the missionaries, they would not urge their suit any further against her; and accordingly, Gov. Lumpkin, in a very *gracious* manner, proclaimed, on the 14th of January, 1833, that "whereas the prisoners had signified to him that they had instructed their counsel to prosecute their suit no further, and should therefore '*leave the question of their continuance in confinement to the magnanimity of the state;*' and taking into view *the triumphant ground* which the state finally occupies in relation to this subject in the eyes of the nation, as has been sufficiently attested through various channels, especially in the recent overwhelming *reëlection of President Jackson*, the known defender of the rights of the state throughout this controversy; and above all, the MAGNANIMITY of Georgia being appealed to, know ye, that I have thought proper to remit the further execution of their sentence, and that they be forthwith discharged." Thus nearly a year had passed since the supreme court had decided that the acts of Georgia were a violation of the laws of the land.*

* The decision was made by Judge Marshall on the 3d March, 1832.

No reflections will ever be required upon this affair from the historian, as they will naturally suggest themselves to the mind of every reader, who has only to consider, that argument had very little to do where Andrew Jackson was concerned.

In the memorial which the chiefs of the Cherokee nation submitted to congress on the 3d of March, 1829, are remarks and reasonings so pertinent and cogent, that it is surprising to us how it could have been disregarded by honorable men. Among other things noticed, they remark that, "It is with no little surprise that we have seen, in a document printed for the use of congress, connected with the subject of Indian emigration, the following sentiments: 'from the ascertained feelings of the chiefs of the southern Indians, there is a fixed purpose, by threats or otherwise, to keep their people from emigrating' And, 'there is no doubt but these people fear their chiefs, and on that account keep back.'" These insinuations, the memorialists say, if meant for them, are the production of culpable ignorance or wilful falsehood. The idea that their people are overawed and in fear of their chiefs, is as ridiculous as it would be to suppose the people of the United States are afraid of their representatives. "The great Washington," they continue, "advised a plan and afforded aid for the general improvement of our nation. President Jefferson followed the noble example, and in concluding an address to a delegation, he said, 'I sincerely wish you may succeed in your laudable endeavors to save the remnant of your nation, by adopting industrious occupations and a *government of regular law.* In this *you may always rely on the counsel and assistance of the United States.*'" But of what avail have been the determination of Washington and the earnest desire of Jefferson?

The "Book of the Troubles and Miseries of the emigrating Indians," has not been published. Hundreds have been swept off by sickness on their rugged road; old and infirm persons have fallen under the fatigues and hardships of their journey; hundreds have been buried beneath the waves of the Mississippi in one awful catastrophe;* wives left husbands on the way, never more to join them; mothers are hurried from the graves of their children. Mrs. Ross, wife of the great chief of that name, languished and died before reaching the unknown land to which she was bound; but I cannot go into these particulars.

On the 19th of July, 1832, a fast was observed in the Cherokee nation. President Ross, in his proclamation recommending it, observes, that "whereas the crisis in the affairs of the nation exhibits the day of tribulation and sorrow, and the time appears to be fast hastening when the destiny of this people must be sealed; whether it has been directed by the wonted depravity and wickedness of man, or by the unsearchable and mysterious will of an all-wise being, it equally becomes us, as a rational and Christian community, humbly to bow in humiliation," &c. This is produced as an ever-standing memorial for all such as may desire to contrast the actions of the Indians with those of Georgia; that they may be able to judge which best deserved the name of a *Christian* community.

Thus, in the year 1832, the Cherokees gave up all hope of receiving justice at the hands of our government, and we see in the Phœnix of June, among others, these observations: "The gigantic silver pipe which George Washington placed in the hands of the Cherokees, as a memorial of his warm and abiding friendship, has ceased to reciprocate; it lies in a corner of the executive chamber, cold, like its author, to rise no more." And in the same paragraph they refer to the value of the gold mines, as follows:

"The value of the Cherokee nation can hardly be set down in figures. It is worth more than one hundred millions of dollars. Let us estimate. From Frogtown, near the source of the Chestatee, commences the gold region, and is termed the limit of Georgia. From this point almost one hundred miles on a straight line south, or towards the western corner of Carroll county, is

* On the 31st of October, 1837, as the steamboat Monmouth, with 600 emigrating Indians, was ascending the Mississippi, it was run into by another vessel, and 311 of those miserable creatures drowned! That such a number should have been crowded into one boat is incredible, and we are informed that the boat was an old, condemned vessel. It was probably hired cheap by the contractors for removing Indians!

one continued bed of gold. The width of this region is not yet known, but at the southern part it is something like thirty miles broad. Millions of dollars' worth of gold have been taken here by thousands of intruders."

Let the oppressors of the Cherokees look well to their motives of action. Are they ignorant of the acts of the Spaniards in the south? or are they acting upon the same principles? If the respective cases be analyzed, the excuse for Georgia is not half as good as for the wholesale murderers of the Mexicans and Peruvians; for there cannot be so strong a motive to action as when the agent is acting under the firm conviction that he is executing the will of God. It was a dark and superstitious age when South America was desolated. The Indians of that country were in the very depths of a bloody superstition; inhumanly sacrificing thousands a year of their innocent countrymen in their religious performances, and with a cruelty that cannot be imagined; for it required ages to find out the various refined modes in which to practise their diabolical executions. They even shocked the Spaniards, who, to put an end to them, thought themselves justified in destroying those who practised them. Gold was, at first, a secondary consideration. What has Georgia to plead at the bar of future history but "gold?" With unprincipled men what will its corrupting influence not do? What has it done to Spain?

The poor Cherokees have said, "Georgia, beware of the pits thine avarice has made;" echo has reverberated it from every hill, and children yet unborn will hear it from their cradles to their graves. To all whom these facts shall come, a voice will speak which cannot be misunderstood. No traveller shall thread the fertile valleys of the ancient Cherokees without feeling deep emotions of sorrow in his breast, that he had not lived at a time when he could have rendered that oppressed people assistance. As a people, we have not done our duty to those Indians. Why did we not rise to a man, and cause justice to be done them? Where is the honest man who is not now sorry that *he* had not done it? And does he not say he *would* do it, were a like case to arise again?

To the "Cherokee Phœnix," the first newspaper ever published by Indians, we have been considerably indebted for many valuable items of intelligence in this part of our work; and we again notice it for the last time, in all probability; forasmuch as Georgia has laid her lawless hand upon it, we can expect no other. In October, 1835, the Georgia guard took possession of that newspaper establishment, and its further issue stopped, unless it would uphold the course of Georgia against the Indians.

At this time Mr. John Ross lived in Tennessee, and was recognized as a citizen of that state. But for some cause or other, that "guard," of infamous memory, then under the command of one Capt. Bishop, proceeded to the residence of Mr. Ross on the 7th of November, made prisoner of him, seized upon all his papers and records of the nation, and marched him into Georgia. Mr. John H. Paine, of New York, happening to be then at the residence of Mr. Ross, was treated in like manner. He had been engaged in the laudable pursuit of material for an historical work on the Indians, and had many papers containing memoranda for that object, of great value to himself, but of none whatever to others; these were also seized. These individuals, however, were not long detained, but they got no redress for the injury and insult, that has ever come to my knowledge. Where the "magnanimity" of Georgia was now, which was so prominent in the case of the missionaries, we leave to the determination of others.

What, then, are the first fruits of this expatriation of the Cherokees? Deadly feuds among them, executions and murders. These have but begun, and how or where they will end, are events hidden in the future. It is well known that the principal men who sold their country, Major *Ridge*, his son, *John Ridge*, Elias Boudinot,* and others, have been executed in pursuance of the laws of the Cherokees, for their wickedness in violating the most vital of their rights and their constitution. Who could have expected any thing different from those Indians? They had been induced to form a code of

* He, it is believed, is the same who was educated at the Missionary school at Cornwall, in Connecticut, and who, about 1825, married a white lady, Harriet R. Gold, of that village.

laws many years ago by Washington and Jefferson, and to live under the operation of those laws until, in 1830, they were forced to abandon them by the interference of Georgia.

It had been an old standing law among the Cherokees, as well as among the Creeks, "that if any persons or person should sell any lands by treaty, without the authority of the nation, they should be punished with death." In 1839, this law was brought up in their legislature, and confirmed as the law of the land. John Ridge himself brought it forward, and Elias Boudinot, editor of the Cherokee Phœnix, published it. It was a law before letters were known among the Cherokees, and was first printed, we believe, in 1829.

Having seen the Cherokees driven beyond the Mississippi, if we would pursue their history we must follow them into that region; but at best we can know but little about their affairs now, the intercourse between them and intelligent white men having, from their remote situation, become unfrequent. Towards the close of the year 1838 the business of emigration was completed, and this was no sooner effected but the white inhabitants bordering on Arkansas began to express great alarm, believing the Indians were making preparations to spread destruction among them. But their fears were without any foundation; the Cherokees having found enough to do for several months to prepare shelters for themselves and families. Yet amidst their busy preparations of this sort, to pacify their white neighbors, they convened the nation in a great council, in which it was solemnly protested that all reports which had been circulated of their hostile intentions towards the whites were without foundation, and utterly false.

The next matter of moment took place in June of last year, 1839. This was no less than the murder of the principal men of the Ridge, or treaty party. Of the parties into which the Cherokees were divided an account has been given. It appears that from the time the Ridges, father and son, and their followers executed the treaty of New Echota with Schermerhorn, their lives were forfeited in the minds of a certain part of the nation, and they only waited a favorable time to put their resolution in execution. It is not our intention to justify the executions of which we are now to give a narration, for be it remembered, that we protest against taking human life under any circumstances whatever, and firmly believe that a community is vastly more injured than benefited by the practice of that law of retaliating murder with murder.

It is matter of historical record, that the Ridges, Boudinot, Bell, Rogers, and others, who signed the treaty of December, 1835, very suddenly changed their minds in respect to the policy of removal. They were as forward as Mr. Ross, or any of that party, in protesting against the acts of Georgia, and as much opposed to making any treaty of sale of their country, up to the time of a certain mission of Schermerhorn, as any of the nation. Therefore it is not strange that the Ross party were surprised at their suddenly coming out and advocating an opposite course. They were immediately accused of bribery and corruption, and whether true or not, the party that remained firm, believed them guilty; and the most we can say concerning their conduct is, there were strong grounds of suspicion against them.

Our information of the massacre of Ridge and others is very indirect, though circumstantial, and is as follows: When it became known to Ross that the lives of certain chiefs were to be taken, he used all the means at his command to prevent it. But a party collected, and on Saturday, the 22d of June, the executioners, to the number of about forty, went to the house of John Ridge early in the morning, before he was up, and took him from his bed, and murdered him in a manner too savage to relate; treating his lifeless body with all the indignity of ancient barbarians. They next proceeded in pursuit of Major Ridge, his father, who had the day before set out to visit some friends in Van Buren, Arkansas. He was overtaken near the foot of Boston Mountain, about 35 miles from his place of destination, and there shot from his horse, and died without hardly knowing why he had been thus savagely dealt with. Thus fell Major Ridge in the sixty-fifth year of his age, and his son at the age of thirty-seven. Of the circumstances of the death of Boudinot, Col. Bell, and two or three others, we are not informed.

Major Ridge once executed a chief for an act of much more doubtful atrocity than that for which he now fell. In 1806, the noted orator DOUBLEHEAD was charged, with others, with the important business of making a treaty, at Tellico, with the United States, for a tract of land to accommodate the seat of government of Tennessee, and for "the first island in the Tennessee, above the mouth of Clinch." In this business, Chuquacuttague, or Doublehead, was charged with bribery; yet nothing was done about it by the nation, and he went unpunished; but in 1817 he was again guilty, and was followed by Major Ridge and others, and in the tavern of one M'Intosh, in the evening, was fallen upon and shot by the hand of Ridge. He escaped with a desperate wound, and was for a short time secreted in a neighboring dwelling, but his pursuers found him, and an Indian named Saunders, one of Ridge's company, sunk his tomahawk into his head, which finished the execution. This was near the agency in Calhoun. Doublehead had himself killed a man in his way thither, for charging him with the crime for which he suffered. This execution is mentioned to show that Ridge was well aware that he had forfeited his life by what he had done at New Echota.

CHAPTER XVII.

THE SEMINOLE WAR RESUMED—*Further account of the causes of the war—Numerous cases of gross imposition—Bad conduct of government officers—A new treaty of removal urged—A deputation visits the west—Their report—Another treaty—Speeches of the chiefs—Examination of the policy of the government, relative to a removal of the Indians—Character of borderers—Review of the manner treaties of sale were procured—The president angry at the Indians' presumption—Barbarous treatment of three Mickasaukies.*

"Let them come with the pipe; we will tread it to dust,
And our arrows of war shall ne'er moulder with rust;
Let them come with their hosts; to the desert we'll flee,
And the drought and the famine our helpers shall be."—PIKE.

THE events of the Seminole war have astonished all to whom the knowledge of them has extended. And the astonishment has been as varied as the wilds of Florida are represented, by those whose misfortune it has been to serve there against their fellow-men. As this war progressed, we wrote down its events in detail, as we have long been wont to do of all occurrences relating to the Indians, but from the conflicting statements, purporting to be from the theatre of their enactment, great difficulty was experienced in arriving at facts and dates.

Nobody could have been much surprised that a war in Florida should break out, if they were at all acquainted with the circumstances which caused it, nor could they have been much surprised, that a hundred men in the midst of the Indian country should have been beset and slain, leaving none to carry the tidings of such disaster. Our only surprise is, that the work had not been done in a more savage manner; that even one could escape by feigning death; and that a monument only of ashes of the slain had not marked the place where they fell. These things astonish us, not the war itself.

We had supposed, like every body else, that there could be but a single campaign, when it was known that the Indians had resisted in good earnest; and when we consider the power of the United States set against a single corner of a territory surrounded with every advantage for warlike operations, we could form no other conclusion but that the poor Indians would be crushed almost at a single blow; and it was not until two distinguished generals had shown that the Seminole was not to be despised, that the war with him became matter of serious consideration at the seat of government. But of these affairs we have already said as much as was necessary.

In bringing down the events of this war to its conclusion, circumstances make it necessary to detail some affairs from the beginning of it, which we have not noticed; having closed our account in the summer of 1836, many facts and documents have since come to hand which could not then be known, and which throw much new light on the subject, as well as furnish much new and important matter.*

Of the origin of the late Seminole war, such facts only have been given as were known to the writer at the earliest period of it. We have now additional sources laid open, and shall proceed, in the next place, to draw from them.

It would be tedious to relate, and irksome to read, the half of what might be gathered of the robberies and enormities committed by infamous white villains in Indian borders; and it is equally insufferable to read of the manner that JUSTICE is there trodden under foot by bodies bearing the name of *court*. Law is all on the side of the white man, and consequently justice is no dweller in such bodies. Indians cannot testify in cases to which they are a party, and they are obliged to submit to whatever decision their *learned guardians* pronounce.†

One Col. *Humphreys* was for some time Indian agent in Florida. In consequence of this man's vociferous avowal of the right of territorial jurisdiction over the Indians, he was elected a member of the legislative council of Florida. Thus much for urging that negro claims should be settled in the territory, instead of their being referred to the decision of the government of the United States. Now such suits could be disposed of with perfect ease, because no Indian could have a hearing except *against his own people*. Some notorious scoundrel had sold negroes to Col. Humphreys, which belonged to a Seminole woman named *Culekeeckowa*. He bought them after application had been made to him as agent, by their owner, for their recovery, of that very villain! Nevertheless, he promised to exert himself for their restoration. He afterwards said he bought them *to prevent* their being sent to Charleston. Some of the negroes that were young when the transfer took place, having grown old enough to be made to understand the nature of the case, went back voluntarily to their real mistress; and the double-dealer *Humphreys* had the audacity to apply to agent Thompson for his interference that he might have them again. Thompson had independence and honesty enough not to comply, the facts being so strong in favor of *Culekeeckowa*, but referred *Humphreys*, together with the facts in the case, to the decision of government.

Another man was employed by a certain Indian woman for the recovery of negroes. She gave him, as he told her, a power of attorney for that purpose. She soon found that, instead of a power of attorney, she had given him a bill of sale of all her negroes!!!!!!!

On another occasion, the chief *Micanopy* requested an individual to draw a form of writing for him, which soon after proved to be a conveyance of a valuable tract of land!

A black, named *Abraham*, who has figured largely in the war, was basely robbed by one of the white border fraternity. The fellow owed *Abraham* a large amount of money, got his receipt for it under pretence that it was a certificate that he owed him, which it was necessary should be sent to Washington before he could pay him! These are a few of the abominations daily practised by individuals; and we shall now pass to others, in which the government itself becomes implicated.

We have spoken plainly of the treaty of Paine's Landing, in the early part of our history of this war; but as new facts have since come to our knowledge, it will be necessary to extend the examination here. It must be re-

---

* There were published in the year 1836 three histories of the Florida war. The first was by Mr. Cohen, the second by a late "staff officer," and the third by "a lieutenant of the left wing." All three of them seem to be very well done, but that by Mr. W. Potter, ("a late staff officer,") if I mistake not the gentleman, is far the most valuable to the historian. To these works I gladly recur, and tender here the authors my acknowledgments for the use I have made of the facts contained in their pages. None of them had appeared when my work was published, and hence I could not profit by them in my previous editions. But for these last five years of the war I have had to gather my materials from the "thousand and one" reports of the day.

† Since writing the above, I have read Gen. *Thompson's* speech to the Indians at a council in Oct. 1834, in which he plainly holds the same language to them.

membered that by the treaty of Camp Moultrie, (18 September, 1823,) the Seminoles had secured to them an annuity of $5,000 for 20 years, and they were to remove within certain boundaries described by the treaty, embracing a tract of land of near 5,000,000 acres. No sooner had they removed within this tract, than white men intruded themselves among them, and committed violence on the persons of several Indians. Nor is this an Indian story;—it was so represented by the agent to Gov. *Duval*, and without the least reason for the outrage. What was done? Why, the agent said he had left a notice with a magistrate to have the offenders *warned off of the reservation in one day from the time the notice should be served.* Thus, instead of seizing at once upon the villains, and bringing them to justice, they are mildly *ordered off of the Indians' lands* in one day! What right had such depredators to any better treatment than is afforded by the tomahawk and scalping-knife? Yet we hear of no retaliation by the Indians. They had no newspapers in which to circulate accounts of *their* wrongs and sufferings;—these are the magnifying glasses of the bad white men.

At the same time, petition after petition was got up among the white inhabitants of Florida, and sent in to the president of the United States, setting forth the wrongs they were daily suffering from the Indians in various shapes, and urging an earlier removal than the former treaty specified. We do not presume but that Indians did sometimes infringe upon their white neighbors, and were often found hunting and fishing beyond the line of the treaty. This is not denied; and the affair at Hogtown in Alachua county, already mentioned, is an instance. Whether these petitions began to flow in before Gen. *Jackson* was president, we are not informed; but if they did, President *Adams* knew what to do with them. Be that as it may, the late president had not been long in the chair of state, when he made known his willingness that another arrangement might be made with the Indians, and appointed Col. *Gadsden* to confer with them, to see what could be done. It happened that this was the most favorable time that could have been fixed upon, namely, the spring of 1832, for such conference, because the crops of the Indians had been cut off, and they were in a state bordering upon starvation; hence they were ready to hear any propositions which promised them immediate relief. Col. *Gadsden* visited *Micanopy*, and on the 8 April had an interview with him, in which little difficulty was experienced in persuading him that his condition, as well as that of his people, would be greatly improved by a removal to the fruitful west. *Micanopy* said, however, that he would defer treating at that time, as his men were dispersed upon their yearly hunting tours, and many of them 150 or 200 miles off; but that he would collect them as soon as he could, and then they would consider the matter together, for he wished them all to hear what their father, the president, had to say to them. Accordingly the 8 May following was fixed upon for the day of council, and Paine's Landing the place of the meeting.

Agreeably to arrangement, the parties met on the 8 of May, 1832, and on the following day, a treaty was signed by such chiefs and head men as were assembled, to the number of fifteen. Of the small number of chiefs who executed this great treaty, we have before remarked, and we have also noted its chief conditions. It is said that the agent had much difficulty in bringing the Indians to any terms, touching a removal; and they finally signed only a conditional treaty, one of the chief articles of which stipulated that a deputation of some competent chiefs of their own should visit the proposed country to which they were to remove, and if, when they returned, and reported the result of their observations to the nation, it should then be thought advisable, they would remove from Florida. The chiefs sent out upon this important embassy, were seven in number, and their names were as follows: JOHN HICKS, representing SAM JONES, (Apiaca, Abica, Arpiucki, &c.); JUMPER, who afterwards fought in the bloody battle at Okeechubee Lake, in which 139 whites were killed and wounded; NEHAUTHULO, representing BLACK DIRT; HOLATA EMATHLA, COA HADJO, (Alligator); CHARLES EMATHLA, YA-HA-HADJO, (Mad Wolf); and *Abraham*, a negro, who accompanied the deputation as interpreter.

What means were taken to cause these chiefs or agents to express their entire approbation of the country they had examined, I will not undertake to say, but certain it is they did sign a writing, in which they say, "We, the undersigned, Seminole chiefs, express ourselves well satisfied with the country examined by us, and we do agree to remove as soon as government will make the necessary arrangements," &c. How much they really understood of this writing, before they signed it, is pretty clearly shown by what they themselves say to agent *Thompson*, when called upon to fulfil their engagement to remove; and from the same source it will be likewise seen how much they understood of the treaty of Moultrie Creek. All that can now be said is, that if they understood what they were signing, when they expressed their satisfaction with the country to which the nation was to remove, they entirely transcended the powers delegated to them by their countrymen.

Although it cannot be denied, that at Paine's Landing a treaty was made, which stipulated that all the Seminoles should, in three years thereafter, remove from the country, under certain conditions, yet it is well known that it was with very great difficulty that the chiefs could be persuaded to execute it, even under its expressed contingencies. On this matter, we will hear the United States commissioner, Col. *Gadsden*, who procured the treaty to be executed. In his communication to the secretary of war, he says, "There is a condition prefixed to the agreement, without assenting to which, the Florida Indians most *positively* refused to negotiate for their removal west of the Mississippi. Even with the condition annexed, there was a reluctance, (which with some difficulty was overcome,) on the part of the Indians, to bind themselves by any stipulations, before a knowledge of facts and circumstances would enable them to judge of the advantages or disadvantages of the disposition the government of the United States wished to make of them. They were finally *induced*, however, to assent to the agreement." By "agreement," does Col. *Gadsden* refer to the treaty itself, or to a separate writing, forwarded to the war office with the treaty?

We have questioned the manner by which the Indian commissioners' signatures were obtained to a certain certificate, acknowledging their satisfaction of the country west of the Mississippi. By another writing, they have been made to express approbation of, and even affection for, Maj. *Phagan*, one of the government agents who accompanied them on that journey. It shall now be shown that these papers speak a very different language from that spoken by the chiefs before their accusers, in open council, afterwards. The council here alluded to, was held at the Seminole agency, immediately after the ratification of the treaty of Paine's Landing by the United States government, viz., in October, 1834.* It was opened by Gen. *Thompson*, in whose speech we find these words: "*You alone have the right to decide whether you will accept the invitation*† *or not; it is left, as it should be, entirely optional with you, and no person but yourselves has any right to say you shall or shall not accede to the proposition.*" Thus it is evident that, although the chiefs had expressed their approbation of the country, a matter of much greater moment had been left open to negotiation. We will now hear the chiefs:—

Micanopy rose and said, "When we‡ were at Camp Moultrie, we made a treaty; and we were to be paid our annuity for twenty years. This is all I have to say."

Jumper, since so celebrated in the war, and a leader in, it is said, the massacre at Fort Mimms, next spoke: "At Camp Moultrie we were told that all difficulties should be buried for 20 years, from the date of the treaty then and

* By the usages of civilized nations, the Indians were under no obligation to abide by the treaty of Paine's Landing, for it was two years after it was concluded before congress ratified it; and all treaties *must be* ratified in a reasonable time—but any time will answer for Indians.

† The Creeks, already removed to the west, had invited the Seminoles to settle among them promiscuously; and it seems the chiefs had given encouragement that they would, when all the neighboring Indians had made peace with them. It will be necessary that this fact be borne in mind by the reader.

‡ He was among the signers of that treaty. I have omitted to mention earlier that Micanopy is grandson to the distinguished King Paine, and that his father's name was Sr Coffee.

there made. Before the 20 years were out, we made a treaty at Paine's Landing. We were told we might go and see the land, but that we were not obliged to remove. When we saw the country, we said nothing, but the whites that went with us *made us sign our hands to a paper*, which you *now say* signified our consent to remove; but we thought the paper said only that *we liked the land*, and when we returned, our nation would decide upon removal. We had no authority to do more. My people cannot say they will go. We are not willing to go. If their tongues say yes, their hearts cry no, and call them liars. The country to which you invite us is surrounded by hostile neighbors, and although it may produce good fruit, the fruit of a bad neighborhood is blood, that spoils the land, and a fire that dries up the brooks. When in the west I said to the agent, 'You say the Seminoles are *rogues*, but you wish to bring us among *worse rogues*, that we may be destroyed by them.' Did they not steal our horses, and were not some of us obliged to return with our packs upon our own backs?"

CHARLES EMATHLA was no friend to a removal at this time, but subsequently consented to go, and having, with three daughters, gone to Camp King, about the 26 November, 1835, to make arrangements for bringing in his cattle, on his return was set upon and shot down in the way, a little in advance of his daughters. Nine balls were found in him, and it is said the deed was done by *Osceola* and some others of the Mickasauky tribe.* He spoke as follows: "Our old speaker was *Hicks.*† He is dead, but I have not forgotten his words. I was not at the treaty of Moultrie Creek. It was not made by children. *Great men* made it, and it is sacred. By it we were to receive the annuity for 20 years,‡ and to enjoy the lands therein defined. The time has not expired; when it does, it is time enough to make a *new* bargain. Our father has often said to me that he loves his children—they love him. When a man is at home, and has his things about him, he sees that himself and family depend upon them. He thinks of these things when he leaves home. My young men and family are all around me. Should I go west, I should lose many on the way. A weak man cannot get there, the fatigue would be so great. None but strong people can go. I am an Indian. There is none but Indian blood in ME. *The agent*, Major Phagan, *that went with us, is a man of violent passions. He quarrelled with us on the way, and after we got there. If he had done his duty, all would have ended well.* If I know my heart, I speak true. If I differ from the agent, he is a free man, and can talk as he pleases. I hope his talk will bring all things right, so that we may all live together hereafter in friendship."

HOLATA EMATHLA said: "The horses that were stolen from us by the Cherokees, when we were viewing the country in the west, were never restored to us. We told the agent the land was good, but the people were bad. We saw them bring scalps to the garrison. We had a meeting with *M'Intosh.*§ He told us that among all their neighbors they had peace; that he and Col. *Arbuckle* were to send out to have a treaty of peace with all the Spanish Indians, and when that was done, a report of it was to be sent to Washington. I am sick. I cannot say all I want to say. I want to talk coolly, and tell the truth in all things. They promised to send word to us when peace was made with all the Indians west of the great river." It had been now about three years, and it does not appear that any news of a treaty had reached the Seminoles; therefore could it be expected they should be

* Here is a slight discrepancy between this and our former relation, (p. 72,) occasioned by a comparison of *Cohen* and *Williams*. It will also be observed, that from the several printed versions of the speeches of the chiefs on this occasion, I have drawn these.

† He was a signer of the treaty of Camp Moultrie, and is said to have been destroyed by the machinations of Jumper in 1825; and that although *Micanopy* was considered the chief of chiefs, yet *Hicks* was much the greatest man. *Hext* he is sometimes called, and to the treaty of Moultrie his name is written *Tokose Mathla*.

‡ Mr. Williams had probably not read that treaty, as he intimates that it stipulated that the Indians were to *remove* at the end of 20 years. The treaty says nothing about a removal, (only on to their 5,000,000 acres,) but stipulates that an *annuity* shall be paid them for 20 years.

§ *Chilly M'Intosh*, son of Gen. *W. M'Intosh*, executed for treason by his own people. See p. 54 of this book.

willing to go before peace was established? This consideration alone was enough to have caused a delay on the part of the government.

The agent had opened the conference with mild language, but he now waxed wroth, and said many hard things to the chiefs; accused one of lying and another of duplicity, and closed by threatenings. Still the chiefs discovered but little irritation, and signified only that they should remain firm in their resolution. In one of the speeches which *Charles Emathla* made at this council, there occurs this passage: "The agent told us yesterday we did not talk to the point. I have nothing to say different from what I have said. At Paine's Landing *the whites forced us into the treaty*. I was there. I agreed to go west, and did go. I went in a vessel, and it made me sick. The Indians and the whites have shed no blood. They stole things from each other They agreed at Paine's Landing, that if blood should be seen in the path, to think it was because a person had snagged his foot."

The policy adopted by the general government of a removal of the Indians is most unquestionably the worst, both for the whites as well as the Indians, that could have been devised. It is next to a system of deliberate murder. To cast one strange tribe upon another is but to put weapons into their hands, and in the language of *Tecumseh*, "to cry stuboy." Their pensions and other effects draw among them from the whites the vilest of knaves, many of whom are obliged to fly their own country for crimes of the darkest hue. It matters not, say many, so long as it is out of our sight and hearing. Is this the manner a parent should treat his children?—Send them forth into the world before they have been instructed in correct principles, and thus abandon them to the haunts of criminals and vile seducers? Had not the authors of this policy foresight enough to discern, that in a very few years tribes so removed would be again surrounded by their own people? That the cry would again and again be raised against their vicinity—that in the very nature of the case there *could* be no other result, so long as a solitary Indian remained on the continent? To write essays in proof of this result is the same as to write an elaborate treatise in the winter to prove that summer would return. How much better would it have been to have let them remain in their own country, where it were easy to protect them, easy to provide against their contamination, by keeping out unprincipled people from among them! how much easier they could have been instructed! how much easier that author of all iniquity, (spirituous liquors,) had been kept from among them! But what are we to expect from a government, when the heads who compose it think nothing of so much importance as the means by which they shall retain their places, and serve those looking to them for rewards for their servile machinations, who have contributed largest to place them there? Washington, Jefferson, Adams, the elder and younger—to their eternal honor be it remembered—advocated no such policy. How can it be but that the Indians on our borders should be bad? It is true with regard to a numerous class of them, but not to the extent that many honest people suppose, who have never dwelt on a border. As a fair illustration of this fact, I will give in the testimony of a gentleman from New England, with whom I met dwelling upon an Indian border, and in the midst of both Indians and whites. I first questioned him with respect to the general character and conduct of the white inhabitants. His answers were just what I supposed they would be. I inquired first about the whites, that he might not think me particularly friendly to the Indians. But when I inquired concerning the latter, his answer was, "They are the only *civil* people here."

The complaints of the white man are carried, as it were, "on the wings of the wind," while that of the poor Indian is drowned in the tempest. A clamor is raised on a frontier, and commissioners are despatched to buy the Indian's lands. He is bewildered with the parade, ostentation, and false show of greatness displayed before him. He puts confidence in what the agents of government tell him, and accedes to their wishes. Still he occupies his country—but very soon learns *that it is not his*,—that he has sold it,—and must now leave it forever! He then, for the first time, begins to realize what he has done. He sees, too late, that he *has done what he had no intention of doing*

It is certainly true that the people of Georgia, South Carolina, and Alabama, expressed great satisfaction at the anticipated relief to be realized when the Indians should be sent from their borders beyond the Mississippi. But are not these very Indians set down in the immediate vicinity of other white people? Whence then comes the benefit to the Indians: and whence the benefits to the whites, too, in the end? Look at the case any way, and I see no point of utility gained to either party. But there is a consideration about which I have heard very little said. It is the consideration that the frontier states and territories have but few votes in a presidential election, while those from which the Indians are removed have many. Now how much this adds to the *justice* of removing Indians I leave my readers to judge. Is it not preposterous in the highest degree to relieve a thousand individuals in Georgia by taking away the Indians from among them, and setting them down in Arkansas, where they can be in the way of but a hundred people? Thus because one state can make more noise than another, its clamors must be hushed at the expense of the other. But cries of distress have already reached the ears of the distant north, from the south-east border, and it requires no prophet to see, that the time is not far distant when these cries will be redoubled, and demand as much from the government, and with as much authority as has already been done by Georgia, South Carolina, Mississippi, or Alabama.

The general government has anticipated a state of things upon the border, which might require no inconsiderable military force to restrain; and hence the late attempt to provide a standing army. And some have shrewdly said, that, as its officers would all be appointed by the president of the United States, and officers and men to be voters too, he had attempted to seize another leading-string of power to continue him in office, or to elect such successor as he should designate, "to follow in his footsteps." However this may be, we decline any opinion on the matter, further than to observe, that a much less army, in all probability, would have protected the Indians in their own country, than will now be required to protect the white inhabitants in the country to which they have been driven.

If, in 1824, there was great fear among the inhabitants of the south-western frontier, from the increased number of Indians forced into their vicinity, what must *now* be their fears, with some 30,000 since turned loose there? Early in 1824, great alarm spread along that region; offence had been given by the whites, and they were for a while in constant agitation, expecting revenge. They said there were not more than 3,000 troops stationed to defend and keep order over nearly 5,000 miles, and to keep in check upwards of 20,000 Indian warriors. If there was need of a standing army in 1824, surely Mr. VAN BUREN ought to have recommended one in 1839.

It is no less absurd than ridiculous, to entertain the idea that we can remove the Indians out of the way of the whites; every citizen who knows any thing of the character and habits of the kind of people hanging upon all Indian borders, will tell us without a moment's hesitation, that numbers of this class will be found in the country in advance of the removing Indians, as completely equipped for defrauding them, as before their departure. We cannot run away from this class of hungry pioneers, for the very good reason that we cannot get beyond them. They know where the emigrants are to be located, a long time before they set out, and any law made to bear on such intruders, is none other than a by-word and a jest with them. They are as familiar with the woods as we are with our closets; and the further we go with the Indians, with proportionate impunity will they set our laws at defiance.*

We have already premised some facts for consideration, touching the number of Indian chiefs† in Florida, who executed the treaties for their people, and those found in arms after the war had begun. We will now ask a moment's attention to a further consideration of this matter. In the year 1821, the agent in Florida made a return to government of such villages or settle-

* See Hon. Mr. *Vinton's* speech, H. R. 1828.

† When the previous part of this fourth book was written, I was not correctly informed relative to the chiefs' standing in regard to one another, and hence a slight discrepancy between the facts before detailed, and the same now under consideration.

ments of Seminoles, as were known to him. This number was THIRTY-FIVE. Of the statistics of some of these towns the agent knew very little; and there were doubtless many others of which he knew nothing. The Mikasaukies he reckoned at 1,000 souls; and concerning several other tribes, he says they contained "a great many souls." Now it is in no wise probable but that one half of these tribes had at least two chiefs or head men, and this would give to the whole nation FIFTY-TWO chiefs. Was it not necessary that a chief from each tribe should have been a party to all treaties, either in his own proper person, or by another duly by him authorized? This same agent reckoned there were 5,000 souls in all. Compare these facts with the well-known one, that only *fifteen* chiefs and sub-chiefs signed the treaty of removal, which is that of Paine's Landing. Not half of the nation could have been represented. If any would dispute this, with the array of evidence now adduced, I will pronounce him wilfully blind, and incapable of reasoning. Look at the treaty of Moultrie Creek; there are the names of more than double the number attached, than were obtained to that of Paine's Landing; and one of the best Seminole chiefs has said, "*The whites forced us into the treaty.*" It is not *very* strange that there were but 15 chiefs at this treaty, or that signed it, for there had been but one month's notice given that any such treaty was on foot.

We shall now show that when a full council of the chiefs was together, nothing like a general consent to a removal could be obtained from them. In March, 1835, when preparations for removal began to be strongly urged by Gen. *Thompson*, at the solicitation of *Jumper*, he gave them until the 22 April, to meet him in council, when he would hear what they had to say touching the matter. At the time appointed, "several hundreds of the chiefs and warriors had assembled," and a talk was read to them from Gen. *Jackson*, enforced and illustrated by the agent and Gen. *Clinch*, all of which amounted to no more than this, "Go you *must*, and go you *shall*, without further delay." Some of the chiefs were in favor of a compliance; but the principal ones were firm in their opposition, and expressed themselves accordingly. These were *Micanopy*, *Jumper*, *Holata Mico*, *Coa Hadjo*. and *Arpiucki*. However, a writing was drawn up, and signed by 16 other chiefs and sub-chiefs, expressive of their willingness to abide by previous treaties, and their wish to remove. This was signed on the 23 April, 1835. It was through the influence of a very influential chief (whose name was *Fucta Lusta Hajo*, or Black-dirt) of the removal party, that this last treaty was made. No sooner had it been effected, than Gen. *Thompson* (acting by precedent, of course) decreed that the five opposing chiefs should no longer be considered or obeyed as chiefs. When this high-handed act had been reported to Gen. *Cass*, secretary at war, he reprobated the proceeding in very strong terms, from reasons too obvious to require detail in this place.

It still remains a question with us, whether an accommodation might not have been brought about, if the officers of government had not persisted too strongly in *their* determination that the Seminoles should settle with the Creeks; but the cry of retrenchment and reform was up, and it was easy to begin with the Indians. It would cost the government much less if they could be included with the Creeks,—a most absurd and blind policy!—The Seminoles were now a great nation. Were they to be lost and absorbed in another? The very idea was revolting to them.

Matters remained in this unsettled state for several months. At length it seems that the principal chiefs, to the number of 25, assembled at the agency on the 19 August, to try once more what could be done by negotiation. *Holata Emathla* was chosen speaker for the Indians, and he delivered himself as follows:—

"My friends, we have come to see you to talk with you on a subject of great importance to us. Hear us, and tell our great father what his children say. We made a treaty at Paine's Landing, by which we agreed to go west of the Mississippi: we were told to send some of our principal chiefs to view the place to which we were to remove. We did so; they found the country good. While there, our chiefs had a talk with Gen. *Stokes* and the commissioners; they were told that the Seminoles and Creeks were of the same family; were to be considered as the same nation, and placed under the same agent. They answered, that the Seminoles were a large nation, and should have their own agent, as before; that if our father, the president, would give us our own agent, our own blacksmith, and our ploughs, we would go; *but if he did not, we should be unwilling to remove;* that we should be among strangers; they might be friendly, or they might be hostile, and we wanted our own agent, whom we knew would be our friend, who would take care of us, would do justice to, and see justice done us by others. They told us our requests were reasonable, and they would do all they could to induce the president to grant them. We have been unfortunate in the agents our father has sent us. Gen. *Thompson*, our present agent, is the friend of the Seminoles. We thought at first that he would be like the others; but we know better now. He has but one talk, and what he tells us is truth. We want him to go with us. He told us he could not go, but he at last agreed to do so, if our great father will permit him. We know our father loves his red children, and won't let them suffer for want of a good agent. This is our talk, which we want you to send to our father, the president, hoping we may receive an early answer."

This talk was despatched to Washington, and that there may be no grounds to question the truth of its contents, I will subjoin an extract from a paper by Gen. *Clinch*, which was transmitted with it. The general says, "In forwarding you the enclosed document, I beg leave to make a few remarks. Although the subject to which it relates is itself of no great importance, yet it may have an important bearing on the present quiet and future happiness of these children of the forest. They are, from peculiar circumstances and long habit, suspicious of the white man. It is hard to induce them to believe that all the efforts and operations of government are intended for their own good. *The question of a separate agency was again and again brought forward by the chiefs, last winter and spring, and appeared to be considered by them of the first importance to their future interests, prosperity, and happiness.*"

Notwithstanding the pathetic appeal of the Indians, and the kind intimations of Gen. *Clinch*, the president would give them no hearing, and they were informed that he was "*very angry*" to think they should have so much presumption.

Meanwhile, some circumstances of a very aggravating nature had taken place. Three poor Mikasaukies, from Long Swamp, were seized by a planter, and tied with a rope by their hands and feet, and confined in his barn, without sustenance, till they were nearly dead. They, or some other Indians, had been accused of purloining from his plantation some of the necessaries of life; the drought of the preceding season having ruined their crops, they were reduced to extreme want. The friends of the three Indians became alarmed from their long absence, and the chief of the village to which they belonged, sought them out and demanded them. The inhuman wretch would not release them. The chief then repaired to his village, and taking several of his men with him, demanded them again, but was again refused. They were in hearing of the distressed cries of their friends, and obeying the promptings of a generous nature, proceeded to the barn, and liberated them by force. They were in a pitiful condition, could neither stand or go; the ropes with which they were tied, had cut through the flesh to the very bones! When their friends were carrying them away, they were fired upon by the owner of the place, and one was wounded. They retaliated only by burning his barn, not suffering him to remove any thing out of it; and whoever knows the circumstances, will only wonder that he had not been confined in, and consumed with it.

CHAPTER XVIII.

CARRYING THE EVENTS OF THE WAR TO THE CLOSE OF THE YEAR 1836

*Review of early difficulties—The Hogtown murder—The insult to Osceola—*MICANOPY*—*KING PAYNE*—Gen. Clinch's expedition—Gen. Scott attacked—Massacre at Char* *lotte Harbor—Fort Micanopy besieged—Death of officers—Lighthouse affair—* BATTLE OF WELIKA—*Creeks and Cherokee affairs—Indians surprised—Murders* —BATTLE OF SAN FELASCO—*Col. Lane's Expedition—His melancholy death—Gov. Call in command*—BATTLES OF THE WAHOO SWAMP—*Gen. Jesup resumes command—His expedition to the Wahoo.*

THE murder of Hogtown, to which we have before alluded, was a serious crisis. It very much hastened hostilities, from the outrageous nature of the case. The additional facts to those we have already given are these. There were eight Indians belonging to the party, and in their wanderings they had killed a cow which did not belong to them, near Deamond's Pond. A part of them, on the 19th of June, being encamped at a sink-hole where there was water, about 3 miles from Kenapaha Pond, are fallen upon by a gang of whites, seven in number, who seized as many of the guns belonging to the Indians as they were able, and then commenced whipping them. Two of the Indians had gone out upon a hunt, and returned while this business was in progress. They made a shot upon the whites, wounding one of them, and in their turn they fired upon the two Indians, killing one, named *Fuxe*, and mortally wounding the other, named *Lechotichee*. Here the rencontre seems to have ended.

A great cry was now raised along the Indian border, and the surviving Indians, who had *done all of this mischief*, were demanded of the chiefs by the agent. They were readily surrendered, the whole surviving six, and thrown into prison, where they remained over thirty days, while their accusers were left at perfect liberty to commit other outrages, and to make preparations for convicting the Indians at the trial which was supposed to await them; but it does not appear that any trial ever took place, and my informant says, that the balance of proof was so much against the whites that they were glad to "dodge the question;" and hence we suppose the Indians were set at liberty. But could any rational man suppose that an outrage of such a flagitious character would pass without retaliation? It followed, but not immediately. On the 11 August, a private, named *Dalton*, carrying the mail between Fort Brook and Fort King, was met on his route and killed. Some seized his horse by the reins, while others dragged him off and shot him. When found, his body bore evidence of savage vengeance, being nearly torn in pieces. The party committing this act are immediately demanded by Gen. *Clinch*, and the chiefs promised they should be surrendered, probably without any intention of so doing. They were Mikasaukies, and having fled among the Redsticks of the Ouithlacooche, could not be found. If the Indians did not avow this murder to be in revenge for that of *Fuxe* and *Lechotichee*, it was known to be so.

The Indians were now, if possible, treated with greater contumely than before, and *Osceola*, about this time, went to the agent to complain of some ruthless villain who had been guilty of grossly illtreating some of his people. It so happened that some white person had, only the preceding day, made a similar complaint against the Indians; which complaints were, it is said, occasioned by the affair at Hogtown. The general therefore, having prejudged the case, as good as told *Osceola* he lied, and that it was his men who were guilty of outrage. An altercation ensued, and this was the time, we are told, that this chief was seized, manacled, and placed in the guard-house of the garrison; the circumstances of which have already been related, agreeably to the then existing information.

We now pass to the events of the war, taking up the subject where it had been suspended in the summer of 1836.

One of the divisions of the army under Gen. Clinch marched from Tampa for Fort Drane on the 14th of April, 1836. After a march of three days, they came within four miles of Fort Cooper, where Major Cooper had been left with his Georgia battalion. Having encamped, Gen. Clinch detached his two mounted companies under Capt. Malone of the Washington corps, with wagons, to Major Cooper, and instructions to join him. When this detachment had proceeded about two or three miles, it was fired upon by Indians concealed in a hommock near the road, and Mr. Howard and Cornet Dunsan of the Washington troops were wounded; the former with three shot, and the latter with one in the leg. Both probably recovered. Capt. Malone immediately sent to Gen. Clinch for a reënforcement, on the arrival of which no Indians were to be found. The detachment then proceeded to Fort Cooper, which had been attacked for 13 days together, but with a loss only of one man, Mr. *Zarock Cook*, of the Morgan Guards.

At the same time Gen. Clinch marched from Tampa, Col. Lindsay left also upon a scout, and while crossing the Hillsborough River, the Indians fired upon him, killing Mr. James Branham of the Alabama volunteers. Gen. Clinch made but a short stay at Fort Cooper, when he returned to Fort King, where he arrived on the 25th; having had one man wounded, a Mr. Bostick of the Jefferson troop. At the same time Col. Goodwin burns a large Indian town on Peas Creek; and only two days after, a company of Indians attack Fort Drane, make prisoners of several negroes, and carry off a number of horses.

Scarcely a day passed at this period without some tale of blood. Gen. Scott, on his march near Ocklawaha, is attacked in his camp on the 22d of April, and two of his men are wounded. Two days after, the general surprises a party of Indians about 23 miles from Volusia, but they all escape, leaving, however, their horses and packs to the victors.

At Charlotte Harbor, on the 28th of April, the Indians make thorough work, killing Dr. Creus, the collector of that port, "and all the people residing there." They next appear with great boldness before St. Marks, but retire without doing any other damage than frightening the people. About the middle of May depredations were committed within two miles of Mandarin, on the St. John's. They killed and scalped a Mr. Motte, a highly respectable gentleman from New York, and burnt his house and other buildings.

On the 7th of June the Indians burn the extensive sugar-works belonging to Gen. Clinch, together with 70 hogsheads of sugar, and a great amount of other property; and at the same time they burn also the sugar-house of Col. M'Intosh, of Oakland. The next day about 150 warriors invest Fort Micanopy, in which was Major Heillman and 70 or 80 men. After some preparations, a sortie was made, and the Indians dispersed. The whites had five men wounded and one killed Major Heillman had been an active and valuable officer, but his term of service expired with his death, which took place at Micanopy on the 27th of the same month; and but a few days before, (June 15th,) Lieut. Wheelock had put an end to his own existence with his rifle. His duties had been so arduous that he was overcome by an aberration of mind, in which condition he committed the fatal act.

On the 23d of July the Seminoles attack and burn the lighthouse on Cape Florida; the keeper, a Mr. J. W. B. Thompson, is most surprisingly delivered from death, though not till he had been forced to drink deep of the cup of its agonies.* On the 1st of August the express rider is cut off between Newnansville and Micanopy.

Some time in June, the unhealthiness of Fort Drane having been represented to Gov. Call, an order was given for its evacuation. About the 18th of July, a train of 22 wagons left that place, with stores and munitions for Fort Defiance, Micanopy, at 8 o'clock in the morning, escorted by 26 dragoons, under Capt. Ashby, and 36 artillerists, detailed from different companies; in all 62 men. They had a five and a half inch howitzer, under the charge of Lieut. Whitly. On the arrival of the train at Welika Pond, within a mile of its destination, as usual, the first notice of Indians was from a salute from their rifles, by which one man was mortally wounded. The place whence the discharge proceeded was scoured, but the Indians had gone. The force moved on, and at about a quarter of a mile from Micanopy, as it was passing a long hommock, a tremendous fire was poured upon the whole column from 250 Indians, as was supposed; their line extending a quarter of a mile. Soon after Capt. Ashby was severely wounded, but continued in action until compelled to retire from loss of blood. The firing brought out to their relief two companies from Micanopy, 31 strong, under Lieuts. Talcott and Temple, who rendered very important service. The Indians stood their ground until dislodged by a charge, which was not until the fight had been considerably pro-

* I have published Mr. Thompson's narrative of the affair in my Collection of Indian Narratives—a very proper appendix to this work.

tracted. Of the whites 11 were killed and wounded; of the ndians' loss no account was obtained.

On the morning of the 8th of August fell Major Williams, near St. Arthur's Bridge, on his way from Black Creek to Nonardsville. There were 200 Indians, it is said, who did this single act, and although Mr. Williams had a son-in-law with him, he was suffered to escape; they were so elated that they had killed the man who struck the first blow in this wretched war, that they thought of no further retaliation at that time. The reader will, doubtless, readily remember the 19th of June, 1835, and the parallel case of Capt. Chubb.

It is a relief, in pursuing general history, to be able to meet with some thing besides scenes of blood, but in particular history we are confined to the course of events, which when they lead us to nothing but the most dreaded scenes, we have no choice; we do not make events, only record them. For a moment our attention will be drawn to the Creek and Cherokee countries.

Much was said about the more northern Indians going down into Florida and joining the Seminoles, and it was even said that the Seminoles had sent a messenger to the shores of the great lakes with invitations to the Indians in those regions to join them. It may be true. We are told that Gen. Gaines did not disbelieve it, but we have never heard that any came down from thence. The Creeks were adjacent, and it was easy for them to effect such a junction. Accordingly, on the 5th of July, a considerable body of them was discovered making their way towards Florida, which the people of Stewart county, Georgia, endeavored to prevent. They followed them about three days, and had about as many skirmishes with them. The final result was, each party was glad to be rid of the other. One of the whites was wounded, and three Indians were said to have been killed; the former being satisfied to display the remainder of their courage on paper.

On the 16th of July, 2,400 Cherokees were shipped at Montgomery, Alabama, for the Arkansas. In such a vast assemblage of people, forced from the land of their fathers, it would be very strange if there were not some who should show an unwillingness to go. How such unwillingness had been manifested we are not informed, but at this time "some 12 or 15" men were "shackled with heavy irons to prevent their rising." One of them was determined not to submit to such felonious indignity, and, wrenching himself from the grasp of his tormentors, seizes a club, and knocking down one with a blow on the head, gives the war-whoop and attempts an escape. Alas! his struggle is fraught with certain death; he is shot down, and instantly expires. Another is pierced with a bayonet, for what no mention is made; he dies in a few hours after. On the evening of the same day three had escaped from those who guarded them. Soon after one was retaken, brought in in a cart, and as he was thus conveyed along the streets, he cut his own throat, and expired without a groan! To such deeds of desperation does this work of expulsion lead.

About the 2d of August, a small party of Indians struck a small settlement on the Oscilla River, which flows into Appalachee Bay, and about 40 miles from Tallahassee, killed two men, took a boy, and burnt a house. Collecting what spoil they could, they decamped; but being immediately followed by Capt. Fisher's company, they abandoned the boy and plunder, and secured themselves in a hommock, and the whites marched back victorious.

On the 16th of this month, Major Pierce, with 110 men, marched from Gary's Ferry to attack a body of Indians, who, he had learned, were in possession of Fort Drane. He was fortunate enough to come upon them undiscovered, but such was the alertness of the Indians, that they escaped with small loss; 4 or 5, being badly wounded, fell into the hands of the whites, who, to add lustre to their exploit, barbarously put some of them to death. Osceola was there, and to his sagacity we may impute the small success of his enemies.

On the 15th of September we meet with a melancholy account of depredations. At 10 o'clock in the morning of this day, a Mr. Higginbotham arrived at Jacksonville from his late residence at Cedar Swamp, a distance of 7 miles, without a hat and almost exhausted. His house had been attacked at daybreak by a party of Indians. He had two men and nine guns, with which before he left they had been able to silence the Indians. A number of citizens immediately volunteered, and marched for the scene of action, under Major Hart. They found Mr. Higginbotham's family safe, and firing having been heard the night before in the direction of a Mr. M'Cormick's, they proceeded there, and found it had been burnt down; and its ruins were yet smoking. Among them they found the remains of a human being. This was 18 miles from Jacksonville. Thence following the Indians' trail, they came to the house of Mr. Lowder, 7 miles farther. It was abandoned by its owners but very recently, as fire was still burning in the kitchen. Here the Indians had done no mischief. Proceeding thence, the detachment, in four miles, came to Mr. Sparkman's, where a tragedy was opened to their view. They found Mrs. Johns, who had lived in Mr. M'Cormick's house, her scalp taken off, and dreadfully wounded with two bullets; yet she was alive, and able to communicate the particulars of the horrid tragedy through which she had passed. She and her husband were about 20 yards from their own door when they discovered the Indians emerging from the corner of a fence close by them. They ran for the house, entered it, and closed the door; at the same moment the Indians fired on the house, and shortly after they hailed them in English, and told them if they would come out they should not be hurt. They not choosing to trust them, the Indians next looked through between the logs of the house, and ordered them, in a peremptory manner, to come out, but they still refused, and begged for their lives. The Indians then charged the house, burst open the door, shot Mr. Johns through the head, and Mrs. Johns as before related; he fell dead, and she fell upon his body. An Indian then seized her, and dragged her out of the house, and soon after dragged her in again; and after tearing the band and comb from her hair, applying his scalping-knife to her head, and fire to her garments, left her; and to make a more sure mark of his vengeance, he next set fire to the house, and then they all drew off. They carried away a portmanteau containing 100 dollars, and every thing else they thought of any value. As soon as they were out of hearing, the wretched woman raised herself up and crept from the burning building; saw the body of her husband lying unscalped. She fainted and fell, again and again, but finally reached the edge of a swamp not far distant, where she got some water, and lay down with hopes no greater than her strength. In this situation she was found by the scout above mentioned, and eventually recovered.

On the morning of the 17 September, a party of about 100 Indians came within a mile of Fort Gilleland, on the Picolata road, took a cart from some teamsters, and carried it off a piece, then set it on fire. Col. John Warren sallied out from the fort with 150 men, in the direction of San Felasco hommock, where he had reason to believe the Indians were posted. One hundred of his men were mounted, and of his number was a company of artillery, with a 24 pound howitzer. He could meet with none of the Indians that day. Early the next morning he sent out spies; but they soon returned with no intelligence of the enemy; yet so well convinced was he that the Indians were at Felasco, that he divided his men into three columns, and marched on in order of battle. When they came within about three quarters of a mile of the hommock, they found the Indians in their own peculiar order of battle; and they rose up and poured upon the whites a sharp though not a destructive fire. And we have very seldom heard of so much manœuvring and fighting, without greater execution, on any former occasion. The battle having lasted an hour and a half, but one of the whites was killed, and four or five wounded; the Indians lost none that their enemy were certain of, though they report that they saw a great many fall. In the first of the onset the Indians made an attempt to turn the left flank of the Americans, "but were charged on with spirit and success by Lieut. Col. Mills's command, and driven into a thick oak scrub, who then dismounting and charging on them, drove through this into the border of the hommock, when the artillery played upon them with considerable effect; after this they retired to the right, and attempted to turn that wing, but a charge from Capt. Walker and Lieut. Bruten's command drove them within the range of the artillery again, which opened upon them with great effect." They made several desperate attempts to maintain their position, and charged twice on the artillery, but were beaten off at all points, and began a retreat. They were pursued a mile and a half into a dense hommock, and then abandoned. Thus ended the battle of San Felasco Hommock, as it was called. The Indians were reckoned at 300 men. Several of the officers under Col. Warren were highly commended for their bravery and good conduct, in his official account of the battle; especially Adj. Gilleland, Capt. D. D. Tompkins of the artillery, Capts. Beekman, Walker, and Ward, Lieuts. Bruten and Hindly.

About this time, the distinguished Creek chiefs, Paddy Carr and Jim Boy, arrive in Florida, with 950 of their warriors, to assist in subduing the Seminoles.

On or before the 28 September, about 50 Indians, supposed to be Creeks, attacked a house, near Orange Pond, and killed a Mr. Uptegrove and his wife. She at first escaped from the house, but they pursued her, overtook and killed her. A Mr. Hunter, living in the same house, escaped to a pond, and by burying himself almost entirely in water for 24 hours, they supposed him to be drowned; by which artifice he preserved his life.

The next day, namely, September 29th, Col. Lane landed at Tampa, with a force of whites and friendly Indians, from Apalachicola. Hearing that the Indians were committing depredations in the neighborhood, he marched immediately, with 12 mounted men and 100 Indians, to beat up their quarters. A rapid march of 12 miles brought them to Indian River, where they discovered the enemy on the opposite side. The friendly Creeks had not come up, and though there were near 200 Indians to oppose them, yet they engaged them, and for 15 minutes the skirmish was sharp and obstinate. The Creeks, under Maj. Watson, now arrived, and the Seminoles began to relax; they, however, maintained their order for a mile and a half, when they separated and fled in every direction, and night ended the pursuit. This battle was on the 30 of September, after which the colonel returned with his command to Tampa. An act of self-devotedness occurred in this fight, not of a very common character on record: A Mr. Kelly was standing near Col. Lane, when he observed an Indian taking deliberate aim at him; having just discharged his own gun, he saw no chance of saving the life of his commander, but by receiving the ball himself, which he did by instantly throwing himself between him and the Indian. Kelly received the ball and fell; happily he was not mortally wounded.

On the 10 of October, Col. Lane set out on another expedition from Tampa, and, on the 14th, after a march of 50 or 60 miles, he came in full view of Oloklikana, or Spotted Lake, which stretched off to the north as far as the eye could reach, dotted here and there with beautifully-wooded islands. Here they fell upon a fresh trail, and soon after a village, but it was abandoned. In another direction their trail led them to a ford, 200 yards over, which they passed by wading and swimming,—having left their horses behind,—beyond which they came to extensive cornfields, some cattle and ponies, and a village; but no Indians yet. Passing the village, the trail led to a marsh, near a mile in extent, covered with soft mud and water; but it was no barrier to the Creeks, and they dashed into it at once, and were followed by the whites. They were often waist high in mud, from which having extricated themselves, found they had reached a fine island, and the trail still continuing southerly. Here were a village, domestic animals and utensils, and the scalps of several white people. Not far from hence they came to another village, which, with the former, contained above a hundred houses. Another half mile brought them to the shore of a pond, skirted with a thick scrub, of near three fourths of a mile in extent. Here the Seminoles had made a stand, and began the attack by a volley of rifle-balls. A fight, now begun, was kept up for about half an hour, when a charge from the Creeks put them to flight, and they were soon covered by a hommock, and were followed no farther. But one of the whites was wounded, and whether any of the Creeks were killed or wounded, we are not told by their white associates. Of the loss of the enemy, they of course knew nothing, which no doubt amounted to the same. The whites destroyed about a hundred cattle and hogs, and they returned to Fort Drane, with about 400 more, on the 19th.

With this expedition terminated the career of an active and valuable officer. Col. Lane complained some of a brain fever, and being left alone in the tent of Capt. Goff for a few minutes, was found by him, on his return, expiring on his own sword. It was supposed he had fallen on it accidentally, in a fit of dizziness; or that in a moment of intellectual aberration, arising from the nature of his illness, he had been his own executioner. This occurred on the 26th, and cast a deep gloom over the whole army.

A few days previous to this, Gov. Call wrote to the secretary of war, informing him that he had taken the general command in Florida, and that Gen. Jesup had, "with great magnanimity," declined it; but that he had proposed to serve under him as a volunteer Some entertained high expectations at the present prospect, and others expressed no favorable opinion of the result of Gov. Call's assumption. Both were common gratuities; and it would have been singular, indeed, if neither had eventuated in favor of the prophet.

On the 28th, Gov. Call commenced active operations. He marched from the Suanee, at Old Town, with 1,375 men, in high hopes of speedily putting an end to the war. The route to Fort Drane was taken, on which seven Indians were killed. Whether they were warriors, old men, women, or children, no mention is made. They reached Fort Drane, October 1st, where the fires of the Indians were still burning. Had it not been for a faithful spy, OSCEOLA and his Mikasaukies would have fallen into Gov. Call's hands. Here he waited until the evening of the 6th, to be joined by Maj. Pierce, who was to supply him with provisions; which he effected with no ordinary efforts, having marched 66 miles in two days, viz., from Black Creek.

With a supply of 8 days' rations, a move was made for the "Cove of the Ouithlacoochee." On the way they fell in with an encampment of Mikasaukies, "killed 13 men, who did not fire a shot, took 4 women prisoners, and 8 children." From these they learned that the Negro Town was but 3 miles above them. Col. Gill was despatched thence with 300 Tennessee volunteers, on the morning of the 13th, but could not reach the town from the depth of water in the creek before it. He accordingly returned with loss having had 3 men killed, and 7 wounded. Among the former was *Indian Billy*, an interpreter, in much esteem by the whites. He was brother-in-law of CHARLES EMATHLA, of whose tragic death we have before given an account.

The main body marched to the river, which was so overflowed that its width was 250 yards, and could not be crossed. The Indians appeared on the opposite bank, and fired upon them, wounding Maj. Gordon, though slightly. Here the expedition was at an end; the army being obliged to retreat to Fort Drane for supplies. At Gen. Gaines's battle-ground they fell in with Col. Lane, as he was returning from his expedition, just recorded.

Little seems to have been done, or attempted, after this, until about the middle of November. On the 11th of that month, the army, consisting of 2,100 men, marched once more from Fort Drane for the Ouithlacoochee. At this time the river was 220 yards wide; yet it was passed on the 13th, though at great peril, four of the regulars being drowned in the way. The army had now arrived at the "Cove," where Indians were expected to be found; but none were visible, and it appeared that the place had been some time abandoned; yet trails were discovered, leading into Ochlawaha and the Wahoo Swamp. The left division, under Gen. Armstrong, met with no opposition in crossing the creek to the Negro Town. It was crossed by Col. Trawsdale's regiment. Instead of one town, they found two, and burnt them both. Here they found an old negro, who told them the Indians had gone to the Wahoo Swamp. He said, also, that when the Tennessee volunteers made an attempt upon the place the previous month, they killed 46 Indians. This was no doubt said to flatter their vanity, for we have no account that half that number of guns were fired at that time.

Gen. Call now made dispositions to pursue the Seminoles, with certainty of success. Col. Pierce, with 250 regulars, the Creek Indian right, and Col. Warren's mounted men, were to pass out of the Cove by the only practicable outlet in that direction, and, after exploring the country south and west of the river, to reunite with the main army, about the 19th or 20th, near Dade's battle-ground; the general, meanwhile, to march by the river in the direction of the Wahoo, with the Tennessee brigade, two companies of artillery, and the Florida foot. Both divisions marched on the 16th. On the 17th, about noon, a large party of the enemy was discovered by the main body, encamped near a hommock. Col. Bradford, with the 1st regiment of Tennessee volunteers, was immediately detached to attack them.

Although the Indians were surprised, they made good their retreat to the hommock, and waited the approach of the troops, who, when dismounting, received the fire of the enemy. They immediately returned it; but the Indians stood their ground until a charge was made, which, as usual, put them to flight. They left 20 of their dead, and all their baggage, on the ground; and, from traces of blood, a far greater number were supposed to have been carried off. The number of Indians engaged were said to amount to about 200. The whites had two killed, and 10 or 12 wounded, which, after being taken care of, the army retreated four miles to a favorable site, and encamped.

On the 18th, the general, having left his baggage-train under a strong guard, marched again, with 550 Tennesseeans, chiefly foot, to the Wahoo Swamp. At about 3 miles from their camp, they fell upon a large Indian trail, which led through two dense hommocks, and over two creeks, into a large field, surrounded on three sides by hommocks. The enemy were retreating to gain securer positions whence to begin the attack, leaving their houses in flames; at length, making a stand, the whites immediately formed their line of attack. The foot, under Col. Trawsdale, were formed in open order to charge into the hommock, while the horsemen, to the right and left, were thrown back to protect the flank, and to act as a corps of reserve. The columns had not received the word to advance, when a tremendous fire was opened upon them, along their whole front, from a hommock. They began slowly to advance, exchanging shots at short intervals. The order being given to charge, it was obeyed with impetuosity; but the Indians did not break and fly as in times past; they stood and fought hand to hand, exchanging life for life,—while at the same time their wings attacked both flanks of the army, and a small body of about 50 fell boldly on its rear. The battle had raged nearly half an hour, when a general charge broke and dispersed them in every direction, leaving 25 of their number dead on the field; while the whites had but three killed and 18 wounded. 600 Seminoles were said to have been engaged in this battle. The hour being late, and the men much exhausted, the army retreated to its appointed place for the meeting of Col. Pierce, near Dade's battle-ground.

On the 21st, the army marched, in three columns, into the swamp, the Tennesseeans and regulars, and Col. Warren's mounted men on the right, the centre under Col. Pierce, and the Creek regiment on the left. When they came to the battle-ground of the 18th, they found it in possession of the Indians. As the Tennesseeans and regulars advanced, a heavy fire was opened upon them, and they did not answer it until they got into the midst of the Indians; then charging them, they gave way and retreated.

As soon as the direction of their retreat was observed by a party in reserve, Col. Pierce, with his division, and the Creek Indians, were ordered to pursue; and soon after, Col. Trawsdale with his regiment, and Col. Warren with the Florida horsemen, were sent to support them. Unfortunately, the greater part of the regulars and Tennesseeans, by taking a trail to the right, became involved in an almost impassable morass, where no horse could move, and where the men were obliged to wade waist-deep in mud and water. A small number of Creek warriors on the left, led by Col. Brown, taking a better path, followed closely upon the enemy, and found them strongly posted in a cypress swamp. The Creeks charged them with great spirit, and their gallant leader, Major Moniac, was killed, as also were several other Creek warriors. It was soon discovered that this party would be overpowered, and the struggle was momentarily becoming more and more desperate, when two companies of Florida militia under Capt. Groves and Lieut. Myrick, three companies of artillery under Maj. Gardner, Capts. Tompkins, Porter, and Lee, and Col. Waire with his mounted men, coming successively into action, enabled the

Creeks to maintain their ground. Still the fight was animated; and it was not until nearly all the force of the whites was brought to bear on this point, that the Indians could be dislodged. Then it would seem they retired more to give their adversary a chance to retreat, than because they were beaten themselves. Thus ended the second battle of the Wahoo Swamp, in which 25 of Gen. Call's army were killed and wounded, nine being of the former number. The Indians left 10 on the field; but the whites said they lost "50 at least."

The army having consumed all their provisions, and being very severely handled, was glad to make the best of its way out of this hostile region; it accordingly returned to its late encampment at 10 o'clock at night, and the next day marched for Volusia.

Where Gen. Jesup was, or what service he was rendering at this period, and for some time previous, I am uninformed; but, on the 24 November, he arrived at Volusia, with 400 mounted Alabama volunteers. He came late from Tampa, and on the way had taken 33 negroes, the former property of Col. Rees, of Spring Garden, whence they had been carried off by the Seminoles. Here Gen. Jesup received orders from the secretary of war, again to resume the command of the army of Florida. Gov. Call had pretty confidently asserted that, in the campaign now just concluded, he should be able to finish the war; but he had only showed the Seminoles that some of his men could fight as well as Indians, and that others could turn their backs with equal dexterity. On the whole, if the Indians had been one to a thousand against the Americans, it would be no very difficult question to settle, which would be sent beyond the Mississippi. When, in October, the Creek deputation visited them, to persuade them to submit to terms, OSCEOLA assured them with firmness, that "the Seminoles would never yield—never, he said; the land is ours; we will fight and die upon it." The Chief HARJO was at the head of the peace deputation of Creeks, and he found Osceola in a great swamp, on the Ouithlacoochee, having then with him about 3,500 people.

Notwithstanding the severe blows which Osceola had had in the Wahoo Swamp, it yet remained the Narraganset of Florida; and such were the accounts from thence, that Gen. Jesup determined to proceed there with a large force. Accordingly, with ten days' provision, he marched on the 12 of December for that point; but, on reaching it, no Indians were found. On the 17th, he marched for Tampa, taking the course of the Ouithlacoochee in his route; and Col. Foster pursued a parallel course on the other side of the same river; a single Indian was the result of all this business; yet no blame can be attached to those who performed it, for what can men do where there is nothing to be done? Something like calculation can be made in marching against men in a fort or city; but where it is known that a people remove their cities and forts as easy as themselves, quite a different calculation is required. Cæsar never fought Indians, or he would have reversed his celebrated saying, "'Tis easier to foil than find them."

CHAPTER XIX.

EVENTS OF THE WAR DURING THE YEAR 1837.

Expedition to Ahapopka—OSUCHEE *killed—Jesup parleys with the chiefs—Col. Henderson's Expedition*—BATTLE OF LAKE MONROE—*Treaty of Fort Dade—Unobserved—Osceola at Fort Mellon—Numbers of the Seminoles—Sudden abduction of emigrants—Jesup requests to be relieved from command—Western Indians applied to—Gen. Hernandez's Expedition—Capture of King Philip—Surprise of the Uchees—Surrender of chiefs—Mediation of Ross—Capture of Osceola and others—View of the affair*—WILD CAT'S *escape*—BATTLE OF OKECHOBEE.

WITH this chapter we begin the events of the year 1837. On the 22 of January, Gen. Jesup put the main body of the army in motion, with the view of attacking another strong-hold of the Indians, which he had learned was upon the head waters of the Oklawaha. The next day he detached Lieut. Col. Cawlfield with his mounted battalion of Alabama volunteers, Capt. Harris's company of marines, and Maj. Morris's Indian warriors, with his own aid, Lieut. Chambers, to attack OSUCHEE, commonly called the Chief *Cooper*, whose rendezvous was then on the borders of Ahapopka Lake. Osuchee was surprised, and, with 3 of his warriors, killed; nine women and children, and 8 negroes taken. The whites lost one Indian, who was mortally wounded. From the captured it was discovered that the main body of the Semi noles had gone southward.

Pursuit was immediately made, and, on the 24th, the army passed a rugged range of mountains, hitherto unknown to the whites, called, by the Indians, *Thlauhatkee*, or White Mountains. On the 27th, the Indians were discovered on the Hatchee-Lustee, in and about the "Great Cypress Swamp;" and a successful charge was made upon them by Lieut. Chambers, with Price's company of Alabama volunteers, by which 25 Indians and negroes, and their horses and baggage, were taken. The captured were chiefly women and children. Col. Henderson pursued the fugitive warriors into a swamp, and across the Hatchee-Lustee River, and thence into a more extensive swamp, where they could not be pursued without great difficulty and more men. Meanwhile, a messenger had been sent to the general, but he was killed in the way; and it was not till another had been sent, that he was informed how matters were progressing with Col. Henderson.

Gen. Jesup sent a prisoner to JUMPER, on the morning of the 28th, endeavoring to get a parley, while he moved on and took a position at Lake Tohopikalega, within a few miles of where it is approached by the Cypress Swamp. Here he took some hundred head of cattle. The prisoner sent out to Jumper, returned the next day, bringing favorable talks from Alligator and Abraham; and two days after, January 31st, Abraham visited the general in his camp; immediately after, he returned to the Indians, and on the 3 February, brought along with him Jumper and Alligator, with two sub-chiefs, one a nephew of Micanopy. These chiefs agreed to meet the general at Fort Dade, with other chiefs, on the 18th following. Jumper and Alligator, it is said, are among the last of the descendants of the Yamassees.

To return to Col. Henderson. On receipt of his message, Gen. Jesup ordered the disposable force of Gen. Armistead's brigade, Maj. Gorham's infantry, and Tustenugge Hajo's Indian warriors, to move on to his support. They soon captured two Indian women, and several negroes, in a pine wood, over a hundred ponies, some plunder, and several fire-arms. The main force of the Indians had fled; but not having much time in advance, were soon overtaken by Maj. Morris on the border of a considerable stream, 20 or 25 yards wide, in the midst of a swamp. The Indians were in possession of the opposite side, and when the warriors came up, they were fired upon, and a considerable skirmish ensued. The creek was difficult to ford, and the Indians had passed it by two trees felled from the opposite banks. These afforded a sure mark for the Indians' rifles, a very few of which could stand against many; but the whites and their Indian allies, being much the more numerous, were able to extend themselves up and down the stream, by which display the Indians were exposed to a cross fire, and soon began to abandon their position. The order being now given to cross the creek, Capt. Morris (major of the 1st Indian battalion) was the first to advance on the log, followed by Lieuts. Searle and Chambers, and Capt. Harris; Lieut. Lee swimming over at the same time. These officers led the van throughout this expedition, and are mentioned with high encomiums on their conduct. Having all crossed the creek, the Indians made several stands against them, but were forced to fly after a few fires. They were followed for a mile or two, and then the pursuit was given up; the detachments returning late at night to the camp of the main army. The result of this affair was the capture of 28 negroes, and Indian women and children. How many warriors were killed, no certain information could be given; but some two or three they saw, lying dead, as they marched along. Of the whites, one was killed at the passage of the creek in the swamp, and three wounded; and in the pursuit another was killed. Thus ended the affairs of one day, namely, January the 27th.

The next affair of importance, which transpired in Florida, was the battle of Lake Monroe. Brevet Col. A. C. W. Fanning had been stationed at that place, and his camp there bore the name of the lake. Early on the morning of the 8 February, 1837, about 300 Seminoles commenced firing upon Col. Fanning's camp with great spirit. Their right rested on the lake above the fort; their left on the shore below, and another line extended around their front. They were taken rather by surprise, many of whom, being new recruits, scarcely knew what they were about; but after wasting a good share of their ammunition, being bent on making a noise by some means, they were got under some sort of regular *modus operandi*, and the action became sharp. Meanwhile, Lieut. Thomas received orders to man a steamboat, lying in the lake under cover of the fort, and to serve a six-pounder, which was on board of her, upon the right of the Indians. This he was enabled to effect, and they were immediately driven from that position; but they hung upon the right and front for near three hours, before they would give up the contest. The brave Capt. Mellon was killed near the beginning of the fight, and 15 others were wounded, some mortally. PADDY CARR was here with his Creeks, and was among the foremost in all danger; and Col. Fanning gives the names of many of his officers who distinguished themselves.

Thus, only ten days before the time assigned to treat with Gen. Jesup, did the Seminoles give a demonstration of the value they set upon a peace with the whites; but, perhaps, the party which attacked Col. Fanning were unacquainted with the arrangement. However, through the mediation of the Creeks, the general got a hearing with HOLATOOCHEE, nephew of Micanopy, JUMPER, ABRAHAM, LITTLE CLOUD, and several others, at Fort Dade, on the 5 March. Micanopy sent as excuse for his non-appearance, that he was old and infirm. Jumper was inquired of respecting the time the Indians would be ready to remove, and from his answer, all the world, if they had heard it, might have known that all the Indians were after, was to gain time; for he replied, that they could not be ready till fall. The general as promptly replied, that "that was out of the question," insinuating also, that if they wished to gain time by such a manœuvre, they were mistaken. Jumper showed some indignation at being thus suspected, and after considerable other talk, the council was adjourned to the next day.

Accordingly, they met again on the 6th, with augmented numbers on the part of the Indians; among whom were representatives of Alligator, Coachochee or Wild Cat, (Philip's son,) his nephew, and Pease Creek John, and a treaty was drawn up and signed. It purported, that hostilities should from that time cease; all the Seminoles to remove immediately beyond the Mississippi; to give hostages to secure its observance; all the Indians to go immediately south of the Hillsborough; Micanopy to be one of the hostages; and, by the 10 April, all were to be ready to remove. To these articles four chiefs put their marks, with Gen. Jesup; and we shall see how they were observed.

To keep up the deception, and make sure of the promised rations, the Indians began to frequent the general's camp, as though in good earnest to fulfil the treaty. By the 26 March, there were there, or had been there, the chiefs, Yaholoochie, (Cloud,) Jumper, Abraham, and Tigertail; and the principal chiefs on the St. John's, Tuskiunia and Emathla, (Philip,) had sent word that they would emigrate if Micanopy said so, and Abiaca (Sam Jones) had been invited by Philip to go to Micanopy to arrange for a removal. Abiaca being chief of the Mikasaukies, his acquiescence was thought of no little consequence. About this time, it was reported that Yaholoochie was commander-in-chief at the battle of the Wahoo Swamp, and that Osceola had been deposed for cowardice in that action. On the 18 March, Micanopy signed a written acknowledgment of, and acquiescence in, the treaty of the 6th; and Gen. Jesup seemed quite sure the war was at an end. Nevertheless, about this time a circumstance occurred which much alarmed the Indians, and whether feigned or real, answered the same end. A report was circulated among them, that as soon as Gen. Jesup had got a sufficient number into his power, he would handcuff and ship them for Arkansas. Thus matters were retarded and moved slow. And, besides, Philip, chief of the

Tohopkolikies, had begun to show himself again, and remained in his stronghold with 400 men. This much lessened the confidence of the general, and he began to make preparations for aggressions. Murders were also almost daily committed in some direction.

However, by the 1 May, Osceola* had come in to Fort Mellon, Lake Monroe; and, by the 8th of that month, there were assembled there, and in the immediate neighborhood, not less than 3,500 men, women, and children, to whom about 1,000 rations had been issued. Many, if not all the chiefs, had liberty to come and go as they pleased, and this could not be objected to; in the first place, because they were to bring in their people, and horses and cattle, to be ready to remove; and, in the next place, had an attempt been made to detain them, all that could would have run away, and it would have been very difficult ever to have got them again. Hence, in this view of the matter,—and we can take no other of it,—a different course would have led at once to a ruin of what appeared to have been so well begun; whereas, by that adopted, there was some prospect of success. Therefore, it is plain that those who condemn Gen. Jesup for his policy, speak unadvisedly.

While the Indians were at Fort Mellon, much information was gathered from them, relative to their numbers and condition. Maj. Gardner said he was assured there were 2,500 Seminoles then able to bear arms, and Col. Harney's information confirmed that conclusion.

All things seemed to promise success to Gen. Jesup's efforts, and he became by the end of May quite confident that the war was at an end. Osceola had slept in the tent of Col. Harney, and great confidence seems to have taken the place of mutual distrust. The general felt quite assured that Osceola would be of great service in bringing in his countrymen, and before the middle of May he had lying at Tampa 24 transports to take off the Indians; but to his great astonishment, on the morning of the 2d of June, he found that nearly all of them had fled into their own wilds and fastnesses. And thus the edifice that had been so long in building had been swept away in one night. Osceola had been some time absent, and had returned with 200 Mikasaukies, and compelled such as were not willing to leave, to go off with him. Micanopy said he had agreed to emigrate, and would do so, and being told that he might choose between compliance and death, he said, "Kill me here then—kill me quickly," but he was forced upon his horse and driven off. Jumper had sold all of his horses, and was forced to march on foot.

Thus stood the affairs of Florida in the beginning of June, 1837. The Indians were sure of a truce till fall, when they would be again in a condition to fight with a better prospect of success than ever. Many of the forces of the whites had gone home, and many were quite as inefficient as though they were there also; as sickness had begun to prevail, and terror and dismay were fast spreading in every direction of that ill-fated land. The general had done every thing he could do, or that any other man in like circumstances could have done, but that did not save him from slanderous tongues; and on the 5th of the same month he wrote to the secretary of war, requesting to be relieved from the command in Florida; but his request was not granted.

An account of the state of affairs in Florida having reached Washington, the secretary of war, on the 22d of July, issued orders for enlisting the western Indians to fight the Seminoles; namely, 400 Shawanese, 200 Delawares and 100 Kikapoos, which were soon after carried into effect; and in September following, there had arrived in Florida upwards of 1,000 southern and western Indians, prepared to act in conjunction with their white allies against the Seminoles.

The first affair of importance in the fall campaign of 1837, was the expedition to Dunlawton, Tomoka, and the Uchees, under Gen. Hernandez. That officer was at Fort Peyton, seven miles south of St. Augustine, on the 4th of September, when four negroes, which had belonged to Major Heriot, came in and delivered themselves up, and informed that many Indians were engaged south of Tomoka, and east of the St. John's, preparing coonti, *(zamia.)* Preparations were immediately made for an expedition in that direction, and

* Some wrote Os-sin-yah-holo, others Assinyohola, but Osceola has obtained.

a force marched from thence on the 7th, under Lieut. Peyton, who volunteered to take the lead on this occasion. It consisted of 170 men, and the same evening they reached Bulow's, 33 miles from Fort Peyton. Here, on the 8th, at daylight, four other negroes gave themselves up, who had belonged to the same master, and at the same time there came along with them an Indian negro, named John, a slave of King Philip, who had run away, on account of an attachment to his master's squaw. He was made to act as a guide. Spies were sent out, who soon returned with the information that there was an encampment of Indians at Dunlawton. This it was determined to beat up, and Lieuts. Peyton and Whitchenst were detached for the purpose, and at midnight they fell upon them with complete success; capturing the whole party, except a son of Philip, a lad of 18, who made his escape. None were killed or wounded on either side. The whites were much elated at this capture, having found that they had taken the arch King Philip,—who had laid waste this part of the country in the beginning of the war,—Tomoka John, and several others, women and children.

On examining Tomoka John, the general learned that at about 10 miles from thence was a company of some 8 or 10 Uchees, under Uchee Billy, and Philip confirmed his statement. It was resolved, without loss of time, to surprise this encampment also. Accordingly, 40 men marched out, with John for a guide, and here also the surprise was complete, with the exception of one man, who escaped under cover of night. But they did not find the Uchees entirely unprepared, and in their resistance they mortally wounded Lieut. M'Neill, a promising young officer. Two Indians were killed, three wounded, and 16 captured. Among the latter was Uchee Billy, whose capture was viewed of no small consequence. In all 5 chiefs were captured during the expedition, making a total of 94 Indians and negroes.

Before the month expired, a son of Philip (probably he who escaped at Dunlawton) came with four others to St. Augustine, with a flag; but they were no sooner come than Gen. Hernandez ordered them into confinement. We have no other particulars, and whether the general had good reasons for such a step, take not upon us to say. It appears that the whites in general were determined to have the Indians, some how or other, and this seems to have been an earnest of what was afterwards enacted. John Hix, or Hext, (Tuckebatche Hajo,) who was supposed to have been killed in an encounter near a year ago, came into Fort King on the 3d of August, and on the 7th there arrived at Black Creek, Coahajo, Yahajo, (brother-in-law of Osceola,) and Honese Tustunnuggee. These captures and surrenders gave great encouragement to the people, and they again counted on a total emigration in a short time.

On the 20th of October, as Lieut. T. B. Adams was escorting an express from Tampa to Fort Foster, he fell in with and took three Indians. One was a prominent chief of Pease Creek, named Holachta-Mico-chee, Hac-te-hal-chee, a sub-chief, and one warrior.

At the same time was prepared at Washington a very sensible talk, by the chief of the Cherokees, JOHN ROSS, which was to be sent to the Seminoles; in which he ardently expressed himself for their welfare, and strongly urged upon them the necessity of coming to a settlement with the whites, and the utter impracticability of continuing in war, with the least prospect of success. This Mr. Ross undertook, by the consent and with the advice of President Jackson, and four trusty Cherokees were soon after despatched with it to Florida. It was addressed to Micanopy, Philip, Coacoochee, (Wild Cat,) Osceola, and other chiefs and warriors, and signed KOOWESKOOWE, alias JOHN ROSS, and a commendatory article, by seven of his head men.

This deputation met the Seminoles in their country, and held a talk with Sam Jones, at the head of 300 Mikasaukies. Nothing seems to have been finally settled, but Abiaca (Jones) said he would treat with the whites if they would not use him ill. However, before this negotiation began, the Seminoles had met with the saddest blow of any, before or since; eight more of their principal men had fallen into the hands of Gen. Jesup, among whom was Osceola himself. This came about as follows:—

About the 18 October, Osceola sent a message to Fort Peyton, that wished to have a talk with Gen Hernandez, and stated that he was but a few miles from there. He had not even ventured thus far, had not the snare been laid by the commander-in-chief of the whites, who, it must ever hereafter be allowed, displayed as much of the Indian in the matter, as Coacoochee had done before, in the abduction of old Micanopy and others, when the general had them nearly ready for Arkansas. For this act of Coacoochee, the general had determined to be revenged; and he declared, "if he (Coacoochee) had been a white man, he would have executed him the moment he came into his hands." Now we have seen that he did, some time before this, fall into his, or Gen. Hernandez's hands. He was the one sent out, or, as the general says, allowed to go out, at the request of old Philip, his father. He it was that brought about this overture of Osceola, which proved so fatal to him, as in the sequel will be seen.

The Indians, having come as near Fort Peyton as they dared, sent word for Gen. Jesup to come out and talk with them; he returned them no answer, but ordered Lieut. Peyton to get them into the fort if he could, and then to seize them. But in this he could not succeed, and Gen. Hernandez was sent out with 200 men, and commenced a parley with them. Gen. Jesup remained in the vicinity of Fort Peyton, and ordered the lieutenant of the fort to proceed to the treaty-ground, to learn whether the Indians "answered Gen. Hernandez's questions satisfactorily or not." He soon returned, and reported that the answers were "evasive and unsatisfactory;" whereupon he ordered Maj. Ashby to capture them, which, with the aid of Hernandez, was done, without the discharge of a gun on either side. Seventy-five Indians were, by this manœuvre, taken with loaded rifles in their hands, disarmed, and confined in the fort; and thus ended this "brilliant" affair, which took place on the 21 October, 1837.

The names of the principal chiefs "grabbed" in this "haul," were, as the interpreters gave them, YOSO-YA-HOLA (Osceola,) COAHAJO (Alligator,) POW-AS-HAJO, JOHN CAVALLO, who had been a hostage with Gen. Jesup, NO-CO-SO-SIA-HOLA, EMATHLA-CHAMY, CO-HI-LO-LUE-HAJO (Doctor,) and HASTORO-MICO.

Severe animadversions have been indulged in, upon the conduct of Gen. Jesup, in thus seizing Osceola and his companions. We have not time nor space for an examination of what has and may be urged for and against the measure. We have followed the general's own account of the affair, and must leave our readers to judge for themselves upon its justness. One remark, however, may not be unimportant, as it may assist in a just decision of the question. The general has said, that, inasmuch as the Indians had grossly deceived him on a former occasion, he would use any means to get the chief actors in that deception into his hands; and we have seen *how* the matter was managed to effect that object. Now, when Indians fight Indians, whatever advantage is gained by circumvention, of one party over another, is just, according to the laws which govern their modes of warfare; but it is a rare circumstance that a party is attacked when coming to another with the offer of peace. We are now considering the whites on *equal* footing with the Seminoles; for we see no other ground that this act of seizure can, in any way, be justified. The general asserts, what we do not clearly discover, that Osceola did not come to treat of peace, but came under that pretence, "falsely," expecting thereby to get some white officer into his power, with whom he might purchase the liberation of Philip. But, as has been observed, we do not see sufficient evidence of such a plot, to authorize the "grab game," as some of the *classical* editors termed it, which was played by the general Much, however, might be added in extenuation of his conduct; he had been a long time in Florida, exerting himself to the utmost to accomplish the wretched business forced upon him; he had been baffled and foiled by the Indians, and derided and shamefully treated by some of his own countrymen. He was now determined to do something, and he performed this signal act when nobody expected it, and his enemies were at once out upon him, because he had acted like the people he was among. No blood was shed; but a very important service was performed. On the whole, we cannot condemn Gen. Jesup, but rather the policy that placed him where he was. Of this we have distinctly spoken in an earlier page, and must waive a further examination.

On the 23 October, 29 "Indians, squaws, and negroes," were captured near Fort Peyton; and, on the 25th, a family of 5 more were taken. They were conveyed to St. Augustine, and imprisoned, where there now were 147 in all, in confinement. Great preparations had been made to pursue the Indians with vigor, and forces had come in from various quarters, so that by the first of December, there were at the various posts in Florida, 8,993 men, of whom 4,637 were regulars, 4,078 volunteers, 100 seamen, and 178 friendly Indians.

Amid all these preparations and watchings, the noted chief Coacoochee (Wild Cat) made his escape from St. Augustine, with 17 warriors and two squaws. Thus the fellow whom Gen. Jesup looked upon with such distrust, had, somehow or other, outwitted his keepers, and joined Sam Jones in his unknown retreat.

The next event which comes within the line of our design, was one of the most sanguinary which has happened since this war began, with the exception of that in which Maj. Dade and his command were cut off. This was the battle of Okeechobee Lake, between a large Indian force under Abiaca and Alligator, and Col. Z. Taylor at the head of about 600 men; the particulars of which are as follows:—

Col. Taylor marched from Fort Gardner on the 19 December, 1837, and, following the meanderings of the Kissimmee River, arrived on the third day at a point on its banks, 15 miles above its entrance into Lake Okeechobee, which name is said to mean *Big Water*. Here he learned from a prisoner, who had fallen into his hands, that Alligator, "with all the war spirits of the Seminoles, Sam Jones, and 175 Mikasaukies," was encamped about 25 miles off, on the east side of Lake Kissimmee. Crossing the river, the colonel left Capt. Monroe, with his company, the pioneers, pontooneers, and a large portion of his Delaware warriors, who declined proceeding, from lameness, occasioned by their feet and legs being badly cut with the saw-palmetto. The next day, taking the captured Indian as a pilot, he moved on with the rest of his force. After passing several cypress swamps and dense hommocks, he reached the vicinity of the Indians' encampment, on the morning of the 25th. Here they were found in one of the strongest places, as well as most difficult of access, of any before known in Florida; but between 12 and 1 o'clock the conflict commenced. The main body of the Indians were posted in a hommock, from which they poured such a destructive fire upon the volunteers, that they were obliged to fall back. They formed in the rear of the infantry, who, coming now into action, "sustained one of the most destructive fires ever experienced from Indians." But they pressed forward, and gained the hommock; the struggle continuing more than an hour, which was sustained with difficulty on the part of the whites, the Indians at one time nearly breaking their line; they were, however, finally routed and driven at every point, leaving 10 of their dead on the field, and numerous traces of blood where others had been dragged away. It was reported afterwards, by the Indians themselves, that they lost 20 in all; and yet this story of blood is not half told. Col. Taylor had 28 killed, and 111 wounded! Every officer of four companies, with one exception, and every orderly sergeant of the same companies, were killed, and the sergeant major was mortally wounded. Col. A. R. Thompson, of the 6th U. S. infantry, received three mortal wounds nearly at the same time; Adjutant J. P. Center, Capt. Vanswearingen, and Lieut. F. J. Brooke, of the same corps, were killed outright; Col. Gentry, of the Missouri volunteers, was killed by a shot through the body, the same ball wounding his son in the arm. Such was the issue of the disastrous battle of Lake Okeechobee, which served two ends; one of which was to reduce the number of Indians in opposition, and to teach the survivors that the whites could and would fight. No prisoners were taken, but some 200 horses and cattle were found.

Skirmishes on a smaller scale continued. Gen. Nelson, of the Georgia volunteers, fell in with a few Indians on the Suanee, on the 26 December, at a place called Wacusape, and we presume, judging from indirect information, came off second best. His horse was killed under him, and he lost his lieutenant, and three horses, and a man or two wounded. He took one Indian and a negro prisoners, and one Indian was reported to have been killed.

About the same time, there was a fight at Charlotte Harbor, in which five Indians were killed, and nine taken. Lieut. Harding was dangerously wounded. And a day or two after, Capt. Winder, with 30 dragoons, surprised and took seven men and 23 women and children, about 40 miles south of Fort McLane, and near Fort McNiell; and 20 miles south-west of Fort Harney, he took 29 more, among whom was a sister of Coahajo. Such were the important operations in Florida, during the year 1837.

CHAPTER XX.

EMBRACING THE EVENTS OF 1838 AND 1839.

Battle of Wacasa Swamp—*Defeat of Lieut. Powell*—Battle of Lucha Hatche—*Gen. Jesup wounded*—Death of Osceola—*His character—Gen. Jesup desires to give up the war, and allow the Indians to live in Florida—Not allowed by the government—His talk with* Toskegee—*Indians seized at Fort Jupiter—Gen. Jesup leaves Florida—Death of* Philip *and* Jumper—*Capt. Ellis's exploit—Indians surprise Capt. Beall—Families murdered—Crews of vessels murdered—Death of* Mushalatubee—*Camp Forbes attacked—Numerous murders—Capt. Russell and Maj. Noel killed—Capt. Rowell defeated—Gen. Macomb takes command in Florida—Endeavors to make a treaty—Lieut. Hulbert killed—Reward for Indians—Massacre at Coloosbatchie—Indians surprised at Fort Mellon—Murders on the Waculla—Bloodhounds to be employed against the Seminoles—Depredations continue.*

New year has come, but not a "happy new year" to Florida; for its first day had only passed, when the sound of the rifle is heard in its desolate coasts, followed by the groans of the wounded and dying. Brig. Gen. Charles Nelson, with a brigade of Georgia volunteers, being charged with the defence of Middle Florida, was, on the 2 January, scouting in the vicinity of Wacasa Swamp, near Fort Fanning, when he discovered Indian signs leading to said swamp: following them up, he was fiercely attacked as he approached it, and immediately the fight became obstinate, and lasted near three hours. At 5 o'clock, P. M., the Indians dispersed, carrying off their killed and wounded. The whites suffered severely; but they claimed a large victory, having captured "15 men and children," and a chief named Chickachoo. Col. Foster, who commanded the left wing, was shot down, but his wound proved slight. Lieut. Jennings was killed. Among the wounded were Col. Ambrister, slightly; Serg. Maj. Jones, badly; Dr. Sheftall of Savannah, badly; with several privates.

We now proceed with an account of a sharp action, near Jupiter Inlet, between a force of about 80 men under Lieut. L. M. Powell, of the navy, and a body of Indians under Toskegee, in which the whites were defeated, and suffered severely in killed and wounded. The action commenced about 4 in the P. M., and continued till half past seven at night, of the 15 January.

On proceeding upon a trail, after landing at Jupiter River, Lieut. Powell captured a squaw, whom he made pilot him to the Indian camp, which he reached after a march of about five miles. He found them prepared for him, and the war-whoop was immediately raised. The whites "charged them through a deep swamp," and the fire became general. Lieut. Harrison, of the navy, was soon shot down at the head of his men, who were left without an officer. Lieut. Fowler, of the artillery, was directed to penetrate the swamp to the right, while the remaining two companies, under Lieut. M'Arthur, of the navy, advanced in line. By these manœuvres the Indians were driven, or retreated, to a large cypress swamp, 700 or 800 yards in the rear. Here they made a determined stand, and here Lieut. M'Arthur was badly wounded, and Dr. Leitner was killed while in the discharge of his duty as surgeon. Night was approaching, and the men were falling fast, when Lieut. Powell ordered a retreat. Lieut. Fowler was shot down in the successful attempt which he made to cover the retreat, and but three officers remained upon their feet at the close of the action. The whites made what haste they could to their boats, all of which they got off except one, which the Indians took, containing ammunition. In this affair the whites had 5 killed, and 30 wounded, many of them severely, and some three several times. The Indians lost 4 or 5. The commander-in-chief in this expedition makes no charges against any engaged in it, in his official account; but an officer, who was twice wounded in the fight, said the sailors were great cowards, and had it not been for the company of artillery under Lieut. Fowler, who covered their retreat, nearly all of them would have been scalped. As it was, about half the wounded were of that class. This fight was on Lucha Hatche, or Turtle River.

Gen. Jesup, thinking the Indians had probably made their head-quarters on the Lucha Hatche, marched with the force under his immediate command from Fort Lloyd, near the head of the St. John, on the 20 January, to see whether Lieut. Powell had just cause for leaving them in full possession there, or not. He came upon them on the 24th, between 11 and 12 o'clock, A. M., and if he had had no more men than the lieutenant had, it is doubtful whether he would have given as good an account, or fared as well; though the general himself says, "that the strength of their position was such, that they ought to have held it much longer than they did;" yet, in forcing them out of it, he was pretty severely wounded, with 30 of his men, and 10 were killed or mortally wounded. Thus had TOSKEGEE handled two considerable forces under separate commanders, and was doubtless as well prepared for a third, as either of those for a second; for he and his men were able to make good their retreat without loss of time, with their all, leaving conjecture only to their enemies of their next locality.

We must now turn our attention, for the last time, to the once feared, and much dreaded, and now no less regretted, chief, OSCEOLA. We left him in prison at St. Augustine, in November last, from which place he was, soon after the escape of COACOOCHEE from thence, sent to Charleston, and confined to the fort in that harbor for safe keeping, until he should be, with others, shipped for the west. But that time never came for him! Death came with that aid which the white man refused! He died in confinement at Fort Moultrie, of a catarrhal fever, on the 30 January, 1838. The portrait of Osceola is difficult to be drawn; some have made him a coward, and others a knave; some have averred that he was but a sub-chief, and without respect among his own people; others have indignantly added, that he was the son of a white man, as though their own blood had degraded him in the scale of being. It might be so. How then ought they to look upon themselves? Doubly degraded in that scale. Others portray his character in unmeasured terms of admiration; making him the greatest of chiefs, ablest of counsellors, and bravest of warriors. We affirm to neither. The circumstance of his being better known when the war began, than other chiefs, gave him a celebrity or notoriety which his deeds did not claim. He had lived more among the white people, and hence was better known to them; and when a depredation was committed, or a battle fought, Osceola was the *supposed* leader of the Indians; and as the report of such occurrences spread, the supposition vanished, and thus arose much of the celebrity of Osceola. Hence it is easy to see how he came so prominently into the van of notoriety. Thus, in our account of the defeat of Major Dade, the authorities then relied upon made us say he was the leader in that wretched disaster; but we are now assured that he was at Camp King that same day, and was the chief actor in that tragedy, and hence could not have been in the fight with Maj. Dade. He lived near Camp King when the war began, after which he removed to Long Swamp, 12 miles to the south-west of it.

But we detract nothing from the just fame of Osceola. He was a great man, and his name will go down to the latest posterity, with as much renown as that of PHILIP of Pokanoket. Both, by fatal errors, were brought prematurely into the hands of their enemies; Philip, by the rash murder of one of his own men, and Osceola by a mistaken estimate of the character of his foes.

We return to Gen. Jesup, whom we left wounded, though safely through the battle of Lucha Hatche. The next day, January 25th, he crossed the river, and encamped on Jupiter Bay, where he erected a stockade, which he named Fort Jupiter. Here he remained until the 5 February, his men being destitute of shoes and other supplies. At this period he marched southward, about 12 miles, when he encamped again; and here an interview was sought with the Indians. It was now looked upon by the general, as well as all his principal officers, as a matter past accomplishment, to subdue the Seminoles, "for years to come." It was, therefore, concluded that it would be best to effect an accommodation with them, and to allow them to retain and live upon that part of Florida "where nobody else could live." Accordingly, he wrote to the secretary of war, on the 11 February, recommending that measure. In answer, the secretary said, that it was not a question now to be considered by the president, whether it would be better to let the Indians remain in the country or not, but that, as a treaty had been ratified, by which the Indians had agreed to remove, it was his duty to see it executed; that, therefore, no arrangements with the Seminoles would be allowed, having for its object their future residence in Florida. Thus a "veto" was set to the humane object of Generals Jesup, Eustace, and others, though they were allowed to make a kind of a truce with them for the ensuing summer, or until the season would allow the whites to fight them again to advantage.

Meanwhile, Gen. Jesup had moved on slowly, and on the 7th, by means of messengers which he sent out, got a parley with a young chief, named Hallec Hajo. This chief told the general that the Indians were in a wretched condition, that they were unwilling to leave the country, but would be contented with any small portion of it, if they might be allowed to continue in it. At this stage of the conference, the general (very abruptly we think) demanded hostages, or a surrender of the arms of the Indians; but the chief gave him to understand that neither would be done. He then requested a conference with Toskegee, the principal chief of the band. The next day Toskegee came, and the interview resulted in an agreement for a meeting at Fort Jupiter, in ten days from that time. What was done at that fort, or whether the general ever got the Indians there or not, he has not told us; but he says, in his communication to the secretary of war, that "the measure which he adopted had resulted in the peaceable surrender of about 1,200 Indians and negroes, of whom 319 were warriors. Had any other course been adopted, it is questionable," he says, "whether 20 warriors could have been killed or taken."

Hence we are to infer, that without gross deception, now-a-days called stratagem, nothing could be effected, of any account, against the Indians of Florida; and what it is probable will be remarked upon hereafter, as worthy of admiration, is the curious fact, that it had taken the government of the country, and all its officers who had been engaged in Florida, three years to find it out. An army could march from one end of that country to another, if they avoided its lakes and swamps; and dogs could, with equal ease, drive all the birds from a rye-field, if there were no brambles in their course; and the latter of these experiments would be of about as much consequence to the owner of the rye-field, as the former to the inhabitants of Florida.

Toskegee had been prevailed upon to lay down his arms, and come into the strong-holds of the white men, to hold a treaty with them, under the assurance that he and his people would be allowed to retain *some little part of their own country*. But we are told, as the Indians probably were afterwards, that they would be permitted to remain in Florida, provided the president would consent to it. They had become quite confident that such would be the fact, for the very good reason, that the officers who made them this promise, were very confident themselves, that it would be acceded to by him. No other conclusion can be drawn from Gen. Jesup's language, in his communication to the secretary of war, before alluded to. Speaking of his overtures for a reservation, he says, "I believed then, and I believe now, that, as commander-in-chief of the army in the field, I had a right to adopt those measures, either of direct hostility, or of policy, which promised to be most useful in the end, taking care not to place the ultimate decision of them beyond the control of my official superiors."

Some time had now intervened since proposals had been made, and it is probable the chiefs had begun to think all was not right; for when, on the 17th March, the general had got his answer from Washington, he notified them to meet him on the 20th, at Fort Jupiter; they did not appear; whereupon Col. Twiggs, by his order, surrounded and captured the whole party, amounting to 513. In a day or two after, negroes enough were taken to make up 678; but in the mean time Passac-mico, a chief, with 14 others, made their escape.

On the 24 March, Gen. Jesup detached Halatoochee, Tustenuc-cocho-conee, and the negro chief ABRAHAM, to Gen. Taylor. These were sent out with messages to their countrymen west of Okeechobee and Pahaiokee, and they prevailed upon Alligator, with 360 Indians and negroes, of whom a hundred were warriors, to surrender to Col. Smith and Gen. Taylor; and soon after Lieut. Anderson captured Pahose-mico, a sub-chief of Toskegee, with his band of 47 persons. Major Lauderdale and Lieut. Powell pursued Appiacca, (Sam Jones,) as Gen. Jesup writes the name, into the everglades, and came up with him on an island, and dispersed his party.

We have now traced events to the month of April, 1838, in which month Gen. Jesup was ordered to proceed to the Cherokee country, and leave Gen. Taylor in command of the forces in Florida. He began operations there in December, 1836, from which time to that now arrived at, there had been taken, with those who surrendered, about 2,400 Indians, above 700 of whom were warriors. Many of the principal chiefs had already been sent out of the country. King Philip, Cloud, and Coahajo, arrived at New Orleans on the 12th of March, but the former never reached his place of destination. King Philip died on board his transport boat in July, 40 miles below Fort Gibson. He was buried on shore with the honors of war; 100 guns being discharged over his grave. JUMPER had preceded him. This chief languished for about two months, at the "Barracks" in New Orleans, when, on a day memorable in our annals, April the 19th, his spirit took its flight. He was buried under arms with much ceremony. Into his coffin were put his rifle, pipe, tobacco, and other equipments, agreeable to the custom of his people. We now return to inquire what is doing in the land whence they came.

A scouting party of volunteers, under Capt. Ellis, found five Indians in a hommock near Santa Fee bridge, all of whom are killed, without injury to his own party. This was on the 10th of May. On the 17th of June, as a detachment of about 30 United States dragoons, under Capt. Beall, were seeking Indians in the neighborhood of San Felasco, near Newnansville, they fell into an ambush, and seven of their number were killed and wounded. Among the former was Capt. Walker. They immediately retreated, and were followed some distance by the Indians. On the 19 July the family of a Mr. Guynn was cut off on the Santa Fee; himself, wife, and infant child were murdered. On the 25th of the same month, a family of the name of Lasley was broken up on the Ocloknee, 15 or 20 miles from Tallahassee. Mr. Lasley and a daughter were killed. In Middle Florida, on the last day of the month, a Mr. Singletary, his wife, and two children were cut off. On the 19th of August, a severe blow was struck on the family of a Mr. Baker, on the east side of the Oscilla. Himself, wife, and a grandchild were killed. And thus we might fill out page after page with such awful details—consequences of a war to be remembered only to be lamented.

Many had supposed, that when so many Indians had been sent out of Florida, but few could be left to trouble their expatriators, but it proved far otherwise. The poor mariner, who had never had any hand in the war, if cast away on any part of that coast, immediately found himself in the midst of Indians. In a terrible tempest, which happened about the 7th of Septem ber, near 40 vessels were wrecked or stranded on its extensive shores. One only we shall particularly name This was the brig Alna, Capt. Thomas, of Portland. After being wrecked, the crew all got safe on shore, except one man, who was washed overboard. The captain, A. J. Plummer, and Wi-

Reed, were killed. S. Cammett and E. Wyer, Jr., though wounded, almost miraculously escaped.

Amidst these events we will pause to notice the death of the great Choktaw chief, MUSHALATUBEE. He died at the agency in Arkansas, September the 30th, of small-pox. He had led his warriors against the Creeks, under Jackson, during the war of 1812.

On the 6th of September, Adj. Gen. R. Jones issued orders for the reassembling of such officers and others, in Florida and the Cherokee country, as had been detached to the north-west, or elsewhere, to be ready for active service. On the 11th, as Capt. Rowell's company of Florida volunteers, about 16, were scouting near the mouth of the Oscilla, they fall upon a camp of Indians under Tigertail. Most of them escape on ponies, but two women were killed.

We meet with very little of importance until the close of this year. On the 28th December an attack was made on Camp Forbes, by a small party of Indians, but they were obliged to retire, leaving two of their number dead behind. The next morning Lieut. Thomas went in pursuit of the party, and came up with them on the Chattahoochee; here again they were dispersed with loss, but how great is not mentioned. On the 4th of January, 1839, some citizens of Magnolia, learning that Indians were in their neighborhood, searched them out, and killed the whole party, six in number. Capt. L. J. Beall, scouting with a company of dragoons near Ahapopka Lake, captured 16 Indians, of which number but two were men. The two men were near relations of Wild Cat and Sam Jones. The latter had given out word that he would hang any Indian who should attempt to surrender.

A party of 10 or 12 Indians went within about 12 miles of Tallahassee, and cut off the family of a Mr. Pendarvis; killing him, his wife, and two children. This was on the 15th of February, and on the 18th they cut off the family of a Mr. White, four miles nearer the same place. Here they killed two persons and desperately wounded Mr. and Mrs. White. On the Thursday previous, the same, or perhaps another party of Indians attacked the house of a Mr. Stokens, of Jefferson county, and though the family escaped, they plundered it of 1,000 dollars in bank notes, and burnt it.

On the 23d of February, about 15 or 20 Indians attack three wagons on the Magnolia road, loaded with provisions for Camp Wacasa, and about 9 miles from that place. Four persons were killed. As Capt. S. L. Russell was ascending the Miami River, in open boats, from Fort Dallas, with a part of his men, they were fired on by Indians concealed, and Capt. Russell is killed, and Major Noel is mortally wounded. This was on the last day of February, viz., the 28th.

On the 1st of March, the Indians which had been collected at St. Augustine were shipped for the west. There were 250 in all, 65 of whom were men. At this time went the long noted negro chief, *Abraham*. Yet murders continued to be every where committed. On the 8th, the house of Edmund Gray, in Jefferson county, 9 miles from Monticello, is beset, Mr. Gray and two children killed and one badly wounded, and the house burned.

In pursuing his business of scouting, Capt. Rowell came upon 50 or 60 Indians near Patterson's Hommock, 5 miles east of the Oscilla. They engaged him, and obliged him to retreat with the loss of two killed and two wounded. This happened on the 18th of March, and on the 3d of April some 10 or 15 Indians went to the residence of Capt. Scott, in Jefferson county, about two miles from Bailey's mills, where they killed one person and wounded two or three more. About the same time the house of a Mr. Rollins is attacked at the head of the St. Mary's, on the edge of the Okefeenoke Swamp. Mrs Rollins was killed, and he made a very narrow escape.

Meanwhile Gen. Macomb had been appointed commander-in-chief of the army in Florida, and on the 5th of April he arrived at its head-quarters on Black Creek. His main instructions appear to have been, to pacify the Indians again, until the return of another season for campaigning. But his prospects were discouraging, for "they were dividing themselves into small parties, penetrating the settlements, committing some murders, and firing from their coverts on the expresses and passengers going from post to post.

And it was believed that no communication could be opened with them. However the general was determined to make the attempt, and finding some prisoners at Gary's Ferry, he treated them kindly for a while, then set them at liberty, with the request that they would proceed to the hostiles and invite them to a parley. At or about the same time Gen. Taylor sent out some of "his Indians, in whose sincerity and honesty he had great confidence;" but these joined the enemy and never returned, and the prisoners returned after some time, and said they could not find their people. In the mean time, on the 22 April, about 100 Tallahassies, under the chief Nea Stoco Matla, marched to Tampa in the night, and forced away about 30 of their countrymen, who were waiting there to be shipped to the west.

At length, on the 17th of May, the general got a number of chiefs together, from the southern part of the peninsula, by the negotiation of Col. Harney, and an amicable arrangement was made, by which they were to remain in the country for the present, or until they could be assured of the prosperous condition of their friends who had emigrated. The general then left Florida.

On the 3 May, five persons were killed on the Santa Fee. On the same day Lieut. Hulbert and a man named O'Driscoll were killed at Fourteen-mile Creek. The express rider between Fort Frank Brooke and Fort Andrews not arriving as usual, Lieut. Hulbert went out with ten men to learn the cause. Being in advance of his men, he fell into an ambush, and was thus cut off. He belonged to New York, and had graduated at West Point.

About sunset on the 28 May, a body of Indians surround the dwelling of Mr. James Osteen, of Alligator, shoot him near his stable, badly wound a Mr Dell, and also a sister of Mr. Osteen. Mrs. Osteen and her children escape to the nearest house. These and numerous other equally horrid affairs happening immediately after the treaty just made, destroyed all confidence in its utility. The people of Florida declared they would take the management of the war into their own hands, and early in June the government of the territory offered a reward of 200 dollars for every Indian killed or taken. And soon after, TIGERTAIL, the chief of the Tallahassies, issued a proclamation declaring the treaty made between Gen. Macomb and Chitto Tustenuggee null and void. It does not appear that the two principal chiefs of the Seminoles, Tigertail and Sam Jones, had any thing to do with Gen. Macomb's treaty.

On the 13 July, between 9 and 10 at night, a small party of Indians attack the family of Mr. G. Chairs, 10 miles from Tallahassee, and kill Mrs. Chairs and two children. On the 23d, Col. Harney was attacked on the Coloosahatchie or Synebal River, and had 13 out of 18 of his men killed. The colonel had gone to this place to establish a trading house, agreeably to the treaty made at Fort King between some of the Seminoles and Gen. Macomb, before spoken of. Thus that treaty (which was only verbal) was either made on the part of the Indians to deceive the general, or some Indians made it without any authority from their nation; the latter was doubtless the fact.

When the news of Col. Harney's surprise reached Fort Mellon, on the 31st, some 50 Indians, who had come into that neighborhood, were alarmed for their safety, and fled; but soon after, about 45 of them came in to talk with Lieut. Hanson, and were surrounded and taken; two men, in attempting to escape, were shot down and killed. About this time, as a company of soldiers were building a bridge in Middle Florida, about two miles from a post on the Suanee, they were surprised by the Indians, and 6 of their number killed. At Fort Wheelock, two or three soldiers are killed while bathing in Orange Lake. On the 27 September, a party fall upon the family of a Mr. Bunch, on the Wakulla, murder Mrs. Bunch and one child, and burn the house. Mr. Whitaker, a near neighbor, is severely wounded.

Early in October, it was announced that 7,000 regular troops were to be sent to Florida, and that Gen. Taylor had been authorized to send to Cuba for a large number of bloodhounds, to enable them to scent out the Indians. When it was known throughout the country that dogs were to be employed against them, there was a general burst of indignation; but though it is a fact that the dogs were procured and brought to Florida, with Spaniards to direct them, yet we believe they entirely failed in the experiment; there being but here and there a solitary instance of their performing the service for which they were intended. If the originators of this dog-scheme had in view the destruction of the Indians in the manner they were destroyed by the followers of Columbus, they deserve not the rights of humanity, but should rather be hunted out of society by beasts as savage as themselves, if such could be found. How much was effected by the hounds, it is difficult to tell, for long before their arrival in the country, the editors of papers in that region had probably concluded upon what course they would pursue, when *official accounts from dogs* should be offered for publication; but occasionally a reckless fellow dropped a paragraph like the following: "The Cuba dogs have proved quite beneficial. They caught five Indians the other day, in Middle Florida, handsomely." In March, (1840,) "Col. Twiggs made a 15 days' scout up the St. Johns River with the bloodhounds. On his return, it was stated that *they were found to be perfectly useless;* all attempts to induce them to take the trail of the Indians proving unsuccessful. These and other trials are evidences sufficient to put an end to all further anxiety on the part of the northern sentimentalists." From such statements we are left to make up such accounts as we may, of what was effected by the bloodhounds They will be noticed in the order of time as we proceed.

During this expedition, two Indians were discovered in a boat and shot one of whom was said to be a brother of Sam Jones.

On the 19 October, a party of dragoons were fired upon while crossing the Oscilla, and had 7 of their number killed. Some Indians, pretending friendship, had encamped about two miles from the fort, on New River; and having become familiar with the soldiers, invited them all to a dance, which they were to have on the night of the 27 September; but three, however, had the temerity to go, and they were all killed. It was supposed they intended or were in hopes of drawing out the whole garrison, which if they had, their fate would have been the same. This was but a retaliation. A baggage-wagon passing between Micanopy and Fort Wheelock, with an escort of seven men, was taken by the Indians on the 3 November; the driver was mortally wounded, and another man severely; killing and wounding some 6 or 7 mules and horses; 50 Indians were said to have done this mischief; but if there had been half that number, it is exceeding doubtful whether either of the seven men would have escaped.

The climate, as well as the Seminoles, continued to do its work also. On the 5 November, Lieut. Rodney died at St. Augustine, and the next day, Quartermaster M'Crabb died at the same place.

On the 9 November, the house of Mr. John Johnson was attacked, on the Oscilla, in which four negroes and one white boy were killed. Four days after, a party took Alfred Oliver's house, on the Ocloknee, 12 miles to the westward of Tallahassee, and killed his son. On the 25th, as Capt. Searle is proceeding in a carriage from St. Augustine to Picolata, he was fired upon, when about 6 miles out, and mortally wounded; a young man, a Polander, who was riding on horseback behind him, was killed upon the spot. On the same day, a Mr. Weedman, with his son, proceeded to visit his farm, three and a half miles only from St. Augustine, on the same road. It was the first time he had made the attempt since the war began, and by it he now lost his life, being shot dead by some concealed Indians; and his son was badly wounded.

During this month, Gov. Call, with some 200 or 300 men, scoured Middle Florida, and "drove up all the Indians" in their lines of march. They presumed they would not "light down again" for some time. However, in a few days after, the house of Maj. J. S. Taylor, about 6 miles from Monticello, was burnt down, but the family escaped. This act was laid to the Indians, and we cannot undertake to say they did not do it, for they certainly were the possessors of the country

CHAPTER XXI.

EVENTS OF THE YEAR 1840.

A train of wagons taken—Lieut. Whedan killed—Dog exploits—Families destroyed—Defeat of Capt. Rains—Lieut. Sanderson's defeat—Col. Riley's exploit—Col. Green's—Col. Harney's—A company of players attacked—Cow Creek skirmish—Indian Key destroyed—Lieut. Arthur's exploit—Eleven families destroyed—Capt. Beall's fight—Lieut. Hanson's battle—Indian hanged—Pacification attempted through a deputation of Seminoles from Arkansas—It fails—Whites taken in aiding Indians—Wild Cat's exploit—Sad accident—Lieut. Judd ambushed—Fort Hanson burnt—Col. Harney's voyage to the Everglades—Hangs nine Indians—The chief CHIAKIKA *killed—Fort Walker attacked—Capt. Davidson dies—Lieut. Sherwood's ambush, and death of Mrs.* MONTGOMERY.

"You plough the Indian's grave; you till his land—
Is there no blood, white man, upon your hand?
Recall the time when first your fathers spread
Upon these icy shores their wintry bed;—
When, powerless exiles on the desert sea,
Their only strength—the spirit to be free."

WE have now arrived at the beginning of the year 1840. On the first day of February of this year, a detachment of men, sent in pursuit of deserters were fired on near Fort Brooke, by which three of the detachment were wounded. A sergeant, whose horse was shot from under him, was supposed to have been killed. Four days after, some 10 or 15 Indians captured a train of 12 wagons, about 10 miles from Gary's Ferry, as they were returning to that place with provisions and stores from the interior. They killed one man, and wounded four or five mules, and made off with the property.

On the 22 February, as Lieut. Whedan, with a detachment of volunteers was in pursuit of Indians upon a fresh trail near the Calico Hills, in the vicinity of Magnolia, he fell into an ambush, and was killed; his men ran away and left him to the Indians.

About a month after, namely, March 18, the Indians made a spirited attempt to add to their stock of provisions. They attacked another train of wagons on its way from Post No. 2 to Micanopy, killed three men and wounded others; but found no booty, as the wagons were only going after stores. This was done in spite of what a company of soldiers could do, who were present as an escort. But a few days previous, (March 8th,) two men are killed between "Charles Old Town" and Micanopy; and, on the 10th, a Methodist minister, named M'Rea, was killed at "Suggs Old Place," between Wahcahota and Micanopy. On the 26 March, some Indians crawled up within 200 yards of the pickets at Fort King, and killed two soldiers.

About the beginning of March, somewhere in Middle Florida, two bloodhounds captured an Indian; one seized him by the throat, while the whites came up and took him. He was greatly terrified, and pointed out where others might be found; and soon after they captured four more. On 13 March, nine dogs were announced as having arrived at Gary's Ferry, and that they were to be *employed* by Col. Twiggs, of the 2d dragoons, on a contemplated expedition to the Ocklawaha. The officers under whom they were to *serve*, were probably desirous to know how much they might depend upon them, and, therefore, on the next *Sunday*, made the following experiment in their tactics. An Indian prisoner was sent out, (without the knowledge of the dogs,) with orders to climb a tree at some five miles' distance. He did so; and the hounds were put upon his trail. The dog *captain*, or leader, went directly to the tree, and attempted to climb it, and had actually got up six feet, when the others arrived. Such was the report of the affair; which report, whether from the principal officer under whose conduct it was performed, or from the chief leader of the dogs, we are uninformed.

Towards the end of April, a small band of Indians attacked a guard of six men, who were convoying a wagon from Fort Fanning to Deadman's Bay

The officer commanding was badly wounded; but the fight was continued several hours, until all their ammunition was spent, when they charged the Indians, and made good their retreat. The attacking party lost one man and "a big negro."

About the same time, the family of a Mr. M'Lane, on the Togolee, was assaulted, and Mrs. M'Lane and three of her children were barbarously murdered. About 8 miles from Blount's Town, the family of a Mr. Lamb was destroyed; and before the end of the month three others met the same fate. On the 28 April, as Capt. Rains was returning from a scout, with 18 men, he was fired upon from an ambush by a large body of Indians, within two miles of Fort King, and had 4 men killed, and 5 wounded; among the latter was the captain, severely. The whites reported that they killed three of the Indians. From another source, the affair of Capt. Rains is related as follows:— Some of his men had been lately killed by the Indians, "as they left the garrison" of Fort King, and he was determined to show them the same kind of play; accordingly, he placed some shells under a blanket, within hearing distance, and in the night he heard an explosion. Next morning, he took 18 men, and marched to the place where the shells had been deposited. He found no Indians, either dead or alive, but traces of blood, pony tracks, and fragments of garments. While examining these, all at once the Indians rose up, as it were, out of the ground, and nearly surrounded him and his little band; the terrible Halec Tustenugge was at their head, and with the most deafening yells rushed to the fight. The whites charged, and the Indians took to the trees, and thus prolonged the battle. At length, Halec, after desperately wounding Capt. Rains, fell himself, and was borne off by his warriors. The captain would doubtless have been despatched by the mighty arm of the chief, had not Serg. Jackson, too, badly wounded, rushed to his rescue, and shot Tustenugge. At this stage of affairs, the fight seems to have ended, and, as usual, the whites hastened away to report a victory. They rated the Indians at 93; but how they came by this minute information, we are not informed. But their bravery and courage are, probably, far less questionable than their statement of the number of their equally brave enemy. The same night, or the next, some Indians went to Stanley's plantation, within three miles of Newnansville, where they killed 12 hogs, cut down the fruit-trees, and burnt the buildings, by which 800 bushels of corn were consumed.

About the same time, a volunteer, named Sanders, was killed, about four miles from Newnansville; and another man, in company with him, was badly wounded.

On the 19 May, as Lieut. Martin and three other men were proceeding from Micanopy to Wakahoota, in charge of a government wagon, they were all cut off. The wagoner escaped, and carrying the intelligence to Micanopy, Lieut. Sanderson sallied out with 17 men, and pursued the Indians. He soon fell in with them, but was defeated, and himself, with 9 men, killed, besides three bloodhounds and their keepers; four other men were missing.

Some time in June, Col. Riley surprised an Indian camp on the Ouithlacoochee, killed two warriors, and took a man, woman, and child, prisoners. The man soon after escaped, and in pursuit of him, Capt. Mason was accidentally shot by his own men. About the same time, Col. Greene fell upon a small party of Indians in Middle Florida, killed three, and a white man with them. Towards the end of the month, Col. Harney returned from a long expedition, in which he captured Wild Cat's mother and daughter, liberated a negro, who had been a prisoner near two years, and was the only survivor of the crew of a vessel wrecked at New Smyrna. He also destroyed 27 cornfields of the Indians.

When Dr. Cotton Mather was about to write the history of a sanguinary massacre, which happened at Durham in New Hampshire, he began with the ominous expression of "*Bloody fishing at Oyster River!*" We have now to record a bloody *tragedy among tragedians* A Mr. Forbes, it appears, was not satisfied with what tragedies he could manufacture elsewhere, but must needs go to that country of tragedies, Florida, with his theatrical corps, as though the people there would prefer counterfeit to the real ones, or had not enough of both; doubtless the whites much preferred the former; but not so with the Indians, where they could have a hand in them. This company of players was in two wagons, passing from Picolata to St. Augustine, on the 23 May, and when within 5 or 6 miles of the latter place, were attacked by a large number of Indians under WILD CAT, and four of them killed. How many were in the company we are not told; but Forbes and the females escaped. The Indians, immediately after, surrounded Fort Searle, danced about it in defiance, and dared the soldiers to come out and fight; but the garrison was too weak to make a sortie. We have to close the relation of this tragedy with a comedy. The Indians had found time, before appearing at Fort Searle, to dress themselves in such of the actors' clothes as they had taken. Wild Cat had got on the turban of Othello; and others had sashes and spangles, which they took care to display to advantage. Wild Cat showed a rich velvet dress to some negroes who afterwards came in, and told them he would not take a hundred head of cattle for it.

At Cow Creek Hommock, near Fort White, there was a skirmish, on the 12 July, between Serg. Zeigler and three or four men, and 21 Indians. A corporal and two soldiers were killed, and the others were wounded.

On the 7 August, there happened a most horrid massacre at Indian Key. Six persons were killed by the Indians in their barbarous manner; among whom was Dr. Henry Perrine, formerly of Connecticut, a scientific gentleman, who had located himself there for the purpose of cultivating some rare plants which he had obtained in South America, while residing there as consul. There were upon Indian Key, at the time of this massacre, 44 people, all of whom had the good fortune to escape, except the six before named. All the houses were burned except one. The number of Indians was said to be 100 or 150.

On the 10 August, word was brought to Fort Barkee, that an encampment of Indians was discovered, about seven miles from thence, on the road to Fort Mitchell. Lieut. B. H. Arthur immediately marched out, with "a company of soldiers," to surprise them. The object was effected; two Indians were killed, one wounded, and 3 rifles taken. Early in the morning of the same day, the house of Mr. Wyley Jones, on the Econfina, about 6 miles north of the St. Joseph's, was attacked and burnt; the Indians shot Mrs. Jones and one of her children; a little daughter of 13 conveyed away four of her younger brothers and sisters to a safe place, and then returned to see what had become of her mother. She found her only time enough to see her expire! and then made a second escape!

About the middle of August, eleven families are said to have been broken up, on the Suanee River, and a great number of people killed. Among them was the family of a Mr. Courcy. He was from home at the time, and on his return, found his wife and six children murdered, and left in the most barbarous manner, here and there lying about the fields where they fell. Of Mr. Howell's family, his wife and one child were killed, and three other children escaped. A Mrs. Green and one child were also murdered. A Mrs. Patrick was shot in her house while preparing a bed for her children! Mr. Thomas Davis and two children, and Mr. Patrick's daughter, all murdered.

On the 4 September, as Capt. B. L. Beall, with 10 or 12 men, was upon a scout, he came suddenly upon about 30 Indians, who all escaped but four; the rest secured themselves in a swamp on Wacoosasa River. One of the prisoners was said to be Holatoochee, a sub-chief of the Mikasaukies. With these prisoners several guns were taken "in good order," and "a large deer-skin full of honey."

But two days after, Lieut. W. K. Hanson had a smart battle with some Seminoles, near Fort Wekahoota. Word being brought to the lieutenant then at that post, that Indians were in the vicinity, he immediately marched out with 35 regulars; and when one and a half miles from the fort, was fired upon from a gloomy hommock, which obliged him to retreat about 300 yards to an open wood, closely pursued by the Indians. Here he made a stand, and continued the fight about half an hour, at which time the Indians, to decoy him, retreated again to the hommock; but Lieut. Hanson, having now five of his men killed and wounded, concluded to retreat while he was at liberty to do so. The firing had brought out a reënforcement under Capt. Haw kins, who not long after charged the hommock, but he found no Indians. The number of Indians supposed to have fought in this skirmish, was stated to be 80. On the morning of the same day, the same Indians, it is said, killed and horribly mutilated a young man named Geiger; his head was severed and carried off.

On the 7 September, the house of a Mr. Dorsey is plundered and burnt;—fortunately, he had lately removed his family to Alabama. About ten days after, Lieut. Saunders, scouting with a party of dragoons in the neighborhood of Fort Mellon, captured a single Indian. This *brave* company first shot their prisoner, and afterwards hung him on a tree.

A more pacific policy, on the part of the government, had been instigated, in a manner not to be passed unheeded, by the public expression; and, consequently, Gen. Armistead was directed to act on the protective system; at the same time, to endeavor by every possible means to influence the Seminoles to go quietly from the land of their fathers. More effectually to carry these views into effect, a deputation of their countrymen had been sent for, beyond the Mississippi, and treated with to visit Florida, and intercede with their friends and brothers to give up the country, and end the controversy. Accordingly, this proposition was acceded to; and fourteen chiefs and others left Arkansas on this embassy, and arrived at Tampa, in Florida, on the 2 November. They came prepared to assure their countrymen that they would be far better off in Arkansas; and as they had been known to have been exceedingly opposed to emigration, and had been forced away from Florida themselves, great reliance was placed upon their endeavors to end the troubles. And to satisfy the whites of their good intentions, they left all their wives and children behind. Among them were the noted chiefs, Alligator, Holatoochee, and Micanopy; and on the morning of the 3d, they commenced their march of 100 miles for Fort King, where they were to have an interview with some of the hostile chiefs.

The deputation arrived at Fort King in about 4 days, viz., on the 6th, and Gen. Armistead on the 7th. Every effort was now made to discuss matters with freedom; and Halec Tustenugge, Tiger-tail, and many others, were waiting in the woods, not far off, when the before-named functionaries arrived. Sundry conferences and talks were had during the following six days; but what was said and done we are not informed; though, judging from what happened immediately after, it could not have been very satisfactory to the Indians, whatever they may have pretended; for, on the night of the 14 November, they all took leave very unceremoniously, and retired into their old fastnesses, as was conjectured, for they said nothing about that, nor did the whites have an opportunity of guessing where they had gone until the next morning. At this conduct of the hostiles, those from Arkansas expressed themselves "utterly astonished." As soon as the general was informed of the escape of the Indians, which was "early the next morning," he wrote to the secretary of war, Mr. Poinsett, in the following desponding strain:—"Thus have ended all our well-grounded hopes of bringing the war to a close by pacific measures; confident in the resources of the country, the enemy will hold out to the last, and can never be induced to come in again. Immediately upon the withdrawal of the Indians, orders were transmitted to commanders of regiments, to put their troops in motion; and before this reaches you, they will be scouting in every direction."

Notwithstanding these efforts at peace-making on the part of the whites, hostilities did not entirely cease on the side of the Indians. On the 17 October, a party went to Col. Gamble's plantation, at Welaune, in Jefferson county, where they fired upon and wounded a negro man, and took a woman, with whom they made off; but, in their flight, meeting with a company of whites, they left her, and she escaped. On the 24th, some bloodhounds led a company of soldiers to a house, in Middle Florida, in which three *white* men were captured, charged with aiding and abetting the Indians.

At Col. Hanson's plantation, about 20 Indians made quite a "business operation," on the 28 October, which, without any other *insurance* than their own peculiar tactics, was, to say the least of it, a very "risky transaction." Such is our judgment upon it, inasmuch as the place where it was done was only *two miles* from St. Augustine. Although they did not succeed to the extent of their wishes, yet they took and carried off all the blankets and other clothing which had been provided for a "large stock of negroes," for the ensuing winter; and when about to fire the buildings, became alarmed by the approach of some neighboring whites, whom a negro had informed of what was going on, and fled without doing further mischief. They had intended to have carried off all the slaves, but were prevented by this circumstance. Wild Cat is said to have led the Indians in this expedition.

People flocked in and garrisoned the place, and watched all night for the return of the Indians, who doubtless had not the most distant idea of repeating their visit. This led to one of those melancholy events, accounts of many of which are already upon our records. The news of the descent upon Col. Hanson's farm was carried immediately to Picolata, which caused Lieut. Graham to march with a small force for that place, hoping to surprise the Indians there, or in its vicinity. Accordingly, he approached it with great caution about 2 o'clock on the morning of the next day, not knowing that guards had been set to receive the Indians, should they return; and, unfortunately, being himself and company taken for Indians, were fired upon, and Serg. Wolcott was mortally, and Lieut. Graham severely wounded.

On the same day, the post rider between Forts Fanning and Macomb was found murdered, quartered, and thrown into a pond.

Every day adds new scenes to the tragedy. On the 1st day of November, as Lieut. Judd, with Mr. Falany and three dragoons, was proceeding from Fort Searle for St. Augustine, they were fired upon when near the eight-mile-post, by Indians concealed in bushes along the road, by which a sergeant and one private were killed, and Mr. Falany and another private severely wounded. Lieut. Judd escaped, as it were, by a miracle. He rode with the wounded soldier till he fell from his horse, then dismounting, dragged him from the path, and the Indians being just upon him, concealed himself in the bushes until they gave up the chase.

About the same time Col. Harney captured 12 Indians (women and children) near Fort Reid, on the St. John's. He found them in possession of 50 blankets, mostly new, pieces of calico, &c., supposed to have been taken from Indian Key, when it was destroyed in August last.

Fort Hanson, 15 miles from St. Augustine, was abandoned about the 5 November, and in two or three hours after was burnt by the Indians.

Early in December, Col. Harney, as much now the terror of the Seminoles as Col. Church was to the Wampanoags, or Daniel Boone to the Kikapoos, undertakes an expedition into the everglades. These much heard of and little known retreats extend over perhaps 100 square miles. They are an expanse of shoal water, varying in depth from one to five feet, dotted with innumerable low and flat islands, generally covered with trees or shrubs. Much of the water is shaded by an almost impenetrable saw-grass, as high as a man's head, but the little channels in every direction are free from it. It had been long supposed, that upon the islands in some part of this district the Indians had their head-quarters, from whence they had issued upon their destructive expeditions. This suspicion amounted to a certainty a little before this, from the testimony of a negro named *John*, who had escaped from a clan in that region and come in at Cape Florida. He had been with the Indians since 1835, at which time he was captured by them from Dr. Grew. Therefore it was determined by Col. Harney to take John as a guide, and endeavor to strike an effectual blow upon them in their own fastness. Accordingly, with 90 men in boats, he set out to traverse that monotonous world, the everglades. John faithfully performed his promise, and led the armament directly to the island where the Indians were, which was at once surrounded, and 38 prisoners taken and 2 killed. It proved to be the band of CHAI-KI-KA, as "noted a rogue" as Tatoson of old. He it was, it is said, who led the party that destroyed Indian Key, and traitorously massacred Col. Harney's men at the Synebal. As direct evidence of the fact, upwards of 2,000 dollars' worth of the goods taken from Dr. Perrine's settlement were identified, and 13 Colt's rifles lost at the Synebal were found; therefore, as an offset to those affairs, nine of the "warriors" were forthwith executed by hanging, and the tenth was preserved for a future guide.

When Col. Harney came upon Chaikika's band, the chief was at a short distance from his people, chopping wood, and on discovering that the foe was upon them, fled with all his might for the high grass. Several soldiers started in pursuit, but he outran them all except a private named Hall. When he found he could not escape from him, and being unarmed, he faced about, and with a smile of submission on his face, threw up his arms, in token of surrender. This availed him nothing. Hall levelled his rifle, which sent a bullet through his skull into his brains, and he fell lifeless into the water but a little distance from the shore of the island! How like the fall of the great Wampanoag chief! Col. Harney had one man killed and five wounded, of whom negro John, the pilot, was one.

There was great rejoicing at the success of Col. Harney all over Florida; and although his summary vengeance upon some of the prisoners called forth imprecations from many, those were drowned by the general burst of approbation; but this was damped in some degree by the loss of a very valuable and meritorious officer, who died immediately after the expedition returned from the everglades. This was Capt. W. B. Davidson, who died at Indian Key on the 24th of the same month, from disease engendered while upon that service.

About this time, or previous to 23 December, Tiger-tail's son and brother, with several others, came in to Fort King and surrendered. The old chief himself was daily expected in also, but that expectation only amounted to a disappointment. Not long after these Indians came in, a party went to Fort Walker, between Micanopy and Newnansville, where they killed three negroes and wounded one white woman, without being molested.

On the morning of the 29 December, a wagon was ordered to proceed from Fort Micanopy to Fort Wacahoota, and notwithstanding "positive orders had been given by the commanding general, forbidding any escort from post to post to consist of less than 30 men," but 11 went on this occasion. They were under the command of Lieuts. Sherwood and Hopson, and "as the morning was fine, a Mrs. Montgomery, wife of Lieut. Montgomery, rode out with them." This company had got scarcely three miles on the way when it fell into an ambush, and Mrs. Montgomery, Lieut. Sherwood, a sergeant-major, and two privates were immediately killed. Lieut. Sherwood and a soldier sacrificed themselves to save Mrs. Montgomery, but it availed her nothing. Her husband arrived on the ground soon after, but she was dead, and a soldier was lying by her side in the agonics of death, but had strength enough to say to her husband, "Lieutenant, I fought for your wife as long as I could," and then expired! Mrs. Montgomery was an accomplished lady from Cincinnati, and had not been married but about three weeks.

About the same time two wagoners were killed on the way from Pilatka to Fort Russell. They started in advance of the escort.—Such are some of the most prominent events of Florida warfare, which brings our account of it to the close of the year 1840.

BIOGRAPHY AND HISTORY

OF THE

INDIANS OF NORTH AMERICA.

BOOK V.

BOOK V.

BIOGRAPHY AND HISTORY OF THE IROQUOIS OR FIVE NATIONS, AND OTHER NEIGHBORING TRIBES OF THE WEST.

Nurslings of nature, I mark your bold bearing,
Pride in each aspect and strength in each form,
Hearts of warm impulse, and souls of high daring,
Born in the battle and reared in the storm.
The red levin flash and the thunder's dread rattle,
The rock-riven wave and the war trumpet's breath,
The din of the tempest, the yell of the battle,
Nerve your steeled bosoms to danger and death.—J. R. DRAKE

CHAPTER I.

Particulars in the history of the IROQUOIS *or* FIVE NATIONS—*Extent of their dominions—Antiquities and traditions—Destroy the* ERIES—*War with the* ADIRONDAKS—*Specimen of their language—Account of the chiefs*—GRANGUELE—BLACKKETTLE—*His bloody wars with the French*—ADARIO—*His singular stratagem to unite his countrymen against the French—Destroys Montreal and near a thousand inhabitants—Dies in peace with the French*—DEKANISORA *a renowned orator*—PEISKARET—*The miraculous stories concerning him. History of the journey of Five Iroquois chiefs to England.*

THE great western confederacy of Indian nations has commonly been styled by the French, *Iroquois*,* but generally by the English, the *Five Nations* † and sometimes the *Six Nations;* but either of the two latter appellations must be considered *only* as such, because we shall show, as we proceed, that they are not numerically true *now*, if they *ever* were. Five may have been the number which originally leagued together, but when that happened, if indeed it ever did, can never be known. It is a tradition that these people came from beyond the lakes, a great while ago, and subdued or exterminated the inhabitants of the country on this side. Even if this were the case, it

* "Le nom d'Iroquois est purement François, et a été formé du terme *Hiro*, qui signifie, *J'ai dit:* et par quel ces sauvages finissent tous leurs discours, comme les Latins faisoient autrefois par leur *Dixi;* et de Koué, qui est un cri, tantôt de tristesse, lorsqu'on le prononce en traînant, et tantôt de joye, quand on le prononce plus court. Leur nom propre est *Agonnonsionni*, qui veut dire *Faiseurs de Cabannes;* parce qu'ils les batissent beaucoup plus solides, que la plûpart des autres sauvages." *Charlevoix*, i. 270—1, (sub anno 1646,) also *Loskiel*, i. 2.—*Heckewelder*—and *Forster's Northern Voyages.*

† "*Ces barbares ne sont qu'une seule nation, et qu'un seul intérêt public. On pourroit les nommer pour la distribution du terrain, les Suisses de ce continent. Les Iroquois sont partager en cinq cantons, sçavoir les Tsonontoüans, les Goyogoans, les Onnotagues, les Onoyouts et les Agniés.*" (Lahontan, i. 35.) By the *Agniés* we are to understand *Mohawks.*

proves nothing of their origin; for there may have been a time when their ancestors went from this side to the country beyond, and so on. The Mohawks, sometimes called *Wabingi*, are said to have been the oldest of the confederacy, and that the "Onayauts" (Oneidas) were the first that joined them by putting themselves under their protection. The Onondagos were the next, then the "Teuontowanos, or Sinikers," (Senecas,) then the "Cuiukguos," (Cayugas.) The Tuscaroras, from Carolina, joined them about 1712, but were not formally admitted into the confederacy until about 10 years after that. The addition of this new tribe gained them the name of the Six Nations, according to most writers, but it will appear that they were called the Six Nations long before the last-named period.*

The Shawanese were not of the confederacy, but were called brothers by them. This nation came from the south, at no very remote period, and the Iroquois assigned them lands on the west branch of the Susquehannah, but looked upon them as inferiors.

The dominions of this "United People" cannot be particularly described, for they were never stationary; at one time they extended beyond the St. Lawrence and the Mississippi, and at another they were circumscribed between them. *Smith*, the historian of New York, says, "Our Indians universally concur in the claim of all the lands [in 1756] not sold to the English, from the mouth of Sorel River, on the south side of Lakes Erie and Ontario, on both sides of the Ohio, till it falls into the Mississippi; and on the north side of those lakes, that whole territory between the Outawais River, and the Lake Huron, and even beyond the straits between that and Lake Erie."

"When the Dutch began the settlement of New York, all the Indians on Long Island, and the northern shore of the sound, on the banks of Connecticut, Hudson, Delaware, and Susquehannah Rivers, were in subjection to the Five Nations; and within the memory of persons now living, acknowledged it by the payment of an annual tribute." As a proof of this it is mentioned that "a little tribe, settled at the Sugar-loaf mountain, in Orange county, to this day, [1756,] make a yearly payment of about £20 to the Mohawks."†

Among the many tribes or nations which they wholly or partially destroyed were the *Eries*, a powerful tribe on the southern shore of the great lake whose name they bore. In the year 1653 they were entirely extirpated, and no remnant of them has since been heard of in existence.‡

When the French settled in Canada in 1611, it was upon the lands of the Adirondaks, above Three Rivers. They found them at war with the Iroquois, then mainly seated along the southern side of Lake Ontario. The Adirondaks, by the assistance of the French, were able to defeat their enemies in every battle, who at length were in danger of a total extermination. Meanwhile the Dutch had begun their trade in the Hudson River, which they profitably carried on in arms with the Iroquois. Being now able to meet the Adirondaks on more equal footing, they continued the war, and with such success, that the Adirondaks, in their turn, became almost destroyed.

The Six Nations did not know themselves by such names as the English apply to them, but the name Aquanuschioni,§ which signified *united people*, was used by them.‖ This term, as is the case with most Indian words, is defined by a knowledge of its etymology. A knowledge of the Indian languages would enable us to know what almost every place in the country has

* In the *British Empire*, iii. 56, it is said, "The Cowetas also, or Creek Indians, are in the same friendship with them."

† Selected from the *well*-selected notes to *Sears's* Poem, entitled *Mineral Waters*.

‡ *Charlevoix*.

§ *Loskiel*, Hist. Mis. i. 2. "They say themselves, that they have sprung and grown up in that very place, like the very trees of the wilderness." *William's Key*. Another name they often gave themselves was, *Ongue-honwe*, which signified, a people surpassing all others. *Hist. Brit. Dominions* in *N. America*. Book iii. 55, (ed. 4to. Lond. 1773.)

‖ At a great assemblage of chiefs and warriors at Albany, in August, 1746, the chief speaker of the Six Nations informed the English commissioners that they had taken in the Messesagues as a seventh nation. *Colden*, Hist. F. Nations, ii. 175.

been noted for; whether hill or mountain, brook or river. It is said by *Colden*,* that New England was called *Kinshon*, by the Indians, which, he says, means a fish;† and that the New England Indians sent to the Iroquois a "model of a fish, as a token of their adhering to the general covenant." The waters of New England are certainly abundantly stored with fish; hence the name of "*the Fishing People.*"

We will here present a specimen of the language of the Six Nations, in the Lord's Prayer, all of whom, except the Tuscaroras, "speak a language radically the same." *So-ung-wau-ne-ha cau-ro-unk-yaw-ga, teh-see-ta-ro-an, sauh-son-e-you-sta, esa, saw-an-e-you, o-ket-tauh-se-la, eh-ne-au-wong, na, cau-ronunk-yawga, naugh-wou-shauga, ne-at-te-weh-ne-sa-lauga, taug-wau-nau-to-ro-no-an-tough-sick, to-an-taug-we-lee-whe-you-staung, che-nee-yeut, cha-qua-tau-ta-leh-whe-you-staun-na, tough-sau, taugh-waus-sa-re-neh, ta-waut-ot-ten-au-gal-ough-toung-ga, nas-aw-ne, sa-che-au-taug-was, co-an-teh-sal-oh-aun-za-ick-aw, esa, saw-au-ne-you, esa, sash-autz-ta, esa, soung-wa-soung, chen-ne-auh-a-aug-wa, au wen.*‡

Perhaps we cannot present the reader with a greater orator than GARANGULA, or, as he was called by the French, GRAND'GUEULE; though *Lahontan*, who knew him, wrote it Grangula. He was by nation an Onondaga, and is brought to our notice by the manly and magnanimous speech which he made to a French general, who marched into the country of the Iroquois to subdue them.

In the year 1684, Mr. *de la Barre*, governor-general of Canada, complained to the English, at Albany, that the Senecas were infringing upon their rights of trade with some of the other more remote nations. Governor *Dongan* acquainted the Senecas with the charge made by the French governor. They admitted the fact, but justified their course, alleging that the French supplied their enemies with arms and ammunition, with whom they were then at war. About the same time, the French governor raised an army of 1700 men, and made other "mighty preparations" for the final destruction of the Five Nations. But before he had progressed far in his great undertaking, a mortal sickness broke out in his army, which finally caused him to give over the expedition. In the mean time, the governor of New York was ordered to lay no obstacles in the way of the French expedition. Instead of regarding this order, which was from his master, the Duke of York, he sent interpreters to the Five Nations to encourage them, with offers to assist them.

De la Barre, in hopes to effect something by this expensive undertaking, crossed Lake Ontario, and held a talk with such of the Five Nations as would meet him.§ To keep up the appearance of power, he made a high-toned speech to *Grangula*, in which he observed, that the nations had often infringed upon the peace; that he wished now for peace; but on the condition that they should make full satisfaction for all the injuries they had done the French, and for the future never to disturb them. That they, the Senecas, Cayugas, Onondagos, Oneidas, and Mohawks, had abused and robbed all their traders, and unless they gave satisfaction, he should declare war. That they had conducted the English into their country to get away their trade heretofore, but the past he would overlook, if they would offend no more; yet, if ever the like should happen again, he had express orders from the king, his master, to declare war.

---

* Hist. Five Nations, i. 109.

† *Kickons*, in Algonkin; *Kegonce*, in Chippeway. *Long's Voyages*, &c. 202, 4to.

‡ *Smith's* Hist. N. York, 40. (ed. 4to.) The above differs somewhat from a copy in Proud's Pa. ii. 301.

§ As it will gratify most of our readers, we believe, to hear the general in his own words, we will present them with a paragraph of his speech to *Grangula* in his own language:—

"Le roi mon maître informé que les cinq Nations, Iroquoises contrevenoient depuis long-tems à la paix, m'aordonné de me transporter ici avec une escorte, et d'envoier Akouessan au village des Onnatagues, pour inviter les principaux chefs à me venir voir. L'intention de ce grand monarque est que nous fumions toi et moi ensemble dans le grand calumet de paix; pourvû que tu me promettes au nom des Tsonontouans, Goyogoans, Onnotagues, Onoyouts et Agniés, de donner une entiere satisfaction et dédommagement à ses sujets, et de ne rien faire à l'avenir, qui puisse causer une facheuse rupture." &c. *Lahontan*, i. 58, 59

Grangula listened to these words, and many more in the like strain, with that contempt which a real knowledge of the situation of the French army, and the rectitude of his own course, were calculated to inspire; and after walking several times round the circle, formed by his people and the French, addressing himself to the governor, seated in his elbow chair, he began as follows:—*

"*Yonnondio*;† I honor you, and the warriors that are with me likewise honor you. Your interpreter has finished your speech. I now begin mine. My words make haste to reach your ears. Harken to them.

"*Yonnondio*; You must have believed, when you left Quebeck, that the sun had burnt up all the forests, which render our country inaccessible to the French, or that the lakes had so far overflown the banks, that they had surrounded our castles, and that it was impossible for us to get out of them. Yes, surely, you must have dreamt so, and the curiosity of seeing so great a wonder has brought you so far. Now you are undeceived, since that I, and the warriors here present, are come to assure you, that the Senecas, Cayugas, Onondagas, Oneidas and Mohawks are yet alive. I thank you, in their name, for bringing back into their country the calumet, which your predecessor received from their hands. It was happy for you, that you left under ground that murdering hatchet that has been so often dyed in the blood of the French.

"*Hear, Yonnondio*; I do not sleep; I have my eyes open; and the sun, which enlightens me, discovers to me a great captain at the head of a company of soldiers, who speaks as if he were dreaming. He says, that he only came to the lake to smoke on the great calumet with the Onondagas. But *Grangula* says, that he sees the contrary; that it was to knock them on the head, if sickness had not weakened the arms of the French. I see *Yonnondio* raving in a camp of sick men, whose lives the Great Spirit has saved, by inflicting this sickness on them.

"*Hear, Yonnondio*; our women had taken their clubs, our children and old men had carried their bows and arrows into the heart of your camp, if our warriors had not disarmed them, and kept them back, when your messenger *Akouessan*‡ came to our castles. It is done, and I have said it.

"*Hear, Yonnondio*; we plundered none of the French, but those that carried guns, powder and balls to the Twightwies§ and Chictaghicks, because those arms might have cost us our lives. Herein we follow the example of the Jesuits, who break all the kegs of rum brought to our castles, lest the drunken Indians should knock them on the head. Our warriors have not beaver enough to pay for all those arms that they have taken, and our old men are not afraid of the war. This belt preserves my words.

"We carried the English into our lakes, to trade there with the Utawawas and Quatoghies,‖ as the Adirondaks brought the French to our castles, to carry on a trade, which the English say is theirs. We are born free. We neither depend on *Yonnondio* nor *Corlear*.¶ We may go where we please, and carry with us whom we please, and buy and sell what we please. If your allies be your slaves, use them as such, command them to receive no other but your people. This belt preserves my words.

"We knock the Twightwies and Chictaghicks on the head, because they had cut down the trees of peace, which were the limits of our country. They have hunted beaver on our lands. They have acted contrary to the customs of all Indians, for they left none of the beavers alive, they killed both male and female. They brought the Satanas into their country, to take part with them, after they had concerted ill designs against us. We have done

* "*Grangula*, qui pendant tout le descours avoit eu les yeux fixament attachez sur le bout de sa pipe, se leve, et soit par une civilité bisarre, ou pour se donner sans façon le tems de méditer sa réponse il fait cinq ou six tours dans nôtre cercle composé de sauvages et de François. Revenu en sa place il resta debout devant le général assis dans un bon fauteuil, et le regarant il lui dit." *Lahontan*, (i. 61, 62.) who was one of those present.

† The name they gave the governors of Canada. Spelt in *Lahontan*, *Onnontio*.

‡ The name they gave Mr. *Le Maine*, which signified a partridge.

§ Iwikties, *Colden*.

‖ Chictaghicks, *Colden*.

¶ The name they gave the governors of New York.

less than either the English or French, that have usurped the lands of so many Indian nations, and chased them from their own country. This belt preserves my words.

"*Hear, Yonnondio;* what I say is the voice of all the Five Nations. *Hear* what they answer. Open your ears to what they speak. The Senecas, Cayugas, Onondagas, Oneidas and Mohawks say, that when they buried the hatchet at Cadarackui, in the presence of your predecessor, in the middle of the fort, they planted the tree of peace in the same place; to be there carefully preserved: that, in the place of a retreat for soldiers, that fort might be a rendezvous for merchants: that, in place of arms and ammunition of war, beavers and merchandise should only enter there.

"*Hear, Yonnondio;* take care for the future, that so great a number of soldiers as appear there do not choke the tree of peace planted in so small a fort. It will be a great loss, if, after it had so easily taken root, you should stop its growth, and prevent its covering your country and ours with its branches. I assure you, in the name of the Five Nations, that our warriors shall dance to the calumet of peace under its leaves; and shall remain quiet on their mats, and shall never dig up the hatchet, till their brother *Yonnondio* or *Corlear* shall, either jointly or separately, endeavor to attack the country which the Great Spirit has given to our ancestors. This belt preserves my words, and this other, the authority which the Five Nations have given me."

Then, addressing himself to the interpreter, he said, "Take courage, you have spirit, speak, explain my words, forget nothing, tell all that your brethren and friends say to *Yonnondio*, your governor, by the mouth of *Grangula*, who loves you, and desires you to accept of this present of beaver, and take part with me in my feast, to which I invite you. This present of beaver is sent to *Yonnondio*, on the part of the Five Nations."

De la Barre was struck with surprise at the wisdom of this chief, and equal chagrin at the plain refutation of his own. He immediately returned to Montreal, and thus finished this inglorious expedition of the French against the Five Nations.

Grangula was at this time a very old man, and from this valuable speech we became acquainted with him; a very *Nestor* of his nation, whose powers of mind would not suffer in comparison with those of a Roman, or a more modern senator. He treated the French with great civility, and feasted them with the best his country would afford, on their departure. We next proceed to notice

BLACK-KETTLE, whom the French called LA CHAUDIERE NOIRE. A war with France, in 1690, brought this chief upon the records of history. In the summer of that year, Major *Schuyler*, of Albany, with a company of Mohawks, fell upon the French settlements at the north end of Lake Champlain. *De Callieres*, governor of Montreal, hastily collected about 800 men, and opposed them, but, notwithstanding his force was vastly superior, yet they were repulsed with great loss. About 300 of the enemy were killed in this expedition. The French now took every measure in their power to retaliate. They sent presents to many tribes of Indians, to engage them in their cause, and in the following winter a party of about 300 men, under an accomplished young gentleman, marched to attack the confederate Indian nations at Niagara. Their march was long, and rendered almost insupportable; being obliged to carry their provisions on their backs through deep snow. *Black-kettle* met them with about 80 men, and maintained an unequal fight until his men were nearly all cut off; but it was more fatal to the French, who, far from home, had no means of recruiting. *Black-kettle*, in his turn, carried the war into Canada during the whole summer following, with immense loss and damage to the French inhabitants. The governor was so enraged at his successes, that he caused a prisoner, which had been taken from the Five Nations, to be burnt alive. This captive withstood the tortures with as much firmness as his enemies showed cruelty. He sung his achievements while they broiled his feet, burnt his hands with red hot irons, cut and wrung off his joints, and pulled out the sinews. To close the horrid scene, his scalp was torn off, and red hot sand poured upon his head.

But this was a day in which that people were able to contend successfully against even European enemies. They had, in 1691, laid a plan to prevent the French from extending their settlements westward, for surprising those already formed, and for intercepting the western Indians as they brought down their peltries to them.

Two armies, of 350 men each, were to march out on this business about November; the first were to attack the fort at the Falls of St. Louis, and the other to proceed by way of Lake Champlain against the settlements. Before they set out, two Indian women, who had been captives among them, made their escape, and gave notice of their object. This, in a great measure, defeated the enterprise. Governor *De Callieres* raised troops, and strengthened every place he was able. The first party was discovered as they approached St. Louis, who, after skirmishing some time with the parties detached against them, retired without gaining any material advantage. The second did little more, and retired, after destroying some houses, and carrying with them some prisoners.

About the end of November, 34 Mohawks surprised some of the French Indians of St. Louis, who were carelessly hunting about Mount Chambly, killing 4 and capturing 8 others. Some escaped, and informed their friends of what had happened, and a company immediately went in pursuit. They overtook them near Lake Champlain, and a hard fight followed. The Catholic Indians rushed upon them with great fury, tomahawk in hand, and although the Mohawks had taken post behind rocks, they were routed, 6 being killed, and five taken. They also liberated all their friends taken at Mount Chambly.

In the beginning of February, 1692, *De Callieres* ordered M. *De Orvillieres* to march, with 300 men, into the peninsula, which terminates at the confluence of the Ottoway and St. Lawrence Rivers, to surprise a company of Iroquois he had been informed was there. It was their hunting-ground during the winter, and the pretext for attacking them was, that they were now there to surprise the settlements, and intercept such as passed up and down said rivers. While on his march, *De Orvilliers* met with an accident which obliged him to return to Montreal, and the command devolved upon Captain *De Beaucourt*. This officer marched to Isle Tonihata, not far from Cataroсouy or Katarokkui, where he surprised 50 Senecas in their cabins, killed 24, and took 6 of them prisoners.

Enough had passed before this to arouse the spirit of vengeance in the great chief of Onondaga, *Black-kettle;* but this last act could not be passed without, at least, an attempt at retaliation. About 100 Senecas were near the Sault de la Chaudiere, on Ottoway River, at this time, and *Black-kettle* soon after joined them with a band of his Onondagos; and they immediately put themselves into an attitude for intercepting their enemies.

Governor *De Callieres* had supposed that by the affair at Tonihata, the Iroquois were sufficiently humbled for the present, and that they were not to be regarded as capable of any considerable undertaking; but he soon discovered the error of his judgment; for 60 friendly Indians, having arrived at Montreal to trade, reported that the way was clear, but requested a guard when they returned. This was granted them. *S. Michel* volunteered upon this service, and put under the command of Lieutenant *De la Gemeraye*, 30 men. He had for his two ensigns, M. *Le Fresniere*, oldest son of the Sieur *Hertel*, and his brother. Having arrived at a place called the Long Falls, on Ottoway River, some marched upon the side of the river, while others endeavored to effect the passage of the falls in the boats. They had no sooner entered upon this business, when the warriors of *Black-kettle*, from an ambush, fired upon them, put the 60 Indians to flight, killing and wounding many of the French. They then rushed upon them with such fury that little time was allowed for resistance, and they fled to their boats for safety; but in their hurry they overturned them, and many were made prisoners. Among these were *S. Michel* and the two *Hertels*. *La Gemeraye* and a few soldiers only escaped.* *Black-kettle's* force on this occasion was computed at 140 men.

Some time now passed without hearing from *Black-kettle*, but on 15 July, 1692, he fell upon the Island of Montreal, as has already been recorded.

* *Colden* says, (i. 134,) that but four escaped in all.

Parties of soldiers collected and went in pursuit, overtook the rear of the Indians, killed 10 men, and retook many prisoners.

Some days after this, as the Sieur *De Lusignan* was passing near the Isles of Richelieu, *Black-kettle* fell upon his party, killed him, and put his men to flight. We hear nothing more of great moment of this famous chief, until the year 1697, in which he was treacherously murdered. He appears at this period to have concluded upon making peace with the French, and messengers had been despatched to Quebec upon that design. In the mean time he was hunting in the neighborhood of Catarocouy, where the French had a garrison, which was then commanded by Captain *Gemeraye*, before mentioned, to whom he gave notice that negotiations were on foot. Notwithstanding, 34 Algonquins, in the French interest, were suffered to go and surprise *Black-kettle* and his 40 hunters, who were not far from Catarocouy, at a place named *Quinte*. They were fallen upon at a time when they thought not of an enemy, and about half of them were slain, among whom was *Black-kettle;* his wife and many others were taken prisoners.*

ADARIO, KONDIARONK, SASTARETSI, and THE RAT, were names of a chief of great renown among the Hurons. The tribe to which he originally belonged was called the Dinondadies or Tionnontatés. His character, as drawn by *Charlevoix*, is as follows: "A man of a great mind, the bravest of the brave, and possessing altogether the best qualities of any known to the French in Canada." Of what we are about to relate concerning him, we have already given a sketch, which being defective in some of the main particulars, it was thought best to add another version of it in this place.

It was with no small difficulty that the French had engaged him in their cause. While on a visit to the governor, in 1688, he had passed his word that he would make war on his detested enemies, the Iroquois, and soon after departed for Michilimakinak, with a chosen band of his Hurons, resolved to distinguish himself by some signal exploit. In his way he passed by Catarocouy. At this place, he learned, to his surprise, that a negotiation was already on foot between the French and Iroquois, and was at the same time informed by the officer in command there, that he would infinitely disoblige M. *De Denonville*, if he should commit the least hostility upon any of the Iroquois, who was immediately to receive their ambassadors at Montreal together with hostages from all the cantons.

Kondiaronk concealed his surprise, and although now convinced that the French would sacrifice him and his allies, yet he made no complaint, and left the place as though to return to his own country. But he had no sooner conceived the design of intercepting the Iroquois ambassadors and hostages, than he set out upon it. Having placed his men in ambush at Famine Creek, he had waited but few days when they arrived. As they were descending the creek in their canoes, *Adario's* warriors fired upon them, killed several, and took the rest prisoners.

The celebrated DEKANISORA, or, as the French called him, *Teganisorens*, of Onondago, was at the head of this embassy, and was among the prisoners. He demanded of *Adario*, how it happened that he could be ignorant that he was an ambassador to their common father, and of his endeavor to bring about a lasting peace. The subtle chief completely subdued his irritable and indignant passions, by expressing far greater surprise than *Dekanisora* himself; protesting that the French were the whole cause of what had happened, for that they had sent him to surprise his party, and had assured him that he could do it with ease, as their numbers were small; and, to drive suspicions from the mind of *Dekanisora* and his people, set them all at liberty, but one, who was to supply the place of one of the Hurons that was killed. At parting, *Adario* spoke to them as follows:—

"Go, my brethren, I untie your bonds, and send you home again, though our nations be at war. The French governor has made me commit so black an action, that I shall never be easy after it, till the Five Nations have taken full revenge."

Some report that, after capturing *Dekanisora*, *Adario* returned to Kadarak-

* This is according to the text of *Charlevoix.*

kui, or Catarocouy, and that, being asked by the French from whence he came, said, "*From preventing peace.*" * They did not at first comprehend his meaning, but soon after, one of his prisoners, that escaped, gave them the history of the affair.

But for what followed, the character of *Adario* would stand well among warriors. He sacrificed his only prisoner, which completed this act of the tragedy; and it seemed necessary to carry out his deep-laid stratagem.

That the Iroquois should have no chance to believe the French innocent of the blood at the River Famine, which they had used great endeavors to effect, by sending emissaries among them, *Adario* went with his prisoner immediately to Michilimakinak, and delivered him to M. *De la Durantaye*, the commander of that post, who as yet had had no knowledge of any negotiation between the Iroquois and his superiors. Whereupon he forthwith caused the poor prisoner to be put to death. The news of this affair, the cunning chief caused to be made known among the cantons, by an old captive he had held a long time in bondage at his village, whom he now set at liberty for this purpose.

The catastrophes that befell the French not long after, and the suffering they endured, are almost without a parallel. †

About 1200 of the chief warriors of the Five Nations landed upon the Island of Montreal, 25 August, 1689, while the French were in perfect security, burnt their houses, sacked their plantations, and slew a vast number of the inhabitants. The English accounts say a thousand persons perished, but this number was no doubt far greater than the truth. In October following they attacked the island again with nearly equal success. These horrid disasters threw the whole country into the utmost consternation, in which the fort at Lake Ontario was abandoned by the garrison, and as soon possessed by the Indians. Here, among other things of great value to them, 28 barrels of gunpowder fell into their hands. Nothing now saved the French from an entire extermination but the ignorance of their enemies in the art of attacking fortified places.

Adario finally died at peace with the French, and almost in the act of concluding it. He had accompanied the heads of several tribes to Montreal, in 1701, to hold a treaty, and, on the 1 August, (that being the first day of public councils,) *Adario* found himself seized by sickness. Every thing was done to relieve him, ("as the governor general," says Charlevoix, "rested his principal hope of success in the treaty, upon him,") but without avail; being carried to l'Hotel Dieu, he died at two o'clock on the following night. At his funeral ‡ the greatest display was made, and nothing was omitted which could inspire the Indians present with a conviction of the great respect in which he was held. On his tomb-stone were engraved these words,

---

* "*Il répondit qu'il venoit de teur la paix; et qu'il ajoûta, nous verrons comment Ononthic se tirera de cette affaire.*"

† Few would wish to read, in English, the cruelties at the sacking of Montreal: the account of them, we agree with Dr. HOLMES, "is too horrid to translate."—"*Ils trouveren tout le mond endormi, et ils commencerent par massacrer tous les hommes; ensuite ils miren le feu aux maisons. Par-là tous ceux, qui y étoient restés, tomberent entre mains de ces sauvages, et essuyerent tout ce que la fureur peut inspirer à des barbares. Ils la pousserent même à des excès, dont on ne les avoit pas encore cru capables. Ils ouvrirent le sein des femmes enceintes, pour en arracher le fruit, qu'elles portoient, ils mirent des enfans tout vivans à la broche, et contraignirent les meres de les tourner pour les faire rôtir. Ils inventerent quantité d'autres supplices inouis, et 200 personnes de tout âge et de tout sexe perirent ainsi en moins d'une heure dans les plus affreux tourmens. Cela fait, l'ennemi s'aprocha jusqu'à une liue de la ville, faisant par tout les mêmes ravages, et exerçant les mêmes cruautes, et quand ils furen las de ces horreurs; ils firent 200 prisonniers, qu'ils emmenerent dans leur villages, où ils les brûlerent.*"

‡ "Le lendemain on fit ses funerailles, qui eurent quelque chose de magnifique et de singulier. M. *de St. Ours*, premier capitaine, marchoit d'abord à la tête de 60 soldats sous les armes. Seize guérriers Hurons, vêtus de longues robes de castor, le visage peint en noir, et le fusil sous le bras, suivoient, marchant quatre à quatre. Le clergé venoit après, et six chefs de guerre portoient le cercueil, qui étoit couvert d'un poële semé de fleurs, sur lequel il y avoit un chapeau avec un plumet, un hausse-col et une épée. Les freres et les enfans du défunt étoient derriere, accompagnés de tous les chefs des nations, et M. *de Vaudreuil*, gouverneur de la ville, qui menoit madame de *Champigny*, fermoit la marche."

"CY GIT LE RAT, CHEF HURON."

Which in English is, "*Here lies the Rat, Chief of the Hurons.*" The encomiums passed by the French upon him that was once their most dreaded enemy, are only equalled by those of their countrymen, *Fontenelle* and *Laharpe*, upon their favorite characters.

His body was a short time exposed before it was interred, dressed in the uniform of an officer, with his arms by his side, because he ranked as a captain, at the time of his death, in the French service.

The intercourse of *Dekanisora* with the French and English was long, and from the fact he was able, for much of the time during their wars, to be on good terms with both nations, we are to suppose that he possessed some skill in the arts of duplicity. He is first mentioned by *Charlevoix* in 1682, at which time he, with four other ambassadors, visited Montreal upon a peace expedition. He was suspected of insincerity by the French, and no reliance appears to have been put upon his pretensions. Twelve years after, *Colden* saw him, and thus speaks of him: "*Decanesora* had for many years the greatest reputation among the Five Nations for speaking, and was generally employed as their speaker, in their negotiations with both French and English: he was grown old when I saw him, and heard him speak; he had a great fluency in speaking, and a graceful elocution, that would have pleased in any part of the world. His person was tall and well made, and his features, to my thinking, resembled much the bustos of *Cicero*." *

If he were an old sachem in 1694, he must have been very old in 1726, for in this year he was at Albany with six other ambassadors, where, on the 14 September, they executed an agreement with the English; the conditions of which were that they should surrender all their hunting-grounds into the hands of Coorakhoo, as they called the King of England, "to be protected and defended by his said majesty, his heirs and successors, to and for the USE of us, our heirs, and the said three Nations." These had before been enumerated, as follows: "*Kanakarighton* and *Shanintsaronwe*, SINNEKE sachems; *Ottsoghkoree*, *Dekanisoree* and *Aenjeucratt*, CAYOUGE sachems; *Raclyakadorodon* and *Sadageenaghtie*, ONONDAGO sachems." †

Charlevoix was unable to ascertain the time of *Dekanisora's* death, although he learned that it happened at the Falls of St. Louis. Under date 1693, he speaks in high terms of him, *Oureouharé* and *Garakonthié*, Iroquois Christians, whom *Dekanisora* had employed secretly to bring about a peace with that nation; but knew not, as to his Christianity, he said, at that time; but was certain that he had professed it. He probably died about 1730.

We will go a little back in this place, to notice a chief of the Adirondaks, of whom the most extraordinary stories are told; even those of *Jack-the-giant-killer* are but little more incredible. And even though Father *Charlevoix* was familiar with them, yet he deemed them as fiction, it will be imagined, from his not relating them in his minute history. The name of PEISKARET was, for sundry years previous to 1646, terrible to the enemies of the Adirondaks. This nation, when Canada was settled by the French, in 1603, resided about 300 miles to the westward of Three Rivers. How long they had been at war with the Iroquois at this time, is not mentioned, but it was continued until the death of *Peiskaret* in 1646, though with interruption and various success; but with this chief perished all opposition, and the Adirondaks figured no more as a nation.

As we have put the reader upon his guard, about receiving the huge stories about *Peiskaret* with too much confidence, it will be expected at our hands, perhaps, that we give a sample of them, as it may be said, "possibly they are true." We might have done this without thus premising, as others have done, upon the authority of *Colden*, (an author of small value, comparatively speaking.) His relation proceeds:—

"An Indian named *Piskaret* was at this time ‡ one of the captains of

* Hist. FIVE NATIONS, i. 156.

† Governor *Thomas Pownal*, Administration of the British Colonies, i. 238, 239.

‡ He mentions no particular time, but that of the settlement of Canada, in 1603; but some time during the war of which we have spoken must be understood.

greatest fame among the Adirondacks; this bold man, with four other captains, set out for Trois Rivières in one canoe, each of them being provided with three muskets, which they loaded with two bullets apiece, joined with a small chain ten inches long. They met with five canoes in Sorel River, each having 10 men of the Five Nations on board. *Piskaret* and his captains, as soon as those of the Five Nations drew near, pretended to give themselves up for lost, and sung their death-song, then suddenly fired upon the canoes, which they repeated with the arms that lay ready loaded, and tore those birch vessels betwixt wind and water.* The men of the Five Nations were so surprised, that they tumbled out of their canoes, and gave *Piskaret* and his companions the opportunity of knocking as many of them on the head as they pleased, and saving the others, to feed their revenge, which they did by burning them alive with the most cruel torments. This, however, was so far from glutting *Piskaret's* revenge, that it seemed rather to give a keener edge to it; for he soon after undertook another enterprise, in which none of his countrymen durst accompany him. He was well acquainted with the country of the Five Nations, and set out about the time the snow began to melt, with the precaution of putting the hinder part of his snow-shoes forward, that if any should happen upon his footsteps, they might think he was gone the contrary way; and for further security, went along the ridges and high grounds, where the snow was melted, that his track might be often lost. When he came near one of the villages of the Five Nations, he hid himself till night, and then entered a cabin, while every body was fast asleep murdered the whole family, and carried their scalps into his lurking-place. The next day the people of the village searched for the murderer in vain. The following night he murdered all he found in another cabin. The inhabitants next day searched likewise in vain for the murderer: but the third night a watch was kept in every house. *Piskaret*, in the night, bundled up the scalps he had taken the two former nights, to carry, as the proof of his victory, and then stole privately from house to house, till at last he found an Indian nodding, who was upon the watch in one of the houses: he knocked this man on the head; but as this alarmed the rest, he was forced immediately to fly. He was, however, under no great concern from the pursuit, being more swift of foot than any Indian then living. He let his pursuers come near him from time to time, and then would dart from them. This he did with design to tire them out, with the hopes of overtaking him. As it began to grow dark, he hid himself, and his pursuers stopped to rest. They not being apprehensive of any danger from a single man, soon fell asleep; and the bold *Piskaret* observing this, knocked them all on the head, and carried away their scalps with the rest. Such stories as these," continues *Colden*, "are told among the Indians, as extraordinary instances of the courage and conduct of their captains."

Before this, as we apprehend, though related afterwards by this author, were the great expeditions of the Iroquois against the Adirondaks. The French took part with the latter from the beginning, and when *Champlain* visited the country, he joined a party of them, and went against the Iroquois, and, with the aid of his fire-arms, overcame them in a battle near Lake Corlar, which was henceforth called Lake Champlain. Two hundred Iroquois were in this fight, and the French kept themselves concealed, until it began, then rushed forward, and immediately put the Iroquois to flight. This was the first time they had seen the effects of guns. This affair was in 1611.

Finally, the Iroquois, having grown conscious of their strength, felt confident that, if they could prevent the French from assisting them, they could withstand them. Therefore, they pretended to be well affected towards their religion, and requested that missionaries should be sent among them. This was done without delay. Their real object was soon apparent; for they treated the Jesuit missionaries only as hostages, and this was the means of making them stand neutral while they carried on their war with the Adirondaks and Quatoghies or Hurons, whom they soon after defeated "in a dreadful battle fought within two leagues of Quebeck."

This expedition turned out so much to their advantage, "the Five Nations

* The author of *Indian Tales* has copied this closely, but gives no credit. *Tales*, ii. 36 &c.

gave out, that they intended next winter * to visit the governor of Canada these visits are always made with much show. Under this pretence they gathered together 1000 or 1200 men. Their outscouts met with *Piskaret* near Nicolet River, and still pretending a friendly visit to the governor of Canada, as their only design, he told them, that the Adirondacks were divided into two bodies, one of which hunted on the north side of St. Lawrence River at Wabmake, three leagues above Trois Rivières, and the other at Nicolet. As soon as they had gained this information, they killed him, and returned with his head to the army. The Five Nations divided likewise into two bodies: they surprised the Adirondacks, in both places, and in both cut them in pieces."

This account is more circumstantial than that given by *Charlevoix*, but, as we have seen, would have been without any value, but for his chronology. He states that, by their previous conduct, the Mohawks had reason to expect, that all the neighboring nations would join to oppose them, and that they sent out parties to observe what was passing among them; that one of these scouts met *Peiskaret* alone, but dared not attack him; being persuaded he would kill at least half of them, as he had often done before. They therefore accosted him as a friend, while some came up behind him, and stabbed him to the heart.

But for the French, the Iroquois had now been complete masters of all the northern and western regions; and some have observed, that had they known the weakness of those white neighbors, at the time they overcame the Algonquins, near Quebec, they might easily have cleared the country of them also.

We will close this chapter with an account of the visit of five Iroquois chiefs to England. The English in America had supposed that if they could convince the Indian nations of the power and greatness of their mother country, they should be able to detach them forever from the influence of the French. To accomplish this object, these chiefs were prevailed upon to make the voyage. They visited the court of Queen *Anne* in the year 1710. None of the American historians seem to have known the names of these chiefs, or, if they did, have not thought it proper to transmit them. *Smith*, in his history of New York, mentions the fact of their having visited England, and gives the speech which they made to the queen, and says it is preserved "in *Oldmixon*," perhaps in the 2d edition of his BRITISH EMPIRE IN AMERICA,† as nothing of the kind is found in his history of England, although he records the circumstance, and ill-naturedly enough too. We think he would hardly have done even this, but for the purpose of ridiculing the friends of the queen. The following is all that he says of them:‡ "Three weeks after the battle of Sarragossa was fought by General *Stanhope*, whose victory made way for the march to Madrid, the news of the victory was brought to the queen by Colonel *Harrison*, the 15 September, O. S., at which time the High-church rabble were pelting General *Stanhope's* proxy, and knocking down his friends at the Westminster election. However, for the successes in Spain, and for the taking of Doway, Bethune and Aire, by the duke of *Marlborough* in Flanders, there was a thanksgiving-day appointed, which the queen solemnized in St. James's chapel. To have gone as usual to St. Paul's, and there to have had Te Deum sung on that occasion, would have shown too much countenance to those brave and victorious English generals, who were fighting her battles abroad, while High-church was plotting, and railing, and addressing against them at home. The carrying of four § Indian Casaques about in the queen's coaches, was all the triumph of the Harleian administration; they were called kings, and clothed, by the

* No one can tell when *next winter* was, that is, what year it was in, by any connection in *Colden's* text; he is so exceedingly loose with regard to dates; but, according to *Charlevoix*, it was in 1646.

† The first edition (which I possess) was printed in 1708.

‡ *Hist. England*, ii. 452. (Fol. London, 1735.)

§ He says *five*, a few lines onward, in his usual random mode of expression, supposing it all the same, doubtless, *as he was only considering Indians!* It will be seen that five was the real number.

play-house tailor, like other kings of the theatre; they were conducted to audience by Sir *Charles Cotterel;* there was a speech made for them, and nothing omitted to do honor to these five monarchs, whose presence did so much honor to the new ministry; which the latter seemed to be extremely fond of, and defrayed all their expenses during their stay here. They were the captains of the four nations, [Five Nations,] in league with the English at New York and New England, and came in person to treat of matters concerning trade with the lords commissioners of plantations; as also of an enterprise against the French, and their confederate Indians in those parts."

Sir *Richard Steele* mentions these chiefs in his Tatler of May 13, 1710, and *Addison* makes them the subject of a number of the Spectator the next year, at a suggestion of Dean *Swift.** Neither of these papers, however, contain many facts respecting them. In the former it is mentioned that one of them was taken sick† at the house where they were accommodated during their stay in London, and they all received great kindness and attention from their host, which, on their departure, was the cause of their honoring him with a name of distinction; which was *Cadaroque*, and signified "*the strongest fort in their country.*" In speaking of their residence, Mr. *Steele* says, "They were placed in *a* handsome apartment at an upholster's in King-street, Covent-garden." There were fine portraits of each of them painted at the time, and are still to be seen in the British Museum.‡

The best and most methodical account of these chiefs was published in the great annual history by Mr. *Boyer*, § and from which we extract as follows: "On the 19 April *Te Yee Neen Ho Ga Prow*, and *Sa Ga Yean Qua Prah Ton*, of the Maquas; *Elow Oh Koam*, and *Oh Nee Yeath Ton No Prow*, ‖ of the river sachem,¶ and the Ganajoh-hore sachem,** four kings, or chiefs of the Six Nations †† in the West Indies, ‡‡ which lie between New England, and New France, or Canada: who lately came over with the West India fleet, and were cloathed and entertained at the queen's expense, had a public audience of her majesty at the palace of St. *James*, being conducted thither in two of her majesty's coaches, by Sir *Charles Cotterel*, master of the ceremonies, and introduced by the duke of *Shrewsbury*, lord chamberlain. They made a speech by their intrepreter, which Major *Pidgeon*, who was one of the officers that came with them, read in English to her majesty, being as follows:—

"Great Queen—We have undertaken a long and tedious voyage, which none of our predecessors §§ could be prevailed upon to undertake. The motive that induced us was, that we might see our great queen, and relate to her those things we thought absolutely necessary, for the good of her, and us, her allies, on the other side the great water. We doubt not but our great

---

* "I intended to have written a book on that subject. I believe he [*Addison*] has spent it all in one paper, and all the under hints there are mine too." *Swift's Letter to Mrs. Johnson, dated London*, 28 April, 1711.

† This was probably the one that died, of whom *Kalm*, in his travels in America, i. 210, makes mention; though I do not find a record of it in any periodical of that day.

‡ Notes to the *Spectator*, ed. in 8 vols. 8vo. London, 1789.

§ "The Annals of Queen *Anne's* Reign, Year the IX. for 1710," 189—191. This is a work containing a most valuable fund of information, and is, with its continuation, a lasting monument to its learned publisher; his being dragged into the Dunciad in one of Pope's freaks notwithstanding.

‖ We have these names in the Tatler, spelt *Tee Yee Neen Ho Ga Row*, *Sa Ga Yeath Rua Geth Ton*, *E Tow Oh Koam*, and *Ho Nee Yeth Taw No Row.*

¶ It is difficult to conceive what is meant by *River Indians* from many of our authors. In the Appendix to *Jefferson's Notes*, 308, they are called River Indians, or Mohickanders, "who had their dwellings between the west branch of Delaware and Hudson's river, from the Kittatinny ridge down to the Rariton." The "Mohiccons" were another tribe about the islands and mouth of the Hudson.

** Probably the chief of Canajohara.

†† *Query.* If, according to *Colden* and others, the Tuscaroras did not join the Iroquois until 1712, and until that time these were called the Five Nations, how comes it that they were known in England by the name of *Six Nations* in 1710?

‡‡ No one can be misled by this error, any more than an Englishman would be by being told that London is situated at the foot of the Rocky Mountains.

§§ None of the Six Nations, must be understood

queen has been acquainted with our long and tedious war, in conjunction with her children, against her enemies the French: and that we have been as a strong wall for their security, even to the loss of our best men. The truth of which our brother *Queder*, Colonel [*Peter*] *Schuyler*, and *Anadagarjaux*, Colonel *Nicholson*, can testify; they having all our proposals in writing We were mightily rejoiced when we heard by *Anadagarjaux*, that our great queen had resolved to send an army to reduce Canada; from whose mouth we readily embraced our great queen's instructions: and in token of our friendship, we hung up the kettle, and took up the hatchet; and with one consent joined our brother *Queder*, and *Anadagarjaux*, in making preparations on this side the lake, by building forts, store-houses, canoes and batteaux; whilst *Aundiasia*, Colonel *Vetch*, at the same time, raised an army at Boston, of which we were informed by our ambassadors, whom we sent thither for that purpose. We waited long in expectation of the fleet from England, to join *Anadiasia*, to go against Quebec by sea, whilst *Anadagarjaux*, *Queder*, and we, went to Port Royal by land; but at last we were told, that our great queen, by some important affair, was prevented in her design for that season. This made us extreme sorrowful, lest the French, who hitherto had dreaded us, should now think us unable to make war against them. The reduction of Canada is of such weight, that after the effecting thereof, we should have free hunting, and a great trade with our great queen's children; and as a token of the sincerity of the Six Nations, we do here, in the name of all, present our great queen with the belts of wampum. We need not urge to our great queen, more than the necessity we really labor under obliges us, that in case our great queen should not be mindful of us, we must, with our families, forsake our country, and seek other habitations, or stand neuter; either of which will be much against our inclinations. Since we have been in alliance with our great queen's children, we have had some knowledge of the Savior of the world; and have often been importuned by the French, both by the insinuations of their priests, and by presents, to come over to their interest, but have always esteemed them men of falsehood; but if our great queen will be pleased to send over some persons to instruct us, they shall find a most hearty welcome. We now close, with hopes of our great queen's favor, and leave it to her most gracious consideration."

We cannot but respond *amen* to Mr. *Oldmixon's* opinion of this speech, namely, that it was made *for* instead of *by* the chiefs; still we thought it proper to print it, and that by so doing we should give satisfaction to more than by withholding it. Our account next proceeds: "On Friday, the 21 April, the four Indian princes went to see Dr. *Flamstead's* house, and mathematical instruments, in Greenwich Park; after which they were nobly treated by some of the lords commissioners of the admiralty, in one of her majesty's yachts. They staid about a fortnight longer in London, where they were entertained by several persons of distinction, particularly by the duke of *Ormond*, who regaled them likewise with a review * of the four troops of life-guards; and having seen all the curiosities in and about this metropolis, they went down to Portsmouth, through Hampton Court and Windsor, and embarked on board the Dragon, one of her majesty's ships, Captain *Martin*, commodore, together with Colonel *Francis Nicholson*, commander-in-chief of the forces designed for an expedition in America. On the 8 May, the Dragon and Falmouth sailed from Spithead, having under convoy about 18 sail, consisting of merchantmen, a bomb-ship and tender, and several transports, with British officers, a regiment of marines, provisions and stores of war; and on the 15 July arrived at Boston in New England."

Little is to be gathered from *Smith's* history of New York relative to those sachems. He gives a speech which they made to the queen, but it is a meagre abridgment of less than half of the one above, and the

* And the chiefs made a speech in return, but our author makes this note upon it "N. B. The speech which was said to have been made by them, on that occasion, to the duke of *Ormond*, is spurious."

rest is omitted entirely. "The arrival of the five sachems in England made a great bruit throughout the whole kingdom The mob followed wherever they went, and small cuts of them were sold among the people." *

The main object of their visit to England was not, nor, in the nature of things, could it be effected. I mean the introduction of Christianity among them. Even these very sachems, who, according to the stories of that day, requested to have missionaries settled with them, were among the first to neglect them when settled among them.† "It might have been imagined," says the author just cited, "the sachems, those petty kings, who were in England in the late Queen's time, should have been so strongly affected with seeing the grandeur, pleasure, and plenty of this nation, that when they came to their own countries, they would have tried to reduce their people to a polite life; would have employed their whole power to expel that rude barbarism, and introduce arts, manners, and religion: but the contrary happened; they sunk themselves into their old brutal life, and though they had seen this great city, [London,] when they came to their own woods, they were all savages again."

There cannot be a wider difference than the two nations, English and French, make in their accounts of the original condition, manners and customs of the Iroquois. While the writers of the former described them as the most barbarous, cruel, and bloody, those of the latter portray them in enviable colors. This difference seems to have entirely arisen from the different relation of the two nations to them. That they were cruel and barbarous to their enemies is agreed by both, and it unfortunately happened that the English were generally their enemies, until the reduction of Canada, in 1760.

CHAPTER II.

Tamany, *a famous ancient Delaware—His history—*Shikellimus*—Favors the Moravian Brethren—His reception of Count Zinzendorf—His death—*Canassatego*—Visits Philadelphia—His speech to the Delawares—Anecdotes of him—*Glikhikan*—His speech to Half-king—His attachment to the Christian Indians—Meets with much trouble from Captain Pipe—Conduct of Half-king—Of Pipe—Glikhikan perishes in the massacre at Gnadenhuetten—*Pakanke*—His history—*Netawatwees*—Becomes a Christian—His speech to Pakanke—His death—*Paxnous*—*Tadeuskund*—His history and death—*White-eyes*—His transactions with the missionaries—*Skenando*—His celebrated speech—Curious anecdote of him—His death.*

Tamany was a name much in print, fifty years since, but of what nation or country, or whether applied to an imaginary or real personage, by any account accompanying it, no one could determine. The truth respecting this has at length come to light.

He was a Delaware chief, of similar renown to the *Basheba* of Kennebeck, and *Nanepashemet* of Massachusetts; and we infer from *Gabriel Thomas*,‡ that possibly he might have been alive as late as 1680 or 1690. He wrote the name *Temeny*.

Mr. *Heckewelder*, in his Historical Account of the Indian Nations, devotes a chapter to this chief and *Tadeuskund*. He spells the name *Tamaned*. The difficulty of gaining information of deceased individuals among the Indians is well known to those conversant with their history. Mr. *Heckewelder* says, "No white man who regards their feelings, will introduce such subjects in conversation with them." This reluctance to speak of the de-

* Hist. New York, 122. ed. 4to. London, 1757. Beautiful full-length portraits of four of these chiefs were done in mezzotinto at the time they were in England, but they were long since of very rare occurrence. I possess the best set of them which I have ever seen. They are usually found in black frames, and are about 20 inches in height by 12 in breadth. The portrait of the one that died was not probably taken, which accounts for our having but four.

† Humphrey's Historical Account Soc. for Prop. Gospel, 309, 310.

‡ "Who resided there [in Pennsylvania] about 15 years," and who published "*An Historical and Geographical Account of Pa.* and *W. Jersey*," 12mo. *London*, 1698.

parted he attributes to "the misfortunes which have befallen some of the most beloved and esteemed personages among them, since the Europeans came among them." It is believed, however, that it had a more remote origin. The same author continues, "All we know of *Tamened* is, that he was an ancient Delaware chief, who never had his equal." *

It is said that when, about 1776, Colonel *George Morgan*, of Princeton, New Jersey, visited the western Indians by direction of congress, the Delawares conferred on him the name of *Tamany*, "in honor and remembrance of their ancient chief, and as the greatest mark of respect which they could show to that gentleman, who they said had the same address, affability and meekness as their honored chief." †

"The fame of this great man extended even among the whites, who fabricated numerous legends respecting him, which I never heard, however, from the mouth of an Indian, and therefore believe to be fabulous. In the revolutionary war, his enthusiastic admirers dubbed him a saint, and he was established under the name of St. *Tammany*, the patron saint of America. His name was inserted in some calendars, and his festival celebrated on the first day of May in every year. On that day a numerous society of his votaries walked together in procession through the streets of Philadelphia, their hats decorated with bucks' tails, and proceeded to a handsome rural place out of town, which they called the *wigwam;* where, after a *long talk* or Indian speech had been delivered, and the calumet of peace and friendship had been duly smoked, they spent the day in festivity and mirth. After dinner, Indian dances were performed on the green in front of the wigwam, the calumet was again smoked, and the company separated."

It was not till some years after the peace that these yearly doings were broken up, which would doubtless have lasted longer but for the misfortune of the owner of the ground where they were held. Since that time Philadelphia, New York, and perhaps other places, have had their *Tamany* societies, *Tamany* halls, &c. &c. In their meetings these societies make but an odd figure in imitating the Indian manner of doing business, as well as in appropriating their names upon one another.

Among the multitude of poems and odes to *Tamany*, the following is selected to give the reader an idea of the acts said to have been achieved by him:—

"Immortal *Tamany*, of Indian race,
Great in the field and foremost in the chase!
No puny saint was he, with fasting pale;
He climbed the mountain, and he swept the vale,
Rushed through the torrent with unequalled might;
Your ancient saints would tremble at the sight;
Caught the swift boar and swifter deer with ease,
And worked a thousand miracles like these.
To public views he added private ends,
And loved his country most, and next his friends;
With courage long he strove to ward the blow;
(Courage we all respect ev'n in a foe;)
And when each effort he in vain had tried,
Kindled the flame in which he bravely died!
To *Tamany* let the full horn go round;
His fame let every honest tongue resound;
With him let every gen'rous patriot vie,
To live in freedom or with honor die." ‡

We are next to speak of a chief, concerning whom much inquiry has been made from several considerations. We mean

Shikellimus, the father of the celebrated *Logan*. He was a Cayuga sachem, and styled by Mr. *Loskiel*, § "first magistrate and head chief of all the Iroquois Indians living on the banks of the Susquehannah, as far as Onondago.

He is the same often mentioned by *Colden*, ‖ under the names *Shickcalamy*. *Shicalamy*, and *Shick Calamy*, and occupies a place next the famous *Canassa*

* Some will doubtless imagine that this was *knowing* a good deal.
† Heckewelder, *ut supra.* ‡ *Carey's* Museum, v. 104. § *Hist. Missions*, ..
‖ *Hist. Five Nations*, ii. 57, 69, 75, 77, 85.

tego. His residence was at Conestoga in Pennsylvania. He was present at a great council held in Philadelphia in 1742, with 91 other chiefs, counsellors and warriors of the Six Nations, to consult about the encroachments of some of the Delawares upon the people of Pennsylvania, as will be found mentioned in the history of *Canassatego.* That he was a man of much consequence among the Five Nations will appear from the fact, that *Canassatego* repeated a speech of his to Governor *Thomas,* when the assault upon *William Webb* was inquired into, "whereby his [the said *Webb's*] jaw-bone was broke, and his life greatly endangered by an unknown Indian." This took place upon the disputed lands in the forks of the Delaware. "*Canassatego* repeating the message delivered to the Six Nations by *Shickcalamy,* in the year 1740, with a string of wampum, said in answer: 'The Six Nations had made diligent inquiry into the affair, and had found out the Indian who had committed the fact; he lived near Asopus, [Æsopus,] and had been examined and severely reproved; and they hoped, as *William Webb* was recovered, the governor would not expect any further punishment, and therefore they returned the string of wampum received from their brethren, by the hand of *Shickcalamy,* in token that they had fully complied with their request.'"

When Count *Zinzendorf,* founder of the sect called Moravians, visited this country, in 1742, he had an interview with this chief at Shamokin. *Conrad Weiser* was present, and *Shikellimus* inquired with great anxiety the cause of the count's visit. *Weiser* told him "that he was a messenger of the living God, sent to preach grace and mercy;" to which he answered, "he was glad that such a messenger came to instruct his nation."

While in the exercise of his pious labors, *Zinzendorf* very narrowly escaped assassination; and, to illustrate the force of superstition upon untutored minds, it will be proper to relate the circumstance. Having arrived on the banks of the Wyoming, the Indians could not believe that he had come solely for their benefit, but had come to the conclusion that his real object was the acquisition of land; and they therefore resolved to put him to death. On a cool evening in September, as he sat alone in his tent, upon a bundle of weeds, which was his bed, the appointed assassins approached his frail mansion. He had a small fire, and was writing at the time; and nothing prevented the easy execution of their commission. A blanket, suspended by the corners, formed the door of his tent, and as the Indians drew this a little aside, they beheld a large rattlesnake which the fire had driven from his covert, laying near the venerable man, but was not seen by him; being too deeply engaged in his subject to notice him or the more dangerous Indians. The rattlesnake being an animal they feared and respected as a kind of Manito, and seeing it in company with the stranger, they doubted not of his divine origin also, and at once shrunk from their object, and returned to report what they had seen to their brethren in their village.* He was now received by the Shawanese, and a mission was begun among them.

Shikellimus was a great friend of the missionaries, and his death was a severe loss to them. He died at his own residence in Shamokin, in 1749. We have already named the chief proper to be proceeded with, on finishing our account of *Shikellimus.*

CANASSATEGO, a chief of the Six Nations, was of the tribe of Onondago. In 1742, there arose a dispute between the Delawares and the government of Pennsylvania, relative to a tract of land in the forks of the Delaware. The English claimed it by right of prior purchase, and the Delawares persisted in their claim, and threatened to use force unless it should be given up by the whites. This tribe of the Delawares were subject to the Six Nations, and the governor of Pennsylvania sent deputies to them to notify them of the trouble, that they might interfere and prevent war. It was on this occasion that *Canassatego* appeared in Philadelphia with 230 warriors. He observed to the governor, "that they saw the Delawares had been an unruly people, and were altogether in the wrong; that they had concluded to remove them, and oblige them to go over the river Delaware, and quit all claim to any lands on this side for the future, since they had received pay for them, and

* Chapman's Hist. Wyoming, 20 to 22.

it is gone through their guts long ago. They deserved, he said, to be taken by the hair of the head, and shaken severely, till they recovered their senses, and became sober; that he had seen with his own eyes a deed signed by nine of their ancestors, above fifty years ago, for this very land, and a release signed not many years since, by some of themselves, and chiefs yet living, (and then present,) to the number of 15 and upwards; but how came you (addressing himself to the Delawares present) to take upon you to sell land at all? We conquered you; we made women of you; you know you are women; and can no more sell land than women; nor is it fit you should have the power of selling lands, since you would abuse it. This land you claim is gone through your guts; you have been furnished with clothes, meat and drink, by the goods paid you for it, and now you want it again, like children as you are. But what makes you sell lands in the dark? Did you ever tell us that you had sold this land? Did we ever receive any part, even the value of a pipe shank, from you for it? You have told us a blind story, that you sent a messenger to us, to inform us of the sale; but he never came amongst us, nor did we ever hear any thing about it. This is acting in the dark, and very different from the conduct our Six Nations observe in the sales of land. On such occasions they give public notice, and invite all the Indians of their united nations, and give them all a share of the presents they receive for their lands.

"This is the behavior of the wise united nations. But we find you are none of our blood; you act a dishonest part, not only in this, but in other matters; your ears are ever open to slanderous reports about your brethren. For all these reasons, *we charge you to remove instantly; we don't give you liberty to think about it.* You are women." They dared not disobey this command, and soon after removed, some to Wyoming and Shamokin, and some to the Ohio.*

When *Canassatego* was at Lancaster, in Pennsylvania, in 1744, holding a talk † about their affairs with the governor, he was informed that the English had beaten the French in some important battle. "Well," said he, "if that be the case, you must have taken a great deal of rum from them, and can afford to give us some, that we may rejoice with you." Accordingly, a glass was served round to each, which they called a *French glass.* ‡

Dr. *Franklin* tells us a very interesting story of *Canassatego*, and at the same time makes the old chief tell another. In speaking of the manners and customs of the Indians, the doctor says, "The same hospitality, esteemed among them as a principal virtue, is practised by private persons; of which *Conrad Weiser*, our interpreter, gave me the following instances. He had been naturalized among the Six Nations, and spoke well the Mohawk language. In going through the Indian country, to carry a message from our governor to the council at Onondago, he called at the habitation of *Canassatego*, an old acquaintance, who embraced him, spread furs for him to sit on, placed before him some boiled beans, and venison, and mixed some rum and water for his drink. When he was well refreshed, and had lit his pipe, *Canassatego* began to converse with him; asked how he had fared the many years since they had seen each other; whence he then came; what occasioned the journey, &c. *Conrad* answered all his questions; and when the discourse began to flag, the Indian, to continue it, said, '*Conrad*, you have lived long among the white people, and know something of their customs: I have been sometimes at Albany, and have observed, that once in seven days they shut up their shops, and assemble in the great house; tell me what that is for; what do they do there?' 'They meet there,' says *Conrad*, 'to hear and learn good things.' 'I do not doubt,' says the Indian, 'that they tell you so; they have told me the same; but I doubt the truth of what they say, and I will tell you my reasons. I went lately to Albany, to sell my skins, and buy blankets, knives, powder, rum, &c. You know I used generally to deal with *Hans*

---

* *Colden* and *Gordon's* Histories.

† The minutes of the conference taken at the time by *Witham Marshe*, occupies 30 pages in the *Coll. Mass. Hist. Soc.* vii. vol.

‡ *Colden's* Hist. Five Nations, ii. 142.

Hanson; but I was a little inclined this time to try some other merchants. However, I called first upon *Hans*, and asked him what he would give for beaver. He said he could not give more than four shillings a pound; but, says he, I cannot talk on business now; this is the day when we meet together to learn *good things*, and I am going to the meeting. So I thought to myself, since I cannot do any business to-day, I may as well go to the meeting too, and I went with him. There stood up a man in black, and began to talk to the people very angrily; I did not understand what he said, but perceiving that he looked much at me, and at *Hanson*, I imagined that he was angry at seeing me there; so I went out, sat down near the house, struck fire, and lit my pipe, waiting till the meeting should break up. I thought too that the man had mentioned something of beaver, and suspected it might be the subject of their meeting. So when they came out, I accosted my merchant. 'Well, *Hans*,' says I, 'I hope you have agreed to give more than 4*s.* a pound.' 'No,' says he, 'I cannot give so much, I cannot give more than three shillings and sixpence.' I then spoke to several other dealers, but they all sung the same song,—*three and sixpence, three and sixpence.* This made it clear to me that my suspicion was right; and that whatever they pretended of meeting to learn *good things*, the purpose was to consult how to cheat Indians in the price of beaver. Consider but a little, *Conrad*, and you must be of my opinion. If they met so often to learn good things, they would certainly have learned some before this time. But they are still ignorant. You know our practice. If a white man, in travelling through our country, enters one of our cabins, we all treat him as I do you; we dry him if he is wet; we warm him if he is cold, and give him meat and drink, that he may allay his thirst and hunger; and we spread soft furs for him to rest and sleep on; we demand nothing in return. But if I go into a white man's house at Albany, and ask for victuals and drink, they say, Get out, you Indian dog. You see they have not yet learned those little *good things* that we need no meetings to be instructed in, because our mothers taught them to us when we were children; and therefore it is impossible their meetings should be, as they say, for any such purpose, or have any such effect: they are only to contrive the cheating of Indians in the price of beaver.'"*

The missionary *Frederic Post*, in his journal of an embassy to the Indians on the Ohio, in 1758, mentions a son of *Canassatego*, whom he calls *Hans Jacob.*

We are not to look into the history of Pennsylvania for a succession of Indian wars, although there have been some horrid murders and enormities committed among the whites and Indians. For about 70 years, their historic page is very clear of such records, namely, from 1682, the arrival of William Penn, until the French war of 1755.

And we will here record the proceedings of *William Penn*, on his taking possession of his lands upon the Delaware, so far as they are connected with our Indian history.

Humanity being a prominent feature in every Quaker who lives up to his profession, we are to expect a display of it in that of Penn; and happily we do not find ourselves disappointed. The force of his example was such, that, for many years, his followers practised the art of peacemaking; and hence no wars occurred, as we have already observed; but as the enlightened mind of *Penn* carried his acts more than one hundred and fifty years in advance of his contemporaries, they acting without the true principle which governed him, soon forgot its importance, and pursued a different course, which brought the evils of war and dissolution.

William Penn had confirmed to him the country since bearing his name, by a royal charter, and having sent over a small colony to take possession of it in 1681, followed himself the next year. His first care on his arrival was to establish a lasting friendship with the Indians. This he effected by the greatest possible care in rendering them strict justice and great kindness, and above all by purchasing the country of them, and paying them to their con-

* The editors of the valuable Encyclopedia Perthensis have thought this anecdote worthy a place in that work, (i. 652.)

tent for it. *Penn* landed at what is now Newcastle, 24 October, and soon began to exchange goods for lands with the Indians. By this intercourse he learned their language,* and thus qualified himself to render them justice in all cases.

The first formed treaty entered into between *Penn* and the Indians was made in Dec. 1682, and took place almost two miles above what is now Chestnut Street, on the same side of the Delaware, in the present township of Kensington, under the wide-spreading branches of an elm-tree, aged at that time 155 years, as since ascertained.† A small cubical marble monument now marks the spot, which, with the adjacent neighborhood, in the days of *Penn*, was called *Shakamaxon*. A street perpetuates this name, not far distant, which runs at right angles to the river. The little monument of which we have made mention, was almost invisible from piles of rubbish, when visited by the writer in April, 1834.‡

In reference to Penn's Treaty, so often the subject of prose in both hemispheres, *Voltaire* has in his peculiar vein observed, that it was the only one made without an oath, and the only one which had not been broken.§

An admirable painting of this treaty, by Sir *Benjamin West*, has often been sketched upon copper, and impressions circulated in various works; there is, however, in all of them, a very glaring want of taste or judgment, arising probably from a false notion of the painter, which is the appearance of handsome houses in the back-ground. There is one of the best sketches of an Indian treaty painted upon the sign of an inn in Beach Street, near the old treaty ground, which I have seen.

It is no wonder the Indians remembered *Penn* so long, and so affectionately, for it was not uncommon for him to perform the engagements of others, who purposely set out upon wronging them. In a speech which a chief of the Six Nations made at a conference, at Lancaster, in June, 1744, he gives the following narrative of one of *Penn's* generous acts in these words:—

"When our brother *Onas*, a great while ago, came to Albany to buy the Susquehannah lands of us, our brother the governor of N. York, who, as we suppose, had not a good understanding with our brother *Onas*, advised us not to sell him any land, for he would make a bad use of it, and pretending to be our friend, he advised us, in order to prevent *Onas's*, or any other persons, imposing on us, and that we might always have our land when we wanted it, to put it into his hands; and he told us he would keep it for our use, and never open his hands, but keep them close shut, and not part with any of it, but at our request. Accordingly we trusted him, and put our lands into his hands, and charged him to keep them safe for our use. But some time after he went to England, and carried our land with him, and there sold it to our brother *Onas* for a large sum of money. And when at the instance of our brother *Onas* we were minded to sell him some lands, he told us we had sold the Susquehannah lands already to the governor of N. York, and that he had bought them from him in England; though when he came to understand how the governor of N. York had deceived us, he very generously paid us for our lands over again."‖

There were several chiefs very noted about this period, on account of their connection with the Moravian Brethren. Among the most noted was

GLIKHIKAN,¶ or *Glikhickan*,** "an eminent captain and warrior, counsellor and speaker of the Delaware chief [*Pakanke*] in Kaskaskunk." It is said that he had disputed with the French Catholic priests in Canada, and con-

---

* His own letter, dated the year following, giving an account of the country, its products, inhabitants, &c. &c. dated 16 August, 1683, and printed in *Blome's America*, 96.

† Holmes's Annals, i. 405. The old elm was blown down by a tempest in 1810, and was then 283 years old. *Ib.* Pieces of its stump are preserved in the cabinets of the curious, along with fragments of the Plymouth Rock, &c.

‡ I was lately informed by Mr. *Duponceau* of Philadelphia, that some important errors existed in the printed accounts of *Penn's Treaty*, and he showed me some manuscripts concerning it which he had lately discovered, and was preparing to have them printed in the Hist. Colls. of Pennsylvania.

§ C'est le seul traité entre ces peuples et les Chrétiens qui n'ait point été juré et qui n'ai point été rompu. *Œuvres*, vol. liv. 415, ed. of 1785, in 91 vols. 12mo.

‖ An Enquiry into the Causes, &c. of the Alienation of the Shawanese and Delawares, 51

¶ *Loskiel.* ** *Heckewelder.*

founded them, and now (1769) made his appearance among the United Brethren for the purpose of achieving a like victory; but as the Brethren's account has it, his heart failed him, and he became a convict to their doctrines In 1770, he quitted Kaskaskunk, to live with the Brethren, greatly against the minds of his friends and his chief. This occasioned great trouble, and some endeavored to take his life. *Pakanke's* speech to him upon the occasion will be seen when we come to the account of that chief. At the time of his baptism, *Glikhikan* received the name of *Isaac.*

The period of the revolutionary war was a distressing time for the Brethren and those Indians who had adhered to their cause. War parties from the hostile tribes were continually passing and repassing their settlements, and often in the most suspicious manner. It was to the famous chief *Glikhikan* that they owed their preservation on more than one occasion. The Indians about the lakes sent deputies to draw the Delawares into the war against the Americans, but they were not received by them. Shortly after, in the year 1777, 200 Huron warriors, with *Half-king* at their head, approached the Moravian settlement of Lichtenau, in their way to attack the settlements upon the frontiers, and caused great consternation among the Brethren; but resolving to show no signs of fear, victuals were prepared for them, and sent out by some of the Christian Indians to meet them. The reception of those sent out was far more promising than was anticipated, and soon after was "sent a solemn embassy to the *Half-king* and other chiefs of the Hurons." *Glikhikan* was at the head of this embassy, and the following is his speech to *Half-king:*—"Uncle! We, your cousins, the congregation of believing Indians at Lichtenau and Gnadenhuetten, rejoice at this opportunity to see and speak with you. We cleanse your eyes from all the dust, and whatever the wind may have carried into them, that you may see your cousin with clear eyes and a serene countenance. We cleanse your ears and hearts from all evil reports which an evil wind may have conveyed into your ears and even into your hearts on the journey, that our words may find entrance into your ears and a place in your hearts. [*Here a string of wampum was presented by Glikhikan.*] Uncle! hear the words of the believing Indians, your cousins, at Lichtenau and Gnadenhuetten. We would have you know, that we have received and believed in the word of God for 30 years and upwards, and meet daily to hear it, morning and evening. You must also know, that we have our teachers dwelling amongst us, who instruct us and our children. By this word of God, preached to us by our teachers, we are taught to keep peace with all men, and to consider them as friends; for thus God has commanded us, and therefore we are lovers of peace. These our treachers are not only our friends, but we consider and love them as our own flesh and blood. Now as we are your cousin, we most earnestly beg of you, uncle, that you also would consider them as your own body, and as your cousin. We and they make but one body, and therefore cannot be separated, and whatever you do unto them, you do unto us, whether it be good or evil." Then several fathoms of wampum were delivered. *Half-king* received this speech with attention, and said it had penetrated his heart, and after he had consulted with his captains, he spoke as follows in answer:—"Cousins! I am very glad and feel great satisfaction that you have cleansed my eyes, ears and heart from all evil, conveyed into me by the wind on this journey. I am upon an expedition of an unusual kind; for I am a warrior and am going to war, and therefore many evil things and evil thoughts enter into my head, and even into my heart. But thanks to my cousin, my eyes are now clear, so that I can behold my cousin with a serene countenance. I rejoice, that I can hear my cousins with open ears, and take their words to heart." He then delivered a string of wampum, and after repeating the part of *Glikhikan's* speech relating to the missionaries, proceeded: "Go on as hitherto, and suffer no one to molest you. Obey your teachers, who speak nothing but good unto you, and instruct you in the ways of God, and be not afraid that any harm shall be done unto them. No creature shall hurt them. Attend to your worship, and never mind other affairs. Indeed, you see us going to war; but you may remain easy and quiet, and need not think much about it, &c." This was rather odd talk for a savage warrior, and verily it seems more like that of one of the European Brethren, but the veracity of *Loskiel* will not be questioned.

Some time after this, a circumstance occurred which threw *Glikhikan* into much trouble and danger. A band of Huron warriors seized upon the missionaries at Salem and Gnadenhuetten, and confined them, and did much mischief. *Michael Jung*, *David Zeisberger* and *John Heckewelder* were the Brethren confined at this time. The savages next pillaged Schoenbrunn, from whence they led captive the missionary *Jungman* and wife, and the sisters *Zeisberger* and *Senseman;* and, singing the death-song, arrived with them at Gnadenhuetten, where were the rest of the prisoners. This was September 4, 1781. It appears that the famous Captain *Pipe* was among these warriors, from what follows. A young Indian woman, who accompanied the warriors, was much moved by the hard treatment of the Brethren, and in the night "found means to get Capt. *Pipe's* best horse, and rode off full speed to Pittsburgh, where she gave an account of the situation of the missionaries and their congregations." This woman was related to *Glikhikan;* on him, therefore, they determined to vent their wrath. A party of warriors seized him at Salem, and brought him bound to Gnadenhuetten, singing the death-song. When he was brought into the presence of the warriors, great commotion followed, and many were clamorous that he should be at once cut to pieces; especially the Delawares, who could not forget his having renounced his nation and manner of living; here, however, *Half-king* interfered, and prevented his being killed. They now held an inquisitorial examination upon him, which terminated in a proof of his innocence, and, after giving vent to their spleen in loading him with the worst of epithets and much opprobrious language, set him at liberty.

The missionaries and their congregations were soon at liberty, but were obliged to emigrate, as they could have no rest upon the Muskingum any longer; war parties continually hovering about them, robbing and troubling them in various ways. They went through the wilderness 125 miles, and settled at Sandusky, leaving their beautiful cornfields just ready to harvest. Their losses and privations were immense. Above 200 cattle and 400 hogs, much corn in store, beside 300 acres just ripening, were among the spoils. "A troop of savages commanded by English officers escorted them, enclosing them at the distance of some miles on all sides." They arrived at their place of destination October 11, and here were left by *Half-king* and his warriors without any instructions or orders.

Many believing Indians had returned to Gnadenhuetten and the adjacent places in 1782. Here, on 8th March of this year, happened the most dreadful massacre, and *Glikhikan* was among the victims. Ninety-six persons were scalped and then cut to pieces. Besides women, there were 34 children murdered in cold blood.* This was done by white men!

Of this horrid and diabolical murder it behoves us to give the facts more in detail. The month of February of the year 1782, having been very favorable to war parties, it was improved by some Sandusky warriors, and some murders were committed in an unlooked for moment upon the frontiers of the whites. The family of a *William Wallace*, consisting of his wife and five or six children, were killed, and one *John Carpenter* † was taken prisoner. These early movements of the Indians led the whites to conclude that they were either done by the Moravians at Muskingum, or that the warriors that committed the murders were quartered among them.‡ Therefore, without further information, a band of about 80 or 90 men suddenly collected upon the frontier of Pennsylvania, and each man having provided himself with his own arms, ammunition and provisions, mostly mounted upon horses, set out under one Colonel *David Williamson* for the devoted congregation at Gnadenhuetten. They rendezvoused and encamped the first night on the Mingo Bottom, on the west side of the Ohio River.§

---

* I have been particular in noticing this affair, as it is not found in such extensively circulated works as the *American Annals*.

† He afterwards made his escape at great peril.

‡ *Doddridge's* Notes on the Indian Wars, 248, 249.

§ Ibid.

Meanwhile Colonel *Gibson*, at Pittsburgh, understanding the object of th crew who had gone forth under *Williamson*, despatched messengers to alarm the Christian Indians, but they arrived too late. However, they received timely notice from another quarter, but their trusting to their innocence to protect them, did in this case prove a fatal error: a white man, who had narrowly escaped from the hands of some warriors, warned them with great earnestness to fly for their lives. These warriors, who had "murdered and impaled a woman and a child, not far from the Ohio, arrived soon after at Gnadenhuetten," where they expressed their well-grounded fears to the Christians, that a party of white people, who were pursuing them, would surely kill them all.* All these warnings were not enough to shake their faith in the protecting arm of their own innocence.

The second day's march of the band of murderers, brought them within ne mile of the middle Moravian town, where they again encamped for the ight. This was on the 6th day of March. The next morning the party as divided into three equal divisions, "one of which was to cross the river bout a mile above the town; their videttes having reported that there were dians on both sides of the river. The other party was divided into three visions, one of which was to take a circuit in the woods, and reach the river ittle distance below the town, on the west side. Another division was to all into the middle of the town, and the third upon its upper end. When the party designed to make the attack on the west side, had reached the river, they found no boats to take them over; but something like a canoe was seen on the opposite bank. The river was high, with some floating ice. A young man of the name of *Sloughter* swam the river, and brought over, not a canoe, but a trough designed for holding sugar water. This trough could carry but two men at a time. In order to expedite their passage, a number of men stripped off their clothes, put them into the trough, together with their guns, and swam by its sides, holding its edges with their hands. When about 16 had crossed the river, the two centinels, who had been posted in advance," † "met young *Schebosch* in the woods, fired at and wounded him so much that he could not escape. He then, according to the account of the murderers themselves, begged for his life, representing that he was *Schebosch*, the son of a white Christian man: But they paid no attention to his entreaties, and cut him in pieces with their hatchets." "One of them broke one of his arms by a shot. A shot from the other centinel killed him. These *heroes* ‡ then scalped and tomahawked him.

"By this time, about 16 men had got over the river, and supposing the firing of the guns, which killed *Shabosh*, would lead to an instant discovery, they sent word to the party designed to attack the town on the east side of the river, to move on instantly, which they did.

"In the mean time, the small party which had crossed the river, marched with all speed, to the main town on the west side of the river. Here they found a large company of Indians gathering the corn, which they had left in their fields the preceding fall, when they removed to Sandusky. On the arrival of the men at the town, they professed peace and good will to the Moravians, and informed them that they had come to take them to fort Pitt, for their safety. The Indians surrendered, delivered up their arms, and appeared highly delighted with the prospect of their removal, and began with all speed to prepare food for the white men, and for themselves on their journey.

"A party of white men and Indians was immediately despatched to Salem, a short distance from Gnadenhuetten, where the Indians were gathering in their corn, to bring them in to Gnadenhuetten. The party soon arrived with the whole number of the Indians from Salem. In the mean time the Indians at Gnadenhuetten were confined in two houses some distance apart, and placed

* *Loskiel*, Hist. Moravians, iii. 176.

† I am following *Doddridge's* Narrative, but the next quotation is from *Loskiel*, iii. 177, and then continues *Doddridge* without any omission.

‡ My author does not italicize this word, but he doubtless would, if he were to give us a new edition of his book, if he did not add at least a half a dozen exclamations to it.

under guards; and when those from Salem arrived, they were divided, and placed in the same houses, with their brethren of Gnadenhuetten.

"The prisoners being thus secured, a council of war was held to decide on their fate. The officers, unwilling to take on themselves the whole responsibility of the awful decision, agreed to refer the question to the whole number of the men. The men were accordingly drawn up in a line. The commandant of the party, Colonel *David Williamson*, then put the question to them in form, 'whether the Moravian Indians should be taken prisoners to Pittsburgh, or put to death?' requesting all who were in favor of saving their lives to step out of the line, and form a second rank. On this, 16, some say 18, stepped out of the rank, and formed themselves into a second line; but alas! this line of mercy was far too short for that of vengeance." Thus was the fate of the Moravian Indians decided on, and they were ordered to prepare for death.

"From the time they were placed in the guard-houses, the prisoners foresaw their fate, and begun their devotions of singing hymns, praying and exhorting each other to place a firm reliance in the mercy of the Savior of men." "The particulars of this dreadful catastrophe are too horrid to relate. Suffice it to say, that in a few minutes these two slaughter-houses, as they were then called, exhibited in their ghastly interior, the mangled, bleeding remains, of those poor unfortunate people, of all ages and sexes; from the aged grey-headed, down to the helpless infant at its mother's breast; dishonored by the fatal wounds of the tomahawk, mallet, war-club, spear and scalping-knife!" Thus was the 8th day of March spent at Gnadenhuetten, in the year 1782!

Only two, who were young persons, escaped this dreadful day's slaughter. One of whom had been knocked down and scalped, and by counterfeiting himself dead, while the murderers had left the place, was enabled to save his life. The other crept unobserved into a cellar, and in the night escaped to the woods.

Whether any of the murderers were called to an account for what they did I do not learn, though they probably were not, owing to the state of anarchy occasioned by the revolutionary war.

PAKANKE was a powerful Delaware chief, whose residence, in 1770, was at a place called Kaskaskunk, about 40 miles north of Pittsburgh. He is brought to our notice by the agency of the missionary *Loskiel*, from whom it appears that he was very friendly to the Brethren at first, and invited them into his country, but when *Glikhikan*, his chief captain and speaker, forsook him, and went to live with them, he was so disconcerted, that he turned against them, and for a time caused them much difficulty. Meeting with *Glikhikan* afterward in public, he spoke to him in an angry tone as follows: "And even you have gone over from this council to them. I suppose you mean to get a white skin! But I tell you, not even one of your feet will turn white, much less your body. Was you not a brave and honored man, sitting next to me in council, when we spread the blanket and considered the belts of wampum lying before us? Now you pretend to despise all this, and think to have found something better. Some time or other you will find yourself deceived." To which *Glikhikan* made but a short and meek reply. Some epidemic disease carried off many of the Indians about this time, and they attributed its cause to their obstinacy in not receiving the gospel. *Pakanke* was among the number at last who accepted it as a remedy. He appears not to have been so credulous as many of his neighbors; for when the acknowledgment of Christianity was concluded upon by many, he remained incredulous; and when a belt of wampum was sent him, accompanied with a message, declaring that "whosoever refused to accept it would be considered a murderer of his countrymen," he affected not to understand its import, and doubtless would not have acknowledged it, but for the impending danger which he saw threatening him. When he went to hear the Brethren preach, he declared his conviction, and recommended his children to receive the gospel. A son of his was baptized in 1775.

NETAWATWEES was head chief of the Delawares, and if we are to judge of him from our scanty records, he will appear to the best advantage "He used to lay all affairs of state before his counsellors for their consideration, without telling them his own sentiments. When they gave him their opinion, he either approved of it, or stated his objections and amendments, always alleging the reasons of his disapprobation." Before the revolution, it was said that he had amazingly increased the reputation of the Delawares; and he spared no pains to conciliate all his neighbors, and reconcile them one to another. His residence, in 1773, was at Gekelemukpechuenk. The Moravian missionaries sent messengers to him, with information of the arrival of another missionary, in July of this year, requesting a renewal of friendship and a confirmation of his former promise of protection. When this was laid before him and his council, they were not much pleased with the information, and the old chief *Netawatwees*, said, "*They have teachers enough already, for a new one can teach nothing but the same doctrine.*" He was, however, prevailed upon to give his consent to their request, and afterwards became a convert to their religion. After he had set out in this course, he sent the following speech to his old friend *Pakanke:* "*You and I are both old, and know not how long we shall live. Therefore let us do a good work, before we depart, and leave a testimony to our children and posterity, that we have received the word of God. Let this be our last will and testament.*" *Pakanke* consented, and was at great pains to send solemn embassies to all such tribes as he thought proper to communicate his determination. *Netawatwees* died at Pittsburgh near the close of 1776.

Netawatwees had been a signer to the treaty of Conestoga in the year 1718, being then young, probably about 25 years of age. The Turtle tribe was the first among the Delawares, and of this he became, by their usages, chief. To him was committed all the tokens of contracts; such as belts of wampum, writings obligatory, with the sign manual of *William Penn*, and others since, down to the time himself, with his tribe, was forced to leave their lands and retire into Ohio.

After having been seated upon the Ohio, at a place convenient for communication with the Wyandots and other warlike nations of the west, he made known to them the wrongs which he and his people had suffered. By advice of the Wyandot chiefs, he settled finally upon Cayahaga River, leaving open the Rivers Muskingum and Big Beaver for any of his nation that were there already, and should afterwards come to settle there. And this was the occasion of *King Beaver's* building a town and settling the Turkey tribe at the mouth of Nemoschilli Creek, since called Tuscarawas. Of this distinguished chief we shall speak more at large in another place.

When Colonels *Bouquet* and *Bradstreet*, in 1763, were penetrating into the Indian country, *Netawatwees*, not without reason, became alarmed for his safety, and could not be prevailed upon to attend the treaty with Colonel *Bouquet*, after the battle of Bushy Rum, notwithstanding the other chiefs did. His residence being in range of the march of *Bouquet's* army, he too late attempted to escape down the Muskingum in a canoe; but being intercepted by some of *Bouquet's* Indian spies, was brought before the colonel, who, because he did not appear at the treaty, publicly deposed him, and put another at the head of his tribe. Upon the conclusion of a peace, however, the first act of importance performed by the Delaware nation was to reinstate *Netawatwees*. He continued in the undisturbed possession of the office until his death, which happened in the second year of the revolution, 1776, at Pittsburgh, when he had attained the age of near 99 years.*

The missionaries, especially, felt his loss with great severity, for his council was of the greatest benefit to them on all trying occasions.

WHITE-EYES, or, as some write, *White-eye*, was "the first captain among the Delawares." There was always great opposition among the Indians against missionaries settling in their country; who, in the language of one of the Moravians, "were a stone of offence to many of the chiefs and to a great part of the council at Gekelemukpechuenk, and it was several times proposed to expel them by force." But "this man [Captain *White-eyes*] kept

* *Heckewelder's* Biographies, &c., in *Philos. Trans.*

the chiefs and council in awe, and would not suffer them to injure the missionaries, being in his own heart convinced of the truths of the gospel. This was evident in all his speeches, held before the chiefs and council in behalf of the Indian congregation and their teachers." *

Upon the death of *Netawatwees*, in 1776, Captain *White-eyes* became chief sachem, to which place his former situation of first counsellor to that chief rendered him highly qualified. But as he was not chief by regular descent, he only accepted the office until a young chief should be of age, who, it seems, was heir apparent. It is said he had long looked forward with anxiety to the time when his countrymen should become Christians, and enjoy the benefits of civilization; "but he did not live to see that time, for while accompanying Gen. *Mackintosh* with his army, to Muskingum, in 1778, or '9, he took the small-pox and died." †

The old chief *Netawatwees* used every art to thwart the endeavors of *White-eyes*, and, as they were rather in a strain bordering upon persecution, were only sure to make the latter more strenuous. He therefore declared "that no prosperity would attend the Indian affairs, unless they received and believed the saving gospel," &c. *White-eyes* was forced about this time to separate himself from the other chiefs. "This occasioned great and general surprise, and his presence being considered both by the chiefs and the people as indispensably necessary, a negotiation commenced, and some Indian brethren were appointed arbitrators. The event was beyond expectation successful, for chief *Netawatwees* not only acknowledged the injustice done to Captain *White-eye*, but changed his mind with respect to the believing Indians and their teachers, and remained their constant friend to his death." ‡

At the breaking out of the revolutionary war, the American congress endeavored to treat with the chiefs of the Six Nations, and accordingly invited the Delawares to send deputies. *White-eyes* attended on the part of the Brethren, and his conduct before the commissioners was highly approved by the missionaries.

Towards the close of the year 1776, the Hurons sent a message to the Delawares, "that they must keep their shoes in readiness to join the warriors." *Nettawatwees* being their head chief, to him, consequently, was the talk delivered. He would not accept the message, but sent belts to the Hurons, with an admonition for their rash resolution, and reminding them of the misery they had already brought upon themselves. Captain *White-eyes* was a bearer of the belts, who in his turn was as unsuccessful as the Huron ambassadors; for when they were delivered to the chiefs in Fort Detroit, in presence of the English governor, he cut them in pieces, and threw them at the feet of the bearers, ordering them, at the same time, to depart in half an hour. He accused *White-eyes* of a connection with the Americans, and told him his head was in danger.

It is not strange that *White-eyes* was treated in this manner, if he took the stand at the commencement of the war, which we suppose from the following circumstance that he did: The Iroquois, being chiefly in the English interest, and considering the Delawares bound to operate with them, ordered hem to be in readiness, as has been just related. Upon this occasion, *White-eyes* said "he should do as he pleased; that he wore no petticoats, as they falsely pretended; he was no woman, but a man, and they should find him to act as such." §

We hear nothing more of importance of this chief until 1780, which was the year of his death. He died at Pittsburgh, in Pennsylvania, of the small-pox. Many others died about this time, among whom was a man who must have been very old, perhaps near 120, as he could well remember when the first house was built in Philadelphia, in 1682, being then a boy.

Although *White-eyes* was so friendly to the Brethren, yet he never fully joined them, stating his political station as a reason.

The Delaware nation perpetuated his name; a chief signed a treaty in

* *Loskiel*, iii. 101—2.
† *Heckewelder's* Biographies, &c., in *Philos. Trans.*
‡ *Loskiel*, iii. 101—2
§ *Heckewelder*, Hist. 22

1814, at Greenville, in Ohio, bearing it.* *White-eyes'* town is frequently mentioned in history. It was the place of his residence, which was near the falls of the Muskingum.

PAXNOUS was head chief of the Shawanese in 1754. At this time, the Christian Indians of the Moravian settlement, Gnadenhuetten, were oppressed by a tribute to the Hurons. This year, *Paxnous* and *Gideon Tadeuskund*, who had become dissenters, came to them, and delivered the following message: "The great head, that is, the council of the Iroquois in Onondago, speak the truth and lie not: they rejoice that some of the believing Indians have moved to Wajomick, [near Wilksburg and the Susquehannah,] but now hey lift up the remaining Mahikans and Delawares, and set them also down in Wajomick; for there a fire is kindled for them, and there they may plant and think of God. But if they will not hear, the great head, or council, will come and clean their ears with a red-hot iron;" that is, set their houses on fire, and send bullets through their heads. The next year, *Paxnous* and 13 others came again, and in the name of the Hurons demanded an answer to the summons he had delivered last year. His wife attended him, and for whom he had great affection, having then lived with her 38 years. She, being touched by the preaching of the Brethren, was no doubt the cause of softening the heart of *Paxnous*, and causing him thenceforth to do much for them. This answer was returned to him to bear to the Hurons: "The Brethren will confer with the Iroquois themselves, concerning the intended removal of the Indians from Gnadenhuetten to Wajomick." *Paxnous*, "being only an ambassador in this business, was satisfyed, and even formed a closer acquaintance with the Brethren." This is sufficient to explain *Paxnous'* partiality for the Brethren. Before they departed, his wife was baptized, and all present, among whom was her husband, were much affected. She declared, as she returned home, "that she felt as happy as a child new born." *Paxnous* also had two sons, who did much for the Brethren.

TADEUSKUND, a noted chief among the Delawares, may be considered next in importance to those above named. He was known among the English, previous to 1750, by the name *Honest-John.* About this time, he was received into the Moravian community, and after some delay, "owing to his wavering disposition," was baptized, and received into fellowship. His baptismal name was *Gideon.* He adhered to the missionaries just as long as his condition appeared to be better, but when any thing more favorable offered, he stood ready to embark in it.

The Christian Indians at Gnadenhuetten were desirous of removing to Wajomick, which offered more advantages than that place, and this was a secret desire of the wild Indians; for they, intending to join the French of Canada, wished to have them out of the way of their excursions, that they might with more secrecy fall upon the English frontiers. It was now 1754.

Meanwhile *Tadeuskund* had had the offer of leading the Delawares in the war, and hence he had been a chief promoter of a removal to Wajomick. The missionaries saw through the plot, and refused to move; but quite a company of their followers, to the number of about 70, went thither, agreeably to the wishes of *Tadeuskund* and his party, and some went off to other places.

Tadeuskund was now in his element, marching to and from the French in warlike style. When *Paxnous*, as has been related, summoned the remaining believers at Gnadenhuetten to remove to Wajomick, *Tadeuskund* accompanied him. As the interest of the French began to decline, *Tadeuskund* began to think about making a shift again. Having lived a considerable part of the year 1758 not far from Bethlehem, with about 100 of his followers, he gave the Brethren there intimations that he wished again to join them; and even requested that some one would preach on his side of the Lehigh. But the hopes of his reclaim were soon after dissipated. And "he now even endeavored to destroy the peace and comfort of the Indian congregation." From the discouraging nature of the affairs of the French, ten Indian nations were induced to send deputies to treat with the English a

* See Hist. Second War, by *S. R Brown,* Appendix, 105.

Easton, which eventuated in a treaty of peace. *Tadeuskund* pretended that this treaty had been agreed to on condition that government should build a town on the Susquehannah for the Indians, and cause those living with the Brethren to remove to it. This his enemies denied. There was some foundation, from their own account, for *Tadeuskund's* pretending to have received full commission to conduct all the Indians within certain limits, which included those of Bethlehem, to Wajomick; and therefore demanded their compliance with his commands. He was liberal in his promises, provided they would comply; saying, they should have fields cleared and ploughed, houses built, and provisions provided: not only so, but their teachers should attend them, to live there unmolested, and the believers entirely by themselves. But, through the influence of their priests, they would not comply, which occasioned some threats from *Tadeuskund*, and he immediately set off for Philadelphia, considerably irritated.

Tadeuskund went to Philadelphia in consequence of an intended general congress of the Indians and English, including all those who did not attend at Easton. When he returned, he demanded a positive answer, and they replied that they would not remove unless the governor and all the chiefs so determined, for that they could not without the greatest inconvenience. This seemed to satisfy him, and he left them.

The great council or congress of English and Indians at Easton above referred to, being of much importance in Indian history, as also illustrative of other eminent characters as well as that of *Tadeuskund*, we will refer its details to a separate chapter.

Tadeuskund was burnt to death in his own house at Wajomick in April, 1763.

Of an execrable murder at Gnadenhuetten we have not spoken, as we have not learned the name of the leaders in or instigators of it; however, it will not be proper to pass it over in detailing the events of our history. It happened in the time of the French and Indian wars, in 1755. Although it is generally spoken of as the massacre of Gnadenhuetten, yet it did not happen in that town, but in a small village on Mahony Creek, about a half a mile from it. On the 24 November, a band of Indians, (their numbers unknown,) who came from the French, fell suddenly upon the place, while the Brethren were at supper, and killed eleven persons; namely, seven men, three women, and one child 15 months old. Only two men, one woman, and a boy, escaped. The slaughter would have been far greater, if the Christian Indians had not been away at that time upon a hunting excursion. Had not a dog given the alarm, as the Indians approached, they would probably have taken all the whites prisoners; but the moment the dog gave the alarm, those within the house sprung to the doors and windows to secure them, which being open, the Indians fired into them, killing one man and wounding several other persons. The poor people succeeded in securing the doors and windows, and then retreated into the garret of the house. This, as they must have expected, they found a wretched retreat! the roof over their heads was soon in flames, and the only persons that escaped were a man and his wife, and a boy, which they effected through the burning roof! One more, a man who had been confined in an out-house by sickness, escaped from a window. All the buildings in the village, the cattle and other animals in the barns, were consumed in the flames! *

The leader of this party, whose name it is as well I cannot give, soon met with a requital for his murders. By the influence of the Governor of Pennsylvania, and Mr. *George Croghan*, the hostile Indians were prevailed upon to meet the whites in a council at Easton, the next year, viz. 1756. This Indian captain sét out to attend the council, and in the way, it seems, he fell in company with *Tadeuskund*. With this chief he contrived, some how or other, to get up a quarrel, in which *Tadeuskund* killed him.†

SKENANDO, though belonging to a later age, may very properly be noticed here. He was an Oneida chief, contemporary with the missionary *Kirkland*, to whom he became a convert, and lived many years of the latter

* *Heckewelder's* Narrative, 44. † Ibid. 51, 52.

part of his life a believer in Christianity. Mr. *Kirkland* died at Paris, N York, in 1808, and was buried near Oneida. *Skenando* desired to be buried near him at his death, which was granted. He lived to be 110 years old, and was often visited by strangers out of curiosity. He said to one who visited him but a little time before his death, "*I am an aged hemlock; the winds of an hundred winters have whistled through my branches; I am dead at the top. The generation to which I belonged has run away and left me.*"

In early life, he was, like nearly all of his race, given to intoxication. In 1775, he was at Albany to settle some affairs of his tribe with the government of New York. One night he became drunk, and in the morning found himself in the street, nearly naked, every thing of worth stripped from him, even the sign of his chieftainship. This brought him to a sense of his duty, and he was never more known to be intoxicated. He was a powerful chief, and the Americans did not fail to engage him on their side in the revolution. This was congenial to his mind, for he always urged the rights of the prior occupants of the soil, and once opposed the Americans on the same principle, for encroachments upon the red men. He rendered his adopted Anglo brethren important services.

From the "Annals of Tryon County,"* we learn that *Skenando* died on the 11 March, 1816. He left an only son. And the same author observes that "his person was tall, well made, and robust. His countenance was intelligent, and displayed all the peculiar dignity of an Indian chief. In his youth he was a brave and intrepid warrior, and in his riper years, one of the noblest counsellors among the North American tribes:" and that, in the revolutionary war, by his vigilance he preserved the settlement of German Flats from being destroyed.

We will close the present chapter with some of the land transactions with the Indians in Pennsylvania.

By his last will, Governor *Penn* devised to his grandson, *William Penn*, and his heirs, 10,000 acres of land to be laid out "in proper and beneficial places in this province, by his trustees." *William Penn*, the grandson, sold out this land to a gentleman, Mr. *William Allen*, a great land-jobber. By a little management *Allen* got this land located, generally, where he desired. One considerable tract included part of Minisink, and no previous arrangement had been made with those Indians. It would be very charitable to suppose, that the trustees intended, and that perhaps they did not doubt, but the same course would be pursued in purchasing of the Indians as had been before, by others; but no sooner had the new proprietor got the lands surveyed to him, than he began to sell it to those that would go on at once and settle it.

Hence we clearly see the road opened for all difficulties. About the same time proposals were published for a land lottery, and by the conditions of these proposals, not the least notice was taken, or the least reserve made, of the rights of the Indians. But on the contrary, such persons as had settled upon lands that did not belong to them, were, in case they drew prizes, to remain unmolested upon the lands of the Indians. By this means much of the land in the Forks of the Delaware, since Easton and vicinity, as well as other places, became taken up, by this kind of gambling, and the Indians were thus crowded from it. They for some time complained, and at length began to threaten, but the event was war and bloodshed.

To still the clamors of these injured people, recourse was had to as great abuses as had already been practised: crimes were sought to be clouded by bold stratagem. The Iroquois were connived with, and they came forward, confirmed the doings of the land-jobbers, and ordered the Delawares to leave their country. They were to choose one of two horns of a wretched dilemma. The power of the Iroquois could not be withstood, backed as it was by the English. They ordered the poor Delawares to remove, or they would destroy them, as in the life of *Canasatego* will be found related.

A sort of claim was obtained to some of the disputed lands, in a similar a manner as Georgia got hers of some of the Creek country not many

---

* By *W. W. Campbell*.

years since. At one time, a party of a deputation having remained upon the ground eleven days after the others had gone home, were by kindnesses prevailed upon to sign a writing, relinquishing all their right to lands upon Delaware. These were Indians of the Six Nations, and had deeded lands on the Susquehannah just before, with those who had gone home. Why the proprietors did not include the lands on Delaware in their first deed, when the deputation were all together, is a good deal singular, but requires no explanation. Yet certain it is, those who remained and gave a writing quit-claiming lands on Delaware, had no consideration for so doing This writing expresses only that they intended in the former deed to include said lands.

That the Delawares or Chihohockies (which was their real name) were, until some time subsequent to 1736, entirely independent of the Iroquois, is beyond a doubt true, although from sinister motives, there were those who maintained that they were always subject to them. It is true, that, when by a long intercourse with the whites they had lost much of their energy and character as a nation, the haughty Six Nations found little difficulty in seducing some tribes of them to join them, and of forcing others to obey them. A circumstance which clearly proves this, is, that in the first treaties of sales of land by the Six Nations to the Pennsylvanians, they did not presume to convey any lands to the east of the sources of the streams that were tributary to the Susquehannah; the assertions of some of the speech-makers among the Six Nations, to the contrary, however.*

The celebrated chief *Tadeuskund*, of whom we have already spoken in detail, gave the following very pointed account of the manner in which the whites had conducted in getting his people's lands fraudulently. It was at the conference in Easton, in November, 1756. *Tadeuskund* was present as the representative of "four nations," viz. the Chihohockies, the Wanamies, the Munseys and Wapingers. Governor *Denny* requested the Indians to state the reasons for their late hostile movements. *Tadeuskund:* "I have not far to go for an instance. This very ground that is under me (striking it with his foot) was my land and inheritance, and it is taken from me by fraud. [This was in the Forks of the Delaware.] When I say this ground, I mean all the land lying between Tohiccon Creek and Wyoming, on the River Susquehannah. I have not only been served so in this government, but the same thing has been done to me, as to several tracts in New Jersey, over the river." On the governor's asking him what he meant by fraud, he answered: "When one man had formerly liberty to purchase lands, and he took the deed from the Indians for it, and then dies; after his death his children forge a deed like the true one, with the same Indian names to it, and thereby take lands from the Indians which they never sold; this is fraud. Also when one king has land beyond the river, and another king has land on this side, both bounded by rivers, mountains and springs which cannot be moved, and the proprietaries, greedy to purchase lands, buy of one king what belongs to another; this likewise is *fraud*."

Then the governor asked *Tadeuskund* whether he had been served so? He said, "*Yes.* I have been served so in this province; all the land extending from Tohiccon, over the great mountain, to Wyoming, has been taken from me by fraud; for when I had agreed to sell land to the old proprietary, by the course of the river, the young proprietaries came and got it run by a *straight course*, by the compass, and by that means took in double the quantity intended to be sold." †

The meaning of *Tadeuskund* will be fully explained in what we are about to lay before the reader. The lands above the Kittatinny Mountains were not intended to be sold by the Delawares, but the whites found means to encroach upon them, and by the aid of the Iroquois, as before noted, were able not only to maintain but to extend their encroachments. It will be well to bear in mind that the lands conveyed to *William Penn* in 1685, included the country from Duck Creek, or Quingquingus to the Kittatinny Hills; and to bear in mind, also, how purchases were made, so as to admit of contention

* See Proud's Pa., ii. 334. † Ibid. ii. 333.

sometimes, doubtless, for the secret intention of taking advantage, and at others from inability to fill certain blanks in the deeds at the time they were given. As for example, when a tract of land was to extend in a certain direction upon a straight line, or by a river, "as far as a man can walk in a day," the point to be arrived at must necessarily be left blank, until at some future time it should be walked. This manner of giving and receiving deeds, it is easy to see, threw into the hands of sordid purchasers, every advantage over the Indians. In one instance they complain that the "walker" *run;* in another, that "he walked after it was night," and so on.

The Indians had deeded lands in this way to *William Penn*, and no advantage was taken on his part; but when he was dead, and others became proprietors, the difficulties arose, of which *Tadeuskund* reminded the whites at Easton; and this will illustrate what has just been given from his speech to Governor *Denny* at that time.

The deed to *William Penn*, to which we in particular refer, was given in 1685, and ran thus:—

"This Indenture witnesseth, that, We, *Packenah, Jarckhan, Sikals, Partquesott, Jervis Essepenauk, Felktroy, Hekellappan, Econus, Machloha, Metthconga, Wissa Powey,* Indian Kings, Sachemakers, right owners of all lands, from Quingquingus, called Duck Creek, unto Upland called Chester Creek, all along by the west side of Delaware river, and so between the said creeks backwards *as far as a man can ride in two days with a horse*, for and in consideration of these following goods to us in hand paid, and secured to be paid, by *William Penn*, proprietary and governor of the province of Pennsylvania and territories thereof, viz. 20 guns, 20 fathoms match-coat, 20 fathoms Stroudwater, 20 blankets, 20 kettles, 20 pounds powder, 100 bars of lead, 40 tomahawks, 100 knives, 40 pairs of stockings, 1 barrel of beer, 20 pounds red lead, 100 fathoms wampum, 30 glass bottles, 30 pewter spoons, 100 awl-blades, 300 tobacco pipes, 100 hands of tobacco, 20 tobacco tongs, 20 steels, 300 flints, 30 pair of scissors, 30 combs, 60 looking-glasses, 200 needles, one skipple of salt, 30 pounds sugar, 5 gallons molasses, 20 tobacco boxes, 100 jews-harps, 20 hoes, 30 gimblets, 30 wooden screw boxes, 100 string of beads.—Do hereby acknowledge, &c. given under our hands, &c. at New Castle, second day of the eighth month, 1685."

We will now proceed to take further notice of *Tadeuskund's* charges at the Easton conference, before spoken of. The manner of *William Allen's* becoming proprietor has been stated. In 1736, deputies from the Six Nations sold the proprietor all the "lands lying between the mouth of Susquehannah and Kittatinny Hills, extending eastward as far as the heads of the branches or springs which run into the said Susquehannah." Hence this grant did not interfere at all with the lands of the Delawares, and may be urged as an evidence, that the Six Nations had no right to them; for, if they had, why were they not urged to sell them before the breaking up of the conference? and not, as we have before mentioned, waited eleven days, until all the head men had gone, and then to have got a release from the few that remained! It is therefore very evident that this could not be done when all were present, or the latter course would not have been resorted to. Notwithstanding the proprietor had grasped at the lands on Delaware, by a partial transaction with a few of a deputation, he, nevertheless, soon manifested that he considered his right as not beyond question, by his assembling the Delaware chiefs the next year, 1737, to treat further upon it. The names of these chiefs were *Monokykickan, Lappawinzoe, Tishekunk* and *Nutimus*.* At this conference a release was obtained from them, the preamble of which set forth,

"That *Tishekunk* and *Nutimus* had, about three years before, begun a treaty at Durham with *John* and *Thomas Penn;* that from thence another

---

* His name signified, *a striker of fish with a spear.* Heckewelder. He was generally called *Pontius Nutamaeus*—an excellent man, who never drank liquor. He was born on the spot where Philadelphia now stands, removed to Ohio about 1745, died on the Muskingum in 1780, aged about 100 years. He had a brother who was called Isaac *Nutimus*, and like him was a very amiable man, and died about the same time. *Ib.*

meeting was appointed to be at Pennsbury the next spring, to which they repaired with *Lappawinzoe*, and several others of the Delaware Indians; that, at this meeting, several deeds were shown to them for several tracts of land which their forefathers had more than 50 years ago sold to *William Penn;* and, in particular, one deed, from *Maykeerikkisho, Sayhoppey* and *Taughhaughsey*, the chiefs or kings of the Northern Indians on Delaware, who for a certain quantity of goods, had granted to *William Penn* a tract of land, beginning on a line drawn from a certain spruce-tree on the River Delaware, by a west-north-west course to Neshameny Creek, from thence back into the woods *as far as a man could go in a day and a half*, and bounded on the west by Neshameny, or the most westerly branch thereof, so far as the said branch doth extend, and from thence by a line [*blank*] to the utmost extent of the day and half's walk, and from thence [*blank*] to the aforesaid River Delaware, and so down the courses of the river to the first mentioned spruce tree; and that this appeared to be true by *William Biles* and *Joseph Wood*, who, upon their affirmation, did declare, that they well remembered the treaty held by the agents of *William Penn* and those Indians;" "that they were now come to Philadelphia with their chief *Monokyhickan*, and several other old men, and upon a former treaty held upon the same subject, acknowledge themselves satisfied that the above described tract was granted by the persons above mentioned, for which reason, they the said *Monokyhickan, Lappawinzoe, Tishekunk* and *Nutimus*, agree to release to the proprietors all right to that tract, and desire that it may be walked, travelled, or gone over by persons appointed for that purpose."

Now it must be borne in mind, that by former treaties the Lechay Hills, which I take to mean the Lehigh Mountains, were to be the boundaries, in all time to come, on the north: meanwhile we will proceed to describe the manner the land was *walked out*, of which we have been speaking.

"The relation which *Thomes Furniss*, sadler, gives concerning the *day an a half's walk*, made between the proprietors of Pennsylvania and the Delawa Indians, by *James Yeates* and *Edward Marshall*."

"At the time of the walk I was a dweller at Newton, and a near neighbo to *James Yeates*. My situation gave him an easy opportunity of acquaintin me with the time of setting out, as it did me of hearing the different senti ments of the neighborhood concerning the *walk;* some alleging it was to be made by the river, others that it was to be gone upon a straight line fron somewhere in Wright's-town, opposite to a spruce-tree upon the river's bank said to be a boundary to a former purchase. When the walkers started I was a little behind, but was informed they proceeded from a chestnut-tree near the turning out of the road from Durham road to *John Chapman's*, and being on horseback, overtook them before they reached Buckingham, and kept company for some distance beyond the Blue Mountains, though not quite to the end of the journey. Two Indians attended, whom I considered as deputies appointed by the Delaware nation, to see the walk honestly performed. One of them repeatedly expressed his dissatisfaction therewith. The first day of the walk, before we reached Durham creek, where we dined in the meadows of one *Wilson*, an Indian trader, the Indian said the *walk* was to have been made up the river, and complaining of the unfitness of his shoepacks for travelling said he expected *Thomas Penn* would have made him a present of some shoes. After this some of us that had horses, walked, and let the Indians ride by turns; yet in the afternoon of the same day, and some hours before sunset, the Indians left us, having often called to *Marshall* that afternoon and forbid him to run. At parting they appeared dissatisfied, and said they would go no farther with us; for as they saw the *walkers* would pass all the good land, they did not care how far or where we went to. It was said we traveled 12 hours the first day, and it being in the latter end of September, or beginning of October, to complete the time, were obliged to walk, in the twilight. *Timothy Smith*, then sheriff of Bucks, held his watch for some minutes before we stopped, and the walkers having a piece of rising ground to ascend, he called out to them, telling the minutes behi and bid them pull up, which they did so briskly, that, immediately upon saying the time was out, *Marshall* clasped his arms about a saplin to supp himself, and thereupon the sheriff asking him what was the matter, he said he was almost gone, and that, if he had proceeded a few poles further, he must have fallen. We lodged in the woods that night, and heard the shouting of the Indians at a cantico, which they were said to hold that evening in a town hard by. Next morning the Indians were sent to, to know if they would accompany us any farther, but they declined it, although I believe some of them came to us before we started, and drank a dram in the company, and then straggled off about their hunting or some other amusement. In our return we came through this Indian town or plantation, *Timothy Smith* and myself riding forty yards more or less before the company, and as we approached within about 150 paces of the town, the woods being open, we saw an Indian take a gun in his hand, and advancing towards us some distance, placed himself behind a log that laid by our way. Timothy observing his motions, and being somewhat surprised, as I apprehended, looked at me, and asked what I thought that Indian meant. I said, I hoped no harm, and that I thought it best to keep on, which the Indian seeing, arose and walked before us to the settlement. I think *Smith* was surprised, as I well remember I was, through a consciousness that the Indians were dissatisfied with the walk, a thing the whole company seemed to be sensible of, and upon the way, in our return home, frequently expressed themselves to that purpose. And indeed the unfairness practised in the walk, both in regard to the way where, and the manner how, it was performed, and the dissatisfaction of the Indians concerning it, were the common subjects of conversation in our neighborhood, for some considerable time after it was done. When the walk was performed I was a young man in the prime of life. The novelty of the thing inclined me to be a spectator, and as I had been brought up most of my time in Burlington, the whole transaction to me was a series of occurrences almost entirely new, and which therefore, I apprehend, made the more strong and lasting impression on my memory.

Thomas Furniss." *

As we have already observed, the end of these affairs was war. The Delawares were driven back, and they joined the French against the English

CHAPTER III.

Of several chiefs spoken of by Washington, in his journal of an embassy to the French of Ohio—Battle near Great Meadows, and death of Jumonville—SHINGIS—MONACATOOCHA—HALF-KING—JUSKAKAKA—WHITE-THUNDER—ALLIQUIPA—CAPTAIN JACOBS—HENDRICK—*His history—Curious anecdote of*—LOGAN—*Cresap's War—Battle of Point Pleasant—Logan's famous speech*—CORNSTOCK—*His history*—RED-HAWK—ELLINIPSICO—*The barbarous murder of these three—Melancholy death of Logan*—PONTIAC—*A renowned warrior—Colonel Rogers's account of him—His policy—Fall of Michilimakinak*—MENEHWEHNA—*Siege of Detroit—Pontiac's stratagem to surprise it—Is discovered—Official account of the affair at Bloody Bridge—Pontiac abandons the siege—Becomes the friend of the English—Is assassinated.*

THE expedition of *Washington* to the French on the Ohio, in 1753, brings to our records information of several chiefs of the Six Nations, of the most interesting kind. He was commissioned and sent as an ambassador to the French, by Governor *Dinwiddie* of Virginia. He kept an accurate journal of his travels, which, on his return to Virginia, was published, and, not long after, the same was republished in London, with a map; the substance of this journal was copied into almost every periodical of importance of that day.

* Causes of the Alienation of the Delaware and Shawanese Indians, &c., 8vo. London, 1759.

SHINGIS was the first chief he visited, who lived in the forks of the Alleghany and Monongahela Rivers, where Pittsburgh now stands. He intended holding a council with the celebrated *Half-king*,* already mentioned, at Loggstown, and such others as could be assembled at short notice, to strengthen them in the English interest. He therefore invited *Shingis* to attend the council, and he accordingly accompanied him to Loggstown. "As soon as I came into town," says *Washington*, "I went to *Monakatoocha*, (as the *Half-king* was out at his hunting cabin, on Little Beaver Creek, about 15 miles off,) and informed him by *John Davidson*, my Indian interpreter, that I was sent a messenger to the French general, and was ordered to call upon the sachems of the Six Nations to acquaint them with it. I gave him a string of wampum and a twist of tobacco, and desired him to send for the half-king, which he promised to do by a runner in the morning, and for other sachems. I invited him and the other great men present to my tent, where they stayed about an hour, and returned." This place was about 140 miles, "as we went, and computed it," says the great writer, "from our back settlements, where we arrived between sunsetting and dark, the twenty-fifth day after I left Williamsburgh."

Half-king, it seems, had, not long before, visited the same place to which *Washington* was now destined; for as soon as he returned to his town, *Washington* invited him privately to his tent, "and desired him to relate some of the particulars of his journey to the French commandant," the best way for him to go, and the distance from that place. "He told me," says *Washington*, "that the nearest and levelest way was now impassable, by reason of many large miry savannas; that we must be obliged to go by Venango, and should not get to the near fort in less than five or six nights' sleep, good travelling." *Half-king* further informed him that he met with a cold reception; that the French officer sternly ordered him to declare his business, which he did, he said, in the following speech:—

"Fathers, I am come to tell you your own speeches; what your own mouths have declared. You, in former days, set a silver basin before us, wherein there was the leg of a beaver, and desired all the nations to come and eat of it; to eat in peace and plenty, and not to be churlish to one another: and that if any such person should be found to be a disturber, I here lay down by the edge of the dish a rod, which you must scourge them with; and if your father should get foolish, in my old days, I desire you may use it upon me as well as others.—Now, fathers, it is you who are the disturbers in this land, by coming and building your towns; and taking it away unknown to us, and by force.—We kindled a fire, a long time ago, at a place called Montreal, where we desired you to stay, and not to come and intrude upon our land. I now desire you may despatch to that place; for, be it known to you, fathers, that this is our land, and not yours.—I desire you may hear me in civilness; if not, we must handle that rod which was laid down for the use of the obstreperous. If you had come in a peaceable manner, like our brothers the English, we would not have been against your trading with us, as they do; but to come, fathers, and build houses upon our land, and to take it by force, is what we cannot submit to."

Half-king then repeated what was said to him in reply by the French, which, when he had done, *Washington* made a speech to him and his council. He acquainted them with the reason of his visit, and told them he was instructed to call upon them by the governor of Virginia, to advise with them, to assure them of the love of the English, and to ask the assistance of some of their young men, to conduct him through the wilderness, to the French, to whom he had a letter from his governor. *Half-king* made this reply:—

"In regard to what my brother the governor had desired of me, I return

---

* He is called a *Huron* by *Loskiel*, Hist. Missions, iii. 123. He was called by the Delawares *Pomoacan*, which in English means *Sweet-house*. *Heckewelder*, Nar. 235. In the letter, or speech, as *Washington* called it, which this chief sent to the governors of Virginia and Pennsylvania, in 1754, his name is set down *Seruniyattha*. See 1 *Coll. Mass. Hist. Soc.* vi. 143.—I will here note, that my friend, JARED SPARKS, Esq., verbally informs me, that he is of opinion, that this is not the same *Half-king* mentioned in *Loskiel*. I am now of the same belief, although it is possible

you this answer." "I rely upon you as a brother ought to do, as you say we are brothers, and one people." "Brother, as you have asked my advice, I hope you will be ruled by it, and stay until I can provide a company to go with you. The French speech belt is not here; I have it to go for to my hunting cabin. Likewise the people, whom I have ordered in, are not yet come, and cannot until the third night from this; until which time, brother, I must beg you to stay."

When Washington told him that his business would not admit of so much delay, the chief seemed displeased, and said it was "*a matter of no small moment, and must not be entered without due consideration.*" Perhaps it will not be too much, to give this Indian chief credit for some of that character which was so well exemplified by *Washington* in all his after-life. And "as I found it impossible," says the narrator, "to get off, without affronting them in the most egregious manner, I consented to stay." Accordingly, *Half-king* gave orders to King *Shingis*, who was present, to attend on Wednesday night with the wampum, and two men of their nation, to be in readiness to set out with us next morning." There was still a delay of another day, as the chiefs could not get in their wampum and young men which were to be sent; and, after all, but three chiefs and one hunter accompanied. "We set out," says *Washington*, "about 9 o'clock, with the *Half-king*, *Juskakaka*,* *White-thunder*, and the hunter; and travelled on the road to Venango, where we arrived the 4th of December." This place is situated at the junction of French Creek with the Ohio. Here the French had a garrison, and another a short distance above it, which was the extent of our discoverer's peregrinations northward. The commanders of these posts used all means to entice *Half-king* to desert the English, and it was with great difficulty that *Washington* succeeded in preventing them. They endeavored to weary him out by making the chiefs delay their departure from day to day, by means of liquor, so that they should be left behind. At length, having out-generalled his complotters, and "got things ready to set off, I sent for the *Half-king*," continues the narrator, "to know whether he intended to go with us, or by water. He told me that *White-thunder* had hurt himself much, and was sick, and unable to walk; therefore he was obliged to carry him down in a canoe;" so, notwithstanding the delays, *Washington* was obliged to go without him; but he cautioned him strongly against believing Monsieur *Joncaire's* pretensions of friendship, and representations against the English. Here ends *Washington's* account of *Half-king*.

And before closing our account of the termination of Washington's journey we will close *our* account of this chief also. In 1754 he accompanied *Washington* in his excursion to dislodge the French from the disputed territory upon the Ohio, and was his constant counsellor, until after the surrender of Fort Necessity at the Great Meadows, on the 4 July. At the surprise of M. de *Jumonville*, on the 28 May previous, he led a company of his warriors, and piloted the English under *Washington* to the place where he was encamped, which was but a few miles from Great Meadows. *Jumonville's* force was small, consisting of but about 33 men. The night previous to the attack, *Half-king*, who was encamped six miles from Great Meadows, having made a discovery of the approach of the French force, sent an express to *Washington*, to inform him that the French were discovered in an obscure retreat. The colonel immediately marched out with 40 men and reached *Half-king's* quarters a little before sunrise. A council was now held by the chiefs of the parties, and it was agreed that the English and Indians should march together and attack the French. They marched in single file through the woods, in the Indian manner, in a most dismal storm of rain; and following the track just explored by *Half-king's* spies, soon found themselves near the party *Jumonville* was in a secure place, half a mile from a road, and surrounded by rocks, and had he not been fallen upon by surprise, it is doubtful whether the attacking party had not found it difficult to have contended successfully

---

* We hear again of this chief in 1794, when, with 58 others, he signed a treaty with the United States at Fort Stanwix. His name is there written *Jishkaaga*, which signified a *green grasshopper*. He was sometimes called *Little-Billy*.

against him. But not being discovered, *Washington* made a good disposition of his men; himself with the English formed the right wing, and *Half-king* at the head of the Indians, the left. The French were found without their arms in their hands, but they flew to them, and a fight of about 15 minutes ensued. None of the party escaped. Eleven of the French were killed, among whom was *M. de Jumonville;* one wounded, and 21 taken prisoners. *Washington* lost but one man, and two or three only were wounded.*

We now return to the narrative of *Washington*, which we had found it necessary abruptly to interrupt.

He now set out for the frontiers with all expedition. He had, he says, the "most fatiguing journey possible to conceive of. From the 1st to the 15th December, there was but one day on which it did not rain or snow incessantly; and through the whole journey, we met with nothing but one continued series of cold, wet weather."

This expedition of *Washington* has in it great interest, more especially from his superior eminence afterwards. It is pleasing to contemplate the "savior of his country" in every adventure and circumstance of his life; and even gratifying to view him with a gun in one hand, a staff in the other, and a pack upon his back; wading through rivers, encountering storms of sleet and snow, and sleeping upon the ground, thus early, for his country's good. He had some very narrow escapes, and, during part of the way on his return, he had but one attendant. One day, as they were passing a place called *Murdering Town*, they were fired upon by one of a war-party of French Indians, who had waited in ambush for them; and although they were within fifteen paces of him, yet they escaped unhurt. They captured the fellow that fired upon them, and kept him until nine at night, then dismissed him, and travelled all night, "without making *any* stop," fearing they should be pursued the next morning by his party. Continuing their course all the next day, they came to the river where they intended to cross. Here the firmness of *Washington* and his companion was thoroughly tried. The river was very high, and filled with floating ice, and there was no way to pass it but by a raft. They had "but one poor hatchet," with the assistance of which, after laboring from morning till sunset, they had a raft ready to launch; on this they set out, but it was soon crushed between the floating ice, and they very narrowly escaped perishing. *Washington* was himself precipitated into the river, where the water was ten feet deep. Fortunately, however, he catched by a fragment of the raft, and saved himself. They finally extricated themselves from their perilous situation, by getting upon the ice which confined their frail bark, and from thence to an island, and finally to the opposite shore. The cold was so intense, that Mr. *Gist* froze his hands and feet. This place was about three miles below the mouth of the Yohogany, where an Indian queen, as *Washington* calls her, lived. He went to see her, he observes, she having "expressed great concern that we passed her in going to the fort. I made her a present of a watch coat, and a bottle of rum, which latter was thought much the best present of the two." Her name was *Alliquippa*. From this place, he pursued his journey home without further accident.

We have mentioned the friendly attention of *Shingis* to our adventurer, who had probably expected he would have attended him on his journey; but *Shingis* went to collect in his men, and did not return. The Indians said it was owing to the sickness of his wife, but *Washington* thought it was fear of the French, which prevented him. But this conjecture does not seem well founded, for he ordered *Kustaloga*, who lived at Venango, to proceed to the French and return the wampum, which was as much as to tell them they wished no further fellowship with them.

The massacres which followed *Braddock's* defeat were horrible beyond description. *Shingis* and Captain *Jacobs* were supposed to have been the principal instigators of them, and 700 dollars were offered for their heads.† Captain *Jacobs* did not long escape, although the reward did not hasten his end. The hostile Indians had their head-quarters at Kitanning on the Allegha-

* SPARKS's Writings of Washington, ii. 451, 452.
† *Watson's* Annals of Philadelphia, 450.

ny River, 44 miles above its confluence with the Monongahela. Here they retired with their prisoners and booty after their expeditions into the frontiers In 1756, Colonel *John Armstrong* was sent with about 300 men against Kittanning. "On 3 September he joined the advanced party at the Beaver Dams, near Frankstown; and on the 7th in the evening, being within 6 miles of Kitanning, the scouts discovered a fire in the road, and reported that there were but 3 or at most 4 Indians at it. It was not thought proper to attempt surprising" them, as it might be a means of alarming the town, if any should escape. Hence Lieutenant *Hogg*, with a file of 12 men, was ordered to watch them, while the main body proceeded to the immediate vicinity of Kitanning. The night being warm, many of the Indians lodged in a cornfield upon the margin of the river, about 100 rods below the town. Here at day-break the attack began. Several Indians were killed in the field, and the town was immediately entered. As they advanced, Captain Jacobs gave the war whoop, retired to his log-cabin, and defended himself with great bravery. Inspired by his intrepidity, his men refused quarter, saying, "*We are men, and will not be prisoners.*" The whites being unable to drive them from their wigwams, Colonel *Armstrong* ordered these to be set on fire. At the same time he received a musket-shot in the shoulder. "When the Indians were told that they would be burnt if they did not surrender, one of them replied, *he did not care, as he could kill 4 or 5 before he died.*" When the fire approached them, some began to sing, and others burst from their houses, and were killed in their flight. Captain *Jacobs*, when defence could no longer avail him, endeavored to escape, with his wife, though a window of his house. This was his last act —he was shot down, and his wife also. A lad, called the *King's Son*, was killed with them. As at Nerigwok, many were killed in the river as they fled.

The Indians were said to have had their houses stored with spare arms and ammunition; for, when they were burnt up, their guns discharged from the heat, and quantities of powder blew up from time to time, which threw some of their bodies to a great height in the air. Eleven prisoners were recovered at this time, who informed their deliverers that a great quantity of goods was also consumed, which had but ten days before been sent them by the French; and that the Indians had boasted that they had powder enough for a ten years' war with the English. They also learned that the party which Lieutenant *Hogg* had been left to watch, instead of being but 3 or 4, consisted of 24 warriors, who were on their way to attack Fort Shirley, having been sent forward by Captain *Jacobs*, while he was to have followed with a strong force the next day. Hence the fate of the lieutenant's party was suspected. On returning to the place, Colonel *Armstrong* found that Lieutenant *Hogg* had attacked the Indians at great disadvantage, in point of numbers, and had been defeated, himself and Captain *Mercer* (afterwards General *Mercer*, who fell at Princeton) severely wounded. At the first fire *Hogg's* party killed 3 of the Indians, who, after maintaining the fight for an hour, killed but 3 of the whites. *Hogg*, being now wounded, was abandoned by his men, but was fortunate enough to be found by the army.* It was at this period, that the dead bodies of some that had been murdered and mangled were sent from the frontiers to Philadelphia, and hauled about the streets, to inflame the people against the Indians, and also against the Quakers, to whose mild forbearance was attributed a laxity in sending out troops. The mob surrounded the house of assembly, having placed the dead bodies at its entrance, and demanded immediate succor. At this time the above reward was offered.

Mr. *Heckewelder* knew *Shingis*, or, as he wrote his name, *Shingask*, † and gave him a good character. He was brother to *King-beaver*, and in the French war was considered the greatest Indian warrior of the day. He was a terror to the whole frontier of Pennsylvania. "Passing one day with him," says Mr Heckewelder, "in the summer of 1762, near by where his two prisoner boys (about 12 years of age) were amusing themselves with his own boys, and he observing me looking that way, inquired what I was looking at. On my replying that I was looking at his prisoners, he said, When I first took them

* *Coll. N. Y. Hist. Soc.* iii. 398—9. 3 *Coll. Mass. Hist. Soc.* iv. 298—9.
† *Level*, or *Bog-meadow*.

they *were* such; but they are now *my* children; eat their victuals out of one and the *same* bowl! which was saying as much as, that they, in all respects, were on an equal footing with *his own* children—alike dear to him." Though of small stature, the same author observes, he had a great mind.

The wife of this chief died in 1762. She was of the highest rank and respectability; and the ceremonies at her funeral, and manner of decoration and interment, described here, would occupy several pages.*

In the time of the French war, when the governor of Pennsylvania sent *C. F. Post* to the distant tribes to persuade them from aiding the French, mention is often made in the journal which he kept,† of *Shingis*, and uniformly to his advantage. The Reverend Mr. *Post* performed two missions, the first at the close of 1758, and the second in 1759. Under date of 28 August, 1758, he writes, "We set out from Sawcunk in company with 20, for Kushcushkee; on the road *Shingas* addressed himself to me, and asked, if I did not think, that if he came to the English they would hang him, as they had offered a great reward for his head. I told him that was a great while ago, 'twas all forgotten and wiped away now." An Indian in the company, called *Shamokin Daniel*, who had been tampered with by the French, understanding what was said, interrupted and said, "Don't believe him, he tells nothing but idle lying stories," and asked, "Why then did the English hire 1200 Indians [meaning the Cherokees] to kill us?" Mr. *Post* protesting it was false, *Daniel* vociferated, G—d d—n you for a fool; did you not see the woman lying in the road that was killed by the Indians that the English hired?" After a few other harsh expressions, *Shingis* told him to be still, for he did not know what he said."

Mr. *Post* dined with *Shingis* on the 29 August, at which time he observed to him, that although the English had offered a great reward for his head, yet he had never thought to revenge himself, but was always very kind to such prisoners as were brought in, and that he would do all in his power to bring about a peace, and wished he could be sure the English were in earnest for peace also.

Although the name of *Shingis* has not generally been as conspicuous as that of Captain *Jacobs*, yet he is said to have been "the greatest Delaware warrior of his time," and that, "were his war exploits on record, they would form an interesting document, though a shocking one." ‡

Hendrick was a gallant Mohawk chief, who took part, with many of his men, against the French, in the year 1755. The French were encouraged by the defeat of General *Braddock*, and were in high expectation of carrying all before them. *Hendrick* joined the English army at the request of General *Johnson*, and met the French, consisting of 2000 men, under General *Dieskau* at Lake George. While the English and Indians were encamped in a slight work, their scouts brought news of the approach of the French, with a great body of Indians upon their flanks. General *Johnson* despatched Colonel *Williams* of Massachusetts, with 1000 men, and *Hendrick* with 200 of his warriors, to give them battle; but falling in with them about four miles from camp unexpectedly, Colonels *Williams* and *Hendrick* were killed, with many other officers and privates of the detachment. The rest fled to the main body with great precipitation, infusing consternation into the whole army.§ The French followed closely, and poured in a tremendous fire, which did very little execution, from the precaution of the English in falling flat upon their faces. They soon recovered from their surprise, and fought with bravery, having advantage not only in numbers, but artillery, of which the French had none.‖ At length the brave *Dieskau* was wounded in the thigh, and his Indians, being terrified at the havoc made by the cannon of the English, fled to the woods, and the regulars were ordered to retreat by their general, which they did in great disorder. General *Dieskau* was found in the pursuit, supporting himself by the stump of a tree. Supposing plunder to be the first object of

* For which see *Heckewelder's* Hist. Ind. Nations, 264, &c.

† Reprinted in "*The Causes of the Alienation,*" &c., and *Proud's* Pa., vol. 2d.

‡ *Heckewelder's* Narrative, 64.

§ The English lost about 200 in this ambush. *Guthrie's* Universal History, x 94.

‖ Ibid.

his captors, as he was attempting to draw his watch to present to them, some one, supposing him to be searching for his pistol, discharged his gun into his hips. Notwithstanding he was thus twice wounded, he lived to reach England, but he died soon after. The French lost 800 men in the attack.

When General *Johnson* was about to detach Colonel *Williams*, he asked *Hendrick's* opinion, whether the force was sufficient. To which he replied, "*If they are to fight, they are too few. If they are to be killed, they are too many.*" And when it was proposed to divide the detachment into three parts, *Hendrick* objected, and forcibly to express the impracticability of the plan, picked up three sticks, and, putting them together, said to the general, "*You see now that these cannot be easily broken; but take them one by one, and you may break them at once.*" But from this valuable counsel very little advantage seems to have been derived.

It was reported at the time, that 38 of *Hendrick's* men were killed, and 12 wounded.* Few historians mention the loss of the Indians; probably considering them as unworthy of record! Such historians *may be forgotten*. At least, they cannot expect to pass under that name in another age.

The Indians were greatly exasperated against the French, "by the death of the famous *Hendrick*," says the same writer, "a renowned Indian warrior among the Mohawks, and one of their sachems, or kings, who was slain in the battle, and whose son, upon being told that his father was killed, giving the usual Indian groan upon such occasions, and suddenly putting his hand on his left breast, swore his father was still alive in that place, and stood there in his son: that it was with the utmost difficulty, General *Johnson* prevented the fury of their resentment taking place on the body of the French general."†

As soon as the battle was over, the Indians dispersed themselves in various directions, with the trophies of victory; some to their homes, to condole with the friends of the slain, and some to the English, to carry the we come news of victory. The different runners brought into Albany above 80 scalps within a very short time after the fight.‡ And thus we are furnished with an early record of the wretched custom which appears to have been fostered, and actually encouraged by all who have employed the Indians as auxiliaries in war. Indeed to employ them, was to employ their practices—they were inseparable. To talk, as some have done, of employing them, and preventing their barbarous customs with the unfortunate captives, all experience shows, is but *to talk* one thing and mean another.

Soon after Sir *William Johnson* entered upon his duties as superintendent of Indian affairs in North America, he received from England some richly embroidered suits of clothes. *Hendrick* was present when they were received, and could not help expressing a great desire for a share in them. He went away very thoughtful, but returned not long after, and called upon Sir *William*, and told him he had dreamed a dream. Sir *William* very concernedly desired to know what it was. *Hendrick* as readily told him he had dreamed that Sir *William Johnson* had presented him with one of his new suits of uniform. Sir *William* could not refuse it, and one of the elegant suits was forthwith presented to *Hendrick*, who went away to show his present to his countrymen, and left Sir *William* to tell the joke to his friends. Some time after, the general met *Hendrick*, and told him he had dreamed a dream. Whether the sachem mistrusted that he was now to be taken in his own net, or not, is not certain: but he seriously desired to know what it was, as Sir *William* had done before. The general said he dreamed that *Hendrick* had presented him with a certain tract of land, which he described, (consisting of about 500 acres of the most valuable land in the valley of the Mohawk River.) *Hendrick* answered, "*It is yours;*" but, shaking his head, said, "Sir *William Johnson*, I will never dream with you again."

John Konkapot, a Stockbridge Indian, was grandson to *Hendrick*, and he informs us that his grandfather was son of the *Wolf*, a Mohegan chief, and that his mother was a Mohawk.§ Reverend *Gideon Hawley*, in a letter to Governor *Hutchinson* (1770) about the Marshpee Indians, has this passage

* *Gent. Magazine* for 1755. † Ibid ‡ Ibid.

§ *Coll. Mass. Hist. Soc.*

"Among *Johnson's* Mohawks, *Abraham* and *Hendrick* were the oldest of their tribe, when they died, and neither of them was 70, at their deaths. I saw a sister of theirs in 1765, who appeared to be several years above 70. At Stockbridge, Captain *Kunkapot* was for many years the oldest man in his tribe." * We have now come to one of the most noted chiefs in Indian story

Logan was called a Mingo † chief, whose father, *Shikellimus*, was chief of the Cayugas, whom he succeeded. *Shikellimus* was attached in a remarkable degree to the benevolent *James Logan*, from which circumstance, it is probable, his son bore his name. The name is still perpetuated among the Indians. For magnanimity in war, and greatness of soul in peace, few, if any, in any nation, ever surpassed *Logan*. He took no part in the French wars which ended in 1760, except that of a peacemaker; was always acknowledged the friend of the white people, until the year 1774, when his brother and several others of his family were murdered, the particulars of which follow. In the spring of 1774, some Indians robbed the people upon the Ohio River,‡ who were in that country exploring the lands, and preparing for settlements. These land-jobbers were alarmed at this hostile carriage of the Indians, as they considered it, and collected themselves at a place called Wheeling Creek, the site on which Wheeling is now built, and, learning that there were two Indians on the river a little above, one Captain *Michael Cresap*, belonging to the exploring party, proposed to fall upon and kill them. His advice, although opposed at first, was followed, and a party led by *Cresap* proceeded and killed the two Indians. The same day, it being reported that some Indians were discovered below Wheeling upon the river, *Cresap* and his party immediately marched to the place, and at first appeared to show themselves friendly, and suffered the Indians to pass by them unmolested, to encamp still lower down, at the mouth of Grave Creek. *Cresap* soon followed, attacked and killed several of them, having one of his own men wounded by the fire of the Indians. Here some of the family of *Logan* were slain. The circumstance of the affair was exceeding aggravating, inasmuch as the whites *pretended no provocation*.

Soon after this, some other monsters in human shape, at whose head were *Daniel Greathouse* and one *Tomlinson*, committed a horrid murder upon a company of Indians about thirty miles above Wheeling. *Greathouse* resided at the same place, but on the opposite side of the river from the Indian encampment. A party of thirty-two men were collected for this object, who secreted themselves, while *Greathouse*, under a pretence of friendship, crossed the river and visited them, to ascertain their strength; on counting them, he found they were too numerous for his force in an open attack. These Indians, having heard of the late murder of their relations, had determined to be avenged of the whites, and *Greathouse* did not know the danger he was in, until a squaw advised him of it, in a friendly caution, "to go home." The sad requital this poor woman met with will presently appear. This abominable fellow invited the Indians to come over the river and drink rum with him; this being a part of his plot to separate them, that they might be the easier destroyed. The opportunity soon offered; a number being collected at a tavern in the white settlement, and considerably intoxicated, were fallen upon, and all murdered, except a little girl. Among the murdered was a brother of *Logan*, and his sister, whose delicate situation greatly aggravated the horrid crime.

The remaining Indians, upon the other side of the river, on hearing the firing, set off two canoes with armed warriors, who, as they approached the shore, were fired upon by the whites, who lay concealed, awaiting their approach. Nothing prevented their taking deadly aim, and many were killed and wounded, and the rest were obliged to return. This affair took place May 24th, 1774.§ These were the events that led to a horrid Indian

* *Coll. Mass. Hist. Soc.* 3. i. 151.

† *Mengwe, Maquas, Maqua*, or *Iroquos* all mean the same.

‡ "In the month of April, 1774, a rumor was circulated, that the Indians had stolen several horses from some land-jobbers on the Ohio and Kentucky Rivers; no evidences of the fact having been adduced, lead to the conclusion that the report was false." *Doddridge's* Notes, 225—6.

§ Facts published in *Jefferson's Notes*.

war, in which many innocent families were sacrificed to satisfy the vengeance of an incensed and injured people.

A calm followed these troubles, but it was only such as goes before the storm, and lasted only while the tocsin of war could be sounded among the distant Indians. On the 12 July, 1774, *Logan*, at the head of a small party of only eight warriors, struck a blow on some inhabitants upon the Muskingum, where no one expected it. He had left the settlements on the Ohio undisturbed, which every one supposed would be the first attacked, in case of war, and hence the reason of his great successes. His first attack was upon three men who were pulling flax in a field. One was shot down, and the two others taken. These were marched into the wilderness, and, as they approached the Indian town, *Logan* gave the scalp halloo, and they were met by the inhabitants, who conducted them in. Running the gantlet was next to be performed. *Logan* took no delight in tortures, and he in the most friendly manner instructed one of the captives how to proceed to escape the severities of the gantlet. This same captive, whose name was *Robinson*, was afterwards sentenced to be burned; but *Logan*, though not able to rescue him by his eloquence, with his own hand cut the cords that bound him to the stake, and caused him to be adopted into an Indian family. He became afterwards *Logan's* scribe, and wrote the letter that was tied to a war club, the particulars of which we shall relate farther onward.

There was a chief among the Shawanese more renowned as a warrior than even *Logan* himself at this time. CORNSTOCK * was his name, and to him seems to have fallen the chief direction of the war that was now begun; the causes of which were doubtless owing to the outrages already detailed, committed by *Cresap* and *Greathouse*, but there can be but little if any doubt, that the several tribes engaged in it, had each been sufficiently injured to justify *their* participation also. The history of the murder of *Bald Eagle* is more than sufficient to account for the part acted by the Delawares. What this man had been in his younger days is unknown to history, but at this time he was an old inoffensive Delaware chief, who wandered harmlessly up and down among the whites, visiting those most frequently who would entertain him best. Having been on a visit to the fort at the mouth of Kanhawa, he was met, as he was ascending alone upon the river in his canoe, by a man, who, it is said, had suffered much from the Indians. It was in the evening, and whether any thing happened to justify violence on the part of either, we have no evidence, but certain it is, the white man killed the chief, and scalped him, and, to give his abominable crime publicity, set the dead body upright in the canoe, and in this manner caused it to drift down the river, where it was beheld by many as it passed them. From the appearance of the old chief, no one suspected he was dead, but very naturally concluded he was upon one of his ordinary visits. The truth of the affair, however, soon got to his nation, and they quickly avowed vengeance for the outrage. †

The Virginia legislature was in session when the news of an Indian war was received at the seat of government. Governor *Dunmore* immediately gave orders for the assembling of 3000 men; one half of whom were to march for the mouth of the great Kanhawa under the command of General *Andrew Lewis*,‡ and the remainder, under the governor in person, was to proceed to some point on the Ohio, above the former, in order to fall upon the Indian towns between, while the warriors should be drawn off by the approach of *Lewis* in the opposite direction. He was then to proceed down the Ohio, and form a junction with General *Lewis* at Point Pleasant, from whence they were to march according to circumstances.

---

* Generally written *Cornstalk*, but in our oldest printed account, it is as in the text. There is no harm in changing the orthography of a word, when we use it for a proper instead of a common substantive.

† *M'Clung*.

‡ His rank was that of colonel, but, being commander-in-chief of that division, was properly called general, to distinguish him from his brother, who was also a colonel, and as having the chief command.

On the 11 September, the forces under General *Lewis*, amounting to 1100 men, commenced their march from Camp Union for Point Pleasant on the Great Kanhaway, distant 160 miles. The country between was a trackless wilderness. The army was piloted by Captain *Matthew Arbuckle*, by the nearest practicable route. The baggage was all transported on pack-horses, and their march took up 19 days.*

Having arrived there upon the last day of the month, an encampment was commenced on the first of October. Here General *Lewis* waited with anxiety to get some tidings of *Dunmore*, for eight or nine days. At the end of this time, no prospect of a junction appearing, news was brought into camp in the morning of the 10 October, by one of two persons who had escaped the rifles of a great body of Indians about two miles up the Ohio, that an attack would be immediately made. These two men were upon a deer hunt, and came upon the Indians without observing them, when one was shot down, and the other escaped to the camp with difficulty. He reported "that he had seen a body of the enemy, covering four acres of ground, as closely as they could stand by the side of each other." †

Upon this intelligence, General *Lewis*, "after having deliberately lighted his pipe," ‡ gave orders to his brother, Colonel *Charles Lewis*, to march with his own regiment, and another under Colonel *William Fleming*, to reconnoitre the enemy, while he put the remainder in a posture to support them. These marched without loss of time, and about 400 yards from camp met the Indians intent upon the same object. Their meeting was somewhere between sun's rising and sun an hour high,§ and the fight in a moment began. The Virginians, like their opponents, covered themselves with trees or whatever else offered, but the latter were more than a match for them, and put them to flight with great slaughter. Colonel *Lewis* was in full uniform, and being, from the nature of his duties, exposed at every point, soon fell mortally wounded.‖ There was no result for which the commander-in-chief was not prepared; for at this critical moment he had ordered up Colonel *Field* with his regiment, which, coming with great resolution and firmness into action, saved the two retreating regiments, and effectually checked the impetuosity of the Indians, who, in their turn, were obliged to retreat behind a rough breastwork, which they had taken the precaution to construct from logs and brush for the occasion.

The point of land on which the battle was fought was narrow, and the Indians' breastwork extended from river to river: their plan of attack was the best that could be conceived; for in the event of victory on their part, not a Virginian could have escaped. They had stationed men on both sides of the river to prevent any that might attempt flight by swimming from the apex of the triangle made by the confluence of the two rivers.

Never was ground maintained with more obstinacy; for it was slowly, and with no precipitancy, that the Indians retired to their breastwork. The division under *Lewis* was first broken, although that under *Fleming* was nearly at the same moment attacked. This heroic officer first received two balls through his left wrist, but continued to exercise his command with the greatest coolness and presence of mind. His voice was continually heard, "Don't lose an inch of ground. Advance, outflank the enemy, and get between them and the river." But his men were about to be outflanked by the body that had just defeated *Lewis;* meanwhile the arrival of Colonel *Field* turned the fortune of the day, but not without a severe loss; Colonel *Fleming* was again wounded,¶ by a shot through the lungs; ** yet he would not retire, and Colonel *Field* was killed as he was leading on his men.

---

* *Doddridge*, 280. † *Withers*, 126. ‡ *M'Clung*, 321.

§ At sun-rise, *Burk*, iii. 393.—Sun an hour high, *Royal Amer. Magazine for November*, 1774.—A little after sunrise, *Doddridge*, 231.—The sun was just rising, *M'Clung*, 322.—Sunrise, *Withers*, 127.

‖ He walked into camp, and expired in his own tent. *Doddridge*.

¶ Mr. *M'Clung* says he was killed, but we cannot find any authority to agree with him. Mr. *Withers* says he was "an active governor of Virginia during the revolutionary war." *Chronicles*, 130.

** *Burk*, iii. 394.

The whole line of the breastwork now became as a blaze of fire, which lasted nearly till the close of the day. Here the Indians under *Logan*, *Cornstock*, *Elenipsico*, *Red-Eagle*, and other mighty chiefs of the tribes of the Shawanese, Delawares, Mingoes, Wyandots and Cayugas, amounting, as was supposed, to 1500 warriors, fought, as men will ever do for their country's wrongs, with a bravery which could only be equalled. The voice of the mighty *Cornstock* was often heard during the day, above the din of strife, calling on his men in these words: "Be strong! Be strong!" And when by the repeated charges of the whites, some of his warriors began to waver, he is said to have sunk his tomahawk into the head of one who was cowardly endeavoring to desert.

General *Lewis*, finding at length that every charge upon the lines of the Indians lessened the number of his forces to an alarming degree, and rightly judging that if the Indians were not routed before it was dark, a day of more doubt might follow, he resolved to throw a body, if possible, into their rear. As the good fortune of the Virginians turned, the bank of the river favored this project, and forthwith three companies were detached upon the enterprise, under the three captains, *Isaac Shelby*, (afterwards renowned in the revolution, and since in the war with Canada,) *George Matthews*,* and *John Steuart*. These companies got unobserved to their place of destination upon Crooked Creek, which runs into the Kanhawa.† From the high weeds upon the banks of this little stream, they rushed upon the backs of the Indians with such fury, as to drive them from their works with precipitation. The day was now decided. The Indians, thus beset from a quarter they did not expect, were ready to conclude that a reinforcement had arrived. It was about sunset when they fled across the Ohio, and immediately took up their march for their towns on the Scioto.

As is common, in reviewing past events, we find much difference of opinion in regard to many of the facts; the loss of the whites in this battle is very variously stated, but that of the Indians no one has presumed to set down but by inference. The morning after the battle, Colonel *Christian*‡ marched to the battle-ground; where his men found and scalped § 21 of their dead, and 12 others were found in places where they were placed for concealment; that many were also thrown into the river is said to have been at the time known. In an account published at the time, it is set down that the killed of the Virginians were "Col. *Charles Lewis*, Major *John Field*, Capt. *John Murray*, *Robert Mc Clenechan*, *Samuel Wilson*, *James Ward*, Lieut. *Hugh Allen*, Ensigns, *Candiff*, *Baker*, and 44 privates;" making the whole number of the killed 55. "Wounded, Captain *W. Fleming*, since dead, *Y. Dickinson*, *Thomas Blueford*, *John Stidman*, Lieuts. *Goodman*, *Robeson*, *Laud*, *Vannes*, and 79 *Privates*;" making in all 87 wounded. We are aware that neither the names or numbers agree with accounts since published, but we have taken the above from the Royal American Magazine, which was published the following month at Boston, into which it seems to have been copied from a Philadelphia print.‖

There was a kind of stratagem used by the whites in this battle which reminds us of that practised at the Pawtucket fight, related in Book III. of our history. The soldiers in Colonel *Fleming's* regiment would conceal themselves behind a tree or some other shelter, and then hold out their hats from behind, which the Indians seeing, would mistake as covering the heads

---

* Probably the same who was a colonel in the Virginia line during the revolution, and once a prisoner. See Contin. *Burk*, 107, 358, also *Withers*, 130.

† *Withers*, 127.

‡ He was not present at the fight, but arrived with a reinforcement, which he had raised from Holston, immediately after it was over. It was this force, it is supposed, that the Indians expected were surrounding them in the rear. They were said to have been acquainted with all circumstances connected with the operations of the Virginians.

§ *Royal Amer. Magazine* for November, 1774.

‖ Dr. *Doddridge*, 231, sets down the killed at 75, and the wounded at 140, and he is doubtless, Mr. *Withers's* authority, who says the same. His list of killed and wounded are also verbatim from *Doddridge*. *Burk*, who wrote twenty years before either, agrees with the *Royal American Magazine* very nearly.

of their enemies, and shoot at them. The hat being at once dropped, the Indian would run out from his covert to scalp his victim, and thus met a sure death from the tomahawk of his adversary.

The chief of the men raised for this service, were, as *Burk* expresses himself, "prime riflemen," and the "most expert woodsmen in Virginia." They were principally from the counties of Augusta, Botetourt, Bedford and Fincastle, and from the enraged settlers who had fled from their frontier settlements to escape the vengeance of the injured Indians. For reasons which were not perfectly understood at that time, Lord *Dunmore* divided the army into two parts, as already stated. The part which *Dunmore* soon after took in the revolutionary events, discovered the real cause of his preposterous proceedings. His pretence of falling upon the backs of the Indians, and coöperating with General *Lewis*, was soon detected as such; for it needed only to be known that he was moving no less than 75 miles from him, and that, therefore, no coöperation could be had. The imputation, however, of the historian *Burk*,* "that the division under *Lewis* was devoted to destruction, for the purpose of breaking the spirits of the Virginians," to render his own influence and reputation brighter and more efficient, is unnatural, and without facts to warrant it. To our mind a worse policy to raise himself could not have been devised. There are two other, far more reasonable conclusions, which might have been offered: The governor, seeing the justness of the Indians' cause, might have adopted the plan which was followed, to bring them to a peace with the least possible destruction of them. This would have been the course of a humane philosophy; or he might have exercised his abilities to gain them to the British interest, in case of a rupture between them and the colonies, which the heads of government must clearly have by this time foreseen would pretty soon follow. Another extraordinary manœuvre of Governor *Dunmore* betrayed either a great want of experience, generalship, or a far more reprehensible charge; for he had, before the battle of Point Pleasant, sent an express † to Colonel *Lewis*, with orders that he should join him near the Shawanee towns, with all possible despatch. These instructions were looked upon as singularly unaccountable, inasmuch as it was considered a thing almost impossible to be accomplished, had there not been an enemy to fear; for the distance was near 80 miles, and the route was through a country extremely difficult to be traversed, and, to use the words of Mr. *Burk*, "swarming with Indians."‡ The express did not arrive at Point Pleasant until the evening after the battle; § but that it had been fought was unknown to the governor, and could in no wise excuse his sending such orders, although the power of the Indians was now broken.

The day after the battle, General *Lewis* caused his dead to be buried, and entrenchments to be thrown up about his camp for the protection of his sick and wounded; and the day following, he took up his line of march, in compliance with the orders of Governor *Dunmore*. This march was attended with great privations and almost insurmountable difficulties. Meanwhile Governor *Dunmore* descended with his forces down the river, from Fort Pitt to Wheeling, where he halted for a few days. He then proceeded down to the mouth of Hockhocking, thence over land to within 8 miles of the Shawanee town Chilicothe, on the Scioto. Here he made preparations for treating with the Indians. Before reaching this place he had received several messages from the Indians with offers of peace, and having now determined to comply, he sent an express to General *Lewis* with an order that he should immediately retreat. This was entirely disregarded by the general, and he continued his march until his lordship in person visited the general in his camp, and gave the order to the troops himself. LEWIS's troops complied

* Hist. Virginia, iii. 396.

† The famous pioneer, *Simon Kenton*, alias *Butler*, was the person sent by *Dunmore* at this time.

‡ Hist. Virginia, iii. 395.

§ This is not agreeable to the statement of Dr. *Doddridge*, who says their arrival was before the battle, and Mr. *Withers* follows him; but I follow Mr. *Burk*, who doubtless had the best means of giving the truth. *Marshall* [Ky. i. 40] agrees with the former.

with great reluctance, for they had determined on a general destruction of the Indians.

A treaty was now commenced, and conducted on the part of the whites with great distrust, never admitting but a small number of Indians within their encampment at a time. The business was commenced by *Cornstock* in a speech of great length, in the course of which he did not fail to charge upon the whites the whole cause of the war; and mainly in consequence of the murder of *Logan's* family. A treaty, however, was the result of this conference; and this conference was the result of the far-famed speech of LOGAN, the Mingo chief; since known in every hemisphere. It was not delivered in the camp of Lord *Dunmore*, for, although desiring peace, *Logan* would not meet the whites in council, but remained in his cabin in sullen silence, until a messenger was sent to him to know whether he would accede to the proposals it contained. What the distance was from the treaty-ground to *Logan's* cabin, we are not told; but of such importance was his name considered, that he was waited on by a messenger* from Lord *Dunmore*, who requested his assent to the articles of the treaty. Logan had too much at heart the wrongs lately done him to accede without giving the messenger to understand fully the grounds upon which he acceded; he therefore invited him into an adjacent wood, where they sat down together. Here he related the events of butchery which had deprived him of all his connections; and here he pronounced that memorable speech, which follows:

"*I appeal to any white to say, if ever he entered* Logan's *cabin hungry, and he gave him not meat; if ever he came cold and naked, and he clothed him not.*

"*During the course of the last long bloody war,* Logan *remained idle in his cabin, an advocate for peace. Such was my love for the whites, that my countrymen pointed as they passed, and said,* 'Logan *is the friend of white men.*'

"*I had even thought to have lived with you, but for the injuries of one man.* Col. Cresap *the last spring, in cold blood, and unprovoked, murdered all the relations of* Logan; *not even sparing my women and children.*

"*There runs not a drop of my blood in the veins of any living creature. This called on me for revenge. I have sought it. I have killed many. I have fully glutted my vengeance. For my country, I rejoice at the beams of peace. But do not harbor a thought that mine is the joy of fear.* Logan *never felt fear. He will not turn on his heel to save his life. Who is there to mourn for* Logan?—*Not one!*"

When Mr. *Jefferson* published his "Notes on Virginia," the facts therein stated implicating *Cresap* as the murderer of *Logan's* family, were by *Cresap's* friends called in question. Mr. *Jefferson* at first merely stated the facts as preliminary to, and the cause of, the "Speech of *Logan*," which he considered as generally known in Virginia; but the acrimony discovered by his enemies in their endeavors to gainsay his statement, led to an investigation of the whole transaction, and a publication of the result was the immediate consequence, in a new edition of the "Notes on Virginia."

There are perhaps still some who doubt of the genuineness of *Logan's* speech and indeed we must allow, that there are some circumstances laid before us in Dr. *Barton's* Medical and Physical Journal, for the year 1808; which look irreconcilable. Without impeaching in the slightest degree the character of Mr. *Jefferson*, such facts are there compared, and disagreements pointed out, as chanced to come in the way of the writer. It appears from the French traveller *Robin*, that, in the time of our revolution, a gentleman of Williamsburg gave him an Indian speech, which bears great resemblance to the one said to be by *Logan*; but differing very essentially in date, and the person implicated in murdering the family of Logan. The work of *Robin* is entitled "New Travels in America," and we have only an English translation

---

* Mr. *John Gibson*, then an officer in *Dunmore's* army, and afterwards a man of considerable distinction

of it.* It is therefore possible that some mistakes may have crept into it, or that *Robin* himself might have misunderstood the date, and even other parts of the affair; however, the probability is rather strong that either the speech of *Logan* had been perverted for the purpose of clearing *Cresap's* character of the foul blot which entirely covered it, by wilfully charging it upon another, or that some old speech of his upon another occasion, had been remodeled to suit the purpose for which it was used. Upon these questions we must leave the reader to decide. *Robin* has the name of the chief, *Lonan*. Some Frenchmen may write it thus, but I have before me those that do not,† and more probably some English pronounced it so, and so *Robin* heard it. The way he introduces the speech, if the introduction be fact, forever destroys the genuineness of the speech of *Logan* of 1774. It is thus:

"Speech of the savage LONAN, in a General Assembly, as it was sent to the Gov$_r$. of Virginia,‡ anno 1754."

Now it is certain, if the speech which we will give below *was delivered in the Assembly of Virginia, in the year* 1754, it could not have been truly delivered, as we have given it, to Lord *Dunmore* in 1774. That the reader may judge for himself, that of 1754 follows.

"LONAN will no longer oppose making the proposed peace with the white men. You are sensible he never knew what fear is—that he never turned his back in the day of battle—No one has more love for the white men than I have. The war we have had with them has been long and bloody on both sides. Rivers of blood have ran on all parts, and yet no good has resulted therefrom to any. I once more repeat it—let us be at peace with these men. I will forget our injuries, the interest of my country demands it. I will forget—but difficult indeed is the task! Yes, I will forget—that Major *Rogers* § cruelly and inhumanly murdered, in their canoes, my wife, my children, my father, my mother, and all my kindred.—This roused me to deeds of vengeance! I was cruel in despite of myself. I will die content if my country is once more at peace; but when *Lonan* shall be no more, who, alas, will drop a tear to the memory of *Lonan!*"

With a few incidents, and reflections, we will close our account of events connected with the history of CRESAP'S WAR.

On the evening before the battle of Point Pleasant, *Cornstock* proposed to his warriors to make peace with General *Lewis*, and avoid a battle, but his advice was not accepted by the council. "Well," said he, "since you have resolved to fight, you shall fight, although it is likely we shall have hard work to-morrow; but if any man shall flinch or run from the battle, I will kill him with my own hand." And it is said he made his word good by putting one to death who discovered cowardice during the fight, as has been mentioned.

After the Indians had retreated, *Cornstock* called a council at the Chilicothe town, to consult on what was to be done. Here he reflected upon the rashness that had been exercised in fighting the whites at Point Pleasant; and asked, "*What shall we do now! the Long-Knives are coming upon us by two routes. Shall we turn out and fight them?*"—No answer was made. He then inquired, "*Shall we kill all our squaws and children, and then fight until we shall all be killed ourselves?*"—As before, all were silent. In the midst of the council-house a war-post had been erected; with his tomahawk in his hand, *Cornstock* turned towards it, and sticking it into the post, he said, "Since you are not inclined to fight, I will go and make peace;" and he forthwith repaired to *Dunmore's* camp.‖

---

* Since the above was written, I have met with the French edition; and, from its imprint I presume both editions were published under the supervision of the author. "*A Philadelphie et se trouve à Paris*, 1782."

† See *Recherches sur les Etats-Unis*, iv. 153—5. The authors of this well-written work should not have withheld their names. It was printed at Paris, in 8vo., 1788.

‡ "11 *Net*" is found in the French copy, and this marginal note to it; "*ce mot signifie apparemment le mois Lunaire ou Solaire.*"

§ In the French copy no person is mentioned. After *Major*, a blank is left. In other respects the speech is tolerably correctly translated.

‖ *Doddridge's* Notes, 239—40.

We have been more minute and particular in these events, in which *Logan* and *Cornstock* were engaged, than in many others; but I trust the reader of this history will not be displeased with such minuteness upon so important an event; especially as no work with which I am acquainted does the subject justice. It was truly a great event, both in respect to the parties engaged, and the consequences necessarily growing out of it, and it has been passed over too slightly by historians.

In respect to the speech of *Logan*, it would be highly gratifying if a few matters connected with it could be settled; but whether they ever will, time only can determine. From the statement of Dr. *Barton*, * before cited, we are led to expect that he had other documents than those he at that time published, going to show that *Cresap* was not the murderer of *Logan's* family, but he never published them, as I can learn, and he has left us to conjecture upon such as we have. Another author, † upon the authority of an officer who was at the time with Lord *Dunmore*, states that he heard nothing of *Logan's* charging *Cresap* with the murder of his kindred during the whole campaign, nor until a long time after. That it was not publicly talked of among the officers is in no wise strange, as *Cresap* himself was one of them; therefore, that this is evidence that no such charge was made by Logan, we think unworthy consideration.

Among other proofs, that the chief guilt lay upon the head of *Cresap* of bringing about a bloody war, since well known by his name, Judge *Innes* of Frankfort, Kentucky, wrote to Mr. *Jefferson*, 2 March, 1799, that he was, he thought, able to give him more particulars of that affair than, perhaps, any other person; that, in 1774, while at the house of Colonel *Preston*, in Fincastle county, Va., there arrived an express, calling upon him to order out the militia, "for the protection of the inhabitants residing low down on the north fork of Holston River. The express brought with him a war club, and a note tied to it, which was left at the house of one *Robertson*, whose family were cut off by the Indians, and gave rise for the application to Colonel *Preston*." Here follows the letter or note, of which Mr. *Innes* then made a copy, in his memorandum-book:—

"*Captain* Cresap, *What did you kill my people on Yellow Creek for? The white people killed my kin at Conestoga,* ‡ *a great while ago; and I thought nothing of that. But you killed my kin again, on Yellow Creek, and took my cousin prisoner. Then I thought I must kill too; and I have been three times to war since; but the Indians are not angry; only myself.*"

It was signed, "*Captain* John Logan."

Not long after these times of calamities, which we have recorded in the life of *Logan*, he was cruelly murdered, as he was on his way home from Detroit. For a time previous to his death, he gave himself up to intoxication, which in a short time nearly obliterated all marks of the great man!

The fate of *Cornstock* is equally deplorable, although in the contemplation of which, his character does not suffer, as does that of *Logan*. He was cruelly murdered by some white soldiers, while a hostage among them. And there is as much, nay, far more, to carry down *his* remembrance to posterity, as that of the tragical death of *Archimedes*. He was not murdered while actually drawing geometrical figures upon the ground, but, while he was explaining the geography of his country by drawings upon the floor, an alarm was given, which, in a few minutes after, eventuated in his death. We will now go into an explanation of the cause and manner of the murder of *Cornstock*. It is well known that the war of the revolution had involved all, or nearly all, of the Indians in dreadful calamities. In consequence of murders committed by the Indians on the frontiers of Virginia, several companies marched to Point Pleasant, where there had been a fort since the battle there in 1774. Most of the tribes of the north-west, except the Shawanees, were determined to fight against the Americans. *Cornstock* wished

* *Med. and Phys. Jour.* part ii. p. 162. † *Withers*, Chronicles, 136.

‡ Alluding, I suppose, to the massacre of the Conestoga Indians in 1763.

to preserve peace, and therefore, as the only means in his power as he had used his powerful eloquence in vain, resolved to lay the state of affairs before the Americans, that they might avert the threatened storm. In the spring of 1777, he came to the fort at Point Pleasant, upon this friendly mission, in company with another chief, called *Red-hawk.* After explaining the situation of things with regard to the confederate tribes, he said, in regard to his own, the Shawanese, "*The current sets* [with the Indians] *so strong against the Americans, in consequence of the agency of the British, that they* [the Shawanese] *will float with it, I fear, in spite of all my exertions.*" Upon this intelligence, the commander of the garrison thought proper to detain him and *Red-hawk* as hostages to prevent the meditated calamities. When Captain *Arbuckle*, the commander of the garrison, had notified the new government of Virginia of the situation of affairs, and what he had done, forces marched into that country. A part of them having arrived, waited for others to join them under General *Hand*, on whom these depended for provisions.

Meanwhile the officers held frequent conversations with *Cornstock*, who took pleasure in giving them minute descriptions of his country, and especially of that portion between the Mississippi and Missouri. One day, as he was delineating a map of it upon the floor, for the gratification of those present, a call was heard on the opposite side of the Ohio, which he at once recognized as the voice of his son, *Ellinipsico*, who had fought at his side in the famous battle of Point Pleasant, in 1774, of which we have spoken. At the request of his father, *Ellinipsico* came to the fort, where they had an affectionate meeting. This son had become uneasy at his father's long absence, and had at length sought him out in his exile here; prompted by those feelings which so much adorn human nature. The next day, two men crossed the Kanhawa, upon a hunting expedition. As they were returning to their boat after their hunt, and near the side of the river, they were fired upon by some Indians, and one of the two, named *Gilmore*, was killed, but the other escaped A party of Captain *Hall's* men went over and brought in the body of *Gilmore*; whereupon a cry was raised, "*Let us go and kill the Indians in the fort.*" A infuriated gang, with Captain *Hall* at their head, set out with this nefarious resolution, and, against every remonstrance, proceeded to commit the deed of blood. With their guns cocked, they swore death to any who should oppose them. In the mean time, some ran to apprize the devoted chiefs of their danger. As the murderers approached, *Ellinipsico* discovered agitation, which when *Cornstock* saw, he said, "*My son, the Great Spirit has seen fit that we should die together, and has sent you to that end. It is his will, and let us submit.*" The murderers had now arrived, and the old chief turned around and met them. They shot him through with seven bullets. He fell, and died without a struggle!

Ellinipsico, though having at first appeared disturbed, met his death with great composure. He was shot upon the seat on which he was sitting when his fate was first disclosed to him.

Red-hawk was a young Delaware chief, and, like *Ellinipsico*, had fought under *Cornstock.* He died with less fortitude: having tried to secrete himself, he was soon discovered and slain. Another Indian, whose name is not mentioned, was mangled and murdered in the most barbarous manner. Suffice it here to say, that this was all that was effected by the expedition, and the forces soon after returned home.

Few, if any, chiefs in history are spoken of in terms of higher commendation than *Cornstock.* Mr. *Withers*, a writer on Indian affairs,* speaks as follows of him:

"Thus perished the mighty *Cornstalk*, sachem of the Shawanees, and king of the northern confederacy, in 1774,—a chief remarkable for many great and good qualities. He was disposed to be at all times the friend of white men, as he ever was the advocate of honorable peace. But when his country's wrongs 'called aloud for battle,' he became the thunderbolt of war, and made her oppressors feel the weight of his uplifted arm." "His noble bearing—his generous and disinterested attachment to the colonies, when the thun-

* In his "*Chronicles*," a work, it is our duty to remark, written with candor

of British cannon was reverberating through the land—his anxiety to preserve the frontier of Virginia from desolation and death, (the object of his visit to Point Pleasant,) all conspired to win for him the esteem and respect of others; while the untimely and perfidious manner of his death, caused a deep and lasting regret to pervade the bosoms even of those who were enemies to his nation; and excited the just indignation of all towards his inhuman and barbarous murderers."

Colonel *Wilson*, present at the interview between the chiefs and Governor *Dunmore* in 1774, thus speaks of *Cornstock*:—"When he arose, he was in no wise confused or daunted, but spoke in a distinct and audible voice, without stammering or repetition, and with peculiar emphasis. His looks, while addressing *Dunmore*, were truly grand and majestic; yet graceful and attractive. I have heard the first orators in Virginia,—*Patrick Henry* and *Richard Henry Lee*,—but never have I heard one whose powers of delivery surpassed those of *Cornstalk*."

Ten years after the bloody affair above related, an able writer * upon those times says, "The blood of the great CORNSTOCK and of his gallant son was mingled with the dust, but their memory is not lost in oblivion." But how few at this day know of his fate, or even that such a chief ever existed! and, at the same time, the same persons would be indignant, were we to suppose them ignorant of the fate of the monster *Pizarro*.

We hear of one son who survived *Cornstock*, who was conspicuous in some early events of the revolution. He was a chief, and known among the whites by the name of the WOLF. He was a hostage, with three others, at Williamsburgh, when Governor *Dunmore* fled on board a man-of-war to escape the fury of the revolutionists. After the governor had got off, he sent for the Indians to come to him, which they did. He then explained to them the reason of his flight, and directed them to fly also, or they would surely be murdered the next day. They fled into the woods, and owing to the darkness of the night, lost one of their companions, and the *Wolf* and another soon after returned to Williamsburgh, and were well received by the inhabitants. The object of the governor was very obvious.

As great a warrior, perhaps, as any who have lived among the nations of the west, we shall in the next place proceed to give an account of. This was

PONTIAK, a chief of the Ottoway nation, whose fame, in his time, was not alone confined to his own continent; but the gazettes of Europe spread it also.

One who knew this chief, and the tribes over whom he had sway, thus speaks of them in 1765:—"The Indians on the lakes are generally at peace with one another, having a wide extended and fruitful country in their possession. They are formed into a sort of empire, and the emperor is elected from the eldest tribe, which is the Ottawawas, some of whom inhabit near our fort at Detroit, but are mostly further westward, towards the Mississippi. *Ponteack* is their present king or emperor, who has certainly the largest empire and greatest authority of any Indian chief that has appeared on the continent since our acquaintance with it. He puts on an air of majesty and princely grandeur, and is greatly honored and revered by his subjects." †

In 1760, Major *Rogers* marched into his country, in fulfilling his orders of displacing the French, after the fall of Quebec.‡ Apprized of his approach, *Pontiak* sent ambassadors to inform him that their chief was not far off, and desired him to halt until he could see him "with his own eyes," and to inform him that he was the king and lord of the country.

Pontiak soon met the English officer, and demanded his business into his country, and how it came about that he dared enter it without his permission When the colonel told him he had no design against the Indians, and only wished to remove the French, their common enemy, and cause of all their trouble, delivering him at the same time several belts of wampum, *Pontiak* replied, "I stand in the path you travel in, until to-morrow morning," and gave him a belt. This communication was understood, and "was as much as to say," says the actor, "I must not march further without his leave."

---

* In *Carey's* Museum, iv. 140. † *Rogers's Account of North America*, 240

‡ *Quebeis* is an Algonquin word, signifying a *Strait*. *Charlevoix*.

The colonel continues: "When he departed for the night, he inquired whether I wanted any thing that his country afforded, and [if I did] he would send his warriors to fetch it. I assured him that any provisions they brought should be paid for; and the next day we were supplied by them with several bags of parched corn, and some other necessaries. At our second meeting, he gave me the pipe of peace, and both of us by turns smoked with it; and he assured me he had made peace with me and my detachment; that I might pass through his country unmolested, and relieve the French garrison; and that he would protect me and my party from any insults that might be offered or intended by the Indians; and, as an earnest of his friendship, he sent 100 warriors to protect and assist us in driving 100 fat cattle, which we had brought for the use of the detachment from Pittsburgh, by the way of Presque-Isle. He likewise sent to the several Indian towns on the south side and west end of Lake Erie, to inform them that I had his consent to come into the country. He attended me constantly after this interview till I arrived at Detroit, and while I remained in the country, and was the means of preserving the detachment from the fury of the Indians, who had assembled at the mouth of the strait, with an intent to cut us off. I had several conferences with him, in which he discovered great strength of judgment, and a thirst after knowledge."

This same officer observes, that he discovered much curiosity at their equipage, and wished to know how their clothes were made, and to learn their mode of war. He expressed a willingness to acknowledge the king of England, though not as his superior, but as his uncle, which he would acknowledge, as he was able, in furs. England was much in his thoughts, and he often expressed a desire to see it. He told Colonel *Rogers* that, if he would conduct him there, he would give him a part of his country.

He was willing to grant the English favors, and allow them to settle in his dominions, but not unless he could be viewed as sovereign; and he gave them to understand, that, unless they conducted themselves agreeably to his wishes, "he would shut up the way," and keep them out. Hence it is fair, within the scope of the most reasonable conjecture, to conclude, that his final disaffection to the English was owing to their haughty carriage, and maltreatment of him and his people.

The principal scenes of his prowess were at Michilimakinak and Detroit. The French finally gave up possession in Canada, in 1760; but many of the Indian nations who had become attached to them were taught, at the same time, to hate the English. *Pontiak* was most conspicuous in his enmity, although, until he had united the strength of many tribes to his, he showed great kindness and friendship towards them. The Miamis, Ottawas, Chippewas, Wyandots, Pottowatomies, Mississagas, Shawanese, Ottagamies, and Winnebagoes, constituted his power, as, in after-time, they did that of *Tecumseh*.

There was more system employed by this distinguished man than, perhaps, by any other of his countrymen upon any similar undertaking, not excepting even *Metacomet* or *Tecumseh*. In his war of 1763, which is justly denominated "*Pontiac's* war," he appointed a commissary, and began to make and issue bills of credit, all of which he afterwards carefully redeemed. He made his bills or notes of bark, on which was drawn the figure of the commodity he wanted for it. The shape of an otter was drawn under that of the article wanted, and an otter was the insignia or arms of his nation. He had also, with great sagacity, urged upon his people the necessity of dispensing altogether with European commodities, to have no intercourse with any whites, and to depend entirely upon their ancient modes of procuring sustenance.*

Major *Gladwin* held possession of Detroit in 1763. Having been despatched thither by General *Amherst*, he had been informed by commissioners who had been exploring the country, that hostile feelings were manifested among the Indians, and he sent men on purpose to ascertain the fact, who, on their return, dissipated all fears.

"In 1763," says Major *Rogers*, "when I went to throw provisions into the

* *Rogers's Concise Account of North America*, 244.

garrison at Detroit, I sent this Indian a bottle of brandy by a Frenchman His counsellors advised him not to taste it, insinuating that it was poisoned and sent with a design to kill him; but *Ponteack*, with a nobleness of mind laughed at their suspicions, saying it was not in my power to kill *him*, who had so lately saved *my* life." *

Several traders had brought news to the fort at Michilimakinak, that the Indians were hostile to the English. Major *Etherington* commanded the garrison, and would believe nothing of it. A Mr. *Ducharme* communicated the information to the major, who was much displeased at it, "and threatened to send the next person who should bring a story of the same kind a prisoner to Detroit."†

The garrison, at this time, consisted of 90 men, besides two subalterns and the commander-in-chief. There were also at the fort four English merchants. Little regard was paid to the assembling of sundry bands of Indians, as they appeared friendly; but when nearly 400 of them were scattered up and down throughout the place, "I took the liberty," says Mr. *Henry*, "of observing to Major *Etherington*, that, in my judgment, no confidence ought to be placed in them; in return, the major only rallied me on my timidity."

On the fourth of June, the king's birth day, the Indians began, as if to amuse themselves, to play at a favorite game of ball, which they called *baggatiway*, which is thus described by Mr. *Henry*:—"It is played with a bat and ball, the bat being about four feet in length, curved, and terminated in a sort of racket. Two posts are placed in the ground, at a considerable distance from each other, as a mile or more. Each party has its post, and the game consists in throwing the ball up to the post of the adversary. The ball, at the beginning, is placed in the middle of the course, and each party endeavors as well to throw the ball out of the direction of its own post, as into that of the adversary's. This farce drew many off their guard, and some of the garrison went out to witness the sport.

"The game of baggatiway, (he continues,) as from the description above will have been perceived, is necessarily attended with much noise and violence. In the ardor of contest, the ball, as has been suggested, if it cannot be thrown to the goal desired, is struck in any direction by which it can be diverted from that designed by the adversary. At such a moment, therefore, nothing could be less liable to excite premature alarm, than that the ball should be tossed over the pickets of the fort, nor that, having fallen there, it should be followed, on the instant, by all engaged in the game, as well the one party as the other, all eager, all striving, all shouting, all in the unrestrained pursuit of a rude athletic exercise." And this was their plan, while in the height of their game, to throw their ball within the pickets of the fort, and then all to rush in, and, in the midst of their hubbub, to murder the garrison; and it succeeded to their wishes. They struck the ball over the stockade, as if by accident, and repeated it several times, running in and out of the fort with all freedom, "to make the deception more complete;" ‡ and then, rushing in in every direction, took possession of the place without the least resistance.

They murdered the soldiers, until their numbers were so diminished, that they apprehended nothing from their resistance; many of whom were ransomed at Montreal afterwards, at a great price. Seventy were put to death, and the other twenty reserved for slaves. A few days after, a boat from Montreal, without knowing what had happened, came ashore with English passengers, who all fell into the hands of the Indians. *Pontiak* was not personally concerned in this affair, but it was a part of his design, and, therefore, is very properly here related. A chief named *Menehwehna* was the commander in that affair. §

It was only 15 days from the time the first blow was struck, before *Pontiak* had taken possession of every garrison in the west except three. No less

* The Abbe *Raynal*, whom we followed in the former editions, (not then possessing *Rogers's* own account,) does not narrate this circumstance faithfully.

† Travels in Canada, by *Alexander Henry*, Esq., from which the following account of the destruction of Michilimakinak is taken.

‡ *Carver's* Travels, 19, 20. edit. 8vo. Lond. 1784.

§ *Henry's* Travels, *ut supra*.

than 10 were, in this short space, reduced. Detroit alone remained in that distant region, and, as will presently be seen, this was brought to the very brink of the most awful precipice of which the imagination can conceive. The names of those captured at this time were Le Boeuf, Venango, Presq'Isle, on or near Lake Erie; La Bay,* upon Lake Michigan; St. Joseph's, upon the river of that name: Miamis, upon the Miami River; Ouachtanon, upon the Ouabache; Sandusky, upon Lake Junundat; and Michilimakinak.†

The garrison at Detroit was closely besieged by *Pontiac*, in person, before the news of the massacre of Fort Michilimakinak arrived there. It was garrisoned by about 300 men, and when *Pontiac* came with his warriors, although in great numbers, they were so intermixed with women and children, and brought so many commodities for trade, that no suspicion was excited, either in the mind of Major *Gladwin*, or the inhabitants. He encamped a little distance from the fort, and sent to the major to inform him that he was come to trade, and, preparatory thereto, wished to hold a talk with him for the purpose of "brightening the chain of peace" between the English and his people. No suspicion was yet entertained, and the major readily consented, and the next morning was fixed upon for the council.

The same evening, a circumstance transpired which saved the garrison from a dreadful massacre. An Indian woman, who had made a pair of moccasins for Major *Gladwin*, out of a curious elk skin, brought them to him, and returned the remainder of the skin. Being much pleased with them, the major wished her to take the skin and make another pair, as he had concluded to give the others to a friend, and what was left to make into shoes for herself. She was then paid for her work, and dismissed. But when those whose duty it was to see that the fort was clear of strangers, and to close the gates for the night, went upon their duty, this woman was found loitering in the area, and, being asked what she wanted, made no reply. The major, being informed of her singular demeanor, directed her to be conducted into his presence, which being done, he asked her why she did not depart before the gates were shut. She replied, with some hesitation, that she did not wish to take away the skin, as he set so great a value upon it. This answer was delivered in such a manner, that the major was rather dissatisfied with it, and asked her why she had not made the same objection on taking it in the first place. This rather confused her, and she said that if she took it away now, she never should be able to return it.

It was now evident that she withheld something which she wished to communicate, but was restrained through fear. But on being assured by Major *Gladwin* that she should not be betrayed, but should be protected and rewarded, if the information was valuable, she said that the chiefs who were to meet him in council the next day had contrived to murder him, and take the garrison, and put all the inhabitants to death. Each chief, she said, would come to the council, with so much cut off of his gun, that he could conceal it under his blanket; that *Pontiac* was to give the signal, while delivering his speech, which was, when he should draw his peace belt of wampum, and present it to the major in a certain manner; and that, while the council was sitting, as many of the warriors as could should assemble within the fort, armed in the same manner, under the pretence of trading with the garrison.

Having got all the information necessary, the woman was discharged, and Major *Gladwin* had every precaution taken to put the garrison into the best possible state for defence. He imparted the discovery to his men, and instructed them how to act at the approaching council; at the same time sending to all the traders in different directions to be upon their guard.

The next morning having arrived, every countenance wore a different aspect; the hour of the council was fast approaching, and the quick step and nervous exercise in every evolution of the soldiers were expressive of

* So called by the French, who built it, because it stood at the extremity of a bay in Michigan, called "Le Baie des Puants," now Green Bay. It was taken by the Menominies: the garrison consisted of 30 men. See *Carver's* Travels, 21, 22.

† *Bouquet's* Ohio Expedition, Int. iii.

an approaching event, big with their destiny. It was heightened in the past night, when a cry was heard in the Indian encampment different from what was usual on peace occasions. The garrison fires were extinguished, and every man repaired to his post. But the cry being heard no more, the remainder of the night was passed in silence.

The appointed hour of ten o'clock arrived, and also as punctual arrived *Pontiac* and his 36 chiefs, followed by a train of warriors. When the stipulated number had entered the garrison, the gates were closed. The chiefs observed attentively the troops under arms, marching from place to place; two columns nearly inclosing the council house, and both facing towards it. On *Pontiac's* entering it, he demanded of Major *Gladwin* the cause of so much parade, and why his men were under arms; he said it was an odd manner of holding a council. The major told him it was only to exercise them. The Indians being seated upon the skins prepared for them, *Pontiac* commenced his speech, and when he came to the signal of presenting the belt, the governor and his attendants drawing their swords half out of their scabbards, and the soldiers clinching their guns with firmness, discovered to the chiefs, by their peculiar attitudes, that their plot was discovered. *Pontiac*, with all his bravery, turned pale, and every chief showed signs of astonishment. To avoid an open detection, the signal in passing the belt was not given, and *Pontiac* closed his speech, which contained many professions of respect and affection to the English. But when Major *Gladwin* commenced his, he did not fail directly to reproach *Pontiac* with treachery; told him he could not do any thing to insnare the English, and that he knew his whole diabolical plan. *Pontiac* tried to excuse himself, and to make Major *Gladwin* believe that he had laid no plot; upon which the major stepped to the chief nearest himself, and, drawing aside his blanket, exposed his short gun, which completed their confusion.

The governor, for such was Major *Gladwin*, ordered *Pontiac* to leave the fort immediately, for it would be with difficulty he could restrain his men from cutting him in pieces, should they know the circumstances. The governor was afterwards blamed for thus suffering them to withdraw, without retaining several of them as hostages for the quiet behavior of the rest; but he, having passed his word that they should come and go without hinderance or restraint, merited, perhaps, less censure for keeping it, and respecting his honor, than those who reproached him.

A furious attack was the next day made upon the fort. Every stratagem was resorted to. At one time they filled a cart with combustibles, and run it against the pickets, to set them on fire. At another, they were about to set fire to the church, by shooting fiery arrows into it; but religious scruples averted the execution,—a French priest telling *Pontiac* that it would call down the anger of God upon him. They had frequently, during the siege, endeavored to cut down the pickets so as to make a breach. Major *Gladwin* ordered his men, at last, to cut on the inside at the same time, and assist them. This was done, and when a breach was made, there was a rush upon the outside towards the breach, and at the same instant, a brass four-pounder, which had been levelled for the purpose, was shot off, which made a dreadful slaughter among them. After this they merely blockaded the fort, and cut off its supplies, and the English were reduced to the greatest distress, and for some time subsisted upon half rations.

There was great difficulty in throwing succor into the garrison at Detroit as there was such an extent of country between it and the other most western posts, in possession of the English. Fort Pitt and Niagara had been besieged, and all communication for a long time cut off; the former had been reduced to great extremities, but they were at length relieved by Colonel *Bouquet*. Captain *Dalyell* was at the same time sent for the relief of Detroit, where he arrived on 29 July, 1763.* A bloody scene was shortly to follow. Captain *Dalyell*, with 247 men, went out of the fort to surprise *Pontiac* in his camp; but the wary chief had runners out, who gave him timely notice, and

* *Bouquet's* Expedition, Introd. iv.

he met them in an advantageous place, and, being vastly superior in numbers, and concealed behind a picket fence, near a bridge where the English were to pass, poured in upon them a dreadful fire. Many fell at the first onset, but they kept their order, and exerted themselves to regain the bridge they had just passed. They effected their purpose, but many fell in the attempt, among whom was Captain *Dalyell*. The famous Major *Rogers*, the second in command, and Lieutenant *Brehm*, with about 200 others, recovered the fort. This bridge, where so many brave men were slain, is called to this day *Bloody Bridge*.

Pontiac ordered the head of Captain *Dalyell* to be cut off and set upon a post. Between eighty and a hundred dead bodies were counted upon the bridge the next morning, which entirely blocked up its passage.

We have thought proper to give this account as it is generally found in our histories, but having been put in possession of the official return of Sir *Jeffery Amherst*, minutely detailing this important affair of Bloody Bridge, we will lay it before the reader, as it appeared at the time. From which it will be seen that the common report is probably erroneous in some of its most important features.

"On the evening of the 30th of July, Captain *Dalyell*, aid-de-camp to General *Amherst*, being arrived here with the detachment sent under his command, and being fully persuaded that *Pontiac*, the Indian chief, with his tribes, would soon abandon his design, and retire, insisted with the commandant, that they might easily be surprised in their camp, totally routed, and driven out of the settlement; and it was thereupon determined, that Captain *Dalyell* should march out with 247 men. Accordingly, we marched about half an hour after two in the morning, two deep, along the great road by the river side, two boats up the river along shore, with a patteraro in each, with orders to keep up with the line of march, cover our retreat, and take off our killed and wounded; Lieutenant *Bean*, of the *Queen's Independents*, being ordered, with a rear guard, to convey the dead and wounded to the boats. About a mile and a half from the fort, we had orders to form into platoons, and, if attacked in the front, to fire by street-firings. We then advanced, and, in about a mile farther, our advanced guard, commanded by Lieutenant *Brown*, of the 55th regiment, had been fired upon so close to the enemy's breastworks and cover, that the fire, being very heavy, not only killed and wounded some of his party, but reached the main body, which put the whole into a little confusion; but they soon recovered their order, and gave the enemy, or rather their works, it being very dark, a discharge or two from the front, commanded by Captain *Gray*. At the same time, the rear, commanded by Captain *Grant*, were fired upon from a house, and some fences about twenty yards on his left; on which he ordered his own and Captain *Hopkins's* companies to face to the left, and give a full fire that way. After which, it appearing that the enemy gave way every where, Captain *Dalyell* sent orders to Captain *Grant*, to take possession of the above-said houses and fences; which he immediately did; and found in one of the said houses two men, who told him, the enemy had been there long, and were well apprized of our design. Captain *Grant* then asked them the numbers; they said, above 300; and that they intended, as soon as they had attacked us in the front, to get between us and the fort; which Captain *Grant* told Captain *Dalyell*, who came to him when the firing was over. And in about an hour after, he came to him again, and told Captain *Grant* he was to retire, and ordered him to march in the front, and post himself in an orchard. He then marched, and about half a mile farther on his retreat, he had some shots fired on his flank; but got possession of the orchard, which was well fenced; and just as he got there, he heard a warm firing in the rear, having, at the same time, a firing on his own post, from the fences and corn-fields behind it. Lieutenant *M'Dougal*, who acted as adjutant to the detachment, came up to him, (Captain *Grant*,) and told him, that Captain *Dalyell* was killed, and Captain *Gray* very much wounded, in making a push on the enemy, and forcing them out of a strong breastwork of cord-wood, and an intrenchment which they had taken possession of; and that the command then devolved upon him. Lieutenant *Bean* immediately came up, and told him, that Captain *Rogers* had desired him to tell Captain *Grant*, that he had taken possession of a house, and that he had better retire with what numbers he had, as he (Captain *Rogers*) could not get off without the boats to cover him, he being hard pushed by the enemy from the enclosures behind him, some of which scoured the road through which he must retire. Captain *Grant* then sent Ensign *Pauli*, with 20 men, back to attack a part of the enemy which annoyed his own post a little, and galled those that were joining him, from the place where Captain *Dalyell* was killed, and Captain *Gray*, Lieutenants *Brown* and *Luke*, were wounded; which Ensign *Pauli* did, and killed some of the enemy in their flight. Captain *Grant*, at the same time, detached all the men he could get, and took possession of the enclosures, barns, fences, &c. leading from his own post to the fort, which posts he reinforced with the officers and men, as they came up. Thinking the retreat then secured, he sent back to Captain *Rogers*, desiring he would come off; that the retreat was quite secured, and the different parties ordered to cover one another successively, until the whole had joined; but Captain *Rogers* not finding it right to risk the loss of more men, he chose to wait for the armed boats, one of which appeared soon, commanded by Lieutenant *Brehm*, whom Captain *Grant* had directed to go and cover Captain *Rogers's* retreat, who was in the next house. Lieutenant *Brehm* accordingly went, and fired several shots at the enemy. Lieutenant *Abbott*, with the other boat, wanting ammunition, went down with Captain *Gray*. Lieutenant *Brown* and some wounded men returned also, which Captain *Grant* supposes the enemy seeing, did not wait her arrival, but retired on Lieutenant *Brehm's* firing, and gave Captain *Rogers*, with the rear, an opportunity to come off: so that the whole from the different posts joined without any confusion, and marched to the fort in good order, covered by the armed boats on the water side, and by our own parties on the country side, in view of the enemy, who had all joined, and were much stronger than at the beginning of the affair, as was afterwards told us by some prisoners that made their escape; many having joined them from the other side the river, and other places. The whole arrived at the fort about eight o'clock, commanded by Captain *Grant*, whose able and skilful retreat is highly commended.

"Return of killed and wounded of the several detachments near the Detroit, July 31, 1763.

"*Of the* 55*th Regiment*:—1 Sergeant, 13 rank and file, *killed;* 1 captain, 2 lieutenants, 1 drummer, 28 rank and file, *wounded.*

"*Of the Royal Americans*:—1 rank and file, *killed;* 1 rank and file *wounded.*

"*Of the* 80*th Regiment*:—2 rank and file *killed;* 3 rank and file *wounded.*

"*Of the Queen's Rangers*:—2 rank and file *killed;* 1 rank and file *wounded.*

"*Names of the officers*:—55*th Regiment:* Captain *Gray*, Lieutenant *Luke*, and Lieutenant *Brown*, wounded.

"N. B.—Captain *Dalyell*, killed, not included in the above."

Hence it appears that but 19 were killed and 42 wounded in the celebrated "Battle of Detroit," but I am inclined to think that this return was made out before the exact state of the troops engaged in it was ascertained. It is evident that Captain *Dalyell* was found to be among the killed after the return was finished, or nearly so. It is unnecessary to apprize the reader, that returns were often made more favorable than strict scrutiny would warrant, from obvious motives.

About this time several small vessels fell into the hands of *Pontiac*, which were destined to supply the garrison, and the men were cruelly treated. The garrison was in great straits, both from the heavy loss of men, as well as from want of provisions and continual watching. In this time of despondency, there arrived near the fort a schooner, which brought them supplies of provisions, but nothing of this kind could be landed without *Pontiac's* knowledge, and he determined, if possible, to seize the schooner: a detachment made the attempt, and, to save herself, the vessel was obliged to tack short about, and proceed in an opposite direction. The Indians followed her in canoes, and, by continually firing into her, killed almost every man, and at length boarded her. As they were climbing up the sides and shrouds in every quarter, the captain, having determined not to fall into their hands alive, ordered the gunner to set fire to the magazine, and blow all up together.

This was heard by a Huron chief, who understood enough English to know what was going forward, and instantly communicated it to his followers. They disengaged themselves from the vessel as fast as possible, and fled from her in a great fright, at considerable distance. Meantime the crew took the advantage of a wind, and arrived safe at the fort. In the pursuit of the vessel, the Indians discovered extreme temerity, often coming so close to the schooner as to be severely burned by the discharge of her guns.

This vessel had been sent from Niagara, and was manned with 18 men, 12 of whom were Mohawk Indians. They arrived at Detroit on the 3 September; and thus was the garrison saved from certain destruction. So sensible was Major *Gladwin* and his officers of their escape from a dreadful fate by the bravery of the crew of this vessel, that they caused silver medals to be struck and presented to each descriptive of the event.*

Many other circumstances are related of this famous siege, but it is believed the preceding are all that are well authenticated.

Pontiac having invested Detroit now for about twelve months, and the news of his operations having been carried to various parts of the British empire, extensive preparations were made to put down the Indian power. Aware of the movements of General *Bradstreet*, who was proceeding for Detroit with an army of 3000 men, he gave up, and sued for peace, which was granted him, and his warriors retired to their hunting-grounds. By some it is reported that he was killed, with many others of his chief men, by the Ioways, in the year 1769, in a war which at that time raged between the Ottowas and that nation. It is also said that he had a son named Sheganaby, who was also a distinguished chief, and who, after the death of his father, revenged his murder by the destruction of almost the entire nation of the Ioways. When the revolution commenced, the Americans sent messages to *Pontiac* to meet them in council. He was inclined to do so, but was prevented from time to time by Governor *Hamilton* of Detroit. He seems now to have laid aside all resentment against the English, and became their friend; and to reward his attachment, the government granted him a liberal pension. It has also been reported that he became suspected in the time of the war, and as he was going to hold a council among the Indians in Illinois, as an agent for the English, a spy attended him to observe his conduct; and that, in a speech, he betrayed the English, and discovered his former enmity against them. When he had finished, the Indian who had accompanied him, plunged a knife into his breast, and thus ended the days of a chief who has been renowned for singular sagacity, daring courage, great spirit of command, and indeed numerous other qualities, found only in those born with such elementary organizations as produce them by their peculiar school of circumstances.

* *Holmes's Annals*, ii. 122.

CHAPTER IV.

CAPTAIN PIPE—*Situation of affairs on the frontiers at the period of the revolution—Sad condition of the Moravian Indians at this period—Half-king engages to take them to Canada—His speech to them—They remonstrate—Half-king inclines not to molest them, but Captain Pipe's counsel prevails, and they are seized—Pipe's conduct thereupon—Missionaries taken to Detroit and examined—Pipe went to accuse them—Changes his conduct towards them, and they are acquitted—Remarkable deliverance—Captain* WHITE-EYES *opposes the conduct of Pipe—His speech to his people—Colonel Broadhead's expedition—Brutal massacre of a chief*—PACHGANTSCHIHILAS—*Surprises the missionaries*—GELELEMEND—BUOKONGAHELAS—*Murder of Major Trueman and others—In the battle of Presque-Isle—His death—His great intrepidity—Further particulars of Captain Pipe—His famous speech—Expedition and defeat of Colonel Crawford, who is burnt at the stake, and many more*—CHIKTOMMO—TOM LEWIS—MESSHAWA—KING-CRANE—LITTLE TURTLE—*Defeats General St. Clair's army—Incidents in that affair—Little-turtle's opinion of General Wayne—Visits Philadelphia—His interview with C. F. Volney—Anecdotes*—BLUE-JACKET—*Defeated by General Wayne in the battle of Presque-Isle.*

PIPE, or *Captain Pipe*,* as he is usually called, from his having been a most conspicuous war-captain among the Delawares, during the period of the revolution, in particular, was chief of the Wolf tribe. His character is a very prominent one, in the memorable troubles among the frontier settlements, at the breaking out of the war. Situated as were the Delawares between the English of Canada and the Americans, it was hardly to be expected but that they should be drawn into that war. They could not well weigh its merits or demerits upon either side. A speech of the renowned *Corn-plant* contains the best commentary upon this matter. The English stood much the best chance of gaining the Indians to their interest, inasmuch as they were profuse in their presents of what was useful to them, as well as ornamental, whereas the Americans required all their resources to carry on the war. The commanding officer at Detroit, believing that the Moravian Indians upon the Susquehannah favored the Americans, ordered them, dead or alive, with their priests, to be brought into Canada. The Iroquois agreed that it should be done, but, unwilling to do it themselves, sent messengers to the Chippeways and Ottawas, to intimate that, if they would do it, "they should have them to make soup of." These two tribes, however, refused, and the *Half-king* of the Hurons undertook it himself. He had been formerly very friendly to the believing Indians, and now pretended that he only concluded to seize upon them, to save them from destruction; and, Mr. *Loskiel* adds, "even the *Half-king* would certainly never have agreed to commit this act of injustice, had not the Delaware, Captain *Pipe*, a noted enemy of the gospel and of the believing Indians, instigated him to do it." *Pipe* and his company of Delawares, joined by *Half-king* and his warriors, and some Shawanese, held a war-feast, roasted a whole ox, and agreed upon the manner of proceeding. The captains only of this expedition knew fully its destination. With such secrecy did they proceed, that the Moravian settlements knew nothing of their approach, until they were in their vicinity. They bore an English flag, and an English officer was among them. It was now 10 August, 1781. *Half-king* sent in a message to Salem, requesting the inhab-

---

* His Indian name, according to *Heckewelder*, was HOPOCAN, and signified a *Tobacco pipe*. This name he bore until about 1763, when that of KOGIESCHQUANOHEL was substituted. This meant, *Maker of Day-Light*. Of the word *pipe*, a more extended notice should be taken. The French writers generally use the name *calumet*, which means the same thing, and, of its origin, Baron *Lahontan*, "Voyages dans L'Amerique," i. 401, observes as follows:—"It is a Norman word, which comes from *chalumeau*, and was introduced into Canada by the people of that nation, on their first coming into this country, by whom it has ever since been used. The Iroquois call it *Ganondaoé*, and the other Indian nations, POAGAN;" this, allowing for the difference between the French and English idioms, will agree tolerably with Mr. *Heckewelder's* HOPOCAN. A chief named *Pipe* signed a treaty at Fort Greenville, in 1814, with 112 others, by which it seems the Delawares perpetuated it. It followed that of *White-eyes*.

itants not to be alarmed, for they should receive no injury, and that he had good words to speak to them, and wished to know at which of the settlements they might hold a council with them. Gnadenhuetten being fixed upon, all assembled there upon 11 August.

Meanwhile, the numbers of *Pipe's* expedition had increased from 140 to 300, and about 10 days after, *Half-king* made the following speech to the believing Indians and their teachers:—

"Cousins: ye believing Indians in Gnadenhuetten, Schoenbrunn, and Salem, I am much concerned on your account, perceiving that you live in a very dangerous spot. Two powerful, angry and merciless gods stand ready opening their jaws wide against each other: you are sitting down between both, and thus in danger of being devoured and ground to powder by the teeth of either one or the other, or both. It is therefore not advisable for you to stay here any longer. Consider your young people, your wives, and your children, and preserve their lives, for here they must all perish. I therefore take you by the hand, lift you up, and place you in or near my dwelling, where you will be safe and dwell in peace. Do not stand looking at your plantations and houses, but arise and follow me! Take also your teachers [priests] with you, and worship God in the place to which I shall lead you, as you have been accustomed to do. You shall likewise find provisions, and our father beyond the lake [the governor at Detroit,] will care for you. This is my message, and I am come hither purposely to deliver it."

The brethren, after taking this into consideration, remonstrated, in feeling language, against such an immediate removal; saying they did not conceive that the danger was so great, as, moreover, they were at peace with all men, and took no part in the war, and that it would bring famine and distress upon them, to set out before their harvest with nothing in their hands, but that they would keep and consider his words, and would answer him the next winter. It was supposed that *Half-king* was willing to comply, but for the importunity of *Pipe* and the English captain.

This affair eventuated in the seizure of the missionaries and their removal to Sandusky, as has been written in the account of *Glikhikan*.

Captain *Pipe* now publicly boasted of his exploit, and said the Indians and their priests were his slaves. They had had but a moment's repose at Sandusky, when the governor at Detroit ordered Captain *Pipe* to conduct them to him. They were glad of an opportunity of seeing the governor face to face, believing they could convince him that they had never assisted the Americans, and accordingly attended *Pipe* thither. Here the missionaries *Zeisberger*, *Senseman*, *Heckewelder* and *Edwards* had to await a kind of trial, and *Pipe* was the evidence against them. On the 9 November, this trial or examination came on, and Captain *Pipe* appeared, and spoke as follows: "*Father, you have commanded us to bring the believing Indians and their teachers from the Muskingum. This has been done. When we had brought them to Sundusky, you ordered us to bring their teachers and some of their chiefs unto you. Here you see them before you: now you may speak with them yourself, as you have desired. But I hope you will speak good words unto them, yea I tell you, speak good words unto them, for they are my friends, and I should be sorry to see them ill used.*" The governor then repeated to *Pipe* the charges he had formerly urged against the brethren, and called on him to prove his assertions. The chief seemed now evidently confused, and said such things might have happened, but they would do so no more, for they were now at Detroit. This did not satisfy the governor, and he peremptorily demanded that *Pipe* should answer positively to the point. This caused him still greater embarrassment, and he asked his counsellors what he should say, but each held down his head in silence, and this occasioned his choosing the only wise course, and he thus ingenuously spoke: "*I said before, that some such thing might have happened, but now I will tell you the plain truth. The missionaries are innocent. They have done nothing of themselves: what they have done, they were compelled to do. I am to blame, and the chiefs that were with me in Goschachguenk: we have forced them to do it, when they refused.*" The governor now declared them innocent, in the presence of the court, and they were permitted to return to their brethren.

One circumstance, illustrative of savage superstition we will notice here. When *Pipe's* warriors were about to force the brethren to leave their dwellings, it was almost unanimously concluded at one time by the chiefs, that the white brethren should be put to death. They, however, would not adventure upon such a deed without the advice of one of their common warriors, who was considered a great sorcerer. His answer was, "he could not understand what end it would answer to kill them." Upon this, the chiefs held a council, in which it was resolved to kill not only the white brethren and their wives, but the Indian assistants also. When they made this resolution known to the sorcerer, he said to them, "Then you have resolved to kill my friends; for most of their chief people are my friends: but this I tell you, that if you hurt any one of them, I know what I will do!" This threat deterred them: thus were the missionaries as well as many others saved.

It is stated by Mr. *Heckewelder*, that, notwithstanding Captain *Pipe* was so eager for the war before its commencement, he soon became sorry for it afterwards. This might have been the case; and yet he was one of the most efficient enemies of the Americans after the peace, as will elsewhere appear. Captain *White-eyes*, or *Koquethagaeehlon*, which was his Indian name,* was his particular friend, and they were both great men of the Delaware nation, having been nearly alike distinguished by their courage on many occasions. No one could have more at heart the welfare of their country, than Captain *White-eyes* had that of the Delaware nation, and it is not pretended, but that as much should be said of Captain *Pipe;* but they were differently circumstanced, and the former was open and fearless in his declarations in favor of the Americans, while the latter secretly favored the British. Thus they were unwillingly opposed to each other, and for about two years, one by his frankness and the other by his clandestine operations strove to unite and strengthen their respective parties.

Meanwhile a circumstance happened, which Captain *Pipe* seized upon for declaring war. *M'Kee*, *Elliot*, *Girty*, and several others, had been held at Pittsburg as tories. Early in the spring of 1778, they made an escape, and fled into the Indian country, and, as they went, proclaimed to that people, that the Americans had determined to destroy them; that therefore their only safety consisted in repelling them; that they must fly to arms, and fight them in every place. *Pipe*, being rather inclined to war, believed all that those exasperated fugitives said; while, on the other hand, *White-eyes* would give no credit to them. Having got many of his men together, Captain *Pipe* addressed them with great earnestness, and with great force of oratory said, "*Every man is an enemy to his country, who endeavors to persuade us against fighting the Americans, and all such ought surely to be put to death.*" Captain *White-eyes* was not idle, and at the same time had assembled the people of his tribe, and the substance of what he said was, "*that if they* [any of his warriors] *meant in earnest to go out, as he observed some of them were preparing to do, they should not go without him. He had, he said, taken peace measures in order to save the nation from utter destruction. But if they believed that he was in the wrong, and gave more credit to vagabond fugitives, whom he knew to be such, than to himself, who was best acquainted with the real state of things; if they had determined to follow their advice, and go out against the Americans, he would go out with them; but not like the bear hunter, who sets the dogs on the animal to be beaten about with his paws, while he keeps at a safe distance; no! he would lead them on, place himself in the front, and be the first who should fall.* THEY *only had to determine on what they meant to do; as for his own mind, it was fully made up, not to survive his nation; and he would not spend the remainder of a miserable life, in bewailing the total destruction of a brave people, who deserved a better fate.*"

This speech was spoken with a pathos and in a manner calculated to touch the hearts of all who listened to it, and its impression was such, that all unanimously came to the determination to obey its instructions and orders and to hear or receive directions from no other person, of any nation or color but Captain *White-eyes*.

* According to Mr. *Heckewelder*. His residence was at the mouth of the Big Beaver

At the same time, Captain *White eyes*, in order to counteract, as much as possible, the evil counsel of the white men just mentioned, despatched runners to the Shawanese towns on the Scioto, where these impostors had gone, with the following speech: "*Grandchildren, ye Shawanese, some days ago, a flock of birds, that had come on from the east, lit at Goschochking, imposing a song of theirs upon us, which song had nigh proved our ruin. Should these birds, which on leaving us, took their flight towards Scioto, endeavor to impose a song on you likewise, do not listen to them, for they lie!*"

A knowledge of the proceedings of Captain *White-eyes* having reached *Pipe*, he knew not what course to take, and, while thus confounded a kind and conciliatory message was received in the Delaware nation, from the American agent of Indian affairs at Pittsburg. It particularly cautioned the people of that nation "*not to hearken to those wicked and worthless men, who had run away from their friends in the night, and to be assured of the real friendship of the United States.*" This completed *Pipe's* confusion. But after pondering a while upon the wrongs to which his countrymen had for a long time been subjected, like the sachem of the Wampanoags, he permitted his warriors to go out, and surprise, and murder all the Americans they could lay their hands upon.

Blood having now begun to flow, barbarities followed in quick succession. Early in the spring of 1781,* Colonel *Broadhead* arrived near the Moravian town of Salem, and notified the inhabitants that he was on an expedition against the hostile Indians, and gave them that timely notice that they might collect their people, if any were abroad, that they might not be taken for enemies. "However," says Mr. *Heckewelder*, "whilst the colonel was assuring me that our Indians had nothing to fear, an officer came with great speed from one quarter of the camp, and reported that a particular division of the militia "were preparing to break off for the purpose of destroying the Moravian settlements up the river, and he feared they could not be restrained from so doing.'" They were, however, by the exertions of the commander-in-chief, aided by Colonel *Shepherd*, of Wheeling, partially prevented from their murderous design. Thus these Christian Indians were situated precisely like many of those of N. E. in Philip's war. But we have no instance to record, of the latter, equal in extent, for diabolical atrocity, to that of the massacre of Gnadenhuetten, elsewhere mentioned.

Meanwhile Colonel *Broadhead* proceeded to Coshocton, a hostile settlement near the forks of the Muskingum; and with such secrecy did he proceed, that not a person escaped. How many fell into the hands of the army is not mentioned; but, not long after, 16 warriors were put to death with shocking manifestations of depravity. There accompanied Colonel *Broadhead's* army a Delaware chief named *Pekillon.*† Sixteen of the captive warriors were designated by him as perpetrators of murders, and they were forthwith tomahawked and scalped. They were executed pursuant to the decree of a court-martial.

Some extenuation has been urged for this revolting transaction, and that alone in which, perhaps, the mind can find any relief. But a short time before *Broadhead's* expedition, a large Indian force, called by the whites an army, collected, and set out for the destruction of North-western Virginia. This army was divided into two parts, and their expectations were wrought up to a very high degree, which, when suddenly blasted, were changed into rage and fury. Having, in their march, taken a large number of captives, they retreated to a place of safety, and there tied them to trees and put them to death in their barbarous manner. This massacre was, however, confined to their male prisoners. Fathers, in presence of their families, were led forth to execution, amid tears and lamentations, which no creature but infuriated man could withstand. This barbarity was the more aggravating when it was contemplated that those who fell into their hands had made no resistance! Nothing, therefore, like just retribution was to be expected from an army of frontier militia, when vengeance was the only pursuit.

---

* *Doddridge*, Notes, 291, says, this "campaign" was in the summer of 1780.

† The same who, afterwards, as I conclude, was a party to *Wayne's* treaty

After every thing had been destroyed in the Indian country through which the Americans passed, they returned to Pittsburg. Before leaving Coshocton, a shocking circumstance occurred, which alone was sufficient to have tarnished the most brilliant exploits. An Indian came to the side of the river over against the encampment, and called to the sentinels, who asked him what he wanted. He answered that he wished to see the "*big captain*" (the name by which Indians commonly designate the commander-in-chief). Colonel *Broadhead* appeared, and asked him what he wanted, who replied, "*To make peace.*" Then, said the colonel, send over some of your chiefs. The Indian interrogatively said, "*May be you kill?*" No, said the colonel, they shall come and go in safety. Hereupon a chief of most elegant appearance crossed to the encampment, and—I hesitate to relate it—while this chief was conversing with the colonel, a monster, of the militia, came up, and with a tomahawk, which he had concealed in his clothes, laid him dead with a single stroke! * The name of this fiend was *Wetzel.* The army soon began its retreat, and Colonel *Broadhead* having put his prisoners, (about 20 in number,) into the care of the soldiers, they immediately began to massacre them! all except a few women and children were killed. These were taken to Pittsburg, and afterwards exchanged for an equal number of white prisoners.† Thus the peace which might have been concluded was unhappily suspended, and the war afterwards might well have been expected to exhibit scenes no less bloody than before.

A chief, called Pachgantschihilas, distinguished himself upon the frontiers, immediately upon the retreat of Colonel *Broadhead's* army; not as many others have, but by magnanimity and address. And subsequently his name was set to many treaties between his nation and the United States, from that of General *Wayne* at Greenville to that of St. Mary's in 1818: if, indeed, *Petchenanalas, Bokongehelas,* and several other variations, stand for the same person. His name, according to *Heckewelder,* signified *a fulfiller,* or *one who succeeds in all he undertakes.* He was a son of a great chief whose name is written *Wewandôchwalend,* which signified *one employed on important messages;* and who in the French war was a great captain, and in peace a great counsellor. He had upon his under lip and chin tatooed the figure of a water lizard, on which account he was often called *Tweegachschasu. Buokongahelas* was head warrior of all the Delawares who lived on the Miami and White Rivers.

Petchenanalas, at the head of 80 warriors, appeared suddenly at Gnadenhuetten, surrounding it before day, allowing no one a chance for escape. Not knowing his object, the people were filled with terror. But he soon dispelled their fears, by telling them that he came to take the chief *Gelelemend,* and a few other head men, whom he would have, either dead or alive. As it happened, not one of those he sought after was there at the time. Having satisfied himself of this fact, the chief demanded that deputies from the three Christian towns should meet to hear what he had to say to them. When the deputies and others had met, he spoke to them as follows:—

"Friends and kinsmen, listen to what I say to you. You see a great and powerful nation divided. You see the father fighting against the son, and the son against the father.—The father has called on his Indian children to assist him in punishing his children, the Americans, who have become refractory. I took time to consider what I should do; whether or not I should receive the hatchet of my father, to assist him. At first I looked upon it as a family quarrel, in which I was not interested. At length it appeared to me, that the father was in the right, and his children deserved to be punished a little.—That this must be the case, I concluded from the many cruel acts his offspring had committed, from time to time, on his Indian children—in encroaching on their lands, stealing their property—shooting at and murdering without cause, men, women, and children:—yes, even murdering those, who at all times had been friendly to them, and were placed for protection under

* Chronicles of Western Settlements, *passim.*
† *Doddridge's* Notes, 293.

the roof of their father's house;* the father himself standing sentry at the door, at the time!—Friends and relatives, often has the father been obliged to settle and make amends for the wrongs and mischiefs done us, by his refractory children; yet these do not grow better. No! they remain the same, and will continue to be so, as long as we have any land left us! Look back at the murders committed by the Long-Knives on many of our relations, who lived peaceable neighbors to them on the Ohio! Did they not kill them without the least provocation?—Are they, do you think, better now, than they were then? No! indeed not; and many days are not elapsed, since you had a number of these very men near your doors, who panted to kill you, but fortunately were prevented from so doing, by the Great Sun,† who, at that time, had by the Great Spirit been ordained to protect you!"

The chief then spoke with respect of their peaceable mode of life, and commended their desire to live in friendship with all mankind; but said, they must be aware of their exposed situation—living in the very road the hostile parties must pass over, in going to fight each other; that they had just escaped destruction from one of these parties; that therefore no time should be lost, but they should go to the country on the Miami, where they would be entirely out of danger.

The Christian Indians replied, that, as they had never injured the Americans, they thought they need not fear injury from them; that if their friends at war wished them well, in truth, they would not make their settlement upon the path they took to go to war, as it would lead their antagonists the same way; and that they could not remove without great detriment; and therefore, as they were then situated, they could not consent to go.

Pachgantschihilas consulted in the mean time with his chief men, and answered very feelingly to what the brethren had said. He observed that he was sorry that they should differ from him in opinion, but that he had no intention to use compulsion, and only requested that those might be permitted to go, whose fears prompted them to it. This was readily assented to, and the council broke up, and the warriors departed. At Salem they made a short stay, where they conducted themselves as they had done at Gnadenhuetten. Here a family of old people joined them, through fear of what *Pachgantschihilas* had predicted, and the event justified the proceeding! The massacre of Gnadenhuetten will ever be remembered with the deepest regret and indignation.

Nothing was feared from the good *Petchenanalas;* but the prowling monsters *M'Kee, Girty, Elliot,* and perhaps others, calling themselves white, were the plotters of the ruin of the innocent people at Gnadenhuetten, which followed not long after.

Our present design makes it expedient that we pass over many events in the chronicles of the frontier wars, that we may be enabled to proceed with more minuteness of detail, in the lives of the eminent chiefs. Although we cannot, by any rule known to us, derive *Buokongahelas* from *Pachgantscihilas* or *Petchenanalas*, yet, as they have as much affinity as *Pometacom* and *Metacomet,* we shall let them pass for the same person, and thus continue our narrative.

Buokongahelas was not only a great, but a noble warrior. He took no delight in shedding blood; and when he raised the hatchet on the side of the British in the revolution, it was for the best of reasons; and would that numerous other allies we could name had acted from as pure motives! Our next notice of *Buokongahelas* is in 1792, when he showed himself no less magnan imous than at Gnadenhuetten and Salem. Colonel *Hardin,* Major *Trueman* and several others, were sent, in May of this year, by *Washington,* with a flag of truce, to the Indian nations of the west, particularly the Maumee towns They having arrived near the Indian town of Au Glaize on the south-wes

* Alluding to the murder of the Conestoga Indians, which was as atrocious as that at Gnadenhuetten, and of which we shall in due course give a relation.

† Referring to what we have just related of Colonel *Daniel Broadhead* and his army.

branch of the Miami of the Lake, fell in with some Indians, who treated them well at first, and made many professions of friendship, but in the end took advantage of them, while off their guard, and murdered nearly all of them. The interpreter made his escape, after some time, and gave an account of the transaction. His name was *William Smally;* and he had been some time before with the Indians, and had learned their manners and customs, which gave him some advantage in being able to save himself. He was at first conducted to Au Glaize, and soon after to "*Buokungahela*, king of the Delawares, by his captors." The chief told those that committed the murder, *he was very sorry they had killed the men. That instead of so doing, they should have brought them to the Indian towns; and then, if what they had to say had not been liked, it would have been time enough to have killed them then. Nothing*, he said, *could justify them for putting them to death, as there was no chance for them to escape.* The truth was, they killed them to plunder their effects. *Buokongahelas* took Mr. *Smally* into his cabin, and showed him great kindness; told him to stay there while he could go safely to his former Indian friends. (He having been adopted into an Indian family, in place of one who had been killed, in his former captivity.) While here with *Buokongahelas*, which was near a month, Mr. *Smally* said the chief would not permit him to go abroad alone, for fear, he said, that the young Indians would kill him.

From another source we learn the names of several of the murdered. "A letter from Paris (in the new French settlement), dated July 17, states, that intelligence had been received at Fort Jefferson, of the death of Major *Trueman*, Mr. *Freeman*, *Debachi* and *Jarrat*. That this information was brought by two prisoners, who were laboring in a cornfield, and made their escape. The one had been taken prisoner at the time General *Harmer* was defeated—the other is *William Duer*, of Capt. *Buchanan's* company of levies. They further inform, that on the 15th June a party of Indians took 8 men prisoners, who were making hay near Fort Jefferson; that when they had moved the prisoners some distance from the fort, they divided them—four were given to the Chippewas, and four to the Shawanese—that the Shawanese burnt the four unfortunately assigned to them—that the Chippewas took theirs home, to the intent of making laborers of them—that the Indians are determined for war, and will not treat, but will kill every white person that attempts to go to them, either with or without a flag—that their present plan is to cut off the escorts of provisions destined to the outposts, and by that means oblige the troops stationed there to surrender; and that for this purpose they kept two spies constantly out." *

It is said that the conduct of the British, at the battle of Presque-Isle, forever changed the mind of this chief, as it did that of many others, in regard to them. *Buokongahelas* said he would henceforth trust them no more. The fort at Maumee was critically situated, but by its own imprudence. The officers of it had told the Indians that if the battle turned against them, they should have protection in the fort. Immediately after, General *Wayne* informed them, that if they did protect the Indians in that event, he would treat them as though found in arms against him; therefore, thinking their own safety of more consequence than keeping their faith with the Indians, they barred the gates, and were idle spectators of those they had basely betrayed, cut down in great numbers by the swords of the horsemen, under their very ramparts!

It would seem from a passage in the Memoirs of General *Harrison*,† that *Buokongahelas* died soon "after the treaty of 1804;" that if he had been alive, Mr. *Dawson* thinks, when *Tecumseh* and the *Prophet* enlisted so many nations against the Americans, he would not have suffered their plans to have been matured. The same author relates an incident of peculiar interest, concerning our subject, which is as follows:—After the fight with *Wayne's* army before mentioned, *Buokongahelas* collected the remnant of his band, and embarked with them in canoes, and passed up the river, to send a flag of

* *Carey's Museum*, xii. 15.

† By Mr. *Dawson*, page 82.

truce to Fort *Wayne*. When the chief arrived against the British fort, he was requested to land, which he did. When he had approached the sentinel, he demanded, "*What have you to say to me?*" He was answered that the commandant desired to speak with him. "*Then he may come* HERE," was the reply. The sentry then said the officer would not do that, and that he would not be allowed to pass the fort, if he did not comply with its rules. "*What shall prevent me?*" said the intrepid chief. Pointing to the cannon of the fort, the sentry said, "Those." The chief replied indignantly, "*I fear not your cannon: after suffering the Americans to defile your spring, without daring to fire on them, you cannot expect to frighten* BUOKONGEHELAS." He reëmbarked, and passed the fort, without molestation. By "defiling their spring," he meant an ironical reproach to the British garrison for their treachery to the Indians. which has been mentioned.

It is said that *Buokongahelas* was present at Fort M'Intosh, at the treaty of 1785; but as his name is not among the signers, we suppose he was opposed to it. General *George R. Clark*, *Arthur Lee*, and *Richard Butler*, were the American commissioners; the former had been a successful warrior against the Indians, which had gained him the respect of *Buokongahelas;* and when he had an opportunity, he passed the others without noticing them, but went and took General *Clark* by the hand, and said, "*I thank the Great Spirit for having this day brought together two such great warriors, as* BUOKONGAHELAS *and* GEN. CLARK."

A separate article in the treaty just named, illustrates the history of several chiefs already mentioned. It is in these words:—"It is agreed that the Delaware chiefs *Kelelamand*, [*Gelelemend, Killbuck*,] or Colonel *Henry; Hengue-pushees*, or the *Big-cat; Wicocalind*, or Captain *White-eyes;* who took up the hatchet for the United States, and their families, shall be received into the Delaware nation, in the same situation and rank as before the war, and enjoy their due portions of the lands to the Wyandot and Delaware nations in this treaty, as fully as if they had not taken part with America."

GELELEMEND, one of the most conspicuous of those noticed in the provisi[on] of the treaty of Fort M'Intosh, we will proceed to consider in this pla[ce.] His name signified *A leader*, but he was called *Killbuck* because the whi[tes] had so called his father, and to distinguish him, junior was added. Up[on] the death of *White-eyes*, he, as that chief had done, accepted the office o[f] chief, until the young heir should be old enough to fill the important pla[ce.] He continued the course of measures carried on by his predecessor, but i[n] spite of all he could do, Captain *Pipe* succeeded in defeating his designs. Such was the power of *Pipe*, that *Gelelemend* and his party were forced through fear to abandon their council-house at Goschochking, and retire under the protection of the Americans near Pittsburg. Here they supposed themselves safe, but they were soon disappointed; "for while the friendly chiefs, together with a number of their people, were peaceably living together on an island just below the town of Pittsburg, they were suddenly surprised and attacked by the murdering party which had returned from killing near a hundred of the Christian Indians, and partly killed and partly put to flight, from whence this chief (*Killbuck*) saved his life only by taking to the river and swimming across to the point, or town, [of Pittsburg] leaving all his property behind; among which was the bag containing all the wampum speeches and written documents of *William Penn* and his successors for a great number of years, which had for so long a time been carefully preserved by them, but now had fallen into the hands of a murdering band of white savages, who killed at the same time the promising young Delaware chief above mentioned." The many services he rendered to Pennsylvania were known and appreciated; which services, however, being obnoxious to the enemy, drew their hatred upon him, so much so, that they ordered any that should meet with him to shoot him dead. He therefore remained concealed some time after the peace with the Indians, with his family at Pittsburg. He finally joined the Christian Indians and lived under their protection; never venturing far from home, lest the Munseys should meet with and kill h[im.] He was baptized by the name of *William Henry*, a name he had been k[nown] known under, and which was that of a distinguished member of congr[ess] conferred by himself. *Killbuck** died in the faith in January, 1811, aged about 80.†

At the time these peaceable Indians were murderously driven from their island, as just noticed, *Big-cat*‡ narrowly escaped the slaughter. He retired to the Miami country, where he afterwards died. He had been an able counsellor, and afterwards a chief of the Turtle tribe.† But to return to Captain *Pipe*.

At one time after an expedition against the Americans, Captain *Pipe* went to Detroit, where he was received with respect by the British commandant, who, with his attendants, was invited to the council-house, to give an account of past transactions. He was seated in front of his Indians, facing the chief officer, and held in his left hand a short stick, to which was fastened a scalp. After a usual pause, he arose and spoke as follows:—

"*Father*, [then he stooped a little, and, turning towards the audience, with a countenance full of great expression, and a sarcastic look, said, in a lower tone of voice,] "*I have said* FATHER, *although, indeed, I do not know* WHY *I am to call* HIM *so, having never known any other father than the French, and considering the English only as* BROTHERS. *But as this name is also imposed upon us, I shall make use of it, and say,* [at the same time fixing his eyes upon the commandant,] *Father, some time ago you put a war hatchet into my hands, saying, 'Take this weapon and try it on the heads of my enemies, the Long-Knives, and let me afterwards know if it was sharp and good.' Father, at the time when you gave me this weapon, I had neither cause nor inclination to go to war against a people who had done me no injury; yet in obedience to you, who say you are my father, and call me your child, I received the hatchet; well knowing, that if I did not obey, you would withhold from me the necessaries of life, without which I could not subsist, and which are not elsewhere to be procured, but at the house of my father.—You may perhaps think me a fool, for risking my life at your bidding, in a cause too, by which I have no prospect of gaining any thing; for it is your cause and not* mine. *It is your concern to fight the Long-Knives;* you *have raised a quarrel amongst yourselves, and* you *ought yourselves to fight it out. You should not compel your children, the Indians, to expose themselves to danger, for* your *sakes.—Father, many lives have already been lost on your account!—Nations have suffered, and been weakened!—children have lost parents, brothers, and relatives!—wives have lost husbands!—It is not known how many more may perish before* your *war will be at an end!—Father, I have said, that you may, perhaps, think me a fool, for thus thoughtlessly rushing on* your *enemy!—Do not believe this, father: Think not that I want sense to convince me, that although you* now *pretend to keep up a perpetual enmity to the Long-Knives, you may before long conclude a peace with them.—Father, you say you love your children, the Indians.—This you have often told them, and indeed it is your interest to say so to them, that you may have them at your service. But, father, who of us can believe that you can love a people of a different color from your own, better than those who have a white skin like yourselves? Father, pay attention to what I am going to say. While you, father, are setting me* [meaning the Indians in general] *on your enemy, much in the same manner as a hunter sets his dog on the game; while I am in the act of rushing on that enemy of yours, with the bloody destructive weapon you gave me, I may, perchance, happen to look back to the place from whence you started me; and what shall I see? Perhaps I may see my father shaking hands with the Long-Knives; yes, with these very people he now calls his enemies. I may then see him laugh at my folly for having obeyed his orders; and yet I am now risking my life at his command! Father, keep what I have said in remembrance.—Now, father, here is what has been done with the hatchet you gave me.* [With these words he handed the stick to the commandant, with the scalp upon it, above mentioned.] *I have done with the hatchet what you ordered me to do, and found it sharp. Nevertheless, I did not do* all *that I* might *have done. No, I did not. My*

* Another of the same name is mentioned by Mr. *Latrobe*, Rambles, ii. 118, whom he saw at New Fairfield in 1832; "a venerable" man "watching the bed of his dying daughter, the last of 12 children."

† *Heckewelder's* Biography of the Delawares, &c., in *Philos. Trans*

‡ *Machingue Puschis*, according to *Heckewelder*.

heart failed within me. I felt compassion for your *enemy.* Innocence [helpless women and children] *had no part in your quarrels; therefore I distinguished—I spared. I took some* live flesh, *which, while I was bringing to you, I spied one of your large canoes, on which I put it for you. In a few days you will recover this* flesh, *and find that the skin is of the same color with your own. Father, I hope you will not destroy* what *I have saved. You, father, have the means of preserving that which with me would perish for want. The warrior is poor, and his cabin is always empty; but your house, father, is always full.*"

After a high encomium upon this speech, which need not be repeated, Mr Heckewelder says, "It is but justice here to say, that *Pipe* was well acquainted with the noble and generous character of the British officer to whom this speech was addressed. He is still living in his own country, an honor to the British name. He obeyed the orders of his superiors, in employing the Indians to fight against us; but he did it with reluctance, and softened as much as was in his power the horrors of that abominable warfare. He esteemed Captain *Pipe*, and, I have no doubt, was well pleased with the humane conduct of this Indian chief, whose sagacity in this instance is no less deserving of praise than his eloquence."

The name of Captain *Pipe* is unfortunately associated with the history of the lamented Colonel *William Crawford*, who perished at the stake, after suffering the most horrible and excruciating tortures possible for Indians to inflict. He was particularly obnoxious to them, from having been many years a successful commander against them. He fell into the hands of the Indians not far from Upper Sandusky, in the latter end of May, 1782. At this time he was arrived there, at the head of a band of about 500 volunteers, who were attacked and put to flight, without having acquitted themselves like soldiers in any degree; except, indeed, some individual instances. At least a hundred were killed and taken, and of the latter, but two are said ever to have escaped.

Captain *Pipe*, if not the principal, was probably one of the chief leaders of the Indians at this time. When the rout of the army began, instead of retreating in a body, they fled in small parties, and thus fell an easy prey into the hands of their pursuers. Colonel *Crawford* became separated from the main body of his soldiers, by his extreme anxiety for his son, and two or three other relations, whom he suspected were in the rear, and therefore waited for them an unreasonable time. He at length fled, in company with a Dr. *Knight* and two others. Unfortunately, after travelling nearly two days, they were, with several others, surprised by a party of Delawares, and conducted to the Old Wyandot Town. Here Captain *Pipe*, with his own hands, painted *Crawford* and *Knight* black in every part of their bodies. A place called the New Wyandot Town was not far off. To this place they were now ordered, and *Pipe* told *Crawford*, that when he arrived there, his head should be shaved; of which, it seems, he did not understand the import. These miserable men were accompanied by *Pipe* and another noted Delaware chief, named *Wingenim*. Several other captives had been sent forward; and in the way, as *Knight* and *Crawford* passed along, they saw four of the mangled bodies of their friends, lying upon the ground, dead and scalped. Nine others had been picked up at the same time the two just named were, and four of these were those murdered in the way. The other five met a like fate, from the hands of Indian squaws and boys at the destined village. Here *Crawford* and *Knight* saw *Simon Girty*, of whom no human being since, we apprehend, has spoken or written without indignation. He is represented to have witnessed the torture of *Crawford* with much satisfaction!

After the colonel was tied to the fatal post, Captain *Pipe* addressed the assembled Indians in an earnest speech, which when he had closed, they all joined in a hideous yell, and fell to torturing the prisoner, which continued for about three hours, when he sunk down upon his face, and with a groan expired.

Dr. *Knight* was reserved for the same fate, and was present, and obliged to hear the agonizing ejaculations of his friend, and at last to see him expire without being able to render him even the assistance of a consoling word!—Indeed the thoughts of his own condition, and the end that awaited him, were as much, nay, more, perhaps, than a rational mind could bear. There seemed no possibility of a deliverance; but it came in an unexpected hour

He was to be sent to the Sawanee Town, and for this purpose was intrusted to a young warrior, who watched him incessantly. The distance was about 40 miles; and, during their march, he found means to knock down his driver and make good his escape. He was 21 days in the wilderness alone, and was nearly famished when he arrived at Fort M'Intosh. At the place to which he was destined by the Indians, Colonel *Crawford's* son, son-in-law, and several others, were put to death about the same time.

Wingenund, *Winganoond*, or *Wingaynoond*, had an interview with Colonel *Crawford* immediately before his execution, and as the substance of what passed between the victim and the chief has been preserved, it shall here be given, not merely for the history which it contains, but as it strikingly brings to view the manner in which an Indian exercises his views of justice in an extraordinary case.

This chief had been known to *Crawford* some time before, and had been on terms of true friendship with him, and kindly entertained by him at his own house; and such acts of kindness all red men remember with gratitude. *Wingenund* dces not appear to have been present when the first preparations were made for burning the prisoner, but resided not far from the fatal spot, and had retired to his cabin that he might not see the sentence of his nation executed upon one calling him his friend; but *Crawford* requested that he might be sent for, cheering his almost rayless mind with the faint hope that he would interpose and save him. Accordingly, *Wingenund* soon appeared in the presence of the bound and naked white man. He was asked by *Crawford* if he knew him, who said, he believed he did, and asked, "Are you not Colonel *Crawford?*" "I am," replied the colonel. The chief discovered much agitation and embarrassment, and ejaculated—"So!—Yes!—Indeed!" "Do you not recollect the friendship that always existed between us, and that we were always glad to see each other?" said *Crawford*. "Yes," said the chief, "I remember all this, and that we have often drank together, and that you have been kind to me." "Then I hope," added *Crawford*, "the same friendship still continues." "It would of course," said *Wingenund*, "were you where you ought to be, and not here." "And why not here?" said the colonel; "I hope you would not desert a friend in time of need. Now is the time for you to exert yourself in my behalf, as I should do for you, were you in my place." "Colonel *Crawford*," replied *Wingenund*, "you have placed yourself in a situation which puts it out of my power and that of others of your friends to do any thing for you." "How so, Captain *Wingenund?*" said the colonel. He added, "By joining yourself to that execrable man, *Williamson* and his party. The man who but the other day murdered such a number of the Moravian Indians, knowing them to be friends; knowing that he ran no risk in murdering a people who would not fight, and whose only business was praying." "But I assure you, *Wingenund*," said *Crawford*, "that had I been with him at the time, this would not have happened. Not I alone, but all your friends and all good men, wherever they are, reprobate acts of this kind." "That may be," said *Wingenund*, "yet these friends, these good men did not prevent him from going out again, to kill the remainder of those inoffensive, yet foolish Moravian Indians! I say *foolish*, because they believed the whites in preference to us. We had often told them that they would be one day so treated by those people who called themselves their friends! We told them that there was no faith to be placed in what the white men said; that their fair promises were only intended to allure us, that they might the more easily kill us, as they have done many Indians before they killed these Moravians." "I am sorry to hear you speak thus," said *Crawford*: "as to *Williamson's* going out again, when it was known that he was determined on it, I went out with him, to prevent him from committing fresh murders." "This," said *Wingenund*, "the Indians would not believe, were even I to tell them so." *Crawford* then asked, "And why would they not believe it? "Because," replied *Wingenund*, "it would have been out of your power to prevent his doing what he pleased." "Out of my power?" exclaimed the colonel, and asked, "Have any Moravian Indians been killed or hurt since we came out?" "None," answered the chief; "but you went first to their town, and finding it empty and deserted, you turned on the path towards us. If you had been in search of warriors only, you would not have gone thither. Our spies watched you closely. They saw you while you were embodying yourselves on the other side of the Ohio. They saw you cross that river—they saw where you encamped at night—they saw you turn off from the path to the deserted Moravian town—they knew you were going out of your way—your steps were constantly watched, and you were suffered quietly to proceed until you reached the spot where you were attacked."

Crawford, doubtless, with this sentence, ended his last rays of hope. He asked, with faint emotion, "What do they intend to do with me?" when *Wingenund* frankly replied, "I tell you with grief. As *Williamson*, with his whole cowardly host, ran off in the night at the whistling of our warriors' balls, being satisfied that now he had no Moravians to deal with, but men who could fight, and with such he did not wish to have any thing to do—I say, as he escaped, and they have taken you, they will take revenge on you in his stead." "And is there no possibility of preventing this?" said *Crawford*—"Can you devise no way to get me off? You shall, my friend, be well rewarded if you are instrumental in saving my life." "Had *Williamson* been taken with you," answered the chief, "I and some friends, by making use of what you have told me, might, perhaps, have succeeded in saving you, but as the matter now stands, no man would dare to interfere in your behalf. The king of England himself, were he to come to this spot, with all his wealth and treasure, could not effect this purpose. The blood of the innocent Moravians, more than half of them women and children, cruelly and wantonly murdered, calls aloud for *revenge*. The relatives of the slain, who are among us, cry out and stand ready for *revenge*. The nation to which they belonged will have *revenge*. The Shawanese, our grandchildren, have asked for your fellow prisoner; on him they will take *revenge*. All the nations connected with us cry out, *revenge! revenge!* The Moravians whom you went to destroy, having fled, instead of avenging their brethren, the offence is become national, and the nation itself is bound to take *revenge!*" "My fate then is fixed," said the wretched man, "and I must prepare to meet death in its worst form." "Yes, colonel," said the chief; "I am sorry for it, but cannot do any thing for you. Had you attended to the Indian principle, that as good and evil cannot dwell together in the same heart, so a good man ought not to go into evil company, you would not be in this lamentable situation. You see, now, when it is too late, after *Williamson* has deserted you, what a bad man he must be! Nothing now remains for you but to meet your fate like a brave man. Farewell, Colonel *Crawford!* they are coming I will retire to a solitary spot."

Accordingly a host of executioners were immediately upon him, and he died by their cruel hands, as we have already written. It is said that *Wingenund* shed tears at parting with his friend, and that ever after, when the circumstance was mentioned, he seemed very sensibly affected.*

Colonel *Crawford's* son was compelled to witness this cruel death of his father, and suffered the same fate immediately after.†

The expedition of Colonel *Crawford* was not so laudably undertaken as many others, in as far as it was directed against the Moravian towns upon the Muskingum, where *many*, who composed it, were determined that the Christian Indians, which they there expected to find, should glut their vengeance by their blood, as those at Gnadenhuetten had done but a short time before.‡

CHIKATOMMO. In 1790, this chief succeeded in capturing many boats upon the Ohio River, killing many of those in them, and taking and destroying a vast amount of property. Among the boats which fell into the hands of *Chikatommo* was one in which was a Mr. *Charles Johnston* of Botetourt county, Virginia, and several others, and from whose narrative we derive much of this information—a book replete with instruction, and one of the most valuable in its kind.§ As this company were descending the Ohio, in an un-

---

* *Heckewelder's* Indian Nations, 281 to 284. † *Columbian Magazine* for 1787, p. 548.

‡ Our chief authority for these events is the valuable CHRONICLES by Mr. *Withers*, before referred to.

§ The author appears to have been prompted to its publication by the misinterpretation of his oral communications by the *Duke de Liancourt;* whom, by the way, we do not find to differ so materially, in his account, from the author as one might apprehend from his state

wieldy flat-bottomed boat, in which were a number of horses and considerable merchandise, two white men appeared upon the shore, and called to them affecting great distress, and begged to be taken on board. Before these two whites showed themselves, however, a smoke was seen above the trees, and for some time held them in doubt on which side of the river it was. They wished to ascertain this fact, as thereby they might keep close in upon the opposite shore, and so escape mischief in the event of an ambushment of Indians. They were thus wary, as the Indians were constantly doing mischief upon the rivers, and had but a short time before destroyed a settlement at a place called Kennedy's Bottom, in Kentucky.

It was before sunrise on the 20 March, that the two white men before mentioned hailed the boat, which was safely out of the reach of fire-arms, having discovered the smoke to be upon the N. W. shore, and therefore they kept upon the S. W. These white men, the more effectually to decoy the boat's crew, said they had been taken prisoners by the Indians at Kennedy's Bottom, and had just escaped from them, and unless they would take them on board they must perish from hunger and cold. The truth was, one or both of them were abandoned wretches, who had leagued with a band of depredators under *Chikatommo*, and thus were the means of destroying many innocent lives in the most atrocious manner. When hailed by them, as we have just said, some in the boat were for listening to them, and some against it. In the mean time, the boat floated fast down the current, and left those on shore considerably in the rear, although they exerted themselves to keep abreast of the boat. Those who were against taking them on board had their objections well grounded; for when these men were asked the occasion of the smoke upon their side of the river, they denied that there had been any, or said they knew of no such thing; and this was urged as a sufficient reason why they should reject the other part of their story. Still, as the boat glided down, those on board debated the subject, and at length concluded, that if there were Indians where they first saw the men, they must then be far up the river, as it was thought impossible that they could have got through the woods so fast as they had floated down; and one of the company, a Mr. *Flinn*, whose kindness of heart brought upon them this calamity, proposed hazarding his own person on shore, without in the least endangering the rest. His plan was as follows: that whereas they must be now out of the reach of the Indians, they should haul in, and barely touch upon the shore, and he would jump out, and the boat should at the same time haul off; so that if Indians should be coming, the boat would have time to get off safe, and as to himself, he could well outrun them, and would get on board the boat again at a certain point below. And thus was the humane plan laid of relieving supposed distress, the sad recompense of which we now proceed to relate.

One circumstance had not been taken into account by this devoted company. The current being rapid, it took them much longer than they had anticipated to gain the shore; and this gave some of the most swift-footed of *Chikatommo's* party time to arrive at the point at the same time with them. Having arrived close to the shore, Mr. *Flinn* had but barely cleared himself from the boat, when a large number of Indians, painted in the most frightful manner, came rushing upon them. Some of the boat's crew seized their guns, and determined to resist, while the others used every means to get their boat from the shore; but every thing seemed to conspire against them. Their boat became entangled in the branches of a large tree, and the whole body of Indians, having arrived, being 54 in number, gave a horrible yell and poured in their whole fire upon the boat. From the protection afforded by the side of the boat, one only was killed, *Dolly Fleming*, and Mr. *Skyles* wounded. All resistance was vain, and the others lay down upon the bottom of the boat, to prevent being immediately killed. The Indians kept up their fire until all the horses were shot down, which added much to the

ment. The chief disagreement appears in such minor points as the spelling of names: thus, in naming the persons captivated, for Skyles he writes *Skuyl;* for Dolly Fleming, *Doly Flamming;* for Flinn, *Phlyn*, &c.

horror of the situation of those upon the bottom of the boat, as they were in great danger of being trampled to death by them before they fell, and afterwards from their strivings. When this was finished, the firing ceased, and Mr. *May* stood up, and held up a white cap in token of surrender; but he fell in a moment after, with a ball shot through his head. Several of the Indians now swam to the boat, and were helped into it by those within. Having now got possession of it, they seemed well pleased, and offered no further violence. All things were now taken on shore, and an immense fire kindled; the dead were scalped, and thrown into the river, and the captives divested of most of their clothes. As several Indians were gathered around Mr. *Johnston* when he was stripped, one, observing that he had on a kind of red vest, approached and said to him in English, "*Oh! you cappatin?*" He said, "*No.*" Then the Indian pointed to his own breast, and said, "*Me cappatin—all dese my sogers.*" This was *Chickatommo.* An Indian, named *Tom Lewis*, discovered much humanity to Mr. *Johnston*, in that he covered him with his own blanket after he had lost his clothes.

Being all stationed about the fire, *Chickatommo* was at one end of it, (it being about 50 feet in length,) who, rising up, made a speech to the multitude. An old Shawanee chief, whose name is not mentioned, made the first speech, at the end of which *Chickatommo* conducted *Johnston* to another Shawanee chief, whose name was *Mes-shaw-a*, to whom he was given or assigned, and informed that he was his friend. At the end of *Chickatommo's* speech, another prisoner was disposed of. The same ceremony was repeated with the third and last. *Johnston, Skyles*, and *Flinn* went to the Shawanese, and *Peggy Fleming* to the Cherokees. This band of robbers appears to have been made up of adventurers from the tribes just mentioned, with the addition of a few Delawares. The latter had none of the prisoners, as they did not wish to be known in the business, thinking it might involve their nation in a war with the United States.

The two white men who had decoyed the boat into the Indians' hands were still with them, and the next day all the captives were ordered to take a position upon the edge of the river, to decoy the first that should be passing. A boat soon appeared, and, repugnant as such an employment was to the feelings of these captives, yet they were obliged thus to do, or suffer a horrible death. *Divine* and *Thomas* were the names of the two whites so often mentioned: the former was the voluntary agent, and, as Mr. *Johnston* expresses it, the one who "alone had devised and carried into effect their destruction;" and, "ingenious in wicked stratagems, seemed to be perfectly gratified to aid the savages in their views, and to feel no scruples in suggesting means for their accomplishment. He fabricated a tale, that we were passengers down the Ohio, whose boat had suffered so great an injury that we were unable to proceed until it was repaired; but that for want of an axe, it was impossible for us to do the necessary work. These unsuspecting canoe-men turned towards us; but the current bore them down so far below us, as to preclude all chance of my putting them on their guard. [Mr. *Johnston* having intended by some sign to have given them warning of what awaited them.] The Indians, as they had acted in our case, ran down the river at such a distance from it, and under cover of the woods, that they were not discovered until the canoe was close to the shore, when they fired into it, and shot every one on board. As they tumbled into the water, their little bark was overset. Two, who were not yet dead, kept themselves afloat, but were so severely wounded that they could not swim off. The Indians leaped into the river, and after dragging them to the shore, despatched them with the tomahawk. The bodies of the four who were killed were also brought to land, and the whole six were scalped. All were then thrown into the river. Nothing I could then learn, or which has since come to my knowledge, has enabled me to understand who these unfortunate sufferers were."

After various successes and encounters upon the river, *Chickatommo* left it, and met a number of his company at an encampment about five miles from it. Here he left the rest, taking with him a select number and some of the Cherokees, with Miss *Fleming*; and the company with whom *Johnston* remained did not join him again for many days. After much delay and interesting incident, they reached the Indian town of Upper Sandusky Here they squandered all their rich booty for whiskey, and, as usual, rioted in drunkenness for several days. *Chickatommo* at this time showed himself very savage to the prisoners, and had he not been prevented by the humane and benevolent *Messhawa*,* would have killed some of them. The unfortunate *Skyles* had some time before left them, and gone in an unknown direction with his cruel master.

A French trader at Sandusky, a Mr. *Duchouquet*, had used endeavors to ransom *Johnston;* but his master for some time would hear nothing of it. At length, having dissipated all his booty, and ashamed to return home in such a state, he concluded to sell *Johnston* for the most he could get; and accordingly 600 silver broaches were paid him, equal in value to 100 dollars, the amount agreed upon. *Chickatommo* and his party then took up their march or Detroit. Not long after this, Mr. *Johnston* returned home by way of that lace. Before he left Sandusky, he was informed of the burning of the illted *Flinn:* he suffered at the stake at the Miami village, and was eaten by s torturers. The Indian who brought the news to Sandusky, said that he mself had feasted upon him.

King-crane, a Wyandot chief, appears conspicuous in this narrative, and ustrates a valuable trait of character in Indian life. When Mr. *Duchouquet* and *Johnston* had arrived at Lower Sandusky, in their way to Detroit, the town was filled with alarm, and they soon learned the occasion to be from the arrival of some Cherokees in the neighborhood, with a female captive. The traders in the place immediately went to their camp, where they found *Peggy Fleming*, who some time before had been separated from *Johnston* and the other captives. Among those who went to see her, was a white man by the name of *Whitaker*, who, having been carried into captivity in his youth, had grown up in all the Indian habits, and being a man of consider able physical powers and enterprise, had become a chief among the Wyandots.† He had been upon the frontiers with the Indians upon trading expeditions, and had lodged at times in Pittsburg in the tavern of Miss *Fleming's* father. She immediately knew him, and besought him, in the most affecting manner, to deliver her from bondage. He went immediately to *King-crane*, and told him that the woman with the Cherokees was his sister, ‡ and begged him to use means for her relief. *King-crane* went without loss of time, and urged the Cherokees to restore her to her brother. They were enraged at the request, and there was danger of their murdering her lest she should be taken from them. He next tried to purchase her; but his benevolent offers were indignantly refused, and their rage was still increased. Resolved to rescue her out of their hands, *King-crane* repaired to their camp early the next morning, accompanied with 8 or 10 young warriors. They found the Cherokees asleep, but the captive—it is shocking to humanity to relate—was without the least attire! extended and lashed to the stake!—ready to be burned!—her body painted all over with black. *King-crane* silently cut the thongs with which she was bound, then awakened the murderers, and threw down upon the ground the price of a captive in silver broaches, (which are current money among them,) and departed. She was soon after sent forward for her home, disguised in the attire of a squaw. The Cherokees prowled about seeking vengeance upon some white person for a few days, and then disappeared.

The reader may wish to know what became of *Skyles:*—he was taken to a place upon the Miami River, where he was doomed to be burnt, but made his escape the night previous to the day on which he was to have suffered. After enduring the most painful fatigues and hunger, from wandering alone in the wilderness, he met with some traders who conveyed him to Detroit, and from thence home to Virginia.

The sequel of the life of the old hard-hearted *Chickatommo* is as follows

* Mr. *Johnston*, throughout his narrative, gives him an excellent character. He was alive after the war of 1812 began, and was one of the followers of *Tecumseh*.

† *Hurons* and *Wyandots* are synonymous terms with most writers.

‡ If ever good came out of evil, we should expect it in a case like this.

For four years succeeding the events above related, he followed his depredating career, and was concerned in opposing the war parties of Americans until the time of General *Wayne's* famous expedition. As that veteran was advancing into the western region, *Chickatommo* met an advance party of his army at the head of a band of his desperate warriors, who were sent forward as the Indian forlorn hope. A sharp skirmish followed, and *Chickatommo* was slain. This was the action near Fort Defiance. *King-crane* was also in arms to oppose General *Wayne;* but in the last war against England, he fought for the Americans, and is supposed to have died three or four years after its close. He was one of the signers of *Wayne's* famous treaty at Fort Greenville, and several others.

We now pass to a chief by far more prominent in Indian history than many who have received much greater notice from historians. This was MISHIKINAKWA, (a name by no means settled in orthography,) which, interpreted, is said to mean the *Little-turtle.* To the different treaties bearing his name, we find these spellings: *Meshekunnoghquoh,* Greenville, 3 Aug. 1795; *Meshekunnoghquoh,* Fort Wayne, 7 June, 1803; *Mashekanahquah,* Vincennes, 21 August, 1805; *Meshekenoghqua,* Fort Wayne, 30 September, 1809; and were we disposed to look into the various authors who have used the name, we might nearly finish out our page with its variations.

LITTLE-TURTLE was chief of the Miamis, and the scenes of his warlike achievements were upon the country of his birth. He had, in conjunction with the tribes of that region, successfully fought the armies of *Harmer* and *St. Clair;* and in the fight with the latter, he is said to have had the chief command; hence a detailed account of that affair belongs to his life.

It is well known that the Americans inveighed loudly against the English of Canada, in most instances, charging them with all the guilt of the enormities committed on their frontiers by the Indians. It is equally well known, at this day, by every judicious inquirer, that they were not so blamable as the Americans reported, nor so innocent as themselves and friends, even long after, pretended. That the British government encouraged depredations upon the frontiers in times of peace, should not too easily be received for truth; still, there is reason to believe that some who held inferior offices under it, were secret abettors of barbarities. In the attack upon General *St. Clair's* army, now about to be related, there was much cause of suspicion against the Canadians, as it was known that many of them even exceeded in that bloody affair the Indians themselves. Mr. *Weld,* the intelligent traveller, says,* "A great many young Canadians, and in particular many that were born of Indian women, fought on the side of the Indians in this action; a circumstance which confirmed the people of the States in the opinion they had previously formed, that the Indians were encouraged and abetted in their attacks upon them by the British. I can safely affirm, however, from having conversed with many of these young men who fought against *St. Clair,* that it was with the utmost secrecy they left their homes to join the Indians, fearful lest the government should censure their conduct."

The western Indians were only imboldened by the battles between them and detachments of General *Harmer's* army, in 1790, and, under such a leader as *Mishikinakwa,* entertained sanguine hopes of bringing the Americans to their own terms. One murder followed another, in rapid succession, attended by all the horrors peculiar to their warfare, which caused President *Washington* to take the earliest opportunity of recommending Congress to adopt prompt and efficient measures for checking those calamities; and 2000 men were immediately raised and put under the command of General *St. Clair,* then governor of the North-Western Territory. He received his appointment the 4th of March, 1791, and proceeded to Fort Washington, by way of Kentucky, with all possible despatch, where he arrived 15 May.† There was much time lost in getting the troops imbodied at this place; General *Butler,* with the residue, not arriving until the middle of September. There were various circumstances to account for the delays, which it is unnecessary to recount here.

---

* *Travels in Canada,* 436—7, 8vo. London, (4 ed.) 1800. † *St. Clair's Narrative,* p. 4.

Colonel *Darke* proceeded immediately on his arrival, which was about the end of August, and built Fort Hamilton, on the Miami, in the country of *Little turtle;* and soon after Fort Jefferson was built, forty miles farther onward. These two forts being left manned, about the end of October the army advanced, being about 2000 strong, militia included, whose numbers were not inconsiderable, as will appear by the miserable manner in which they not only confused themselves, but the regular soldiers also.

General *St. Clair* had advanced but about six miles in front of Fort Jefferson, when 60 of his militia, from pretended disaffection, commenced a retreat; and it was discovered that the evil had spread considerably among the rest of the army. Being fearful they would seize upon the convoy of provisions, the general ordered Colonel *Hamtramk* to pursue them with his regiment, and force them to return. The army now consisted of but 1400 effective men, and this was the number attacked by *Little-turtle* and his warriors, 15 miles from the Miami villages.

Colonel *Butler* commanded the right wing, and Colonel *Darke* the left. The militia were posted a quarter of a mile in advance, and were encamped in two lines. They had not finished securing their baggage, when they were attacked in their camp. It was their intention to have marched immediately to the destruction of the Miami villages. Of this their movements apprized the Indians, who acted with great wisdom and firmness. They fell upon the militia before sunrise, 4 November, who at once fled into the main camp, in the most disorderly and tumultuous manner: many of them, having thrown away their guns, were pursued and slaughtered. At the main camp the fight was sustained some time, by the great exertions of the officers, but with great inequality; the Indians under *Little-turtle* amounting to about 1500 warriors. Colonels *Darke* and *Butler*, and Major *Clark*, made several successful charges, which enabled them to save some of their numbers by checking the enemy while flight was more practicable.

Of the Americans, 593 were killed and missing, beside *thirty-eight* officers; and 242 soldiers and twenty-one officers were wounded, many of whom died. Colonel *Butler* was among the slain. The account of his fall is shocking. He was severely wounded, and left on the ground. The well-known and infamous *Simon Girty* came up to him, and observed him writhing under severe pain from his wounds. *Girty* knew and spoke to him. Knowing that he could not live, the colonel begged of *Girty* to put an end to his misery. This he refused to do, but turned to an Indian, whom he told that the officer was the commander of the army; upon which he drove his tomahawk into his head. A number of others then came around, and after taking off his scalp, they took out his heart, and cut it into as many pieces as there were tribes in the action, and divided it among them. All manner of brutal acts were committed on the bodies of the slain. It need not be mentioned for the information of the observer of Indian affairs, that *land* was the main cause of this as well as most other wars between the Indians and whites; and hence it was very easy to account for the Indians filling the mouths of the slain with earth after this battle. It was actually the case, as reported by those who shortly after visited the scene of action and buried the dead.

General *St. Clair* was called to an account for the disastrous issue of this campaign, and was honorably acquitted. He published a narrative in vindication of his conduct, which, at this day, few will think it required. What he says of his retreat we will give in his own words.* "The retreat was, you may be sure, a precipitate one; it was in fact a flight. The camp and the artillery were abandoned; but that was unavoidable, for not a horse was left alive to have drawn it off, had it otherwise been practicable. But the most disgraceful part of the business is, that the greatest part of the men threw away their arms and accoutrements, even after the pursuit, which continued about four miles, had ceased. I found the road strewed with them for many miles, but was not able to remedy it; for, having had all my horses killed, and being mounted upon one that could not be pricked out of a walk, I could not get forward myself, and the orders I sent forward, either to halt

* *Penn. Gazette*, of that year

the front, or prevent the men from parting with their arms, were unattended to."

The remnant of the army arrived at Fort Jefferson the same day, just before sunset, the place from which they fled being 29 miles distant. General *St. Clair* did every thing that a brave general could do. He exposed himself to every danger, having, during the action, eight bullets shot through his clothes. In no attack related in our records, did the Indians discover greater bravery and determination. After giving the first fire, they rushed forward with tomahawk in hand. Their loss was inconsiderable; but the traders afterwards learned among them that *Little-turtle* had 150 killed and many wounded.* "They rushed on the artillery, heedless of their fire, and took two pieces in an instant. They were again retaken by our troops: and whenever the army charged them, they were seen to give way, and advance again as soon as they began to retreat, doing great execution, both in the retreat and advance. They are very dextrous in covering themselves with trees; many of them however fell, both of the infantry and artillery." "Six or eight pieces of artillery fell into their hands, with about 400 horses, all the baggage, ammunition, and provisions." †

Whether the battle-ground of General *St. Clair* were visited by the whites previous to 1793 I do not learn; but in December of that year a detachment of General *Wayne's* army went to the place, and the account given of its appearance is most truly melancholy. This detachment was ordered to build a fort there, which having done, it was called Fort Recovery. Within a space of about 350 yards were found 500 skull bones, the most of which were gathered up and buried. For about five miles in the direction of the retreat of the army the woods was strewed with skeletons and muskets. The two brass cannon, which composed *St. Clair's* artillery, one a *three*, and the other a six-pounder, were found in a creek adjacent.‡

The following song has been often reprinted, and although not the best of poetry, is considered a valuable relic of those days. It is headed thus:-

SAINCLAIRE'S DEFEAT.

§ 'Twas November the fourth, in the year of ninety-one,‖
We had a sore engagement near to Fort Jefferson;
Sinclaire was our commander, which may remembered be,
For there we left nine hundred men in t' West'n Ter'tory.

At Bunker's Hill and Quebeck, where many a hero fell,
Likewise at Long Island, (it is I the truth can tell,)
But such a dreadful carnage may I never see again
As hap'ned near St. Mary's, upon the river plain.

Our army was attacked just as the day did dawn,
And soon were overpowered and driven from the lawn
They killed Major *Ouldham*, *Levin* and *Briggs* likewise,
And horrid yells of sav'ges resounded thro' the skies.

Major *Butler* ¶ was wounded the very second fire;
His manly bosom swell'd with rage when forc'd to retire;
And as he lay in anguish, nor scarcely could he see,
Exclaim'd, "Ye hounds of hell, O! revenged I will be."

We had not been long broken when General *Butler* found
Himself so badly wounded, was forced to quit the ground.

---

* *Penn. Gazette*, of that year.

† Letter from Fort Hamilton, dated six days after the battle.

‡ Massachusetts Magazine for 1794, p. 191.

§ When I began to copy these lines, I did not intend to change a word in them, but soon found my resolution shaken; the lines were of such unequal lengths, and the rhyme so bad, could not endure it, and, therefore, when the syllables were too many, some were dropped and when too few, some were added; but the sense is in no wise impaired. The copy I use I found in Baltimore in 1817. They were printed in 1815.

‖ That is, 1791.

¶ *Richard Butler* was of Nottingham, in New Hampshire, where some of his relatives yet remain.

"My God!" says he, "what shall we do; we're wounded every man;
Go charge them, valiant heroes, and beat them if you can."

He leaned his back against a tree, and there resigned his breath,*
And like a valiant soldier sunk in the arms of death;
When blessed angels did await, his spirit to convey;
And unto the celestial fields he quickly bent his way.

We charg'd again with courage firm, but soon again gave ground,
The war-whoop then redoubled, as did the foes around.
They killed Major *Ferguson*, which caused his men to cry,
"Our only safety is in flight; or fighting here to die."

"Stand to your guns," says valiant *Ford*, "let's die upon them here
Before we let the sav'ges know we ever harbored fear."
Our cannon-balls exhausted, and artill'ry-men all slain,
Obliged were our musketmen the en'my to sustain.

Yet three hours † more we fought them, and then were forc'd to yield,
When three hundred bloody warriors lay stretch'd upon the field.
Says Colonel *Gibson* to his men, "My boys, be not dismay'd;
I'm sure that true Virginians were never yet afraid.

"Ten thousand deaths I'd rather die, than they should gain the field;"
With that he got a fatal shot, which caused him to yield.
Says Major *Clark*, "My heroes, I can here no longer stand,
We'll strive to form in order, and retreat the best we can."

The word, Retreat, being past around, there was a dismal cry,
Then helter skelter through the woods, like wolves and sheep they fly.
This well-appointed army, who but a day before,
Defied and braved all danger, had like a cloud pass'd o'er.

Alas! the dying and wounded, how dreadful was the thought,
To the tomahawk and scalping-knife, in mis'ry are brought.
Some had a thigh and some an arm broke on the field that day,
Who writhed in torments at the stake, to close the dire affray.

To mention our brave officers, is what I wish to do;
No sons of Mars e'er fought more brave, or with more courage true
To Captain *Bradford* I belonged, in his artillery,
‡ He fell that day amongst the slain, a valiant man was he.

It has been generally said, that had the advice of *Little-turtle* been taken at the disastrous fight afterwards with General *Wayne*, there is very little doubt but he had met as ill success § as General *St. Clair* ‖ did before him. He was not for fighting General *Wayne* at Presque-Isle, and inclined rather to peace than fighting him at all. In a council held the night before the battle, he argued as follows: "*We have beaten the enemy twice under separate commanders. We cannot expect the same good fortune always to attend us. The Americans are now led by a chief who never sleeps: the night and the day are alike to him. And during all the time that he has been marching upon our villages, notwithstanding the watchfulness of our young men, we have never been able to surprise him. Think well of it. There is something whispers me, it would be prudent to listen to his offers of peace.*" For holding this language he was reproached by another chief with cowardice, which put an end to all further discourse. Nothing wounds the feelings of a warrior like the reproach of cowardice; but *Little-turtle* stifled his resentment, did his duty in the battle, and its issue proved him a truer prophet than his accuser

* This was probably a report, but is doubtless incorrect.

† This is not fact.

‡ It would have been agreeable if our poet had given us a kind of catalogue of *all* such as were killed at this time, of any note. Captain *Newman* was among the number. *Elliot's Works*, 135.

§ *Little-turtle* told Mr. *Volney* circumstances which gave him that opinion. See his *Travels in America*, ed. Lond. 1804.

‖ General *Arthur St. Clair* was of Edinburgh, Scotland. He came to America in the fleet which brought over Admiral *Boscawen*, in 1755, and having served through the revolutionary and Indian wars, died at his farm near Greensburgh, Pa. 31 Aug. 1818. *Amer. Mon Mag.* ii. 469, (N. Y. 1818.)

believed.* His residence was upon Eel River, *about* 20 miles from Fort Wayne, where our government built him a house, and furnished him with means of living, much to the envy of his countrymen. Therefore what had been bestowed upon *him*, to induce others to a like mode of life by their own exertions, proved not only prejudicial to the cause, but engendered hatred against him in the minds of all the Indians. He was not a chief by birth, but was raised to that standing by his superior talents. This was the cause of so much jealousy and envy at this time, as also a neglect of his counsel heretofore. The same author,† from whom we get the facts in the preceding part of this paragraph, says, "*Meshecunnaqua*, or the *Little-turtle*, was the son of a Miami chief, by a Mohecan woman. As the Indian maxim, with regard to descents, is precisely that of the civil law in relation to slaves, that the condition of the woman adheres to the offspring, he was not a chief by birth," &c.

Little-turtle was alike courageous and humane, possessing great wisdom. "And," says my author, "there have been few individuals among aborigines who have done so much to abolish the rites of human sacrifice. The grave of this noted warrior is shown to visitors, near Fort Wayne. It is frequently visited by the Indians in that part of the country, by whom his memory is cherished with the greatest respect and veneration." ‡

The grave of his great opponent was also in the same region; but his remains were not long since removed to the seat of his family. Ever after his successful expedition, the Indians called him the *Big-wind;* § or *Tornado;* some, however, on particular occasions, called him *Sukach-gook*, which signified, in Delaware, a black-snake; because, they said, he possessed all the art and cunning of that reptile. ‖ We hear yet of another name, which, though it may not have been his fault that acquired it, is less complimentary than the two just named. It is well known that the British bestowed a great many more presents upon the Indians than the Americans did; but *some* of the latter made large pretensions about what they *would* do. General *Wayne*, the Indians said, made great promises to them of goods, but never got ready to fulfil them, (probably from being disappointed himself by the failure of his government in not forwarding what was promised;) therefore they called him General *Wabang*,¶ which signified General *To-morrow*.**

When the philosopher and famous traveller *Volney* was in America, in the winter of 1797, *Little-turtle* came to Philadelphia, where he then was. *Volney* sought immediate acquaintance with the celebrated chief, for highly valuable purposes, which in some measure he effected. He made a vocabulary of his language, which he printed in the appendix to his Travels. A copy in manuscript, more extensive than the printed one, is said to be in the library of the Philosophical Society of Pennsylvania.

Having become convinced that all resistance to the whites was vain, *Little-turtle* brought his nation to consent to peace, and to adopt agricultural pursuits. And it was with the view of soliciting Congress, and the benevolent society of Friends, for assistance to effect this latter purpose, that he now visited Philadelphia. While here, he was inoculated for the small-pox, and was also afflicted with the gout and rheumatism.

At the time of Mr. *Volney's* interview with him for information, he took no notice of the conversation while the interpreter was communicating with Mr. *Volney*, for he did not understand English, but walked about, plucking out his beard and eyebrows. He was dressed now in English clothes. His skin, where not exposed, Mr. *Volney* says, was as white as his; and on speaking upon the subject, *Little-turtle* said, "I have seen Spaniards in Louisiana, and found no difference of color between them and me. And why should there be any? In them, as in us, it is the work of the *Father of colors*, the *Sun*, that burns us. You white people compare the color of your face with that of your bodies." Mr. *Volney* explained to him the notion of many

* *Schoolcraft's* Travels. † *Dawson*, Mems. *Harrison*. ‡ *Schoolcraft's* Travels.
§ Pa. Gazette. ‖ *Heckewelder's* Narrative
¶ Or, according to Mr. *W. J. Snelling*, it should be written *Wabunk*.
** *Weld's Travels*, 424.

that his race was descended from the Tartars, and by a map showed him the supposed communication between Asia and America. To this *Little-turtle* replied, "*Why should not these Tartars, who resemble us, have come from America? Are there any reasons to the contrary?* Or why should we not both have been born in our own country?" It is a fact that the Indians give themselves a name which is equivalent to our word *indigene*, that is, *one sprung from the soil*, or natural to it.*

Baron *Lahontan*,† after describing the different dances, or dances for different occasions, among the Indians of Canada, adds the following in a note:—"*Toutes ces danses peuvent être comparées à la pyrrhique de Minerve, car les sauvages observent, en dansant d'une gravité singulière, les cadences de certaines chansons, que les milices Grecques d'Achilie, apelloient hyporchematiques. Il n'est pas facile de sçavoir si les sauvages les ont aprises des Grecs, ou si les Grecs les ont aprises des sauvages.*" It is, perhaps, from such passages that *Lahontan* has been branded with the name of infidel;‡ but truly there can be nothing irreligious in such deductions, inasmuch as it is conceded on all hands that the geological formations of the new world have required as much time for their perfection as those of the old. Mr. *Volney* comes within the same pale, when he compares the Spartans to the Five Nations. In contrasting the states of Lacedæmon with modern France, he says, "*Maintenant que j'ai vu les sauvages d'Amérique, je persiste de plus en plus dans cette comparaison, et je trouve que le premiere livre de Thucydide, et tout ce qu'il dit des mœurs des Lacédémoniens, convienent tellement aux cinq nations, que j'appellerais volontiers les Spartiates, les Iroquois de l'ancien monde.*"§

When Mr. *Volney* asked *Little-turtle* what prevented him from living among the whites, and if he were not more comfortable in Philadelphia than upon the banks of the Wabash, he said, "*Taking all things together, you have the advantage over us; but here I am deaf and dumb. I do not talk your language; I can neither hear, nor make myself heard. When I walk through the streets, I see every person in his shop employed about something: one makes shoes, another hats, a third sells cloth, and every one lives by his labor. I say to myself, Which of all these things can you do? Not one. I can make a bow or an arrow, catch fish, kill game, and go to war: but none of these is of any use here. To learn what is done here would require a long time.*" "*Old age comes on.*" "*I should be a piece of furniture useless to my nation, useless to the whites, and useless to myself.*" "*I must return to my own country.*"

At the same time, (1797,) among other eminent personages to whom this chief became attached in Philadelphia, was the renowned *Koskiusko*. This old Polish chief was so well pleased with *Little-turtle*, that when the latter went to take his final leave of him, the old "war-worn soldier" and patriot presented him with a beautiful pair of pistols, and an elegant robe made of sea-otter's skin, of the value of "several" hundred dollars.

Little-turtle died in the summer of 1812, at his residence, but a short time after the declaration of war against England by the United States. His portrait, by Stewart, graces the walls of the war-office of our nation. The following notice appeared in the public prints at the time of his death: "Fort Wayne, 21 July, 1812. On the 14 inst. the celebrated Miami chief, the *Little-turtle*, died at this place, at the age of 65 years.‖—Perhaps there is not left on this continent, one of his color so distinguished in council and in war. His disorder was the gout. He died in a camp, because he chose to be in the open air. He met death with great firmness. The agent for Indian affairs had him buried with the honors of war, and other marks of dis-

* See *Volney's* Travels, *ut supra*. † *Memoires de L' Amerique* ii. 109.

‡ No one presumes to pronounce Father *Hennepin* an infidel, and he denies, (after living much among the Indians,) that they have any notion, or belief, of what Christians call *Deity*. But Mr. *Beverly* (Hist. Virginia, 169.) says, "Baron *Lahontan*, on the other hand, makes them have such refined notions, as seem almost to confute his own belief of Christianity."

§ Œuvres de *C. F. Volney*, t. 6. 129. (Paris, 1826.)

‖ There was a chief of the same name among the Miamis in 1818, who is mentioned in the treaty made with those Indians on 6 October, at St. Marys. The passage in the treaty is as follows:—To *Meshenoqua* or the *Little-turtle*, one section of land on the south side of the Wabash, where the portage path strikes the same." *Indian Treaties*, 314.

tinction suited to his character.' He was, generally, in his time, styled the Messissago chief,* and a gentleman who saw him soon after *St. Clair's* defeat, at Montreal, says he was six feet high, "about 45 years of age, of a very sour and morose countenance, and apparently very crafty and subtle. His dress was Indian moccasins, a blue petticoat that came half way down his thighs; an European waistcoat and surtout; his head was bound with an Indian cap that hung half way down his back, and almost entirely filled with plain silver broaches, to the number of more than 200; he had two ear-rings to each ear, the upper part of each was formed of three silver medals, about the size of a dollar; the lower part was formed of quarters of dollars, and fell more than 12 inches from his ears—one from each ear over his breast, the other over his back; he had three very large nose jewels of silver, that were curiously painted. The account he gave of the action [with the Americans, 4 Nov.] was, that they killed 1400 of them, with the loss of nine only of their party, one of whom killed himself by accident." The person who gave this account said this chief was in Canada for the purpose of raising all the Indian force he could to go out again in the spring against the whites.

Mr. *Dawson* relates a pleasant anecdote of *Little-turtle*, which happened while he was sitting for his portrait in Philadelphia. A native of the Emerald Isle was sitting for his at the same time, who prided himself upon his ability at joking. *Little-turtle* was not backward in the same business, and they passed several meetings very pleasantly. One morning, *Little-turtle* did not take much notice of his friend, and seemed rather sedate, which was construed by the Hibernian into an acknowledgment of victory on the part of the chief, in their joking game, and accordingly began to intimate as much. When *Little-turtle* understood him, he said to the interpreter, "*He mistakes; I was just thinking of proposing to this man, to paint us both on one board, and there I would stand face to face with him, and blackguard him to all eternity.*"

Among the chiefs associated in command, in the wars of which we have been speaking with the famous *Mishikinakwa*, was another of nearly equal note, familiarly called *Blue-Jacket* by the whites, but by his own nation, *Weyapiersenwaw*. He was the most distinguished chief of the Shawanese, and we hear of him at Fort Industry, on the Miami of the Lake, as late as 1805 By some particular arrangement, the chief command seems to have devolved on him of opposing General *Wayne*. He was more bloody and precipitate than *Mishikinakwa*, and possessed less discrimination and judgment. He was among the last of the chiefs who came in to treat with General *Wayne*. The Shawanese held out as long as they could, and came in very slowly. On the 24 June, a boy, who had been a captive among them, (having been lately retaken,) confidently asserted that the Shawanese would not make peace. But one month after, 23 July, *Blue-Jacket* made his appearance, and it was duly noticed by a gentleman at the time, who kept a journal of important matters at Greenville. He then adds, "deputations from all the late hostile tribes north of the Ohio are, consequently, now at this place."†

We find this notice of Blue-jacket in August, 1792. "By a gentleman immediately from Montreal, we learn that about four weeks since, the famous Indian partisan, known by the name of Captain *Blue-Jacket*, was at Detroit, with about 2000 men, waiting for the Americans to come out into the woods: it is believed at Montreal, that in case the Americans do not go out, they will be divided into small parties to harass our frontiers."‡ The tribes which furnished warriors to oppose the Americans were the Wyandots, Miamis, Pottowattomies, Delawares, Shawanese, Chippeways, Ottaways, and a few Senecas. *Blue-Jacket* was the director and leader of this mighty band of warriors.

In the treaty of 29 September, 1817, at the "Foot of the Rapids" of the Miami of the Lakes, with the Wyandots, Senecas, Delawares, Shawanese,

* Those of this tribe in the vicinity of Lake Ontario, are of a much darker complexion than the other Indians of the west. *Weld*, Travels in America, 451.

† See *Elliot's* Works, 141, 142.

‡ *Carey's* Museum, xii. 113

&c. there is a paragraph which it is presumed has reference to a daughter of this chief. It proposes to give "To *Nancy Stewart*, daughter of the late Shawanee chief *Blue-Jacket*, one section of land, to contain six hundred and 40 acres, on the Great Miami river below Lewistown, to include her present improvements, three quarters of the said section to be on the S. E. side of the river, and one quarter on the N. W. side thereof."*

From the time General *St. Clair* was defeated, in 1791, murders were continued upon the frontier, and all attempts on the part of government to effect a peace, proved of no avail; and lastly the ambassadors sent to them were murdered, and that too while the army was progressing towards their country.

After building Fort Greenville, upon the Miami, six miles above Fort Jefferson, General *Wayne* took possession of the ground where General *St. Clair* had been defeated, and there erected a fort, to which he gave the name of Recovery, in which the army spent the winter of 1793-4. Many censures were passed upon the general for his slow progress; but he knew much better what he was doing than newspaper writers did what they were writing, when they undertook to censure him, as the event proved.

It was the 8 August, 1794, when the army arrived at the confluence of the rivers Au Glaize and Maumee, where they built Fort Defiance. It was the general's design to have met the enemy unprepared, in this move; but a fellow deserted his camp, and notified the Indians. He now tried again to bring them to an accommodation, and from the answers which he received from them, it was some time revolved in his mind, whether they were for peace or war; so artful was the manner in which their replies were formed.† At length, being fully satisfied, he marched down the Maumee, and arrived at the rapids, 18 August, two days before the battle. His army consisted of upwards of 3000 men, 2000 of whom were regulars. Fort Deposit was erected at this place, for the security of their supplies. They now set out to meet the enemy, who had chosen his position upon the bank of the river, with much judgment. They had a breastwork of fallen trees in front, and the high rocky shore of the river gave them much security, as also did the thick wood of Presque Isle. Their force was divided, and disposed at supporting distances for about two miles. When the Americans had arrived at proper distance, a body was sent out to begin the attack, "with orders to rouse the enemy from their covert with the bayonet; and when up, to deliver a close fire upon their backs, and press them so hard as not to give them time to reload."‡ This order was so well executed, and the battle at the point of attack so short, that only about 900 Americans participated in it. But they pursued the Indians with great slaughter through the woods to Fort Maumee, where the carnage ended. The Indians were so unexpectedly driven from their strong hold, that their numbers only increased their distress and confusion; and the cavalry made horrible havoc among them with their long sabres. Of the Americans, there were killed and wounded about 130. The loss of the Indians could not be ascertained, but must have been very severe. The American loss was chiefly at the commencement of the action, as they advanced upon the mouths of the Indians' rifles, who could not be seen until they had discharged upon them. They maintained their coverts but a short time, being forced in every direction by the bayonet. But until that was effected, the Americans fell fast, and we only wonder that men could be found thus to advance in the face of certain death.

This horrid catastrophe in our Indian annals is chargeable to certain white men, or at least mainly so; for some days before the battle, General *Wayne* sent a flag of truce to them, and desired them to come and treat with him. The letter which he sent was taken to Colonel *M'Kee*, who, it appears, was their ill-adviser, and he, by putting a false construction upon it, increased the rage of the Indians: he then informed them that they must forthwith fight the American army. Some of the chiefs, learning the truth of the letter, were for peace; but it was too late. *Little-turtle* was known to have been in favor of making peace, and seemed well aware of the abilities of the American

* Indian Treaties, 90. † *Marshall's* Washington, v. 481. ed. 4to. ‡ *Schoolcraft*.

general; but such was the influence of traders among them, that no arguments could prevail. Thus, instances without number might be adduced, where these people have been destroyed by placing confidence in deceiving white men.

The night before the battle, the chiefs assembled in council, and some proposed attacking the army in its encampment, but the proposal was objected to by others; finally the proposition of fighting at Presque Isle prevailed.

In this battle all the chiefs of the Wyandots were killed, being nine in number. Some of the nations escaped the slaughter by not coming up until after the defeat. This severe blow satisfied the western Indians of the folly of longer contending against the Americans; they therefore were glad to get what terms they could from them. The chiefs of twelve tribes met commissioners at Fort Greenville, 3 August, 1795, and, as a price of their peace, gave up an extensive tract of country south of the lakes, and west of the Ohio; and such other tracts as comprehended all the military posts in the western region. The government showed some liberality to these tribes, on their relinquishing to it what they could not withhold, and as a gratuity gave them 20,000 dollars in goods, and agreed to pay them 9000 dollars a year forever; to be divided among those tribes in proportion to their numbers.*

CHAPTER V.

Life of THAYANDANECA, *called by the whites,* BRANT—*His education—Visits England—Commissioned there—His sister a companion to Sir Wm. Johnson—His letter to the Oneidas—Affair with Herkimer at Unadilla—Cuts off Herkimer and 200 men at Oriskana—Anecdote of Herkimer—Burns Springfield—Horrid affair of Wyoming—Incidents—Destroys Cherry Valley—Barbarities of the tories—Sullivan's depredations among the Five Nations—Brant defeated by the Americans Newtown—Destruction of Minisink, and slaughter of 100 people—Destruction Harpersfield—Brant's letter to M'Causland—Marriage of his daughter—Her husband killed—Brant becomes the friend of peace—Visits Philadelphia—His marria —Lands granted him by the king—His death—His son John—Traits of charac —One of his sons killed by him, in an attempt to kill his father—Account of Bran arrival in England—Some account of his children.*

COLONEL JOSEPH BRANT was an Onondaga of the Mohawk tribe, whose Indian name was *Thayendaneca,*† or *Tayadanaga,*‡ signifying *a brant.*§ But as he was seldom called by that name after he became known to the whites, it was generally forgotten. He received a very good English education at "Moor's charity school," at Lebanon, in Connecticut, where he was placed by Sir *William Johnson,* in July, 1761. His age, at this time, we have not learned.

The story that he was but half Indian, the son of a German, has been widely spread, but is denied by his son, and now believed to be a falsehood, ignorantly circulated. This error might have arisen either from the known fact of his being of rather a lighter complexion than his countrymen in general, or from his having married a woman who was a half-breed.‖

Brant went to England in 1775, in the beginning of the great revolutionary rupture, where he was received with attention, and doubtless had there his mind prepared for the part he acted in the memorable struggle which ensued.

---

* The terms of this treaty were the same as were offered to them before the battle, which should be mentioned, as adding materially to our good feelings towards its authors. It is generally denominated *Wayne's* treaty. It is worthy of him.

† *Carey's* Museum, v. 13. ‡ Annals Tryon County, 15.

§ Generally written *Brandt* by those who are unacquainted with the meaning of his Indian name.

‖ It has been mentioned to me by a gentleman, (the editor of WASHINGTON'S WRITINGS,) that he had no doubt of the fact that *Brant* was the *son* of Sir *William Johnson.* I am not satisfied upon the subject, and, therefore, note the opinion of one which claims primary sideration on all subjects connected with our history. The only author, that I recollect, has circulated a printed opinion of this kind, is *Chapman.* See *Hist. Wyoming,* 121

He had a colonel's commission in the English army upon the frontiers, which consisted of such of the Six Nations and tories, as took part against the country. General Sir *William Johnson* was agent of Indian affairs, and had greatly ingratiated himself into the esteem of the Six Nations. He lived at the place since named from him, upon the north bank of the Mohawk, about 40 miles from Albany. Here he had an elegant seat, and would often entertain several hundreds of his red friends, and share all in common with them. They so much respected him, that, notwithstanding they had the full liberty of his house, yet they would take nothing that did not belong to them. The better to rivet their esteem, he would, at certain seasons, accommodate himself to their mode of dress, and, being a widower, took as a kind of companion a sister of *Brant*, by the name of *Molley*. He had received honors and emoluments from the British government, and the Indians received also, through his agency, every thing which, in their opinion, conduced to their happiness. Hence it is not strange that they should hold in the greatest reverence the name of their "great father," the king, and think the *few* rebels who opposed his authority, when the revolution began, most ungratefully wicked, and unworthy all mercy. Sir *William* died in 1774, about a year before the battle of Bunker's Hill.

The *Butlers, John* and *Walter*, whose names are associated with the recollection of the horrid barbarities upon Cherry-valley and Wyoming, lived at Caughnewaga, four miles south-easterly from the village of Johnston, and upon the same side of the Mohawk.

In 1775, in a letter to the Oneidas, our chief subscribes himself "secretary to *Guy Johnson*." This was early in the summer of that year, and hence he was immediately from England. Colonel *Guy Johnson* was son-in-law of Sir *William*. The letter was found in an Indian path, and was supposed to have been lost by the person who was intrusted with it. It was in the Mohawk language, the translation of which commences thus: "*Written at* Guy Johnson's, *May*, 1775. *This is your letter, you great ones or sachems.* Guy Johnson *says he will be glad if you get this intelligence, you Oneidas, how it goes with him now, and he is now more certain concerning the intention of the Boston people.* Guy Johnson *is in great fear of being taken prisoner by the Bostonians. We Mohawks are obliged to watch him constantly*," &c.

After this, *Brant* accompanied *Guy Johnson* when he fled to Canada. The two *Butlers* were also in the train. Being now in a place of safety, and the means in their hands, plots of destruction were put in execution in rapid succession.

Having had some disagreement with *Johnson, Brant* came again to the frontiers. Some of the peaceable Mohawks had been confined, to prevent their doing mischief, as were some of the Massachusetts Indians in *Philip's* war. *Brant* was displeased at this, for he said, if the distant Indians should come down, they would destroy them indiscriminately with the whites. He was accompanied by a band of 70 or 80 warriors, who, in their rambles, visited Unadilla, where they assembled the inhabitants, and told them that they stood in need of provisions, and if they did not give them some, they should take it by force; a refusal, therefore, would have been worse than useless. *Brant* further observed, "*that their agreement with the king was strong, and that they were not such villains as to break their covenant with him.*" General *Herkimer* marched up to Unadilla, in July, with 380 men, where he found *Brant* with 130 of his warriors. Here he had an interview with him, in which he held the following language:—"*That the Indians were in concert with the king, as their fathers and grandfathers had been. That the king's belts were yet lodged with them, and they could not falsify their pledge. That* General Herkimer *and the rest had joined the Boston people against their king. That Boston people were resolute, but the king would humble them. That Mr.* Schuyler, *or general, or what you please to call him, was very smart on the Indians at the treaty at German Flatts; but was not, at the same time, able to afford them the smallest article of clothing. That the Indians had formerly made war on the white people all united; and now they were divided, the Indians were not frightened.*" Colonel *Cox*, who accompanied *Herkimer*, said, if war was his determination, the matter was ended. *Brant* then spoke to his warriors, and they shouted, and ran to their place of encampment, seized their arms, fired several guns, and, after giving the war-whoop, returned in warlike array. General *Herkimer* then told *Brant* he did not come to fight, and the chief motioned for his men to remain quiet. Perhaps, as a worthy author observed upon a transaction in *Philip's* war, it is better to omit the cause of the conduct of *Herkimer*, than too critically to inquire into it. His men vastly outnumbered the Indians, and his authority was ample; but his motives were no doubt pure, and his courage must not now be called in question, as will appear from what is to be related. To put the most favorable construction upon his neglecting to break down the power of *Brant*, is to suppose that he was impressed with the belief that the Indians would not join with the English in committing hostilities; if this were the case, he too late discovered the error of his judgment.

After the general had said that *he did not come to fight*, *Brant*, with an air of importance, said, "*If your purpose is war, I am ready for you.*" A tempest, which came up suddenly, separated the parties, and each retired peaceably. This is said to be the last talk held by any of the Americans with the Six Nations, previous to hostilities, except with the Oneidas; all, save a very few of whom remained neutral.

Towards the autumn of this year, (1777,) *Brant* was under the direction of General *St. Leger*, who detached him with a considerable body of warriors for the investment of Fort Stanwix. Colonel *Butler* was commander-in-chief, with a band of tories. The inhabitants in the valley of the Mohawk determined to march for the relief of Colonel *Gansevoort*, who commanded the fort, which they did, in two regiments, with General *Herkimer* at their head. As is usual with militia, they marched in great disorder, and when the general ordered scouting parties to march, as security against surprise, upon the flanks of the main body, they accused him with cowardice, which, most unwarrantably, had more influence upon his mind, than the safety of his army. A catastrophe ensued, which, though not so momentous in that day, as was that of *Lothrop* in 1676, nor so complete a victory on the part of the Indians, yet it was a severe fight, in which 200 Americans were slain.* The place of attack was selected by *Brant* or *Butler*, and was a ravine of a broad bottom, nearly impassable, except a rough track covered with logs of from 12 to 15 feet in length, laid transversely,† which extended across it. General *Herkimer* arrived at this place about two hours before mid-day, August 6. He might reasonably have expected an ambush, but his first intimations of the vicinity of an enemy were the terrifying yells of the Indians, and the still more lasting impressions of their rifles. The advanced guard were all cut off. Such as survived the first fire, were hewn down with the tomahawk. The fatal causeway was semicircular, and *Brant* and his forces occupied the surrounding heights. These are the principal events in the battle of Oriskana. A surgeon, Dr. *Moses Younglove*, was taken prisoner in this battle, and after his return from captivity, he wrote a poem upon the affair, from which we extract the following:—

> "The time and place of our unhappy fight,
> To you at large were needless to recite:
> When in the wood our fierce inhuman foes,
> With piercing yell from circling ambush rose,
> A sudden volley rends the vaulted sky;
> Their painted bodies hideous to the eye,
> They rush like hellish furies on our bands,
> Their slaughter weapons brandish'd in their hands."

Running down from every direction, they prevented the two regiments from forming a junction, one of them not having entered the causeway; and a part of the assailants fell upon those without, and the remainder upon those within it. The former fared worse than the latter, for in such

* Their whole loss was about 400, says *Marshall*, Life Washington, v. 261.

† All who have travelled, even within a few years, in this part of the state of New York, cannot but well remember the "*Corduroy*" roads. Such was the *road* over this memorable ravine.

cases a flight has almost always been a dismal defeat. It was now the case. The other regiment, hemmed in as they were, saw, in a moment, that,

To fight, or not to fight, was death.

They, therefore, back to back, forming a front in every direction, fought like men in despair. This, Dr. *Younglove* thus forcibly depicts :—

"Now, hand to hand, the contest is for life,
With bay'net, tom'hawk, sword, and scalping knife
Now more remote the work of death we ply,
And thick as hail the show'ring bullets fly;
Full many a hardy warrior sinks supine;
Yells, shrieks, groans, shouts and thund'ring volleys join;
The dismal din the ringing forest fills,
The sounding echo roars along the hills."

The poet thus presents to our view the attacking parties :—

"Of two departments were the assailing foes;
Wild savage natives lead the first of those;
Their almost naked frames, of various dyes,
And rings of black and red surround their eyes·
On one side they present a shaven head;
The naked half of the vermilion red;
In spots the party-color'd face they drew,
Beyond description horrible to view;
Their ebon locks in braid, with paint o'erspread;
The silver'd ears depending from the head;
Their gaudry my descriptive power exceeds,
In plumes of feathers, glitt'ring plates and beads."

He thus speaks of the tories :—

"These for the first attack their force unite,
And most sustain the fury of the fight;
Their rule of warfare, devastation dire,
By undistinguish'd plunder, death and fire;
They torture man and beast, with barbarous rage
Nor tender infant spare, nor rev'rend sage."

And *Butler* is noticed as follows :—

"O'er them a horrid monster bore comman ,
Whose inauspicious birth disgrac'd our land;
By malice urg'd to ev'ry barb'rous art;
Of cruel temper, but of coward heart."

With such bravery did they fight in this forlorn condition, that the Indians began to give way; and, but for a reinforcement of tories, under Major *Watson*, they would have been entirely dispersed.* This reinforcement is thus characterized by the surgeon :—

"The second was a renegado crew,
Who arm and dress as Christian nations do,
Led by a chief who bore the first command;
A bold invader of his native land."

The sight of this reinforcement greatly increased the rage of the Americans. It was composed of the very men who had left that part of the country at the commencement of the war, and were held in abhorrence for their loyalty to the king. The fight was renewed with vigor, and the reinforcement fought also with bravery, until about thirty of their number were killed.

* Dr. *Gordon* says the tories and Indians got into a most wretched confusion, and fought one another; and that the latter, at last, thought it was a plot of the whites on both sides, to get them into that situation, that they might cut them off.

Major *Watson*, their leader, was wounded and taken prisoner, but left upon the battle-ground.

In the mean time, General *Herkimer* had got forward to the fort an express, which informed Colonel *Gansevoort* of his situation. He immediately detached Colonel *Marinus Willet* with 207 men, who succeeded in rescuing the remnant of this brave band from destruction. He beat the enemy from the ground, and returned to the fort with considerable plunder. Such were the events of the battle of Oriskana.

General *Herkimer* died of a wound which he received in this fight. Near its commencement, he was severely wounded in the leg, and his horse was killed. He directed his saddle to be placed upon a little knoll, and resting himself upon it, continued to issue his orders. On being advised to remove to a place of greater safety, he said, "*No—I will face the enemy;*" and, adds the historian of Tryon county, "In this situation, and in the heat of the battle, he very deliberately took from his pocket his tinderbox, and lit his pipe, which he smoked with great composure."

The Indians, as well as the Americans, suffered dreadfully in this fight. And our poet writes,

"Such was the bloody fight: and such the foe:
Our smaller force return'd them blow for blow;
By turns successfully their force defy'd,
And conquest wav'ring seem'd from side to side."

Brant's loss being about 100 men; we are inclined to think the loss of the Indians exaggerated in these lines:—

"Not half the savages returned from fight;
They to their native wilds had sped their flight."

The Senecas alone lost 30, and the tories about 100. The regiment which fled suffered severely, but would have suffered still more, had not their pursuers been apprized of the desperate case of their fellows engaged in the ravine, which caused them to abandon the pursuit. The commanding officer, Colonel *Cox*, was killed, and the command devolved upon Lieutenant Colonel *Campbell* and Major *Clyde*, who conducted the retreat.

The scene in the night following the battle is thus strikingly presented by Dr. *Younglove*, the eye-witness:—

"Those that remain'd a long encampment made,
And rising fires illumin'd all the shade:
In vengeance for their num'rous brothers slain,
For torture sundry prisoners they retain;
And three fell monsters, horrible to view,
A fellow pris'ner from the sentries drew;
The guards before received their chief's command,
To not withhold from the slaught'ring band;
But now the sufferer's fate they sympathize,
And for him supplicate with earnest cries.
I saw the general* slowly passing by,
The sergeant on his knees, with tearful eye,
Implor'd the guards might wrest him from their hands,
Since now the troops could awe their lessen'd bands.
With lifted cane the gen'ral thus replies,
(While indignation sparkles from his eyes:)
'Go! sirrah! mind your orders giv'n before!
'And for infernal rebels plead no more!'
For help the wretched victim vainly cries,
With supplicating voice and ardent eyes;
With horror chill'd, I turn away my face,
While instantly they bear him from the place.
Dread scene!—with anguish stung I inly groan,
To think the next hard lot may be my own."

The poet next describes his dream, in which he was carried to the battle-ground; and then thus opens the morning scene:—

* *Butler.*

"When savages, for horrid sport prepar'd,
Demand another pris'ner from the guard,
We saw their fear'd approach, with mortal fright,
Their scalping-knives they sharpen'd in our sight,
Beside the guard they sat them on the ground,
And view'd, with piercing eyes, the prisoners round."

"At length, one rising seized me by the hand;
By him drawn forth, on trembling knees I stand;
I bid my fellows all a long adieu,
With answering grief, my wretched case they view.
They led me bound along the winding flood,
Far in the gloomy bosom of the wood;
There, (horrid sight!) a pris'ner roasted lay,
The carving-knife had cut his flesh away."

After enduring every thing but death in his captivity, Dr. *Younglove* returned home in safety.

In 1778, a fort was built at Cherry-valley, where families for considerable extent about took up their abode, or retired occasionally for safety. *Brant* intended to destroy this, and came into the neighborhood for the purpose It happened that, at the time he chose to make the discovery of the strength of the garrison, the boys were assembled in a training, with wooden guns, for amusement: not having a clear view of them from the foliage of the trees which intervened, *Brant* thought them to be men. It was his design to have made the attack the following night; but on this discovery, he gave up the design. He still remained in the neighborhood; secreted behind a large rock near the main road to the Mohawk, and about two miles north of the fort in the valley. Here he waited to intercept some unwary passenger, and gain more certain intelligence. Near this place is the little cascade called by the natives, *Tekaharawa*. The inhabitants of the valley were in expectation of a company of soldiers from the Mohawk, to reinforce them, and the same day Lieutenant *Wormwood* came from thence, and informed them that Colonel *Klock* would arrive the next day with the party. Near night he set out to return, accompanied by one *Peter Sitz*, the bearer of some despatches. He was a young officer, of fine personal appearance, and was to return the next day with one of the companies of soldiers. He had been out of sight but a few minutes, when, as he passed the ambush of *Brant*, his warriors fired upon him, and he fell from his horse. The chief, springing from his hiding-place, tomahawked him with his own hands. *Wormwood* and his companion were ordered to stand, but not obeying, occasioned their being fired upon. *Brant* was acquainted with Lieutenant *Wormwood* before the war, and afterwards expressed sorrow at his fate, pretending that he took him to be a continental officer. His horse immediately running back to the fort, with blood upon the saddle, gave some indication of what had happened. His companion, *Sitz*, was taken prisoner.

In June, the same summer, *Brant* came upon Springfield, which he burned, and carried off a number of prisoners. The women and children were not maltreated, but were left in one house unmolested. About this time, great pains were taken to seize the wary chief, but there was no Captain *Church*, or, unlike *Philip* of Pokanoket, *Brant* had the remote nations to fly to without fear of being killed by them. Captain *M'Kean* hunted him for some time, and, not being able to find him, wrote an insulting letter for him, and left it in an Indian path. Among other things, he challenged him to single combat, or to meet him with an equal number of men; and "that if he would come to Cherry-valley, and have a fair fight, they would change him from *a Brant* into *a Goos*." This letter, it is supposed, *Brant* received, from an intimation contained in one which he wrote about the same time to a tory. To this man (*Parcifer Carr*, of Edmeston) he writes from Tunadilla [Unadilla] under date 9 July, 1778,—"*Sir: I understand by the Indians that was at your house last week, that one* Smith *lives near with you, has little more corn to spare. I should be much obliged to you, if you would be so kind as to try to get as much corn as* Smith *can spared; he has sent me five skipples already, of which I am much obliged to him, and will see him paid, and would be very glad if you could spare one or two your men to join us, especially* Elias. *I would be glad to see him, and I* *wish you could sent me as many guns you have, as I know you have no use for them, if you any; as I mean now to fight the cruel rebels as well as I can; whatever you will able to sent'd me, you must sent'd by the bearer. I am your sincere friend and humble ser't.* JOSEPH BRANT. *P. S. I heard that Cherry-valley people is very bold, and intended to make nothing of us; they called us wild geese, but I know the contrary.*" This we suppose to be a fair specimen of the composition of the chief who afterwards translated the Gospel according to *John* into the Mohawk language, also the Book of Common Prayer; copies of which are in the library of Harvard college.*

The next event of importance in which *Brant* was engaged, was the destruction of Wyoming,† one of the most heart-rending records in the annals of the revolutionary war. In that horrid affair, about 300 settlers were killed or carried into captivity; from the greater part of whom no intelligence was ever obtained.

It was known early in the spring of 1778, that a large force was collecting at Niagara for the object of laying waste the frontiers of Pennsylvania, Virginia and New York, and even as early as February, General SCHUYLER wrote to congress to inform them that such was his belief. In March he wrote again to congress, saying, "A number of Mohawks, and many of the Onondagoes, Cayugas, and Senecas, will commence hostilities against us as soon as they can; it would be prudent, therefore, early to take measures to carry the war into their country; it would require no greater body of troops to destroy their towns than to protect the frontier inhabitants."‡ But congress had more than their hands full in other directions, and nothing was done. In the beginning of July, the tory and Indian force, amounting together to about 1600 men, were discovered in possession of Fort Wintermoot,§ a short distance from the village of Wyoming. Here was also a fort, at which were collected near 400 men for the defence of the country, who were under the immediate command of Colonel *Zebulon Butler*.‖ On the 3 July, a council of war was held upon the propriety of marching out and attacking the tory and Indian army, and it was finally agreed that the enemy should be sought. Accordingly the Americans marched out upon this expedition the same day. Having sent forward spies, they had not proceeded far, when they were discovered by two Indians, who were, doubtless, upon the same business. The scouts fired each upon the other, and then hastened to their respective head-quarters. Both parties were immediately in motion, and joined battle near a thick swamp. The Indians and tories, being the more numerous, outflanked the Americans, and *Brant*, at the head of his furious warriors, issuing from the swamp, turned their left flank, and creating thereby a confusion, which greatly favored his kind of warfare, and enabled him to make dreadful havoc among them.

The Americans were in two lines, and it was the line commanded by Colonel *Dennison* that *Brant* successfully encountered. *Butler*, at the same time, was gaining some advantage over the other line, under his cousin *Zebulon*, which, added to the raging disaster in the left, became immediately a flight. Colonel *Dennison's* order to fall back, by which he designed to make an advantageous evolution, was distorted, by the terrified troops, into an order for flight; and all was in a few moments lost. And from Judge *Marshall* we add as follows:—"The troops fled towards the river, which they endeavored to pass, in order to enter Fort Wilkesbarre, [in the village of that name on the opposite side of the Susquehannah.] The enemy pursued 'with the fury of

---

* It would seem from Mr. *Weld*, (Travels in America, 485,) that he translated those works before the war; but I have heard it said that they were the production of the chief *John Norton*; my authority, however, I do not remember.

† This name is said to signify *a field of blood*, from a great battle fought there by the Indians before its settlement by the whites. This derivation, however, is not according to *Heckewelder*, but I must refer the curious philologist to *Chapman's Hist. Wyoming*, p. 10, or to his authority, since printed in the *Trans. Amer. Philos. Soc.*

‡ *Gordon's* American Revolution, iii. 184.

§ This was garrisoned by a company of men, who had been suspected of *toryism*, and it now appeared that they had not only given up the fort, but joined the hostile party. *Marshall's Washington*, iii. 557.

‖ He was cousin to *John Butler*, the leader of the tories. *Marshall*, ibid. 556, and iv. Appendix, 13.

devils; and of the 400 who had marched out on this unfortunate parley only about 20 escaped," among whom were the commanding officers.

The fort at Wyoming was now closely besieged, and seeing no chance of escape, Colonel *Butler* proposed a parley with his *friend* and namesake, which was assented to. The place of meeting was appointed at some distance from the fort, and the Americans marched out in considerable force, to prevent treachery, to the place appointed; but when they arrived there, they found nobody with whom to parley. The commander of the tories has been branded with gross infamy, for this piece of treachery with his kinsman; for he feigned fear from his approach, and had retired as they advanced, displaying meanwhile the flag of truce. The unwary Americans were, by this treacherous stratagem, led into an ambush in nearly the same manner as were *Hutchinson* and *Wheeler*, at Wickabaug Pond, in *Philip's* war. They were, in a moment, nearly surrounded by *Brant's* warriors, and the work of death raged in all its fury.* The tories "were not a whit behind the very chiefest" of them in this bloody day. A remnant only regained the fort, out of several hundreds that went forth. They were now more closely besieged than before; and the more to insult the vanquished, a demand was sent in to them to surrender, "accompanied by 196 bloody scalps, taken from those who had just been slain." When the best terms were asked of the besiegers, the "infamous *Butler*" replied in these two words, "*the hatchet.*" This was the only *truth* we hear of his uttering. It was *the hatchet*, indeed—a few only fled to the surrounding wilderness, there to meet a more lingering death by famine. These were chiefly women and children.

Thus passed *the fourth of July*, 1778, in the before flourishing settlement of Wyoming, on the eastern branch of the Susquehannah. *Barlow* knew well, in his early day, who was forever to be branded with infamy for the acts of this memorable tragedy. He says,—

"His savage hordes the murderous *Johnson* leads,
Files through the woods and treads the tangled weeds
Shuns open combat, teaches where to run,
Skulk, couch the ambush, aim the hunter's gun,
Whirl the sly tomahawk, the war-whoop sing,
Divide the spoils, and pack the scalps they bring."

Columbiad, vi. 389, &c

Having now got full possession of Wyoming, and, observes Dr. *Thacher*, "after selecting a few prisoners, the remainder of the people, including women and children, were enclosed in the houses and barracks, which were immediately set on fire, and the whole consumed together. Another fort was near at hand, in which were 70 continental soldiers; on surrendering without conditions, these were, to a man, butchered in a barbarous manner; when the remainder of the men, women and children were shut up in the houses, and the demons of hell glutted their vengeance in beholding their destruction in one general conflagration." The houses of the tories were spared. As though they could not exercise their cruelty enough upon human beings, they fell upon the beasts in the field—shooting some, wounding and mangling others, by cutting out their tongues, &c. and leaving them alive. Well does *Campbell* make his Oneida chief to say, (who comes as a friend to warn the settlement of the approach of the combined army of tories and Indians,)

"'But this is not a time,'—he started up,
And smote his breast with woe-denouncing hand—
'This is no time to fill thy joyous cup:
The mammoth comes—the foe—the monster *Brandt*,
With all his howling desolating band;—
These eyes have seen their blade, and burning pine,
Awake at once and silence half your land.
Red is the cup they drink; but not with wine:
Awake and watch to-night! or see no morning shine.

* There is much incongruity in relation to the affairs of Wyoming. *Chapman* distinctly states that *Brant* commanded the right wing of the army under *Butler*, when he was met by the forces that marched out to meet them; but it has lately been denied that *Brant* was ever at Wyoming during these affairs.

"'Scorning to wield tne natchet for his bribe,
'Gainst *Brandt* himself I went to battle forth:
Accursed *Brandt! he left of all my tribe*
Nor man, nor child, nor thing of living birth:
No! not the dog, that watched my household hearth,
Escaped, that night of blood, upon our plains!
All perished!—I alone am left on earth!
To whom nor relative nor blood remains,
No!—not a kindred drop that runs in human veins!'"

Gertrude of Wyoming

The tories, as was often the case, were attired like Indians, and, from every account, it appears that they exceeded them in ferocity.

Dr. *Thacher* gives us the following examples of horror, which were of notoriety at the time, and "promulgated from authentic sources. One of the prisoners, a Captain *Badlock*, was committed to torture, by having his body stuck full of splinters of pine knots, and a fire of dry wood made round him, when his two companions, Captains *Ranson* and *Durkee*, were thrown into the same fire, and held down with pitchforks, till consumed. One *Partial Terry*, the son of a man of respectable character, having joined the Indian party, several times sent his father word that *he hoped to wash his hands in his heart's blood.* The monster, with his own hands, *murdered his father, mother, brothers and sisters*, stripped off their scalps, and cut off his father's head!" *

It was upon such scenes as these, that the mind of the poet just cited had dwelt, which caused him to wield the pen of denunciation with such effect upon the memory of *Brant.* That *Butler* was the far greater savage, none can dispute, and Mr. *Campbell* has long since acknowledged his too great severity upon the character of the former. We should explain here, that a son of Colonel *Brant*, a chief Mohawk, of the name of *Ahyonwaeghs*, called by the English *John Brant*, was in London in 1822, and furnished Mr. *Campbell* with documents, which, in the poet's own words, "changed his opinion of his father." This passage was contained in a long and interesting letter upon the subject, to *Ahyonwaeghs*, which appeared at that time in the newspapers.

With Wyoming were destroyed Wilkesbarre and Kingston, upon the other side of the Susquehannah. Though Wyoming is generally understood to be the place destroyed, it should be remembered that in the valley bearing that name, there were three other towns, which were all destroyed, as well as Wyoming.† These towns were settled by emigrants from Connecticut, and when destroyed contained more than 1000 families, and had furnished the continental army with more than 1000 men, who were generally the young and active part of the population.‡ The opposite sides which the inhabitants took in the great revolutionary question, created the most violent rancor in the bosoms of both parties, and hence the barbarities which ensued.

In November following, Cherry-valley met with a fate similar to Wyoming. At this time, *Brant* was returning to winter-quarters, when he was met by a tory captain, and persuaded to engage in one expedition more. This was *Walter Butler*, son of *John*, the *hero* of Wyoming. He went to Canada with *Guy Johnson*, in 1775, as has been mentioned; and now some circumstances brought him among the frontier settlements of New York. What his object was, we are not informed; but it was, doubtless, that of a spy. However, he was taken up on suspicion, at least, and confined in jail at Albany; falling sick, he was removed to a private dwelling, from whence he soon found means to escape. Joining his father at Niagara, he succeeded in detaching a part of his regiment upon an incursion. Meeting with *Brant*, as was just mentioned, they returned to the frontier. It is said that *Brant* was at first

* *Thacher's* Journal.

† The settlement of Wyoming consisted of eight townships, each five miles square. *Annual Reg.* for 1779, page 9. "Each containing a square of five miles," is the language of the Register; but it is thought unlikely that these towns were so small. Writers, and good writers too, often commit mathematical errors of this kind; not distinguishing between miles *square*, and *square* miles: Thus, the difference between five square miles, and five miles square, *i. e.* $5^2-5=20$ square miles, the true difference between the two quantities.

‡ *Marshall*, iii. 555.

displeased with the project, understanding that Captain *Walter* had been put in office over him by his old general, *Walter's* father, but stifled his resentment. Their whole force was 700 men, 500 of whom were the warriors of *Brant*.

Colonel *Ichabod Alden*, of Massachusetts, was in command at Cherry-valley, and to his misguided judgment is to be attributed the disaster which ensued. But, like *Waldron* of Cochecho, he was doomed to escape the disgrace. He was early apprized of the march of *Brant*, and when urged to receive the inhabitants into the fort, observed that there was no danger, as he would keep out scouts who would apprize them of the approach of an enemy in season to remove. Scouts were accordingly sent out; one of which, either forgetting the business they were upon, or, what was equally reprehensible, made a large fire and lay down to sleep. *Brant's* warriors were not misled by so luminous a beacon, and the whole were made prisoners. This was on the night of the 9 November, 1778. The prisoners now in the hands of *Brant* were obliged to give the most exact intelligence concerning the garrison. On the morning of the 11, favored by a thick and hazy atmosphere, they approached the fort. Colonels *Alden* and *Stacia* quartered at the house of a Mr. *Wells*. A Mr. *Hamble* was fired upon as he was coming from his house to the fort, by a scout, which gave the first notice of the enemy. He escaped, and gave the alarm to Colonel *Alden*, who, strange as it may appear, was still incredulous, and said it was nothing more than some straggling Indians. The last space of time was thus lost!—and, in less than half an hour, all parts of the place were invested at once. Such of the soldiers as were collected being immediately all killed or taken, the poor inhabitants fell an easy prey. Colonel *Alden* was among the first victims. Like *Chopart*, in the massacre at Natchez, he fled from his house, and was pursued by an Indian with his hatchet, at whom the colonel endeavored several times to discharge his pistol; but it missing fire, and losing time in facing about for this purpose, the Indian was sufficiently near to throw his tomahawk with deadly effect. He did so. Colonel *Alden* fell upon his face, and his scalp was in a moment borne off in triumph. "A tory boasted that he killed Mr. *Wells* while at prayer." His daughter, a young lady of great amiableness, fled from the house to a pile of wood for shelter; but an Indian pursued her, who, coming near, composedly wiped his long knife, already bloody, upon his leggins, then returning it to his belt, seized her by the arm, and with a blow of his tomahawk ended her existence. She could speak some Indian, and begged her murderer to spare her life, and a tory interceded, who stood near, urging that she was his sister; but he would hear to neither. Other transactions in this affair, of still greater horror, we must pass in silence.

Between 30 and 40 prisoners were carried off; but the fort, containing about 200 soldiers, was not taken, although several trials were made upon it.

Brant was the only person engaged in this tragedy of whom we hear any acts of clemency; one of which was the preservation of a poor woman and her children, who, but for him, would have met the tomahawk. He inquired for Captain *M'Kean*, (who wrote him the letter before mentioned,) saying he had now come to accept his challenge. Being answered that "Capt. *M'Kean* would not turn his back upon an enemy," he replied, "I know it. He is a brave man, and I would have given more to have taken him than any other man in Cherry-valley; but I would not have hurt a hair of his head."

Brant had seen and heard so much of what is called *civilized warfare*, that he was afraid of the traduction of his character, and always said that, in his councils, he had tried to make his warriors humane; and to his honor it is said, (but in proportion as his character is raised, that of the white man must sink,) that where he had the chief command, few barbarities were committed.

The night before *Brant* and *Butler* fell upon Cherry-valley some of the tories who had friends there, requested liberty to go in secretly and advise them to retire. *Butler*, though some of his own friends were among the inhabitants, refused, saying, "that there were so many families connected, that the one would inform the others, and all would escape. He thus sacrificed his friends, for the sake of punishing his enemies." This, whether reported by *Brant* to magnify his own humanity, by a contrast with the depravity of his associate, is not known, but it may have been the fact.

But this midnight assassin did not escape his retribution; he was killed by an Oneida Indian, on 30 October, 1781, under the following circumstances: Colonel *Willet* having been ordered with about 400 men to make an expedition into the country of the Mohawk, he surprised a party of 600 tories, and 130 Indians at Johnston, and drove them into the woods, and severely distressed them by cutting off their retreat to their boats. About this time Colonel *Willet* was joined by 60 Oneida Indians, and he shortly after came up with a party which formed the rear of the British and Indians, and killed and took prisoners the most of them. *Walter Butler* was among the vanquished, and being wounded by one of *Willet's* Indians, cried for quarter; upon which the Indian screamed out with a dreadful voice, "Sherry Valley," at the same time cleaving his head with his tomahawk! *

Whether the following interesting affair belongs to *Walter* or *John Butler*, or whether it happened at Wyoming or at Cherry-valley, it equally affects the character of *Brant*. It is said, that *Butler*, on entering a house, ordered a woman and child to be killed, whom they found in a bed; but *Brant* said, "*What? kill a woman and child! No! that child is not an enemy to the king, nor a friend to the congress. Long before he will be big enough to do any mischief, the dispute will be settled.*"†

The depredations of the Indians and tories at Wyoming and other places in that region, caused General *Washington* to order General *Sullivan* with 2500 men into the Indian country. Considerable delay was experienced, and the forces were not concentrated at Wyoming until a year after it was destroyed. On 22 July, a company of Pennsylvania militia who had marched from this place to Lackawaxen to protect the settlers there, were attacked by 140 Indians and 40 or 50 of them were killed or made prisoners.‡

It was said that this summer, (1779,) 160,000 bushels of their corn was destroyed. As soon as it was known that *Sullivan* was advancing into the country, *Brant* and *Butler*, with 600 Indians, and *Johnson*, with 200 tories, took a position on his route, to cut him off. *Sullivan* came upon them, August 29, at a place called *Newtown*, on Tioga River,§ where they had entrenched themselves, and immediately attacked them. The battle lasted about two hours, when, by a successful movement of General *Poor*, at the head of his New Hampshire regiment, *Brant's* warriors were thrown into confusion, and the whole were put to flight.‖ Few were killed, and they made no other stand against the Americans during the expedition.¶ The historian adds, "They utterly destroyed 40 villages, and left no single trace of vegetation upon the surface of the ground."** All their cattle were either killed or brought off, many of which they had before taken from the Americans. "None of the bounties of nature, none of the products of human industry, escaped the fury of the Americans."†† Upon this business the same author writes, that "the officers charged with the execution of these devastations, were themselves ashamed of them; some even ventured to remonstrate that they were not accustomed to exercise the vocation of banditti." General *Poor*, doubtless, was the efficient man in this expedition, but the ostentation of *Sullivan* gained him the *honor!* of it. Thus were the

---

* *Marshall's* Washington, iv. Appendix, 13.—*Allen's* Biog. Dict. Article, *Butler, John.*

† *Allen*, ibid.

‡ *Chapman*, 131.

§ *Chapman's* Hist. Wyoming, 132.

‖ Nine only of the Indians were killed; of the Americans, four. It is said to be owing to the sagacity of *Brant*, that his whole force escaped falling into the hands of the Americans. *Annals Tryon Co.* 125.

¶ *Botta*, Hist. Rev. ii. 206.

** Ibid. Some of the officers thought it too degrading to the army to be employed in destroying fruit-trees, and remonstrated to Gen. *Sullivan* against the order. He replied "The Indians shall see that there is malice enough in our hearts to destroy every thing that contributes to their support." *Gordon*, Amer. Rev. iii. 21

†† *Gordon*, Amer. Rev. iii. 207.

Five Nations chastised for acting as they had been taught by the white people; yea, by the Americans themselves.*

The following summer, (23 July, 1779,) Colonel *Brant*, with 60 of his warriors and 27 white men, came suddenly upon Minisink, in Orange county, New York, where they killed sundry of the inhabitants and made others captives. They burnt ten houses, twelve barns, a garrison and two mills, and then commenced their retreat. The militia from Goshen and places adjacent, to the number of 149, collected, pursued, and came up with them, when a most bloody battle was fought. The Indians were finally victorious, and 30 only, out of the 149 whites, escaped. Some were carried into captivity, and the rest were killed. Not being sufficiently cautious, they fell into an ambush, and so fought at great disadvantage.†

In 1821, a county meeting was held, by which it was voted that the bones of the slain should be collected, and deposited under a suitable monument at the same time ordered to be erected.‡ In 1822, the committee appointed to collect the bones "which had been exposed to the suns and snows for 43 years," had found those of 44 persons, which were, with much formality, publicly interred.§

In the spring of 1780, *Brant* surprised Harpersfield, with a company of his warriors, and a few tories. He took 19 prisoners, and killed several others. On 2 August following, he fell upon Canajoharrie, with about 400 mixed warriors, killed 16 people, took about 55 prisoners, chiefly women and children; they killed and drove away, at the same time, about 300 cattle and horses, burnt 53 houses, and as many barns, besides out-houses, a new and elegant church, a grist-mill and two garrisons.

Doubtless there were many other warlike scenes in which *Brant* was engaged personally; but we have already dwelt longer upon them than we intended.

European writers, for a long time, contended that the N. American Indians had, naturally, no beards.‖ A Mr. *M'Causland* took the trouble of writing to *Brant*, after the revolution, to get the truth of the matter. The following is *Brant's* letter to his inquiry:—"*Niagara, 19 April, 1783. The men of the Six Nations have all beards by nature; as have likewise all other Indian nations of North America, which I have seen. Some Indians allow a part of the beard upon the chin and upper lip to grow, and a few of the Mohawks shave with razors, in the same manner as Europeans; but the generality pluck out the hairs of the beard by the roots, as soon as they begin to appear; and as they continue this practice all their lives, they appear to have no beard, or, at most, only a few straggling hairs, which they have neglected to pluck out. I am, however, of opinion, that if the Indians were to shave, they would never have beards altogether so thick as the Europeans; and there are some to be met with who have actually very little beard.*¶

Jos. Brant Thayendanegea."

A daughter of Colonel *Brant* married a Frenchman, who in June, 1789, was killed by a party of Indians, while peaceably travelling up the Wabash River. He was in company with nine others, four of whom were killed and three wounded. When the hostile party came up to them, and discovered

---

* See the speech of *Big-tree, Corn-plant,* and *Half-town,* to which nothing need be added by way of commentary upon such affairs.

† *Gordon's* America, iii. 22. ‡ *Spafford's* Gaz. 328.

§ *Holmes's* Amer. Annals, ii. 302.

‖ Even the great luminary *Voltaire* fell into this error. He says, "*Les Iroquois, les Hurons, et tous les peuples jusqu'à la Floride, parurent olivâtres et sans aucun poil sur le corps excepté la tête.*" That is, all from the 60° of N. latitude. Voyez *Œuvres complètes* iv. 708, ed. Paris, 1817, 8vo. See also *Raynal*, viii. 210.

A gentleman, Mr. *W. J. Snelling*, who resided among the western Indians for some time, says, *It is not an error* that the Indians have no beard; that the "Saques and Foxes have but very few hairs upon their faces, nor have they any instrument for extirpating it; and what makes the fact certain is, they have no hair on the concealed parts of their bodies." According to Lawson, *Account of the Indians of North Carolina*, 190, 191, the same is true with regard to them. *Lawson* travelled much among the southern Indians.

¶ This is the case with many of the whites.

the son-in-law of *Brant*, they assisted in drawing the arrows from the wounded, and then went off.*

When the Indians upon the southern and western frontier were showing themselves hostile, in 1791, Colonel *Brant* used his exertions to prevent hostilities, by visiting such tribes as appeared hostile. His name appears in many important transactions of those times. The boundary line between the United States and the Indian nations had not been satisfactorily established, which was the cause of much trouble. A gentleman in Canada wrote to another in the state of New York, under date of 2 August, 1791, wherein Colonel *Brant* is thus mentioned: "Capt. *Joseph Brant*, after having attended for some time the councils of the western Indians at the Miami River, set off a few days ago for Quebec, attended with several of the chiefs from that quarter; as they avowedly go to ask Lord *Dorchester's* advice, and as we well know his and government's strong desire for peace, we would gladly hope that it may be the means of bringing on an accommodation."

In 1792, his arrival in Philadelphia is thus publicly noticed in the Gazette of that city:—"Capt. *Joseph Brant*, the principal warrior chief of the Six Nations, arrived in this city on Wednesday evening last, (June 20.) It is said his errand is a visit to a number of his acquaintance residing here, and to pay his respects to the president of the United States." He left there about the beginning of July, upon another peace excursion among the western tribes, which still remained hostile.

When General *Wayne* was marching into the Indian country, in 1793, many of the tribes were alarmed, having heard that his army consisted of 8000 men. Learning, also, that commissioners accompanied the army, authorized to treat of peace, and wishing to know the strength of the Americans, thirty chiefs of different tribes were despatched upon this important business. Colonel *Brant* was one of these 30 Indian ambassadors. If the Americans would make the Ohio the boundary, they wished peace. The whole cause of General *Wayne's* war appears to have been about the lands lying west of the Ohio and Alleghany Rivers. We have no doubt *Brant* secretly, if not openly, advocated the establishment of this boundary; yes, and we must acknowledge that if he did, it was from the best of reasons. We know that *Tecumseh* labored incessantly for this boundary. Rightly did they conceive of the mighty wave of population rolling westward, southward and northward. Truly, they must have been blind not to have seen that it was about to engulf them forever! When they had met the commissioners, and found them inflexible in their determination, *Brant*, with most of the chiefs of the Six Nations, gave up the point as hopeless, preferring peace, on any terms, to war. But the Wyandots, Delawares, Shawanees and Miamis would not agree to it.

Mention will be found in the account of *Farmers-brother* of a great council held by the chiefs of most of the western nations at Niagara, in April, 1793. In this council it was agreed that peace should be maintained; and "they unanimously agreed to meet the Americans in a grand council, to be holden the June following, upon the south side of Lake Erie; and for the purpose of making the peace more permanent and extensive, they have appointed *Brant* who is now their king of kings, to go and convene all those tribes who live to the north-west of Lake Ontario. He accordingly, the day after, set out for that purpose." The Indians did not assemble until July, from the difficulty of their journeys and other causes, which is generally the case with meetings of this kind. The council was held at Sandusky, and Colonel *Brant* set out from Niagara for that place in May. Before leaving, he had frequent conversations with a gentleman of respectability, to whom he gave it as his opinion, that no peace could take place, until the Ohio and Muskingum should make the boundary between the Americans and the red men. He still expressed good feelings towards the United States, and hoped that they would see it to be their interest to agree to that boundary, as he firmly believed war would ensue should they refuse. He even said, that, in case hey would not consent to make these rivers the boundary, he should take

* *Carey's* Museum, vi. 178

part against them. It was not agreed to; but we do not hear that the old chief was actually engaged in the hostilities that followed.

How much the English of Canada influenced the measures of the Indians, it is difficult to determine;* but men like *Pontiac*, *Brant* and *Tecumseh* could easily see through such duplicity as was practised by a few unprincipled speculators, as *M'Kee*, *Girty* and *Elliot*. They had, doubtless, conceived that if the Ohio and Muskingum were made the boundary, it would be an easy matter for them to possess themselves of the country from thence to the lakes, and thus enlarge the extent of Canada. They knew well that if the Indians possessed this tract of country, it would be no difficult matter to purchase it from them by means of a few trifling articles, comparatively of no consideration, and that worst of calamities, ardent spirits! In this they were disappointed, and, with the battle of Presque Isle, resigned their hopes, at least for a season. They urged upon the Indians what they must have been well assured of—their destruction!

Much has been said and written of the cold-blooded atrocities of *Brant*, but which, in our opinion, will be much lessened on being able to come pretty near the truth of his history. Every successful warrior, at least in his day, is denounced by the vanquished as a barbarian. *Napoleon* was thus branded by all the world—we ask no excuse for our chief on this score—all wars are barbarous, and hence those who wage them are barbarians! This we know to be strong language; but we are prepared to prove our assertion. When mankind shall have been cultivated and improved to that extent which human nature is capable of attaining,—when the causes of avarice and dissension are driven out of the human mind, by taking away the means which excite them,—then, and not till then, will wars and a multitude of attending calamities cease.

As a sample of the stories circulating about Colonel *Brant*, while the affairs of Wyoming and Cherry-valley were fresh in the recollections of all, we extract from *Weld's* Travels the following:—†

"With a considerable body of his troops he joined the forces under the command of Sir *John Johnston*." "A skirmish took place with a body of American troops; the action was warm, and *Brant* was shot by a musket ball in his heel; but the Americans, in the end, were defeated, and an officer with about 60 men were taken prisoners. The officer, after having delivered up his sword, had entered into conversation with Colonel *Johnston*, who commanded the British troops, and they were talking together in the most friendly manner, when *Brant* having stolen slily behind them, laid the American officer lifeless on the ground with a blow of his tomahawk. The indignation of Sir *John Johnston*, as may be readily supposed, was roused by such an act of treachery, and he resented it in the warmest terms. *Brant* listened to him unconcernedly, and when he had finished, told him, that *he was sorry for his displeasure, but that, indeed, his heel was extremely painful at the moment, and he could not help revenging himself on the only chief of the party that he saw taken.*"

Upon this passage the author of the Annals of Tryon County‡ observes: "I have heard a story somewhat similar told of him, but it was said that the officer was killed to prevent his being retaken by the Americans, who were in pursuit." This we should pronounce very *dis*-similar to the story

* We will hear a great writer and traveller upon this subject, whose means of forming a correct judgment, it is presumed, will not be questioned. "Je remarquerai à cette occasion sans m'étendre davantage sur ce sujet, que toute la politque de l'Angleterre avec les Indiens est absolument dans les mains des agens, qui seuls en entendent la langue; et qui seuls sont les distributeurs des presens;" &c. *Voyage dans les Etats-unis en* 1795, *etc. Par La Rochefoucauld-Liancourt*, ii. 78. The duke was at Newark, U. C., at this time, where he witnessed a business assemblage of Indians. After a dance, which they held before their audience with the governor of Canada, the duke says that, "Pendant ces jeux, l'agent s'est approché du général avec un des chefs, et lui a dit que sa nation de Tuscorora le consultait pour savoir si elle irait à un conseil tenu par les Indiens Oneydas à Onondago pour vendre leurs terres de reserve, que l'Etat de New Yorck désirait acheter. Le gouverneur a répondu trés-vaguement à cette question; l'agent a traduit comme il a voulu cette réponse; mais il a repliqué au gouverneur de la part des Indiens qui comme ils croyaient être plus agréables au roy d'Angleterre en n'y allant pas; ils n'iraient pas." Ibid. 77.

† Page 486, octavo ed. London, 1800.

‡ In the Appendix, p. 15.

told by Mr. *Weld.* But there was, no doubt, some circumstance out of which a story has grown, the truth of which, we apprehend, is now past find ing out.

Colonel *Brant* was married, in the winter of 1779, to a daughter of Colonel *Croghan* by an Indian woman. He had lived with her some time *ad libitum*, according to the Indian manner, but at this time being present at the wedding of a Miss *Moore*, at Niagara, (one of the captives taken from Cherry-valley,) insisted on being married himself; and thus his consort's name was no longer Miss *Croghan*, but Mrs. *Brant*. The ceremony was performed by his companion-in-arms, Colonel *John Butler*, who, although he had left his country, yet carried so much of his magistrate's commission with him, as to *solemnize* marriages *according to law*.

King *George* conferred on his famous ally a valuable tract of land situated upon the west shore of Lake Ontario, where he finally settled and lived after the English fashion. His wife, however, would never conform to this mode of life, but would adhere to the custom of the Indians, and on the death of her husband, which happened 24 November, 1807, she repaired to Grand River, there to spend her days in a wigwam, with some of her children, while she left behind others in a commodious dwelling.* A son, of whom we have spoken, with a sister, lately occupied this mansion of their father, and constituted an amiable and hospitable family. This son, whose name is *John*, is a man of note, and is the same who was in England in 1822, as has been mentioned, and the same, we conclude, who has been returned a member of the colonial assembly of Upper Canada. His place of residence was in the county of Haldiman, in Brantford, so called, probably, in honor of the old chief.† Several other places are mentioned as having been the residence of *Brant*—Unadilla, or Anaquaqua, (which is about 36 miles south-west from the present site of Cooperstown,) and Niagara. He resided at these places before the Mohawks removed to Canada, which was soon after the war of the revolution was ended. They made their principal residence upon Grand River, which falls into Lake Erie on the north side, about 60 miles from the town of Newark, or Niagara. At one time, he had no less than 30 or 40 negroes, who took care of his horses and lands. "These poor creatures," says Mr. *Weld*, "are kept in the greatest subjection, and they dare not attempt to make their escape, for he has assured them, that if they did so, he would follow them himself, though it were to the confines of Georgia, and would tomahawk them wherever he met them. They know his disposition too well not to think that he would adhere strictly to his word." The same author says that *Brant* received presents, which, together with his half-pay as captain, amounted to £500 *per annum*.

An idea of the importance of this chief, in 1795, may be formed from the circumstance, that a gentleman considered himself a loser to the amount of £100, at least, by not being able to arrive at Niagara in season to attend to some law case for him. Contrary winds had prevented his arrival, and the business had been given to another.‡

"Whenever the affairs of his nation shall permit him to do so, *Brant* declares it to be his intention to sit down to the further study of the Greek language, of which he professes himself to be a great admirer, and to translate from the original, into the Mohawk language, more of the New Testament; yet this same man, shortly before we arrived at Niagara, killed his own son, with his own hand. The son, it seems, was a drunken, good-for-nothing fellow, who had often avowed his intention of destroying his father. One evening, he absolutely entered the apartment of his father, and had begun to grapple with him, perhaps with a view to put his unnatural threats in execution, when *Brant* drew a short sword, and felled him to the ground. He speaks of this affair with regret, but, at the same time, without any of that emotion which another person than an Indian might be supposed to feel. He

* *Buchanan's* Sketches, i. 36.

† Mr. *Campbell's* Annals of Tryon County has been one of our main sources of information throughout this account, especially of the revolutionary period.

‡ *Weld* Travels, 487.

consoles himself for the act, by thinking that he has benefited the nation, by ridding it of a rascal." *

With regard to the dress of the sachem, there has been some contradiction. Mr. *Weld*, though he did not see him, says he wore his hair in the Indian fashion, as he also did his clothes; except that, instead of the blanket, he wore a kind of hunting frock. This was in 1796. But it was reported, that, in 1792, *Brant* having waited on Lord *Dorchester*, the governor of Canada, upon some business, his lordship told him, that as he was an officer in the British service, he ought to lay aside the Indian dress, and assume that of an English captain; and that, if he persisted in wearing an Indian dress, he should stop his pay. It is added that thereupon he changed his dress.†

When Colonel *Brant* arrived at any principal city, his arrival was publicly announced in the gazettes with great minuteness. Although we have given some specimens of these, we will add one more:—

"New York, June 20, 1792. On Monday last arrived in this city, from his settlement on Grand River, on a visit to some of his friends in this quarter, Captain *Joseph Brandt*, of the British army, the famous Mohawk chief, who so eminently distinguished himself during the late war, as the military leader of the Six Nations. We are informed that he intends to visit the city of Philadelphia, and pay his respects to the president of the U. States," ‡ General *Washington*, which he did. We have before mentioned his visit to that city.

The very respectable traveller § *Rochefoucauld* thus notices our chief: "At 24 miles from this place, (Newark, U. C.) upon Grand River, is an establishment which I had been curious to visit. It is that of Colonel *Brant*. But the colonel not being at home, and being assured that I should see little else than what I had already seen among those people, I gave over my intention. Colonel *Brant* is an Indian who took part with the English, and having been in England, was commissioned by the king, and politely treated by every one. His manners are half European. He is accompanied by two negro servants, and is in appearance like an Englishman. He has a garden and farm under cultivation; dresses almost entirely like an European, and has great influence over the Indians. He is at present [1795] at Miami, holding a treaty with the United States, in company with the Indians of the west. He is equally respected by the Americans, who extol so much his character, that I regret much not to have seen him." ‖

The great respect in which *Brant* was held in England will be very apparent from a perusal of the following letter,¶ dated 12 December, 1785: "Monday last, Colonel *Joseph Brant*, the celebrated king of the Mohawks, arrived in this city, [Salisbury,] from America, and after dining with Colonel *de Peister*, at the head-quarters here, proceeded immediately on his journey to London. This extraordinary personage is said to have presided at the late grand congress of confederate chiefs of the Indian nation in America, and to be by them appointed to the conduct and chief command in the war which they now meditate against the United States of America. He took his departure for England immediately as that assembly broke up; and it is con-

---

* *Weld*, Travels, 489. † Apollo for 1792. ‡ American Apollo, 297.

§ Duke *de Liancourt*, Travels, ii. 81, before cited, from whom we translate this.

‖ This French traveller seems to have been in advance of history, in as far as he thus early sets in their proper light the characters of the heroes of Wyoming. After speaking of the influence of Indian agents over those people, as we have extracted in a previous note, he thus consigns to Colonel *Butler* the place which he is doubtless to hold in all after-time in the annals of his country:—" *L'agent anglais dont* il est ici queston, est le Colonel *Buttler*, fameux par ses incendies, ses pillages et ses meurtres dans la guerre d'Amerique. Il est lui-même Américain d'auprès de Wilkesbarre; [one of the towns in the valley of Wyoming;] son prétendu loyalisme qu'il a su se faire payer de brevets et de traitemens, lui a fait commettre plus de barbaries, plus d'infamies contre sa patrie, qu'à qui que ce soit. Il conduisait les Indiens, leur indiquait les fermes, les maisons à brûler, les victimes à scarpeler, les enfans à dechirer. L'Angleterre a recompensé son loyalisme de *cinq mille* acres de terre pour lui, d'une quantité pareille pour ses enfans, d'une pension de deux à trois cents livres sterlings, d'une place d'agent auprès des Indiens, qui lui en vaut cinq cents autres, avec la facilité de puiser à volonté dans les magasins de présens." *Rochefoucauld*, ut supra, (ii. 78—9.)

¶ There is no name to this letter; but it was written in Salisbury, Eng., and thence se[illegible] London, where it was published.

jectured that his embassy to the British court is of great importance. This country owes much to the services of Colonel *Brant* during the late war in America. He was educated at Philadelphia, [at the Moor's charity school in Lebanon, Connecticut,] is a very shrewd, intelligent person, possesses great courage and abilities as a warrior, and is inviolably attached to the English nation."

It has been denied that *Brant* was in any way engaged in the massacres at Wyoming, but it seems hardly possible that so many should have been deceived at that time; and, moreover, we do not find that it was denied until almost every one of that age had left the stage of action. Those who deny that he was at Wyoming should, at least, prove an alibi, or they cannot expect to be believed.*

Brant was said to have been 65 years old at his death. A daughter of his married *William J. Ker*, Esq. of Niagara, and he had several other children besides those we have mentioned. The son who visited England in 1822, and another named *Jacob*, entered *Moor's* school at Hanover, N. H. in 1801, under the care of Dr. *Wheelock*. The former son, *John*, died about two years since, in the winter of 1831.

CHAPTER VI.

Facts in the history of the Seneca nation—SAGOYEWATHA, *or* RED-JACKET—*His famous speech to a missionary—His interview with Colonel Snelling—British invade his country—Resolves to repel them—His speech upon the event—Governor Clinton's account of him—Witchcraft affair—Complains of encroachments—One of his people put to death for being a witch—He defends the executioner—His interview with Lafayette—Council at Canandaigua—Farmers-brother—Red-jacket visits Philadelphia—His speech to the governor of Pennsylvania—Speech of Agwelondongwa or Good-peter—Narrative of his capture during the revolutionary war*—FARMERS-BROTHER, *or* HONAYAWUS—*Visits Philadelphia*—PETER-JAQUETTE—*Visits France—Account of his death—Memorable speech of Farmers-brother—His letter to the secretary of war—Notice of several other Seneca chiefs*—KOYINGQUATAH, *or* YOUNG-KING—JUSKAKAKA, *or* LITTLE-BILLY—ACHIOUT, *or* HALF-TOWN—KIANDOGEWA, *or* BIG-TREE—GYENTWAIA, *or* CORN-PLANT—*Address of the three latter to President Washington—Grant of land to Big-tree—His visit to Philadelphia, and death—Further account of Corn-plant—His own account of himself—Interesting events in his life—His sons.*

THE Senecas were the most important tribe among the Iroquois, or Five Nations, and, according to *Conrad Weiser*, they were the fourth nation that joined that confederacy. He calls them † "Ieuontowanois or Sinikers," and says, "they are styled by the Mohawks and Onondagos, brothers;" and that their title in councils is Onughkaurydaaug. The French call them Tsonnonthouans, from their principal castle, or council-house, the name of which, according to *Colden*, is Sinondowans. ‡ Other particulars of this nation will be related as we proceed in detailing the lives of its chiefs. Among these perhaps, the most illustrious was

SAGOYEWATHA, § called by the whites, *Red-jacket*. His place of resi-

* In a late criminal trial which has much agitated New England, reasonable people said, the defendant, out of respect to public opinion, ought to make it appear where he was at the time a murder was committed, although in law he was not bound so to do. An advocate for his innocence told the writer, that "he was not *obliged* to tell where he was," and it was nobody's business; and, therefore, we were bound, according to law, to believe him innocent. This we offer as a parallel case to the one in hand. But it happens we are not "bound by law" to believe our chief entirely innocent of the blood shed at Wyoming.

† American Mag.

‡ Hist. Five Nations, i. 42.

§ The common method of spelling. Governor *Clinton* writes, *Saguoaha*. Written to the treaty of "Konondaigua," (Nov. 1794,) *Soggooyawauthau*; to that of Buffalo Creek (June, 1802,) *Soogooyawautau*; to that of Moscow, (Sept. 1823,) *Sagouata*. It is said to signify "*One who keeps awake*," or simply, *Keeper-awake*. "*Sō-gwē'-ē'-wau''-tŏh*; is wide awake, and keeps every body else awake, a very appropriate name for the Cic

dence was, for many years previous to his death, (which happened 20 January 1830, at his own house,) about four miles from Buffalo, and one mile north of the road that leads through the land reserved for the remnant of the Seneca nation, called the *Reservation.* His house was a log-cabin, situated in a retired place. Some of his tribe are Christians, but *Red-jacket* would never hear to any thing of the kind. He was formerly considered of superior wisdom in council, and of a noble and dignified behavior, which would have honored any man. But, like nearly *all* his race, he could not withstand the temptation of ardent spirits, which, together with his age, rendered him latterly less worthy notice. Formerly, scarce a traveller passed near his place of residence, who would not go out of his way to see this wonderful man, and to hear his profound observations.

In the year 1805, a council was held at Buffalo, in the state of New York, at which were present many of the Seneca chiefs and warriors, assembled at the request of a missionary, Mr. *Cram,* from Massachusetts. It was at this time that *Red-jacket* delivered his famous speech, about which so much has been said and written, and which we propose to give here at length, and *correctly;* as some omissions and errors were contained in it as published at the time. It may be taken as genuine, at least as nearly so as the Indian language can be translated, in which it was delivered, for *Red-jacket* would not speak in English, although he understood it. The missionary first made a speech to the Indians, in which he explained the object for which he had called them together; namely, to inform them that he was sent by the missionary society of Boston to instruct them "how to worship the *Great Spirit,*" and not to get away their lands and money; that there was but one religion, and unless they embraced it they could not be happy; that they had lived in darkness and great errors all their lives; he wished that, if they had any objections to his religion, they would state them; that he had visited some smaller tribes, who waited their decision before they would consent to receive him, as they were their "older brothers."

After the missionary had done speaking, the Indians conferred together about two hours, by themselves, when they gave an answer by *Red-jacket,* which follows:—

"*Friend and brother,* it was the will of the Great Spirit that we should meet together this day. He orders all things, and he has given us a fine day for our council. He has taken his garment from before the sun, and caused it to shine with brightness upon us; our eyes are opened, that we see clearly; our ears are unstopped, that we have been able to hear distinctly the words that you have spoken; for all these favors we thank the Great Spirit, and him only.

"*Brother,* this council fire was kindled by you; it was at your request that we came together at this time; we have listened with attention to what you have said; you requested us to speak our minds freely; this gives us great joy, for we now consider that we stand upright before you, and can speak what we think; all have heard your voice, and all speak to you as one man; our minds are agreed.

"*Brother,* you say you want an answer to your talk before you leave this place. It is right you should have one, as you are a great distance from home, and we do not wish to detain you; but we will first look back a little, and tell you what our fathers have told us, and what we have heard from the white people.

"*Brother, listen to what we say.* There was a time when our forefathers owned this great island.* Their seats extended from the rising to the setting sun. The Great Spirit had made it for the use of Indians. He had created the buffalo, the deer, and other animals for food. He made the bear and the beaver, and their skins served us for clothing. He had scattered

of the west. His English appellation had its origin from the circumstance of his wearing, when a child, a *red jacket.*" *Alden's Account of Missions,* 162.—This is a very natural derivation; but from what circumstance some of the Indians derived their names, it would be hard to divine: thus, *Red-jacket* had an uncle whose name meant a *heap of dogs,* ib. 164.

* A general opinion among all the Indians that this country was an island.

them over the country, and taught us how to take them. He had caused the earth to produce corn for bread. All this he had done for his red children because he loved them. If we had any disputes about hunting grounds, they were generally settled without the shedding of much blood: but an evil day came upon us; your forefathers crossed the great waters, and landed on this island. Their numbers were small; they found friends, and not enemies; they told us they had fled from their own country for fear of wicked men, and come here to enjoy their religion. They asked for a small seat; we took pity on them, granted their request, and they sat down amongst us; we gave them corn and meat; they gave us poison * in return. The white people had now found our country, tidings were carried back, and more came amongst us; yet we did not fear them, we took them to be friends; they called us brothers; we believed them, and gave them a larger seat. At length their numbers had greatly increased; they wanted more land; they wanted our country. Our eyes were opened, and our minds became uneasy. Wars took place; Indians were hired to fight against Indians, and many of our people were destroyed. They also brought strong liquors among us: it was strong and powerful, and has slain thousands.

"*Brother*, our seats were once large, and yours were very small; you have now become a great people, and we have scarcely a place left to spread our blankets; you have got our country, but are not satisfied; *you want to force your religion upon us.*

"*Brother, continue to listen.* You say that you are sent to instruct us how to worship the *Great Spirit* agreeably to his mind, and if we do not take hold of the religion which you white people teach, we shall be unhappy hereafter; you say that you are right, and we are lost; how do we know this to be true? We understand that your religion is written in a book; if it was intended for us as well as you, why has not the Great Spirit given it to us, and not only to us, but why did he not give to our forefathers the knowledge of that book, with the means of understanding it rightly? We only know what you tell us about it; how shall we know when to believe, being so often deceived by the white people?

"*Brother*, you say there is but one way to worship and serve the Great Spirit; if there is but one religion, why do you white people differ so much about it? why not all agree, as you can all read the book?

"*Brother*, we do not understand these things; we are told that your religion was given to your forefathers, and has been handed down from father to son. We also have a religion which was given to our forefathers, and has been handed down to us their children. We worship that way. *It teacheth us to be thankful for all the favors we receive; to love each other, and to be united; we never quarrel about religion.*

"*Brother*, the Great Spirit has made us all; but he has made a great difference between his white and red children; he has given us a different complexion, and different customs; to you he has given the arts; to these he has not opened our eyes; we know these things to be true. Since he has made so great a difference between us in other things, why may we not conclude that he has given us a different religion according to our understanding; the Great Spirit does right; he knows what is best for his children; we are satisfied.

"*Brother*, we do not wish to destroy your religion, or take it from you; we only want to enjoy our own.

"*Brother*, you say you have not come to get our land or our money, but to enlighten our minds. I will now tell you that I have been at your meetings, and saw you collecting money from the meeting. I cannot tell what this money was intended for, but suppose it was for your minister, and if we should conform to your way of thinking, perhaps you may want some from us.

"*Brother*, we are told that you have been preaching to white people in this place; these people are our neighbors, we are acquainted with them; we will wait a little while and see what effect your preaching has upon them.

* Spirituous liquor is alluded to, it is supposed.

If we find it does them good, makes them honest, and less disposed to cheat Indians, we will then consider again what you have said.

"*Brother*, you have now heard our answer to your talk, and this is all we have to say at present. As we are going to part, we will come and take you by the hand, and hope the Great Spirit will protect you on your journey, and return you safe to your friends."

The chiefs and others then drew near the missionary to take him by the hand; but he would not receive them, and hastily rising from his seat, said, "that there was no fellowship between the religion of *God* and the works of the *Devil*, and, therefore, could not join hands with them." Upon this being interpreted to them, "they smiled, and retired in a peaceable manner."

The Indians cannot well conceive how they have any participation in the guilt of the crucifixion; inasmuch as they do not believe themselves of the same origin as the whites; and there being no dispute but that they committed that act. *Red-jacket* once said to a clergyman who was importuning him on this subject,

"*Brother, if you white men murdered the Son of the* Great Spirit, *we Indians had nothing to do with it, and it is none of our affair. If he had come among us, we would not have killed him; we would have treated him well. You must make amends for that crime yourselves.*" *

Red-jacket took part with the Americans in the war of 1812, but was not distinguished for that prodigality of life which marked the character of *Tecumseh*, and many others, but, on all occasions, was cool and collected. He had become attached to Colonel *Snelling* during the war, and when he heard that that officer was ordered to a distant station, he went to take his farewell of him. At that interview he said,

"*Brother, I hear you are going to a place called* Governor's Island. *I hope you will be a governor yourself. I understand that you white people think children a blessing. I hope you may have a thousand. And, above all, I hope, wherever you go, you may never find whisky more than two shillings a quart.*"†

Grand Island, in Niagara River, just above the famous Niagara Falls, is owned by the Senecas. When it was rumored that the British had taken possession of it, in their last war with the Americans, *Red-jacket* assembled his people, to consult with Mr. *Granger*, their agent. After having stated to him the information, the old chief made the following profound speech:—

"*Brother, you have told us that we had nothing to do with the war that has taken place between you and the British. But we find the war has come to our doors. Our property is taken possession of by the British and their Indian friends. It is necessary now for us to take up the business, defend our property, and drive the enemy from it. If we sit still upon our seats, and take no means of redress, the British (according to the customs of you white people) will hold it by conquest. And should you conquer the Canadas, you will claim it upon the same principles, as [though] conquered from the British. We, therefore, request permission to go with our warriors, and drive off those bad people, and take possession of our lands.*" Whereupon, such of the Senecas as had an inclination, were permitted to join the American army.

In one action *Red-jacket* acted a conspicuous part, and is most honorably mentioned by the commanding general. The action took place near Fort George, on the 17 August, 1813, between about 300 volunteers and Indians, supported by 200 regulars. These surprised the British and Indian camp at day light, killed 75 and took 16 prisoners. The success of the expedition was almost entirely owing to a stratagem of the Indians, who, when they had formed their plan of attack, decoyed their brethren, on the British side into an ambush, by giving a war-whoop which they mistook for that of their friends. General *Boyd*, who commanded here, says, "The principal chiefs who led the warriors this day, were FARMER'S BROTHER, RED-JACKET,

---

* "This occurred in a conversation between *Red-jacket* and the Reverend Mr. *Brackenridge*; *Tommy-Jemmy*, *Jack-Berry* and myself were present. I heard the remark, and will vouch for it." *W. J. Snelling*.

† N. E. Galaxy, 13 July, 1833.

LITTLE BILLY, POLLARD, BLACK SNAKE, JOHNSON, SILVERHEELS, Captain HALF-TOWN, Major HENRY O. BALL, (Corn-planter's son,) and Captain COLD, chief of Onondago, who was wounded. In a council which was held with them yesterday, they covenanted not to scalp or murder; and I am happy to say, that they treated the prisoners with humanity, and committed no wanton cruelties upon the dead." "Their bravery and humanity were equally conspicuous. Already the quietness in which our pickets are suffered to remain, evinces the benefit arising from their assistance."*

Governor *De Witt Clinton*, in his most valuable discourse before the Historical Society of New York, thus notices *Red-jacket*:—"Within a few years, an extraordinary orator has risen among the Senecas; his real name is *Saguoaha*. Without the advantages of illustrious descent, and with no extraordinary talents for war, he has attained the first distinctions in the nation by the force of his eloquence." *Red-jacket* having, by some means, lost the confidence of his countrymen, in order, as it is reported, to retrieve it, prevailed upon his brother to announce himself a prophet, commissioned by the Great Spirit to redeem them from their miserable condition.—It required nothing but an adroit and skilful reasoner to persuade the ignorant multitude, given to the grossest superstition, of his infallibility in the pretended art or mystery. If good ever came out of evil, it did at this time. The Onondagas were, at that period, the most drunken and profligate of all the Iroquois. They were now so far prevailed upon as almost entirely to abstain from ardent spirits, became sober and industrious, and observed and respected the laws of morality. This good effect was not confined to the Onondagas, but shed its benign influence through the nations adjacent. But as this reform was begun in hypocrisy, it necessarily ended with its hypocritical author. The greatest check, perhaps, which can be thrown in the way of imposture, is its own exposition. In this case, like witchcraft among us in former times, it was stayed by its own operations. Many were denounced as witches, and some would have been executed but for the interference of their white neighbors. *Red-jacket* was denounced in a great council of Indians, held at Buffalo Creek, as the chief author of their troubles. He was accordingly brought to trial, and his eloquence saved his life, and greatly increased his reputation. His defence was near three hours long. And, in the language of Governor *Clinton*, "the iron brow of superstition relented under the magic of his eloquence: he declared the prophet [his brother] an impostor and a cheat; he prevailed; the Indians divided, and a small majority appeared in his favor. Perhaps the annals of history cannot furnish a more conspicuous instance of the triumph and power of oratory, in a barbarous nation, devoted to superstition, and looking up to the accuser as a delegated minister of the Almighty. I am well aware that the speech of *Logan* will be triumphantly quoted against me, and that it will be said, that the most splendid exhibition of Indian eloquence may be found out of the pale of the Six Nations. I fully subscribe to the eulogium of Mr. *Jefferson*, when he says, 'I may challenge the whole orations of *Demosthenes* and *Cicero*, and of any more eminent orator, if Europe has furnished more eminent, to produce a single passage superior to the speech of *Logan*.' But let it be remembered that *Logan* was a *Mingo* chief," that is, an Iroquois.

The time is not far distant, if not already arrived, when the name of *Red-jacket* will be heard, in the most august assemblies, to give weight to the mightiest efforts of eloquence. In the debate on the Indian bill, in 1830, in congress, Mr. *Crockett*,† of Tennessee, said, "I am forcibly reminded of the remark made by the famous *Red-jacket*, in the rotunda of this building, when he was shown the panel which represented in sculpture the first landing of the Pilgrims, with an Indian chief presenting to them an ear of corn, in token of friendly welcome. The aged Indian said, '*That was*

* *Niles' Register*, iv. 418, and v. 7.—*Branan's Official Letters*, 200.—*Shallus's Tables*, ii. 120.

† The pitiful crusade in which this brave man lost his life, will as long be remembered for its unjustifiable origin, as the many valuable but misguided men who have been sacrificed in it. Having joined the army of Texas, Colonel *Crockett* was there murdered with the rest of a garrison which fell into the hands of the Mexicans; this present year, 1836.

good.' He said he knew they came from the Great Spirit, and he was willing to share the soil with his brothers. But when he turned round to view another panel, representing *Penn's* treaty, he said, '*Ah! all's gone now.*' There was a great deal of truth in this short saying."

Nothing seems more to have troubled the peace of *Red-jacket* than the intrusion of missionaries among his people. With the merits or demerits of the manner in which particular creeds have been forced upon the Indians in general, we have nothing to do, but we will refer the reader to Mr. *Buchanan's* Sketches,* where, in our opinion, every sectarian will glean some useful hints upon that head.

Red-jacket and his council, in 1821, made a formal complaint to the governor of New York, of the arbitrary conduct of some teachers among his people, and of their undue influence generally. Considering it to contain a most important and valuable piece of information, we will give it entire:—

"Brother *Parish*, I address myself to you, and through you to the governor. The chiefs of Onondaga have accompanied you to Albany, to do business with the governor; I also was to have been with you, but I am sorry to say that bad health has put it out of my power. For this you must not think hard of me. I am not to blame for it. It is the will of the Great Spirit that it should be so. The object of the Onondagas is to purchase our lands at Tonnewanta. This and all other business that they may have to do at Albany, must be transacted in the presence of the governor. He will see that the bargain is fairly made, so that all parties may have reason to be satisfied with what shall be done; and when our sanction shall be wanted to the transaction, it will be freely given. I much regret that, at this time, the state of my health should have prevented me from accompanying you to Albany, as it was the wish of the nation that I should state to the governor some circumstances which show that the chain of friendship between us and the white people is wearing out, and wants brightening. I proceed now, however, to lay them before you by letter, that you may mention them to the governor, and solicit redress. He is appointed to do justice to all, and the Indians fully confide that he will not suffer them to be wronged with impunity. The first subject to which we would call the attention of the governor, is the depredations that are daily committed by the white people upon the most valuable timber on our reservations. This has been a subject of complaint with us for many years; but now, and particularly at this season of the year, it has become an alarming evil, and calls for the immediate interposition of the governor in our behalf. Our next subject of complaint is, the frequent thefts of our horses and cattle by the white people, and their habit of taking and using them whenever they please, and without our leave. These are evils which seem to increase upon us with the increase of our white neighbors, and they call loudly for redress. Another evil arising from the pressure of the whites upon us, and our unavoidable communication with them, is the frequency with which our chiefs, and warriors, and Indians, are thrown into jail, and that, too, for the most trifling causes. This is very galling to our feelings, and ought not to be permitted to the extent to which, to gratify their bad passions, our white neighbors now carry this practice. In our hunting and fishing, too, we are greatly interrupted by the whites. Our venison is stolen from the trees where we have hung it to be reclaimed after the chase. Our hunting camps have been fired into, and we have been warned that we shall no longer be permitted to pursue the deer in those forests which were so lately all our own. The fish, which, in the Buffalo and Tonnewanta Creeks, used to supply us with food, are now, by the dams and other obstructions of the white people, prevented from multiplying, and we are almost entirely deprived of that accustomed sustenance. Our great father, the president, has recommended to our young men to be industrious, to plough, and to sow. This we have done, and we are thankful for the advice, and for the means he has afforded us of carrying it into effect. We are happier in consequence of it. *But another thing recommended to us, has created great confusion*

* Vol. i. chap. ix.

among us, and is making us a quarrelsome and divided people; and that is, the introduction of preachers into our nation. These black coats contrive to get the consent of *some* of the Indians to preach among us, and wherever this is the case, confusion and disorder are sure to follow, and the encroachments of the whites upon our lands are the invariable consequence. The governor must not think hard of me for speaking thus of the preachers. I have observed their progress, and when I look back to see what has taken place of old, I perceive that whenever they came among the Indians, they were the forerunners of their dispersion; that they always excited enmities and quarrels among them; that they introduced the white people on their lands, by whom they were robbed and plundered of their property; and that the Indians were sure to dwindle and decrease, and be driven back in proportion to the number of preachers that came among them. Each nation has its own customs and its own religion. The Indians have theirs, given to them by the Great Spirit, under which they were happy. It was not intended that they should embrace the religion of the whites, and be destroyed by the attempt to make them think differently on that subject from their fathers.* It is true, these preachers have got the consent of some of the chiefs to stay and preach among us, but I and my friends know this to be wrong, and that they ought to be removed; besides, we have been threatened by Mr. *Hyde*, who came among us as a school-master and a teacher of our children, but has now become a black coat, and refused to teach them any more, that unless we listen to his preaching and become Christians, we will be turned off our lands. We wish to know from the governor if this is to be so; and if he has no right to say so, we think *he* ought to be turned off our lands, and not allowed to plague us any more. We shall never be at peace while he is among us. Let them be removed, and we will be happy and contented among ourselves. We now cry to the governor for help, and hope that he will attend to our complaints, and speedily give us redress.

RED-JACKET."

"This letter was dictated by *Red-jacket*, and interpreted by *Henry Obeal*,† in the presence of the following Indians: *Red-jacket's* son, *Corn-planter*, *John-cobb*, *Peter*, *Young-kings-brother*, *Tom-the-infant*, [*Onnonggaiheko*,] *Blue-sky*, [*Touyocauna*,] *John-sky*, *Jemmy-johnson*, *Marcus*, *Big-fire*, *Captain-Jemmy*."

The success this petition met with, it is presumed, was full and satisfactory to him, in respect to one particular; for no ministers, for some time afterwards, were admitted upon the reservation.

In the spring of 1821, a man of *Red-jacket's* tribe fell into a languishment and died. His complaint was unknown, and some circumstances attended his illness which caused his friends to believe that he was bewitched. The woman that attended him was fixed upon as the witch, and by the law, or custom, of the nation, she was doomed to suffer death. A chief by the name of *Tom-jemmy*, called by his own people *Soo-nong-gise*, executed the decree by cutting her throat. The Americans took up the matter, seized *Tom-jemmy*, and threw him into prison.‡ Some time after, when his trial came on, *Red-jacket* appeared in court as an evidence. The counsel for the prisoner denied that the court had any jurisdiction over the case, and after it was carried through three terms, *Soo-nong-gise* was finally cleared. *Red-jacket* and the other witnesses testified that the woman was a witch, and that she had been tried, condemned and executed in pursuance of their laws, which had been established from time immemorial; long before the English came into the country. The witch doctrine of the Senecas was much ridiculed by some of the Americans, to which *Red-jacket* thus aptly alludes in a speech which he made while upon the stand:—

"*What! do you denounce us as fools and bigots, because we still continue to believe that which you yourselves sedulously inculcated two centuries ago? Your divines have thundered this doctrine from the pulpit, your judges have pronounced*

---

* A happy illustration of the force of education. † Son of *Corn-planter*, or *Corn-plant*.

‡ Information of a gentleman (*W. J. Snelling*, Esq.) who was on the spot, and saw him brought to Buffalo. This was the next day after the murder, and the blood was yet upon his hands.

it from the bench, your courts of justice have sanctioned it with the formalities of law, and you would now punish our unfortunate brother for adherence to the superstitions of his fathers! Go to Salem! Look at the records of your government, and you will find hundreds executed for the very crime which has called forth the sentence of condemnation upon this woman, and drawn down the arm of vengeance upon her. What have our brothers done more than the rulers of your people have done? and what crime has this man committed by executing, in a summary way, the laws of his country, and the injunctions of his God?" Before *Red-jacket* was admitted to give evidence in the case, he was asked if he believed in future rewards and punishments, and the existence of God. With a piercing look into the face of his interrogator, and with no little indignation of expression, he replied: "*Yes! much more than the white men, if we are to judge by their actions.*" Upon the appearance of *Red-jacket* upon this occasion, one observes: "There is not, perhaps, in nature, a more expressive eye than that of *Red-jacket;* when fired by indignation or revenge, it is terrible; and when he chooses to display his unrivalled talent for irony, his keen sarcastic glance is irresistible." *

When *Lafayette*, in 1825, was at Buffalo, among the persons of distinction who called upon him, was *Red-jacket.* Of the old chief, M. *Levasseur* observes: † This extraordinary man, although much worn down by time and intemperance, preserves yet, in a surprising degree, the exercise of all his faculties. He had ever remembered *Lafayette* since 1784, at which time he, with others, met a great council of all the Indian nations at Fort Schuyler, when the interest of all those nations, friends and enemies, was regulated with the United States. He asked the general if he recollected that meeting. He replied that he had not forgotten that great event, and asked *Red-jacket* if he knew what had become of the young chief, who, in that council, opposed with such eloquence the "burying of the tomahawk." *Red-Jacket* replied, "*He is before you.*" His speech was a master-piece, and every warrior who heard him was carried away with his eloquence. He urged a continuation of the war against the Americans, having joined against them in the revolution. The general observed to him that time had much changed them since that meeting. "Ah!" said *Red-jacket*, "time has not been so severe upon you as it has upon me. It has left to you a fresh countenance, and hair to cover your head; while to me..... behold.....!" and taking a handkerchief from his head, with an air of much feeling, showed his head, which was almost entirely bald.‡

At this interview, was fully confirmed what we have before stated. *Levasseur* continues: *Red-jacket* obstinately refuses to speak any language but that of his own country, and affects a great dislike to all others; although it is easy to discern that he perfectly understands the English; and refused, nevertheless, to reply to the general before his interpreter had translated his questions into the Seneca language. The general spoke a few words in Indian, which he had learned in his youth, at which *Red-Jacket* was highly pleased, and which augmented much his high opinion of *Lafayette.*

The author of the following passage is unknown to us; but presuming it to be authentic, we quote it. "More than 30 years § have rolled away since a treaty was held on the beautiful acclivity that overlooks the Canandaigua ||

* Niles's Weekly Register, vol. xx. 359, 411.

† In his *Lafayette en Amérique*, tome ii. 437-8.

‡ "*Les assistants ne purent s'empêcher de sourire de la simplicité de l'Indien, qui semblait ignorer l'art de réparer les injures du temps; mais on se garda bien de détruire son erreur; et peut-être fit-on bien, car il eût pu confondre une perruque avec une chevelure scalpée, et concevoir l'idée de regarnir sa tête aux dépens de la tête d'une de ses voisons.*" *Ibid.* —This attempt at facetiousness by Mons. *Levasseur* is entirely a failure, and in very bad taste. Had it had reference to an obscure person, it would have been different. For a parcel of white ignoramuses to make themselves merry at the simple but dignified appearance of the old chief, only shows them off in their true light; and the assertion that he covered his own head at the expense of that of his neighbor, too nearly classes the writer with his companions.

§ This writer, I conclude, wrote in 1822. I copy it from *Miscellanies selected from the Public Journals*, by Mr. *Buckingham.*

|| Signifying, in the Seneca language, *a town set off.* The lake received its name from the town upon its shore.—*Spafford's Gaz.*

Lake. The witnesses of the scene will never forget the powers of native oratory. Two days had passed away in negotiation with the Indians for a cession of their lands. The contract was supposed to be nearly completed, when *Red-jacket* arose. With the grace and dignity of a Roman senator, he drew his blanket around him, and, with a piercing eye, surveyed the multitude. All was hushed. Nothing interposed to break the silence, save the gentle rustling of the tree tops, under whose shade they were gathered. After a long and solemn, but not unmeaning pause, he commenced his speech in a low voice and sententious style. Rising gradually with the subject, he depicted the primitive simplicity and happiness of his nation, and the wrongs they had sustained from the usurpations of white men, with such a bold but faithful pencil, that every auditor was soon roused to vengeance, or melted into tears. The effect was inexpressible. But ere the emotions of admiration and sympathy had subsided, the white men became alarmed. They were in the heart of an Indian country—surrounded by more than ten times their number, who were inflamed by the remembrance of their injuries, and excited to indignation by the eloquence of a favorite chief. Appalled and terrified, the white men cast a cheerless gaze upon the hordes around them. A nod from the chiefs might be the onset of destruction. At this portentous moment, *Farmers-brother* interposed. He replied not to his brother chief, but, with a sagacity truly aboriginal, he caused a cessation of the council, introduced good cheer, commended the eloquence of *Red-jacket*, and, before the meeting had reassembled, with the aid of other prudent chiefs, he had moderated the fury of his nation to a more salutary review of the question before them. Suffice it to say, the treaty was concluded, and the Western District, at this day, owes no small portion of its power and influence to the counsels of a savage, in comparison with whom for genius, heroism, virtue, or any other quality that can adorn the bawble of a diadem, not only *George* the IV. and *Louis le Desiré*, but the German emperor and the czar of Muscovy, alike dwindle into insignificance." We can add nothing to this high encomium.

Red-jacket was of the number who visited Philadelphia in 1792, as will be found mentioned in the account of *Jaquette;* at which time he was welcomed by the governor of Pennsylvania to that city, and addressed by him, in behalf of the commonwealth, in the council-chamber. The following is the closing paragraph of the governor's speech: "Brothers! I know the kindness with which you treat the strangers that visit your country; and it is my sincere wish, that, when you return to your families, you may be able to assure them that the virtues of friendship and hospitality are also practised by the citizens of Pennsylvania." He had before observed that the government had furnished every thing to make them comfortable during their stay at Philadelphia. This was upon the 28 March, 1792, and on 2 April following, they met again, when *Red-jacket* spoke in answer to the governor as follows:—

"Brother, Onas* Governor, open unprejudiced ears to what we have to say. Some days since you addressed us, and what you said gave us great pleasure. This day the Great Spirit has allowed us to meet you again, in this council-chamber. We hope that your not receiving an immediate answer to your address, will make no improper impression upon your mind. We mention this lest you should suspect that your kind welcome and friendly address has not had a proper effect upon our hearts. We assure you it is far otherwise. In your address to us the other day, in this ancient council-chamber, where our forefathers have often conversed together, several things struck our attention very forcibly. When you told us this was the place in which our forefathers often met on peaceable terms, it gave us sensible pleasure, and more joy than we could express. Though we have no writings like you, yet we remember often to have heard of the friendship that existed between our fathers and yours. The picture † to which you drew our atten-

* *Onas* was the name the Indians gave *William Penn,* and they continue the same name to all the governors of Pennsylvania.

† A fine picture representing *Penn's* treaty with the Indians.

tion, brought fresh to our minds the friendly conferences that used to be held between the former governors of Pennsylvania and our tribes, and showed the love which your forefathers had of peace, and the friendly disposition of our people. It is still our wish, as well as yours, to preserve peace between our tribes and you, and it would be well if the same spirit existed among the Indians to the westward, and through every part of the United States. You particularly expressed that you were well pleased to find that we differed in disposition from the Indians westward. Your disposition is that for which the ancient Onas Governors were remarkable. As you love peace, so do we also; and we wish it could be extended to the most distant part of this great country. We agreed in council, this morning, that the sentiments I have expressed should be communicated to you, before the delegates of the Five Nations, and to tell you that your cordial welcome to this city, and the good sentiments contained in your address, have made a deep impression on our hearts, have given us great joy, *and from the heart I tell you so.* This is all I have to say."

When *Red-jacket* had finished, another chief, called *Agwelondongwas*, (and sometimes *Good-peter*,*) addressed the assembly. His speech is much in the style of *Red-jacket's*, and was chiefly a repetition, in other words, of it. It was short, and contained this passage: "What is there more desirable than that we, who live within hearing of each other, should unite for the common good? This is my wish. It is the wish of my nation, although I am sorry I can't say so of every individual in it; for there are differences of opinions among us, as well as among our white brethren."

Since we have here introduced *Dominie Peter*, we will so far digress as to relate what follows concerning him. He was one of those who took part against the Americans in the revolutionary war, and when hostilities commenced, he retired and joined the remote tribes towards Canada. Colonel *John Harper* (one of the family from whom Harpersfield, New York, takes its name) was stationed at the fort at Schorrie, in the state of New York. Early in the spring of 1777, in the season of making maple sugar, when all were upon the look-out to avoid surprise by the Indians, Colonel *Harper* left the garrison and proceeded through the woods to Harpersfield; thence by an Indian path to Cherry-valley. In his way, as he was turning the point of a hill, he saw a company of Indians, who, at the same time, saw him. He dared not attempt flight, as he could expect no other than to be shot down in such attempt. He, therefore, determined to advance and meet them without discovering fear. Concealing his regimentals as well as he could with his great coat, he hastened onward to meet them. Before they met him, he discovered that *Peter* was their chief, with whom he had formerly traded much at Oquago, but who did not know him. *Harper* was the first to speak, as they met, and his words were, "*How do you do, brothers?*" The chief answered, "*Well.—How do you do, brother? Which way are you bound?*" The colonel replied, "*On a secret expedition. And which way are you bound, brothers?*" They answered without hesitation or distrust, thinking, no doubt, they had fallen in with one of the king's men, "*Down the Susquehannah, to cut off the Johnstone settlement.*" This place, since called *Sidney Plains*, consisted of a few Scotch families, and their minister's name was *Johnstone;* hence the name of the settlement. The colonel next asked them where they lodged that night, and they told him, "At the mouth of Scheneva's Creek." After shaking hands, they separated. As soon as they were out of sight, *Harper* made a circuit through the woods with all speed, and soon arrived at the head of Charlotte River, where were several men making sugar. This place was about ten miles from Decatur Hill, where he met the Indians. He ordered them to take each a rope and provisions in their packs, and assemble at Evan's Place, where he would soon meet them: thence he returned to Harpersfield, and collected the men there, which, including the others and himself, made 15, just equal to *Peter's* force. When they arrived at Evan's Place, upon the Charlotte, *Harper* made known his project. They set off, and before day the next morning, came into the neighborhood of the In

* And often *Domine-peter*. 2 Coll. N. Y. Hist. Soc. 74.

dians' camp. From a small eminence, just at dawn of day, their fire was seen burning, and *Peter*, amidst his warriors, lying upon the ground. All were fast asleep. *Harper* and his companions each crept silently up, with their ropes in their hands, man to man; and each, standing in a position to grasp his adversary, waited for the word to be given by their leader. The colonel jogged his Indian, and, as he was waking, said to him, "*Come, it is time for men of business to be on their way.*" This was the watchword; and no sooner was it pronounced, than each Indian felt the warm grasp of his foe. The struggle was desperate, though short, and resulted in the capture of every one of the party. When it was sufficiently light to distinguish countenances, *Peter*, observing Colonel *Harper*, said, "*Ha! Colonel Harper. Now I know you! Why did I not know you yesterday?*" The colonel observed, "*Some policy in war, Peter.*" To which *Peter* replied, "*Ah! me find em so now.*" These captives were marched to Albany, and delivered up to the commanding officer. By this capital exploit no doubt many lives were saved.*

As has been noted, *Red-jacket* died at his residence near Buffalo, on the 20th of January, 1830, aged about 80 years. In 1833, a grandson of his was chosen chief of the Senecas.

The famous Seneca chief, called the FARMERS-BROTHER, is often mentioned in the accounts of *Red-jacket.* His native name was *Ho na-ya-wus.*

In 1792, FARMERS-BROTHER was in Philadelphia, and was among those who attended the burial of Mr. *Peter Jaquette*, and is thus noticed in the Pennsylvania Gazette of 28 March, of that year: "On Monday last, the chiefs and warriors of the Five Nations assembled at the state-house, and were welcomed to the city of Philadelphia in an address delivered by the governor. Three of the chiefs made a general acknowledgment for the cordial reception which they had experienced, but postponed their formal answer until another opportunity. The room in which they assembled was mentioned as the ancient council-chamber, in which their ancestors and ours had often met to brighten the chain of friendship; and this circumstance, together with the presence of a great part of the beauty of the city, had an evident effect upon the feelings of the Indians, and seemed particularly to embarrass the elocution of the *Farmers-brother.*" This last clause does not correspond with our ideas of the great chief.

Through his whole life, *Farmers-brother* seems to have been a peacemaker. In the spring of the next year, there was a great council held at Niagara, consisting of the chiefs of a great many nations, dwelling upon the shores of the western lakes. At this time, many long and laborious speeches were made, some for and others against the conduct of the United States. *Farmers-brother* shone conspicuous at this time. His speech was nearly three hours long, and the final determination of the council was peace. We know of no speeches being preserved at this time, but if there could have been, doubtless much true history might have been collected from them. He seems not only to have been esteemed by the Americans, but also by the English.†

Of *Peter Jaquette*, whom we have several times incidentally mentioned, we will give some account before proceeding with *Honayawus.* He was one of the principal sachems of the Oneidas. This chief died in Philadelphia, 19 March, 1792. He had been taken to France by General *Lafayette*, at the close of the revolutionary war, where he received an education. Mr *Jaquette*, having died on Monday, was interred on the following Wednesday. "His funeral was attended from *Oeler's* hotel to the Presbyterian burying-ground in Mulberry-street. The corpse was preceded by a detachment of the light infantry of the city, with arms reversed, drums muffled, music playing a solemn dirge. The corpse was followed by six of the

* Annals of Tryon Co. 8vo. N. York, 18.

† "Le village de Buffalo est habité par les Senecas. Le chef de cette nation est *Brothers farmer*, estimé par toutes les tribus comme grand guerrier et grand politique, et fort caressé à ce titre par les agens anglais et les agens Américains. Buffalo est le chef lieu de la nation Seneca." *Rochefoucauld, Voyage dans l'Amérique en* 1795, 6, and 7, t. i. 299.

chiefs as mourners, succeeded by all the warriors; the reverend clergy of all denominations; secretary of war, and the gentlemen of the war department; officers of the federal army, and of the militia· and a number of citizens." *

One of the most celebrated speeches of *Farmers-brother* was delivered in a council at Genesee River, in 1798, and after being interpreted, was signed by the chiefs present, and sent to the legislature of New York. It follows:—

"*Brothers*, as you are once more assembled in council for the purpose of doing honor to yourselves and justice to your country, we, your brothers, the sachems, chiefs and warriors of the Seneca nation, request you to open your ears and give attention to our voice and wishes.—You will recollect the late contest between you and your father, the great king of England. This contest threw the inhabitants of this whole island into a great tumult and commotion, like a raging whirlwind which tears up the trees, and tosses to and fro the leaves, so that no one knows from whence they come, or where they will fall.—This whirlwind was so directed by the Great Spirit above, as to throw into our arms two of your infant children, *Jasper Parrish* and *Horatio Jones*.† We adopted them into our families, and made them our children. We loved them and nourished them. They lived with us many years. *At length the Great Spirit spoke to the whirlwind, and it was still.* A clear and uninterrupted sky appeared. The path of peace was opened, and the chain of friendship was once more made bright. Then these our adopted children left us, to seek their relations; we wished them to remain among us, and promised, if they would return and live in our country, to give each of them a seat of land for them and their children to sit down upon.—They have returned, and have, for several years past, been serviceable to us as interpreters. We still feel our hearts beat with affection for them, and now wish to fulfil the promise we made them, and reward them for their services. We have, therefore, made up our minds to give them a seat of two square miles of land, lying on the outlets of Lake Erie, about three miles below Black-rock, beginning at the mouth of a creek known by the name of *Scoyguquoy-descreek*, running one mile from the River Niagara up said creek, thence northerly as the river runs two miles, thence westerly one mile to the river, thence up the river as the river runs, two miles, to the place of beginning, so as to contain two square miles.—We have now made known to you our minds. We expect and earnestly request that you will permit our friends to receive this our gift, and will make the same good to them, according to the laws and customs of your nation.—Why should you hesitate to make our minds easy with regard to this our request? To you it is but a little thing; and have you not complied with the request and confirmed the gifts of our brothers the Oneidas, the Onondagas and Cayugas to their interpreters? And shall we ask and not be heard? We send you this our speech, to which we expect your answer before the breaking up our great council fire."

A gentleman ‡ who visited Buffalo in 1810, observes that *Farmers-brother* was never known to drink ardent spirits, and although then 94 years old, walked perfectly upright, and was remarkably straight and well formed; very grave, and answered his inquiries with great precision, but through his interpreter, Mr. *Parrish*, before named. His account of the mounds in that region will not give satisfaction. He told Dr. *King* that they were thrown up against the incursions of the French, and that the implements found in them were taken from them; a great army of French having been overthrown and mostly cut off, the Indians became possessed of their acoutrements which, being of no use to them, were buried with their owners.

He was a great warrior, and although "eighty snows in years" when the war of 1812 began, yet he engaged in it, and fought with the Americans.

* Pennsylvania Gazette.

† Taken prisoners at the destruction of Wyoming by the tories and Indians under *Butler* and *Brant*.

‡ Dr. *William King* the celebrated electrician, who gives the author this information verbally.

He did not live till its close, but died at the Seneca village, just after the battle of Bridgewater, and was interred with military honors by the fifth regiment of United States infantry. He usually wore a medal presented him by General *Washington.* In the revolution, he fought successfully against the Americans. Perhaps there never flowed from the lips of man a more sublime metaphor than that made use of by this chief, in the speech given above, when alluding to the revolutionary contest. It is worth repeating: "*The Great Spirit spoke to the whirlwind, and it was still.*"

This celebrated chief was engaged in the cause of the French, in the old French war, as it is termed, and he once pointed out the spot to a traveller, where, at the head of a band of his warriors, he ambushed a guard that accompanied the English teams, employed between the Falls of Niagara and Fort Niagara, which had then recently surrendered to the English under Sir *William Johnson.* The place of the ambush is now called the Devil's Hole, and is a very noted place to inquisitive visitors of that romantic region, as it is but three and a half miles below the great Falls, and upon the American shore. It is said of this place, that "the mind can scarcely conceive of a more dismal looking den. A large ravine, made by the falling in of the perpendicular bank, darkened by the spreading branches of the birch and cedar, which had taken root below, and the low murmuring of the rapids in the chasm, added to the solemn thunder of the cataract itself, contribute to render the scene truly awful. The English party were not aware of the dreadful fate that awaited them. Unconscious of danger, the drivers were gayly whistling to their dull ox-teams. *Farmers-brother* and his band, on their arrival at this spot, rushed from the thicket which had concealed them, and commenced a horrid butchery." So unexpected was the attack that all presence of mind forsook the English, and they made little or no resistance. The guard, the teamsters, the oxen and the wagons were precipitated down into the gulf. But two of the men escaped; a Mr. *Stedman,* who lived at Schlosser, above the falls, who, being mounted on a fleet horse, effected his escape; and one of the soldiers, who was caught on the projecting root of a cedar, which sustained him until the Indians had left the place. He soon after got to Fort Niagara, and there gave an account of what had happened. The small rivulet that runs into the Niagara through the Devil's Hole, was, it is said, colored with the blood of the slain on that unfortunate day, and it now bears the name of Bloody-Run.

Farmers-brother fought against the Americans in the Revolution, and was no inconsiderable foe; but his acts were probably mostly in council, as we hear of no important achievements by him in the field.

The following remarkable incident should not be omitted in the life of this chief. In the war of 1812, a fugitive Mohawk from the enemy had endeavored to pass for a Seneca, and accordingly came among those under *Red-jacket* and *Farmers-brother.* The latter discovered him, and immediately appeared in his presence, and thus accosted him. "*I know you well. You belong to the Mohawks. You are a spy. Here is my rifle—my tomahawk—my scalping-knife. Say, which I shall use. I am in haste.*" The young Mohawk knew there was no reprieve, nor time to deliberate. He chose the rifle. The old chief ordered him to lie down upon the grass, and with one foot upon his breast, he discharged his rifle into his head.*

The following letter will, besides exhibiting the condition of the Senecas, develop some other interesting facts in their biographical history.

"To the Honorable *William Eustis,* secretary at war.

"The sachems and chief warriors of the Seneca nation of Indians, understanding you are the person appointed by the great council of your nation to manage and conduct the affairs of the several nations of Indians with whom you are at peace and on terms of friendship, come, at this time, as children to a father, to lay before you the trouble which we have on our minds.

* *Buckingham's Miscellanies,* i. 33, 34.

"Brother, we do not think it best to multiply words: we will, therefore, tell you what our complaint is.—Brother, listen to what we say: Some years since, we held a treaty at Bigtree, near the Genesee River. This treaty was called by our great father, the president of the United States. He sent an agent, Col. *Wadsworth*, to attend this treaty, for the purpose of advising us in the business, and seeing that we had justice done us. At this treaty, we sold to *Robert Morris* the greatest part of our country; the sum he gave us was 100,000 dollars. The commissioners who were appointed on your part, advised us to place this money in the hands of our great father, the president of the United States. He told us our father loved his red children, and would take care of our money, and plant it in a field where it would bear seed forever, as long as trees grow, or waters run. Our money has heretofore been of great service to us; it has helped us to support our old people and our women and children; but we are told the field where our money was planted is become barren.—Brother, we do not understand your way of doing business. This thing is very heavy on our minds. We mean to hold our white brethren of the United States by the hand; but this weight lies heavy; we hope you will remove it.—We have heard of the bad conduct of our brothers towards the setting sun. We are sorry for what they have done; but you must not blame us; we have had no hand in this bad business. They have had bad people among them. It is your enemies have done this. —We have persuaded our agent to take this talk to your great council. He knows our situations, and will speak our minds.

[Subscribed with the marks of]

Farmer's Brother, [*Honayawus*,]	Wheelbarrow,
Little Billy, [*Gishkaka*,]	Jack-berry,
Young King, [*Koyingquautah*,]	Twenty Canoes, [*Cachaunwasse*,]
Pollard, [*Kaoundoowand*,]	Big-kettle, [*Sessewa*?]
Chief-warrior, [*Lunuchshewa*,]	Half-town, [*Achiout*,]
Two-guns,	Keyandeande,
John Sky,	Captain-cold,
Parrot-nose, [*Soocoowa*,]	Esq. Blinkney,
John Pierce, [*Teskaiy*,]	Capt. Johnson, [*Talwinaha*.]
Strong, [*Kahalsta*,]	

"N. B. The foregoing speech was delivered in council by *Farmers-Brother*, at Buffalo Creek, 19 Dec. 1811, and subscribed to in my presence by the chiefs whose names are annexed.

Erastus Granger."

Eight thousand dollars * was appropriated immediately upon receipt of the above.

Little-billy, or *Gishkaka*, is the same of whom we have spoken in a preceding chapter, and called by *Washington*, *Juskakaka*.

Young-king, the third signer of the above talk, was engaged in fighting for the Americans in the last war with England, and by an act of congress was to be paid yearly, in quarterly payments, 200 dollars, during life. The act states that it was "a compensation for the brave and meritorious services which he rendered" in that war, "and as a provision for the wound and disability which he received in the performance of those services." This was in the spring of 1816.

Of *Pollard*, or Captain *Pollard*, we shall have occasion elsewhere to say more.

Jack-berry was sometimes interpreter for *Red-jacket*.

Half-town was very conspicuous in the affairs of the Senecas, but as he is generally mentioned, in our documents, in connection with *Corn-plant*, or *Corn-planter*, and *Big-tree*, we had designed to speak of the three collectively.

We find among the acts of the Pennsylvania legislature of 1791, one "for

* "In lieu of the dividend on the bank shares, held by the president of the U States in trust for the Seneca nation, in the bank of the U. States."

† Or *Kiandogewa*, *Kayenthoghke*, &c.

‡ *Benson's* Memoir, before the N. Y. Hist. Soc. page 20. Also Amer. Magazine.

granting 800 dollars to *Corn-planter*, *Half-town* and *Big-tree*, Seneca chiefs, in trust for the Seneca nation." At this time much was apprehended from an Indian war. Settlers were intruding themselves upon their country, and all experience has shown that whenever the whites have gone among them, troubles were sure to follow. Every movement of the Indians was looked upon with jealousy by them at this period. *Half-town* was the "white man's friend," and communicated to the garrisons in his country every suspicious movement of tribes of whom doubts were entertained. It is evident that hostile bands, for a long time, hovered about the post at Venango, and, but for the vigilance of *Half-town*, and other friendly chiefs, it would have been cut off. In April this year, (1791,) *Corn-plant* and *Half-town* had upwards of 100 warriors in and about the garrison, and kept runners out continually, "being determined to protect it at all events." Their spies made frequent discoveries of war parties. On the 12 August, 1791, *Half-town* and *New-arrow* gave information at Fort Franklin, that a sloop full of Indians had been seen on Lake Erie, sailing for Presque Isle; and their object was supposed to be Fort Franklin; but the conjecture proved groundless.

The Indian name of *Half-town* was *Achiout*. We hear of him at Fort Harmer, in 1789, where, with 23 others, he executed a treaty with the United States. The commissioners on the part of the latter were General *Arthur St. Clair*, *Oliver Wolcut*, *Richard Butler* and *Arthur Lee*. Among the signers on the part of the Senecas were also *Big-tree*, or *Kiandogewa*, *Corn-planter*, or *Gyantwaia*, besides several others whose names are familiar in history. *Big-tree* was often called *Great-tree*, which, in the language of the Five Nations, was *Nihorontagowa*,* which also was the name of the Oneida nation.† *Big-tree* was with General *Washington* during the summer of 1778, but returned to the Indian nations in the autumn. He proceeded to the Senecas, and used his eloquence to dissuade them from fighting under *Brant* against the Americans. The Oneidas were friendly at this time, and *Big-tree* was received among them with hospitality, in his way, upon this mission. Having staid longer than was expected among the Senecas, the Oneidas sent a messenger to him to know the reason. He returned answer that when he arrived among his nation, he found them all in arms, and their villages, Kanadaseago and Jennessee, crowded with warriors from remote tribes; that they at first seemed inclined to hearken to his wishes, but soon learning by a spy that the Americans were about to invade their country, all flew to arms, and *Big-tree* put himself at their head, "*determined to chastise*," he said, "*the enemy that dared presume to think of penetrating their country*." But we do not learn that he was obliged to maintain that hostile attitude, and doubtless returned soon after.

CORN-PLANTER was a warrior at *Braddock's* defeat, but whether a chief I do not learn; we will, however, according to our design, give an account of that signal disaster, in this connection. The French having established themselves upon the Ohio, within the territory claimed by the English, and built a fort upon it, as low down as the confluence of that river with the Monongahela, the latter were determined to dispossess them. This was undertaken by a force of about 2200 men under the command of General *Edward Braddock*. With about 1300 of these he proceeded on the expedition, leaving the rest to follow under Colonel *Dunbar*.‡ Through nearly the whole course of his march, he was watched by spies from Fort Duquesne, (the name of the French fort on the Ohio,) and the earliest intelligence of his movements was carried there by Indian runners with the utmost despatch. When it was told among the Indians that the army was marching upon them in solid columns, they laughed with surprise, and said, one to another, "*We'll shoot 'em down, all one pigeon!*" § and it will always be acknowledged that, in this, the Indians were not mistaken.

The French, it seems, formed but a small part of the force that defeated

---

* Or *Kiandogewa*, *Kayenthoghke*, &c.

† *Benson's* Memoir, before the N. Y. Hist. Soc. page 20. Also Amer. Magazine

‡ Account of the Ohio Defeat, p. 4, 4°. Boston, 1755.

§ *Withers's Chronicles*, 53, 54

Braddock's army; the Indians planned and executed the operations chiefly themselves, and their whole force is said not to have exceeded 400 men; but from the accounts of the French themselves, it is evident there were about 600 Indians, and not far from 250 French,* who marched out to meet *Braddock.*

Early in the morning of the 9 July, 1755, the English army arrived at a fording-place on the Monongahela, at the junction of the Youghiogany, which it passed in fine order, and pursued its march upon the southern margin of the river, to avoid the high and rugged ground on the north, which they would have had to encounter upon the other side of it. *Washington* often said afterwards, "that the most beautiful spectacle which he had ever beheld was the display of the British troops on this eventful morning." They were in full uniform, and marched in the most perfect order, and dreamed of nothing but an easy conquest. About noon they arrived at their second crossing place, which was distant only 10 miles from Fort Duquesne. It was here that the Indians and French had intended to commence their attack; but owing to some delay, they did not arrive in season, and therefore took a position further in advance, and awaited the approach of the English.

The French were commanded by M. *de Beaujeu,* who had for his lieutenant, M. *Dumas.* The place chosen for the ambush was the best possible, and the Indians never showed greater courage and firmness. It is said by the French, that they were for some time opposed to going out to fight the English, but that after several solicitations from M. *Beaujeu,* they consented, but the Indian account is as we have before stated.

Immediately on crossing the river the army were formed in three divisions, which was the order of march. A plain, or kind of prairie, which the army had to cross, extended from the river about half a mile, and then its route lay over an ascending ground, of very gentle ascent, covered with trees and high prairie grass. At the commencement of this elevation began a ravine, which, as it extended up the rising ground, formed a figure resembling nearly that of a horse-shoe, and about 150 yards in extent. Into this inclosure two divisions of the army had passed when the attack began.

Notwithstanding *Washington* had urged upon the general the propriety of keeping out scouting parties to avoid surprise, yet he would take no advice, and it is said, that on one occasion, he boisterously replied, "that it was high times for a young Buckskin to teach a British general how to fight!" Such was his contempt for scouting parties, that he accepted with cold indifference the services of *George Croghan,* who had offered himself with 100 Indians for the important business of scouring the woods. The consequence was, the Indians, one after another, left the army in its march, much to the regret of *Washington* and other provincial officers, who knew how to appreciate their value.

When the first division of the army had nearly ascended the hill, as the rising ground was called, the Indians broke the silence of the morning with a most appalling yell, and at the same moment poured a most deadly fire from their coverts upon the devoted column. The first shocks were sustained with firmness, and the fire was returned, by which a few Indians were killed, and the French commander-in-chief, M. *de Beaujeu,* mortally wounded. It is said that the Indians now began to waver, and but for the good conduct of M. *Dumas,* second in command, would have fled; but by his exertions order was restored, and the firing, which had not ceased, was redoubled.

The advanced column was commanded by Lieutenant-Colonel *Gage,* since so well known as governor of Massachusetts, in 1775. This column was about 100 yards in advance of the second, which had just begun to ascend the hill when the attack began, and the main body, under the general in person, was but a few rods in the rear of this, and on hearing the firing he pressed forward to support the engaged party.

Meanwhile the extensive line of Indians upon the right flank made an onset from their section of the ravine, and from their superior numbers, the shock could not be withstood, and the column was immediately broken, and

* *Sparks's Washington,* ii. 468—76.

† Ib. c. 1, 469.

began to retreat in disorder down the hill—confusion and dismay ensued—no exertions of the officers could prevent the panic from spreading among the regular troops, and the fight was afterwards continued in the utmost irregularity. Imboldened by the confusion of the English, the Indians now rushed upon them with their tomahawks, which, after near two hours, terminated the battle, and the field was left in their possession. Not only the field of battle, but all the killed and many of the wounded, all the artillery, (eleven pieces of cannon,) all the general's baggage, and even private papers, and all the ammunition and provisions, fell into the hands of the victors.

All but the Virginians fought for some time in the most wretched confusion; but the officers were mournfully sacrificed—sometimes charging the enemy in a body by themselves, hoping by their example to draw out their men in a manner to repel their adversaries; but all to no purpose: and it is not doubted but that the confused multitude of regulars killed many of their companions, as they often fired fifty or a hundred in a huddle together, seemingly for no other object but to get rid of their ammunition. The Virginians fought in the Indian manner, behind trees and coverts; and it was owing to their good conduct that any of the wretched army escaped.

After having five horses shot under him, General *Braddock* received a wound in his lungs, of which he died on the 13th of July, 4 days after the battle, at Fort Cumberland, whither he had arrived with a part of his shattered army. *Washington* had been suffering, for some time before arriving at the fatal battle-field, from a fever; and in a letter which he wrote to his mother, dated July 18th, he thus speaks of himself:—"The Virginia troops showed a good deal of bravery, and were nearly all killed; for I believe, out of three companies that were there, scarcely 30 men are left alive. Captain *Peyrouny*, and all his officers down to a corporal, were killed. Captain *Polson* had nearly as hard a fate, for only one of his were left. In short, the dastardly behavior of those they call regulars exposed all others, that were inclined to do their duty, to almost certain death, and at last, in despite of all the efforts of the officers to the contrary, they ran, as sheep pursued by dogs, and it was impossible to rally them." "Sir *Peter Halket* was killed in the field, where died many other brave officers. I luckily escaped without a wound, though I had 4 bullets through my coat, and two horses shot under me. Captains *Orme* and *Morris*, two of the aids-de-camp, were wounded early in the engagement, which rendered the duty harder upon me, as I was the only person then left to distribute the general's orders, which I was scarcely able to do, as I was not half recovered from a violent illness, that had confined me to my bed and wagon for above 10 days."

We know of no battle, in which so great a proportion of officers fell. There were 86 engaged in it, and 63 were killed and wounded, of whom 26 were killed. Besides those already named, there were among the wounded Colonel *Burton*, Sir *John St. Clair*, Colonel *Orme*, and Major *Sparks*. Of the private soldiers there were killed and wounded 714, half of whom were killed, or fell into the hands of the Indians, and suffered a cruel death afterwards. Mr. *John Field*, then a lieutenant, and Mr. *Charles Lewis*, two distinguished officers afterwards, escaped the carnage of *Braddock's* field to fall in a more fortunate place. They were colonels under General *Andrew Lewis*, and were killed in the battle of Point Pleasant, as will be found mentioned in the life of *Logan*.

In the year 1790, *Big-tree*, *Corn-plant* and *Half-town* appeared at Philadelphia, and, by their interpreter, communicated to President *Washington* as follows:—

"*Father:* The voice of the Seneca nations speaks to you; the great counsellor, in whose heart the wise men of all the *thirteen fires* [13 U. S.] have placed their wisdom. It may be very small in your ears, and we, therefore, entreat you to hearken with attention; for we are able to speak of things which are to us very great.

"When your army entered the country of the Six Nations, we called you the *town destroyer;* to this day, when your name is heard, our women look behind them and turn pale, and our children cling close to the necks of their mothers"

"When our chiefs returned from Fort Stanwix, and laid before our council what had been done there, our nation was surprised to hear how great a country you had compelled them to give up to you, without your paying to us any thing for it. Every one said, that your hearts were yet swelled with resentment against us for what had happened during the war, but that one day you would consider it with more kindness. We asked each other, *What have we done to deserve such severe chastisement?*

"*Father:* when you kindled your 13 fires separately, the wise men assembled at them told us that you were all brothers; the children of one great father, who regarded the red people as his children. They called us brothers, and invited us to his protection. They told us that he resided beyond the great water where the sun first rises; and that he was a king whose power no people could resist, and that his goodness was as bright as the sun. What they said went to our hearts. We accepted the invitation, and promised to obey him. What the Seneca nation promises, they faithfully perform. When you refused obedience to that king, he commanded us to assist his beloved men in making you sober. In obeying him, we did no more than yourselves had led us to promise." "We were deceived; but your people teaching us to confide in that king, had helped to deceive us; and we now appeal to your breast. *Is all the blame ours?*

"*Father:* when we saw that we had been deceived, and heard the invitation which you gave us to draw near to the fire you had kindled, and talk with you concerning peace, we made haste towards it. You told us you could crush us to nothing; and you demanded from us a great country, as the price of that peace which you had offered to us: *as if our want of strength had destroyed our rights.* Our chiefs had felt your power, and were unable to contend against you, and they therefore gave up that country. What they agreed to has bound our nation, but your anger against us must by this time be cooled, and although our strength is not increased, nor your power become less, we ask you to consider calmly—*Were the terms dictated to us by your commissioners reasonable and just?*"

They also remind the president of the solemn promise of the commissioners, that they should be secured in the peaceable possession of what was left to them, and then ask, "*Does this promise bind you?*" And that no sooner was the treaty of Fort Stanwix concluded, than commissioners from Pennsylvania came to purchase of them what was included within the lines of their state. These they informed that they did not wish to sell, but being further urged, consented to sell a part. But the commissioners said that "*they must have the whole;*" for it was already ceded to them by the king of England, at the peace following the revolution; but still, as their ancestors had always paid the Indians for land, they were willing to pay them for it. Being not able to contend, the land was sold. Soon after this, they empowered a person to let out part of their land, who said congress had sent him for the purpose, but who, it seems, fraudulently procured a *deed* instead of a *power* to lease; for there soon came another person claiming all their country northward of the line of Pennsylvania, saying that he purchased it of the other, and for which he had paid 20,000 dollars to him and 20,000 more to the United States. He now demanded the land, and, on being refused, threatened immediate war. Knowing their weak situation, they held a council, and took the advice of a white man, whom they took to be their friend, but who, as it proved, had plotted with the other, and was to receive some of the land for his agency. He, therefore, told them they must comply. "Astonished at what we heard from every quarter," they say, "with hearts aching with compassion for our women and children, we were thus compelled to give up all our country north of the line of Pennsylvania, and east of the Genesee River, up to the great forks, and east of a south line drawn up from that fork to the line of Pennsylvania." For this he agreed to give them 10,000 dollars down, and 1000 dollars a year forever. Instead of that, he paid them 2500 dollars, and some time after offered 500 dollars more, insisting that that was all he owed them, which he allowed to be yearly. They add,

"*Father:* you have said that we were in your hand, and that by closing it you could crush us to nothing. Are you determined to crush us? If you are, tell us so; that those of our nation who have become your children, and have determined to die so, may know what to do. In this case, one chief has said, he would ask you to put him out of his pain. Another, who will not think of dying by the hand of his father, or his brother, has said he will retire to the Chataughque, eat of the fatal root, and sleep with his fathers in peace."

"All the land we have been speaking of belonged to the Six Nations. No part of it ever belonged to the king of England, and he could not give it to you."

"Hear us once more. At Fort Stanwix we agreed to deliver up those of our people who should do you any wrong, and that you might try them and punish them according to your law. We delivered up two men accordingly. But instead of trying them according to your law, the lowest of your people took them from your magistrate, and put them immediately to death. It is just to punish the murder with death; but the Senecas will not deliver up their people to men who disregard the treaties of their own nation."

There were many other grievances enumerated, and all in a strain which, we should think, would have drawn forth immediate relief. In his answer, President *Washington* said all, perhaps, which could be said in his situation; and his good feelings are manifest throughout: still there is something like evasion in answering some of their grievances, and an omission of notice to others. His answer, nevertheless, gave them much encouragement. He assured them that the lands obtained from them by fraud was not sanctioned by the government, and that the whole transaction was declared null and void; and that the persons who murdered their people should be dealt with as though they had murdered white men, and that all possible means would be used for their apprehension, and rewards should continue to be offered to effect it. But we have not learned that they were ever apprehended. The land conveyed by treaty, the president informed them, he had no authority to concern with, as that act was before his administration.

The above speech, although appearing to be a joint production, is believed to have been dictated by *Corn-planter*. It, however, was no doubt the sentiments of the whole nation, as well as those of himself, *Half-town* and *Big-tree*. Of this last-named chief we will here speak as follows:—In 1791, an act passed the legislature of Pennsylvania, "to empower the governor to grant a patent to *Big-tree*, a Seneca chief, for a certain island in the Alleghany River." He lamented the disaster of *St. Clair's* army, and was heard to say afterwards, *that he would have two scalps for General Butler's*, who fell and was scalped in that fight. *John Deckard*, another Seneca chief, repeated the same words. Being on a mission to Philadelphia, in April, 1792, he was taken sick at his lodgings, and died after about 20 hours' illness. Three days after, being Sunday, the 22d, he was buried with all requisite attention. The river *Big-tree* was probably named from the circumstance of this chief having lived upon it. His name still exists among some of his descendants, or others of his tribe, as we have seen it subscribed to several instruments within a few years. To return to *Corn-planter*.

His Indian name, as we have before noted, was *Gyantwaia;* and most of our knowledge concerning him is derived from himself, and is contained in a letter sent from him to the governor of Pennsylvania; and, although written by an interpreter, is believed to be the real production of *Corn-planter*. It was dated "Alleghany River, 2d mo. 2d, 1822," and is as follows:—

"I feel it my duty to send a speech to the governor of Pennsylvania at this time, and inform him the place where I was from—which was at Conewaugus,* on the Genesee River.

"When I was a child, I played with the butterfly, the grasshopper and the frogs; and as I grew up, I began to pay some attention and play with the Indian boys in the neighborhood, and they took notice of my skin being a different color from theirs, and spoke about it. I inquired of my mother the cause, and she told me that my father was a residenter in Albany.† I still

---

* This was the Iroquois term to designate a place of Christian Indians; hence many places bear it. It is the same as *Caughnewaga*.

† It is said (Amer. Reg. ii. 228) that he was an Irishman.

eat my victuals out of a bark dish. I grew up to be a young man, and married me a wife, and I had no kettle or gun. I then knew where my father lived, and went to see him, and found he was a white man, and spoke the English language. He gave me victuals whilst I was at his house, but when I started to return home, he gave me no provision to eat on the way. He gave me neither kettle nor gun, neither did he tell me that the United States were about to rebel against the government of England.

"I will now tell you, brothers, who are in session of the legislature of Pennsylvania, that the Great Spirit has made known to me that I have been wicked; and the cause thereof was the revolutionary war in America. The cause of Indians having been led into sin, at that time, was that many of them were in the practice of drinking and getting intoxicated. Great Britain requested us to join with them in the conflict against the Americans, and promised the Indians land and liquor. I myself was opposed to joining in the conflict, as I had nothing to do with the difficulty that existed between the two parties. I have now informed you how it happened that the Indians took a part in the revolution, and will relate to you some circumstances that occurred after the close of the war. General *Putnam*, who was then at Philadelphia, told me there was to be a council at Fort Stanwix; and the Indians requested me to attend on behalf of the Six Nations; which I did, and there met with three commissioners, who had been appointed to hold the council. They told me they would inform me of the cause of the revolution, which I requested them to do minutely. They then said that it had originated on account of the heavy taxes that had been imposed upon them by the British government, which had been for fifty years increasing upon them; that the Americans had grown weary thereof, and refused to pay, which affronted the king. There had likewise a difficulty taken place about some tea, which they wished me not to use, as it had been one of the causes that many people had lost their lives. And the British government now being affronted, the war commenced, and the cannons began to roar in our country. General *Putnam* then told me, at the council at Fort Stanwix, that, by the late war, the Americans had gained two objects: they had established themselves an independent nation, and had obtained some land to live upon: the division line of which, from Great Britain, run through the lakes. I then spoke, and said that I wanted some land for the Indians to live on, and General *Putnam* said that it should be granted, and I should have land in the state of New York for the Indians. General *Putnam* then encouraged me to use my endeavors to pacify the Indians generally; and, as he considered it an arduous task to perform, wished to know what I wanted for pay therefor. I replied to him, that I would use my endeavors to do as he had requested, with the Indians, and for pay thereof, I would take land. I told him not to pay me money or dry goods, but land. And for having attended thereto, I received the tract of land on which I now live, which was presented to me by Governor *Miflin*. I told General *Putnam* that I wished the Indians to have the exclusive privilege of the deer and wild game, which he assented to. I also wished the Indians to have the privilege of hunting in the woods, and making fires, which he likewise assented to.

"The treaty that was made at the aforementioned council, has been broken by some of the white people, which I now intend acquainting the governor with. Some white people are not willing that Indians should hunt any more, whilst others are satisfied therewith; and those white people who reside near our reservation, tell us that the woods are theirs, and they have obtained them from the governor. The treaty has been also broken by the white people using their endeavors to destroy all the wolves, which was not spoken about in the council at Fort Stanwix, by General *Putnam*, but has originated lately.

"It has been broken again, which is of recent origin. White people wish to get credit from Indians, and do not pay them honestly, according to their agreement. In another respect, it has also been broken by white people, who reside near my dwelling; for when I plant melons and vines in my field, they take them as their own. It has been broken again by white people using their endeavors to obtain our pine-trees from us. We have very few pine-trees on our land, in the state of New York; and white people and Indians often get into dispute respecting them. There is also a great quantity of whisky brought near our reservation by white people, and the Indians obtain it and become drunken. Another circumstance has taken place which is very trying to me, and I wish the interference of the governor.

"The white people, who live at Warren, called upon me, some time ago, to pay taxes for my land; which I objected to, as I had never been called upon for that purpose before; and having refused to pay, the white people became irritated, called upon me frequently, and at length brought four guns with them and seized our cattle. I still refused to pay, and was not willing to let the cattle go. After a time of dispute, they returned home, and I understood the militia was ordered out to enforce the collection of the tax. I went to Warren, and, to avert the impending difficulty, was obliged to give my note for the tax, the amount of which was 43 dollars and 79 cents. It is my desire that the governor will exempt me from paying taxes for my land to white people; and also cause that the money I am now obliged to pay, may be refunded to me, as I am very poor. The governor is the person who attends to the situation of the people, and I wish him to send a person to Alleghany, that I may inform him of the particulars of our situation, and he be authorized to instruct the white people in what manner to conduct themselves towards the Indians.

"The government has told us that when any difficulties arose between the Indians and white people, they would attend to having them removed. We are now in a trying situation, and I wish the governor to send a person authorized to attend thereto, the forepart of next summer, about the time that grass has grown big enough for pasture.

"The governor formerly requested me to pay attention to the Indians and take care of them. We are now arrived at a situation that I believe Indians cannot exist, unless the governor should comply with my request, and send a person authorized to treat between us and the white people, the approaching summer. I have now no more to speak."*

Whether the government of Pennsylvania acted at all, or, if at all, what order they took, upon this pathetic appeal, our author does not state. But that an independent tribe of Indians should be taxed by a neighboring people, is absurd in the extreme; and we hope we shall learn that not only the tax was remitted, but a remuneration granted for the vexation and damage.

Corn-plant was very early distinguished for his wisdom in council, notwithstanding he confirmed the treaty of Fort Stanwix of 1784; five years after, at the treaty of Fort Harmer, he gave up an immense tract of their country, and for which his nation very much reproached him, and even threatened his life. Himself and other chiefs committed this act for the best of reasons. The Six Nations having taken part with England in the revolution, when the king's power fell in America, the Indian nations were reduced to the miserable alternative of giving up so much of their country as the Americans required, or the *whole* of it. In 1790, *Corn-plant*, *Half-town* and *Big-tree*, made a most pathetic appeal to congress for an amelioration of their condition, and a reconsideration of former treaties, in which the following memorable passage occurs:—

"*Father:* we will not conceal from you that the great God, and not men, has preserved the *Corn-plant* from the hands of his own nation. For they ask continually, "Where is the land on which our children, and their children after them, are to lie down upon? You told us that the line drawn from Pennsylvania to Lake Ontario, would mark it forever on the east, and the line running from Beaver Creek to Pennsylvania, would mark it on the west, and we see that it is not so; for, first one, and then another, come and take it away by order of that people which you tell us promised to secure it to us.' He is silent, for he has nothing to answer. When the sun goes down, he opens his heart before God, and earlier than the sun appears, again upon the hills he gives thanks for his protection during the night.

* *Buchanan's* Sketches.

For he feels that among men become desperate by the injuries they sustain, it is God only that can preserve him. He loves peace, and all he had in store he has given to those who have been robbed by your people, lest they should plunder the innocent to repay themselves. The whole season, which others have employed in providing for their families, he has spent in endeavors to preserve peace; and this moment his wife and children are lying on the ground, and in want of food."

In President *Washington's* answer, we are gratified by his particular notice of this chief. He says, "The merits of the *Corn-plant*, and his friendship for the United States, are well known to me, and shall not be forgotten; and, as a mark of esteem of the United States, I have directed the secretary of war to make him a present of *two hundred and fifty dollars*, either in money or goods, as the *Corn-plant* shall like best."

There was, in 1789, a treaty held at Marietta, between the Indians and Americans, which terminated "to the entire satisfaction of all concerned. On this occasion, an elegant entertainment was provided. The Indian chiefs behaved with the greatest decorum throughout the day. After dinner, we were served with good wine, and *Corn-planter*, one of the first chiefs of the Five Nations, and a very great warrior, took up his glass and said, '*I thank the Great Spirit for this opportunity of smoking the pipe of friendship and love. May we plant our own vines—be the fathers of our own children—and maintain them.*'"*

In 1790, an act passed the legislature of Pennsylvania, for "granting 800 dollars to *Corn-planter*, *Half-town* and *Big-tree*, in trust for the Seneca nation, and other purposes therein mentioned." In February, 1791, *Corn-plant* was in Philadelphia, and was employed in an extremely hazardous expedition to undertake the pacification of the western tribes, that had already shown themselves hostile. The mission terminated unfavorably, from insurmountable difficulties.† There were many, at this time, as in all Indian wars, who entertained doubts of the fidelity of such Indians as pretended friendship. *Corn-plant* did not escape suspicion; but, as his after-conduct showed, it was entirely without foundation. In the midst of these imputations, a letter written at Fort Franklin says, "I have only to observe that the *Corn-plant* has been here, and, in my opinion, he is as friendly as one of our own people. He has advised me to take care; '*for*,' said he, '*you will soon have a chance to let the world know whether you are a soldier or not.*' When he went off, he ordered two chiefs and ten warriors to remain here, and scout about the garrison, and let me know if the bad Indians should either advance against me, or any of the frontiers of the United States. He thinks the people at Pittsburgh should keep out spies towards the salt licks, for he says, by and by, he thinks, the bad Indians will come from that way."

In 1792, the following advertisement appeared, signed by *Corn-plant*: "My people having been charged with committing depredations on the frontier inhabitants near Pittsburgh, I hereby contradict the assertion, as it is certainly without foundation, and pledge myself to those inhabitants, that they may rest perfectly secure from any danger from the Senecas residing on the Alleghany waters, and that my people have been and still are friendly to the U. States."

About the time *Corn-plant* left his nation to proceed on his mission to the hostile tribes, as three of his people were travelling through a settlement upon the Genesee, they stopped at a house to light their pipes. There happened to be several men within, one of whom, as the foremost Indian stooped down to light his pipe, killed him with an axe. One of the others was badly wounded with the same weapon, while escaping from the house. They were not pursued, and the other, a boy, escaped unhurt. (The poor wounded man, when nearly well of the wound, was bitten by a snake, which caused his immediate death.) When *Corn-plant* knew what had happened, he charged his warriors to remain quiet, and not to seek revenge, and was

* *Carey's* Museum, v. 415.

† "Causes of the existing Hostilities," &c. drawn up by the sec'y of war, General *Knox*, in 1791

heard only to say, "*It is hard, when I and my people are trying to make peace for the whites, that we should receive such reward. I can govern my young men and warriors better than the thirteen fires can theirs.*" How is it that this man should practise upon the maxims of *Confucius*, of whom he never heard? (*Do ye to others as ye would that they should do unto you*;) and the monster in human form, in a gospel land, taught them from his youth, should show, by his actions, his utter contempt of them, and even of the divine mandate?

In 1816, the Reverend *Timothy Alden*, then president of Alleghany college, in Meadville, Pennsylvania, visited the Seneca nation. At this time, *Corn-plant* lived seven miles below the junction of the Connewango with the Alleghany, upon the banks of the latter, "on a piece of first-rate bottom land, a little within the limits of Pennsylvania." Here was his village,* which exhibited signs of industrious inhabitants. He then owned 1300 acres of land, 600 of which comprehended his town. "It was grateful to notice," observes Mr. *Alden*, "the present agricultural habits of the place, from the numerous enclosures of buck-wheat, corn and oats. We also saw a number of oxen, cows and horses; and many logs designed for the saw-mill and the Pittsburgh market." *Corn-plant* had, for some time, been very much in favor of the Christian religion, and hailed with joy such as professed it. When he was apprized of Mr. *Alden's* arrival, he hastened to welcome him to his village, and wait upon him. And notwithstanding his high station as a chief, having many men under his command, he chose rather, "in the ancient patriarchal style," to serve his visitors himself; he, therefore, took care of their horses, and went into the field, cut and brought oats for them.

The Western Missionary Society had, in 1815, at *Corn-plant's* "urgent request," established a school at his village, which, at this time, promised success.

Corn-plant received an annual annuity from the U. States of 250 dollars, besides his proportion of 9000 divided equally among every member of the nation.

Gos-kuk-ke-wa-na-kon-ne-di-yu, commonly called the *Prophet*, was brother to *Corn-plant*, and resided in his village. He was of little note, and died previous to 1816.† *Corn-plant*, we believe, was, when living, like all other unenlightened people, very superstitious. Not long since, he said the Good Spirit had told him not to have any thing to do with the whites, or even to preserve any mementoes or relics they had from time to time given him; whereupon, among other things, he burnt up his belt and broke his elegant sword. He often mentions his having been at *Braddock's* defeat. *Henry Obeale*, his son, he sent to be educated among the whites. He became a drunkard on returning to his home, and is now discarded by his father. *Corn-plant* has other sons; but he says no more of them shall be educated among the whites, for he says, "*It entirely spoil Indian.*" And although he countenances Christianity, he does not do it, it is thought, from a belief of it, but probably from the same motives as too many whites do.‡

The following story, *M. Bayard* says,§ was told him by *Corn-planter*. We have often heard a similar one, and as often a new origin; but never before that it originated with *William Penn*. However, as our author observes, as we have more respect for truth than great names, we will relate it. *Penn* proposed to the Indians to sell him as much land as he could encompass with the hide of a bullock. They, supposing he meant only what ground would be covered by it, when it was spread out, and looking upon what was offered as a good price, consented to the proposition. *Penn*, like *Didon*, cut the skin into a line of immense length, to the astonishment of the venders, who, in silent indignation, religiously observed their contract. The quantity of land encompassed by the line is not mentioned; but, more or less, the Indians had passed their word, and they scorned to break it, even

* Formerly called *Obaletown*. See Pa. Gaz. 1792, and *Stanbury's* Jour.

† Amer. Register for 1816, vol ii. 226, &c.

‡ Verbal account of *E. T. Foote*, Esq. of Chatauque co. N. Y. who possesses much valuable information upon matters of this kind.

§ *Voyage dans l'Intérieur des Etats-Unis*, et cet. ps. 206. 207

though they would have been justified by the discovery of the fraud. We do not vouch for the truth of this matter, nor do we believe *William Penn* ever practised a trick of the kind. No doubt some person did; and perhaps *Corn-planter* had been told that it was *Penn*.

We have now to record the death of the venerable *Corn-plant*. He died at his residence on the Seneca reservation, on the 7th of March last, 1836 aged upwards of 100 years.

Teaslaegee, or *Charles Corn-planter*, was a party to the treaty of Moscow, N. Y. in 1823. He was probably a son of *Koeentwahk*, or *Gyantwaia*.

CHAPTER VII.

TECUMSEH—*His great exertions to prevent the whites from overrunning his country—His expedition on Hacker's Creek—Coöperation of his brother, the Prophet—Rise of the difficulties between Tecumseh and Governor* Harrison—*Speech of the former in a council at Vincennes—Fearful occurrence in that council*—WINNEMAK—*Tecumseh visited by Governor Harrison at his camp—Determination of war the result of the interview on both sides—Characteristic anecdote of the chief—Determines, in the event of war, to prevent barbarities—Battle of Tippecanoe—Battle of the Thames, and death of Tecumseh—Description of his person—Important events in his life*—PUKEESHENO, *father of Tecumseh—His death—Battle of Magaugo—Specimen of the Shawanee language—Particular account of* ELLSKWATAWA, *or the* PROPHET—*Account of* ROUND-HEAD—*Capture and massacre of General Winchester's army at the River Raisin*—MYEERAH, *or the* CRANE, *commonly called* WALK-IN-THE-WATER—TEYONINHOKERAWEN, *or* JOHN NORTON—LOGAN *the Shawanee*—BLACK-BIRD—*Massacre at Chicago*—WAWNAHTON—BLACK-THUNDER—ONGPATONGA, *or* BIG-ELK—PETALESHARO—METEA.

TECUMSEH, by birth a Shawanee, and brigadier-general in the army of Great Britain, in the war of 1812, was born about 1770, and, like his great prototype, *Pometacom*, the Wampanoag, seems always to have made his aversion to civilization appear a prominent trait in his character; and it is not presumed that he joined the British army, and received the red sash and other badges of office, because he was fond of imitating the whites; but he employed them, more probably, as a means of inspiring his countrymen with that respect and veneration for himself which was so necessary in the work of expulsion, which he had undertaken.

The first exploit in which we find *Tecumseh* engaged was upon a branch of Hacker's Creek, in May, 1792. With a small band of warriors, he came upon the family of *John Waggoner*, about dusk. They found *Waggoner* a short distance from his house, sitting upon a log, resting himself after the fatigues of the day. *Tecumseh* directed his men to capture the family, while himself was engaged with *Waggoner*. To make sure work, he took deliberate aim at him with his rifle; but fortunately he did not even wound him, though the ball passed next to his skin. *Waggoner* threw himself off the log, and ran with all his might, and *Tecumseh* followed. Having the advantage of an accurate knowledge of the ground, *Waggoner* made good his escape. Meanwhile his men succeeded in carrying off the family, some of whom they barbarously murdered. Among these were Mrs. *Waggoner* and two of her children. Several of the children remained a long time with the Indians.

This persevering and extraordinary man had made himself noted and conspicuous in the war which terminated by the treaty of Greenville, in 1795. He was brother to that famous impostor well known by the name of the *Prophet*, and seems to have joined in his views just in season to prevent his falling into entire disrepute among his own followers. His principal place of rendezvous was near the confluence of the Tippecanoe with the Wabash, upon the north bank of the latter. This tract of country was none of his, but had been possessed by his brother the *Prophet*, in 1808, with a motley band of about 1000 young warriors from among the Shawanese, Delawares, Wyandots, Potowatomies, Ottowas, Kikkapoos and Chippeways. The

Miamies were very much opposed to this intrusion into their country, but were not powerful enough to repel it, and many of their chiefs were put to death in the most barbarous manner, for remonstrating against their conduct. The maladministration of the *Prophet*, however, in a short time, very much reduced his numbers, so that, in about a year, his followers consisted of but about 300, and these in the most miserable state of existence. Their habits had been such as to bring famine upon them; and but for the provisions furnished by General *Harrison*, from Vincennes, starvation would doubtless have ensued.* At this juncture, *Tecumseh* made his appearance among them; and although in the character of a subordinate chief, yet it was known that he directed every thing afterwards, although in the name of the *Prophet*. His exertions now became immense to engage every tribe upon the continent in a confederacy, with the open and avowed object of arresting the progress of the whites.

Agreeably to the direction of the government, Governor *Harrison* purchased of the Delawares, Miamies, and Pottowatomies, a large tract of country on both sides of the Wabash, and extending up the river 60 miles above Vincennes. This was in 1809, about a year after the *Prophet* settled with his colony upon the Wabash, as before stated. *Tecumseh* was absent at this time, and his brother, the *Prophet*, was not considered as having any claim to the country, being there without the consent of the Miamies. *Tecumseh* did not view it in this light, and at his return was exceedingly vexed with those chiefs who had made the conveyance; many of whom, it is asserted, he threatened with death. *Tecumseh's* displeasure and dissatisfaction reached Governor *Harrison*, who despatched a messenger to him, to state "that any claims he might have to the lands which had been ceded, were not affected by the treaty; that he might come to Vincennes and exhibit his pretensions, and if they were found to be solid, that the land would either be given up, or an ample compensation made for it."† This, it must be confessed, was not in a strain calculated to soothe a mighty mind, when once justly irritated, as was that of *Tecumseh*. However, upon the 12 August, 1810, (a day which cannot fail to remind the reader of the fate of his great archetype, *Philip, of Pokanoket*,) he met the governor in council at Vincennes, with many of his warriors; at which time he spoke to him as follows:—

"It is true I am a Shawanee. My forefathers were warriors. Their son is a warrior. From them I only take my existence; from my tribe I take nothing. I am the maker of my own fortune; and oh! that I could make that of my red people, and of my country, as great as the conceptions of my mind, when I think of the Spirit that rules the universe. I would not then come to Governor *Harrison*, to ask him to tear the treaty, and to obliterate the landmark; but I would say to him, Sir, you have liberty to return to your own country. The being within, communing with past ages, tells me, that once, nor until lately, there was no white man on this continent. That it then all belonged to red men, children of the same parents, placed on it by the Great Spirit that made them, to keep it, to traverse it, to enjoy its productions, and to fill it with the same race. Once a happy race. Since made miserable by the white people, who are never contented, but always encroaching. The way, and the only way to check and to stop this evil, is, for all the red men to unite in claiming a common and equal right in the land, as it was at first, and should be yet; for it never was divided, but belongs to all, for the use of each. That no part has a right to sell, even to each other, much less to strangers; those who want all, and will not do with less. The white people have no right to take the land from the Indians, because they had it first; it is theirs. They may sell, but all must join. Any sale not made by all is not valid. The late sale is bad. It was made by a part only. Part do not know how to sell. It requires all to make a bargain for all. All red men have equal rights to the unoccupied land. The right of occupancy is as good in one place as in another. There cannot be two occupations in the same place. The first excludes all others. It is not so in hunting or travelling; for there the same ground will serve many, as they may follow each

* Memoirs of *Harrison*.

† *M'Afee*

other all day; but the camp is stationary, and that is occupancy. It belongs to the first who sits down on his blanket or skins, which he has thrown upon the ground, and till he leaves it no other has a right."*

How near this is to the original is unknown to us, but it appears too much Americanized to correspond with our notions of *Tecumseh;* nevertheless it may give the true meaning. One important paragraph ought to be added, which we do not find in the author from which we have extracted the above; which was, "that the Americans had driven them from the sea-coasts, and that they would shortly push them into the lakes, and that they were determined to make a stand where they were." † This language forcibly reminds us of what the ancient Britons said of their enemies, when they besought aid of the Romans. "The barbarians (said they) drive us to the sea, and the sea beats us back upon them; between these extremes we are exposed, either to be slain with the sword, or drowned in the waves." ‡

Tecumseh, having thus explained his reasons against the validity of the purchase, took his seat amidst his warriors. Governor *Harrison*, in his reply, said, "that the white people, when they arrived upon this continent, had found the Miamies in the occupation of all the country on the Wabash, and at that time the Shawanese were residents of Georgia, from which they were driven by the Creeks. That the lands had been purchased from the Miamies, who were the true and original owners of it. That it was ridiculous to assert that all the Indians were one nation; for if such had been the intention of the Great Spirit, he would not have put six different tongues into their heads, but have taught them all to speak a language that all could understand. That the Miamies found it for their interest to sell a part of their lands, and receive for them a further annuity, the benefit of which they had long experienced, from the punctuality with which the seventeen fires [the seventeen United States] complied with their engagements; and that the Shawanese had no right to come from a distant country and control the Miamies in the disposal of their own property." The governor then took his seat, and the interpreter proceeded to explain to *Tecumseh* what he had said, who, when he had nearly finished, suddenly interrupted him, and exclaimed, "*It is all false;*" at the same time giving to his warriors a signal, they seized their war clubs, and sprung upon their feet, from the green grass on which they had been sitting. The governor now thought himself in imminent danger, and, freeing himself from his arm-chair, drew his sword, and prepared to defend himself. He was attended by some officers of his government, and many citizens, more numerous than the Indians, but all unarmed; most of whom, however, seized upon some weapon, such as stones and clubs. *Tecumseh* continued to make gestures and speak with great emotion; and a guard of 12 armed men stationed by the governor in the rear were ordered up. For a few minutes, it was expected blood would be shed. Major *G. R. Floyde*, who stood near the governor, drew his dirk, and *Winnemak* cocked his pistol, which he had ready primed; he said *Tecumseh* had threatened his life for having signed the treaty and sale of the disputed land. A Mr. *Winas*, the Methodist minister, ran to the governor's house, and, taking a gun, stood in the door to defend the family.

On being informed what *Tecumseh* had said, the governor replied to him, that "he was a bad man—that he would have no further talk with him—that he must return to his camp, and set out for his home immediately." Thus ended the conference. *Tecumseh* did not leave the neighborhood, but, the next morning, having reflected upon the impropriety of his conduct, sent to the governor to have the council renewed, and apologized for the affront offered; to which the governor, after some time, consented, having taken the precaution to have two additional companies of armed men in readiness, in case of insult.

Having met a second time, *Tecumseh* was asked whether he had any other grounds, than those he had stated, by which he could lay claim to the land in question; to which he replied, "No other." Here, then, was an end of all argument. The indignant soul of *Tecumseh* could not but be enraged at

* Hist. Kentucky. † Mem. *Harrison.* ‡ *Seller's* England.

the idea of an "equivalent for a country," or, what meant the same thing, a *compensation* for land, which, often repeated, as it had been, would soon *amount to a country!* "The behavior of *Tecumseh*, at this interview, was very different from what it had been the day before. His deportment was dignified and collected, and he showed not the least disposition to be insolent. He denied having any intention of attacking the governor, but said he had been advised by white men"* to do as he had done; that two white men had visited him at his place of residence, and told him that half the white people were opposed to Governor *Harrison*, and willing to relinquish the land, and told him to advise the tribes not to receive pay for it; for that the governor would be soon put out of office, and a "good man" sent in his place, who would give up the land to the Indians. The governor asked him whether he would prevent the survey of the land: he replied that he was determined to adhere to the *old boundary*. Then arose a Wyandot, a Kikkapoo, a Pottowattomie, an Ottowas, and a Winnebago chief, each declaring his determination to stand by *Tecumseh*, whom they had chosen their chief. After the governor had informed *Tecumseh* that his words should be truly reported to the president, alleging, at the same time, that he knew the land would not be relinquished, and that it would be maintained by the sword, the council closed.

The governor wished yet to prolong the interview, and thought that, possibly, *Tecumseh* might appear more submissive, should he meet him in his own tent. Accordingly he took with him an interpreter, and visited the chief in his camp the next day. The governor was received with kindness and attention, and *Tecumseh* conversed with him a considerable time. On being asked by the governor if his determination really was as he had expressed himself in the council, he said, "Yes;" and added, "that it was with great reluctance he would make war with the United States—against whom he had no other complaint, but their purchasing the Indians' land; that he was extremely anxious to be their friend, and if he (the governor) would prevail upon the president to give up the lands lately purchased, and agree never to make another treaty, without the consent of all the tribes, he would be their faithful ally, and assist them in all their wars with the English," whom he knew were always treating the Indians like dogs, clapping their hands and hallooing *stu-boy;* that he would much rather join the seventeen fires; but if they would not give up said lands, and comply with his request in other respects, he would join the English. When the governor told him there was no probability that the president would comply, he said, "Well, as the great chief is to determine the matter, I hope the Great Spirit will put sense enough into his head, to induce him to direct you to give up this land. It is true, he is so far off he will not be injured by the war. He may sit still in his town, and drink his wine, whilst you and I will have to fight it out." He had said before, when asked if it were his determination to make war unless his terms were complied with, "*It is my determination; nor will I give rest to my feet, until I have united all the red men in the like resolution.*"

Thus is exhibited the determined character of *Tecumseh*, in which no duplicity appears, and whose resentment might have been expected, when questioned, again and again, upon the same subject. Most religiously did he prosecute this plan; and could his extraordinary and wonderful exertions be known, no fiction, it is believed, could scarcely surpass the reality. The tribes to the west of the Mississippi, and those about Lakes Superior and Huron, were visited and revisited by him previous to the year 1811. He had raised in these tribes the high expectation that they should be able to drive the Americans to the east of the Ohio. The famous *Blue-jacket* was as sanguine as *Tecumseh*, and was his abettor in uniting distant tribes.

The following characteristic circumstance occurred at one of the meetings at Vincennes. After *Tecumseh* had made a speech to Governor *Harrison*, and was about to seat himself in a chair, he observed that none had been placed for him. One was immediately ordered by the governor, and, as the interpreter handed it to him, he said, "Your father requests you to take

* Memoirs of *Harrison*.

a chair." "*My father?*" says *Tecumseh*, with great indignity of expression, "*the sun is my father, and the earth is my mother; and on her bosom I will repose;*" and immediately seated himself, in the Indian manner, upon the ground.*

The fight at Tippecanoe followed soon after. This affair took place in the night of Nov. 6, 1811, in which 62 Americans were killed, and 126 wounded. *Tecumseh* was not in this fight, but his brother, the *Prophet*, conducted or ordered the attack. During the action, he was performing conjurations on an eminence not far off, but out of danger. His men displayed great bravery, and the fight was long and bloody. *Harrison* lost some of his bravest officers. The late Colonel *Snelling*, of Boston, then a captain, was in this fight, and took prisoner with his own hands an Indian chief, the only Indian taken by the Americans. The name of the captured chief we do not learn, but from his fear of being taken for a Shawanee, it is evident he was not of that tribe. When he was seized by Capt. *Snelling*, he ejaculated, with hurried accents, "*Good man, me no Shawanee.*" † The chiefs *White-lion* (*Wapamangwa*,) *Stone-eater* (*Sanamahhonga*,) and *Winnemak*, were conspicuous at this time. The latter had been the pretended friend of the governor, but now appeared his enemy. He was killed the next year by the lamented *Logan*.

Just before hostilities commenced, in a talk Governor *Harrison* had with *Tecumseh*, the former expressed a wish, if war must follow, that cruelty to prisoners should not be allowed on either side. *Tecumseh* assured him that he would do all in his power to prevent it; and it is believed he strictly adhered to this resolution. Indeed, we have one example, which has never been called in question, and is worthy the great mind of this chief. When Colonel *Dudley* was cut off, and near 400 of his men, not far from Fort Meigs, by falling into an ambush, *Tecumseh* arrived at the scene of action when the Americans could resist no longer. He exerted himself to put a stop to the massacre of the soldiers, which was then going on; and meeting with a Chippeway chief who would not desist by persuasion nor threats, he buried his tomahawk in his head. ‡

It is said that *Tecumseh* had been in almost every important battle with the Americans, from the destruction of General *Harmer's* army till his death upon the Thames. He was under the direction of General *Proctor*, in this last great act of his life, but was greatly dissatisfied with his course of proceedings, and is said to have remonstrated against retreating before the Americans in very pointed terms. *Perry's* victory had just given the Americans the command of Lake Erie; and immediately after, *Proctor* abandoned Detroit, and marched his majesty's army up the River Thames, accompanied by General *Tecumseh*, with about 1500 warriors. *Harrison* overtook them near the Moravian town, Oct. 5, 1813, and, after a bloody battle with the Indians, routed and took prisoners nearly the whole British army; *Proctor* saving himself only by flight. After withstanding almost the whole force of the Americans for some time, *Tecumseh* received a severe wound in the arm, but continued to fight with desperation, until a shot in the head from an unknown hand laid him prostrate in the thickest of the fight. § Of his warriors 120 were left upon the field of battle.

Thus fell *Tecumseh*, in the forty-fourth year of his age. He was about five feet ten inches in height, of a noble appearance, and a perfectly symmetrical form. "His carriage was erect and lofty—his motions quick—his eyes penetrating—his visage stern, with an air of *hauteur* in his countenance, which arose from an elevated pride of soul. It did not leave him even in death." He is thus spoken of by one who knew him.

At the battle of the Thames, a chief by the name of *Shane* served as a guide to Colonel *Johnson's* regiment. He informs us that he knew *Tecumseh* well, and that he once had had his thigh broken, which not being properly set, caused a considerable ridge in it always after. This was published in a Kentucky newspaper, lately, as necessary to prove that the Indian killed by

---

* *Schoolcraft.* † Information of his son, *W. J. Snelling*, Esq. of Boston.

‡ *James*, i. 291—*Perkins*, 221.

§ The story that he fell in a personal rencounter with Colonel *Johnson*, must no longer be believed. Facts are entirely opposed to such a conclusion. Indeed, we cannot learn that the colonel ever *claimed* the *honor* of the achievement.

Colonel *Johnson* was *Tecumseh.* From the same paper it would seem, that, even on the day of battle, it was doubted by some whether the chief killed were *Tecumseh,* and that a critical inquest was held over his body; and although it was decided to be he, yet to the fact that the colonel killed him, there was a demur, even then. But, no doubt, many were willing it should so pass, thinking it a matter of not much consequence, so long as *Tecumseh,* their most dreaded enemy, was actually slain; and, perhaps, too, so near the event, many felt a delicacy in dissenting from the report of Colonel *Johnson's* friends; but when time had dispelled such jealousy, those came out frankly with their opinion, and hence resulted the actual truth of the case.

That the American soldiers should have dishonored themselves, after their victory, by outraging all decency by acts of astonishing ferocity and barbarity upon the lifeless body of the fallen chief, is grievous to mention, and cannot meet with too severe condemnation. Pieces of his skin were taken away by some of them as mementoes! * He is said to have borne a personal enmity to General *Harrison,* at this time, for having just before destroyed his family. The celebrated speech, said to have been delivered by the great "Shawanese warrior" to General *Proctor,* before the battle of the Thames, is believed by many not to be genuine. It may be seen in every history of the war, and every periodical of that day, and not a few since, even to this. Therefore we omit it here. The speech of *Logan,* perhaps, has not circulated wider. Another, in our opinion, more worthy the mighty mind of *Tecumseh,* published in a work said to be written by one who heard it,† is now generally (on the authority of a public journal ‡) discarded as a fiction.

Among the skirmishes between the belligerents, before General *Hull* surrendered the north-western army, *Tecumseh* and his Indians acted a conspicuous part.

Malden, situated at the junction of Detroit River with Lake Erie, was considered the Gibraltar of Canada, and it was expected that General *Hull's* first object would be to possess himself of it. In a movement that way, Colonel *M'Arthur* came very near being cut off by a party of Indians led by *Tecumseh.* About 4 miles from Malden, he found a bridge in possession of a body of the enemy; and although the bridge was carried by a force under Colonel *Cass,*§ in effecting which, 11 of the enemy were killed, yet it seems, that in a "few days afterwards" they were in possession of it again, and again the Americans stood ready to repeat the attack. It was in an attempt to reconnoitre, that Colonel *M'Arthur* "advanced somewhat too near the enemy, and narrowly escaped being cut off from his men" ‖ by several Indians who had nearly prevented his retreat.

Major *Vanhorn* was detached on the 4 August from Aux Canards, with 200 men, to convoy 150 Ohio militia and some provisions from the River Raisin. In his second day's march, near Brownstown, he fell into an ambush of 70 Indians under *Tecumseh,* who, firing upon him, killed 20 men; among whom were Captains *M'Culloch,*¶ *Bostler, Gilcrease,*** and *Ubry:* 9 more were wounded. The rest made a precipitate retreat.

Major *Vanhorn* having failed in his attempt, Colonel *Miller* was sent on the 8th of August, with 600 men to protect the same provisions and transports. The next day, August 9th, about 4 o'clock in the afternoon, the van-guard, commanded by Captain *Snelling,* was fired upon by an extensive line of British and Indians, at the lower end of the village of Magaugo, 14 miles from Detroit. The main body was half a mile in the rear when the attack began. Captain *Snelling* maintained his position in a most gallant manner, under a heavy fire, until the line was formed and advanced to his relief. The force against which the Americans were now contending was made up

---

* We have often heard it said, but whether in truth we do not aver, that there are those who still own razor straps made of it.

† *John Dunn Hunter.* ‡ North American Review.

§ Since governor of Michigan, and now secretary of war.

‖ Brackenridge, Hist. War, 31.

¶ In this officer's pocket, it is said, was found a letter written for his wife, giving an account of his having killed an Indian, from whose head he tore the scalp with his teeth

** *Gilchrist,* commonly written.

of a body of 500 Indians under *Tecumseh*, *Walk-in-the-water*, *Marpot*, and the since famous *Black-hawk*, and a considerable number of whites under Major *Muir*. They were formed behind a breastwork of felled trees. When Colonel *Miller* had brought his men into line, the enemy sprang from their hiding-places, and formed in line of battle, and a fierce and appalling strife ensued. The British and Indian force was one third greater than the American, but nothing could withstand them, when led on by such officers as *Miller* and *Snelling*, and the ground was disputed inch by inch for near two miles, to the village of Brownstown. Here the British took to their boats, and the Indians to the woods, and thus the battle closed. It was owing to a disobedience of orders on the part of the cavalry, that the British escaped entire destruction; for Colonel *Miller* ordered them to rush upon them and cut them up when their guns were unloaded, and their ranks were in confusion, but they would not, although Captain *Snelling* offered to lead them in person. In this affair the Indians and British lost 100 killed and 200 wounded, and the Americans had 18 killed and 58 wounded.*

A British writer upon the late war,† after having related the battle of the Thames, in which *Tecumseh* fell, says: "It seems extraordinary that General *Harrison* should have omitted to mention, in his letter, the death of a chief, whose fall contributed so largely to break down the Indian spirit, and to give peace and security to the whole north-western frontier of the U. States. *Tecumseh*, although he had received a musket-ball in the left arm, was still seeking the hottest of the fire," when he received the mortal wound in the head, of which he in a few moments expired. The error, which for some time prevailed, of his being shot by Colonel *Johnson*, is copied into this author's work. The following descriptions, though in some respects erroneous, are of sufficient value to be preserved.

Tecumseh was endowed "with more than the usual stoutness, possessed all the agility and perseverance, of the Indian character. His carriage was dignified; his eye penetrating; his countenance, which, even in death, betrayed the indications of a lofty spirit, rather of the sterner cast. Had he not possessed a certain austerity of manners, he could never have controlled the wayward passions of those who followed him to battle. He was of a silent habit; but, when his eloquence became roused into action by the reiterated encroachments of the Americans,‡ his strong intellect could supply him with a flow of oratory, that enabled him, as he governed in the field, so to prescribe in the council. Those who consider that, in all territorial questions, the ablest diplomatists of the U. States are sent to negotiate with the Indians, will readily appreciate the loss sustained by the latter in the death of their champion. The Indians, in general, are full as fond as other savages of the gaudy decoration of their persons; but *Tecumseh* was an exception. Clothes and other valuable articles of spoil had often been his; yet he invariably wore a deerskin coat and pantaloons. He had frequently levied subsidies to, comparatively, a large amount; yet he preserved little or nothing for himself. It was not wealth, but glory, that was *Tecumseh's* ruling passion. Fatal day! when the 'Christian people' first penetrated the forests, to teach the arts of 'civilization' to the poor Indian. Till then water had been his only beverage, and himself and his race possessed all the vigor of hardy savages. Now, no Indian opens his lips to the stream that ripples by his wigwam, while he has a rag of clothes on his back, wherewith to purchase rum; and he and his squaw and his children wallow through the day, in beastly drunkenness. Instead of the sturdy warrior, with a head to plan, and an arm to execute vengeance upon the oppressors of his country, we behold the puny, besotted wretch, squatting on his hams, ready to barter his country, his children, or himself, for a few gulps of that deleterious compound, which, far more than the arms of the United States, [Great Britain and France,] is hastening to extinguish all traces of his name and character. *Tecumseh*, himself, in early life, had been addicted to intemperance; but no sooner did his judgment

* *Sketches of the War*, i. 22. † *James*, i. 287, &c.

‡ As though the English of Canada had never been guilty of encroachments!

decide against, than his resolution enabled him to quit, so vile a habit Beyond one or two glasses of wine, he never afterwards indulged."

It was said not to be from good will to the Americans, that he would not permit his warriors to exercise any cruelty upon them, when fallen into their power, but from principle alone. When Detroit was taken by the British and Indians, *Tecumseh* was in the action at the head of the latter. After the surrender, General *Brock* requested him not to allow his Indians to ill-treat the prisoners; to which he replied, "*No! I despise them too much to meddle with them.*"

Some of the English have said that there were few officers in the U. States' service so able to command in the field as *Tecumseh*. This it will not us behove to question; but it would better have become such speech-makers, if they had added, "in his peculiar mode of warfare." That he was a more wily chief than *Mishikinakwa*, may be doubted; that either had natural abilities inferior to those of General *Wayne*, or General *Brock*, we see no reason to believe. But this is no argument that they could practise European warfare as well as those generals. It is obvious, from his intercourse with the whites, that *Tecumseh* must have been better skilled in their military tactics than most, if not all, of his countrymen, whether predecessors or contemporaries.

A military man,* as we apprehend, says, "He [*Tecumseh*] was an excellent judge of position, and not only knew, but could point out the localities of the whole country through which he had passed." "His facility of communicating the information he had acquired, was thus displayed before a concourse of spectators. Previously to General *Brock's* crossing over to Detroit, he asked *Tecumseh* what sort of a country he should have to pass through in case of his proceeding farther. *Tecumseh*, taking a roll of elm-bark, and extending it on the ground by means of four stones, drew forth his scalping-knife, and with the point presently etched upon the bark a plan of the country, its hills, woods, rivers, morasses, and roads; a plan which, if not as neat, was, for the purpose required, fully as intelligible as if *Arrowsmith* himself had prepared it. Pleased with this unexpected talent in *Tecumseh*, also with his having, by his characteristic boldness, induced the Indians, not of his immediate party, to cross the Detroit, prior to the embarkation of the regulars and militia, General *Brock*, as soon as the business was over, publicly took off his sash, and placed it round the body of the chief. *Tecumseh* received the honor with evident gratification, but was, the next day, seen without his sash. General *Brock*, fearing something had displeased the Indian, sent his interpreter for an explanation. The latter soon returned with an account that *Tecumseh*, not wishing to wear such a mark of distinction, when an older, and, as he said, abler, warrior than himself was present, had transferred the sash to the Wyandot chief *Round-head*."

The place of this renowned warrior's birth was upon the banks of the Scioto River, near what is now Chillicothe. His father's name was *Pukeesheno*, which means, *I light from flying*. He was killed in the battle of Kanhawa, in 1774. His mother's name was *Meetheetashe*, which signifies, *a turtle laying her eggs in the sand*. She died among the Cherokees. She had, at one birth, three sons:—*Ellskwatawa*, which signifies, *a door opened*, was called the *Prophet*; *Tecumseh*, which is, *a tiger crouching for his prey*; and *Kumskaka*, *a tiger that flies in the air*. †

We will here present the reader with a specimen of the Shawanee language, in the *Lord's Prayer*.

Coe-thin-a, spim-i-key yea-taw-yan-oe, o-wes-sa-yeg yey-sey-tho-yan-ae: Day-pale-i-tum-any-pay-itch tha-key, yea-issi-tay-hay-yon-ae issi-nock-i-key, yoe-ma assis-key-kie pi-sey spim-i-key. Me-li-na-key oe noo-ki cos-si-kie ta-wa-it-thin oe yea-wap-a-ki tuck-whan-a; puck-i-tum-i-wa-loo kne-won-ot-i-they-way. Yea-se-puck-i-tum-a ma-chil-i-tow-e-ta thick-i ma-chaw-ki tus-sy-neigh-puck-sin-a wa-wun-si-loo wau po won-ot-i-they ya key-la tay pale-i-tum-any way wis-sa kia was-si-cut-i-we-way thay-pay-we-way.‡

---

* Mr James, *ut supra*. † *Schoolcraft*. ‡ Carey's Museum, vi 318, (for 1789.)

In 1826, the only surviving son of *Tecumseh*, whose name is *Puchethei*, which signifies *crouching or watching his prey*, left the Ohio to settle beyond the Mississippi.* This son, when his father was slain, was fighting by his side. "The prince regent," says Mr. *James*, "in 1814, out of respect to the memory to the old, sent out as a present to the young *Tecumseh* a handsome sword;" and then closes this paragraph with this most savage lamentation: "Unfortunately, however, for the Indian cause and country, faint are the prospects that *Tecumseh* the son will ever equal, in wisdom or prowess *Tecumseh* the father." †

ELLSKWATAWA. Although we have given some important facts in the life of this impostor, there are some circumstances which claim to be related. After the termination of the war of 1812, he received a pension from the government of Great Britain, and resided in Canada. In 1826, he was prevailed upon to leave that country, and went, with others, to settle beyond the Mississippi. At the same time also went the only surviving son of *Tecumseh*.

Much has been said and written about the *Prophet*; and, as is generally the case, the accounts vary, in proportion to their multiplicity. From a well-written article in a foreign periodical,‡ it is said that, during the first 50 years of his life, he was remarkable for nothing except his stupidity and intoxication. In his 50th year, while in the act of lighting his pipe, he fell back in his cabin, upon his bed; and, continuing for some time lifeless, to all appearances, preparations were made for his interment; and it was not until the tribe was assembled, as usual on such occasions, and they were in the act of removing him, that he revived. His first words were, "*Don't be alarmed. I have seen heaven. Call the nation together, that I may tell them what has appeared to me.*" When they were assembled, he told them that two beautiful young men had been sent from heaven by the Great Spirit, who spoke thus to him: —The Great Spirit is angry with you, and will destroy all the red men: unless you refrain from drunkenness, lying and stealing, and turn yourselves to Him, you shall never enter the beautiful place which we will now show you." He was then conducted to the gates of heaven, from whence he could behold all its beauties, but was not permitted to enter. After undergoing several hours' tantalization, from extreme desire of participating in its indescribable joys and pleasures, he was dismissed. His conductors told him to tell all the Indians what he had seen; to repent of their ways, and they would visit him again. My authority says, that, on the *Prophet's* visiting the neighboring nations, his mission had a good effect on their morals, &c. But this part of his story, at least, is at variance with facts; for none would hear to him, except the most abandoned young warriors of those tribes he visited, and their miserable condition in colonizing themselves upon the Wabash, in 1811, is well known. §

There was an earthquake said to have taken place in the Creek country in December, 1811.‖ The *Prophet* visited the Creeks in the previous August, and "pronounced in the public square, that shortly a lamp would appear in the west, to aid him in his hostile attack upon the whites, and, if they would not be influenced by his persuasion, the earth would ere long tremble to its centre. This circumstance has had a powerful effect on the minds of these Indians, and would certainly have led them, generally, to have united with the northern coalition, had it not been for the interposition of travellers." This statement was made by a Mr. *Francis M'Henry*, in the Georgia Journal, to contradict that ever any such earthquake did take place, and by which we

* Johnson's Ind. Nar. 217. † Military Occurrences, i. 293.

‡ The New Monthly Magazine.

§ This famous vision of the *Prophet* will compare in strangeness with that of *Keposh*, head chief of the Delaware nation, related by *Loskeil*, (ii. 114.) He lay to all appearance dead for three days. In his swoon, he saw a man in white robes, who exhibited a catalogue of the people's sins, and warned him to repent. In 1749, he was about 80 years of age, and was baptized by the name of *Solomon*. We have related in Book III. an account of *Squando's* vision; and others might be mentioned.

‖ "The earthquakes, which, in 1811, almost destroyed the town of New Madrid of the Mississippi, were very sensibly felt on the upper portion of the Missouri country, and occasioned much superstitious dread amongst the Indians." *Long's Expedition*, i. 272.

earn that that part of the superstitious world really believed that it had, and that places had been actually sunk. The same communicant says, "I have only to state that I have comfortably reposed in houses where newspapers have announced every disappearance of earth." He states also, upon the authority of "a Mr. *Chadbury*, an English gentleman, from Quebec," that, "at the age of 15, this Indian disappeared from his relatives, and was considered as finally lost. That he strolled to Quebec, and from thence to Montreal, where, taken as a pilot to Halifax, he remained several years; and in this space received an education qualifying him to act the part already known." The comet of 1811 was viewed by many, throughout the country, as a harbinger of evil, and it was upon this seeming advantage that the *Prophet* * seized to frighten his red brethren into his schemes. †

He was said to have been killed on the 18 November, 1812, when the Mississinaway towns were destroyed on the Wabash by a detachment under Colonel *Campbell;* but this was only a rumor of the day.

ROUND-HEAD was a Wyandot, and fought against the Americans in the last war. He was very conspicuous in the battle at Frenchtown upon the River Raisin. The Indian force in this affair was about 1000.‡ General *Winchester's* quarters were at 1 or 200 yards from the main army when the fight commenced, and, in an endeavor to render it assistance, was fallen upon by the Wyandots, and himself and attendants captured. *Round-head* seized upon General *Winchester* with his own hands. It was a severe cold morning, 22 January, 1813, and the ground was covered with snow.

Our chief, in a manner truly characteristic, obliged the general to divest himself of his great coat and all his uniform. With nothing but his shirt to protect him from the cold, *Round-head* conducted him to a fire, but not until he had got on the general's cocked hat, uniform coat, vest, &c. It was in this condition, that Colonel *Proctor* found him; and it was not without much persuasion that the stern warrior relinquished his important captive and it was with still more reluctance, that he gave up the uniform, in which he had so short a time to strut about and show himself to his countrymen.§

This was a most disastrous expedition for the Americans: 538 were captured according to the British account, which does not differ materially from the American; ‖ and 300 killed in the battle, and massacred by the Indians immediately after.

In Colonel *Proctor's* official account of this affair, he speaks in high terms of the conduct of the Indian chiefs and warriors. His words are: "The zeal and courage of the Indian department were never more conspicuous than on this occasion, and the Indian warriors fought with their usual bravery."

Colonel *Proctor* has been much censured for his conduct at the River Raisin. It was said that he agreed to the terms asked for by General *Winchester*, and then paid no attention to their observance, but rather countenanced the Indians in their barbarities, thinking thereby to strike the Americans with dread, that they might be deterred from entering the service in future. But the British historians say that "the whole of the left division surrendered at discretion," and not "on condition of their being protected from the savages, being allowed to retain their private property, and having their side-arms returned to them," as stated by General *Winchester:* for, Mr. *James* adds, "had this been the understanding, one may suppose that some writing would have been drawn up; but, indeed, Gen. *Winchester* was not in a condition to dictate terms. Stripped to his shirt and trowsers, and suffering exceedingly from

* *Lambert,* who published three volumes of travels in America in 1810, (London,) in speaking of the *Prophet,* says, "Thus we find, that prophets are not confined to our own happy island: but I make no doubt, that many of our *sealed* countrymen and countrywomen, who are running after *Joanna Southcott* from one end of the kingdom to the other, will (if they should ever read this speech) turn up their nose at the Indian, and quote a text from Revelations to prove that he is a *false* prophet." *Lambert,* i. 396.

† Halcyon Luminary, i. 205, &c. New York, (June,) 1812.

‡ Perkins's Late War, 100.

§ *James,* Milit. Occurrences, i. 191

‖ Thomson has 522. *Hist. Sketches,* 104.

the cold, the American general was found by Col. *Proctor*, near to one of the Indian fires, in possession of the Wyandot chief *Round-head*."

So, according to the judgment of this historian, Colonel *Proctor* was under no obligation to keep his word, because there was "no writing" with his name to it. The historian that will even set up a defence for treachery may calculate with certainty upon the value posterity will set upon his work We want no other than Colonel *Proctor's* own account from which to condemn him of, at least, great want of humanity. We do not pretend that the Americans were always free from the same charges; but we would as soon scorn their extenuation as that of their enemies.

Round-head was present with General *Brock* and *Tecumseh* when they took possession of Detroit, on the 15 August, 1812. When about to cross the river to lay siege to Detroit, General *Brock* presented *Tecumseh* with his red sash. This chief had too much good sense to wear it, well knowing it would create jealousy among the other chiefs, who considered themselves equal with him; he therefore presented it to *Round-head*, as has been mentioned in the life of *Tecumseh*.

Whether this chief were more wise than *Tecumseh*, in the last affair in which the latter was engaged, we are unable to say; but it appears highly probable that the conduct of General *Proctor* was the cause of his being abandoned by most, if not all the Wyandots, previous to the battle of the Thames.* As *Round-head* was their chief, to him will be attributed the cause of their wise proceeding.

The following letter, written after the battle of the River Raisin, (we conclude,) is worthy of a place here.

"*The Hurons, and the other tribes of Indians, assembled at the Miami Rapids, to the inhabitants of the River Raisin.—Friends, listen! You have always told us you would give us any assistance in your power. We, therefore, as the enemy is approaching us, within 25 miles, call upon you all to rise up and come here immediately, bringing your arms along with you. Should you fail at this time, we will not consider you in future as friends, and the consequences may be very unpleasant. We are well convinced you have no writing forbidding you to assist us. We are your friends at present.*

Round-head ⌗ his mark.
Walk-in-the-water ⓢ his mark †"

WALK-IN-THE-WATER also signalized himself in these events. His native name is *Myeerah*. He is a Huron, of the tribe of the Wyandots, and, in 1817, resided on a reservation in Michigan, at a village called Maguaga, near Brownstown. Mr. *Brown*, in his valuable Western Gazetteer, justly styles this famous chief one of "nature's nobles." The unfortunate General *Hull* mentions him as one of the principal "among the vast number of chiefs who led the hostile bands" of the west when the war of 1812 commenced. The Kaskaskias Wyandots, in 1814, were nearly equally divided between a chief called *Tarhe*, which signifies the *Crane*, and *Myeerah*. The former was called the grand chief of the nation, and resided at Sandusky. He was a very venerable and intelligent chief. In 1812, *Myeerah* told some American officers who were sent to the Indians to secure their favor, that the American government was acting very wrong to send an army into their country, which would cut off their communication with Canada. The Indians, he said, were their own masters, and would trade where they pleased; that the affair of the Wabash was the fault of General *Harrison* entirely. He commanded the Indian army with *Round-head* at the battle of the River Raisin.

After the battle of the Thames, in which also *Walk-in-the-water* was a conspicuous commander, he went to Detroit to make peace, or rather to ask it of General *Harrison*. In crossing from Sandwich with a white flag, many were attracted to the shore to see him, where also were drawn up the Kentucky volunteers. All were struck with admiration at his noble aspect and fearless

* General *Harrison's* official letter, among *Brannan's Official Doc.* p. 237
† *English Barbarities*, 132.

carriage, as he ascended the bank and passed through the ranks of the soldiers. The greatest firmness attended his steps, and the most dignified *nonchalance* was upon his countenance, notwithstanding his condition was now calculated to discover humiliation and deep depression. Only a few days before, he had fought hand to hand with these same volunteers, whose ranks he now passed through.

We have not heard of the death of the heroic and truly great chief *Myeerah*; but, whether alive or dead, our veneration is the same. It was said of his contemporary, *Tecumseh*, that in the field he was an *Achilles*, and in the council an *Agamemnon*. At least, we think, as much may in truth be said of *Myeerah*. The sequel of the life of *Tarhe* will be found in a former chapter, where he figures under the name of King *Crane*. In 1807, a treaty was made at Detroit between the Chippeways, Ottowas, Pottowattomies and Wyandots and the United States. Two chiefs besides *Myeerah* signed on behalf of the last-named tribe. His name to that treaty is written *Miere*. The next year, 1808, another treaty was made at Brownstown with the same tribes, with the addition of two delegates from the Shawanees. Three besides *Myeerah* signed at this time. He was also, we believe, a party to the treaty made at Fort Industry in 1805, on the Miami of the Lake.

Less is known of the history of the two next chiefs, of which we shall say something, than of many others less distinguished.

TEYONINHOKERAWEN was a Mohawk chief, who is generally known under the appellation of *John Norton*. "This interesting Indian, about two years ago, [1804 or 5,] visited England, where numerous traits of an amiable disposition and a vigorous intellect produced the most pleasing impressions on all who were introduced to him. A proof of his possessing, in a high degree, the qualities of a good temper and great mental quickness, occurred at the *upper rooms*, at Bath, where he appeared in the dress of his country. A young Englishman, who had been in America, accosted the chief with several abrupt questions respecting his place of abode, situation, and the like. To these *Norton* returned answers at once pertinent and modest. The inquirer, however, expressed himself dissatisfied with them, and hinted, in almost plain terms, that he believed him to be an impostor. Still the American suppressed his resentment, and endeavored to convince the *gentleman* that this account of himself might be depended upon. 'Well, but,' returned the other, 'if you really are what you pretend to be, how will you relish returning to the savages of your own country?' '*Sir*,' replied Norton, with a glance of intelligence, '*I shall not experience so great a change in my society as you imagine, for I find there are savages in this country also.*' Animated with the spirit of genuine patriotism, this generous chieftain was unweariedly occupied, during the intervals of his public business, in acquiring every species of useful knowledge, for the purpose of transporting it to his own country, for the benefit of his people; and what the friends to the happiness of men will hear with still greater admiration and pleasure, he was also engaged, under the auspices of Mr. *Wilberforce* and Mr. *Thornton*, in the laborious employment of translating the Gospel of St. John into his native tongue."* Whether that published by the American Bible Society be the same translation, I am not positive, but believe it is. The following is the 3d verse of Chap. i. *Yorighwagwegon ne rode weyenòkden, ok tsi nikon ne kaghson yagh oghnahhoten teyodon ne ne yagh raonhah te hayàdare.*

From the London Monthly Repository it appears, that *Norton* was educated "at one of the American universities. There is an excellent portrait of him presented by the respectable Robert Barclay, hung up in the Bath Agricultural Society's great room; for he was made an honorary member while here." And the same writer adds:—"I have a pamphlet published by him while in England, entitled 'An address to the Six Nations,' recommending the Gospel of St. John, one side in English, the other in Mohawk language, in which are discovered sentences very similar to the Welsh; for instance,

---

* *Janson's* Stranger in America, 278, 4to, London, 1807.

INDIAN. O Niyoh toghsa eren teshàwighe ne sagraciane wahoni.
WELSH. O Nhaw naddug erom dy devishaid grâce am whahani.
ENGLISH. O God, take not from us thy grace, because we have erred from thy ways." *

Some of the words which seem to be corresponding and analogous to the eye, in the two first languages, are not so in meaning; in fact there is no analogy whatever between the Welsh and Indian languages.

In 1808, this chief was the bearer of a long and exceedingly excellent talk from the Senecas west of the Ohio, to the Indians of the interior of Canada, about 100 miles from Niagara Falls. It was from a Prophet named SKANYADARIO.†

We learn also from Mr. *Jansen* that when *Teyoninhokerawen* was in England, he "appeared to be about 45 years of age;" tall, muscular, and well proportioned, possessing a fine and intelligent countenance. His mother was a Scotch woman, and he had spent two years in Edinburgh, in his youth, namely, from his 13th to his 15th year, read and spoke English and French well. He was married to a female of his own tribe, by whom he had two children. He served in the last war with the English, as will presently be related.

Because this chief spent a few years in Scotland when young, some historians ‡ have asserted that he was not an Indian, but a Scotchman; and a writer § of a sketch of the late Canada war says he was related to the French. Of this we have no doubt, as it is not uncommon for many of those who pass for Indians to have white fathers. We should think, therefore, that, instead of his mother's being a Scotch woman, his father might have been a Frenchman, and his mother an Indian.

Of *Norton's* or *Teyoninhokerawen's* exploits in the last war, there were not many, we presume, as there are not many recorded. When Col. *Murray* surprised Fort Niagara, on the 19 Dec. 1813, *Norton* entered the fort with him, at the head of a force of about 400 men. ‖ Fort Niagara was garrisoned by about 300 Americans, of whom but 20 escaped. All who resisted, and some who did not, were run though with the bayonet. We only know that *Norton* was present on this occasion.

On the 6 June, 1814, General *Vincent* and *Norton*, with a considerable force,¶ attacked an American camp ten miles from Burlington Bay, at a place called Fifty Mile Creek. The onset was made before day on a Sunday morning. The invaders seized upon seven pieces of cannon, and turned them upon their enemies. The night was very dark, and the confusion was very great. The American Generals *Chandler* and *Winder*, one major, five captains, one lieutenant, and 116 men, were taken prisoners. Nevertheless the Americans fought with such resolution that the attacking party were obliged to abandon their advantage, leaving 150 of their number behind them. They, however, carried off two pieces of cannon and some horses.

LOGAN was a great Shawanee chief, who was more brave than fortunate. He was no connection of *Logan* of 1774, but was equally great, and, in the hands of a *Jefferson*, would have been equally celebrated. Shortly after General *Tupper's* expedition to the Miami Rapids, Captain *James Logan*, as he was called by the English, was sent by General *Harrison* in the direction of those rapids, with a small party of his tribe, to reconnoitre. He met with a superior force of the enemy near that place, by which he was so closely pursued that his men were obliged to break and flee for safety in the true Indian manner. *Logan*, with two of his companions, Captain JOHN and BRIGHT-HORN, arrived safe at General *Winchester's* camp. When he gave an account here of what had happened, accusers in the army stood ready to charge him with treachery, and a design of aiding the enemy. He felt the false charge

* *Monthly Repository*, iii. 715, London, 1809. † *Ibid.* 709.
‡ *James*, Military Occurrences, ii. 16. § Mr. *M. Smith*, who lived then in Canada.
‖ Some American historians say, "British and Indians;" but Mr. *James* (ii. 16.) says there was but one "Indian," and he was a Scotchman!
¶ The number of rank and file was 704, of the Americans about 3000.

with cutting severity, but without any inclination for revenge. On the contrary, he determined to prove by some unequivocal announcement that he was not thus to be taken as a spy.

Accordingly, on 22 November, with the two men above named, he set out, resolved either to bring in a prisoner or a scalp, or to hazard his life in the attempt. When he had proceeded down the Miami about 10 miles, on the north side, he met with Captain *Elliot*, (son of him of infamous memory, before mentioned in this book of our history,) accompanied by five Indians. As this party was too strong for *Logan* and his two brave companions, four of them being on horseback, he therefore determined to pass them, pretending to be of the British party, and advanced with confident boldness and a friendly deportment. But it unfortunately happened, that the noted *Winnemak*, of whom mention has been made in the life of *Tecumseh*, and who had fought at the head of the Pottowattomies in the battle of Tippecanoe, knew him and denounced him as a spy. *Logan*, however, persisted that he was the friend of the British, and was then on his way to the Rapids to give information of the situation of the Americans. After conversing a while, he proceeded on his way, and *Winnemak*, with his companions, turned and followed with him. *Winnemak* and his party closely watched the others, and when they had proceeded about eight miles, he proposed to Captain *Elliot* to seize and tie them; but he said it was not necessary, for if they attempted to escape they could be shot down, or easily run down with their horses. *Logan*, overhearing this, communicated it to his companions, and it was agreed to make an attack upon them, although they were five to three. Until now, *Logan* had intended to go on with them till night, and then escape.

No sooner was the resolution taken than the fight began. When they had all fired three rounds apiece, the advantage was in favor of the three; having driven their adversaries considerable distance, and cut them off from their horses. *Elliot* and *Winnemak* had both fallen mortally wounded, and a young Ottowa chief was killed. Towards the close of the fight, both *Logan* and *Bright-horn* were badly wounded. As soon as *Logan* was shot, he ordered a retreat, and, seizing the enemies' horses, they effected it to *Winchester's* camp. Captain *John* escaped unhurt, and after taking the scalp of the Ottowa chief, followed, himself, and arrived there the next morning.

Logan had now indeed established his reputation, but he lost his life! His wounds proved mortal two days after. In General *Winchester's* letter to General *Harrison*, he says, "More firmness and consummate bravery have seldom appeared on the military theatre." "He was buried with all the honors due to his rank, and with sorrow as sincerely and generally displayed as ever I witnessed." Thus wrote Major *Hardin* to Governor *Shelby*:—

"His physiognomy was formed on the best model, and exhibited the strongest marks of courage, intelligence, good-humor and sincerity. He had been very serviceable to our cause, by acting as a pilot and a spy. He had gone with General *Hull* to Detroit, and with the first Kentucky troops who marched for the relief of Fort Wayne."

Winnemak, while in conversation with *Logan* before the fight, declared that he commanded all the Indians in that quarter; and boasted that he had caused the massacre of *Wells* and those who had surrended at the battle of Chicago, after having gone with *Wells*, as a friend, to guard the garrison of that place to Fort Wayne.

In 1786, General *Logan*, of Kentucky, took *Logan*, then a boy, prisoner, and kept him some time. After sending him to school till he had acquired considerable education, he gave him his liberty and his own name. He was ever afterwards friendly to the whites. His mother was own sister to *Tecumseh* and the *Prophet*. He said that in the summer preceding his death, he had talked a whole night with *Tecumseh*, trying to persuade him against fighting against the States; but *Tecumseh* urged him as strongly to join the British. His wife (probably before she was known to *Logan*) was taken prisoner by Colonel *Hardin*, in 1789, and had remained in his family until the treaty of Greenville. In the army *Logan* had formed an attachment to Major *Hardin*, son-in-law of General *Logan*, whom, before he died, he requested to see that what was due him for his services should be faithfully paid over to his family which was done. His family resided at Wapoghoognata, which was called Logan's village.*

BLACK-BIRD was a Pottowattomie chief, who made himself notorious by the massacre of the garrison of Fort Dearborn. Before it was known in the western region of the upper lakes, that war had been declared by the United States, Indian and Canadian forces were collected at several points ready for the word to be given. That act seems to have been anxiously looked for by the Indians, as well as some of their advisers, who seem to have been much better prepared to meet the emergency of war than those who declared it.

Mackanaw, or as it is generally written, Michillimakinak, was garrisoned at this time with only 58 effective men, and the first news they had of the declaration of war was the appearance of 500 Indians and about the same number of Canadians ready to attack them. The fort was therefore surrendered by Lieutenant *Hanks*, on the 17 of July, 1812.

When General *Hull* heard of the fate of Michillimakinak, he rightly judged that Fort Dearborn, now Chicago, would be the next object of attack. Accordingly he despatched orders to Captain *Heald*, then in command there, to evacuate the place with all haste. But before this message reached him, *Black-bird*, with a host of his warriors, was prepared to act according to circumstances. A large number of the neighboring Indians, who had pretended friendship, hearing that the place was to be evacuated, came there to receive what could not be carried away.

On the 13 July, Captain *Wells*, of Fort Wayne, arrived at Fort Dearborn, with about 30 Miamies, to escort Captain *Heald* to Detroit. They marched from the fort on the 15 July, with a guard of Miamies in front, and another in the rear, under Captain *Wells*. They marched upon the shore of the lake, and when they had proceeded about one mile, they discovered Indians prepared to attack them from behind the high sand-bank which bounded the beach of the lake. Captain *Heald* then ascended the bank with his men, and a fight was immediately begun by the Indians. The Indians being vastly numerous, Captain *Heald* saw that it was useless to contend, and immediately retreated to a small eminence in the adjacent prairie, and not being followed by the Indians, was out of the reach of their shot. Meantime the Indians got possession of all their horses and baggage.

The Indians, after a short consultation, made signs for Captain *Heald* to advance and meet them. He did so, and was met by *Black-bird*, who, after shaking hands with him, told him, if he would surrender, the lives of the prisoners should be spared. There was no alternative, and after all their arms were surrendered, the party was marched back to the Indian encampment, near the fort, and divided among the different tribes. The next morning, they burned the fort, and left the place, taking the prisoners with them. Captain *Heald's* force was 54 regulars and 12 militia. In the fight on the bank of the lake, 26 of regulars and all of the militia were killed; besides two women and 12 children. Eleven women and children were among the captives. Captain *Wells* and many other officers were killed, and Captain *Heald* and his wife were both badly wounded, and were taken to the mouth of the St. Joseph's, where they were taken into the family of an Indian trader. Soon after, *Black-bird* set out with his warriors for the capture of Fort Wayne, and Captain *Heald* hired a Frenchman to take him to Michillimakinak. He was afterwards exchanged. What other successes this chief had during the war is unknown.

Black-hawk, in speaking of the capture and treatment of Captain *Heald* and his men, says,† it was owing to their *not keeping their word* with the Indians. The night before the fort was abandoned by the whites, they threw all the powder they could not carry with them into the well, which they had promised to give them.

The next chief we introduce chiefly to illustrate a most extraordinary mode of doing penance among the nations of the west.

---

* Taken principally from *Niles's Register*, and *Darnall's Narrative*.
† In his Life, written by himself, p. 42.

WAWNAHTON,* a bold and fearless chief, of the tribe of Yankton,† (whose name, translated, is "*he who charges the enemy*,") was considerably noted in the last war with Canada. "He had," says my author, "killed seven enemies in battle with his own hand, as the seven war-eagle plumes in his hair testified, and received nine wounds, as was shown by an equal number of little sticks arranged in his coal-black hair, and painted in a manner that told an Indian eye whether they were inflicted by a bullet, knife or tomahawk, and by whom. At the attack on Fort Sandusky, in the late war, he received a bullet and three buck shot in his breast, which glanced on the bone, and passing round under the skin, came out at his back." This, and other extraordinary escapes, he made use of, like the famous *Tuspaquin*, two ages before, to render himself of greater importance among his nation. At this time he was supposed to be about 30 years of age, of a noble and elegant appearance, and is still believed to be living.‡

Major *Long's* company considered *Wawnahton* a very interesting man, whose acquaintance they cultivated with success in the neighborhood of Lake Traverse. They describe him as upwards of six feet high, and possessing a countenance that would be considered handsome in any country. He prepared a feast for the party, as soon as he knew they were coming to his village. "When speaking of the Dacotas, we purposely postponed mentioning the frequent vows which they make, and their strict adherence to them, because one of the best evidences which we have collected on this point connects itself with the character of *Wanotan*, and may give a favorable idea of his extreme fortitude in enduring pain. In the summer of 1822, he undertook a journey, from which, apprehending much danger on the part of the Chippewas, he made a vow to the sun, that, if he returned safe, he would abstain from all food or drink for the space of four successive days and nights, and that he would distribute among his people all the property which he possessed, including all his lodges, horses, dogs, &c. On his return, which happened without accident, he celebrated the dance of the sun; this consisted in making three cuts through his skin, one on his breast, and one on each of his arms. The skin was cut in the manner of a loop, so as to permit a rope to pass between the flesh and the strip of skin which was thus divided from the body. The ropes being passed through, their ends were secured to a tall vertical pole, planted at about 40 yards from his lodge. He then began to dance round this pole, at the commencement of this fast, frequently swinging himself in the air, so as to be supported merely by the cords which were secured to the strips of skin separated from his arms and breast. He continued this exercise with few intermissions during the whole of his fast, until the fourth day about 10 o'clock, A. M., when the strip of skin from his breast gave way; notwithstanding which he interrupted not the dance, although supported merely by his arms. At noon the strip from his left arm snapped off: his uncle then thought that he had suffered enough," and with his knife cut the last loop of skin, and *Wanotan* fell down in a swoon, where he lay the rest of the day, exposed to the scorching rays of the sun. After this he gave away all his property, and with his two squaws deserted his lodge. To such monstrous follies does superstition drive her votaries!

In Tanner's Narrative, there is an interesting account of an expedition of an uncle of *Wawnahton*, at the head of 200 Sioux, against the Ojibbewas. *Wawnahton* was himself of the party, but he had not then become so distinguished as he was afterwards. They fell upon a small band of Crees and Assinneboins, and after a fight of near a whole day, killed all the Ojibbewas but one, the *Little-claw*, two women and one child, about 20 in number. This happened not far from Pembina.§ In 1822, he very much alarmed that post, by murdering some Assinneboins in its neighborhood.‖

BLACK-THUNDER, or *Mackkatananamakee*, was styled the celebrated patriarch of the Fox tribe. He made himself remembered by many from an

* *Wanotan*, in *Long's* Exped. to St. Peters, i. 448.
† *Yanktoan*, (*Long*, *ib.* 404,) which signifies *descended from the fern leaves*.
‡ Facts published by *W. J. Snelling*, Esq. It is said by *Keating*, in *Long's* Exped. i. 448, that he was about 28 years of age. This was in 1823.
§ *Tanner's* Narrative, 138. ‖ *West's* Red River Colony, 84.

excellent speech which he made to the American commissioners, who had assembled many chiefs at a place called the Portage, July, 1815, to hold a talk with them upon the state of their affairs; particularly as it was believed by the Americans that the Indians meditated hostilities. An American commissioner opened the talk, and unbecomingly accused the Indians of breach of former treaties. The first chief that answered, spoke with a tremulous voice, and evidently betrayed guilt, or perhaps fear. Not so with the upright chief *Black-thunder.* He felt equally indignant at the charge of the white man, and the unmanly cringing of the chief who had just spoken. He began:—

"My father, restrain your feelings, and hear calmly what I shall say. I shall say it plainly. I shall not speak with fear and trembling. I have never injured you, and innocence can feel no fear. I turn to you all, red-skins and white-skins—where is the man who will appear as my accuser? Father, I understand not clearly how things are working. I have just been set at liberty. Am I again to be plunged into bondage? Frowns are all around me; but I am incapable of change. You, perhaps, may be ignorant of what I tell you; but it is a truth, which I call heaven and earth to witness. It is a fact which can easily be proved, that I have been assailed in almost every possible way that pride, fear, feeling, or interest, could touch me—that I have been pushed to the last to raise the tomahawk against you; but all in vain. I never could be made to feel that you were my enemy. *If this be the conduct of an enemy, I shall never be your friend.* You are acquainted with my removal above Prairie des Chiens.* I went, and formed a settlement, and called my warriors around me. We took counsel, and from that counsel we never have departed. We smoked, and resolved to make common cause with the U. States. I sent you the pipe—it resembled this—and I sent it by the Missouri, that the Indians of the Mississippi might not know what we were doing. You received it. I then told you that your friends should be my friends—that your enemies should be my enemies—and that I only awaited your signal to make war. *If this be the conduct of an enemy, I shall never be your friend.*—Why do I tell you this? Because it is a truth, and a melancholy truth, that the good things which men do are often buried in the ground, while their evil deeds are stripped naked, and exposed to the world.†—When I came here, I came to you in friendship. I little thought I should have had to defend myself. I have no defence to make. If I were guilty, I should have come prepared; but I have ever held you by the hand, and I am come without excuses. If I had fought against you, I would have told you so: but I have nothing now to say here in your councils, except to repeat what I said before to my great father, the president of your nation. You heard it, and no doubt remember it. It was simply this. My lands can never be surrendered; I was cheated, and basely cheated, in the contract; I will not surrender my country but with my life. Again I call heaven and earth to witness, and I smoke this pipe in evidence of my sincerity. If you are sincere, you will receive it from me. My only desire is, that we should smoke it together—that I should grasp your sacred hand, and I claim for myself and my tribe the protection of your country. When this pipe touches your lip, may it operate as a blessing upon all my tribe.—*May the smoke rise like a cloud, and carry away with it all the animosities which have arisen between us.*"‡

The issue of this council was amicable, and, on the 14 Sept. following, *Black-thunder* met commissioners at St. Louis, and executed a treaty of peace.

ONGPATONGA,§ or, as he was usually called, *Big-elk,* was chief of the Mahas, or Omawhaws, whose residence, in 1811, was upon the Missouri.‖ Mr

---

* The upper military post upon the Mississippi, in 1818.

† "This passage forcibly reminds us of that in *Shakespeare*:"

'The evil that men do lives after them;
The good is often interred with their bones."

‡ Philadelphia Lit. Gazette.

§ *Ongue-pon-we,* in Iroquois, was "men surpassing all others." *Hist. Five Nations.*

‖ "The O'Mahas, in number 2250, not long ago, abandoned their old village on the south

Brackenridge visited his town on the 19 May of that year, in his voyage up that river. His "village is situated about three miles from the river, and contains about 3000 souls, and is 836 miles from its mouth."* We shall give here, as an introduction to him, the oration he made over the grave of *Black buffalo*, a Sioux chief of the Teton tribe, who died on the night of the 14 July, 1811, at "Portage des Sioux," and of whom Mr. *Brackenridge* remarks:† "The *Black-buffalo* was the Sioux chief with whom we had the conference at the great bend; and, from his appearance and mild deportment, I was induced to form a high opinion of him." After being interred with honors of war, *Ongpatonga* spoke to those assembled as follows:—"Do not grieve. Misfortunes will happen to the wisest and best men. Death will come, and always comes out of season. It is the command of the Great Spirit, and all nations and people must obey. What is passed, and cannot be prevented, should not be grieved for. Be not discouraged or displeased then, that in visiting your father‡ here, [the American commissioner,] you have lost your chief. A misfortune of this kind may never again befall you, but this would have attended you perhaps at your own village. Five times have I visited this land, and never returned with sorrow or pain. Misfortunes do not flourish particularly in our path. They grow every where. What a misfortune for me, that I could not have died this day, instead of the chief that lies before us. The trifling loss my nation would have sustained in my death, would have been doubly paid for by the honors of my burial. They would have wiped off every thing like regret. Instead of being covered with a cloud of sorrow, my warriors would have felt the sunshine of joy in their hearts. To me it would have been a most glorious occurrence. Hereafter, when I die at home, instead of a noble grave and a grand procession, the rolling music and the thundering cannon, with a flag waving at my head, I shall be wrapped in a robe, (an old robe perhaps,) and hoisted on a slender scaffold to the whistling winds,§ soon to be blown down to the earth; ‖ my flesh to be devoured by the wolves, and my bones rattled on the plain by the wild beasts. Chief of the soldiers, [addressing Col. *Miller*,] your labors have not been in vain. Your attention shall not be forgotten. My nation shall know the respect that is paid over the dead. When I return, I will echo the sound of your guns."

Dr. *Morse* saw *Ongpatonga* at Washington in the winter of 1821, and discoursed with him and *Ishkatappa*, chief of the republican Paunees, "on the subject of their civilization, and sending instructors among them for that purpose." The doctor has printed the conversation, and we are sorry to acknowledge that, on reading it, *Big-elk* suffers in our estimation; but his age must be his excuse. When he was asked who made the red and white people, he answered, "The same Being who made the white people, made the red people; *but the white are better than the red people.*" This acknowledgment is too degrading, and does not comport with the general character of the American Indians. It is not, however, very surprising that such an expression should escape an individual surrounded, as was *Ongpatónga*, by magnificence, luxury, and attention from the great.

Big-elk was a party to several treaties made between his nation and the United States, previous to his visit to Washington in 1821.

PETALESHAROO was not a chief, but a *brave* of the tribe of the Paunees. (A brave is a warrior who has distinguished himself in battle, and is next in importance to a chief.¶) He was the son of *Letelesha*, a famous chief, commonly called the *Knife-chief*, or *Old-knife*. When Major *Long* and his company travelled across the continent, in 1819 and '20, they became acquainted with *Petalesharoo*. From several persons who were in *Long's*

---

side of the Missouri, and now dwell on the Elk-horn River, due west from their old village 80 miles west-north-west from Council Bluffs." *Morse's* Indian Report, 251.

* Brackenridge, *ut sup.* 91. † Jour. up the Missouri, 240.

‡ Governor *Edwards* or Colonel *Miller*.

§ It is a custom to expose the dead upon a scaffold among some of the tribes of the west See *Brackenridge*, Jour., 186.; *Pike's* Expedition; *Long's* do.

‖ The engraving at the commencement of Book II. illustrates this passage.

¶ *Long's* Expedition, i. 356; and Dr. *Morse's* Indian Report, 247.

company, Dr. *Morse* collected the particular of him which he gives in his INDIAN REPORT as an anecdote.

In the winter of 1821, *Petalesharoo* visited Washington, being one of a deputation from his nation to the American government, on a business matter.

This *brave* was of elegant form and countenance, and was attired, in his visit to Washington, as represented in the engraving. In 1821, he was about 25 years of age. At the age of 21, he was so distinguished by his abilities and prowess, that he was called the "*bravest of the braves.*" But few years previous to 1821, it was a custom, not only with his nation, but those adjacent, to torture and burn captives as sacrifices to the great Star. In an expedition performed by some of his countrymen against the Iteans, a female was taken, who, on their return, was doomed to suffer according to their usages. She was fastened to the stake, and a vast crowd assembled upon the adjoining plain to witness the scene. This *brave*, unobserved, had stationed two fleet horses at a small distance, and was seated among the crowd, as a silent spectator. All were anxiously waiting to enjoy the spectacle of the first contact of the flames with their victim; when, to their astonishment, a *brave* was seen rending asunder the cords which bound her, and, with the swiftness of thought, bearing her in his arms beyond the amazed multitude; where placing her upon one horse, and mounting himself upon the other, he bore her off safe to her friends and country. This act would have endangered the life of an ordinary chief; but such was his sway in the tribe, that no one presumed to censure the daring act.

This transaction was the more extraordinary, as its performer was as much a son of nature, and had had no more of the advantages of education than the multitude whom he astonished by the humane act just recorded.

This account being circulated at Washington, during the young chief's stay there, the young ladies of Miss *White's* seminary in that place resolved to give him a demonstration of the high esteem in which they held him on account of his humane conduct; they therefore presented him an elegant silver medal, appropriately inscribed, accompanied by the following short but affectionate address: "Brother, accept this token of our esteem—always wear it for our sakes, and when again you have the power to save a poor woman from death and torture, think of this, and of us, and fly to her relief and her rescue." The *brave's* reply:—"*This* [taking hold of the medal which he had just suspended from his neck] *will give me more ease than I ever had, and I will listen more than I ever did to white men. I am glad that my brothers and sisters have heard of the good act I have done. My brothers and sisters think that I did it in ignorance, but I now know what I have done. I did it in ignorance, and did not know that I did good; but by giving me this medal I know it.*"

Some time after the attempt to sacrifice the Itean woman, one of the warriors of *Letelesha* brought to the nation a Spanish boy, whom he had taken. The warrior was resolved to sacrifice him to Venus, and the time was appointed. *Letelesha* had a long time endeavored to do away the custom, and now consulted *Petalesharoo* upon the course to be pursued. The young *brave* said, "I will rescue the boy, as a warrior should, by force." His father was unwilling that he should expose his life a second time, and used great exertions to raise a sufficient quantity of merchandise for the purchase of the captive. All that were able contributed, and a pile was made of it at the lodge of the *Knife-chief*, who then summoned the warrior before him. When he had arrived, the chief commanded him to take the merchandise, and deliver the boy to him. The warrior refused. *Letelesha* then waved his war-club in the air, bade the warrior obey or prepare for instant death. "*Strike*," said *Petelesharoo*, "*I will meet the vengeance of his friends.*" But the prudent and excellent *Letelesha* resolved to use one more endeavor before committing such an act. He therefore increased the amount of property, which had the desired effect. The boy was surrendered, and the valuable collection of goods sacrificed in his stead.* This, it is thought, will be the

* Long, *ut supra*, 35–78.

last time the inhuman custom will be attempted in the tribe. "The origin of this sanguinary sacrifice is unknown; probably it existed previously to their intercourse with the white traders."* They believed that the success of their enterprises, and all undertakings, depended upon their faithfully adhering to the due performance of these rites.

In his way to Washington, he staid some days in Philadelphia, where Mr. *Neagle* had a fine opportunity of taking his portrait, which he performed with wonderful success. It was copied for Dr. *Godman's* Natural History, and adorns the second volume of that valuable work.

METEA, chief of the Pottowattomies, is brought to our notice on account of the opposition he made to the sale of a large tract of his country. In 1821, he resided upon the Wabash. To numerous treaties, from 1814 to 1821, we find his name, and generally at the head of those of his tribe. At the treaty of Chicago, in the year last mentioned, he delivered the following speech, after Governor *Cass* had informed him of the objects of his mission.

"My father,—We have listened to what you have said. We shall now retire to our camps and consult upon it. You will hear nothing more from us at present. [This is a uniform custom of all the Indians. When the council was again convened, *Metea* continued.] We meet you here to-day, because we had promised it, to tell you our minds, and what we have agreed upon among ourselves. You will listen to us with a good mind, and believe what we say. You know that we first came to this country, a long time ago, and when we sat ourselves down upon it, we met with a great many hardships and difficulties. Our country was then very large; but it has dwindled away to a small spot, and you wish to purchase that! This has caused us to reflect much upon what you have told us; and we have, therefore, brought all the chiefs and warriors, and the young men and women and children of our tribe, that one part may not do what the others object to, and that all may be witness of what is going forward. You know your children. Since you first came among them, they have listened to your words with an attentive ear, and have always hearkened to your counsels. Whenever you have had a proposal to make to us, whenever you have had a favor to ask of us, we have always lent a favorable ear, and our invariable answer has been 'yes.' This you know! A long time has passed since we first came upon our lands, and our old people have all sunk into their graves. They had sense. We are all young and foolish, and do not wish to do any thing that they would not approve, were they living. We are fearful we shall offend their spirits, if we sell our lands; and we are fearful we shall offend you, if we do *not* sell them. This has caused us great perplexity of thought, because we have counselled among ourselves, and do not know how we can part with the land. Our country was given to us by the Great Spirit, who gave it to us to hunt upon, to make our cornfields upon, to live upon, and to make down our beds upon when we die. And he would never forgive us, should we bargain it away. When you first spoke to us for lands at St. Mary's, we said we had a little, and agreed to sell you a piece of it; but we told you we could spare no more. Now you ask us again. You are never satisfied! We have sold you a great tract of land, already; but it is not enough! We sold it to you for the benefit of your children, to farm and to live upon. We have now but little left. We shall want it all for ourselves. We know not how long we may live, and we wish to have some lands for our children to hunt upon. You are gradually taking away our hunting-grounds. Your children are driving us before them. We are growing uneasy. What lands you have, you may retain forever; but we shall sell no more. You think, perhaps, that I speak in passion; but my heart is good towards you. I speak like one of your own children. I am an Indian, a red-skin, and live by hunting and fishing, but my country is already too small; and I do not know how to bring up my children, if I give it all away. We sold you a fine tract of land at St. Mary's. We said to you then it was enough to satisfy your children, and the last we should sell: and we thought it would be the last you would ask for. We have now told you what we had to say. It is

* Long, *ut supra*, 357–8

what was determined on, in a council among ourselves; and what I have spoken, is the voice of my nation. On this account, all our people have come here to listen to me; but do not think we have a bad opinion of you. Where should we get a bad opinion of you? We speak to you with a good heart, and the feelings of a friend. You are acquainted with this piece of land—the country we live in. Shall we give it up? Take notice, it is a small piece of land, and if we give it away, what will become of us? The Great Spirit, who has provided it for our use, allows us to keep it, to bring up our young men and support our families. We should incur his anger, if we bartered it away. If we had more land, you should get more, but our land has been wasting away ever since the white people became our neighbors, and we have now hardly enough left to cover the bones of our tribe. You are in the midst of your red children. What is due to us in money, we wish, and will receive at this place; and we want nothing more. We all shake hands with you. Behold our warriors, our women, and children. Take pity on us and on our words."

Notwithstanding the decisive language held by *Metea* in this speech, against selling land, yet his name is to the treaty of sale. And in another speech of about equal length, delivered shortly after, upon the same subject, the same determination is manifest throughout.

At this time he appeared to be about forty years of age, and of a noble and dignified appearance. He is allowed to be the most eloquent chief of his nation. In the last war, he fought against the Americans, and, in the attack on Fort Wayne, was severely wounded; on which account he draws a pension from the British government.*

At the time of the treaty of Chicago, of which we have made mention, several other chiefs, besides *Metea*, or, as his name is sometimes written, *Meeteya*, were very prominent, and deserve a remembrance. Among them may be particularly named

KEEWAGOUSHKUM, a chief of the first authority in the Ottowa nation. We shall give a speech which he made at the time, which is considered very valuable, as well on account of the history it contains, as for its merits in other respects. INDIAN HISTORY by an Indian, must be the most valuable part of any work about them. *Keewagoushkum* began :—

"My father, listen to me! The first white people seen by us were the French. When they first ventured into these lakes, they hailed us as children; they came with presents and promises of peace, and we took them by the hand. We gave them what they wanted, and initiated them into our mode of life, which they readily fell into. After some time, during which we had become well acquainted, we embraced their father, (the king of France,) as our father. Shortly after, these people that wear red coats, (the English,) came to this country, and overthrew the French; and they extended their hand to us in friendship. As soon as the French were overthrown, the British told us, 'We will clothe you in the same manner the French did. We will supply you with all you want, and will purchase all your peltries, as they did.' Sure enough! after the British took possession of the country, they fulfilled all their promises. When they told us we should have any thing, we were sure to get it; and we got from them the best goods.—Some time after the British had been in possession of the country, it was reported that another people, who wore white clothes, had arisen and driven the British out of the land. These people we first met at Greenville, [in 1795, to treat with General *Wayne*,] and took them by the hand.—When the Indians first met the American chief, [*Wayne*,] in council, there were but few Ottowas present; but he said to them, 'When I sit myself down at Detroit, you will all see me.' Shortly after, he arrived at Detroit. Proclamation was then made for all the Indians to come in.—We were told, [by the general,] 'The reason I do not push those British farther is, that we may not forget their example in giving you presents of cloth, arms, ammunition, and whatever else you may require.' Sure enough! The first time, we were clothed with great liberality. You gave us strouds, guns, ammunition, and many other things we stood in need

* *Schoolcraft's* Travels.

of, and said, 'This is the way you may always expect to be used.' It was also said, that whenever we were in great necessity, you would help us.—When the Indians on the Maumee were first about to sell their lands, we heard it with both ears, but we never received a dollar.—The Chippewas, the Pottowattomies, and the Ottowas *were, originally, but one nation.* We separated from each other near Michilimackinac. We were related by the ties of blood, language and interest; but in the course of a long time, these things have been forgotten, and both nations have sold their lands, without consulting us."—"Our brothers, the Chippewas, have also sold you a large tract of land at Saganaw. People are constantly passing through the country, but we received neither invitation nor money. It is surprising that the Pottowattomies, Ottowas, and Chippewas, who are all one nation, should sell their lands without giving each other notice. Have we then degenerated so much that we can no longer trust one another?—Perhaps the Pottowattomies may think I have come here on a begging journey, that I wish to claim a share of lands to which my people are not entitled. I tell them it is not so. We have never begged, and shall not now commence. When I went to Detroit last fall, Governor *Cass* told me to come to this place, at this time, and listen to what he had to say in council. As we live a great way in the woods, and never see white people except in the fall, when the traders come among us, we have not so many opportunities to profit by this intercourse as our neighbors, and to get what necessaries we require; but we make out to live independently, and trade upon our own lands. We have, heretofore, received nothing less than justice from the Americans, and all we expect, in the present treaty, is a full proportion of the money and goods."

"A series of misfortunes," says Mr. *Schoolcraft*, "has since overtaken this friendly, modest, and sensible chief. On returning from the treaty of Chicago, while off the mouth of Grand River, in Lake Michigan, his canoe was struck by a flaw of wind and upset. After making every exertion, he saw his wife and all his children, except one son, perish. With his son he reached the shore; but, as if to crown his misfortunes, this only surviving child has since been poisoned for the part he took in the treaty."

The result of this treaty was the relinquishment, by the Ottowas, Chippewas, and Pottowattomies, of a tract of country in the southern part of the peninsula of Michigan, containing upwards of 5,000,000 acres, and for which they received of the United States, in goods, 35,000 dollars; and several other sums were awarded to the separate tribes, to some yearly forever, and to others for a limited term of years. Some of the chiefs who attended to the treaty were opposed to this sale, and hence the reason that *Keewagoushkum's* son was poisoned.

CHAPTER VIII.

BLACK-HAWK'S *war—Historical account of the tribes engaged in it—Treaty between them—Murders among the Sioux and Chippewas—*RED-BIRD*—Taken for murder—Dies in prison—Trial and execution of Indians—*BLACK-HAWK*—The Sacs murder 28 Menominies—Indians insulted—Their country sold without the consent of a large party—This occasions the war—Ordered to leave their country—General* Gaines *drives them beyond the Mississippi—Conclude a Treaty—Treaty broken—Sacs return again to their village—Determine on war—General* Atkinson *marches against them—They retreat up Rock River.*

IT will be necessary, in this chapter, to give some account of such tribes of Indians as will often be mentioned as we proceed. We shall, however, confine ourselves to such tribes as took part in the late war in the neighborhood of the Lakes Michigan and Superior, more especially; and firstly, of the Winnebagos. This tribe inhabit the country upon the Ouisconsin, a river that rises between the Lakes Superior and Michigan, and which disembogues itself into the Mississippi, near the S. W. angle of the N. W. territory. They were found seated here when the country was first visited by whites, about

150 years ago, and here they still remain. In 1820, they were supposed to number 1550 souls, of whom 500 were men, 350 women, and 700 children, and lived in ten towns or villages.* A body of Winnebago warriors was in the fight at Tippecanoe, under the impostor *Ellskwatawa*. *Sanamahhonga*, called *Stone-eater*, and *Wapamangwa*, or *White-loon*, were leaders of the Winnebago warriors. The latter was one that opposed General *Wayne* in 1794, but was reconciled to the Americans in 1795, by the treaty of Greenville. He also treated with General *Harrison*, in 1809, at Fort Wayne, and again at Greenville in 1814; but he was active in the war of 1812, and on the British side. Winnebago Lake, which discharges its waters into Green Bay, was probably named from this tribe of Indians, or, what is quite as probable, they received their name from the lake.

Secondly, the Menominies. This tribe inhabits a river bearing their name, and is situated about one degree north of the Winnebagos, from whom they are separated by a range of mountains. They numbered in 1820, according to some, about 355 persons, of whom not more than 100 were fighters; but this estimate could apply only, it is thought, to the most populous tribe.

Thirdly, the Pottowattomies, or Pouteouatamis. This nation was early known to the French. In the year 1668, 300 of them visited Father *Allouez*, at a place which the French called Chagouamigon, which is an island in Lake Superior. There was among them at this time an old man 100 years old, of whom his nation reported wonderful things; among others, that he could go without food 20 days, and that he often saw the Great Spirit. He was taken sick here, and died in a few days after.†

The country of the Pottowattomies is adjacent to the south end of Lake Michigan, in Indiana and Illinois, and in 1820 their numbers were set down at 3400. At that time the United States paid them yearly 5700 dollars. Of this, 350 dollars remained a permanent annuity until the late war.

Fourthly, the Sacs and Foxes. These are usually mentioned together, and are now really but one nation. They also had the gospel taught them about 1668, by the Jesuits. They live to the west of the Pottowattomies, generally between the Illinois and Mississippi Rivers, in the state of Illinois. The chief of the Sauks, or Sacs, for at least 14 years, has been *Keokuk*. Of him we shall particularly speak in due course. The Sacs and Foxes were supposed to amount, in 1820, to about 3000 persons in all; one fifth of whom may be accounted warriors.

Thus we have taken a view of the most important points in the history of the tribes which were engaged in the late border war under *Black-hawk*, and are, therefore, prepared to proceed in the narration of the events of that war. It will be necessary for us to begin with some events as early as 1823; at which period a chief of the Winnebagos, called *Red-bird*, was the most conspicuous. This year, the United States' agents held a treaty at Prairie du Chien, with the Sacs, Foxes, Winnebagos, Chippeways, Sioux, &c., for the purpose, among other things, of bringing about a peace between the first-named tribe and the others, who were carrying on bloody wars among themselves; the treaty stipulated that each tribe should confine itself to certain boundaries, which were designated; and as parties from them all were constantly visiting the United States' forts, upon business, or various other occasions, it was agreed that any party should be protected from insult or injury from any other Indians while upon such visits. It would not seem, however, that the makers of the treaty could have supposed that any such agreement would avail much, where deep hatred existed between any of the parties; for the very circumstance of protection being offered, would lead directly to difficulty, by placing one party in a situation exactly to accommodate another, in their peculiar method of surprise; nor could any one have supposed that any fear of punishment from the whites would have been equal to the gratification of revenge. Yet the motives of the whites were good, however little was effected by them.

As was expected, frequent murders happened among the Indians; and it was

* Dr. *Morse* rated them at 5000. *Ind. Report*, Ap. 362

† *Charlevoix*, Hist. de la Nouv. France, i. 395.

not often that those guilty of them could be found or recognized. At length, in the summer of 1827, a party of 24 Chippewas, on a tour to Fort Snelling, were surprised by a band of Sioux, who killed and wounded eight of them. The commandant of Fort Snelling captured four of them, whom he delivered into the hands of the Chippewas, who immediately shot them, according to the directions of the commandant. A Sioux chief, named RED-BIRD, resented the proceedings of the commandant, and resolved upon a further retaliation upon the Chippewas. Accordingly, he led a war party against them soon after, but was defeated; and upon his return home from the expedition, his neighbors derided him, as being no *brave*.

What were the grounds of *Red-bird's* enmity in the first place is now unknown, nor is it important to be inquired into in our present business; but certain it is, he had, or conceived that he had, just cause for his attack upon the Chippewas; his last and unsuccessful expedition against them, however, was to revenge the execution of those at Fort Snelling, who, he had been told, were executed for the murder of a family of seven persons, named *Methode*, near Prairie des Chiens. This, however, was not very likely the case.

As he could not get revenge of the Chippewas, *Red-bird* resolved on seeking it among the whites, their abettors; therefore, with two or three other desperadoes, like himself, of whom *Black-hawk* was probably one, he repaired to Prairie des Chiens, where, on the 24 July, 1827, they killed two persons and wounded a third. We hear of no plunder taken, but with a keg of whisky, which they bought of a trader, they retired to the mouth of Bad-axe River. Six days after, July 30, with his company augmented, *Red-bird* waylaid two keel-boats that had been conveying commissary stores to Fort Snelling. One came into the ambush in the day time, and, after a fight of four hours, escaped with the loss of two killed and four wounded. It was midnight before the other fell into the snare, and, owing to the darkness, escaped without much injury.

Notice has probably been taken by *Black-hawk*, in his narrative, of these events; but as he relates every thing without any regard to dates, it is impossible to assign some of his incidents to their proper places in history.

Not long after these events, in September, 1827, General *Atkinson* marched into the Winnebago country, with a brigade of troops, regulars and militia, and succeeded in making prisoners of *Red-bird*, and six other Winnebagos, who were held in confinement at Prairie du Chien until a trial could be had on them. On the 25 October, 1828, at a special term of the United States' Circuit Court, they were tried, all except *Red-bird*, who had died in prison. *Waniga* or the *Sun*, and *Chik-hong-sic*, the *Little-bull*, were each tried on two indictments; one for the murder of *Registre Gagnier*, as accomplices of *Red-bird*, in the murder of which mention has already been made. On the second indictment, *Chik-hong-sic* was tried for the murder of *Solomon Lipcap*; and *Waniga* on the same, as his accomplice. On the third indictment, *Waniga* was tried for scalping *Louisa Gagnier* with intent to kill. On the first indictment, both were brought in guilty. On the second, *Chik-hong-sic* was brought in guilty, and *Waniga* was acquitted. On the third, *Waniga* was found guilty, and *Chik-hong-sic* was acquitted. They were sentenced to be executed on the 26 of the following December.

The two charged with the murder of Mr. *Methode* and family were acquitted by a *nolle prosequi*. *Black-hawk*, or *Kara-zhonsept-hah*, as his name was then written, and *Kanonekah*, the *Youngest of the Thunders*, were among the prisoners charged with the attack on the boats the preceding year; but the charge not being sustained for want of evidence, they were discharged, as was also a son of *Red-bird*.

Thus it appears a year had passed since these Indians were captured, before they were brought to trial. Such a delay of justice was to the friends of the imprisoned Indians ten times as insufferable, if possible, as any punishment could have been, inflicted in any reasonable time after a crime had been committed. They cannot understand why, if one be guilty, he should not at once be punished, as it seldom happens, with Indians, that they deny an act when guilty: the most of them scorn to do it. Hence, the white people's keeping them imprisoned, they think an act of great cowardice; presuming they dare not punish the culprit. It has sometimes happened, that after an Indian had been imprisoned for a long time, and been discharged for want of evidence, although at the time of his capture there were no doubts of his guilt, even upon his own confession, he has been shot by some skulking white borderer on his way to his home. This, to the friends of such Indian, is the most abominable crime; and these things had all happened in Illinois before the end of 1828.

BLACK-HAWK, as we have just seen, was captured and held some time in durance for attacking the boats, which, it seems, could not be proved against him, as he was discharged; but if there were doubts of his guilt before, there can be none now, according to his own confession, which, it would seem, he had too much craft to acknowledge before his trial.

Matters continued in a ruffled state for about three years, though acts of violence seem not often to have occurred. In 1831, it was the general opinion on the frontiers, that the Indians intended to forbear no longer; and it was rightly judged by General *Atkinson*, that efforts had been, or were being made by some of them to unite all the Indians from Rock River to Mexico in a war. That this was the truth of the case we will hear *Black-hawk* in evidence. He says, "Runners were sent to the Arkansas, Red-River and Texas—not on the subject of our lands, but a secret mission, which I am not, at present, permitted to explain."

The difference between the Sacs and Foxes, and Menominies and Sioux, was one great cause of the troubles previous to the war of 1832. The whites used their endeavors to bring about a peace between them, and finally effected it, although at the very time murders were committed by one party upon the other, while on their way to attend a treaty for their own benefit. But such is their thirst for revenge, that they will take it at the hazard of themselves and all their connections. *Black-hawk* himself relates, that on a certain time, which, I believe, was in the summer of 1830, the chiefs of the Foxes were invited to attend a treaty at Prairie du Chien for the settlement of their differences with the Sioux. Nine of the head men of the Foxes, with one woman in their company, set out to attend the treaty, who, on their way, were met by a company of Sioux, near the Ouisconsin, and all of them, except one man, were killed.

This murder went unrevenged until the next year, when a band of Sioux and Menominies, who were encamped within a mile of the fort at Prairie du Chien, were attacked by some Foxes from *Black-hawk's* party, and 28 of them were killed. The whites now demanded the murderers, but *Black-hawk* said they had no right to make such a demand, for it was an affair between the Indian nations, over whom they had no authority; and besides, he said, when the Menominies had murdered the Fox chiefs, the year before, they made no such demand for the murderers.

According to the treaty of the 15th of July, 1830, at Prairie du Chien, the Sacs and Foxes sold their country to the United States, and the Sioux, Omahahs, Ioways, Ottoes, and several other tribes and bands, participated in the sale; but *Black-hawk* had nothing to do with it. *Keokuk*, or the *Watchful-fox*, at this time headed the party of Sacs that made the treaty; when *Black-hawk* knew what was done, it very much agitated and displeased him; but *Keokuk* had pleased the whites, and sold his country, as the ill-advised *M'Intosh* had done. The next summer, 1831, *Black-hawk* says, that while on a visit to the Indian agent at Rock Island, he heard, for the first time, "talk of our having to leave my village. The trader (he says) explained to me the terms of the treaty that had been made, and said we would be obliged to leave the Illinois side of the Mississippi, and advised us to select a good place for our village, and remove to it in the spring." This trader was the adopted brother of the principal Fox chief, whom he had persuaded to leave his village and build another on the west side of the Mississippi. *Keokuk* had consented to go and was using all his influence to induce others to go with him.

A party now began to organize itself in opposition to that of *Keokuk*. They called upon *Black-hawk* for his opinion about it; and, says the old chief "I gave it freely—and after questioning *Quàsh-quà-me* about the sale of the lands, he assured me that he never had consented to the sale of our village. I now promised this party to be their leader, and raised the standard of opposition to *Keokuk*, with a full determination not to leave my village."

The Sac village was on the point of land formed by Rock River and the Mississippi. The tribe had here usually about 700 acres of planting land, which extended about two and a half miles up the Mississippi. According to the tradition of the Indians, a village had stood here about 150 years. The whole extent of the Sac country on the Mississippi, was from the mouth of the Ouisconsin to the Portage des Sioux, almost to the entrance of the Missouri, in length near 700 miles.

About the time of the treaty of which we have been speaking, some outrages were committed upon the Indians by the whites in kind like the following:—One of *Black-hawk's* men having found a hive of bees in the woods, in a hollow tree, took it to his wigwam. Some whites, having learned the circumstance, repaired to the Indian's wigwam and demanded the honey as theirs, and he gave it up to them. They not only took the honey, but made plunder of all the skins he had got during his winter's hunt, and carried them off also. The case of the Indian was exceeding hard, for he owed the skins to his trader. Therefore he could not pay him, nor could he get necessaries for his family, in consequence of his inability to meet his former contract.

About this time *Black-hawk* met with gross ill treatment from some whites who met him in the woods a-hunting. They fell upon him, and beat him so severely that he was lame for some time after it. The whites pretended he had done them an injury. Such outrages, added to those of a public nature, had driven the Indians to desperation, and finally determined *Black-hawk* to act on the offensive. But he was sadly deceived in his real strength when he came to trial; for he had been assured that the Chippewas, Ottowas, Winnebagos and Pottowattomies all stood ready to help and second him. *Neapope*, who had been among some of them, was either deceived himself, or he intentionally deceived his chief. But the *Prophet*, *Wabokieshiek*, w doubtless the greatest deceiver. He sent word to *Black-hawk* that he h received wampum from the nations just mentioned, and he was sure of the coöperation. Besides this strong encouragement, it was also told to th principal Sac chiefs, that their British father at Malden stood ready to he them, in case of wrong being offered them by the whites; but this wa without doubt, a stratagem of the *Prophet*, or *Neapope*, the bearer of th intelligence. The chiefs of the whites at Malden and other places, had bee visited by *Black-hawk* or his head men, and, on being told their situation in respect to being obliged to leave their country, these friends of the Indians honestly told them that, if they had not sold their country, it could not be taken from them.

When the old chief, *Black-hawk*, found that *Keokuk* had sold the Sac village, with the rest of their country on the east side of the Mississippi, he saw and conversed with him about it, and *Keokuk* was so well convinced that he had done what he had no right to do, that he promised to go to the whites, and use all his endeavors to get it back again by giving any other part of the country for it: *Black-hawk* said he would give up even the *lead-mines*, if they could only be allowed to enjoy their old village, and the little point of land on which were the beautiful cornfields which their wives had cultivated, for years, undisturbed, and the adjacent burying-grounds of their honored dead.

With strong hopes that something would be effected for them, the Sacs set out upon their usual winter's hunt, in the fall of 1830, and meanwhile the whites came on and possessed their beloved village! When the Indians returned, they saw families of intruders in their own wigwams and lodges, that they had left the fall previous—the wives and children of the poor Indians were now upon the banks of their own Mississippi, but without a home or lodge to cover them! This was insufferable to *Black-hawk*—where is the white man that could endure such things? There are none that could, even the most servile slave.

The Sacs were encamped on the west bank of the Mississippi, having r[e]turned from their hunting-grounds earlier than usual, on account of inf[or]mation of the state of things in their village. The ice had not left the M[ississippi]

sissippi; but before it was time to plant corn, the firm resolution of the chiefs was taken, that their village they would again possess. They acted in accordance with their resolution, and went on and took possession. The whites were alarmed, and doubting of their ability to drive off the Indians *then*, said they would *live and plant together;* but took care to seize upon all the best planting land. The Indians were determined not to be the first to commit any hostile act, and submitted to great insults; some of their women being shamefully beaten by their white neighbors for the most trifling offence, to which their new situation had unavoidably subjected them, and one young man was actually beaten to death, or so that he soon after died; nevertheless, to the shame of those whites be it told, there is no account which has ever come to me that the Indians attempted to retaliate.

Other evils were experienced while the poor Sacs endeavored to live with the whites in their own village. Ardent spirits were brought in, and used to cheat the Indians out of their personal property, their guns, and articles with which they hunted.

In the fall of 1830, the Indians had been told that they must not come again to the east side of the river. Meantime the lands of the Sac village had been sold, or a part of them, and all the Indians were ordered to leave them. *Black-hawk* and his band, however, would not obey, and some of them remained on the unsold lands, while the others were on their hunting expeditions. And early in the spring of 1831, after having used every means for a reconciliation, without giving up their village, the Sacs in a body recrossed the river to their old cornfields, and in a menacing manner took possession; but if we can believe *Black-hawk*, he did not mean to be provoked into a war by any thing less than the life-blood of some of his people; which he said the whites dare not take, at least so long as he remained on the government's land; for by an article of the treaty which had caused these troubles, the Indians were not obliged to leave the lands so long as they remained unsold. But the settlers cried out against the *encroachments of the Indians* upon them, which soon became so loud and clamorous that Governor *Reynolds* forthwith taking the *responsibility*, declared the state of Illinois invaded by hostile Indians, although it does not appear that any of them were upon other lands than those owned by the United States.

Accordingly, on the 28 May, 1831, Governor *Reynolds* wrote from Belleville, the capital of the state of Illinois, to General *Gaines*, the military commander of the western department, that he had received undoubted information that the section of the state near Rock Island was at that time invaded by a hostile band of the Sac Indians, headed by *Black-hawk;* and that in order to repel said invasion, and to protect the citizens of the state, he had called on 700 of the militia of the said state, to be mounted and ready for that service. He therefore, "as executive of the state of Illinois," respectfully solicited his coöperation. General *Gaines* said in answer, the next day, that he had ordered six companies of regular troops to proceed from Jefferson Barracks the day following, May 30, for the Sac village, and if necessary he would add two companies more from Prairie du Chien. This force he considered sufficient to put down the "hostile Sacs;" but, he said, if the Indian force had been augmented by other Indians, then he would correspond with his excellency by express, and avail himself of his offer of the 700 mounted volunteers.

Governor *Reynolds* had just before (26 May) written to General *Clark*, the superintendent of Indian affairs at St. Louis, and among other things said, he had considered it necessary to order out troops "to *protect* the citizens" of the state "near Rock Island *from invasion* and depredation;" but from his letter to *Gaines*, dated only two days after, the state was actually *invaded*. Hence it appears, that in something less than two days, by thinking the matter over, the governor had, in his mind, changed the *fear* of invasion into *actual* invasion. In the same letter he goes on: The object of the government of the state is to protect those citizens by removing said Indians, "peaceably if they can, but forcibly if they must." "I consider it my duty to inform you of the above call on the militia, and that in or about 15 days, a sufficient force will appear before these Indians to remove them, *dead* or *alive*, over the west side of the Mississippi." Whether his excellency did not mean to stop with his Indians short of the Western Ocean, I cannot say, but certainly he says nothing of leaving them any where *on lands* on the west side of the Mississippi; he, however, humanely adds, "But to save all this disagreeable business, perhaps a request from you to them, for them to remove to the west side of the river, would effect the object of procuring peace to the citizens of the state." General *Clark* replied, two days after, that every effort on his part "had been made to effect the removal from Illinois of *all* the tribes who had ceded their lands."

Hence no alternative now remained but to proceed on with an army to drive off the Indians. Accordingly General *Gaines* proceeded to the country in dispute, and by his prudent management succeeded in settling the difficulty, which, as matters immediately afterwards turned out, seems to have amounted to but little; and as General *Gaines's* account of his expedition agrees very well with what *Black-hawk* has since said about it, we lay it before the reader. It is contained in a letter dated Rock Island, 20 June, 1831.

"I have visited the Rock River villages, with a view to ascertain the localities, and, as far as possible, the disposition of the Indians. They confirm me in the opinion I had previously formed, that, whatever may be their *feelings* of hostility, they are resolved to abstain from the use of their tomahawks and fire-arms except in self-defence. But few of their warriors were to be seen—their women and children, and their old men appeared anxious, and at first somewhat confused, but none attempted to run off. Having previously notified their chiefs that I would have nothing more to say to them, unless they should desire to inform me of their intention to *move forthwith*, as I had directed them, I did not speak to them, though within 50 yards of many of them. I had with me on board the steam-boat some artillery, and two companies of infantry. Their village is immediately on Rock River, and so situated that I could from the steam-boat destroy all their bark houses (the only kind of houses they have) in a few minutes, with the force now with me, probably without the loss of a man. But I am resolved to abstain from firing a shot without some bloodshed, or some manifest attempt to shed blood, on the part of the Indians. I have already induced nearly one third of them to cross the Mississippi to their own land. The residue, however, say, as the friendly chiefs report, that they *never will move;* and what is very uncommon, their women urge their hostile husbands to fight rather than to move and thus to abandon their homes."

Thus stood matters previous to the arrival of the Illinois militia; neither party wishing to do any thing to bring on hostilities. On the 7th June, *Black-hawk* met General *Gaines* in council, and plainly told him he would not remove, and to let him know he was not afraid of his forces, went to the council-house at the head of his band, armed and painted as though they expected to be attacked; the consequence was, nothing was effected thus far. But the general was satisfied that the reports of other tribes having engaged to assist them were entitled to little credit. That the general well understood the affairs of the Sacs at this time, no doubt will be entertained, on comparing his account with the statement of *Black-hawk* in his life. "Several other tribes," observes the general, "such as the Winnebagos, Pottowattomies, and Kikapoos, have been invited by these Sacs to assist them; but I cannot positively ascertain that more than 200 have actually joined, and it is very doubtful whether these will remain true to their offending allies."

As General *Gaines* found he could not effect a compliance with his demands, he concluded to wait for the militia, who, on the 25 June, promptly arrived. These the Indians thought it not proper to oppose, knowing well that border militia would submit to no restraint from their officers; they therefore fled across the Mississippi to avoid being massacred; and on the following day, June 26, the army took possession of the Sac village, without the firing of a gun on either side. On the 27th, *Black-hawk* caused a white flag to be displayed to show his disposition to have a parley, which soon after ensued, and this ended in a treaty.

In his despatch to the secretary of war, General *Gaines* said he was of opinion that "these Indians were as completely humbled, as if they had been chastised in battle, and less disposed to disturb the frontier inhabitants;"

and that Governor *Reynolds* was of the same opinion. But in this they were both mistaken, although when the treaty was made, *Black-hauk* without doubt intended strictly to observe it; yet he could not foresee what would happen. He had been promised corn to supply the wants of his people, instead of that which they had been obliged to abandon; but what they received was far from sufficient, and they began to feel the encroachment of famine. In this state of things, a party of Sacs, as the old chief says, went over the river *to steal corn from their own fields!* and thus began a new series of troubles which ended in bloodshed.

Black-hawk, with his chief men, had signed the treaty, and it was broken the same year by both parties. It was dated on the 30 June, 1831, five days after the "flight," and among the signers we recognize, besides MUCATA-MUHI-EATAK (*Black-hawk*), as his name was then written, PASHEPAHO (*Stabbing-chief*), WEESHEAT (*Sturgeon-head*), KAKEKAMAH (*All-fish*), and several others. It was in the course of the same summer, that the party from *Black-hawk's* band killed the 28 Menomonies, of which we have before given an account, and although the whites considered it their concern, seem not to have undertaken to revenge it until the spring of 1832; and the probability is, they would hardly then have undertaken it, had not some of the Sacs intruded themselves again into their old village, by which a new cry was raised against them. Be this as it may, General *Atkinson* set out for the Upper Mississippi, about the first of April, at the head of the sixth regiment of United States infantry, at whose approach *Black-hawk* and his party abandoned their camp on the Mississippi, where Fort Madison had been built, and ascended Rock River. It was in this direction he expected to be reinforced by the Pottowattomies, Winnebagos, and Kikapoos, but who in the end declined the hazardous and unequal conflict.

As *Black-hawk* moved leisurely up Rock River, he received several expresses from General *Atkinson*, ordering him in a peremptory manner to leave the country; but he constantly said he would not, and said he was going to the *Prophet's* village to make corn, to which he had been invited, and the whites might attack him if they dared; that they might come on if they chose, but they would not find him unprepared; yet he would not begin with them.

Meanwhile General *Atkinson*, not judging it expedient to pursue the Indians up Rock-River, made a stand at Dixon's Ferry. and waited for a reinforcement.

CHAPTER IX.

March of Major Stillman—*Kills some of* BLACK-HAWK'S men—Stillman's *defeat—Talk with the Winnebagos—Menomonies join the whites—Settlement on Indian Creek destroyed—Captivity of two young women—Murders—Plum River settlement broken up—Congress orders out troops—Murders near Galena—Indians cut off by* General Dodge—Snider's *defeat*—Stevenson's *defeat—Attack on the fort at Buffalo Grove—On that at Apple River—Defeat of* Major Dement—*Murder at Cincinawa Mound—Ravages of the cholera among the regular troops—Battle of the Ouisconsin—Action with the steam-boat Warrior—Battle of the 2d of August, and end of the war.*

BEFORE the arrival of General *Atkinson* at Ogee's or Dixon's Ferry, General *Whitesides* had proceeded there with a considerable body of mounted men, and a march of discovery was resolved upon. Accordingly, about the 13th of May, a company of 270 men proceeded on towards Sycamore Creek, under Major *Stillman*. BLACK-HAWK being apprized of the march of this detachment, sent out three young warriors with a white flag to meet them, and invite them to his camp; but the whites, paying no regard to the flag, took the bearers of it prisoners. Five others had been sent after the first, to see what ensued, and to report what might take place. These five were discovered and pursued by a small party of the whites, and, being overtaken, two of them were killed, and the rest escaped. It was now near night, on the 14th of May. The party that had killed the two Indians returned to the main body, which, it seems, was preparing to encamp for the night when this circumstance took place; all immediately mounted their horses and rushed forward in confusion. It does not appear that *Black-hawk* had any thoughts that the whites would attack him, for he had not but about 40 of his men with him at this time, the others being out upon a hunting excursion; but when his spies returned, and reported that two of their number had been barbarously murdered, the war-whoop was sounded, and the best preparations were made, that the time would allow to meet the invaders.

When they approached Sycamore Creek, the whites proceeded to cross it in the same disorderly manner they came to it, although the country was very favorable for ambushes. The Indians stood firm, and were doubtless sure of a victory, seeing the enemy pass the creek man by man as they arrived; and when a sufficient number had crossed, the Indians rushed upon them with their usual fury of attack. The whites say the Indians "showed themselves on every quarter, mounted and armed. They commenced the attack with guns," and continued it with knives and tomahawks. Their situation became in a moment desperate, and Major *Stillman*, who was in the rear, learning the situation of the advance column, immediately ordered a retreat, but none was effected—it was a most disorderly and wretched flight! scarce two flying together; and it was owing to the smallness of *Black-hawk's* force that any were so fortunate as to escape.

Thus *Black-hawk* with about 40 men had put 270 to flight, and dispersed them in such a manner, that it was reported at first by themselves, that 60 or 70 had been killed; but, as it proved afterwards, it was their great fear of the Indians, that had driven them so far from their companions, that they did not all arrive at Dixon's Ferry for several days after the fight, although the battle-ground was only 30 miles from that place. They generally came in, one at a time, as they had crossed Sycamore Creek on the evening of the 14th; and in the end, all but 12 were accounted for, and 11 of these were found afterwards on the battle-ground and interred. A letter from that country says, "The dead that were found were cut and mangled in a most shocking and indecent manner; their hearts cut out, heads off, and every species of indignity practised upon their persons. One alone escaped this treatment: he was found dead, with his head nearly cut off, embraced by the arms of an Indian who had been shot through the body, but yet had strength enough remaining to tomahawk the man who had shot him, and partly to cut off his head, dying in the very act—his last convulsive struggle being an embrace of his enemy even in death." From *Black-hawk's* own account, it appears he lost but three men in the whole transaction, and that these were killed who were sent out to meet the whites in their approach to Sycamore Creek.

Hence it appears that the whites were guilty of the first blood shed in this war.

The affair of Sycamore Creek caused a dire alarm to be sounded throughout the western region. *Black-hawk's* 40 warriors were magnified into 1500, and only the next day after *Stillman's* defeat, Governor *Reynolds* issued a proclamation calling on the militia to assemble at Hennepin, on Illinois River, by the 10 of June, to the number of 2000 men; which number, he said, he "considered necessary to subdue those Indians, and drive them out of the state."

Although the news of Major *Stillman's* disaster flew over the country among the whites with great rapidity, yet it is mentioned as a circumstance well worthy of remark, that messengers from the hostile Sacs, bearing to the Missouri Indians the news of their victory, arrived at the Des Moines Rapids 24 hours before the express sent by Governor *Reynolds* at the same place.

About the time the proclamation of the 15th of May was issued, calling for 2000 militia, an attempt was made by the whites to secure or draw off the Winnebagos, and prevent their joining the war party. On the 26 May, Mr. *Gratoit*, a sub-Indian agent, held a council at the head of the Four Lakes with a number of the Winnebago chiefs, and they all signified their desire of remaining at peace with the white people. At this council, the chief, called the *Little-black*, made a speech, and among other things said

"Father, what you have heard of us is from forked tongues, and what you have heard of *Man-eater* is false. *Man-eater* is sick; but he has sent his sister and daughter here to speak for him. Father, since I knew you, I have always heard your counsel, and did what you told me. My father, the Great Spirit, has sent you both here. You have taken me by the hand, and you have held it fast in yours. We hope, in the name of the Great Spirit, and all our women and children, that you will hold it fast, and we will hold on to you so hard that you cannot shake us off. My father, I ask nothing but a clear sky over our heads, which have been hanging down lately, and the sky has been dark, and the wind has been blowing continually, and trying to blow lies in our ears, but we turn our ears from it; but when we look towards you, the weather is clear, and the wind does not blow. My father, our young men do not travel much, for they are afraid of the Sacs, and afraid they will be taken for Sacs by the troops. My father, we wish you to give us a paper like the one General *Atkinson* gave us, that we may show it to the whites whom we meet, that they may know we are friends and for peace."

As soon as the troubles began, there were many of the Menomonies and Sioux, who, thirsting for the blood of the Sacs, came and offered themselves to the whites, to fight for them, but their services were refused; now they had had a fight, and being beaten, they were glad to call upon the Indians for assistance, and it was granted. Yet it should not be supposed that it was from any love they bore towards the whites that they were glad to fight for them, but from their natural inclination to war, and to seek revenge for injuries they had received from the Sacs during their former troubles. Consequently several hundreds of them were soon upon the march in various directions to surprise those belonging to the war party, and others attached themselves to the army.

Blood had now been shed, and no one had any right to expect but that the Indians would retaliate upon any whites, according to their manner, whether in arms or the cradle. There was a small settlement upon Indian Creek, near its confluence with Fox River, about 25 miles from the town of Hennepin, the rendezvous of the army. On the 20th* of May, this settlement was fallen upon by a small band of warriors, led by a Pottowattomie, who, after killing 15 persons, took considerable plunder, and proceeded to *Black-hawk's* camp.

The Indians gave as a reason for their attack upon this place, that not long before, a man who lived there by the name of *Hall*, had severely beaten the Pottowattomie who led the party that committed the murder. Yet the family of this man, if not the man himself, had been told by a friendly Indian, that a party would come and murder them, and advised them to fly for their lives. They immediately did so, but as vengeance had decreed, they appear to have returned again very soon, as they were there found and murdered, as before stated. Two daughters of Mr. *Hall* were led away captive, one about 16, and the other about 18 years of age; two brothers of these young women, who were at work in the field when the massacre began, made their escape and arrived safe at Dixon's Ferry. *Black-hawk* said the young women would have been killed by the Pottowattomies when they were taken, but were spared at the intercession of two of his men, who were with them. The following account was written immediately after they were delivered from captivity, by a person at Dixon's Ferry, where they were delivered, and is probably correct.

"Of the Misses *Halls*, whose case seems to interest every body, (and who are now at Galena,) it may not be uninteresting to hear the following, as the best information that could be collected from the Indians who succeeded in procuring their liberation. After the bloody scene of despatching such of the family as were about the house, (to which they could not avoid being eye-witnesses,) those young women were each placed on a horse, which was led by a man—other men walked alongside, to guard and keep them from falling off

* The editor of the *American Annual Register* is under a great mistake in placing this affair a month earlier. It changes the whole aspect of affairs; making the Indians the first murderers, which is not fact.

in difficult passes.—At night a lodge was set apart, and blankets spread for them, and elderly squaws made to sleep on each side, by whom they were taken care of. Such food as the Indians had, was offered to them; but they cried and wept, and were too unwell to eat or be comforted. All of which the young women say is true, and that the Indian men offered no insult to them. They also confirm what is stated of *Black-hawk's* camp, as seen in going through a narrow passage, where their horses mired in the mud:—more of the camp, it is supposed, they were not allowed to see. It seems there was more difficulty in procuring the liberty of one than the other: a young warrior claimed her as his prize, and was very unwilling to give her up; but after using all the arguments they were capable of, the Winnebagos say they had to use threats, which, together with an addition of ten horses to the offer, obtained his consent. The young warrior cut from Miss *Hall's* head a lock of her hair; which, by the by, has no affinity to a similar act among whites, but is to be kept as a trophy of his warlike exploits. The price paid by the Winnebagos is stated to be forty horses, wampum and trinkets,—in all to the amount of 2000 dollars."

Black-hawk was now in the neighborhood of Four Lakes, at the head sources of Rock River, about 60 miles from Fort Winnebago, and General *Atkinson* was in pursuit of him; but before he reached his place of retreat, he had retraced his steps, and was next discovered on the Ouisconsin.

About this time, a travelling preacher of the denomination called Dunkards was killed on the road to Chicago. His head was severed from his body, and carried off as a trophy. He was noted for his odd appearance; his beard being represented as near a yard in length. He had been informed that suspicious Indians were in the neighborhood, and a family, at whose house he stopped, retreated towards the settlements on receiving the information; but the Dunkard preacher thought proper to abide in the deserted house over night, and was killed.

On the 22 May, a party of spies having been sent out by General *Atkinson*, with despatches for Fort Armstrong, were attacked by the Indians, and four of them were killed. *St. Vrain*, an Indian agent, was among the number. They were all scalped, and their scalps were carried to *Black-hawk's* camp. *St. Vrain* had been odious to the Sacs from the part he took concerning their removal.

About this time, a man by the name of *Smith* was murdered near the Blue Mounds on the Galena frontier, and Mr. *Winters*, a mail contractor at Galena, was killed near Dixon's Ferry. The body of another man was found near the same place, but it was so disfigured that it was not known.

On the 6th June, a small settlement at the mouth of Plum River, 30 miles from Galena, was attacked, and the people retreated to a block-house, which they had wisely taken the precaution to erect. This the Indians tried to take for about an hour, but could not effect their object, and drew off. The inhabitants then went down the river in a boat to Galena. Whether any persons were killed, I do not find.

By the beginning of June, there were so many troops spread over the Indian country, that *Black-hawk's* party found but few opportunities to murder the frontier inhabitants. And although there were about 3000 men in arms to combat 500 Indians, yet congress ordered 600 mounted rangers to be raised "for the defence of the frontiers."

On the 14th of June, five persons were killed not far below Hamilton's Fort, near Galena, and on the 16th one man was killed within a mile of the same place. General *Dodge* being in the neighborhood, marched with 30 of his mounted men immediately in pursuit. When about three miles on his way, he discovered 12 Indians, whom he took to be the party who had committed the murders, and he pursued them with great spirit. Immediately after crossing East Pichetoneka Creek, the Indians buried themselves in a thick swamp The whites dismounted, and after securing their horses, and placing a small guard to watch for any that might attempt to escape, rushed in after the retreating Indians. They presently came up with them, and began an indiscriminate slaughter. No resistance was made, and every Indian was killed or murdered in a few minutes. Not satisfied with this, they tore off the scalps of every one, and bore them off in triumph.

On the same day, Captain *Snyder* met with and defeated a small Indian force near Kellog's Grove. Four of the Indians were said to have been killed, and one of the whites was mortally wounded. In their return march, they were attacked by an ambush and defeated, having three of their men killed and mortally wounded. The whites now escaped by flight.

On the 18th of June, as Captain *Stevenson* with a small force was scouting near where General *Dodge* cut off the 12 Indians, he was met by a force under *Black-hawk*, and a fierce contest ensued. The whites fought well, but they were defeated. At one time, Captain *Stevenson* was left almost alone by his party, and was severely wounded; but they rallied again, and effected a retreat, with the loss of three only of their number. The fight was close and desperate for a short time, in which bayonets, knives and tomahawks were chiefly used.

An attempt was made on the 24 of June, by a considerable body of warriors, to surprise the fort at Buffalo Grove, on Rock River, only about 12 miles to the northward of Dixon's Ferry. It was guarded by 150 militia, who were prepared to meet them, and a considerably sharp contest ensued. Sixteen of the Indians were killed before they retreated. But few of the whites were wounded. The garrison was in great fear of being cut off, having expended all their ammunition before a reinforcement arrived, which had been sent for while the attack was going on.

About this time, as *Black-hawk* was approaching a small fort on Apple River, about 12 miles from Galena, he fell in with four men who had been sent express to this place. They did not discover the Indians until fired upon, when they fled for the fort, and the Indians pursued them; one of the men, a Mr. *Welsh*, was wounded before reaching the fort, and another man was killed in the fort, who had raised his head above the pickets to make discovery. The Indians contented themselves by taking away a considerable quantity of flour, and a number of cattle and horses. They would doubtless have burnt the fort and buildings, and killed all the people, but from fear that the light of them would be seen by some large body of white soldiers, who might pursue and overtake them.

On the 25th of June, a pretty severe fight took place between a company of spies under Major *Dement* and a band of Indians, not far from Kellog's Grove. He had arrived there only the evening before, and being informed that an Indian trail was discovered in the neighborhood, set off immediately with 30 mounted men to attack them. He had not proceeded far before the Indians appeared, and confidently attacked him. The Indian yell so frightened the horses that they were thrown into confusion, and soon began a retreat. The Indians pursued them a considerable distance, and lost nine of their number, two of whom were chiefs. Five of the whites were killed, and they lost about 30 of their horses.

On the 29th of June, three men were attacked in a field at the Cincinaway Mound, about 10 miles from Galena, and two of them were killed. Major *Stevenson* marched immediately in pursuit of the murderers. On arriving at the Mound he found the bodies of the two men, *John Thompson* and *James Boxley*, both shockingly mutilated. The heart of the former was taken out, and both were scalped. Having left a few men to bury the dead, Major *Stevenson* followed the trail of the party to the Mississippi, where he found they had stolen a canoe and effected their escape across the river.

Mention has been made of the prompt action of congress for the relief of the frontiers. "General *Scott* was ordered from the sea-board with nine companies of artillery, and their cannon were to be drawn from the coast; nine companies of infantry were ordered from the lakes, and two companies from Baton Rouge, to put an end to the war. Such was the promptness with which these orders were executed, that five out of the six companies of artillery ordered from Fort Monroe in the Chesapeake arrived in 18 days at Chicago, 1800 miles distant in the interior of the country. Unfortunately this detachment was attacked by the cholera on the route, and the whole were rendered unfit to take the field before they arrived at the scene of action." Accordingly General *Scott* informed General *Atkinson* that he could not coöperate with him without endangering the troops already in the field, and therefore directed him to act without reference to his forces.

The scenes of horror occasioned by this most singular disease will doubtless be told of in after-times with an effect which has not been surpassed in that of the histories of the plagues in ancient days. Several of the companies before mentioned were entirely broken up. Of a corps of 208 men under Colonel *Twiggs*, but nine were left alive. Mr. *John Norvell*, at Detroit, wrote on the 12th July, to the editor of the Pennsylvania Enquirer, concerning its ravages in that region, as follows :—

"I regret to add, that the intelligence from the regular troops is disastrous. Of the three companies of artillery under Colonel *Twiggs*, and two or three more companies of infantry with them, few remain. These troops, you will recollect, landed from the steam-boat Henry Clay below Fort Gratiot. A great number of them have been swept off by the disease. Nearly all the others have deserted. Of the deserters, scattered all over the country, some have died in the woods, and their bodies been devoured by the wolves. I use the language of a gallant young officer. Others have taken their flight to the world of spirits, without a companion to close their eyes, or console the last moments of their existence. Their straggling survivors are occasionally seen marching, some of them know not whither, with their knapsacks on their backs, shunned by the terrified inhabitants as the source of a mortal pestilence. Colonel *Twiggs* himself, and Surgeon *Everett*, are very low. They were still living at the latest accounts from Fort Gratiot, and sanguine hopes were entertained of their recovery. No other officers have yet been assailed, except Lieutenant Clay.

"You will remember that the troops under Colonel *Cummings*, several of whom died here, embarked on board the steam-boat William Penn, on Sunday last, for Chicago. The sickness among them increased as they proceeded to Fort Gratiot, and became so great by the time they arrived there, that they were disembarked, and have returned to the vicinity of this city, and encamped at Springwells, about three miles below town. Seventeen or eighteen of them have died, and some still remain sick, probably never to recover. One half of the command of General *Scott*, ordered to Chicago by the lakes, will never reach him; a large portion of them dying; a still larger number deserting from an overwhelming dread of the disease, and the residue obliged to march back again."

In pursuing the thread of events in our narrative, we left General *Atkinson* in pursuit of *Black-hawk*, whose camp was said to be at the Four Lakes. General *Atkinson* had got this information from a Pottowattomie Indian, named WAPANSETH, whom, with several others, he had employed for the purpose. He said the old chief's camp was "inaccessible on all sides, except through a narrow pass, which was muddy, being otherwise surrounded by water or swamps. It was a little above the junction of a small creek, called Whitewater, with the principal stream of Rock River, and between the two." But, as we have already noted, when the army arrived at the Four Lakes, *Black-hawk* had gone; and so well did he manage his retreat that the whites were deceived as to the direction he had taken.

"Gen. Atkinson, expecting, when he marched, to meet the enemy in a short time, had taken with him but a small quantity of provisions, in consequence of which he was obliged to halt and divide his forces at Lake Cosh-ko-nong (one of the four) above named. He himself with the regulars, some 650 strong, remained at the lake; the militia, consisting of three brigades, under Generals *Posey*, *Dodge* and *Henry*, about 2000 men, were ordered to march to Fort Winnebago, on the Ouisconsin, where stores were hourly expected. It was the intention of the commander-in-chief to consolidate his forces, and renew the pursuit as soon as he had obtained sufficient stores."

Instead of crossing the country to escape beyond the Mississippi, as was expected, *Black-hawk* descended the Ouisconsin to escape in that direction; by which means General *Dodge* came upon his trail and commenced a vigorous pursuit. The old chief had received encouragement that in the country to which he had retreated, he should not only receive additional forces by which he could withstand all the Americans could bring against him, but also provisions in abundance. He found too late that he had been deceived in both particulars; he was obliged to fly from *Atkinson's* army, without provisions, nor had he time to procure any upon the way. *Dodge* was immediately upon his trail, but did not overtake him until near a hundred miles pursuit.

On the 21 of July, General *Dodge*, with about 900 men besides Indians came up with *Black-hawk* on the Ouisconsin, 40 miles from Fort Winnebago, over against the old Sac village, and it was only by the superior management of the old warrior chief, that himself or any of his people escaped capture. A great number of Indians belonged to *Dodge's* army, who contributed much to the successful result of the affair. The whites came upon the Indians as they were about to cross the river, and the time being evening, may account for their not being all cut off; for immediately after the attack began, it was so dark that the whites could not continue it without disadvantage to themselves. A letter dated at Fort Howard, 25 July, gives the following account of the affair:—

"Last evening we received the intelligence of a battle having been fought between Gen. *Dodge* and his division, and the Sacs and Foxes, in which the former were victorious. The particulars, as stated in Capt. *Plimpton's* letter to Capt. *Clark*, are these: *Parquett*, with a few Winnebagos, left the Portage a few days since, to proceed to Gen. *Dodge's* army, and guide them to the Sac camp. On Saturday morning last, 21st inst., Gen. *Dodge* sent his adjutant to report to Gen. *Atkinson* of his movements. He had not proceeded far before he came upon the Sacs' and Foxes' trail, directing their course to the Ouisconsin river. He immediately returned and reported the circumstance to Gen. *Dodge*, who pursued and overtook them about sundown of the same day, (Saturday) on the left bank of the Ouisconsin, and about 40 miles from Fort Winnebago, when the fight ensued; the Indians at the same time retreating. The night being very dark, they found it impossible to pursue them. They had found, when *Parquett* left them, which was early the next morning, 16 Indians killed, and but one white man killed, and four wounded. *Parquett* thinks not less than 40 Indians fell in the engagement."

We have the official account of the battle by General *Dodge;* but as it contains no additional facts, and is less minute than this, it was not thought worth while to insert it.

The truly deplorable condition of the Indians at this time cannot well be conceived of. In their pursuit of them before the battle, the whites found numbers dead in the way—emaciated, and starved to death! When overtaken by Gen. *Dodge*, they were not estimated to be but about 300 men, besides women and children, and although the affair of the 21st is called a battle, it does not seem that it can scarcely deserve that name, for if there had been any thing more than a show of resistance, more of the whites would have been killed.

The Indians report that they were attacked about a mile from the river: the approach of the army was discovered, and *Black-hawk*, with only 50 or 60 men, met them, to give the remainder time to cross to an island. *Neapope*, who had been ordered to march in the rear with about 20 warriors, to give notice when the whites were discovered, had been passed by them by an unexpected route, and *Black-hawk* heard no more from him until after the war. He found there was no chance of success by continuing it, deserted his braves, went to the Winnebago village, and soon after became a prisoner to the whites. Meanwhile General *Atkinson* had marched from Coshconong, and following in the trail of *Dodge*, had arrived within two days' march of the place where the fight had been with the Indians, and was immediately ready to coöperate with him. After receiving the news of the battle, he marched to the Blue Mounds on the Ouisconsin, opposite to where the fight had been.

The Indians were surprised that they were not pursued; but for want of boats or canoes, or the means of constructing rafts, they could not even cross to the island to which the Indians had escaped for two days after, and in the mean time they escaped. That they were not pressed harder on the night of the battle, General *Dodge* urged in excuse, that his men were worn down with fatigue, having marched 40 miles that day.

Among the prisoners taken by General *Dodge's* party, was the wife of the warrior called the BIG-LAKE. She was a sister of *Keokuk*, and her husband had been killed in the fight. Although the whites were satisfied before, they were now informed by this squaw of *Black-hawk's* final resolution; which was, for such of his men as had good horses to proceed with him and strike the Mississippi above Prairie du Chien, while the remainder should proceed by the Ouisconsin; and a place of rendezvous was appointed for all to meet on the west side of the great river. This squaw also stated that before the battle on the Ouisconsin, in which she was taken, 200 of *Black-hawk's* men had been killed.

General *Dodge* having recommended a cannon to be placed on the bank of the river, at a suitable place below the battle-ground, to cut off such as should attempt an escape in that direction, marched with his army on the 23d, and joined General *Atkinson* at the Blue Mounds, and every thing was immediately put in readiness to pursue the main body of the Indians under *Black-hawk*.

As was intended, many fell into the hands of the whites as they descended the Ouisconsin. Some of the boats conveying these poor wretches were overset, and many of those in them were drowned; the greater number, however, fell into the hands of their enemies in their passage. Many of the children were found to be in such a famished state that they could not be revived.

Several untoward circumstances now transpired to prevent the escape of the main body under *Black-hawk*. The first was his falling in with a steam-boat on the 1st of August, just as they were preparing to cross the Mississippi, by which means that day was lost. And upon the next day, the whole army of whites under General *Atkinson* came upon them, which completed their destruction. As in the affair of the 21 of July on the Ouisconsin, *Black-hawk* did not wish to fight, but to escape; and when the steam-boat fell in with him he used every means to give the captain of her to understand that he desired to surrender. He displayed two white flags, and about 150 of his men approached the river without arms, and made signs of submission; but whether, as was said by the whites, the interpreter on board was so frightened that he could not convey the meaning of those on shore to the captain of the boat, or whether, as it would seem, the whites were determined to *kill* Indians, we will not take upon us to decide, but lay before the reader the account of the affair by Captain *I. Throcmorton*, of the boat, which is as follows:—

"Prairie du Chien, 3 Aug. 1832. I arrived at this place on Monday last, [30 July,] and was despatched, with the Warrior alone, to Wapashaw's village, 120 miles above, to inform them of the approach of the Sacs, and to order down all the friendly Indians to this place. On our way down, we met one of the Sioux band, who informed us that the Indians (our enemies) were on Bad-axe River, to the number of 400. We stopped and cut some wood, and prepared for action. About 4 o'clock on Wednesday afternoon, [1 Aug.] we found the *gentlemen* [Indians] where he stated he had left them. As we neared them, they raised a white flag, and endeavored to decoy us; but we were a little too old for them; for instead of landing, we ordered them to send a boat on board, which they declined. After about 15 minutes' delay, giving them time to remove a few of their women and children, we let slip a six-pounder loaded with canister, followed by a severe fire of musketry; and if ever you saw straight blankets, you would have seen them there. I fought them at anchor most of the time, and we were all very much exposed. I have a ball which came in close by where I was standing, and passed through the bulk-head of the wheel-room. We fought them for about an hour or more, until our wood began to fail, and night coming on, we left, and went on to the Prairie. This little fight cost them 23 killed, and, of course, a great many wounded. We never lost a man, and had but one man wounded, (shot through the leg.) The next morning, before we could get back again, on account of a heavy fog, they had the whole [of General *Atkinson's*] army upon them. We found them at it, walked in, and took a hand ourselves. The first shot from the Warrior *laid out three.* I can hardly tell you any thing about it, for I am in great haste, as I am now on my way to the field again. The army lost eight or nine killed, and seventeen wounded, whom we brought down. One died on deck last night. We brought down 36 prisoners, women and children. I tell you what, *Sam*, there is no fun in fighting Indians, particularly at this season, when the grass is so very bright. Every man, and even my cabin-boy, fought well. We had 16 regulars, 5 riflemen, and 20 of ourselves. Mr. *How*, of Platte, Mr. *James G. Soulard*, and one of the *Rolettes*, were with us, and fought well."

Lieutenant *Kingsbury*, an officer in command of the United States' troops on board the Warrior at the time of the fight, reported that, about 40 miles above Prairie du Chien, a great number of the Sacs and Foxes were seen, who hoisted a white flag, but would not send a canoe on board, although they were told that, in case they did not, they should be fired upon, which was immediately done. They seemed much alarmed when the six-pounder was discharged upon them, and all immediately covered themselves with trees and whatever offered. Five or six were supposed to have been killed.

Early on the morning of the next day, August 2, the whole combined army, amounting to 1600 men, came up with the Indians; and the following are the particular details of that whole transaction, as published at Galena, four days after it happened, namely, August 6.

"The whole army under General *Atkinson*, embracing the brigades commanded by Generals *Henry*, *Posey*, and *Alexander*, and squadron under command of General *Dodge*, all crossed over to the north side of the Ouisconsin at Helena, on the 28th and 29th ult. They took up a line of march in a northerly direction, in order to intersect the Indian trail. At the distance of about five miles, the great trail was discovered, leading in a direction N. of W. towards the Mississippi, and supposed to be about four days old. General *Atkinson*, seeing the direction of the enemy, knew well that it would require all diligence and expedition to overtake them before they would cross the Mississippi, and hence commenced from that time a *forced march;* leaving all baggage wagons, and every thing else which was calculated to retard the pursuit.

"The country through which the enemy's trail led our army between the Ouisconsin Bluffs and the Kickapoo River was one continued series of mountains. No sooner had they reached the summit of one high and almost perpendicular hill, than they had to descend on the other side equally steep to the base of another. Nothing but a deep ravine, with muddy banks, separated these mountains. The woods, both upon the top of the highest mountains, and at the bottom of the deepest hollows, was of the heaviest growth. The under-bushes were chiefly thorn and prickly ash. This is a short description of the route, and shows the difficulties of the pursuit. Notwithstanding all this, our army gained on the enemy daily, as appeared from the enemy's encampments. The tedious march thus continued was met by our brave troops without a murmur; and as the Indian signs appeared more recent, the officers and men appeared more anxious to push on. On the fourth night of our march from Helena, and at an encampment of the enemy, was discovered an old Sac Indian, by our spies, who informed them that the main body of the enemy had, on that day, gone to the Mississippi, and intended to cross on the next morning, Aug. 2d. The horses being nearly broken down, and the men nearly exhausted from fatigue, General *Atkinson* ordered a halt for a few hours, (it being after 8 o'clock,) with a determination to start at 2 o'clock for the Mississippi, about ten miles distant. At the precise hour the bugles sounded, and in a short time all were ready to march.

"General *Dodge's* squadron was honored with being placed in front; the infantry followed next; General *Henry's* brigade next; General *Alexander's* next; and General *Posey's* formed the rear-guard. General *Dodge* called for, and as soon received, 20 volunteer spies to go ahead of the whole army.

"In this order the march commenced. They had not, however, gone more than five miles, before one of our spies came back, announcing their having come in sight of the enemy's picket-guard. He went back, and the intelligence was quickly conveyed to General *Atkinson*, then to all the commanders of the brigades; and the celerity of the march was instantly increased. In a few minutes more, the firing commenced at about 500 yards ahead of the front of the army, between our spies and the Indian picket guard. The Indians were driven by our spies from hill to hill, and kept up a tolerably brisk firing from every situation commanding the ground over which our spies had to march; but being charged upon and routed from their hiding-places, they sought safety by retreating to the main body on the bank of the river, and joining in one general effort to defend themselves there or die on the ground.

"Lest some might escape by retreating up or down the river, General *Atkinson* very judiciously ordered General *Alexander* and General *Posey* to form the right wing of the army, and march down to the river above the Indian encampment on the bank, and then move down. General *Henry* formed the left wing, and marched in the main trail of the enemy. The U. S. infantry, and General *Dodge's* squadron of the mining troops, marched in the centre. With this order our whole force descended the almost perpendicular bluff, and came into a low valley, heavily timbered with a large growth of under-brush, weeds and grass.—Sloughs, deep ravines, old logs, &c. were so plentiful as to afford every facility for the enemy to make a strong defence. General *Henry* first came upon and commenced a heavy fire, which was returned by the enemy. The enemy, being routed from their first hiding-places, sought others. General *Dodge's* squadron and the U. S. troops soon came into action, and, with General *Henry's* men, rushed into the strong defiles of the enemy, and killed all in their way, except a few who succeeded in swimming a slough of the Mississippi, 150 yards wide. During this time the brigades of Generals *Alexander* and *Posey* were marching down the river, when they fell in with another part of the enemy's army, and killed and routed all that opposed them.

"The battle lasted upwards of three hours. About 50 of the enemy's women and children were taken prisoners, and many, by accident in the battle, were killed. When the Indians were driven to the bank of the Mississippi, some hundreds of men, women, and children, plunged into the river, and hoped by diving, &c. to escape the bullets of our guns; very few, however, escaped our sharp-shooters.

"The loss on the side of the enemy never can be exactly ascertained, but, according to the best computation, they must have lost in killed upwards of 150. Our loss in killed and wounded was 27.

"Some had crossed the river before our arrival; and we learn by a prisoner, that *Black-hawk*, while the battle waxed warm, had stolen off, and gone up the river on this side. If he did, he took nothing with him; for his valuables, many of them, together with certificates of good character, and of his having fought bravely against the United States during the last war, &c., signed by British officers, were found on the battle-ground.

"It is the general impression in the army and at this place, that the Sacs would be glad to conclude a peace on almost any terms we might propose. On the morning of the 4th inst. a party of Sioux came to our camp, and begged premission to go on the back trail and have a fight with them. On the same day, our whole army started to go down to Prairie du Chien, (about 40 miles,) and wait further orders.

"General *Atkinson*, accompanied by Generals *Dodge* and *Posey*, with tho U. S. infantry, arrived at the Prairie on the evening of the 4th, on board the S. B. Warrior, and will remain until the mounted volunteers arrive. The Winnebagos, at Prairie du Chien, are daily bringing in Sac prisoners and scalps.

"On the same day, a party of 15 men from Cassville, under command of Captain *Price*, were reconnoitring the country between that place and the Ouisconsin, and fell upon a fresh Sac trail making towards the Mississippi. They rushed with full speed of horses, and soon came upon, killed and took prisoners to the number of 12.

"General *Scott* and staff left here this morning for Prairie du Chien, in the steam-boat Warrior, to join General *Atkinson*."

This was the finishing stroke to the war with the Sacs and Foxes, although *Black-hawk* himself had made his escape. General *Atkinson* immediately directed *Keokuk* to send out some of his Indians to demand a surrender of all the warriors that had escaped, and if possible to capture *Black-hawk*, and bring him in either alive or dead.

Respecting his last battle, *Black-hawk* has said, that when the whites came upon his people, they tried to give themselves up, and made no show of resistance until the soldiers began to slaughter them, and then his braves determined to fight until they were all killed. With a small party he went to the Winnebago village at Prairie la Cross. Here he told the chief he desired to give himself up to the whites, and let them kill him, if they wished to do so. The squaws at this place made him a dress of white deerskins, preparatory to his departure for Prairie du Chien, to which it appears he went voluntarily with those that had been sent out after him.

The Sioux, of whom we have made mention, that had permission to go out after the flying Sacs on the 3d of August, were about 100 in number. They soon after met with the flying band on the west side of the Mississippi, and indiscriminately murdered about 120 of the poor half-starved creatures who had escaped from the whites through so many perils.

A most distressing incident is related as having taken place in the battle of the 2 August, which it may not be improper to lay before the reader, that examples of the horrors of war may not be wanting. "When our troops charged the enemy in their defiles near the bank of the Mississippi, men, women, and children, were seen mixed together, in such a manner as to render it difficult to kill one, and save the other. A young squaw of about 19 stood in the grass at a short distance from our line, holding her little girl in her arms, about four years old. While thus standing, apparently unconcerned, a ball struck the right arm of the child above the elbow, and, shattering the bone, passed into the breast of its poor mother, who instantly fell dead to the ground. She fell upon the child, and confined it to the ground also. During the whole battle, this babe was heard to groan and call for relief, but none had time to afford it. When, however, the Indians had retreated from that spot, and the battle had nearly subsided, Lieutenant *Anderson*, of the United States' army, went to the place and took from under the dead mother her wounded daughter, and brought it to a place selected for surgical aid. It was soon ascertained that its arm must come off; and the operation was performed upon the little sufferer without drawing from it a tear or a shriek." At the last accounts it was doing well. When we are told that this Indian child was sucking a piece of dry biscuit during the whole time of the amputation, it almost causes a disbelief of the whole story; but such are the facts given.

Although no further depredations could be feared from the Sacs, yet on the 9 August, six Indians approached a block-house on Cedar Creek, which runs into Henderson's River, about 10 miles north of Warren court-house, and shot, tomahawked and scalped a young man named *William Martin*. They left behind them a pair of leggins and a loaded gun, and fled, as was supposed, over the Mississippi. A company of 15 rangers went in immediate pursuit, but could not come up with them. It was soon after discovered that this murder was committed by some of *Keokuk's* band, and he gave up his nephew as the perpetrator of it.

CHAPTER X.

Particulars in the lives of the chief men—NEAPOPE—*His account of himself—Surrender of* BLACK-HAWK—*Speeches on the occasion—His speech on the same—Particulars in his early history*—WABOKIESHIEK, *the Prophet—Treaty of September*, 1832—*Account of* Black-hawk's *companions—Arrival of the Indians at Washington*—Black-hawk's *interview with the President.*

NEAPOPE was second in command to *Black-hawk*, and in all the expeditions against the whites; he was taken prisoner in the fight with the Sioux, and at his examination afterwards by General *Scott*, about the murders which had been committed on the whites, he gave this account of himself:—

"I always belonged to *Black-hawk's* band. Last summer I went to Malden; when I came back, I found that by the treaty with General *Gaines*, the Sacs had moved across the Mississippi. I remained during the winter with the Prophet, on Rock River, 35 miles above the mouth. During the winter, the Prophet sent me across the Mississippi, to *Black-hawk*, with a message, to tell him and his band to cross back to his village and make corn; that if the Americans came and told them to move again, they would shake hands with them. If the Americans had come and told us to move, we should have shaken hands, and immediately have moved peaceably. We encamped on Syracuse Creek. We met some Pottowattomies, and I made a feast for them. At that time I heard there were some Americans [under Major *Stillman*] near us. I prepared a white flag to go and see them, and sent two or three young men on a hill to see what they were doing. Before the feast was finished, I heard my young men were killed. This was at sunset. Some of my young men ran out; two killed, and the Americans were seen rushing on to our camp. My young men fired a few guns, and the Americans ran off, and my young men chased them about six miles."

Neapope further said, that the Pottowattomies of the village immediately left them, and that no Kikapoos joined them, but those who were originally with *Black-hawk;* but the Winnebagos did, and brought in scalps frequently; that, at last. when they found the Sacs would be beaten, they turned against them. It was also given in by some of those examined at this time, that *Black-hawk* said, when the steam-boat Warrior approached them, that he pitied the women and children, and began to make preparations to surrender to the whites, and for that purpose sent out a white flag to meet the boat, which immediately fired upon them. Then said he, "*I fired too.*" The truth of this will not be questioned, inasmuch as the facts agree with the captain of the Warrior's own account. Hence the inference is clear, that much blood might have been saved, but for the precipitancy of those who only sought a fight with the Indians.

Parties of the friendly tribes were so continually on the alert, that it seemed very probable the principal chiefs would soon fall into their hands. These expectations were soon realized; for at 11 o'clock, 27 August, *Black-hawk* and his Prophet were delivered to General *Street* at Prairie du Chien. They were brought by two Winnebagoes, *Decorie* and *Chaetar*, and, when delivered, were dressed in a full dress of white-tanned deerskins. Soon after they were seated in the presence of the officer, *Decorie*, called the *One-eyed*, rose and spoke thus to him:—

"My father, I now stand before you. When we parted, I told you I would return soon; but I could not come any sooner. We have had to go a great distance, [to the Dalle, on the Ouisconsin, above the Portage.] You see we have done what you sent us to do. These [pointing to the prisoners] are the two you told us to get. We have done what you told us to do. We always do what you tell us, because we know it is for our good. Father, you told us to get these men, and it would be the cause of much good to the Winnebagoes. We have brought them, but it has been very hard for us to do so. That one, *Mucatamishkakaekq*, [meaning *Black-hawk*,] was a great way off. You told us to bring them to you alive: we have done so. If you had told us to bring their heads alone, we would have done so, and it would have been less difficult than what we have done.—Father, we deliver these men into your hands. We would not deliver them even to our brother, the chief of the warriors, but to you; because we know you, and we believe you are our friend. We want you to keep them safe; if they are to be hurt, we do not wish to see it. Wait until we are gone before it is done.—Father, many little birds have been flying about our ears of late, and we thought they whispered to us that there was evil intended for us; but now we hope these evil birds will let our ears alone.—We know you are our friend, because you take our part, and that is the reason we do what you tell us to do. You say you love your red children: we think we love you as much if not more than you love us. We have confidence in you, and you may rely on us. We have been promised a great deal if we would take these men,—that it would do much good to our people. We now hope to see what will be done for us.—We have come in haste; we are tired and hungry. We now put these men into your hands. We have done all that you told us to do."

General *Street* said, in answer:—

"My children, you have done well. I told you to bring these men to me, and you have done so. I am pleased at what you have done. It is for your good, and for this reason I am pleased. I assured the great chief of the warriors, [General *Atkinson*,] that if these men were in your country, you would find them, and bring them to me, and now I can say much for your good. I will go down to Rock Island with the prisoners, and I wish you who have brought these men, especially, to go with me, with such other chiefs and warriors as you may select. My children, the great chief of the warriors, when he left this place, directed me to deliver these, and all other prisoners, to the chief of the warriors at this place, Colonel *Taylor*, who is here by me.—Some of the Winnebagoes south of the Ouisconsin have befriended the Saukies, [Sacs,] and some of the Indians of my agency have also given them aid. This displeaseth the great chief of the warriors and your great father the president, and was calculated to do much harm.—Your great father, the president at Washington, has sent a great war-chief from the far east, General *Scott*, with a fresh army of soldiers. He is now at Rock Island. Your great father, the president, has sent him and the governor and chief of Illinois to hold a council with the Indians. He has sent a speech to you, and wishes the chiefs and warriors of the Winnebagoes to go to Rock Island to the council on the tenth of next month. I wish you to be ready in three days, when I will go with you.—I am well pleased that you have taken the *Black-hawk*, the Prophet, and others prisoners. This will enable me to say much for you to the great chief of the warriors, and to the president, your great father. My children, I shall now deliver the two men, *Black-hawk* and the Prophet, to the chief of the warriors here; he will take care of them till we start to Rock Island."

Colonel *Taylor*, having taken the prisoners into his custody, addressed the chiefs as follows:—

"The great chief of the warriors told me to take the prisoners when you shall bring them, and send them to Rock Island to him. I will take them and keep them safe, but I will use them well, and send them with you and General *Street*, when you go down to the council, which will be in a few days. Your friend, General *Street*, advises you to get ready and go down soon, and so do I. I tell you again I will take the prisoners; I will keep them safe, but I will do them no harm. I will deliver them to the great chief of the warriors, and he will do with them and use them in such manner as shall be ordered by your great father, the president."

Chaetar, the other Winnebago, next spoke, and said, "My father, I am young, and do not know how to make speeches. This is the second time I ever spoke to you before people.—I am no chief; I am no orator; but I have been allowed to speak to you. If I should not speak as well as others, still you must listen to me. Father, when you made the speech to the chiefs *Waugh kon Decorie Carramani*, the One-eyed *Decorie*, and others, 'tother day, I was there. I heard you. I thought what you said to them, you also said to me. You said, if these two [pointing to *Black-hawk* and the Prophet] were taken by us and brought to you, there would never more a black cloud hang over your Winnebagoes. Your words entered into my ear, into my brains, and into my heart. I left here that same night, and you know you have not seen me since until now. I have been a great way; I had much trouble; but when I remembered what you said, I knew what you said was right. This made me continue and do what you told me to do. Near the Dalle, on the Ouisconsin, I took *Black-hawk*. No one did it but me. I say this in the ears of all present, and they know it—and I now appeal to the Great Spirit, our grandfather, and the earth, our grandmother, for the truth of what I say. Father, I am no chief, but what I have done is for the benefit of my nation, and I hope to see the good that has been promised to us. That one *Wa-bo-kie-shiek*, [the *Prophet*,] is my relation—if he is to be hurt, I do not wish to see it. Father, soldiers sometimes stick the ends of their guns into the backs of Indian prisoners when they are going about in the hands of the guard. I hope this will not be done to these men."

The following is said to be the speech which *Black-hawk* made when he surrendered himself to the agent at Pairie du Chien:—

"You have taken me prisoner with all my warriors. I am much grieved, for I expected, if I did not defeat you, to hold out much longer, and give you more trouble before I surrendered. I tried hard to bring you into ambush, but your last general understands Indian fighting. The first one was not so wise. When I saw that I could not beat you by Indian fighting, I determined to rush on you, and fight you face to face. I fought hard. But your guns were well aimed. The bullets flew like birds in the air, and whizzed by our ears like the wind through the trees in the winter. My warriors fell around me; it began to look dismal. I saw my evil day at hand. The sun rose dim on us in the morning, and at night it sunk in a dark cloud, and looked like a ball of fire. That was the last sun that shone on *Black-hawk*. His heart is dead, and no longer beats quick in his bosom.—He is now a prisoner to the white men; they will do with him as they wish. But he can stand torture, and is not afraid of death. He is no coward. *Black-hawk* is an Indian.

"He has done nothing for which an Indian ought to be ashamed. He has fought for his countrymen, the squaws and papooses, against white men, who came, year after year, to cheat them and take away their lands. You know the cause of our making war. It is known to all white men. They ought to be ashamed of it. The white men despise the Indians, and drive them from their homes. But the Indians are not deceitful. The white men speak bad of the Indian, and look at him spitefully. But the Indian does not tell lies; Indians do not steal.

"An Indian, who is as bad as the white men, could not live in our nation; he would be put to death, and eat up by the wolves. The white men are b schoolmasters they carry false looks, and deal in false actions; they sm in the face of the poor Indian to cheat him; they shake them by the hand gain their confidence, to make them drunk, to deceive them, and ruin c wives. We told them to let us alone, and keep away from us; but they f lowed on, and beset our paths, and they coiled themselves among us, like t snake. They poisoned us by their touch. We were not safe. We lived danger. We were becoming like them, hypocrites and liars, adulterers, la drones, all talkers, and no workers.

"We looked up to the Great Spirit. We went to our great father. We were encouraged. His great council gave us fair words and big promises; but we got no satisfaction. Things were growing worse. There were no deer in the forest. The opossum and beaver were fled; the springs were drying up, and our squaws and papooses without victuals to keep them from starving; we called a great council, and built a large fire. The spirit of our fathers arose and spoke to us to avenge our wrongs or die. We all spoke before the council fire. It was warm and pleasant. We set up the war-whoop, and dug up the tomahawk; our knives were ready, and the heart of *Black-hawk* swelled high in his bosom, when he led his warriors to battle. He is satisfied. He will go to the world of spirits contented. He has done his duty. His father will meet him there, and commend him.

"*Black-hawk* is a true Indian, and disdains to cry like a woman. He feels for his wife, his children and friends. But he does not care for himself. He cares for his nation and the Indians. They will suffer. He laments their fate. The white men do not scalp the head; but they do worse—they poison the heart; it is not pure with them.—His countrymen will not be scalped, but they will, in a few years, become like the white men, so that you can't trust them, and there must be, as in the white settlements, nearly as many officers as men, to take care of them and keep them in order.

"Farewell, my nation! *Black-hawk* tried to save you, and avenge your wrongs. He drank the blood of some of the whites. He has been taken p oner, and his plans are stopped. He can do no more. He is near his e His sun is setting, and he will rise no more. Farewell to *Black-hawk*."

It is somewhat singular that the old chief should ever have been taken alive, and he probably never would have been by the whites. When it was reported currently that he had sacrificed himself in the stand that he made upon the banks of the Mississippi, in the end of July, as has been related, *Spenser's* famous lines were the first to discover themselves to our mind, upon the great event.

> "Unto the mighty stream him to betake,
> Where he an end of battle and of life did make."
>
> FAIRY QUEEN.

But we were soon glad to learn that the report, like the lines of *Spenser*, was only poetry.

It can be scarcely necessary to add that the prisoners were set at liberty, and the offenders were ordered again to be sought after.

On the 7 September, the Indian prisoners and their guards went on board the steam-boat Winnebago, and were conveyed down the river to Jefferson Barracks, ten miles below St. Louis. There were, besides *Black-hawk* and the *prophet*, eleven chiefs or head men of the Sacs and Foxes, together with about fifty less distinguished warriors. These were landed just above the lower rapids, on their pledge of remaining peaceable. Two days before, a boat had conveyed to the barracks six or seven warriors, among whom was *Neapope*. On their arrival at the barracks, all of them were put in irons.

Black-hawk is not so old a man as was generally supposed. Some, who knew him well, said he was not above 48, although the toils of wars had made him appear like one of 70.* He was by birth a Pottowattomie, but brought up by the Sacs. His height is about six feet. As to his physiognomy, it is unnecessary for us to add concerning it here, as that may be better had from an inspection of the engraving of him, as our likeness is said, by many who have seen him, to be excellent.

Like other Indian names, his is spelt in as many ways as times used by different writers. At a treaty which he made with the United States in 1829, at Prairie du Chien, it is written *Hay-ray-tshoan-sharp*. In a description of him about the time he was taken, we find him spelt *Mus-cata-mish-ka-kaek;* and several others might be added.

The *Prophet*, or *Wabokieshiek*, (White-cloud,) is about 40 years old, and nearly six feet high, stout and athletic. He was by one side a Winnebago, and the other a Sac or Saukie, and is thus described:—He "has a large, broad face, short, blunt nose, large, full eyes, broad mouth, thick lips, with a full suit of hair. He wore a white cloth head-dress, which rose several inches above the top of his head; the whole man exhibiting a deliberate savageness; not that he would seem to delight in honorable war, or fight, but marking him as the priest of assassination or secret murder. He had in one hand a white flag, while the other hung carelessly by his side. They were both clothed in very white dressed deerskins, fringed at the seams with short cuttings of the same." This description, though written long before any painting was made of him, will be found, we think, to correspond very well with the engraving of him which we have given.

It is said by many, and is evident from *Black-hawk's* account, that *Wabokieshiek* was the prime mover of this war, and had powwowed up a belief among his people, that he was able to conjure such kind of events as he desired; and that he had made *Black-hawk* believe the whites were but few, and could not fight, and therefore might easily be driven from the disputed lands. It seems, however, rather incredible that *Black-hawk* should have believed that the Americans *were few and could not fight*, when it is known that he was opposed to them in the last war, and must, therefore, have been convinced of the falsity of such a report long before this war.

In September, a treaty was made by the United States with the Winneba-

---

* In the account of his life, published by Mr. *J. B. Patterson*, in 1834, *Black-hawk* says he was born in 1767, on Rock River; and hence, in 1832, he was in his 65th year. His father's name was PYESA. His great-grandfather's name was NA-NA-MA-KEE, or *Thunder*, who was born in the vicinity of Montreal, "where the Great Spirit first placed the Sac nation"

goes, and another with the Sacs and Foxes. The former ceded all their lands south of the Ouisconsin, and east of the Mississippi, amounting to 4,600,000 acres of valuable lands. The treaty with the Sacs and Foxes was on the 21 of that month, and 6,000,000 acres were acquired at that time, "of a quality not inferior to any between the same parallels of latitude." It abounds in lead ore, and the Indians say in others.

For these tracts the United States agreed to make the following considerations:—"To pay an annuity of 20,000 dollars for 30 years; to support a black smith and gunsmith in addition to those then employed; to pay the debts of the tribes; to supply provisions; and, as a reward for the fidelity of *Keokuk* and the friendly band, to allow a reservation to be made for them of 400 miles square * on the Ioway River, to include *Keokuk's* principal village."

By the same treaty, *Black-hawk*, his two sons, the *Prophet*, *Naopope*, and five others, principal warriors of the hostile bands, were to remain in the hands of the whites, as hostages, during the pleasure of the president of the United States. The other prisoners were given up to the friendly Indians.

A gentleman who visited the captive Indians at Jefferson Barracks, Missouri, speaks thus concerning them:—"We were immediately struck with admiration at the gigantic and symmetrical figures of most of the warriors, who seemed, as they reclined in native ease and gracefulness, with their half-naked bodies exposed to view, rather like statues from some master-hand, than like beings of a race whom we had heard characterized as degenerate and debased. We extended our hands, which they rose to grasp, and to our question, 'How d'ye do?' they responded in the same words, accompanying them with a hearty shake." "They were clad in leggins and moccasins of buckskin, and wore blankets, which were thrown around them in the manner of the Roman toga, so as to leave their right arms bare." "The youngest among them were painted on their necks, with a bright vermilion color, and had their faces transversely streaked with alternate red and black stripes. From their bodies, and from their faces and eyebrows, they pluck out the hair with the most assiduous care. They also shave, or pull it out from their heads, with the exception of a tuft of about three fingers' width, extending from between the forehead and crown to the back of the head; this they sometimes plait into a queue on the crown, and cut the edges of it down to an inch in length, and plaster it with the vermilion, which keeps it erect, and gives it the appearance of a cock's-comb."

The same author says, the oldest son of *Black-hawk*, *Nasinewiskuk*, called *Jack*, but for want of "that peculiar expression which emanates from a cultivated intellect," could have been looked upon by him "as the living personification of his *beau ideal* of manly beauty." He calls *Black-hawk Mack-atama-sic-ac-ac*, and states his height at about five feet eight inches, and that he should judge his age to be 50. Those who have known him for years, say his disposition is very amiable; that he is endowed with great kindness of heart, and the strictest integrity; that, like *Mishikinakwa*, he was not a chief by birth, but acquired the title by bravery and wisdom.

Naseuskuck, or the *Thundercloud*, is the second son of *Black-hawk*, and accompanied him in his captivity. He is said not to be very handsome.

Opeekeeshieck, or *Wabokieshiek*, the Prophet, of whom we have already given some particulars, carries with him a huge pipe, a yard in length, with the stem ornamented with the neck feathers of a duck, and beads and ribands of various colors. To its centre is attached a fan of feathers. He wears his hair long all over his head.

NE-A-POPE, *Naopope*, *Naapope*, &c., or *Broth*, of whom we have also several times spoken, was brother to the Prophet, and "some years his junior;" and our informant adds, "he resembles him in height and figure, though he is not so robust, and his face is more sharp: in wickedness of expression they are *var nobile fratrum*." "When Mr. *Catlin*, the artist, was about taking the portrait of *Naapope*, he seized the ball and chain that were fastened to his leg, and raising them on high, exclaimed, with a look of scorn, '*Make me so, and*

* So says our authority, (*Niles's Register*,) but we very much doubt this enormous space 40 miles square gives 1600 square miles, which perhaps might have been the truth But when 160,000 square miles are considered, all probability is outraged

show me to the great father." On Mr. *Catlin's* refusing to paint him as he wished, he kept varying his countenance with grimaces, to prevent him from catching a likeness.

"*Poweeshieck*, or *Strawberry*, is the only Fox among them, the rest being all Sacs. He is the son of the chief *Epanoss:* his parents dying while he was an infant, he was adopted by *Naapope*. He is 19 years of age."

"*Pomahoe*, or *Fast-swimming-fish*, is a short, thick set, good-natured old brave, who bears his misfortunes with a philosophy worthy of the ancients."

The following act of congress we extract, as it throws light upon subsequent details:—"For the expenses of 12 prisoners of war of the Sac and Fox tribes, now in confinement, and to be held as hostages, under the seventh article of the treaty of 21 Sept. 1832, embracing the cost of provisions and clothing, compensation to an interpreter, and cost of removing them to a place of safety, where they may be kept without being closely confined, the sum of 2500."

On the 22 April, (1833,) the captive Indians arrived at Washington, and the next day *Black-hawk* had a long interview with President *Jackson*. The first words with which it is said he accosted the president were, "I AM A MAN, AND YOU ARE ANOTHER."

The president, after a few brief observations, directed the articles of dress provided for them to be exhibited to them, and told *Black-hawk* that the whole would be delivered to him to be distributed as, in his judgment, he should think best. He then told them they must depart immediately for Fort Monroe, and remain there contented, until he gave them permission to return to their country. That time, he said, depended upon the conduct of their people; that they would not be set at liberty, until all the articles of the treaty had been complied with, and good feelings were evinced by their countrymen. The Prophet then said:—

"We expected to return immediately to our people. The war in which we have been involved, was occasioned by our attempting to raise provisions on our own lands, or where we thought we had a right so to do. We have lost many of our people, as well as the whites. Our tribes and families are now exposed to the attacks of our enemies, the Sioux and the Menominies. We hope, therefore, to be permitted to return home to take care of them."

Black-hawk spoke some time to the president, giving a clear and comprehensive history of the rise of the war, and, towards the close, said:—

"We did not expect to conquer the whites; no. They had too many houses—too many men. I took up the hatchet, for my part, to revenge injuries which my people could no longer endure. Had I borne them longer without striking, my people would have said, *Black-hawk* is a woman; he is too old to be a chief—he is no Sac. These reflections caused me to raise the war-whoop. I say no more of it; it is known to you. *Keokuk* once was here; you took him by the hand, and when he wished to return to his home, you were willing. *Black-hawk* expects, that, like *Keokuk*, we shall be permitted to return too."

The president added, that he was well acquainted with the circumstances which led to the disasters to which they had alluded. It was unnecessary to look back upon them. He intended now to secure the observance of peace. They need not feel any uneasiness, he said, about their own women and children. They should not suffer from the Sioux and Menominies. He would compel the red men to be at peace with one another. That when he was satisfied that all things would remain quiet, then they would be permitted to return. He then took them by the hand, and dismissed them.

It is said, that, while in Washington, the Indians expressed more surprise and pleasure at the portraits of the Indian chiefs in the war department than any thing else that was shown them.

On Friday, 26 April, the captives were conducted from Washington towards Fort Monroe, which is upon a small island, at Old Point Comfort, on the west side of the Chesapeake Bay, in Virginia.

Before closing the present chapter, a few other interesting matters shall be laid before our readers. We have just given the description of the Indians while at Jefferson Barracks, by one who visited them there not long after their confinement. We now intend to give what the author of Knickerbocker says of them soon after. Mr. *Irving's* account is contained in a letter, dated Washington, 18 Dec. 1832.—"From St. Louis I went to Fort Jefferson, about 9 miles distant, to see *Black-hawk*, the Indian warrior, and his fellow-prisoners—a forlorn crew—emaciated and dejected—the redoubtable chieftain himself, a meagre old man upwards of 70. He has, however, a fine head, a Roman style of face, and a prepossessing countenance."

Since we are upon descriptions, the following will not be thought out of place, perhaps, although we had reserved it for our next chapter. It is from the pen of the editor of the U. States Literary Gazette, Philadelphia. "We found time, yesterday, to visit the *Black-hawk*, and his accompanying Indian chiefs, and the Prophet, at Congress Hall Hotel. We went into their chamber, and found most of them sitting or lying on their beds. *Black-hawk* was sitting in a chair, and apparently depressed in spirits. He is about 65, of middling size, with a head that would excite the envy of a phrenologist—one of the finest that Heaven ever let fall on the shoulders of an Indian. The Prophet has a coarser figure, with less of intellect, but with the marks of decision and firmness. His face was painted with red and white. The son of *Black-hawk* is a noble specimen of physical beauty—a model for those who would embody the idea of strength. He was painted, and his hair cut and dressed in a strange fantasy. The other chiefs had nothing in particular in their appearance to distinguish them from other natives of the forest. The whole of the deputation visited the water works yesterday, [June 11 or 12,] and subsequently were taken to the Cherry-hill Prison, and shown the manner in which white men punish. The exhibition of arms and ships at the navy-yard, led the *Hawk* to remark *that he suspected the great father was getting ready for war.*"

It was remarked by some in Philadelphia that *Black-hawk's* "pyramidal forehead" very much resembled that of Sir *Walter Scott*. Others observed that his countenance strongly reminded them of their late worthy benefactor, *Stephen Girard*. In Norfolk it was noticed that the old warrior very much resembled the late President *Monroe*.

CHAPTER XI.

From the time of the setting out of BLACK-HAWK *and his five* companions from Fortress Monroe, 5 June,* 1833, *to their arrival on the Upper Mississippi, on the first of August following; prefaced by some reflections upon the events of the war.*

IT is not difficult to perceive, without a formal commentary, that in the late Indian war, much blood was shed which might have been avoided. Twice had the despairing Indians displayed the white flag, to give notice of their willingness to surrender; but, like the wretched Hallibees, the rifle was the only answer they received. When Major *Stillman* was on his march to Sycamore Creek, a few Indians were sent from *Naopope's* camp with friendly intentions, and under a white flag; but such was the carriage of the whites, no interview could be had, and they were obliged to fly to save their lives, which all, it seems, were not fortunate enough to do. This, it will be said, is Indian talk—it is even so. What say the whites? They say, the Indians whom they first discovered were only a decoy. This is mere assertion, and proves nothing on their own side, neither does it disprove the Indian account. Is it not plain that *Black-hawk* caused a white flag to be exhibited before he was attacked by the steam-boat Warrior? He had resolved to fight no more, if he could get terms of peace; but his flag was at once fired upon; then says the old chief, "*I fired too;*" and the whites expected nothing else, and too many of them, it would seem, desired nothing else. But we reflect no more upon this matter.

The reader has, in the last chapter, been conducted through the principal,

* An anonymous author, of whom we have made considerable use in this chapter, gives us their names, &c. as follows.—

Mac-cut-i-misk-e-ca-cac,............*Black-hawk.*	Pamaho, *Prophet's brother,*.............*Fish Fin.*
Na-she-escuck, *his son,*..........*Loud Thunder.*	Po-we-zhick, *Prophet's adopted son,*..*Strawberry*
Wa-be-ke-zhick, *the Prophet,*........*Clear Day.*	Napope, *the warrior*..............*Strong Soup*

and all the important events of the war, and accompanied the chiefs of the Indians engaged in it to Fortress Monroe, in Virginia. We are now to observe what passed in their travels from hence through several of our great cities, and thence to their wilderness homes in the distant west.

Having been conducted to Fort Monroe, the captives found themselves in a kind of elegant confinement; and instead of balls and chains to their ankles, were kindly treated, and saw nobody but friends. This state of things, however, must have become, in a short time, exceedingly irksome; but an early order for their liberation prevented such result. For, on the 4 June, 1833, orders came for their being liberated; and the next day, Major *John Garland* set off with them in a steam-boat for Baltimore, by Norfolk, Gosport, Portsmouth, &c.

During their short stay at Monroe, the Indians became much attached to its commander, Colonel *Eustis*, and on the afternoon of the same day that the order of release arrived, *Black-hawk* went and took his leave of him, and at parting made the following speech:—

"Brother, I have come on my own part, and in behalf of my companions, to bid you farewell. Our great father has at length been pleased to permit us to return to our hunting-grounds. We have buried the tomahawk, and the sound of the rifle will hereafter only bring death to the deer and the buffalo. Brother, you have treated the red men very kindly. Your squaws have made them presents, and you have given them plenty to eat and drink. The memory of your friendship will remain till the Great Spirit says it is time for Black-Hawk to sing his death-song.—Brother, your houses are as numerous as the leaves upon the trees, and your young warriors, like the sands upon the shore of the big lake, which rolls before us. The red man has but few houses, and few warriors, but the red man has a heart which throbs as warmly as the heart of his white brother. The Great Spirit has given us our hunting grounds, and the skin of the deer which we kill there is his favorite, for its color is white, and this is the emblem of peace. This hunting-dress and these feathers of the eagle are white. Accept them, my brother; I have given one like this to the *White-otter*. Accept of it as a memorial of Black-hawk. When he is far away, this will serve to remind you of him. May the Great Spirit bless you and your children—farewell."

Colonel *Eustis*, in his reply, said, the fortune of war had placed him in his hands, and as it was not the practice of the whites to attack an unarmed foe, he was safe; but that if he had met him in the field of battle, his duty would have required him to have taken his life. He rejoiced, he said, at his prospect of speedily returning to his friends, and hoped he would never again trouble his white neighbors. To which *Black-hawk* added, "*Brother, the Great Spirit punishes those who deceive us, and my faith is now pledged.*"

On leaving Fort Monroe, the Indians were taken to Portsmouth and Gosport, to see the navy-yard, the dry-dock, and men-of-war. At Gosport, they went on board the 74 Delaware, where they could not but express much astonishment at the vastness of the "big canoe," as they called it, and its extraordinary uncouth furniture. *Black-hawk* seemed the most to admire the ship, and wished to see the *chief* who commanded it, and especially the man that built it; for he wished, he said, "*to take him by the hand.*" When they left the ship, they passed around under her bow, which terminates in a colossal statue of an Indian warrior. This the Indians beheld with considerable emotions of surprise and evident demonstrations of high gratification.

At Norfolk, the rush to see the Indians was very great, and many could not be gratified even with a sight of them. This great curiosity in the very vicinity where they had been for near 10 weeks, will not be thought strange, when it is considered, that no one expected their immediate removal, and therefore few had been to see them; thinking they could do so when some more convenient time offered.

Having taken lodgings at the hotel in Norfolk, the Indians were aware of the great curiosity of the people, and therefore they exhibited themselves upon the balcony, from whence *Wabokieshiek*, the Prophet, made the following address:—

"The Great Spirit sent us here, and by the same fiat we are now happily about to return to our own Mississippi, and our own people. It affords us much happiness to rejoin our friends and kindred. We would shake hands with all our white friends assembled, and offer our best wishes for their prosperity. Should any of them go to our country on the Mississippi, we would take pleasure in requiting the many kindnesses we have received from their people here. We will go home with peaceable dispositions towards our white brethren, and endeavor to make our conduct hereafter more satisfactory to them. We bid you all farewell, as it is the last time we may see each other."

Black-hawk then said a few words, expressing the same sentiments; and one o'clock having arrived, they departed. This was 5 June.

When the steam-boat was near Baltimore, it was discovered that there had been a robbery committed on board; and when this became known to *Black-hawk*, he showed considerable concern, fearing some of his party should be suspected; and when the boat lay to at considerable distance from the wharf, to make search for the money, he said, "*he desired that himself and company should be searched, for he would let the whites know that the Sacs did not steal.*"

President JACKSON had arrived in Baltimore, and after *Black-hawk's* arrival he had an interview with him. The Indians were conveyed in the steamboat Columbus, and arrived about 11 o'clock in the forenoon of the next day, after leaving Norfolk, namely, 6 June. Among the crowds who visited them were many ladies, to whom, generally, the Indians said, "*Pretty squaws, pretty squaws.*"

The Indians and the president attended the theatre the same night, and it was remarked, that the attention of the house was pretty nearly equally divided between them. On the next day occurred the interview between them, of which mention has just been made; at which time, among other things, the president said to the old chief:—

"When I saw you in Washington, I told you, that you had behaved very badly, in raising the tomahawk against the white people." He added, that his conduct last year had caused him to send out his warriors against him, and that he and those with him had been surrendered to him to be kept during his pleasure, or until he should think there would be no danger from letting him go. "I told you," he continued, "I would inquire whether your people wished you should return, and whether, if you did return, there would be any danger to the frontier. General *Clark* and General *Atkinson*, whom you know, have informed me that *Sheckak*, your principal chief, and the rest of your people, are anxious you should return, and *Keokuk* has asked me to send you back. Your chiefs have pledged themselves for your good conduct."—"You will see the strength of the white people. You will see that our young men are as numerous as the leaves in the woods. What can you do against us?"—"When you go back, listen to the counsels of *Keokuk* and the other friendly chiefs."

To this the Prophet said a few words, as follows:—

"Father, my ears are open to your words; I am glad to hear them; I am glad to go back to my people. I want to see my family. I did not behave well last summer. I ought not to have taken up the tomahawk. But my people have suffered a great deal. When I get back, I will remember your words. I will not go to war again. I will live in peace. I will hold you by the hand."

Black-hawk intended to have made a long speech at this time; but the president was unable to hear him out, on account of the great fatigues he had undergone, and the old chief was, therefore, very short. He said, "*My heart is big, for I have much to say to my great father,*" and closed, after many expressions of affection and respect for him. The warmth of the weather and the great crowd that surrounded the hotel in which the Indians were lodged, caused them to retire to Fort M'Henry, about 3 miles below the city The landlord said the crowd was so great about his house, that they had carried away his banisters, windows, and he was fearful, if they remained longer, that his whole house would be carried away also

They visited the Washington monument, among other places, while at Baltimore, and were at first afraid to ascend in it, upon its circular steps; saying it was the *Manitou* of the white people. At length *Naopope* said he would venture up. *Black-hawk* observed, that then they would all go; for if it fell down, he said they would not be safer on the ground at its base than if they were in it.

They visited the circus also, while here, and were much better pleased with the performances there, than at the theatre. The elegant horses pleased them far more than the stars and garters of the mock lords and ladies of the theatre, and it was very natural they should. To see a lady ride upon one foot, while the horse was running at his utmost speed, was matter of fact to them, and excited the greatest admiration. But to see a fellow popping out from behind a curtain, strutting about the stage, uttering to himself some unintelligible nonsense, could not interest any one similarly situated. They said they believed those who rode in the circus could hunt buffalo even better than the Sacs.

Considerable inconvenience was experienced from the meeting of two such conspicuous characters as the PRESIDENT of the United States and *Black-hawk*, at the same time, in populous places; and it was announced in a Philadelphia paper, of 9 June, that Major *Garland* had arrived there, but had left the Indians in Baltimore, and that they would not proceed to N. York until the day after the president. Accordingly they did not arrive in Philadelphia until 10 June, when they were conducted to lodgings in Congress Hall. The next day there was a great military display, accompanied by an immense procession, and the whole passed up Third Street, opposite Congress Hall, by which means the Indians had a fine opportunity to see and contemplate their numbers. Pointing to the soldiers, *Black-hawk* asked if they were the same that were in his country last summer.

Having visited all places of amusement and curiosity in Philadelphia, the Indians departed for N. York, where they arrived in a steam-boat of the People's Line, about 5 o'clock, 14 June, on Friday. The arrival of *Lafayette*, in 1825, could not have attracted a greater crowd than was now assembled at and in the vicinity of Castle Garden. As it happened, Mr. *Durant*, the aeronaut, had just got ready to ascend in his balloon from the garden. The steam-boat, therefore, rounded to, that the passengers might witness the ascension. When it was known on shore that the Indians were on board, the cheering and clapping became tremendous; and it was not a little augmented from those on board the numerous craft in the river. Those in the boat answered as well as their numbers would admit. The Indians, at first, were some terrified, supposing they had at last come to an enemy, and that the noise about them was the war-whoop of the whites, but were soon undeceived.

Soon after the balloon had cleared the walls of the castle, and Mr. *Durant* had unfurled his flag, *Black-hawk* was asked what he thought of it. To which he answered:—

"*That man is a great* BRAVE. *I don't think he'll ever get back. He must be a Sac.*" Another said, "*If he is a Sac, he'll get none of his brothers to follow in his trail. None of 'em will ever see the smoke of his wigwam. He will have to live alone—without any squaw.*"

When the balloon had attained a vast height, and almost out of the old chief's sight, (which had become considerably impaired,) he exclaimed, "*I think he can go to the heavens; to the Great Spirit.*" *Pomahoe* then said, "*I think he can see the country of the English.*" The Prophet, or *Wabokieshiek*, having been asked what he thought of the balloon, said, "*I can't form any idea, but think he can go up to the clouds if he will. Should think he could see the Great Spirit now.*"

We can only conjecture what might have been passing in their minds at this strange sight. They were struck with wonder, and no doubt were ready to exclaim, "What cannot the white people do? Why can they not send an army in that way to hurl down destruction upon their enemies? They surely will do it. If they can ascend to the Great Spirit, *they must be Great Spirits too!*"

On their landing, such was the density of the crowd, that for a time it seemed impossible to effect a passage for them. After some time, however, by the aid of the police officers, they were taken up in carriages, and carried to their lodgings at the Exchange Hotel in Broad Street. The spacious square and street adjacent were instantly filled by the people, whose eagerness to see the strangers was so great, that it seemed almost impossible to prevent a forcible entrance into the house. Whereupon the directors of the Indians let *Black-hawk* show himself several times at a window; and immediately after, the multitude quietly dispersed, without carrying away banisters or windows, as had been complained of in Baltimore. Thus ended Friday.

On Saturday evening, they were conducted to the Bowery Theatre, and on Monday, the papers of the city announced that they would visit Castle Garden that evening, the Park Theatre on Tuesday, Niblo's on Wednesday, Richmond Hill Theatre on Thursday, Vauxhall Garden on Friday, and, on Saturday, leave for Albany. Thus were the doings of every evening of their stay allotted, which, we believe, came to pass accordingly. Of the manner in which the daytime was spent, we shall, in the next place, proceed to give some account.

On Monday, 17 June, the Hon. *John A. Graham* met the Indians, at their quarters, and made a speech to them, which is as well adapted to the Indian manner, as any thing we have seen. He began:

"Brothers, open your ears. You are brave men. You have fought like tigers, but in a bad cause. We have conquered you. We were sorry, last year, that you raised the tomahawk against us; but we believe you did not know us then as you do now. We think, that in time to come, you will be wise, and that we shall be friends forever. You see that we are a great people—numerous as the flowers of the field, as the shells on the sea-shore, or the fish in the sea. We put one hand on the eastern, and, at the same time, the other on the western ocean. We all act together. If, sometimes, our great men talk loud and long at our council fires, but shed one drop of white men's blood, our young warriors, as thick as the stars of the night, will leap on board our great boats, which fly on the waves, and over the lakes—swift as the eagle in the air—then penetrate the woods, make the big guns thunder, and the whole heavens red with the flames of the dwellings of their enemies. Brothers, the president has made you a great talk. He has but one mouth. That one has sounded the sentiments of all the people. Listen to what he has said to you. Write it on your memories. It is good, very good. BLACK-HAWK, take these jewels, a pair of topaz ear-rings, beautifully set in gold, for your wife or daughter, as a token of friendship, keeping always in mind that women and children are the favorites of the Great Spirit. These jewels are from an old man, whose head is whitened with the snows of 70 winters; an old man, who has thrown down his bow, put off his sword, and now stands leaning on his staff, waiting the commands of the Great Spirit. Look around you, see all this mighty people, then go to your homes, open your arms to receive your families. Tell them to bury the hatchet, to make bright the chain of friendship, to love the white men, and to live in peace with them, as long as the rivers run into the sea, and the sun rises and sets. If you do so, you will be happy. You will then insure the prosperity of unborn generations of your tribes, who will go hand and hand with the sons of the white men, and all shall be blessed by the Great Spirit. Peace and happiness, by the blessing of the Great Spirit, attend you. Farewell."

When this was ended, *Black-hawk* said, "*Brother, we like your talk. We will be friends. We like the white people. They are very kind to us. We shall not forget it. Your counsel is good. We shall attend to it. Your valuable present shall go to my squaw. It pleases me very much. We shall always be friends.*"

The following circumstance is said to have occurred, while the Indians were in New York: One day, after dinner, a gentleman got admittance to their room, whose object was to communicate to them some religious instruction. He began with *Black-hawk's* son; but when the young fellow understood by the interpreter what his object was, he said, "*I lazee*," and, covering his face with his blanket, stretched himself out upon a sofa, and went to sleep.

The Cherokee Phœnix was shown to *Black-hawk*, in New York, by a gentleman, who gave the chief to understand that it was the first and only newspaper printed in Indian. After explaining the great use of papers to him, the chief was well pleased, said he knew the Cherokee tribe well, but did not know they had such a thing among them as a newspaper. He requested the gentleman to make the name of *Black-hawk* on it, which he did, and gave it to him; when the old chief carefully folded it up and laid it away, saying he would show it to his people when he got home.

On Thursday, 20 June, the Indians were shown the famous arsenal in White Street. The great cannon, mortars and shells, on the first floor, filled them with astonishment and awe, in spite of their philosophical indifference. On visiting the second floor, their countenances were seen to enliven. The sight of 10,000 stand of small arms, all as bright as polishing could make them, with all the bayonets fixed, was evidently more agreeable to them than the great, unwieldy cannon below. Their admiration was greatly heightened on being shown the operation of Mr. *Hiddon's* new patent artillery lock. It had been fitted for the occasion, on the beautiful brass 3 pounder, which Gov *Tompkins* gave the state in 1814. This gun being placed in the yard, and charged with a blank cartridge, Gen. *Arcularius*, of the arsenal, drew the string attached to the lock, and the discharge was instantaneous. Here again they could not conceal their astonishment, which was much raised by the mysterious operation of the lock. The cannon being again charged, *Black-hawk* was invited to pull the string and discharge it; but he declined from timidity, and all the rest followed his example. At length the Prophet stepped forward, with a great air of resolution, and discharged it. The report startled him a little; but the moment after, finding himself unharmed, he laughed heartily. Then all the rest ventured to discharge it. When Mr. *Hiddon* showed them the fulminating wafer, upon which his lock acts, "the vacant seriousness and gravity," says one present, "with which they returned it, as a matter quite too profound for their comprehension, was irresistibly comic."

Several of the captives had been attacked with an inflammation in their eyes, accompanied with some fever, supposed to have been brought on by the fatigues they had experienced during their journey. But while they remained in New York, they had nearly recovered.

When it was announced in the papers, that the Indians would not proceed any farther north, great disappointment was felt here; but we heard no one complain. All seemed sensible that to show them about from place to place, was inflicting a punishment upon them which could in no wise benefit us. There might be *one* exception, for we were informed that a gentleman had made large arrangements here for writing *Black-hawk's* life. But whether it were the old chief's good or bad fortune that prevented him from falling into the ambush of that biographer, we do not undertake to say; but there may be those cold-hearted beings, who are glad that both *Black-hawk* and the public have escaped.

On Saturday, 22 June, they left New York for Albany, where they arrived the next day at evening. Here, as we should expect, the crowd was far more savage than had been witnessed any where in the journey, and it was near three hours before a landing for them could be effected; and even then only by disguising them. *Black-hawk* was not recognized until he had got almost to the tavern where he and his party were to lodge. One observes, that Albany, at this time, was more like an Indian camp, than the residence of civilized beings. Some urged, that if *Black-hawk* had been permitted to have shown himself to the multitude, and addressed them, they would at once have ceased their boisterous clamors. It is said he was about to do so, but his son would not consent to it.

Whether the conduct of the populace was such, after they were in their quarters, as to cause alarm for their safety, is not mentioned; but certain it is, they set off from Albany in the night, 24 June, and proceeded west upon the railroad.

When they had got upon the grand canal, and seen how they were transported by means of locks, some of the party said *it must be the work of a*

MANITOU, *for it was the first river they ever saw go over hills and across other rivers.*

The interview of our travellers, the Sacs and Foxes, with their countrymen, the Senecas, cannot fail to be interesting to all our readers. Having arrived at Buffalo on Friday, 28 June, they remained there until Sunday morning. The next morning after their arrival, they rode over to Black Rock, where they viewed the union of the grand canal with the lake at that place. From this place they had a full view of the Canada shore, and *Black-hawk* immediately pointed out Fort Erie, and seemed well acquainted with the adjacent country; he having been there in the time of the last war with England, in the British service, and at the time "*when the Americans walked into Fort Erie,*" as he expressed the capture of it. After the battle of Lake Erie, he said, he was obliged to return with his band to his own country. In the afternoon of the same day, the party visited the Senecas, who had collected at the council house, on their reservation, to receive them. They were addressed by the chief, Capt. *Pollard*, or *Karlundawana*, of whom we have already spoken, an old and very respectable man. After expressing the pleasure which it gave him and his people to meet the chiefs of the Sacs and Foxes, and after alluding to the present state of the aborigines, he counselled his visitors to return home with a peaceable mind; to cultivate the earth, and no more to fight against so powerful a people as the whites. *Black-hawk* replied as follows:—

"*Our aged brother of the Senecas, who has spoken to us, has spoken the words of a good and wise man. We are strangers to each other, though we have the same color; and the same Great Spirit made us all, and gave us this country together. Brothers, we have seen how great a people the whites are. They are very rich, and very strong. It is folly for us to fight with them. We shall go home with much knowledge. For myself, I shall advise my people to be quiet, and live like good men. The advice which you gave us, brother, is very good, and we tell you now we mean to walk the straight path in future, and to content ourselves with what we have, and with cultivating our lands.*

The Prophet added a few sentences, but nothing worthy of notice, except he said he wished all the tribes of Indians could be collected upon one spot, west of the Mississippi.

From Buffalo the Indians were conveyed by water to Detroit, where they arrived July. Here a curiosity was evinced by the inhabitants to see them; not exactly such as had been shown in the Atlantic cities, but with that cold indifference, their near vicinity to the late scenes of blood was calculated to call forth. A writer has remarked, that they were soon seen walking the streets "unknowing and unknown," and newspapers from that region say they were burnt in effigy. *Black-hawk* had often been there in times past, and when he visited the former residence of Gov. *Cass*, he said, "*This is the old council ground. I have heard much good counsel here; but my trail led to the opposite shore, and my ears were closed.*"

From Green Bay they were to pass through the country of the Menominies and Winnebagoes* to Chicago. As these tribes are bitter enemies to the Sacs and Foxes, troops were detached from that place to attend them.

Having left Chicago, as they passed up Fox River and down the Ouisconsin, *Black-hawk* would point out the spots, where, once, he said, had stood the fine villages of the Sacs. His depression at the sight was evident, and he seemed much to regret their emigration beyond the Mississippi.

It was about the first of August, 1833, that the captives arrived at Fort Armstrong, on the Upper Mississippi, where we are presently to take our leave of them. The Prophet had been set at liberty a little before at Prairie

* This tribe is divided into five families—the Decorie, Black-leg, &c. *One-eyed Decorie*, before mentioned, is one of their most conspicuous chiefs. He appeared about 50 years old in 1826. Mr. *W. J. Snelling* saw him at the Portage in that year, accompanied by a wife of 15.

The name *Winnebago* is supposed to be that of a kind of duck, found on the lake of the same name, in great abundance.

du Chien; he having declared his conviction of the power of the Americans, and that now he would return and live in peace. "His return," says our informant, "is attended with as many unpleasant associations as that of any of the party. The village over which he once presided has been broken up; his wigwam has been burnt to the ground; his family without a protector, and he must find a home in the village of some neighboring chieftain."

The Indians were at first gloomy and taciturn, on entering their own forests, but in a short time they began to be more communicative, and at length would laugh and talk about the jokes and odd manœuvres they had seen among the whites.

Being now at Rock Island, where it was concluded to dismiss the party, they were considerably disappointed in not meeting with some of their friends, from whom they might gain intelligence of their families. Meanwhile they examined their bundles and packages, containing the presents they had received during their journey. These were by no means inconsiderable, and were said, by those who saw them, to be in value of at least 1,000 dollars; which, when their friends arrived, were liberally distributed among them. They had not been long in suspense when this happened. A band of Foxes arrived the next day after them, who gave the desired intelligence. To an observer of nature, their meeting must have been exceedingly interesting. Notwithstanding their long separation, their first interviews were nearly the same as though it had been but of a day's continuance. But they very soon discovered to the spectators, that they had met with those who were capable of enjoying again their society; and the freedom of early life began gradually to show itself.

"Fort Armstrong, Rock Island, Illinois, was selected as the most appropriate place for the liberation of *Black-hawk* and his party. It being the most central point from the surrounding villages, a greater number of Indians could be there assembled at a short notice, than at any other point on the Mississippi. With most of the party, their return was the return of happy days, and of those manners and customs which they had looked forward to with much anxiety, during their long and arduous journey. But with *Black-hawk* it was the revival of those scenes associated with his former greatness and power—when no white man crossed his trail, or encroached upon his hunting grounds. He is now hailed not as a chieftain, nor as a warrior, but as a Sac, divested of his honors, an humble suppliant for the sympathies and hospitalities of his tribe.

"It was understood, on their arrival, that *Keocuck*, the principal chiet of the tribe, was absent with most of his band, upon a buffalo hunt, and it was doubtful whether he had yet returned. A courier, however, was despatched to his village, with instructions, if returned, to request his immediate attendance, with as many of his tribe as could conveniently accompany him. The messenger returned the same night, saying that *Keocuck* was encamped about 20 miles below, with a large number of his tribe, and would arrive during the day. About noon, the dull monotony of the Indian drum, accompanied with occasional shouts, was heard, which announced his approach. He led the van, with two large canoes, lashed side by side, with a large canopy extended over him and his three wives, where he sat in all his dignity, with the American flag waving over the bow. About 20 canoes followed in his train, each containing from 4 to 8 of his companions, who made the 'welkin ring' with their wild and savage songs. They proceeded up the river at a moderate rate, and encamped on the opposite side from *Black-hawk's* camp. After remaining about two hours to arrange their toilets, they again commenced their songs, making their way directly across the river. *Keocuck* was the first to land, decorated, as well as the rest of the party, with all their medals, and in all the paraphernalia which distinguishes the braves from the common Indians. After the party had landed, he turned to them and said, '*The Great Spirit has sent our brother back. Let us shake hands in friendship.*' He then proceeded towards *Black-hawk*, who was seated with his party, in front of their tent, leaning upon his cane, apparently lost in deep reflection. He extended his hand, which the old man seemed to shake with some cordiality. Having saluted the rest of the party, he took his seat in their imme diate vicinity. His companions followed the example, and scattered themselves upon the ground. Not a murmur was heard among the crowd. No one presumed to break the silence, until the chieftain had spoken. Fifteen minutes elapsed before a word was uttered by any one, when *Keocuck* asked *Black-hawk* how long he had been upon the road? '*That he had been expecting him, and was coming up in the expectation of meeting him.*' Pipes were soon introduced, and passed among both parties, as an interchange of good feeling. After smoking and talking, alternately, for about an hour, a general move was made for their departure. *Keocuck* arose, shook hands with all the party, saying, '*to-morrow he should return.*'" They now crossed the river in silence, and the night was spent in songs and dances. On the next day, by appointment, was to be opened the grand council.

"A commodious room in the garrison was prepared for the reception of both parties. About 10 o'clock, *Keocuck* was announced by the incoherent and guttural strains of more than 100 savages. When they arrived at the garrison, they followed silently in, preceded by their chief, who was shown to the room, where he was to be elevated upon the ruins of an indiscreet old man, with whom he had been struggling many years for supremacy. He took his seat with *Parsheparho*, (the stabbing chief,) chief of the Sacs, upon one side, and *Wapella*, (the little prince,) chief of the Foxes, upon the other He told his young braves to sit immediately behind him; and all maintained the most profound silence during the interview. *Keocuck*, they said, would speak for all of them.

"*Black-hawk* and his party soon made their appearance. As they entered the room, the chiefs arose and shook hands with them. They passed round, and took their seats immediately opposite. *Black-hawk* and his son appeared quite dejected. They manifested some reluctance to the proposed council, the day previous; and that morning, as it would have too much importance attached to it, the son felt keenly his situation. It was as humiliating to him as it was to his father. Maj. *Garland* was the first to break the silence in council. He told them that he was grateful to find so much good feeling existing in the tribe towards *Black-hawk* and his party. He felt confident, from what he had witnessed since his arrival, that they would hereafter live in peace. He had but little to say, as the president's speech to *Black-hawk* and party, at Baltimore, said all, which should be read to them. It was interpreted to them by an able interpreter, to which the whole company responded, at the termination of each sentence."

Keocuck then arose, shook hands with the most important personages present, and commenced:—

"I have listened to the talk of our great father. It is true we pledged our honors, with those of our young braves, for their liberation. We thought much of it; our councils were long; their wives and children were in our thoughts. When we talked of them, our hearts were full. Their wives and children came to us, which made us feel like women; but we were men. The words which we sent to our great father was one word, the word of all. The heart of our great father was good; he spoke like the father of children. The Great Spirit made his heart big in council. We receive our brothers in friendship; our hearts are good towards them. They once listened to bad counsel; now their ears are closed. I give my hand to them; when they shake it, they shake the hands of all. I will shake hands with them, and then I am done."

Maj. *Garland* then told them, that he wished it distinctly understood by all present, that the president considered, and should in future acknowledge *Keocuck* as the principal chief of the nation; that he wished and expected *Black-hawk* to *listen* and *conform* to his counsels; and that if any discordant feeling now existed, it must be buried here; that the two bands that had heretofore existed in the tribe must be broken up. From the misapplication of some word on the part of the interpreter, *Black-hawk* understood him, that he *must* conform to the counsels of *Keocuck*. The old man became completely infuriated. The spirit and vigor of his youth broke forth like a volcano; he rose to speak, but was so much excited, he could scarcely articulate. He said:—

"I am a man—an old man—I will not conform to the counsels of any one. I will act for myself—no one shall govern me—I am old—my hair is gray—I once gave counsels to my young men—am I to conform to others? I shall soon go to the Great Spirit, where I shall rest. What I said to our great father in Washington, I say again—I will always listen to him. I am done."

The feeling which he evinced, caused a momentary excitement among all present; it was his last expiring struggle. The nature of the remark was explained to him—that the president *requested* him to listen to *Keocuck.* He made no reply; he sat completely absorbed in his own feelings, when *Keocuck*, in a suppressed tone, said to him, "*Why do you speak so before the white men? I will speak for you; you trembled; you did not mean it.*" He consented when *Keocuck* arose and said:—

"Our brother, who has again come to us, has spoken; but he spoke in wrath—his tongue was forked—he spoke not like a man, a Sac. He knew his words were bad; he trembled like the oak, whose roots have been washed by many rains. He is old; what he said, let us forget. He says he did not mean it; he wishes it forgotten. I have spoken for him. What I have said is his own words—not mine. Let us say he spoke in council to-day—that his words were good. I have spoken."

Col. *Davenport*, who commands at Rock Island, then told *Black-hawk* that he was gratified to meet him—that once he was his enemy, but now he met him as a friend—that he was here by the commands of his great father, and should always be glad to see him. If he wished for advice at any time, he should be always ready to give it to him; he had had, during his absence, frequent talks with his tribe, who were anxious for his return; and could assure him, that his nation entertained for him and his party the most friendly feeling.

Maj. *Garland* told him, that he was now at liberty to go where he pleased; that he, and all the Americans, were pleased with his and his party's uniform good conduct while among them; that they were convinced that their hearts were good, but they had listened to bad counsels. They had seen the power of the white men, and had taken their great father by the hand, who had restored them to their families, upon his and his tribe's faithful assurances of peace and friendship.

Black-hawk, after reflecting upon what he had said, requested that if his remarks were put upon paper, a line might be drawn over it—he did not mean it.

Wapella, chief of the Foxes, said he had nothing to say. "I am not," said he, "in the habit of talking—I think—I have been thinking all day—*Keocuck* has spoken—I am glad to see my brothers—I will shake hands with them. I am done." A general shaking of hands was commenced by the chief, which was an indication that the council was adjourned sine die.

The impetuosity of *Black-hawk's* speech was undoubtedly influenced by the presence of his son, who evidently governed his speech and actions during their tour through the United States. He appeared anxious that his father should maintain his former stand, in spite of all opposition, and no doubt gave instructions to that effect. The old man's pride was deeply wounded; yet he would have submitted to any degradation, rather than to have been committed in the presence of so large a number of the most conspicuous men of the nation. He felt convinced that he had erred, and endeavored to atone for it, during the day, by saying, "*he did not know what he said.*"

That evening, Maj. *Garland* invited the principal chiefs, together with *Black-hawk*, to his quarters, as it would afford a good opportunity to ascertain, explicitly, the feeling which existed among them towards their fallen foe. About seven o'clock they arrived. They took their seats in silence, passed the pipe for all to take a whiff, and in return quaffed a glass of champagne, which seemed to have a peculiar relish. *Parsheparho* shook hands with all present, and commenced:—

"We met this morning; I am glad to meet again. That wine is very good; I never drank any before. I have thought much of our meeting today, it was one that told us we were brothers,—that we were Sacs. We had just returned from a buffalo-hunt; we thought it was time for our brothers to be here, as our fathers at St. Louis told us this was the moon. We started before the rising sun to meet you; we have met, and taken our brothers by the hand in friendship. They always mistrusted our counsels, and went from the trail of the red men, where there was no hunting grounds, nor friends returned, and found the dogs howling around their wigwams, and wives looking for their husbands and children. They said we counselled like women; but they have found our counsels were good. They have been through the country of our great father. They have been to the wigwams of the white men; they received them in kindness, and made glad their hearts. We thanked them; say to them that *Keocuck* and *Parsheparho* thank them. Our brother has promised to listen to the counsels of *Keocuck*. What he said in council to-day, was like the Mississippi fog—the sun has shone, and the day is clear—let us forget it; he did not mean it. His heart is good, but his ears have been open to bad counsels. He has taken our great father by the hand, whose words are good. He listened to them, and has closed his ears to the voice which came across the great waters. He now knows that he ought to listen to *Keocuck*. He counselled with us, and our young braves, who listened to his talk. We told our great father that all would be peace. He opened his dark prison, and let him see the rising sun once more, gave him to his wives and children, who were without a lodge. Our great father made straight his path to his home. I once took the great chief of the Osages prisoner. I heard the cries of his women and children; I took him out by the rising sun, and put him upon the trail to his village; 'There,' said I, 'is the trail to your village; go, and tell your village, that I, *Parsheparho*, the chief of the Sacs, sent you.' We thank our great father; say to him that I wish to see him; I reach out my right hand; he is a great way off, but I now shake him by the hand; our hearts are good towards him; I will see him before I lie down in peace; may the Great Spirit be in his councils; what our brother said to-day, let us forget. I am done."

Keocuck, after going through the usual ceremonies, said, "We feel proud that you have invited us here this evening to drink a glass with you; the wine which we have drank, we never tasted before; it is the wine which the white men make, who know how to make any thing; I will take another glass, as I have much to say; we feel proud that we can drink such wine; to-day we shook hands with our brothers, whom you brought to us; we were glad to see them; we have often thought of our brothers; many of our nation said they would never return; their wives and children often came to our wigwams, which made us feel sad; what *Parsheparho* has said, is true; I talked to our young men, who had the hearts of men; I told them that the Great Spirit was in our councils; they promised to live in peace; those who listened to bad counsels, and followed our brothers, have said their ears are closed, they will live in peace; I sent their words to our great father, whose ears were open, whose heart was made sad by the conduct of our brothers; he has sent to their wigwams; we thank him; say to him that *Keocuck* thanks him; our brothers have seen the great villages of the white men; they travelled a long road, and found the Americans like the grass; I will tell our young men to listen to what they shall tell them. Many years ago I went through the villages of our great father; he had many, that were like the great prairies; but he has gone, another is our father, he is a great war chief, I want to see him, I shall be proud to take him by the hand, I have heard much of him, his head is gray, I must see him; tell him that as soon as the snow is off of the prairie, I shall come. What I have said, I wish spoken to him, before it's put upon paper, so that he shall hear it as I have said it; tell him that *Keocuck* spoke it; what our brother said in council to-day, let us forget; he told me to speak; I spoke his words. I have spoken."

Black-hawk then said, in a very calm and dejected manner, "I feel that I am an old man; once I could speak, but now I have but little to say; to-day we met many of our brothers, we were glad to see them; I have listened to what my brothers have said, their hearts are good; they have been like Sacs since I left them; they have taken care of my wife and children, who had no wigwam; I thanked them for it; the Great Spirit knows that I thank them;

before the sun gets behind the hills to-morrow I shall see them, I want to see them; when I left them, I expected soon to return; I told our great father, when in Washington, that I would listen to his counsels; I say so to you, I will listen to the counsels of *Keocuck;* I shall soon be far away, I shall have no village, no band, I shall live alone. What I said in council to-day I wish forgotten. If it has been put upon paper, I wish a mark to be drawn over it. I did not mean it. Now we are alone, let us say we will forget it. Say to our great father and Gov. *Cass*, that I will listen to them. Many years ago I met Gov. *Cass* in councils, far across the prairies, to the rising sun. His counsels were good. My ears were closed; I listened to the great father across the great waters. My father listened to him whose band was large. My band was once large. Now I have no band. I and my son, and all the party, thank our great father for what he has done. He is old, I am old; we shall soon go to the Great Spirit, where we shall rest. He sent us through his great villages. We saw many of the white men, who treated us with kindness. We thank them; say to them we thank them. We thank you and Mr. *Sprague* for coming with us; your road was long, and crooked. We never saw so many white men before. When you was with us, we felt as though we had some friends among them. We felt safe; you knew them all. When you come upon the Mississippi again, you shall come to my wigwam. I have none now. On your road home, you pass where my village once was. No one lives there now; all are gone. I give you my hand; we may never meet again; I shall long remember you. The Great Spirit will be with you, and your wives and children. Before the sun rises I shall go to my family My son will be here to see you, before we go. I will shake hands with my brothers here, then I am done."

The party separated with a most perfect understanding among themselves, and in fellowship and good feeling; but *Black-hawk* was cast down, his pride was wounded, and he departed in silence.

CHAPTER XII.

From the time Black-hawk was set at liberty in his own country, in 1833, to his death, on October 3d, 1838, with other important matters connected with the Indians in the west.

"In pain and peril, when thy years were few,
And death's dark shadow on thy pathway fell,
Thou to the greatness of thy trial grew,
Bade fortune, friends, and blighted hope farewell."—S. L. Fairfield.

For about three years after the liberation of Black-hawk, few incidents of importance seem to have transpired. The first we shall notice is the death of a great Winnebago chief, some of whose family have passed under our notice in a former chapter, from the conspicuous part he acted in the capture of Black-hawk. His name was Schachipkaka, or Decorie. He died in Wisconsin, on the 20th of April, 1836, in his 90th year. Died also, at the Seneca reservation, Major Berry, aged 74. He fought with the Americans in the war of 1812, and died a pensioner. His place of residence was known as Jack Berry's town. He was a distinguished chief. And on the 29th of the same month died that celebrated pioneer of the west, Simon Kenton, aged 82. He, it will be recollected, it was who was engaged as a pilot to the army of Lord Dunmore, in 1774, being then about nineteen years of age. He afterwards spent many years in a most wretched captivity among the Miami Indians, and finally made some escapes, which, it seems to us, that nothing short of miraculous interference could have brought about.

On the 24th of May, 1836, a treaty of cession was made at Washington, between a delegation of chiefs and others of the Chippewas, and the United

States, by which all the reservations heretofore held by them in the state of Michigan is relinquished.

A report was current among us in the summer of this year, that a sanguinary battle had been fought on the 20th of June, at a noted place on the Red River, called the Cross Timbers, between 25 Shawanees and 350 Camanches; that the battle lasted a whole day, and eventuated in the defeat of the latter, who lost 77 of their number.

On the 19th of November, 1836, a large war party of Sioux surprised five lodges of Foxes, on the lower Ioway, 15 or 20 miles from where the line of the "Black-hawk purchase" crosses it, and killed about 20 of them. One of the Foxes, a young man, though severely wounded in the neck, made his escape, and carried the news to Poweeshieck's village.

In May, 1837, died at the Huron village, LORETTE, or GRAND LOUIS, whose Indian name is Tandarelion, aged 74. He had been a great hunter and an upright man, though at times intemperate. A man who had a grudge against another, endeavored to hire him to shoot his enemy, but Lorette replied, "Je ne suis pas en guerre avec lui," "I have no cause of war with that man," and turned scornfully from him. And on the 13th of the following June, another respected chief paid the debt of mortality.

CAPT. GEORGE, principal chief of the ancient and once famous tribe of the Onondagas, died, aged 70. He was one of the most able orators of the Six Nations, not only possessing the confidence of his own, but all the confederate tribes, and was greatly esteemed by the white people.

In the order of time, the next event of importance was a severe battle between the Sacs and Foxes, and Sioux. And what makes it to be the more lamented is, in consequence of the criminal negligence of our government. When the Sacs and Foxes sold us the best portions of Illinois, Missouri, and Wisconsin, amounting to 26,500,000 acres, which included all the lead mines, for the sum of THREE CENTS PER ACRE, certain provisions were to be made them; certain grounds were to be put in cultivation, certain amour of money paid at certain times, and, especially, they were promised protecti from their bloody enemies, the Sioux, when hunting upon certain groun allowed to them. But none of the promises made them had been performe and famine forced them, when they could wait for us no longer, to go unpr tected into the wilderness to hunt for game.

The battle, of which we are to give an account, happened about the 2d of August, 1837, and the history we have of it is derived from the chief of the Sacs and Foxes, who was mortally wounded in it. He had been to St. Louis to see what could be done for his people, and he says, "when I returned, I found our people starving at the village. I divided all the provisions I had received from our trader among them, and powder and lead to enable us to make a hunt to supply our families until our corn was ripe, or that our great father had paid our money to enable our traders to furnish us." Having divided his tribe into two parties, that they might hunt to better advantage, one was to proceed along the dividing country between the Ioway and Red Cedar Rivers, and the other to advance up the right bank of Cedar River. At the head of the latter division was the chief of whom mention has been made, whose name was WAU-COSH-AU-SHE. He had in his company about 170 people, of whom but 40 were men, the rest women and children. They found no game for many days, and, says the old chief, "we had to depend on fish, which we caught from the Cedar, to keep our people from dying with hunger." He was in great expectation, that, if he could reach a belt of wooded country, between the Wapesepineca and Cedar, to find plenty of game. Accordingly he sent out some of his young men in advance, and followed as well as he was able with the rest, but his pioneers soon returned, and informed him that the Winnebagoes were hunting there. "This was bad news," says Waucoshaushe, "in our starving condition, and we could not return, for we had nothing to return to," and their nearest hope was about the mouth of Otter River. He therefore bent his course thither.

On arriving on the confines of that country, he encamped, and sent o some hunters, but, as before, they soon returned, and reported that the ground was in possession of the Sioux; and, he asks, "What was now to done? My number of fighting men was small; but to retreat was impossible; for we must have been discovered by the Sioux, and followed; and whenever you turn your back on an enemy, you are sure of defeat. My braves agreed with me, that we should immediately start on the trail, leave our women and children at the camp, and go and ascertain their strength; that if we found them not too strong, to drive them out of our hunting-grounds. We followed their trail across Otter River, and then it took a direction into the prairie, towards where the sun sets. About midnight, we thought we discovered the Sioux lodges. We raised the war-cry, and rushed upon them; but found no Sioux there, only sand-hills instead of lodges. They were encamped in a hollow; and by this mistake we were discovered. We might now have retreated; but, reflecting on our condition,—our families starving, our hunting-grounds possessed by our enemies, and the remembrance of our friends they had murdered last winter on the Ioway,—determined us to follow them as far as the *line*.

"We had not proceeded far, when the Sioux fired on us. I, with my party, rushed into their camps, and, after fighting desperately for some time, found they were in too strong a force for us. All that could, retreated out of the camps, and, taking a position back of a small rise, within gunshot of their camps, fired upon them until our ammunition was exhausted. We then retreated to our camp,—where we had left our women and children,—bringing *thirteen* wounded with us, and leaving *eleven* killed on the field."

Such is the account of the battle, by an actor in it. As soon as he could, Waucoshaushe sent two of his braves with this account, to the agency, at Rock Island, where they arrived on the 8 of August. The chief closed his talk in the following words: "My father, I am one of the wounded, and expect *never to see you again*. I have followed your advice, and done the best I could for my nation, and *I do not fear to die*. We have with the greatest difficulty reached our village, and fear that many of our people will die of hunger. Father, I have no more to say."

What was done for these poor, distressed Indians, I have no account, but doubt not it might be quickly told! However, a delegation of Sacs and Foxes, and another of Sioux and Ioways, visited Washington in the end of the following September; but we hear nothing of any redress for the former; yet the government bought of the Sioux 5,000,000 of acres of their land, on the east side of the Mississippi, at *twenty cents an acre*. These same Indians were induced to travel through our great cities by advice of the president, who wished to make them acquainted with our power and consequence; and they accordingly arrived in Boston, the extent of their journey on the coast, on the 27 October, 1837. They consisted of both deputations,—in all, 35. Among the Sacs and Foxes were the well-known and celebrated old ex-chief, BLACK-HAWK, his son NASHEESKUK, (Loud Thunder,) KEOKUK, and WAPELLA. On Saturday morning, the whole party had an audience of the mayor, Mr. S. A. Eliot, the aldermen, and common council of the city, in Faneuil Hall. The Sacs and Foxes arrived first, in carriages, and were seated on the right of the elevated platform; and the Sioux, arriving immediately after, were seated on the left. As each party entered, a band of music, stationed for the occasion, played martial airs. The mayor then welcomed them in a short speech, through their interpreters. Gov. Everett was present, and, being introduced to them, invited them to an audience in the State-House, on Monday; for which civility Keokuk presented him with a bow and arrows. They were then shown the armories in the upper hall of the same building, where they expressed high gratification at seeing so many bright guns fit for use. They then returned to their lodgings in Concert Hall.

On Sunday morning, a part of the Sac and Fox delegation visited the navy-yard, and in the afternoon the Sioux and Ioways were there. They were presented by Capt. Percival to Com. Downes, who conducted them over the yard, much to their entertainment. The ships of war most astonished them, and we are not sure they understood the use of that grand affair, the dry dock; they approached and looked down its sides with evident feelings of awe. To a handsome address from Com. Downes, they made an appropriate reply, and returned to their quarters. In the evening, some attended the oratorios at Boylston Hall and the Masonic Temple. On Monday, they held a levee at Faneuil Hall, under the direction of the city marshal, for the especial accommodation of the ladies, which was closed at eleven o'clock, when preparations were made for meeting the governor at the State-House, agreeably to previous arrangements.

As but a very small portion of the community could be admitted to the "Indian council" in the representatives' chamber, notice was given in the newspapers to such as might expect admission, that "passes" had been provided for them, and were to be had between 9 and 11, A. M., at the offices of the adjutant general and city auditor. These "passes" were cards, on which was printed, "PASS TO THE REPRESENTATIVES' CHAMBER, 30TH OCTOBER, 1837."

Meanwhile, the Sioux left the city, and proceeded on their journey west. It was evidently unpleasant to both parties to meet at the same time and place, as the war between them, of which we have taken notice, had not ceased, and, for aught they knew to the contrary, the friends of each were falling by the hand of the other, in the country from which they were thus temporarily absent.

The hour having arrived for the Indians to make their appearance in the hall of the State-House, it was crowded to overflowing, as was every avenue leading to it. The governor occupied the speaker's chair, with his aids and council around him, when the chiefs came in and took seats in the adjacent area. The governor then arose, and, in explanation, stated the object of their visit. "They are," said he, "a most respectable deputation from the Sac and Fox tribes, which are in amity with our government. The object of their mission to Washington, was to form a treaty explanatory of the great treaty made in 1836, defining the boundaries between their territory and that of the United States. Their lands are situated between the Mississippi and Missouri. The united tribes comprise about 5000, of whom about 1400 are braves. They are the descendants of the Algonquins, or Lennape, and speak the same language as that anciently spoken by the Indians of this region." Some persons in the galleries showing a disposition to manifest their ridiculous conceptions, when the Indians came in, the governor observed to the audience, that any such demonstrations by laughing, however seemingly ludicrous any appearance might be, would be highly improper, and the Indians might construe such exhibition of mirth into disrespect.

The interpreter was then requested to inform them that the governor bade them a hearty welcome to the hall of council of their white brethren. "We have," said he, "before heard of the Sacs and Foxes, by our travellers; and we have been told the names of their great men and chiefs; and now we are glad to see them with our eyes. We are called the people of Massachusetts; it is the name of the red people who once lived here. In former times, the red man's wigwam stood on our very fields, and his council-fire was kindled on this spot. When our forefathers came to this country, they were but a small band. The red man stood on the rock on the sea-side, and looked at them. He might have pushed them off, and drowned them; but he took them by the hand, and said, 'Welcome.' Our forefathers were hungry, and the red man gave them corn and venison. They were cold, and the red man spread his blanket over them, and made them warm. We are now grown great and powerful; yet we remember the kindness of the red man to our forefathers.

"Brothers! our faces are white, and yours are red; but our hearts are alike. You dwell between the Mississippi and Missouri; they are mighty streams. One stretches out to the east, and the other away to the west, even to the Rocky Mountains; but still they make but one river, and they run together to the sea. Brothers! we dwell in the east, and you live in the far west; but we are one family. Brothers! as you passed through the hall below, you stopped to look upon the image of our great father, Washington; it is a cold stone, and cannot speak; but our great father loved the red man, and he commanded us to love you. He is dead; but his voice made a deep print in our hearts, like the footsteps of the great buffalo in the clay of the prairie"

Keokuk had his son with him, about 14 years old. The governor alluded to him, when he said, "May the Great Spirit preserve the life of your son. May he grow up by your side, like the tender sapling by the side of the mighty oak. May you long flourish together; and when the mighty oak is fallen in the forest, may the young tree take its place, and spread out its branches over his people. Brothers! I have made you a short talk, and once more bid you welcome to our council hall."

Keokuk said in reply, "I am very much gratified at the pleasure of shaking hands with the great chief of the country, and others about him. The Great Spirit, as you have said, made us the same; we only speak different languages. Brother! I am very happy to be able to say, before I die, that I have seen the house where your fathers used to speak with ours, as we now do with you, and hope the Great Spirit is pleased at the sight. I hope he will long keep peace between the white and red men."

Wapella next spoke. He said, "I am very happy to meet my friends in the land of our forefathers. I recollect, when a little boy, of hearing my forefathers say, that at this place the red man first took the white man by the hand. I am very happy that this island can support so many white men as have come on to it; I am glad they can find a living, and happy they can be contented with living on it. I am glad to hear the white men call us their brothers; it is true they are the oldest; but where I live my tribe is the oldest among the red men. I shall go home and tell my brethren that I have been to this great place, and it shall not be forgotten by me nor my children."

Waacashaashee then came forward, and said, "I have just listened to the words spoken by you and my chiefs about our forefathers. I have long wished to see the shores where my fathers took the white men by the hand, and I shall not forget it."

Poweeshieck next spoke as follows: "You have heard what my chiefs have to say. They are much gratified with their visit to this town. This is the place where our tribe once lived. I have often heard my father and grandfather say that they once lived by the sea coast, where the white man first came. I wish I had a book,* and could read in it all these things. I have been told that this is the way you get all your knowledge. I think the Americans are among the greatest of the white people, that very few can overpower them. It is so with the Sacs, though I say it.† They call me a great man where I live, and I am very happy that two such great men as you and I should meet and shake hands together."

Next came the Indian who wore a buffalo skin all over him, its head on his own, with horns erect. His name we could not get hold of; but he said, "I am much pleased with the conversation our chiefs have had with you. I am glad you noticed *Mausanwout*, Keokuk's son. He will succeed his father, and be a chief. The chiefs who have spoken to you are all village chiefs; for my part, I have nothing to do with the villages; but I go to war, and fight for the women and children."

Appanoseokemar next spoke: "I am very happy to shake hands with you. I do it with all my heart. Although we have no paper to put down words on, we shall not forget this good council. I am a brave, and have my arms in my hands. They are all my defence; but I wish to leave them in this house for the white man to remember the red man of the far west. My presents may not be agreeable, but they are given with a good heart." And, divesting himself of all his clothes, wampum belt, moccasins, &c., except a blanket, he gave them and his arms to the governor.

Black-hawk's turn now came. His voice was very shrill, and he was the only one among them with any of the costume of the whites about him. He began, "I like very well to hear you talk of the Great Spirit. He made us both of one heart, though our skins are of different complexions. The first white men that came to this island were French. They were our brothers as

* They probably knew no difference in books, and supposed that any book would read as might be desired. They look upon them as a kind of oracle, and suppose one as good as a thousand, having no idea of their different contents. One might get such an idea from a certain hymn of Dr. Watts, but it is original with the Indians.

† This caused a pleasing sensation in the house.

you are. When at the president's village, your people put medals about our necks. The French used to do so by our fathers. The Great Spirit is pleased at our talking together. I am a man. You are a man. None of us are any thing more. I live between the Mississippi and Missouri. I have now got to be an old man. It is surprising to me how so many people can live in so small a place as this village is. I cannot see where they get venison and corn enough to live upon; but if they like it, I am satisfied.* I cannot shake hands with all my friends, but by shaking hands with you, I mean it for all."

Keokuk then presented his son to the governor, who caused his own son to shake the hand of that of the chief apparent. Then came forward a brave, who said his father was a Frenchman; he presented the governor with a pipe. His excellency then informed the Indians that some presents had been prepared for them, in the balcony in front of the hall, and that they should proceed there and receive them, which was accordingly done. The presents consisted of guns, swords, trinkets, and clothes for their women and children, &c. To the son of Keokuk the governor gave an elegant little rifle, and observed that he hoped he would soon be able to shoot buffaloes with it.

All these affairs took up much time, especially the speeches, as the interpreters had to repeat them sentence by sentence, as they were delivered, to both parties of Indians. At the end of each sentence delivered to the Indians, they would simultaneously utter assent to it in an inexpressible sound, something like what might be derived from a peculiar pronunciation of the letters *a-ugh-yah*, which must be done in the same breath, and a gradual raising of the voice. And there was such a dissimilarity in language between one portion of the chiefs and the others, that two interpreters were necessarily employed.

Agreeably to notice given, the Indians withdrew from the balcony of the State-House to the senate chamber, where they partook of a collation, and then appeared on the common, where they performed a mock war dance, to the great amusement of the immense multitude. In the evening, they visited the Tremont Theatre, where Forrest took a benefit in the "Banker of Bogota." The Sioux had before attended the National Theatre. On Tuesday, the 31st, they left the city, taking their journey west.

Indian deputations were things new to this generation, in Boston, and when some began to think they were satisfied with seeing one, another was announced; and, on the 20 November, there arrived in the Providence cars 26 chiefs, from a country far beyond that from whence came the preceding ones. They were said to represent the Grand Pawnees, Pawnee Loupes, and Republican Pawnees, Otoes, and Omahas. The name of the principal chief is Odderussin, a descendant of the ancient Mohawks. They were lodged at Concert Hall also, and the next day visited the navy-yard, theatre in the evening, and on Wednesday left the city. They were dressed entirely in the far forest costume, and fantastically painted; and some of them were of immense stature, and appeared as though they had endured the frosts of countless winters.

Scenes of wretchedness have been recorded in our early pages, occasioned by malignant diseases, among Indians of our own land. We are now to relate the doings of death on a broader scale, in the regions of the Upper Missouri. In October last, (1837,) the small-pox was still raging over that vast country. Up to the first of that month, the Mandans were reduced from 1,600 to 31 souls; the Minetarees from 1,000 to 500, and they were still dying fast. The Ricarees, who had recently joined them, were hunting by themselves, when the disease was raging among their friends, and were not seized by the horrid malady until a month after. They numbered 3,000, and half of them were in a few days swept away, and hundreds of the survivors were killing themselves in despair; some with their own spears and other instruments of war, and some by casting themselves down the high precipices along the Missouri. The great nation of Assinnaboines, 10,000 strong; the Crees, 3,000, are nearly all destroyed. The Black Feet had known no such foe be-

* None of the reporters did justice to the old chief's speech; but my ears did not deceive me. These last two sentences were omitted by all.

fore; it had reached the Rocky Mountains, and swept away the people in a thousand lodges. They were reckoned at 60,000 strong. It is impossible to be accurate in these details, but such are the accounts from the west; and they are to this day, 1841, uncontradicted. Here is a commentary upon our policy of settling the border Indians among the wild tribes in the west! of which we have expressed our opinion in an earlier part of this work.

Proceeding in the order of events, we next find Black-hawk, his noted son *Nasheuskuk*, and his wife, a handsome squaw of the Sac tribe, attending a ball, by invitation, at Fort Madison, in Wisconsin, in honor of Washington's birthday, 22 February, 1838. On the 4th of the July following, Black-hawk was again present at the same place, where a celebration was enacted. At the table, Mr. J. G. Edwards honored him by the following sentiment: "*Our illustrious guest. May his declining years be as calm as his previous life has been boisterous from warlike events. His present friendship to the whites fully entitles him to a seat at our board.*" To which Black-hawk made the following very sensible reply: "It has pleased the Great Spirit that I am here to-day. The earth is our mother, and we are now permitted to be upon it. A few snows ago, I was fighting against the white people—perhaps I was wrong—but that is past, it is buried; let it be forgotten. I love my towns and cornfields on the Rock River,—it was a beautiful country. I fought for it, but now it is yours. Keep it as the Sacs did. I was once a warrior, but I am now poor. Keokuk has been the cause of what I am—do not blame him. I love to look upon the Mississippi; I have looked upon it from a child. I love that beautiful river; my home has always been upon its banks. I thank you for your friendship. I will say no more."

Now we have approached the closing scene of the celebrated Black-hawk. How long he had had his camp on the Des Moines, we are not informed; but about this time we find him there, and there he died, on the 3 of October, 1838, aged 73. When it was known that the spirit of the old chief had departed, many, whites as well as Indians, assembled at his lodge, and performed his last request, which was, that he might be buried as all Sac chiefs anciently were, and it was in accordance done. No grave was made; but his body was placed upon the ground in a sitting position, with his cane between his knees, and grasped in his hands; slabs or rails were then piled up about him. Such was the end of Black-hawk. Here, however, his bones did not long rest in peace, but they were stolen from their place of deposit some time in the following winter; but, about a year after, it was discovered that they were in possession of a surgeon, of Quincy, Illinois, to whom some person had sent them to be wired together. When Gov. Lucas, of Ioway, became acquainted with the facts, they were, by his requisition, restored to his friends.

> "What fiend could thus disturb the peaceful dead?
> Remembrance pointing to what last he said:—
>
> 'Prepare the hollow tomb, and place me low,
> My trusty bow and arrows by my side;
> For long the journey is that I must go,
> Without a partner and without a guide.'"—Freneau

CHAPTER XIII.

Monakattooatha, *or* Scaroyada, *at Braddock's defeat—His son killed there—His coolness in battle—His great concern for the frontier settlements after the defeat—Visits Philadelphia—Speech to the Governor and Assembly—His counsel neglected—His friendship continues—Incidents of the war in Pennsylvania—Murdered people carried to Philadelphia—John Churchman.*—Treaty of Fort Stanwix.

Having in a former chapter given but a passing notice of a very prominent chief, we shall in this place proceed with his biography. Monakattoocha, or, according to Peter Williamson, who knew him, Monckatoathy, was also called SCARROOYDA, and Scaroyada. We believe him to have been a Wyandot, as he, and also a son of his, were often employed upon messages between that nation and the government of Pennsylvania; yet the anonymous author of "A Brief View of the Conduct of Pennsylvania for the year 1755," says he was an Iroquois, and had for a long time lived among "our friendly Indians about Shamokin, and other places on the Susquehannah." He was one of the few warriors who escaped the perils of Braddock's bloody field; having fought on the side of the English, he was among those who stood by that unfortunate general to the last. His son, a bold and intrepid warrior, whom we have just mentioned, lost his life there, though not by the enemy, it is believed, but by his own friends, in their random discharges amongst themselves in their amazed condition. Scaroyada sincerely lamented him, especially as he had been killed by his own people, whom he was faithfully endeavoring to serve. When no more could be done, and a retreat was ordered, finding he had fired away all his ammunition, he coolly lighted his pipe, and seating himself under the branches of a tree, began smoking as though the day had gone the other way.

When the border war broke out anew in October, about three months after Braddock's defeat, it excited great alarm throughout Pennsylvania, and although there was a continual domestic warfare between the general assembly and their governor, R. H. Morris, yet Scaroyada was not forgotten by the latter, who recommended that he and *Andrew Montour*, an interpreter, should be rewarded to their satisfaction for their trouble and great service.

The friendly Indians were situated between the English and hostile party, and they applied to the governor for liberty to leave their country and go out of the way of the war parties. Scaroyada, Montour, and Col. Conrad Weiser were employed to persuade them to join the English in the war. How the chief viewed the crisis of this period, may better be learned from his own account than from any other source. Several families having been murdered in the most revolting manner, Scaroyada proceeded to Philadelphia with Col. Weiser and two other chiefs. "A mixture of grief, indignation, and concern sat upon their countenances." Scaroyada immediately demanded an audience of the governor and all the members of the assembly, to whom, when assembled, he thus addressed himself:—

"Brethren, we are once more come among you, and sincerely condole with you on account of the late bloodshed, and the awful clouds that hang over you and over us. Brethren, you may be assured that these horrid actions were committed by none of those nations that have any fellowship with us; but by certain false-hearted and treacherous brethren. It grieves us more than all our other misfortunes, that any of our good friends the English should suspect us of having false hearts.

"Brethren, if you were not an infatuated people, we are yet about 300 warriors firm to your interest; and if you are so unjust to us, as to retain any doubts of our sincerity, we offer to put our wives, our children, and all we have, into your hands, to deal with them as seemeth good to you, if we are found in the least to swerve from you. But, brethren, you must support and assist us, for we are not able to fight alone against the powerful nations who are coming against you; and you must this moment resolve, and give us an explicit answer what you will do; for those nations have sent to desire us, as old friends, either to join them, or to go out of their way and shift for ourselves. Alas! brethren, we are sorry to leave you! We remember the many tokens of your friendship to us—but what shall we do? We cannot stand alone, and you will not stand with us.

"Brethren, the time is precious. While we are here consulting with you, we know not what may be the fate of our brethren at home. We do, therefore, once more invite and request you to act like men, and be no longer as women, pursuing weak measures, that render your names despicable. If you will put the hatchet into our hands, and send out a number of your young men in conjunction with our warriors, and provide the necessary arms, ammunition, and provisions, and likewise build some strong houses for the protection of our old men, women, and children, while we are absent in war we shall soon wipe the tears from your eyes, and make these false-hearted brethren repent their treachery and baseness towards you and us

"But we must at the same time solemnly assure you, that if you delay any longer to act heartily in conjunction with us, or think to put us off, as usual, with uncertain hopes, you will see our faces under this roof no more. We must shift for our own safety, and leave you to the mercy of your enemies, as an infatuated people, upon whom we can have dependence no longer."

Tears were standing in the old chief's eyes when he finished his speech but he was doomed to suffer yet greater perplexity, from the delay of the assembly to act upon the matter. This appeal of the chiefs was made on a Saturday, and an adjournment was immediately moved and carried, and no action could be had at that time. On the following Tuesday the assembly met again, but several days passed and nothing was done. The Friends had a majority of members in that body, and they would not believe that war on any conditions was to be tolerated; and thus the good intentions of Scaroyada were thrown away, and the war was carried on with success by the enemy.

Notwithstanding the neglect shown him on this occasion, we find him busily engaged in November following in his humane purpose of warding off the calamities from the frontier families. At one time he learned that a party of Delawares and Shawanees were preparing to strike a blow on the English border, and he forthwith repaired to Harris's Ferry, and gave the information in time to prevent the intended mischief. We hear no more of Scaroyada until 1757, in which year he raised a company of Mohawks, and in May marched to the relief of Fort Augustus. In 1742 mention is made of a chief named Skanarady, who was acting a conspicuous part among the Cayugas. He may be the same person, but of that we have no other evidence than the approximation in the spelling of the names. It may be mentioned that one of the chiefs, Cayenquiloquoas, who went to Philadelphia with Scaroyada in 1755, had two sons in an academy in that city, where they had been placed the year before to be educated. They were supported by the province.

We will in this place recur again to an incident in the war of 1755, as it was a fulfilment of the prediction of Scaroyada, which probably gave Pennsylvania more alarm, and caused her greater consternation than any other in her whole history; not even excepting the war of the revolution, or the "Western Insurrection."

The author of the view of that province in 1755, closes his work with this "POSTSCRIPT. I send you," he writes, "the following postscript to my long letter. The scalping continues! Yesterday [December 14th] the Dutch brought down for upwards of 60 miles, in a wagon, the bodies of some of their countrymen who had been just scalped by the Indians, and threw them at the State-House door, *cursing the Quakers' principles, and bidding the committee of assembly behold the fruits of their obstinacy, and confess that their pretended sanctity would not save the province without the use of means*, at the same time threatening, *that if they should come down on a like errand again, and find nothing done for their protection, the consequences should be fatal.* A Dutch mob is a terrible thing; but methods are taking to pacify them, and prevent it."

The manner in which this serious affair is spoken of by honest John Churchman, in his life and travels, deserves to be noticed, as well for its addition to the stock of historical facts, as showing how it was viewed by one of the strictest of the Friends' party. "The Indians," he says, "having burnt several houses on the frontiers of this province, also at Gnadenhutten, in Northampton county, and murdered and scalped some of the inhabitants, two or three of the dead bodies were brought to Philadelphia in a wagon, with an intent, as was supposed, to animate the people to unite in preparations for war, to take vengeance on the Indians, and destroy them. They were carried along several of the streets, many people following, cursing the Indians, also the Quakers because they would not join in war for destruction of the Indians. The sight of the dead bodies and the outcry of the people were very afflictive and shocking to me: standing at the door of a friend's house, as they passed along, my mind was much humbled, and turned much inward, when I was made secretly to cry, *What will become of Pennsylvania?*" The good man also said to himself, that the sins of drunkenness, pride, profaneness, and other wickedness, had not only polluted the borders where the murders were committed, but Philadelphia likewise, and that in the day of retribution blood would be required here also

Severe reflections were indulged in relative to the conduct of some of the Quakers. *Nathaniel Grubb*, member of the assembly, and a prominent character among them, was sent into the interior to learn the truth respecting the ravages complained of; he is reported to have said that "those killed by the Indians were only some *Scotch-Irish*, who could well enough be spared;" and such, it was further reported, was "the common language of many of that sect." But these charges are to be taken with large allowances.

CHAPTER XIV.

Early western history—Incidents of battles—ESTILL'S DEFEAT—*Simon Girty—Siege of Bryant's station*—DANIEL BOONE—BATTLE OF THE BLUE LICKS—*Its disastrous issue—Massacre of Major Doughty's men—Harmer's Campaign*—COL. HARDIN—*His first defeat—Narrow escapes of individuals*—MAJOR WYLLYS—*Second defeat—Majors Fontaine and Wyllys killed—Battle near Fort Recovery—Chiefs* UNDERWOOD AND SALLAD—MCMAHON'S DEFEAT AND DEATH—*Gallant action of Lieut Drake—Capt. Hartshorne killed—Fate of the chief* SALLAD—PIOMINGO.

"Of all men, saving Sylla the man-slayer,
  Who passes for in life most lucky
Of the great names, which in our faces stare,
  The General Boon, backwoodsman of Kentucky,
Was happiest among mortals anywhere;
————————The present case in point I
Cite is, that Boon lived hunting up to ninety

'Tis true he shrank from men, even of his nation,
  When they built up into his darling trees,—
He moved some hundred miles off, for a station
  Where there were fewer houses and more ease."—BYRON

As the tide of emigration rolled westward, farther and farther was carried from the Atlantic shores the van billow, which broke in blood as it rolled onward, and which will not cease until it has met its kindred wave, progressing from the western ocean, and both shall have swept down and buried in their course those forms of humanity, in whose name there will remain a charm forever; and which will strike the imagination stronger and stronger, as the times in which they were are seen through the dim distance of ages. We can yet view upon the hills of the west, as the sun sinks beyond them, the figure of one of the race, with his bow in his hand, and its production by his side, in his way to his humble wigwam in the glen to which its smoke above the tops of the lofty trees directs him. Is there a landscape in nature like this? Who that has even *read* of the Indian can efface it from his memory? But it is our ruling maxim not to indulge in descriptions merely to delight the imagination, but to give our space entirely to facts which should be remembered, leaving poetry to those writers better skilled in it.

We shall here proceed to the detail of the events of one of the most sanguinary battles, considering the numbers engaged, ever fought in the west.

On the 22 March, 1782, a company of 25 Wyandots attacked Estill's station, in Kentucky, killed one man and took a negro prisoner. The owner of the station, Capt. JAMES ESTILL,* a bold pioneer, was at the time absent engaged in scouting in defence of his neighbors, and having received intelligence of the attack upon his own house, hastened in pursuit of the party which had made it. Their trail led across Kentucky River, thence towards the Ohio, which Capt. Estill followed with ardor; and when he came within about two miles of Little Mountain, now the village of Mount Sterling, the Indians were discovered on the right bank of Hinkston's branch of Licking River. They immediately threw themselves into a position of defence, and Capt. Estill whose men numbered the same as those of the Indian chief, drew up his in-

* In all the editions of Boone's Narrative it is *Ashton*, but it is an error. A county perpetuates the name of the brave Estill.

front of them on the opposite side. All now depended on the greatest exercise of skill; for neither could claim to be better marksmen than the other if the whites were good, so were the Wyandots. They waited for the Kentuckians to begin the battle, which they immediately did, and on the first fire the chief of the Indians was severely wounded. This so disconcerted his men that many of them were for making a rapid retreat; but his voice rallied them to their posts, and the strife was now urged with the utmost determination on both sides. Each was confident in his own superiority in skill over his adversary, and for some time but few fell, owing to the covered positions both parties held.

At length it was apparent to the chiefs that it would require a long time to decide the contest by that mode of action, and each waited impatiently for the other to make some advances by which advantage might be gained. It is unnatural for a white man to lie by a deer's path all day, waiting for it to pass, at the end of which he is quite as uncertain whether it will come in the course of another, or, perhaps, not till the end of ten days. It may be as unnatural for the Indian; but he will wait day in and day out without half the uneasiness which a white man feels. Thus, at the memorable battle of the Little Mountain, the whites would not wait for a change of position by the Indians, and therefore resolved to make one themselves. Experienced tacticians seldom divide their forces. The Indian chief kept his imbodied; but the Kentuckian divided his, and it proved his ruin.

Capt. Estill despatched Lieut. Miller, with six men, with orders to cross the river, and come upon the backs of the Indians, while he would occupy them in front. Accordingly, Miller marched out on this design; and, to deceive the Indians, the captain extended his line in front, with the view of closing in on the flanks of the Indians the moment Lieut. Miller should divert them in his direction. Unhappily for the whites, that time never came; Miller was easily defeated; or, as some * say, came no more into action. Yet Estill was enabled to continue the fight for more than an hour; meanwhile, his centre became weak, and being furiously charged by the Indians, his men broke and dispersed. Each man shifted for himself as well as he could; Capt. Estill, and his second lieutenant, South, both escaped from the field of battle; but they fell by the tomahawk in their flight. Four only escaped from that sanguinary strife,—excepting those under Miller,—and those four were all wounded.

The Indians were supposed to have lost half their number; but they were imboldened by this success, and other depredations followed.

In the following August, that noted fiend and miscreant, Simon Girty, now twice a savage in disposition, came down upon Kentucky at the head of above 500 Indians, from the tribes of the Wyandots, Miamies, Pottowattomies, Shawanees, and Cherokees. Their object was the destruction of Bryant's station, on the Elk Horn, which fortunately had news of their approach in time to prepare for them. Nevertheless, Girty, relying on his numbers, determined to reduce it. A spring near the fort, which supplied it with water, was unprotected, and he stationed a considerable body near it, in concealment, to cut off such as should venture to it during the siege. Another party was ordered to post themselves in full view in front of the garrison, by which feint it was expected the main strength of it would be drawn out; in which event a third party was to storm a certain gate, and, if possible, force it, and thereby gain possession.

The attack commenced in front; but Girty's design was fathomed by the shrewd backwoodsmen. They at once saw that but a small party began the onset, and rightly judged a much greater one lay concealed in their rear. They now determined to attempt a stratagem on Girty's camp, and with what success we shall next proceed to state. Thirteen young men were sent out to attack the Indians in front, while the remainder of the garrison (about 30) were prepared to receive the party in the rear. Girty was completely deceived by the manœuvre, for supposing the main body had gone in pursuit

* Gov. Morehead, in his admirable address in Commemoration of the First Settlement of Kentucky

of the small party in front, he rushed up with great fury to execute this part of his plan. At the same moment the garrison opened upon him a most deadly fire. This was entirely unexpected, and "the whole Indian army" fled with the utmost precipitation, leaving the 13 brave men, who had made the sortie, at liberty to rejoin their friends. But the siege was not to terminate here; the fugitives returned in a short time, under cover of logs and fences, and for several hours kept up a continual firing upon the garrison.

Meanwhile, word had been received at Lexington, that Bryant's fort was in imminent danger, and a party of about 50 men, horse and foot, set off to relieve it. The besieging Indians, being aware of their march, ambushed the road near the garrison, and were exulting in the prospect of cutting off the whole party; but such was the dexterity of that company of men, that they succeeded in dashing through the whole body of Indians, with the loss only of six of their number; and even those were lost, as it were, by accident. The company approached the garrison in two divisions at the same time, and the party first attacked did not lose a man, while the other, instead of proceeding directly to the fort, tacked and marched for the relief of their friends, and thereby came directly into the hands of the Indians, who had now nothing to do but to turn their arms upon them. In this affair Girty was knocked down by the force of a ball which lodged in his shot-pouch, without doing him any injury.

Girty, being now well aware that a further waste of time and ammunition would be of no avail, resolved, as a last resort, to try the effect of a gasconade. Accordingly, crawling up as near the fort as he could find a covert, he hailed those within, and demanded a surrender; said they now had an opportunity to save their lives; but if they held out longer, he could not be accountable for their safety. And, besides, he said, he hourly expected two pieces of cannon, and a thousand more Indians, who, when arrived, would make deplorable havoc of every man, woman, and child; that now was their only chance of escaping that scene of blood. And, after extolling their bravery and courage, he closed with the announcement of the name of SIMON GIRTY, and that what had been promised was *upon his honor;* and demanded whether the garrison knew him.

A young man, named Reynolds, was appointed to reply to him, which he did in a style of taunt which will long be remembered in Kentucky story. "Know you?" said Reynolds; "Ay, that we do. I have a good-for-nothing dog named *Simon Girty*. Bring up your reënforcements and artillery, and be d——d to you; we will not fight you with guns, but have prepared switches with which to drive you out of the fort if you should get in;" with much more in like kind. If Girty was not satisfied before, he became so now; and, on the following morning, the whole army marched off towards their own country. Thus ended the celebrated siege of Bryant's station, August 17th, after about 36 hours' duration.

The country had become alarmed over a wide extent, and, on the next day after the termination of the siege, a large number of men had assembled on the ground, eager to pursue the Indians. Among them were several officers of known valor, the chief of whom were Col. JOHN TODD of Lexington, Lieut. Col. TRIGG of Harrodsburgh, Lieut. Col. BOONE of Boonesborough, and Majs. HARLAN, MCGARY, and LEVI TODD. Col. Logan had been notified, and was believed to be on his march to join them; but such was the ardor of the men now assembled, though no more than 182, to have a fight with those Indians, whom they believed 600 strong, that they would not be restrained, and they marched on the evening of the same day, on their trail. This irrational impetuosity, it should be remembered, did not extend to such men as Daniel Boone,* who coolly gave it as his opinion, that it was not prudent to pursue until a reënforcement should arrive; but this sage counsel was scouted by some, while others attributed it to cowardice. Like Little Turtle, before the

* The writer of the life of "Boon," in the "American Portrait Gallery," has not noticed the distinguished part he acted in the battle of the Blue Licks. This justly-celebrated man died in the house of his son, Maj. N. Boone, of Montgomery county, 26 September, 1820, in his 85th year.

battle of Miami, Boone bore the insult in silence, but did his duty in the battle which ensued.

As this devoted band marched along, it was apparent to every man of experience which composed it, that the enemy expected pursuit, for they had, in many ways, left traces of their march, which an enemy not courting pursuit would never have made. Boone, and others of his mind, who had doubted the propriety of the proceeding, hoped that the impetuous party would come to their reason as they approached the scene of danger, which doubtless would have been the case, but for the mad act of one man, and that was a Maj. McGary.

After a march of about 40 miles, they came to Licking River, at the since well-known point called the *Blue Licks;* and as the hill opened to their view on the opposite side, a few Indians were discovered slowly ascending it, and leisurely disappeared on the other side. Here a council of war was called, and Col. Todd, the commander-in-chief, called on Col. Boone for his advice. It was given with candor, and caution was strongly recommended, as it had been before leaving Bryant's, on the preceding day. This course of the commander ought to have silenced all clamors, especially as none could but acknowledge the wisdom of Col. Boone. He well understood the nature of the adjacent country; he had made salt at the lick; hunted in its vicinity; and it was there he fell into the hands of the Indians in 1778, and suffered a long captivity. These considerations availed little. Spies were sent out; but they returned without making any discovery. Boone described a ravine, in which he did not doubt the Indians lay concealed, and proposed two measures; one of which he thought should be adopted. The first was to wait for a reënforcement; but if they would not consent to that, he advised that a part of their force should be detached up the river, to cross it and surprise the Indians; while the remainder should make a feint in front of their position. Here all deliberations were suspended by the war-whoop, not from the Indians, but McGary, who, spurring his horse into the river, in defiance of all subordination, called out for *all that were not cowards to follow him—he would show them the Indians.* The miserable "example was contagious among the fiery spirits;" and though a part remained with Todd and Boone for a short time, all were soon over the river, and, says Boone,* "we discovered the enemy lying in wait for us. On this discovery, we formed our columns into one single line, and marched up in their front within about 40 yards, before there was a gun fired. Col. Trigg commanded on the right, myself on the left, Maj. McGary in the centre, and Maj. Harlan the advance party in front. From the manner in which we had formed, it fell to my lot to bring on the attack. This was done with a very heavy fire on both sides, and extended back of the line to Col. Trigg, where the enemy was so strong that they rushed up and broke the right wing at the first fire. Thus the enemy got into our rear, and we were compelled to retreat with the loss of 77 of our men,† and 12 wounded." Such is the summary account of that sanguinary battle by Col. Boone himself, a most conspicuous actor in it.

The right wing was dreadfully cut to pieces. Col. Trigg was killed, with most of his men, while Boone sustained himself manfully in his position. Maj. Harlan, whom no danger could daunt, maintained his ground until but three of his men were left, when he fell mortally wounded. The tomahawk was now resorted to by the savages, and the remainder of the little army gave way, one wing after another, and a dismal rout ensued. Some regained their horses, while others fled on foot. They were a mile from the lick where they had crossed the river; and when they arrived there, the Indians in great numbers were upon them. No pen can describe the scene now begun. Col. Todd was here numbered with the slain. Boone very narrowly escaped, conveying away his son by a secret path, who, to his lasting sorrow, he soon found was mortally wounded, and he was obliged to leave him in the way.

---

* In a letter to the governor of Virginia, dated on the 30 August following the battle, appended to Gov. Morehead's discourse.

† The Indians were said to have lost the same number; but it is improbable. They burnt at the stake several of the whites who fell alive into their hands.

The flying party met Col. Logan with the expected reënforcement, before they arrived at Bryant's station. That veteran officer shed tears when he heard of the blind fate of so many valuable men. With Col. Boone, and such others as would join him, he marched for the battle-ground of the 19th, and arrived there on the 21st; from whence, after burying the dead, he returned to the settlements. "The news of this grievous disaster went like a dagger to the hearts of the people of Kentucky." But its strength was to be exerted under more favorable auspices in future. Gen. Clark destroyed the Indian town of Chillicothe, and several other villages on the Miami, immediately after, which terminated the war in Kentucky. In this expedition, too, Boone was conspicuous.

Passing over minor events of border warfare, we come next to the detail of Harmer's campaign, one of the most extraordinary incidents in western history. With the war of the revolution that with the Indians closed, only to be revived according to circumstances on their part, or when it suited their convenience. Various acts of hostility were kept up, growing out of what the Indians with truth were made to believe were infringements upon their rights and privileges. That both parties had cause of complaint will not be denied; but that both had an equal chance for redress, is a question no one will seriously propound. The Indians were by no means on equal footing in this respect; and hence the cause of their frequently attempting redress by retaliation. In fact, few of them knew any other remedy. The complaints from the western frontiers had become so loud in 1790, that congress requested the secretary of war, Gen. Knox, to collect what information he could, relative to depredations by the Indians upon the inhabitants of that region. An able report was the result of the investigation, in which it was stated that within two years last, upwards of 1,500 persons had been killed or carried into captivity, and a great amount of property destroyed. Among other mischiefs, was an attack upon a company of government soldiers, under the following circumstances:—

In the month of April, 1790, Maj. John Doughty and Ensign Sedam went, with 15 men, in boats, upon some public business to the friendly Chikasaws. Having performed their mission, and, as they were ascending the Tennessee River, 40 Indians approached them in canoes, under a white flag. They were admitted on board; and nothing but a friendly disposition being manifested, presents were distributed to them, and they left in seeming good faith; but no sooner had they put off from their friends, than they poured in upon them a destructive fire. The Americans were almost entirely unprepared for such a salutation; but they returned it as soon as their circumstances would allow, and the fight continued for some time; and, notwithstanding the great inequality of numbers, finally succeeded in beating off the Indians, though not until they had killed all but four of the company. Such are the incidents of the massacre of Maj. Doughty's men. This, with other events of a less atrocious character, caused the appointment of Gen. Josiah Harmer, then commanding at Fort Washington, to be placed at the head of a force, to be led against the Indians on the Miami; an account of which, in the next place, we shall proceed to give in detail.

Gen. Harmer was considered an able tactician, and was an officer of the late revolutionary army; and it was expected that he would find little difficulty in breaking up the haunts of the Indians, and subduing them, if they attempted to meet him in a general battle. He had 320 regular troops put under him, with orders to call upon Kentucky and Pennsylvania for quotas of militia to increase his force to 1,500 men. About the close of September, the requisite number of men having arrived, the army marched from Fort Washington for the Indian country. Col. Hardin was detached, with 600 men, with orders to proceed in advance of the main body; and, after a march of 17 days, he arrived at the Great Miami village, October 16. He found it deserted and in flames. It was situated at the confluence of the St. Joseph's and St. Mary's Rivers—a site now included in Allen county, Indiana. About 5 acres were enclosed by pickets, within which the army encamped. In the burning buildings, great quantities of grain were discovered; and, on further search, abundance more was found in holes in the ground. At the same time, a detachment of 300 men, under Col. Trotter and Maj. Rhea, marched out upon discovery. They found 5 villages, all burnt, and saw about 30 Indians. Thinking these a decoy, they did not attack them. The next day, which was the 17 October, Maj. Fontaine, aid-de-camp to Gen. Harmer, with a party of 200 foot and about 50 horsemen, proceeded to find Indians. Numerous signs were discovered; and, at some 6 or 7 miles from camp, he fell in with a party, and was defeated with a loss of 70 men. Others state that there were but 170 men in all, 30 of whom were regulars under Lieut. Armstrong and Ensign Hartshorn; that 23 of the latter were killed or taken, and seven escaped by flight. Lieut. Armstrong saved himself by plunging into a slough, and remaining most of the night up to his neck in mud and water. Ensign Hartshorn made an equally narrow escape. In his flight he stumbled over a log, which, as he fell, he observed contained a cavity of sufficient magnitude to admit his body. He crawled into it, and eventually escaped unobserved. While he lay in the hollow tree, he witnessed from a knot-hole the burning and dreadful torture of several of his comrades on the same ground where they had been defeated. Ensign Hartshorn is believed to be the same who fell afterwards in the battle at Fort Recovery.

Never did Indians gain a more complete victory, and never was a plan better laid to insure it. They drew the army after them by their trail; then, dividing themselves into two parties, marched back, on each side of it, to a heath or plain, and there lay concealed in the bushes, while their pursuers came directly into the snare. "The militia," Gen. Harmer said, "shamefully and cowardly threw away their arms and ran, without scarcely firing a gun;" and thus the regulars were left to fight the whole force of the Indians, which could not have been less than a thousand warriors; and it is matter of surprise how even seven of the whites should have escaped.

This defeat was on the 17 October; and the next day Harmer arrived with the main body at the Great Miami village, having lost several of his scouting parties on his march. Among these was Sergeant Johonnet, who published a narrative of his captivity, after his escape, which is one of the most interesting of the kind.

We are at great loss to account for the movements the general next made. Why he began a retreat without any further operations, it is difficult to see. Perhaps he had decided in his own mind that any further efforts would be useless, and, without holding a council of his officers, had determined to return home. If such was his resolution, and had he kept it, he would have saved many valuable lives, if he had lost his reputation; yet, as the case turned, he not only lost his reputation, but what was of far greater moment to the country, many valuable lives with it.

Whether conscious that he was grossly reprehensible for what he had done, or not, we can only infer the fact from the circumstances; for he gives us no journal of his marches from place to place, and we next find him about 8 miles on his way home, on the evening of 21 October. Here he made a stand, and again detached Col. Hardin, with about 400 men, of whom 60 only were regulars, with orders to return to the Great Miami village, which, it seemed, the general had already been informed, was in possession of the Indians, and to bring on an engagement with them. Under Col. Harden went, at this time, Maj. Wyllys of Connecticut, Maj. Fontaine, Maj. McMullen, and Col. Hall. They marched in the course of the same night, and about day, on the 22d, came to the village in four divisions, to each of which was assigned a different point of attack. They did not find the Indians unprepared; but were met by them with a bravery and valor not to be overcome. By one account, it is said the fight lasted three hours; that, during it, Maj. McMullen drove a party of the Indians into the Miami. Maj. Wyllys, with about 60 men, was cut off by a band of warriors, who came upon him in the rear, under cover of a field of thick hazels. Maj. Fontaine, having ordered his men to retreat, himself, "in a frenzy of courage," rode directly back into the thickest of the enemy, "cutting and slashing," till he was wounded, and carried off by two of his men; but he was overtaken, killed, and scalped. Maj. Wyllys was left mortally wounded. He requested to be helped upon his horse, "that he might give them another charge; but, in the hurry of the retreat, it could not be done;" and Lieut. Frothingham, of his command, was left among the slain.

A retreat was made in tolerable order; and because the whites were not pursued, Harmer pretended to claim a victory! But Indians will never leave plunder to pursue a flying foe, who has left all behind him.

There fell in this miserably conducted expedition, 214 men, of whom 183 were killed in battle, and 31 wounded; several of these died of their wounds. The proportion of officers was very great; besides those already named, there were lost, Capts. Tharp, Scott, and McMutrey; Lieuts. Sanders, Worley, Clark, and Rogers; Ensigns Sweet, Bridges, Arnold, Higgins, and Threlkeld.

On reviewing the conduct of Gen. Harmer in this affair, it would seem that he was either crazy, or utterly devoid of judgment. It must have been apparent to every subaltern of his command, that the first battle with the Indians had not only increased their boldness, but their numbers also. Then, at the very time, the troops are marched off the ground, leaving them in full triumph; and when at a safe distance from danger, a fifth part is sent back into the very jaws of destruction. With these glaring facts in full view, it is difficult to comprehend on what ground a court martial could *honorably* exonerate Gen. Harmer of all blame; nor is it any easier to discover how he could have been acquitted of unofficerlike conduct with *honor*.

In the battles with the Indians during this expedition, many of them fought on horseback, having their horses equipped with a bunch of bells hanging down the left side of their heads, and two narrow strips of red and white cloth as a sort of pendants. The Indians themselves were painted red and black, in a manner "to represent infernal spirits." Their most hideous and terrific appearance, added to the noise of the bells and the flapping of the pendent strips of cloth, rendered them so formidable to the horses of the militia, that they shrunk back in dismay, and it was with the greatest difficulty they could be brought to the charge.

The accounts of Harmer's campaign are of the most conflicting character, no two agreeing in its important details. His official account of it is one of the most meagre documents of the kind to be found any where. The most we can learn from it is, that he had been somewhere to fight Indians, and had got back again to Fort Washington, and had lost 183 men. But where, or when, or how it was done, he has left us to conjecture. Judge Marshall has unaccountably placed it under 1791, and Shallus, who is generally to be relied on, places his march from Fort Washington, and all his battles (which, by the way, he never fought any) under the date of 30 September.

I am aware that this account of Harmer's campaign differs considerably from those before printed, but the main facts were long since obtained from persons engaged in it, and may be received as substantially correct.

The next prominent event in western history occurred during the campaign of Gen. Wayne, and has been referred to as THE ACTION NEAR FORT RECOVERY.

Fort Recovery was so named because it was built on the ground where Gen. St. Clair had been defeated; and hence that ground was *recovered* out of the hands of the savages. This fort became immediately very noted in history, from a bloody battle fought in its vicinity, on the 30th of June, 1794.

Fort Recovery was one of those advanced posts upon which Gen. Wayne depended, in the event of his being obliged to retreat out of the Indian country, upon any unforeseen disaster. It was on a small branch of the Wabash, (mistaken by Gen. St. Clair for the St. Mary's,) about 23 miles from Greenville, and about 80 or 90 from Fort Washington, (Cincinnati,) and is upon the southern border of Mercer county, Ohio, not 3 miles from the line dividing Ohio from Indiana. It had been built in the winter of 1793, and in June, 1794, the general ordered a quantity of provisions to be deposited there, as a link in the chain of his supplies. It was not until the 29th of this month that a convoy was ready to proceed thither from Fort Greenville.

Meanwhile two distinguished Indian chiefs, with a few followers, had marched for Fort Recovery, to learn what they could, in the way, of the vicinity of the enemy. These two chiefs were named CAPT. UNDERWOOD and Capt. Bobb Sallad; the former a Chikasaw, and the latter a Choctaw They performed their service faithfully, and arrived at Recovery the same evening that the convoy did, but whether before or after, is not mentioned; yet the value of their service upon this occasion was lost from want of a proper arrangement; for on hailing the fort, they were taken for the enemy, and speaking a different language from the western Indians, could make no communication to those within, and hence were obliged to retire with mortification. They were prepared to communicate the important intelligence, that "a large army" of Indians was hovering about the fort, and were to be expected immediately to attack it. It was discovered afterwards, that the Indians had learned the weakness of the garrison, and determined on carrying it by storm, thus proving the value of the information which was lost; the important post, Recovery, being then defended by but about 100 men, under Capt. Gibson. Of these, 30 were infantry, under the immediate command of Lieut. Drake, who, in the battle which followed, acted a most conspicuous part.

The convoy consisted of 300 pack-horses, 80 riflemen under Capt. Hartshorn, and 50 dragoons under Capt. Taylor; the whole under Major J. McMahon. They arrived the same evening at their place of destination, without accident. On the morning of the last day of June, as the convoy was about to resume its return march, it was fiercely attacked by a numerous body of Indians, 3,000 or upwards, as was afterwards ascertained. Previous to marching, the pack-horsemen had spread themselves along their road, and were grazing their horses, and some were nearly a mile from the fort when the onset begun. On hearing the firing, Major McMahon, supposing the Indians but few, took only the 50 dragoons, and pushed forward to the point of attack. Near the extremity of the line of pack-horses, he found himself almost encompassed by Indians, who, showing themselves of a sudden, seemed to cover the ground for a great distance. With their deafening yells they poured an incessant fire upon the devoted band with deadly effect. Among the first killed was the commander, who was shot dead from his horse. Capt. Taylor, with the remainder of the troops, came immediately to the rescue, but finding himself surrounded by the great numbers of the enemy, endeavored to cut his retreat through them, and was likewise slain, as was also Cornet Terry. Capt. Hartshorn, who commanded the riflemen, received a severe wound in the knee, and notwithstanding he was carried some distance by his men, he was finally overtaken and killed. They gained an eminence and continued the fight.

In the meantime the remnant of dragoons and other fugitives had gained the cleared ground adjacent to the fort, and were contending at most fearful odds with their victorious enemy. Seeing their desperate situation, Capt. Gibson permitted Lieut. Drake, at his own request, to make a sally from the fort in aid of his companions. "He accordingly sallied out, at the head of his own men and a portion of the riflemen, skilfully interposed his detachment between the retreating troops and the enemy, opened upon them a hot fire, arrested their advance, and thus gave an opportunity to the wounded to effect their escape, and to the broken and retreating companies to reform and again to face the enemy. Throughout the whole affair, Drake's activity, skill, and extraordinary self-possession, were most conspicuous. The enemy observed it as well as his friends. The numerous shots directed at him, how ever, were turned aside by providential interference, until he had accom plished all that he had been sent to perform. He then received a ball through his body and fell; a faithful corporal came to his assistance, and with his aid he reached the fort; and those two were the last of the retreating party that entered it—Drake making it a point of honor that it should be so." *

Lieut. Drake was not mortally, though very severely wounded, but never entirely recovered. He returned home to Connecticut in the summer of 1796, on a furlough, and died there shortly after, from the immediate effects of the yellow

* From a communication of our present worthy chief magistrate, Gen. Harrison, by which he illustrated in the most happy manner, that it was no proof of cowardice for an officer to decline fighting a duel; Drake having before refused to accept a challenge from, notwithstanding he had been grossly insulted by, another officer.

fever, it is said, which he had contracted in passing through Philadelphia, in his way. The brave Capt. Hartshorn, as has been mentioned, was wounded, and could not travel. He requested his men to leave him and take care of themselves, and immediately a British officer (the notorious Capt. M'Kee) came to him, and told him to surrender and he should be well treated. But he had determined never to fall alive into the hands of the Indians, and at the same moment aimed a blow at M'Kee with his rifle, which knocked him off his horse; and before he recovered, his negro servant and an Indian were upon Capt. Hartshorn, and had despatched him. Lieut. Marks, of Capt. Hartshorn's company, was surrounded and alone. He fought, and kept off the Indians with his spontoon until it was broken to pieces, and then jumping over the heads of some, and knocking down with his fist one that had taken him prisoner, escaped.

In this protracted and desperate fight, 25 of the Americans were killed and 40 wounded, and all the pack-horses lost; on many of which the Indians conveyed away their dead and wounded; but their actual loss was never known. Several other American officers deserve especial notice; as Ensign Dodd of Lieut Drake's command, and Lieut. Michael of Capt. Hartshorn's. Michael had been detached with a chosen party, all of whom were killed but three; himself escaping in a similar manner to that of Lieut. Marks. The Indians closely besieged the fort all that day and night, and the next day till about noon, when they drew off. The Indians displayed great bravery, often advancing in solid column within the range of the guns of the fort.*

The well-known chiefs, LITTLE TURTLE and BLUE JACKET, were among the foremost leaders of the Indians in this battle. Of Capt. Underwood, we have no further account; but the sequel of the life of his companion is soon told. He had about this time been sent upon an excursion, and meeting with a party of the enemy, defeated them; pursued one into the midst of a large encampment, where he despatched him; but, at the same time, lost his own life.

There were, in Gen. Wayne's army, 20 warriors out of the tribe of Cho taws. PIOMINGO, who had been with St. Clair, was also of the number. I is believed to have been the same, afterwards called Gen. COLBURT, in whi suggestion, if we are correct, he was the son of a Scottish gentleman by Indian woman, whose father was killed in an affair near the mouth of tl Ohio, in 1781. His services under Gen. St. Clair have been touched upo and for those under Gen. Washington, he received a sword, and a commissi of major; and Gen. Jackson gave him a sword also, and a colonel's commis sion. Having been always in the interest of the government of the United States, he supported the emigration principle; and that his example might have weight, he went himself to Arkansas, in 1836, with the Ridge party. But his years there were few, as doubtless they must have been in the land of his nativity, for in 1839 he had attained his 95th year, which ended his earthly career. He died there in November of that year.

PIOMINGO was a true Indian. His men having taken a prisoner who had been engaged in St. Clair's defeat, he ordered him to immediate execution; and that no warrior should be disgraced by the act, an old man was appointed to shoot him. He had joined Gen. St. Clair's army with 21 men.

CHAPTER XV.

EVENTS OF THE INDIAN WAR OF 1763 AND 1764, ON THE OHIO.

Siege of Fort Pitt—Ably defended by Capt. ECUYER—*Col. Henry Bouquet ordered to march to its relief—Extreme danger of the undertaking—Throws succor into Fort*

* I have been thus circumstantial in detailing this important event in our Indian wars, because it has not been done by any writer; several have, however, noticed it, but their accounts are very incomplete. My chief authorities are, "*A Letter dated at Fort Greenville, few days after the battle,*" *The Western Review*, and *Withers's Chronicles*.

Ligonier, as does Capt. Ourry—*Fort Bedford besieged*—Battle of Bushy Run—*A second battle—End of the campaign—An army raised for another—Col. Bouquet commands it—Col. Bradstreet to coöperate by the lakes—Indians completely subdued and sue for peace—Surrender 206 captives.*

Westward the waves of population roll,
Like the wild pyramid of awful flame.
Sweeping the broad prairie without control,
Urged by fierce tempests which no might can tame

In this chapter it is proposed to detail those events of Pontiak's war not before particularly considered. We have seen the termination of the siege of Detroit, and we will now return into the distant south, to another besieged fort, upon the Ohio, named Pitt, in honor of the great statesman, William Pitt. It had been closely invested for many days, when Pontiak gave up the siege of Detroit, and all communication was cut off from it, when an order was given for an attempt to throw supplies into it by marching through the wilderness. This fort stood upon a narrow tongue of land made by the confluence of the Monongahela with the Ohio, and such was the boldness of the Indians that "they had posted themselves under the banks of both rivers, by the very walls of the fort, and continued, as it were, buried there, from day to day, with astonishing patience; pouring in an incessant storm of musketry and fire arrows;" by which they had counted upon starving or burning out at length the beleaguered garrison.

Fort Pitt was commanded by Capt. Ecuyer, an officer who did himself much credit on the occasion, for he had not only the wily chiefs of forty bands of savages to provide against, but the flood-gates of heaven had been opened against him; by which the swollen rivers had nearly destroyed the foundation of his fortress. He was 200 miles, by any travelled path, from all settlements, and could send no account of his distressed condition beyond the walls of the fort.

Gen. Amherst was acquainted with the fate of some of the outposts, and he had thrown succors into Detroit; but whether Fort Pitt was in the hands of the Indians or the English, there was nothing beyond conjecture. Such was the condition of things when he magnanimously determined to send a force to its relief. He had only the shattered remainder of the 42d and 77th regiments, just returned from the West Indies, that he could spare for the enterprise, and it was hazarding not a little to attempt it with men worn down with hard service and disease; when those in high spirits and sound health could scarcely hope to pass Braddock's fatal fields with safety.

The forces destined for the expedition were ordered to rendezvous at Carlisle in Pennsylvania, and Col. Henry Bouquet was appointed to lead them. Melancholy forebodings occupied the minds of the frontier inhabitants; a great number of plantations had been plundered and burnt, mills destroyed, "and the full ripe crops stood waving in the fields, ready for the sickle, but the reapers were not to be found." But about 500 effective men were all that the colonel could count upon, and it was feared that they would meet with a defeat, which would leave the inhabitants in a vastly worse condition than if the expedition had not been undertaken. And such was the despondency of the people, that, notwithstanding a deposit of provisions had been ordered at Carlisle early in the season, when Col. Bouquet arrived there in July, he found nothing had been done; and instead of finding supplies for his men, he found the wretched inhabitants expecting them of him, and he actually bestowed some upon them out of his own stores. Yet in spite of these discouragements, he was ready, in about eighteen days, to take up his line of march.

Meanwhile, Fort Ligonier, far advanced into the wilderness, and west of the Alleghany Mountains, was in the greatest danger of falling into the hands of the Indians, and all haste was made by Col. Bouquet to reach it with the army to prevent such a catastrophe. This was of especial importance, inasmuch as that fort contained a large quantity of military stores, and was in a ruinous condition, as well as weakly garrisoned, notwithstanding two other small forts had been abandoned to strengthen it: namely, one "at the crossings of the Juniata," and the other at Stony Creek

Not being able to march with the main body as soon as he deemed it necessary, Col. Bouquet determined to send thirty men in advance through the woods to join the garrison. "For an object of that importance, every risk was to be run," it was said; and they set out on their hazardous journey with small hopes from their friends. Contrary to what might have been expected, as well as former experience, this little band succeeded, by forced marches, without being discovered by the Indians, until they had got within sight of the fort, by throwing themselves into it; and although fired upon, escaped uninjured. Their having been anticipated, however, in their benevolent work, detracts nothing from the honor of its performance; nor is Capt. Ourry the less to be commended for having encouraged twenty volunteers to march from Fort Bedford, where he commanded, upon the same difficult service. These few brave woodsmen met with a success proportionate to their courage. "Here the distressed families, scattered for twelve or fifteen miles around, fled for protection, leaving most of their effects a prey to the savages."

Fort Bedford was as closely invested as Ligonier; and about this time a party of eighteen men were surprised in its very neighborhood and all cut off. This happened but a few days previous to the arrival of Col. Bouquet at that place, which was on the 25 July, 1763. Fort Bedford was 100 miles beyond the frontier, and the same distance from Fort Pitt.

As soon as the Indians became acquainted with the march of the English army, they broke up the siege of Fort Pitt, and proceeded to waylay the route they knew it must take. There were many formidable leaders among them at this period, as KIKYUSKUNG, the WOLF, Delaware chiefs; but the most savage and dreaded were Shawanese, whose names have not reached us. The colonel marched from Fort Bedford on the 28 July, and having to pass several dangerous defiles, he prudently determined to leave his wagons and proceed only with pack-horses. Turtle Creek, along which he was to pass, was commanded the whole way by high and craggy hills. This place he intended to have passed on the night of the 29 July, by a forced march, thereby, if possible, to have eluded the vigilance of his wily adversary; but this he was not able to effect; and we will give, in his own words, Col. Bouquet's account of the attack made upon his men on their march. His official despatch was dated at Edge Hill, twenty-six miles from Fort Pitt, 5 August, 1763; and is as follows:—

"The 2d instant the troops and convoy, intended for Fort Pitt, arrived at Ligonier, where I could obtain no intelligence of the enemy; the expresses sent since the beginning of July, having been either killed, or obliged to return, all the passes being occupied by the enemy. On the 4th, proceeded with the troops, and about 340 horses laden with flour. I intended to have halted to-day at Bushy Run, a mile beyond this camp, and, after having refreshed the men and horses, to have marched in the night over Turtle Creek, a very dangerous defile of several miles, commanded by high and craggy hills; but at one o'clock this afternoon, after a march of seventeen miles, the savages suddenly attacked our advanced guard, which was immediately repulsed by the two light infantry companies of the 42d regiment, who drove the savages from their ambuscade, and pursued them a good way. They immediately returned to the attack, and the fire being obstinate on our front, and extending along our flanks, we made a general charge with the whole line, to dislodge the savages from the heights; in which attempt we succeeded, though without obtaining by it any decisive advantage; for as soon as they were driven from one post, they appeared on another, till, by continual reënforcements, they were at last able to surround us, and attack the convoy left in our rear. This obliged us to march back to protect it. The action then became general, and though we were attacked on every side, and the savages exerted themselves with uncommon resolution, they were constantly repulsed with loss. We also suffered considerably: Capt. Lieut. Graham and Lieut. M'Intosh are killed, and Capt. Graham wounded. Of the Royal American regiment, Lieut. Dow, who acted as deputy quartermaster-general, is shot through the body. Of the 77th, Lieut. Donald Campbell, and Mr. Peebles, a volunteer, are wounded; in all, above sixty are killed and wounded. The action has lasted from one o'clock till night, and we expect to begin again at daybreak."

Thus ended the first battle "near Bushy Run," and both armies were determined on another as soon as they could distinguish friend from foe, at the earliest return of daylight. Accordingly, "in the morning," says Col. Bouquet, "the savages surrounded our camp, at the distance of about 500 yards, and by shouting and yelping quite round that extensive circumference, thought to have terrified us with their numbers: they attacked us early, and under favor of an incessant fire, made several bold efforts to penetrate our camp; and though they failed in the attempt, our situation was not the less perplexing, having experienced that brisk attacks had little effect upon an enemy who always gave way when pressed, and appeared again immediately: our troops were, besides, extremely fatigued with the long march, and as long action of the preceding day, and distressed to the last degree by a total want of water, much more intolerable than the enemy's fire."

Such was the commencement of the second battle near Bushy Run; at this stage of which many had been killed and wounded, and some had fallen into the Indians' hands. Nothing seemed to be gained, but every thing wore an unfavorable aspect. Tied to their convoy, the whites could neither pursue the foe nor continue their march, and many of their horses were killed, and their drivers had taken refuge in the woods. At length the colonel put in practice a stratagem, which probably was the only means he could have adopted to have saved his army from a total defeat. He saw that the Indians became every moment more and more imboldened, and to repulse them effected nothing, while to him it would soon amount to certain defeat; he therefore made a feigned retreat, and so masterly was it performed, that the Indians were completely deceived, and they pressed forward in a body from their coverts to gain the centre of the circular encampment, while one of the wings of the army, under Major Campbell, seconded by Capt. Basset, suddenly closed in upon them from a point of the hill where he could not be observed, pouring in at the same time a tremendous fire, and then charging them with impetuosity. Many of them were killed, and though they returned the fire, their ardor was damped, and victory was no longer doubtful. The whole army was upon them before they could reload, and numbers were cut off by a cross fire before they could regain their trees.

The battle having now closed, the army was enabled to encamp and take a little repose, of which it was in extreme need. On mustering, it was found that 115 had been killed, wounded, and missing of the regular troops, fifty of which were of the former number. Of the Indians they learned sixty were killed. Four days after Col. Bouquet arrived at Fort Pitt, without any other accident than a few scattering shot from unseen Indians; and here he was obliged to end this campaign, not having sufficient force to pursue the enemy beyond the Ohio, nor any prospect of a reënforcement.

The next year it was determined to send out a larger force under the same excellent commander, which should be able to strike an effectual blow upon the Indians in their strong-holds, or awe them into submission. Pennsylvania was to raise 1,000 men; Virginia was called upon, and 200 friendly Indians tendered their services. With these, part of two regiments of regulars were to be joined, and the whole were expected at Carlisle ready to march by July; but it was the beginning of August before they were ready, and then no men from Virginia appeared, and the friendly Indians never came. Virginia excused herself by saying it had already 700 men in the field, and those were insufficient to protect its own frontier.

Meanwhile, as soon as the spring returned, the Indians fell anew upon the back settlements of Pennsylvania and Virginia, and spread a deplorable ruin over a great extent of country, killing and carrying away the inhabitants with their wonted barbarity.

Gen. Gage was now commander-in-chief in the colonies, and he ordered Col. Bradstreet, with a strong force, to act in conjunction with Col. Bouquet, by proceeding by way of the lakes, and falling upon the backs of the Wyandots, Ottawas, and Miamies.

Col. Bouquet marched from Carlisle on the 9 August, 1764, and reached Fort Loudon on the 13th. In this march of four days, desertions had become alarming among the Pennsylvania troops, notwithstanding they had been warned, both by the commander and Gov. Penn, of the ruin it would create, and the condign manner in which it would be punished. The latter gentleman had accompanied Col. Bouquet to Carlisle, and there appropriately addressed the troops before they began their march. Nevertheless the Pennsylvania troops had decreased from 1,000 to 700 men, and the colonel was obliged to apply to the governor and commissioners to complete his complement. And by the exertions of Gov. Fauquier of Virginia, the quota of men from that province were enabled to join the expedition at Pittsburgh.

Before leaving Fort Loudon, Col. Bouquet received despatches from Col Bradstreet, acquainting him that he had concluded a peace with the Delawares and Shawanese; but Col. Bouquet had no faith in their pretensions, and on communicating with Gen. Gage, the treaty was rejected by him, and offensive measures were not relaxed.

As soon as the army had arrived at Fort Pitt, ten Indians were observed on the north side of the Ohio, who signified a desire for a conference. This the colonel looked upon as a stratagem made use of by them to get information of his strength and intentions. Three of the party were induced to visit the fort; and not being able to satisfy the whites of their good intentions, they were held as spies, and their associates fled. On the 20 September the colonel sent one of the three out with a message to his countrymen, informing them that he had heard of the treaty with Col. Bradstreet, but he had learned too, that since then they had committed several murders; that he was now prepared to distress them to the utmost, if they did not immediately stop their depredations, and give assurances of their sincerity by leaving the path open to Detroit, and safely returning the messengers he was now to send to Col. Bradstreet; and if the said messengers were detained or injured, he would put his hostages to death, and show no mercy in future to any of them. Twenty days were allowed them to perform the mission.

This talk had a salutary influence on the minds of the chiefs; they had become pretty well assured that Col. Bouquet was not to be trifled with, nor caught asleep; and on the 1 October, an Onondaga and one Oneida came to Fort Pitt, pretending friendship, claiming to be friends under the ancient league between the Five Nations and English. They offered him a little friendly advice, as that his force was too small to think of doing any thing against so numerous an enemy as were the Indians, and that if he would wait a little they would all come and make peace with him; and especially if he would set at liberty those he held as hostages. But Col. Bouquet understood Indian talk quite as well as they understood him, probably, when he told them he should now proceed to Tuscarawas, and, if they had any thing further to say, they might meet him there; but as to delay, that was out of the question. And the next day, October the 2d, he was ready to take up his line of march, and his entire force consisted of 1,500 men. Before leaving, he found it necessary to shoot two soldiers for desertion. All the women, except one to each corps, and two nurses for the general hospital, were ordered to return to the settlements, and every other encumbrance was avoided before taking up the line of march.

On the 6th the army reached Beaver Creek, and here a soldier joined it, who had been taken near Fort Bedford, and now escaped from his captors. He informed the colonel that the Indians had watched the army, and were surprised at its numbers. Two miles farther on was found the skull of a child set upon a pole. On the 9th trees were seen, on the bark of which were many hieroglyphical characters painted, said to have been done by the Indians to denote their war exploits. On the 13th the army arrived at Tuscarawas, and here the colonel found the two men who had been sent to Col. Bradstreet with despatches, before spoken of. They stated that they had been made prisoners by the Delawares, who carried them to one of their towns, 16 miles from Tuscarawas, where they kept them until the army reached here; and now, "making a virtue of necessity," set them at liberty, and ordered them to tell "the great white captain" that the head men of the Delawares and Shawanese were coming as soon as possible to treat with him. On the 15th they encamped on Margaret's Creek, and soon after a deputation of six Indians arrived, and informed Col. Bouquet that the chiefs were in council ready to treat with him, about eight miles off. He returned answer that he would meet them the next day at a bower at some distance from his own camp, and in the interim fortified his position, trusting nothing in their protestations of friendship.

On the 17 October the colonel marched to the bower, making the best display he could of his best troops, and soon after the Indians arrived, and were as follows: Kiyashuta, chief of the Senecas, with 15 warriors; Custaloga, chief of the Wolf tribe of the Delawares, and Beaver, chief of the Turkey tribe of the same nation, with 20 warriors; Keissinautchtha, a chief of the Shawanese, and 6 warriors. The Indian speakers were Kiyashuta, Turtle-heart, Custaloga, and Beaver. These severally spoke, but we know not that their speeches have been preserved; but what they said went only to excuse themselves, and cast the blame on their young men, and the western nations, over whom they had no control; but "they sued for peace in the most abject manner," promising to deliver up all their prisoners without delay. The colonel then dismissed them, and told them he would meet them again the next day, but owing to the weather the meeting was deferred to the 20th. He then told them their excuses amounted to nothing; recounted to them the outrages they had committed, as killing and captivating the traders sent among them at their own request; attacking Fort Pitt, which had been built by their consent, murdering four men, who had been sent to them with messages; their attacking his troops last year; their falsifying their promise to Col. Bradstreet, of delivering up their captives to him by the 10 of last month, &c; that they might rest assured that the army would not leave their country until his terms were complied with, and 12 days were allowed them to deliver the prisoners in, which was to be done at Wakatamake. All persons were required, "Englishmen, Frenchmen, women and children; whether adopted, married, or living among them under any denomination or pretence whatsoever; and to furnish horses, clothing and provisions, to carry them to Fort Pitt." When they had fully complied with these terms, "they were to be informed on what terms they might have peace."

It should have been observed, that at the first meeting, on the 17th, the Delaware chiefs delivered up 18 white prisoners, and 83 small sticks, indicating the number still remaining in their hands. Meanwhile Col. Bouquet determined to march further into their country, knowing that his success in getting prisoners depended much on the presence of his army; and on the 25 October he arrived within a mile of the Forks of Muskingum, where, instead of Wakatamake, the prisoners were to be delivered; this position being very convenient for the Indians, most of their principal towns lying around it. Besides, it was a position from whence an effectual blow might be struck at any moment. Here convenient houses were built for the reception of the captives. On the 28 October, Peter, the Caughnawaga chief, and 20 others of that nation, arrived from Sandusky, bringing a letter from Col. Bradstreet, by which it appeared he had ascended the River Sandusky as far as he could in canoes, but had not effected any treaty or received any prisoners, and was about to leave that part of the country.

By the 9 November, there were delivered to Col. Bouquet 206 captives, of which 90 were Virginians, and 116 belonged to Pennsylvania: among them there were 125 women and children There yet remained with the Shawanese about 100 more, which, from their scattered condition, could not be had, but hostages were taken for their safe delivery the next spring. The separating of these captives from the Indians, and their meeting with their friends and relatives, (many of whom were present,) was a scene past description; children brought up among the Indians clung to their adopted mothers, and the mothers to them, flying with fear from their own parents. The Indian has by many been denied that paternal affection so common to humanity; but had such witnessed this scene, their opinions would have changed. Some would not be separated from their white captives, and even followed the army in its march to Philadelphia. Thus ended one of the most brilliant Indian expeditions upon record; not brilliant by reason of sanguinary battles, but from far more glorious deeds of humanity.

That the Indians were completely humbled by the firm and resolute conduct of Col. Bouquet, has been remarked; but we cannot, with justice to the subject, submit it, without letting the chiefs be fully heard. Notwithstanding the Shawanese had, by their deputy, assented to the demands of the colonel, as far as they could under present circumstances, they were considered "still out in rebellion," and remained to be treated with. They had shown "a dilatoriness and sullen haughtiness in all their conduct, which rendered it very suspicious." Accordingly, a separate conference was had with them on the 12 November, when there appeared the chiefs, KEISSINAUTCHTHA and NIMWHA, with the RED HAWK, LAVISSIMO, BENSIVASICA, EWEECUNWEE, KEIGLEIGHQUE, and 40 warriors. There were also present, the Caughnawaga, Seneca, and Delaware chiefs. RED HAWK was chief speaker of the Shawanese, and he thus addressed the English:—

"Brother, listen to us, your younger brothers. As we see something in your eyes that looks dissatisfaction, we now clear them. You have credited bad stories against us. We clean your ears, that you may hear better hereafter. We wish to remove every thing bad from your heart, that you may be as good as your ancestors. [*A belt.*] We saw you coming with an uplifted tomahawk in your hand. We now take it from you, and *throw it up to God* Let him do with it as he pleases. We hope never to see it more. Brother, as you are a warrior, take hold of this chain [*handing a belt*] of friendship, and let us think no more of war, in pity of our old men, women, and children. We, too, are warriors."

The remarkable figure made use of in this speech, of *throwing the hatchet up to God*, is new; and it was remarked by Thomas Hutchins, who heard it, that by it the speaker wished probably to be understood that, by this disposition of it, it would be out of the reach of bad men, and would be given only to the party in future, to whom the right of revenge belonged; whereas if it were buried in the ground, any miscreant might dig it up.

The English did not much like the talk of RED HAWK; they saw no supplication, but a manly independence, which they ought to have admired, rather than reprobated. That the Indians, especially the Shawanese, did not acknowledge themselves entirely in the wrong, is evident from their producing at this time, through their speaker, the treaty made with Pennsylvania in 1701, and three messages or letters from that government, of different dates, by which they undoubtedly intended to show that the English had been guilty of barbarities as well as the Indians. However, RED HAWK promised, on behalf of his nation, that all the prisoners should be delivered up at Fort Pitt the next spring.

Col. Bouquet finding no more prisoners could be obtained, owing, as has been stated, to their being scattered with their masters upon very distant hunting grounds, gave up his campaign, and returned to Philadelphia, where he arrived in the beginning of January, 1765. Before leaving "these remote parts," however, the colonel gave the Indians a talk, in which he observed, that what the Shawanese had said would have been agreeable to him, provided their acts had corresponded with it. He reminded them that they had promised, at Tuscarawas, a month before, that all the prisoners should be delivered to him at his present encampment in 10 days, and demanded what right they had to expect better terms than the Delawares and others, who had, without delay, brought in their captives. This was rather unreasonable on the part of the colonel, inasmuch as he was well aware that he was pressing an impossibility. "But," he says, "I will cut this matter short with you; and before I explain myself further, I insist on your immediate answer to the following questions: 1st. Will you collect and deliver up all the prisoners, taken in this or former wars, whether French, English, or negroes, and without any exception or evasion whatsoever? 2d. Will you deliver 6 hostages into my hands as security for the performance of your promise, and as a guaranty that your people shall commit no more hostilities on his majesty's subjects?"

BENSIVASICA said the Shawanese would comply, excepting as regarded the French; but over them they had no control, and the English might do with them as they pleased; but he believed they had nearly all returned to their own country. And here it will be proper to remark that the captives were delivered at Fort Pitt agreeable to this treaty. After the hostages were delivered, Col. Bouquet remarked to them, "that though he had brought the tomahawk in his hand, yet as they had now submitted, he would not let it fall on their heads, but let it drop to the ground," and exhorted them to be kind to the prisoners, and said he should send along with them some of the friends of the captives, to aid in the collection of them. At the same time the chiefs of the other tribes present, severally addressed the Shawane chiefs, whom they called grandchildren and nephews, and urged them "to perform their promises, and be strong in doing good, that this peace might be everlasting." These transactions occurred on the 12 November, 1764.

In the narration of the delivery of captives on the 9 of the same month, the relation of a captive was passed over, which shall here be given. A Mr. Smallman, who had been a major of Pennsylvania troops, and had been made prisoner in the summer of 1763, near Detroit, by the Wyandots, who delivered him to the Shawanese, was among those surrendered at that time. He proved of great service to the whites, as well as Indians, on this occasion, by being able to confirm much of the information given by the latter. He told Col. Bouquet that all the Indians who had heard of his demand had come on immediately with their captives. It had been reported among the Shawanese that the object of the English was to put them all to death. As soon as this news came to be circulated among them, they began to prepare to kill all the captives; and a French trader among them, who had many barrels of powder and ball, offered it all to them to go out and fight the English army. When they were about to commence murdering the prisoners, the message from the colonel was received, stating that he only wanted the captives and to make peace with them, and thus a horrid tragedy was prevented. Soon after, when many prisoners had been collected, and marched as far as Wakautamikie, news came that a soldier had been killed near the camp of the army at Muskingum. This the Indians thought would blast all their hopes of mercy, and they again resolved to put the captives to death; and when they had even got them into a small compass for that purpose, another express arrived from Col. Bouquet, which assured them that he had no suspicion that they had any knowledge of the murder, and thus a second calamity was happily averted.

Several eminent chiefs, it will have been perceived, make their appearance in this part of our work, and to them we can add the name of Hopocan, or Capt. Pipe. He was one of the two Indians whom we have mentioned as having been detained as spies at Fort Pitt; the name of the other was Capt John. These were set at liberty when the 206 captives were given up. Of the melancholy and barbarous murder of Red Hawk, notice has been taken.

The causes of this war were well known in England, and the complaints of the Indians were acknowledged "to have been too well founded." They had long watched the progress of settlements upon the Susquehannah, and the building of forts in their country, against treaty stipulations. They had not only submitted to this, but to treatment the most insolent. They resolved, in the spring of 1763, to drive back their oppressors; not, however, without first remonstrating in respectful terms to the English, in one of their capitals, through a deputation of their chiefs. Here they declared that whatever deeds might be produced by one J. H. Lydias of Albany, or others, pretending to claim lands upon the Susquehannah, they were utterly false, and would not be allowed; and that they would defend them to the last extremity. The result we have seen.

Thus we have traced the events of Pontiak's war to its close—a glorious termination, inasmuch as it was a bloodless one. Many years of comparative peace ensued; indeed the troubles with the Indians were not very serious for the next ten years. Cresap's war was the next, which terminated in the sanguinary battle of Point Pleasant. Then succeeded the calamities of the Revolution, from which the Indians never recovered.

CONDITION IN 1859, OF THE INDIAN TRIBES REMOVED FROM THEIR ORIGINAL LANDS.

The Indian tribes west of the Mississippi occupy the territory bounded by the Red river and the Nebraska, between the 34th and 40th degrees of north latitude, and the 94th and 100th degrees of west longitude. The Cherokees hold 15,000,000 acres on the north bank of the main channel of the Arkansas river, and an adjoining tract of 300,000 acres; the Choctaws and Chickasaws own jointly 15,000,000 acres; and the Creeks and Seminoles 13,140,000 acres. Adjacent, on the east, are the Quappas, possessing 96,000 acres of land; the Senecas, owning 67,000 acres; and the mixed Senecas, holding 100,000 acres. The latest census returns present an aggregate population of 97,657, exclusive of the indigenous tribes within the same area of territory, which number 7,355 persons; but, as these returns are not of recent date, and as the tribes have, meanwhile, been increasing and prospering, the gross population of the four most important tribes, the Choctaws, Cherokees, Chickasaws, and Creeks, with the affiliated Seminoles, may now be estimated to exceed 100,000 souls. Mr. Schoolcraft, who explored this territory in 1819, thus narrates its peculiar characteristics and advantages:

"Geologically viewed, its surface consists of a drift deposit of sand, loam, clay, marl, and comminuted gravel, arising from the broken down silurian series, in which the leading strata of sandstone, limestone, and slate, are the parent elements. Over this, deposits of leaves, of the decayed forms of organic life, and of carbonaceous matter from the forests, have formed a rich mould, making the soil mellow and easy to cultivate. Much of it is level, or lying in gentle slopes, unencumbered with a heavy forest, difficult to be removed by the axe. It is, nevertheless, well watered, and there is a full supply of timber for building fences, and for firewood.

"Among the advantages of the country may be mentioned the saline formation. Salt springs exist in many localities, and this geological trait is attended with the usual accompaniment of this formation, namely gypsum and coal. The discovery of efflorescent bodies of salt on the prairies, originated the once prevalent opinion that masses of rock-salt were deposited beneath the soil. Through these beds, which lie on gently sloping hills and in valleys, the Red river, the Washitaw, the Arkansas, and the Kanzas, flow out of, or from the direction of, the Rocky mountains, and, with their numerous affluents, water the entire country; the Missouri washes its borders for several hundred miles; the Red river bounds its southern line to the distance of six degrees of longitude; and the States of Missouri and Arkansas lie between its eastern limits and the Mississippi.

"Geographically, this great tract of arable land is bounded by the Ozark hills, or mountains, a very broad midland range, resting on azoic rocks, extending from the Hot Springs of Arkansas, to the head waters of the River St. Francis, of Missouri. At both terminal points there arises a series of these rocks; that at the south, consisting of slate, schist, and quartz; and at the north, of granite, sienite, trap, and porphyry. Superimposed upon these, and frequently concealed altogether for a considerable distance, are the characteristic sandstone and limestone formations of the region. Through these the Red river, Washitaw, Arkansas, White river, and St. Francis, pursue their way to the Mississippi, producing rapids, but no striking falls. Connected with this central upheaval of the old rocky strata, are developments of mineral wealth.

"Of the climatic phenomena of the Indian territories, thus bounded, we cannot speak from instrumental observations. It may suffice to observe that travellers, official agents, and missionary teachers, all concur in describing the climate as mild, genial, and favorable to the growth of all the varieties of cereals and esculents. The cotton plant thrives, and is cultivated in the southern portion. Wheat and Indian corn are its staples; and grazing is nowhere more profitably pursued. Its water-power is sufficient for the purposes of mills and manufactories."

The industrial condition and resources, the governmental polity and moral status of the four principal tribes cannot be better exhibited to the reader, than as set forth in the language of Mr. Armstrong, the western superintendent of Indian affairs. We will quote from his report to the government in detail:

Choctaws and Chickasaws. — The Indians of the former tribe have long since justly acquired for themselves, not only from the Government of the United States, but from the citizens with whom they have intercourse, a name for honesty and fidelity, at least not surpassed by any of our Indian tribes. They have, by a steady attention to their own business, since they emigrated to their present homes, greatly increased in wealth; they have not been unmindful, at the same time, of educating the rising generation, and they have, by these means, added to the general intelligence and standing of the nation. This favorable change is indicated more clearly on Red river than with that portion of the nation on the Arkansas; and the wealth as well as the intelligence of the nation are confined mainly to the two districts on Red river.

The Choctaws may be considered as an agricultural and stock-raising people—farms on Red river will compare with any in the States. They have great advantages over other tribes, as a portion of their country is located in the cotton region. The past year they cultivated this valuable staple to a considerable extent; they have eight or ten cotton gins, and shipped between 700 and 800 bales of cotton. Many of the Choctaws live in comfortable houses, and, with very few exceptions, even the poorer class have good, substantial log cabins. They own large stocks of horses, cattle, hogs, and sheep, which constitute the wealth of those who may be termed the poorer class. It is rare indeed to find a family that has not a good supply of stock; and the richer class, in addition to stock, own, many of them, a number of slaves, who are engaged generally in cultivating cotton. The manufacture of salt is carried on at two points in the Choctaw nation. The works owned by Col. David Folsom, a Choctaw of respectability and energy, are perhaps the most extensive; about twenty bushels a day are manufactured — a supply equal to the demand, which no doubt will be increased as the article is wanted.

The Choctaws have mechanics in the nation, in addition to those furnished by the United States. These consist of four blacksmiths, two of whom are native Choctaws, and all the strikers or assistants are youths selected from the nation. There is also a millwright, who has been engaged in erecting mills for the Choctaws. Trade is carried on at suitable and convenient places in the nation. The most extensive trading is at Doaksville, within a mile of Fort Towson. There are five stores at this place, three of which are owned, in part, by Choctaws; the other two are exclusively owned by citizens of the United States. The stocks of goods are large, and the assortments such as are usual in stores — sugar and coffee being used by all classes in the nation to an extent at least equal to the whites. It may not be uninteresting to state, that the village of Doaksville is one of the most orderly and quiet towns that may be found in the West. In addition to the five stores, there are a resident physician, a good tavern, blacksmith's shop, wagon-maker, and wheelwright; a church has also been erected, in which there is preaching usually once or twice every Sabbath, by the missionaries who reside in the neighborhood; a temperance society is also organized, which numbers a large portion of the most respectable Choctaws and Chickasaws, as well as our own population. I have been at this village a week at a time, without seeing anything like ardent spirits or a drunken Indian.

The Choctaws and Chickasaws, to a great extent, may be regarded as one people; they speak the same language, and intermarried with each other, even before the emigration of the Chickasaws. By an arrangement between the tribes, the Chickasaws obtained what is now called the Chickasaw district of the Choctaw nation, making a fourth district, entitling them to an equal representation in the general council, which passes all laws for the government of the people. They enjoy equal privileges, according to the treaty, to settle in whatever district they may choose, and each to vote and be eligible to any office within the gift of the people. The only difference is, that each tribe manages its own annuities or public moneys without any interference from the other. The country owned by the Choctaws, according to the treaty and the patent received from the department, commences near Fort Smith, running up the Arkansas to the mouth of the Canadian, up the same to the limits of the United States, and with those limits to Red river, down the same to where a due south line, from the beginning near Fort Smith, will strike the Red river, which is the dividing line between the State of Arkansas and the Choctaws. The line from the Canadian to the Red river has not been run.

The Choctaws are governed by written laws and a constitution; elections are held annually for members to the general council. The nation is divided into four districts (one being the Chickasaw). Each district elects, by the qualified voters, a chief, who holds his office for four years, and is eligible for two terms. These chiefs receive a salary from the United States of $250 each, per annum, by treaty stipulation. The general council, consisting of forty members, convenes on the first Monday in October; a speaker and a clerk is elected; the speaker is addressed as is customary in legislative bodies, and the whole business of the council is conducted with the utmost decorum. Each chief delivers a message in person to the council, recommending such laws as he may deem conducive to the interests of the people, and as there is but one representative body, all laws that are passed by the council are submitted to the chiefs; if approved, the same become laws; if not, the bills are returned to the council, and if passed by two-thirds, become laws. The council-house, a large and commodious building, with committee-rooms, and also seats for spectators, was erected under the treaty stipulations. Much interest is manifested by the people in electing councillors, and also when they meet together; they usually remain in session from ten to fifteen days, and receive a per-diem pay of $2. Judges are nominated by the chief of the district, and receive a small compensation; and trial by jury is guaranteed in all capital offences; but there is no law enforcing the collection of debts.

It will be seen that the Choctaws have materially bettered their condition by an exchange of country; are fast approximating to our own laws and institutions; and feel a deep interest in the success and prosperity of our own people, as well as the perpetuity of our Government. They have school funds sufficient to educate a large portion of the people, beside annuities from the United States, and also an investment of $500,000, at five per cent., in bonds of the State of Alabama, for the benefit of the whole people. They have also other sources of wealth. Their laws are generally respected, and when violated, punishment is inflicted. It is very rare that acts of violence take place between themselves; every individual feels safe in his own property; and travellers pass through the nation with as much safety as they do in any country.

The Chickasaws number about 5000. They have settled promiscuously among the Choctaws; lately they are beginning to move up to the district assigned them, which they did not do at first, owing to the scarcity of provisions and the exposed situation of the frontier. The Chickasaws have obtained greater pecuniary advantages by the exchange of their country than any of the tribes. Their lands were surveyed and sold at a time when speculation was at its highest, and when the most enormous prices were paid. The funds thus arising were invested for the benefit of the nation, after each head of a family had obtained a reservation. Some profited by receiving large amounts; but in most cases, the money having been easily obtained, was as freely spent. It is, however, the home the Chickasaws obtained from the Choctaws that compensates them. They are now fairly settled in a country at least as fertile as the one they left, and removed, to a great extent, from the evils that were fast destroying them as a people. They unite with the Choctaws in forming the fourth district, and come into the general council of the nation with a representation corresponding to their population. The Chickasaws have ample national funds to extend the mechanic arts, as well as education, among their people. Some of the more wealthy are planting cotton, and, with few exceptions, the people are getting around them small stocks of horses, cattle, and hogs, which, with care and attention, in a country so well adapted to stock-raising, will soon greatly increase.

Cherokees. — This people combine more intelligence than any of the tribes. They have intermarried more with the whites, have had the advantages of education, and, by their location, have had an opportunity of observing more immediately the customs and manners of a civilized people than any other of the Indian tribes. There are many intelligent and well-educated Cherokees.

The nation consists of about 18,000 souls, spread over an extent of country sixty miles square, comprising several varieties of soil. Estimating one warrior to every five souls, would give 3600. They are improving in intellectual condition; have executive, legislative, and judicial departments; an organized government; a principal and assistant chief, elective every four years; a council and committee, organized somewhat upon the principle of the House of Representatives and Senate of the United States — the former consisting of twenty-four members, and the latter of sixteen, elective every two years. They sit annually, and are usually in session from three to four weeks. The judiciary is composed of a supreme bench, a circuit court, and a district court; the first consisting of five members, the second of four, and the latter of eight. They have written laws, and a criminal code. The circuit court sits spring and fall; the supreme court once a year; the district court whenever an emergency arises. They have juries, and hear pleadings. The judges of the circuit and district benches are appointed more for their probity and personal worth than on account of their legal attainments, and will compare, in point of moral worth, with any similar body in the United States. They are rigid in the execution of their laws; generally impartial in the administration of justice, as yet necessarily in a rude state. As many as four executions have taken place in one year. The people are very tenacious of the management and regulation of their internal affairs.

There are about 2000 professors of the Christian religion, consisting of Baptists, Methodists, and Presbyterians: the former, comprising much the largest class, may be considered the first both for intelligence and general integrity. The greater part of the Cherokee people are half-breeds, or what are known to be the middle class, who are ardent and enterprising, and passionately fond of gaming. When not under the influence of ardent spirits, they are hospitable and well disposed; but, when under such influence, their worst passions seem to be roused. They have a school fund of their own, which they are wisely appropriating to the diffusion of knowledge throughout the nation, by appointing trustees to superintend the disbursements.

The Cherokees are not naturally disposed to labor; but there is a manifest change in this particular, both from necessity and inclination, and they are now engaged in agricultural pursuits. Their country is well watered, and supplies abundantly all the products known to that latitude, such as corn, wheat, rye, oats, tobacco, and hemp. Within the limits of the nation, there are two abundant and valuable salt springs; one of them is leased to a Cherokee for an inconsiderable sum, but is not worked to much advantage, either to the proprietor or the nation. Stone coal of the finest quality abounds in two adjacent sections.

The Cherokees have received from the Government of the United States large sums of money; some have profited by the money received, while others have lavished theirs away, leaving only a desire to be supplied, without any disposition to do so by their own labor. Their country is well adapted to raising corn, wheat, oats, &c., with the usual varieties of garden vegetables, and farms, as well as neat houses, are found in many parts of the nation, exhibiting signs of wealth and intelligence unusual in an Indian country. A large portion of the country is well watered, is generally divided into woodland and prairie, and the lands are rich and very productive. Large stocks of cattle, horses, hogs, and sheep, are owned by the natives, and many have also paid attention to planting orchards, which are very unusual in an Indian country. Salt water is found in great abundance, and the Grand Saline, if judiciously managed, is capable of supplying a large portion of our own population with salt. Stone coal is to be found in several places, and if the country was examined, it would, no doubt, exhibit great resources of wealth in minerals and salt water.

They are furnished by the United States with four blacksmiths and assistants, iron, and steel; also, a wheelwright and wagon-maker; independent of whom they have mechanics of different kinds in the nation. They also hold a large fund for educational purposes, placed by treaty under the control of the national council, which, if properly applied, will go far to educate a large portion of the people. They are governed by a constitution and laws adopted and passed by the people. Debts are collected in the usual way, by issuing executions; letters of administration are also granted on estates of deceased persons in the nation; and, indeed, all the forms and regulations are observed, usually in use in the States. In government the Cherokees are in advance of any of their red brethren.

Creeks.—These are more numerous than any of the tribes, numbering at least 20,000. The census of the nation has not been taken since the emigration, the annuity not being paid to the heads of families. As a people, they have less education and intelligence than either the Choctaws or Cherokees; but lately they have given better evidences of a disposition to encourage education than at any previous time. Many of the Creeks have separate fields; but their ancient custom of making a town field is still, to a great extent, observed. They raise large quantities of corn, melons, pumpkins, beans, and are cultivating rice to some extent, which is said to grow well, and will be a great accession to their living. They have four blacksmiths and assistants, with iron and steel furnished by treaty stipulations, and also a wheelwright and wagon-maker. Possessing but few, if any, native mechanics, they rely mainly for their work upon mechanics furnished by the Government. They have quite a large annuity, which is paid to the chiefs, and by them divided among the different towns, in accordance with existing laws, and their own request, which at least makes it satisfactory to the chiefs. They have commenced passing regular laws, which are recorded by the clerks appointed for that purpose; but they do not elect representatives, their chiefs being the law-makers generally. The principal chief, Rolly M'Intosh, is a man of undoubted attachment to the United States Government, and the same may be said of most of the chiefs. The certainty that the country they own is really theirs, does much to reconcile old feelings.

The late emigrants, or what are termed the *Upper Creeks*, although very much dissatisfied for a length of time after their removal to their new homes, owing mainly to their sufferings from sickness, and the great mortality that prevailed among them, are now a happy, healthy, and contented people, are much in advance of the *Lower Creeks* (or early emigrants) in the variety, quality, and quantity of their agricultural products, as well as in the management of their farms, and have larger and better stocks of domestic animals. They are likewise much in advance of the Lower Creeks in domestic or household manufactures, making quantities of cotton cloth from the raw material, planted and cultivated upon their own farms; have also several useful native mechanics among them, such as carpenters, wheelwrights, loom-makers, smiths, &c.; and all reside in good comfortable houses of their own construction.

Seminoles.—This tribe have from time to time removed, until it is now understood they have generally emigrated. Unfortunately for the Seminoles, the chief of each party, as they landed at or near Fort Gibson, endeavored to settle away from the others. This was done by the chiefs, with the hope of keeping around them a party of which they were the head, fearing that if they become united, some other more favored leader would supersede them, and by this means they were scattered not only in the Creek but also in the Cherokee country. Micanopy, and other leading Seminoles, settled on the D Fork of the Canadian, in the country assigned them. Efforts have been made to concentrate the Seminoles at this point; but this is difficult to do, and does not meet with much favor from the Creeks. They are willing for them to settle in any part of the Creek nation promiscuously, giving as a reason that the Seminoles themselves are not suited, from their present feelings, to locate in a body, and become quiet and orderly neighbors. That portion of the Seminoles who settled on the Deep Fork of the Canadian have raised a surplus of corn, beans, pumpkins, and melons, all of which grow to great perfection, and a few have raised small patches of rice. The labor, however, is principally performed by their negroes, who were participants in the Florida war, but who have thus far conducted themselves with great propriety.

Whatever may have been the importance or distinction of the Seminole chiefs in Florida, they seem to lose their greatness in the crowd of other Indians who are engaged in the cultivation of the soil.

The twenty-one tribes transferred from the old States and settled in the territory partially included in Kansas, comprise the Delawares, Shawnees, Wyandots, Miamies, Weas, Piankashaws, Ottowas, Chippewas, Pottawattamies, Kickapoos, Sacs and Foxes, Senecas, mixed Senecas and Shawnees, Peorias Kaskaskias, Iowas, Stockbridges or Mohicans, Munsees, and portions of the Iroquois, forming together an aggregate population of 30,893. The indigenous tribes residing in the territory are the Quappas, Osages, Kanzas, Pawnees, and Arapahoes, numbering 7358. The Otoes, Omahaws, Missouries, Cheyennes, and some other indigenous tribes, have not been enumerated.* The local agents, writing to the head of the Bureau of Indian Affairs, a short time after the period of colonization, present a report of the condition of the Indians under their jurisdiction, from which we make a few extracts.

Quappas.—This tribe have greatly changed their habits within a few years; from having been a whiskey-drinking, squalid, poverty-stricken race, they have become temperate, frugal, and industrious, directing their attention to agriculture, and to the general improvement of their condition. They are now well clothed, and have enough to eat. This change is in part owing to the fact, that the venders of spirits in the Cherokee settlements north of the Quappas, whence their supplies were principally drawn, have abandoned the trade, in consequence of the opposition of some of their more respectable neighbors. A great deal of credit is, however, due to the Quappas themselves, for they could, if so disposed, procure liquor from the whites; but they have listened to better counsels, and resisted the temptation.

Mixed Senecas and *Shawnees.*—These Indians have never been as much inclined to intemperance as some of the other bands, and there has not been so great a change among them. They continue to raise corn, wheat, oats, garden vegetables, &c., and, on the whole, are improving rather than otherwise.

The country occupied by these tribes is high, rolling, healthy, and finely watered; containing springs of the best water in every direction, sometimes gushing out of the solid rock in streams large enough to turn a mill. Where it is fit for cultivation at all, the land is fertile; but much of it is hilly and barren, worthless except for the timber. The lands on the water-courses are of the best quality, well suited to the cultivation of tobacco, hemp, corn, and the small grains, and the upland prairies are scarcely inferior; but there is a much greater quantity of good land than the present occupants will ever use. The heavily-timbered bottoms on the Pomme de Terre and the Neosho afford not only good winter range for cattle, but an abundance of marsh for hogs. The Quappas have a coal-bank immediately on the Neosho, the coal in which is bituminous, of good quality, easily obtained, and the supply apparently inexhaustible. In the vicinity of this coal there are several tar-springs, or rather springs of sulphur-water and mineral tar, or petroleum, together; the latter substance rising with the water, and separating from it immediately after it issues from the earth.

Osages.—This tribe has made but little perceptible improvement in agri

* History, Condition, and Prospects of the Indian Tribes, Vol. VI.

..ltural pursuits, though some ten or twelve families of Pa-ha-sca's (George White Hare) and Clermont's bands, have lately fenced and ploughed their fields. They are still living, with few exceptions, in large towns, where it will be impossible to make much progress in stock-raising or farming; Tab-hu-sca, the principal chief, and a bad man, being much opposed to the farming operations of his people. They have adopted a short code of penal laws for the government of their people, which forbid, not the introduction, but the sale, of ardent spirits in their country, under the penalty of the destruction of the spirits, and lashes on the offender. The people meet in general council once in each and every year, assisted by their agent and interpreter, for the purpose of law-making, &c.

Shawnees.—This tribe own a tract of country twenty-five miles north and south, and one hundred east and west, bounded on the east by the State of Missouri, and on the north by the Kanzas river, which, in point of soil, timber, and water, is equalled by but few tracts of the same size in any country; though there is, however, hardly a sufficient proportion of timber for the prairie. The Shawnees have become an agricultural people; their buildings and farms being similar to those of the whites in a new-settled country; enclosed by rail fences, and most of them in good form; each string of fence being straight, sufficiently high to secure their crops, and many of them staked and ridered. They all live in comfortable cabins, perhaps half or more being built of good hewn logs, and neatly raised, with outhouses, stables, and barns.

Delawares.—The Delawares own a tract of country sixty miles east and west, and about twenty-four miles north and south, bounded on the south by the Kanzas river, and on the east by the Missouri river, or State of Missouri. The soil, timber, and water, are generally very good. Like the Shawnees, they depend for a subsistence mainly on their farms, which, with their horses, are nearly or quite equal to those of the Shawnees. They cultivate Indian corn, wheat, oats, beans, peas, pumpkins, potatoes, cabbage, turnips, and many other vegetables in abundance, and raise a great number of horses, cattle, and hogs.

Kickapoos.—The Kickapoos own a tract of country immediately north of the Delawares, about sixty miles east and west, by thirty north and south, bounded on the east by the Missouri river, or State of Missouri, and on the south by the Delaware country. They raise a large surplus of Indian corn; also beef and pork for sale.

Stockbridges.—By permission, this little band of Stockbridges settled on the Delaware lands, near the Missouri river, and about seven miles below Fort Leavenworth, some time in February, 1840, since when they have built for themselves a number of neat log cabins, opened several small farms, and raise more Indian corn than they need for their own use. They grow pumpkins, beans, peas, cabbage, potatoes, and many other vegetables, and have made good root-houses to preserve them; all of which they have effected with very little means.

Christian Indians.—The Christian Indians came with, and at the same time as the Stockbridges, settled among the Delawares, built comfortable little cabins, and made small farms.

Kanzas.—The Kanzas Indians, located on the Kanzas river, about eighty miles above its mouth, make many excuses for not turning their attention to agricultural pursuits; the principal one being, that they are afraid to work, for fear the Pawnees will come on them and kill them all off. They raise but little grain, in fact, not enough to subsist them; and their only dependence for a subsistence is on the buffalo, and what few deer and turkeys they can kill. They follow the chase.

Ottoes and Missourias.—These Indians are in a most deplorable situation, notwithstanding they have had the assistance of the Government extended to them for many years, and that, during certain periods they bid fair to follow the example of some of their more advanced red brethren of the west in the pursuits of agriculture and civilization—having been furnished with teachers, blacksmiths, and farmers, for these purposes; but the evil spirit found its way, through various channels, into their lodges, and generated among them discontent, jealousy and strife, which eventually terminated in butchery and bloodshed. This state of things produced in their minds a settled prejudice against the spot which they then occupied, on the north side of the river Platte, under the impression that an evil spirit hovered over and around them; and, acting under this belief, they, in a moment of drunkenness and riot, set fire to their village, which was soon reduced to ashes. Their farm, which was located contiguous to the village, suffered a similar fate; the greater part of the fences having been torn down and burnt, and the whole is now lying waste and uncultivated. They have totally abandoned this ill-fated spot, and settled, rather temporarily, in various lodges or villages on the south side of the River Platte. The village of the Missourias stands on the prairie, on the bank of the river, while the Ottoe villages, four in number, are located a short distance from the river, between a point five miles above its mouth, and one eighteen miles higher up.

Omahas.—These Indians follow the chase as usual, and claim the country bounded by the Missouri river on the east, by Shell creek on the west, by the River Platte on the south, and on the north by the Poncas country. The Elkhorn, which runs in a southerly direction and empties into the Platte about twenty miles above its mouth, is the largest stream which passes through their territory. Their favorite village once stood near the Missouri river, and about one hundred miles above Fort Leavenworth; but several years since they were driven from this location by the Sioux, and since then have settled temporarily on the Elkhorn, where they now suffer from extreme indigence, not using even ordinary savage exertion in the culture of corn.

Pawnees.—The four principal chiefs, with a number of their respective bands, have removed to their new homes on the Loup fork of the Platte. They generally evince a peaceable and friendly disposition, though they have an unsettled difficulty with the Ottoes, growing out of murders heretofore committed by the latter on some of their people.

Kaskaskias, Weas, Piankashaws, and Pottawattamies.—These tribes have made but little change in their condition; owning some cattle and hogs, work-oxen, farming utensils, &c., and depending entirely on agricultural pursuits for a subsistence; though if it were not for the ruinous practice pursued by those lawless individuals who are settled immediately on the line of the State of Missouri, and, in violation of the State laws, furnish them with whiskey, their improvement would be rapid.

Ottowas.—This people is still advancing in agricultural pursuits; they may be said to have entirely abandoned the chase; all of them live in good, comfortable log cabins; have fields enclosed with rail-fences; and own domestic animals. Out of their annuity they have erected a good horse-mill; many of them are sowing wheat, and ere long they will raise grain enough to supply themselves with flour and meal for their own consumption.

Iowas.—This tribe is located on the waters of the Namaha, a tributary of the Missouri, and their principal village is situated one mile above the mouth of the Great Namaha. These Indians are much given to intemperance, and while under the influence of liquor act very ill toward each other, as well as toward the whites.

Sacs and Foxes.—These Indians are a proud, independent people, pursuing the chase during the hunting season. They are not so much given to intemperance as the Iowas, and entertain much more respect and love for the white man than do the latter; frequently boasting of their friendship to the whites, and their peaceable disposition toward their red brothers.

Some years later, the chief officer of the Indian Bureau at Washington, makes use of the following language, after having visited personally the colonized tribes:

"The condition of the Indians located west of Missouri and Iowa is not as prosperous, or their advance in civilization as rapid, as the official reports annually received from that part of the country would authorize us to expect. In several tribes are to be found some educated, intelligent men; and many are able, by the cultivation of the earth, to subsist themselves. Among these classes there are some sincere professors of religion; but the mass of the

Indians are indolent and intemperate, and many of them are degraded and debased.

"The transplanting of these Indians, and the dedication of their present country to their use, and for their future home, was an emanation of the purest benevolence, and the dictate of humanity. Vast sums of money have been expended by the Government for the sustenance, comfort, and civilization of these unfortunate people, and the missionary has occupied that field of labor long and faithfully; but, notwithstanding all that has been done by the Government and good men, the experiment has measurably failed. Located generally on large tracts of land, separated into small and distinct bands, roaming at will, and wandering in idleness, the mass of these tribes are in a degraded state, with no hope of a considerable degree of reformation (even with such improvements as are practicable in their present management), without a change of residence."

APPENDIX.

But little change occurred in the status of the various Indian tribes until the discovery of gold in California. Then, the migration of Americans to that rich country brought the men in transit over the plains and the mountains right in contact with several powerful tribes, of whom little had been popularly known.

Before reverting to the annals of any of these tribes, we will follow the fortunes of the Cherokees, and other partially civilized tribes.

The troubles breaking out upon the election of President Lincoln placed the Cherokees and their affiliated tribes in a very peculiar and distressing situation. The lands which they occupied were surrounded by slave States, most of which were actually or sympathetically in alliance with the Confederate government. Some of the most prosperous and influential of those Indians were themselves the owners of black slaves, and the active agents of the Southern Confederacy lost no opportunity of impressing upon the Indians that it was the object of the United States to release all slaves. A large number of the Indians accordingly threw in their lot with the Southerners. A powerful minority, however, struggled hard to retain their fellow-countrymen in loyalty to the Union. Among the latter was the principal chief, John Ross. But in spite of all the powerful arguments of Ross and other loyal Indians, first the Choctaws, then the Chickasaws, and finally the Cherokees, enlisted under the Confederates. The wife of Ross was the last person who yielded to the Secession torrent, and she, personally, prevented the Confederate flag from being hoisted over the Council House. These Indians contributed several regiments toward the Southern quota, but, as ever with their people, failed to make any great mark upon battle-fields where regular military organization prevails. It must be said in their favor, that at the outset of the war the United States was unable to give those tribes any kind of physical support, and they only saw a probability that all their lands, crops, dwellings, and slaves would be confiscated by the then victorious Southerners. At the end of the war these tribes resumed their former relation to the general government.

The annexed will be found a reliable statement of the present condition of the following named tribes:

The Delewares have a reservation in Kansas. They number about 1,000, and each individual has a personal property of at least $1,000. The bulk of these people have taken kindly to civilization. Many of them are thrifty farmers, while others are traders in cattle and goods, dealing with Indians and whites on the prairies and mountains.

The Missouri Iowas devote themselves almost entirely to agriculture; reverting to hunting only as a pastime. They number something over 300, and have quite a large sum secured to each individual.

The Kicapoos have at times been on the verge of starvation. But they took diligently to farming; raising wheat and other food. They have a reserve fund of $40,000 among 350 of them.

The Omahas are among the most prosperous of the Indians. They have fine farms, on which they cultivate corn, wheat, and sorghum. They have also extensive pasture lands. They have a regular police force, and give much attention to schools.

The Pottawatomies have some 30 miles square of property belonging to them, in a fine healthy situation, on the Kansas river. They number more than 4,000 souls, and are prosperous. They have not entirely abandoned the chase. Schools and churches are flourishing.

The Sacs and Foxes, once a most powerful and warlike tribe, still cling to the garb and many of the primitive usages of their race. They number over 1,300 individuals, and eke out their subsistence by annually hunting the buffalo and depending upon the yearly sums paid them by the government.

The Shawnees, always an intelligent people, number nearly 1,000. The property held by the tribe is estimated to be worth about two millions of dollars. They appear to be progressively improving in all the best points of civilized life.

The Winnibagoes number about 2,200, and have property worth at least $70,000. Each family has a farm of 80 acres; each male unmarried, 40 acres.

One band of the Sioux, the Yanctounnais, have always been fierce and untamable, preferrring to continue their roving habits. This section of the Sioux amount to nearly 4,000, and yield very reluctantly to any proffers from the government looking to the sale of their lands.

Another large party of the Sioux take kindly to a more civilized state of existence, cultivate farms and assume many of the ways of the whites, dwelling in houses and dressing in the fashion of the neighboring whites. The Sioux proper are calculated to be little short of 7,000. Their wealth is counted largely in horses and cattle.

THE SIOUX WAR.

A large force of Indians, composed in the main part of Sioux, with an addition of many wandering portions of other warlike tribes, had located themselves in a very advantageous position upon the Big Little Horn river, in the Yellowstone country, in the year 1876. On the 25th of May, of that year, General Custer, who had greatly distinguished himself as a cavalry officer during the civil war, was ordered by his superiors to hunt up and attack this Indian force. The situation of the savages was not at all well known, and the customary scouting does not appear to have been done. The sad result of this neglect we know too well—the immediate particulars of the action we know only by surmise. The gallant Custer, in this instance, instead of surprising, was himself surprised. Riding at the head of five hundred as brave men as ever bestrode a war-horse, he rushed right into a deathly vortex. The soldiers, to a man, were shot, brained, or stabbed. Not one individual remained alive to rehearse the dreadful scene. Dumb evidence enough remained to inform spectators of the bloody field that the heroic Custer, and his no less heroic officers and soldiers, fought bravely, and only fell before the onslaught of the Indians, who greatly outnumbered them. A wily Sioux chief, with the strange name of Sitting Bull, is presumed to have been the leader of the Indians. While this fight with Custer was going on, the Sioux, either by extraordinary luck for them, or most wonderful strategy, contrived to find employment for two or three other detachments of cavalry, so that they could not come to Custer's aid. The prudence of Major Reno, and the fortunate arrival of General Terry, possibly saved the rest of the expedition from the same fate.

Apart from the fatal rencontre with Sitting Bull, the Sioux had several other encounters with United States troops, which resulted in a different manner. General Crook, who commanded about 2,000 men, during eight months of 1876, marched over 3,000 miles, in a very rough country. During this campaign, Crook's force killed and captured over 700 Indians, wounded 500, and destroyed 400 lodges, which sheltered at least 3,000 persons.

Under the leadership of Sitting Bull, the Indians managed to elude all plans laid to prevent their escape, and contrived, with little loss, to get across the line into the neighboring British possessions. Here they have since remained. So far they have scornfully rejected all offers made by our government for their return to our jurisdiction. It is but justice to remark that the Canadian government and our own are in perfect accord upon this subject, the former having given the Indians peremptory orders to remain peaceful, and not attempt to make any raids across the border.

The Cheyennes and Arapahoes, ranging between the upper Arkansas, Texas, and Colorado, are a very bold, warlike people.

The Pah-Ute tribe, occupying a part of Nevada Territory, during the war prevented any interruption with the coach and telegraph service. They might have given us a great deal of trouble had they struck at these important lines of communication and travel.

The Washoe Indians have not the least aspirations toward a better mode of life. They look to the natural, unartificial products of the soil and various insects to enable them to drag out their ill-fed existence.

The Navajoes and Apaches, who live in New Mexico, are seldom really at peace with our people. They are a martial race, admirable horsemen, skillful in the use of arms. They frequently make incursions upon the defenceless villages of Mexico, often recrossing the border with much spoil and many captives. These two tribes, together, it is estimated by the best authorities, count about 20,000.

The Pueblos and Mohuache Utahs are not so savage in their nature, and during our late war evidenced, by word and deed, a friendly feeling toward us. These two tribes united fall little short of 20,000 individuals.

The Utah Indians originally numbered at least 17,000 people. The Mormons are accused of having used these Indians to make depredations upon the whites opposed to their peculiar tenets.

The California Indians, in spite of the self-sacrificing missions long kept up by the first Spanish settlers, have failed to make anything like satisfactory advances in civilization. They are a poor, degraded specimen of the Indian race, proving that something else is needed to elevate man than a fertile soil and a glorious climate.

THE MODOCS AND THE MODOC WAR.

In the year 1867, the Modocs, a small, but brave tribe, living on the boundaries between California and Oregon, began to give much trouble to the settlers. Their hostile speeches and movements, however, excited but little apprehension, as they were not deemed any way formidable, on account of the pancity of their numbers.

One Modoc Jack acquired popularity with his tribe by his wisdom in council and by his rash bravery in the field.

The Modocs resided on Lost River.

The chief was Schonches; and although his father had been shot and killed by the whites—in which respect he resembled Modoc Jack—yet he was willing to lead a quiet life.

Troubles between the Indians and the whites became quite common. The whites continued to settle the country in the region of Lost River, near the boundary of Upper California and Oregon, until a disposition prevailed to send the Indians to a reservation. The Indian Commissioner, about the year 1864, made an effort to get the Modocs upon the Yinax reservation on Martin River, in Oregon, fifty miles north of Lost River.

This at once raised up two parties among the Modocs—Schonches, the chief, being in favor of going to the reservation, while Jack opposed it.

Jack exhorted the Modocs to resist the palefaces, until he fired them with enthusiasm.

Finally, after a great deal of talk, Schonches consented to go to the reservation, and he set out with about thirty warriors, with their squaws and pappooses.

The rest of the tribe remained, intending to fight it out with the whites to the last, and these chose Jack for chief. Then it was that Jack drew upon himself the notice of the whites: his fame began to be carried abroad.

Captain Jack was a stern, dignified man.

Besides Jack were several other noted characters, who united with him in opposing the encroachments of the palefaces. Among these were Scar-faced Charley, the next noted one of the tribe. Shack Nasty Jim, a youngster of not over twenty or twenty-two. Hocker Jim, though quite young, looked as if he could be guilty of anything.

When it was found that Jack was placed at the head of the Modocs, great efforts were made to prevail upon him and the rest of the tribe to remove to the reservation where Schonches had gone, but Jack and others only went to examine the place. They expressed their preference for the plentiful supply of fish in Lost River; and so they went back to their old home.

But the troubles continued. The borderers hated the Indians, and they made no secret of it, while, on the other hand, the Indians regarded the borderers as interlopers on their domain.

In the fall of 1867, Mr. Lindsay Applegate induced Captain Jack and his band to accept the hospitality of Uncle Sam, and they consequently moved up to Yinax reservation. They remained there until January, and then returned to their quarters on Lost River. The Modocs since that time lived in this locality.

The first treaty was made with Ike, an Indian, who claimed the right over that section of the country. A second treaty was made with Big Jack, and finally a third with Captain Jack, Schonches and others. A consideration was paid the Indians on each occasion. Mr. Odincal, the present Indian Commissioner, annoyed by the perpetual complaints of Oregon settlers, determined to remove the Modoc Indians to Yinax reservation. A combined movement was consequently made on Thanksgiving Day. There was a brisk fight between the United States troops and Captain Jack's band, in which upward of fifty Indians and several soldiers were killed, and many wounded. In the meantime the settlers had nearly prevailed on the Curly-headed Doctor's band to go to the reservation, as they stated that Captain Jack's party had surrendered; but hearing the firing on the other side of the river, they refused to go, and presently both sides began firing. The citizens finally retreated, leaving one of their party dead on the field, and the Indians state the whites killed a squaw and two pappooses in the fight. This party then broke loose over the country and murdered some twelve or thirteen white settlers, and then going round the northern end of Tule or Rhett Lake, joined Captain Jack in the Lava Beds. Captain Jack and his party had retreated there immediately after their fight with the soldiers, but kept on the California side of the river, and went into the Lava Beds from the southern side. They did not murder any citizens on their retreat, and, in fact, told a settler named Samuel Watson to go home, as they only wanted to fight with soldiers, not settlers.

The Indians all started off one night and joined Captain Jack in the Lava Beds, reinforcing his command. Captain Jack refused to go back to the reservation. The principal Peace Commissioners sent to the Modocs were Mr. Meacham, Rev. Dr. Thomas, and Mr. Dyer. The labors of these Peace Commissioners proved abortive, and Captain Jack persisted in remaining with his tribe, in the Lava Beds.

These Lava Beds present a strange appearance. If one could imagine a smooth, solid sheet of granite, ten miles square and five hundred feet thick, covering resistless mines of gunpowder scattered at irregular intervals under it—that these mines are exploded simultaneously, rending the whole field into rectangular masses from the size of a match-box to that of a church, heaping the masses high in some places and leaving deep chasms in others. Following the explosion, the whole thing is placed in one of Vulcan's crucibles and heated up to a point where the whole begins to fuse and run together, and then suffered to cool. The roughness of the upper surface remains as the explosion left it, while all below is honeycombed by the crevices caused by the cooling of the melted rock.

From the top of one of these stone pyramids an Indian can shoot a man without even exposing a square inch of himself.

The country along the line separating California from Oregon, in which the lava beds are situated, has been the theatre of military operations against the Indians at different times during the past twenty years. It has been traversed by emigrants who settled in the neighborhood and it is well and favorably known as a cattle range.

The Lava Beds cover an area of 100 square miles. They appear to have been brought into existence by upheavals from below. The largest cave is known as Ben Wright's cave. It contains fifteen acres of open space under ground, in which there is a good spring and many openings through which a man can crawl, the main entrance being about the size of a common window. In this cave Jack and his followers fortified themselves.

In the Lava Beds, are a number of small plots abundantly supplied with bunch grass.

The troops were well posted, so as to prevent the Indians escaping. Their only line of retreat would seem to be in a southerly direction into the Pitt River Mountains. The tribes in that quarter are of a warlike character, and have given the government considerable trouble in times past. In 1858 and 1859 their ambushes were so effective and their manner of warfare so advantageous that at first very little progress was made in reducing them to submission.

The troops, in pursuing the Modocs, had to follow them on foot, and in passing through the gulches and crevices must expect to find the enemy on the high bluffs above them at every point, or making their way through concealed passages to secure retreat. The cannon and howitzer commanded all approaches to and from the cave.

The peculiar geological features of the lake country in California resemble the county Antrim, in Ireland, in which is located the celebrated Giant's Causeway.

In this delightful country Jack lived like an Italian bandit.

Our allies, the Warm Spring Indians, are a band of friendly Indians brought from the Warm Springs reserve in Oregon, and were entrusted with an important duty. They acted as scouts and also to intercept any movement of the Modocs to escape in a southerly direction. These Indians are known as the confederated bands in Middle Oregon, and comprise seven of the Walla Wallas, Wacos, Teninoz and Deschutes tribes, numbering 626 men, women and children. Their leader, Donald McKenzie, no doubt a half-breed, was well acquainted with the mode of warfare Jack and his party adopted. The Warm Springs reservation contains over a million acres, located in the central part of the State, and the tract of country is such that nobody wants it, The tillable portion occupied by the Indians consists of five hundred acres, and though even this portion is not very good land, many of the families, by reason of their industry, have succeeded measurably in their farming operations, and are considered self-sustaining.

The trouble with the Modoc Indians commenced as far back as 1872. At that time the Modocs were prowling around Lost River, on the banks of which romantic stream they had their camp. They were great cattle thieves, and annoyed the Oregonian settlers terribly, and occasionally a settler would kill a Modoc, or *vice versa.*

The government finally came to the conclusion to put the Modocs in the Klamath reservation. They were informed of this action of their Great Father at Washington, but they positively refused to go. They wanted to stay where they were.

When the government was told of the Modoc stand, it was decided to use force, as long as moral suasion didn't work.

So on the 28th day of November, 1872, Major Jackson, of Company B, First Cavalry, with thirty-five men, moved on their camp at Lost River.

The Modocs were a band of seventy-five, armed with Springfield rifles, revolvers and bowie knives.

A fight took place at Lost River, which resulted in a victory for the United States over the Modoc nation.

Captain Jack lost fifteen braves, and Uncle Sam lost one soldier. After the fighting Jack, his band, squaws and pappooses retreated to the Lava Beds.

Skirmishing was kept up from that time until January.

The government of the United States sent a Peace Commission, composed of Mr. A. B. Meacham, Jesse Applegate, Samuel Chase, and Oliver Applegate, Indian Agent at Yinax, as clerk, which met at Fairchild's ranche about the middle of February, 1873. Mr. Steele and Mr. Fairchild, both old settlers were engaged to assist them in their negotiations with Captain Jack.

After much unsatisfactory discussion in council the following terms were offered to the Modocs through Mr. Steele:

First—To surrender to General Canby and receive full amnesty for the past.

Second—To be removed to Angel Island, where they are to be fed with soldiers' allowance and clothed until a new home can be provided for them and they are able to support themselves in it.

Third—To be furnished by General Canby with transportation for their women and children to the island, and thence to their new home, perhaps in Arizona.

Fourth—General Canby is of the opinion that he can promise that Jack and some of his head men should go to visit the President, and that the President will permit them to select for themselves a new home in a warmer climate.

They had a long talk over the matter; but from the first evinced a marked dislike to leaving the home of their forefathers, and finally sent back word by Mr. Steele that they would only live in their own country.

General Canby was opposed to granting the claims of the Modocs, and gave the following reasons:

First—They cannot live there without stealing, as their country produces nothing for their support.

Second—If the government intends to feed them it will cost 200 per cent. more in the Lava beds than on any other reservation of a more appropriate nature.

Third—The country will be perpetually disturbed by quarrels between the Oregon settlers and the Indians; and

Fourth—Such acquiescence to all their wishes, after the United States troops had received a whipping, would be an encouragement to the Snakes and Pitnes, already disaffected, to make war and demand their own terms.

The second Commission, composed of Meacham, Judge Roseborough, Mr. Thomas, and Mr. Dyar, was as unsuccessful as the previous one. Several interviews were held with the Indians, and Mr. Meacham sent a dispatch to Washington, in which he stated the principal impediment to peace negotiations was the fear that the Indians indicted by the Jackson County Grand Jury would be given up for punishment.

There were at this time about six hundred United States troops in the neighborhood, stationed in different detachments. General Canby, commander of the district of the Pacific, and the United States Peace Commissioners, used every means in their power to arrange peace with the Modocs.

In their efforts in this direction they were not aided by the Governor of Oregon, who strongly protested against a peace. The Governor was in favor of a war of extermination against the savages. Captain Jack, among other audacious acts, burned a log hut in view of the troops. A message was sent to the Indians stating that the President of the United States, General Grant, had heard about the war and was very sorry his children were fighting.

The Modocs refused all offers of peace, and the Commission proved a total failure. A. B. Meacham, of the Commission, telegraphed these facts to Washington.

On the 20th of March, 1873, it was decided to surround the Indian camp, and reinforcements were ordered to the Lava Beds.

About the first of April there was a conference with the Modocs, which lasted several hours, and, at the request of Captain Jack, only Judge Roseborough, Mr. Meacham, and Mr. John Fairchild were present. There were ten or twelve of the leading Modocs with Captain Jack. Judge Roseborough commenced the talk by explaining to the Indians the position they were in, and how he had come from Yreka to try and make peace. Captain Jack and John Schonchin, in reply, reiterated their determination to remain where they were. They gave up the claim to Lost River, and said they would be satisfied to remain in the Lava Beds.

The U. S. cavalry then commenced reconnoitering with a view to active aggressive movements. The Indians said they would have "no more talk." Captain Jack was very defiant.

The Indians built rock fortifications and otherwise prepared themselves for a desperate resistance. The U. S. troops were held in readiness to move on the Lava Beds in force.

General Canby, Mr. Meacham and Dr. Thomas paid a visit to the Indian chiefs. General Edward Richard Spigg Canby of the United States Army was born in Kentucky in the year 1819. He graduated at West Point in 1839 and served in the Florida war from that year to 1842, and was made Assistant Adjutant-General with the rank of Captain, March 3, 1847, and was distinguished at Cerro Gordo. He was appointed Brigadier-General U. S. Army, July 28, 1866. During the reconstruction campaign he commanded successively the Fifth and First Military Districts, and was finally in command of the department of Columbia, with headquarters at Portland, Oregon.

Mr. Meacham is a prominent citizen in Oregon, and a friend of Attorney-General Williams, at whose suggestion he was appointed one of the Peace Commissioners to visit the Modocs and see if some arrangement could not be made by which a war with this band could be averted.

Rev. Eleazar Thomas, D. D., of the California Conference, was the Presiding Elder of the Methodist Church in the Petaluma Circuit, State of California.

In the latter part of March the prospect of peace with the Modoc Indians was not very promising, as they appeared to grow more independent every day, and consequently more grasping in their demands.

As General Canby was evidently getting rather tired of peace manipulations the troops would soon be moved into position surrounding the Lava Beds, and then some aggressive movement would be made in order to impress the Modocs with an idea of the number of soldiers that could be brought against them.

General Canby now received a message from the Indians, that Captain Jack and Schonchin would talk with Generals Canby and Gillem at the juniper tree, half way between the foot of the bluffs and their present position. Jack did not show any very great eagerness for an interview, and thought Gen. Canby had better come where he was. But, when two hostages were left behind, he seemed better satisfied and started to meet the Genera's, acccompanied by Scar-Faced Charley, Steamboat Frank, the Curly-Headed Doctor, and three others.

The interview took place. Captain Jack was not very well satisfied with it; he said that he wanted peace, and the interview proved abortive.

Such was the state of affairs when the Modocs pretended they were going to remove to the reservation. A day was appointed and agreed to for the surrender to take place. Wagons were sent by the Commissioners to convey Captain Jack's baggage over the rough ground; but no signs of the Indians were discoverable. Days passed, and at length an Indian appeared, who complained that Captain Jack and his fellows were fearful of the troops, and that they wanted to go to their old Lost River Reservation. The troops under General Canby now moved forward again and commenced to encircle the savages in their fortress. The circle was drawn gradually closer, and the Indians again professed a desire for peace conferences. They saw the troops drawing closer and closer, and now set up a new demand. They objected altogether to leaving the lava beds, and wanted the troops sent away. Notwithstanding this preposterous demand the Peace Commissioners listened to the palaver of the braves. Several interviews took place.

The Commissioners, together with General Canby, had labored hopefully, and had apparently gained several points over the Indians looking to a peaceful solution of this question.

For some time, all the Modoc schemes of treachery had been thwarted through the fidelity of the interpreter, Mrs. Riddle, who was a Modoc woman. Terms were agreed on for a meeting which were satisfactory to Dr. Thomas and Gen. Canby, but not to Mr. Meacham or Mr. Dyar, or to Mrs. Riddle, who expressed her apprehensions that mischief was breeding in the Modoc camp. But Gen Canby said that the Modocs dared not molest them, as his forces commanded the situation, and Dr. Thomas declared that where God called him to go, he would go, trusting to His care.

On the afternoon of April 10th, 1873, five Indians and four squaws came into the camp and were made presents of clothing and provisions by the Peace Commissioners, and a message was sent out by the Commissioners asking for a talk next morning at a point about a mile from the picket line. Later in the evening Bogus Charley came in and told the picket that he could take his gun; that he (Charley) did not intend to go back any more. The picket brought him in and took him to the tent of General Canby, where Charley left his gun and remained at the tent of Frank Riddle during the night. Next morning Boston Charley came in and told the Commission that Captain Jack and five other Indians would meet the Commission outside the lines. Boston Charley and Bogus Charley then mounted a horse and started for the Lava Beds. About an hour after their departure, General Canby started for the place appointed. The party arrived at the appointed place, and were closely watched by the signal officer, Lieutenant Adams, from the signal station on the hill overlooking the camp.

It was between ten and eleven o'clock in the morning when the Peace Commission party — comprising Gen. Canby, Mr. A. B. Meacham, Dr. Thomas, Mr. Dyar, Riddle, the interpreter, and squaw, and Bogus Charley and Boston Charley—went out to the designated spot. There they met Captain Jack, John Schonchin, Black Jim, Shack Nasty Jim, Ellen's Man, and Hawker Jim. They had no guns with them, but each carried a pistol at his belt. This, however, was not much noticed, as in previous interviews they had their guns with them. They sat down in a kind of broken circle, and General Canby, Meacham, and Dr. Thomas sat together, faced by Captain Jack and Schonchin. Mr. Dyar stood by Jack, holding his horse, with Hawker Jim and Shack Nasty Jim to his left.

Meacham opened the talk, and gave a long history of what they wanted to do for them, after which General Canby and Dr. Thomas both talked for some time. The Commissioners reaffirmed that the soldiers would never be withdrawn until the difficulty was settled, still extending the offer of amnesty, a suitable and satisfactory home, and ample provision for their welfare in the future. The reply from Jack and Schonchin—both chiefs—was: "Take away your soldiers, and we will talk about it."

Captain Jack then talked in an apparently good, serious strain, and when he finished stepped back to the rear, near where Meacham's horse was hitched. Jack asked for Hot Creek and Cottonwood, the places occupied by Fairchild and Dorris, for a reservation. Mr. Meacham told Jack that it was not possible to give him what he asked. John Schonchin then began to talk. He told Mr. Meacham to say no more; that he had said enough on that subject, and while Schonchin was speaking, Capt. Jack was heard to say "All ready!" At the same time Mr. Dyar heard a cap miss fire, and, looking around, he saw Captain Jack to his left, with his pistol pointed at General Canby. This was the signal for a general massacre, and a dozen pistols were fired inside of half a minute. Mr. Dyar, after hearing the cap miss fire, turned and fled, followed closely by Hawker Jim, who fired two shots after him. Dyar, finding that Hawker Jim was gaining upon him, turned and drew his derringer, whereupon Hawker Jim retreated and made the best of his way to the Modoc camp.

Captain Jack fired again on General Canby, who ran off to the left; but the ball of Jack's pistol struck him under the eye, and he fell dead to the ground. Meacham was shot at by Schonchin and wounded in the head. He tried to draw his derringer, when two Indians ran up and knocked him down. Boston Charley and another Indian fired at Dr. Thomas. The first discharge brought him to his knees, and the second killed him. Riddle ran off, and it appears they did not fire at him, but they knocked his squaw down. Dyar, Riddle and the squaw returned in safety to the camp.

About half an hour after the party of General Canby had reached the place of meeting with Jack and the other savages, a cry from the signal station was heard, saying that the Indians had attacked the Peace Commission, and that an engagement had commenced between the Indians and Col. Mason. In a moment the troops were under arms, and deployed as skirmishers, under the command of Col. Green, and orders were given to forward, double-quick. Very shortly afterward Mr. Dyar returned and stated that the Indians had attacked them, and that he thought he was the only one who had escaped; but in a few moments after Riddle and his squaw were seen within the picket. Col. Miller and Major Throckmorton's two batteries, that were leading the skirmish line, rushed out, and, after about five minutes' tramp over the broken rocks, they arrived at the scene of the massacre.

In the distance were seen three of the perpetrators of the murders, running round the edge of the lake on their way back to their rocky fastness. About a hundred yards to the west of the place of meeting was found Mr. A.

B. Meacham, badly wounded with a pistol-shot over the left eye. He was immediately attended to and carried back for medical treatment. Fifty yards further on was the body of the Rev. Dr. Thomas, lying on his face and stripped to the waist. Life was extinct from pistol-shot wounds in his head. The body of General Canby, the hero of many a fight, was stripped of every vestige of clothing, and lay about one hundred yards to the southward, with two pistol-shots in his head.

Pausing only to cast a glance on the body of the man they both loved and respected, the troops dashed on and the two leading batteries were within a mile of the murderers when the bugle-call sounded a "halt." Lieutenant Egan and Major Wright's companies of the Twelfth Infantry were behind the artillery, and then came the cavalry.

General Gillem and Colonel Green and staff were up with the men, but as soon as they found that the Indians had all got back to their stronghold the troops were ordered to fall back with the intent of commencing active operations on the next day. That the Indians intended a general massacre is sufficiently evident.

Nothing of note transpired until April 26th, when a reconnoitering party, composed of Companies K and A, Fourth Artillery, and Company E, Twelfth Infantry, left camp at half past seven o'clock in the morning, in the direction of the stronghold of the Modocs. They were commanded by Captain E. Thomas of the Fourth Artillery. A dozen Warm Spring Indians were expected to co-operate on Captain Thomas' left. The troops having formed a line of skirmishers, advanced without molestation until they arrived at the foot of the bluff south of the Lava Beds, having, meanwhile, signaled to the camp that no Indians were to be found. On reaching the bluff the Modocs opened a severe fire, causing the troops to seek such shelter as they could find in the crevices, chasms, etc. As usual, the foe was unseen. The first position soon became untenable, owing to the fact that the Indians were able to deliver both a cross-fire and an enfilading fire, the enemy enjoying every advantage of position and knowledge of the ground. They were also well armed.

In more than one instance a Modoc has been known to have two or more Spencer rifles, enabling him to keep up a rapid fire from his natural or artificial breastwork of rock. The surface of the ground in many places is torn up by volcanic actions, which form crevices, and these are adaptable to the purposes of either hiding or for points of defence. In several instances the soldiers, knowing nothing of the topography, have come unawares on such fissures, and before they could escape were confronted with a wily Indian, rifle leveled and finger on the trigger. Death, or at least a dangerous wound, is the result.

It was impossible to estimate the number of Modocs wounded. It was reported that the Warm Spring Indians took four scalps. This may be the whole or it may be only a portion of the killed, the Modocs being very careful to destroy as far as possible all traces of their casualties, carrying their wounded into caves and burning the dead bodies. The wounded were supposed to be hidden in caves, but few of them have ever been found. Justice to the memory of the gallant dead compels the record of the following well-authenticated facts: When Captain Thomas found himself and his men surrounded by his vindictive foe, true to his nature as a soldier, he sought to cheer the soldiers on to the bitter end, and obtain, if possible, life for life, and to sell their lives dearly, saying: "Men we are surrounded; we must fight and die like men and soldiers."

In his noble efforts to sustain the courage of his small command he was ably seconded by Lieutenant Howe and Lieutenant Wright. After receiving a mortal wound, he buried his gold watch and chain among the rocks and emptied his revolver among the enemies before dying.

If living he would also write in terms of well-deserved praise of the conduct of Lieutenant Harris, who was similarly situated. Captain Thomas, with a portion of his Battery K, Fourth Artillery, set an example of bravery and determination to his men, uttering some such sentiments as those already quoted. Not that it required such expressions to stimulate the men to deeds of bravery, when every man would willingly have followed either officer wherever they chose to lead; yet it showed the mutual confidence existing between them. Since they were to fall, it is a pity it had not been when opposed to worthier foes. Yet it is a mournful consolation that each, Captain Thomas, Lieutenant Howe, and Lieutenant Wright, the sons of soldiers, met a soldier's death in defence of the Government and laws of the country. Of the men killed or wounded it is perhaps sufficient to say they showed their bravery with their blood—the former with their lives, the latter in total or partial disability. The victory of the Modocs was complete. The news of this defeat created quite a sensation in army circles, where the three young officers who were killed were well known. Army officers attributed this disaster to the inefficiency of the cavalry, which was dismounted because of the epizootic.

The two batteries of artillery and the one company of infantry that were ordered to advance into the Lava Beds with such fatal results, were intended as a reconnoitering party, to find out whether the Modocs had really absconded. The suspicion that they had, and a too confident presumption that they would not fight in a body, may explain the disastrous blunder of exposing two companies of brave soldiers to be shot down like dogs by an unseen foe lying in ambush. It seems too apparent that the Indians practiced successful feints upon General Gillem. They made him believe, or at least suspect, they had fled and scattered, and thereby disarmed his wariness and entrapped him into an ambuscade. We accordingly lost, in killed and wounded, more soldiers than the whole number of fighting Modocs. On their part there was no random firing. They were all expert marksmen, and from their places of concealment every shot told. After this defeat of our troops, General Davis arrived and took command of the Modoc expedition. He sent out scouting parties, had his men disciplined in Indian dodges, and put his first grand movement in operation.

About this time it was discovered that the Modocs had escaped from their stronghold by three routes, and finally encamped on Snow Mountain, twenty miles south of Sorass Lake. Fights without any decided results were taking place occasionally, causing the loss and wounding of our troops. But, notwithstanding those successes of the Modocs, it seemed that the peace men in the Modoc camp were dissatisfied, and preferred to trust to the good faith of the palefaces. Accordingly, fifty-five members of Captain Jack's band of Modocs surrendered to our army. Fifteen of these were warriors, and the rest were women and children. Captain Jack then had twenty warriors left, and he resolved to fight to the end, being relieved of two obstacles, viz.: the women and children, and the peace party among the Modocs.

After a series of reverses befalling our soldiers operating in the Lava Fields, their bravery was crowned with success. Deserted and in despair, the Modoc chief surrendered, a prisoner of war, and with three captured companions, upon trial by court-martial, was condemned to death and soon after publicly hanged.

THE NEZ PERCES WAR.

The Nez Perces Indians are the insignificant, as far as numbers go, remains of a once numerous and powerful tribe, who roamed as their choice dictated over a vast country on the Pacific side of the Rocky Mountains. For years they had been on friendly terms with the whites. They had abandoned hunting to a great extent, and were yearly relying more and more on agriculture and grazing for a living. Close investigation fails to discover, on either side, an adequate reason for the violent outbreak which occurred. As usual, both sides accuse the other. So peaceful were the Nez Perces that many people on this side of the Rocky Mountains hardly knew of their existence. As we have the advantage of telling the story, the Indians appear, of course, to be in fault. What we do know is, that Chief Joseph, who was the leading man among the Nez Perces, was ordered to give up some lands which he had held from a long line of ancestors. He resolutely refused to do so. General Howard, commanding in that military division, tried to take them by force. The Indians made a stout resistance. When the chief found himself greatly outnumbered, and learned that large reinforcements were advancing to the help of Howard, he formed the bold resolution of retreating almost across the continent, in hopes of forming a coalition with the Sioux and other Indians then at war with the United States — a resolve as brave as that of Cortez when he burned his ships on the shores of Mexico. Chief Joseph set out on this retreat in the presence of superior numbers, led by an educated military officer. He successfully foiled all efforts to outflank him or bring him to an engagement, only turning upon his pursuers when it seemed necessary for him (Joseph) to fight. This retreat was not like that of Braddock's, for instance: it never became a rout. But Joseph carried nearly all his large stock of cattle and horses with him, this, too, through hundreds of miles of the most difficult campaigning country upon earth. Eventually he only surrendered to very superior numbers, and then not to his pursuer, General Howard, but to the gallant Indian-fighter, General Miles, this officer having been apprised by telegraph, in a roundabout way, where to station his troops in order to intercept this swarthy Xenophon. What adds greatly to the deservedly great fame of Chief Joseph, is that he treated prisoners humanely, and never scalped or otherwise mutilated the dead. Joseph and his remaining people were well treated by General Miles, and placed temporarily on reservations, while their future homes were determined on.

THE UTE WAR OF 1879.

The unexpected outbreak of the Utes at the White River agency seems to have been brought about, as far as can be ascertained, by local causes. The Indian agent, Mr. Meeker, wished them to engage in farming, and many of them were uncompromisingly hostile to anything in the way of labor, which might assist in making them self-supporting. As soon as a knowledge of the trouble was communicated by the Indian Bureau to the military authorities, a force which was deemed more than sufficient by the agent was sent from the nearest post, under command of Major Thornburgh, Fourth Infantry. Before the troops reached the agency, the agent, Mr. Meeker, and most of his employees were murdered by the Indians, who then came out and attacked Major Thornburgh's force at a point eighteen miles distant from the agency.

The narrative of the Ute massacre at the White River agency, in the northwestern portion of Colorado, the fight with Major Thornburgh's men, and the relief of the beleaguered survivors by a company of colored cavalry is, in a few words, one of the most thrilling and romantic stories of Indian life. For quickness of action, baseness of motive, and cruelty of execution, it far surpasses any episode in Indian warfare.

This story opens with an encounter on the 29th of September, 1879, between the Ute Indians and Major Thornburgh's command, which had been ordered to the relief of Indian agent Meeker. The field of battle was admirably chosen for defense by the Indians, and had it not been for Major Thornburgh's advance guard, commanded by Lieutenant Cherry, discovering the ambuscade, the entire command would have been annihilated. He saw a small party of Indians disappear over a hill half a mile in front, and at once divided his party to reconnoitre, and only discovered the Indians when he had flanked their position by about 200 yards. Lieutenant Cherry rode back at full speed with one or two men who were with him, and notified Major Thornburgh, who had already begun the descent into the deep ravine which was intended to engulf the command. The Indians were dismounted and lying down along the crest of the high, steep ridge for a hundred yards from the point where the deadly assault would have commenced. The troops were withdrawn a short distance, dismounted, and deployed in line of battle, with orders to await the attack of the Indians. Lieutenant Cherry was here ordered by Thornburgh to take a detachment of fifteen picked men and make a reconnoissance and communicate if possible with the Indians, as it was thought that they only desired to oppose his approach to their agency, and would have a big talk if they could be communicated with. Cherry moved out at a gallop with his men from the right flank, and noticed a like movement of about twenty Indians from the left of the Indian position. He approached to within a couple of hundred yards of the Indians, and took off his hat and waved it, but the response was a shot fired at him, wounding a man of his party, and killing his horse. This was the first shot, and was instantly followed by a volley from the Indians.

The work had now begun in real earnest, and seeing the advantage of the position he held, Lieutenant Cherry dismounted his detachment and deployed along the crest of the hills to prevent the Indians flanking his position, or to cover the retreat, if it was found necessary to retire upon the wagon train, which was then coming up slowly, guarded by Lieutenant Paddock, Company D, Fifth Cavalry. Orders were sent to park the wagons and cover them with the company guarding them. The two companies in the advance were Captain Payne's, Company F, Fifth Cavalry, and Captain Lawson's, Company E, Third Cavalry, which were dismounted and deployed as skirmishers, Captain Payne on the left and Captain Lawson on the right. From Lieutenant Cherry's position he could see the Indians were trying to cut him off from the wagons, and at once sent word to Major Thornburgh, who then withdrew the line slowly, keeping the Indians in check until opposite the point which his men held, when, seeing that the Indians were concentrating to cut off his retreat, Captain Payne, with Company F, Fifth Cavalry, was ordered to charge the hill, which he did in gallant style, his horse being shot under him and several of his men wounded. The Indians having been driven from this point, the company was rallied on the wagon-train. Major Thornburgh then gave orders to Lieutenant Cherry to hold his position and cover Captain Lawson's retreat, who was ordered to fall back slowly with the horses of his company. Cherry called for volunteers of twenty men, who responded promptly and fought with desperation. Nearly every man was wounded before he reached the camp. Two men were killed. Cherry brought every wounded man in with him. Captain Lawson, the brave old veteran, displayed the greatest coolness and courage during this retreat, sending up ammunition to Cherry's men when, once, they were nearly without it. Major Thornburgh started back to the wagon-train after giving his final orders to Captain Payne to charge the hill and to Captain Lawson and Lieutenant Cherry to cover the retreat. He was shot dead when barely half way there, as his body was seen by one of Captain Lawson's men, life extinct, lying on his face.

Captain Payne, then in command, at once set about having the wounded horses shot, to be used for breastworks, dismantling the wagons of boxes and bundles of bedding, corn and flour-sacks, which were quickly piled up for fortifications. Picks and shovels were used vigorously for digging intrenchments. Meantime, a galling fire was concentrated upon the command from all the surrounding bluffs which commanded the position. Not an Indian could be seen, but the incessant crack of their Sharp and Winchester rifles dealt fearful destruction among the horses and men.

On October 1st, the besieged men were suddenly alarmed by heavy and responsive firing, but approaching their position. Sharper and nearer came the rattling, desultory discharges, and soon afterwards, dismounted and leading their horses, which fell fast under the Ute rifles, they saw a colored troop of cavalry approach and force its way into the barricade. It proved to be Captain Dodge's company, numbering forty-five men, of the Ninth (colored) Cavalry. Their approach had been most dangerous and difficult, but hearing of the situation they had persisted, without halting and without fear. During the remainder of the six days' siege, they shared the perils and discomforts with patience that cannot be too highly praised.

At five o'clock on the morning of the 5th, General Merritt relieved the command, having marched his men about 170 miles over "the worst road ever traveled" in a little more than forty-eight hours. He found the command much as reported in the original dispatches. The casualties were twelve killed and forty-three wounded. All the animals of the command were killed, except twelve mules and three horses of the four companies of cavalry.

The funeral of Major Thornburgh took place at Omaha on October 22d, under Masonic management. A halt was ordered in the march of the troops after the fugitive Utes, confidence being placed in the ability of General Adams, the special agent, to effect a peace, with the tribe. General Charles Adams came into General Merritt's camp on the morning of the 24th with the women and children of the Meeker and Price families.

The last letter written by Mr. Meeker before his death was to Major Thornburgh, dated one o'clock, September 29th, three hours after the attack had commenced and Thornburgh's death, stating that "all was quiet at the agency and that Douglass had the United States flag flying above his house." The last authentic accounts state that Douglass took no part in the fight, and that he was guarding Mrs. Meeker and the other women from injury. It will surprise many who have had faith in the fidelity of Douglass to read Miss Meeker's assertions of his treachery and brutality as detailed in her narrative. Jack, to whose camp Mrs. Price and her children were conveyed, after the captives were separated, is one of the war chiefs of the White River band, and is supposed to have been one of the leaders in the attack at the agency. He is next in rank to Douglass, and is noted for his shrewdness and cunning.

The history of the prisoners during their captivity forms a most pathetic chapter. After the killing of Agent Meeker the women attempted to escape into the brush from the burning buildings. Mrs. Meeker was fired at, with the result of a flesh-wound in the hip four inches in length. Miss Meeker and Mrs. Price were called to: "Indians no shoot white women. Stop! Indians no hurt." They were then mounted—Miss Meeker, with Mrs. Price's eldest child, four years old, tied behind her; Mrs. Price, with her infant in her arms, and Mrs. Meeker, who is sixty-four years of age, and lame from her wound.

When they struck the camp at midnight, Mrs. Meeker was dismounted, and fell to the ground unable to move, and the Indians surrounded her and added to the misery of the situation by jeering and taunting "the old white squaw." The next morning they were separated, Douglass retaining the charge of Mrs. Meeker, and Persune taking Miss Meeker, while Mrs. Price and children were in the charge of an Uncompahgre Ute. The sufferings of Mrs. Meeker were indescribable during her stay with Douglass, whose squaw abused her by neglect, pushing, striking, and taunts.

On one occasion Douglass threw down blankets and compelled Miss Meeker to dismount, saying that they were going into camp. He then said that they were going to stab them, and exhibited the butcher knives to be used for the purpose. Then he placed a musket to her forehead and said: "Indian going to shoot." The courageous girl never flinched, and laughed at the burly savage. He asked her if she was afraid, and her ready response, "I am not afraid of Indians or death," elicited the admiration of the Indians. They turned upon Chief Douglass with derision, and he slunk from the presence of the brave woman.

Soon after this they were placed in charge of Chief Johnson, and through the instrumentality of Johnson's squaw their condition was very much improved and further indignities prevented.

After their rescue by General Adams, their condition was made still more comfortable. Their costume, as they appeared on their arrival at Denver, October 30th, after a journey of five hundred miles by stage or ponies, is thus described: Miss Josie's costume was the most striking. Her dress was made of an Indian blanket, plain skirt, and long jacket-waist with tight sleeves. The blanket stuff was dark-brown, the broad yellow stripes in the goods acting as a border around the bottom of the dress and the flowing waist. Her feet were incased in moccasins, and by her side lay a broad white sombrero. Miss Meeker, though by no means a handsome young lady, is bright and attractive in appearance. She is a blonde, and naturally of fair complexion, though now sunburned. Her hair is cut short to the neck.

Mrs. Price is a young lady yet. Though but twenty-three years of age, she has been married several years. She is naturally bright and active, but just now the death of her husband and her terrible experience has saddened her. Mrs. Price was dressed in a plain woolen dress, which she said she wore when taken captive. She, however, exchanged it for a "blanket" dress similar to that worn by Miss Meeker, and saving it, reassumed it when she reached Alamosa. Mrs. Price also wore a sombrero.

Mrs. Meeker wore, when she arrived, a long wrapper and a hood, with which she was provided at Los Pinos. The two little children, May and Johnnie, wore their agency clothes, sadly tattered and torn.

The "blanket" suits of Miss Meeker and Mrs. Price were made by them while in camp on Grand River, their captors furnishing the material, thread, needles, etc.

HISTORICAL AND MYTHOLOGICAL TRADITIONS OF THE ALGONQUINS.

WITH A TRANSLATION OF THE WALUM-OLUM, OR BARK RECORD OF THE LENNI LENAPE.*

By E. G. Squier.

The Algonquins were a numerous family of North American Indians, once spread over all the northern part of the Rocky Mountains, and south of the St. Lawrence. Their language was heard from the bay of Gaspe to the valley of the Des Moines, from Cape Fear to the land of the Esquimaux; from the Cumberland river, of Kentucky, to the western banks of the Mississippi. It was spoken, though not exclusively, in a Territory that extended through sixty degrees of longitude and more than twenty degrees of latitude. All the tribes of New England were Algonquins; the tribes in Maine, the great tribe of the Delaware Indians, the Creeks in the region of the Great Slave Lake, and the Ottawas and Pottawatomies in Michigan claimed the same origin. Traces of the primitive Algonquin language appear in the names of places, such as Alleghany, Connecticut. At present the Algonquins do not number more than two hundred warriors, included in the tribe of the Chippewas.

The discovery of America, in the fifteenth century, constitutes a grand era in the history of the world. From it we may date the rise of that mental energy and physical enterprise, which has since worked such wonderful changes in the condition of the human race. It gave a new and powerful impulse to the nations of Europe, then slowly rousing from the lethargy of centuries. Love of adventure, hope, ambition, avarice—the most powerful incentives to human action—directed the attention of all men to America. Thither flocked the boldest and most adventurous spirits of Europe ; and half a century of startling events sufficed to lift the veil of night from a vast continent, unsurpassed in the extent and variety of its productions, abounding in treasures, and teeming with a strange people, divided into numberless families, exhibiting many common points of resemblance, yet differing widely in their condition, manners, customs, and civil and social organizations.

Along the shores of the frozen seas of the north, clothed with the furs of the sea-monsters whose flesh had supplied them with food, burrowing in icy caverns during the long polar nights, were found the dwarfed and squalid Esquimaux. In lower latitudes, skirting the bays and inlets of the Atlantic, pushing their canoes along the shores of the great lakes, or chasing the buffalo on the vast meadows of the west, broken up into numerous families, subdivided into tribes, warring constantly, and ever struggling for ascendency over each other, were the active and fearless hunters, falling chiefly within the modern extended denominations of the Algonquin and Iroquois families. Still lower down, in the mild and fertile regions bordering the Gulf of Mexico, more fixed in their habits, half hunters, half agriculturists, with a systematized religion, and a more consolidated civil organization, and constituting the connecting link between the gorgeous semi-civilization of Mexico, and the nomadic state of the northern families, were the Floridian tribes, in many respects one of the most interesting groups of the continent. Beneath the tropics, around the bases of the volcanic ranges of Mexico, and occupying her high and salubrious plains, Cortez found the Atzecs and their dependencies—nations rivaling in their barbarous magnificence the splendors of the oriental world—far advanced in the arts, living in cities, constructing vast works of public utility, and sustaining an imposing, though bloody religious system. Passing the nations of Central America, whose architectural monuments challenge comparison with the proudest of the old world, and attest the advanced condition and great power of their builders, Pizarro found beneath the equa-

* Reprinted from *The American Whig Review* (New York), for February, 1849.

tor a vast people, living under a well-organized and consolidated government, attached to a primitive Sabianism, fixed in their habits and customs, and happy in their position and circumstances. Still beyond these to the southward, were the invincible Araucanians, together with numerous other nations, with distinctive features, filling still lower places in the scale of advancement, and finally subsiding into the squalid counterparts of the Esquimaux in Patagonia.

These numerous nations, exhibiting contrasts so striking, and institutions so novel and interesting, it might be supposed, would have at once attracted the attention of the learned of that day, and insured at their hands a full and authentic account of their government, religion, traditions, customs, and modes of life. The men, however, who subverted the empires of Montezuma and the Incas were bold adventurers, impelled for the most part by an absorbing avarice and unfitted by habit, as incapable, from education and circumstances, of transmitting to us correct or satisfactory information respecting the nations with which they were acquainted. The ecclesiastics who followed in their train, from whom more might have been expected, actuated by a fierce bigotry, and eager only to elevate the symbol of their intolerence over the emblems of a rival priesthood, misrepresented the religious conceptions of the Indians, and exaggerated the bloody observances of the aboriginal ritual, as an apology, if not a justification, for their own barbarism and cruelty. They threw down the high altars of Atzec superstition, and consecrated to their own mummeries the solar symbols of the Peruvian temples. They burned the pictured historical and mythological records of the ancient empire in the public square of Mexico; defaced the sculptures on her monuments, and crushed in pieces the statues of her gods. Yet the next day, with an easy transition, they proclaimed the great impersonation of the female, or productive principle of nature, who in the Mexican, as in every other system of mythology, was the consort of the Sun, to be no other than the Eve of the Mosaic record, or the Mother of Christ; they even tracked the vagrant St. Thomas in the person of the benign Quetzalcoatl, the Mexican counterpart of the Hindoo Buddha and the Egyptian Osiris!

All these circumstances have contributed to throw doubt and uncertainty over the Spanish accounts of the aboriginal nations. Nor were the circumstances attending European adventure and settlements, in other parts of the continent, much more favorable to the preservation of impartial and reliable records. The Puritan of the north and the gold-hunter of Virginia and Carolina, looked with little interest and less complacency upon the "wilde salvages" with which they were surrounded and of whom Cotton Mather wrote, that, "Although we know not *when* nor *how* they first became inhabitants of this mighty continent, yet we may guess the devil decoyed these miserable salvages hither, in hopes that the gospel of the Lord Jesus Christ would never come to destroy his absolute empire over them."

The Jesuits and other enthusiasts, the propagandists of the Catholic faith among the northern tribes, were more observant and correct, but their accounts are very meagre in matters of the most consequence, in researches concerning the history and religion of the aborigines. All treated the religious conceptions and practices and transmitted traditions of the Indians with little regard. Indeed it has been only during the last century, since European communication with the primitive nations of Southern Asia, and a more intimate acquaintance with oriental literature, have given a new direction to researches into the history of mind and man, that the true value of the religious notions and the recorded or transmitted traditions of various nations, in determining their origins and connections, and illustrating their remote history, has been ascertained. And even now there are few who have a just estimation of their importance in these respects. It may however be claimed, in the language of an erudite American that "of all researches which most effectually aid us to discover the origin of a nation or people, whose history is either unknown, or deeply involved in the obscurity of ancient times, none are perhaps attended with such important results, as the analysis of their theological dogmas, and their religious practices. To such matters mankind adheres with the greatest tenacity, and though both modified and corrupted in the revolutions of ages, they still preserve features of their original construction when language, arts, sciences and political establishments no longer retain distinct lineaments of their ancient constitutions."

The traveler Clarke, maintaining the same position, observes, "that by a proper attention to the vestiges of ancient superstition, we are sometimes enabled to refer a whole people to their original ancestors, with as much if not more certainty, than by observations made upon their languages, because the superstition is engrafted upon the stock, but the language is liable to change." However important is the study of military, civil and political history, the science is incomplete without mythological history, and he is little imbued with the spirit of philosophy, who can perceive in the fables of antiquity nothing but the extravagance of a fervid imagination.[1] It is under this view, in the absence of such information derivable from early writers, as may form the basis of our inquiries into the history of the American race, its origin, and the rank which it is entitled to hold in the scale of human development, that the religious conceptions and observances, and authentic traditions of the aboriginal nations, become invested with new interest and importance. And although the opportunities for collecting them, at this day, are limited, and much care and discrimination is requisite to separate that which is original from what is derivable, still they perhaps afford the safest and surest means of arriving at the results desired. Not that I would be understood as undervaluing physical or philological researches, in their bearings upon these questions; for if the human mind can ever flatter itself with having discovered the truth, it is when many facts, and these facts of different kinds, unite in producing the same result.

Impressed with these views, I have, in pursuing investigations in another but cognate department of research, taken considerable pains to collect from all available sources, such information as seemed authentic, relating not only to the religious ceremonies and conceptions, but also to the mythological and historical traditions of the aborigines of all parts of the continent. An analysis and comparison of these have led to some most extraordinary results, which it would be impossible, in the narrow scope of this paper, to indicate with necessary fullness. It may be said generally, that they exhibit not only a wonderful uniformity and concurrence in their elements and more important particulars, but also an absolute identity, in many essential respects, with those which existed among the primitive nations of the old world, far back in the monumental and traditional periods.

Among the various original manuscripts which, in the course of these investigations, fell into my possession, I received through the hands of the executors of the lamented Nicollet, a series by the late Prof. C. S. Rafinesque —well known as a man of science and of an inquiring mind, but whose energies were not sufficiently concentrated to leave a decided impression in any department of research. A man of unparalleled industry, an earnest and indefatigable collector of facts, he was deficient in that scope of mind joined to severe critical powers, indispensable to correct generalization. While, therefore, it is usually safe to reject his conclusions, we may receive his facts, making proper allowances for the haste with which they were got together.

Among these manuscripts ("*rudis indigestaque moles*"), was one entitled the *Walum Olum* (literally, *painted sticks*), or painted and engraved traditions of the Lenni-Lenape, comprising five divisions, the first two embodying the traditions referring to the creation and a general flood, and the rest comprising a record of various migrations, with a list of ninety-seven chiefs, in the order of their succession, coming down to the period of the discovery. This manuscript also embraces one hundred and eighty-four compound mnemonic symbols, each accompanied by a sentence or verse in the original language, of which a literal translation is given in English. The only explanation which we have concerning it, is contained in a foot note, in the hand of Rafinesque, in which he states that the manuscript and wooden originals were obtained in Indiana in 1822, and that they were for a long time inexplicable, "until with a deep study of the Delaware, and the aid of Zeisberger's manuscript dictionary in the library of the Philosophical Society, a translation was effected." This translation, it may here be remarked, so far as I have been able to test it, is a faithful one, and there is slight doubt that the original is what it professes to be, a genuine Indian record. The evidence that it is

---

1 "The existence of similar religious ideas in remote regions, inhabited by different races, is an interesting subject of study; furnishing as it does, one of the most important links in the great chain of communication which binds together the distant families of nations."—*Prescott's Mexico.*

so, is however rather internal and collateral than direct.[1] The traditions which it embodies coincide, in most important respects, with those which are known to have existed, and which still exist, in forms more or less modified, among the various Algonquin tribes, and the mode in which they are recorded is precisely that which was adopted by the Indians of this stock, in recording events, communicating intelligence, etc., and which has not inaptly been denominated *picture-writing*.

The scope of this system of picture-writing, and the extent to which it was applied, have not been generally understood nor fully recognized. Without, however, going into an analysis of the system, its principles and elements—an inquiry of much interest—it may be claimed, upon an array of evidence which will admit of no dispute, that under it the Indians were not only able to communicate events and transmit intelligence, but also to record chants and songs, often containing abstract ideas—allusions to the origin of things, the power of nature, and to the elements of their religion. "The Indians," says Heckewelder, "have no alphabet, nor any mode of representing words to the eye, yet they have certain hieroglyphics, by which they describe facts in so plain a manner, that those who are conversant with their marks, can understand them with the greatest ease—as easily, indeed, as they can understand a piece of writing."[2] This writer also asserts that the simple principles of the system are so well recognized, and of so general application, that the members of different tribes could interpret with the greatest facility the drawings of other and remote tribes. Loskiel has recorded his testimony to the same effect. He says: "The Delawares use hieroglyphics on wood, trees and stones, to give caution, for communication, to commemorate events and preserve records. Every Indian understands their meaning, etc."[3] Mr. Schoolcraft also observes of the Ojibwas, that "every path has its blazed and figurated tree, conveying intelligence to all that pass, for all can understand these signs, which," he adds, "are taught to the young as carefully as our alphabet." Testimony might be accumulated upon this point, to an indefinite extent, were it necessary to our present purpose.

Most of the signs used in this system are representations of things: some however were derivative, others symbolical, and still others entirely arbitrary. They however were not capable of doing more than to suggest classes of ideas, which would not be expressed in precisely the same words by different individuals. They were taught in connection with certain forms of expression, by which means they are made essentially *mnemonic*—a simple or compound sign, thus serving to recall to mind an entire sentence or a series of them. A single figure, with its adjuncts, would stand for the verse of a song, or for a circumstance which it would require several sentences to explain.

Thus the famous *Metäi song* of tho Chippeways, presented by Mr. Catlin, although embracing but about thirty signs, occupied, in the slow, monotonous chant of the Indians, with their numerous repetitions, nearly an hour in its delivery. James observes, respecting the recorded Indian songs—"They are usually carved on a flat piece of wood, and the figures suggest to the minds of those who have learned the songs, the ideas and the order of their succession. The words are not variable, but must be taught; otherwise, though from an inspection of the figure the idea might be comprehended, no one would know what to sing." Most of the Indian lore being in the hands of the priests or medicine-men, the teaching of these songs was almost entirely monopolized by them. They taught them only to such as had distinguished themselves in war and the chase, and then only upon the payment of large prices. Tanner states that he was occupied more than a year in learning the great song for "medicine hunting," and then obtained his knowledge only at the expense of many beaver skins. After the introduction of Christianity, among some of the Western tribes, prayers were inscribed on pieces of wood, in mnemonic symbols, in the making and teaching of which to their followers, some of the Christian chiefs obtained a profitable monopoly.

[1] Since the above was written, a copy of Rafinesque's *American Nations*, published in 1836, has fallen under my notice. It is a singular jumble of facts and fancies, and it is perhaps unfortunate for the manuscript, spoken of in the text, that it falls in such a connection. The only additional information we have respecting it, is that it was "obtained by the late Dr. Ward of Indiana, of the remnant of the Delawares on the White River."

[2] *Hist. Acct. of the Indian Nations*, p. 118.

[3] *Hist. United Brethren in America*, p. 25.

Admitting then, as we must do upon this evidence, that the Algonquins had the means of imperfectly recording their traditions, songs, etc., we can readily understand how these might be taught by father to son, and perpetuated in great purity through a succession of priests—the sages of the aboriginal races. The fact that they were recorded, even in the rude way here indicated, would give them a degree of fixedness, and entitle them to a consideration which they would not possess if handed down in a simple oral form.[1]

In illustration of the manner in which the manuscript is written, the first two songs or chants are presented as they appear in the original. We have first, the original sign; second, the suggested verse or sentence in the Delaware dialect; and third, a literal translation of the same in English.

SONG I.—THE CREATION.

1. Say ewitalli wemiguma wokgetaki.[2]
At first there all sea-water above land.

2. Hackung-kwelik owanaku wakyutali
Above much water foggy (was) and (or also) there
Kitanitowitessop.[3]
Creator he was.

3.[4] Sayewis[5] hallemiwis[6] nolemiwi Kitanitowit-
First-being, Eternal-being, invisible Creator
essop.
he was.

4. Sohalawak kwelik hakik owak
He causes them much water much land much air (or
awasagamak.
clouds) much heaven.

5. Sohalawak gishuk nipanum alankwak.
He causes them the Sun the moon the stars.

6. Wemi-sohalawak yulik yuch-aan.
All he causes these well to move.

7. Wich-owagan kshakan moshakwat
With action (or rapidly) it blows (wind) it clears up
kwelik kshipelep.
great waters it ran off.

8. Opeleken mani-menak delsin-epit.
It looks bright made islands is there at.

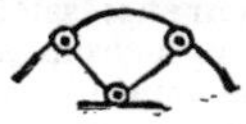

9. Lappinup Kitanitowit manito manitoak.
Again when Creator he made spirits or makers.

10. Owiniwak Angelatawiwak chichankwak
First beings also and Angels Souls also
wemiwak.
and all.

[1] "Were it not," says Dr. Barton, in his paper on the *Origin of the American Nations*, published in the *Transactions of the Philosophical Society*—"Were it not for the traditions of many of the American nations, we might for ever remain in doubt concerning their real origin. These traditions are entitled to much consideration; for, notwithstanding the rude condition of most of the tribes, they are often perpetuated in great purity, as I have discovered by much attention to their history."

[2] The terminal *aki* is a contraction of *hakki*, land, and frequently denotes *place* simply.

[3] Written *Getanitowit* by Heckewelder, p. 422.

[4] Figure 3 is a representation of the sun, which was the Algonquin symbol of the Great Spirit.

[5] The termination *wiss* or *iss* makes according to Mr. Schoolcraft, whatever precedes it personal (*Algic Res.*, vol. i, p. 201). The better translation would therefore be, "The First," "The Eternal," &c.

[6] *Allowini*, more, and *wulik*, good, enter into most designations of the Supreme.—Heck., p. 422.

11. Wtenk-manito 'jinwis[1] lennowak mukom.
After he made beings men and grandfather.

12. Milap netami-gaho owini-gaho.
He gave them the first mother first-being's-mother.

14. Namesik-milap tulpewik awesik cholensak.
Fishes he gave him turtles beasts birds.

14. Makimani-shak sohalawak makowini n'akowak amangamek.
Bad Spirit but he causes them bad beings black snakes monsters (or large reptiles).

15. Sohalawak uchewak sohalawak pungusak.
He causes them flies he causes them gnats.

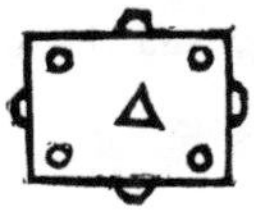

16. Nitisak wemi-owini w'delsinewuap.
Friends all beings were then.

17. Kiwis, wunand wishi-manitoak essopak.
Thou being good God good spirits were there.

18. Nijini netami lennowak nigoha netami okwewi nantinewak.
The beings the first men mothers first wives little spirits (fairies).

19. Gattamin netami mitzi nijiti nantiné.
Fat fruits the first food the beings little spirits.

20. Wemi wingi-namenep weni-ksin elan-damep wullatemanuwi.
All willingly pleased all easy think-ing happy.

---

[1] In the Chippeway, according to McKenzie and Long *ninnee* or *inini* means *man*. Mr. Schoolcraft states that *ininee* is the diminutive form of the word, signifying *little-men*, as Puck-wudj-*ininee*, "vanishing little men," the fairy-men of Algonquin story. The cognate term of the text seems to have a slightly differeni meaning: it is translated *beings*, and is written *nijini* or *'jini*, beings; *owini*, first beings, *mako-wini*, evil beings, etc. In the Delaware dialect *lenno* or *lenna* meant man, and is so translated in the text. The true designation of the Delawares was "Lenni-Lenape," which is usually understood to mean "Original" or "True men." It is not impossible that it is compounded of "*nijini*," beings, and *lenno*, men; literally men-beings. This compound may have been suggestive of something superior to men in general or collectively.

21. Shukand elikimi mekenikink wakon
But then while secretly on earth snake god[1]
powako init'ako.
priest-snake worship snake.

22. Mattalugas pallalugas maktatin owagan
Wickedness crime unhappiness actions.
payat-chikutali.
coming there then.

23. Wactapan-payat wihillan mboagan.
Bad weather coming distempers death.

24. Wonwemi wiwunch-kamik atak-kitahikan
This all very long aforetime beyond great waters
netami-epit.
first land at.

PARAPHRASE OF THE ABOVE SONG.

1. At the first there were great waters above all the land,
2. And above the waters were thick clouds, and there was God the Creator:
3. The first being, eternal, omnipotent, invisible, was God the Creator.
4. He created vast waters, great lands, and much air and heaven;
5. He created the sun, the moon and the stars;
6. He caused them all to move well.

7. By his power he made the winds to blow, purifying, and the deep waters to run off:
8. All was made bright and the islands were brought into being.

9. Then again God the Creator made the great Spirits,
10. He made also the first beings, angels and souls:
11. Then made he a man being, the father of men;
12. He gave him the first mother, the mother of the early born,
13. Fishes gave he him, turtles, beasts and birds.

14. But the Evil Spirit created evil beings, snakes and monsters:
15. He created vermin and annoying insects.
16. Then were all beings friends:
17. There being a good god, all spirits were good—
18. The beings, the first men, mothers, wives, little spirits also.
19. Fat fruits were the food of the beings and the little spirits:
20. All were then happy, easy in mind and pleased.

21. But then came secretly on earth the snake-(evil) god, the snake-priest and snake-worship:
22. Came wickedness, came unhappiness.
23. Came then bad weather, disease and death.

24. This was all very long ago, at our early home.

The grand idea of a Supreme Unity, a Great, Good, Infinite and Eternal Creator, so clearly indicated in the foregoing song, may be regarded by many as the offspring of European intercourse, or as a comparatively late engraftment upon Algonquin tradition. Without denying that the teachings of the early missionaries had the effect of enlarging this conception, and of giving it a more definite form, it may at the same time be unhesitatingly claimed that the idea was an original one with the Indian mind. The testimony of the earliest travelers and of the earliest missionaries themselves, furnishes us

[1] The snake among the Algonquins was symbolical of evil or malignant force.

abundant evidence of the fact. "Nothing," says Charlevoix, "is more certain than that the Indians of this continent have an idea of a Supreme Being, the First Spirit, the Creator and Governor of the world." [1] And Loskiel, not less explicit in his testimony, observes, "The prevailing opinion of all these nations is, that there is one God, a great and good Spirit, who created the heavens and the earth; who is Almighty; who causes the fruits to grow, grants sunshine and provides his children with food." [2] Says Schoolcraft, "They believe in the existence of a Supreme Being, who created material matter, the earth and heavens, men and animals, and filled space with subordinate spirits, having something of his own nature, to whom he gave part of his power." From this great and good being, it was believed, no evil could come; he was invested with the attribute of universal beneficence, and was symbolized by the sun. He was usually denominated *Kitchi-Manitou* or *Gitchy-Monedo*, literally, Great, Good Spirit. Various other names were employed to designate him under his various aspects, as *Waskeánd*, Maker; *Waosemigoyan*, Universal Father.

Subordinate to this Supreme, Good Being, was an Evil Spirit, *Mitchi-Manitou*, or *Mudje-Monedo* (Great Bad Spirit), who, according to Mr. Schoolcraft, was a subsequent creation, and not coexistent with the Kitchi-Manitou. This seems implied in the song, where he is first spoken of after the creation of men and beings. Great power was ascribed to him, and he was regarded as the cause and originator of all the evils which befall mankind. Accordingly his favor was desired, and his anger sought to be averted by sacrifices and offerings. The power of the Mitchi-Manitou was not, however, supposed to extend to the future life.[3] He is represented in the text as the creator of flies and gnats, and other annoying insects, an article of belief not exclusively Indian. While the symbol of the Good Spirit was *the Sun*, that of the chief of the Evil Spirits was *the Serpent*, under which form he appears in the Chippeway tradition of his contest with the demi-god Manabozho.

The idea of a destruction of the world by water seems to have been general amongst the Algonquin nations. The traditionary details vary in almost every instance where they have been recorded, but the traditionary event stands out prominently. The catastrophe is in all cases ascribed to the Evil Spirit; who, as already observed, was symbolized as a great Serpent. He is generally placed in antagonism to Manabozho, a powerful demi-god or intermediate spirit. These two mythological characters have frequent conflicts, and the flood is usually ascribed to the final contest between them. In these cases the destruction of the world is but an incident. As recorded in the *Walum Olum*, it originates in a general conflict between the Good Spirits, "the beings," and the Evil Spirit, *Maskinako*. The variation is, however, unimportant, for in this, as in all the other versions of the tradition, Manabozho appears in the character of Preserver. The concurrence in the essential parts of the several traditions, is worthy of remark.

SONG II.—THE DELUGE.

1. Wulamo maskan-ako-anup lennowak
   Long ago powerful snake when men also
   makowini essopak.
   bad beings had become.

2. Maskanako shingalusit nijini-essopak
   Strong snake enemy beings had become
   shawalendamep ekin-shingalan.
   became troubled together hating.

[1] *Canada*, vol. ii, p. 141.
[2] *United Brethren in America*, p. 34.
[3] *Carver's Travels*, p. 381.

3. Nishawi palliton nishawi machiton, nishawi
Both fighting both spoiling both
matta lungundowin.
not peaceful (or keeping peace).

4. Mattapewi wiki nihanlowit mekwazuan.
Less men with dead keeper fighting.

5. Maskanako gichi penauwelendamep
Strong snake great resolved
lennowak owini palliton.
men beings to destroy (fight).

6. N'akowa petonep, amangam petonep
Black snake he brought, monster he brought
akopehella petonep
rushing snake water he brought.

7. Pehella-pehella, pohoka-pohoka, eshohok
Much water rushing, much go to hills, much
eshohok palliton-palliton.
penetrating, much destroying.

8. Tulapit menapit Nanaboush,
At Tula (or turtle land) at that island Nanabush
maska-boush, owinimokom linowimokom
(strong) of beings the grandfather of men
the grandfather.

9. Gishikin-pommixin tulagishatten-lohxin.
Being born creeping at Tula he is ready to
move and dwell.

10. Owini linowi wemoltin pehella gahani
Beings men all go forth flood water
pommixin nahiwi tatalli
creeping (floating?) above water which
tulapin.
way (where) turtle-back.

11. Amangamek makdopamek alendguwek
Monsters of the sea they were many some of
metzipannek.
them they did eat.

12. Manoti-dasin mokol-wichemass papal
Spirit daughters boat helped come, come
payat payat wemichemap.
coming coming all helped.

13. Nanaboush, Nanaboush, wemimokom
Nanabush, Nanabush, of all the grandfather,
winimokom linnimokom tula-
of beings the granfather, of men the grand-
mokom.
father, of turtles the grandfather.

14. Linapima tulapima tulapewi tapitawi.
Man then turtle then turtle they altogether.

15. Wishanem tulpewi pataman
Frightened (startled?) turtle he praying
tulpewi paniton wuliton.
turtle he let it be to make well.

16. Kshipehelen penkwihilen kwamipokho
Water running off it is drying plain and moun-
sitwalikho maskan wagan
tain path of cave powerful or dire action
palliwi.
elsewhere.

PARAPHRASE.

1. Long ago came the powerful serpent (*Maskanako*), when men had become evil.
2. The strong serpent was the foe of the beings, and they became embroiled, hating each other.
3. Then they fought and despoiled each other, and were not peaceful.
4. And the small men (*Mattapewi*) fought with the keeper of the dead (*Nihanlowit*).
5. Then the strong serpent resolved all men and beings to destroy immediately.
6. The black serpent, monster, brought the snake-water rushing.
7. The wide waters rushing, wide to the hills, everywhere spreading, everywhere destroying.
8. At the island of the turtle (*Tula*) was Manabozho, of men and beings the grandfather—
9. Being born creeping, at turtle land he is ready to move and dwell.
10. Men and beings all go forth on the flood of waters, moving afloat, every way seeking the back of the turtle (*Tulapin*).
11. The monsters of the sea were many, and destroyed some of them.
12. Then the daughter of a spirit helped them in a boat, and all joined, saying, Come help!
13. Manabozho, of all beings, of men and turtles, the grandfather!
14. All together on the turtle then, the men then, were all together.
15. Much frightened, Manabozho prayed to the turtle that he would make all well again.
16. Then the waters ran off, it was dry on mountain and plain, and the great evil went elsewhere by the path of the cave.

The allusion to the turtle, in the tradition, is not fully understood. The turtle was connected, in various ways with the mythological notions of the upper Algonquins. According to Charlevoix and Hennepin, the Chippeways had a tradition that the mother of the human race, having been ejected from heaven was received upon the back of a tortoise, around which matter gradually accumulated, forming the earth.[1] The great turtle, according to Henry, was a chief spirit of the Chippeways, the "spirit that never lied," and was often consulted in reference to various undertakings. An account of one of these ceremonies is given by this author.[2] The island of *Michilimakanak* (literally, great turtle) was sacred to this spirit, for the reason, probably, that a large

[1] Charlevoix, vol. ii. p. 143; Hennepin, p. 55.
[2] Henry's Travels, p. 168.

hill near its centre was supposed to bear some resemblance, in form, to a turtle.[1] The turtle tribe of the Lenape, says Heckewelder, claim, a superiority and ascendency, because of their relationship to the great turtle, the Atlas of their mythology, who bears this great island (the earth) on his back.[2]

With these few illustrative observations, which might be greatly extended, I pass to the second or historical portion of the traditional record, with the simple remark that the details of the migrations here recounted, particularly so far as they relate to the passage of the Mississippi and the subsequent contest with the Tallegwi or Allegwi, and the final expulsion of the latter, coincide, generally, with those given by various authors, and well known to have existed among the Delawares.

The traditions, in their order, relate first to a migration from the north to the south, attended by a contest with a people denominated Snakes, or Evil, who are driven to the eastward. One of the migrating families, the *Lowaniwi*, literally northlings, afterwards separate and go to the snow land, whence they subsequently go to the east, towards the island of the retreating Snakes. They cross deep waters, and arrive at *Shinaki*, the land of Firs. Here the *Wunkenapi*, or Westerners, hesitate, preferring to return.

A hiatus follows, and the tradition resumes, the tribes still remaining at *Shinaki* or the Fir land.

They search for the great and fine island, the land of the Snakes, where they finally arrive, and expel the Snakes. They then multiply and spread towards the south, to the *Akolaki* or beautiful land, which is also called Shoreland, and Big-fir land. Here they tarried long, and for the first time cultivated corn and built towns. In consequence of a great drought, they leave for the *Shillilakiny* or Buffalo land. Here, in consequence of disaffection with their chief, they divide and separate, one party, the *Wetamowi*, or the Wise, tarrying, the others going off. The *Wetamowi* build a town on the *Wisawana* or Yellow river (probably the Missouri), and for a long time are peaceful and happy. War finally breaks out, and a succession of warlike chiefs follow, under whom conquests are made, north, east, south and west. In the end *Opekasit* (literally east looking) is chief, who, tired with so much warfare, leads his followers towards the the sun-rising. They arrive at the *Messussipi*, or Great river (the Mississippi), where, being weary, they stop, and their first chief is *Yagawanend*, or the Hut-maker, under whose chieftaincy it is discovered that a strange people, the *Tallegwi*, possess the rich east land. Some of the *Wetamowi* are slain by the Tallegwi, and then the cry of *palliton! palliton!!* war! war!! is raised, and they go over and attack the *Tallegwi*. The contest is continued during the lives of several chiefs, but finally terminates in the *Tallegwi* being driven southward. The conquerers then occupy the country on the Ohio below the great lakes—the *Shawanipekis*. To the north are their friends, the *Talamatun*, literally *not-of-themselves*, translated Hurons. The Hurons, however, are not always friends, and they have occasional contests with them.

Another hiatus follows, and then the record resumes by saying that they were strong and peaceful at the land of the Tallegwi. They built towns and planted corn. A long succession of chiefs followed, when war again broke out, and finally a portion under *Linkewinnek*, or the Sharp-looking, went eastward beyond the *Talegachukung* or Alleghany mountains. Here they spread widely, warring against the *Mengwi* or Spring-people, the *Pungelika*, Lynx or Eries, and the *Mohegans* or Wolves. The various tribes into which they became divided, the chiefs of each in their order, with the territories which they occupied, are then named—bringing the record down until the arrival of the Europeans. This latter portion we are able to verify in great part from authentic history.

SONG III.—MIGRATIONS.

1. After the flood the true men (*Lennapewi*) were with the turtle, in the cave house, the dwelling of Talli.
2. It was then cold, it froze and stormed, and

[1] Ib., 37, 110.
[2] Heckewelder, p. 246.

3. From the northern plain, they went to possess milder lands, abounding in game.
4. That they might be strong and rich, the new comers divided the lands between the hunters and tillers (*Wikhichik, Elowichik*).
5. The hunters were the strongest, the best, the greatest.
6 They spread north, east, south and west;
7. In the white or snow country (*Lumowaki*), the north country, the turtle land and the hunting country, were the turtle men or *Linapiwi*.
8. The Snake (evil) people being afraid in their cabins, the Snake priest (*Nakopowa*) said to them, let us go away.
9. Then they went to the east, the Snake land sorrowfully leaving.
10. Thus escaped the Snake people, by the tremblIng and burned land to their strong island (*Akomenaki*).
11. Free from opposers, and without trouble, the Northling (*Lowaniwi*) all went forth separating in the land of snow (*Winiaken*).
12. By the waters of the open sea, the sea of fish, tarried the fathers of the White-eagle (tribe?) and the White-wolf.
13. Our fathers were rich; constantly sailing in their boats, they discovered to the eastward the Snake island.
14. Then said the Head-beaver (*Wihlamok*) and the Great-bird, let us go to the Snake land.
15. All responned, let us go and annihilate the Snakes.
16. All agreed, the northerlings, the easterlings, to pass the frozen waters.
17. Wonderful! They all went over the waters of the hard, stony sea, to the open the Snake waters.
18. In vast numbers, in a single night, they went to the eastern or Snake island; all of them marching by night in the darkness.
19. The northerlings, the easterlings, the southerlings (*Shawanapi*), the Beaver-men (*Tamakwapis*), the Wolf-men, the Hunters or best men, the priests (*Powatapi*), the *Wiliwapi*, with their wives and daughters, and their dogs.
20. They all arrived at the land of Firs (*Shinaking*), where they tarried; but the Western men (*Wunkenapi*) hesitating, desired to return to the old Turtle land (*Tulpaking*).

It may be suggested that the account of the second migration, across frozen waters, is so much in accordance with the popular prejudice, as to the mode in which the progenitors of the American race arrived in America, that it throws suspicion on the entire record. It is not impossible, indeed, that the original tradition may have been slightly modified here by the dissemination of European notions among the Indians. McKenzie, however, observes of the traditions of the northern Chippeways: "The Indians say that they originally came from another country, inhabited by a wicked people, and had traversed a great lake, which was shallow, narrow and full of islands, where they sufferred great hardships and much misery, it being always winter, with ice and deep snows. * * * They describe the deluge when the waters spread over the whole earth, except the highest mountain, on the top of which they were preserved."[1]

The preceeding songs have something of a metrical character, and there is in some of the verses an arrangement of homophones which has a very pleasing effect. For instance, the last verse of the above song is as follows;

Wemipayat guneunga shinaking
Wunkenapi chanelendam payaking
Allowelendam kowiyey-tulpaking.

How far this system was carried it is difficult to say, but it is not unlikely that most of the transmitted songs or chants had something of this form.

The next song resumes, after the lapse of an indefinite period, as follows:

---

1 *McKenzie*, p. 113.

SONG IV.—THE CHRONICLE.

1. Long ago our fathers were at *Shinaki* or Fir land.
2. The White Eagle (*Wapalanewa*) was the path-leader of all to this place.
3. They searched the great and fine land, the island of the Snakes.
4. The hardy hunters and the friendly spirits met in council.
5. And all said to *Kalawil* (Beautiful-head) be thou chief (*sakima*) here.
6. Being chief he commanded they should go against the Snakes.
7. But the Snakes were weak and hid themselves at the Bear hills.
8. After Kalawil, *Wapagokhas* (White-owl) was sakima at Fir land.
9. After him *Jantowit* (Maker) was chief.
10. And after him *Chilili* (Snow-bird) was sakima. The south, he said
11. To our fathers, they were able, spreading, to possess.
12. To the south went Chilili; to the east went *Tamakwi* (the Beaver).
13. The South land (*Shawanaki*) was beautiful, shore-land, abounding in tall firs.
14. The East land (*Wapanaki*) abounded in fish; it was the lake and buffalo land.
15. After Chilili, *Agamek* (Great warrior) was chief.
16. Then our fathers warred against the robbers, Snakes, bad men, and stony men, *Chikonapi, Akhonapi, Makatapi, Assinapi* (Assiniboins ?)
17. After Agamek came ten chiefs, and than were many wars, south, east and west.
18. After them was *Langundowi* (the Peaceful) sakima, at the *Aholaking* (Beautiful land).
19. Following him *Tasukamend* (Never bad), who was a good or just man.
20. The chief after him was *Pemaholend* (Ever-beloved), who did good.
21. Then *Matemik* (Town-builder), and *Pilwihalen.*
22. And after these, in succession, *Gunokeni*, who was father long, and *Mangipitak* (Big-teeth).
23. Then followed *Olumapi* (Bundler-of-sticks), who taught them pictures (records).
24. Came then *Takwachi* (Who-shivers-with-cold), who went southward to the Corn land (*Minihaking*).
25. Next was *Huminiend* (Corn-eater), who caused corn to be planted.
26. Then *Alko-ohit* (the Preserver), who was useful.
27. Then *Shiwapi* (Salt-man), and afterwards *Penkwonowi* (the Thirsty) when
28. There was no rain, and no corn, and he went to the east, far from the great river or shore.
29. Passing over a hollow mountain (*Oligonunk*) they at last found food at *Shililaking*, the plains of the Buffalo land.
30. After *Penkwonowi*, came *Mekwochella* (the Weary), and *Chingalsawi* (the Stiff).
31. After him *Kwitikwund* (the Reprover), who was disliked and not willingly endured.
32. Being angry, some went to the eastward, and some went secretly afar off.
33. The wise tarried, and made *Makaholend* (the Beloved) chief.
34. By the *Wisawana* (Yellow river) they built towns, and raised corn on the great meadows.
35. All being friends, *Tamenend* (the Amiable, literally *beaver-like*) became the first chief.
36. The best of all, then or since, was *Tamenend*, and all men were his friends.
37. After him was the good chief, *Maskansisil* (Strong-buffalo), and
38. *Machigokhos* (Big-owl), and *Wapikicholen* (White-crane).
39. And then *Wingenund* (the Mindful or Wary), who made feasts.
40. After him came *Lapawin* (the White), and *Wallama* (the Painted), and
41. *Waptiwapit* (White-bird), when there was war again, north and south.
42. Then was *Tamaskan* (Strong-wolf), chief, who was wise in council and
43. Who made war on all, and killed *Maskensini* (Great-stone).
44. *Messissuwi* (the Whole) was next chief, and made war on the Snakes (*Akowini*).

45. *Chitanwulit* (Strong-and-good) followed, and made war on the northern enemies (*Lowanuski*).
46. *Alkouwi* (the Lean) was next chief, and made war on the Father-snakes (*Towakon*).
47. *Opekasit* (East-looking) being next chief, was sad because of so much warfare,
48. Said, let us go to the sun-rising (*Wapagishek*); and many went east together.
49. The great river (*Messussipu*) divided the land, and being tired, they tarried there.
50. *Yagawanend* (Hut-maker) was next *sakima*, and then the *Tallegwi* were found possessing the east.
51. Followed *Chitanitis* (Strong-friend), who longed for the rich eastland.
52. Some went to the east, but the *Tallegwi* killed a portion.
53. Then all of one mind exclaimed, war, war!
54. The *Talmatan* (Not-of-themselves), and the *Nitilowan*, all go united (to the war).
55. *Kinnehepend* (Sharp-looking) was their leader, and they went over the river.
56. And they took all that was there, and despoiled and slew the *Tallegwi*.
57. *Pimokhasuwi* (Stirring-about) was next chief, and then the *Tallegwi* were much too strong.
58. *Tenchekensit* (Open-path) followed, and many towns were given up to him.
59. *Paganchihilla* was chief, and the *Tallegwi* all went southward.
60. *Hattanwulatou* (the Possessor) was *sakima*, and all the people were pleased.
61. South of the lakes they settled their council-fire, and north of the lakes were their friends the *Talamatan* (Hurons?)
62. They were not always friends, but conspired when *Gunitakan* was chief.
63. Next was *Linniwalamen*, who made war on the *Talamatan*.
64. *Shakagapewi* followed, and then the *Talamatan* trembled.

SONG V.—THE CHRONICLE CONTINUED.

1. All were peaceful, long ago, at the land of the *Tallegwi*.
2. Then was *Tamaganend* (Beaver-leader) chief at the White river (*Wapalaneng*, Wabash).
3. *Wapushuwi* (White-lynx) followed, and much corn was planted.
4. After came *Walichinik*, and the people became very numerous.
5. Next was *Lekhihitin*, and made many records (*walum-olumin*, or painted-sticks).
6. Followed *Kolachuisen* (Blue-bird), at the place of much fruit or food (*Makeliming*).
7. *Pematalli* was chief over many towns.
8. And *Pepomahemen* (Paddler), at many waters (or the great waters).
9. And *Tankawon* (Little-cloud) was chief, and many went away.
10. The *Nentegos* and the *Shawanis* went to the south lands.
11. *Kichitamak* (Big-beaver) was chief at the White lick (*Wapahoning*).
12. The Good-prophet (*Onowatok*) went to the west.
13. He visited those who were abandoned there and at the south-west.
14. *Pawanami* Water-turtle) was chief at the *Talegahonah* (Ohio) river.
15. *Lakwelend* (Walker) was next chief, and there was much warfare.
16. Against the *Towako* (Father Snakes), against the *Sinako* (Stone or Mountain Snakes), and against the *Lowako* (North Snakes).
17. Then was *Mokolmokoni* (Grandfather-of-boats) chief, and he warred against the Snakes in boats.
18. *Winelowich* (Snow-hunter) was the chief at the North land (*Lowashkin*).
19. And *Linkwekinuk* (Sharp-seer) was Chief at the Alleghany mountains (*Talegachukang*).
20. And *Wapalawikwan* (East-settler) was chief east of the *Tallegwi* land.
21. Large and long was the east land;
22. It had no enemies (snakes), and was a rich and good land.

23. And *Gikenopalat* (Great-warrior) was chief towards the north ;
24. And *Hanaholend* (Stream-lover) at the branching stream (*Saskwihanang* or Susquehanna).
25. And *Gattawisi* (the Fat) was sakima at the Sassafras land, (*Winaki*).
26. All were hunters from the big Salt water (*Gishikshapipek*, Chesapeake, or literally Salt sea of the sun), to the again (or other) sea.
27. *Makliuawip* (Red-arrow) was chief at tide water (*Lapihaneng*.)
28. And *Wolomenap* was chief at the Strong falls (*Maskekitong*, Trenton?)
29. And the *Wapenend* and the *Tumewand* were to the north.
30. *Walitpallat* (Good-fighter) was chief, and set out against the north.
31. Then trembled the *Mahongwi* (the Iroquois ?) and the *Pungelika* (Lynx like, or Eries).
32. Then the second *Tamenend* (Beaver) was chief, and he made peace with all.
33. And all were friends, all united under this great chief.
34. After him was *Kichitamak* (Great-good-beaver) chief in the Sassafras land.
35. *Wapahakey* (White-body) was chief at the Sea shore (*Sheyabi*).
36. *Elangonel* (the Friendly) was chief, and much good was done.
37. And *Pitemunen* was chief, and people came from somewhere.
38. At this time from the east sea came that which was white (vessels ?)
39. *Makelomush* was chief and made all happy.
40. *Wulakeningus* was next chief, and was a warrior at the south.
41. He made war on the *Otaliwako* (Cherokee snakes or enemies), and upon the *Akowetako* (Coweta ? snakes).
42. *Wapagamoski* (White-otter) was next chief, and made the *Talamatans* (Hurons) friends.
43. *Wapashum* followed, and visited the land of *Tallegwi* at the west.[1]
44. There were the *Hiliniki* (Illinois), the *Shawanis* (Shawanoes), and the *Kenowiki* (Kenhawas ?)
45. *Nitispayat* was also chief, and went to the great lakes.
46. And he visited the *Wemiamik* (Beaver-children, or Miamis), and made them friends.
47. Then came *Packimitzin* (Cranberry-eater), who made the *Tawa* (Ottawas) friends.
48. *Lowaponska* was chief, and visited the Noisy place (*Ganshowenik*).
49. And *Tashawinso* was chief at the Sea shore (*Shayabing*.
50. Then the children divided into three parts, the *Unamini* (Turtle tribe), the *Minsimini* (Wolf tribe), the *Chikimini* (Turkey tribe).
51. *Epallahchund* was chief, and fought the *Mahongwi*, but failed.
52. *Laugomuwi* was chief, and the *Mahongwi* trembled.
53. *Wangomend* was chief, yonder between. (?)
54. The *Otawili* and *Wasiotowi* were his enemies.
55. *Wapachikis* (White-crab) was chief, and a friend of the Shore people.
56. *Nenachipat* was chief towards the sea.
57. Now from north and south came the *Wapagachik* (White-comers).
58. Professing to be friends, in big-birds (ships). Who are they ?

Here stop the pictured records. There is, however, a fragment in the original manuscripts, which may be taken as a continuation, and concerning which Rafinesque says nothing more than that it "was translated from the Lenape by John Burns." The references, so far as I am able to verify them, are historically correct. It is here given in its original form, with no attempt at paraphrase. It resumes with an answer to the question which concludes the last song, "who are these *Wapsinis?*"

SONG IV.—THE MODERN CHRONICLE.

1. Alas, alas ! we now know who they are, these *Wapsinis* (East-people), who came out of the sea to rob us of our lands. Starving wretches ! they came with smiles, but soon became snakes (or enemies).

[1] "At present," says Loskiel, "the Delawares call the whole country as far as the entrance of the river Wabash into the Ohio, *Alligewi-nengk*, that is, a land into which they came from distant parts."—*Hist. United Brethren*, p. 127.

2. The *Walumolum* was made by *Lekhibit* (the writer), to record our glory. Shall I write another to record our fall? No! Our foes have taken care to do that; but I speak what they know not or conceal.
3. We have had many others chiefs since that unhappy time. There were three before the friendly *Mikwon* (*Miquon* or Penn) came. *Mattanikum*[1] (Not-strong) was chief when the *Winakoli* (Swedes) came to *Winaki*; *Nahumen* (Raccoon) when the *Sinalwi* (Dutch) came, and *Ikwahon* (Fond-of-women) when the *Yankwis* (English) came. *Miquon* (Penn) and his friends came soon after.
4. They were all received and fed with corn; but no land was ever sold to them: we never sold any land. They were allowed to dwell with us, to build houses and plant corn, as friends and allies. Because they were hungry and we thought them children of *Gishaki* (or Sun-land), and not serpents and children of serpents.
5. And they were traders, bringing fine new tools, and weapons, and cloth, and beads, for which we gave them skins and shells and corn. And we liked them and the things they brought, for we thought them good and made by the children of *Gishaki*.
6. But they brought also fire-guns, and fire-waters, which burned and killed; also baubles and trinkets of no use, for we had better ones before.
7. After Mikwon, came the sons of *Dolojo-sakima* (King George), who said, more land, more land we must have, and no limit could be put to their steps.
8. But in the north were the children of *Lowi-sakima* (King Louis), who were our good friends, friends of our friends, foes of our foes; yet with *Dolojo* wished always to war.
9. We had three chiefs after Mikwon came—*Skalichi*, who was another *Tamenend*, and *Sasunam-Wikwikhon* (Our-uncle-the-builder), and *Tutami* (Beaver-taker), who was killed by a *Yankwako* (English-snake), and then we vowed revenge.
10. *Netatawis* (First-new-being) became chief of all the nations in the west. Again at *Talligewink* (Ohio, or place of Tallegwi) on the river Cuyahoga, near our old friends the *Talamatans*. And he called on all them of the east (to go to war).
11. But *Tadeskung* was chief in the east at *Mahoning*, and was bribed by *Yankwis*; then he was burnt in his cabin, and many of our people were killed at *Hickory* (Lancaster) by the land-robber *Yankwis*.
12. Then we joined *Lowi* in war against the *Yankwis*; but they were strong, and they took *Lowanaki* (North-land, Canada) from *Lowi*, and came to us in *Talegawink*, when peace was made, and we called them *Kichikani* (Big-knives).
13. Then *Alimi* (White-eyes) and *Gelelenund* (Buck-killer) were chiefs, and all the nations near us were friends, and our grand-children again.
14. When the Eastern-fires began to resist *Dolojo*, they said we should be another fire with them. But they killed our chief *Unamiwi* (the Turtle) and our brothers on the Muskingum. Then *Hopokan* (Strong-pipe) of the Wolf tribe was made chief, and he made war on the *Kichikani-Yankwis*, and became the friend of *Dolojo*, who was then very strong.
15. But the Eastern-fires were atronger; they did not take *Lowinaki*, but bebecame free from *Dolojo*. We went to *Wapahani* (White river) to be further from them; but they followed us everywhere, and we made war on them, till they sent *Makhiakho* (Black snake, General Wayne), who made strong war.
16. We next made peace and settled limits, and our chief was *Hackingpouskan* (Hard-walker), who was good and peaceful. He would not join our brothers, the *Shawanis* and *Ottawas*, nor *Dolojo* in the next war.
17. Yet after the last peace, the *Kichikani-Yankwis* came in swarms all around us, and they desired also our lands of *Wapahani*. It was useless to resist, because they were getting stronger and stronger by joining fires.
18. *Kithtilkand* and *Lapanibit* were the chiefs of our two tribes when we

[1] *Note by Rafinesque.* "*Mattanikum* was chief in 1645. He is called *Matta-horn* by Holm, who by a blunder, has made his name half Swedish. *Horn* is not Lenapi. Mattawikum means *Not-Horned*, without horns, emblem of having little strength."

resolved to exchange our lands, and return at last beyond the *Masispek*, near to our old country.

19. We shall be near our foes the *Wakon* (Osages), but they are not worse than the *Yankwisakon* (English snakes) who want to possess the whole Big-island.
20. Shall we be free and happy, then, at the new *Wapahani?* We want rest, and peace, and wisdom.

So terminate these singular records. It is unfortunate that they lack that kind of authentication, which depends upon a full and explicit account of the circumstances under which they were found, transcribed and translated. Rafinesque was not particular in these matters, and his carelessness and often extravagant assumptions, have rendered his name of little weight in matters of research. Still, upon neither of these grounds may we reject these records. As already observed, they have the internal evidence of genuineness, and are well supported by collateral circumstances. Some of these circumstances were presented at the outset, and need not be recapitulated. Rafinesque himself has anticipated, and thus disposes of one objection, not among the least formidable: "That so many generations and names can be remembered, may appear doubtful to some; but when symbolical signs and paintings are accompanied with songs, and carefully taught from generation to generation, their retention and perpetuation is not so remarkable." To this may with propriety be added the subjoined observations of Loskiel: "The Delawares delight in describing their genealogies, and are so well versed in them, that they mark every branch of the family with the greatest precision. They also add the character of their forefathers: such an one was a wise and intelligent counsellor; a renowned warrior, or a rich man, etc. But though they are indifferent about the history of former times, and ignorant of the art of reading and writing, yet their ancestors were well aware that they stood in need of something to enable them to convey their ideas to a distant nation, or preserve the memory of remarkable events. To this end they invented something like hieroglyphics, and also strings and belts of wampum, etc."[1]

I have alluded to the general identity of the mythological traditions here recorded, with those which are known to have been, and which are still current among the nations of the Algonquin stock. The same may be observed of the traditions which are of a historical character, and particularly that which relates to the contest with the people denominated the *Tallegwi*. The name of this people is still perpetuated in the word *Alleghany*, the original significance of which is more apparent, when it is written in an unabbreviated form, *Tallegwi-henna*, or *Tallegwi-hanna* literally river of the Tallegwi. It was applied to the Ohio (the present name is Iroquois, and literally rendered by the French *La Belle Rivière*), and is still retained as the designation of its northern or principal tributary. The traditionary contest between the Lenape and the Tallegwi is given by Heckewelder, and is adduced in further illustration of the general concurrence above mentioned. The details vary in some points, but I am inclined to give the first position to the tradition as presented in the *Walumolum;* it being altogether the most simple and consistent. It must be observed, that Mr. Heckewelder's diffuse account is much condensed in the following quotations, and that part which refers to the wars with the Cherokees, etc., is entirely omitted.

"The Lenni-Lenape (according to the traditions handed down to them from their ancestors) resided many hundred years ago, in a very distant country, in the western part of the American continent. For some reason, which I do not find accounted for, they determined on migrating to the eastward, and accordingly set out together in a body. After a very long journey, and many nights' encampment ('night's encampmeut' is a halt of a year in a place), they at length arrived on the *Namaesi-sipu*,[2] where they fell in with the Mengwi (Iroquois), who had likewise emigrated from a distant country, and had struck upon this river higher up. Their object was the same with that of the Delawares; they were proceeding to the eastward, until they should

[1] United Brethren in America, p. 24.

[2] This differs from the foregoing record, and is undoubtedly incorrect. It is difficult to derive Mississippi from *namaesi-sipu* which is made up of *namaesi*, a fish, and *sipu*, river. The etymology is clearly *messu*, *messi*, or *michi*, signifying *great*, or as Mr. Gallatin suggests, the *whole* and *sipu*, river.

find a country that pleased them. The spies which the Lenape had sent forward for the purpose of reconnoitering, had long before their arrival discovered that the country east of the Mississippi was inhabited by a very powerful nation, who had many large towns built on the great rivers flowing through the land. These people (as I was told) called themselves *Tallegwi* or *Talligewi*. Col. John Gibson, however, a gentleman who has a thorough knowledge of the Indians, and speaks several of their languages, is often of opinion that they were called *Alligewi*." * * * * * *

"Many wonderful things are told of this famous people. They are said to have been remarkably tall and stout, and there are traditions that there were giants among them. It is related, that they had built to themselves regular fortifications or entrenchments, from whence they would sally out, but were generally repulsed. * * * When the Lenape arrived on the banks of the Mississippi, they sent a message to the *Alligewi*, to request permission to settle themselves in their neighborhood. This was refused them; but they obtained leave to pass through the country, and seek a settlement further to the eastward. They accordingly commenced passing the Mississippi, when the *Alligegwi* discovering their great numbers became alarmed, and made a furious attack upon those who had crossed. Fired, at their treachery, the Lenape consulted on what was to be done; whether to retreat, or try their strength against their oppressors. While this was going on the Mengwi, who had contented themselves with looking on from a distance, offered to join the Lenape, upon condition that they should be entitled to a share of the country, in case the combination was successful. Their proposal was accepted, and the confederates were able, after many severe conflicts, to drive the Alligewi down the Mississippi river. The conquerors divided the country between themselves; the Mengwi selecting the lands in the vicinity of the great lakes, and on their tributary streams, while the Lenape took possession of the country below them. For a long period of time, some say many hundred of yhars, the two nations lived peaceably, and increased their numbers with great rapidity. Ultimately some of the most adventurous among them crossed the mountains towards the rising sun, and falling on streams running to the eastward, followed them to the great Bay river (Susquehanna), and thence to the bay (Chesapeake) itself. As they pursued their travels, partly by land and partly by water, sometimes near and sometimes on the great-salt-water lake (as they call the sea), they discovered the great river which we call the Delaware; and still further to the eastward, the *Sheyibbi* country, now called New Jersey. Afterwards they reached the stream now called the Hudson. The reports of the adventurers caused large bodies to follow them, who settled upon the four great rivers, the Delaware, Hudson, Susquehanna and Potomac, making the Delaware, which they call *Lenapewihittuck* (the river of the Lenape) the centre of their possessions.

"They add that a portion of their people remained beyond the Mississippi, and still another portion tarried between the Mississippi and the mountains. The largest portion, they supposed, settled on the Atlantic. The latter were divided into three tribes, two of which were distinguished as *Unâmis*, or Turtle, and *Wnalachtgo*, or Turkey. These chose the lands lying nearest the coast. Their settlements extended from the *Mohicanittuck* (river of the *Mohicans* or Hudson) to beyond the Potomac. * * * The third great tribe, the *Minsi* (which we have corrupted into *Monseys*), or tribe of the wolf, lived back of the others, forming a kind of bulwark, and watching the nations of the *Mengwi*. They were considered the most active and warlike of all the the tribes. They extended their settlements from the *Minisink*, where they had their council-fire, quite to the Hudson on the east, and westward beyond the Susquehanna, and northward to the head waters of that stream and the Delaware. * * * From the above three divisions or tribes, comprising together the body of the people called Delawares, sprung many others, who, having for their own convenience chosen distinct spots to settle in, and increasing in numbers, gave themselves names, or received them from others. * * * Meanwhile trouble ensued with the *Mengwi*, who occupied the southern shores of the lakes and resulted in fierce and sanguinary wars. The reverses of the *Mengwi* induced them to confederate, after which time the contests with the Lenape were carried on with vigor until the arrival of the French in Canada;"

It will be seen that there is a difference between the traditions, as given by Heckewelder, and the *Walum-olum* in respect to the name of the confederates against the *Tallegwi*. In the latter the allies are called *Talamatan*, literally Not-of-themselves, and which, in one or two cases, is translated *Hurons*, with what correctness I am not prepared to say. Heckewelder calls them *Mengwi*, Iroquois. This must be a mistake, as the *Mengwi* are subsequently and very clearly alluded to in the *Walum-olum*, as distinct from the *Talamatan*.

It is remarkable that the traditions of almost all the tribes, on the eastern shore of the continent, refer, with more or less distinctness, to a migration from the westward. "When you ask them," says Lawson, speaking of the Carolina Indians, "whence their fathers came, that first inhabited the country, they will point to the westward and say, 'Where the sun sleeps, our fathers came thence.'" Most of the nations speak of the passage of the Mississippi river. The Natchez, who assimilated more nearly to the central American and Peruvian stocks (the *Toltecan* family), informed Du Pratz that they once dwelt at the south-west, "under the sun." The Muscogulges or Creeks, according to Bartram's manuscript, assert that they formerly lived beyond the Mississippi, and that they relinquished that country in obedience to a dream in which they were directed to go to the country where the sun rises. They claim that they crossed the river in their progress eastward, about the period that De Soto visited Florida. The Cherokees (a cognate tribe) have a similar tradition. They assert that "a long time ago all the Indians traveled a great distance and came to a great water. Upon arriving there, and immediately before or immediately after crossing, it is not remembered which, a part went north and another part south. Those who went northwards settled in two towns called *Ka-no-wo-gi* and *Nu-ta-gi;* the others at *Ka-ga-li-u*, or old town, and because they took the lead in the journey were considered the grandfathers of the Indians." Roger Williams informs us that the south-west, or *Sawaniwa*, was constantly referred to by the Indians of New England. "From thence, according to their traditions, they came. There is the court of their great god, *Cawtantowit;* there are all their ancestors' souls; there they also go when they die, and from thence came their corn and beans, out of *Cantantowit's* field."

It will thus be seen that the general tenor and some of the more important details of the traditions of the Indians of the Algonquin stock, as they have been presented to us by various authorities, are the same with those of the foregoing remarkable records. These records are peculiar, chiefly as giving us a greater number of details than we before possessed.

A BRIEF HISTORY OF THE BLACKFEET INDIANS.

The Blackfeet originally inhabited that region of country watered by the Saskatchawain and its tributaries, never extending their war parties farther south than the head waters of the Marias river, or farther east than the head waters of the Milk river, a tributary of the Missouri, into which it empties about one hundred and fifty miles above the Yellowstone river.

The cause of their separation and dispersion over a wider range of country grew out of a civil war regarding the claims of two ambitious chiefs, each claiming sovereign powers, and each having different-colored banners or flags —the one red, the other black. The warriors being divided, enrolled themselves under the two banners, and after many skirmishes and assassinations, a pitched battle ensued, which resulted in the disastrous defeat of the black chief.

The original tribe is now divided into three bands—the Blood Indians, Blackfeet, and Peigans. The Blood Indians still remain in the north, though a portion of them make an annual visit to their relatives on the Missouri, when their friendly feelings are such as to justify it. The Peigans formed a treaty of alliance and friendship with the Flatheads, which, with few interruptions, has been kept in good faith up to the present time.

The section of country that may now be considered as claimed and occupied by the three bands, generally known as the Blackfeet Nation, extends from the waters of the Hudson Bay, south to the head waters of the Missouri river, and to the northern sources of the Yellowstone river.

Their only occupations, beyond the social circle, are war and hunting. War, however, absorbs all other considerations, and this will be the case, so long as their present laws and regulations exist. As soon as a youth is capable of using the bow and arrow, he enlists under the wolf-skin banner of some favorite war chief, and joins in the first campaign against their hereditary enemies, the Crows and Assiniboins. These war parties frequently last for one or more years, it being considered disgraceful to return without scalps; and on one occasion, a war party, consisting of 300 young men, were absent for four years, without seeing or hearing from their own people. The cause of this extraordinary perseverance may be traced to their fundamental laws, one of which prohibits a youth to marry, or have a lodge of his own, until he has taken a scalp, or performed some other military exploit that will entitle him to rank as a brave. Neither is he permitted to sit in council, or be present at a feast; and, what is still more mortifying to youth, he is not allowed to join in a war or scalp-dance, when all the belles of the tribe are seen in gayest feathers, jingling bells, and fancy paints.

The laws or regulations by which a Blackfoot camp is governed, are well adapted to their peculiar condition, being legislative, judicial, and military. The chiefs, as a general rule, are elective, though great respect is paid to hereditary chiefs; but they have little or no power, unless they have distinguished themselves as warriors, and are supported by a band of braves. In every camp there is a military police, which consists of all the unmarried who rank themselves as braves, and a lodge for their accommodation is erected in the centre of the camp, which is generally of a circular form. When any matter of sufficient importance occurs, the subordinate chiefs are summoned to attend at the lodge of the head chief, where the subject is gravely discussed, and the decision made known to the war chief, whose duty it is to assemble his soldiers, and carry the orders of the chief into immediate execution. Though these orders from the chief sometimes condemn to death a father or a brother of one or more of the soldiers, yet they never hesitate to obey. On one occasion a wife of one of the chiefs being condemned for infidelity to be stripped of all her clothing, her nose cut off, to be whipped out of the camp, and to become the slave of any one who chose to take her, two of her brothers assisted in carrying the sentence into execution.

All questions of peace or war, of the time for raising the camp, or in regard to the regulations for a general hunt, are decided upon by the chiefs, and carried into execution by the soldiers. Notwithstanding the camp might be in a state of starvation, and there were plenty of buffalo or other game in sight, no one, not even the head chiefs, would be allowed to disturb them, without the consent of the council. The policy of this is obvious, as one individual might frighten off a herd of buffalo sufficient to feed the whole camp.

The Blackfoot has always been regarded as a treacherous, blood-thirsty savage; but this is a mistake, growing out of ignorance of his true character. It is true, they killed and scalped a great many of the mountain trappers; but they found them trespassing on their hunting-grounds, and killing off the game upon which they relied for subsistence; and any other tribe, or even civilized nation, would have retaliated for much less cause of provocation. Those who have long resided among them, have always found them frank, generous, and hospitable — ready at all times to repay any kindness they might receive from the whites.

INDIANS OF CALIFORNIA.*

The men are generally tall — living in a state of nature, so far as dress goes, not even possessing that natural article of clothing, a breech clout. The dress of the female consists mostly of a Talé skirt, fastened around the waist with a cord, and extending loosely to a little below the knees. They wear their hair long behind, but so cut in front as to shade their eyes; tattoo their

* History, Condition, and Prospects of the Indian Tribes, Appendix to Vol. V.

chins with three lines; and wear ornaments in their ears, formed of the leg bones of fowls, ornamented with carving, and used also as a pipe.

The tribes living in the valley of the San Joaquin river inhabit houses formed of mats laid on a framework of willow or cotton-wood; but the Sacramento tribes construct a more permanent habitation, made of a framework of heavy timber, covered with mud and grass—the floor being about two feet below the level of the ground. There are but two openings, a door for entrance, and a hole at the top, for the escape of the smoke of their fires, which they build on the ground. The men are indolent, doing only the lighter labor, such as making their arms and nets, while the women collect the grass seeds, acorns, &c., for their subsistence, in which occupation they are attended by one or more of the elders of the villages.

Their food consists of grass seeds and acorns, pounded together, mixed with water, and baked in the sand, whereby all the deleterious properties of the acorn, as well as its bitter taste, are removed. Grasshoppers and crickets also form a part of their subsistence, and these they collect by setting fire to the prairies in a circle, when, moving in a body towards the centre, they drive the insects into the flames, by which their legs are burned off. They are then collected, and pounded with deer tallow, or any kind of grease they may have, and used for food. As soon as the acorns commence falling, they collect great quantities of them, which they put up in cylindrical stacks, from eight to ten feet high, made of willows bound together by cords of wild hemp.

Their weapons for war and the chase consist of bows and arrows; the former being made of a kind of cedar, covered on the back with the sinews of a horse or elk, which make them very strong and elastic; the latter are chiefly of cane—those used in the chase having a point of hard wood, those intended for war are pointed with small heads of flint, beautifully barbed.

They are superstitious, knowing but little of the Christian religion, except what they have learned from association, either with the whites, or with other Indians who have been educated at the old Catholic mission, under Spanish rule. The first fish of the season they offer to the Deity, on a platform erected in the middle of a stream; the fish being hung on a high pole, decorated with feathers and other ornaments, beside which the medicine man takes his place, and harangues for nearly the whole day, after which the fish is left to decay.

Every village has its sweat-house, which is generally built near the edge of a stream, so that when individuals have perspired sufficiently within its walls, they may have the pleasure of an immersion in the cold water, which is their usual mode of relieving fatigue.

The tribes of California are divided into small bands, speaking different languages, and warring on each other, though living but a few miles apart. Their general domestic habits vary but little, feeding upon the same kind of food, and preparing it in the same manner. In their disposition they are cowardly; treachery and theft, as with most Indians, forming part of their creed. Their animal food consists of the game of the country, except the grizzly bear, which the uncivilized ones will not eat. Horses, both wild and tame, form, particularly among those residing near the coast settlements, their principal animal diet.

In the manufacture of their baskets and socks they manifest much neatness and taste, particularly in those covered with feathers, which generally consist of those of the summer duck, and scalps of the red-headed woodpecker, bound round the top with beads of their own manufacture. They are also very expert in weaving blankets of feathers, many of which have really beautiful figures worked on them.

SUPERSTITIONS OF THE DAKOTAH INDIANS.

According to the Rev. Gideon H. Pond, of Minnesota, "Every Dakotah warrior looks to the wakan-man as almost his only resource. From him he receives a spear and tomahawk, constructed after the model furnished from the armory of the gods, and also those paints which serve as an armature for his body. To obtain these things, the proud applicant is required to become a servant to the *Zuya-wakan*, while the latter goes through those painful and exhausting performances which are necessary preparatory to the bestowal of them; such as vapor-baths, fastings, chants, prayers, &c. The implements of destruction being thus consecrated, the person who is to receive them, wailing most piteously, approaches the war-prophet and presents the pipe to him as to a god; while in the attitude of prayer, he lays his hands upon his sacred head, and penetrated with a sense of his own impotency, sobs out his request in substance as follows: 'Pity thou one who is poor and helpless—a woman in action—and bestow on me the ability to perform manly deeds.' The prophet then presents the weapons desired, saying, 'Go thou, try the swing of this tomahawk and the thrust of this spear, and witness the power of the god to whom they belong; but when in victory thou shalt return, forget not to perform thy vows.' Each warrior is required to paint himself for battle in the same manner as his arms have been painted by the prophet; and must never paint in the same manner at any other time, except it may be in the performance of extraordinary religious rites. In this manner every young man is enlisted for life into the service of the war-prophet. These weapons are preserved as sacredly by the Dakotah warriors as was the 'ark of the covenant,' by the Israelites, are carefully wrapped up in a cloth cover, together with plumes and sacred pigments, laid outside of the tent every day, except in the storm, and must never be touched by a female who has arrived at the age of puberty. Every warrior feels that his success, both in war and hunting, depends entirely upon the strictnesss with which he conforms to the rules and ceremonies imposed upon him by the *wakan warrior*. The 'armor feasts' are of almost daily occurrence in the Dakotah camp, when the fruits of the chase are sufficient to supply them, at which time these arms are always religiously exhibited. Thus the influence of the medicine-man, as a warrior, pervades the whole community, and it is hardly possible to over-estimate it; though, however, vastly weakened by coming in contact with civilization and Christianity. The medicine-men themselves seem to be well aware of the fact, that the dissemination of knowledge among the people tends directly to the destruction of their influence.

"In the capacity of a doctor, or *wapiya*, the influence of the Dakotah medicine-man has scarcely any limits, as health is hardly more necessary to the happiness of the Indian than the wakan-man is for the preservation of health. It is believed that they have in their bodies animals (gods), which have great powers of suction, and which serve as suction-pumps, such as the lizard, bull-frog, leech, tortoise, garter-snake, &c. Other gods confer on them vocal powers, and their chants and prayers are the gifts of inspiration.

"If the doctors are long without practice, they suffer great inconvenience from the restlessness of the gods within them, to pacify whom they sometimes take blood from the arm of some person and drink it. When one of them, having been respectfully and reverently called upon, and liberally prepaid, is about to operate upon a suffering patient—'a little ox struggling on the earth'—he has him placed upon a blanket on the ground, in a tent, with the body chiefly naked, and also generally strips off his own clothes, except the middle-cloth. After chants, prayers, the rattling of the gourd-shell, and innumerable other trite ceremonies, making a variety of indescribable noises, and muttering something like the following, 'The god told me that having this, I might approach even a skeleton and set it on its feet,' he gets down upon his knees, and applying his mouth to the affected part of the patient, sucks with an energy which would seem to be almost superhuman—the gourd-shell still rattling violently. In this manner the god which is in the doctor pumps the disease from the sufferer. After sucking thus for a considerable time, the doctor rises on his feet in apparent agony, groaning so as to be heard a mile if the atmosphere is clear, beating his sides, writhing, and striking the earth with his feet so as almost to make it tremble, and holding a dish of water to his mouth, he proceeds with a sing-song bubbling to deposit in the dish that which has been drawn from the sick person. This laborious and disgusting operation is repeated at short intervals, for hours, and the operator is thus enabled not only to relieve the sufferer, but also to discover the sin on account of which he has been afflicted, the spirit of which he sees rush into the lodge, and violently lay hold of the unfortunate sinner, as if he would rend him to atoms. The doctor now makes an image of the offended animal whose enraged spirit he saw, and causes it to be shot by three or four persons in quick succession, when the god that is in him, leaping out, falls upon, not the image, but the spirit of the animal which the image represents, and kills it. Now the sick man begins to convalesce, unless other offended spirits appear to afflict him; but sometimes the doctor is overcome by these spirits and the patient dies, unless one of greater *wakan* powers can be obtained; for they are *wakan* to different degrees, corresponding to the strength of this attribute as it exists in the gods by whom they are respectively inspired. It seems to be the general impression that there are wakan-men who are able to subdue any foe to health till the superior gods order otherwise; but it is difficult to obtain their aid; for if they are not properly respected at all times, and well remunerated for their services, they let the sufferers perish without exerting their power to save them—doing their work deceitfully. It is also believed that they can inflict diseases as a punishment for sins committed against themselves, that death is often the effect of their *wakan* power, and that when they thus kill a person, they cut off the tip of his tongue and preserve it as a memento of the fact. The people stand in great fear of these medicine-men, and when sick will give all they possess, and all they can obtain on credit, to secure their services; frequently giving a horse for a single performance. They are always treated with the greatest respect, and generally furnished with the best of everything; and if there are impostors, this fact turns decidedly to the advantage of those who are believed to be true. There are from five to twenty-five of these men and women at each of the villages, most of whom have a fair reputation and considerable employment; and that, notwithstanding these Indians are now receiving so much aid from our own people who follow the medical profession. I do not believe that an individual Dakotah can be found, who does not believe that these jugglers can heal diseases without the help of vegetable or mineral medicines, except as this faith has been destroyed by the introduction among them of science and Christianity; and, even at this day, the persons who do not employ them as *wakan* jugglers are very few indeed."

MYTHOLOGY OF THE SIX NATIONS.*

"An unlimited expanse of water once filled the space now occupied by the world we inhabit, and here was the abode of total darkness, which no ray of light ever penetrated. At this time the human family dwelt in a country situated in the upper regions of the creation, abounding in everything conducive to the comfort and convenience of life; the forests were full of game; the lakes and streams swarmed with fish and fowl; while the earth and fields spontaneously produced a profusion of vegetables for the use of man; an unclouded sun enlivened their days, and storms and tempests were unknown in that happy region.

"The inhabitants were strangers to death, and its harbingers, pain and disease; while their minds, freed from the corroding passions of jealousy, hatred, malice, and revenge, were perfectly happy.

"At length, however, an event occurred which interrupted their tranquillity, and introduced care and anxiety, till then unknown. A certain young man, of high position, was observed to withdraw himself from the circle of their social amusements; the solitary recesses of the grove became his favorite walks; care and chagrin were depicted in his countenance; and his body, from long abstinence, presented to the view of his friends the mere skeleton of a man. Anxious friends again and again vainly solicited to know the cause of his grief, until, debilitated both in body and mind, he yielded to the importunities of his associates, and promised to disclose the cause of his troubles, on condition that they would dig up by the roots a certain white

* Paper by James Dean, Esq., of Oneida County, New York, in History, &c., of Indians, Vol. VI.

pine tree, lay him on his robes near the edge of the hole, and seat his wife by his side. Complying with his request, the fatal tree was taken up by the roots; in doing which the earth was perforated, and a passage opened to the abyss below, when the robe was placed by the side of the opening, and the youth laid thereon; his wife taking her seat by his side. The multitude, eager to learn the cause of such strange and unusual conduct, pressed around; when, on a sudden, to their horror and astonishment, he seized upon the woman, then enciente, and precipitated her headlong into the darkness below; then, rising from the ground, he informed the assembly that he had for some time suspected the chastity of his wife, and that having now disposed of the cause of his mental suffering, he should soon recover his usual health and vivacity.

"All the birds and amphibious animals which now inhabit the earth, then occupied the watery waste, to which the woman in her fall was hastening. The loon first discovered her coming, and called a council to prepare for her reception. Observing that the animal which approached was a human being, they knew that earth was indispensably necessary for her accommodation, and the first subject of deliberation was, who should support the burden. The sea bear first presented himself for a trial of his strength, when instantly the other animals gathered around, and seated themselves on his back; but the bear, unable to support the weight, sunk beneath the surface of the water, and was judged by the whole assembly unequal to the task of supporting her, and her prerequisite, the earth. Several others in succession presented themselves as candidates for the honor, and with similar ill-success. Last of all, the turtle modestly advanced, tendering his broad shell as the basis of the earth, now about to be formed. The beasts then made trial of its strength to bear weight, and finding their united pressure unable to sink the turtle below the surface, adjudged to him the honor of supporting the world. A foundation being thus provided, the next subject of deliberation was, how to procure earth, which, it was concluded, must be obtained from the bottom of the sea. Several of the most expert divers went in quest of it; but invariably, when they rose to the surface of the water, they were dead. The mink at length took the dangerous plunge, and when, after a long absence, his carcass floated to the surface, a critical examination discovered a small quantity of earth in one of his claws, which he had scratched from the bottom, and this being carefully preserved, was placed on the back of the turtle. In the meantime, the woman continued falling, and at length alighted on the back of the turtle, on which the earth had already grown to the size of a man's foot, and on this she stood with one foot covering the other. Shortly after she had room for both feet, and was soon able to sit down. The earth continued to expand, and soon formed a small island, skirted with willow, and other aquatic plants and shrubbery; and at length it stretched out into a widely-extended plain, interspersed with rivers and smaller streams, which, with gentle current, rolled forward their tributary waters to the ocean. Atahentsic, the woman, then repaired to the sea-shore, erected a habitation, and settled in her new abode, where, not long after, she became the mother of a daughter, and was supported by the spontaneous productions of the earth until the child arrived at adult years, when the latter was solicited in marriage by several animals, changed into the form of young men. The loon first presented himself as a suitor, in the form of a tall, well-dressed, fine-looking young man, but after due consultation with the mother, his suit was rejected. Several others presented themselves, and were rejected by the mother; until, at length, the turtle, with his short neck, short bandy legs, and humped back, offered himself as a suitor, and was received. After she had laid herself down to sleep, the turtle placed upon her abdomen two arrows in the form of a cross, one headed with a flint, the other with the rough bark of a tree, and took his leave. In due time she became the mother of two sons, called, in Iroquois, Yoskiki and Thoitsaron; but died in giving them birth. When the time arrived for the children to be born, they consulted together about the best mode of egress from their place of confinement, and the youngest determined to make his exit by the natural passage, whilst the other resolved to take the shortest route, by breaking through the walls of his prison; in effecting which he consequently destroyed his mother, thus giving the first evidence of his malignant disposition. The grandmother, enraged at her daughter's death, resolved to destroy the children, and, taking them in her arms, threw them both into the sea, but scarcely had she reached her wigwam, when the children appeared at the door. The experiment of drowning them was several times repeated, but in vain.

"Discouraged by her ill success, she determined to let them live. Then, dividing the corpse of her daughter into two parts, she threw them upwards towards the heavens, when the upper part became the sun and the lower part the moon, which is the reason why the latter has always presented the form of the human face. At this time began the succession of day and night in our world. The children speedily became men, and expert archers. The elder, whose name, in Oneida, was *Thau-wisk-a-lau* (a term expressive of the greatest degree of malignity and cruelty), used the arrow of the turtle pointed with flint, and killed with it the largest beasts of the forest; while the younger, whose name, in the same dialect, was *Tau-lou-ghy-au-wan-goon* (a name denoting unbounded goodness and benevolence), had the arrow headed with bark; but the former was, on account of his malignant disposition, and his skill and success in hunting, a favorite with his grandmother. They lived in the midst of plenty, but would not permit the younger brother, whose arrow was not sufficiently powerful to destroy anything but birds, to share in their abundance. As this young man was one day wandering along the shore, he saw a bird, perched upon a bough projecting over the water, which he attempted to kill; but his arrow, till that time unerring, flew wide of the mark and sank in the sea. He determined to recover it; and, swimming to the place where it fell, plunged to the bottom, when, to his astonishment, he found himself in a small cottage, in which a venerable old man was sitting, who received him with a smile of fraternal complacency, and thus addressed him: 'My son, I welcome you to the habitation of your father. To obtain this interview, I have directed all the circumstances which have conspired to bring you hither. Here is your arrow, and here is an ear of corn, which you will find pleasant and wholesome food. I have watched the unkindness both of your grandmother and your brother, and while he lives the earth can never be peopled; you must, therefore, take his life. When you return home, you must traverse the whole earth; collect all the flint-stones into heaps which you find, and hang up all the bucks'-horns, as these are the only things of which your brother is afraid, or which can make any impression upon his body, which is made of flint. They will furnish you with weapons, always at hand, wherever he may direct his course.' Having received these and other instructions from his father, he returned to the world, and began immediately to obey his father's directions, which being done, the elder resolved on a hunting excursion. On their way to the hunting-ground, he inquired of the younger what were the objects of his greatest aversion. He informed him (falsely) that there was nothing so terrific to him as beech-boughs and bulrushes, and inquired in turn of *Thau-wisk-a-lau* what he most dreaded; he answered, nothing so much as flint-stones and bucks'-horns, and that nothing else could injure him; and that lately he had been much annoyed by them wherever he went. Having arrived at their place of destination, the elder went in quest of game, leaving the younger to attend to the menial occupation of erecting his hut, and preparing such other accommodations as he required. After an absence of some time, the elder returned exhausted with fatigue and hunger, and partaking of a hearty repast, prepared by his brother, he retired to his wigwam to sleep; but when he had fallen into a profound slumber, the younger kindled a large fire at its entrance. After a time, the elder found himself extremely incommoded by the heat; and the flinty materials of his body, expanding by its intensity, were exploding in large scales from his carcass. In a great rage, and burning for revenge, he broke through the fire in front of the hut, hastened to a neighboring beech, armed himself with a large bough, and returned to chastise and destroy his brother; but finding that his repeated and violent blows had no effect upon his brother, who pelted him with flint-stones and belabored him with bucks'-horns, which caused the flinty scales to fall from his body in copious showers, he betook himself to a neighboring marsh, where he supplied himself with a bundle of bulrushes, and returned to the contest, though with the same ill success. Finding himself deceived, and failing of his purpose, he sought safety in flight. As he fled, the earth trembled. A verdant plain, bounded by the distant ocean, lay before him; behind him, the earth sunk in deep valleys and frightful chasms, or rose into lofty mountains or stupendous precipices; the streams ceased to roll forward their waters, and, bursting their barriers, poured down the cliffs in cataracts, or foamed through their rocky channels to the ocean. The younger brother followed the fugitive with vigorous steps, wounding him continually with his weapons, and at length, in a far distant region, beyond the savannahs of the west, he breathed his last, loading the earth with his flinty form.

"The great enemy of the race of the turtle being destroyed, they came up out of the ground in human form, and for some time multiplied in peace, and spread extensively over its surface. Atahentsic, the grandmother, roused to furious resentment for the loss of her darling son, and resolving to be revenged, for many days successively, caused the rain to descend in torrents from the clouds, until the whole surface of the earth, and even the highest mountains, were covered; but the inhabitants fled to their canoes, and escaped the impending destruction. The disappointed grandmother caused the rains to cease, and the waters to subside, when the inhabitants returned to their former places of abode. Determining to effect her purpose in another manner, she covered the earth with a deluge of snow, to escape which new evil they betook themselves to their snow-shoes, and thus eluded her vengeance. Chagrined at length by these disappointments, she gave up the idea of destroying the whole human race at once, and determined to wreak her vengeance upon them in a manner which, although less violent, should be more efficacious. Accordingly, she has ever since been employed in gratifying her malignant disposition, by inflicting upon mankind all those evils which are suffered in this present world. Tarenyawagon, in Oneida, *Tau-lou-ghy-au-wan-goon*, on the other hand, displays the infinite benevolence of his nature by bestowing on the human race the blessings they enjoy, all of which flow from his bountiful providence. This personage afterwards dwelt among his brethren under the name of Hiawatha. The name Tarenyawagon, literally translated, is 'the Holder, or Supporter of the Heavens.' Hiawatha was the minister of Tarenyawagon, and agent of his good will to mankind."

NOTES, ADDITIONS, AND CORRECTIONS.

P. 47.—The whole of the letter of *Gov. Bradstreet* is now printed in the *New Eng. Hist. and Genealog. Reg.* ii. 150.

P. 51.—Murder of Miss McCrea. Among the many versions of this tragedy there is one in *Barber's Hist. Coll. of New York*, pp. 569, 570, which *may be* worth consulting; it *would be*, doubtless, had he informed us how he got his information. Perhaps from people in the neighborhood of the murder. We do not like inferences when easily avoided.

P. 69.—This early voyage to New England has been reprinted entire, in 3 *Coll. Mass. Hist. Soc.* vol. viii.

P. 83.—Respecting the visit of *Sir Francis Drake* to the coast of New England before the settlement of Plimouth, our account is pretty full. The conclusion there arrived at, that *Drake* did actually land somewhere in the neighborhood of Cape Cod, we thought our authorities clearly justified. But some critical writers since my work was published, questioning the fact, I am ready to confess that the subject is not, nor did I ever consider it, settled *beyond* a doubt; yet, after all, it may be quite as difficult to settle it the other way, namely, that he *did not* land in New England.

P. 111.—On this, and the pages immediately before and after it, notices are contained of several chiefs and others who were living between Boston and Salem when the English came. The most of them had more or less to do with all the whites who settled near them, and especially with those who settled at and about *Saugus*, afterwards called *Lynn*. This circumstance brought their history particularly under the investigation of the accomplished historian of that town, Alonzo Lewis, Esq. Our text was written before the appearance of his second edition, to which is added a great amount of the most valuable information, of which we were not in possession. Therefore, instead of making a long note here, of extracts, corrections, &c., we must refer our readers to the work of Mr. Lewis, where the numerous facts will be found, clothed in the easy and polished style of that writer.

P. 111.—Concerning SAGAMORE JOHN, we have a note as early as 1631. In his *letter to the countess of Lincoln*, *Gov. Dudley* says, "John is a handsome young man—conversant with vs, affecting English Aparell and howses, and speaking well of our God."—*James*, the brother of *John*, "commanded not above 30 or 40 men." *Dudley, ib.*

P. 122.—"The most common pronunciation of the name of *Miantonomo* will appear, I imagine, in the following couplet from *S. Danforth's* Almanack for 1649:

'And by thy fall comes in the English wo
If it may be by Miantonomo.'"

MS. note by John Farmer.

P. 182.—CAPT. TOM, alias Wattasacompanum. Some of the proceedings against this man have of late been brought to light. His case is one of most melancholy interest, and his fate will ever be deeply regretted; inasmuch as the proof against him, so far as we can discover, would not at any other time have been deemed worthy of a moment's serious consideration. The younger *Eliot* pleaded earnestly for him, that he might even have a new trial, but without avail. In our MS. "Chronicles of the Indians," we have this entry: "22 June, 1676. Death warrant signed for *Captain Tom's* execution." It is directed to "*Edward Mitchelson*, Marshall Generall," who is ordered to see that "Captain Tom Indian and Jno. Oultuck, Indian enemys be hanged on this day after ye lecture till they be dead."

P. 183.—SAMPSON OCCOM. There was a portrait taken of this distinguished Indian while he was in England, painted by *M. Chamberlain*, from which a fine mezzotinto engraving was made by *J. Spilsbury*, and published on a folio sheet. It is thus entitled: "The Reverend Mr. Samson Occom, the first Indian minister that ever was in Europe, and who accompanied the Rev. Nath'l Whitaker, D. D., in an application to Great Britain for Charities to support ye Rev. Dr. Wheelock's Indian Academy, and Missionaries among ye Native Savages of N. America." Published according to act of Parliament, Sept. 20,

1768, by Henry Parker, at No. 82 in Cornhill, London. ***Portrait in possession of the author.***

P. 218.—The following curious document is added, to throw some light on the Narraganset expedition of Dec. 1675 :—

"Whereas at the fireinge of Majo^r^ Appletons Tent at Narragansitt Diuers armes and Clothes were lost by the fire belonging to perticuler persons, a list of whom is taken and in the hands of Capt. Swayne, then Leiut. to Majo^r^ Appleton, who heretofore haue rec. no satisfaction for the same, This Court [Gen. Ct. of Ms.] Doth order that repayration be made by the Country to the persons Damnifyed by the s^d^ fire, and that the Committees of Militia in the severall Townes, doe allow Damage vpon the Accounts afforesd, and enter them amongst the Disbursements of the s^d^ townes. The Deputyes haue past this Desiring the Consent of o^r^ Honor^d^ Magistrates hereto.

William Torrey, Cleric.

15 Sept. 1676. Consented to by the magists. Edw. Rawson, Secrety."

P. 222.—Following other *printed* accounts of the war, we gave the name of "Captain *Crowell*," which should be "*Cowell*." *James Cowell* was of Boston, before and after this war. In our MS. "CHRONICLES," above cited, we have a circumstantial account of the affair which at this time brought him to the notice of the historians. The account is by himself, as he gave it in a deposition, at the trial of *Capt. Tom*, and is as follows :—

"As I was returning from Marlborough to Boston, in the Contoryes searvice, and had 18 men under my conduct, and about 3 miles from Sudbury wee ware Suprysed with divors hundred of Indians, whereof this Indian *Tom* was one, none by a grombleing sign or noyse y^t^ he made; as in my Judgement was ye cause of our bejng ffyored vpon; at which tjme fower of my Company was killed and one wounded; beside ffive horses were disinabled, [being] shot. Vpon Capt. Wadsworth's ingadgen wjth [y^e^] Indians, I wentt backe and buryed ye ffower men which ware killed, whereof was *Thomas* [*Har*] and *Hopkinses* son of Roxbury, Goodman, a son of *Robert Wayles* of Dorchister." "Sworn in Court, 19 June, 1676."

P. 263.—MATOONAS. The following characteristic reflections and observations of Dr. *Increase Mather*, which the consideration of the acts and fate of this chief seemed to excite in his mind, are extracted, as worthy of preservation in this connection :—

"*How often have we prayed, that the Lord would remember the cruelty, treachery, and above all the blasphemy of these heathen!*—This prayer has been heard in Heaven. As for their cruelty, God hath remembered that, many of them falling into the hands of the *Mohawks* or other Indians, who fought in our quarrel, used their enemies after their own kind. And it hath been observed, that the vengeance from the Lord did pursue them presently upon the perpetration of some horrid acts of barbarous cruelty towards such as fell into their murderous hands. And as for their treachery, God hath retaliated that upon them; as for the perfidious *Narragansets*, *Peter* Indian was false and perfidious to them, upon a disgust received amongst them, and directed our army where to find them. Treacherous *Philip*, one of his own men ran away from him, and told Capt. *Church* where that grand enemy had hid himself, the issue of which was, another Indian shot a bullet into the treacherous heart of that covenant-breaking infidel. Yea, many of those cloudy and deceiptful Indians who were taken by Capt. *Church*, would frequently destroy and betray their bloudy and false-hearted comrades. *Matoonas*, who was the first Indian that treacherously shed innocent English blood in *Massachusetts* Colony, he some years before pretended to something of religion, being a professor in general (though never baptized, nor of the in-churched Indians) that so he might the more covertly manage the hellish design of revenge that was harbored in his divelish heart."

P. 263.—"The murder at Woburn here referred to by Hubbard, apparently as perpetrated a little before Philip's war, was not improbably the same as one committed in the west part of Woburn, now Burlington, the story of which has been transmitted there by tradition from time immemorial, and is briefly as follows: On a certain Sabbath, an Indian concealed himself in a hop house, the site of the kiln of which is still pointed out, about a mile from Burlington meeting-house, close to the north side of the road to Bedford, between the houses of Deacon George McIntire and of Miss Ruth Wilson. When he supposed the neighbors generally had gone to meeting, he came out from his lurking-place, and went to the house which then stood on the spot where Miss Wilson's now is. Upon entering, he asked for cider of a young woman that had been left at home.

In compliance with his request, she went to draw some; but upon her return, he knocked her in the head as she reached the top of the cellar stairs. The cellar door was dashed with her blood, the stain of which was never wiped off; and when the house came to be taken down, not far from a century ago, to build another on its site, this blood-stained door was removed as it was to the barn, and there, and at a house in the neighborhood to which it was subsequently conveyed, it continued for years to be exhibited as a memorial of this instance of savage cruelty." [Tradition in the Wilson family, &c.]—*MS. Letter from Rev. Samuel Sewall, of Burlington, Ms., to the Author.*

P. 264.—In the History of Framingham, Ms., by the Rev. Mr. Barry, will be found many important facts relative to the destruction of the family of *Thomas Eames*, of Sudbury, which that diligent author derived from original MSS. We have many others, shedding further light, in our MS. Chronicles above referred to, but our limits do not allow of their admission here. A few items from himself are all we can at present add.

Thomas Eames came to New England about 1634. He served in the Pequot war, after which he was "maimed by the hand of God in his limbs." He was born in the year 1616, and in 1668, was "the father of many children," "but had not one foote of land in ye countray of his owne," and was "very poore." His fortune seems to have been much improved not long after, for when his house was destroyed by the Indians, in 1676, he says, "Yea, I am now left destitute, and bereaved of almost all comforts of my life, and of euery bitt of my estate, which the other day amounted to no less than aboue 350 pounds. And being very lame and aged, and have half a dozen children, each under a dozen years of age." This was about the close of Philip's war, at which time he asks the General Court to grant him the land which had been possessed by those Indians that had destroyed his family; "seeing," he says, "the ten owners and inhabitants yrof are not now extant, 6 of them burned my house and family, 3 of whome haue been hanged, and the others are all fled vnto ye enemy." The government granted him 200 acres of land, but he did not live long to enjoy it. He died on the 25th of January, 1680, æt. 64. For an account of his posterity, consult the *History of Framingham.*

P. 280.—The treaty entered into by the chiefs of the Eastern Indians and English in the midst of Philip's war, seems not to have fallen within the notice of the chroniclers, either of that time or since. Possibly Hubbard *may* refer to in his *Indian Wars.* It being a document of great importance, is here inserted entire, from the *Massachusetts Archives.*

"Pascataqua River, Cochecho, 3 July [1676.]

At a meeting of ye Come appointed by ye Hond Genl. Ct. for to treat ye Inds. of the Eastern Parts in order for ye procuring an Honll Peace with ym. Wee wth ye mutll consent of ye Sagamores Underwritten in behalfe of themselues and ye men—Indians belonging to them being about 300 in Number, have agreed as followeth:

1ly. That hence forwards none of ye said Indians shall offer any violence to ye persons of any English, nor doe any Damage to theyrs Estates in any kind whatsoever. And if any Indian or Indians shall offend herein, they shall bring or cause to bee brought ye offender to some English authority, there to be prosecuted by ye English Lawes according to ye Nature of ye Offence.

2ly. That none of said Indians shall entertain at any time any of our enemies, but shall giue psent notice to ye Comte when any come among them, ingaging to goe forth wth ye English against them (if desired) in order to ye seizing of them. And if any of sd Indians shall themselues at any time bring such or Enemies vnto vs, they shall for their reward haue £3. for each they shall so bring in.

3ly. The Indians performing on their part, as is before expressed, wee ye comittee doe ingage in ye behalfe of ye English not to offer any violence to any of their persons or estates, and if any injury be offered to said Indians by any English, they [their] complaints to Authority, ye offender shall be prosecuted by English Lawes according to yr nature of ye offence. In witness to each and all ye prmises we haue mutually shaken hands and subscribed our names.

Comittee { Richard Waldern, Nic: Shapleigh, Tho: Daniell

Wanalanset, *Sagamore*
Sampson Aboquacemoka
Mr. Wm. Sagamore
Squando *Sagamore*
Dony
Serogumba
Samll Numphow
The mark ⊙ Warockomee."

P. 303.—A more precious document than the subject of this note, we seldom have the satisfaction of laying before the public. It elucidates a passage in New England's history of the deepest interest; and had we space, much explanatory matter might be given.

"Honoured Mother

After my duty and my wifes presented to yourselfe these may inform you of [our] present health of our present being when other of our friends are by the barbarous heathen cut off from having a being in this world The Lord [of] late hath renewed his witnesses against vs, and hath dealt very bitterly with us in that we are deprived of the societie of our nearest friends by the breaking in of the adversarie against vs; On Friday last in the morning your own son with your two sons in Law Anthony and Thomas Bracket and their whole families were killed and taken by the Indians, we know not how, tis certainly known by us that Thomas is slain and his wife and children carried away captiue, and of Anthony and his family we haue no tidings and therefore think that thay might be captivated the night before because of the remoteness of their habitation from neighborhood, Gm Corban and all his family Gm Lewis and his wife, James Ross and all his family, Gm Durham, John Munjoy, and Daniel Wakely, Benjamin Hadwell and all his family are lost, all slain by sun an hour high in the Morning and after, Gm Wallis his dwelling house and none besides his is burnt there are of men slain 11, of women and children 23 killed and taken, we that are alive are forced upon Mr. Andrews his Island to secure our own and the liues of our families we haue but little provision and are so few in number tha we are not able to bury the dead till more strength come to us, the desire of the people to your selfe is that you would be pleased to speak to Mr. Munjoy and Deacon Philips that they would entreat the Governour that forthwith aid might be sent to vs either to fight the enemie out of our borders that our English Corn may be inned in whereby we may comfortably liue or remoue vs out of Danger that we may provide for our selues elsewhere having no more at present but desiring your prayers to God for his preservation of us in these times of danger, I rest Your dutifull Son

Thaddeus Clark.

ffrom Casco-bay 16. 6. 76. remember my Love to my Sister &c.

These ffor his honoured Mother Mrls Elizabeth Harvey living in Boston."

P. 312.—"I have understood that the town of Moultonborough was named in honor of Gen. *Jonathan Moulton*, of Hampton, who was a principal proprietor." *MS. note of John Farmer in a copy of the 3d Ed. of the* Book of the Indians.

P. 313.—Prof. Upham, of Bowdoin College, is the author of the ballad there given. *Farmer, as above cited.*

P. 522.—CAPT. WHITEEYES. In the Narrative of Richard Bard's Adventures among the Indians will be found some interesting details for an enlargement of the life of this chief. See *Loudon's Selection of Ind. Nars.* ii. 57—71.

P. 531.—HALFKING. Besides the different Indian names which we have given for this chief, another has been published in the "*History of Western Pennsylvania.*" He is there called *Tanacharison,* where it is also stated that he died at Harris Ferry, (Harrisburg,) Oct. 1st, 1754. In another part of the same work, (p. 71,) it is stated that he died at the house of *John Harris,* of that place, and was buried by him.

P. 572.—Note ‡. In the Boston Courier of 31th August, 1843, it is mentioned that the *Capt. Newman,* who fell in *St. Clair's* defeat, was of Boston; that he was of the class of 1766, in the Latin school, while of the same class were *Isaac Coffin,* since *Admiral Sir Isaac,* Dr. *Jona. Homer,* late of Newton, Dr. *James Freeman,* &c.

P. 683. In our note stating the age and death of *Daniel Boone,* we have made an alteration in conformity to information received from Rev. J. M. Peck. It now agrees with what he has since published in his excellent life of the old *Pioneer,* and corresponds very nearly with the facts in *Niles's Register,* printed at the time.

INDIAN LANGUAGES OF THE PACIFIC STATES AND TERRITORIES.*

BY ALBERT S. GATSCHET.

A few decenniums of research in our newly acquired western dominions have acquainted us with the singular fact that clusters of very numerous, and for the larger part narrowly circumscribed areas of languages exist in these vast and remote regions. In California, and north of it, one stock of language is generally represented by several, sometimes by a large number of dialects and sub-dialects; but there are instances, as in Shasta and in Klamath, where a stock is represented by one idiom only, which never had diverged into dialects, or the sub-dialects of which have become extinct in the course of time. Although certain resemblances between them may be traced in their phonological morphological character, they are totally distinct in their radicals, and by this criterion we are enabled to attempt their classification by stocks or families. Any other than a *genealogical* classification is at present impossible, for we do not possess even the most necessary grammatical data for the majority of the languages spoken along the Pacific coast.

For the western languages, and those of the great Interior Basin, our main sources of information are (and will be for many years to come) vocabularies of one hundred to two hundred terms each. Those obtained and published frequently bear the stamp of dilettantism, sometimes that of profound ignorance of linguistic science on the part of word-collectors, who wholly underrated the great difficulty of taking down a set of disconnected words in a totally unknown and phonetically unwieldy idiom. These word-gatherers would have fared much better, and collected more reliable material, if they had taken short sentences of popular import or texts containing no abstract ideas. For an Indian is not accustomed to think of terms incoherent, or words disconnected from others, or of abstract ideas, but uses his words merely as integral parts of a whole sentence, or in connection with others. This is the true cause of the large incorporative power of the American tongues, which in many of them culminates in an extended polysynthetism, and embodies whole sentences in one single verbal form.

At a time when the principal languages and dialects of Asia, Africa and Australasia, the living as well as the extinct, are being investigated with uncommon ardor; myths, popular songs, dirges and speeches collected, published and commented upon with erudition and corresponding success, very few of the American languages, north and south, have been the object of thorough research. There is no scarcity of thorough linguists among us, but the reason for their want of activity in this direction simply lies in the want of proper encouragement from the authorities, the publishers, the press and the public. This is very discouraging, we confess; but it shall not hinder us from examining somewhat closer this topic, and from trying to get at the true facts.

The general public is very ignorant of languages and linguistics, and as a rule confounds linguistics with philology. Many people have a horror of philology because the Latin and Greek paradigms which they had to study in college classes recall to them the dreariest days of compulsory education, juvenile misery and birch-rod executions. From these two languages they infer, superficially enough, that the study of all other foreign tongues must involve similar mental torments. Others believe that the Indian languages are not real tongues, deserving to be termed so; but only thwarted productions of the diseased heathen mind, because they do not agree with classical models nor with the grammar of the primeval language of the world, the Hebrew, "which was spoken in Paradise."

The majority, however, suppose that any Indian language is simply a gibberish not worth bothering about; they ought to remember that every language, even the most harmonious and perfect, is a gibberish to those who do

* Reprinted from *The Magazine of American History* (New York), for March, 1877.

not understand it, sounding unpleasantly to their ears, because they are unaccustomed to its cadences and phonetic laws. The mastering of a language is the only remedy against a certain repugnance to it on the side of the listener.

A further objection which is sometimes raised against studying the tongues of the red man, consists in the erroneous assertion that they have no literature of their own. This statement is founded on a profound ignorance of existing facts, and moreover, is only the expression of the old-fashioned, mistaken idea that languages should be studied only on account of their literatures, thus confounding philology with linguistics. Indians never did and do not write down their mental productions, simply because they do not trace their immediate origin from the Eastern races, from whom we have received the priceless gift of alphabetical writing; but that they really possess such productions, as well as the Malays, Polynesians and South Africans, no one can doubt who has read of Indian prophets, orators and story-tellers, with their fluency and oratorical powers, who has listened to their multiform, sometimes scurrilous mythological tales or yarns, heard their war-shouts, the words accompanying their dancing tunes, or in the darkness of the night overheard some of their lugubrious, heart-moving dirges sung by wailing women, as they slowly marched in file around the corpse of some relative, the whole scene lit up by the flickering flames of the lurid camp-fires. A volume of Schoolcraft's Indians contains a large number of Odjibway songs, and the author of this article has himself obtained over seventy most interesting and popular songs from the Cayuses, Warm Springs, Klamaths, Taos, Iroquois and Abnákis, in their original form. So the white race alone is to blame for its imperfect knowledge of the unwritten, often highly poetical productions of an illiterate race.

The science of linguistics is of so recent a date, that few men have yet grasped its real position among the other sciences. We must henceforth consider it as a *science of nature*, and reject the old conception of it as a science of the human mind. Stylistics and rhetorics of a language may be called the province of the human mind, but language itself is a product of nature, produced through human instrumentality. Man does not invent his language, any more than a bird does its twittering, or a tree its leaves. It requires a whole nation to produce a language, and even then such nation must start from phonetic elements already understood.

The innumerable agencies which give to a country its climate will also, by length of time, shape man and his language. Nothing is fortuitous or arbitrary in human speech and its historical developments; the most insignificant word or sound has its history, and the linguist's task is to investigate its record. Thus every language on this globe is perfect, but perfect only for the purpose it is intended to fulfill; Indian thought runs in another, more concrete direction than ours, and therefore Indian speech is shaped very differently from indogermanic models, which we, in our inherited and unjustified pride, are prone to regard as the only models of linguistic perfection. The Indian neglects to express with accuracy some relations which seem of paramount importance to us, as tense and sex, but his language is largely superior to ours in the variety of its personal pronouns, in many forms expressing the mode of action, or the idea of property and possession, and the relations of the person or persons addressed to the subject of the sentence.

Another prejudice against the Indian tongues is derived from the filthy or uninviting appearance of the red-skinned man himself. It is true that most Indians seem very miserable, disgusting, poor, silly, even grotesque and comical; yet this is partly due to the state of degradation to which he has been reduced by the land-grabbing Anglo-American settler, who has deprived him of his former, natural ways of subsistence; but it is also a characteristic of his cinnamon-complexioned race, and has been so for times immemorial. In the numerous settlements, where the condition of the Indian has undoubtedly undergone a great change for the better, through the advent of the white population, he seems just as miserable, shy, sad and filthy as before. To draw conclusions from the exterior appearance of a people on their language, and to suppose that a man not worth looking at cannot speak a language worth studying, would be the acme of superficiality, and worthy only of those who in their folly trust to appearances alone.

Pursuant to these intimations, I judge that the only means of bringing about a favorable change in public sentiment concerning the tongues of our aborigines, is a better understanding of the real object and purpose of linguistic science. Languages are living organisms, natural growths, genuine productions of race and country, and scientifically speaking, it is as important to investigate them as to describe minutely a curious tree, a rare plant, a strange insect or aquatic animal. But to gather information on them with success, a much more accurate method of transcription or transliteration than those generally used by word-collectors must be adopted. The old nonsensical method of using the English orthography, so utterly unscientific and unbearable to the sight of every instructed man, has at last been discarded almost universally. Only scientific alphabets must be here employed, and an alphabet can be considered as such only when *one* sound is constantly expressed by *one and the same* letter only. Such alphabets have been proposed by G. Gibbs, Professors Richard Lepsius, Haldeman, Alex. Ellis, and many others, and it would be a fitting subject for a congress of linguists to decide which system is the most appropriate for transcribing Indian tongues. Cursive Latin characters must be used, and in some cases, altered by diacritical marks, to convey peculiar meanings; the invention of new alphabetic systems or syllabaries like those of Sequoyah, and the hooks and crooks recently used for transcribing Cree and other northern tongues are not a help to science, because they are not *readily* legible or reducible to the accepted old-world systems of transcribing languages. A debate may also be started by a linguistic congress, what term should be employed instead of *Indian*, which is unsatisfactory in many respects; a thorough remodeling of the terminology used in Indian grammars would form another fruitful theme of discussion. Our indogermanic ideas of grammar must be entirely disregarded if we would write a correct grammatical sketch of some Indian language.

The vocabularies,* in the shape as we possess them now, are useful in many respects. They do not give us much information about the structure of the languages, but serve at least for classifying purposes, and the small number of them which bear the stamp of accuracy in their notation of the accent and the use of a scientific alphabet, at least give a foothold for Indian phonology.

But men of science need a great deal more than this. Language is a living organism, and to study it, we must not only have the loose bones of its body, but the life-blood which is throbbing in its veins and forms the real essence of human speech. Not the stems or words alone, but the inflectional forms, the syntactical shaping of the spoken word and the sentence itself are desideratums mostly craved for. Linguists must therefore, as reliable grammars and full dictionaries (all the words properly accentuated!) cannot be expected at once, place their hopes in collections of *texts* illustrating the native customs and manners, the religious beliefs, superstitions, scraps of Indian history, speeches, dialogues, songs and dirges, descriptions of manufactured articles, and of the houses, tools, implements and dress of each nation and tribe visited.

These texts should be given *in the Indian language*, and accompanied by a very accurate, and if possible, an interlinear and verbal translation of the items. All the commentaries and remarks needed for a full understanding of the texts should be added to it. The more material is furnished in this way, the better our linguists will be enabled to disclose the hidden scientific treasures stored up in these curious, but now almost unknown, forms of human speech, and to present them to the world, in the shape of grammars, dictionaries and anthologies of aboriginal prose and poetry. To the ethnologist such texts will be just as valuable as to the historian and the linguist.

THE LANGUAGES OF THE WESTERN SLOPE.

A most singular fact disclosed by the topography of language-stocks all over the world is the enormous difference of the *areas* occupied by the various families. In the eastern hemisphere, we see the Uralo-Altaic, the Chinese, the Indogermanic, Semitic and Dravidian, the Pullo and the Congo-

* In 1875, the 29th year from its foundation, the Smithsonian Institution, in Washington, had collected texts, phraseology, and 771 vocabularies of about 200 words each, but for unknown reasons had published only a small portion of this enormous linguistic material.

Kafrian or Ba'-ntu family of languages, extending over areas much wider or as wide as the Tinné, Shóshoni, Algónkin, Dakóta, Cháhta-Máskoki and Guarani stock, while small areas are, perhaps, as numerous in the eastern hemisphere as in the western. Their size evidently depends on the configuration and surface-quality of the lands, which again determine the mode of the subsistence of their inhabitants.

The natives of a country, when not influenced by the civilization of the white race, will in barren plains, steppes, prairies and woodland, generally become hunters; on the shores of the sea and on the banks of the larger rivers, they will resort to fishing, and sometimes, when settled on the coast, turn pirates or form smaller maritime powers, while the inhabitants of tablelands will till the fields, plant fructiferous trees, or collect esculent roots for their sustenance. Of these three modes of sustenance we see frequently two combined in one tribe. The fishers live peacefully and in *small* hordes, because large settlements, on *one* spot of a river bank at least, could not be supplied at all seasons of the year with a sufficient supply of fish from the river. Hunters become, from their nomadic habits, accustomed to a restless, adventurous life, and in their thus acquired warlike disposition will constantly threaten their weaker neighbors; if opportunity offers itself will declare war, overwhelm and enslave or destroy them, and thereby extend the dominion of their own language over a wider area. Agricultural pursuits bear in themselves the germs of steadiness, of order and progress; countries settled and improved by agriculturists will gradually, when the population becomes more dense, consolidate into oligarchies or monarchies, generally of a despotic character. Such political bodies have frequently absorbed neighboring communities engaged in similar pursuits, and turned with them into powerful empires, as in the case of the Aztecs, Mayas, Chibchas and Quichhuas, in the western hemisphere. For obvious reasons pastoral pursuits were almost entirely unknown in America, but were powerful agents of culture in Asia and Europe, since they facilitated the transition from the hunter or nomadic state to the state of agriculturists.

California and portions of the Columbia river basin, with their numerous rivers and the enormous quantity of salmon, trout and lamprey eel ascending annually their limpid waters, were essentially countries occupied by fisher-tribes, and before the advent of the white man, are supposed to have harbored a dense native population. Among these fisher-tribes we also find the smallest areas of languages; six of them are crowded on the two banks of the Klamath river and many more around the Sacramento, although these streams do not exceed in length, respectively, 250 and 400 miles. To produce or preserve so many small language families, totally distinct from each other in their radicals, these tribes must have lived during very long periods in a state of comparative isolation, and have remained almost untouched by foreign invaders, protected as they were by the sea-coast, and by the high-towering wall of the snow-capped Sierra Nevada.

In the wide basin of the upper Columbia river several tribes hunting the bear, buffalo, elk, deer and antelope, roam over the thinly populated prairies, and occupy enormous tracts of barren and sage-brush plains. Hunting tribes need a wide extent of territory, and when it is refused to them they will fight for it. Thus originate the constant wars of extermination among many of these tribes, and their encroachments over others in regard to territory. Of this we find the most conspicuous instances among the nomadic tribes roving between the Rocky mountains and the Mississippi river.

In their morphological character the languages of America do not differ materially from the Asiatic tongues of agglutinative structure, except by their more developed power of polysynthetism. But in many of their number this faculty remains only in an embryonic state, and by dint of a far-going analysis, some of them approach the structure of our modern European analytic languages. Still, in a number of others, the incorporative tendency prevails in a high degree; they are synthetic as much as the Latin, Greek or Gothic—many of them superlatively so. They use not only prefixes and affixes, as we do, but also infixes, viz.: particles, or particle-fragments, inserted into the stem. As a general thing, American languages are not sex-denoting, though we find a distinction of sex in the dual of the Iroquois *verb*, and in some Central American verb-inflections, where *he* is distinguished from *she* in the personal pronoun. A true substantive verb *to be* is not found in any American language,* and the word-stems have not undergone that process of thorough differention between noun and verb which we observe in German, English, and French. These three languages we call accentuating, since the quantity of their syllables is of relative importance only, the influence of the accentuation being paramount. In many American languages we observe, on the contrary, that accent shifts from syllable to syllable, though only in a restricted number of words, and that instead of the accent length and brevity of the syllables receive closer attention. Such idioms we may call quantitating languages, for their system of prosody does not seem to differ much from those of the classical languages.

No plausible cause can as yet be assigned for the frequent perhaps universal, interchangeability of *b* with *p*, *d* with *t* and *n*, *g* with *k*, *χ*, and the lingual *k*, *m* with *b* and *v* (*w*), *hh* with *k*, *χ*; but as there is nothing fortuitous in nature or in language, a latent cause *must* exist for this peculiarity. No preceding or following sound seems to have any influence on this alternating process, and the vowels alternate in a quite similar manner.

From these general characteristics, to which many others could be added, we pass over to those peculiarities which are more or less specific to the languages of the Pacific slope. It is not possible to state any absolute, but only some relative and gradual differences between these western tongues and those of the east, of which we give the following:

The generic difference of animate, inanimate, and neuter nouns, is of little influence on the grammatical forms of the Pacific languages. A so-called *plural* form of the transitive and intransitive verb exists in Selish dialects, in Klamath, Mutsun, San Antonio (probably also in Santa Barbara,) and in the Shóshoni dialects of Kauvuya and Gaitchin. Duplication of the entire root, or of a portion of it, is extensively observed in the formation of frequentative and other derivative verbs, of augmentative and diminutive nouns, of adjectives (especially when designating colors), etc., in the Selish and Sahaptin dialects, in Cayuse, Yakon, Klamath, Pit River, Chokoyem, Cop-éh, Cushna, Santa Barbara, Pima, and is very frequent in the native idioms of the Mexican states. The root or, in its stead, the initial syllable, is redoubled regularly, or frequently, for the purpose of forming a (distributive) plural of nouns and verbs in Selish dialects, in Klamath, Kizh, Santa Barbara, and in the Mexican languages of the Pimas, Opatas (including Heve), Tarahumaras, Tepèguanas, and Aztecs.

A definite article *the*, or a particle corresponding to it in many respects, is appended to the noun, and imparts the idea of actuality to the verb in Sahaptin, Klamath, Kizh, Gaitchin, Kauvuya, Mohave. In San Antonio this article is placed *before* the noun. The practice of appending various classifiers or determinatives to the cardinal numerals, to point out the different qualities of the objects counted, seems to be general in the Pacific tongues, for it can be traced in the Selish proper, in the Nisqualli (a western Selish dialect), in Yákima, in Klamath, in Noce or Noze, and in Aztec. In De la Cuestas' Mutsun grammar, however, no mention is made of this synthetic feature.

The phonological facts most generally observed throughout the coast lands, from Puget sound to San Diego, are as follows; Absence of the labial sound *F* and of our rolling *R* (the guttural *kh* or *χ* is often erroneously rendered by *r*): comparative scarcity of the medial or soft mutes as initial and final consonants of words; frequency of the *k*, or croaking, lingual *k*, identical with the *c castañuelas* of the south; sudden stops of the voice in the midst of a word or sentence; preponderance of clear and surd vowels over nasalized vowels. From all the information obtainable at present, we can properly infer that all the above mentioned peculiarities will by future investigators be discovered to exist also in many *other* tongues of our Pacific states. In the northern sections the consonantic elements predominate to an enormous degree, sometimes stifling the utterance of the vowels; many southern tongues, on the contrary, show a tendency towards vocalism, though the consonantic frame of the words is not in any instance disrupted or obliterated by the vocalic element, as we observe it in Polynesia. Languages, with a sonorous, sweet, soft, and vocalic utterance, and elementary vocalism, are the Mohave, Hualapai, Meewoc, Tuólumne, and Wintoon (and Kalapupa further north), while the dialects

* Full and detailed information concerning the structure prevailing in American languages will be found in Prof. J. H. Trumbull's article on *Indian Languages*, in Johnson's New Cyclopædia, vol. II. New York, 1875.

of the Santa Barbara stock seem to occupy an intermediate position between the above and the northern languages.

Unnumbered tongues have in the course of centuries disappeared from the surface of these western lands, and no monuments speak to us of their extent, or give a glimpse at the tribes which used them. Many others are on the verge of extinction: they are doomed to expire under the overpowering influx of the white race. Other languages labor under the continued influence of linguistic corruption and intermixture with other stocks, and the Chinook jargon seems to make havoc among the tongues of the Columbia river. To transmit these languages to posterity in their unadulterated state, is not yet altogether impossible in the decennium in which we live, and would be a highly meritorious undertaking. It would be equivalent almost to rescuing these remarkable linguistic organisms from undeserved oblivion.

In the subsequent pages I attempt to give a synoptical survey of our Pacific language-stocks west of the Rocky mountains (excluding the pueblos of New Mexico and Arizona), based on the writings of such predecessors as George Gibbs, Latham, H. H. Bancroft, Stephen Powers, and I have taken pains to carefully compare their data with the linguistic material available. For obvious reasons, I have found myself frequently constrained to dissent from them, and I claim the decision of men of undoubted competency concerning the correctness of my classifications.

Shóshoni.—The Shóshoni family borders and encircles all the other stocks of the Pacific slope of the United States, on the *eastern side*, and my enumeration, therefore, commences with the dialects of this populous and widely-scattered inland nation. The natives belonging ro this race occupy almost the whole surface of the great American inland basin, extending from the Rocky mountains to the Sierra Nevada. To the northeast, and all along the western border, they have crossed these towering land-marks, constructed by nature itself, but do not appear to have interfered considerably with the original distribution of the tribes in the Californian valleys and mountain recesses. The dispositions evinced by them are more of a passive and indolent than of an aggressive, offending or implacable nature, though they are savages in the truest sense of the word; some bands of Utahs, for instance, really seem too low-gifted ever to become a cause for dread to peaceful neighbors. We do not yet understand any of their numerous dialects thoroughly, but as far as the southern dialects are concerned, a preponderence of surd and nasalized *a*, *o* and *u* vowels over others is undoubted. They all possess a form for the plural of the noun; the Comanche, even one for the dual. Their dialects are sketched in the rough as follows:

Snake.—This dialect received its name irom the Shóshoni, Lewis, or Snake river, on whose shores one of the principal bands of Snake Indians was first seen. Granville Stuart, in his *Montana as it is* (New York, 1865), gives the following ethnological division: *Washakeeks*, or Green river Snakes, in Wyoming; *Tookarikkah*, or Salmon river Snakes (literally, Mountain-sheep eaters), in Idaho. These two bands he calls genuine Snakes. Smaller bands are those of the *Salt Lake Diggers* in Utah, the *Salmon Eaters* on Snake river, the root-digging *Bannocks* or *Panasht*, on Boisé, Malheur and Owyhee rivers, and a few others, all of whom differ somewhat in their mode of speech. Snakes of the *Yahooshkin* and *Walpahpe* bands were settled recently on Klamath reserve in Oregon, together with a few Piutes.

Utah (*Yutah, Eutaw, Ute;* Spanish, *Ayote*), is spoken in various dialects in parts of Utah, Wyoming, and Arizona territories, and in the western desert regions of Colorado, where a reservation of Confederated Utes has been established, with an area of twelve millions of acres. To draw an accurate limit between the numerous bands of the Utahs and those of the Snakes and Payutes seems to be impossible at present, since all of them show the same national characteristics; I give the names of some of the more important bands of Utah Indians, which no doubt differ to a certain degree in their sub-dialects: *Elk Mountain Utahs* in southeastern Utah; *Pah-Vants* on Sevier lake, southeast of Salt lake; *Sampitches*, on Sevier lake and in Sampitch valley; *Tash-Utah* in northern Arizona; *Uinta-Utahs* in Unitah valley reserve; *Weber-Utahs*, northeast of Salt Lake; *Yampa-Utahs*, south of the Uinta-Utahs.

Payute (*Pah-Utah, Pi-Ute*—literally, River Utah; Utah, as spoken on Colorado river), a sonorous, vocalic dialect, spoken throughout Nevada, in parts of Arizona and California. The dialect of the Southern Payutes on Colorado river closely resembles that of the neighboring *Chemehuevis*, but differs materially from that spoken in northern Nevada, and from the dialect of Mono and Inyo counties, California. Other Payute tribes are the Washoes and Gosh-Utes.

Kauvuya (*Cáwio;* Spanish, *Cahuillo*). This branch of the Shóshoni stock prevails from the Cabezon mountains and San Bernardino valley, California, down to the Pacific coast, and is at present known to us in four dialects: *Serrano*, or mountain dialect, spoken by Indians who call themselves Takhtam, which means men, people; *Kauvuya*, in and around San Bernardino valley; *Gaitchin* or *Kechi*, a coast dialect in use near the missions of San Juan Capistrano and San Luis Rey de Francia; *Netēla* is another name for it; *Kizh*, spoken in the vicinity of the mission of San Gabriel by a tribe calling itself Tobikhar, or settlers, and of San Fernando mission, almost extinct. The two last mentioned dialects considerably differ among themselves, and from the mountain dialects of the Takhtam and Kauvuyas.

Comanche, formerly called *Hietan*, *Jĕtan*, *Na-uni*, in northern Texas, in New Mexico and in the Indian Territory. They are divided into three principal sections, and their language resembles in a remarkable degree that of the Snakes.

Various Shóshoni dialects have largely influenced the stock of words of a few idioms, which otherwise are foreign to this family. We mean the Pueblo idioms of New Mexico, the Moqui of Arizona, and the Kiowa, spoken on Red river and its tributaries. There exists a deep-seated connection between the Shóshoni stock and several languages of northern Mexico in the radicals, as well as in the grammatical inflections, which has been pointed out and proved in many erudite treatises by Professor T. C. E. Buschmann, once the collaborator of the two brothers Alexander and William von Humboldt.

YUMA.—The Indians of the Yuma stock are scattered along the borders of the Lower Colorado and its affluents, the Gila river and the Bill Williams fork. Their name is derived from one of the tribes—the Yumas—whom their neighbors frequently call Cuchans or Ko-u-tchans. Some dialects, as the Mohave, possess a large number of sounds or phonetic elements, the English *th* amongst them, and are almost entirely built up of syllables which contain but one consonant followed by a vowel. The verb possesses a plural form. At present we know of about seven dialects: *Mohave* (Spanish *Mojave*), on Mohave river and on Colorado river reservation; *Hualapai*, on Colorado river agency; *Maricopa*, formerly Cocomaricopa, on Pima reservation, Middle Gila river; *Tonto*, Tonto-Apaches or *Gohun*, on Gila river and north of it; *Cocopa*, near Fort Yuma and south of it; *Cuchan* or Yuma, on Colorado river; their former seats were around Fort Yuma; *Diegeño* or *Comoyei*, around San Diego, along the coast, on New river, etc.

Scattered tribes are the kóninos, and the Yavipais or Yampais, east of the Colorado river. The term *opa*, composing several of these tribal names, is taken from the Yuma, and means *man;* the definite article *-tch* joined to it forms the word *ĕpach* or *Apache*, man, men, people.

PIMA.—Dialects of this stock are spoken on the middle course of the Gila river, and south of it on the elevated plains of southern Arizona and northern Sonora (Pimería alta, Pimería bá ja). The Pima does not extend into California, unless the extinct, historical *Cajuenches*, mentioned in Mexican annals, spoke one of the Pima (or Pijmo, Pimo) dialects. *Pima*, on Pima reserve, Gila river, a sonorous, root-duplicating idiom; *Névome*, a dialect probably spoken in Sonora, of which we possess a reliable Spanish grammar, published in Shea's Linguistics; *Pápago*, on Pápago reserve in southwestern Arizona. The Pima language bears a close relationship to the various dialects of the Opata family and to a number of languages spoken in the interior Mexican states.

SANTA BARBARA.—We are not cognizant of any national name given to the race of Indians who spoke the intricate dialects of this language-family. Its northern dialects differ as much from the southern as Minitaree does from Santee-Dakota, or Scandinavian from the dialects of southern Germany.

The southern dialects are: *Santa Inez*, near Santa Inez mission; liturgic specimens, translations of parts of catechisms, etc., of this dialect, and of that of Santa Barbara mission, were forwarded to the Smithsonian Institution by Mr. Alex. S. Taylor, of Santa Barbara city; *Santa Barbara*, around Santa Barbara mission, closely related to *Kasuá* or *Kashwáh* (Spanish *Cieneguita*), three miles from Santa Barbara mission; *Santa Cruz island*, this dialect reduplicated the root in forming the plural of nouns, and probably extended over the other islands in its vicinity; it is extinct now.

The northern dialects are: *San Luis Obispo;* stock of words largely mixed with Mutsun terms: the Indian name of the locality was Tixilini; *San Antonio*, spoken at or near San Antonio mission, known to us through Padre Sitjar's dictionary. The plural of nouns is formed in more than twelve different ways, and the phonology is quite intricate.

MUTSUN.—This name, of unknown signification, has been adopted to designate a family of dialects extending from the environs of San Juan Bautista, Cal., in a northwestern direction up to and beyond the bay of San Francisco and the straits of Karquines, in the east reaching probably to San Joaquin river. It is identical with the language called *Runsien* or *Rumsen*, and shows a great development of grammatical forms. Its alphabet lacks the sounds of *b, d, f*, and of our rolling *r*. We can distinguish the following dialects: *San Juan Bautista;* Padre F. Felipe Arroyo de la Cuesta has left us a grammar and an extensive phraseological collection in this idiom, which were published by John G. Shea, in two volumes of his Linguistic Series; *Mission of Carmelo*, near the port of Monterey, the Eslenes inhabited its surroundings; *Santa Cruz*, north of the bay of Monterey, vocabulary in *New York Historical Magazine*, 1864 (Feb.), page 68; *La Soledad mission*—if this dialect, of whose grammatical structure we know nothing, really belongs to the Mutsun stock, it is at least largely intermixed with San Antonio elements; the tribe living around the mission was called Sakhones; *Costaño*, on the bay of San Francisco, spoken by the five extinct tribes of the Ahwastes, Olhones, Altahmos, Romonans, Tulomos. See Schoolcraft's Indians, vol. II, page 494.

Under the heading of "Mutsun" I subjoin here a series of dialects spoken north of the bay of San Francisco, which, judging from the large number of Mutsun words, probably belong to this stock, but show also a large amount of Chocuyem words, which dialect is perhaps not, according to our present information, a Mutsun dialect. This point can be decided only when its grammatical elements, as verbal inflection, etc., will be ascertained.

The dialects, showing affinities with Mutsun, are as follows: *Olamentke*, spoken on the former Russian colony about Bodega bay, Marin Co., vocabulary in Wrangell, Nachrichten, etc., St. Petersburg, 1839, and reprinted by Prof. Buschmann; *San Rafael mission*, Marin Co., vocabulary taken by Mr. Dana, printed in Hale's Report of Exploring Expedition, and in *Transactions of American Ethnological Society*, II, page 128; the words are almost identical with those of Chocuyem; *Talatui* or *Talantui*, on Kassima river, an eastern tributary of the Sacramento, is clearly a dialect of Chocuyem; vocabulary by Dana, *Tr. Am. Ethn. Soc.*, vol. II; *Chokuyem* or *Tchookoyem* was the name of a small tribe once inhabiting Marin county, north of the Golden Gate; their language extended across San Antonio creek into Sonoma valley, Sonoma Co. G. Gibbs' vocabulary, published in Schoolcraft, III, 428-sq, discloses the singular fact that almost all Chocuyem words are *dissyllabic*, and frequently begin and terminate in vowels. A Lord's prayer in Chocuyem was published in Duflot de Morfras' Explorations, II, 390, and reproduced by Bancroft; the name of the tribe living around the mission of San Rafael was Youkiousmé, which does not sound very alike, nor very different from Chocuyem. Some of the more important terms agreeing in the Chocuyem and in the Mutsun of San Bautista, are as follows:

ENGLISH.	CHOCUYEM.	MUTSUN.
head	móloh	mogel
teeth	ki-iht	sit, si-it
foot	coyok	coro
house	kotchâ	kuka, ruca
white	pahkiss	palcasmin
black	mūlūtá	humulusmin
I, myself	kani	can
thou	mī	men
two	osha	utsgin
father	api	appa
mother	enu	anan

The supposition that the Chocuyem belongs to the Mutsun stockis greatly strengthened by the mutual correspondence of these terms, but cannot be stated yet as existing on this ground alone, for the terms for most numerals, parts of human body, and those for fire, water, earth, sun, moon, and star disagree entirely.

The Chocuyem stock probably included also the Petaluma or Yolhios, as well as the Tomalo and other dialects spoken beyond the northern limit of Marin county. From a notice published by Alex. S. Taylor, Esq., we learn that Padre Quijas, in charge of Sonoma mission from 1835 to 1842, composed an extensive dictionary of the idiom spoken in the vicinity of this religious establishment.

YOCUT.—This tribe lives in the Kern and Tulare basins, and on the middle course of the San Joaquin river. Consolidated in 1860 into one coherent body by their chief, Pascual, the Yocuts show more national solidarity than any other California nation. In the *Overland Monthly*, Mr. Stephen Powers gave a sketch of this remarkable tribe, and described at length one of their terrific nocturnal weeping dances, called Kotéwachil. The following tribes and settlements may be mentioned here: *Taches* (*Tatches*), around Kingston; *Chewenee*, in Squaw valley; *Watooga*, on King's river; *Chookchancies*, in several villages; a *King's river tribe*, whose vocabulary is mentioned in Schoolcraft's Indians, vol. IV, 413–414; *Coconoons*, on Merced river, their vocabulary in Schoolcraft, IV, 413; a tribe formerly living at Dent's Ferry, on Stanislaus river, in the Sierra Nevada of Calaveras county, vocabulary given by Alex. S. Taylor in his *California Farmer*. In former years many individuals of the Yocut nation were carried as captives to San Luis Obispo, on the coast, and were put to work in the service of the mission.

MEEWOC.—Stephen Powers (*Overland Monthly*, April, 1873), calls the Meewoc tribe the largest in California in population, and in extent. "Their ancient dominion reached from the snow-line of the Sierra Nevada to the San Joaquin river, and from the Cósumnes to the Fresno: mountains, valleys and plains were thickly peopled." Bands of this tribe lived in a perfectly naked state in the Yosemite valley, when this spot first came into notice. The language is very homogeneous for a stretch of one hundred and fifty miles, and the radicals and words are remarkably vocalic. Meewoc, mi-ua, mivie, is the word for Indian, and *osoamit*, whence Yosemite, which means the grizzly bear; *wakálumni* is a river, hence Mokélumne was formed by corruption; *kossumi* a salmon, hence Cósumnes river. Some of the Meewoc bands were called by the following names, which probably represent as many dialects or sub-dialects: *Choomteyas*, on middle Merced river; *Cawnees*, on Cósumne river; *Yulónees*, on Sutter creek; *Awnaees*, in Yosemite valley; *Chowchillas*, on middle Chowchilla river; *Tuólumne*, on Tuólumne river. Their vocabulary was taken by Adam Johnson, and published in Schoolcraft's Indians, IV. 413. *Four Creek Indians;* vocabulary published in the San Francisco *Wide West* in July, 1856, under the name of Kahwéyah, but differing considerably in the words given by Mr. Powers. Some further Meewoc bands are called after the cardinal points of the compass.

MEIDOO.—The Meidoo nation formerly extended from Sacramento river to the snow-line, and from Big Chico creek to Bear river, the cognate Neeshenams from Bear river to the Cósumnes, where the language changed abruptly. The Meidoos are a joyful, merry and dance-loving race. Their language is largely made up of vocalic elements; vowels and n's terminate more than one-half of their words. We possess vocabularies of the following bands: *Yuba*, opposite the mouth of Yuba river, a tributary of Feather river. A collection of some forty words was made by Lieut. Edward Ross, and published in *Historical Magazine* of New York, 1863, page 123. *Cushna*, on mountains of South Yuba river, Nevada county. Vocabulary by Adam Johnson, an Indian agent, published in Schoolcraft, II, page 494. *Pujuni*, or Bushumnes, on western bank of Sacramento river. *Secumnes*, also west of Sacramento river. Short vocabularies of both dialects were collected by Mr. Dana, and reprinted in *Tr. Am. Ethnol. Soc.*, vol. II. *Neeshenam*, south of Bear river; Powers separates them as a distinct nation from the Meidoos; but from the words given, it appears that both speak dialects of the same language. Their bands are partly called after the points of the compass. Of other Meidoo tribes or bands, we mention the *Otákumne*, in the Otakey settlement; the *Ollas*, opposite mouth of Bear river, and the *Concows* or Cancows, in Concow valley. Mr. Powers gives the names of about a dozen more. Perhaps the little tribe of the undersized *Noces* or *Nozes*, in Round mountain, Oak run and vicinity, should be classified here, because a few of their numerals, which almost all end in *mona*, agree with those of the Cushnas. Mr. Powers supposes these and the ferocious *Mill Creek Indians* to be of foreign origin.

WINTOON.—The timid, superstitious, and grossly sensual race of the Wintoons is settled on both sides of upper Sacramento and upper Trinity rivers, and is found also in the lower course of Pit river. Stephen Powers calls their language rich in forms and synonyms; their dialect, studied by Oscar Loew, forms the plurals of its nouns by means of a final *-t* preceded by a reduplicated vowel of the root. Loew's vocabulary, published with one of the Uinta-Utah and thirteen others by the author of this article in his recent publication, *Zwölf Sprachen aus dem Südwesten Nord-Amerikas; Weimar*, 1876 (150 pages), offers a few words of very difficult guttural pronunciation; but in general the language (called Digger in that vocabulary) is of a soft and sonorous character.

Some of the more noteworthy Wintoon tribes are as follows: *Dowpum Wintoons*, on Cottonwood creek, the nucleus of this race: *Noemocs* or southern people; *Poomeocs* or eastern people; *Nome Lakees* or western talkers; *Wikainmocs*, on extreme upper Trinity river and Scott mountain; *Normocs*, on Hay Fork: *Tehámas*, near Tehāma Town; *Mag Reading Wintoons*, vocabulary taken about 1852, by Adam Johnson, and published in Schoolcraft, IV, p. 414. *Cop-ēh.* A tribe of this name was found at the head of Putos creek, the words of which are mostly dissyllabic, and partake of the vocalic nature of southern languages.

Stephen Powers calls by the name *Patween* a race inhabiting the west side of the middle and lower Sacramento, Caché and Putos creek, and Napa valley. Physically, the Patweens do not differ from the Wintoons. Their complexion varies from brassy bronze to almost jet-black, they walk pigeon-toed, and have very small and depressed heads, the arch over their eyes forming sometimes a sharp ridge. They are socially disconnected and have no common name; but their language does not differ much in its dialects, and belongs, as far as we are acquainted with it, to the Wintoon stock. Powers (*Overland Monthly*, December, 1874, p. 542, sqq.) classes under this heading a number of clans or bands, of which we mention: *Suisuns*, in Suisun valley, Solano Co.; *Ululatos*, in Ulatus creek, near Vacaville; *Lewytos* and *Putos*, in Putos creek; *Napas*, in Napa valley; *Lolsels*, east of Clear lake; *Corusies*, near Colusa, on Sacramento river; *Chenposels*, on Caché creek; *Noyukies*, intermarried with Wintoons, on Stony creek; *Guilulos* or *Guillilas*, in Sonora valley. A Lord's prayer given in their dialect, by Duflot de Mofras, II, p. 391, differs entirely from the Chocuyem, hence the Guilulo may belong to the Patween stock. The words of the *Napa* root-diggers, collected by Major Bartlett, and another vocabulary of the Napa have not yet been been published by the Smithsonian Institution.

YUKA.—The Yuka or Uka language extends over a long and narrow strip of territory parallel for a hundred miles to the Pomo dialects and the coast, in and along the coast range. The area of the Pomo language, however, breaks across that of the Yuka from the west at Ukiah and surrounds Clear lake. The revengeful race of the Yukas, who are conspicuous by very large heads placed on smallish bodies, originally dwelt in Round valley, east of Upper Eel river. Nome Cult, meaning western tribe, is the Wintoon name for this solitary and fertile valley, which has become the seat of an Indian reservation. Of the Yuka we have a short vocabulary by Lieut. Edward Ross, in *New York Historical Magazine* for April, 1863. Surd vowels, perhaps nasalized, are frequent; also the ending *-um*, *-un*, which is probably the plural termination of nouns. No connection with the Chokuyem is perceptible, but a faint resemblance with the Cushna can be traced in a few words. Other tribes speaking Yuka are the *Ashochemies* or *Wappos*, formerly inhabiting the mountain tract from the Geysers down to Calistoga Hot springs; the *Shumeias*, at the head of Eel river; and the *Tahtoos*, on the middle and south forks of Eel river, and at the head of Potter valley

POMO.—The populous, unoffending Pomo race is settled along the coast, on Clear lake and on the heads of Eel and Russian rivers; a portion of them now inhabit the reservation of Round valley, together with their former tormentors, the Yukas. Those of the interior show more intelligence and a stronger physical constitution than the coast Pomos. The Cahto Pomos and the Ki Pomos, on Eel river, have adopted the Tinné dialect of the Wi Lakee, which is closely allied to the Hoopa. Powers considers as the nucleus of the numerous Pomo tribes the Pome Pomos, living in Potter valley, a short distance northwest of Clear lake. The language rapidly changes from valley to valley; but the majority of the dialects are sonorous, and the vocalic element preponderates.

We enumerate the following bands: *Pome Pomos,* earth people, in Potter valley. *Ballo Ki Pomos,* Wild Oat valley people, in Potter valley. *Choan Chadēla Pomos,* Pine-pitch people, in Redwood valley. *Matomey Ki Pomos,* Wooded valley people, around Little lake. *Usàls* or *Camalèl Pomos,* on Usal creek. *Shebalne Pomos,* neighbor people, in Sherwood valley. *Gallinomeros,* below Healdsburg; a few grammatical informations given in H. H. Bancroft's Native Races, vol. III, part second. *Yuka-i* or *Ukiah,* on Russian river (not to be confounded with Yuka in Round valley); vocabulary by G. Gibbs in Schoolcraft, vol. III (1853). *Choweshak,* at the head of Eel river; Gibbs' vocabulary in Schoolcraft, III, pp. 434, sqq. *Batemdikaie,* at the head of Eel river, called after the valley in which they live; vocabulary in Schoolcraft, III, 434, sqq. *Kulanapo,* on southwest shore of Clear lake; vocabulary in Schoolcraft, III, 428. Bancroft has called attention to the fact that many words of this and other dialects, spoken south of it, correspond to Polynesian and Malay terms, but on account of the uncertain nature of Oceanic consonantism, he is unwilling to draw any ethnological deductions from this coincidence. Kulanapo agrees pretty closely with Choweshah and Batemdikaie, but differs somewhat from Chwachamaju. *Chwachamaju,* to the north of Bodega bay. The words in Wrangell's vocabulary (see Olamentke, *mutsun*) appear to agree more closely with Yuka-i than with any other Pomo dialect.

WISHOSK.—Spoken on a very small area around the mouth of Eel river, on the sea-coast, and called so from the Indian name for Eel river. We know of two sub-dialects almost entirely identical, and showing a rather consonantic word-structure. Vocabularies were collected with care by George Gibbs, and published in Schoolcraft, III, p. 422. *Weeyot,* or *Veeard,* on mouth of Eel river; *Wishosk* on northern part of Humboldt bay, near mouth of Mad river; *Patawat,* identical with G. Gibbs' Kowilth, or Koquilth; and about a dozen other settlements speaking dialects of the same language. Proceeding through the basin of the Klamath river, we meet with a number of small, socially incoherent, bands of natives, engaged in salmon or trout fishing on the shores of this stream and of its tributaries. Some do not possess any tribal name, or name for their common language, and were in a bulk called Klamath river Indians, in contradistinction to the Klamath lake Indians, E-ukshiknit on the head of Klamath river. These latter I call here Klamaths.

EUROK.—The Euroc tribe inhabits both banks of the Klamath river, from its mouth up to the great bend at the influx of the Trinity river. The name simply means down (down the river), and another name given them by their neighbors, Pohlik, means nearly the same. Their settlements frequently have three or four names. Requa is the village at the mouth of the Klamath river, from which they set out when fishing at sea. The language sounds rough and guttural; the vowels are surd, and often lost between the consonants, as in mrpr, *nose;* chlh, chlec, *earth;* wrh-yenex, *child.* In conversation, the Eurocs terminate many words by catching sound (-h'-) with a grunt; with other Indians we observe this less frequently. They are of darker complexion than the Cahroks, and in 1870 numbered 2,700 individuals in the short stretch of forty miles along the river.

WEITS-PEK.—In Schoolcraft we find a vocabulary named after the Indian encampment at Weits-pek, a few miles above the great bend of Klamath river, on the North shore, whose words totally disagree with Eurok, Cahrok, Shasta, or any other neighboring tongue.

CAHROK.—*Cahrok* or *Carrook,* is not a tribal, but simply a conventional name, meaning above, upwards (up the Klamath river, as Eurk means down, and Modoc—probably—at the head of the river). The Cahrok tribe extends along Klamath river from Bluff creek, near Weits-pek, to Indian creek, a distance of eighty miles. Pehtsik is a local name for a part of the

Cahroks; another section of them, living at the junction of Klamath and Salmon (or Quoratem) rivers, go by the name of Ehnek. Stephen Powers thinks that the Cahroks are probably the finest tribe in California; that their language much resembles the Spanish in utterance, and is not so guttural as the Euroc. In Schoolcraft we find vocabularies from both tribes.

TOLEWA.—The few words of the Tolewa, or Tahlewah language, on Smith river, between Klamath and Rogue rivers, which were given to G. Gibbs by an unreliable Indian from another tribe, show a rough and guttural character, and differ entirely in their radicals from any other language spoken in the neighborhood.

SHASTA.—At the time of the Rogue river war the Shastas, or Shasteecas, became involved in the rebellion of their neighbors, and after their defeat the warriors of both tribes were removed, with their families, to the Grand Ronde and Siletz reserves in Oregon. Hence, they almost entirely disappeared from their old homes in the Shasta and Scott valleys, which are drained by affluents of the Klamath river, and also from their homes on Klamath river, from Clear creek upwards. Nouns form their plurals by adding oggára, ukára, *many*, and the language does not sound disagreeably to our ears. We know this vocalic tongue only through a few words, collected by Dana; the Smithsonian Institution owns three vocabularies. The Scott's valley band was called Watsahéwa; the names of other bands were T-ka, Iddoa, Hoteday, We-ohow.

PIT RIVER.—The Pit river Indians, a poor and very abject-looking lot of natives, live on upper Pit river and its side creeks. In former years they suffered exceedingly from the raids of the Modocs and Klamath Lakes, who kidnapped and kept them as slaves, or sold them at the slave-market at Yánex in southern Oregon. Like the Pomos and most other Californians, they regard and worship the coyote-wolf as the creator and benefactor of mankind. Powers calls their language "hopelessly consonantal, harsh, and sesquipedalian, very unlike the sweet and simple tongues of the Sacramento river." Redoubling of the root seems to prevail here to a large extent. A few words from a sub-dialect are given by Mr. Bancroft, which do not differ materially from the Palaik (or mountaineer) vocabulary printed in *Transactions of Am. Ethnol. Soc.*, vol. II, p. 98. After a military expedition to their country, General Crook ordered a removal of many individuals of this tribe to the Round valley reserve, where they are now settled. *Pú-su, Pú-isu* is the Wintoon name of the Pit river Indians, meaning eastern people. According to Mr. Powers' statement (*Overland Monthly*, 1874, pp. 412, sgg.), the Pit river Indians are sub-divided in: *Achomáwes* in the Fall river basin; from *achoma* river, meaning Pit river. *Hamefcuttelies*, in Big valley. *Astakaywas*, or *Astakywich*, in Hot spring valley; from *astakày*, hot spring. *Illmawes*, opposite Fort Crook, south side of Pit river. *Pácamallies*, on Hat creek.

KLAMATH.—The watershed between the Sacramento and Columbia river basin consists of a broad and mountainous table land rising to an average height of four to five thousand feet, and embellished by beautiful sheets of fresh water. The central part of this plateau is occupied by the Klamath reservation, which includes lakes, prairies, volcanic ledges, and is the home of the Klamath stock of Indians, who inhabit it together with the two Shóshoni tribes mentioned above. The nation calls itself (and other Indians) *Máklaks*, the encamped, the settlers, a term which has been transcribed into English *Múckalucks*, and ought to include all the four divisions given below. About 145 Modocs were, after the Modoc war of 1873, removed to Quápaw agency, Indian Territory. The language is rich in words and synonyms, only slightly polysynthetic, and lacks the sounds *f* and *r*. They divide themselves into: *Klamaths*, or *Klamath Lakes*, *E-ukshikni*, from e-ush, *lake;* on Big Klamath lake. *Modocs*, originally inhabiting the shores of Little Klamath lake, now at Yánex. The Pit Rivers call them Lútuam; and they call the Pit Rivers, *Móatuash*, or southern dwellers. *Kómbatuash*, grotto or cave dwellers, from their abode in the Lava Bed caves—a medley of different races. Some *Mólele* or Molále, renegades of the Cayuse tribe, have recently become mixed with Rogue Rivers and Klamaths, and have adopted the Klamath language in consequence. No Klamath sub-dialects exist, the idioms of all these tribes being almost identical. Klamaths and other southern Oregonians communicate with other tribes by means of the Chinook jargon.

THE TINNÉ FAMILY.—The Tinné family of languages, which extends from the inhospitable shores of the Yukon and Mackenzie rivers to Fraser river, and almost to Hudson's bay, sent in bygone centuries a powerful offshoot to the Rio Grande del Norte and the Gila rivers, now represented by the Apache, Lipan, and Návajo. Other fragments of the Tinné stock, represented by less populous tribes, wandered south of the Columbia river, and settled on the coast of the Pacific ocean; they were the Kwalhioqua, Tlatskanai, Umpqua, Rogue Rivers (or Rascal Indians), and the Hoopa. Following them up in the direction from south to north, we begin with the Hoopa.

Hoopa.—The populous and compact Hoopa (or better, Húpô) tribe has its habitation on the Trinity, near its influx into Klamath river, California, and for long years kept in awe and submission the weaker part of the surrounding tribes and clans, exacting tributes, and even forcing their language upon some of them, as upon the Chimalaquays on New river, the Kailtas on Redwood creek, and upon the two Pomo bands above mentioned. Powers holds their language to be copious in words, robust, strong in utterance, and of martial simplicity and rudeness. The *Wylakies*, or *Wi Lakees*, near the western base of Shasta butte, speak a Hoopa dialect No information is at hand to decide whether the *Lassics* on Mad river, the *Tahahteens* on Smith river, and a few other tribes, speak, as the assumption is, Tinné dialects or not.

Rogue River.—The *Tototen*, *Tootooten*, or *Tututamys* tribe, living on Rogue river, and its numerous side creeks, Oregon, speak a language which is, like the majority of Oregonian and northern tongues, replete of guttural and croaking sounds. According to Dr. Hubbard, whose vocabulary is published in Taylor's *California Farmer*, this nation comprised in 1856 thirteen bands, consisting in all of 1,205 individuals. (See article *Shasta*). The appearance of the numerals, the terms for the parts of the human frame, many other nouns, and the pronoun, *mine*, *my* (ho, hwo, hu), induced me to compare them with the Tinné languages. They differ considerably from Hoopa and Taculli, but singularly agree with Apache and Návajo, and Tototen has, therefore, to be introduced as a new offshoot of the coast branch into the great Tinné or Athapascan family of languages. The Smithsonian Institution owns two vocabularies, inscribed "Rogue River," two "Tootooten," and one "Toutouten."

Umpqua.—The Umpquas live in and around Alsea sub-agency, on the sea coast, together with the Alsea, Sayústkla and Coos Indians. Their idiom is softer than the other branches of the Tinné stock. Further north we find two other small tribes of the same origin, whose languages were studied only by Horatio Hale, of Wilkes' exploring expedition. One of them was the *Tlatskanai*, south of Columbia river; the other, the *Kwalhioqua*, at the outlet of this stream, both extremely guttural. On account of the smallness of the tribes speaking them, these idioms have probably become extinct; their owners merged into other tribes, and were identified with them beyond recognition. They roved in the mountains at some distance from the coast and the Columbia, living on game, berries, and esculent roots.

YAKON.—Before 1848, the Yakon tribe was settled on the Oregon coast, south of the Tillamuks, numbering then about seven hundred individuals. In the collection of fifty Yakon words, given in *Transactions of Am. Ethn. Soc.*, II, part 2d, pp. 99 sqq., we discover very few monosyllables, but many clusters of consonants, not easily pronounced by English speaking people, as kwotχl, *fingers;* pusuntχlχa, *three.*

CAYUSE.—The national appellation of the Cayuses, whose home is in the valley of Des Chutes river, Oregon, is *Wayíletpu*, the plural form of *Wa-ílet*, one Cayuse man. The Wayíletpu formerly were divided into Cayuses and Moléles, but the latter separated, went south and joined other tribes (see Klamath), or were removed to the Grand Ronde reserve. The Cayuses are rapidly assimilating, or identifying themselves, with the Walawalas on and around Umatilla agency, about seventy miles east of Des Chutes river outlet, and a majority of them have forgotten already their paternal idiom. Judging from the Cayuse words printed in the *Transactions of Am. Ethn. Society*, II, p. 97, this language prefers consonantic to vocalic endings, and possesses the aspirate *th* and *f*. The occurrence of both sounds, especially of *f*, is not uncommon in Oregonian languages.

KALAPUYA.—The original seats of this tribe were in the upper Willamette valley. The laws of euphony are numerous in this language, whose utterance is soft and harmonious; thus it forms a remarkable contrast with all the surrounding languages, the sounds of which are uttered with considerable pectoral exertion. The personal pronoun is used also as a possessive; no special termination exists for the dual or plural of nouns. *Yamkalli*, on head of Willamette river, is a dialect of Kalapuya.

CHINOOK.—The populous, Mongol-featured nation of the Chinooks once dwelt on both sides of the Lower Columbia; but after the destruction of four-fifths of their number in 1823 by a terrible fever-epidemy, a part of the survivors settled north, and now gradually disappear among the Chehalis. The pronunciation is very indistinct, the croakings in lower part of the throat frequent, the syntaxis is represented as being a model of intricacy. To confer with the Lower, the Upper Chinooks had to use interpreters, although the language of both is of the same lineage. The dialects and tribes were distributed as follows: *Lower Chinook*, from mouth of Columbia river up to Multnomah island, Clatsop; *Chinook proper;* Wakiakum; Katlámat. *Middle Chinook*—Multnomah, Skilloot. *Upper Chinook*—Watálla or Watχlála, showing a dual and a plural form in the inflection of the noun; Klakamat, south-east of Portland, a tribe once dispossessed of its homes by the Moléles; the idiom of the Cascade Indians, and of the extinct Waccanessisi. Following the authority of George Gibbs, I mention also as an Upper Chinook dialect the Wasco or Cathlasco language. From their original homes east of the Dalles, the Wascoes were removed to the Warm Spring agency.

CHINOOK JARGON.—The location of the Chinooks in the central region of western border commerce, and on the outlet of the international roadway of Columbia river, rendered the acquisition of the Chinook, or Tsinúk language very desirable for the surrounding tribes. But the nature of this language made this a rather difficult task, and so a trade language gradually formed itself out of Chinook, Chehali, Selish, Nootka, and other terms, which, on the advent of the whites, were largely increased by French, and in a less degree by English words. The French words were derived from the Canadian and Missouri patois of the fur traders. Two-fifths of the jargon terms were taken from Chinook dialects, and as the inflectional forms, prefixes and affixes of these unwieldy idioms were dropped altogether, and replaced by particles or auxiliaries, the acquisition of the jargon became easy. A comprehensive sketch of this idiom will be found in the preface to George Gibbs' *Dictionary of the Chinook Jargon*, New York, 1863 (in Shea's Linguistics).

We have similar instances of medley jargons from very disparate languages in the Lingua Franca of the Mediterranean ports, in the Pidgin English of Canton, the Negro-English-Dutch of Surinam, the Slavé on the Upper Yukon river, in a Sahaptin slave-jargon, and in the numerous women-languages of South America.

SAHAPTIN.—This name belongs to a small affluent of the Kooskooskie or Clearwater river, and has been adopted to designate the stock of languages spoken in an extensive territory on the middle and lower Columbia river, and on its tributaries, Yákima, Paluse, Clearwater and Snake rivers. The morphological part of the Sahaptin grammar is rich and well developed, and polysynthetism is carried up to a high degree. The exterior of the race recalls the bodily structure, not the complexion, of the Mongolian type of mankind. The easternmost tribe is:

Nez-Percés, the most numerous and powerful Sahaptin tribe, settled on a reserve in northern Idaho (about 2,800 Indians), or roaming in the neighborhood. A sketch of their grammar was published in *Transactions of American Ethn. Society*. The western and northern Sahaptin tribes are the following: *Wála-wála* (rivermen), on Umatilla agency, in northeastern Oregon. *Palús* or Paloose, on Palús river and Yákima reservation; *Yákama* or Yákima, on Yákima reserve, Washington Territory. Rev. Pandosy wrote a Grammar, Texts and Dictionary of this dialect, which were published in Mr. Shea's Linguistic Series. From their habitat they are called Pshuanwappum, dwellers in the stony country. *Klikitat*, on Yákima reserve and vicinity, formerly roaming through the woodlands around Mount St. Helens. *Umatilla*, on Oregon side of Columbia river and on Umatilla agency. No vocabularies. *Warm Spring Indians* on west side of Middle Des Chutes river. They call themselves Tishχáni-hhláma, after a locality on that water-course, or Milli-hhláma, from the thermal sources surging on the territory of their reservation (*milli*, bubbling, or tepid, *hhláma* belonging to, pertaining). A slave jargon exists among the Nez-Percé Indians, which originated through their intercourse with prisoners of war, and contains expressions for *eye, horse, man, woman*, and other most common terms, which are entirely foreign to Sahaptin.

SELISH.—The Selish family extends from the Pacific ocean and the straits of Fuca, through America and partly through British territory to the Rocky mountains and the 113. meridian. This race is most densely settled around Puget sound, and its main bulk resides north of Columbia river. By joining into one name their westernmost and easternmost dialect, their language has been called also Tsihaili-Selish, or Chehâli-Selish. A large number of words of this truly northern and superlatively jaw-breaking language are quite unpronounceable to Anglo-Americans and Europeans—i. e., tsatχlsh, *shoes;* skaiχlentχl, *woman*, in Tsihaili; shitχltso, *shoes*, in Atnah. This stock abounds in inflectional and syntactical forms, and redoubles the root or part of it extensively, but always in a *distributive* sense. It divides itself into a large number of dialects and subdialects, among which we point out the subsequent ones as probably the most important, going from west to north, and then to the east; *Nsietshawus* or *Tillamuk* (Killamuk), on Pacific coast, south of Columbia river; *Tsihaili, Chehâli;* on or near Pacific coast, Washington Territory: has three subdialects; *Tsihaili* proper on Chehali river and in Puyallup agency; *Quiantl, Quaiantl* or *Kwantlen; Quêniauitl.* A few *Chehalis* and Chinooks inhabit Shoalwater bay. *Cowlitz* or *Ká-ualitsk*, spoken on Puyallup agency. Their ancient home is the valley of the Cowlitz river, a northern tributary of the Lower Columbia river. *Soaiatlpi*, west of Olympia city. This tribe once included the Kettlefalls Indians. *Nisqualli, N'skwâli;* east of Olympia, on Nisqualli river, settled there in company with the Squaxins, on Puyallup agency. *Clallam* (*S'Clallum*), on S'Kokomish agency, northwest of Oylmpia city. Twana, in same locality. *Dwamish*, partly settled on Tulalip sub-agency. *Lummi*, on Nootsak or Lummi river, near the British boundary. This dialect is largely impregnated with Nootka and other foreign elements. The *Shushwap, Suwapamuck* or *Southern Atnah* belongs to the Selish stock, but does not extend from middle course of Fraser river and its affluents so far south as to reach American territory. It closely resembles Selish proper. The eastern Selish dialects are: *O'Kinakane* (*Okanagan*), with the subdialect *St'lakam*, on Okanagan river, a northern tributary of Upper Columbia river and on Colville reserve, which is located in the northeastern angle of Washington Territory. *Kullespelm, Kallispelm*, or Pend d'Oreille of Washington Territory, on Pend d'Oreille river and Lake Callispelm. The Upper Pend d'Oreille are settled on Flathead or Jocko reservation, Montana. *Spokane*, on Colville reserve and vicinity; three subdialects; Sngomenei, Snpoilschi, Syk'eszilni. *Skitsuish* or Coeur d'Alène; on a reservation in northern Idaho. *Selish* proper or Flathead. The tribe speaking it resides on Flathead reservation, and is called so without any apparent deformity of the head. The dialect lacks the sounds b, d, f, r; it has been studied by a missionary, Rev. Gregory Mengarini, who at present is writing a second edition of his *Grammatical linguae Selicae;* the first edition was published in New York, 1861 (in Shea's Linguistics). *Piskwaus* or *Piskwas*, on middle Columbia river and on Yákima reservation, Washington Territory.

NOOTKA.—The only dialect of this stock spoken within the limits of the United States is that of the *Makah*, Classet or Klaizzaht tribe in Neah bay near Cape Flattery. The Smithsonian Institution published in 1869 a very elaborate ethnological sketch of this fisher-tribe, written by James G. Swan. Nootka dialects are mainly in use on Vancouver's island, which is divided in four areas of totally different families of languages.

KOOTENAI.—The Kootenai, Kitunaha, or Flatbow language, is spoken on Kootenay river, an important tributary of Upper Columbia river, draining some remote portions of Idaho, Montana and the British possessions. A Lord's prayer in Kootenai is given in Bancroft's *Native Races*, vol. III, p. 620.

In bestowing the greatest care and accuracy on the compositon of this topographical survey of Pacific languages, my principal purpose was to give a *correct division*, of the idioms into stocks, and their dialects and subdialects, and I shall be very grateful for suggestions correcting my statements, if any should be found erroneous. To have given another location for a tribe than the one it occupies at present, cannot be considered as a grave error, for many American tribes are nomadic, and shift constantly from one prairie, pasture, or fishing place to another, or are removed to distant reservations by government agents. For want of information, I was unable to classify the Hhána in Sacramento valley, the Hagnaggi on Smith river, California, the Chitwout or Similkameen on the British-American border, and a few other tongues; but, in spite of this, I presume that the survey will be useful for orientation on this linguistic field, where confusion has reigned supreme for so many generations.

For the better guidance of students in ethnology and linguistics, I propose to classify all the Indian dialects in a very simple and clear manner, by adding to their dialect name that of the stock or family, as it is done in zoölogy and botany with the genera and species. In the same manner as the Mescaleros and Lipans are called Mescalero-Apaches and Lipan-Apaches, we can form compound names, as: Warm Spring Sahaptin Piskwaus Selish, Watχlála Chinook, Kwalhioqua Tinné, Hoopa Tinné, Dowpum Wintoon, Gallinomero Pomo, Coconoon Yocut, Kizh Shoshoni (or Kizh Kauvuya), Comoyei Yuma, Ottare Cherokee, Séneca Iroquois, Abnáki Algónkin, Delaware Algonkin, and so forth. The help afforded to linguistic topography by this method would be as important as the introduction of Linnean terminology was to descriptive natural science, for genera and species exist in human speech as well as among animals and plants.

The *thorough* study of *one* Indian tongue is the most powerful incentive to instructive and capable travelers for collecting as much linguistic material as possible, and as accurately as possible, chiefly in the shape of texts and their translations. It is better to collect little information accurately, than much information of an unreliable nature. The signs used for emphasizing syllables, for nasal and softened vowels, for explosive, lingual, croaking, and other consonantic sounds, must be noted and explained carefully; and the whole has to be committed to such publishers or scientific societies as are *not in the habit* of procrastinating publications. Stocks and dialects become rapidly extinct in the west, or get hopelessly mixed, through increased inter-tribal commerce, so that the original shape, pronunciation and inflection can no longer be recognized with certainty. The work must be undertaken in no distant time by zealous men, for after "the last of the Mohicans" will have departed this life, there will be no means left for us to study the most important feature of a tribe—its language—if it has not been secured in time by alphabetical notation.

COMPARATIVE VOCABULARIES OF THE SEMINOLE AND MIKASUKE TONGUES.*

BY BUCKINGHAM SMITH.

These words were recently taken down in Washington from the mouth of a Seminole delegation from Arkansas—Foos-harjo, an educated Indian, and Johnson, a black, speaking the Mvskoke, and Chocot-harjo, the Mikasuke, the last communicating through the Mvskoke, and sometimes himself writing out the words in his own tongue. The Indians were born in Florida, the negro in Alabama.

Major Caleb Swan, U. S. A., in a report to the department of war respecting the Seminoles in the year 1790–1, states that they were inhabiting country in Alabama, Florida, and the state of Georgia; and, according to tradition, that they came originally in roving bands from the northwest with

* Reprinted from *The Historical Magazine* (Morrisania, N. Y.), for August, 1866.

the name Seminole; that subsequently they conquered the Alabamas, and, according to their policy, united that people to their own nation, called Mvskoke; that later, the Apalaches were added, and, at the time of writing, he speaks of their having *Mikasuka* and some other permanent villages on the Apalachicola river. The language had then undergone so great change among the wandering hordes, still called Seminoles, that it was hardly understood by the Creeks (Mvskokes inhabiting fixed settlements), or, in general, even by themselves. It must be remembered, that, at the time he writes, the nation had already added to their number the remnants of the Alabamas or Coosadas, Uchees, Natches, Hitchitis, and Shauanos, with their several languages, six constituting the number spoken by the members of the confederacy.

The Hitchitis resided on the Flint and Chatahooche rivers. They are near of kin to the Mikasukes, to judge from the words of a small vocabulary taken by Mr. Gallatin from a Chelaqui, reprinted here with numerals taken at Tampa by Capt. Casey, and entitled: "Hitchittee or Chel-o-kee Dialect, spoken by several tribes of the great Muskokee Race." Those speaking the Mikasuke in Florida probably went from Georgia with the Mvskoke family, and some of them, at the time of the cession of the province to the United States by Spain, were living at a well-known lake bearing their name. From names borne by geographical objects, they appear to have widely extended their wanderings over the peninsula.

Whatever may be the theoretic history of the early migration of the Seminoles or Mvskokes, this much seems certain: the meaning of the word *seminole* is *wanderer, strayed off*, and is applied to the nomadic Mvskoke; that, while traditions among an unlettered people become vague and uncertain in less than three generations from the time of the event they would commemorate, names preserved in the narratives of the march of Hernando de Soto, attest that the Mvskoke language was in use among the Indians of Georgia, over three centuries since.

ENGLISH.	SEMINOLE.	MIKASUKE.	HITCHITEE.
Sound of the vowels: *a* as in far, *e* as in they, *i* as in marine, *o* as in go, *v* as in gun.			
man	hvnvnwa	navkni	nuckenih
woman	hokte	taikee	hohlagih
old woman		konchaka	
boy	chipane	ahlehloce	aucheanbotche
girl	choktoche	taikoche	autech auchee
infant	istoche, hipoachee	iatoche	
my father (said by son)	chalskee	tate	ilgih
my father (said by daughter)	"	chalhke	
my mother (said by son)	chvtskee	hoache	ahgih
my mother (said by daughter)	"	"	
my husband	chahee	vnnvk'ne	enukenih
my wife	chahaiua	chahvlke	chahulgih
my son (said by father)	chvpuchee	achóche	auchee
my son (said by mother)	chvtshusua	"	
my daughter (said by father)	chvtshuste	achostaike	auchooouhgtda
my daughter (said by mother)	chvtshusua	"	
my elder brother	chvtslaha	chachaie	
my younger brother	chachose	chaiapose	
sister	chauanua	hamóchaca	
my elder sister	hoktala	chafvnke	
my younger sister	chanunua manitka	chafvn ochapaca	
an Indian	iste chate	iatketesché	
people	iste	iaton	
head	icá	iose	
hair	ica isé	ios hiske	
face	itothlofá	tafokee	
forehead	icahoma iuinha	thlafeele	
ear (his)	ihustsko	hakehobe	
eye (his)	itolhuá	eté	
nose	iupo	ebé	
mouth	ichukua	eichi	
tongue	tolasua	cholase	

ENGLISH.	SEMINOLE.	MIKASUKE.	HITCHITEE.
teeth	inútee	enote	
beard	chukhisse	choske	
neck	nvkua	nokbe	
arm	sakpa	thlokfe	
hand	inke	elbe	
fingers	uisaka	ilbe uisake	
thumb	inkitski	ilbeke	
nails	inkikosusua	ilbakose	
body	ina	achakné	
chest	ohokpe	chonoke	
belly	nulhke	lvmpé	
female breasts	ipisi	moache	
leg	ele	eele	
foot	ile	elepalase	
toes	ileuasaka	cuesake	
bone	fane	efone	
heart	chafike	chonosbé	chifegaut
blood	chata	pechekche	bitchikchee
town, village	talofa	oelé	ochgiliohgih
chief	miko	míkei	mickee
warrior	tusikyavlge *(all)*	tusikiahlhe	tustenuggee
friend	anhise	achame	ahchormih
house	choko	chiki	chickee
bread	tvklaike	pvlvste	
kettle	chalkvs hvtke	ieckhahatkee	
bow	ichokotakse	iftchekotokbi	
arrow	thí	slakee	
axe, hatchet	pochusua	chiafe	
knife	islafka	eskvlvfkee	
canoe	pithlochee	pithlochee	
moccasins	*chuse* iste libika	*chuse* ueléé *(buckskin)*	
pipe	iche pakua	taloobe	
tobacco	ichí	akchvmé	
sky	aholoche	hossóte	
sun	hasse	haase	hahsohdih
moon	hoslibu	haso tale	hahsodalih
star	cochochompa	oache ke	ohwohchikee
day	nitta	nihtaki	uhbuksee
night	nihli	nihthlaki	mohsoostee
morning	huthijutki	hampole	
evening	iatké	opivs	
spring	tasahchi	lvkhachoslas	
summer	miske	lvkhache	
autumn			
winter	slafo	sláfi	
wind	hotalí	fapliche	
thunder	tinitkí	tohohkahche	toknoukkee
lightning	atoiohattí	lamalecheeche	
rain	oské	okóbache	
snow	etote	eptivele	
fire	tootka	été	edih
water	oiva	ohke	okkee
ice	etote	epte	
earth, land	icána	iakne	
sea	oihatka	okatke	
river	oislako	okichobe	
lake	okhasse	alope, okelose	
valley	oihossi, panofa	penatké	
prairie	hiakpo	hiatlé	
hill, mountain	ican halue	iacnebeké	
island	otí, houitska	okantakle	
stone, rock	cható	talé	
salt	okchanva	okchahni	ochchahnih
iron		kochone	
forest	ituvlkate	pahayóke	
tree, wood	itú	ahí	ahlee
leaf	tuisí	ahihíske	
bark	itohulhpe	ahehnlbe	
grass	pahe	pahe	
pine	chole	chole	
maize	ache	aspe	usppe
squash	tahaia	chicoie	
flesh, meat	apesua	akné	
dog	ita	efé	
buffalo	ianasa	ianasé	
bear	noposé	iansé	nogasaut
wolf	iahá	oba hosé	ohboorhoose
fox	cholá	cholé	
deer	echo	eché	echee
elk	chopieká	eichhoke	
beaver	eichhasua	posafe	
rabbit, hare	chofe	chokfé	
tortoise	locha	iokche	

ENGLISH.	SEMINOLE.	MIKASUKE.	HITCHITEE.
horse	cholako	cauaie	
fly	chana	choane	
mosquito	okieha	hoskotone	
snake	chittoo	chinté	
rattlesnake	chĭttoo miko	chintmike	
bird	fosua	foosé	
egg	itshostake	onase	
feathers	tafa	hiské	
wings	italhpa	tolokbé	
goose	sasakua	hoshalé	
duck (mallard)	fochó	fooché	
turkey	pínuá	faiti	
pigeon	pachí	pachi	
fish	thathlo	thlathle	
name	ochifka	ochilké	
white	hvtké	hvtké	
black	lvste	loóche	
red	chate	ketesché	
light blue	holatte	onotbé	
yellow	lané	lakvne	
light green	pahi *lanomi (looks like)*	pahetalukchome	
great, large	slakke	choobe	
small, little	chukki	uikchosis	
strong	yikchi	uante	
old	achùli	naknosi	
young	mvnitti	ojahbí	
good	héintle	heintlos	
bad	holouak	humpikos	
dead	ilí	eie	
alive	uinaki	fisahke	
cold	kasuppi	kabalekosche	
warm, hot	haye	haieche	
I	aní	aní	
thou	chiimi	chihni	
he	imi	inihni	
we	pomi	pohni	
ye	chintaki	chénoche	
they	imetahke	inenohche	
this	hiamá	iyale	
that	ma	mamé	
all	omulka	laapké	
many, much	anachome	anakapen	
who	istaimut	nohloté	
far	opaie	opvnke	
near	ahele	auelosis	
here	yama	yalé	
there	ma	mamí	
to-day	mochanetta	emanetaki	
yesterday	paksangke	opiahchama	
to-morrow	pakse	paksaka	
yes	encá	hó	
no	ecosche	mates	
one	hvmkin	thlamen	thlah' hai
two	hokolen	toklan	to kai
three	totchinen	tochínan	to chay
four	oosten	citaken	see tah
five	chaskepen	cháskepvn	chah kee
six	ipaken	ípaken	ee pak
seven	colapaken	colapaken	ko lapah
eight	chinapaken	tosnapaken	tos nap pah
nine	ostapaken	ostapaken	os ta pah
ten	palen	pokolen	po kolin
eleven	hvmkon talaken	tklauaikvn	po thlah' wai kan
twelve	hokolokaken	toklauaican	
twenty	pale hokolen	poco toklan	po ko to ko lin
thirty	" totchinen	" totchinan	
forty	" osten	" sitaken	
fifty	" chaskepen	" cháskepen	
sixty	" ipaken	" lepaken	
seventy	" kola paquen	" kolapaken	
eighty	" chinapaken	" tosnapaken	
ninety	" ostapaken	" lostapaken	
one hundred	chokpi hvmkin [kin	chokpi thlamen	chok pee thlah'min
one thousand	chokpi thloko hvm-	" chobí thlamen	
to eat	hvmpita	empike	
to drink	iskíta	iskéke	
to run	litkita	isthnitkikí	
to dance	litkita	isthnitkikí	
to sing	iahaikita	hopvnke	
to sleep	nochita	nocheke	
to speak	opoonaita	apvnke	
to see	hechita	hechéke	
to love	anokichita	anokachike	

ENGLISH.	SEMINOLE.	MIKASUKE.	HITCHITEE.
to kill	ille ichita	illi chike	
to sit	laikita	chokoliki	
to stand	hoythlita	hachaleke	
to go	ayeta	athleki	
to come	atita	onteke	
to walk	yakapita	chaiake	
to work	atotketá	takalskake	
to steal	holskopita	okepeke	
to lie	laksitá	olaske	
to give	emeta	emekeke	
to laugh	apilita	haiakeki	
to cry	hacaihkita	hilaihkiki	
alligator	hvlpata	hvlpati	
slave	salvfki	anope	
cane	coha	othlane	
pumpkin	chase	chokse	
turtle	olakaa	ilakue	
wildcat	coaki	koosi	
ravine	panasofki		
brier-root flour	kuntí	kantiki	
high	hvlui	abvnti	
low	kunchapí	iakne	
flute	fíhpa	conbokachichiki	
gourd	iphipi	iphipi	
ghost		solope	
opossum	sokha hatka	sokeasikeni	
raccoon	uulko	shaue	
persimmon	sata	othkofé	
hawk	aiú	akale	
owl	opá	opaké	
tiger	kacha	koachobe	
bean	taláko	shalale	

PROPER NAMES, WITH THEIR SIGNIFICATIONS.

Istopoga, *iste atepogo*, person drowned. Sem.

Okichobe, *oki chobe*, water big. Mik.

Halpatioka, *hvlpati oka*, alligator many. Mik.

Wekiwa, water spring. Sem.

Pilatka, *waca ak pilatka*, driving many cows across. Sem.

Pithlo-chokco, boat-house (ship). Sem.

Oclawaha, water muddy in there. Mik.

Tohopkilige, *tohopki laiki*, fort site. Sem.

Locktshapopka, *locktsha popka*, acorn to eat. Sem.

Hichepoksasa, *hihepok sassa*, pipe many. Sem.

Wekiwache, *oiva vche*, water. Sem.

Homosasa, *homo sassa*, pepper many. Sem.

Echashotee, *echas hotee*, beaver his house. Sem.

Choko-chate, house red. Sem.

Choko-liska, house old. Sem.

Panasoffke, *pane sofke*, valley deep. Sem.

Withlacooche, *oiva slakke uche*, water long, narrow. Sem.

Chase-howi ska, pumpkin kay. Sem.

Alaqua (hiliqua?), sweet gum. Sem.

Fenholloway, *fenholoue*, young turkey. Sem.

Oklokne, *okeloknee*, much bent. Sem.

Etawa, one polling (a boat). Sem.

Etenaiah, scrub. Sem.

Econholloway, *icana halue*, earth high. Sem.

THE LORD'S PRAYER IN MIKASUKE.*

In the last number of *The Historical Magazine* was published some vocabularies of the Indian languages, to which is now added the Lord's Prayer, given by one of the chiefs. As he did not speak English, and as the letters did not appear to be the same as ours, and perhaps, if identical, not sounded the same, it was sent to Washington to be verified, and is now printed as it comes, rewritten by the competent ability of George Gibbs, Esq., who says, beyond this: "I tried to get something approaching a literal

* From *The Historical Magazine* for September, 1866.

INDEX.

NOTE.—The names of Indians are printed in CAPITALS; and all names of tribes and Indian names of places are set in *Italic* type. This method of distinguishing articles the author has found, by experience, greatly to relieve the eyes.

Not only names of tribes, nations, and countries are *italicized*, but such English names are printed in the same letter as have been given to tribes, nations, and places inhabited by Indians.

A few baptismal or Christian names, and some names of places, will be found in brackets. Those are additions, and are not found in the body of the work.

A.

Anecdotes, Ind. 34—45, 516, 596.
Androscoggin, signification of, 318; dispersion of the tribe of, 316.

B.

F.

G.

I.

J.

K.

L.

M.

N.

O.

P.

Q.

R.

S.

T.

U.

V.

W.

INDEX TO APPENDIX.

9 781428 6333

Printed in the USA
CPSIA information can be obtained
at www.ICGtesting.com
LVHW050906211023
761739LV00006B/164